Restaurant

G   B

This 15th edition published 2007
© Automobile Association Developments Limited 2007.
Automobile Association Developments Limited retains the copyright in the current edition © 2007 and in all subsequent editions, reprints and amendments to editions. The information contained in this directory is sourced entirely from the AA's information resources. All rights reserved. No part of this publication may be reproduced, stored in a retrieval system, or transmitted in any form or by any means - electronic, photocopying, recording or otherwise - unless the written permission of the Publishers has been obtained beforehand. This book may not be sold, resold, hired out or otherwise disposed of by way of trade in any form of binding or cover other than that in which it is published, without the prior consent of all relevant Publishers.
The contents of this book are believed correct at the time of printing. Nevertheless, the Publisher cannot be held responsible for any errors or omissions, or for changes in the details given in this Guide, or for the consequences of any reliance on the information provided by the same. This does not affect your statutory rights. Assessments of AA inspected establishments are based on the experience of the Hotel and Restaurant Inspectors on the occasion(s) of their visit(s) and therefore descriptions given in this Guide necessarily dictate an element of subjective opinion which may not reflect or dictate a reader's own opinion on another occasion. See page 6 for a clear explanation of how, based on our Inspectors' inspection experiences, establishments are graded. If the meal or meals experienced by an Inspector or Inspectors during an inspection fall between award levels the restaurant concerned may be awarded the lower of any award levels considered applicable. The AA strives to ensure accuracy of the information in this Guide at the time of printing. Due to the constantly evolving nature of the subject matter the information is subject to change. The AA will gratefully receive any advice from our readers of any necessary updated information.

Please contact
Advertisement Sales: advertisingsales@theaa.com
Editorial Department: lifestyleguides@theaa.com

Front cover photograph courtesy of Forest Pines Golf and Country Club Hotel, Scunthorpe, Lincolnshire
Photographs in the gazetteer provided by the establishments.
Typeset/Repro: Keenes, Andover
Printed by Trento Srl, Italy.
Restaurant descriptions have been contributed by the following team of writers: Cathy Fitzgerald, Sarah Gilbert, David Hancock, Julia Hynard, Denise Laing, Melissa Riley-Jones, Allen Stidwill, Derryck Strachan, Mark Taylor and Kate Trew

Published by AA Publishing, a trading name of Automobile Association Developments Limited, whose registered office is Fanum House, Basing View, Basingstoke, Hampshire RG21 4EA.
Registered number 1878835.
A CIP catalogue for this book is available from the British Library.
ISBN-10: 0-7495-5299-9
ISBN-13: 978-0-7495-5299-2
A03282

Maps prepared by the Mapping Services Department of The Automobile Association.
Maps © Automobile Association Developments Limited 2007.

 This product includes mapping data licensed from Ordnance Survey® with the permission of the Controller of Her Majesty's Stationery Office.
© Crown copyright 2007.
All rights reserved.
Licence number 100021153.

 This product includes mapping based upon data licensed from Ordnance Survey of Northern Ireland® reproduced by permission of the Chief Executive, acting on behalf of the Controller of Her Majesty's Stationery Office.
© Crown copyright 2007.
Permit number 60240.

Republic of Ireland mapping based on Ordnance Survey Ireland Permit number MP000106.
© Ordnance Survey Ireland and Government of Ireland.

Contents

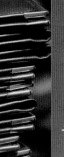

How to Use the Guide

1 **Map reference** is for the atlas section at the back of the Guide. The map page number is followed by the National Grid Reference. To find a location, read the first figure horizontally and the second figure vertically within the lettered square. For Central London and Greater London, there is an 8-page map section starting on page 252.

2 **Place name** Restaurants are listed in country and county order, then by town and then alphabetically within the town. There is an index by restaurant at the back of the book and a similar one for the Central & Greater London sections on pages 248-251 with plan references.

3 **Restaurant name.**

4 ◉ **The AA Rosette Award**
Main entries have been awarded one or more Rosettes, up to a maximum of five. See page 6 for an explanation of how they are graded.

5 **Food style** of the restaurant is in bold italics, followed by a short summary statement.

6 **Photographs** Restaurants awarded AA Rosettes are invited to enhance their entry with up to two photographs.

7 **The names of the chef(s) and owner(s)** are as up-to-date as possible at the time of going to press, but changes in personnel often occur, and may affect both the style and quality of the restaurant.

8 **Prices** are for fixed lunch and dinner (where available) and à la carte dishes. Service charge information (see also opposite). Note: Prices quoted are a guide only, and are subject to change without notice.

9 **Notes** Additional information e.g. availability of vegetarian dishes, civil weddings, air con.

10 **Rooms** If the establishment is in either of the AA's accommodation schemes, the number of rooms and the rating are shown. See page 7 for further details.

11 **Directions** are given wherever they have been supplied by the establishment.

12 **Neighbourhood restaurants**. These are not AA inspected but are well worth trying.

13 **Parking details**.

14 **Children** Menu, portions, age restrictions etc.

15 **Number of seats** in the restaurant, followed by private dining room (Pr/dining room).

16 **Number of wines** under and over £20, and available by the glass.

17 **Daily opening and closing times**, the days of the week it is closed and seasonal closures. Note that opening times are liable to change without notice.

It is wise to telephone in advance to avoid disappointment.

18 **Description** of the restaurant and the food that it serves.

19 **E-mail address and website**.

20  **toptable**. Online Booking Service. For explanation, see right.

21 **V** Indicates a **vegetarian menu**. Restaurants with some vegetarian dishes available are indicated under Notes.

22 **NOTABLE WINE LIST** Indicates **notable wine list**. See pages 14-15 for wine information.

23 **NEW** Indicates that an entry is new to the Guide this year.

24 Indicates the use of **local produce**. See also feature about local British produce on pages 16-17.

All establishments take major credit cards, except where we have specified otherwise.

All information is correct at the time of print but may change without notice. Details of opening times and prices may be omitted from an entry when the establishment has not supplied us with up-to-date information. This is indicated where the establishment name is shown in italics.

Service Charge
We asked restaurants the following questions about service charge: (Their responses appear under Prices in each entry.)
- Is service included in the meal price, with no further charge added or expected?
- Is service optional – charge not automatically added to bill?
- Is service charge compulsory, and what percentage?
- Is there a service charge for larger groups, minimum number in group, and what percentage?

Many establishments automatically add service charge to the bill but tell the customer it is optional.

Smoking Regulations
From July 2007 smoking is now banned in all public places in the United Kingdom and Ireland. The proprietor can designate one or more bedrooms with ventilation systems where the occupants can smoke, but communal areas must be smoke-free. Communal areas include the interior bars and restaurants in pubs and inns.

toptable.co.uk Online Restaurant Booking Service
free online restaurant & party booking

We continue our relationship with toptable, Europe's largest online booking service. During 2007 they will seat over 1.6 million diners. Readers of the AA Restaurant Guide will be able to take advantage of their experience and expertise with free online booking and hundreds of great offers. As you read through the Guide you'll see that some establishments feature the 'computer' symbol which indicates that they are bookable online.
All you have to do is log onto the AA website, **www.theAA.com**, and follow the links through to the restaurant pages. Enter the restaurant name, and, if it's bookable online, you'll see the BOOK NOW! button. Click on this and you'll be able to make bookings 24 hours a day, as well as using the unique features, including 360° images, to give you a real feel for the style of the place.
Register to use the service and you'll receive the very latest special offers by email.

Neighbourhood Restaurants
We've also included some neighbourhood restaurants in this year's Guide which are bookable online. They have the computer symbol too, and you can find them in the same way as above or use the website address quoted in their entry.

Please note - it is possible that during the currency of the Guide more restaurants will sign up for the online booking service, and also that some, due to change of hands or other reasons, may withdraw.

Facilities for Disabled Guests
The **Disability Discrimination Act** (access to Goods and Services) means that service providers may have to consider making adjustments to their premises. For further information see **disability.gov.uk/dda**. The establishments in this Guide should all be aware of their responsibilities under the Act. Always phone in advance to ensure that the establishment you have chosen has appropriate facilities.
See also **holidaycare.org.uk**.

Website Addresses
Website addresses are included where they have been supplied and specified by the respective establishment. Such websites are not under the control of The Automobile Association Developments Limited and as such The Automobile Association Developments Limited has no control over them and will not accept any responsibility or liability in respect of any and all matters whatsoever relating to such websites including access, content, material and functionality. By including the addresses of third-party websites the AA does not intend to solicit business or offer any security to any person in any country, directly or indirectly.

How the AA Assesses for Rosette Awards

The AA's Rosette award scheme was the first nationwide scheme for assessing the quality of food served by restaurants and hotels. The Rosette scheme is an award, not a classification, and although there is necessarily an element of subjectivity when it comes to assessing taste, we aim for a consistent approach throughout the UK. Our awards are made solely on the basis of a meal visit or visits by one or more of our hotel and restaurant Inspectors, who have an unrivalled breadth and depth of experience in assessing quality. They award Rosettes annually on a rising scale of one to five.

So what makes a restaurant worthy of a Rosette Award?

For our Inspectors, the top and bottom line is the food. The taste of a dish is what counts, and whether it successfully delivers to the diner the promise of the menu. A restaurant is only as good as its worst meal. Although presentation and competent service should be appropriate to the style of the restaurant and the quality of the food, they cannot affect the Rosette assessment as such, either up or down. The summaries below indicate what our Inspectors look for, but are intended only as guidelines. The AA is constantly reviewing its award criteria, and competition usually results in an all-round improvement in standards, so it becomes increasingly difficult for restaurants to reach award level. For more detailed Rosette criteria, please visit **www.theAA.com**.

◉ One Rosette
- Excellent restaurants that stand out in their local area
- Food prepared with care, understanding and skill
- Good quality ingredients

Around 50% of restaurants have one Rosette.

◉◉ Two Rosettes
- The best local restaurants
- Higher standards
- Better consistency
- Greater precision apparent in the cooking
- Obvious attention to the quality and selection of ingredients

About 40% of restaurants have two Rosettes.

◉◉◉ Three Rosettes
- Outstanding restaurants demanding recognition well beyond local area
- Selection and sympathetic treatment of highest quality ingredients
- Timing, seasoning and judgement of flavour combinations consistent
- Excellent intelligent service and a well-chosen wine list

Around 10% of restaurants have three Rosettes.

◉◉◉◉ Four Rosettes
Dishes demonstrate:
- intense ambition
- a passion for excellence
- superb technical skills
- remarkable consistency
- appreciation of culinary traditions combined with desire for exploration and improvement
- Cooking demands national recognition

Twenty-five restaurants have four Rosettes.

◉◉◉◉◉ Five Rosettes
- Cooking stands comparison with the best in the world
- Highly individual
- Breathtaking culinary skills
- Setting the standards to which others aspire
- Knowledgeable and distinctive wine list

Six restaurants have five Rosettes.

AA Accommodation Ratings

Where AA Star ratings appear under the 'Rooms' heading in the Restaurant Guide, the establishment has been inspected under one of the AA's nationally recognised Classification Schemes. These ratings ensure that your accommodation meets the AA's high standards of cleanliness, with an emphasis on professionalism, proper booking procedures and efficient service.

Quality Standards

In association with VisitBritain, VisitScotland and VisitWales, the AA has developed common Quality Standards for rating accommodation. Both hotels and guest accommodation are rated with Stars, and a descriptive 'designator' is used to define the style of the establishment. The designators have been abbreviated in the Restaurant Guide.

Abbreviations are as follows:

HL	Hotel
TH	Townhouse Hotel
SH	Small Hotel (less than 20 bedrooms)
CHH	Country House Hotel
GA	Guest Accommodation
RR	Restaurant with Rooms
B&B	Bed & Breakfast (six or fewer paying guests)
GH	Guest House (more than six paying guests)
INN	Inn
FH	Farmhouse

★★ Star Classification

There are a number of minimum entry requirements which must be fulfilled before a hotel or guest accommodation establishment can be rated by the AA. Star ratings are affected by quality, facilities and the provision of services. The criteria for the Hotel Scheme and the Guest Accommodation Scheme are slightly different, but for both Classification Schemes Stars are awarded on a rising scale of one to five, from simpler, more informal places to the very finest and most luxurious.

The hotels that are the very best in their Star rating are indicated by Red Stars.

★ Guest Accommodation – Yellow stars

Establishments within the AA Guest Accommodation scheme that are the very best of the three-, four- and five-Star ratings are indicated by Yellow Stars.

If you would like to know more about the Classification Schemes and how the AA inspects accommodation, or what to expect at each rating level, please visit www.theAA.com

AA Restaurants of the Year
for England, London, Scotland and Wales

Potential Restaurants of the Year are nominated by our team of full-time Inspectors based on their routine visits. In selecting a Restaurant of the Year, we look for somewhere that is exceptional in its chosen area of the market. Whilst the Rosette awards are based on the quality of the food alone, Restaurants of the Year takes into account all aspects of the experience.

England

Tanners Restaurant
Plymouth, Devon
Page 137 ◉◉

Housed in Plymouth's oldest building, this restaurant offers modern style in an impressive 15th-century setting that blends flagstones, beams, vaults and an ancient well with contemporary art. The Pilgrim Fathers may have eaten their last meal in England in the courtyard here, but it's a foregone conclusion it wouldn't have included dishes cooked with such flair. With a separate vegetarian menu available, careful sourcing of local produce is all important. Think roast partridge served with bubble-and-squeak and a thyme sauce, or perhaps seared fillet of brill teamed with smoked salmon croquettes and a horseradish velouté. This is a popular venue thanks to consistent standards and the owners' TV appearances: the Tanner brothers have also opened a sibling contemporary brasserie - the Barbican Kitchen - in the city's Plymouth Gin Distillery building.

London

Trinity Restaurant
London, SW4
Page 315 ◉◉◉

Trinity sees chef-restaurateur Adam Byatt return to his Clapham roots after a sojourn in the bright lights of WC2 - ex Thyme and Origin at Covent Garden's Hospital media complex, he was originally of the much-acclaimed Thyme in Clapham Park Road. Here he's landing back in the Old Town area on the edge of leafy Clapham Common, and has created an exciting, buzzy, neighbourhood venture. Set well back from the road, it catches the eye and the light with its smart exterior and large window frontage. Inside there's a sophisticated, friendly atmosphere, the room decked out with white-clothed tables, elegant cream and chocolate-coloured walls, comfortable cane-backed chairs and soft lighting; all providing a contemporary backdrop to the polished, modern French cooking. High technique, clear flavours and creative presentation add to the wow-factor.

Scotland

The Horseshoe Inn
Eddleston, Scottish Borders
Page 639 ◉◉◉

A converted village blacksmiths' houses the luxurious fine-dining Bardoulet's restaurant plus a bistro/bar and lounge areas. The décor is striking – a combination of traditional with a modern twist; vibrant colours juxtapose soft-toned fabrics, with fabulous table appointments, gilt-edged mirrors and character stone floors all adding to the ambience. Staff are refreshingly helpful, knowledgeable, relaxed but attentive, while the highly accomplished kitchen under Patrick Bardoulet draws on his native homeland to deliver a modern French approach with a nod to traditional Scottish fare. Quality, local fresh seasonal ingredients are combined with flair and vision, while technical skills and execution are top drawer. Think a loin of roe deer served with onion roasted in liquorice, celeriac purée, potato croquette and game jus, or meunière of Dover sole with parsnip purée, razor clams and samphire.

Wales

Carlton Riverside
Llanwrtyd Wells, Powys
Page 684 ◉◉◉

Now home to the friendly and enthusiastic Gilchrists (the husband-and-wife team previously at Carlton House), this small, character, three-storey restaurant with rooms is set right beside the river bridge in the centre of town. The stylish, intimate restaurant combines quality contemporary fabrics and furnishings with the charm of the house and river views. It's all very soothing, with comfort provided by high-backed chocolate-brown leather chairs and cream napery, and the diligent and attentive service of Alan Gilchrist. Wife Mary Ann looks after the cooking, her confident, one-women act undertaken with panache, underlining her obvious passion and talent. Her fixed-price menus (the Chef's Menu a no-choice affair, while the Irfon Menu offers a compact selection) make a virtue of simplicity, the wonderful straightforward approach driven by stunningly fresh, local seasonal produce.

AA Chefs' Chef 2007-08

This is the annual poll of all the chefs in The Restaurant Guide. Around 1,900 of the country's top chefs vote to recognise the achievements of one of their peers from a shortlist chosen by the AA's team of Inspectors.

Michael Caines OBE

This year's AA Chefs' Chef is Michael Caines - a chef who is no stranger to the restaurant and hotel industry, and no stranger to the food-keen public either.

Michael has been at Gidleigh Park Hotel, in Devon, since 1994, where he is now executive chef and winner of four AA Rosettes. He is also a director of Abode Hotels.

He has made a huge impact on the culinary world in a relatively short time. Amongst numerous accolades, Michael has cooked at 10 Downing Street for Tony Blair, and participated in the 'Great British Menu' competition, broadcast on BBC2, for the honour of cooking for the Queen's 80th birthday celebrations. In 2006 he was awarded an MBE for services to the hospitality industry - an award that acknowledges not just what he has achieved in Abode and the Michael Caines Restaurants, but more importantly, what he is contributing to the whole profession.

Born in Exeter in 1969, Michael gained his passion for food from his mother, who he used to enjoy helping in the kitchen. In 1987 he was Student of the Year at Exeter Catering College, going on to spend three influential years under his mentor Raymond Blanc at Le Manoir aux Quat' Saisons. From there he moved to France, working alongside two super-star French chefs - the late Bernard Loiseau in Saulieu, and Joël Robuchon in Paris.

In 1994, very shortly after his arrival at Gidleigh Park, Michael suffered a terrible car accident, in which he lost his right arm. Remarkably, he was back in the kitchen part-time within two weeks, and full-time after just one month.

Andrew Brownsword, owner of Gidleigh Park, says, 'Michael is so enthusiastic and inspirational. We share the same values in food, hospitality and life in general.'

Michael opened his own restaurant at the Royal Clarence Hotel in 1999, and then established Abode Hotels with Andrew Brownsword in 2003.

Cooking is Michael's passion. He is not only a hugely talented chef, but is also a dedicated and energetic manager, and an inspirational leader. 'I both love to cook and I love to help my chefs to develop their own talents and reach their potential,' he says. The fact that four of his protégés now run their own Abode kitchens is testament to that dedication. He is also active outside his own kitchens, being involved in charities and food festivals in his native South West.

'The challenge to be the best remains and continues to motivate me. The kitchen is where I am most at home, where I feel at my most creative.'

'The dining concepts that we have created in our Abode venues reflect my belief that good food is not just for an exclusive elite, but for everybody.'

It is not surprising that Michael's peers have voted him AA Chefs' Chef 2007-08.

Previous Winners

Andrew Fairlie
Andrew Fairlie @ Gleneagles, Scotland p630

Germain Schwab
Winteringham Fields (former chef), Lincolnshire p246

Raymond Blanc
Le Manoir aux Quat' Saisons, Great Milton, Oxfordshire p418

Shaun Hill
The Glasshouse, Worcester, Worcestershire p523

Heston Blumenthal
The Fat Duck, Bray, Berkshire p30

Jean-Christophe Novelli
A Touch of Novelli at The White Horse, Harpenden, Hertfordshire p214

Gordon Ramsay
Restaurant Gordon Ramsay, London SW3 p312

Rick Stein
The Seafood Restaurant, Padstow, Cornwall p75

Marco Pierre White

Kevin Viner

Find it with theAA.com

www.theAA.com

Go to **theAA.com** for maps and the **Route Planner** to help you find AA listed guest houses, hotels, pubs and restaurants – more than 12,000 establishments

Simply enter your postcode and the establishment postcode given in this guide and click **Get route**. Check your details and you are on your way. Or, search on the home page for a Hotel/B&B or a Pub/Restaurant by location or establishment name. Scroll down the list of finds for the interactive map and local routes.

You can also do postcode searches on www.ordnancesurvey.co.uk and www.multimap.com, and the latter provides useful aerial views of your destination.

Discover new horizons with Britain's largest travel publisher

AA Wine Awards

Winning selection of wines - Sketch / Menu	Wine selection	Price
Appetiser – slow-poached loin of rabbit with marinated foie gras, butternut squash sorbet, apple crème fraîche	1998 Sylvaner, Domaine Weinbach, Alsace	£25 per bottle
Portland crab and alfalfa shoots in a cannelloni of sugarsnap jelly, oyster beignets, pickled baby squid	2005 O Rosal, Terras Gauda, Rias Baixas	£34 per bottle
Saddle of Lakeland venison, braised oxtail, veal tongue and sweetbreads with juniper-scented Swiss chard	2003 Bandol Domaine de Terrebrune	£50 per bottle
St Nectaire, Fourme au Maury, Comté and Langres with caramelised pear and apple jelly	2001 Rivesaltes, Ambré Domaine Chênes	£32 per bottle
Single estate bitter chocolate negus with bergamot, salted caramel biscuit cigar, milk ice cream, Earl Grey brûlée	2004 Maury, Mas Amiel	£28 per half bottle
Coffee and petits fours	1979 Digestif: Armagnac Dartigalongue	£9 per measure

The AA Wine Award

This year's AA Wine Awards attracted, as ever, a very large response with over 1,000 entries. Three national winners were chosen – Sketch (Lecture Room & Library), England; Killiecrankie House Hotel, Scotland; and The Bell at Skenfrith, Wales. Sketch was the Overall Winner, and one of their wine team wins an all expenses paid trip to Willi Opitz's vineyards at Illmitz in Austria's Burgenland.

All 1,800 or so rosetted restaurants in last year's Guide were invited to submit their wine lists. From these, the panel selected a shortlist of around 160 establishments who are highlighted in the Guide with the **Notable Wine List** symbol.

The shortlisted establishments were then asked to choose wines from their list (within a budget of £50 per bottle) to accompany a menu designed by Michael Wignall, chef of the Devonshire Arms Country House Hotel & Spa in North Yorkshire, the 2007 England and Overall Winner.

The final judging panel included the AA Chief Inspector, Jeremy Rata (last year's winner), an independent wine journalist and our wine sponsor.

Other lists that reached the final consideration were Knockinaam Lodge at Portpatrick, The Crown at Whitebrook, The Greyhound at Battersea and The Ledbury, both in London.

Notable Wine Lists
So what makes a wine list notable?

Clearly we want to see high-quality wines, with diversity/coverage across grapes and/or countries and style, and the best individual growers and vintages. The list should be well presented, ideally with some helpful notes and, to reflect the demand from diners, a good choice of wines by the glass.

What upsets the judges are spelling errors, wines under incorrect regions, lack of vintage information, split vintages (no excuse in this word processor world), lazy purchasing (all the wines from a country coming from just one grower or negociant) and sloppy or confusing layout. Sadly, too many restaurants still provide ill-considered wine lists.

To reach the final shortlist, we are looking for a real passion for wine, which should come across to the diner, a fair pricing policy (depending, of course, on the style of restaurant), an interesting coverage (not necessarily a large list), which might include a specialism, such as sherries or different-sized bottles.

Wine List Trends

We asked our restaurateurs two questions this year. One question was about upcoming wine areas and the other asked about the areas where the greatest sales increase had been noticeable.

New Zealand was the country showing the largest increase in sales, followed by Italy, Spain, Chile and Argentina - probably no surprises there.

The upcoming wine growing regions were more interesting. Portugal led the field, with Argentina and Chile following. Next were England and Slovenia (Kent was specifically named by three entries).

Fascinating - so watch this space as global warming makes its mark in southern England.

The AA Wine Awards are sponsored by
T&W Wines Ltd
5 Station Way, Brandon
Suffolk IP27 0BH
Tel: 01842 814414
email: contact@tw-wines.com
web: www.tw-wines.com

Winner for
England & Overall Winner

Sketch (Lecture Room & Library)
London W1   Page 353

This one-time HQ of Christian Dior comes brimful of surprises, outrageous flamboyancy and refinement. A collaboration between Mourad Mazouz and Parisian super-chef Pierre Gagnaire that offers a multi-level food-based extravaganza, which includes the vibrant, ground-floor Gallery brasserie, plus the cool Parlour tea room by day, hyper-trendy bar by night.

An outstanding wine list from all perspectives - beautifully presented, with helpful and accurate comments in a clear and inviting layout. There are 5 pages of wines by the glass – with many affordable choices; a fine selection of grand wines e.g. Yquem; 7 pages of Champagnes (including 22 rosé); a range of sizes, including magnums, jeroboams and double-magnums. With a sherries list, and good German wines there is a fine diversity across Old and New Worlds.

Winner for
Scotland

Killiecrankie House Hotel
Perth & Kinross, Killiecrankie   Page 633

A relaxing country hotel, built as a dower house in 1840, and set in mature landscaped gardens overlooking the River Garry and the Pass of Killiecrankie. The hotel maintains consistently high standards and a sound reputation for accomplished modern Scottish cooking. The compact fixed-price dinner menu changes daily and is driven by fresh local produce, including game and fish as well as herbs and vegetables from the kitchen garden.

In the final shortlist for the last few years and now, finally, the winner. The wine list has personality all through it and is constantly evolving. There are good notes and tips, an eclectic selection and some wonderful value. The personal choice shines through, with some especially fine choices from Italy, Spain and the US.

Winner for
Wales

The Bell at Skenfrith
Skenfrith, Monmouthshire   Page 673

Standing beside the River Monnow in a lovely village setting, this stylishly refurbished former coaching inn still retains much charm and character. Beams, flagstone floor and big fires blend with plain walls and simple wooden tables that contribute to the understated elegance, backed by relaxed, friendly and efficient service. The menu follows a modern British approach, with keen attention to seasonality and the use of quality local produce - with the herbs used in the kitchen's well-presented dishes grown in The Bell's own garden.

A previous wine award winner that continues to show great enthusiasm. The list offers great wines by the glass, a fine selection of Cognacs, well written notes and superb value. 'It creates a feeling of trust.'

Local British Produce *by Mark Taylor*

A few years ago, chefs and restaurateurs prided them-selves on sourcing ingredients from far-flung corners of the globe. They would search the ends of the earth for out-of-season Mexican asparagus, African runner beans, New Zealand lamb and French apples. How times change. Now, the buzz words are 'local' and 'seasonal' and if it's not local and seasonal, then it has to be 'organic' or 'free-range'. Ideally, it will be all of these things.

Consumer demand for locally-produced food is continuing to rise. You only have to look at the enormous growth in numbers of farmers' markets, farm shops and box schemes to see that the pendulum has swung back towards sourcing as much local and British produce as possible.

According to research, a quarter of the adult population now claims to have a commitment to buying locally-reared and grown produce. Their reasons for doing so are because they want to support the local economy and also because they believe that buying their food direct from the farmer or grower means it must be fresher, and tastier and healthier. As a nation, we are also becoming more and more conscious of the importance of buying food that is environmentally friendly and sustainable. We are all aware that we must endeavour to reduce our carbon footprint and one of the most significant ways of doing this is by buying our food locally and in season. It sounds obvious, but buying strawberries grown locally in July or the first crop of English asparagus in May will be infinitely better for the environment than produce that has been grown in hothouses the other

side of the world and air-freighted thousands of miles to Britain. They will, of course, also taste considerably better than their imported equivalents - much of which will be days, rather than hours, old before it reaches our plates.

Research shows that nearly two-thirds of UK consumers are more likely to buy from a business they think is taking action to tackle climate change and therefore reducing its carbon footprint. Nearly three-quarters of UK consumers are concerned about climate change and their own carbon footprint and two-thirds want to know the carbon footprint of the products and services they buy. Two-thirds of UK consumers are more likely to buy products with a low carbon footprint, which is why they increasingly favour purchasing their food and drink from a farmers' market, where the stallholders have travelled just a few miles to sell their produce.

Appropriately, this edition of the AA Restaurant Guide sees the launch of its first Regional Food Awards. The awards have been sponsored by Food from Britain, the market development consultancy commissioned by the government to support the growth of quality regional food producers and increase exports of UK food and drink. Food from Britain works with over 700 UK food and drink companies every year to grow their business across the world and its website has a database of 4,000 regional producers for consumers and the hospitality industry to tap into.

In the Guide, we are highlighting with a strawberry icon those restaurants that buy regionally, cook seasonally and go that bit further when it comes to reducing food miles and forging strong working relationships with their local suppliers.

The purpose of these awards is to showcase and encourage the use of quality regional ingredients from across the UK by AA-recommended restaurants, and also to widen awareness of quality regional products among consumers.

The awards will go to those establishments which

invest time and effort into sourcing and demonstrating a skilful use of local and regional ingredients, especially those which are distinctive to the area. These are establishments which adopt a clear and effective marketing of local and regional produce on their menus and websites, and also by training their staff about the importance of sourcing British produce. And, of course, the awards also reflect quality cooking of these regional ingredients in establishments which have achieved at least one AA Rosette.

So, what does 'regional' mean in the context of these awards?

The AA and Food from Britain want to recognise restaurants which are committed to local purchasing wherever it is possible and relevant.

It would be unreasonable and short-sighted to expect innovative, ingredient-driven chefs and restaurateurs not to buy Amalfi lemons, Sicilian tomatoes and Indian mangoes when available because they are arguably the finest in the world, but we would expect them to buy their staple and core seasonal ingredients from local growers and suppliers. We would expect a restaurant on the Cornish or Devon coast to buy its fish direct from the markets of Newlyn or Brixham, rather than go through a middleman who buys it from the same market, sends it off to be processed and then dispatches it to the restaurant.

Similarly, we would expect a restaurant in Wales to source its lamb from a local farm, rather than buy in cheaper, frozen cuts from New Zealand.

Of course, a restaurant in the land-locked Midlands will struggle to find local seafood, but in those instances, we would expect seafood to be sourced from British markets before looking elsewhere.

British food has seen a remarkable renaissance in recent years and we are now respected by many of our European neighbours for the diverse and delicious range of food produced here.

According to Food from Britain, consumers are willing to pay more for locally-produced food. Around 70% of British consumers want to buy regional produce and 49% want to buy more than they do now, so there is a consumer demand for locally-sourced food. There is the added benefit that it supports the local community and a restaurant or gastro-pub is likely to get more local recommendations if it's buying from the farmer next door or the market gardener down the road.

'Intelligent cooking and shopping have always been a cornerstone of the AA Rosette awards, and this is now highlighted even more by our Regional Food Awards' says The AA Chief Inspector Peter Birnie.

If you are aware of any restaurants which are fine examples of this flag-waving approach to sourcing British produce, please let us know. We will check them out for the next edition of the AA Restaurant Guide and see if they are worthy contenders for the coveted strawberry icon.

By supporting local farmers and producers, we are not just keeping local industry alive and kicking, but also helping to support the environment by reducing the food miles that our own food travels. The shorter the distance food travels from field to plate, the better.

Ever mindful of their customers' needs and moods, an increasing number of restaurants are now trying to buy as intelligently and sustainably as they can.

The food and drink manufacturing industry is the largest manufacturing sector in the UK, with a turn-over of £70bn, accounting for 15% of the total manufacturing sector. Food and drink remains the biggest spending category in the country. In 2005, consumer spending on food and drink was nearly £153.8bn - 20% of UK consumer expenditure.

There has never been a better time to eat fresh local produce in our restaurants and launch of our Regional Food Awards is another way of recognising the renaissance of British food.

The Top
Ten Per Cent

Each year all the restaurants in the AA Restaurant Guide
are awarded a specially commissioned plate that marks
their achievement in gaining one or more AA Rosettes.
The plates represent a partnership between the AA and
Villeroy & Boch two quality brands working together to
recognise high standards in restaurant cooking.

Restaurants awarded three, four or five AA Rosettes
represent the Top Ten Per Cent of the restaurants in this
Guide. The pages that follow list those establishments
that have attained this special status

Villeroy & Boch
1748

Villeroy & Boch in the restaurant

Villeroy & Boch is Europe's best selling tableware brand
and, with its renowned tiles and bathrooms division,
the company is also the world's leading ceramics
manufacturer. At prestigious restaurants and hotels
around the globe, Villeroy & Boch is the first choice of
discerning chefs and restaurant managers, who choose
Villeroy & Boch china, glassware and cutlery for its
stunning design and uncompromising quality.

Villeroy & Boch in your home

Villeroy & Boch is no stranger to the domestic dining
table either! Since 1748, brides and grooms have
chosen the brand as much for the reputation and status
of the name as for the quality and diversity of the
designs. But the appeal of Villeroy & Boch is not limited
to wedding lists. China cutlery and glass bearing the
Villeroy & Boch name is simply chosen by people who
want the best!

Villeroy & Boch in the future

Each year Villeroy & Boch brings an array of
exciting new designs to its diverse range of tableware
collections. Among new additions this year are two
premium collections with luxurious gold enhancements.
'Golden Garden' is an elegant oriental design featuring a
floral pattern. An opulent Art Deco design 'Vivian' offers
sumptuous hues of chocolate and gold and a wide range
of plates, platters and dishes ideal for entertaining.
Villeroy & Boch also continues to develop the signature
NewWave collection with an asymmetrical wave design
which is now available with an African pattern.

Villeroy & Boch for every occasion and every home

Formal or relaxed, patterned or plain, cutlery, glass and
china from Villeroy & Boch suits every occasion and
every budget. It will give lasting pleasure time and again,
and is available from quality stores throughout the UK.
Call 0208 875 6060 or visit www.villeroy-boch.com for
more information.

The Top Ten Per Cent

LONDON
ⓐⓐⓐⓐⓐ

Foliage
Mandarin Oriental Hyde Park
66 Knightsbridge, SW1
020 7235 2000

Pétrus
The Berkeley, Wilton Place, Knightsbridge, SW1
020 7235 1200

Restaurant Gordon Ramsay
68 Royal Hospital Road, SW3
020 7352 4441

Tom Aikens
43 Elystan Street, SW3
020 7584 2003

ENGLAND
ⓐⓐⓐⓐⓐ

BERKSHIRE
The Fat Duck
High Street, BRAY, SL6 2AQ
01628 580333

OXFORDSHIRE
Le Manoir aux Quat' Saisons
GREAT MILTON, OX44 7PD
01844 278881

LONDON
ⓐⓐⓐⓐ

The Capital
Basil Street, SW3
020 7589 5171

Aubergine
11 Park Walk, SW10
020 7352 3449

Locanda Locatelli
8 Seymour Street, W1
020 7935 9088

Pied à Terre
34 Charlotte Street, W1
020 7636 1178

Sketch (Lecture Room & Library)
9 Conduit Street, W1
0870 777 4488

The Square
6-10 Bruton Street, W1
020 7495 7100

LONDON, GREATER
ⓐⓐⓐⓐ

Chapter One
Farnborough Common, Locksbottom,
BROMLEY, BR6 8NF
01689 854848

ENGLAND
ⓐⓐⓐⓐ

BERKSHIRE
Waterside Inn
Ferry Road, BRAY, SL6 2AT
01628 620691

The Vineyard at Stockcross
Stockcross, NEWBURY, RG20 8JU
01635 528770

CAMBRIDGESHIRE
Midsummer House
Midsummer Common, CAMBRIDGE, CB4 1HA
01223 369299

CUMBRIA
L'Enclume
Cavendish Street, CARTMEL, LA11 6PZ
01539 536362

DERBYSHIRE
Fischer's Baslow Hall
Calver Road, BASLOW, DE45 1RR
01246 583259

DEVON
Gidleigh Park
CHAGFORD, TQ13 8HH
01647 432367

GLOUCESTERSHIRE
Le Champignon Sauvage
24 Suffolk Road, CHELTENHAM, GL50 2AQ
01242 573449

GREATER MANCHESTER
Juniper
21 The Downs, ALTRINCHAM, WA14 2QD
0161 929 4008

LINCOLNSHIRE
Winteringham Fields
WINTERINGHAM, DN15 9PF
01724 733096

NOTTINGHAMSHIRE
Restaurant Sat Bains with Rooms
Lenton Lane, NOTTINGHAM, NG7 2SA
0115 986 6566

RUTLAND
Hambleton Hall Hotel
Hambleton, OAKHAM, LE15 8TH
01572 756991

YORKSHIRE, NORTH
The Burlington Restaurant
The Devonshire Arms Country House Hotel & Spa
BOLTON ABBEY, BD23 6AJ
01756 710441

JERSEY
⊛⊛⊛⊛

Bohemia
The Club Hotel & Spa, Green Street, ST HELIER, JE2 4UH
01534 880588

SCOTLAND
⊛⊛⊛⊛

CITY OF EDINBURGH
Restaurant Martin Wishart
54 The Shore, Leith, EDINBURGH, EH6 6RA
0131 553 3557

HIGHLAND
The Boath House
Auldearn, NAIRN, IV12 5TE
01667 454896

PERTH & KINROSS
Andrew Fairlie @ Gleneagles
AUCHTERARDER, PH3 1NF
01764 694267

NORTHERN IRELAND
⊛⊛⊛⊛

CO BELFAST
Deanes
34-40 Howard Street, BELFAST, BT1 6PF
028 9033 1134

REPUBLIC OF IRELAND
⊛⊛⊛⊛

DUBLIN
Restaurant Patrick Guilbaud
Merrion Hotel, 21 Upper Merrion Street
01 676 4192

LONDON
⊛⊛⊛

EC1
Club Gascon
57 West Smithfield
020 7796 0600

EC2
Aurora at Great Eastern Hotel
Liverpool Street
020 7618 7000

Rhodes Twenty Four
Tower 42, Old Broad Street
020 7877 7703

N7
Morgan M
489 Liverpool Road, ISLINGTON
020 7609 3560

NW1
Odette's
130 Regent's Park Road
020 7586 8569

SE3
Chapter Two
43-45 Montpelier Vale,
Blackheath Village
020 8333 2666

SW1
Nahm
The Halkin Hotel, Halkin Street
020 7333 1234

La Noisette
164 Sloane Street
020 7750 5000

One-O-One
Sheraton Park Tower, 101 Knightsbridge
020 7290 7101

Zafferano
15 Lowndes Street
020 7235 5800

SW3
Rasoi Restaurant
10 Lincoln Street
020 7225 1881

SW4
Trinity Restaurant
4 The Polygon, Clapham Old Town
020 7622 1199

SW17
Chez Bruce
2 Bellevue Road, Wandsworth Common
020 8672 0114

W1
Angela Hartnett at The Connaught
Carlos Place
020 7592 1222

Arbutus Restaurant
63-64 Frith Street
020 7734 4545

L'Escargot – The Picasso Room
48 Greek Street
020 7439 7474

Le Gavroche Restaurant
43 Upper Brook Street
020 7408 0881

Gordon Ramsay at Claridge's
Brook Street
020 7499 0099

The Greenhouse
27a Hay's Mews
020 7499 3331

The Grill (Dorchester Hotel)
Park Lane
020 7629 8888

Hakkasan
No 8 Hanway Place
020 7927 7000

Lindsay House Restaurant
21 Romilly Street
020 7439 0450

Maze
London Marriott Grosvenor Hotel,
10-13 Grosvenor Square,
020 7107 0000

Nobu
The Metropolitan, 19 Old Park Lane
020 7447 4747

Roka
37 Charlotte Street
020 7580 6464

Theo Randall, InterContinental London
1 Hamilton Place, Hyde Park Corner
020 7318 8747

Umu
14-16 Bruton Place
020 7499 8881

W4
La Trompette
5-7 Devonshire Road, CHISWICK
020 8747 1836

W6
The River Café
Thames Wharf, Rainville Road
020 7386 4200

W8
Royal Garden Hotel, Tenth Floor Restaurant
2-24 Kensington High Street
020 7361 1910

W11
The Ledbury
127 Ledbury Road, NOTTING HILL
020 7792 9090

Notting Hill Brasserie
92 Kensington Park Road
020 7229 4481

WC1
Pearl Restaurant & Bar
Renaissance Chancery Court,
252 High Holborn
020 7829 7000

WC2
L'Atelier de Joël Robuchon
13-15 West Street
020 7010 8600

Clos Maggiore
33 King Street, COVENT GARDEN
020 7379 9696

JAAN Restaurant
Swissôtel, The Howard, Temple Place
020 7836 3555

LONDON, GREATER
ⓐⓐⓐ
The Glasshouse
14 Station Road, KEW TW9 3PZ
020 8940 6777

ENGLAND
ⓐⓐⓐ
BERKSHIRE
Fredrick's Hotel, Restaurant & Spa
Shoppenhangers Road, MAIDENHEAD, SL6 2PZ
01628 581000

L'Ortolan
Church Lane, SHINFIELD, RG2 9BY
01189 888 500

BUCKINGHAMSHIRE
Hartwell House Hotel, Restaurant & Spa
Oxford Road, AYLESBURY, HP17 8NR
01296 747444

The Hand & Flowers
126 West Street, MARLOW, SL7 2BP
01628 482277

Macdonald Compleat Angler
Marlow Bridge, MARLOW, SL7 1RG
0870 4008100

Oak Room at Danesfield House
Henley Road, MARLOW, SL7 2EY
01628 891010

Waldo's Restaurant, Cliveden
Cliveden Estate, TAPLOW, SL6 0JF
01628 668561

CHESHIRE
The Arkle
Chester Grosvenor & Spa
Eastgate, CHESTER, CH1 1LT
01244 324024

CO DURHAM
Seaham Hall Hotel – The White Room Restaurant
Lord Byron's Walk, SEAHAM, SR7 7AG
0191 516 1400

CORNWALL & ISLES OF SCILLY
Restaurant Nathan Outlaw
Marina Villa Hotel
17 Esplanade, FOWEY, PL23 1HY

Well House Hotel
St Keyne, LISKEARD, PL14 4RN
01579 342001

The Seafood Restaurant
Riverside, PADSTOW, PL28 8BY
01841 532700

St Martin's on the Isle
Lower Town, ST MARTIN'S, TR25 0QW
01720 422092

Hotel Tresanton
Lower Castle Road, ST MAWES, TR2 5DR
01326 270055

CUMBRIA
Rampsbeck Country House Hotel
WATERMILLOCK, CA11 0LP
017684 86442

Gilpin Lodge Country House Hotel & Restaurant
Crook Road, WINDERMERE, LA23 3NE
015394 88818

Holbeck Ghyll Country House Hotel
Holbeck Lane, WINDERMERE, LA23 1LU
015394 32375

Linthwaite House Hotel & Restaurant
Crook Road, WINDERMERE, LA23 3JA
015394 88600

The Samling
Ambleside Road, WINDERMERE, LA23 1LR
015394 31922

DERBYSHIRE
The Old Vicarage
Ridgeway Moor, RIDGEWAY, S12 3XW
0114 247 5814

DEVON
22 Mill Street
22 Mill Street, CHAGFORD, TQ13 8AW
01647 432244

The New Angel
2 South Embankment, DARTMOUTH, TQ6 9BH
01803 839425

The Horn of Plenty
GULWORTHY, PL19 8JD
01822 832528

The Masons Arms Inn
KNOWSTONE, EX36 4RY
01398 341231

Lewtrenchard Manor
LEWDON, EX20 4PN
01566 783222

Bovey Castle
MORETONHAMPSTEAD, TQ13 8RE
01647 445000

Hotel Endsleigh
Milton Abbot, TAVISTOCK, PL19 0PQ
01822 870000

Corbyn Head Hotel & Orchid Restaurant
Sea Front, TORQUAY, TQ2 6RH
01803 213611

The Elephant Bar & Restaurant
3/4 Beacon Terrace, TORQUAY TQ1 2BH
01803 200044

DORSET
Sienna Restaurant
36 High West Street, DORCHESTER, DT1 1UP
01305 250022

**Summer Lodge Country House Hotel,
Restaurant & Spa**
EVERSHOT, DT2 0JR
01935 482000

Stock Hill Country House Hotel & Restaurant
Stock Hill, GILLINGHAM, SP8 5NR
01747 823626

GLOUCESTERSHIRE
Cotswold House
The Square, CHIPPING CAMPDEN, GL55 6AN
01386 840330

Lords of the Manor
UPPER SLAUGHTER, Cheltenham, GL54 2JD
01451 820243

5 North Street
5 North Street, WINCHCOMBE GL54 5LH
01242 604566

HAMPSHIRE
Le Poussin at Whitley Ridge Country House Hotel
Beaulieu Road, BROCKENHURST, SO42 7QL
01590 622354

36 on the Quay
47 South Street, EMSWORTH, PO10 7EG
01243 375592

Chewton Glen Hotel
Christchurch Road, NEW MILTON, BH25 6QS
01425 275341

JSW
20 Dragon Street, PETERSFIELD, GU31 4JJ
01730 262030

Avenue Restaurant
Lainston House Hotel,
Sparsholt, WINCHESTER, SO21 2LT
01962 863588

HEREFORDSHIRE
Castle House
Castle Street, HEREFORD, HR1 2NW
01432 356321

HERTFORDSHIRE
The Grove
Chandler's Cross, RICKMANSWORTH, WD3 4TG
01923 296015

KENT
Apicius
23 Stone Street, CRANBROOK, TN17 3HF
01580 714666

Read's Restaurant
Macknade Manor, FAVERSHAM, ME13 8XE
01795 535344

Thackeray's
TUNBRIDGE WELLS, TN1 1EA
01892 511921

LANCASHIRE
Northcote Manor
Northcote Road, LANGHO, BB6 8BE
01254 240555

The Longridge Restaurant
104-106 Higher Road, LONGRIDGE, PR3 3SY
01772 784969

LINCOLNSHIRE
Harry's Place
17 High Street, Great Gonerby,
GRANTHAM, NG31 8JS
01476 561780

MERSEYSIDE
Fraiche
11 Rose Mount, Oxton Village,
BIRKENHEAD, CH43 5SG
0151 652 2914

NORFOLK
Morston Hall
Morston, Holt, BLAKENEY, NR25 7AA
01263 741041

SHROPSHIRE
Mr Underhills
Dinham Weir, LUDLOW, SY8 IEH
01584 874431

Overton Grange Country House & Restaurant
Old Hereford Road, LUDLOW, SY8 4AD
01584 873500

Old Vicarage Hotel and Restaurant
WORFIELD, WV15 5JZ
01746 716497

SOMERSET
Bath Priory Hotel and Restaurant
Weston Road, BATH, BA1 2XT
01225 331922

Cavendish Restaurant
Dukes Hotel, Great Pulteney Street, BATH, BA2 4DN
01225 787960

Andrews on the Weir
Porlock Weir, PORLOCK, TA24 8PB
01643 863300

Little Barwick House
Barwick Village, YEOVIL, BA22 9TD
01935 423902

SUFFOLK
The Bildeston Crown
104 High Street, BILDESTON, IP7 7EB
01449 740510

Hintlesham Hall Hotel
HINTLESHAM, IP8 3NS
01473 652334

SURREY
The Latymer
Pennyhill Park Hotel & Spa,
London Road, BAGSHOT, GU19 5EU
01276 471774

Drake's Restaurant
The Clock House, High Street, RIPLEY, GU23 6AQ
01483 224777

SUSSEX, WEST
Queens Room at Amberley Castle
AMBERLEY, BN18 9LT
01798 831992

Ockenden Manor
Ockenden Lane, CUCKFIELD, RH17 5LD
01444 416111

Gravetye Manor Hotel
EAST GRINSTEAD, RH19 4LJ
01342 810567

The Camellia Restaurant at South Lodge Hotel
Brighton Road, LOWER BEEDING, RH13 6PS
01403 891711

WARWICKSHIRE
Mallory Court Hotel
Harbury Lane, Bishop's Tachbrook,
ROYAL LEAMINGTON SPA, CV33 9QB
01926 330214

WEST MIDLANDS
Simpsons
20 Highfield Road, Edgbaston,
BIRMINGHAM, B15 3DU
0121 454 3434

WILTSHIRE
The Bybrook at the Manor
CASTLE COMBE, SN14 7HR
01249 782206

Lucknam Park
COLERNE, SN14 8AZ
01225 742777

The Harrow Inn at Little Bedwyn
LITTLE BEDWYN, SN8 3JP
01672 870871

Whatley Manor
Easton Grey, MALMESBURY, SN16 0RB
01666 822888

YORKSHIRE, NORTH
Samuel's at Swinton Park
MASHAM, Ripon, HG4 4JN
01765 680900

Yorke Arms
RAMSGILL, HG3 5RL
01423 755243

Judges Country House Hotel
Kirklevington, YARM, TS15 9LW
01642 789000

YORKSHIRE, WEST
Box Tree
35-37 Church Street, ILKLEY, LS29 9DR
01943 608484

Anthony's Restaurant
19 Boar Lane, LEEDS, LS1 6EA
0113 245 5922

JERSEY
◉◉◉
Ocean Restaurant at the Atlantic Hotel
Le Mont de la Pulente, St Brelade, JE3 8HE
01534 744101

Longueville Manor
ST SAVIOUR, JE2 7WF
01534 725501

SCOTLAND
◉◉◉
ABERDEENSHIRE
Darroch Learg Hotel
Braemar Road, BALLATER, AB35 5UX
013397 55443

ANGUS
Castleton House Hotel
Castleton of Eassie, GLAMIS, DD8 1SJ
01307 840340

England

ENGLAND

BEDFORDSHIRE

BEDFORD
MAP 12 TL04

⚛️⚛️ Woodlands Manor Hotel

British, European NEW

Victorian manor-house experience with accomplished cuisine

☎ 01234 363281 Green Ln, Clapham MK41 6EP
e-mail: reception@woodlandsmanorhotel.com
web: www.signaturegroup.co.uk

Sitting in acres of well-tended grounds, this Victorian manor offers a warm welcome. Traditional-styled public areas include a cosy bar, while the smart restaurant is a tall, roomy affair with gold-themed décor, appropriately decked out with chandeliers, long drapes, clothed tables and high-backed chairs in coordinated colours. The cooking takes a modern approach, delivering quality ingredients in intelligently straightforward, well-executed dishes of clean-cut flavours. Expect mains such as loin of lamb with confit garlic, thyme and rosemary jus served with fine beans and potato fondant, with a hot plum and apple soufflé accompanied by Tahitian vanilla ice cream to tempt for dessert.

Times: 12.30-2/7.30-9.30, Closed L Sat **Rooms:** 32 (32 en suite) ★★★ HL **Directions:** From A6 to Clapham turn right into Green Lane

🖥️ Knife & Cleaver

☎ 01234 740 387 The Grove, Houghton Conquest MK45 3LA
web: www.knifeandcleaver.com

Modern cooking with emphasis on seasonal and local produce, in 17th-century inn with links to John Bunyan. At the time of going to press, Knife & Cleaver was awarded one rosette, see Late Entries.

Villa Rosa

☎ 01234 269259 Ram Yard MK40 1AL

Bustling, family-run Italian.

MILTON ERNEST
MAP 11 TL05

⚛️⚛️ The Strawberry Tree

Traditional British

Innovative cuisine using carefully-sourced produce in a lovely thatched cottage

☎ 01234 823633 3 Radwell Rd MK44 1RY
e-mail: strawberrytree_restaurant@yahoo.co.uk

A 17th-century thatched cottage which was originally divided into three, with a sweet shop at the front, laundry in the middle and cottage at the back. Run as a tea shop for ten years, the restaurant was then developed and refurbished, retaining original features like the bread oven, flagstone floors and inglenook fireplaces. Here you can enjoy carefully-sourced local produce like Lincoln Red beef, Suffolk lamb and organic vegetables and herbs. Try a starter of celery and celeriac soup with a lasagne of wild mushrooms, followed by breast of local pheasant with smoked bacon, roast parsnips, pumpkin, bread sauce and cep mushroom sauce. Dessert might feature white chocolate and lime parfait with mascarpone sorbet and passionfruit.

Times: 12-1.45/7-9, Closed 2 wks Jan & Sep, Sun-Tue, Closed L Sat **Directions:** M1 junct 13, 4M N of Bedford on A6

WOBURN
MAP 11 SP93

⚛️ The Inn at Woburn

Modern British

Seamless blend of old and modern in lovely market town

☎ 01525 292292 George St MK17 9PX
e-mail: enquiries@theinnatwoburn.com
web: www.theinnatwoburn.com

The original inn and courtyard-style extension are full of character with sage green paintwork and old stock brickwork set off by old-fashioned street lamps. The restaurant is named Olivier's after the chef and offers an interesting carte, a few specials and vegetarian options. Typical main courses might include loin of Woburn venison and quince jus with braised Savoy cabbage, turnip purée and Parmentier potatoes, or grilled tuna medallions with ratatouille, fennel couscous and sauce vièrge. If it's wine by the glass you'd prefer, there are more than 15. Look out for gourmet evenings.

Chef: Olivier Bertho **Owners:** Bedford Estates **Times:** 12-2.30/6-10.15 **Prices:** Fixed L £10.50-£12.50, Starter £3.25-£8.25, Main £9.25-£14.95, Dessert £4.25-£6.25, Service optional **Wine:** 15 bottles over £20, 23 bottles under £20, 18 by the glass **Notes:** Gourmet D monthly £50, Vegetarian available, Civ Wed 60, Air con **Seats:** 40, Pr/dining room 90 **Children:** Menu, Portions **Rooms:** 57 (57 en suite) ★★★ HL **Directions:** 5 mins from M1 junct 13. Follow signs to Woburn. Inn in town centre at x-rds, parking to rear via Parm St **Parking:** 80

☼☼ Paris House Restaurant

French V

Classical French cooking in an English park

☎ 01525 290692 Woburn Park MK17 9QP
e-mail: gail@parishouse.co.uk
web: www.parishouse.co.uk

Built in 1878 for the Paris Exhibition, this stunning black and white timbered house was dismantled and rebuilt on the Woburn Estate by the 9th Duke of Bedford. Over time it fell into disrepair, until the early 1980s when it was renovated and reopened in its present incarnation as a fine-dining restaurant. Chef-patron Peter Chandler rules the roost, greeting customers in friendly style, and delivering the culinary goods with aplomb. King prawns are flambéed in Pernod and garlic butter to start, while a fillet of sea bass main arrives with red wine and pancetta, and breast of corn-fed chicken is served with crayfish sauce. The pricey carte and short menu du jour are supplemented by a gastronomic menu.

Chef: Peter Chandler **Owners:** Mr P Chandler **Times:** 12-2.30/7-10.15, Closed 26 Dec, 1-17 Jan, Mon, Closed D Sun **Prices:** Fixed L £25-£55, Fixed D £55, Service optional **Notes:** Fixed L 3 courses, Vegetarian menu **Seats:** 48, Pr/dining room 16 **Children:** Menu, Portions **Directions:** M1 junct 13. From Woburn take A4012 Hockliffe, 1.75m out of Woburn village on left **Parking:** 24

BERKSHIRE

ASCOT MAP 06 SU96

☼ Macdonald Berystede Hotel & Spa

British, International

Elegant dining room offering classical, seasonal cuisine

☎ 01344 623311 Bagshot Rd, Sunninghill SL5 9JH
e-mail: general.berystede@macdonald-hotels.co.uk
web: www.berystede.com

A smart hotel with state-of-the-art leisure facilities, the Macdonald Berystede occupies an impressive, extended Victorian mansion a short canter from Ascot racecourse. The large and elegant Hyperion restaurant (named after a famous racecourse) overlooks the roof terrace (perfect for fair-weather dining), the spa and manicured grounds. The kitchen takes a modern approach with a strong classical base. The quality of the ingredients is evident in a main course of 21-day hung beef fillet, served with fondant sweet potato, spinach, braised chicory and morel jus, and to follow perhaps a rich dark chocolate tart with fudge sauce and chocolate sorbet.

Times: 12.30-2/7-9.45, Closed L Sat **Rooms:** 126 (126 en suite) ★★★★ HL **Directions:** Join A30 from M3 junct 3, A322 then left onto B3020 to Ascot or M25 - junct 13, follow signs for Bagshot. At Sunningdale turn right onto A330

BRACKNELL MAP 05 SU86

☼☼ Rowans at Coppid Beech

European, Pacific Rim V

Enjoyable dining in Alpine-style hotel

☎ 01344 303333 John Nike Way RG12 8TF
e-mail: welcome@coppid-beech-hotel.co.uk
web: www.coppidbeech.com

This popular modern hotel was built to resemble a Swiss chalet and stands beside a dry-ski slope. It boasts a health club, ice rink and

'Apres' night club, as well as a choice of restaurants: the basement Bier Keller with its brasserie-style menu, and the fine-dining Rowans. The latter is a bright, modern affair with a timber ceiling and crystal chandeliers. The modern British carte with European and Pacific Rim influences shows plenty of imagination and is extensive enough to suit most tastes. Typical choices may include a steak from the grill menu, or a more ambitious main such as Hendred Estate venison loin with turned root vegetables, rösti potato and cranberry and chocolate sauce.

Chef: Paul Zolik **Owners:** Nike Group Hotels Ltd **Times:** 12-2.15/7-10.30 **Prices:** Fixed L £17.95, Fixed D £24.95, Starter £4.95-£10.95, Main £14.25-£26, Dessert £5.25-£6.75, Service optional **Wine:** 72 bottles over £20, 29 bottles under £20, 10 by the glass **Notes:** Fixed L 3 courses, Sun L 3 courses £17.95, Vegetarian menu, Dress Restrictions, Smart casual, shirt & tie, no jeans/T-shirts, Civ Wed 300, Air con **Seats:** 120, Pr/dining room 20 **Children:** Menu, Portions **Rooms:** 205 (205 en suite) ★★★★ HL **Directions:** From M4 junct 10 follow A329(M) (Bracknell/Wokingham) to 1st exit. At rdbt take 1st exit to Binfield (B3408); hotel 200yds on right **Parking:** 350

Sultan Balti House

☎ 01344 303330 7 Great Hollands Square, Great Hollands RG12 8UX

Step from a shopping arcade into a verdant Indian orange grove. Wide menu specialises in Balti, and dishes exhibit freshness and quality.

BRAY MAP 06 SU97

☼☼☼☼☼ The Fat Duck

see page 30

☼☼ Hinds Head Hotel

British

Fine British pub food, destination dining

☎ 01628 626151 High St SL6 2AB
e-mail: info@hindsheadhotel.co.uk
web: www.hindsheadhotel.co.uk

The Hinds Head wants to be a local village pub, but as part of Heston Blumenthal's stable it will always invite interest from much further afield as gastronomes beat a path to its 15th-century door. A fascinating place with uncertain origins, perhaps a former hunting lodge or guest house for the local abbot, the inn was no stranger to celebrity in the past with guests including Prince Philip on his stag night. The main dining area on the ground floor is a light restaurant, and there's plenty of oak panelling, beams, leather chairs and real fires too. The menu is quite different to that at The Fat Duck - make no mistake, this is pub food - with traditional British dishes like pea and ham soup, oxtail and kidney pudding, Lancashire hot pot, and puddings like sherry trifle, treacle tart and banana Eton Mess.

Chef: Heston Blumenthal **Owners:** Heston Blumenthal & James Lee **Times:** 12-2.30/6.30-9.30, Closed 25-26 Dec, Closed D Sun **Prices:** Starter £5.50-£9.50, Main £10.50-£18.50, Dessert £4.95, Group min 8 service 10% **Wine:** 64 bottles over £20, 10 bottles under £20 **Seats:** 90, Pr/dining room 22 **Children:** Portions **Directions:** M4 junct 8/9, at rdbt take exit to Maidenhead Central, next rdbt take exit Bray & Windsor, after 0.5m take B3028 to Bray **Parking:** Car park across road

The Fat Duck

BRAY   MAP 06 SU97

Modern British 🍷NOTABLE WINE LIST 🖥️

The epitome of contemporary dining

☎ 01628 580333   High St SL6 2AQ
web: www.fatduck.co.uk

Who could have predicted that the well-groomed,
Thames-side village of Bray would become home to
British gastronomy. First with the Roux brothers at the
Waterside Inn (see entry) bringing French classicalism to
Britain (and training a whole generation of big name chefs),
and now Heston Blumenthal's Fat Duck, leading the way in
innovative gastronomy. Two small cottages on the main village
road seem an unassuming and unlikely international
destination of culinary discovery and home to one of the
world's best chefs, but The Fat Duck oozes understated quality
and chic. Oak beams and low ceilings are complemented by
modern art and coloured-glass screens, which combine
effortlessly with the Tudor building. Comfortable chairs and
white napery are backed by impeccable service (a real feature
of The Fat Duck experience), which is professional,
enthusiastic and friendly - with staff eager to share their
knowledge without a hint of condescension.
Blumenthal is a chef par excellence as well as a true culinary
pioneer, and a leading exponent of the scientific approach to
cuisine. Whilst there's nothing bizarre about the ingredients he
uses, it's this combination of flavours that sometimes raises
eyebrows or catches the headlines; witness a new tasting-
menu dish called Sound of the Sea (a seafood offering eaten
while listening to an iPod playing just that). But it's not just
the exciting combinations that are a hallmark of this stunning
experience, it's Heston's absolute precision and clarity of
flavour and balance that sets him apart. For the full-on show,
look to the tasting menu with its eight or so courses and
various head-turning tasters and inter-courses, though there is
also a good-value lunch option and carte, which might deliver
a best end of lamb with purée of onion and thyme, hot pot of
lamb neck, sweetbread and oyster, or perhaps a galette of
rhubarb with neroli-scented yogurt mousse, crystallised
coconut and rhubarb sorbet. Wow! An extensive wine list
rounds off the package in style. So just sit back and enjoy the
journey with a culinary alchemist at the helm.

Chef: Heston Blumenthal
Owners: Fat Duck Ltd
Times: 12-1.45/7-9.45,
Closed 2 wks at Xmas,
Mon, Closed D Sun
Prices: Fixed D £80-
£84.75, Service added but
optional 12.5%
Wine: 100 bottles over
£20, 17 by the glass
Notes: Tasting menu £115,
Vegetarian menu, Air con
Seats: 40
Children: Portions
Directions: M4 junct 8/9
(Maidenhead) take A308
towards Windsor, turn left
into Bray. Restaurant in
centre of village on right
Parking: Two village car
parks

Waterside Inn

BRAY MAP 06 SU97

French 🍷 NOTABLE WINE LIST

A gastronomic Thames-side legend delivering classic French cuisine

☎ 01628 620691 Ferry Rd SL6 2AT
e-mail: reservations@waterside-inn.co.uk
web: www.waterside-inn.co.uk

Though Bray may have become the epicentre of British gastronomy, this corner of the village will be forever France. Since 1972, the celebrated Waterside and the Roux family - a name synonymous with fine food - have been offering their special blend of classic-French-cuisine-meets-quintessential-English setting here. The Roux personnel may have changed, with son Alain having assumed the mantle of chef-patron from his father Michel in 2001, but standards at the Waterside never falter. Service here is impeccable and as good as it gets; traditional maybe, slick, polished, professional and knowledgeable, but unstuffy, friendly and genuine, and the valet parking adds just another touch of pampering. The lovely timbered building on the water's edge sports a classic, elegant dining room and, while most tables have a view of the river, the tiered terrace at the back is a magical setting to sip champagne and nibble canapés on a warm summer day watching Thames life go by.

Inside, the colour scheme is green and gold, with hand-painted frescos of flowers and lots of mirrors giving an illusion of space. Large plate-glass windows offer diners those views over the Thames, while tables come clothed in heavy white linen set off by fresh orchids, and vases of fresh lilies further complement the room's garden theme. Like the service, the food still remains rooted in classical French, so expect impeccable ingredients, luxury, high skill and clear flavours to be delivered on a repertoire of five-course menu Exceptionnel and a lengthy and appealing carte. Think grilled tender rabbit fillets served on a celeriac fondant with Armagnac sauce and glazed chestnuts, or fillet of sole filled with a soft broad bean mousse, served with baby leeks and a light champagne and sorrel sauce, with perhaps a warm golden plum soufflé to finish. The extensive and equally classy wine list stays as patriotically Gallic as the food, while peripherals like breads, amuse-bouche, pre-desserts and petits fours all hold form through to the end.

Chef: Michel Roux, Alain Roux
Owners: Michel Roux & Alain Roux
Times: 12-2/7-10, Closed 26 Dec for 5 wks, Mon, Closed L Tue, D Tue ex Jun-Aug
Prices: Fixed D £91, Starter £22-£39.50, Main £38.50-£52, Dessert £19.50-£31, Service added but optional 12.5%
Wine: 700+ bottles over £20, 4 bottles under £20, 8 by the glass
Notes: Sun L 3 courses £42-£56, Fixed D 5 courses, Vegetarian available, Dress Restrictions, Smart casual, Civ Wed 70, Air con
Seats: 75, Pr/dining room 8
Children: Min 12 yrs, Menu
Directions: M4 junct 8/9, A308(Windsor) then B3028 to Bray. Restaurant clearly signed
Parking: 20

ENGLAND

BRAY CONTINUED

⚜ Monkey Island Hotel

Modern

Fine dining in idyllic island setting

☎ 01628 623400 Old Mill Ln SL6 2EE

e-mail: salesco@monkeyisland.co.uk

web: www.monkeyisland.co.uk

This unique island hotel was once a fishing lodge used by monks and it extended over hundreds of years to form an idyllic retreat. Accessed only by footbridge, boat or helicopter, to dine here offers an experience before you've even set foot in the restaurant. The light and airy Pavilion dining room is situated at the head of the island and has wonderful upstream Thames-side views. In summer, lunches and afternoon teas are served on the outside terrace. A team of chefs prepare contemporary international cuisine like confit of duck marinated in orange and honey served with creamed potato and parsnip, baby vegetables and a red wine jus, and to finish, perhaps crème brûlée with a chocolate-dipped tuile biscuit.

Chef: Gary Devereaux, Raj Maharjan **Owners:** Metropolitan Hotels International **Times:** 12-2.30/7-9.30 **Prices:** Fixed L £30, Fixed D £40, Starter £9.50-£12, Main £22-£29.50, Dessert £8.50-£9.95, Service added but optional 10% **Wine:** 61 bottles over £20, 10 bottles under £20, 7 by the glass **Notes:** Fixed L 4 courses, Fixed D 6 courses, Dress Restrictions, Smart casual, no trainers or shorts, Civ Wed 120 **Seats:** 80, Pr/dining room 120 **Children:** Menu, Portions **Rooms:** 26 (26 en suite) ★★★★ HL **Directions:** M4 junct 8/9, A308 towards Windsor, before flyover turn left towards Bray village, turn right at Crown pub then follow signs **Parking:** 100

⚜⚜ The Riverside Brasserie

French

Brasserie dining beside Thames-side marina

☎ 01628 780553 Bray Marina SL6 2EB

e-mail: grrydws@aol.com

web: www.riversidebrasserie.co.uk

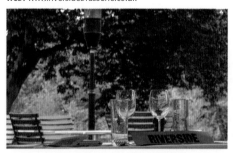

Housed in a simple, café-like building in Bray marina, this contemporary, no-frills riverside eatery functions as a pit-stop for boats on the Thames, and draws the summer crowds for leisurely alfresco lunches on the waterside decked terrace. Expect wooden floors, an open-to-view kitchen, a relaxed atmosphere, and unpretentious yet accomplished brasserie fare. Using top-notch ingredients, clean, well-presented dishes mix classics such as braised belly pork with celeriac remoulade or rib-eye steak with triple-cooked chips and bone marrow sauce, with more innovative, Mediterranean-inspired ideas, for example spaghetti with cockles, and confit of sea bream on crushed potatoes with fennel purée. Classic puddings include chocolate tart and apple crumble.

Times: 12-3/6.30-10 **Directions:** Off A308, signed Bray Marina

⚜⚜⚜⚜ Waterside Inn

see page 31

Slice Restaurant

☎ 01628 788999 Old Mill Ln SL6 2BG

New concept of Italian cuisine, combining chic city cuisine and traditional wholesome rural dining.

CHIEVELEY   MAP 05 SU47

⚜⚜ The Crab at Chieveley

Modern British V

Award-winning seafood restaurant

☎ 01635 247550 Wantage Rd RG20 8UE

e-mail: info@crabatchieveley.com

web: www.crabatchieveley.com

A deceptively simple cooking style belies the abundance of skill to be found in the kitchen at this former downland pub, but don't be fooled - expect top-notch cooking conjured from the freshest fish and seafood available. Tastefully transformed into a well-appointed hotel, there's a cosy bar and two dining areas: a formal room with red and chocolate coloured leather seating, and a more relaxed space with polished wooden tables. This former winner of the AA award for best seafood offers an extensive menu that will delight fish fanciers. Typically dishes include baked monkfish with lentils and pancetta, whole plaice with caper beurre noisette, or roast turbot with red wine jus. Finish with vanilla pannacotta and passionfruit jelly with a refreshing blackcurrant sorbet.

Chef: David Horridge **Owners:** David & Jackie Barnard **Times:** 12/11 **Prices:** Fixed L £10-£17.50, Fixed D £29.50-£33, Service optional, Group min 6 service 10% **Wine:** 8 bottles under £20, 14 by the glass **Notes:** Fish tasting menu available, Vegetarian menu, Vegetarian menu, Civ Wed 60, Air con **Seats:** 120, Pr/dining room 50 **Children:** Menu, Portions **Rooms:** 14 (14 en suite) ★★★★ RR **Directions:** M4 junct 13 to Chieveley, School Rd to B4494, turn right to Wantage **Parking:** 80

see advert opposite

The Crab at Chieveley

Tel: 01635 247550
Fax: 01635 247440
Email: info@crabatchieveley.com
www.crabatchieveley.com

If it's the freshest seafood and home grown ingredients, matched with a magnificent wine list and an atmosphere that is warm and welcoming, The Crab at Chieveley should definitely be your next stop!

This 'fairytale for grown ups' serves up everything you could wish for in an intimate dinner for two or that something different for larger parties and special occasions.

Coupled with 15 opulent Famous Rooms, named and designed after exotic resorts around the world, some boasting private outdoor hot tubs, The Crab is not just a leading seafood restaurant it is also an excuse to enjoy the best in food and wine.

COOKHAM — MAP 06 SU88

◉◉ Malik's

Indian, Bangladeshi

Genuine Indian cooking in a very English setting

☎ 01628 520085 High St SL6 9SF

web: www.maliks.co.uk

The setting for this award-winning Indian restaurant is an ivy-covered former coaching inn on the River Thames in the village of Cookham. The intimate interior comprises white-clothed tables set on wooden floors, each decorated with flowers and large church candles in black stands, and an open fire burns in winter. The extensive menu includes a good choice of tandoori, vegetarian and traditional dishes, from kormas to vindaloos, and some speciality options such as seafood bhuna, with king scallops, squid, cuttle fish and tiger fish in the Bengali chef's special stock. Desserts such as pear simmered in a cinnamon syrup are complemented by more familiar Indian ice creams. There's also a range of banquets to choose from for private parties.

Chef: Malik Ahmed, Shapon Miah **Owners:** Malik Ahmed **Times:** 12-2.30/6-11.00, Closed 25-26 Dec, Closed L Eid festival **Prices:** Fixed D £25-£30, Starter £3.95-£7.95, Main £7.25-£15.95, Dessert £3.50-£6.95, Service added but optional 10% **Wine:** 42 bottles over £20, 10 bottles under £20, 4 by the glass **Notes:** Sun L buffet £9.95, Vegetarian available, Dress Restrictions, Smart dress **Seats:** 70, Pr/dining room 30 **Children:** Portions **Directions:** M4 junct 7, take A4 towards Maidenhead, 2m **Parking:** 26

COOKHAM DEAN — MAP 05 SU88

◉◉ The Inn on The Green

Modern European 🖳

Modern classics at a boutique hotel

☎ 01628 482638 The Old Cricket Common SL6 9NZ

e-mail: reception@theinnonthegreen.com

web: www.theinnonthegreen.com

This small, picturesque hotel nestles in a rural Berkshire village, surrounded by National Trust countryside. Its sophisticated décor and lavish furnishings - deep red velvet sofas sit beside enormous leather armchairs - combine to create a relaxed and intimate atmosphere. The restaurant is comprised of three individually-styled dining areas: an airy conservatory leading on to a courtyard where alfresco dining is enjoyed in warm weather, the wood-panelled Stublie Room, and the Lamp Room, a modern creation with exposed brickwork and a magnificent chandelier. Expect imaginative modern French classics with international influences from a kitchen that doesn't disappoint. Try entrecote steak, fried egg and wild mushrooms with bordelaise jus, or maize-fed chicken, buttered chicory, shallot and parsley roasting juices and Merlot wine.

Chef: Garry Hollihead **Owners:** Andy Taylor, Mark Fuller & Garry Hollihead **Times:** 1-4/7-10, Closed Mon, Closed L Tue-Sat, D Sun **Prices:** Fixed L £25.50, Fixed D £21.95-£25, Starter £9-£16, Main £13-£28, Dessert £6-£12, Service added but optional 12.5% **Wine:** 40 bottles over £20, 4 bottles under £20, 10 by the glass **Notes:** Civ Wed 100, Air con **Seats:** 60, Pr/dining room 35 **Children:** Portions **Rooms:** 9 (9 en suite) ★★★★ RR **Directions:** From Marlow or Maidenhead follow Cookham Dean signs. In Cookham Dean turn into Hills Lane; into National Trust road by War Memorial **Parking:** 50

FRILSHAM — MAP 05 SU57

◉ The Pot Kiln

Traditional British, French NEW 🌶

Small gastro-pub serving simple, country-style food

☎ 01635 201366 RG18 0XX

e-mail: info@potkiln.org

This small, charmingly unpretentious country pub - hidden away down a narrow country lane - is a food-focused affair owned by TV chef and presenter Mike Robinson. Off a tiny bar you will find the L-shaped dining room with warming winter fires and walls hung with hunting, shooting and fishing prints. Unclothed wooden tables add to the relaxed atmosphere, while the kitchen takes a country-style approach, strongly influenced by meat and game. Regularly-changing menus reflect the seasons and ingredient quality, and, while the cooking may be straightforward, presentation comes modern-bistro styled. Think slow-roast pork belly with caramelised beetroot, or perhaps rabbit bourguignon with green beans.

Chef: Mike Robinson **Owners:** Mike Robinson **Times:** 12-2.30/7-9.30, Closed 25 Dec, Closed D Sun **Prices:** Fixed L £18.50, Starter £6-£8.50, Main £13-£18, Dessert £6, Service added but optional 10% **Wine:** 51 bottles over £20, 8 bottles under £20, 6 by the glass **Notes:** Fixed L Mon-Thu **Seats:** 48 **Children:** Portions **Directions:** From Yattendon follow Frilsham signs, cross over motorway, along Bucklebury Road. Pub on right

HUNGERFORD   MAP 05 SU36

The Bear Hotel

Rosettes not confirmed at time of going to press

British, International NEW

Ambitious modern cooking in historic hotel

☎ 01488 682512   41 Charnham St RG17 0EL
e-mail: info@thebearhotelhungerford.co.uk
web: www.thebearhotelhungerford.co.uk

Dating back to the early 13th century, this hotel was once owned by King Henry VIII and visited by Queen Elizabeth I. It's also where the future William III met the Commissioners of James II in his bedchamber to receive the English Crown. Although it has retained its dark wooden beams, the hotel is now contemporary and stylish, with a restaurant serving British cuisine with international influences. Typical dishes include cider-baked Crottin goat's cheese tart with peppered pears, followed by line-caught sea bass with saffron potatoes and lobster and fennel jus, and rhubarb and toffee crème brûlée for dessert.

Times: 12-2/7-9, Closed L Sat, D Sun   **Rooms:** 31 (31 en suite) ★★★ HL

The Swan Inn

☎ 01488 668326   Craven Rd, Inkpen RG17 9DX

Rambling 17th-century inn where almost all food is prepared on the premises, using fresh GMO-free organic produce.

HURLEY   MAP 05 SU88

◉◉ Black Boys Inn

Traditional French

A popular choice for French cuisine

☎ 01628 824212   Henley Rd SL6 5NQ
e-mail: info@blackboysinn.co.uk
web: www.blackboysinn.co.uk

Behind the traditional façade of this 16th-century inn, smart modern décor with chic pastel shades and polished wooden tables comes together with solid beams and original floorboards. More a restaurant with rooms than village pub, this family-run establishment is a popular local haunt and attracts an appreciative crowd even on mid-week evenings. Its appealing menu is rooted in French cuisine, with a number of authentic continental delicacies coming courtesy of a weekly trip to Paris. Such attention to detail also characterises the presentation of dishes, with hearty portions delivered to the table in beautiful style. Kick off with kiln-roast River Dart smoked trout and crayfish with watercress purée perhaps, before tucking into steamed Cornish monkfish with scallops, Toulouse cassoulet and Xérès vinegar.

Chef: Simon Bonwick   **Owners:** Adrian & Helen Bannister   **Times:** 12-2/7-9, Closed 2 wks Xmas, 2 wks Aug, BHs, Mon, Closed D Sun   **Prices:** Starter £7.50-£8.95, Main £12.50-£17.50, Dessert £6.25, Service optional   **Wine:** 58 bottles over £20, 16 bottles under £20, 34 by the glass   **Seats:** 45, Pr/dining room 12   **Children:** Min 12yrs   **Rooms:** 8 (8 en suite) ★★★★ RR   **Directions:** M40 junct 4, A404 towards Henley, then A4130. Restaurant 3m from Henley-on-Thames   **Parking:** 45

HURST   MAP 05 SU77

◉◉ The Castle Inn

British, French

Fine dining in an ancient building

☎ 0118 934 0034   Church Hill RG10 0SJ
e-mail: info@castlerestaurant.co.uk
web: www.castlerestaurant.co.uk

Step back in time as you stand outside this 500-year-old building opposite the village church. Inside, the décor has been brought right up to date with a modern, minimalist feel; the restaurant has exposed brick walls, chocolate brown chairs and oakwood floors. There's a lively bar with dark green furnishings and low coffee tables and an upstairs gallery room overlooks beautiful countryside. Rustic French cuisine and classic British dishes form the bulk of the menu, with terrine de campagne and moules marinière typical starters. Mains range from straightforward fare (steak and ale pie with hand-cut chips) to more complex options such as roast suckling pig with sage and onion stuffing, baked apple and cider jus.

Chef: Jerome Leopold   **Owners:** Amanda Hill   **Times:** 12-2/6.30-9.30   **Prices:** Fixed L £10, Fixed D £15, Starter £4.50-£7, Main £10-£16, Dessert £5-£6, Group min 10 service 10%   **Wine:** 42 bottles over £20, 16 bottles under £20, 7 by the glass   **Notes:** ALC only at wknds   **Seats:** 80, Pr/dining room 40   **Children:** Portions   **Directions:** M4 junct 10, A329(M) towards Reading (E). Take first exit to Winnersh/Wokingham. Continue for 1m, at Sainsbury's turn left into Robin Hood Lane. Continue for 1.5m and go straight when approaching sharp left bend towards St Nicholas Church   **Parking:** 43

LAMBOURN   MAP 05 SU37

◉◉ The Hare Restaurant @ The Hare & Hounds

Modern European

Assured cooking in stylishly converted pub

☎ 01488 71386   RG17 7SD
e-mail: cuisine@theharerestaurant.co.uk
web: www.theharerestaurant.co.uk

This smartly painted former pub is located at a crossroads just outside the horse-racing village of Lambourn. Rambling dining rooms sport a bright, modern and stylish décor, with slate floors, exposed beams, rustic wooden tables, and squashy leather sofas by the log fire. This is a relaxing and informal setting in which to sample some ambitious cooking that combines British with modern European influences. Sensibly compact menus (including a tasting option) are well balanced, using top-notch ingredients and interesting combinations to produce some adventurous dishes; perhaps halibut and frogs' legs with rosemary risotto balls and tomato cassonade, or veal cheek and bavette with swede purée and young onions. The lunch menu offers good value.

CONTINUED

Fredrick's Hotel, Restaurant & Spa

MAIDENHEAD MAP 06 SU88

Modern British, French

Accomplished cooking at a luxurious retreat

☎ 01628 581000 Shoppenhangers Rd SL6 2PZ
e-mail: eat@fredricks-hotel.co.uk
web: www.fredricks-hotel.co.uk

An oasis of calm only minutes from the M4, this luxury hotel knows a thing or two about pampering its guests. Luxurious rooms and a swanky spa would be reason enough to visit, but add exquisite cuisine from an experienced kitchen and you're in for a treat. The elegant restaurant is traditionally styled in blues and golds with a backdrop of striking artwork and views over the terrace, patio and well-tended gardens. Enjoy aperitifs in the bar or on the patio in summer, and then take your seat for some accomplished cooking.

Expect classic French and British dishes with a contemporary touch from a kitchen that likes to dot its menus with luxury ingredients and high-quality produce. A selection of old favourites such as grilled Dover sole or tournedos au poivre should suit those in the mood for familiar fare, while the more adventurous might try suprême of John Dory with scallops and blood orange sauce, or saddle of wild venison with a cep and nut crust and potato gratin.

Chef: Brian Cutler
Owners: FW Lösel
Times: 12-2.30/7-10,
Closed 25 Dec, 1 Jan,
Closed L Sat
Prices: Fixed L £25.50,
Fixed D £43.50, Starter
£14.50-£18.50, Main
£25.50-£36, Dessert
£11.50, Service optional
Wine: All bottles over £20,
6 by the glass
Notes: Fixed L 2 or 3
courses, Sun L 3 courses
£36.50 incl coffee,
Vegetarian available, Dress
Restrictions, Smart casual,
Civ Wed 120, Air con
Seats: 60, Pr/dining room
140
Children: Portions
Rooms: 34 (34 en
suite)★★★★ HL
Directions: From M4 junct
8/9 take A404(M), then
turning (junct 9A) for Cox
Green/White Waltham. Left
on to Shoppenhangers Rd,
restaurant 400 mtrs on
right
Parking: 90

Chef: Tristan Lee Mason **Owners:** Paul Whitford & Helen Windridge
Times: 12-2/7-9.30, Closed 2 wks Xmas, 2 wks summer, Mon, Closed D
Sun **Prices:** Fixed L £19, Fixed D £43, Service optional, Group min 10
service 10% **Wine:** 70 bottles over £20, 7 bottles under £20, 8 by the glass
Notes: Tasting menu 7 courses £65 **Seats:** 50, Pr/dining room 24
Children: Portions **Directions:** M4 junct 14, A338 towards Wantage, left
onto B4000 towards Lambourn, restaurant 3m on left **Parking:** 30

MAIDENHEAD   MAP 06 SU88

◉◉◉ Fredrick's Hotel, Restaurant & Spa

see opposite

◉ The Royal Oak at Paley Street

British, French

Village gastro-pub with celebrity connections

☎ 01628 620541 Paley St, Littlefield Green SL6 3JN
e-mail: royaloakmail@aol.com
web: www.theroyaloakpaleystreet.com

Jointly owned by TV presenter Michael Parkinson and his son, Nick, this
whitewashed village pub south of Maidenhead has a reputation for great
music, with Jamie Cullum, Katie Melua and Amy Winehouse among the
artists to have played here. Oak beams, polished wood floors, a gallery
of framed photos and blazing log fires create a convivial setting, aided by
quality piped jazz. Choose a bar snack (kippers, oysters and Guinness, or
a bacon sarnie) or something more substantial, such as pork cutlet with
red cabbage and apple sauce, or skate wing with capers, lemon and
parsley - either way, expect pub food at its honest and hearty best.

Chef: Dominic Chapman **Owners:** Nick Parkinson **Times:** 12-3/6-12,
Closed 1 Jan, Closed D Sun **Prices:** Starter £4.50-£9.50, Main £9.50-£15,
Dessert £4.95, Service optional **Wine:** 80 bottles over £20, 20 bottles
under £20, 7 by the glass **Seats:** 50 **Children:** Portions **Directions:** M4
junct 8/9. Take A308 towards Maidenhead Central, then A330 to Ascot. After
2m, turn right onto B3024 to Twyford. Second pub on left **Parking:** 70

MARSH BENHAM   MAP 05 SU46

◉ Red House

British, French

Anglo-French dining in countryside restaurant

☎ 01635 582017 RG20 8LY
web: www.theredhousepub.com

This well-presented thatched, 18th-century country dining pub started
life long ago as a bakery. There's a bar and an L-shaped dining room
with delightful countryside views. Bookcases line the dining room and
tables are well spaced; the formal look balanced by friendly and

efficient service. Expect generous modern European menus of
unpretentious dishes with clear flavours and the occasional French
and international accent. Roasted Cornish cod with casserole of beans
and calamari is a fine example of the fare.

Red House

Times: 11.30-2.30/7-9.30, Closed Xmas, New Year, Closed D Sun
Directions: 400yds off A4, 3m from Newbury, 5m from Hungerford

NEWBURY   MAP 05 SU46

◉◉ Donnington Valley Hotel & Spa

British, French 🍷 NOTABLE WINE LIST

Modern dining in impressive golfing hotel

☎ 01635 551199 Old Oxford Rd, Donnington RG14 3AG
e-mail: general@donningtonvalley.co.uk
web: www.donningtonvalley.co.uk

A smart, modern golfing hotel, with extensive conference facilities and
lovely grounds. The Wine Press restaurant is an impressive contemporary
dining area with a raised gallery around the outside looking down on to
the central restaurant area. The wine theme extends to a well-balanced
list with a large number of wines offered by the glass. When it comes to
the food, the emphasis is firmly on fresh produce, locally sourced and
simply prepared. Both classic and modern dishes are offered on a varied
menu, with a good choice of shellfish, fish, meat and vegetarian dishes.
Expect a classic moules marinière or calves' liver served with smoked
bacon, spinach, mash and black pudding.

Chef: Kelvin Johnson **Owners:** Sir Peter Michael **Times:** 12-2/7-10
Prices: Fixed L £20, Fixed D £27, Starter £7-£11, Main £10-£27, Dessert £8-
£10, Service optional **Wine:** 190 bottles over £20, 34 bottles under £20,
20 by the glass **Notes:** Sun L 1-3 courses £15-£21, Vegetarian available, Civ
Wed 85, Air con **Seats:** 120, Pr/dining room 130 **Children:** Menu,
Portions **Rooms:** 111 (111 en suite) ★★★★ HL **Directions:** M4 junct
13, A34 towards Newbury. Take immediate left signed Donnington Hotel.
At rdbt take right, at 3rd rdbt take left, follow road for 2m, hotel on right
Parking: 150
AA Hotel of the Year for England

The Vineyard at Stockcross

NEWBURY MAP 05 SU46

Modern V

Superb blend of innovation and tradition in the kitchen and setting

☎ 01635 528770 Stockcross RG20 8JU
e-mail: general@the-vineyard.co.uk
web: www.the-vineyard.co.uk

Chef: John Campbell, Peter Eaton
Owners: Sir Peter Michael
Times: 12-2/7-9.45
Prices: Fixed L £15-£25, Fixed D £35-£40, Service optional
Notes: Vegetarian menu, Civ Wed 60, Air con
Seats: 86, Pr/dining room 60
Children: Menu, Portions
Rooms: 49 (49 en suite)★★★★★ HL
Directions: M4 junct 13 join A34 Newbury bypass southbound, take 3rd exit signed Hungerford/Bath road interchange. Take 2nd exit at 1st and 2nd rdbts signed Stockcross, 0.6 mile on right
Parking: 100

Oddly, there's actually no vineyard here at Stockcross, instead it takes its name and inspiration from proprietor Sir Peter Michael's winery in California. But there's a dramatic steel 'grapevine' balustrade that wraps its way around the bright, stylish, split-level dining room, to offer a nod to this contemporary hotel's personality. And there are also two dazzling wine lists; one magnificent tome devoted appropriately to California, the other volume takes on the rest of the world.

However, this little slice of California in the Berkshire countryside is nothing if not individual, mixing the contemporary with a dash of country-house décor, and, its ultimate jewel in the crown, the platform for renowned chef John Campbell's inspired modern cuisine. Opulence reigns at this plush modern venue, though it's not over the top, with calming colours and a pleasing sense of space. Art and sculpture are another important facet of The Vineyard experience, as demonstrated by the contemporary 'Fire and Water' sculpture outside, which makes a dramatic statement, especially at night, with its flaming torches set on a large pond. Public areas provide the backdrop for a fine art collection, and there are two comfortable lounges for aperitifs or coffee. Service is expectedly slick and professional but with a friendly touch, while dining tables are attractively set in homage to John Campbell's poised, contemporary and striking cooking. Campbell's style is based on the state-of-the-art scientific approach, delivering an exciting blend of flavours, textures and top-notch ingredients. So expect innovative and visually striking dishes to thrill the palate and senses on crisply-scripted menus; think John Dory with clam risotto, or perhaps beef fillet slow-cooked with braised rib and beetroot, and to finish, perhaps 'jelly and ice cream' (port, coffee and Muscovado).

NEWBURY CONTINUED

◉ Regency Park Hotel

Modern British

Brasserie cooking with eye-catching views

☎ 01635 871555 Bowling Green Rd, Thatcham RG18 3RP
e-mail: info@regencyparkhotel.co.uk
web: www.regencyparkhotel.co.uk

Situated in this smart, stylish hotel, the Watermark restaurant overlooks pretty waterfall gardens and is an airy, modern place to dine. Open all day for breakfast, lunch and dinner, it's a serene setting, with large windows, crisp linen, and an attentive waiting team who work hard to make guests feel at home. Expect a brasserie-style menu of contemporary British and French dishes designed to suit all tastes: starters such as mussels in a white wine and parsley cream sauce perhaps, followed by pan-fried calves' liver and crispy bacon with grain mustard mash, or corn-fed chicken with sun-blushed tomato and black olive risotto. Desserts include crispy almond and date fritters with honey-whipped cream.

Chef: Laurent Guyon **Owners:** Pedersen Caterers **Times:** 12.30-2/7-10, Closed L Sat **Prices:** Starter £6.95, Main £10-£14.50, Dessert £6.75, Service optional **Wine:** 24 bottles over £20, 26 bottles under £20, 12 by the glass **Notes:** Vegetarian available, Civ Wed 100 **Seats:** 100, Pr/dining room 140 **Children:** Menu, Portions **Rooms:** 109 (109 en suite) ★★★★ HL **Directions:** M4 junct 13, follow A339 to Newbury for 2m, then take the A4 (Reading), the hotel is signed **Parking:** 210

◉◉◉◉ The Vineyard at Stockcross

see opposite

READING ⸱⸱⸱⸱ MAP 05 SU77

◉◉ Forburys Restaurant

French 🍷 NOTABLE WINE LIST

Contemporary restaurant in the Forbury Square development

☎ 0118 957 4044 & 0118 956 9191 1 Forbury Square, The Forbury RG1 3BB
e-mail: forburys@btconnect.com
web: www.forburys.com

Designed by the same architect responsible for Canary Wharf, the building has floor-to-ceiling windows overlooking Forbury Square and a terrace with heated umbrellas overlooking Forbury Gardens. The colour scheme within is sand and cream with brown leather seating and oak floors, and there's space enough for a private dining room and a contemporary-style bar in stainless steel and leather. The cooking style is French and, in addition to the seasonal carte, a good-value market menu

is available at lunch and dinner. Popular dishes include pan-fried scallops with cauliflower mash, pea broth and pancetta chips, or roasted rump of Welsh lamb with braised root vegetables and warm balsamic dressing, with pistachio and chocolate chip soufflé to finish. Great wine list.

Chef: Jose Cau **Owners:** Xavier Le-Bellego **Times:** 12-2.15/6-10, Closed 26-28 Dec, 1-2 Jan, Closed D Sun **Prices:** Fixed L £14.95-£18.95, Fixed D £18.95, Starter £7-£11, Main £12.50-£22.50, Dessert £5-£8.95, Service optional, Group min 4 service 12.5% **Wine:** 120 bottles over £20, 9 bottles under £20, 11 by the glass **Notes:** Tasting menu available, Vegetarian available, Air con **Seats:** 80, Pr/dining room 16 **Children:** Min 6 yrs, Portions **Directions:** M4 junct 11, 3m to town centre, opposite Forbury Gardens **Parking:** 40

◉◉ Millennium Madejski Hotel Reading

Modern French V 🖳

Contemporary food in striking, modern stadium complex

☎ 0118 925 3500 Madejski Stadium RG2 0FL
e-mail: sales.reading@mill-cop.com
web: www.millennium-hotels.com

Part of the Madejski Stadium complex that houses Reading Football Club and London Irish Rugby Club, the fine-dining Cilantro is a stylish, modern restaurant serving contemporary French dishes. The buzzy atmosphere is made more enjoyable by the friendly and efficient service. Have an aperitif in the Atrium bar before trying starters like braised pork belly with pineapple confit, pineapple jelly and Jerusalem artichoke. Main courses might deliver roasted quail served with pan-fried scallops, avocado purée and vitaloc potato, while a pear Tatin with beetroot sorbet and crumbled roquefort cheese might provide the finale. A seven-course menu gourmand (plus a separate vegetarian version) bolsters the upbeat package.

Chef: John O'Reilly **Owners:** Madejski Hotel Co **Times:** 7-10, Closed 25 Dec, 1 Jan, BHs, Sun, Closed L all week **Prices:** Fixed D £45-£47.50, Service optional **Wine:** 64 bottles over £20, 36 bottles under £20, 12 by the glass **Notes:** Tasting menu £52.50, Vegetarian menu, Dress Restrictions, Smart casual, Air con **Seats:** 55, Pr/dining room 12 **Children:** Min 12 yrs, Portions **Rooms:** 200 (200 en suite) ★★★★ HL **Directions:** 1m N from M4 junct 11 and 2m S from Reading town centre **Parking:** 100

L'Ortolan

SHINFIELD MAP 05 SU76

French V 💻

Serious fine dining in stylish listed building

☎ 0118 988 8500 Church Ln RG2 9BY
e-mail: info@lortolan.com
web: www.lortolan.com

This listed 17th-century converted vicarage will be known to many gourmands from its previous incarnations, receiving plaudits under Nico Ladenis and more recently John Burton Race. Today's highly talented incumbent, Alan Murchison, is a worthy successor, having in fact worked with Burton Race and also the likes of Raymond Blanc in the past. His modern French-focused cuisine - underpinned by classical foundations - now draws its own acclaim.
L'Ortolan's interior under Murchison is an altogether modern, design-focused affair, chic and sophisticated, stylish and uncluttered. The long dining room is enhanced by a small bar and conservatory, while two first-floor private dining rooms further complete the package, alongside confident, professional and friendly service. The kitchen focuses on high-quality seasonal produce, delivered via an excellent-value lunch jour, plus an appealing carte and seven-course gourmand offering. Clean, refined flavours, interesting combinations, polished presentation and obvious skill feature in sometimes complex dishes. Think seared scallops with smoked salmon, Oscietra caviar and celeriac cream to start, followed by a ballotine of organic salmon, herb crème fraîche, purple potato mousse and horseradish relish, and maybe pistachio, prune and Armagnac soufflé with its own ice cream for dessert. Peripherals like excellent breads and amuse-bouche deliver with style, too.

Chef: Alan Murchison
Owners: Alan Murchison Restaurants Ltd
Times: 11.45-2/7-10, Closed 2 wks Xmas/New yr, Mon/Sun
Prices: Fixed L £20-£49, Service added but optional
Wine: 350 bottles over £20, 5 bottles under £20, 10 by the glass
Notes: Tasting menu 7 courses £60, £99 incl wine, Vegetarian menu, Civ Wed 50
Seats: 64, Pr/dining room 20
Children: Menu, Portions
Directions: From M4 junct 11 take A33 towards Basingstoke. At 1st rdbt turn left, after garage turn left, 1m turn right at Six Bells pub. Restaurant 1st left (follow English Tourist Board Signs)
Parking: 45

READING CONTINUED

⊛ Novotel Reading Centre

Modern, International NEW

Brand new city-centre hotel with accomplished cooking

☎ 0118 952 2600   25b Friar St RG1 1DP
e-mail: h5432-fb@accor.com

This modern, city-centre hotel offers a stylish and relaxed vibe. The bar area comes open-planned and decked out with high leather seats, while the spacious, airy restaurant continues the theme. Large, bright artwork catches the eye, while some tables are designed with the business guest in mind, and have TV screens discreetly placed at the table. The kitchen's seasonal menu has something for everyone, offering varying size portions (taster, starter or main), while the accomplished cooking delivers quality ingredients with robust flavours and attractive presentation. Expect a classic côte de boeuf with béarnaise sauce, and a vanilla pannacotta finish.

Chef: Miguel Oliveira **Owners:** Novotel, Accor UK **Times:** 12/11 **Prices:** Fixed L £8.95-£28, Fixed D £14.45-£33, Starter £4.95-£7.50, Main £5.50-£20.50, Dessert £4-£5, Service optional **Wine:** 8 bottles over £20, 15 bottles under £20, 19 by the glass **Notes:** Buffet L available Mon-Fri, Vegetarian available, Air con **Seats:** 86, Pr/dining room 60 **Children:** Portions **Rooms:** 178 (178 en suite) ★★★★ HL **Directions:** Within short distance of M4 **Parking:** 18

Loch Fyne Restaurant

☎ 0118 918 5850   The Maltings, Bear Wharf, Fobney St RG1 6BT

Quality seafood chain.

LSQ2 Bar and Brasserie

☎ 0118 987 3702   Lime Square, 220 South Oak Way, Green Park RG2 6UP

Modern British fare in business park location.

Pepe Sale

☎ 0118 959 7700   3 Queens Walk RG1 7QF

Buzzing Italian/Sardinian.

SHINFIELD   MAP 05 SU76

⊛⊛⊛ L'Ortolan

see opposite

SLOUGH   MAP 06 SU97

⊛ The Pinewood Hotel

Modern European

Simple but appealing dining in a luxury small hotel

☎ 01753 824848   Uxbridge Rd, George Green SL3 6AP
e-mail: info@pinewoodhotel.co.uk
web: www.bespokehotels.com

Striking design is backed up with good levels of comfort at this new hotel just outside Slough. The Eden Brasserie specialises in food cooked on a wood-burning oven and stove, including pizzas and dishes from Greece, Israel and Morocco. There are some excellent breads, straight from the oven, and good garlicky houmous. Start with seared tiger prawns, couscous and saffron cream sauce, and follow up with chicken tagine with dried apricots and roasted almonds in a good combination of colours and textures. Finish with a generous portion of warm lemon syrup cake, or choose from the selection of cheeses served with quince jelly and pickled walnuts.

Times: 12-3/6-10 **Rooms:** 49 (49 en suite) ★★★★ HL **Directions:** Telephone for directions

SONNING   MAP 05 SU77

⊛⊛ The French Horn

Traditional French V   NOTABLE WINE LIST

Classical dining on the Thames

☎ 0118 969 2204   RG4 6TN
e-mail: info@thefrenchhorn.co.uk
web: www.thefrenchhorn.co.uk

Nestled on the banks of a sleepy stretch of the Thames, this restaurant has a long-standing reputation for quality cuisine. Take a drink in the cosy bar where a spit-roast duck turns above the fire promising good things to come, and then move through to the elegant dining room where you'll find tables set with quality ware, many with views of the river. A classical English and French menu with innovative touches suits the formal setting; start with pan-fried scallops served on a relish of cucumber and tomato with coriander and curry dressing perhaps, and then tuck into whole grilled or pan-fried Dover sole, tournedos de boeuf au vin rouge, finishing with chocolate soufflé.

Chef: G Company **Owners:** Emmanuel Family **Times:** 12-1.45/7-9.15, Closed 26-30 Dec **Prices:** Fixed L £25, Fixed D £39.50, Starter fr £9.50, Main £19.50-£38, Dessert £9.50, Service included **Wine:** 450 bottles over £20, 14 by the glass **Notes:** Vegetarian menu, Dress Restrictions, No shorts **Seats:** 70, Pr/dining room 24 **Children:** Portions **Rooms:** 21 (21 en suite) ★★★ HL **Directions:** From Reading take A4 E to Sonning. Follow B478 through village over bridge, hotel on right, car park on left **Parking:** 40

STREATLEY   MAP 05 SU58

⊛⊛ Cygnetures

British, International

Fine-dining hotel restaurant with a gorgeous Thames-side vista

☎ 01491 878800   The Swan at Streatley, High St RG8 9HR
e-mail: sales@swan-at-streatley.co.uk
web: www.swanatstreatley.co.uk

Built to service the ferry crossings before the Goring bridge was constructed, this charming 17th-century inn was apparently the site where Jerome K Jerome wrote *Three Men in a Boat*. It's easy to see why he was attracted to the beautiful Thames-side location; diners at the Cygnetures restaurant enjoy spectacular views of the river while sampling the contemporary European and international flavours of the menu. The new chef maintains high standards, drawing inspiration from the finest ingredients. Try a typical starter like giant crevettes with lemon mayonnaise, followed by a main course of crispy fillet of sea bass, globe artichokes, wild mushrooms and aged balsamic vinegar. Sweets are spot on too - iced cherry parfait with hot chocolate sauce.

CONTINUED

STREATLEY CONTINUED

Owners: John Nike Group **Times:** 12.30-2/7-10 **Prices:** Fixed L £15-£18, Fixed D £26.95-£32.95, Starter £5.95-£10.95, Main £15-£25.95, Dessert £5.95-£6.95, Service optional **Wine:** 89 bottles over £20, 31 bottles under £20, 18 by the glass **Notes:** Sun L 3 courses £18, Dress Restrictions, Smart casual, Civ Wed 150 **Seats:** 70, Pr/dining room 130 **Children:** Menu, Portions **Rooms:** 45 (45 en suite) ★★★★ HL **Directions:** Follow A329 from Pangbourne, on entering Streatley turn right at lights. Hotel on left before bridge **Parking:** 120

WINDSOR   MAP 06 SU97

◉◉ Mercure Castle Hotel

Modern European 🖾

Fine dining in centrally-located hotel with castle views

☎ 0870 4008300 01753 851577 High St SL4 1LJ

web: www.mercure-uk.com

Prominently situated opposite Sir Christopher Wren's Guildhall, this 16th-century former coaching inn is one of the oldest buildings in Windsor. Enjoying fine views of Windsor Castle, it's a popular venue for functions and weddings, from small dinners up to formal evening balls. The elegant contemporary-style restaurant is decorated in shades of aubergine and soft beige, and offers comprehensive modern international cuisine that makes the most of the finest seasonal produce, sourced from a range of suppliers countrywide. Cooking is thoughtful and innovative with a variety of classical dishes and modern interpretations on the seasonally-changing menus, complemented by an extensive wine list. Take a pan-fried fillet of red mullet, with oriental crab and sweet chilli dressing to start, and follow with lemon sole and lobster paupiette, served with a fricassée of baby vegetables and caviar.

Chef: Imad Abdul-Razzak **Times:** 12-2.30/6.30-9.45 **Prices:** Fixed L £14.50-£15.95, Fixed D £21.50, Starter £7.25-£9.95, Main £14-£21.50, Dessert £5.50-£7.50, Service added but optional 12.5% **Wine:** 67 bottles over £20, 22 bottles under £20, 14 by the glass **Notes:** Dress Restrictions, Smart casual, Civ Wed 80, Air con **Seats:** 60, Pr/dining room 300 **Children:** Menu, Portions **Rooms:** 108 (108 en suite) ★★★★ HL **Directions:** M25 junct 13 take A308 towards town centre then onto B470 to High St. M4 junct 6 towards A332, at rdbt first exit into Clarence Rd, left at lights to High St **Parking:** 112

◉◉ Sir Christopher Wren's House Hotel & Spa

Modern British

Relaxed fine dining with unbeatable views

☎ 01753 861354 Thames St SL4 1PX

e-mail: reservations@wrensgroup.com

web: www.sirchristopherwren.co.uk

Wren himself may well have approved of the Thames-side views from Strok's restaurant overlooking Eton Bridge at his one-time home; watch the sun set behind the riverbank trees from the champagne terrace. Soft downlights, flickering candles, modern and contemporary with a hint of traditional elegance is the style. The European menu with Mediterranean twists takes a modern approach with classical influences. Quality ingredients meet skilful, balanced dishes with understated presentation; think a tian of goat's cheese and roasted pepper with shaved truffle salad to open, perhaps followed by a seared scallop and crayfish risotto with Avruga caviar, or noisettes of lamb served with confit celeriac and carrots, and veal sweetbreads.

Chef: Stephen Boucher **Owners:** The Wrens Hotel Group **Times:** 12.30-2.30/6.30-10 **Prices:** Fixed L £21.50, Fixed D £28.80, Starter £7.25-£8.25, Main £18.75-£23.25, Dessert £6.50-£9.50, Service optional **Wine:** 60 bottles over £20, 5 bottles under £20, 6 by the glass **Notes:** 1st Sun each mth 3 course jazz L £34.50, Vegetarian available, Dress Restrictions, Smart casual preferred, Civ Wed 100, Air con **Seats:** 65, Pr/dining room 100 **Children:** Portions **Rooms:** 95 (95 en suite) ★★★★ HL **Directions:** Telephone for directions **Parking:** 14

🖾 Thai Square

☎ 01753 868900 29 Thames St SL4 1PR

web: www.theaa.com/travel/index.jsp

In a prime position opposite the famous castle, and with décor that combines the best of modern European and Thai design with traditional Thai artefacts. Warm, charming service.

YATTENDON   MAP 05 SU57

◉ Royal Oak Hotel

Modern European

Extensive menu and a setting to suit all occasions

☎ 01635 201325 The Square RG18 0UG

e-mail: info@royaloakyattendon.com

web: www.royaloakyattendon.com

Standing on the square of a pretty Berkshire village, within easy reach of the M4, this 16th-century inn has been attracting diners since Oliver Cromwell reputedly ate here on the eve of the Battle of Newbury. There are three separate dining venues - the brasserie, the formal restaurant and the walled garden - each serving the same menu. There's a choice of hot and cold starters, and several speciality pasta and risotto dishes. Mains take in roast partridge with Anna potatoes, root vegetables and red wine jus, or pan-fried red mullet with spinach and dill sauce.

Chef: Simon Rudd **Owners:** William Boyle **Times:** 12-2.15/7-10, Closed 1 Jan **Prices:** Fixed L £12, Starter £5.50-£9, Main £14.50-£18.50, Dessert £5.95-£7, Service added but optional 10% **Wine:** 6 by the glass **Notes:** Dress Restrictions, Smart casual preferred **Seats:** 60, Pr/dining room 10 **Children:** Portions **Rooms:** 5 (5 en suite) ★★ HL **Directions:** M4 junct 12, follow signs to Pangbourne, left to Yattendon, or M4 junct 13 follow signs to Hermitage, after Post Office turn right to Yattendon **Parking:** 25

BRISTOL

BRISTOL   MAP 04 ST57

◉ Arno's Manor Hotel

British, Mediterranean

Atmospheric hotel dining

☎ 0117 971 1461   470 Bath Rd, Arno's Vale BS4 3HQ
e-mail: arnos.manor@forestdale.com
web: www.forestdale.com

This historic 18th-century hotel was once the home of a wealthy merchant. The chapel has been transformed into a comfortable lounge and the refurbished restaurant is housed in an atmospheric conservatory-style area, created by placing a glass-domed roof over an internal courtyard. The menu is lengthy and features popular favourites alongside modern British fare. You might find starters like duck confit salad with beetroot dressing, and main courses like venison with Brussels sprout purée with port and pancetta sauce.

Times: 7-10   **Rooms:** 73 (73 en suite) ★★★ HL

◉◉ Bells Diner

Modern European 🖥

Inventive European cuisine in rustic surroundings

☎ 0117 924 0357   1-3 York Rd, Montpellier BS6 5QB
e-mail: info@bellsdiner.com
web: www.bellsdiner.com

This former grocery shop, at the heart of one of Bristol's oldest districts, continues to serve a loyal clientele. The intimate, rustic restaurant recently received a sympathetic refurbishment, but retains some of the original shop fittings and Shaker-style décor. Inventive European cooking remains the central focus with classic flavour combinations using modern and traditional techniques. Investment in new equipment reflects the owner's commitment to developing and evolving the menu to the highest standard. With a tasting menu available, typical dishes might include a starter of beef carpaccio with beetroot sorbet and horseradish cream. For a main course, try sea trout with asparagus, broad beans, peas, and liquorice sabayon. Desserts include banana soufflé with toffee ice cream.

Times: 12-2.30/7-10.30, Closed 24-30 Dec, Sun, Closed L Mon & Sat
Directions: Telephone for further details

◉ Bordeaux Quay

European NEW 🐌

Enthusiastic seasonal cuisine in modern waterside warehouse restaurant

☎ 0117 906 5550   V-Shed, Cannons Rd BS1 5UH
web: www.bordeaux-quay.co.uk

Decked out over two floors and set around a wide central atrium (with ground-floor bar and deli, and smart first-floor restaurant), this modern warehouse restaurant overlooks the waterfront in the centre of the city. Light and airy, the high-ceilinged, open-plan restaurant cultivates the contemporary theme, with bags of elegant wood and a nod to industrial pipe work. The kitchen takes an equally modern, intelligently straightforward line, using carefully-sourced regional produce. Think a tranche of halibut delivered with spinach, morels and a butter sauce, and perhaps treacle tart with vanilla ice cream to finish.

Times: 12.30-3/6.30-10.30 (last orders 10), Closed Sun

◉ The Bowl Inn

Modern British NEW

Carefully prepared dishes in traditional surroundings

☎ 01454 612757   16 Church Rd, Lower Almondsbury BS32 4DT
e-mail: reception@thebowlinn.co.uk
web: www.thebowlinn.co.uk

Nestling on the edge of the Severn Vale, this popular whitewashed 16th-century village inn comes brimful of history and all the traditional trappings. Lilies restaurant continues the theme, with beamed ceilings, country furniture and tables donned with linen cloths. It's an intimate, relaxed and friendly affair, while the bar offers a more informal menu and range of cask ales. The kitchen takes a modern approach, using the best local and free-range produce; take an assiette of Oakleaze Farm pork served with choucroute and a red wine and marjoram sauce, or perhaps pan-fried halibut with a clam, leek and potato broth.

Chef: Ricky Stephenson, David Jones   **Owners:** P Alley   **Times:** 12-2.30/6-9.30, Closed 25 Dec   **Prices:** Starter £4.95-£6.95, Main £11.95-£19.95, Dessert £5.25, Service optional   **Wine:** 5 bottles over £20, 27 bottles under £20, 9 by the glass   **Notes:** Vegetarian available, Dress Restrictions, Smart casual   **Seats:** 60, Pr/dining room 25   **Children:** Menu, Portions   **Rooms:** 13 (15 en suite) ★★ HL   **Directions:** M5 junct 6 towards Thornbury, take 3rd left into Over Ln, then 1st right into Sundays Hill and next right into Church Rd   **Parking:** 60

◉ The Bristol Marriott Royal

Traditional British

Stylish venue offering seasonal British cuisine

☎ 0117 925 5100   College Green BS1 5TA
e-mail: bristol.royal@marriotthotels.co.uk
web: www.marriott.co.uk

Right in the city centre, next to the cathedral and the historic harbour, this stunning hotel has an array of impressive facilities. The restaurant is truly spectacular with high sandstone walls, balconies and a stained-glass wall. Tables are classically dressed with white linen, silver cutlery and sparkling glassware. Quintessentially British dishes are offered as in a starter of tomato and Blue Vinney cheese tart, followed by pot-roasted Gloucestershire chicken, candied apple with Taunton cider

CONTINUED

BRISTOL CONTINUED

sauce and fondant potato. Finish off the meal with a steamed chocolate sponge with mint choc chip ice cream perhaps. There's also a Champagne Bar opposite the restaurant.

Times: 12-2.30/7-10, Closed Sun, Mon, BHs **Rooms:** 242 (242 en suite) ★★★★ HL **Directions:** Next to cathedral by College Green

◉◉ Culinaria

Mediterranean

Simple, Mediterranean cuisine to eat in or take away

☎ 0117 973 7999 1 Chandos Rd, Redland BS6 6PG

web: www.culinariabristol.co.uk

Culinaria is a great concept combining the popularity of restaurant dining with the takeaway option of enjoying a meal in your own home. The traditional bistro restaurant serves simple, beautifully executed dishes in a contemporary setting, while in another room the deli and takeaway serve a growing customer base, offering chilled and frozen dishes to warm at home. Mediterranean-style cooking sees scallops with tomato risotto and pesto to start, with main courses ranging from monkfish with green peppercorn sauce to pheasant braised with celery, port, chestnuts and orange sauce. Desserts may include chocolate St Emilion. Both restaurant and takeaway menus change weekly and are updated on the restaurant website.

Chef: Stephen Markwick **Owners:** Stephen & Judy Markwick **Times:** 12-2/6.30-9.30, Closed Xmas, New Year, BHs, Sun-Tue, Closed L Wed-Thur **Prices:** Starter £6-£7.50, Main £11.95-£15.50, Dessert £6-£6.50, Service optional **Wine:** 13 bottles over £20, 20 bottles under £20, 4 by the glass **Notes:** Vegetarian available **Seats:** 30 **Children:** Portions **Parking:** On street

◉ Glass Boat Restaurant

British, European

Accurate cooking in a unique riverside setting

☎ 0117 929 0704 Welsh Back BS1 4SB

e-mail: bookings@glassboat.co.uk

web: www.glassboat.co.uk

The name sums it up; a glass-topped barge - anchored in the city centre's historic docks close to the famous Bristol Bridge - proves a popular draw for lunch or romantic candlelit dinner to the backdrop of waterfront life. Original wooden floors, simple table settings and nicely worn fixtures offer further character. The crowd-pleasing, modern-focused menu comes awash with the flavour of the Mediterranean, the cooking honest and appealing, and service friendly and efficient. The menu may include roast fillet of halibut with tagliatelle, piperade and a herb crust, or perhaps Welsh Black beef fillet served with Sardalaise potato, sauté cep and a Madeira sauce.

Chef: Matthew Woods **Owners:** Arne Ringer **Times:** 12-2.30/6.30-11, Closed 24-26 Dec, 1 Jan, Closed L Sat, D Sun **Prices:** Fixed L £10.45-£20, Fixed D £22.50, Starter £4.50-£9.95, Main £14.50-£19.95, Dessert £7.25-£7.50, Service added but optional 10% **Wine:** 100 bottles over £20, 40 bottles under £20, 8 by the glass **Notes:** Civ Wed 120, Air con **Seats:** 120, Pr/dining room 40 **Directions:** Moored below Bristol Bridge in the old centre of Bristol **Parking:** NCP

◉◉ Goldbrick House

Traditional, Italian NEW

Stylish, modern city-centre dining with quality ingredients and balanced flavours

☎ 0117 945 1950 69 Park St BS1 5PB

e-mail: info@goldbrickhouse.co.uk

web: www.goldbrickhouse.co.uk

Converted from two Georgian townhouses and a Victorian factory, Goldbrick incorporates an informal café-bar with upstairs champagne and cocktail bar, restaurant and terrace. The fine-dining restaurant has a stylish, contemporary simplicity to its design and period features are treated with sensitivity, while table service here is suitably relaxed and friendly but professional. The kitchen's approach fits the surroundings, mixing British and Italian classics (the chef hails from Sardinia) with a contemporary twist, the intelligently straightforward approach driven by quality, locally-sourced produce and well-balanced flavours. Take halibut bouillabaisse with white beans, fennel and Fowey mussels, or perhaps fillet of beef with potato and cep gratin and roasted shallots, while dessert might feature panettone bread-and-butter pudding with rum-and-raisin ice cream, or iced touron semi-fredo washed down with one of the recommended dessert wines.

Chef: Piero Boi **Owners:** Dougal Templeton, Alex Reilley & Mike Bennett **Times:** 12-3/6-10.30, Closed D Sun **Prices:** Fixed L £12, Fixed D £30, Starter £5.50-£9.50, Main £13-£22.50, Dessert £6-£7.50, Service added but optional 10% **Wine:** 42 bottles over £20, 18 bottles under £20, 20 by the glass **Notes:** Vegetarian available, Civ Wed 100 **Seats:** 180, Pr/dining room 16 **Children:** Menu, Portions **Directions:** M32, follow signs for city centre. Left side of Park St, going up the hill towards museum **Parking:** On street, NCP

◉ Hotel du Vin & Bistro

French, European

Relaxed and friendly French bistro style

☎ 0117 925 5577 The Sugar House, Narrow Lewins Mead BS1 2NU

e-mail: info@bristol.hotelduvin.com

web: www.hotelduvin.com

This city-centre hotel is housed in a Grade II listed converted 18th-century sugar refinery. The bistro-style restaurant has a pleasant, lively feel with hop garlands adorning the windows, walls full of wine pictures and heavy wood floors and tables. The menu includes a good selection of vegetarian options and a 'simple classics' selection offering favourites like coq au vin or Chateaubriand for two. All the dishes show attention to detail and good quality ingredients. Typical mains might include beef bourguignon, finishing with chocolate and walnut brownie with espresso ice cream. Naturally, the wine list is a highlight.

Times: 12-2/6-10 **Rooms:** 40 (40 en suite) ★★★★ TH **Directions:** From M4 junct 19, M32 into Bristol. With Bentalls on left take right lane at next lights. Turn right onto opposite side of carriageway. Hotel 200yds in side road

⊚ riverstation

Modern European
Riverside dining location with a buzz

☎ 0117 914 4434 The Grove BS1 4RB
e-mail: relax@riverstation.co.uk
web: www.riverstation.co.uk

Housed in a former police station, this chic waterside eatery has an arresting modern décor of glass, wood and steel. Downstairs there's a popular café/deli serving light meals and hot and cold snacks, while upstairs the airy restaurant caters to a smarter crowd lured by the buzzy ambience as much as the cooking. The modern menu offers good quality fresh food, simply prepared. Try seared gravad lax to start perhaps, served with pickled cucumber salad, and then tuck into pan-fried halibut with olive oil mash, curly kale and red wine sauce, or rack of lamb with white bean and mint houmous, roast cherry tomatoes and saffron oil.

Chef: Peter Taylor **Owners:** J Payne & P Taylor **Times:** 12-2.30/6-10.30, Closed Xmas, 1 Jan **Prices:** Fixed L £12.50-£15.50, Fixed D £28, Starter £5.50-£11, Main £12.50-£19, Dessert £4-£6.50, Service optional, Group min 8 service 10% **Wine:** 56 bottles over £20, 12 bottles under £20, 10 by the glass **Seats:** 120, Pr/dining room 26 **Children:** Portions **Directions:** On the dock side in central Bristol **Parking:** Pay & display, meter parking opposite

⊚ Rodney Hotel

British, French NEW
Smart hotel restaurant offering a compact menu

☎ 0117 973 5422 4 Rodney Place, Clifton BS8 4HY
e-mail: rodney@cliftonhotels.com
web: www.cliftonhotels.com

This small hotel in the city's popular Clifton Village area boasts a smart bar and remodelled, stylish, modern restaurant. Think wooden floors, walls donned with local photographs and friendly and relaxed service. The short menu suits the surroundings changing seasonally to reflect the best quality produce. Simple but carefully-prepared dishes are delivered from an equally small kitchen; take pork medallions served with a warm cabbage salad, broccoli, butternut squash purée and a sherry vinegar sauce, and to finish, perhaps a rich chocolate tart with red wine-poached pear.

Rooms: 31 (31 en suite) ★★ HL

⊚ Thistle Bristol

Modern European NEW
Modern cooking in stylish hotel brasserie

☎ 0870 333 9130 Broad St BS1 2EL
e-mail: bristol@thistle.co.uk
web: www.thistlehotels.com/bristol

Behind the traditional façade of the Thistle Bristol hotel, the simple, clean and modern lines in the refurbished Tyrells Restaurant afford it a brasserie feel. With floors that are partly wooden and partly tiled, modern artwork and light fittings adorn the walls and fresh flowers decorate the tables. With good skill and presentation levels, the kitchen uses quality ingredients in simple, modern European dishes.

You could start with chicken liver and foie gras parfait with perry jelly and toasted brioche, and move on to confit leg of Gressingham duck with casserole of smoked pork, tomato and haricot beans.

Times: 12.30-2.30/7-9.15, Closed L Sat **Rooms:** 182 (182 en suite) ★★★★ HL

The Boars Head

☎ 01454 632278 The Main Rd, Aust BS35 4AX

Cosy candlelit pub with delightful ambience serving very good fresh fish dishes and excellent Sunday lunch.

🍴 Howards Restaurant

☎ 0117 926 2921 1a-2a Avon Crescent, Hotwells BS1 6XQ
web: www.theaa.com/travel/index.jsp

Lively restaurant, with an easy flair, offering a well-priced bistro menu.

Severnshed

☎ 0117 925 1212 The Grove, Harbourside BS1 4SE

Riverside open-plan setup with mainly organic brasserie-style menu.

Wagamama

☎ 0117 922 1188 63 Queens St, Clifton BS8 1QL

Relaxed, Japanese noodle-based eaterie.

BUCKINGHAMSHIRE

AMERSHAM   MAP 06 SU99

⊚⊚ The Artichoke

Modern French
Smart high-street restaurant with refined cooking

☎ 01494 726611 9 Market Square, Old Amersham HP7 0DF
e-mail: info@theartichokerestaurant.co.uk
web: www.theartichokerestaurant.co.uk

This smart eatery occupies a 16th-century house in old Amersham's pretty market square and teams ancient beams and a vast open fireplace with modern art and modish Italian leather chairs. It's a friendly, unfussy place to dine, staffed by a knowledgeable waiting team who deliver a top-notch menu of modern French cuisine, complete with tasting option. High-quality local ingredients are much in evidence and arrive on the plate in creative combinations that delight. Start with a salad of hand-dived Isle of Skye scallops, Jerusalem artichoke purée, apple, pancetta and thyme jus, and then move on to a main such as roast saddle of Highland venison with beetroot fondant, creamed Savoy, glazed onions and orange venison jus. There is a tiny courtyard for alfresco dining in summer.

Chef: Laurie Gear **Owners:** Laurie & Jacqueline Gear **Times:** 12-2/6.45-10, Closed 1 wk Xmas, 2 wks Aug BH, 1 wk Apr, Sun, Mon **Prices:** Fixed L £18.50, Fixed D £38, Starter £11, Main £20, Dessert £9, Service added but optional 12.5% **Wine:** 76 bottles over £20, 5 bottles under £20, 8 by the glass **Notes:** Tasting menu available, Vegetarian available, Smart casual **Seats:** 25 **Children:** Portions **Directions:** M40 junct 2. 1m from Amersham New Town **Parking:** On street, nearby car park

AYLESBURY   MAP 11 SP81

◉◉◉ Hartwell House Hotel, Restaurant & Spa
see below

BLETCHLEY   MAP 11 SP83

◉ The Crooked Billet

Modern British, French 🍷 NOTABLE WINE LIST

Popular village pub serious about its food

☎ 01908 373936   2 Westbrook End, Newton Longville MK17 0DF

e-mail: john@thebillet.co.uk
web: www.thebillet.co.uk

The Crooked Billet

Originally built around 1665 as a farmhouse, this thatched village pub with a separate restaurant boasts oak beams and wooden floors. The pub's lunchtime menu offers a range of sandwiches, wraps and burgers, plus traditional pub dishes, while in the evening the restaurant's offering includes a six-course tasting menu. Seasonal produce arrives fresh each morning from local and national suppliers. The cheeseboard is particularly noteworthy with choices from Longman Dairy and individual UK cheesemakers, complemented by a fine wine list and an enormous selection of wines by the glass.

Chef: Emma Gilchrist **Owners:** John & Emma Gilchrist **Times:** 12.30-2.30/7-10, Closed 25 Dec, Closed L Mon-Sat, D Sun **Prices:** Starter £4.50-£11, Main £10-£24.50, Dessert £5-£10, Service optional **Wine:** 300 bottles over £20, 20 bottles under £20, 300 by the glass **Notes:** Tasting Menu 8 courses £60-£75, with wine £85-£95 **Seats:** 50 **Children:** Portions **Directions:** M1 junct 14 follow A421 towards Buckingham. Turn left at Bottledump rdbt to Newton Longville. Restaurant on right as you enter the village **Parking:** 30

◉◉◉

Hartwell House Hotel, Restaurant & Spa

AYLESBURY   MAP 11 SP81

British V 🍷 NOTABLE WINE LIST

An imposing setting for a special occasion or treat

☎ 01296 747444   Oxford Rd HP17 8NR

e-mail: info@hartwell-house.com
web: www.hartwell-house.com

It once was home to the exiled king of France Louis XVIII for many years in the early 19th century, but this stately home, with its magnificent public rooms and landscaped grounds, is now open to all. A dramatic Gothic hall and staircase with carved Jacobean figures set the scene, followed by a series of elegant day rooms decorated with oak panelling, fine paintings and antiques.
The restaurant is a graceful, high-ceilinged affair and makes an understated backdrop for the talented kitchen's elaborate creations; expect thoughtful and imaginative cuisine with a classical foundation, distinguished by technical genius and quality ingredients. A ballotine of foie gras is a typical starter, served with prune and Armagnac chutney and smoked goose salad, while mains might include venison loin with a gingerbread crust, port wine shallots, almond potatoes and a bitter chocolate praline sauce, or pan-fried sea bass on parsley mash with red and white wine mustard sauces. Take a stroll around the garden if there's time - as well as serpentine walks, a picturesque lake

and 18th-century statues, they contain a luxurious spa with a buttery for light meals and snacks.

Chef: Daniel Richardson **Owners:** Historic House Hotels **Times:** 12.30-1.45/7.30-9.45 **Prices:** Fixed L £23, Fixed D £39, Starter £9-£13.50, Main £23-£29, Dessert £9-£10.50, Service included **Wine:** 300 bottles over £20, 11 bottles under £20, 10 by the glass **Notes:** Tasting menu £67.50, Sun L £32.50, Vegetarian menu, Dress Restrictions, Smart casual, No jeans, tracksuits or trainers, Civ Wed 60 **Seats:** 56, Pr/dining room 30 **Children:** Min 6 yrs, Portions **Rooms:** 46 (46 en suite)★★★★ HL **Directions:** 2m SW of Aylesbury on A418 (Oxford road) **Parking:** 50

BUCKINGHAM   MAP 11 SP63

⊛⊛ Villiers Hotel Restaurant & Bar

Modern British

Stylish brasserie-style restaurant serving appealing modern cuisine

☎ 01280 822444 3 Castle St MK18 1BS
e-mail: reservations@villiershotels.com
web: www.oxfordshire-hotels.co.uk

Originally a coaching inn dating back to Cromwellian times, the hotel comes steeped in history and has been tastefully modernised over the years. A completely new look sees the restaurant achieving a modern, brasserie style and vibe. Simple modern cooking to match provides some classics, alongside new and interesting combinations, with pasta and rice options available as starter or main portions. Expect to kick off with the likes of crispy pork belly teamed with seared scallops and apple purée or a classic chicken liver and foie gras parfait with pear chutney and sultana toast, perhaps followed by seared lamb's liver served with celeriac purée, smoked bacon and Savoy cabbage. Dessert might feature an Indian vanilla crème brûlée or prune and Armagnac tart with praline cream.

Chef: Paul Stopps **Owners:** Oxfordshire Hotels Ltd **Times:** 12-2.30/6-9.30 **Prices:** Fixed L £17.95-£25, Starter £3.95-£7.95, Main £8.95-£21.50, Dessert £4.95-£6.25, Service optional **Notes:** Vegetarian available, Civ Wed 150, Air con **Seats:** 70, Pr/dining room 150 **Rooms:** 46 (46 en suite) ★★★★ HL **Directions:** Town centre - Castle Street is to the right of Town Hall near main square **Parking:** 46

DINTON   MAP 05 SP71

⊛ La Chouette

Belgian

Quirky Belgian restaurant

☎ 01296 747422 Westlington Green HP17 8UW

The menu at this rustic Belgian restaurant announces several of the dishes as 'superb', offers 'surprise' desserts, and describes a grey shrimp salad as 'bloody good'. Luckily there's no fall to go with all this culinary pride - just an accomplished range of traditional dishes designed to suit most tastes. The setting is the delightful village of Dinton, and a former pub that stands on the green and retains a wealth of original 16th-century features including stone walls, wooden beams and a large inglenook fireplace. You might kick off with scallops with chicory perhaps, and then tuck into grilled fillet of Scottish salmon with a sorrel sauce, or leg of lamb with seasonal vegetables.

Chef: Frederic Desmette **Owners:** M F Desmette **Times:** 12-2/7-9, Closed Sun, Closed L Sat **Prices:** Fixed L £14, Fixed D £29.90, Starter £9-£17, Main £10-£17, Dessert £5-£7, Service added but optional 12.5% **Wine:** 2 by the glass **Notes:** Fixed L 3 courses, D 4 courses, Menu dégustation £37 **Seats:** 35 **Children:** Portions **Directions:** On A418 at Dinton **Parking:** 20

GREAT MISSENDEN   MAP 06 SP80

Annie Baileys

Modern British

Ever-popular rural restaurant

☎ 01494 865625 Chesham Rd, Hyde End HP16 0QT
e-mail: david@anniebaileys.com
web: www.anniebaileys.com

Named after a local Victorian landlady, this popular rural restaurant is an informal and friendly place to take a relaxing meal or enjoy a drink at the bar or by the fire. The interior has a country-cottage feel, combined with a Mediterranean colour scheme. The Mediterranean theme extends to the food, presented on a brasserie-style menu with something for everyone. Starters double as light bites and might include slow-roasted tomatoes with grilled goat's cheese or honey-roast figs in Parma ham. Follow with sea bass served with a crayfish risotto, and be sure to leave room for desserts such as Annie Baileys 'Baileys' crème brûlée or caramel fudge brownie with honeycomb ice cream.

Chef: Andrew Fairall **Owners:** Open All Hours (UK) Ltd **Times:** 12-2.30/7-9.30, Closed D Sun **Prices:** Fixed L £13.50-£14.95, Starter £5-£7.95, Main £10.50-£18.95, Dessert £5-£7.50, Service optional **Wine:** 10 bottles over £20, 20 bottles under £20, 16 by the glass **Notes:** Vegetarian available **Seats:** 65 **Children:** Portions **Directions:** Off A413 at Great Missenden. On B485 towards Chesham **Parking:** 40

HADDENHAM   MAP 05 SP70

Green Dragon

British

Quality food in a village inn atmosphere

☎ 01844 291403 8 Churchway HP17 8AA
e-mail: paul@eatatthedragon.co.uk
web: www.eatatthedragon.co.uk

The picturesque location of this 17th-century pub, close to the church and duck pond, has attracted several TV film crews. Although it's a gastro business, customers who just want a drink are welcome and the village beer is certainly worth sampling. Lunchtime options range from sandwiches to light meals, plus the popular Sunday lunch, and there's a simple dinner menu available on Tuesday and Thursday priced for two courses. Dishes might include salmon and prawn fishcake with lemon and garlic mayonnaise, followed by smoked haddock with saffron-crushed potatoes, and for dessert, apricot tart Tatin with vanilla ice cream. Produce is generally locally sourced, apart from fresh fish from Devon, served within a day of the catch.

Green Dragon

Times: 12-2/6.30-9.30, Closed 25 Dec, 1 Jan, Closed D Sun
Directions: From M40 take A329 towards Thame, then A418. Turn 1st right after entering Haddenham

IVINGHOE   MAP 11 SP91

The King's Head

Modern British, French V

Charming inn with bags of character and traditional dining

☎ 01296 668388 LU7 9EB
e-mail: info@kingsheadivinghoe.co.uk
web: www.kingsheadivinghoe.co.uk

This 17th-century, ivy-clad inn is a former posting house and oozes old-world charm. The exposed beams, whitewashed walls and antiques add to the traditional feel, with open fireplaces in the cosy bar areas and wooden furniture, low ceilings and candlelight in the intimate restaurant. The menu is a mix of modern and classic French and English, delivered with refreshing simplicity backed by flambé and carving at the table and desserts chosen from the sweet trolley. Expect the likes of calves' liver and bacon with roasted tomato and crispy bacon, or perhaps pan-fried fillet of sea bream with Parmentier potatoes, peas and chorizo, often accompanied by live music.

ENGLAND

Chef: Jonathan O'Keeffe **Owners:** G.A.P.J. Ltd **Times:** 12-2.30/7-9.30, Closed 27-30 Dec, Closed D Sun **Prices:** Fixed L £18.95, Fixed D £36-£46, Starter £7.25-£12.25, Main £20-£24, Dessert £6.95, Service added but optional 12.5% **Wine:** 80 bottles over £20, 8 bottles under £20, 2 by the glass **Notes:** Fixed L 3 courses, Fixed D 4 courses, Vegetarian menu, Dress Restrictions, No jeans, trainers or shorts, Air con **Seats:** 55, Pr/dining room 40 **Children:** Portions **Directions:** From M25 junct 20 take A41 past Tring. Turn right onto B488 (Ivinghoe), hotel at junct with B489 **Parking:** 20

Chef: Trevor Bosch, Donald Joyce **Owners:** Trevor & Annie Bosch **Times:** 12-2.30/7-9.30, Closed D Sun **Prices:** Fixed L £14.50, Starter £4.50-£9.50, Main £14.25-£26.50, Dessert £5, Service optional, Group min 8 service 10% **Wine:** 58 bottles over £20, 29 bottles under £20, 12 by the glass **Notes:** Tasting menu Mon-Fri £35.00 5 courses, Sun L £19.95-24.95, Vegetarian available, Air con **Seats:** 75, Pr/dining room 14 **Children:** Portions **Directions:** Beside B4011, 2m NW of Thame **Parking:** 30

LONG CRENDON — MAP 05 SP60

⊛ The Angel Restaurant
Mediterranean, Pacific Rim
Gastro-pub with a friendly atmosphere

☎ 01844 208268   47 Bicester Rd HP18 9EE
e-mail: angelrestaurant@aol.com
web: www.angelrestaurant.co.uk

A 17th-century coaching inn, now operating as a gastro-pub, The Angel retains its original wattle-and-daub walls, exposed beams and fireplaces. The menu, with Mediterranean and Pacific Rim influences, offers imaginative dishes prepared from local produce. Fish is a strength with blackboard specials taking advantage of the latest catch. Recommendations include crispy duck and bacon salad with hoisin dressing or seared fillet of sea bass on chargrilled vegetables and sweet chilli sauce, with pear and apple strudel and vanilla custard for dessert. Excellent table service is managed by attentive, yet unobtrusive staff.

MARLOW — MAP 05 SU88

⊛⊛⊛ The Hand & Flowers
see page 50

⊛⊛⊛ Macdonald Compleat Angler
see below

⊛⊛⊛ Oak Room at Danesfield House
see page 51

⊛⊛⊛
Macdonald Compleat Angler

MARLOW — **MAP 05 SU88**
Modern British
Assured cooking in new fine-dining restaurant overlooking the Thames

☎ 0870 400 8100   Marlow Bridge SL7 1RG
e-mail: general.compleatangler@macdonald-hotels.co.uk
web: www.macdonald-hotels.co.uk/compleatangler-hotel.co.uk

Idyllically situated on the banks of the River Thames, this elegant Georgian hotel overlooks the rushing waters at Marlow weir and was named after Izaak Walton's famous book on angling. Whether enjoying a cosy fireside drink in the 350-year-old cocktail bar in winter, perhaps a champagne picnic aboard one of the hotel's private boats, or aperitifs on the terrace on warm summer days, the location is perfect. The two redesigned and refurbished restaurants provide contrasting styles of cooking: Dean Timpson at The Compleat Angler is the intimate, fine-dining option, delivering modern British food in a formal but friendly setting, while Bowaters restaurant is a more informal venue offering more traditional fare. The stylish décor at Dean Timpson's combines a rich, vibrant colour scheme of purple, white and silver with lush maple woods and polished oak panels, offset with a clever use of fabrics and brocades to create a sleek,

sophisticated environment with a luxurious feel that's still cosy and welcoming. The accomplished kitchen's approach is delivered via a good-value market menu for lunch, an extensive carte for both lunch and dinner, and also the signature Gastronome's Tasting Menu that offers seven imaginatively-conceived courses accompanied by selected wines. Timpson's philosophy of simplicity in style is reflected in clean-flavoured, attractively presented dishes based around classical themes, featuring bags of technical skill and focusing on local, seasonal ingredients with an emphasis on quality. For mains, why not try grilled fillet of cod with crayfish, parmesan gnocchi and crayfish sauce, while chilled strawberry consommé with mascarpone and balsamic ice cream might catch the eye at dessert.

Chef: Dean Timpson, Mark Constable **Owners:** Macdonald Hotels **Times:** 12-2.30/7-10, Closed L Mon-Tue, D Sun-Mon **Prices:** Fixed L £24.50, Service added but optional 12.5% **Wine:** 270 bottles over £20 **Notes:** Fixed L 3 courses, Sun L £39, Tasting menu available, Dress Restrictions, Smart casual, No jeans or trainers, Civ Wed 100 **Seats:** 80, Pr/dining room 64 **Children:** Menu, Portions **Rooms:** 64 (64 en suite) ★★★★ HL **Directions:** A404 to rdbt, take Bisham exit, 1m to Marlow Bridge, hotel on right **Parking:** 60

The Hand & Flowers

MARLOW MAP 05 SU88

British, French

Unpretentious gastro-pub offering first-rate cooking

☎ 01628 482277 126 West Street SL7 2BP
web: www.thehandandflowers.co.uk

Don't be fooled by first impressions, this unassuming whitewashed pub on the edge of town is a class act, and with chef-patron Tom Kerridge in the kitchen (ex Adlard's in Norwich (see entry) and Monsieur Max at Hampton) it has a fine pedigree. Low wooden beams and exposed brick and stone walls help retain the country pub feel, with some modern art thrown in to add a contemporary twist. Plain, solid-wood furniture (no cloths), subdued lighting and relaxed, friendly service from an enthusiastic young team (led by wife Beth), all help maintain the warm, unstuffy atmosphere.

Tom's cooking is intelligently simple and elegant, with flavour and skill top of his agenda. The style is modern-focused Anglo-French, with fresh, top-quality produce of the utmost importance, while presentation is equally simple and true to each dish. Expect dishes such as potted Dorset crab with cucumber and dill chutney, followed by Highland Dornach cannon of lamb with parsley crust, with perhaps praline parfait, pineapple sorbet and nougat to finish. At lunchtime, a three-dish bar menu is also offered, and there's a patio for summer alfresco dining.

Chef: Tom Kerridge
Owners: Tom & Beth Kerridge
Times: 12-2.30/7-9.30, Closed 25-26 Dec, Closed D Sun
Prices: Starter £5-£9.50, Main £15.50-£21, Dessert £6.50, Service optional, Group min 6 service 10%
Wine: 28 bottles over £20, 23 bottles under £20, 11 by the glass
Seats: 50
Children: Portions
Directions: M40 junct 4/M4 junct 8/9 follow A404 to Marlow
Parking: 30

Oak Room at Danesfield House

MARLOW MAP 05 SU88

Modern British V 🖥

Stunning cuisine in fairytale surroundings

☎ 01628 891010 Henley Rd SL7 2EY
e-mail: adooley@danesfieldhouse.co.uk
web: www.danesfieldhouse.co.uk

Set within 65 acres of magnificent grounds in the beautiful Chiltern Hills, Danesfield is the third house to enjoy the magnificent view here over the River Thames since 1664; the present property was built in 1899 as a family home. Constructed of white stone with castellated towers, tall chimneys and raised terraces, it has all the hallmarks of a fairytale castle. The Oak Room restaurant was redesigned with a light, airy feel in 2005 by Anouska Hempel - its bleached wood panelling, soft shades of fawn and latte and top-notch napery give a luxurious yet relaxing impression as you enter. Nothing prepares you, however, for the stunning culinary experience, where new chef Adam Simmonds (ex Ynyshir Hall, see entry) shows off his fine kitchen pedigree. The modern approach is underpinned by a classical theme to produce top-quality, innovative cooking using high-quality seasonal produce and some serious technical skill. Clean flavours and presentation allow each dish a unique taste experience; take pan-fried fillet of cod served with parsnip purée, braised salsify, razor clams, curry jelly and goat's cheese, and to finish, perhaps a wild strawberry mousse with ice cream, nettle pannacotta, meringue and crystallised nettle leaves. Once you've eaten here, you'll certainly want to repeat the experience.

Chef: Adam Simmonds
Times: 12-2/7-9.30, Closed Xmas, New Year, BHs, Sun, Closed L Mon-Wed, D Sun
Prices: Fixed L £29.50, Fixed D £55, Service added 12.5%
Notes: Fixed L 3 courses, Tasting menu £70, Vegetarian menu, Dress Restrictions, Smart casual, Civ Wed 100
Seats: 30, Pr/dining room 14
Children: Min 12 yrs, Portions
Rooms: 87 (87 en suite) ★★★★ HL
Directions: M4 junct 4/A404 to Marlow. Follow signs to Medmenham and Henley. Hotel is 3m outside Marlow
Parking: 100

MARLOW CONTINUED

⊛⊛ The Vanilla Pod

Modern British, French

Cottage restaurant offering imaginative modern cuisine

☎ 01628 898101 31 West St SL7 2LS
e-mail: info@thevanillapod.co.uk
web: www.thevanillapod.co.uk

The former home of TS Eliot, poet and critic, this cosy cottage is located in the town centre, with the recently refurbished dining room at the rear overlooking a small courtyard. Contemporary design complements the rustic room with its bright Mediterranean décor, beamed walls and ceiling. The atmosphere is intimate and welcoming, with polite, professional and knowledgeable service. Modern cooking combines British style and French influences, with a deft touch and well-judged ingredients, in dishes of seared scallops with a purée of white beans and bourbon vanilla foam, or carpaccio of beetroot with goat's cheese and aged balsamic vinegar, followed by fore rib of beef with boulangère potatoes and red wine shallot sauce, and maybe bitter chocolate fondant and milk chocolate parfait to finish.

Chef: Michael Macdonald **Owners:** Michael & Stephanie Macdonald **Times:** 12-2.30/7-11, Closed 23 Dec-3 Jan, 22 Aug-6 Sep, Sun-Mon **Prices:** Fixed L £15.50, Fixed D £40, Service optional **Wine:** 64 bottles over £20, 6 bottles under £20, 8 by the glass **Notes:** Tasting menu 8 courses £45, Smart casual **Seats:** 34, Pr/dining room 8 **Directions:** From M4 junct 8/9 or M40 junct 4 take A404, A4155 to Marlow. From Henley take A4155 **Parking:** On West Street

Villa D'Este

☎ 01628 474798 2 Chapel St SL7 1DD

Popular local Italian restaurant serving familiar favourites and attracting loyal clientele.

MILTON KEYNES   MAP 11 SP83

⊛⊛ Lanes Restaurant, Mercure Parkside Hotel

Modern European NEW

Stylish hotel dining meets creative cooking

☎ 0870 1942128 01908 661919 Macdonald Parkside Hotel, Newport Rd, Woughton on the Green MK6 3LR

Set in a rural location on the outskirts of town, Parkside provides stylish, modern-vogue hotel dining. Deep, high-backed seating and

double-clothed tables with crisp napery deliver the comforts, while legions of staff offer attentive, professional service. The accomplished kitchen deals in quality produce, its repertoire carte and daily-changing market menu providing classic and contemporary combinations that catch the eye and showcase high skill, clean, clear flavours and good presentation. Take a tasting of spring lamb with dauphinoise potato, crushed peas and vièrge dressing, or baked fillet of cod with crab and saffron risotto and red pepper coulis, while desserts might feature a hot chocolate fondant with gingerbread ice cream and marinated oranges.

Chef: Brett Lambourne-Paynter **Owners:** Macdonald Hotels **Times:** 12-2/7-10, Closed L mid wk days **Prices:** Fixed L £15-£25, Fixed D £30-£50, Starter £4.50-£8, Main £13-£23, Dessert £4.50-£8, Service included **Notes:** Civ Wed 125 **Seats:** 50, Pr/dining room 50 **Children:** Menu, Portions **Rooms:** 49 (49 en suite) ★★★ HL **Parking:** 80

TAPLOW   MAP 06 SU98

⊛⊛ Berry's at Taplow House Hotel

Modern British

Skilful modern British cooking at a luxurious hotel

☎ 01628 670056 Berry Hill SL6 0DA
e-mail: reception@taplowhouse.com
web: www.taplowhouse.com

This Georgian mansion combines period charm with country-house comfort and sits amid 6 acres of leafy gardens. There's a champagne terrace for summer drinks, or a whisky bar for those who'd rather sup a malt by the fire, while the elegant, high-ceilinged Berry's restaurant offers pretty views from well-spaced tables. The kitchen's modern British approach - underpinned by classical French themes - uses prime local produce, the carte offering wine selections with each dish. Expect a rare fillet of British beef with wild mushroom risotto, caramelised root vegetables and a red wine sauce, while a hot chocolate fondant - served with white chocolate ice cream and milk chocolate sauce - might head-up desserts.

Chef: Neil Dore **Owners:** Taplow House Hotel Ltd **Times:** 12-2/7-9.30, Closed L Sat **Prices:** Fixed L £19.95, Fixed D £31.95, Starter £7.50, Main £18.50, Dessert £5.95, Service included **Wine:** 36 bottles over £20, 8 bottles under £20, 10 by the glass **Notes:** Tasting menu £45, Sun L 3 courses £19.95, Dress Restrictions, Smart casual, Civ Wed 90, Air con **Seats:** 40, Pr/dining room 90 **Children:** Portions **Rooms:** 32 (32 en suite) ★★★★ HL **Directions:** From Maidenhead follow A4 towards Slough, over Thames, 3m turn right at lights into Berry Hill, or M4 junct 7 towards Maidenhead, at lights follow signs to Berry Hill **Parking:** 100

Waldo's Restaurant, Cliveden

TAPLOW   MAP 06 SU98

Modern British V ♦ NOTABLE WINE LIST

Enjoyable classical cuisine in sumptuous surroundings

☎ 01628 668561   Cliveden Estate SL6 0JF
e-mail: reservations@clivedenhouse.co.uk
web: www.clivedenhouse.co.uk

Set amid 376 acres of magnificent formal gardens and parkland, stately homes don't come much statelier than this. A jewel in the National Trust crown, Cliveden's lofty façade and luxurious interior are a testament to its long history as a hub of pleasure, power and politics, while the chalk cliffs that gave the estate its name afford visitors to the house panoramic views over the beautiful Berkshire countryside and the River Thames.
Waldo's is named after the sculptor of the famous Fountain of Love which graces the house's sweeping driveway, and manages to be a delightfully unstuffy place to dine, in spite of its venerable reputation and the opulent setting. Expect a menu of modern British and French dishes, rooted in classical cuisine and distinguished by careful consideration for the seasonality and origin of ingredients. Pan-roast Orkney scallops are a typical starter, served with truffle-flavoured pumpkin purée and a butter sauce, while mains might include pan-fried Cornish sea bass with a ravioli of red chard, candied tomatoes and balsamic vinegar dressing, or steamed fillet of Scottish turbot with poached native oyster, herb-mashed potato, tomato and chive cream sauce. Desserts such as whole roasted figs, with goat's cheese ice cream, spicy fig sauce and an oatmeal tuile will not disappoint, or try blackcurrant-poached pear with golden beetroot Tatin and liquorice ice cream. The wine list also impresses, and with sommeliers happy to spend as much time over the selection of a glass as a bottle, you're guaranteed a memorable tipple.

Chef: Daniel Galmiche, Ben Webb
Owners: von Essen Hotels
Times: 7-9.30, Closed Xmas, New Year, 2 wks Aug, Sun & Mon, Closed L all week
Prices: Fixed D £68, Service optional
Wine: 600 bottles over £20, 8 by the glass
Notes: Vegetarian menu, Dress Restrictions, Jacket & tie, Civ Wed 120, Air con
Seats: 28, Pr/dining room 12
Children: Min 12 yrs
Rooms: 39 (39 en suite)★★★★★ CHH
Directions: M40 junct 2 onto A355, right into Burnham Rd/Littleworth Rd. Follow signs for Wooburn/Taplow, then for Cliveden
Parking: 60

TAPLOW CONTINUED

⊚⊚ The Terrace Dining Room, Cliveden

Mediterranean, French 🏵️ NOTABLE WINE LIST

Fine dining in elegant surroundings

☎ 01628 668561 Cliveden Estate SL6 0JF
e-mail: reservations@clivedenhouse.co.uk
web: www.clivedenhouse.co.uk

One of England's finest country houses, Cliveden was once home to
Lady Nancy Astor, who entertained the likes of Winston Churchill,
Charlie Chaplin and George Bernard Shaw at the house. Nowadays,
the hoi polloi is welcome too and visitors flock to explore the
estate's parkland and to sample its renowned cuisine. The Terrace
Dining Room is a particular treat: south-facing, it catches the sun and
offers views across the gardens to the Thames. Its chandeliers, wood
panelling and fine works of art create an elegant backdrop to some
imaginative interpretations of classic French cuisine. Start with
lobster carpaccio with lime and pink peppercorns, roasted tiger
prawns and rosemary, before tucking into fillet of John Dory à la
plancha with star anise, fennel and curry purée and a light curry
sabayon.

Chef: Daniel Galmiche **Owners:** von Essen Hotels **Times:** 12-2.30/7-9.30
Prices: Fixed L £27.50, Fixed D £59, Service optional **Wine:** All bottles
over £20, 8 by the glass **Notes:** Sun L 3 courses £49.00, Vegetarian
available, Dress Restrictions, Smart casual L, Jacket & shirt D, Civ Wed 120
Seats: 80, Pr/dining room 60 **Children:** Menu, Portions **Rooms:** 39 (39
en suite) ★★★★★ CHH **Directions:** M40 junct 2 right, onto A355 right
into Burnham Rd/Littleworth Rd. Follow signs for Wooburn/Taplow, then for
Cliveden **Parking:** 60

⊚⊚⊚ Waldo's Restaurant, Cliveden

see page 53

WOOBURN COMMON   MAP 06 SU98

⊚ Chequers Inn

British, French

Cosy inn with simple style

☎ 01628 529575 Kiln Ln HP10 0JQ
e-mail: info@chequers-inn.com
web: www.chequers-inn.com

This former 17th-century coaching inn is a real haven, with its deep
cosy sofas, quiet corners, open fires, and prerequisite oak beams and
flagstone floors. An extensive menu of pub grub is served in the bar,

or classier fare is available in the conservatory, a pleasant room away
from the hustle and bustle, that's decked with greenery and an eclectic
mix of memorabilia. Superb ingredients are the key to its success;
they're handled simply by a confident kitchen and arrive at the table in
dishes like whole plaice with seared scallops and saffron and fennel
risotto, or fillet of beef with roast and puréed parsnips in a wild
mushroom and peppercorn sauce.

Chef: Tarik Benchan **Owners:** PJ Roehrig **Times:** 12-2.30/7-9.30, Closed
D 25 Dec, 1 Jan **Prices:** Fixed L £13.95, Fixed D £27.95, Starter £6.95-
£9.95, Main £14.95-£24.95, Dessert £5.75-£6.50, Service optional
Notes: Sun L £26.95, Vegetarian available **Seats:** 60, Pr/dining room 60
Children: Portions **Rooms:** 17 (17 en suite) ★★★ HL
Directions: Telephone for directions **Parking:** 50

CAMBRIDGESHIRE

BABRAHAM   MAP 12 TL55

⊚ The George Inn

Modern British NEW

*Restored coaching inn offering an exciting range of
dishes*

☎ 01223 833800 High St CB22 3AG
e-mail: george@inter-mead.com
web: www.georgeinnbabraham.co.uk

This smart gastro-pub is full of character. A coaching inn since 1774,
following a fire in 2003 the inn has been beautifully restored, retaining
original features alongside contemporary furnishings. There is also a
new barn-style restaurant. Service in the two dining rooms is relaxed
and professional with black-clad staff sporting long aprons. The lunch
menu offers ciabattas and a range of main courses like dressed
Cromer crab. The evening menu has some exotic starters like
tempura-fried salmon nori roll with ginger mirin and coriander
dressing, while main courses might include tandoori-marinated
chicken breast with lime and coriander wild rice. There is a beautiful
terrace for alfresco dining.

Chef: Mark Edgeley **Owners:** G A Wortley **Times:** 11.30-3/5.30-11,
Closed D Sun nights in winter **Prices:** Starter £5.95-£8.95, Main £14.95-
£22.95, Dessert £5.95-£7.95, Service optional, Group min 10 service 10%
Wine: 19 bottles over £20, 14 bottles under £20, 8 by the glass
Notes: Sun lunch menu, Vegetarian available, Civ Wed 40 **Seats:** 115,
Pr/dining room 40 **Children:** Menu, Portions **Directions:** At junct of A11
& A1307 take A1307 towards Cambridge. Turn left after 200mtrs
Parking: 40

see advert opposite

BRAMPTON MAP 12 TL27

The Grange Hotel

Rosettes not confirmed at time of going to press

Modern European

Modern cuisine in impressive, historic building

☎ 01480 459516 115 High St PE28 4RA
e-mail: info@grangehotelbrampton.co.uk
web: www.grangehotelbrampton.co.uk

A historic building on the village high street, which has in its time been the HQ of the American Eighth Airforce and a girls' school. Overlooking the garden, the restaurant is light and airy with comfortable seating and classic décor. A modern menu, supplemented by blackboard specials, is served throughout the bar and restaurant by relaxed, friendly staff. Local food is sourced carefully so you'll find sausages, bacon, pork and venison from the Denham estate. Typical dishes include terrine of guinea fowl with roasted chicory to start, followed by noisettes of lamb with fondant potato, roasted yam, mushroom purée and a basil sauce, or seared tuna with caramelised fennel, roast cherry tomatoes and crushed potatoes. As we went to press we were informed of a change of ownership at this hotel. Please visit www.theAA.com for further information.

Times: 12-2/6.30-9.30, Closed BHs, Sun **Rooms:** 7 (7 en suite)
Directions: 0.5m E from A1/A14 junct 21 on B1514. Close to Brampton racecourse, 1.5m W from Huntingdon

CAMBOURNE MAP 12 TL35

⊛⊛ The Cambridge Belfry

Modern

Modern setting for classic European cuisine

☎ 01954 714995 Back St CB3 6BW
e-mail: cambridge@marstonhotels.com
web: www.marstonhotels.com

A modern hotel offering great views over the lake and business park. Lighter meals are available in the brasserie, but the Bridge restaurant is the real draw, a contemporary space with sleek lines, polished tiles, and dramatic splashes of deep red. Expect an eclectic menu rooted in classic European cuisine and notable for good use of local produce in season. Crab cakes are a typical starter, served with soba noodles and a ginger and soy dressing, while mains might include a tender piece of Gloucester Old Spot pork belly with celeriac purée, Savoy cabbage, sauté potatoes and roasted root vegetables. To finish, try the pineapple up-side-down cake with cocoa citrus sorbet and coconut foam. Service is relaxed but attentive.

Chef: Kiran Selvarajan **Owners:** QHotels **Times:** 12.30-2.30/7.30-9, Closed L Sat **Prices:** Starter £4.95-£8.95, Main £10.95-£23, Dessert £5.50-£8.50, Service optional **Wine:** 35 bottles over £20, 24 bottles under £20, 12 by the glass **Notes:** Vegetarian available, Civ Wed 120, Air con
Seats: 120, Pr/dining room 160 **Children:** Menu, Portions **Rooms:** 120 (120 en suite) ★★★★ HL **Directions:** Telephone for directions
Parking: 200

THE GEORGE INN AT BABRAHAM

The George Inn can easily be found in the High Street in Babraham, 4 miles to the south-east of Cambridge. It is also very accessible from the M11 and A11. Originally built as a coaching inn on the London to Norwich road, The George Inn has been substantially re-built following an extensive fire in 2003. Now offering a superb range of meals both in the Bar and Restaurant, The George Inn is the ideal place to meet friends or business colleagues for a meal. For great food, extensive wine list and outstanding hospitality call in at The George Inn!

The George Inn,
High Street, Babraham, Cambridge CB22 3AG
Tel 01223 833 800
www.georgeinnbabraham.co.uk

CAMBRIDGE MAP 12 TL45

⊛ Best Western Cambridge Quy Mill Hotel

Modern European

Listed property with a modern take on traditional fare

☎ 01223 293383 Newmarket Rd, Stow Cum Quy CB5 9AG
e-mail: cambridgequy@bestwestern.co.uk
web: www.bw-cambridgequymill.co.uk

Set in open countryside, this 19th-century former watermill and miller's house is convenient for Cambridge. The restaurant occupies the dining room, kitchen and buttery of the old house, and the private dining room features a waterwheel behind glass. Most menus (set menu, specials, light bites and desserts) are available in the restaurant, bars, conservatory and terrace, while the chef's recommendation menu is available in the restaurant in the evening. Traditional dishes are presented in a modern context: chicken liver parfait with kumquat compôte, toasted brioche and mulled wine jelly or confit belly of pork, gratin potato, blood orange and fennel marmalade and a soured apple sauce.

Chef: Guiseppe Mazzone **Owners:** David Munro **Times:** 12-2.30/7-9.45, Closed 27-31 Dec **Prices:** Fixed L £18-£21, Fixed D £24-£27, Starter £4.75-£8.50, Main £14-£22, Dessert £3.25-£5.75, Service optional, Group min 8 service 10% **Wine:** 20 bottles over £20, 10 bottles under £20, 10 by the glass **Notes:** Vegetarian available, Dress Restrictions, Smart dress/smart casual - no shorts (men), Civ Wed 80 **Seats:** 48, Pr/dining room 80
Children: Menu, Portions **Rooms:** 49 (49 en suite) ★★★ HL
Directions: Turn off A14 at junct 35, E of Cambridge, onto B1102 for 50yds, hotel entrance opposite church **Parking:** 90

ENGLAND

Midsummer House

CAMBRIDGE MAP 12 TL45

French, Mediterranean ♦NOTABLE WINE LIST 🖳

Seriously sophisticated, inspired cooking from a high-flyer

☎ 01223 369299 Midsummer Common CB4 1HA
e-mail: reservations@midsummerhouse.co.uk
web: www.midsummerhouse.co.uk

Chef: Daniel Clifford
Owners: Midsummer House Ltd
Times: 12-1.30/7-9.30,
Closed Etr, 1 wk late Aug,
2 wks from 25 Dec, Mon,
Closed L Tue, D Sun
Prices: Main £60-£70,
Service added but optional
12.5%, Group service
12.5%
Wine: 900 bottles over
£20, 12 by the glass
Notes: Tasting menu £70-
£80, ALC 3 courses
Seats: 54, Pr/dining room
20
Children: Portions
Directions: Park in
Pretoria Rd, then walk
across footbridge.
Restaurant on left
Parking: On street

Set in a handsome Victorian villa, on the romantically
named Midsummer Common beside the River Cam, this
delightful, high-flying restaurant is home to some seriously
stylish food. The airy, elegant, conservatory-style dining room
is stylishly decked out with white walls, Indian slate floors
and large, well-spaced tables dressed in crisp white linen and
a single white lily. The atrium-style glass roof, windows and
large mirrors deliver a feeling of light and space, while cream
leather chairs follow the natural colour theme, with the room
appropriately opening on to a pretty, secluded walled garden
of fragrant herbs cultivated for the kitchen. Upstairs there's a
private dining room, and a sophisticated bar and terrace for
alfresco drinks with river views. Predominantly French service
is polished and attentive, the team as enthusiastic about
Daniel Clifford's innovative cooking as the chef himself.
Clifford's quest for culinary perfection has taken the restaurant
to another level over the past few years; his is cooking at its
best, modern-focused but underpinned by classical French
technique, seriously sophisticated with dishes arriving dressed to thrill. Superb-quality
ingredients, advanced technique and technical prowess add wow-factor to the carte and tasting
menu and allow flavours to shine, while unexpected texture contrasts and combinations hit the
spot. Take seared hand-dived scallops with celeriac and truffle purée, Granny Smiths and apple
caramel, followed up with a stunning slow-roast fillet of beef, shallot marmalade, celeriac purée
and essence of port. Excellent peripherals such as freshly baked breads, home-made
chocolates, foams and shooters are all top-drawer, duly complemented by a superb wine list.

CAMBRIDGE CONTINUED

⊛⊛ Graffiti at Hotel Felix

Modern British

Enjoyable brasserie dining in stylish hotel

☎ 01223 277977 Whitehouse Ln CB3 0LX
e-mail: help@hotelfelix.co.uk
web: www.hotelfelix.co.uk

Originally built for a local surgeon, this beautifully refurbished Victorian mansion is set in 3 acres of landscaped gardens. It retains many original features and the décor throughout is simple and contemporary in style. The Graffiti restaurant is a stylish dining venue, decked out with raspberry-coloured chairs and modern art. Expect a brasserie-style menu comprising mainly Mediterranean-inspired fare with a smattering of British dishes given a modern twist. Take Cornish spider crab spring rolls with coriander, spring onion and coconut shavings, followed by medallions of slow-roasted rump beef with oxtail ravioli, creamed potatoes and honey-roast vegetables. Mandarin parfait with toasted marshmallows, fromage frais sorbet and a citrus filo might prove an interesting finale.

Chef: Ian Morgan **Owners:** Jeremy Cassel **Times:** 12-2/6.30-10.30
Prices: Fixed L £12.50, Starter £5.50-£10.50, Main £13.50-£18.50, Dessert £5.50-£6.75, Service optional, Group min 10 service 10% **Wine:** 40 bottles over £20, 18 bottles under £20, 13 by the glass **Notes:** Civ Wed 75
Seats: 45, Pr/dining room 60 **Children:** Portions **Rooms:** 52 (52 en suite) ★★★★ HL **Directions:** M11 junct 12. From A1 N take A14 turning onto A1307. At City of Cambridge sign turn left into Whitehouse Lane
Parking: 90

⊛⊛⊛⊛ Midsummer House

see opposite

⊛ 22 Chesterton Road

Modern British

Accomplished cooking and intimate dining

☎ 01223 351880 22 Chesterton Rd CB4 3AX
e-mail: davidcarter@restaurant22.co.uk
web: www.restaurant22.co.uk

A relaxed, candlelit Victorian dining room with tables cosily close together and the atmosphere of a private house, which is precisely what this once was. Academics, families and business people are equally at home here. The kitchen's monthly-changing fixed-price modern British menu with French influences takes a modern approach, and is short but versatile, with an optional fish and cheese course. Sound skills and an emphasis on quality, fresh local ingredients and flavour ensure consistent results; think a roast loin of venison served with braised red cabbage, pommes Parmentier and celeriac, and perhaps a rum pannacotta with poached pear and ginger shortbread to finish.

Chef: Martin Cullum, Seb Mansfield **Owners:** Mr D Carter **Times:** 7-9.45, Closed 25 Dec & New Year, Sun-Mon, Closed L all wk **Prices:** Fixed L £26.50, Fixed D £26.50, Service optional **Wine:** 40 bottles over £20, 30 bottles under £20, 4 by the glass **Notes:** Fixed L 3 courses, Air con
Seats: 26, Pr/dining room 12 **Children:** Min 10 yrs, Portions
Directions: Telephone for directions **Parking:** On street

Anatolies

☎ 01223 312412 Bridge St CB2 1UJ

This Turkish restaurant is set in the basement of the building and has a charcoal grill and even live belly dancing entertainment.

Loch Fyne Restaurant & Oyster Bar

☎ 01223 362433 The Little Rose, 37 Trumpington St CB2 1QY

Quality seafood chain.

DUXFORD MAP 12 TL44

⊛⊛ Duxford Lodge Hotel

British, European

A sedate setting for imaginative cuisine

☎ 01223 836444 Ickleton Rd CB22 4RT
e-mail: admin@duxfordlodgehotel.co.uk
web: www.duxfordlodgehotel.co.uk

CONTINUED

DUXFORD CONTINUED

Formerly an officers' mess in the First and Second World Wars, this attractive red-brick hotel is a good place for dinner after a day at the Imperial War Museum, just a few minutes drive away in Duxford. With Douglas Bader and Winston Churchill as former guests, pictures of brightly coloured parrots liven up the restaurant, an intimate affair with neatly-clothed tables and large windows on to the garden. The classically-trained chef knows his stuff and likes to deliver intriguing combinations. Start with confit chicken terrine, followed perhaps by rib-eye steak with dauphinoise potatoes, parsnip purée and green peppercorn jus, and round things off with almond and cherry tart and a drink in the cosy lounge bar. Popular, so book ahead.

Chef: Jason Burridge **Owners:** Mr Hemant Amin **Times:** 12-2/7-9.30, Closed 26-30 Dec **Prices:** Fixed L £12.50-£14, Fixed D £27-£30, Starter £8.50-£13.25, Main £14.25-£24, Dessert £5.95-£7.95, Service optional **Wine:** 30 bottles over £20, 23 bottles under £20, 7 by the glass **Notes:** Sun L 2 courses £13.50, 3 courses £17.95, Dress Restrictions, Smart dress/smart casual, Civ Wed 46, Air con **Seats:** 45, Pr/dining room 24 **Children:** Portions **Rooms:** 15 (15 en suite) ★★★ HL **Directions:** M11 junct 10, take A505 E, then 1st right at rdbt to Duxford; take right fork at T-junction, entrance 70 yds on left **Parking:** 30

ELY   MAP 12 TL58

⑯ The Anchor Inn

Modern British

Riverside inn serving imaginatively presented local produce

☎ 01353 778537 Sutton Gault, Sutton CB6 2BD
e-mail: anchorinn@popmail.bta.com
web: www.anchor-inn-restaurant.co.uk

The Anchor was built in 1650, originally to provide shelter for workers digging the New Bedford River, as part of the mass draining of the Fens. Uneven tiled floors, antique pine furniture and roaring fires in winter welcome you to the historic inn. Food is an interesting mixture of traditional English dishes and those with European and international influences. Grilled dates wrapped in bacon on a mild grain mustard cream sauce, or loin of Denham Estate venison with root vegetable gâteau and port, orange, red wine and cranberry sauce are fine examples of the fare.

Chef: Adam Pickup **Owners:** Adam Pickup & Carlene Bunten **Times:** 12-3.30/7-11 **Prices:** Fixed L £10.95, Starter £4.95-£7, Main £9.50-£19.95, Dessert £4.95-£7, Service optional, Group min 10 service 10% **Wine:** 21 bottles over £20, 32 bottles under £20, 12 by the glass **Notes:** Sun L 2 courses £17.50, 3 courses £21.50, Vegetarian available **Seats:** 70 **Children:** Menu, Portions **Rooms:** 4 (4 en suite) **Directions:** Signed off B1381 in Sutton village, 7m W of Ely via A142 **Parking:** 16

HUNTINGDON   MAP 12 TL27

⑯⑯ Old Bridge Hotel

Modern British ⏑ NOTABLE WINE LIST

Hotel with uncompromising standards and a choice of dining venues

☎ 01480 424300 PE29 3TQ
e-mail: oldbridge@huntsbridge.co.uk
web: www.huntsbridge.com

Once a private bank, this 18th-century ivy-clad townhouse hotel stands guard over the old bridge into Huntingdon. There's a choice of two dining venues: the lively and informal Terrace restaurant, serving the full menu, good-value lunches and snacks, and the smart Dining Room restaurant, serving the full à la carte on Friday and Saturday evenings and used for private dining the rest of the week. The chef's love of traditional, rustic French cuisine is reflected in modern British dishes that speak with a strong French accent. Start with confit sea trout with fennel purée and beetroot, followed perhaps by braised oxtail with parsnip purée, washed down with a tipple from the excellent wine list.

Chef: Gareth Thorpe **Owners:** J Hoskins **Times:** 12-2/6.30-9.30 **Prices:** Fixed L £14.75, Starter £4.95-£10, Main £11-£23, Dessert £4.95-£8, Service optional **Wine:** 220 bottles over £20, 45 bottles under £20, 16 by the glass **Notes:** Civ Wed 80, Air con **Seats:** 100, Pr/dining room 40 **Children:** Menu, Portions **Rooms:** 24 (24 en suite) ★★★ HL **Directions:** Off A1 near junct with A1/M1 link and A604/M11 **Parking:** 60

KEYSTON   MAP 11 TL07

⑯ Pheasant Inn

British, French ⏑ NOTABLE WINE LIST

Gastronomic delights in a charming village inn

☎ 01832 710241 Village Loop Rd PE28 0RE
e-mail: pheasant.keyston@btopenworld.com
web: www.huntsbridge.com

This beautiful thatched inn is located in a sleepy farming village, with old farming equipment displayed as a decorative feature. Wooden polished tables and pine settles give a rustic feel, although still comfortable and spacious. Monthly-changing menus have individually priced dishes, supplemented by blackboard specials. Smaller portions and a separate children's menu are also available. Modern British and French cooking shows imagination and technical expertise, with starters like beetroot, fig and goat's cheese tart, or crisp salmon fishcake with agretti and rocket pesto followed by a main course like Portland crab and crayfish open ravioli with roast pineapple, chilli and coriander dressing.

Chef: Jay Scrimshaw **Owners:** John Hoskins **Times:** 12-2.30/6-9.30 **Prices:** Fixed L £12.95, Starter £5.75-£8.95, Main £12.50-£19.75, Dessert £4.95-£7.95, Service optional, Group min 10 service 10% **Wine:** 60 bottles over £20, 20 bottles under £20, 12 by the glass **Seats:** 80, Pr/dining room 30 **Children:** Menu, Portions **Directions:** 0.5m off A14, clearly signed, 10m W of Huntingdon, 14m E of Kettering **Parking:** 40

ENGLAND

MADINGLEY
MAP 12 TL36

⊛ Three Horseshoes Restaurant

Italian ♨ NOTABLE WINE LIST

Modern Italian dining in village setting

☎ 01954 210221 High St CB3 8AB
e-mail: 3hs@btconnect.co.uk
web: www.huntsbridge.com

Despite its quintessentially English location - with a garden stretching down to the village cricket pitch - this 16th-century thatched gastro-pub has a decidedly relaxed, continental feel, complete with table service. The daily-changing menus have Italian and Mediterranean influences and may include the likes of Jerusalem artichoke soup with truffle oil, followed by an excellent roast chicken stuffed with mascarpone and rosemary, served with olive mashed potatoes and slow-cooked cime di rape with crispy pancetta. To finish, try pears cooked in Valpolicella and vanilla. The well-chosen wine list includes recommendations for dessert wines.

Chef: Richard Stokes **Owners:** Huntsbridge **Times:** 12-2/6.30-9.30, Closed 1-2 Jan, Closed D Sun **Prices:** Starter £5-£9, Main £15-£25, Dessert £5-£8, Service optional, Group min 10 service 10% **Wine:** 10 by the glass **Seats:** 65 **Children:** Portions **Directions:** M11 junct 13, turn left, then next right and continue to end of road, and at mini-rdbt turn right **Parking:** 50

PETERBOROUGH
MAP 12 TL19

⊛ Best Western Orton Hall Hotel

Modern British

Historic old building serving modern cuisine

☎ 01733 391111 Orton Longueville PE2 7DN
e-mail: reception@ortonhall.co.uk
web: www.bw-ortonhall.co.uk

Previously the home of the Marquis of Huntly, this impressive, tastefully-restored 17th-century manor house is set in 20 acres of parkland in the conservation village of Orton Longueville. Retaining many of its period features, the elegant Huntly restaurant, with oak panelling and exquisite stained glass, exudes an air of warmth and intimacy. The kitchen's approach, however, is firmly rooted in the present day, its well-balanced, fixed-price repertoire delivering accomplished British dishes with a modern twist, as in smoked haddock soup with a soft poached egg, or fillet of beef with oxtail tortellini. Finish with a classic sticky toffee pudding served with an orange and butterscotch sauce.

Chef: Kevin Wood **Owners:** Abacus Hotels **Times:** 12.30-2/7-9.30, Closed 25 Dec, Closed L Mon-Sat **Prices:** Fixed D £27-£32, Starter £5.50-£7, Main £16-£19.95, Dessert £5.50, Service optional **Wine:** 23 bottles over £20, 42 bottles under £20, 6 by the glass **Notes:** Sun L 3 courses £15.95, Civ Wed 90 **Seats:** 34, Pr/dining room 40 **Rooms:** 65 (65 en suite) ★★★ HL **Directions:** Telephone for directions **Parking:** 200

Gaston Café Bar & Restaurant

☎ 01733 344170 44 Broadway PE1 1RS

An open-plan, modern informal dining room. Watch the pizzas being made.

Loch Fyne Restaurant & Oyster Bar

☎ 01832 280298 The Old Dairy, Elton PE8 6SH

Quality seafood chain.

ST NEOTS
MAP 12 TL16

⊛ The George Hotel & Brasserie

Modern British NEW

Stylish, busy brasserie in former coaching inn

☎ 01480 812300 High St, Buckden PE19 5XA
e-mail: mail@thegeorgebuckden.com
web: www.thegeorgebuckden.com

This venerable coaching inn may date to the 17th century, but it has had a stylish refurbishment to bring it right up to date. Each of its chic bedrooms is individually designed in homage to a famous George, from Washington to Best, while its ground-floor brasserie is a bustling modern affair that caters to casual diners throughout the day. Brown leather stools perch at the long metal bar, while polished wooden tables gleam beneath sparkling glassware; it's a convivial setting, perfectly complemented by a menu of modern British cuisine. Braised venison arrives with parsnip mash, black pudding and sauce bordelaise, while sea bass is served with squid, risotto nero, chilli and rocket.

Chef: Haydn Laidlow **Owners:** Richard & Anne Furbank **Times:** 12-2.30/7-9.30 **Prices:** Starter £5.50-£8.50, Main £12.50-£21.50, Dessert £5.50-£6.50, Service optional **Wine:** 35 bottles over £20, 35 bottles under £20, 16 by the glass **Notes:** Vegetarian available, Dress Restrictions, Smart dress **Seats:** 60, Pr/dining room 30 **Children:** Portions **Directions:** Off A1, S of junct with A14 **Parking:** 25

SIX MILE BOTTOM
MAP 12 TL55

⊛ Swynford Paddocks

Modern European

Historic country-house hotel with reliable cooking

☎ 01638 570234 CB8 0UE
e-mail: info@swynfordpaddocks.com
web: www.swynfordpaddocks.com

Set in 64 acres of parkland, this impressive country-house hotel has associations with both the races (at nearby Newmarket) and Lord Byron, who lends his name to the sumptuous fine-dining restaurant overlooking the impeccable front lawn. The food is modern British with Mediterranean influences, with an emphasis on satisfying, flavoursome fare. Take a starter of red mullet and herb risotto,

CONTINUED

SIX MILE BOTTOM CONTINUED

followed by fillet of sea bass with prawn and sesame mousse, pak choi and light soy broth, or perhaps pancetta-wrapped pheasant breast with confit potato, Savoy cabbage and redcurrant and juniper. Finish with an assiette of pear, or banana and caramel pannacotta.

Swynford Paddocks

Chef: Paul Buckley **Owners:** Paul & Lucie Smith **Times:** 11.30-3/6.30-10, Closed Sat (if sole occupancy wedding) **Prices:** Fixed L £15-£20, Starter £5.75-£9.50, Main £15-£29, Dessert £6.25-£9.50, Service optional **Wine:** 34 bottles over £20, 28 bottles under £20, 10 by the glass **Notes:** Tasting menu available, Vegetarian available, Dress Restrictions, No jeans/trainers at dinner, Civ Wed 120 **Seats:** 30, Pr/dining room 50 **Children:** Menu, Portions **Rooms:** 15 (15 en suite) ★★★ HL **Directions:** M11 junct 9, take A11 towards Newmarket, then onto A1304 to Newmarket, hotel is 0.75m on left **Parking:** 100

STILTON   MAP 12 TL18

⊚ Bell Inn Hotel

British, French

Charming inn with bags of character

☎ 01733 241066 Great North Rd PE7 3RA

e-mail: reception@thebellstilton.co.uk

web: www.thebellstilton.co.uk

Set in a delightful village on the outskirts of Peterborough, this wonderfully agreeable inn is steeped in history and possessed of numerous original features. The imaginative and consistent food is served in the atmospheric village bar and elegant, beamed first-floor restaurant, as well as the smart bistro - you can also eat alfresco in the courtyard. With quality produce at its core, the restaurant menu might deliver steamed fillet of brill with green herb and olive oil mash, crab claws, crevettes and a garlic beurre blanc, or beef and ale stew with stilton dumplings, with perhaps a classic glazed lemon tart with limoncello ice cream to finish.

Chef: Robin Devonshire **Owners:** Mr L A McGivern **Times:** 12-2/7-9.30, Closed 25 Dec, Closed L Sat, D Sun **Prices:** Fixed L £26.95-£31.90, Fixed D £26.95-£31.90, Starter £3.25-£4.95, Main £10.95-£15.95, Dessert £4.75, Service included **Wine:** 30 bottles over £20, 30 bottles under £20, 8 by the glass **Notes:** Fixed L 3 courses, Sun L 3 courses £16.95, Vegetarian available, Civ Wed 90, Air con **Seats:** 60, Pr/dining room 20 **Children:** Min 5 yrs **Rooms:** 22 (22 en suite) ★★★ HL **Directions:** 1m N A1(M) junct 16 follow signs to Stilton. Hotel on High Street in centre of village **Parking:** 30

WANSFORD   MAP 12 TL09

⊚⊚ Bentley's Restaurant

Modern French V

Stylish restaurant offering imaginative cooking

☎ 01780 782223 The Haycock Hotel PE8 6JA

e-mail: sales@thehaycock.co.uk

web: www.thehaycock.co.uk

Set amid attractive landscaped grounds in the heart of the peaceful village of Wansford, this charming 17th-century coaching inn has a wealth of character. The intimate Bentley's Restaurant comes decked out with well-spaced tables, upholstered chairs, crisp white linen and plush drapes, while the accompanying service from smartly uniformed staff is well informed and professional. The kitchen has pedigree and displays highly accomplished technical skills, the modern French cuisine reflecting influences from both America and Spain. Imaginative dishes might include a starter of seared foie gras with brioche and Cabernet Sauvignon caramel, followed perhaps by salt marsh lamb with sweetbreads, shallots, creamed potato and parsley jus.

Chef: Nigel Godwin **Owners:** Philip & Judith Carter **Times:** 12-2.30/7-10, Closed 1st week Jan, Sun, Mon, Closed D 25 & 31 Dec **Prices:** Fixed L £26.95, Starter £12.95-£16.95, Main £24.95-£28.95, Dessert £10.95-£14.95, Service optional **Notes:** Fixed L 3 courses, Tasting menu £68, Vegetarian menu, Dress Restrictions, Smart casual, Civ Wed 150 **Seats:** 30, Pr/dining room 12 **Children:** Menu, Portions **Rooms:** 48 (48 en suite) ★★★ HL **Directions:** In village centre accessible from A1/A47 intersection **Parking:** 200

WISBECH   MAP 12 TF40

⊚ Crown Lodge Hotel

Modern, Traditional NEW

Contemporary brasserie-style restaurant with grill-inspired dining

☎ 01945 773391 Downham Rd, Outwell PE14 8SE

e-mail: crownlodgehotel@hotmail.com

web: www.thecrownlodgehotel.co.uk

The open-plan brasserie-style restaurant here has a relaxed, contemporary vibe. Darkwood tables come laid with trendy crockery and cutlery, while fashionable darkwood flooring and screens to section off the large open-plan bar-lounge area press all the right style buttons. Staff are smartly turned out, with service professional but suitably relaxed, while the kitchen's equally modern approach (showcasing a selection of grills) suits the surroundings and makes use of quality, locally-sourced and properly aged produce. Think chargrilled chicken marinated in tandoori yogurt scented with honey and coriander, or a ubiquitous sticky toffee pudding with toffee sauce and vanilla ice cream.

Times: 12/6.30, Closed 25-26 & 31 Dec, 1 Jan **Rooms:** 10 (10 en suite) ★★★ HL **Directions:** 5m SE of Wisbech on A1122, close to junct with A1101

ENGLAND

CHESHIRE

ALDERLEY EDGE MAP 16 SJ87

◎◎ The Alderley Restaurant

Modern British V

Imaginative cooking at a country-house hotel

☎ 01625 583033 Macclesfield Rd SK9 7BJ

e-mail: sales@alderleyedgehotel.com

web: www.alderleyedgehotel.com

Built for one of Cheshire's cotton merchants, this country house has been modernised and extended to form a pleasant hotel. Its airy, split-level restaurant is popular with well-heeled locals and has also been known to cater to the members of the Manchester United football team. Star-spotting aside, there are plenty of reasons to visit, including a comfortable décor comprised of high-backed leather chairs and smartly appointed tables. And the food's good too, distinguished by imaginative touches, exciting use of flavours and sourcing of local produce. Mains might include sautéed calves' liver with stuffed onion and Cabernet Sauvignon vinegar, while desserts are decadent creations such as hot melting chocolate fondant with tangerine ice cream. Separate vegetarian menu available.

Chef: Chris Holland **Owners:** J W Lees (Brewers) Ltd **Times:** 12-2/7-10, Closed 1 Jan, Closed L 31 Dec, D 25-26 Dec **Prices:** Fixed L £13.50, Starter £6-£10.50, Main £16-£24, Dessert £6.50, Service optional **Wine:** 450+ bottles over £20, 30 bottles under £20, 7 by the glass **Notes:** Tasting menu 6 courses £47.50, Vegetarian menu, Dress Restrictions, Smart casual, Civ Wed 150, Air con **Seats:** 65, Pr/dining room 150 **Children:** Menu, Portions **Rooms:** 50 (50 en suite) ★★★ HL **Directions:** A538 to Alderley Edge, then B5087 Macclesfield Rd **Parking:** 82

ALSAGER MAP 15 SJ75

◎ Best Western Manor House Hotel

Traditional V

Good variety of dishes using choice ingredients

☎ 01270 884000 Audley Rd ST7 2QQ

e-mail: mhres@compasshotels.co.uk

web: www.compasshotels.co.uk

Developed from a former farmhouse, the hotel combines modern style with original features. Ostler's restaurant, in the 17th-century coaching inn, features oak beams and a period fireplace. Choose between the daily fixed-price and seasonal carte menus of British and French dishes using locally-sourced produce. Speciality flambé dishes like steak Diane and crêpes Suzette are offered alongside innovative

combinations such as mutton suet pudding with apricot couscous and rosemary jus, or grilled red mullet with winter kale crab cake and chilli in coconut broth. A separate vegetarian menu offers the likes of baked aubergine with feta cheese, or steamed mushroom and shallot pudding.

Chef: Ian Turner **Owners:** Compass Hotels Ltd **Times:** 12-2/7.15-9.30, Closed 27-30 Dec, Closed L Sat, D Sun **Prices:** Fixed L £13.50-£15.50, Fixed D £24-£26, Service optional **Wine:** 5 by the glass **Notes:** Fixed L 3 courses, D 4 courses, Sun L £15.50, Vegetarian menu, Dress Restrictions, Smart casual, Civ Wed 200 **Seats:** 90, Pr/dining room 28 **Children:** Menu, Portions **Rooms:** 57 (57 en suite) ★★★ HL **Directions:** M6 junct 16, follow A500 towards Stoke on Trent. Leave A500 on 1st slip road, turn left & follow road for 3m. Hotel on left **Parking:** 150

BURWARDSLEY MAP 15 SJ55

◎ The Pheasant Inn

Traditional British

Sandstone inn with cosy bar, restaurant and rooms

☎ 01829 770434 Higher Burwardsley CH3 9PF

e-mail: info@thepheasantinn.co.uk

web: www.thepheasantinn.co.uk

Nestling in the Peckforton Hills with stunning views over the Cheshire plain to the Welsh hills, this delightful 300-year-old sandstone inn boasts a wealth of original features including timber frames, a stone-flagged conservatory, open fires, and a courtyard for alfresco dining. Service is relaxed and friendly, and creative dishes are served either in the traditional beamed bar, where light bites and sandwiches are also available, or in the stylish restaurant. Try a starter like warmed fillet of smoked trout with horseradish cream, while main courses might include pot-roast pheasant with root vegetables, mustard mash and red wine sauce.

Chef: Hany Osman, David Blythe **Owners:** Sue & Harold Nelson **Times:** 12/10, Closed D Mon (no food 3-6pm) **Prices:** Starter £4-£9, Main £9-£19, Dessert £4.50-£5.90, Service optional **Wine:** 31 bottles over £20, 17 bottles under £20, 8 by the glass **Notes:** Vegetarian available **Seats:** 100, Pr/dining room 20 **Children:** Menu, portions **Rooms:** 12 (12 en suite) ★★ HL **Directions:** A41 from Chester towards Whitchurch. After 6m turn left for Tattenhall. In village signs for Burwardsley. Top of hill left at PO **Parking:** 70

CHESTER MAP 15 SJ46

◎◎◎ The Arkle

see page 62

◎ La Brasserie at The Chester Grosvenor & Spa

Modern International

Enjoyable brasserie dining in Chester's ancient heart

☎ 01244 324024 Eastgate CH1 1LT

e-mail: hotel@chestergrosvenor.co.uk

web: www.chestergrosvenor.co.uk

The more informal of the Chester Grosvenor's two eateries, this chic restaurant aims to evoke the bustling brasseries of fin-de-siècle Paris. Art deco mirrors hang above leather banquettes and sleek granite tabletops, smartly set with quality appointments. Brasserie classics

CONTINUED

ENGLAND

CHESTER CONTINUED

such as cassoulet or bouillabaisse form the mainstay of the menu, but there's also more imaginative fare on offer: lemon roast chicken with bacon, charred sweetcorn fondue and sage butter, for example, or a duck mixed grill. A range of lighter snacks is also available, including Alsace beer and onion soup, hickory-smoked duck confit with apple tarte fine and foie gras, and smoked salmon crumpet with scrambled eggs and chives.

Chef: Simon Radley **Owners:** Grosvenor - Duke of Westminster
Times: 12/10.30, Closed 25-26 Dec **Prices:** Fixed D £35, Starter £5.95-£12.95, Main £12.95-£21.95, Dessert £4.50-£5.25, Service optional, Group min 8 service 12.5% **Wine:** 40 bottles over £20, 9 bottles under £20
Notes: Dress Restrictions, Smart casual, Civ Wed 120, Air con **Seats:** 80
Children: Menu, Portions **Directions:** 2m from M53, located in city centre

◉ Rowton Hall Country House Hotel

Traditional British

Magnificent Georgian country-house hotel with fine dining

☎ 01244 335262 Whitchurch Rd, Rowton CH3 6AD
e-mail: reception@rowtonhallhotelandspa.co.uk
web: www.rowtonhall.co.uk

History buffs might be interested to know that this cosy country-house hotel stands on the site of a major battle in the English Civil War, but these days you're more likely to encounter a jogger in the award-winning gardens than a cavalier, thanks to Rowton's impressive health

facilities which include a beauty suite, pool and gym. Inside, surviving period features include an impressive Robert Adams fireplace, extensive oak panelling and a hand-carved, self-supporting fireplace. Take your seat in the Langdale restaurant and choose from an extensive selection of complex dishes, such as roasted monkfish in pancetta with Burgundy risotto, calamari and a ginger beurre blanc, or seared organic salmon with creamed cauliflower, asparagus and a broad bean velouté.

Rowton Hall Country House Hotel

Chef: Matthew Lloyd **Owners:** Mr Wigginton **Times:** 12-2/7-9.30
Prices: Fixed L £13-£18.50, Fixed D £13-£26.50, Starter £5.95-£9.50, Main £13.50-£23, Dessert £6-£7.50, Service optional **Notes:** Fixed L 3 courses, Dress Restrictions, Casually elegant, Civ Wed 170, Air con **Seats:** 57, Pr/dining room 120 **Children:** Portions **Rooms:** 37 (37 en suite)
★★★★ HL **Directions:** M56 junct 12 take A56 to Chester. At rdbt turn left on A41 to Whitchurch. Approx 1m and follow signs for hotel **Parking:** 170

◉◉◉

The Arkle

CHESTER MAP 15 SJ46

Modern French V

Gorgeous hotel restaurant with magnificent modern French cooking

☎ 01244 324024 Chester Grosvenor & Spa, Eastgate CH1 1LT
e-mail: hotel@chestergrosvenor.co.uk
web: www.chestergrosvenor.co.uk

With over 600 bins to choose from, this fine-dining restaurant has one of the most extensive wine cellars in the country. The cuisine is based on classical French with a modern twist, it's innovative, assured, and firmly rooted in the changing seasons. The setting, in one of the area's grandest city-centre hotels, is a dining room named after the famous steeplechase horse owned by the late Anne, Duchess of Westminster. Prints of the eponymous steed adorn the wall, while the colour scheme takes its lead from the black and gold racing colours of the owner and creates an elegant art deco feel. Stylish modern furniture completes the picture. The menu is a teasing wash of flavours that should give you plenty to ponder: Landaise duck with a hot peppercorn crust, ravioli, sweet beetroot and sour cream, for example, or turbot 'Caesar' with grilled lettuce hearts, smoked bacon emulsion,

croûtons and parmesan froth. Tongue-in-cheek modesty sees a starter of frogs' legs and English snail, with wild cress and crayfish tails described as 'pond life', while tranche of foie gras is accompanied by runny yolk, black truffle and 'salty duck bits'.

Chef: Simon Radley **Owners:** Grosvenor - Duke of Westminster
Times: 7-9.30, Closed 1 wk Jan, Sun, Mon, Closed L all week **Prices:** Fixed D £55, Service added but optional 12.5%, Group service 12.5% **Wine:** 600 bottles over £20, 5 bottles under £20, 15 by the glass **Notes:** Menu Gourmande £65, Vegetarian menu, Dress Restrictions, Jacket in The Arkle, No jeans or trainers, Civ Wed 120, Air con **Seats:** 45 **Children:** Min 12 yrs **Rooms:** 80 (80 en suite)★★★★★ HL **Directions:** Chester city centre (Eastgate St) adjacent to the Eastgate Clock and Roman walls

CREWE   MAP 15 SJ75

⍟⍟ Crewe Hall

Modern British

Fine dining in the sumptuous setting of a Jacobean manor

☎ 01270 253333 Weston Rd CW1 6UZ
e-mail: crewehall@qhotels.co.uk
web: www.qhotels.co.uk

The stateliest of homes, Crewe Hall stands in 500 acres of mature grounds and was once owned by the Queen. It dates from the 17th century, but the interior was destroyed by fire in 1866 and replaced in elaborate Victorian style with stained glass, oak panelling and marble fireplaces. A more recent addition is the west wing, including a brasserie with a unique revolving bar. However, the fine-dining option is the Ranulph restaurant, an elegant room located in the historic hall with well-spaced tables and crisp linen. The menu offers modern dishes with classical influences. Expect the likes of halibut fillet with local asparagus and langoustines, or perhaps crispy sea bass with tagliatelle and a spaghetti of vegetables, served with crab and tomato and cracked pepper dressing.

Chef: Russ Brown, Lisa Collis, A Hollinshead **Owners:** QHotels
Times: 12-2.30/7-9.30, Closed Mon, Closed L Tue-Sat, D Sun **Prices:** Fixed D £38-£42, Starter £7-£12, Main £18-£25, Dessert £5-£10, Service optional
Wine: 90 bottles over £20, 10 bottles under £20, 12 by the glass
Notes: Traditional Sun L, Dress Restrictions, Smart casual, Civ Wed 250
Seats: 45, Pr/dining room 180 **Rooms:** 65 (65 en suite) ★★★★ HL
Directions: From M6 junct 16 take A500 towards Crewe. At 1st rdbt take last exit, at next rdbt take 1st exit, then right into drive after 0.5m
Parking: 250

⍟ Hunters Lodge Hotel

Modern British

Seasonal menus in an 18th-century former farmhouse

☎ 01270 539100 Sydney Rd, Sydney CW1 5LU
e-mail: info@hunterslodge.co.uk
web: www.hunterslodge.co.uk

An idyllic retreat, this Georgian property is set amid 16 acres of south Cheshire countryside, offering elegant accommodation, impressive leisure facilities and a popular bar serving informal meals. The serious dining takes place in the spacious beamed restaurant, from a menu reflecting both British and European trends. Specialities include tempura of king prawns with a caviar of aubergines, balanced by a robust main course of braised shoulder of lamb in a sauce of Oakham's beer with champ potatoes, or pan-flashed monkfish with crab croquette, mussels and spinach. Finish with a trio of banana, including a brûlée, crumble, and moist banana pudding, washed down with a recommended pudding wine.

Chef: David Wall **Owners:** Mr A Panayi **Times:** 12-2/7-9.30, Closed BHs, Closed D Sun **Prices:** Fixed D £19.50, Starter £7, Main £14-£23.50, Dessert £7, Service optional **Wine:** 26 bottles over £20, 27 bottles under £20, 21 by the glass **Notes:** Civ Wed 130 **Seats:** 60, Pr/dining room 30
Children: Menu, Portions **Rooms:** 57 (57 en suite) ★★★ HL
Directions: 1m from station, follow signs to Leighton Hospital
Parking: 200

⍟ πr²

Modern NEW

Contemporary brasserie in modern wing of stately home

☎ 01270 253333 Crewe Hall, Weston Rd CW1 6UZ
e-mail: crewehall@qhotels.co.uk
web: www.qhotels.co.uk

This imposing Jacobean manor now boasts two AA-recognised eateries. Ranulph's restaurant in the main house is the fine-dining option, but for a more relaxed and informal experience head to the modern extension, where πr² does a brisk trade in classy brasserie fare. Its spacious modern interior includes a unique revolving bar that rewards you with a different view at every sip as well as comfortable seating and an open kitchen. Grill and vegetarian options supplement an already lengthy menu of accomplished cuisine: dive in with crab and ginger fishcakes with Thai jelly and chilli jam, followed by braised pork belly with apple dauphinoise and black and white puddings.

Times: 12/10, Closed L Sun

NANTWICH   MAP 15 SJ65

⍟⍟ Rookery Hall

Modern British NOTABLE WINE LIST

Classic cooking in a grand château setting

☎ 01270 610016 Main Rd, Worleston CW5 6DQ
e-mail: rookeryhall@handpicked.co.uk
web: www.handpicked.co.uk

This magnificent Georgian mansion, set in 38 acres of gardens, wooded parkland and meadows bordered by the River Weaver, bears more than a passing resemblance to a French château. With its mellow sandstone walls, polished mahogany panelling, ornamental

CONTINUED

NANTWICH Continued

ceilings, sumptuous leather sofas, rich brocades, and stained glass, the place oozes warmth and comfort. The impressive restaurant is the perfect setting for romantic candlelit dining. Modern British cooking with international influences delivers some originally-themed dishes and interesting flavour combinations, as in grilled black pudding with creamed leeks and poached hen's egg, followed by a fillet of Cheshire beef with horseradish potato purée, and warm chocolate fondant with caramelised milk ice cream for dessert. Service is smooth, efficient and unobtrusive.

Chef: Gordon Campbell **Owners:** Hand Picked Hotels/Julia Hands **Times:** 12-2/7-9.30, Closed L Sat **Prices:** Fixed L £15.50, Fixed D £32, Starter £6.95-£12.95, Main £15.50-£25, Dessert £5.50-£7, Service optional **Wine:** 160 bottles over £20, 8 bottles under £20, 10 by the glass **Notes:** Dress Restrictions, Smart casual, No jeans or trainers, Civ Wed 66 **Seats:** 50, Pr/dining room 60 **Children:** Menu, Portions **Rooms:** 70 (70 en suite) ★★★★ HL **Directions:** On B5074 N of Nantwich, 1.5m on right towards Worleston **Parking:** 100

PRESTBURY   MAP 16 SJ87

⊛⊛ White House Restaurant

Modern British

Chic modern restaurant with a good track record

☎ 01625 829336   SK10 4DG
e-mail: enquiries@thewhitehouseinprestbury.com
web: www.thewhitehouseinprestbury.com

Housed in a former farmhouse, this chic restaurant, modishly littered with contemporary paintings, sculptures and etched-glass screens, rubs shoulders with mullioned, leaded windows, stone fireplaces and limed oak beams. A straightforward menu is available in the bar, while the dining room offers more challenging fare; it's all served up courtesy of a long-serving chef who knows his stuff and consistently delivers quality modern cuisine. Take best end of Welsh lamb served with a cannellini bean and smoked sausage cassoulet, or perhaps pan-fried Cornish sea bass teamed with herb and lemon risotto and tempura anchovies. For dessert a bread-and-butter soufflé pudding or warm chocolate and pear tart with mascarpone ice cream might catch the eye.

Chef: James Roberts **Owners:** Shade Down Ltd **Times:** 12-2/7-10, Closed 25 Dec-1 Jan, Closed L Mon, D Sun **Prices:** Fixed L £14.25, Fixed D £15.95-£19.95, Starter £3.75-£12.95, Main £12.75-£22.50, Dessert £3.95-£7.95, Service optional **Wine:** 12 by the glass **Notes:** Vegetarian available,Air con **Seats:** 70, Pr/dining room 40 **Children:** Menu, Portions **Directions:** Village centre on A538 N of Macclesfield **Parking:** 11

PUDDINGTON   MAP 15 SJ37

⊛ Macdonald Craxton Wood

Modern

Stylish hotel for fine dining

☎ 0151 347 4000 Parkgate Rd, Ledsham CH66 9PB
e-mail: info@craxton.macdonald-hotels.co.uk
web: www.macdonaldhotels.co.uk

A smart establishment set in extensive grounds, the hotel offers excellent leisure facilities and an impressive conservatory, lounge and bar. The Garden Room restaurant is handsomely furnished and enjoys lovely garden views. The carte menu provides a wide choice of dishes prepared from excellent produce. A typical selection might include tournedos of Scottish beef with a pavé of mushroom and potato and truffle rarebit, or steamed red snapper with saffron and prawn risotto, seared scallop, and champagne and scallop roe beurre blanc. Vegetarian options feature the likes of open lasagne of ricotta cheese with peas and fresh mint.

Chef: Rob Pritchett **Owners:** Macdonald Hotels Plc **Times:** 12.30-2/7-9.30, Closed L Sat **Prices:** Fixed D £25-£30, Service included **Notes:** Dress Restrictions, No jeans, Civ Wed 300, Air con **Seats:** 56, Pr/dining room 40 **Children:** Menu, Portions **Rooms:** 72 (72 en suite) ★★★★ HL **Directions:** From end of M56 W take A5117 Queensferry, right at 1st rdbt onto A540 (Hoylake). Hotel 200yds after next traffic lights **Parking:** 200

RAINOW   MAP 16 SJ97

⊛ The Highwayman

British NEW

Traditional inn with modern approach to food and service

☎ 01625 573245 Whaley Bridge Rd SK10 5UU

From the outside, The Highwayman looks like the stereotypical country inn, but inside it's a successful marriage of old-style pub and modern makeover. Here, character stone floors, open fires and low ceilings blend with leather sofas and, in the small dining room, wooden tables and leather chairs. Service takes a modern approach - attentive, knowledgeable and helpful - while the kitchen follows a traditional path with some interesting twists, driven by quality local produce and intelligent simplicity. Take Gloucestershire Old Spot pork belly served with black pudding, creamed cabbage and roasting juices, and perhaps glazed lemon curd tart with iced lemon parfait to finish. (Lunch is a simpler affair.)

Chef: Gareth Davies, Matthew Wray, Luke Jackson **Owners:** Thwaites **Times:** 12-2.30/5-9 **Prices:** Starter £3.95-£6.95, Main £9.25-£18.95, Dessert £4.95, Service optional **Wine:** 2 bottles over £20, 18 bottles under £20, 6 by the glass **Notes:** Sun L 2 courses £14.50, 3 courses £17.95 **Seats:** 50, Pr/dining room 24 **Children:** Portions **Directions:** Main road between Macclesfield & Whaley Bridge. Situated between Rainow and Kettleshulme **Parking:** 22

ENGLAND

SANDIWAY   MAP 15 SJ67

⊛⊛ Nunsmere Hall Country House Hotel

Modern British

Traditional fine dining in elegant surroundings

☎ 01606 889100 Tarporley Rd CW8 2ES
e-mail: reservations@nunsmere.co.uk
web: www.nunsmere.co.uk

Dating back to 1900, this grand country-house hotel with 60-acre lake and extensive grounds was originally owned by the Brocklebank family, renowned for the Cunard-Brocklebank shipping line. The Crystal restaurant offers an elegant and intimate dining experience, overlooking the south-facing terrace and sunken garden. Modern British and European-style cooking is accomplished and makes fine use of quality fresh ingredients. A tasting menu is available for the whole table to sample, or expect carte dishes like thyme-roasted turbot with pomme Anna, braised celery and rioja jus, or perhaps a loin of venison with celeriac rösti, chestnut purée and sauce Robert, and to finish, maybe citrus fruit and camomile pannacotta with warm poppy seed cake and citrus sorbet.

Chef: Paul Robertson **Owners:** Mr & Mrs M S McHardy **Times:** 12-2/7-10 **Prices:** Fixed L £22.50, Starter £8-£12, Main £17.50-£28, Dessert £8-£12, Service added but optional 10%, Group service 5% **Wine:** 115 bottles over £20, 12 bottles under £20, 13 by the glass **Notes:** Tasting menu £55, Vegetarian available, Dress Restrictions, No jeans, trainers or shorts, Civ Wed 100 **Seats:** 60, Pr/dining room 45 **Children:** Min 12 yrs, Portions **Rooms:** 36 (36 en suite)★★★★ HL **Directions:** From M6 junct 19 take A56 for 9 miles. Turn left onto A49 towards Tarporley. Hotel is 1m on left **Parking:** 80

WILMSLOW   MAP 16 SJ88

⊛⊛ Stanneylands Hotel

Modern British

Country-house hotel with an engaging cooking style

☎ 01625 525225 Stanneylands Rd SK9 4EY
e-mail: enquiries@stanneylandshotel.co.uk
web: www.stanneylandshotel.co.uk

Within easy reach of Manchester airport and the city centre, this traditional country-house hotel is set in 4 acres of beautifully maintained grounds. Tastefully refurbished, the elegant panelled restaurant has well-appointed tables, and is a popular venue for locals and visitors alike. Relax over a drink in one of the modern lounges before tucking into a starter of baked sage gnocchi with purées of root vegetable and a parmesan tuile. Follow with a main course of lightly smoked potato-crusted fillet of sea bass with roasted sweet onions and fennel marmalade, or vegetarians may opt for cannelloni of leek with honey and cumin-roasted butternut squash and stilton fondue. Desserts include some unusual choices, as in baked beetroot and olive oil cake with feta cheese sorbet and lemon jelly.

Chef: Ernst Van Zyl **Owners:** Mr L Walshe **Times:** 12.30-2.30/7-9.30, Closed D Sun **Prices:** Fixed L £13.50, Fixed D £27.50, Starter £5.55-£9.95, Main £14.55-£22.95, Dessert £6, Service optional **Notes:** Fixed D 4 courses, Sun L 4 courses £18.95, Dress Restrictions, Smart casual, Civ Wed 100 **Seats:** 60, Pr/dining room 120 **Children:** Portions **Rooms:** 56 (56 en suite) ★★★★ HL **Directions:** From M56 junct 5 follow signs for Cheadle. At lights turn right, through Styal, left at Handforth sign, follow into Stanneylands Rd **Parking:** 110

CORNWALL & ISLES OF SCILLY

BODMIN   MAP 02 SX06

⊛ Trehellas House Hotel & Restaurant

Traditional British

Welcoming setting for great local food

☎ 01208 72700 Washaway PL30 3AD
e-mail: enquiries@trehellashouse.co.uk
web: www.trehellashouse.co.uk

There has been a change of hands at this 18th-century former posting inn and the experienced new proprietors have a natural talent for hosting. The building retains many original features, and an interesting choice of dishes is offered in the impressive slate-floored restaurant. Wild mushroom risotto makes a good starter, creamy yet nutty with plenty of mushrooms in evidence, followed perhaps by your pick of fish and shellfish delivered daily from Fowey. For dessert, generously-filled baked apple and cinnamon pie is served with organic vanilla ice cream, or there's a good selection of Cornish cheeses including Yarg and St Endellion brie.

Times: 7-8.30, Closed Xmas & New Year, Sun (non-res), Closed L all week **Rooms:** 12 (12 en suite) ★★ SHL **Directions:** 4m from Bodmin on A389 to Wadebridge, adjacent to Pencarrow

BOSCASTLE   MAP 02 SX09

⊛⊛ The Bottreaux, Restaurant, Bar & Rooms

Modern British

Local produce in a modernised 200-year-old building

☎ 01840 250231   PL35 0BG
e-mail: info@boscastlecornwall.co.uk
web: www.boscastlecornwall.co.uk

Named after the founders of the village, this hotel and restaurant combines 17th-century stables (now the bar), with a former village store (now the restaurant), and the hotel rooms above. The restaurant specialises in fish and seafood dishes in a comfortable setting with modern leather chairs, wooden flooring and simple white-clothed tables. Local Cornish produce is at the heart of the imaginative menu. You might try a starter of crab linguine with chilli, basil and garlic, or Thai-style fishcakes with melon, cucumber and basil salsa, followed by pan-fried fillet of lemon sole with clams in saffron cream and tomatoes. The desserts are truly wicked and include peach and almond tarte with Amaretto glaze or a selection of Cornish cheeses.

Times: 6.30-11, Closed 2 weeks in low season, Mon, Closed L all week **Rooms:** 8 (8 en suite) ★★★★ RR **Directions:** From A30, take A39 towards North Cornwall, and follow signs to Boscastle/Tintagel

BOSCASTLE CONTINUED

◎◎ The Wellington Hotel

Modern British

Imaginative cooking in quaint Cornish village

☎ 01840 250202 The Harbour PL35 0AQ
e-mail: info@boscastle-wellington.com
web: www.boscastle-wellington.com

Following the devastation of the Boscastle floods in 2004, the Roberts family has brought this old lady of a hotel back from ruin. The stylish, modern Waterloo restaurant, with a little help from the BBC's *Changing Rooms* team, provides the perfect setting for son Scottie's imaginative cooking driven by quality produce from the abundant local larder. Take herb-baked cod served with roast fennel, crispy potato cake and dill butter, or perhaps roast pork loin with carrot purée, rösti potato and a cider jus. Service is friendly and relaxed without losing any efficiency. Booking is essential as the restaurant has a fairly limited number of tables, though bar meals are also available.

Chef: Scott Roberts **Owners:** Paul Roberts **Times:** 6.30-9.30, Closed Thu **Prices:** Starter £4.50-£8, Main £10-£20, Dessert £6-£7, Service optional **Wine:** 15 bottles over £20, 41 bottles under £20, 8 by the glass **Seats:** 35, Pr/dining room 28 **Children:** Menu, Portions **Rooms:** 15 (15 en suite) ★★ HL **Directions:** M5, A30, A39 to Camelford, then B3266 to Boscastle. Hotel is situated at the base of village by the harbour **Parking:** 15

CALLINGTON   MAP 03 SX36

◎◎ Langmans Restaurant

Modern British V ✋

Accomplished cuisine in a 16th-century former bakery

☎ 01579 384933 3 Church St PL17 7RE
e-mail: dine@langmansrestaurant.co.uk
web: www.langmansrestaurant.co.uk

You'll find a friendly, relaxed atmosphere at this former bakery, with stylish modern sofas in the bar and crisply-clothed, candlelit tables in the dining room. The building is Grade II listed, tucked away off the main street, and takes its name from Thomas Langman, master baker from 1907. Everything from bread rolls to petits fours is freshly prepared on the premises by the chef owner. Local and organic produce is used wherever possible to produce dishes like fillet of brill with winter vegetables and roast garlic foam, or fillet of Cornish beef with cep sauce. An irresistible dark chocolate 'nemesis' might prove your downfall at dessert. Staff are well trained and fully briefed on the menu and wine list.

Chef: Anton Buttery **Owners:** Anton & Gail Buttery **Times:** 7.30-12, Closed Sun-Wed, Closed L all week **Prices:** Fixed D £33, Service optional **Wine:** 30 bottles over £20, 56 bottles under £20, 11 by the glass **Notes:** Fixed D 6 courses, Tasting menu available, Vegetarian menu, Dress Restrictions, Smart casual preferred **Seats:** 20 **Children:** Min 12 yrs **Directions:** From the direction of Plymouth into Callington town centre, left at lights and second right into Church St **Parking:** Town centre car park

---

CONSTANTINE   MAP 02 SW72

◎ Trengilly Wartha Inn

Traditional, International NEW

Village inn serving good Cornish produce

☎ 01326 340332 Nancenoy TR11 5RP
e-mail: reception@trengilly.co.uk
web: www.trengilly.co.uk

This traditional inn with comfortable rooms and bags of character is set in a charming location by the River Helford. The kitchen specialises in home-made food prepared from fresh, locally-sourced ingredients. Typical dishes might feature local sea bass fillets served with a pesto cream sauce, new potatoes and vegetables, while a chocolate mocha tart or chestnut parfait may provide the finish. The restaurant comes separate from the bar with a lounge connecting the two, while a comprehensive wine list and an imaginative range of bar meals bolster the act.

Chef: Nick Tyler, Richard Penna **Owners:** William & Lisa Lea **Times:** 12-2.15/7-9.30, Closed 25 Dec **Prices:** Fixed D £29, Starter £4-£9, Main £7.20-£26.50, Dessert £4.50, Service optional **Wine:** 27 bottles over £20, 113 bottles under £20, 15 by the glass **Seats:** 25 **Children:** Menu, Portions **Rooms:** 8 (8 en suite) ★★★ INN **Directions:** Between Falmouth and Helston off the former B3291 Penryn-Gweek road **Parking:** 30

FALMOUTH   MAP 02 SW83

◎ Falmouth Hotel

Modern British NEW

Beachfront hotel where seafood is a speciality

☎ 01326 312671 Castle Beach TR11 4NZ
e-mail: reservations@falmouthhotel.com
web: www.falmouthhotel.com

This spectacular beachfront Victorian hotel ticks all the boxes, with its wonderful sea views, inviting lounges, beautiful leafy grounds, impressive leisure facilities and choice of dining options. The Trelawney restaurant is the mainstay of the dining action, where the kitchen makes intelligent use of the abundant Cornish larder on its appealing fixed-price menus, which include a gourmet seafood option awash with the fruits of the sea. Dishes are simple and clean flavoured, allowing the fresh, local seasonal produce to shine. Think pan-fried sea bream mizuna, or medallions of herb-crusted monkfish perhaps.

Chef: Andi Andreou **Owners:** Richardson Hotels of Distinction **Times:** 12.30-2/7-9.30, Closed L Mon-Sat **Prices:** Fixed L £9.99-£12.95, Fixed D £19.95-£37.95, Service optional **Wine:** 21 bottles over £20, 29 bottles under £20, 7 by the glass **Notes:** Fixed Sun L 3 courses, Dress Restrictions, Smart casual, no sportswear, Civ Wed 250 **Seats:** 150, Pr/dining room 40 **Children:** Menu, Portions **Rooms:** 69 (69 en suite) ★★★ HL **Directions:** A39 Western Terrace, over rdbt onto Melvill Rd. Continue to next rdbt, hotel on right

ENGLAND

◉ The Flying Fish Restaurant Bar

Modern British

Relaxed dining by the sea

☎ 01326 312707 St Michael's Hotel and Spa,
Gyllyngvase Beach, Seafront TR11 4NB
e-mail: info@stmichaelshotel.co.uk
web: www.stmichaelshotel.co.uk

The décor of this stylish hotel has a contemporary nautical theme.
Giant sails flap at the entrance, flying fish skim across the restaurant
ceiling, while reception is done up as a yacht, complete with decking
and gentle seaside sound effects. The restaurant is a fun place to eat,
offering stunning ocean views from window tables and a south-facing
sun terrace. Fresh local fish is the mainstay of the menu, offering
Falmouth mussels with West Country cider or Cornish smoked
mackerel with sweet potato cakes. Non-fish options include chicken
marinated in Cornish mead with prosciutto, bubble-and-squeak and
thyme jus.

Chef: Fiona Were **Owners:** Nigel & Julie Carpenter **Times:** 12-2/7-9
Prices: Fixed D £21, Starter £4.25-£6.75, Main £9.50-£16.95, Dessert £4.75-
£6.75, Service optional **Wine:** 13 bottles over £20, 19 bottles under £20,
12 by the glass **Notes:** Vegetarian available, Dress Restrictions, Smart
casual, Civ Wed 100 **Seats:** 90, Pr/dining room 30 **Children:** Menu,
Portions **Rooms:** 61 (61 en suite) ★★★ HL **Directions:** Please
telephone for directions **Parking:** 30

◉ Harbourside Restaurant

Modern British

Contemporary-style restaurant with great harbour views

☎ 01326 312440 The Greenbank, Harbourside
TR11 2SR
e-mail: sales@greenbank-hotel.co.uk
web: www.greenbank-hotel.co.uk

Harbourside Restaurant

Once a base for packet ship captains, this lovely old hotel still has its
own private pier for guests arriving by boat. Its airy restaurant makes
the most of the spectacular waterside views with its huge picture
windows, and sustains the maritime theme. Accomplished cooking is
the order of the day here: sea salt-roasted chump of lamb with a
kidney skewer perhaps, served with hotpot potatoes, seasonal
vegetables and red wine sauce, or spiced pollack fillet with Puy lentil
and smoked bacon salsa, roast red pepper sauce, and an oyster and
nettle emulsion. Desserts are creative and might include rhubarb and
vanilla bavarois with deep-fried custard and roasted rhubarb, or apple
jelly with parsnip ice cream and mint syrup.

Chef: Keith Brooksbank **Owners:** Greenbank Hotel (Falmouth) Ltd
Times: 12-2/7-9.30, Closed L Sat **Prices:** Fixed L £14.95-£15.95, Fixed D
£24.50-£27, Service optional **Wine:** 20 bottles over £20, 42 bottles under
£20, 10 by the glass **Notes:** Fixed L 3 courses, Dress Restrictions, Smart
casual, Civ Wed 90 **Seats:** 60, Pr/dining room 16 **Children:** Portions
Rooms: 58 (58 en suite) ★★★ HL **Directions:** Approaching Falmouth
from Penryn, take left along North Parade. Follow sign to Falmouth Marina
and Greenbank Hotel **Parking:** 60

◉◉ The Terrace Restaurant

Modern International

Modern hotel dining with sea views

☎ 01326 313042 The Royal Duchy Hotel, Cliff Rd TR11 4NX
e-mail: info@royalduchy.co.uk
web: www.brend-hotels.co.uk

Situated in a prime seafront location, with uninterrupted views across
the bay and historic Pendennis Castle, the Royal Duchy is a relaxed,
welcoming and well-maintained hotel. The comfortably-furnished
dining room comes with traditional table settings and glamorous
touches like chandeliers and a grand piano, while the cuisine focuses
on top-quality local and seasonal ingredients using lots of fresh local
seafood. Strong combinations and clarity of flavours demonstrate a

CONTINUED

FALMOUTH CONTINUED

passion for food and accurate cooking. International dishes feature starters like pan-roasted quail with beetroot, Savoy cabbage and quail broth, or crab lasagne with wild mushroom velouté, while mains might feature grilled Cornish plaice with spinach and shellfish bisque, or roast turbot with bouillabaisse, clams and tempura oyster. A range of sandwiches, focaccias, omelettes and jackets, as well as some traditional dishes like home-made steak pie, are also available.

Chef: Dez Turland **Owners:** Brend Hotel Group **Times:** 12.30-2/7-9, Closed L Mon-Sat **Prices:** Fixed L £15.50, Fixed D £35, Starter £9.95, Main £21.95, Dessert £9.95, Service optional **Notes:** Fixed L 3 courses, Fixed D 4 courses, Vegetarian available, Dress Restrictions, Jacket & tie, Civ Wed 150, Air con **Seats:** 100, Pr/dining room 24 **Children:** Menu, Portions **Rooms:** 43 (43 en suite) ★★★★ HL **Directions:** At Pendennis Castle end of Promenade **Parking:** 40

FOWEY   MAP 02 SX15

◎◎ Fowey Hotel

Modern European V 🖳

Super views and elegant dining

☎ 01726 832551 The Esplanade PL23 1HX
e-mail: info@thefoweyhotel.co.uk
web: www.richardsonhotels.co.uk

Perched on the bank of the Fowey River estuary, this grand old hotel has watched the fishing boats and lazy yachts sail by for more than a century now. Just a short drive from the Eden Project, it stands in the pretty village of Fowey, and has a local reputation for accomplished cuisine. Plush drapes and rich wall coverings adorn the restaurant and, with its glorious outlook, window tables are at a premium. A commitment to local produce inevitably means plenty of fish - roast monkfish with saffron-infused potatoes perhaps, served with spinach and butternut squash and chive butter sauce - but meat dishes are also worthy of praise and might include rack of lamb with potato purée, spring greens, celeriac and mint jus.

Chef: Mark Griffiths **Owners:** Keith Richardson **Times:** 12-3/6.30-9 **Prices:** Fixed D £34, Starter £7, Main £19.95, Dessert £7, Service optional **Wine:** 14 bottles over £20, 29 bottles under £20, 7 by the glass **Notes:** Fixed D 4 courses, Sun L 3 courses £15, Vegetarian menu, Dress Restrictions, Smart casual, No torn denim, trainers, shorts **Seats:** 60 **Children:** Menu, Portions **Rooms:** 37 (37 en suite) ★★★★ HL **Directions:** From A390 take B3269 for approx 5m, follow signs for Fowey and continue along Pavillion Rd for 0.75m, 2nd right **Parking:** 13

◎◎ Hansons

British, French

Family-friendly hotel serving local produce

☎ 01726 833866 Fowey Hall, Hanson Dr PL23 1ET
e-mail: info@foweyhall.com
web: www.luxuryfamilyhotels.com

This majestic hotel occupies a prime hillside location in Fowey, enjoying exceptional views over the estuary across to Polruan. Built in 1899 by the Lord Mayor of London, the grand Queen Anne château-inspired façade does not disappoint, with an equally impressive lounge and reception hall, rich architectural detailing, Baroque plasterwork and vaulted ceilings. Hansons restaurant follows the theme, with oak panelling, gold gilt mirrors and heavy drapes offset with cream and pink contemporary décor and floor-to-ceiling windows overlooking the croquet lawn. Elegant tables feature wooden tub chairs with leather cushions, and there's an unmistakably romantic feel to the place, particularly in the evening with candlelight. Chef Glynn Wellington creates modern country-house style dishes using the best of local ingredients. You can see the mussel beds in the river from the restaurant and these - as well as local lobster, fish and shellfish - are the mainstays of a daily-changing menu. Try a starter like Fowey Hall bouillabaisse - a modern interpretation of the classic dish (using langoustine, John Dory, scallop, bass and mullet) demonstrating great depth of flavour and excellent saucing. Main courses include seared beef fillet with griddled chicory and parsley salsa, and to finish, pannacotta with rhubarb compôte will not disappoint. Definitely one to watch.

Chef: Glynn Wellington **Owners:** Andrew Davis **Times:** 12-2.15/7-10 **Prices:** Fixed L £15.95-£20.45, Fixed D £35, Service optional **Wine:** 56 bottles over £20, 19 bottles under £20, 7 by the glass **Notes:** Vegetarian available, Civ Wed 50 **Seats:** 60, Pr/dining room 20 **Children:** Menu, Portions **Rooms:** 36 (36 en suite) ★★★ HL **Directions:** Into town centre, pass school on right, 400yds turn right onto Hanson Drive **Parking:** 35

The Old Quay House

British, European

Fresh local produce served in a stylish waterfront location

☎ 01726 833302 28 Fore St PL23 1AQ
e-mail: info@theoldquayhouse.com
web: www.theoldquayhouse.com

Beautifully restored boutique hotel in an idyllic waterfront location. The terrace on the old quay itself juts out into the harbour and you can dine or take drinks here or in the new, chic bar area called the 'Q' Bar. With amazing views, the stylish, light restaurant is decorated in neutral tones with unusual plaques and artworks adorning the walls. Accomplished cuisine sees influences from France, Italy and Britain, with the emphasis firmly on good use of fresh locally-sourced produce. Begin with ravioli of Cornish crab with sautéed spinach and tarragon bisque, move on to pan-fried sea bass with wild mushroom fricassée and creamed spinach, or rump of Roseland lamb with a tomato and coriander dressing, and finish with steamed ginger pudding. Well worth the drive through Fowey's steep and winding streets.

Chef: Ben Bass **Owners:** Jane & Roy Carson **Times:** 12.30-2.30/7-9, Closed L Mon to Fri (Oct to May) **Prices:** Starter £6.50-£10, Main £13-£19, Dessert £6-£7, Service optional, Service added 10%, Group min 6
Wine: 15 bottles over £20, 15 bottles under £20, 5 by the glass **Seats:** 38
Children: Min 12 yrs **Rooms:** 12 (12 en suite) ★★ HL
Directions: From A390 through Lostwithiel, take left onto B3269 to Fowey town centre, on right next to Lloyds TSB bank

Restaurant Nathan Outlaw

see below

Food for Thought

☎ 01726 832221 The Quay PL23 1AT
Modern European menu in smart modern eatery.

HELSTON   MAP 02 SW62

New Yard Restaurant

Modern British 🐽

Fresh local food in an 18th-century stable yard

☎ 01326 221595 Trelowarren, Mawgan TR12 6AF
e-mail: newyardrestaurant@trelowarren.com
web: www.trelowarren.com

The stunning medieval manor house on the Trelowarren estate near the Lizard peninsula provides the backdrop for this restaurant, which occupies a delightful carriage house in the stable yard next to a gallery, pottery and weaving studio. Most of the ingredients are sourced within a 10-mile radius, with an emphasis on local fish and shellfish, plus game, herbs and fruit supplied by the estate. Typical dishes include fresh fish of the day, a salad of local meat, smoked fish and cheeses, or New Yard burger with fries. Afternoon tea is also served.

Chef: Greg Laskey **Owners:** Sir Ferrers Vyvyan **Times:** 12-2.15/7-9.30, Closed Mon, Closed D Sun **Prices:** Fixed L £13.50, Fixed D £20, Starter £5.50-£11.50, Main £11.50-£15, Dessert £5.50-£7.95, Service optional
Wine: 17 bottles over £20, 45 bottles under £20, 5 by the glass
Notes: Fixed L 3 courses, Vegetarian available **Seats:** 45
Children: Portions **Directions:** 5m from Helston **Parking:** 20

Restaurant Nathan Outlaw

FOWEY   MAP 02 SX15

European

Stunning views with Nathan Outlaw's imaginative cooking - a winning combination

☎ 01726 833315 Marina Villa Hotel, 17 Esplanade PL23 1HY
e-mail: enquiries@marinavilla.com
web: www.themarinahotel.co.uk

The jewel in the crown at the Marina Villa Hotel - set on the narrow streets of town and backing on to the River Fowey, with stunning views across the water to Polruan and out to sea - is this eponymous restaurant. The spacious hallway's stairs lead down to the lower-ground dining room, with its bar and lounge areas. Picture windows make the best of those views, while purple banquette seating or high-backed chairs provide the comforts, set to a backdrop of clothed tables, stylish cutlery and glassware and attentive, friendly service. Nathan, a Cornish phenomenon (previously at the Black Pig at Rock and more recently at St Ervan Manor, Padstow), opened his restaurant here back in February 2007 to showcase his fine pedigree.
In competition with the views, the imaginative cuisine has eye appeal, too, the modern, intelligently simple approach delivering promised flavours and fine balance, driven by quality produce. Take lamb with

garlic potatoes, young carrots and rosemary, or brill with leeks and mustard and brown shrimps, and to finish, perhaps a bitter chocolate fondant served with coffee ice cream. Ancillaries, like canapés, bread, amuse-bouche and pre-desserts all hit top form, too.

Chef: Nathan Outlaw **Owners:** Mr S Westwell **Times:** 12-2/7-9.30, Closed Mon (Tue out of season), Closed L Tue (in season), Wed (out of season) **Prices:** Fixed L £15, Starter £9-£14, Main £18-£24, Dessert £7-£11, Service optional, Group min 6 service 10% **Wine:** 65 bottles over £20, 15 bottles under £20, 10 by the glass **Notes:** Smart casual, Civ Wed 45
Seats: 40 **Children:** Min 10 yrs **Rooms:** 18 (18 en suite)★★ HL
Directions: Please telephone for directions **Parking:** 16

LISKEARD
MAP 02 SX26

◎◎◎ Well House Hotel

see below

MARAZION
MAP 02 SW53

◎ Mount Haven Hotel

Modern British
Local produce in light, stylish surroundings

☎ 01736 710249 Turnpike Rd TR17 0DQ
e-mail: reception@mounthaven.co.uk
web: www.mounthaven.co.uk

This stylish hotel has a stunning location looking out across St Michael's Mount. White walls, tables and crockery and pale-coloured chairs create a light, airy atmosphere in the dining room, while the terrace allows guests to absorb the wonderful views during pre-dinner drinks. Fresh fish dominates the main courses, unsurprisingly given the location, and, like the meat dishes, is refreshingly uncomplicated. Menu choices may include starters like smoked haddock chowder with paprika croûtons or baked Cornish Blue and leek soufflé, followed by braised hake with pancetta or rack of Cornish lamb with Parmentier potatoes and rosemary and mint jus.

Chef: Julie Manley **Owners:** Orange & Mike Trevillion **Times:** 12-2.30/6.45-8.45, Closed last wk Dec-end Jan **Prices:** Fixed L £13.50, Fixed D £15-£30, Starter £5-£8, Main £12-£18, Dessert £5-£6, Service optional, Group min 8 service 10% **Wine:** 11 bottles over £20, 35 bottles under £20, 6 by the glass **Notes:** Dress Restrictions, Smart casual **Seats:** 50 **Children:** Portions **Rooms:** 18 (18 en suite) ★★ HL **Directions:** From centre of Marazion, up hill E, hotel 400yds on right **Parking:** 30

MAWGAN PORTH
MAP 02 SW86

◎ Bedruthan Steps Hotel

Modern British
Atlantic views and full-flavoured food with visual impact

☎ 01637 860555 TR8 4BU
e-mail: office@bedruthan.com
web: www.bedruthan.com

Smartly refurbished family hotel in a glorious setting overlooking a fine beach and the clear Atlantic waters - between Newquay and Padstow. Enjoy alfresco summer drinks on grassed terraces before dining in the spacious and comfortable Indigo Bay restaurant. Cool

---

◎◎◎

Well House Hotel

Modern
Culinary hideaway in a tranquil valley

☎ 01579 342001 St Keyne PL14 4RN
e-mail: enquiries@wellhouse.co.uk
web: www.wellhouse.co.uk

Hidden away along a secluded country lane in a tranquil Cornish valley, this idyllic hotel is just 30 minutes from the Eden Project. Sitting in lovely grounds, it retains its country-house ambience, with modern additions such as the all-weather tennis court, swimming pool and croquet lawn. The perfect venue for a foodie getaway, the spacious restaurant has a muted modern colour scheme and large bay windows that offer views to the garden beyond, while crisp linen, sparkling cutlery and quality glassware adorn the tables.
The cooking is assured - the menu changes daily and features a well-balanced selection of modern British dishes distinguished by carefully-sourced local ingredients and a mature simplicity that allows nothing unnecessary to find its way onto the plate. Starters might include twice-baked parmesan soufflé with caramelised baby pear, while mains are straightforward creations uncluttered by superfluous flavours, such as fillet of black bream, crab cake, chive and tomato velouté, or perhaps a trio of Cornish seafood - scallops, turbot and John Dory with saffron foam. Finish with sabayon-glazed summer pudding with mascarpone sorbet, or maybe a refreshing assiette of citrus desserts.

Owners: Richard Farrow **Times:** 12-3/6.30-10 **Prices:** Fixed L £21.95, Fixed D £37.50, Service optional **Notes:** Vegetarian available, Dress Restrictions, Smart casual **Seats:** 34 **Children:** Menu **Rooms:** 9 (9 en suite) ★★ HL **Directions:** A38 to Liskeard and A390 to town centre, then take B3254 to St Keyne 3m. In village take left fork at church signed St Keyne. Hotel 0.5m on left **Parking:** 30

and contemporary, with white linen, candles and orchids, it's the place to watch the setting sun while savouring some accomplished cooking. Appealing menus use fresh local produce and dishes are well presented, perhaps taking in roast rump of Cornish lamb served with champ and a rosemary and garlic sauce, or sea bass baked with Thai spices and accompanied by steamed coconut rice and a fragrant shellfish broth.

Bedruthan Steps Hotel

Chef: Adam Clark **Owners:** Mrs Stratton & Mrs Wakefield **Times:** 12-2/7.30-9.30, Closed Xmas **Prices:** Fixed D £32, Starter £7-£9, Main £16-£20, Dessert £6.50, Service included **Notes:** Fixed D 4 courses, Vegetarian available, Dress Restrictions, No jeans, T-shirts, beach wear, Civ Wed 200 **Seats:** 200, Pr/dining room 150 **Children:** Min 7 yrs, Menu, Portions **Rooms:** 101 (101 en suite) ★★★★ HL **Parking:** 100

see advert

MAWNAN SMITH   MAP 02 SW72

⊛ Budock Vean - The Hotel on the River

British V

Cornish produce in smart hotel surroundings

☎ 01326 252100 & 250230   TR11 5LG
e-mail: relax@budockvean.co.uk
web: www.budockvean.co.uk

The high-ceilinged restaurant with its beams and minstrels' gallery has local musicians playing each evening, and provides an ideal setting for a special occasion. Top-quality local produce is imaginatively prepared and presented without undue complication. Recommendations include a starter of warm salad of monkfish, king prawns and sautéed potatoes with chilli and lime coriander dressing, followed by roast fillet of beef with fondant potato, wild mushrooms, spinach and Madeira jus. A fitting dessert would be plum and almond clafoutis served with clotted cream ice cream.

Chef: Darren Kelly **Owners:** Barlow Family **Times:** 12.30-2.30/7.30-9, Closed 3 wks Jan, Closed L Mon-Sat **Prices:** Fixed L £16.95, Fixed D £31.50, Starter £6.25-£18, Main £7-£32.50, Dessert £6, Service optional **Wine:** 47 bottles over £20, 35 bottles under £20, 6 by the glass **Notes:** Fixed L 3 courses, Fixed D 5 courses, Vegetarian menu, Dress Restrictions, Jacket & tie, Civ Wed 60, Air con **Seats:** 100, Pr/dining room 40 **Children:** Min 7 yrs, Menu, Portions **Rooms:** 57 (57 en suite) ★★★★ CHH **Directions:** Telephone for directions **Parking:** 100

Bedruthan Steps Hotel

Mawgan Porth   Cornwall   TR8 4BU
Tel: 01637 860555   Fax: 01637 860714
www.bedruthan.com   e-mail: office@bedruthan.com

The Indigo Bay Restaurant has stunning views over the North Cornwall coast and is a wonderful setting for a Bedruthan's dining experience. The table d'hôte menu offers plenty of choice for the discerning diner. Cornish produce features prominently and the style is a modern approach to classic dining. Menus change with the seasons to ensure that diners get the best and freshest food Cornwall can offer.

⊛ Meudon Hotel

Traditional British

Accomplished cooking at a friendly Cornish hotel

☎ 01326 250541   TR11 5HT
e-mail: wecare@meudon.co.uk
web: www.meudon.co.uk

A family of hoteliers now in their fifth generation have run the Meudon for 41 years - their fourth hotel in the village. Dine beneath a fruiting vine in a conservatory restaurant with views of sub-tropical gardens that run down to a private beach. Fresh seafood comes daily from Newlyn, oysters from Helford and cheese from a farm 2 miles away. A classic fixed-price menu of English fare might include grilled fillet of bass with crab meat and rosemary crust, or pan-sautéed suprême of wild Duchy pheasant over a mushroom duxelle with cranberry, in a Merlot and game sauce. Finish with frangipane tart served with a pearl of vanilla ice cream, or choose from the range of Cornish cheeses. Continued

ENGLAND

MAWNAN SMITH Continued

Chef: Alan Webb **Owners:** Mr Pilgrim **Times:** 12.30-2/7.30-9, Closed Jan **Prices:** Fixed L £16.50-£25, Fixed D £29.50-£33, Starter £6-£7.50, Main £15-£18, Dessert £6.50 **Wine:** 80 bottles over £20, 39 bottles under £20, 5 by the glass **Notes:** Fixed L 3 courses, Dress Restrictions, Smart dress **Seats:** 60 **Children:** Menu, Portions **Rooms:** 29 (29 en suite) ★★★ CHH **Directions:** From Truro take A39 towards Falmouth. At Hill Head rdbt turn left. Hotel is 4m on left **Parking:** 30

⊛ Trelawne Hotel

Modern British V

Imaginative British cooking in popular hotel with magnificent views

☎ 01326 250226 TR11 5HS
e-mail: info@trelawnehotel.co.uk
web: www.trelawnehotel.co.uk

Situated in a designated Area of Outstanding Natural Beauty, this small family-run hotel is surrounded by attractive lawns and gardens and enjoys superb views over Falmouth Bay and the surrounding countryside. A relaxed and friendly atmosphere prevails in the spacious restaurant, where quality local produce is used to create imaginative, modern British dishes. Organic produce is sourced whenever the market allows, with all meat and vegetables coming from local farms. Seared Newlyn scallops with Parma ham, red chard and cucumber acknowledges the culinary heritage of the region, as does baked Newlyn cod with silver skin anchovies, parsley purée and lime. Finish with organic Cornish ice cream, or perhaps a selection of West Country cheeses.

Chef: Martin Jones, Oliver Wyatt **Owners:** G P Gibbons **Times:** 7-9, Closed 30 Nov-20 Feb, Closed L all week **Prices:** Starter £5.50-£8.50, Main £9.95-£17.50, Dessert £5.50-£7.50, Service optional **Wine:** 6 bottles over £20, 49 bottles under £20, 5 by the glass **Notes:** Vegetarian menu, Dress Restrictions, Smart casual **Seats:** 30 **Children:** Min 10 yrs, Menu, Portions **Rooms:** 14 (14 en suite) ★★★ HL **Directions:** From Truro take A39 towards Falmouth. Right at Hillhead rdbt, take exit signed Maenporth. After 3m, past Maenporth Beach, hotel at top of hill **Parking:** 20

MOUSEHOLE   MAP 02 SW42

⊛⊛ The Cornish Range Restaurant with Rooms

Modern British

Atmospheric restaurant with great seafood

☎ 01736 731488 6 Chapel St TR19 6SB
e-mail: info@cornishrange.co.uk
web: www.cornishrange.co.uk

A vibrant restaurant with rooms, this former pilchard-processing factory has a long-standing association with the sea and, as you would expect, fish and seafood play a prominent part on the menu, with the freshest produce landed locally at Newlyn and delivered daily. Interiors are decorated in earthy tones, with sturdy chairs and tables, soft lighting, flowers and local contemporary artwork giving a rustic, almost Mediterranean feel to the dining room. The accomplished kitchen's modern approach delivers consistency, interest and diner appeal; take roast turbot fillet teamed with a smoked bacon and mussel stew and buttered new potatoes, or perhaps whole grilled Dover sole served with crab and dill butter. There's also a sub-tropical garden for alfresco dining.

Chef: Keith Terry **Owners:** Richard O'Shea, Chad James & Keith Terry **Times:** 10.45-2.15/6-9.30 **Prices:** Fixed D £17.50, Starter £4.50-£8, Main £12-£22.50, Dessert £3.95-£5.50, Service optional **Wine:** 14 bottles under £20, 5 by the glass **Notes:** Fixed D 2 courses, Vegetarian available **Seats:** 60 **Children:** Portions **Rooms:** 3 (3 en suite) ★★★★ RR **Directions:** Mousehole is 3m S from Penzance, via Newlyn. Follow rd to far side of harbour **Parking:** Harbour car park

◉◉ The Old Coastguard Hotel

Modern British 🖥

Popular summer alfresco destination with stunning sea views

☎ 01736 731222   The Parade TR19 6PR
e-mail: bookings@oldcoastguardhotel.co.uk
web: www.oldcoastguardhotel.co.uk

As the name might suggest, this commanding hotel and restaurant overlooks the sea - but what the name doesn't reveal is how splendid those sea views are and just how quaint and absorbingly lovely the location is, situated in what Dylan Thomas described as 'the most beautiful village in England'. The simple, clean-lined, contemporarily styled décor inside provides a suitably unobtrusive backdrop to enjoy those views over Mount's Bay and the accomplished cuisine. Fish - most from nearby Newlyn - features heavily on a modern menu that might include dishes such as lobster ravioli with a spiced guacamole and tomato and tarragon consommé, or perhaps wild sea bass fillet with a brandade of cod, roasted salsify and broccoli purée.

Chef: Barnaby Mason, Jonathan Blair, Simon Harris   **Owners:** A W Treloar   **Times:** 12-2.30/6-9.30, Closed 25 Dec (reservations only)   **Prices:** Starter £7-£9.50, Main £9.50-£19.50, Dessert £5.50-£6.95, Service optional   **Wine:** 33 bottles over £20, 18 bottles under £20, 11 by the glass   **Notes:** Sun L roast available Nov-Apr, Dress Restrictions, Smart casual preferred   **Seats:** 80   **Children:** Menu, Portions   **Rooms:** 21 (21 en suite) ★★ HL   **Directions:** A30 to Penzance. From Penzance take coast road through Newlyn to Mousehole. Inn 1st large building on left on entering village, after car park   **Parking:** 15
see advert

NEWQUAY   MAP 02 SW86

◉ Headland Hotel

Modern British

Elegant dining with wonderful sea views

☎ 01637 872211   Fistral Beach TR7 1EW
e-mail: office@headlandhotel.co.uk
web: www.headlandhotel.co.uk

Perched on a rocky headland surrounded by the sea on three sides, this imposing Victorian hotel is just the place to get away from the hustle and bustle of town. Views over Fistral Beach and the stunning coastal scenery are the perfect backdrop for relaxed dining in the Sand Brasserie, or in the more formal restaurant where you can watch surfers pit their wits against the waves. Quality ingredients feature on the modern British fixed-price menus, which change daily and not surprisingly focus on fish and shellfish. Expect the likes of seared scallops and pan-fried monkfish to start, followed perhaps by pan-fried medallions of Cornish beef, and tiramisù with a coffee and Amaretto biscuit for dessert.

Chef: Chris Wyburn-Ridsdale   **Owners:** John & Carolyn Armstrong   **Times:** 12.30-2/7-9.45, Closed 25-26 Dec, Closed L Mon-Sat   **Prices:** Fixed

D £26-£28, Starter £5-£6, Main £6-£29, Dessert £4-£5.50, Service included   **Wine:** 79 bottles over £20, 51 bottles under £20, 13 by the glass   **Notes:** Dress Restrictions, Smart casual, Civ Wed 200   **Seats:** 250, Pr/dining room 40   **Children:** Min 3 yrs, Portions   **Rooms:** 104 (104 en suite) ★★★★ HL   **Directions:** A30 onto A392 towards Newquay, follow signs to Fistral Beach, hotel is adjacent   **Parking:** 200

PADSTOW   MAP 02 SW97

◉ Margot's

Modern British

Friendly family-run bistro serving good fresh food

☎ 01841 533441   11 Duke St PL28 8AB
e-mail: enquiries@margots.co.uk
web: www.margots.co.uk

There are just nine tables in this cheerful little shop-fronted bistro, with the genial chef-proprietor combining serving and cooking, a formula that's proven both efficient and popular. The restaurant walls are hung with paintings by local artists, most of them for sale. The menu changes constantly according to the local produce available, and includes fish fresh from the harbour. Cooking is accurate and straightforward, with dishes such as Devon smoked duck breast with truffle oil and cucumber, or guinea fowl with spring onion mash and mustard cream sauce. Save room for dessert - sticky toffee pudding with butterscotch sauce perhaps, or saffron-poached pear with jelly and clotted cream.

Chef: Adrian Oliver   **Owners:** Adrian & Julie Oliver   **Times:** 12-2/7-9, Closed Nov, Jan, Sun-Mon   **Prices:** Fixed D £26.95, Starter £5.50-£7.50, Main £14-£20, Dessert £4.50-£7.50, Service optional   **Wine:** 10 bottles over £20, 16 bottles under £20, 5 by the glass   **Notes:** Tasting menu 5 courses £32   **Seats:** 20   **Children:** Portions   **Directions:** Telephone for directions

ENGLAND

PADSTOW CONTINUED

◉ The Metropole

Modern British 🖥️

Enjoyable British dining in an elegant hotel

☎ 01841 532486 Station Rd PL28 8DB
e-mail: info@the-metropole.co.uk
web: www.richardsonhotels.co.uk

This grand old hotel was a favourite haunt of the Prince of Wales in the 1930s and its public rooms still retain the elegance of a bygone era. Lighter snacks are available in the café bar, but to really get the measure of the place you should plump for the restaurant, an elegant affair boasting enjoyable cuisine and wonderful views over the Camel estuary. Expect modern British mains such as Cornish beef with a steak and truffle suet pudding, horseradish mash and pancetta jus, or pork with a caramelised pear, buttered Savoy and grain mustard sauce, and save room for desserts like amaretti crème brûlée with plum compôte.

Chef: Adam Warne **Owners:** Richardson Hotels Ltd **Times:** 6.30-9.00, Closed L Mon-Sat **Prices:** Fixed D £29.95-£35.95, Service included **Wine:** 21 bottles over £20, 26 bottles under £20, 8 by the glass **Notes:** Dress Restrictions, No jeans, shorts, swimwear **Seats:** 70 **Children:** Menu, Portions **Rooms:** 58 (58 en suite) ★★★★ HL **Directions:** M5/A30 past Launceston, follow signs for Wadebridge and N Cornwall. Then take A39 and follow signs for Padstow **Parking:** 40

◉◉ No. 6

Modern British V NEW

Contemporary surroundings meet ambitious modern cuisine

☎ 01841 532093 Middle St PL28 8AP
e-mail: enquiries@number6inpadstow.co.uk
web: number6inpadstow.co.uk

Smack bang next to Rick Stein's Café, No. 6 is certainly a worthy addition to Padstow's culinary heritage. This Georgian townhouse, once known as a smugglers' den, has been stylishly refurbished in contemporary style, with polished-wood tables, smart cutlery and glassware and white linen napkins. Service is friendly and unstuffy, the atmosphere relaxed and informal. Paul Ainsworth (who previously worked at London high-flyer Pétrus, see entry) shows his kitchen pedigree in accomplished, attractively presented modern dishes that use top-notch ingredients. Expect a starter like Looe Bay scallops served with Stornoway black pudding, carrots, star anise, vanilla and foraged herbs, perhaps followed up by glazed 'Jimmy Butler' belly pork and cheek, with king prawns, rosemary, butternut squash and shallots.

Chef: Paul Ainsworth, David Boulton **Owners:** Paul Ainsworth, David Boulton, Chris Mapp, Molly Christensen **Times:** 6.30-10, Closed Jan, 23-27 Dec, Closed L Etr, Mother's & Father's Day **Prices:** Fixed D £25-£30, Starter £8-£14, Main £16.50-£25, Dessert £7.50, Service added but optional 10% **Wine:** 53 bottles over £20, 8 bottles under £20, 17 by the glass **Notes:** Fixed D between 5.30-6.45, Tasting menu 8 courses, Vegetarian menu, Dress Restrictions, Smart casual **Seats:** 40, Pr/dining room 24 **Children:** Portions **Directions:** A30 follow signs for Wadebridge then sign to Padstow

◉ St Petroc's Bistro

French

Rick Stein's bustling seafood bistro

☎ 01841 532700 4 New St PL28 8EA
e-mail: reservations@rickstein.com
web: www.rickstein.com

Built by a friend of Sir Walter Raleigh, Rick Stein's renowned bistro is the fifth oldest building in Padstow, although its current look is thoroughly modern with clean white walls adorned with modern paintings. The open fire is a big draw in winter, while in summer there's the option of eating alfresco under a huge canopy. The emphasis is on fish and dishes featured in Stein's TV series. Remarkable ingredients are the star of the show here: try chargrilled squid with roasted red pepper and rocket, then continue with whole grilled, lemon sole scored with anchovy butter, or bourride of plaice, sea bass and salt cod.

Chef: David Sharland, Julian Lloyd **Owners:** R & J Stein **Times:** 12-2/7-10, Closed 24-26 Dec, 1 May **Prices:** Food prices not confirmed for 2008. Please telephone for details **Wine:** 22 bottles over £20, 13 bottles under £20, 11 by the glass **Seats:** 54 **Children:** Menu, Portions **Rooms:** 14 (14 en suite) ★★ SHL **Directions:** Follow one-way around harbour, 1st left, situated 100 yds on right

◉◉◉ The Seafood Restaurant

see opposite

◉ Treglos Hotel

British

Seaside hotel with bay views and fish on the menu

☎ 01841 520727 PL28 8JH
e-mail: stay@tregloshotel.com
web: www.tregloshotel.com

Set on the spectacular north Cornwall coast, the hotel enjoys wonderful views over Constantine Bay. It has been in the Barlow family for over 30 years and maintains a tradition of high standards. Dinner is served in a spacious restaurant with a conservatory extension, and seafood is a speciality along with vegetables from the garden. Dishes might include cream of pumpkin, orange and cardamom soup, followed by baked fillet of beef on artichokes and baby onions with lemon dressing, or courgettes with wild mushroom duxelle, glazed with Cornish Welsh rarebit. Finish with hot Bakewell tart served with plum compôte and vanilla pod ice cream.

Times: 12.15-2.15/7.30-9.15, Closed mid Nov-Mar **Rooms:** 42 (42 en suite) ★★★★ HL **Directions:** Take B3276 (Constantine Bay). At village stores turn right, hotel 50yds on left

The Seafood Restaurant

PADSTOW   MAP 02 SW97

International Seafood

Rick Stein's famous restaurant

☎ 01841 532700   Riverside PL28 8BY

e-mail: reservations@rickstein.com

web: www.rickstein.com

Rick Stein says on the menu that he has never regarded his restaurant as a gastronomic temple, but perhaps this statement ought to be reviewed, given that so many pay homage to the cooking made popular by his many TV series. At the door, crowds huddle to read the menu displayed outside this his flagship Padstow enterprise, an empire which now runs to the St Petroc's Hotel and Bistro, a café, deli, pâtisserie, fish and chip shop and seafood cookery school.
The small frontage here belies its tardis-like interior, with a spacious front conservatory for aperitifs overlooking the estuary and fishing boats. Otherwise, it's straight into the light-and-airy dining room's linen-clothed tables and white walls decked out with large, colourful paintings, which, in turn, contrast with the black uniforms of the well-orchestrated, attentive staff.
Superbly fresh and intelligently-simply prepared, well-conceived fish cookery from an accomplished team is the admirable style, with an ethos for using the finest local produce. The approach, via a daily-

changing carte and six-course tasting option, comes dotted with luxury items, a crowd-pleasing blend of classic (bouillabaisse of brill, gurnard, Dover sole, langoustine and mussels) and modern (monkfish vindaloo with raita and kachumber salad), all backed by a notable wine list.

Chef: S Delourme, David Sharland   **Owners:** R & J Stein   **Times:** 12-2/7-10, Closed 24-26 Dec, 1 May, Closed D 31 Dec   **Prices:** Starter £9.50-£22.50, Main £17.50-£45, Dessert £8.50, Service optional   **Wine:** 162 bottles over £20, 6 bottles under £20, 13 by the glass   **Notes:** Tasting menu 6 courses £65, Air con   **Seats:** 104   **Children:** Min 3 yrs+, Menu, Portions   **Rooms:** 20 (20 en suite) ★★★★★ RR   **Directions:** Follow signs for town centre. Restaurant on riverside   **Parking:** Pay & display opposite

Rick Stein's Café

☎ 01841 532700   10 Middle St PL28 8AP

Fish in the Stein style, mostly deliciously simple sometimes bold and striking. No lunch bookings taken, so arrive early.

Stein's Fish & Chip Shop

☎ 01841 532700   South Quay

Traditional fish and chips on the quayside where you can watch the fish being landed.

PENZANCE   MAP 02 SW43

◎◎ The Abbey Restaurant

Modern V

Skilful cooking in a modern setting with harbour views

☎ 01736 330680   Abbey St TR18 4AR

e-mail: kinga@theabbeyonline.com

web: www.theabbeyonline.com

References to its former incarnation as a 1960s nightclub include the bright red walls and tub seating in the restaurant's bar and lounge. The upstairs dining room is more refined with white walls, sculpture and good views of the harbour and St Michael's Mount. Top-quality ingredients are sourced from local producers, and seasonality is paramount. Produce is simply cooked with an emphasis on flavour and no unnecessary embellishment, in dishes like a light starter of pan-fried skate with grilled fennel, roasted tomato and chive butter

sauce, or a main course of equally excellent fish - fillet of brill - with asparagus risotto and a punchy salsa verde. For dessert, take white chocolate and Bailey's pannacotta with malted chocolate ice cream and caramel rum bananas.

The Abbey Restaurant

Chef: Ben Tunnicliffe   **Owners:** B & K Tunnicliffe   **Times:** 12-1.30/6.30-10.30, Closed Mid Dec-End Jan, Mon-Tue (Feb-Mar), Closed L Tue-Thu   **Prices:** Fixed L £25-£30, Fixed D £25-£30, Starter £6-£12, Main £16-£25, Dessert £5-£7.50, Service optional   **Wine:** 45 bottles over £20, 36 bottles under £20, 8 by the glass   **Notes:** Fixed L 3 courses, Vegetarian menu, Air con   **Seats:** 30   **Children:** Menu, Portions   **Directions:** In centre of Penzance turn into Chapel Street opposite Lloyds TSB Bank, 500 yds & turn left at Admiral Benon public house, onto Abbey St   **Parking:** On street

ENGLAND

PENZANCE CONTINUED

⊛⊛ The Bay Restaurant

Modern British ⟡

Contemporary restaurant with fabulous views

☎ 01736 366890 Hotel Penzance, Britons Hill TR18 3AE
e-mail: table@bay-penzance.co.uk
web: www.bay-penzance.co.uk

An Edwardian property with stunning views over the harbour, this restaurant/café/gallery business has been tastefully redesigned. The effects are most notable in the airy modern Bay Restaurant, which opens on to a deck overlooking Mounts Bay. The focus on style is not limited to the décor but is also apparent in the award-winning cuisine based on fresh Cornish produce. Dishes offered from the sea, land and garden might include smoked paprika-roasted sea bass with cannellini bean purée and saffron velouté, pan-fried fillet of Cornish beef with black truffle-crushed potatoes, buttered baby carrots and tarragon hollandaise, or deep-fried fennel beignet with a warm Puy lentil and sweet potato salad. For dessert, expect the likes of warm panettone bread-and-butter pudding with an orange and Flora Muscat anglaise.

Chef: Ben Reeve, Katie Semmens **Owners:** Yvonne & Stephen Hill
Times: 11-2/6.15-11, Closed L Oct-Apr **Prices:** Fixed L £12-£14, Fixed D £28-£30, Starter £5-£8, Main £13-£21, Dessert £5.50-£7.50, Service optional, Group min 8 service 10% **Wine:** 15 bottles over £20, 16 bottles under £20, 10 by the glass **Notes:** Tasting menu available, Vegetarian available, Dress Restrictions, Smart casual, no shorts, Air con **Seats:** 60, Pr/dining room 12
Children: Menu, Portions **Rooms:** 24 (24 en suite) ★★★ HL
Directions: Approaching Penzance from A30, at 'Tesco' rdbt take first exit towards town centre. Britons Hill is third turning on right **Parking:** 13

⊛ Harris's Restaurant

Modern, Traditional

Simple freshly cooked food in a charming little restaurant

☎ 01736 364408 46 New St TR18 2LZ
e-mail: contact@harrissrestaurant.co.uk
web: www.harrissrestaurant.co.uk

Purveyors of food have occupied this site since 1860 and the current establishment has been in the Harris family for over 30 years. The restaurant is located on the ground floor, and has a fine pressed metal ceiling and a decorative spiral staircase leading to the upstairs bar, where lighter lunches are also served. Service, like the atmosphere, is friendly and relaxed. Grilled scallops on salad leaves with fresh herb dressing might be followed by crab florentine, served with fresh spinach and a creamy sauce and gratinated with freshly grated parmesan. The lemon tart is a good example of the classic dessert.

Chef: Roger Harris **Owners:** Roger & Anne Harris **Times:** 12-2/7-9.30, Closed 3 wks winter, 25-26 Dec, 1 Jan, Sun, Mon (winter), Closed L Mon
Prices: Starter £6.50-£8.50, Main £15.95-£27.50, Dessert £6.50-£7.50, Service added but optional 10% **Wine:** 25 bottles over £20, 27 bottles under £20, 6 by the glass **Notes:** Dress Restrictions, Smart casual
Seats: 40, Pr/dining room 20 **Children:** Min 5 yrs **Directions:** Located down narrow cobbled street opposite Lloyds TSB **Parking:** On street, local car park

⊛ The Navy Inn

Modern British

Penzance local with an ambitious kitchen

☎ 01736 333232 Lower Queen St TR18 4DE
e-mail: keir@navyinn.co.uk

Just a short walk from Penzance promenade with its stunning views, this friendly pub has a brightly coloured exterior to match its name and a reputation for great food. It's decked out in shabby-chic style with wooden floors, open fires, and an array of marine artefacts. Working with the best of local ingredients, The Navy's accomplished kitchen conjures an eclectic mix of dishes ranging from typical pub grub (think chicken, bacon and mushroom pie), to more ambitious fare like roasted fillets of monkfish wrapped in Parma ham and served with pears and Cornish blue cheese.

Times: 12-10, Closed D 25 Dec **Directions:** In town centre, follow Chapel St for 50yds, turn right into Queen St and follow to the bottom of road

⊛⊛ The Summer House

Mediterranean

Mediterranean style and Cornish produce

☎ 01736 363744 Cornwall Ter TR18 4HL
e-mail: reception@summerhouse-cornwall.com
web: www.summerhouse-cornwall.com

Once home to one of Cornwall's leading artists, this listed Regency house is now a delightful restaurant with stylish rooms. The philosophy is simple - great food, beautiful surroundings and an informal, happy atmosphere. The restaurant has a Mediterranean theme that spills out into a walled garden full of terracotta pots and palm trees. The chef-patron Ciro Zaino spent years managing some of London's famous hotel restaurants but he has found true inspiration in Cornwall's fine larder, providing a daily-changing menu of fresh choices including lots of local fish and seafood. Think fillets of red mullet served with tomatoes, black olives and fresh basil, or perhaps a rack of lamb with a crust of mustard and aromatic herbs, and to finish, maybe a warm apple tart with crème Chantilly and a hint of Calvados.

Chef: Ciro Zaino **Owners:** Ciro & Linda Zaino **Times:** 7-9.30, Closed Nov-Feb, Mon-Wed, Closed L all week **Prices:** Fixed D £29.50, Service added 10% **Wine:** 6 by the glass **Seats:** 22 **Children:** Min 8 yrs **Rooms:** 5 (5 en suite) ★★★★★ GA **Directions:** Into Penzance on A30. Along harbour past open-air bathing pool & the Promenade to Queens Hotel. Turn right immediately after hotel & restaurant 30mtrs on left **Parking:** 5

PERRANUTHNOE   MAP 02 SW52

⊛ The Victoria Inn

Modern British NEW
Simply great food served in a friendly village inn

☎ 01736 710309 TR20 9NP
e-mail: enquiries@victoriainn-penzance.co.uk
web: www.victoriainn-penzance.co.uk

A popular village inn, just a short stroll from the beach, where top-notch produce is handled with care and reverence by a chef with a good pedigree. The mismatched furniture fits the bill perfectly in the bar and restaurant. The confident cooking style produces rustic, punchy dishes at lunch and dinner. Daily specials, locally-baked breads and excellent fish are among the highlights. Try a starter like foie gras and chicken liver parfait with beetroot chutney and brioche. Look out for mains like roasted monkfish rolled in fresh herbs and served with a prawn and dill risotto. Chocolate and walnut brownie for dessert is a truly wicked indulgence.

Chef: Stewart Eddy **Owners:** Stewart & Anna Eddy **Times:** 12-2.30/6.30-9, Closed 25 Dec, 1 Jan, Mon (off season), Closed D Sun **Prices:** Starter £4.50-£7.95, Main £8.95-£15.95, Dessert £4.75 **Wine:** 4 bottles over £20, 23 bottles under £20, 6 by the glass **Notes:** Vegetarian available **Seats:** 60 **Children:** Menu, Portions **Rooms:** 3 (3 en suite) ★★★ INN **Directions:** A30 to Penzance, A394 to Helston. After 2m turn right into village of Perranuthnoe, pub is on right as you enter **Parking:** 10

PORTHLEVEN   MAP 02 SW62

⊛ Kota Restaurant with Rooms

British, Pacific Rim NEW
Modern British cooking with an Asian twist

☎ 01326 562407 Harbour Head TR13 9JA
e-mail: kota@btconnect.com
web: www.kotarestaurant.co.uk

Situated in an idyllic Cornish coastal village overlooking the Harbour Head, the Kota Restaurant is housed in a former 18th-century corn mill. The décor is in a modern French bistro style, using light colours and wood to create a relaxed atmosphere, while the style of cooking is modern British with Asian influences, using locally-sourced and organic produce wherever possible. 'Kota' is Maori for 'shellfish', so not surprisingly there's a strong emphasis on fish. Tuck into a starter of hearty Thai red curry mussel stew with crispy fried shallots, followed by a main course of tempura-battered cod with mushy pea purée, served with wasabi tartare, home fries and Kota salad.

Chef: Jude Kereama **Owners:** Jude & Jane Kereama **Times:** 12-2.30/6-9, Closed 25 Dec, Jan, Sun (off season), Closed L Mon-Wed (off season) **Prices:** Fixed L £12, Fixed D £12, Starter £4.50-£8.75, Main £11.50-£17.95, Dessert £4.50-£5.50, Service optional, Group min 6 service 10% **Wine:** 30

bottles over £20, 23 bottles under £20, 13 by the glass **Notes:** Fixed D 2 courses, Tasting menu available **Seats:** 40 **Children:** Menu, Portions **Rooms:** 2 (2 en suite) ★★★ RR **Directions:** Take B3304 from Helston to Porthleven, restaurant situated on harbour head opposite slipway **Parking:** On street

PORTLOE   MAP 02 SW93

⊛ The Lugger Hotel

Modern European V NEW
Picturesque harbour setting for accomplished fare

☎ 01872 501322 & 501238 TR2 5RD
e-mail: office@luggerhotel.com
web: www.luggerhotel.com

The aptly-named Lugger (a small ship with lugsails to all you landlubbers) sits on the water's edge in this archetypal Cornish fishing village. Originally a 16th-century inn, reputedly the haunt of smugglers, it has been transformed into today's hotel. The restaurant has stunning views over the harbour, while the kitchen deals in fresh local produce, much of it delivered right to the kitchen door - smack on the harbour slip-road - with seafood (including crab and lobster) delivered direct from the boat. Otherwise expect the likes of roast fillet of cod with spring onion and bacon mash, chorizo and a mild curry oil vinaigrette.

Chef: Franz Hornegger **Owners:** Oxford Hotels **Times:** 12-2.30/7-9.30 **Prices:** Fixed L £21, Fixed D £37.50, Service optional **Wine:** 80 bottles over £20, 10 bottles under £20, 6 by the glass **Notes:** Fixed L 3 courses, Fixed D 4 courses, Vegetarian menu **Seats:** 54 **Children:** Min 12 yrs **Rooms:** 22 (22 en suite) ★★★ HL **Directions:** M5, exit onto A30. Take A390 St Austell to Truro road onto the B3287 to Tregony. Then A3078 St Mawes road, in 2m fork left for Veryan/Portloe, turn left at T-junct for Portloe **Parking:** 24

PORTSCATHO   MAP 02 SW83

Driftwood

Rosettes not confirmed at time of going to press
Modern European
Unique, relaxing location for exquisite cuisine

☎ 01872 580644 Rosevine TR2 5EW
e-mail: info@driftwoodhotel.co.uk
web: www.driftwoodhotel.co.uk

Perched on the side of a cliff overlooking the English Channel and Atlantic beyond, Driftwood does minimalism with soul, teaming a chic modern décor with an incomparable view and its own private beach. You can hear the waves from the garden as you enjoy an alfresco breakfast or aperitif. Expect accomplished cooking with a light, contemporary feel, conjured from the finest seasonal produce available. The ingredients are good and what the kitchen does to them is even better, the sum of each dish exceeding its individual components as clever combinations surprise and delight the palate. Starters might include scallops served with asparagus, duck egg, morels, and golden raisins, followed by roasted Terras duck breast with a pastilla of its leg, endive and orange and port jus, and perhaps prune and Armagnac soufflé to finish. At the time of going to press there was a recent appointment of a new chef.

Chef: Christopher Eden **Owners:** Robinsons **Times:** 7-9.30, Closed Xmas, Jan, Closed L all week **Prices:** Fixed D £39, Service optional **Wine:** 40 bottles over £20, 9 bottles under £20, 6 by the glass **Seats:** 36 **Rooms:** 15 (15 en suite) ★★★ HL **Directions:** 5m from St Mawes off the A3078, signposted Rosevine **Parking:** 30

PORTSCATHO CONTINUED

◉ Rosevine Hotel - Didiers Restaurant

European V

Classically-based flair with breathtaking sea views

☎ 01872 580206 TR2 5EW
e-mail: info@rosevine.co.uk
web: www.rosevine.co.uk

Set on the beautiful Cornish coast, this Georgian comfortable family-run hotel sits in pretty sub-tropical gardens with views over Porthcurnick beach and across the bay to Porthscatho. Its airy restaurant is decked out in heavy fabrics and shades of gold and cream, there's a grand piano for evening entertainment and French doors opening on to the patio. Expect a modern approach with a classic theme on the concise daily-changing menu, with local fish and seafood a speciality. Think roasted line-caught sea bass served with roasted shallot and saffron compôte, crushed chive potatoes and a bouillabaisse sauce, and perhaps a classic crêpe Suzette flambéed at the table to finish.

Chef: Didier Bienaime **Owners:** The Makepeace Family **Times:** 12-3/7.15-9.30, Closed Jan **Prices:** Fixed L £20-£26, Fixed D £38, Starter £6.95-£14, Main £17.50-£40, Dessert £7.95-£12, Service optional **Wine:** 40 bottles over £20, 6 bottles under £20, 20 by the glass **Notes:** Fixed L 3 courses, Fixed D 4 courses, Vegetarian menu, Dress Restrictions, Smart casual **Seats:** 50 **Children:** Menu, Portions **Rooms:** 17 (17 en suite) ★★★ CHH **Directions:** Off A3078, hotel signed on right, 2m after Ruan High Lanes **Parking:** 40

PORTWRINKLE MAP 03 SX35

◉ Whitsand Bay Hotel & Golf Club

Modern British NEW ◔

Luxurious setting to dine in style

☎ 01503 230276 PL11 3BU
e-mail: whitsandbayhotel@btconnect.com
web: www.whitsandbayhotel.co.uk

This imposing Victorian stone hotel, resplendent with oak panelling, stained-glass windows and a sweeping staircase, was moved brick by brick from Torpoint and retains many original features. The elegant dining room doesn't disappoint as comfortable high-backed leather chairs and subtle cream and brown décor give a restrained air of luxury. The modern British menu focuses on Cornish local produce including excellent fish from Looe. Starters might include pan-fried Cornish scallops, black pudding, cauliflower fritters and oxtail sauce, while main courses feature the likes of roast saddle of Cornish lamb, leek and pistachio farle, colcannon and glazed carrots and turnips.

Chef: Tony Farmer **Owners:** Chris, Jennifer, John, Tracey & Paul Phillips **Times:** 12-3/7-9 **Prices:** Fixed L £11.50, Fixed D £26.95, Service optional **Wine:** 20 bottles over £20, 28 bottles under £20, 5 by the glass **Notes:** Dress Restrictions, Smart dress, no jeans, T-shirts, Air con **Seats:** 70 **Children:** Min 12 yrs, Menu, Portions **Rooms:** 32 (32 en suite) ★★★ HL **Directions:** M4/M5 onto A38 for Plymouth, continue over Tamar Bridge into Cornwall. At Trerulefoot rdbt turn left to Polbathic. After 2m turn right towards Crafthole, Portwrinkle. Hotel on right

ROCK MAP 02 SW97

◉◉ The St Enodoc Hotel Restaurant

Modern British, European V

Contemporary cooking in bright modern hotel

☎ 01208 863394 The St Enodoc Hotel PL27 6LA
e-mail: info@enodoc-hotel.co.uk
web: www.enodoc-hotel.co.uk

A striking location above the Camel estuary, stunning views across to Padstow, and a fresh, contemporary décor draw discerning guests to this chic hotel on Cornwall's rugged north coast. Housed in a conservatory-style extension, with big windows and an eclectic collection of local art, the split-level bar and restaurant opens out on to a panoramic terrace. Great emphasis is placed on local seasonal produce, notably seafood, meat and vegetables, and highlights the daily-changing menu. Begin with baked marinated mackerel with walnut butter and green salad, move on to roast fillet of Newlyn monkfish with spiced red lentil dahl, cherry tomato salsa and crispy onions, and finish with poached pear frangipane tart with vanilla crème fraîche ice cream.

Chef: Rupert Brown **Owners:** Linedegree Ltd **Times:** 12.30-2.30/7-10, Closed 2 mths (late Dec, Jan, early Feb) **Prices:** Starter £5.50-£8.50, Main £14.95-£19.95, Dessert £5.50-£8.50, Service added but optional 12.5% **Wine:** 35 bottles over £20, 15 bottles under £20, 10 by the glass **Notes:** Sun L available, Vegetarian menu, Dress Restrictions, Smart casual, Air con **Seats:** 55, Pr/dining room 30 **Children:** Menu, Portions **Directions:** M5/A30/A39 to Wadebridge. B3314 to Rock **Parking:** 60

ST AGNES   MAP 02 SW75

◉ Valley Restaurant

Modern International NEW

Carefully-cooked and presented cuisine in relaxed surroundings

☎ 01872 562202 Rose-in-Vale Country House Hotel, Mithian TR5 0QD
e-mail: reception@rose-in-vale-hotel.co.uk
web: www.rose-in-vale-hotel.co.uk

It's all in the name really, a lovely Georgian country manor-house hotel delightfully secreted away in a wooded valley bathed in peace and tranquility. The spacious Valley Restaurant follows the theme, with relaxed, informal yet efficient service, linen-dressed tables and sweeping bay windows overlooking the gardens. The compact, fixed-price modern menus change daily to make the best of the abundant local larder and deliver carefully-cooked, well-presented dishes, allowing the main ingredient to shine through. Take Cornish beef fillet served with dauphinoise potato and sautéed wild mushrooms, or perhaps grilled fillets of red mullet with wilted nutmeg spinach and caper butter.

Chef: Colin Hankins, James Leon **Owners:** James & Sarah Evans **Times:** 12-2/7-9, Closed L Sat-Wed (winter) **Prices:** Fixed L £5-£20, Fixed D £25-£30, Service optional **Wine:** 10 bottles over £20, 25 bottles under £20, 5 by the glass **Notes:** Vegetarian available, Civ Wed 100 **Seats:** 80, Pr/dining room 12 **Children:** Min 7 yrs, Portions **Directions:** A30 S. At Chiverton Cross rdbt take 3rd exit and at the next rdbt take 3rd exit signed B3277 towards St Agnes. After 0.3m follow brown tourist info signs to Rose-in-Vale **Parking:** 50

ST AUSTELL   MAP 02 SX05

◉ Carlyon Bay Hotel

Modern, Traditional

Sweeping sea views and a fine-dining restaurant

☎ 01726 812304 Sea Rd, Carlyon Bay PL25 3RD
e-mail: info@carlyonbay.co.uk
web: www.carlyonbay.com

An imposing art deco style hotel, purpose-built in 1929 in a fantastic cliff-top location. The restaurant has sea views from its modern but traditionally-styled dining room that offers a choice of daily-changing fixed-price or carte options. Modern British cuisine is inspired here by the Cornish coast and quality local produce, with starters like a classic Cornish shellfish terrine served with saffron and mussel dressing on the menu. Mains might feature rack of local lamb with ham hock and parsnip purée, while Cornish mead bread-and-butter pudding with clotted cream ice cream might catch the eye at dessert. Formal table service is delivered by friendly, professional staff.

Chef: Paul Leakey **Owners:** PR Brend Hoteliers Ltd **Times:** 12-2/7-9.30 **Prices:** Fixed L £15.50-£17.50, Fixed D £35, Starter £2.95-£7.50, Main £4.50-£17, Dessert £5.50-£8.50, Service optional **Wine:** 115 bottles over £20, 66 bottles under £20, 27 by the glass **Notes:** Fixed D 4 courses, Vegetarian available, Dress Restrictions, Smart dress, Civ Wed 140, Air con **Seats:** 180, Pr/dining room 70 **Children:** Menu, Portions **Rooms:** 87 (87 en suite) ★★★★ HL **Directions:** A390 towards St Austell; from town follow Charlestown then Carlyon Bay/Crinnis. Hotel at end of Sea Rd near Cornwall Coliseum **Parking:** 60

◉ Revival

International

Fresh, exciting cooking in historic Charlestown Harbour

☎ 01726 879053 Charlestown Harbour PL25 3NJ
e-mail: info@cornwall-revival.co.uk
web: www.cornwall-revival.co.uk

Contemporary style blends with interesting old features at this white-painted building (a former sail and rope store) set alongside the port. The terrace is a great place for fair-weather aperitifs, while inside is light and airy, with burgundy chairs, white tablecloths and attentive service delivering the comforts. Punchy flavours, quality ingredients and a confident kitchen impress, alongside a deserved reputation for fresh fish and seafood. Lunch is a lighter affair (with a more café-bar buzz), while dinner cranks up a gear and transforms things to a restaurant vibe. Think blackened freshly-caught sea bass served with asparagus, fine beans, new potatoes and a béarnaise sauce.

Chef: Grady Boone **Owners:** Ashley Waller, Angela Husband **Times:** 10-2.45/6.30-10, Closed Mon, Closed D Sun **Prices:** Fixed D £28, Starter £4-£8, Main £16-£20, Dessert £5-£8, Service optional **Wine:** 33 bottles over £20, 19 bottles under £20, 7 by the glass **Notes:** ALC minimum prices for lunch, Dress Restrictions, Smart casual **Seats:** 40 **Children:** Portions **Directions:** Follow signs for Charlestown from St Austell bypass, restaurant on right, next to square rig ships **Parking:** Pay & display nearby

ST IVES   MAP 02 SW54

◉ Alba Restaurant

Modern European V

Sea views and fresh local produce

☎ 01736 797222 Old Lifeboat House, Wharf Rd TR26 1LF
e-mail: julia.stevens@tiscali.co.uk
web: www.thealbarestaurant.com

Formerly a lifeboat house, the restaurant is on the water's edge with huge picture windows making the most of the harbourside views. Bright modern art adorns the newly-decorated warm painted walls in the contemporary interior. The cooking style here is intelligently straightforward, the kitchen's modern approach showcasing fresh local and seasonal produce, with fish fittingly the order of the day. A fixed-price menu is available at lunch and dinner (before 7pm) to bolster the cartes, while specials add to the appealing repertoire. Imaginative offerings might include the likes of a fillet of John Dory served with a pistou of spring vegetables and haricots blanc, and perhaps a classic chocolate fondant with pistachio ice cream to close. Organic meat and vegetarian options available.

CONTINUED

ST IVES CONTINUED

Chef: Grant Nethercott **Owners:** Harbour Kitchen Co Ltd **Times:** 11.30-2/5-9.45, Closed 25-26 Dec **Prices:** Fixed L £13, Fixed D £16, Starter £4.95-£7.95, Main £12.95-£19.50, Dessert £4.95-£5.95, Service optional, Group min 6 service 10% **Wine:** 26 bottles over £20, 38 bottles under £20, 33 by the glass **Notes:** Fixed-price menus before 7.30pm in season or 7pm rest of year, Vegetarian menu, Air con **Seats:** 60 **Children:** Menu, Portions **Directions:** First building onto St Ives harbour front, opposite the new Lifeboat House

◉ Garrack Hotel & Restaurant

Modern British

Relaxed, traditional hotel dining with great fish choices

☎ 01736 796199 & 792910 Burthallan Ln, Higher Ayr TR26 3AA

e-mail: aarest@garrack.com

web: www.garrack.com

Enjoying a peaceful, elevated position with fine views across the harbour and Porthmeor Beach, the Garrack is a well-established hotel with a cosy bar, comfortable lounge and L-shaped traditional, country-house style restaurant. A wide range of dishes features on the modern British carte, including fresh lobster priced by live weight per kilo. Expect large fish portions, perhaps roast monkfish with chilli, shallot and coriander relish, or wild sea bass with smoked fish kedgeree, while meat-eaters can tuck into the likes of roast saddle of St Just lamb served with dauphinoise and fennel pesto, or gâteau of Penwith beef with blue cheese, in a red wine and tarragon jus.

Chef: Neil O'Brien **Owners:** Kilby family **Times:** 6.30-9, Closed L all week **Prices:** Fixed D £25, Starter £6.95-£9, Main £12.95-£19, Dessert £5.95-£9.50, Service optional **Wine:** 16 bottles over £20, 65 bottles under £20, 6 by the glass **Notes:** Early supper menu 6.30-7 aimed at families & older guests, Vegetarian available, Dress Restrictions, Smart casual **Seats:** 40 **Children:** Menu, Portions **Rooms:** 18 (18 en suite) ★★★ HL **Directions:** From Tate Gallery & Porthmeor Beach car park follow road uphill to top. Burthallan Lane & Garrack Rd signs on right **Parking:** 36

◉ Porthminster Beach Restaurant

Modern International V

Contemporary cooking right on the beach

☎ 01736 795352 Porthminster TR26 2EB

e-mail: pminster@btconnect.com

web: www.porthminstercafe.co.uk

A former tea room in original 1930s art deco style, this beachside restaurant has a distinctly Mediterranean feel, with terracotta tiles, unclothed wooden tables and great artwork from Anthony Frost. Window tables are understandably popular, and there is a sunny patio with heating when needed. Locally caught seafood - the freshest possible - dominates the menus. Dishes are modern, eclectic and exciting, including the likes of grilled Helford River oysters in chorizo and wasabi aïoli, crab and smoked pollack lasagne with Oscietra caviar, or turbot tronçon with guanja, rosemary sauce and crispy sweetbreads.

Chef: M Smith **Owners:** Jim Woolcock, David Fox, Roger & Tim Symons, M Smith **Times:** 12-3.30/6, Closed 25-26 Dec **Prices:** Starter £6.99-£10.99, Main £15.99-£23.99, Dessert £4.50-£4.99, Service optional **Wine:** 13 bottles over £20, 15 bottles under £20, 9 by the glass **Notes:** Vegetarian menu **Seats:** 60 **Children:** Portions **Directions:** On Porthminster Beach, beneath the St Ives Railway Station **Parking:** 300yds (railway station)

◉ Sands Restaurant

Traditional Mediterranean

Traditional beachside hotel with enjoyable dining

☎ 01736 795311 Carbis Bay Hotel, Carbis Bay TR26 2NP

e-mail: carisbayhotel@btconnect.com

web: www.carbisbayhotel.co.uk

Built in 1894 by famous Cornish architect, Sylvanus Trevail, this comfortable hotel stands back from its own private beach on the golden sands of Carbis Bay; guests can enjoy the excellent views from the conservatory. The spacious restaurant offers a traditional, no nonsense British/European menu with contemporary touches, and an emphasis on flavour and seasonality. With dishes based on the best of local produce, friendly, attentive staff help you choose from starters like wild mushroom soup with tarragon cream followed by guinea fowl suprême with apricots and bacon and mixed bean and vegetable cassoulet.

Chef: Alan Haag **Owners:** Mr M W Baker **Times:** 12-3/6-9, Closed 3 wks Jan **Prices:** Fixed L £11.95-£14.95, Fixed D £20-£25, Starter £5-£10, Main £11-£19, Dessert £5, Service optional **Wine:** 15 bottles over £20, 20 bottles under £20, 8 by the glass **Notes:** Dress Restrictions, Smart casual, Civ Wed 150 **Seats:** 150, Pr/dining room 40 **Children:** Menu, Portions **Rooms:** 40 (40 en suite) ★★★ HL **Directions:** A3074 to Carbis Bay, turn right along Porthrepta Rd to the sea. The restaurant is on Carbis Bay beach **Parking:** 100

◉ The Wave Restaurant

Modern Mediterranean 🖵

Modern cuisine close to picturesque beaches

☎ 01736 796661 17 St Andrews St TR26 1AH

web: www.wave-restaurant.co.uk

Tucked away in a quiet street a pebble's throw from St Ives harbour, this popular modern, stylish restaurant has a Mediterranean feel to it. With two separate dining areas, clean lines and lots of local artwork add to the intimacy of the place, which is friendly and owner-run. The Mediterranean feel extends to the food, which is also dotted with Asian influences; think Thai salad of sweet pork to start, then pan-fried line-caught local sea bass served with a lemon risotto cake, chargrilled asparagus, Cornish crab and tomato and vanilla dressing, while a saffron and honey bread-and-butter pudding might catch the eye at dessert.

The Wave Restaurant

Chef: S M Pellow **Owners:** Mr & Mrs Cowling, Mr & Mrs Pellow **Times:** 6-9.30, Closed end Nov-beg Mar, Sun, Closed L all week **Prices:** Fixed D £12.95, Starter £4.50-£8.95, Main £12.95-£17.95, Dessert £5.50, Service optional **Wine:** 4 bottles over £20, 20 bottles under £20, 8 by the glass **Notes:** Fixed D 2 courses 6-7.15pm, Dress Restrictions, Smart casual, no swimwear or bare chests **Seats:** 50 **Children:** Menu, Portions **Directions:** Located just outside the town centre, 100yds from the parish church **Parking:** Station car park

Onshore
☎ 01736 796000 Wharf Rd TR26
Quality, wood-baked pizza.

🖳 Russets
☎ 01736 794700 18a Fore St TR26 1AB
web: www.theaa.com/travel/index.jsp
The focus of this Cornish favourite is high quality seafood. There are classic dishes, newer inventions and diverse global influences.

ST MAWES
MAP 02 SW83

◉◉◉ Hotel Tresanton
see below

◉◉ Idle Rocks Hotel
Modern European V
Innovative cooking at the water's edge

☎ 01326 270771 Harbour Side TR2 5AN
e-mail: reception@idlerocks.co.uk
web: www.idlerocks.co.uk

Set on the edge of the harbour wall in this quaint fishing village, Idle Rocks enjoys fantastic views over the bay. The aptly-named, modern split-level Water's Edge restaurant echoes the surroundings, decked out in shades of blue, gold and sand with lightwood floors and picture windows that allow all diners a view. And summer dining on the terrace is just perfect. The talented kitchen takes a modern approach - underpinned by classic technique - and features top-notch local produce and clean flavours on the appealing, daily-changing menus. Take slow-roast best end of lamb served with braised shoulder suet pudding with tomato and tarragon, and perhaps a roquefort pannacotta with Granny Smith sorbet and jelly to close.

Chef: Damian Broom **Owners:** E K Richardson **Times:** 12-3/6.30-9 **Prices:** Food prices not confirmed for 2008. Please telephone for details **Wine:** 50 bottles over £20, 50 bottles under £20, 21 by the glass **Notes:** Vegetarian menu, Dress Restrictions, Smart casual **Seats:** 70 **Children:** Portions **Rooms:** 27 (27 en suite) ★★★ HL **Directions:** From St Austell take A390 towards Truro, turn left onto B3287 signed Tregony, through Tregony, left at T-junct onto A3078, hotel is on left on waterfront **Parking:** 5

Hotel Tresanton

ST MAWES
MAP 02 SW83

Modern Mediterranean
Small boutique hotel reinventing seaside dining

☎ 01326 270055 Lower Castle Rd TR2 5DR
e-mail: info@tresanton.com
web: www.tresanton.com

Perched just above the sea, fashionable Tresanton is an idyllic place to dine or stay - with its magical views over the bay to the Roseland Peninsula and St Anthony's Lighthouse, it is hard not to be seduced. But add Olga Polizzi's much admired stylish, urban-retro design (she's sister of Sir Rocco Forte), and you have a stunning original gem. The dining room comes appropriately surrounded by glass to make the best of those views and has a two-tiered decked terrace. Like the hotel, it is design-led and very stylish with a calm, cool Mediterranean air, fine mosaic floor and nautical themes - think dark blue seating for instance. An impeccable team of front-of-house staff, both in appearance and skill, fit the bill perfectly too.
The accomplished kitchen's approach majors on cracking, high-quality ingredients - sourced locally wherever possible - simply cooked with integrity to maximise freshness and flavour, with the fruits of the sea an obvious strength. Take sea bass served with scallops, langoustine, courgette and peas, or perhaps a pannacotta dessert - accompanied by summer fruits - on the sensibly compact, appealing, fixed-price repertoire. And aperitifs on the terrace on a warm summer's day just can't be beaten.

Chef: Paul Wadham **Owners:** Olga Polizzi **Times:** 12-2.30/7-9.30 **Prices:** Fixed L £21-£25, Fixed D £39-£40, Starter £7-£10, Main £14-£20, Dessert £7-£10, Service optional **Wine:** 79 bottles over £20, 5 bottles under £20, 7 by the glass **Notes:** Sat brunch, Vegetarian available, Civ Wed 50 **Seats:** 50, Pr/dining room 40 **Children:** Min 6 yrs D, Menu **Directions:** On the waterfront in town centre **Parking:** 30

ST MAWES *Continued*

◉ Rising Sun Hotel

Traditional

Smart harbour-side hotel dining

☎ 01326 270233   TR2 5DJ
e-mail: info@risingsunstmawes.co.uk
web: www.risingsunstmawes.com

Looking out across the quaint harbour and the Fal estuary, this stylish small hotel is a popular venue in pretty St Mawes. Gig-rowers and locals fill the lively bar, while the refined restaurant and conservatory brasserie, which take full advantage of the views, are frequented by tourists and the yachting fraternity. An imaginative menu features the pick of the local catch, as well as fresh Cornish produce. Examples are white crab cakes with strawberry dressing to start, followed by pink organic duck breast served with red wine sauce and fruit compôte, and for dessert, raspberry oatmeal meringue or chocolate tipsy cake.

Chef: Ann Long **Owners:** Mr R J Milan **Times:** 12-2/7-9, Closed L Mon-Sat **Prices:** Fixed D £33.50, Service optional **Wine:** 12 bottles over £20, 33 bottles under £20, 12 by the glass **Seats:** 50 **Children:** Min 6 yrs, Portions **Rooms:** 8 (8 en suite) ★★ HL **Directions:** On harbour front **Parking:** 8

ST MERRYN   MAP 02 SW87

◉◉ Ripley's

British, French

Unpretentious eatery serving accomplished cuisine

☎ 01841 520179   PL28 8NQ

Set in a quaint Cornish village just outside Padstow, this popular restaurant has a relaxed rustic feel. Simple contemporary décor highlights features like stone-flag flooring, lightwood furniture and unstained oak beams. The dining area at the rear is small and intimate, darkwood flooring continuing the natural contemporary style. Friendly, unfussy service is a real attraction, as is Paul Ripley's (ex Rick Stein's Seafood Restaurant, Padstow, see entry) straightforward, beautifully prepared food, which makes the best use of top-notch local produce. Think leg of Cornish lamb with honey-roasted shallots (vegetables are ordered and priced separately; perhaps duck fat- and rosemary-roasted red Duke of York potatoes and a cauliflower gratin), and to finish, chocolate tart with Bailey's cream.

Times: 12-2/7-9.30, Closed 2 wks Xmas, BHs, Sun-Mon, Closed L, Limited lunch opening, phone for details

---

SCILLY, ISLES OF
BRYHER   MAP 02 SV81

◉◉ Hell Bay

Modern British V

Stunning location, stunning seafood

☎ 01720 422947   TR23 0PR
e-mail: contactus@hellbay.co.uk
web: www.hellbay.co.uk

Located on the smallest of the Scilly Isles, and perfect for a relaxing break, this hotel overlooks the constantly changing Atlantic seascape. Subtle lighting creates a warm atmosphere in the evenings, and the cream walls are a perfect foil for the original oil paintings. The freshest of island and Cornish produce appears on the menu, from top-quality seafood (perhaps pan-fried sea bream accompanied by a bubble-and-squeak potato cake, creamed Savoy, shallots and a vermouth fondue) to the likes of a rump of lamb served with Parmentier potatoes, baby beetroot and a port and apricot jus. The daily-changing fixed-price menu might also feature a fig and frangipane tartlet with Chantilly cream and red wine reduction to close.

Chef: Glenn Gatland **Owners:** Tresco Estate **Times:** 12-3/6.30-9.30, Closed Jan-Feb **Prices:** Food prices not confirmed for 2008. Please telephone for details **Wine:** 32 bottles over £20, 17 bottles under £20 **Notes:** Vegetarian menu, No jeans, T-shirts in eve, Civ Wed 60 **Seats:** 75, Pr/dining room 20 **Children:** Menu, Portions **Rooms:** 25 (25 en suite)★★★ HL **Directions:** Helicopter from Penzance to Tresco, St Mary's. Plane from Southampton, Bristol, Exeter, Newquay or Land's End

---

ST MARTIN'S   MAP 02 SV91

◉◉◉ St Martin's on the Isle

see opposite

ST MARY'S   MAP 02 SV91

◉ St Mary's Hall Hotel

International NEW

Stunning modern restaurant offering international dishes

☎ 01720 422316   Church St, Hugh Town TR21 0JR
e-mail: recp@stmaryshallhotel.co.uk
web: www.stmaryshallhotel.co.uk

This elegant townhouse was originally built by Count Leon de Ferrari. The restaurant (Café de Ferrari) has been named after him and given an appropriately metropolitan feel using leather, glass, granite and natural wood, supplemented by a brasserie and modern bar. There is a very hands-on approach to service from the family who own the hotel, and their friendly staff. The menu takes you on a tour of international cuisine featuring a range of dishes which might include steak as easily as sushi, while still representing a feel for local produce in the use of seafood and shellfish.

Times: 12-2/6-8, Closed Xmas, Sun (exc residents) **Rooms:** 20 (20 en suite) ★★★ HL

TRESCO   MAP 02 SV81

◉◉ Island Hotel

British

Island living, seafood a speciality

☎ 01720 422883   TR24 0PU
e-mail: islandhotel@tresco.co.uk
web: www.islandhotel.co.uk

This delightful colonial-style hotel is uniquely situated on its own private island, offering a truly memorable seaside location. Furnished in contemporary style, the restaurant is light and airy, enjoying stunning sea views and forming an elegant backdrop for displays of original art. Carefully-prepared, imaginative modern British cuisine is the order of the day, drawing inspiration from international sources and local ingredients, particularly seafood. Think grilled marinated Scottish salmon with olive oil, basil and caramelised vinegar as a starter, while for mains why not make the most of the superb locally-caught fish and go for poached fillet of brill in red wine with pomme

Continued

ENGLAND

St Martin's on the Isle

ST MARTIN'S   MAP 02 SV91

Modern British V

Highly accomplished cooking in idyllic island paradise

☎ 01720 422092 Lower Town TR25 0QW
e-mail: stay@stmartinshotel.co.uk
web: www.stmartinshotel.co.uk

This attractive waterfront hotel, complete with its own sandy beach, enjoys an idyllic position overlooking the islands of Tean and Tresco. The elegant, first-floor Tean restaurant - decked out in natural tones to reflect the surroundings - has a split-level lounge where guests and diners can also enjoy those stunning views. Tables are well spaced and appointments are stylish and simple, set with seasonal flower displays.

A highly accomplished kitchen team provides cuisine to match the impressive location, with daily-changing menus driven by the abundance of the local larder, particularly fish and seafood, where freshness, quality and seasonality are showcased. Expect a light modern touch that allows intense, clean flavours to shine in dishes like line-caught sea bass with butter-roasted local lobster and a pea velouté, or perhaps best end and braised shoulder of Bodmin lamb served with pea and mint purée, baby leeks and a rosemary sauce, and to finish, maybe an iced apricot parfait with toasted almond ice cream and poached apricots.

Chef: Kenny Atkinson
Owners: Peter Sykes
Times: 12.30-2/7-10, Closed Nov-Feb, Closed L all week
Prices: Fixed D £39.50, Service included
Wine: 50 bottles over £20, 25 bottles under £20, 20 by the glass
Notes: Vegetarian menu, Dress Restrictions, Smart casual, Civ Wed 100
Seats: 60
Children: Min 9 yrs, Menu, Portions
Rooms: 30 (30 en suite)★★★ HL
Directions: By helicopter or boat from Penzance to St Mary's - flights from Bristol, Exeter, Southampton, Newquay or Land's End. Then 20 min launch transfer to St Martin's

TRESCO CONTINUED

purée and wild mushrooms. For dessert, succumb to warm chocolate tart with orange and mascarpone ice cream, or if you have room, a selection of West Country cheeses with tomato and sultana chutney.

Chef: Peter Marshall **Owners:** Mr R Dorrien-Smith **Times:** 12-2.30/7-9, Closed 5 Nov-1 Mar, Closed L all week **Prices:** Fixed D £38, Service optional **Notes:** May-Sep Sun D buffet, Dress Restrictions, Smart casual, no jeans or T-shirts **Seats:** 150, Pr/dining room 25 **Children:** Menu, Portions **Rooms:** 47 (47 en suite)★★★ HL **Directions:** 20 minutes from Penzance by helicopter **Parking:** No cars on island

◎◎ New Inn

British

Traditional coaching inn with a contemporary restaurant

☎ 01720 422844 TR24 0QQ
e-mail: newinn@tresco.co.uk
web: www.tresco.co.uk

Steeped in history, The New Inn is owned by the same estate that owns the other three main hotels on Tresco and the island itself, which is the only privately owned land in the Scillies. There's stacks of old-world character here in the bar and lounges, although the restaurant has a modern 'New England' style - light and airy, with stained-wood floors, panelled walls and brightly coloured table settings. The cooking takes a modern approach driven by quality local produce - especially seafood - with the accomplished dishes boasting simple flavours. Take salmon fishcakes with chive-fish cream and spinach to start, perhaps followed by roast Cornish pork loin cutlet served with wild mushrooms, sautéed new potatoes, onions and broad beans.

Chef: Stephen Marsh, Pete Hingston **Owners:** Mr R Dorrien-Smith **Times:** 7-9, Closed L all week **Prices:** Starter £4.50-£7.50, Main £8.50-£20, Dessert £4.50-£6, Service optional **Wine:** 10 bottles over £20, 27 bottles under £20, 13 by the glass **Notes:** Vegetarian available **Seats:** 40 **Children:** Menu, Portions **Rooms:** 16 (16 en suite) ★★ HL **Directions:** 250yds from harbour (private island, contact hotel for details)

TALLAND BAY   MAP 02 SX25

Terrace Restaurant at Talland Bay Hotel
see below

TRURO   MAP 02 SW84

◎◎ Alverton Manor

British

Contemporary Cornish cooking in converted convent

☎ 01872 276633 Tregolls Rd TR1 1ZQ
e-mail: reception@alvertonmanor.co.uk
web: www.alvertonmanor.co.uk

Set in 6 acres of well-tended gardens, this Grade II listed former convent has been converted into a modern hotel with an elegant dining room. Gothic windows, ornate wooden staircases and large windows make the most of its elevated, city-centre position. Service is thoughtful and attentive. The aspiring modern cooking is driven by fresh local produce (organic where possible), delivering well-presented, clean-cut dishes. Think steamed halibut served with a

---

Rosettes not confirmed at time of going to press

Terrace Restaurant at Talland Bay Hotel

TALLAND BAY   MAP 02 SX25

Modern British V

Refined cuisine in wonderful location

☎ 01503 272667 PL13 2JB
e-mail: reception@tallandbayhotel.co.uk
web: www.tallandbayhotel.co.uk

As we went to press we were informed that a new head chef was about to be appointed, therefore the AA Rosette award has been suspended until the next inspection. Please visit www.theAA.com for further information. Spectacular sea views and direct access to the coastal path from the end of the garden are just some of the attractions at this friendly, family-run hotel. The traditional wood-panelled dining room makes the most of views of the sea and garden, but even these won't distract diners once they see the menu.

Chef: Paul Hart **Owners:** Mr & Mrs G Granville **Times:** 12.30-2/7-9, Closed L Mon-Sat (Oct-mid Apr) **Prices:** Fixed L £12-£18, Fixed D £25, Starter £5-£12, Main £14-£29, Dessert £6-£9, Service optional **Wine:** 50 bottles over £20, 20 bottles under £20, 12 by the glass **Notes:** Fixed L 3 courses, Vegetarian menu, Dress Restrictions, Smart casual minimum **Seats:** 40 **Rooms:** 23 (23 en suite) ★★★ CHH **Directions:** Signed from x-rds on A387 between Looe and Polperro **Parking:** 20

shellfish ragout and lobster tortellini, or perhaps seared calves' liver teamed with potato purée and a red onion marmalade and balsamic jus, and to finish, maybe a warm pear tarte Tatin with yogurt parfait and mulled wine syrup.

Alverton Manor

Times: 11.45-1.45/7-9.15, Closed L Sat **Rooms:** 32 (32 en suite) ★★★ HL **Directions:** From Truro bypass take A39 to St Austell. Just past the church on left

◎◎ Probus Lamplighter Restaurant

Modern British V

Local favourite with a sound reputation

☎ 01726 882453 Fore St, Probus TR2 4JL

e-mail: maireadvogel@aol.com

web: www.lamplighter-probus.co.uk

This veteran establishment has fed locals and tourists alike since the 1950s, and has a reputation for top-notch cooking. It's a warm and cosy venue with log fires, beams, comfy sofas, and two candlelit dining areas - a harmonious mix of old and new. Modern British dishes predominate; expect good-quality local ingredients brought together in combinations designed to tempt and intrigue, while offering clean, balanced flavours. Think line-caught turbot teamed with champ potato and a spinach and wild mushroom broth, or perhaps Gressingham duck breast with crisp confit leg served with a soy, honey, whisky and ginger glaze and Sarladaise potatoes on a fixed-price repertoire.

Chef: Robert Vogel **Owners:** Robert & Mairead Vogel **Times:** 7-10, Closed Sun-Mon, Closed L all week **Prices:** Fixed D £28.90 **Wine:** 16 bottles over £20, 17 bottles under £20, 6 by the glass **Notes:** Vegetarian menu, Dress Restrictions, Smart casual **Seats:** 32, Pr/dining room 8 **Children:** Portions **Directions:** 5m from Truro on A390 towards St Austell **Parking:** On street & car park

◎◎ Tabb's

Modern British NEW

Contemporary dining in former pub championing local produce

☎ 01872 262110 85 Kenwyn St TR1 3BZ

web: www.tabbs.co.uk

Husband-and-wife team Nigel and Melanie Tabb have moved their eponymous restaurant to this city-centre location from its previous incarnation (in an old blacksmith's shop on the coast at Portreath) with great effect. The one-time pub has been completely refurbished and now offers a very contemporary vibe; think black slate floors, lilac walls, high-backed leather chairs in cream and lilac, and white linen-

clothed tables. The cooking is cranked up a gear too in line with the surroundings, and takes an exciting modern approach with emphasis on using quality local produce (suppliers come credited on the appealing menu). Expect pan-fried loin of wild Cornish venison with creamed leeks, fricassée of wild mushrooms and rosemary jus, or perhaps grilled fillet of brill with home-made black pasta.

Chef: Nigel Tabb **Owners:** Nigel & Melanie Tabb **Times:** 12-2.30/6.30-9.30, Closed 25 Dec, 1 Jan, 1 wk Jan, Sun, Mon, Closed L Sat **Prices:** Starter £5.95-£8.95, Main £12.50-£20.50, Dessert £5.50-£6.50, Service optional **Wine:** 17 bottles over £20, 20 bottles under £20 **Seats:** 30 **Children:** Portions **Directions:** Down hill past train station, right at mini rdbt, 200yds on left **Parking:** Parking 200yds

---

TYWARDREATH   MAP 02 SX05

◎ Trenython Manor

Modern British

Imaginative cuisine in Palladian setting

☎ 01726 814797 Castle Dore Rd PL24 2TS

e-mail: enquiries@trenython.co.uk

web: www.trenython.co.uk

Dating from the 1800s, there is something distinctly different about Trenython, a classic English manor house designed by an Italian architect. The impressive dining room with carved oak panelling looks out across the gardens towards St Austell Bay. Modern British cooking is the order of the day with a fixed-price dinner menu rich in appeal. Think sea bass with a pine nut crust served with parsnip purée and crushed potato and chives, or perhaps a stem ginger and cinnamon sponge pudding to finish, served with crème anglaise. There's a more relaxed bistro for lunch.

Chef: Alan Ward **Owners:** Club La Costa **Times:** 12-2.30/7-9.30 **Prices:** Fixed L £12.50-£15.95, Fixed D £29-£35, Starter £5-£11.50, Main £9.50-£21.95, Dessert £4.50-£6.95, Service optional **Wine:** 15 bottles over £20, 17 bottles under £20, 2 by the glass **Notes:** Vegetarian available, Civ Wed 75 **Seats:** 64, Pr/dining room 30 **Children:** Menu, Portions **Rooms:** 23 (23 en suite) ★★★ CHH **Directions:** From Exeter join A30 towards Cornwall, then B3269 to Lostwithiel. Take A390 St Austell/Fowey, follow Fowey signs for approx 4m. The hotel is then signed **Parking:** 50

VERYAN   MAP 02 SW93

◎ Nare Hotel

Traditional British

Traditional dining experience in seaside hotel with great views

☎ 01872 501279 Carne Beach TR2 5PF

e-mail: office@narehotel.co.uk

web: www.narehotel.co.uk

Recently redecorated, this delightful hotel on the popular holiday destination of the Roseland Peninsula offers a relaxed, country-house atmosphere in a spectacular coastal setting with terraces and lawns, the lounges, bar and restaurants offering wonderful views across Gerran's Bay. The nautically-themed Quarterdeck restaurant offers a more contemporary dining experience than the formal dining room. Both offer traditional dishes with a modern twist, with an emphasis on locally-landed fish and seafood including Portloe crab and Bigbury Bay oysters, with flambé specials such as veal masala, scampi Newburg and crêpes Suzette.

Continued

ENGLAND

VERYAN Continued

Chef: Malcolm Sparks **Owners:** T G H Ashworth **Times:** 12.30-2.30/7.30-10, Closed L Mon-Sat **Prices:** Fixed L £19, Fixed D £24, Starter £5-£12, Main £12-£72, Dessert £5-£5.50, Service optional **Wine:** 300 bottles over £20, 200 bottles under £20, 18 by the glass **Notes:** Nare Oyster Boat £72 for 2 people, Vegetarian available, Dress Restrictions, Jacket and tie, Air con **Seats:** 75 **Children:** Min 7 yrs, Menu, Portions **Rooms:** 39 (39 en suite) ★★★★ CHH **Directions:** Through Veryan village passing New Inn on left, continue 1 mile to the sea **Parking:** 70

WATERGATE BAY   MAP 02 SW86

⊕ The Brasserie

Modern European

Dine in comfort with superb views after a day on the beach

☎ 01637 860543 Watergate Bay Hotel, The Hotel and Extreme Academy TR8 4AA
e-mail: life@watergatebay.co.uk
web: www.watergatebay.co.uk

You can enjoy fantastic beach and sea views from the spacious decking of the bar and lounge of this modern, stylish hotel or from the Brasserie restaurant. The beach is home to the 'Extreme Academy' hosting sports competitions and lessons in watersports like kite surfing, traction surfing, and just plain old surfing. The imaginative modern menu changes seasonally and makes good use of local produce, particularly seafood, in dishes such as céviche of scallops, oysters, sorrel and poppy seeds as a starter or grilled turbot with lobster and oxtail risotto, tomato foam and tarragon.

Chef: Tom Bradbury **Owners:** Watergate Bay Hotel Ltd **Times:** 7-10, Closed L all week **Prices:** Fixed D £26.75-£30.25, Service optional **Wine:** 25 bottles over £20, 21 bottles under £20, 9 by the glass **Notes:** Children under 12yrs menu 2 courses £14.95, 3 courses £17.95, Civ Wed 50, Air con **Seats:** 140, Pr/dining room 16 **Children:** Menu, Portions **Rooms:** 67 (67 en suite) ★★★ HL **Directions:** 2nd right off A30 after The Victoria Inn onto A3059 straight across rdbt following airport signs. Turn right after 1.5m at B3276 T-junct, turn left to bay **Parking:** 70

⊕ Fifteen Cornwall

Modern British, Italian NEW ✋

Italian-influenced cooking Jamie Oliver style with wonderful views

☎ 01637 861000 On the Beach TR8 4AA
web: www.fifteencornwall.co.uk

Two flags at the end of a pay-and-display car park mark the entrance down to this much-heralded restaurant, its first-floor level above the bay allowing window tables superb ocean views. Like Jamie Oliver's blueprint London outlet, Fifteen Cornwall supports disadvantaged youngsters in building a career in the industry. The contemporary new-build beachside restaurant is a relaxed open-plan affair with wood floors and stylish décor, while staff outfits sport the Fifteen logo. The sunny Mediterranean-style cooking comes rooted in Italy, driven by simplicity and quality seasonal produce; take line-caught Cornish hake with fennel and green mammoth olive 'al forno'. At lunch there's a short daily-changing menu, while dinner is a six-course tasting affair. There's breakfast available too.

Times: 12-2.30/6.30-9.45

ZENNOR   MAP 02 SW43

⊕ The Gurnard's Head

British NEW ✋

Honest modern cooking in relaxed, friendly inn

☎ 01736 796928 Treen TR26 3DE
e-mail: enquiries@gurnardshead.co.uk
web: www.gurnardshead.co.uk

This large old inn, looking out to the Atlantic, has had a sympathetic remodelling to bring it a fresh new look. Inside there's a modern face, yet the décor reflects an endearing natural style, with wooden floorboarded restaurant and solid wooden tables. Service is relaxed and friendly, while the kitchen's modern approach makes the most of the abundant quality local larder on a sensibly compact menu that focuses on an honest, home-cook style. Expect simply-presented cooking with fresh vibrancy in dishes like slow-cooked belly of pork with choucroute, or a chocolate tart and black olive caramel finish.

Times: 12-2.30/6.30-9.30 **Rooms:** 7 (7 en suite) ★★★ INN

CUMBRIA

ALSTON   MAP 18 NY74

⊕ Lovelady Shield House

Modern British

Family-run hotel with an ambitious kitchen

☎ 01434 381203 CA9 3LF
e-mail: enquiries@lovelady.co.uk
web: www.lovelady.co.uk

Hidden away along a tree-lined drive in the heart of the Pennines, this delightful country-house hotel boasts a cosy bar with an impressive array of fine malts, as well as several comfortable lounges. Take an aperitif by the fire, before moving through to the restaurant, an elegant room decorated with antiques and paintings. There you'll find a daily-changing menu of modern British and classical French dishes, including mains such as tranche of smoked sea-loch trout with creamy dill tagliatelle and deep-fried squid, or cider-braised pork belly with Bramley apple compôte, haggis, and swede and carrot mash. Round things off with warm treacle tart, espresso jelly and cinnamon ice cream.

Chef: Barrie Garton **Owners:** Peter & Marie Haynes **Times:** 12-2/7-8.30, Closed L Mon-Sat **Prices:** Fixed D £37.50, Service optional **Wine:** 98 bottles over £20, 29 bottles under £20, 6 by the glass **Notes:** Fixed D 4 courses, Dress Restrictions, No jeans or shorts, Civ Wed 40 **Seats:** 24, Pr/dining room 10 **Children:** Min 7 yrs, Menu, Portions **Rooms:** 10 (10 en suite) ★★★ CHH **Directions:** 2m E of Alston, signed off A689 at junct with B6294 **Parking:** 20

AMBLESIDE

MAP 18 NY30

◎◎ Drunken Duck Inn

Modern British ▮ NOTABLE WINE LIST

Great local produce in a fantastic Lakeland setting

☎ 015394 36347 Barngates LA22 0NG
e-mail: info@drunkenduckinn.co.uk
web: www.drunkenduckinn.co.uk

It may be a 400-year-old coaching inn, but this stylish place has become an institution with a reputation for great food, ales and comfortable rooms. The restaurant is relaxed and informal with two traditional areas and one more modern. The emphasis is on top quality local produce with all suppliers listed. Barngates Brewery at the Duck brews up to six beers using its own water supply from the nearby fells. In the restaurant, modern and traditional British cuisine sees starters like pressed pork belly, poached quail's eggs and pickled chanterelles. For a main course, try braised leg of Kendal lamb with pomme purée, French green beans and Cabernet Sauvignon jus, or loin of wild deer with rosehip, chocolate and stout.

Chef: Nick McCue **Owners:** Stephanie Barton **Times:** 12-2.30/6-9.30
Prices: Starter £7.25-£8.95, Main £12.95-£24.95, Dessert £6.50-£6.95, Service optional **Wine:** 12 by the glass **Seats:** 60 **Children:** Portions
Rooms: 11 (11 en suite) ★★★★★ INN **Directions:** Take A592 from Kendal, follow signs for Hawkshead (from Ambleside), in 2.5m sign for inn on right, 1m up hill **Parking:** 40

◎ The Log House

Modern Mediterranean NEW

Norwegian-style log-house restaurant with flavour-driven modern fare

☎ 015394 31077 Lake Rd LA22 0DN
e-mail: nicola@loghouse.co.uk
web: www.loghouse.co.uk

The exterior of this idiosyncratic, Norwegian-style log cabin certainly catches the eye. Aptly named, it was originally imported at the turn of the century by renowned artist Alfred Heaton Cooper as his studio. Today it is a popular split-level restaurant and bar, decked out with lightwood floors, terracotta walls, wooden chairs and clothed tables creating a modern feel. The atmosphere is suitably relaxed and service professional yet friendly. The kitchen deals in quality seasonal produce and honest, flavour-driven food, with a colourful nod to the Mediterranean; take Cumbrian lamb loin with sautéed potatoes, kalamata olives, green beans, salsa verde and lamb jus.

Chef: Heath Calman **Owners:** Nicola & Heath Calman **Times:** 12-3/6-10, Closed 7 Jan-7 Feb, Mon **Prices:** Fixed L £21.95, Starter £4.95-£7.95, Main £12.95-£17.95, Dessert £5.50, Service optional **Wine:** 17 bottles over £20, 26 bottles under £20, 5 by the glass **Notes:** Fixed L 3 courses **Seats:** 40
Children: Menu, Portions **Rooms:** 3 (3 en suite) ★★★★ RR
Directions: M6 junct 36. Situated on A591 on left, just beyond garden centre **Parking:** 3

◎ Regent Hotel

British

Long-established hotel with a contemporary flavour

☎ 015394 32254 Waterhead Bay LA22 0ES
e-mail: info@regentlakes.co.uk
web: www.regentlakes.co.uk

Well known locally for its award-winning display of summer flowers, this family-run hotel is beautifully located at Waterhead Bay on the shores of Lake Windermere. The contemporary restaurant overlooks a pretty Italianate courtyard and the walls are hung with modern art. The brasserie-style menu showcases Cumbrian produce with dishes like chargrilled prime fell-bred sirloin steak served with chasseur sauce and chips, or grilled Lakes speciality home-made venison and cranberry sausages with red onion sauce, and for dessert double Jersey ice cream with raisins soaked in Pedro Ximenez sherry. Children are made welcome and a separate children's menu is available.

Times: 12-2/6.30-8, Closed Xmas wk **Rooms:** 30 (30 en suite) ★★★ HL
Directions: 1m S of Ambleside at Waterhead Bay

AMBLESIDE Continued

◉ Rothay Manor

Traditional British

Fine dining in the Lakes

☎ 015394 33605 Rothay Bridge LA22 0EH
e-mail: hotel@rothaymanor.co.uk
web: www.rothaymanor.co.uk

Built as a summer residence for a prosperous Liverpool merchant in 1825, this elegant country-house hotel has a Grade II listed Regency façade and has been in the current owner's family for 40 years. The interior retains many original features and is furnished in sedate style with antiques and floral displays, while outside a revolving summer house is a feature of the pretty garden. The friendly, family-run concern offers a mainly traditional English menu, taking in the likes of local Cartmel Valley oak-smoked salmon, Cumbrian fell-bred lamb and elderflower and damson gin jelly, or grilled fillet of sea bass with prawns and saffron sauce, with perhaps apple tarte Tatin for dessert. A separate children's menu is available.

Chef: Jane Binns **Owners:** Nigel & Stephen Nixon **Times:** 12.30-1.45/7.15-9, Closed 3-25 Jan **Prices:** Fixed L £9.50-£18.50, Fixed D £36, Starter £3.80-£5, Main £7.50-£10.50, Dessert £4.50, Service optional **Wine:** 91 bottles over £20, 63 bottles under £20, 8 by the glass **Notes:** ALC L only, Fixed L 3 courses, Dress Restrictions, Smart casual, Air con **Seats:** 65, Pr/dining room 34 **Children:** Min 7 yrs D, Menu, Portions **Rooms:** 19 (19 en suite) ★★★ HL **Directions:** From Ambleside, follow signs for Coniston (A593). Hotel is 0.25 mile SW from the centre of Ambleside opposite the rugby club **Parking:** 35

APPLEBY-IN-WESTMORLAND MAP 18 NY62

◉ BW Appleby Manor Country House Hotel

Modern British V

Accomplished cuisine in relaxed country-house hotel

☎ 017683 51571 Roman Rd CA16 6JB
e-mail: reception@applebymanor.co.uk
web: www.applebymanor.co.uk

Two very different styles distinguish the separate parts of this restaurant, one featuring wood panelling and the original fireplace, and the other a light-and-airy conservatory. Both share views over the manor-house gardens and the surrounding fells, and there's a welcoming atmosphere throughout. The accomplished food comes in interesting combinations of traditional and modern British cooking. Daily specials pad out the carte, which might feature an assiette of

Cumbrian wild rabbit (sauté loin, braised leg and mini rabbit pie) served with a bubble-and-squeak potato cake, buttered beans, diced carrots and rabbit jus, while dessert might feature a ubiquitous sticky toffee pudding with custard. Impressive cheese trolley.

Chef: Chris Thompson **Owners:** Dunbobin Family **Times:** 12-2/7-9, Closed 24-26 Dec **Prices:** Starter £4.95-£8.95, Main £12.50-£18.50, Dessert £4.50-£5.95, Service optional **Wine:** 31 bottles over £20, 50 bottles under £20, 6 by the glass **Notes:** Vegetarian menu, Dress Restrictions, Smart casual **Seats:** 96, Pr/dining room 20 **Children:** Menu, Portions **Rooms:** 30 (30 en suite) ★★★ HL **Directions:** M6 junct 40 take A66 for Scotch Corner for 12m, take turn for Appleby. Manor 1.5m on right **Parking:** 60

BARROW-IN-FURNESS   MAP 18 SD26

◉ Clarence House Country Hotel & Restaurant

British, International

Enjoyable dining in comfortable conservatory surroundings

☎ 01229 462508 Skelgate LA15 8BQ
e-mail: info@clarencehouse-hotel.co.uk
web: www.clarencehouse-hotel.co.uk

Cosy country-house hotel that likes to feed its guests well. Kick off the day with a hearty English breakfast, while away the hours over a genteel afternoon tea, and then round things off with a delicious meal in the airy orangery-style restaurant. Long windows make the most of pretty views over St Thomas' valley, and there's a terrace for alfresco dining in the summer. There's a good mixture of straightforward local dishes as well as British and European items on the menu, with French onion soup, Welsh mussels and Scottish cock-a-leekie all making an appearance, alongside Stavely lamb, Cumbrian beef and North West coastal fish.

Chef: Mr Alan Forsyth **Owners:** Mrs Pauline Barber **Times:** 12-2/7-9, Closed 25-26 Dec, Closed D Sun **Prices:** Fixed L £12.95, Fixed D £32.95, Starter £5.95-£8.95, Main £17.25-£22.95, Dessert £6.50, Service included **Wine:** 29 bottles over £20, 25 bottles under £20, 8 by the glass **Notes:** Fixed D 5 courses, Sun L 4 courses £15.95, Vegetarian available, Dress Restrictions, Smart dress, Civ Wed 100 **Seats:** 100, Pr/dining room 14 **Children:** Portions **Rooms:** 19 (19 en suite) ★★★ HL **Directions:** Telephone for directions **Parking:** 40

BASSENTHWAITE
MAP 18 NY23

◉ Lake View Restaurant at Armathwaite Hall

British, International V
Classic cuisine in a genteel setting

☎ 017687 76551 Armathwaite Hall CA12 4RE
e-mail: reservations@armathwaite-hall.com
web: www.armathwaite-hall.com

Hidden away in 400 acres of peaceful deer park, this imposing 17th-century mansion is a haven of civilised living. Antiques and ornate wood panelling set a genteel tone, while roaring log fires keep things cosy. The restaurant is a grand affair overlooking nearby Bassenthwaite Lake (there's a new conservatory option too), offering a concise, daily-changing menu that mixes classic dishes, such as small fillet steaks flambéed at the table with brandy, mushrooms and cream, with more adventurous creations like a loin of pork with couscous, kumquat jam and a rich pork jus.

Chef: Kevin Dowling **Owners:** Graves Family **Times:** 12.30-1.45/7.30-9.15 **Prices:** Fixed L £21.95, Fixed D £41.95, Service optional **Wine:** 46 bottles over £20, 34 bottles under £20, 6 by the glass **Notes:** Fixed L 4 courses, Fixed D 6 courses, Vegetarian menu, Dress Restrictions, Smart casual, no jeans/T-shirts/trainers, Civ Wed 80 **Seats:** 80, Pr/dining room 25 **Children:** Portions **Rooms:** 42 (42 en suite) ★★★★ CHH **Directions:** From M6 junct 40/A66 to Keswick then A591 towards Carlisle. Continue for 7m and turn left at Castle Inn **Parking:** 100

◉ The Pheasant

Modern British V
Good honest food in traditional inn

☎ 017687 76234 CA13 9YE
e-mail: info@the-pheasant.co.uk
web: www.the-pheasant.co.uk

Dating back to the 16th century, this large former coaching inn close to Bassenthwaite Lake boasts many traditional features, with log fires, oak-panelled rooms and polished parquet floors. Privately owned, it has a relaxed atmosphere and the restaurant benefits from a sound menu of modern British dishes conjured from fresh, high-quality local ingredients. Expect assured cooking in a trio of wild boar (crispy belly, pan-fried loin and sausage) served with red cabbage, root vegetables, herb mash and a truffle jus, or a roasted fillet of halibut with creamed leeks, fine green beans, saffron potato and shellfish velouté.

Chef: Malcolm Ennis **Owners:** Trustees of Lord Inglewood **Times:** 12-2/7-9, Closed 25 Dec **Prices:** Fixed L £19.95, Fixed D £30.95, Service

optional, Group min 8 service 10% **Notes:** Vegetarian menu, Dress Restrictions, Smart casual, No jeans, T-shirts, trainers **Seats:** 45, Pr/dining room 12 **Children:** Min 8 yrs D **Rooms:** 15 (15 en suite) ★★★ HL **Directions:** M6 junct 40, take A66 (Keswick and North Lakes). Continue past Keswick and head for Cockermouth. Signed from A66 **Parking:** 40

BORROWDALE
MAP 18 NY21

◉ Borrowdale Gates Country House Hotel

Modern British V
Ambitious cuisine in a peaceful Cumbrian setting

☎ 017687 77204 CA12 5UQ
e-mail: hotel@borrowdale-gates.co.uk
web: www.borrowdale-gates.com

Tucked away in an idyllic location in the heart of the Borrowdale Valley, this welcoming hotel maintains a genuine country-house atmosphere. Its elegant restaurant boasts magnificent views of the dramatic Lakeland scenery, so book ahead for a window table. Utilising the best local produce, the combination of traditional British fare with a modern French twist creates an excellent balance of flavours in dishes such as twice-baked cheese soufflé with a saffron-poached pear and walnut salad, followed by a pavé of Harryman-reared sirloin of beef wrapped in smoked butter, and Cumbrian air-dried ham with crispy celeriac and butterbean purée. Finish with a decadent marbled dark chocolate and peppermint soufflé with chocolate crisps.

Chef: Mike Wilkinson **Owners:** Green Symbol Ltd **Times:** 12-2/6.30-8.45, Closed L open on request **Prices:** Fixed L £17.50-£22, Fixed D £28-£35, Starter £8.95-£10.75, Main £21-£26, Dessert £8.50-£10, Service optional **Wine:** 58 bottles over £20, 15 bottles under £20, 6 by the glass **Notes:** Vegetarian menu, Dress Restrictions, Smart casual, Civ Wed 60 **Seats:** 53 **Children:** Portions **Rooms:** 27 (27 en suite) ★★★ CHH **Directions:** B5289 from Keswick, after 4m turn right over bridge to Grange. Hotel 400yds on right **Parking:** 25

BORROWDALE CONTINUED

⊛ Hazel Bank Country House

British, European

Victorian house with sweeping views and good honest food

☎ 017687 77248 Rosthwaite CA12 5XB
e-mail: enquiries@hazelbankhotel.co.uk
web: www.hazelbankhotel.co.uk

Set in the heart of Lakeland, with a backdrop of mountain peaks and lush gardens sweeping down towards Rosthwaite village, this traditional Victorian residence offers magnificent views over Borrowdale and fine fell walking across Langdale Pikes. The elegant dining room, with warm burgundy and beige décor, well-appointed tables and attentive service, has a friendly, informal house-party atmosphere with all guests taking their place for dinner at 7pm. Traditional British dishes with European influences are thoughtfully prepared using locally produced ingredients, and may include grilled sea bass on a bed of Camargue red rice and sauce antibiose, or beef in port and Guinness marinade with crispy parsnip cakes.

Chef: Brenda Davies **Owners:** Glen & Brenda Davies **Times:** 7, Closed 25-26 Dec, Closed L Mon-Sun **Prices:** Fixed D £32.50, Service optional
Wine: 9 bottles over £20, 45 bottles under £20, 5 by the glass
Notes: Fixed D 4 courses, Vegetarian available, Dress Restrictions, Smart casual, No shorts or jeans **Seats:** 22 **Children:** Min 12 yrs **Rooms:** 8 (8 en suite) ★★★★★ GH **Directions:** From M6 junct 40, leave the A66 and take the B5289 to Borrowdale. Just before Rosthwaite turn left over hump-back bridge **Parking:** 12

⊛ Leathes Head Hotel

Modern British

Solid cooking in restaurant with fabulous views

☎ 017687 77247 CA12 5UY
e-mail: enq@leatheshead.co.uk
web: www.leatheshead.co.uk

Once an Edwardian gentleman's residence, this family-run hotel is a haven of peace and tranquillity. It's located in pretty gardens in one of the most beautiful areas of England - the picturesque Borrowdale Valley. There are comfy lounges for pre-dinner drinks, plus an elegant restaurant that makes the most of the stunning fell views. Take your seat for some flavourful, unpretentious cuisine using well-sourced ingredients. Baked fillet of Scottish salmon with a cucumber and lime cream sauce, or grilled Ullswater lamb cutlets with cured Cumberland sausage and a rich port wine jus are fine examples of the fare. Round things off with hot date and walnut pudding with dairy ice and maple syrup.

Times: 7.30-8.15, Closed mid Nov-mid Feb **Rooms:** 12 (12 en suite)
★★★ HL **Directions:** 3.75m S of Keswick on B5289, set back on the left

---

BRAITHWAITE   **MAP 18 NY22**

⊛ The Cottage in the Wood

Modern British ❦

Good food and service in marvellous, tranquil surroundings

☎ 017687 78409 Whinlatter Pass CA12 5TW
e-mail: relax@thecottageinthewood.co.uk
web: www.thecottageinthewood.co.uk

Located in the heart of the Whinlatter Forest, this former 17th-century inn has superb views down the valley to the Skiddaw Mountain Range. Diners at this charming cottage-style hotel can enjoy a daily-changing, fixed no-choice menu (three courses during the week, four at the weekend) underpinned by the best of seasonal and local produce (the proprietors know many of the farmers). The modern British cooking is peppered with European/Mediterranean influences - start with spiced William pear with Blengdale Blue strudel and enjoy a main of roasted loin of Galloway beef with wild mushroom casserole and caramelised shallots.

Chef: Liam Berney **Owners:** Liam & Kath Berney **Times:** 7-9.30, Closed Jan, Mon, Closed L all week **Prices:** Fixed D £24, Service optional
Wine: 12 bottles over £20, 6 bottles under £20, 6 by the glass **Seats:** 26
Children: Min 7 yrs, Portions **Rooms:** 10 (10 en suite) ★★ HL
Directions: M6 junct 40. Take A66 signed Keswick, 1m after Keswick take B5292 signed Braithwaite, hotel 2m from Braithwaite **Parking:** 10

BRAMPTON   **MAP 21 NY56**

⊛⊛ Farlam Hall Hotel

Modern British

The epitome of modern English country-house style

☎ 016977 46234 Hallbankgate CA8 2NG
e-mail: farlam@relaischateaux.com
web: www.farlamhall.co.uk

A beautiful Victorian country house with earlier origins, dating back to the 'manor' of Farlam around 1428. Landscaped Victorian gardens include an ornamental lake and stream. The fine furnishings and fabrics of the interior recall an earlier age when the house was home to a large family, who frequently entertained guests. The classic dining room - with huge bay windows - has lovely garden views and makes a fine setting for the traditional English china, crystal glasses and silver cutlery. English country-house cooking is the style, using quality ingredients on an intelligently compact dinner menu. Expect a fillet of halibut grilled with butter and herbs, served with buttered spinach and a saffron and red pepper sauce, while to finish, perhaps a passionfruit mousse with passionfruit ice cream.

Chef: Barry Quinion **Owners:** Quinion & Stevenson Families **Times:** 8-8.30, Closed 25-30 Dec, Closed L all week **Prices:** Fixed D £38.50-£40, Service optional **Wine:** 47 bottles over £20, 9 bottles under £20, 10 by the glass **Notes:** Fixed D 4 courses, Dress Restrictions, Smart dress, No shorts **Seats:** 40, Pr/dining room 20 **Children:** Min 5 yrs, Portions **Rooms:** 12 (12 en suite)★★★ HL **Directions:** On A689, 2.5m SE of Brampton (not in Farlam village) **Parking:** 25

CARTMEL   MAP 18 SD37
◉ Aynsome Manor Hotel
British
Country-house hotel with traditional cuisine and ambience

☎ 01539 536653   LA11 6HH
e-mail: info@aynsomemanorhotel.co.uk
web: www.aynsomemanorhotel.co.uk

Built in 1512, there's an old-fashioned sense of refinement at this beautifully situated country house. A dress code of jacket and tie is required for gentlemen diners, tables are set with a well-rehearsed formality and soup is served in tureens. That said, the candlelit Georgian dining room enjoys a jolly, house-party atmosphere when the hotel is full - at other times there's never any sense of stuffiness. The food likewise follows traditional lines and uses the best local produce; take pan-fried Cartmel Valley guinea fowl with buttered Savoy cabbage and a foie gras cream sauce, for example.

Chef: Gordon Topp **Owners:** P A Varley **Times:** 1/7-8.30, Closed 25-26 Dec, 2-28 Jan, Closed L Mon-Sat, D Sun (ex residents) **Prices:** Fixed D £23-£23.50, Service optional **Wine:** 25 bottles over £20, 60 bottles under £20, 6 by the glass **Notes:** Sun L 4 courses £15-£15.50, Dress Restrictions, Smart dress **Seats:** 28 **Children:** Min 5 yrs, Menu, Portions **Rooms:** 12 (12 en suite) ★★ CHH **Directions:** Leave A590 signed Cartmel. Take left at junctions. Hotel on right 0.5m before reaching Cartmel village **Parking:** 20

◉◉◉◉ L'Enclume
see page 92

CASTLE CARROCK   MAP 18 NY55
◉ The Weary at Castle Carrock
Modern British
Refurbished country inn with contemporary charm and cuisine

☎ 01228 670230   CA8 9LU
e-mail: relax@theweary.com
web: www.theweary.com

The frontage of this almost 300-year-old inn gives no indication of the transformed, stylish, contemporary interior. The conservatory restaurant is split into two sections - an elegant dining room and a bar/lounge with sofas and tub chairs. Subtle lighting, contemporary seating, rich colours and an understated décor create an effective backdrop for original modern art and fine artefacts. The cooking is simple and straightforward, the modern, seasonal British menu based on quality local produce. Expect the restaurant menu to feature the likes of oven-baked lamb loin served with rosemary-infused sweet potato mash and redcurrant jus, and perhaps a trio of steamed puddings.

Chef: Gill Boyd **Owners:** Ian & Gill Boyd **Times:** 12-2.30/5.30-9, Closed Mon, Closed L Tue-Fri **Prices:** Starter £4.95-£7.25, Main £10.95-£17.95, Dessert £4.55-£7.95, Service optional **Wine:** 25 bottles over £20, 39 bottles under £20 **Notes:** Vegetarian available **Seats:** 85, Pr/dining room 14 **Children:** Menu, Portions **Rooms:** 5 (5 en suite) ★ ★ ★ ★ RR **Directions:** M6 junct 43 onto A69 towards Hexham for 2m, at x-rds take right filter lane and turn right, onto B-road for 4m to Castle Carrock **Parking:** 8

COCKERMOUTH   MAP 18 NY13
◉ The Trout Hotel
International
Classic dishes in a lovely riverside setting

☎ 01900 823591   Crown St CA13 0EJ
e-mail: enquiries@trouthotel.co.uk
web: www.trouthotel.co.uk

Ideally situated on the River Derwent, next door to Wordsworth's House, the hotel dates in parts from 1670 and many period features have been retained. The Derwent restaurant has recently been refurbished in classical style and there are separate lounges for pre-dinner drinks and coffee. Local produce is a feature of the menu, which includes venison, lamb and Dovenby pheasant. Start with tiger prawns in garlic butter with braised rice, followed by Cumbrian fell-bred fillet of beef served with Byron potatoes and peppercorn sauce, or for a lighter alternative try steamed lemon sole. The Terrace Bar and Bistro serves food all day and has a sheltered patio area.

Chef: Alex Hartley **Owners:** Mr N Mills **Times:** 12-2/7-9.30, Closed L Mon-Sat **Prices:** Fixed L £15.95, Fixed D £28.95, Starter £8.95-£14.95, Main £17.95-£35, Dessert £4.95-£6.95, Service optional **Wine:** 15 bottles over £20, 26 bottles under £20, 14 by the glass **Notes:** Fixed L 3 courses, Fixed D 4 courses, Civ Wed 60, Air con **Seats:** 60, Pr/dining room 20 **Children:** Menu, Portions **Rooms:** 47 (47 en suite) ★★★ HL **Directions:** M6 junct 40, follow A66 to Cockermouth, hotel situated next to Wordsworth's House **Parking:** 50

◉ Quince & Medlar
☎ 01900 823579   13 Castlegate CA13 9EU

Imaginative and very good value vegetarian cooking in the centre of town.

CROSTHWAITE   MAP 18 SD49
◉ The Punchbowl Inn at Crosthwaite
Modern, Traditional
Historic, elegantly refurbished inn with refined cooking

☎ 01539 568237   Lyth Valley LA8 8HR
e-mail: info@the-punchbowl.co.uk
web: www.the-punchbowl.co.uk

Located in the stunning Lyth Valley beside the ancient village church, this historic inn (sibling to The Drunken Duck Inn, Ambleside, see entry) has been sympathetically but stylishly remodelled, yet retains bags of character. Witness oak beams, open fireplaces and an elegant restaurant that takes on a minimalist formula, enhanced by artwork, leather chairs, white linen and polished wood floors. Service is professional and well informed, while the kitchen shows pedigree, too, its accomplished modern approach utilising well-sourced, local ingredients on an appealing repertoire. Mini steak-and-kidney pie with

CONTINUED

91

L'Enclume

CARTMEL MAP 18 SD37

Modern French NOTABLE WINE LIST

Exhilarating, innovative cuisine to stir a quiet Lakeland village

☎ 015395 36362 Cavendish St LA11 6PZ
e-mail: info@lenclume.co.uk
web: www.lenclume.co.uk

Chef: Simon Rogan
Owners: Simon Rogan, Penny Tapsell
Times: 12-1.30/7-9.30, Closed 1st wk Jan, Mon
Prices: Fixed L £18, Starter £13-£16, Main £23-£27, Dessert £10, Service optional
Wine: 138 bottles over £20, 9 bottles under £20, 8 by the glass
Seats: 35
Children: No children
Directions: 10m from M6 junct 36 follow signs for A590 W, turn left for Cartmel before Newby Bridge
Parking: 7

Home to Simon Rogan's bold and inventive cooking and trademark 'Taste and Texture' menus, this one-time village blacksmiths (enclume translating as anvil) dating back to the 13th century and set in the southern Lakeland, seems an unlikely location for one of the most avant-garde restaurants in the country. Now a smart restaurant with rooms, this northern star is decorated in slick, understated fashion, while retaining original features and a relaxed atmosphere - there's no stuffiness or pomposity here. Exposed ceiling beams, flagstone floor and uneven whitewashed walls are married with dramatic modern artwork, clothed tables and simple but striking flower arrangements. A small conservatory at the back - a real suntrap on sunny days - is the place for aperitifs, while gazing up at the priory and out over the riverside garden. Simon's cuisine has a modern French base, but a highly individual and unorthodox voice; this is bold, precise, sophisticated and complex contemporary cuisine, yet shows restraint. The unique trademarks here are Simon's 'Taste and Texture' menus; three-course fixed-price lunch menu; at dinner, offerings range from the carte menu, seven-course Introduction menu or eleven-course Tour menu. These incorporate many unusual herbs and plants that are a signature of his cooking; think poor man's pepper and sweet cicely, for instance. Stunning flavours, temperatures and textures arrive in well-judged sequence and leave the senses stimulated but not overwhelmed. Innovative and unusual combinations (with some humorous dish names) flow with rhythm and balance, while technique and presentation skills ooze artistry. Think a loin of lamb with kataifi, salsify, plum and cassia, and to finish, perhaps a white chocolate pudding 'gin and tonic'. There's a three-course carte too (predominantly grown-up versions of the Taste and Texture repertoire), and a good value lunch menu. The front-of-house team reflects the quality of the dining experience, highly professional, necessarily well informed, but friendly, while the wine list is extensive and impressive, with a good choice by the glass.

CROSTHWAITE CONTINUED

crispy potatoes, steamed sea bream with samphire and prawn broth, and Valhrona chocolate fondant with Horlicks ice cream and beetroot syrup show the style.

Chef: Craig McMeekin **Owners:** Paul Spencer, Steph Barton, Richard Rose, Amanda Robinson **Times:** 12-2/6.30-9 **Prices:** Starter £5.50-£12.95, Main £12.50-£24, Dessert £5.25-£7.25, Service optional, Group min 10 service 10% **Wine:** 120 bottles over £20, 10 bottles under £20, 14 by the glass **Notes:** Vegetarian available **Seats:** 30 **Children:** Portions **Rooms:** 9 (9 en suite) ✦✦✦✦✦ INN **Directions:** 6m from Kendal **Parking:** 40

ELTERWATER   MAP 18 NY30

◉ Purdeys

Traditional British NEW

Enjoyable dining in old mill styled restaurant

☎ 015394 37302 & 38080 Langdale Hotel & Country Club LA22 9JD
e-mail: purdeys@langdale.co.uk
web: www.langdale.co.uk

Founded on the site of an abandoned 19th-century gunpowder works, this modern hotel is set in 35 acres of woodland and waterways. Extensive public areas include an elegant bar with an interesting selection of snuff. But the main restaurant, Purdeys, is where the real action takes place, designed in the style of an old mill with oak floors, local stone and water features creating an interesting and unique atmosphere. The kitchen deals mainly in traditional British fare, cooked and presented with care and utilising fresh, local produce; take roasted Lakeland rump of lamb with spring greens, rösti potato and redcurrant jus or locally-sourced loin of pork with braised potato, sage and apple tart and sautéed leeks.

Chef: Matt Hockney **Owners:** Langdale Leisure **Times:** 6.30-9.30, Closed L Group L booking essential **Prices:** Fixed D £27.50, Service optional **Wine:** 22 bottles over £20, 40 bottles under £20, 9 by the glass **Notes:** Vegetarian available, Dress Restrictions, Smart casual, Civ Wed 60 **Seats:** 80, Pr/dining room 40 **Children:** Menu, Portions **Parking:** 50

GLENRIDDING   MAP 18 NY31

◉ The Inn on the Lake

Modern French NEW

Lakeside setting for traditional-style dining experience

☎ 017684 82444 Lake Ullswater CA11 0PE
e-mail: info@innonthelakeullswater.co.uk
web: www.innonthelakeullswater.co.uk

As the name suggests, this attractive, grand hotel is set on the edge of a lake, namely Ullswater, and even has its own traditional pub in the grounds called the Ramblers Bar. The restaurant is in the traditional mould, with clothed tables, full-length curtains, upholstered chairs and coordinated patterned carpet and, of course, fabulous views over the water. In line with the surroundings, service has a traditional note, while the kitchen follows suit, dealing in well-executed fare utilising quality local ingredients. Take roasted belly pork with roasted vegetables and thyme, black pudding, wild mushrooms, foie gras and duchess potatoes.

Owners: Charles & Kit Graves **Times:** 12.30-2/7-9, Closed L Sat **Prices:** Fixed L £12.95-£13.95, Fixed D £29.95-£31.95, Service optional **Wine:** 27 bottles over £20, 28 bottles under £20, 8 by the glass **Notes:** Dress Restrictions, Smart casual, Civ Wed 110 **Children:** Menu, Portions **Rooms:** 46 (46 en suite) ★★★ HL **Directions:** M6 junct 40, A66 Keswick, A592 Windermere

GRANGE-OVER-SANDS   MAP 18 SD47

◉ Clare House

Modern British V

Satisfying country-house cooking in relaxing surroundings

☎ 015395 33026 & 34253 Park Rd LA11 7HQ
e-mail: info@clarehousehotel.co.uk
web: www.clarehousehotel.co.uk

Overlooking Morecambe Bay, this family-run Victorian hotel has lovely, well-tended gardens. Retaining a wealth of period features throughout, the dining room has elegant high ceilings, open fireplaces, deep yellow walls, polished mahogany furniture and traditional settings. Efficient and friendly service keeps regulars coming back. Simple, effective traditional and modern dishes populate the menu at this dinner-only affair. Take roast fillet of beef served with wild mushroom and parmesan polenta, hasselbach potatoes, glazed shallots and Madeira sauce, and perhaps baked ginger parkin to finish, with a rhubarb compôte, hot spiced syrup and ginger custard. Dinner is at 6.45pm prompt.

Chef: Andrew Read, Mark Johnston **Owners:** Mr & Mrs D S Read **Times:** 6.45-7.15, Closed Dec-Apr, Closed L Mon-Sun **Prices:** Fixed D £28, Service included **Wine:** 7 bottles over £20, 30 bottles under £20, 2 by the glass **Notes:** Fixed D 4 courses, Vegetarian menu **Seats:** 32 **Children:** Menu, Portions **Rooms:** 18 (18 en suite)★ HL **Directions:** From M6 take A590, then B5277 to Grange-over-Sands. Park Road follows the shore line. Hotel on left next to swimming pool **Parking:** 16

GRASMERE   MAP 18 NY30

◉ Grasmere Hotel

Traditional European

Traditional country-house hotel with fine food

☎ 015394 35277 Broadgate LA22 9TA
e-mail: enquiries@grasmerehotel.co.uk
web: www.grasmerehotel.co.uk

A former Victorian gentleman's residence overlooking the River Rothay, this traditionally decorated mansion house retains many

CONTINUED

ENGLAND

GRASMERE Continued

original features including attractive wood panelling in the lounge areas, a wonderful staircase and a stunning acanthus chandelier in the dining room. Service is an intriguing part of the experience with diners congregating in the lounge for drinks, before being called through to eat at one sitting. Cooking is very much in the country-house vein with a daily-changing traditional European menu and local produce featured throughout. Think a shoulder of Herdwick lamb slow cooked in a minted stock and finished with a port and redcurrant reduction.

Chef: Mr P Hetherington **Owners:** Stuart & Janet Cardwell **Times:** 7, Closed Jan-early Feb, Closed L all week **Prices:** Fixed D £29.50, Service optional **Wine:** 10 bottles over £20, 40 bottles under £20, 8 by the glass **Notes:** Fixed D 4 courses, Dress Restrictions, No jeans or shorts **Seats:** 30 **Children:** Min 10 yrs **Rooms:** 13 (13 en suite) ★★ HL **Directions:** Off A591 close to village centre **Parking:** 13

◎◎ Rothay Garden Hotel & Restaurant

Modern European V

Delightful hotel with stunning scenery and fine dining

☎ 015394 35334 Broadgate LA22 9RJ
e-mail: stay@rothaygarden.com
web: www.rothaygarden.com

Situated on the outskirts of Grasmere village, and set amidst large riverside gardens with spectacular views across the fells, this delightful Lakeland hotel offers a choice of relaxing lounges, a cosy bar with inglenook fireplace and a light and airy conservatory restaurant for fine dining. Service is relaxed and professional, from long-serving, friendly staff. The daily-changing seasonal menu offers a variety of modern dishes, including some more traditional fare. Try for example braised shin of Lakeland lamb with rosemary and mint champ and macédoine of root vegetables, or opt for traditional Finnan haddie sausage with seared scallops and celeriac remoulade with mild curry cream. Round things off with sticky toffee pudding, toffee sauce and cinder toffee ice cream.

Chef: Andrew Burton **Owners:** Chris Carss **Times:** 12-1.45/7.30-9, Closed L 24, 25, 31 Dec, 1 Jan **Prices:** Fixed L £15.50, Fixed D £32.50-£35, Service optional **Wine:** 87 bottles over £20, 43 bottles under £20, 9 by the glass **Notes:** Fixed L 3 courses, Fixed D 4 courses, Vegetarian menu, Dress Restrictions, Smart casual, No jeans or T-shirts **Seats:** 60 **Children:** Min 5 yrs **Rooms:** 25 (25 en suite) ★★★ HL **Directions:** From N M6 junct 40, A66 to Keswick, then S on A591 to Grasmere. From S M6 junct 36 take A591 through Windermere/Ambleside to Grasmere. At N end of village adjacent to park **Parking:** 35

◎◎ Wordsworth Hotel

British, International V

Impressive culinary display in the heart of Lakeland

☎ 015394 35592 LA22 9SW
e-mail: enquiry@thewordsworthhotel.co.uk
web: www.thewordsworthhotel.co.uk

You can't go far in Grasmere without running into Wordsworth - this traditional hotel, a former hunting lodge, is located next to the churchyard where the poet is buried. With the backdrop of towering fells, guests and diners alike can enjoy a pleasant haven away from the tourist throngs and enjoy some fine traditional British cooking (with a few splashes of Mediterranean colour). The fixed-price menu, in the light, airy traditional-styled Prelude restaurant, is never less than impressive with quality, local produce throughout and some interesting ingredient combinations. All the cooking is characterised by good flavours and textures, and first class presentation. Start with carpaccio of Gressingham duck breast with plum chutney and shallot confit and then move on to roast crown and red leg partridge with honey-roasted vegetables and juniper jus.

Chef: Brian Maidment **Owners:** Mr Gifford **Times:** 12.30-2/7-9.30 **Prices:** Fixed D £39.50, Service optional **Notes:** Fixed D 4 courses, Vegetarian menu, Dress Restrictions, Smart casual, jacket preferred, Civ Wed 100, Air con **Seats:** 65, Pr/dining room 18 **Children:** Min 8 yrs, Menu, Portions **Rooms:** 37 (37 en suite) ★★★★ HL **Directions:** From Ambleside follow A591 N to Grasmere. Hotel in town centre next to church **Parking:** 50

HAWKSHEAD   MAP 18 SD39

◉ Queen's Head Hotel

British, International

Charming old-world inn serving honest fare

☎ 015394 36271 0800 137263 Main St LA22 0NS

e-mail: enquiries@queensheadhotel.co.uk

web: www.queensheadhotel.co.uk

Full of character, this centrally-located, 16th-century former coaching inn features flagstone floors, a wood-panelled bar, low oak-beamed ceilings and an open fire. Generous, uncomplicated and carefully prepared meals are served in the bar and pretty dining room. Good use is made of quality local ingredients in a lengthy menu bolstered by daily specials. Honey-roasted Barbary duck with wild berry jus, local Graythwaite pheasant with Huntsman sauce and lamb King Henry (slow-roasted shoulder of lamb with orange demi-glaze) are fine examples of the fare.

Chef: Steve Joseph **Owners:** Anthony Merrick **Times:** 12-2.30/6.15-9.30 **Prices:** Starter £3.95-£6.55, Main £10.25-£18.50, Dessert £3.50-£4.75, Service optional **Wine:** 8 bottles over £20, 40 bottles under £20, 14 by the glass **Notes:** Vegetarian available, Dress Restrictions, Smart casual, Air con **Seats:** 38, Pr/dining room 20 **Children:** Menu, Portions **Rooms:** 14 (12 en suite) ★★ HL **Directions:** Village centre **Parking:** NCP permits issued

◉◉ West Vale Country House & Restaurant

Traditional

Fine dining in a classic country house

☎ 01539 442817 Far Sawrey LA22 0LQ

e-mail: dee.pennington@btconnect.com

web: www.westvalecountryhouse.co.uk

Built as a Victorian gentleman's residence, this charming Lakeland stone-built house sits in the heart of Beatrix Potter country, on the edge of the beautiful village of Far Sawrey. With stunning views of Grizedale Forest and The Old Man of Coniston, its elegant style and warm ambience combine with impeccable service and hospitality. The restaurant continues the theme, with well-spaced tables, white linen and quality tableware. Dishes are classical with a modern approach, the daily-changing menu featuring the best of local produce. Try a starter of seared chicken livers with blueberries and port, followed by roast rack of Cumbrian fell-bred lamb with minted mash drizzled with pan gravy, and a hot chocolate mousse with coconut ice cream finale.

Chef: Glynn Pennington **Owners:** Dee & Glynn Pennington **Times:** 12-2/7-8, Closed Jan **Prices:** Fixed D £34, Starter £4.75-£5.95, Main £15.45-£23.50, Dessert £3.75-£6.50, Service included **Wine:** 8 bottles over £20, 6 bottles under £20, 4 by the glass **Notes:** Fixed D 4 courses, Vegetarian available, Dress Restrictions, Smart casual **Seats:** 24 **Children:** Portions **Rooms:** 7 (7 en suite) ★★★★★ GH **Directions:** Please telephone for directions **Parking:** 7

HOWTOWN   MAP 18 NY41

◉◉ Sharrow Bay Country House Hotel

British, International V 🍷NOTABLE WINE LIST

Elegant lakeside country-house dining with stunning views

☎ 017684 86301 Sharrow Bay CA10 2LZ

e-mail: info@sharrowbay.co.uk

web: www.sharrowbay.co.uk

Popularly described as the 'original country-house hotel', Sharrow Bay's Italianate façade - set smack on the shores of Ullswater - brings a touch of the Italian Lakes to Cumbria. Décor is opulent and in typical English country-house mode, brimful of antiques, soft furnishings and fresh flowers. Take a stroll in the extensive grounds, or enjoy the views from a table in the elegant restaurant, where the classic country-house cooking continues the theme. Tip-top local produce is delivered in accomplished dishes that blend traditional and modern ideas; take a

CONTINUED

HOWTOWN CONTINUED

fillet of sea bass with wild mushroom fricassée, parsnip purée and a juniper berry and rosemary sauce, and perhaps a classic apple tarte Tatin with cinnamon ice cream to finish.

Chef: Colin Akrigg, Mark Teasdale **Owners:** Sharrow Bay Hotels Ltd **Times:** 1/8 **Prices:** Fixed L £32, Fixed D £39.50, Service optional **Wine:** 708 bottles over £20, 38 bottles under £20, 19 by the glass **Notes:** Fixed L 3 courses, Fixed D 6 courses, Vegetarian menu, Dress Restrictions, Smart casual, Civ Wed 35, Air con **Seats:** 55, Pr/dining room 40 **Children:** Min 13 yrs **Rooms:** 22 (24 en suite)★★★ HL **Directions:** M6 junct 40. From Pooley Bridge fork right by church towards Howtown. At x-rds turn right and follow lakeside road for 2m **Parking:** 30

KENDAL   MAP 18 SD59

◎◎ Best Western Castle Green Hotel in Kendal

British, Modern European
Modern restaurant with the kitchen on view

☎ 01539 734000 Castle Green Ln LA9 6BH
e-mail: reception@castlegreen.co.uk
web: www.castlegreen.co.uk

This popular hotel offers a relaxed stay in a peaceful Lakeland setting overlooking fells and castle ruins, but is also conveniently situated for both the town centre and the M6. The smart modern dining room has been decorated in muted shades that provide a perfect foil for the dramatic scenery outside the large plate-glass windows. The ambitious cooking is showcased on the modern menu, where nursery favourites like apple crumble served with apple fritters and caramel ice cream can be found alongside globally-inspired dishes along the lines of perfectly cooked roasted scallops with cauliflower and Parma ham. You can watch the chef at work through a window into the state-of-the-art theatre kitchen.

Chef: Justin Woods **Owners:** James & Catherine Alexander **Times:** 12-2/6-10 **Prices:** Main fr £18.95, Service included **Wine:** 23 bottles over £20, 27 bottles under £20, 12 by the glass **Notes:** ALC £23.95 2 courses, £27.95 3 courses, Vegetarian available, Dress Restrictions, Smart casual, Civ Wed 100, Air con **Seats:** 80, Pr/dining room 200 **Children:** Menu, Portions **Rooms:** 100 (100 en suite) ★★★ HL **Directions:** From Kendal High St, take A684 towards Sedbergh, hotel is last on left leaving Kendal **Parking:** 200

KESWICK   MAP 18 NY22

◎◎ Dale Head Hall Lakeside Hotel

Modern British
Immaculate lakeside hotel dining

☎ 017687 72478 Lake Thirlmere CA12 4TN
e-mail: onthelakeside@daleheadhall.co.uk
web: www.daleheadhall.co.uk

Dating back to the 16th century, this country-house hotel is immaculately maintained and sits in mature gardens that run down to the shores of Lake Thirlmere. With Helvellyn as a backdrop, the scene's set for stunning views that can be enjoyed from many of the hotel's comfortable public rooms. The atmospheric restaurant has exposed stone and low beams, and there is also a smaller dining room looking towards the lake. The menu changes daily and offers a choice of two dishes at each of four courses, such as home-cured gravad lax with chive and potato salad, followed by best end of salt marsh lamb with garlic mash and tapenade sauce. Desserts are indulgent treats and might include warm dark chocolate tart with orange caramel syrup, or lemon and raspberry syllabub with hazelnut shortbread.

Times: 7.30-8, Closed Jan **Rooms:** 12 (12 en suite) ★★★ CHH **Directions:** 5m from Keswick on A591

◎◎ Highfield Hotel & Restaurant

Modern European
Ambitious cooking in friendly Lakeland hotel

☎ 017687 72508 The Heads CA12 5ER
e-mail: info@highfieldkeswick.co.uk
web: www.highfieldkeswick.co.uk

Country house in style, this lovely Victorian hotel retains many original features - think balconies, turrets, bay windows and veranda - and comes set on the edge of town with Lakeland views and a relaxed, friendly atmosphere. The restaurant continues the theme, with original ceiling roses and cornice, while taking advantage of the views. And, while traditional may sum up the setting, the cooking takes a modern approach - classical in style but with contemporary twists. The ambitious, daily-changing, dinner-only menu comes peppered with quality Cumbrian produce in the form of smoked mackerel and lemon crab cakes with Chardonnay dressing, followed by roast loin and pan-fried cutlet of fell lamb with roast parsnip and honey mustard mash and thyme jus.

Chef: Gus Cleghorn **Owners:** Howard & Caroline Speck **Times:** 6.30-8.30, Closed Jan-Early Feb, Closed L all week **Prices:** Fixed D £32.50-£37, Service optional **Wine:** 22 bottles over £20, 41 bottles under £20, 7 by the glass **Notes:** Fixed D 4 courses, Dress Restrictions, Smart casual, Air con **Seats:** 40 **Children:** Min 8 yrs, Portions **Rooms:** 18 (18 en suite) ★★ SHL **Directions:** M6 junct 40, follow signs for Keswick, approaching Keswick, ignore first sign. Continue on A66, at Peach rdbt turn left. At next T-junct turn left, and continue to mini-rdbt and take right exit then third right onto the Heads **Parking:** 23

◉ Lyzzick Hall Country House Hotel

European

Quality cooking accompanied by Lakeland views

☎ 017687 72277 Under Skiddaw CA12 4PY
e-mail: info@lyzzickhall.co.uk
web: www.lyzzickhall.co.uk

Perched in the foothills of Skiddaw overlooking Keswick, this cosy Lakeland hotel boasts beautiful views all year round. The restaurant has a classical décor with quality table settings and fresh flowers. Nothing is too much trouble for its friendly staff, while the kitchen team conjure a menu of accomplished fare from the finest ingredients Cumbria has to offer. Dishes are modern in style, and feature the odd nod to the Mediterranean and beyond - you might start with spinach and white butterbean soup perhaps, and move on to baked cod fillet wrapped in Lakeland pancetta served with buttered leeks and saffron and chive sauce.

Chef: Chris Cooper **Owners:** Mr & Mrs Fernandez **Times:** 12-2/7-9, Closed Jan **Prices:** Food prices not confirmed for 2008. Please telephone for details **Notes:** Fixed D 4 courses, Vegetarian available, Dress Restrictions, Smart casual **Seats:** 75 **Children:** Menu, Portions **Rooms:** 31 (31 en suite) ★★ CHH **Directions:** Leave Keswick towards Carlisle, at main rdbt take 2nd exit signed A591 Carlisle, Lyzzick Hall 1.5m on right **Parking:** 60

◉◉ Swinside Lodge

British, European V

Delightful country house with indulgent food and service

☎ 017687 72948 Grange Rd, Newlands CA12 5UE
e-mail: info@swinsidelodge-hotel.co.uk
web: www.swinsidelodge-hotel.co.uk

Just five minutes stroll from the shores of Derwentwater, this Georgian house is a hidden gem. Staff make you feel as welcome as an old friend, and the country-house furnishings are equally inviting. The intimate dining room is decked out in red with fresh flowers, candles and clothed tables. Take your seat for a four-course, dinner-only menu of modern British dishes that make the most of quality produce from local farmers and the kitchen garden. The daily-changing set menu lets you know you're in safe hands; the cooking here is creative, skilful and great value for money. Kick off with salmon with celery, apple and cucumber remoulade, and then tuck into Cumbrian beef with rösti potato, caramelised onions and Madeira jus.

Chef: Clive Imber **Owners:** Eric & Irene Fell **Times:** 7-10.30, Closed 25 Dec, Closed L Mon-Sun **Prices:** Fixed D £35, Service optional **Wine:** 10 bottles over £20, 12 bottles under £20, 3 by the glass **Notes:** Fixed D 4 courses, Vegetarian menu **Seats:** 18 **Children:** Min 12 yrs, Portions **Rooms:** 7 (7 en suite) ★★ CHH **Directions:** M6 junct 40 take A66 to Cockermouth, ignore exits to Keswick, next left to Portinscale. Follow country road for 2m (do not leave this road). Hotel on right **Parking:** 12

◉◉ Underscar Manor

British, French

Formal fine dining in a beautiful country house

☎ 017687 75000 Applethwaite CA12 4PH
web: www.underscar.co.uk

Dating back to 1856, this listed Victorian, Italianate-style property sits on a flank of Skiddaw and offers picture-postcard views of Keswick, Derwentwater and the surrounding fells. Its lavish restaurant is traditionally furnished and requires men to wear jackets in the evening, although the atmosphere is friendly and relaxed. Take your seat for some ambitious cooking rooted in classical cuisine. Careful presentation and the use of quality local ingredients impress in seasonal dishes such as breast of local pheasant wrapped in Parma ham for example, served with wild mushrooms, clapshot and Calvados sauce, or roast rump of Lakeland lamb with provençale vegetables, hotpot potatoes and piquant sauce.

Chef: Robert Thornton **Owners:** Pauline & Derek Harrison & Gordon Evans **Times:** 12-1/7-8.30 **Prices:** Fixed L £22, Fixed D £38, Starter £9.50-£13.50, Main £22-£23, Dessert £7-£10, Service optional **Wine:** 100 bottles over £20, 4 bottles under £20, 5 by the glass **Notes:** Fixed D 5 courses, Vegetarian available, Dress Restrictions, Smart casual, no T-shirts or trainers **Seats:** 55 **Children:** Min 12 yrs **Directions:** Exit M6 at junct 36 on to Keswick, follow for 17 miles (don't turn off in to Keswick). At rdbt take 3rd exit and turn immediately right at sign for Underscar Manor **Parking:** 40

Morrel's

☎ 017687 72666 34 Lake Rd CA12 5DQ

Relaxed, informal restaurant, handy for the theatre.

ENGLAND

KIRKBY LONSDALE — MAP 18 SD67

◉ *The Whoop Hall*

Modern, Traditional
Modern restaurant offering traditional dishes

☎ 015242 71284 Burrow with Burrow LA6 2HP
e-mail: info@whoophall.co.uk
web: www.whoophall.co.uk

Originally a 17th-century coaching inn, Whoop Hall is now a fully-fledged hotel. Here Connor's restaurant is a bright room on two floors, with a galleried area above. The lightwood furniture and stone-tiled floor give a modern feel. A light bites menu offers a choice of fillings for sandwiches, baguettes, jackets or tortillas, alongside salads, chips and pasta. The main menu offers traditional dishes like moules marinière, and horseshoe gammon topped with a fried egg and fresh pineapple with fries.

Times: 12-6/6-10 **Rooms:** 24 (23 en suite) ★★ HL **Directions:** Please telephone for directions

NEAR SAWREY — MAP 18 SD39

◉ Ees Wyke Country House

British, French NEW
Glorious country-house setting for fine local fare

☎ 015394 36393 LA22 0JZ
e-mail: mail@eeswyke.co.uk
web: www.eeswyke.co.uk

This Georgian country house nestles into the hillside, offering stunning views over Esthwaite Water and the surrounding countryside. Cosy day rooms boast warming log fires in the colder months, an ideal place to relax before or after dinner. Period features have been preserved in the spacious dining room, which looks towards the lake. British dishes with European influences feature on an interesting and varied menu, offering up the best of local produce. Try for example noisettes of wonderful local lamb, pan-fried and served with wine jus, mint and just a hint of garlic.

Chef: Richard Lee **Owners:** Richard & Margaret Lee **Times:** 7.30 **Prices:** Fixed D £32, Service included **Wine:** 24 bottles over £20, 41 bottles under £20, 5 by the glass **Notes:** Fixed D 5 courses **Seats:** 16 **Children:** Min 12 yrs **Rooms:** 8 (8 en suite) ★★★★★ GH **Directions:** On B5285 between Hawkshead and the Windermere Ferry **Parking:** 12

NETHER WASDALE — MAP 18 NY10

◉ *Low Wood Hall Hotel*

European
Fresh modern dishes in Victorian country-house style

☎ 019467 26100 CA20 1ET
e-mail: enquiries@lowwoodhall.co.uk
web: www.lowwoodhall.co.uk

This Victorian hotel is tucked away in a remote valley with beautiful landscaped gardens, surrounded by 5 acres of woodland. The conservatory restaurant offers glorious views and looks very romantic when candlelit at night. Built in the 1860s for a local brewer, Thomas

Dalzell and his family, the house retains many features from the Victorian era, including gasoliers in the lounges, tiled and pine stripped floors and marble fireplaces. The chef serves up modern classic dishes using fresh local ingredients including herbs from the kitchen garden. The menu changes daily to reflect seasonal availability and produce from local suppliers.

Times: 7-9, Closed L all wk **Rooms:** 13 (13 en suite) ★★ HL **Directions:** Exit A595 at Gosforth & bear left for Wasdale, after 3m turn right for Nether Wasdale

NEWBY BRIDGE — MAP 18 SD38

◉◉ Lakeside Hotel

Modern British V
Fine dining in picturesque Lakeland shore setting

☎ 015395 30001 Lakeside, Lake Windermere LA12 8AT
e-mail: sales@lakesidehotel.co.uk
web: www.lakesidehotel.co.uk

Set on the peaceful southern shore of Lake Windermere, next to the steamer dock, this is an impressive, family-run hotel where guests and diners can expect high standards of service. Dinner is served in the elegant, oak-panelled Lakeview restaurant, with its fresh flowers, floor-length tablecloths and sparkling glassware, but more informal meals can be enjoyed in the contemporary John Ruskin's brasserie. Cooking is accomplished, with traditional British and European dishes prepared and presented with flair and expertise - classical dishes with a modern twist. Take a fillet of John Dory served with peas à la Français, braised gem lettuce, fondant potatoes and crispy pancetta, and to finish, perhaps a pistachio soufflé with dark chocolate truffle mousse. Staff are professional and highly skilled.

Chef: Duncan Collinge **Owners:** Mr N Talbot **Times:** 12.30-2.30/6.45-9.30, Closed 23 Dec-10 Jan **Prices:** Fixed L £27, Fixed D £45, Service included **Wine:** 120 bottles over £20, 15 bottles under £20, 12 by the glass **Notes:** Fixed L 3 courses, Fixed D 6 courses, Vegetarian menu, Dress Restrictions, Smart casual, no jeans, Civ Wed 80, Air con **Seats:** 70, Pr/dining room 30 **Children:** Menu, Portions **Rooms:** 77 (77 en suite) ★★★★ HL **Directions:** M6 junct 36 follow A590 to Newby Bridge, straight over rdbt, right over bridge. Hotel within 1m **Parking:** 200

⚜ Swan Hotel

Modern British

Moor up for some comfort cooking

☎ 015395 31681   LA12 8NB
e-mail: enquiries@swanhotel.com
web: www.swanhotel.com

Set beside the river Leven at the southern end of Lake Windermere, this 17th-century coaching inn boasts a choice of eateries. Revells restaurant is the main draw, a traditional dining room with smartly turned out waiting staff and panoramic views. Mains are hearty, comforting creations such as chargrilled fillet of Scottish beef with Meaux mustard mash and beetroot gravy, or a baked open winter vegetable pie with neeps, tatties and roast shallots in cheddar cream sauce, while desserts include old favourites (citrus sponge pudding) and classier fare such as baked toffee and pecan tart with pistachio ice cream.

Chef: Brent Farnworth **Owners:** Sharon Bardsley **Times:** 12-2.30/7-10, Closed D Sun **Prices:** Fixed L £15, Fixed D £30, Starter £4.50, Main £9.50, Dessert £5.25, Service optional **Wine:** 35 bottles over £20, 27 bottles under £20, 10 by the glass **Notes:** Vegetarian available, Dress Restrictions, No jeans, Civ Wed 140, Air con **Seats:** 70, Pr/dining room 26
Children: Menu, Portions **Rooms:** 55 (55 en suite) ★★★★ HL
Directions: M6 junct 36, at rdbt take 1st exit. A590 to Barrow for approx 16m, then follow signs for Newby Bridge **Parking:** 100

PENRITH   MAP 18 NY53

⚜ Edenhall Country Hotel

Modern British

Formal dining in a friendly village hotel - don't forget your tackle

☎ 01768 881454 Edenhall CA11 8SX
e-mail: info@edenhallhotel.co.uk
web: www.edenhallhotel.co.uk

Originally a bolt-hole for fishermen taking advantage of the nearby River Eden, this cosy retreat has become just as popular with walkers enjoying the Lakeland area. Set in pretty grounds, it has a large dining room blessed with huge windows that overlook the garden and surrounding countryside, and delivers a cosmopolitan array of dishes based around the best of local Cumbrian produce. Start with a simple tomato and basil soup, and then tuck into chargrilled collops of fell-bred beef fillet with a mushroom and onion pudding, roast potatoes, creamed celeriac and bordelaise sauce, or roast breast of Barbary duck with pak choi noodles and spicy plum sauce.

Chef: Colin Sim **Owners:** Clare Simmons/Tony Simpson **Times:** 6-9, Closed L all week (bar meals only) **Prices:** Starter £3.95-£6.45, Main £9.95-£14.95, Dessert £4.95-£5.95, Service optional **Wine:** 3 bottles over £20, 22 bottles under £20, 4 by the glass **Notes:** Civ Wed 60
Seats: 60, Pr/dining room 25 **Children:** Menu, Portions **Rooms:** 25 (25 en suite) ★★ HL **Directions:** M6 junct 40, take A66 towards Scotch Corner. At rdbt follow signs to Alston (A686). Edenhall is 3m on right **Parking:** 60

⚜ The Martindale Restaurant

Traditional British NEW ♨

Fine regional ingredients at modern hunting lodge-style hotel

☎ 01768 868111 North Lakes Hotel & Spa, Ullswater Rd CA11 8QT
e-mail: nlakes@shirehotels.com
web: www.shirehotels.com

Striking interior design, featuring timber beams, traditional Lakeland stone, wooden floors and impressive fireplaces, catches the eye at this contemporary hunting lodge-styled hotel with excellent leisure facilities. The Martindale restaurant is where the main dining action takes place, the accomplished kitchen's straightforward, ingredient-led approach making fine use of quality local produce. The Cumbrian starter table (buffet selection of hors d'oeuvre) proves a highlight, while mains might feature slow-cooked Stainton belly pork and confit of duck, with bramley apple mash, Savoy cabbage and cider sauce, and traditional-style desserts could include the ubiquitous sticky toffee pudding.

Chef: Mr Mike Haddow **Owners:** Shire Hotels Ltd **Times:** 12.15-1.45/7-9.15, Closed L Sat, Sun **Prices:** Fixed L £15.50, Starter £5.50-£8, Main £14.25-£23, Dessert £6-£7.25, Service optional **Wine:** 41 bottles over £20, 17 bottles under £20, 14 by the glass **Notes:** Vegetarian available, Civ Wed 200 **Seats:** 112 **Children:** Menu, Portions **Rooms:** 84 (84 en suite) ★★★★ HL **Directions:** M6 just off junct 40 **Parking:** 120

SEASCALE   MAP 18 NY00

⚜ Cumbrian Lodge

International

Homely restaurant with wonderful speciality dishes

☎ 019467 27309 Gosforth Rd CA20 1JG
e-mail: cumbrianlodge@btconnect.com
web: www.cumbrianlodge.com

Built in 1874, this pleasant village restaurant housed the same family until 1999. Now a restaurant with rooms, Cumbrian Lodge has been sensitively refurbished with modern, minimalist décor, modern art on the walls and crisp linen-clothed tables. The quality bistro-style menu features a mix of traditional British dishes with European and Asian influences. Start with moules marinière or home-made wild mushroom and chicken liver pâté and then move on to Thai-style chicken or steak Diane. The house speciality is Geschnetzeltes Schweinefleisch - thinly sliced pork fillet sautéed in butter, wine and cream served with a heavenly rösti potato.

Chef: R Hickson & A Carnall **Owners:** David J Morgan **Times:** 12-2/6.30-9.30, Closed Xmas, New Year, BHs, Sun, Closed L Mon & Sat
Prices: Starter £5.95, Main £9.95-£18.95, Dessert £4.50, Service optional
Wine: 17 bottles over £20, 19 bottles under £20, 15 by the glass **Seats:** 32 **Rooms:** 6 (6 en suite) ★★★★ RR **Directions:** From A595 onto B5344, hotel on left after 2m **Parking:** 17

TEBAY   MAP 18 NY60

◉ Westmorland Hotel & Restaurant

Traditional British

Friendly modern hotel overlooking rugged moorland

☎ 015396 24351   Near Orton CA10 3SB
e-mail: reservations@westmorlandhotel.com
web: www.westmorlandhotel.com

There are picture-postcard views of the fells just half a mile from the M6 at this modern hotel. The split-level Bretherdale restaurant - designed using natural materials that reflect its setting - affords nearly every table a scenic outlook through its huge windows, while right outside there's a cascading water feature. Imaginative modern cooking might deliver a fillet of Cumbrian pork served with smoked cheese mash and leek and prune compôte. There are close ties here with the local farming community - lamb and beef come from the hotel's own farm just 3 miles away, and an award-winning farm shop is part of the complex.

Chef: Graham Evans **Owners:** Westmorland Ltd **Times:** 6.30-9, Closed 1 Jan, Closed D 31 Dec **Prices:** Starter £5.75-£6.15, Main £12-£20, Dessert £4.50-£5, Service optional **Wine:** 4 bottles over £20, 32 bottles under £20, 8 by the glass **Notes:** Set menus can be provided for pre-booked groups, Dress Restrictions, Smart casual, no jeans or T-shirts, Civ Wed 120, Air con **Seats:** 100, Pr/dining room 40 **Children:** Menu, Portions **Rooms:** 51 (51 en suite) ★★★ HL **Directions:** Accessed from the Westmorland Motorway Services between J38 & J39 of M6 **Parking:** 60

TEMPLE SOWERBY   MAP 18 NY62

◉◉ Temple Sowerby House Hotel & Restaurant

Modern British

Intimate setting for ambitious cooking

☎ 017683 61578   CA10 1RZ
e-mail: stay@templesowerby.com
web: www.templesowerby.com

Dating back to 1727, this Grade II listed country-house hotel - once the village's principal dwelling - is situated in the heart of the Eden Valley. Complete with open fire, smartly dressed tables and candles, the charming oak-beamed restaurant is the perfect setting in which to enjoy some adventurous dishes that showcase the kitchen's innovative techniques and bold mix of contemporary and British cooking styles. There's a firm emphasis on seasonal, local and home-grown produce. Take butter-roasted haunch of venison with redcurrant samosa, pommes dauphine and a rosemary and Madeira sauce, or pan-fried fillet of sea bream on crushed ratte potatoes with fennel salad and bacon foam. Desserts tempt with the likes of rum pannacotta with gingerbread and caramelised garden pears, or perhaps hot chocolate and hazelnut fondant with toffee sauce and malted milk ice cream. In fine weather, the terrace is a splendid spot for pre-dinner drinks.

Chef: Ashley Whittaker **Owners:** Paul & Julie Evans **Times:** 7-9, Closed 8 days Xmas, Closed L all week **Prices:** Starter £5-£8, Main £15-£21, Dessert £6-£8, Service optional **Wine:** 30 bottles over £20, 10 bottles under £20, 6 by the glass **Notes:** Dress Restrictions, Smart casual preferred, Civ Wed 40 **Seats:** 24, Pr/dining room 24 **Children:** Min 12 yrs **Rooms:** 12 (12 en suite) ★★★ HL **Directions:** On A66, 7m E of Penrith in village centre **Parking:** 20

WATERMILLOCK   MAP 18 NY42

◉◉ Macdonald Leeming House

Modern British

A taste of Cumbria in sumptuous country house with a view

☎ 0870 4008131   CA11 0JJ
e-mail: leeminghouse@macdonald-hotels.co.uk
web: www.macdonald-hotels.co.uk

Set in a stunning location, in 20 acres of landscaped grounds on the shores of Ullswater, Macdonald Leeming House dates from the 1800s and retains many original features. Beautiful views over the lake and its backdrop of mountain fells enhance the ornate but informal surroundings in the Regency-style restaurant. Classical dishes are given a modern, lighter twist, revealing imagination and flair, and a willingness to experiment with the best seasonal produce that Cumbria has to offer. Dishes may include salmon terrine with honey, lemon and dill dressing to start, followed by roast Lakeland lamb stuffed with fruit and served with a Burgundy and onion gravy, with Bailey's cream cheesecake and apricot coulis for dessert.

Chef: John Badley **Owners:** Macdonald Hotels **Times:** 12-2/6.30-9 **Prices:** Fixed L £14.50, Fixed D £40, Service added but optional 12.5% **Wine:** 75 bottles over £20, 11 bottles under £20, 13 by the glass **Notes:** Fixed D 4 courses, Dress Restrictions, Smart casual, no jeans or T-shirts, Civ Wed 30 **Seats:** 60, Pr/dining room 24 **Children:** Menu, Portions **Rooms:** 41 (41 en suite) ★★★★ HL **Directions:** M6 junct 40, continue on A66 signed Keswick. At rdbt follow A592 towards Ullswater, at T-junct turn right, hotel 3m on left **Parking:** 50

◉◉◉ Rampsbeck Country House Hotel

see opposite

WINDERMERE   MAP 18 SD49

◉◉ Beech Hill Hotel

British, French

Modern cuisine and stunning lake views

☎ 015394 42137   Newby Bridge Rd LA23 3LR
e-mail: reservations@beechhillhotel.co.uk
web: www.beechhillhotel.co.uk

The great views over Lake Windermere and wonderful summer sunsets are not the only draws at this hotel dining room. Rich furnishings, smart interior designs and oak panelling make an elegant statement that is also hard to resist. After drinks on the terrace or in the lounge, guests need no prompting to order from the popular Simple Taste of the Lakes or five-course Gourmet menu. The cooking takes account of Cumbrian produce in peak condition, with several dimensions to each dish: diver-caught scallops with fresh peas, crisp lettuce and pancetta and sweet pea and parmesan foam might be followed by roast wild salmon with wild Scottish mushrooms, new potatoes and lentil sauce, with chilled lemon posset and home-made shortbread to finish.

Times: 7-9, Closed L all week **Rooms:** 57 (57 en suite) ★★★ HL **Directions:** M6 junct 36, take A591 to Windermere, left onto A592 to Newby Bridge, hotel 4m on right

Rampsbeck Country House Hotel

WATERMILLOCK MAP 18 NY42

Modern British, French V

Innovative modern cooking in lakeside hotel

☎ 017684 86442   CA11 0LP
e-mail: enquiries@rampsbeck.co.uk
web: www.rampsbeck.co.uk

Overlooking Lake Ullswater, this idyllic 18th-century country house is set in 18 acres of parkland with attractive gardens, hedges and paths running down to the shore. It boasts many original features - including carved fireplaces - and comes furnished with period and antique pieces. There are three delightful and comfortable lounges plus a small traditional bar (that opens out on to a terrace on warm summer days), as well as the attractive, candlelit restaurant with its large windows that make the best of those views. Tables are well spaced and service nicely traditional, though appropriately friendly and attentive, while the cooking proves a real highlight.
The kitchen's innovative, modern approach uses fresh, top-quality produce in thoughtful, well-judged combinations. Expect clean flavours and interesting textures in complex dishes, like ballotine of pork with chicken and pancetta, served with parsnip purée and a natural jus, or perhaps pan-fried fillet of halibut with confit beetroot, braised onions and pancetta with a red wine reduction, while a baked pear wrapped in sablé biscuit with white sabayon and prune and Armagnac ice cream might feature at dessert.

Chef: Andrew McGeorge
Owners: Mr & Mrs T Gibb
Times: 12-1.15/7-8.30, Closed 5 Jan-9 Feb, L booking only
Prices: Fixed L £29, Fixed D £39.50, Service optional
Wine: 44 bottles over £20, 59 bottles under £20, 6 by the glass
Notes: Fixed L 3 courses, Vegetarian menu, Dress Restrictions, Smart casual, no jeans or shorts, Civ Wed 65
Seats: 40, Pr/dining room 15
Children: Min 7 yrs, Portions
Rooms: 19 (19 en suite)★★★ HL
Directions: M6 junct 40, A592 to Ullswater, T-junct turn right at lake's edge. Hotel 1.25m
Parking: 30

WINDERMERE CONTINUED

🏵 Best Western Burn How Garden House Hotel

British, French

Formal dining overlooking pretty gardens

☎ 015394 46226 Back Belsfield Rd, Bowness LA23 3HH
e-mail: info@burnhow.co.uk
web: www.burnhow.co.uk

There's a relaxed country-house feel to this delightful Victorian hotel, set in its own leafy grounds within walking distance of both the lakeside and town centre. Creative dinners can be enjoyed in the airy dining room, which overlooks the mature garden. Locally-sourced ingredients feature on both the carte and daily specials menu, and dishes include grilled fell-bred prime beef fillet, served with field mushrooms, caramelised baby onions and red wine jus, or Cartmel Valley venison steak navarine with roasted root vegetables. If you have room, round things off with the Cumbrian cheeseboard, or take a dessert like dark chocolate truffle ravioli with rum bananas and vanilla ice cream.

Chef: Jane Kimani **Owners:** Michael Robinson **Times:** 6.30-8.30, Closed Xmas, Closed L all week **Prices:** Fixed D £28, Starter £4.50-£6.50, Main £13.75-£18, Dessert £4-£6, Service optional **Notes:** Vegetarian available **Seats:** 40 **Children:** Min 5 yrs, Menu, Portions **Rooms:** 28 (28 en suite) ★★★ HL **Directions:** 7m from M6. Follow A590 to A591 (Windermere to Bowness) **Parking:** 28

🏵🏵 Fayrer Garden Hotel

Modern British, Traditional

Country-house dining overlooking Lake Windermere

☎ 015394 88195 Lyth Valley Rd,
Bowness on Windermere LA23 3JP
e-mail: lakescene@fayrergarden.com
web: www.fayrergarden.com

This former Edwardian gentleman's residence is set in 5 acres of beautiful gardens and has spectacular views over the lake. The interior is decorated in the country-house style, and the Terrace restaurant has sumptuous fabrics and drapes, crisp linen on the tables and formal settings. Generously priced, five-course, daily-changing menus use local seasonal ingredients that keep locals and visitors returning. The traditional British approach comes with a few modern twists; take a suprême of guinea fowl with a wild mushroom tart, baby vegetables and a thyme and Madeira sauce, or skate wing served with ratatouille, a quenelle of tapenade mash, crisp air-dried ham and a tomato coulis. Finish with a Bramley apple cheesecake.

Chef: Edward Wilkinson **Owners:** Mr & Mrs Wildsmith **Times:** 7-8.30, Closed 1st 2wks Jan, Closed L all week **Prices:** Fixed D £25-£35, Service optional **Wine:** 50 bottles over £20, 50 bottles under £20, 9 by the glass **Notes:** Fixed D 4 courses, Dress Restrictions, Smart casual, no jeans or T-shirts, Civ Wed 60, Air con **Seats:** 60, Pr/dining room 20 **Children:** Min 5 yrs, Portions **Rooms:** 29 (29 en suite) ★★★ HL **Directions:** M6 junct 36, onto A591. Past Kendal, at rdbt turn left onto B5284 (signposted Crook Bowness & Ferry) and continue for 8m, then turn left onto A5074 for 400yds **Parking:** 40

🏵🏵🏵 Gilpin Lodge Country House Hotel & Restaurant

see page 104

🏵🏵🏵 Holbeck Ghyll Country House Hotel

see page 105

🏵🏵 Jerichos

Modern British

Warm and intimate restaurant serving creative food

☎ 015394 42522 Birch St LA23 1EG
e-mail: enquiries@jerichos.co.uk
web: www.jerichos.co.uk

Friendly and unpretentious with a great atmosphere, Jerichos is a modern restaurant off the main street in the centre of town. A warm, rich décor, linen tablecloths, tall chairs, an open-to-view kitchen and walls lined with prints of jazz players create an upbeat vibe. The accomplished, innovative cooking sings to an equally modern tune, with an emphasis on simplicity and flavour; take pan-fried organic corn-fed chicken breast with chorizo and thyme-roasted provençale vegetables, spiced orange couscous and a port wine sauce, or perhaps a white chocolate pannacotta finish, served with a summer fruit coulis, shortbread sablé and peach sorbet. Wine recommendations appear on menus, while the wine list comes helpfully grouped by food type rather than by country.

Chef: Chris Blaydes, Tim Dalzell **Owners:** Mr & Mrs C Blaydes **Times:** 6.45-10, Closed 2 wk end Nov-1st wk Dec, Xmas, 1 Jan, Mon (Apr-Dec), Sun (Jan-Mar), Closed L Tue-Sun **Prices:** Starter £3.95-£9, Main £14.50-£19, Dessert £5.95-£6.50, Service optional **Wine:** 33 bottles over £20, 35 bottles under £20, 9 by the glass **Seats:** 36, Pr/dining room 30 **Children:** Min 12 yrs **Directions:** M6 junct 36, then A591.

🏵 Langdale Chase Hotel

European V

Dining with a view in stunning lakeside setting

☎ 015394 32201 Langdale Chase LA23 1LW
e-mail: sales@langdalechase.co.uk
web: www.langdalechase.co.uk

Situated in the heart of the Lake District, this late-Victorian mansion has plenty to please the discerning guest - a lakeside setting, splendid gardens and oak-panelled public areas with carved fireplaces. Picture windows in the dining room take full advantage of stunning westerly views to the distant fells, and terraced gardens lead down to the shores of Lake Windermere. An interesting daily fixed-price menu is offered at lunch and dinner and may include a tian of avocado and prawns with an avocado salsa, or a croissant and whisky butter pudding with anglais sauce.

Chef: Daniel Hopkins **Owners:** Mr TG Noblett **Times:** 12-2/7-9
Prices: Fixed L £18.95, Fixed D £34, Service optional **Wine:** 24 bottles
over £20, 14 bottles under £20, 7 by the glass **Notes:** Fixed L 3 courses,
Vegetarian menu, Dress Restrictions, Smart casual, Civ Wed 120, Air con
Seats: 80, Pr/dining room 36 **Children:** Menu, Portions **Rooms:** 27 (27
en suite) ★★★ HL **Directions:** 2m S of Ambleside & 3m N of
Windermere **Parking:** 60

⊚ Lindeth Fell Country House Hotel
Modern British
A tranquil haven in the Lakes

☎ 015394 43286 & 44287 Lyth Valley Rd,
Bowness-on-Windermere LA23 3JP
e-mail: kennedy@lindethfell.co.uk
web: www.lindethfell.co.uk

Perched on the wooded slopes above Windermere, this friendly hotel
occupies a former gentleman's residence and sits in pretty gardens full
of colourful rhododendrons and azaleas. Its spacious dining rooms
extend along the lakeside of the house giving diners panoramic views
to go with the kitchen's tempting modern British fare. The concise
menu changes daily and offers three or four choices for each course:
roast loin of lamb with honey shallots and rosemary gravy is a typical
main and might feature alongside seared salmon fillet with buttered
tagliatelle, prawns and a lemon and dill sauce, with desserts such as
raspberry, whisky and caramel syllabub, or brown sugar meringue
with butterscotch sauce.
Times: 12.30-1.45/7.30-9, Closed 3 wks in Jan **Rooms:** 14 (14 en
suite)★★★ CHH **Directions:** 1m S of Bowness-on-Windermere on
A5074

⊚ Lindeth Howe Country House Hotel
Modern British
Accomplished fare in the former home of a famous author

☎ 015394 45759 Lindeth Dr, Longtail Hill LA23 3JF
e-mail: hotel@lindeth-howe.co.uk
web: www.lindeth-howe.co.uk

The former family home of Beatrix Potter is now a charming country-
house hotel set on a hill overlooking the valley, Lake Windermere and
distant fells. The bright, conservatory-style restaurant overlooks the
secluded gardens and provides an elegant setting in which to enjoy
well-presented modern cooking. Take canapés and aperitifs in the
lounge or on the terrace while perusing the daily-changing four-course
dinner menu, perhaps showcasing a baked loin of Cumbrian lamb
with herb crust served with basil-flavoured mash potato, aubergine
caviar and a redcurrant jus. A glazed lemon tart, with pineapple and
Malibu compôte, might provide the finish.

Lindeth Howe Country House Hotel

Chef: Graham Gelder **Owners:** Lakeinvest Ltd **Times:** 12-2.30/7-9
Prices: Fixed L £10-£15, Fixed D £30-£35, Service optional **Wine:** 29
bottles over £20, 37 bottles under £20, 8 by the glass **Notes:** Vegetarian
available, Dress Restrictions, Smart casual, no jeans or T-shirts **Seats:** 70,
Pr/dining room 20 **Children:** Min 7 yrs, Menu, Portions **Rooms:** 36 (36
en suite) ★★★ HL **Directions:** 1m S of Bowness onto B5284, signed
Kendal and Lancaster. Hotel 2nd driveway on right **Parking:** 50

⊚⊚⊚ Linthwaite House Hotel
see page 106

⊚⊚ Macdonald Old England Hotel
Classic British, International V NEW
Stylish modern dining room with stunning lake views

☎ 0870 400 8130 Church St, Bowness LA23 3DF
e-mail: general.oldengland@macdonald-hotels.co.uk
web: www.macdonald-hotels.co.uk

The Old England combines Victorian elegance with the latest modern-
day facilities and nestles in an enviable position smack on the shores
of Lake Windermere. The stylish, modern Vinand restaurant comes
decked out with white walls, white linen, patterned carpet and
upholstered chairs, their neutral, contemporary tones offering a
perfect backdrop for the stunning lake views through its large
windows. The kitchen follows the theme, its equally modern approach
delivering carefully presented, intelligently uncomplicated dishes of
balance and flavour. Take a starter of kitchen-smoked Graythwaite
venison with wild honey and thyme-scented butternut squash, and to
follow, perhaps seared rump of Cumbrian lamb served with a parsnip
and potato sauté, spinach, black pudding and roasting juices.

Chef: Mark Walker **Owners:** Macdonald Hotels **Times:** 6.30-9, Closed L
all week **Prices:** Starter £5-£14, Main £15-£25, Dessert £5-£12, Service
optional **Wine:** 69 bottles over £20, 15 bottles under £20, 13 by the glass
Notes: Vegetarian menu, Dress Restrictions, Smart casual, Civ Wed 150, Air
con **Seats:** 160, Pr/dining room 12 **Children:** Min 4 yrs, Menu, Portions
Parking: 100

❀❀❀ Gilpin Lodge Country House Hotel & Restaurant

WINDERMERE MAP 18 SD49

Modern British V

A culinary paradise in the Lakes

☎ 015394 88818 Crook Rd LA23 3NE
e-mail: hotel@gilpinlodge.co.uk
web: www.gilpinlodge.co.uk

Positioned in the beautiful rural setting of the Lake District, this luxurious family-run hotel is as elegant as it is relaxing. Surrounded by acres of woodland, moor and award-winning gardens, it sits in leafy tranquillity just a short drive from Windermere. Each of the 14 bedrooms is immaculately decorated in chic contemporary style, while dinner - the highlight of any stay - is served in four intimate dining rooms, at tables elegantly dressed with fresh flowers, gleaming silver and crisp white linen.

The modern British food is bold, imaginative, and technically daring, yet firmly rooted in classical cuisine. Gilpin Lodge consistently impresses, handling the best and freshest of local ingredients with deft simplicity to ensure intense flavours on the plate. Expect an imaginative selection of dishes; nettle and blackberry smoked venison with pickled mouli and baby vegetables to start perhaps, followed by best-end of Herdwick lamb with fondant potato, confit vegetables, shallot purée and a rosemary jus. Round things off in style with praline parfait with caramelised pastry and passionfruit sorbet.

Chef: Chris Meredith
Owners: The Cunliffe Family
Times: 12-2/6.45-9
Prices: Fixed L £20, Fixed D £47, Service optional
Wine: 230 bottles over £20, 14 by the glass
Notes: Fixed L 5 courses, Vegetarian menu, Dress Restrictions, Smart Casual
Seats: 60, Pr/dining room 20
Children: Min 7 yrs
Rooms: 20 (20 en suite)★★★★ HL
Directions: M6 junct 36 & A590, then B5284 for 5m
Parking: 40

Holbeck Ghyll Country House Hotel

WINDERMERE MAP 18 SD49

Modern British V

Classical cuisine in former hunting lodge

☎ 015394 32375 Holbeck Ln LA23 1LU
e-mail: stay@holbeckghyll.com
web: www.holbeckghyll.com

Built in the 19th century as a hunting lodge and set in pretty gardens on a hillside above Lake Windermere, breathtaking views over the Lake and the Langdale Fells are just two of the many attractions of this sumptuous hotel and restaurant. The rooms come appropriately decorated in luxurious country-house style with deep sofas and antiques, while a brace of elegant, classically-styled dining rooms (one oak-panelled, the other with French doors leading on to the terrace) take full advantage of the scenery. The terrace provides opportunities for alfresco drinks, lunches or early evening meals on warm summer days.

The professionalism and attentiveness of the staff are exemplary, and the kitchen's modern approach is underpinned by a classical theme, in harmony with the surroundings, delivering a repertoire of fixed-price, compact menus (bolstered by a gourmet option on Fridays and Saturdays) that aren't short on appeal or imagination. An intelligent simplicity allows the high-quality produce to shine in well-presented, clear-flavoured dishes - think roasted turbot served with creamed leeks, crisp ham and a red wine sauce - while elaborate desserts might be headed-up by an assiette of lemon, though the chocolate plate might catch the eye, too. An extensive wine list, with a good range of half-bottles, and a fine selection of cheeses make this a class act.

Chef: David McLaughlin
Owners: David & Patricia Nicholson
Times: 12.30-2/7-9.30
Prices: Fixed L £22.50, Fixed D £49.50, Service optional
Wine: 19 bottles under £20
Notes: Gourmet menu £60, Vegetarian menu, Dress Restrictions, Smart casual, no jeans or T-shirts, Civ Wed 65
Seats: 50, Pr/dining room 20
Children: Min 8 yrs, Portions
Rooms: 23 (23 en suite)★★★★ CHH
Directions: 3m N of Windermere on A591. Past Brockhole Visitor Centre. Turn right into Holbeck Lane. Hotel is 0.5m on left
Parking: 25

Linthwaite House Hotel

WINDERMERE MAP 18 SD49

Modern British V

Fine-tuned cooking and stunning views

☎ 015394 88600 Crook Rd LA23 3JA
e-mail: stay@linthwaite.com
web: www.linthwaite.com

Built in 1901, this elegant Edwardian country house is situated on a sublime hilltop setting in 14 acres of gardens and woods in the heart of the Lake District. Enviable views look out over Lake Windermere to the fells beyond, and a new conservatory ensures that diners soak up the scenery whatever the weather. The décor is a refined combination of period chic with a clean, modern colour scheme and plenty of natural light.

Sourcing the very best of local produce, chef Simon Bolsover's kitchen has clearly moved up a gear and shows high aspirations, with menus full of ambitious dishes that consistently hit their target. There's no over-complication though, with clean flavours and technical precision to the fore. Expect the likes of pan-roasted cod teamed with wild boar pancetta, pod peas and braised baby gem lettuce, or perhaps salt marsh lamb rump served with marjoram-crushed peas, roasted baby carrots 'Jacqueline' and chargrilled sweetbreads. While a pear tarte Tatin with apple crumble ice cream could head-up desserts, a deep-fried jam sandwich with pear sorbet and pistachio glacé might catch the eye too.

Chef: Simon Bolsover
Owners: Mike Bevans
Times: 12.30-2/7-9.30, Closed Xmas (non-residents)
Prices: Fixed L £11-£13.95, Fixed D £47, Service optional
Wine: 100 bottles over £20, 10 bottles under £20, 13 by the glass
Notes: Fixed D 4 courses, Vegetarian menu, Dress Restrictions, Smart casual, Civ Wed 56
Seats: 60, Pr/dining room 16
Children: Min 7 yrs D, Menu, Portions
Rooms: 27 (27 en suite)★★★ CHH
Directions: Take 1st left off A591 at rdbt NW of Kendal (B5284). Follow for 6m, hotel is 1m after Windermere Golf Club on left
Parking: 40

ENGLAND

WINDERMERE Continued

◎◎ Miller Howe Hotel

Modern British 🍷 NOTABLE WINE LIST

Fantastic location with stunning views and a well-earned reputation for fine dining

☎ 015394 42536 Rayrigg Rd LA23 1EY
e-mail: lakeview@millerhowe.com
web: www.millerhowe.com

This magnificent Edwardian country-house hotel has outstanding views over Lake Windermere and Langdale Pikes. The interiors have a traditional feel with many period features, although the two-tiered dining room itself with its honey colours, gilded ceilings, tiled floors and wrought ironwork manages to evoke a sense of the Mediterranean. The food is described as modern British with a twist, but there are influences from all over Europe, especially French, incorporated in sophisticated and accomplished dishes. The menu gourmand is an enjoyable way of sampling all the delights on offer and might include seared salmon with crispy black pudding and herb beurre blanc to start followed by a main of roast lamb saddle with crispy sweetbreads, red cabbage, fondant potatoes and lamb jus.

Chef: Darren Cornish **Owners:** Martin & Helen Ainscough
Times: 12.30-1.45/6.45-8.45 **Prices:** Fixed L £19, Fixed D £35, Service added but optional 10% **Wine:** 100 bottles over £20, 10 bottles under £20, 8 by the glass **Notes:** Gourmet D 6 courses £42.50, Sun L 3 courses £25, Dress Restrictions, Smart casual, Civ Wed 64, Air con **Seats:** 64, Pr/dining room 30 **Children:** Portions **Rooms:** 15 (15 en suite) ★★★ HL **Directions:** M6 junct 36. Follow the A591 bypass for Kendal. Enter Windermere, continue to mini rdbt, take left onto A592. Miller Howe is 0.25m on right **Parking:** 40

The Samling

WINDERMERE   MAP 18 SD49

Modern British V

Impressive dining in Lakeland hillside retreat

☎ 015394 31922 Ambleside Rd LA23 1LR
e-mail: info@thesamling.com
web: www.thesamling.com

Set high above Lake Windermere in its own 67-acre estate, this lovely 18th-century house was once home to Wordsworth's landlord. Today, the hotel's emphasis is firmly on comfort and relaxation - the individually furnished bedrooms, sumptuous drawing room and small library make it ideal for those in search of peace and quiet, and who feel like being spoilt by unstuffy, helpful staff. This unashamedly modern approach also extends to the food, which is served in two small dining areas with views out on to the garden and lake. Local seasonal ingredients provide the basis for simply presented, creative dishes in modern British style. There's no shortage of vision or skill in this kitchen. Good clear flavours characterise appetisers and starters such as pan-fried scallops with red pepper sabayon and saffron oil. Main courses might include a carefully braised shoulder and roasted best end of salt marsh lamb - complemented by confit swede, dauphinoise potatoes and rosemary. Finish with the delights of warm plum fritters, with mascarpone and plum sabayon.

Chef: Nigel Mendham **Owners:** Tom Maxfield **Times:** 12.30-2/7-10, Closed L Mon-Sun (ex bookings) **Prices:** Fixed L £38, Service optional **Wine:** 97 bottles over £20, 15 by the glass **Notes:** Fixed L 3 courses, ALC £55, Gourmand tasting menu £67, Vegetarian menu, Civ Wed 20 **Seats:** 22 **Children:** Min 12 yrs, Menu, Portions **Rooms:** 11 (11 en suite)★★★ HL **Directions:** On A591 towards Ambleside. 1st on right after Low Wood Hotel. 2m from Windermere **Parking:** 15

ENGLAND

WINDERMERE CONTINUED

◉◉ Storrs Hall Hotel

Modern British

Accomplished, imaginative cuisine in luxurious country surroundings

☎ 015394 47111 Storrs Park LA23 3LG
e-mail: storrshall@elhmail.co.uk
web: www.elh.co.uk/hotels/storrshall

This imposing Georgian mansion is set in 17 acres of landscaped grounds on the shores of Lake Windermere. There are numerous comfortable lounges and a smart bar in which to enjoy pre-dinner drinks and canapés, all furnished with fine art and antiques of the period. Ask for a window table as the spacious dining room affords wonderful views over the lake. The food is bold and imaginative, using quality seasonal ingredients throughout with dishes like roast breast of wood pigeon, beetroot and walnut remoulade or pressed terrine of skate, potato and parsley, followed by roast loin of Swalesdale lamb with tomato and basil risotto. A dish like Kendal Mint Cake cheesecake with Grasmere gingerbread ice cream is a firm reminder of exactly where you are.

Chef: Craig Sherrington **Owners:** English Lakes Hotels **Times:** 12.30-2/7-9 **Prices:** Fixed L £19.75-£22.75, Fixed D £39.50, Service included **Wine:** 177 bottles over £20, 26 bottles under £20, 6 by the glass **Notes:** Fixed L 3 courses, tasting menu and themed eves available, Vegetarian available, Dress Restrictions, Smart casual, no jeans or trainers, Civ Wed 90 **Seats:** 64, Pr/dining room 40 **Children:** Min 12 yrs, Portions **Rooms:** 30 (30 en suite) ★★★★ HL **Directions:** On A592, 2 miles S of Bowness on the Newby Bridge Road **Parking:** 50

WORKINGTON   MAP 18 NY02

◉ Washington Central Hotel

Modern British

Relaxing, upmarket dining with renowned hospitality

☎ 01900 65772 Washington St CA14 3AY
e-mail: kawildwchotel@aol.com
web: www.washingtoncentralhotelworkington.com

Hospitality is a key factor in the appeal of this modern, town-centre hotel and restaurant, which is popular with visitors to the Lake District and locals alike. An open and varied approach is taken to classic British and European food, which combines an interest in modern adaptations with consideration for individual preferences. Typical starters include seared king scallops served over Scotch pancakes with tomato relish and saffron oil, or cod fillet marinated in basil and orange, while for mains expect the likes of prime Lakeland fell-bred lamb on rosemary mash, chargrilled asparagus spears and red wine

jus, or for a lighter dish try chargrilled salmon fillet with Parmentier potatoes and peppered strawberries. For special occasions, ask about dining in the clock tower.

Washington Central Hotel

Chef: Michael Buckley **Owners:** William Dobie **Times:** 12-2/7-9.30, Closed 25 Dec, Closed L BHs, D 1st Sat Jan **Prices:** Fixed L £18.50, Fixed D £27.50, Service optional **Wine:** 16 bottles over £20, 40 bottles under £20, 10 by the glass **Notes:** Fixed L 3 courses, Fixed D 4 courses, 7 course L or D £40, Vegetarian available, Dress Restrictions, Smart casual, no jeans or trainers, Civ Wed 350 **Seats:** 45, Pr/dining room 40 **Children:** Menu, Portions **Rooms:** 46 (46 en suite) ★★★ HL **Directions:** M6 junct 40, follow A66 to Workington **Parking:** 10

DERBYSHIRE

ASHBOURNE   MAP 10 SK14

Bramhall's of Ashbourne

Rosettes not confirmed at time of going to press

Modern British

Imaginative cooking in a relaxed bistro setting

☎ 01335 346158 6 Buxton Rd DE6 1EX
e-mail: info@bramhalls.co.uk
web: www.bramhalls.co.uk

An authentic bistro with bags of charm, this establishment occupies two converted cottages in the heart of historic Ashbourne. It's a hub of local gastronomy with a reputation for imaginative cooking at pocket-friendly prices, and offers an eclectic menu with its roots in country cuisine. At the time of going to press we understood there was a change of ownership taking place. Please visit www.theAA.com for further details.

Times: 12-2.30/6.30-9.30, Closed 25-26 Dec, 1 Jan, Closed D Sun (Dec-Apr) **Rooms:** 10 (8 en suite) **Directions:** From Ashbourne Market Square take Buxton road N. Restaurant 30yds on left

@@ Callow Hall

British, French

Dining in country-house luxury

☎ 01335 300900 Mappleton Rd DE6 2AA
e-mail: reservations@callowhall.co.uk
web: www.callowhall.co.uk

Five minutes drive from the centre of Ashbourne, this creeper-clad Victorian mansion makes an ideal retreat. Standing at the end of a tree-lined drive in 44 acres of woods and garden, it overlooks the Dove Valley. Period features abound throughout, most notably in the 'William Morris' dining room with its warm red décor. The kitchen relies heavily on local produce and fresh fish when preparing the traditional British menus. The result is honest, full-flavoured dishes, such as home-smoked organic Scottish salmon with dressed Brixham crab, followed by fillet of Whitby cod on leek and saffron mash with mussels and vermouth fume, and hot bread and almond pudding with Amaretto ice cream to finish. The traditional Sunday lunches are excellent.

Chef: David & Anthony Spencer **Owners:** David, Dorothy, Anthony & Emma Spencer **Times:** 12.30-1.30/7.30-9, Closed 25-26 Dec, Closed L Mon-Sat, D Sun (ex residents) **Prices:** Fixed L £25, Fixed D £42, Starter £7.50-£10.75, Main £17.50-£22.50, Dessert £7.50, Service optional **Wine:** 125 bottles over £20, 45 bottles under £20, 26 by the glass **Notes:** Fixed L 3 courses, Fixed D 4 courses, incl coffee, Dress Restrictions, Smart casual **Seats:** 70, Pr/dining room 40 **Children:** Portions **Rooms:** 16 (16 en suite) ★★★ CHH **Directions:** A515 through Ashbourne in Buxton direction, left at Bowling Green Pub, 1st right Mappleton Rd **Parking:** 30

@@ The Dining Room

Modern British ☺

Imaginative modern cuisine in intimate surroundings

☎ 01335 300666 33 St John St DE6 1GP
web: www.thediningroomashbourne.co.uk

Dating back to 1604, The Dining Room is full of character, with the original cast-iron range still in place, wood-burning stove and low-

beamed ceilings. The intimate, six-table restaurant is chic with muted tones, serving up modern British cuisine with some global influences using locally-sourced, organic seasonal produce. The carte starts with a choice of appetisers, followed by a starter like home oak-smoked foie gras with gooseberry relish. A refreshing sorbet makes way for a main course like peppered Ellastone steak with confit seasonal vegetables and lemon and green pea purée. Desserts need to be ordered with the other courses, and might include hay-baked Braeburn apple tart or Wakefield rhubarb '3 ways'. There is also an impressive 13-course tasting menu on Saturday evenings and an award-winning cheeseboard.

Chef: Peter Dale **Owners:** Peter & Laura Dale **Times:** 12.30/7.30, Closed 2 wks 26 Dec, 1 wk Sep, 1 wk Mar, BH Mon, Sun-Mon **Prices:** Fixed D £36, Starter £10, Main £20, Dessert £6, Service optional **Wine:** 35 bottles over £20, 10 bottles under £20, 2 by glass **Notes:** Tasting menu 12 courses £40, Vegetarian available, Smart casual, Air con **Seats:** 16 **Children:** Min 12 yrs **Directions:** On A52 Derby to Leek road **Parking:** Opposite restaurant (evening)

ASHFORD-IN-THE-WATER   MAP 16 SK16

@@ Riverside House Hotel

Modern French V

Fine dining in opulent surroundings on the Wye

☎ 01629 814275 Fennel St DE45 1QF
e-mail: riversidehouse@enta.net
web: www.riversidehousehotel.co.uk

This gracious Georgian country house - once a shooting lodge - is set in its own grounds on the banks of the River Wye in the lovely Peak District village of Ashford-in-the-Water. The property is full of character and diners can relax in luxurious comfort surrounded by exquisite fabrics, beautiful artwork and rich furnishings in the Riverside restaurant. An imaginative choice of intelligently straightforward dishes might include salmon and langoustine ravioli with carrot and cardamom sauce to start, followed by roast corn-fed chicken wrapped in Parma ham, served with a potato fondant and buttered cabbage, and passionfruit crème brûlée and biscotti to finish. Lighter food is also served in the Conservatory restaurant.

Chef: John Whelan **Owners:** Penelope Thornton **Times:** 12-2.30/7-9.30 **Prices:** Fixed D £44.95, Starter £6.50-£8, Main £10-£20, Dessert £6-£7.95, Service optional **Wine:** 200 bottles over £20, 26 bottles under £20, 32 by the glass **Notes:** ALC L only, Sun L menu £28.95, Tasting menu £60-£120, Vegetarian menu, Dress Restrictions, Smart casual, Jacket & tie preferred, Civ Wed 30 **Seats:** 40, Pr/dining room 30 **Children:** Min 16 yrs **Rooms:** 14 (14 en suite) ★★★ HL **Directions:** M1 junct 29 take A619 and continue to Bakewell. 2m from the centre of Bakewell on A6 towards Buxton. In Ashford village located on Fennel St **Parking:** 25

BAKEWELL   MAP 16 SK26

◉ The Prospect

Modern British

Comfortable, town-centre restaurant with good atmosphere

☎ 01629 810077 Theme Court, Bridge St DE45 1DS
e-mail: theprospect@btinternet.com

Reclaimed antique oak panelling mixes well with polished tabletops and modern place settings at this former forge, and a brand new bar and lounge area create the perfect setting for pre- or post-dinner drinks. The kitchen's no-nonsense approach uses the freshest local ingredients, delivering dishes that are modern in style with Mediterranean and Asian influences, yet firmly rooted in the British tradition. You might start with smoked mackerel, salmon and sorrel fishcakes with aïoli and lemon dressing, and then follow with Elton Estate venison Wellington with sweet potato purée, braised red cabbage and Cumberland sauce, with a delicious bread-and-butter pudding and apricot coulis to finish.

Chef: Darren Goodwin **Owners:** Darren Williams **Times:** 12-2.30/6.30-12, Closed 25-26 Dec, 1 Jan, Easter Sun, Mon **Prices:** Fixed L £12, Fixed D £17.50, Starter £4-£6, Main £13.50-£20, Dessert £4.50-£6, Service optional **Wine:** 18 bottles over £20, 31 bottles under £20, 19 by the glass **Seats:** 60, Pr/dining room 16 **Children:** Portions **Directions:** From A6 (Matlock to Buxton road), follow signs for Baslow. Theme Court is opposite The Queens Arms pub **Parking:** Across road

◉ Renaissance Restaurant

Traditional European

Beautifully appointed restaurant in the town centre

☎ 01629 812687 Bath St DE45 1BX
web: www.renaissance-restaurant.com

Recently refurbished, this comfortable stone-built townhouse in the centre of Bakewell has painted stone walls and ceiling beams. Three eating options are available: the full menu, changed monthly and priced for three courses with some supplements; a good-value set menu from Tuesday to Thursday evening; and a lunchtime bistro serving traditional French dishes with a European twist. The main menu includes classics such as a flavoursome roquefort soufflé with beurre blanc, and lamb shank with parsnip purée and rich red wine sauce, with delightful crêpes Suzette to finish. Service is excellent.

Chef: E Piedaniel, J Gibbard **Owners:** E Piedaniel **Times:** 12-2/7-10, Closed Xmas & New Year, 2wks Jan, 2wks Aug, Mon, Closed D Sun **Prices:** Fixed L £8, Fixed D £18.50-£20, Starter £3.50-£5, Main £10-£15, Dessert £5, Service included **Wine:** 6 bottles over £20, 23 bottles under £20, 10 by the glass **Notes:** Sun L 2 courses £14.95, Vegetarian available **Seats:** 50, Pr/dining room 25 **Children:** Portions **Directions:** From Bakewell rdbt in town centre take A6 Buxton exit. 1st right into Bath St (one-way) **Parking:** Town centre

◉ Rutland Arms Hotel

Traditional, British

Enjoyable dining in welcoming, traditional hotel

☎ 01629 812812 The Square DE45 1BT
e-mail: rutland@bakewell.demon.co.uk
web: www.bakewell.demon.co.uk

This imposing 19th-century stone-built hotel - in whose kitchens the Bakewell pudding was invented - is a local landmark at the heart of town. Its Four Seasons restaurant is classically traditional in style, with polished granite fireplace, lofty ceilings, chandeliers and several clocks, evoking an endearing air of a bygone era. By contrast, the accomplished cooking is up-to-date, showcasing Peak District fare - smoked salmon tian with crème fraîche, followed by rack of lamb with buttered leeks and redcurrant and orange jus and, of course, traditional Bakewell pudding to finish, served with clotted cream and fresh berry compôte.

Rutland Arms Hotel

Chef: Brian Lee **Owners:** David Donegan **Times:** 12-2/7-9 **Prices:** Fixed L £10.95-£13.95, Fixed D £28.50-£34, Starter £4.50-£8.50, Main £8-£18, Dessert £4.50-£6.50, Service optional **Wine:** 6 bottles over £20, 24 bottles under £20, 6 by the glass **Notes:** Vegetarian available, Dress Restrictions, Smart dress **Seats:** 80, Pr/dining room 32 **Children:** Menu, Portions **Rooms:** 35 (35 en suite) ★★★ HL **Directions:** On A6 in Bakewell centre opposite war memorial. Parking opposite side entrance **Parking:** 30

BASLOW   MAP 16 SK27

◉◉ Cavendish Hotel

Modern International

Luxurious surroundings for sumptuous cooking

☎ 01246 582311 Church Ln DE45 1SP
e-mail: info@cavendish-hotel.net
web: www.cavendish-hotel.net

Situated on the edge of the Chatsworth Estate, this Regency-style hotel has a smart contemporary restaurant. Antiques and original artworks strike a classy note and are a reminder that the Duke and Duchess of Devonshire had a hand in the design; there's a real sense of luxury here and service is excellent, combining friendliness with helpful advice. The cooking style balances technique and flavour well and presentation is minimalist with some precise garnishing and restrained artistry. Expect a modern menu with some interesting twists on classic dishes: foie gras brûlée as a starter perhaps, or roasted red pepper and parmesan strudel as a main. The wine list offers a good choice too, clearly listed by drinking style.

Chef: Chris Allison, Ben Handley **Owners:** Eric Marsh **Times:** 12.30-2.30/6.30-10 **Prices:** Fixed L £29.50, Fixed D £38.50, Service added 5% **Wine:** 40 bottles over £20, 12 bottles under £20, 6 by the glass **Notes:** Vegetarian available, Dress Restrictions, No trainers, T-shirts **Seats:** 50, Pr/dining room 10 **Children:** Portions **Rooms:** 24 (24 en suite) ★★★ HL **Directions:** M1 junct 29 follow signs for Chesterfield. From Chesterfield take A619 to Bakewell, Chatsworth & Baslow **Parking:** 40

◉◉◉◉ Fischer's Baslow Hall

see opposite

Fischer's Baslow Hall

BASLOW MAP 16 SK27

Modern European

Sophisticated cuisine in memorable setting

☎ 01246 583259 Calver Rd DE45 1RR
e-mail: reservations@fischers-baslowhall.co.uk
web: www.fischers-baslowhall.co.uk

Chef: Max Fischer/ Rupert Rowley
Owners: Mr & Mrs M Fischer
Times: 12-2/7-10, Closed 25-26 Dec, Closed L Mon, D Sun (ex residents)
Prices: Fixed L £20, Fixed D £65, Service optional
Wine: 117 bottles over £20, 4 bottles under £20, 6 by the glass
Notes: Tasting menu £60, Sun L £35, Dress Restrictions, No jeans, sweatshirts or trainers, Civ Wed 40
Seats: 40, Pr/dining room 20
Children: Min 12 yrs, Portions
Rooms: 11 (11 en suite)★★★ HL
Directions: From Baslow on A623 towards Calver. Hotel on right
Parking: 40

A chestnut tree-lined drive leading up to this fine Grade II listed manor house - built at the turn of the 20th century and set in 5 acres of marvellous gardens bordering the Chatsworth Estate - seems an appropriately fitting curtain-raiser to some outstanding cooking. Baslow is full of charm at every turn, an intimate country-house hotel personally run by its dedicated owners Max and Susan Fischer, and there's plenty of cosseting at hand, with the likes of log fires and comfortable sofas adding to the welcoming approach. A lavish use of fabrics, antiques and pictures all add to the appeal, and, while service is polished and formal, it's suitably friendly, too. The dining room has an elegant classical edge, complemented by fine china, cutlery and glassware, and proves the real focus of the house.

Max Fischer is a dedicated chef-patron and has developed a strong brigade of disciplined chefs led by head chef Rupert Rowley. Their approach - via a fixed-price medley of carte, lunch, jour and tasting menu - is modern European, but underpinned by classical French technique. This is serious cooking; precision, high skill, accuracy, clear flavours and the very best of local ingredients (aided by the Hall's own kitchen garden, and with a strong emphasis on organic and naturally-reared produce) all delivered in consistent style on the plate. Think caramelised belly pork served with Chinese cabbage, pan-fried John Dory and peanut brittle, perhaps followed by a breast of guinea fowl with crayfish cannelloni, spicy cabbage and a crayfish reduction, with maybe a 'taste of blood orange' dessert finish - soufflé, parfait, sorbet and macaroon. Peripherals like breads, canapés, amuse-bouche, pre-desserts and petits fours are a delight, too, while the superbly maintained gardens - Max's other love - with their hidden corners and potager, offer the perfect pre- or post-meal stroll to complete the Baslow Hall experience.

BASLOW CONTINUED

⊚⊚ Rowley's Restaurant & Bar

Modern British, Traditional NEW

Contemporary setting for fine local produce and quality cuisine

☎ 01246 583880 Church Ln DE45 1RY
e-mail: info@rowleysrestaurant.co.uk
web: www.rowleysrestaurant.co.uk

Next door to the village's pretty church, this old country pub has been turned into a modern bar and restaurant by the team behind nearby Fischer's Baslow Hall (namely Max and Susan Fischer and their head chef Rupert Rowley, see entry). This sibling venue offers an informal mix of stone-flagged bar area alongside the chic, more contemporary feel of its three dining areas upstairs. With mainly aubergine-coloured walls, banquette seating and modern lightwood furniture complete the picture. At lunch, the ground floor and bar are also used, while the food is an appealing mix of modern and traditional British, with emphasis on high-quality local produce presented with style but without frivolity. Lunch ranges from lite bites to prime steaks, while dinner could deliver pan-fried calves' liver served with black pudding mash, fine beans, bacon and onion gravy, or stuffed rolled loin of rabbit wrapped in Parma ham.

Chef: Robin Allison, James Grant **Owners:** Susan & Max Fischer, Rupert Rowley **Times:** 12-2.30/6-10, Closed 1-9 Jan, Closed D Sun **Prices:** Fixed L £14.50, Starter £6-£9.50, Main £10.50-£22, Dessert £4.50-£6, Service optional **Wine:** 7 bottles over £20, 15 bottles under £20, 6 by the glass **Notes:** Sun L 2 courses £16, 3 courses £20, Vegetarian available **Seats:** 64, Pr/dining room 18 **Children:** Menu, Portions **Parking:** 17

BELPER MAP 11 SK34

⊚ Shottle Hall Country House Hotel

Modern British NEW

Country-house setting for quality modern cooking

☎ 01773 550577 White Ln, Shottle DE56 2EB
e-mail: info@shottlehall.co.uk
web: www.shottlehall.co.uk

This delightfully refurbished hotel stands in extensive grounds - as the country-house tag might suggest - and is located on the edge of the famous Chatsworth Estate. Stylish décor and furnishings further develop the theme, and there's a separate bar, while the restaurant provides a contemporary dining experience, complete with floor-to-ceiling windows and starlight roof. The kitchen's seasonal menus showcase quality local ingredients, including Chatsworth venison and locally-grown vegetables. The approach is modern with some classical spin; take Derbyshire fillet of beef roasted in cep butter with a red wine jus and twice-cooked chips, or nose-to-tail Peak lamb, with apple and Calvados tarte Tatin to finish.

Chef: Dean Crews **Owners:** Joanne & Steve Nicol **Times:** 12-2/7-9, Closed D Sun **Prices:** Fixed L £15.95-£17.95, Fixed D £31.95-£35.95, Starter £4.50-£8, Main £12.50-£24.95, Dessert £5.25-£7.95 **Wine:** 36 bottles over £20, 16 bottles under £20, 8 by the glass **Notes:** Fixed 3 course Sun L £19.95, Dress Restrictions, Smart casual, no jeans, Civ Wed 80 **Seats:** 60, Pr/dining room 20 **Children:** Portions **Rooms:** 8 (8 en suite) ★★★ HL **Directions:** 0.3m from A517, 2m from Belper **Parking:** 60

BREADSALL MAP 11 SK33

⊚ Priory Restaurant

International

Fine dining at an ancient priory

☎ 01332 832235 Marriott Breadsall Priory, Moor Rd DE7 6DL
e-mail: christopher.tay@marriotthotels.com
web: www.marriott.co.uk

Dating back to 1240, the Breadsall Priory is the oldest property in the world to house a branch of the Marriott chain. Tastefully converted into a country-house hotel, it's surrounded by 400 acres of beautifully-landscaped grounds which include a charming ornamental lake and golf course. Inside, the restaurant is set amid the exposed beams and archways of the old wine cellar and oozes character. It's a popular venue with a crowd-pleasing menu that delivers classically-based cooking with dashes of innovation, using the best local, seasonal produce to hand. Try carrot and ginger soup to start, followed by slow-roast pork belly, stuffed with apricots and walnuts, and served with garlic mash and apple compôte.

Chef: Karl J Kenny **Owners:** Royal Bank of Scotland **Times:** 7-10, Closed L Mon-Sat (private functions only) **Prices:** Fixed L £16-£22, Fixed D £32-£36, Starter £6-£8, Main £11.50-£25, Dessert £6-£7, Service optional **Wine:** 40 bottles over £20, 20 bottles under £20, 10 by the glass **Notes:** Fixed L 3 courses, Vegetarian available, Dress Restrictions, Shirt with collar, long trousers required, Air con **Seats:** 104 **Children:** Menu, Portions **Rooms:** 112 (112 en suite) ★★★★ HL **Directions:** M1 junct 25, A52 to Derby, then signs to Chesterfield. Right at 1st rdbt, left at next. Follow A608 to Heanor Rd, after 3m left then left again **Parking:** 200

BUXTON MAP 16 SK07

⊚ Best Western Lee Wood Hotel

British, International

Family-run hotel with elegant conservatory dining

☎ 01298 23002 The Park SK17 6TQ
e-mail: leewoodhotel@btinternet.com
web: www.leewoodhotel.co.uk

This fine hotel was created in 1860 from three separate houses and is the oldest established hotel in Buxton, owned by two generations of the Millican family. Lunch and dinner are served in the large, airy, conservatory-style Elements restaurant and bar overlooking the garden - there's a patio area for alfresco summer dining, too. A wide choice of dishes from around the globe are prepared from fresh, often local produce, and cooked with imagination. Take a starter of twice-baked goat's cheese and cauliflower soufflé served with a fine herb salad and spiced melon chutney, and perhaps a mains of calves' liver with smoked bacon, caramelised apples and baby onion jus.

Chef: Darren Clarke **Owners:** Mr J C Millican **Times:** 12-2.15/7.15-9.30 **Prices:** Fixed L £13.50-£17.95, Fixed D £22.50-£29.50, Starter £4.95-£8.95, Main £11.95-£21, Dessert £4.95-£8, Service added but optional 10% **Wine:** 7 bottles over £20, 27 bottles under £20, 6 by the glass **Notes:** Vegetarian available, Dress Restrictions, Smart casual preferred, Civ Wed 120 **Seats:** 80, Pr/dining room 120 **Children:** Portions **Rooms:** 40 (40 en suite) ★★★ HL **Directions:** M1 junct 24, A50 towards Ashbourne, A515 to Buxton. From Buxton town centre follow A5004 Long Hill to Whaley Bridge. Hotel approx 200mtrs beyond University of Derby campus **Parking:** 50

CHESTERFIELD — MAP 16 SK37

◉ The Old Post Restaurant

Modern European

Converted shop with bold cuisine

☎ 01246 279479 43 Holywell St S41 7SH
e-mail: theoldpostrestaurant@btopenworld.com
web: www.theoldpostrestaurant.co.uk

Just a few minutes drive from the eastern edge of the Peak District, close to the town's church with its crooked spire, this intimate, split-level restaurant is housed in two 18th-century buildings rumoured to be the oldest in Chesterfield. Formerly a butcher's, grocer's, Victorian laundry and later a post office, the new incarnation delivers ambitious modern European cooking. Everything is made on the premises, with the adventurous kitchen producing dishes with bold flavours and beguiling presentations. Take a fillet of North Sea redfish braised in lobster butter, served with tomato, baby onion and potato ragout and dauphinoise potatoes, while a trio of crème brûlée (mocha chocolate and Tia Maria, creamed rice condé and white chocolate and lavender) might head-up desserts.

Chef: Hugh Cocker **Owners:** Hugh & Mary Cocker **Times:** 12-2/7-9.30, Closed 26 Dec, 1 Jan, Mon, Closed L Sat, D Sun **Prices:** Fixed L £11.25, Fixed D £26.50, Starter £6-£7.50, Main £16.95-£21.75, Dessert £6.10-£7.25, Service optional **Wine:** 5 bottles over £20, 24 bottles under £20, 4 by the glass **Notes:** Fixed D 4 courses, Dress Restrictions, Smart casual **Seats:** 24 **Directions:** M1 junct 29, follow signs for town centre and central parking. Pass 'Crooked Spire' church on left and use Holywell Cross Car Park. Restaurant opposite **Parking:** Car park opposite

DARLEY ABBEY — MAP 11 SK33

◉◉ Darleys Restaurant

Modern British V

Accomplished cuisine delivered in a former cotton mill

☎ 01332 364987 Darley Abbey Mill DE22 1DZ
e-mail: info@darleys.com
web: www.darleys.com

Located in part of an old cotton mill overlooking the River Derwent, this sophisticated restaurant is contemporary in style with an open-plan layout and neutral tones of leather, suede and silk, quality table settings and polished glassware. Additional seating is available outside on the decked terrace overlooking the weir, where afternoon tea is also served. Deftly-prepared modern dishes are created from top-quality local ingredients, such as roast quail salad with pomegranate dressing, followed perhaps by peppered loin of venison with juniper

sauce, or fillet of turbot with squid ink linguine and saffron and mussel chowder. For an unusual finish try rice pudding 'fritter' with roast pineapple and rum syrup.

Darleys Restaurant

Chef: Jonathan Hobson **Owners:** Jonathan & Kathryn Hobson **Times:** 12-2/7-10, Closed BHs, 1st 2 wks Jan, Closed D Sun **Prices:** Fixed L £14.95, Starter £6.90-£8.50, Main £17.25-£19.50, Dessert £6.25, Service optional **Notes:** Sun L £17.95, Vegetarian menu, Air con **Seats:** 70 **Children:** Portions **Directions:** A6 N from Derby (Duffield Rd). After 1m turn right into Mileash Lane, down to Old Lane, turn right and follow road over bridge. Restaurant on right **Parking:** 12

DERBY — MAP 11 SK33

◉◉ Masa Restaurant and Wine Bar

Modern British V NEW

Contemporary wine bar-restaurant in 200-year-old chapel

☎ 01332 203345 The Old Chapel, Brook St DE1 3PF
e-mail: enquiries@masarestaurantwinebar.com
web: www.masarestaurantwinebar.com

The sensitive and stylish refurbishment of this one-time Wesleyan chapel in the town centre - which saw its last service in 2002 - deserves high praise indeed, retaining many original features and bags of character alongside contemporary good looks. The ground floor comes decked out as a spacious bar, while the galleried restaurant has well-spaced tables on different levels. The skilled kitchen shows obvious pedigree (chef Kevin Stone previously worked at Darleys Restaurant at Darley Abbey, see entry), with its intelligent handling of quality produce in slick, clean-flavoured, balanced and well-presented dishes. Take a roasted fillet and braised belly of pork served with black pudding, Savoy cabbage and mustard cream, and perhaps a brioche summer pudding finale.

Chef: Kevin Stone **Owners:** Didar & Paula Dalkic **Times:** 12-2.30/6-9.30 **Prices:** Fixed L £14.50, Fixed D £21, Starter £5-£8.50, Main £12.50-£19.50, Dessert £5.50-£6.50, Service added but optional 10% **Wine:** 20 bottles over £20, 19 bottles under £20, 12 by the glass **Notes:** Vegetarian menu, Dress Restrictions, Smart casual, Black tie when specified, Air con **Seats:** 120 **Children:** Portions **Directions:** 8m from M1 junct 25. Brook St off inner ring road near BBC Radio Derby

ETWALL — MAP 10 SK23

◉ The Blenheim House

British

Modern cooking in village location

☎ 01283 732254 56-58 Main St DE65 6LP

e-mail: info@theblenheimhouse.com

web: www.theblenheimhouse.com

In a lovely village setting, parts of this house date back to the 1700s and feature traditional wooden flooring and beams. There is a large bar area where meals are also served. The stylish restaurant consists of several rooms and features quality table settings. Modern British cooking with classical roots is the basis for a menu featuring good local produce. Try a starter like confit of salmon and crab salad served on blinis, followed perhaps by spit-roast chicken with fries and tarragon sauce. Classic desserts include the likes of lemon posset and banoffee pie.

Chef: Richard Strydom **Owners:** Peter Simpson **Times:** 12-2.30/6-9.30, Closed D Sun **Prices:** Fixed L £12.95, Starter £3.95-£7.95, Main £9.95-£18.95, Dessert £5.95-£6.95, Service optional, Group min 8 service 8% **Wine:** 39 bottles over £20, 26 bottles under £20, 8 by the glass **Notes:** Sun L £12.95-£15.95, Vegetarian available, Dress Restrictions, Smart casual **Seats:** 80, Pr/dining room 32 **Children:** Menu, Portions **Rooms:** 9 (9 en suite) ★★ HL **Directions:** Off A516 in Etwall's main street **Parking:** 20

FROGGATT — MAP 16 SK27

◉ The Chequers Inn

Modern European

A popular country inn for those in need of fresh air and gratifying food

☎ 01433 630231 S32 3ZJ

e-mail: info@chequers-froggatt.com

web: www.chequers-froggatt.com

This roadside inn has its origins in the 16th century and, while there are modern touches throughout, the building still retains its historic charm. There's a printed menu with regularly-changing blackboard specials; food tends toward modern European cooking and British favourites done with aplomb and featuring local ingredients extensively. Take calves' liver served with buttered mash and grape chutney, or perhaps a swordfish steak with wild mushrooms and artichoke. Those interested in food history should try the Bakewell pudding - it was invented nearby and there's usually a great version on the menu here - while other homely offerings might include lemon tart or fruit Pavlova.

Chef: Philip Ball **Owners:** Jonathan & Joanne Tindall **Times:** 12-2/6-9.30, Closed 25 Dec **Prices:** Starter £4.50-£6.50, Main £9.25-£18, Dessert £5-

£6.50, Service optional **Wine:** 11 bottles over £20, 29 bottles under £20, 9 by the glass **Notes:** Vegetarian available **Seats:** 90 **Rooms:** 5 (5 en suite) ★★★★ INN **Directions:** On the A625 in Froggatt, 0.75m from Calver **Parking:** 50

GRINDLEFORD — MAP 16 SK27

◉ The Maynard

Modern British NEW

Imaginative food in a contemporary setting

☎ 04133 630321 Main Rd S32 2HE

e-mail: info@themaynard.co.uk

web: www.themaynard.co.uk

Set in the heart of Derbyshire's beautiful Peak National Park, this imposing Victorian building has recently undergone a tasteful refurbishment. The restaurant's subtle lighting and contemporary décor complement the huge picture windows that offer panoramic views of the stunning Derwent Valley. Friendly and efficient staff serve modern British food, prepared with skill and imagination, using seasonal, locally-sourced produce - organic wherever possible. Take coriander and lime crab wonton with sweet sesame dressing to start, and follow with pan-fried sea bass accompanied by crayfish sausage and tarragon potatoes. A traditional Bakewell tart or Black Forest brownie might feature on the tempting dessert menu.

Chef: Marcus Jefford, Ben Hickinson **Owners:** Paul Downing **Times:** 12-2/7-9, Closed L Sat **Prices:** Fixed L £12-£15, Fixed D £22-£36, Starter £5-£7, Main £12-£19, Dessert £5-£6, Service optional **Wine:** 6 bottles over £20, 8 bottles under £20, 4 by the glass **Notes:** Vegetarian available, Smart casual, Civ Wed 140, Air con **Seats:** 50, Pr/dining room 140 **Children:** Portions **Rooms:** 10 (10 en suite) ★★★★ GA **Parking:** 60

HATHERSAGE — MAP 16 SK28

◉◉ Best Western George Hotel

Modern International

Modern comforts and sophisticated cooking at historic inn

☎ 01433 650436 Main Rd S32 1BB

e-mail: info@george-hotel.net

web: www.george-hotel.net

Set in the heart of a pretty town, this grey-stone former coaching inn reputedly played host to Charlotte Brontë and was rewarded with a mention in *Jane Eyre*. Sympathetically refurbished to retain many original features, the restaurant is a light-and-airy affair along modern minimalist lines, decked out in beige and brown with bold artwork and spacious tables - just the venue to enjoy the accomplished modern cooking of a kitchen that prides itself on the freshness of its approach as well as its ingredients. Mains might include calves' liver with Parma ham, maple-roasted figs, potato rösti and Madeira sauce, George's seafood mixed grill with clam and tomato linguine, or cod with a white onion, chorizo and rocket tart and vine tomato dressing.

Chef: Ben Handley **Owners:** Eric Marsh **Times:** 12-2.30/7-10, Closed D 25 Dec **Prices:** Starter £6.25-£10.95, Main £14-£22, Dessert £6.25-£7.95, Service included **Wine:** 27 bottles over £20, 15 bottles under £20, 8 by the glass **Notes:** 'Early bird' menu Mon-Fri 6.30-7.30pm 3 courses £16, Vegetarian available, Civ Wed 45 **Seats:** 45, Pr/dining room 80 **Children:** Portions **Rooms:** 22 (22 en suite) ★★★ HL **Directions:** In village centre on junction of A625/B6001 **Parking:** 45

⊛ The Plough Inn
Modern English
Destination dining in a great location

☎ 01433 650319   Leadmill Bridge S32 1BA
e-mail: sales@theploughinn-hathersage.co.uk
web: www.theploughinn-hathersage.co.uk

In its time, this stone-built 17th-century property has been a corn mill, lead smelting house and farm. These days it enjoys popularity as a roadside inn with an idyllic location beside the river at Leadmill Bridge, complete with its own beer garden. Sound English pub cooking is on offer alongside cask ales and fine wines. Quality produce is simply and accurately cooked and presented in honest style, exemplified in a hearty meal of curried parsnip soup, followed by roast salmon fillet with rocket mash and citrus beurre blanc, and for dessert orange and crème brûlée with home-made shortbread.

Times: 11.30-2.30/6.30-9.30, Closed 25 Dec   **Rooms:** 5 (5 en suite)
★★★★ INN   **Directions:** 1m from Hathersage village on B6001, 12m from Sheffield city centre via A625

HIGHAM   MAP 16 SK35

⊛ Santo's Higham Farm Hotel
International
Modern cuisine in a romantic setting

☎ 01773 833812   Main Rd DE55 6EH
e-mail: reception@santoshighamfarm.demon.co.uk
web: www.santoshighamfarm.co.uk

The restaurant is located within a sympathetically converted 15th-century farmhouse with views over the Amber Valley. Stylish monogrammed carpet has recently been laid throughout, and the restaurant has new deep red padded suede chairs and crisp white table linen. Exposed stonework and oil-filled candles add to the relaxed and intimate dining experience. A strong emphasis on locally-sourced produce, simply cooked, permeates the modern menu, which draws on influences from around the globe in dishes like lobster gratin, Chateaubriand, or roasted ginger-spiced duck breast, rounded off with a dessert of marmalade cheesecake, or perhaps warm chocolate and hazelnut brownie.

Chef: Raymond Moody   **Owners:** Santo Cusimano   **Times:** 12-2/7-9.30, Closed L Mon-Sat, D Sun   **Prices:** Fixed D £22.50-£25.50, Starter £5.50-£7.50, Main £16.50-£20, Dessert £5.50-£6.50, Service added but optional 5%   **Wine:** 26 bottles over £20, 23 bottles under £20, 3 by the glass   **Notes:** Vegetarian available, Dress Restrictions, Smart casual, Civ Wed 70   **Seats:** 50, Pr/dining room 34   **Children:** Portions   **Rooms:** 28 (28 en suite) ★★★ HL   **Directions:** M1 junct 28, A38 towards Derby, then A61 to Higham, left onto B6013   **Parking:** 100

see advert above

MARSTON MONTGOMERY   MAP 10 SK13

ENGLAND

MARSTON MONTGOMERY CONTINUED

◉ The Crown Inn

British, European

Modern brasserie in a converted Georgian farmhouse

☎ 01889 590541 Riggs Ln DE6 2FF
e-mail: info@thecrowninn-derbyshire.co.uk
web: www.thecrowninn-derbyshire.co.uk

Georgian farmhouse features, including beamed ceilings and fireplaces, combine with contemporary furnishings and décor at this modern brasserie. Local painters' work hung on earthy coloured walls complements sumptuous leather sofas and armchairs. The menu offers traditional dishes prepared and presented with imaginative flair. Locally-sourced produce is used wherever possible and an inspiring specials menu delivers interesting and unusual dishes. Recommendations include twice-baked stilton soufflé with pickled pear salad, with maybe monkfish and scallop medallions with roasted provençal linguini and baked ratatouille to follow, and white chocolate and passionfruit 'tear drop', or banoffee bread-and-butter pudding for dessert.

Chef: Leighton Bradbury **Owners:** Janice & Craig Southway **Times:** 12-2.30/7-9.30, Closed 25 Dec, 1 Jan, Closed D Sun **Prices:** Fixed L £11.95, Starter £4.25-£6.95, Main £10.95-£17.95, Dessert £3.95-£5.25, Service optional **Wine:** 11 bottles over £20, 25 bottles under £20, 7 by the glass **Notes:** Sun L menu available, Special menus for significant dates **Seats:** 40 **Children:** Menu, Portions **Rooms:** 7 (7 en suite) ★★★★ INN **Directions:** From Ashbourne take A515 towards Lichfield, after 5m turn right at Cubley x-rds then follow signs to Marston Montgomery for 1m, take left into Marston Montgomery. The Crown Inn is in centre of village **Parking:** 16

see advert on page 115

MELBOURNE   MAP 11 SK32

◉ *The Bay Tree*

Modern British

Imaginative cuisine in contemporary village setting

☎ 01332 863358 4 Potter St DE73 8HW
e-mail: enquiries@baytreerestaurant.co.uk
web: www.baytreerestaurant.co.uk

Expect robust modern brasserie-style cuisine at this smart but unpretentious village-centre eatery. The 17th-century building has been extended to create a new bar. The spacious, informal dining room is smartly decorated in warm yellow with timber floors and modern artwork on the walls. Dishes have a rustic style and attention is given to presentation, depth of flavour and use of good-quality produce. Dishes include Thai fishcakes with plum and spring onion garnish, and crispy Lunesdale duckling with Saint Clements sauce. For a special treat, try the champagne breakfast.

The Bay Tree

Times: 10.30-3/6.30-10.30 **Directions:** Telephone for directions

---

MORLEY   MAP 11 SK34

◉ The Morley Hayes Hotel - Dovecote Restaurant

Modern British

Converted 17th-century farmhouse serving creative modern cooking

☎ 01332 780480 Main Rd DE7 6DG
e-mail: enquiries@morleyhayes.com
web: www.morleyhayes.com

This charming 18th-century former farmstead is now a friendly hotel complete with an 18-hole championship golf course, so there's no excuse for arriving without a hearty appetite. Taking its name from the converted dovecote which it occupies, the brightly lit dining room oozes character from its vaulted ceiling and exposed beams to its original brickwork walls. After a pre-dinner drink in the piano bar, guests have a choice of menus to peruse: one leans towards the luxurious, while the other is more simply conceived and cooked. Smoked salmon terrine with a confit lemon and herb salad is a typical starter, followed by Derbyshire fillet of beef with beetroot, caramelised shallots and horseradish mash.

Chef: Nigel Stuart **Owners:** Robert & Andrew Allsop/Morley Hayes Leisure Ltd **Times:** 12-2/7-9.30, Closed 1 Jan, Closed L Sat **Prices:** Fixed L £11.45-£14.45, Fixed D £15.95-£32.95, Starter £5.25-£6.75, Main £15.25-£19.45, Dessert £5.25-£6.75, Service optional **Wine:** 22 bottles over £20, 34 bottles under £20, 7 by the glass **Notes:** Sun L £18.75, Dress Restrictions, Smart casual, Air con **Seats:** 100, Pr/dining room 24 **Children:** Menu, Portions **Rooms:** 32 (32 en suite) ★★★★ HL **Directions:** Please telephone for directions **Parking:** 250

RIDGEWAY   MAP 16 SK48

◉◉◉ The Old Vicarage

see opposite

The Old Vicarage

RIDGEWAY MAP 16 SK48

Modern British

Memorable dining in striking house and gardens

☎ 0114 247 5814 Ridgeway Moor S12 3XW
e-mail: eat@theoldvicarage.co.uk
web: www.theoldvicarage.co.uk

Built in 1846, The Old Vicarage is approached by a sweeping gravel drive set in rolling lawns and fine specimen trees, woodland and a wild flower copse. The welcome is equally warm and friendly, the décor pleasingly unfussy country-house, while cosy lounges and open fires beckon to sip aperitifs and nibble canapés, and on warm summer days the terrace comes into play for outdoor dining. The main dining room comes in soft pastel shades with modern watercolours bringing the room to life. Bright and sunny in summer and warm and cosy in winter with log fires and candlelight, it's decked out with parquet flooring and crisp white linen tablecloths. The conservatory dining area opens out on to the terrace and lovely views, while the kitchen's modern focus is admirably inspired by top-quality, seasonal produce from local and specialist suppliers, as well as the kitchen garden itself.

Expect some unusual blends of flavours, but the precision cooking is not tied to fashion or gimmicks. Sound combinations, accomplished skills and clear flavours abound in dishes like lavender-smoked fillet of Whitby cod with spinach and truffle frittata, Ridgeway honey and chive flower foam, or perhaps roast fillet of Aberdeen Angus beef on cinnamon-braised shin with Seville orange and fondant potato.

Chef: T Bramley, N Smith
Owners: Tessa Bramley
Times: 12.30-2/6.30-9.30, Closed 10 days Xmas/New Year, 2 wks Aug & BHs, Sun & Mon, Closed L Sat
Prices: Fixed L £30, Fixed D £55, Service optional
Notes: Tasting menu 7 courses £65, Civ Wed 50
Seats: 40, Pr/dining room 22
Children: Portions
Directions: Please telephone for directions
Parking: 18

ROWSLEY
MAP 16 SK26

❀❀ East Lodge Hotel
Modern British
Country-house hotel dining in romantic setting

☎ 01629 734474 DE4 2EF
e-mail: info@eastlodge.com
web: www.eastlodge.com

The hotel enjoys a romantic setting in 10 acres of beautiful grounds. Peruse the menu in the conservatory lounge area, overlooking the gardens, before entering the modern, country-look restaurant. The emphasis is on local produce and cooking is sound with clear flavours and no unnecessary embellishment. A starter of nicely caramelised scallops comes with smooth pumpkin purée, and loin of lamb, pink and tender, is served on wilted spinach with caramelised button onions, carrot purée, dauphinoise potatoes and a rich jus. Desserts are a highlight, as in a superb rhubarb sponge pudding served with fresh sauce anglaise and a lovely rhubarb compôte, or honeycomb parfait with banana tart and chocolate sorbet. A good choice of dishes is also offered for vegetarians.

Chef: Dean Sweeting **Owners:** Elyzian Hospitality Ltd **Times:** 12-2/7-9.30 **Prices:** Fixed L £15, Fixed D £35, Service optional **Notes:** Sun L 3 courses £23.95, Vegetarian available, Dress Restrictions, Smart casual, no jeans or trainers, Civ Wed 66, Air con **Seats:** 50, Pr/dining room 36 **Children:** Min 12 yrs, Menu, Portions **Rooms:** 12 (12 en suite) ★★★ HL **Directions:** On A6, 5m from Matlock & 3m from Bakewell, at junct with B6012 **Parking:** 40

❀❀ The Peacock at Rowsley
Modern British V
Ambitious cooking at a chic hotel

☎ 01629 733518 Bakewell Rd, DE4 2EB
e-mail: reception@thepeacockatrowsley.com
web: www.thepeacockatrowsley.com

Once again under the ownership of the Haddon Hall estate, this chic little establishment (the former dower house) has undergone a contemporary makeover - a clever fusion of ancient manor with ultra-modern boutique-hotel styling. The mix is easy on the eye, its cool interiors enriched with original features and period furnishings. The dining room follows the theme, backed by well-drilled, hospitable service and garden views. Highly accomplished, flavourful dishes come dressed to thrill and testify to the kitchen's ambition and technical skill. The enticing repertoire takes a modern approach, and making a decision can be tricky; perhaps scallops with confit potatoes, seaweed and fish sauce, or beef fillet with horseradish croquette, broad beans and delicious chips.

Chef: Mathew Rushton **Owners:** Rutland Hotels **Times:** 12-2/7-9, Closed D 24-26 Dec **Prices:** Fixed L £21.50-£25, Starter £5.50-£11.50, Main £22.50-£27.50, Dessert £7.25-£7.50, Service optional **Wine:** 35 bottles over £20, 20 bottles under £20, 15 by the glass **Notes:** Fixed L 3 courses, Fixed Sun D 3 courses £25.00, Vegetarian menu, Civ Wed 20 **Seats:** 40, Pr/dining room 20 **Children:** Min 10 yrs, Menu, Portions **Rooms:** 16 (16 en suite) ★★★ HL **Directions:** M1 junct 29 (Chesterfield), 20 mins to Rowsley **Parking:** 25

STRETTON
MAP 16 SK36

❀ The White Bear
British, French NEW
Accomplished modern cooking at friendly pub-restaurant

☎ 01246 863274 Main Rd DE55 6ET

The outside of this converted pub - set beside the A61 - doesn't prepare you for the revelation inside; for the savvy locals beat a path to this pub-restaurant's door. Inside you will find stone floors, stone and rough-cast walls, leaded windows and wooden tables set with candles. Service is warm and friendly from wife Stephanie, while chef-patron husband Jason (Wardill) - who has worked in many top northern restaurants - shows his pedigree via an appealing modern repertoire that suits their gastro-pub market. Using fresh, quality local produce, think roasted cod fillet with a tiger prawn and chorizo risotto and fennel and ginger butter sauce.

Chef: Jason Wardill **Owners:** Jason Wardill **Times:** 12-2/5.30-9.30, Closed 1 wk Jan, 2 wks Oct, Mon, Closed L Sat, D Sun **Prices:** Fixed L £14.50, Fixed D £16.50, Starter £5.50-£6.50, Main £10.95-£16.95, Dessert £4.75-£5.50, Service optional **Wine:** 6 bottles over £20, 19 bottles under £20, 7 by the glass **Notes:** Sun L available **Seats:** 40 **Directions:** 15 min from M1 junct 29. On A61 between Clay and Shirland **Parking:** 30

THORPE
MAP 16 SK15

❀ Izaak Walton Hotel
Traditional British
Fisherman's paradise serving modern cuisine

☎ 01335 350555 Dovedale DE6 2AY
e-mail: reception@izaakwaltonhotel.com
web: www.izaakwaltonhotel.com

A converted 17th-century farmhouse, named after the famous author of *The Compleat Angler*, with its own two-mile stretch of the River Dove for excellent fishing and views of the Dovedale Valley. The restaurant is traditionally decorated and offers outstanding views of Thorpe Cloud in the Peak District National Park. Modern cooking is exemplified in dishes like pan-fried quail with swede mash in a redcurrant jus, or rump steak with kidney pie, bubble-and-squeak and thyme gravy, followed by a caramelised apple tart with cardamom ice cream. The bar features fishing memorabilia and pictures, and bar meals are served here.

Chef: James Harrison **Owners:** Mr & Mrs J W Day **Times:** 12-2.30/7-9.30 **Prices:** Fixed L £21, Fixed D £32-£35, Service optional **Notes:** Fixed L 3 courses, Vegetarian available, Dress Restrictions, Smart casual, Civ Wed 80 **Seats:** 120, Pr/dining room 20 **Children:** Menu, Portions **Rooms:** 35 (35 en suite) ★★★ HL **Directions:** Telephone for directions **Parking:** 80

DEVON

ASHBURTON   MAP 03 SX77

◉ Agaric

Modern British

Honest cooking in an inviting setting

☎ 01364 654478 30 North St TQ13 7QD
e-mail: eat@agaricrestaurant.co.uk
web: www.agaricrestaurant.co.uk

This cosy restaurant with rooms nestles in the bustling village of Ashburton, with its many antique shops. Located in a Georgian listed building, it comes complete with an open fireplace, granite wall and beautiful courtyard garden, while a large carved wooden mushroom pays deference to the restaurant's theme. A wood-fired oven delivers tasty pizzas and bread, doubling as a smoker for fish and meat; wild ingredients like samphire, mushrooms and laver are picked locally. The daily-changing menu matches the unpretentious setting: expect straightforward, honest dishes such as pan-fried fillet of Devon beef with roasted shallots, red wine and horseradish cream, or duck with spiced plum sauce and squash and apple filo.

Chef: Nick Coiley **Owners:** Mr N Coiley & Mrs S Coiley **Times:** 12-2/7-9.30, Closed 2 wks Aug, Xmas, 1wk Jan, Mon-Tue, Closed L Sat, D Sun **Prices:** Fixed L £12.95-£14.95, Starter £4.95-£8.95, Main £13.95-£17.95, Dessert £5.95-£6.95, Service optional **Wine:** 16 bottles over £20, 9 bottles under £20, 2 by the glass **Seats:** 30 **Children:** Portions **Directions:** Opposite town hall. Ashburton off A38 between Exeter & Plymouth **Parking:** Car park opposite

◉◉ Holne Chase Hotel

Traditional British ♨ NOTABLE WINE LIST ✿

Peaceful country retreat offering fine dining

☎ 01364 631471 Two Bridges Rd TQ13 7NS
e-mail: info@holne-chase.co.uk
web: www.holne-chase.co.uk

An original Domesday manor, Holne Chase was used as a hunting lodge for Buckfast Abbey for many years until it became a hotel in 1934. The traditionally styled restaurant offers fantastic views over the lawn and terrace, while in winter log fires burn and candlelight casts a warm glow over the soft décor. Seasonally influenced menus make full use of local ingredients, including fish from Brixham and Looe, local game, home-grown vegetables from the Victorian walled kitchen garden and produce from the owners' farm. Expect clean flavours in appealing dishes, like braised and glazed blade of Widecombe beef with mash potato and honey-glazed vegetables, or perhaps a pan-fried fillet of red mullet layered with ratatouille and served with baby leaf spinach and a balsamic reduction.

Chef: Joe Bartlett **Owners:** Sebastian & P Hughes West Country Hotels Ltd **Times:** 12-2/7-8.45, Closed L Mon **Prices:** Fixed L £20-£25, Fixed D £35, Service optional **Wine:** 25 bottles over £20, 20 bottles under £20, 6 by the glass **Notes:** Fixed L 3 courses, Light L £5.50-£9.50, Dress Restrictions, Smart casual, Civ Wed 60 **Seats:** 75, Pr/dining room 12 **Children:** Min 12 yrs D, Menu, Portions **Rooms:** 17 (17 en suite) ★★★ CHH **Directions:** Travelling N & E, take 2nd Ashburton turn off A38. 2m to Holne Bridge, hotel is 0.25m on right. From Plymouth take 1st Ashburton turn **Parking:** 40

ASHWATER   MAP 03 SX39

◉◉ Blagdon Manor Hotel & Restaurant

Traditional British V

Confident cooking in delightful Devon retreat

☎ 01409 211224 EX21 5DF
e-mail: stay@blagdon.com
web: www.blagdon.com

Dating back to the 16th century, this Grade II listed traditional Devon longhouse on the Devon/Cornwall border has been added to over the years and is now a relaxed country-house hotel. Set within 20 acres, the hotel retains many original features, including heavy oak beams, slate flagstones and a freshwater well. Service is formal but friendly and the atmosphere is relaxed. Popular with locals, the main restaurant is candlelit and cosy, and leads through to the light and airy conservatory extension. The traditional British cuisine makes the most of high-quality local produce, as in a tian of Dorset coast crab with smoked salmon roulade and avocado, followed by a tasting of West Country lamb. Tempting desserts include hot chestnut soufflé with cranberry sorbet.

Chef: Stephen Morey **Owners:** Stephen & Liz Morey **Times:** 12-2/7-9, Closed 2 wks Oct, 2 wks Jan, Mon (ex residents), Closed L Tue, D Sun **Prices:** Fixed L £17, Fixed D £35, Service optional **Wine:** 21 bottles over £20, 9 bottles under £20, 4 by the glass **Notes:** Sun L £23.50, Vegetarian menu, Dress Restrictions, Smart casual **Seats:** 24, Pr/dining room 16 **Children:** Min 12 yrs **Rooms:** 7 (7 en suite) ★★★ HL **Directions:** From A388 towards Holsworthy, 2m N of Chapman's Well take 2nd right towards Ashwater. Next right by Blagdon Lodge. Hotel 2nd on right **Parking:** 12

AXMINSTER
MAP 04 SY29

◉◉ Fairwater Head Country House Hotel

British, European

Country-house dining with stunning views

☎ 01297 678349 Hawkchurch EX13 5TX
e-mail: info@fairwaterheadhotel.co.uk
web: www.fairwaterheadhotel.co.uk

This charming hotel occupies an Edwardian country house set in attractive gardens surrounded by rolling countryside. It offers cosy public rooms and a more contemporary Garden restaurant overlooking the Axe Valley. The kitchen draws on the best of Devon's produce especially beef, pork and lamb, sourced from local farmers, and the menu offers a mixture of traditional English fare with some more modern European dishes. Highlights include delicious home-made breads along with carefully prepared dishes such as oven-baked fillet of cod with crushed spring onion-scented new potatoes, roast peppers and sauce vierge, or pink-roasted rack of lamb, fondant potatoes, glazed root vegetables and claret jus from the menu gourmand.

Chef: Andre Moore, Anthony Muir **Owners:** Sarah Leydet **Times:** 12-2/7-9 **Prices:** Fixed D £27.50, Starter £4.50-£5.75, Main £6.50-£12.95, Dessert £4.50-£5.75, Service optional, Group min 15 service 10% **Notes:** Fixed D 4 courses, Sun L 3 courses £16.50, Vegetarian available **Seats:** 70, Pr/dining room 18 **Children:** Portions **Rooms:** 16 (16 en suite) ★★★ HL **Directions:** Turn off B3165 Crewkerne to Lyme Regis road, hotel signed from Hawkchurch **Parking:** 40

BEER
MAP 04 SY28

◉ Steamers

Modern, Seafood NEW

Popular village restaurant offering superb seafood

☎ 01297 22922 New Cut, Fore St EX12 3JH
e-mail: info@steamersrestaurant.co.uk
web: www.steamersrestaurant.co.uk

This former chandlery and village bakery has been skilfully converted into a characterful restaurant with interconnecting bar area. With a location like this, seafood has to be at the heart of the menu with its own daily-changing selection, but you'll also find chicken, lamb, beef or duck dishes. Fish is treated with a mixture of British and international influences, creating starters like River Teign mussels in a peppered tomato cream. Main courses might include sautéed fillet of local wild sea bass with king prawns, or a simple grilled whole plaice with lemon and herb butter. Sunday lunch is extremely popular.

Chef: Andy Williams **Owners:** Steamers Ltd **Times:** 12-2/6.30-9.30, Closed 25 & 26 Dec, Mon in winter, Closed D Sun in winter **Prices:** Starter £4.50-£8.95, Main £10.95-£17.95, Dessert £4.95-£5.95, Service optional **Wine:** 15 bottles over £20, 30 bottles under £20, 8 by the glass **Notes:** Sun L 2 courses £12.95-£14.95, 3 courses £15.95-£19.50, Air con **Seats:** 65 **Children:** Menu, Portions **Directions:** Just off A3052 between Sidmouth and Lyme Regis **Parking:** On street & council car park 150mtrs

BIDEFORD
MAP 03 SS42

◉ Yeoldon Country House Hotel

British

Modern cooking in traditional country-house setting

☎ 01237 474400 Durrant Ln, Northam EX39 2RL
e-mail: yeoldonhouse@aol.com
web: www.yeoldonhousehotel.co.uk

A charming Victorian country house in a tranquil location, offering superb views over the River Torridge. The recently refurbished ground floor restaurant has an air of casual elegance, making the most of the views with large windows. There's an intelligent simplicity to the cooking style, the accomplished kitchen delivering well-executed, honest, unpretentious British dishes using fresh, local produce. From the daily-changing menu, look out for celery, watercress and stilton soup, guinea fowl supreme with caramelised orange and ginger stuffing, and lemon tart with lemon meringue ice cream.

Chef: Brian Steele **Owners:** Brian & Jennifer Steele **Times:** 7-8, Closed Xmas, Sun, Closed L all week **Prices:** Fixed D £30, Starter £6-£8, Main £16-£18, Dessert £6, Service included **Wine:** 7 bottles over £20, 32 bottles under £20, 3 by the glass **Notes:** Civ Wed 60 **Seats:** 30 **Children:** Portions **Rooms:** 10 (10 en suite) ★★ HL **Directions:** A361 to Bideford. Go over Torridge Bridge and at rdbt turn right. Take 3rd right into Durrant Lane. Hotel 0.25m **Parking:** 30

BRANSCOMBE
MAP 04 SY18

◉ The Masons Arms

Traditional British

Popular village inn with bags of character and a wonderful beach nearby

☎ 01297 680300 EX12 3DJ
e-mail: reception@masonsarms.co.uk
web: www.masonsarms.co.uk

Set in a pretty chocolate-box village a stone's throw from one of Devon's loveliest beaches, this former 14th-century cider house is a real destination gastro-pub with oodles of old-world charm and a thoughtful approach to food. The décor is enjoyably rustic, but uncluttered. In the summer the extensive outdoor seating, busy bar and two restaurant areas are usually packed with happy diners enjoying imaginative dishes such as lamb chops with sweet potato mash, minted peas and red wine jus, or confit of duck with apple and pear bubble-and-squeak, carrots and pancetta jus. Desserts might include iced chocolate and amaretti biscuit terrine with chocolate sauce. There are open fires in winter with regular spit-roasts.

Chef: R Reddaway, S Garland **Owners:** Mr & Mrs C Slaney **Times:** 12-2/7-9, Closed L all week **Prices:** Fixed D £27.50, Service optional **Wine:** 18 bottles over £20, 30 bottles under £20, 13 by the glass **Notes:** Vegetarian available, Dress Restrictions, No shorts or jeans **Seats:** 70, Pr/dining room 20 **Children:** Min 14 yrs **Rooms:** 22 (22 en suite) ★★ HL **Directions:** Village off A3052 between Sidmouth and Seaton **Parking:** 45

BROADHEMBURY   MAP 03 ST10

◉ Drewe Arms

Modern, Seafood

Classic seafood dining pub

☎ 01404 841267   EX14 3NF

Grade II listed inn, dating from 1228, with an abundance of appealing features, including a large garden and an attractive, sleepy thatched village setting. Inside there are oak beams, open fires and a welcoming atmosphere. The food is 98 per cent fresh fish and seafood, with the focus on simplicity and freshness. Take a fillet of brill served with a remoulade sauce, or fillet of turbot with hollandaise, while a marmalade bread-and-butter pudding or rhubarb crumble could catch the eye at dessert. Open sandwiches and light meals are also served.

Chef: Andrew Burge **Owners:** Andrew Burge **Times:** 12-2/7-9, Closed 25 Dec, Closed D Sun **Prices:** Fixed L £15-£30, Fixed D £20-£35, Starter £8.50, Main £20, Dessert £6, Service optional, Group min 10 **Wine:** 20 bottles over £20, 5 bottles under £20, 8 by the glass **Seats:** 50, Pr/dining room 20 **Children:** Portions **Directions:** M5 junct 28, take A373 Cullompton to Honiton. Follow signs for 5.2m **Parking:** 40

BURRINGTON   MAP 03 SS61

◉◉ Northcote Manor

Modern British V

Accomplished cooking in historic country house

☎ 01769 560501   EX37 9LZ
e-mail: rest@northcotemanor.co.uk
web: www.northcotemanor.co.uk

An idyllic setting, impressive grounds and the warmth and natural friendliness of the staff make this lovely gabled manor house a delightful place to visit. Built in 1716, the house has a long and varied history, dating back to its origins as a Benedictine monastery, and bright murals depicting the colourful history adorn the comfortable, refurbished dining room. Good sourcing of quality, local seasonal produce, including game from nearby shoots, highlights the daily fixed-price dinner menus. Dishes are well executed, well presented and show good combinations of natural flavours. So expect the likes of venison Wellington served with garlic and thyme potatoes and wilted pak choi, and for dessert, perhaps a 'study of Northcote Manor apples'.

Chef: Richie Herkes **Owners:** J Pierre Mifsud **Times:** 12-2/7-9 **Prices:** Fixed L £10-£18.50, Fixed D £38, Starter £7.50, Main £21, Dessert £9.50, Service optional **Wine:** 40 bottles over £20, 6 bottles under £20, 9 by the glass **Notes:** Vegetarian menu, Dress Restrictions, Smart casual preferred, Civ Wed 80 **Seats:** 34, Pr/dining room 14 **Children:** Portions **Rooms:** 11 (11 en suite)★★★ CHH **Directions:** M5 junct 27 towards Barnstaple. Left at rdbt to South Molton. Do not enter Burrington village. Follow A377, right at T-junct to Barnstaple. Entrance after 3m, opp Portsmouth Arms railway station and pub **Parking:** 30

22 Mill Street

CHAGFORD   MAP 03 SX78

Modern European

Laid-back neighbourhood restaurant in quaint moor setting

☎ 01647 432244 22 Mill St TQ13 8AW
web: www.22millstreetrestaurant.co.uk

Hidden by a cream and green shop front, this unassuming restaurant is located in the pretty Dartmoor town of Chagford. The modern but simply decorated interior immediately makes guests feel at home, with rich earthy colours, stone floors and striking original artwork. The highly regarded chef-proprietor's culinary offerings are as unpretentious as the service - he takes on front-of-house duties himself, which makes for an engaging eating experience. The menu focuses on intensity of flavour and quality of produce, with modest but attractive presentation; a lot of effort clearly goes in to balancing the elements at work in each dish and in the menu as a whole - the results certainly have that wow-factor. Typical is the superb starter of saffron lasagne of crab and red peppers, followed by roast squab pigeon with braised lentils, smoked bacon and red wine. On no account miss pudding - the chef clearly enjoys creating special dessert plates and they are undoubtedly a highlight. Try the hot chocolate fondant with poached pears and vanilla ice cream. The breads alone

are worth the trip - especially the addictive buttermilk bread.

Chef: D Walker **Owners:** Duncan Walker **Times:** 12.30-1.45/7.30-9, Closed 2 wks Jan, 10 days Jun, Sun-Mon, Closed L Tue **Prices:** Fixed L £23, Fixed D £38.50, Service included **Wine:** 50 bottles over £20, 10 bottles under £20, 4 by the glass **Seats:** 22 **Children:** No children **Directions:** Please telephone for directions **Parking:** On street

ENGLAND

Gidleigh Park

CHAGFORD MAP 03 SX78

Modern European V ♦ NOTABLE WINE LIST

The epitome of modern, luxury country-house fine dining

☎ 01647 432367   TQ13 8HH
e-mail: gidleighpark@gidleigh.co.uk
web: www.gidleigh.com

The twisting, 1.5-mile drive along a private lane to this globally acclaimed, black-and-white mock-Tudor Dartmoor retreat is so worth the effort - magically set in extensive gardens traversed by the tumbling River Teign, it's nothing short of idyllic! And, though Gidleigh has been stylishly transformed and rejuvenated by a multi-million pound, 11-month refurbishment programme during 2006 (and now in the secure hands of Andrew Brownsword, chef Michael Caines' business partner in the Abode group), it has cleverly lost none of its timeless charm and homely atmosphere - a quite stunning achievement! There are now three dining rooms all with a different style - the more contemporary room comes with a glass wine wall and oak floor, while the Teign is a light room with access out on to the garden terrace and the Meldon is oak panelled and traditional in style. The name Michael Caines alone draws people from far and wide to experience the exquisite, modern, classically-inspired seasonal cuisine. The imaginative cooking showcases fresh, tip-top quality local ingredients, plentiful of luxury and intricate presentation, his kitchen's approach via fixed-price lunch, dinner and tasting option. Think roast best end of Dartmoor lamb served with fondant potato, onion and thyme purée, tomato fondue and a tapenade jus and perhaps a passionfruit mousse with pineapple, mango and paw paw, rice pudding ice cream and a coconut tuile to finish. The cheeseboard is a cracking feature, the wine list superb, while peripherals like canapés, breads, amuse-bouche and petits fours all hit top form too. The rejuvenated Gidleigh really is a must-visit destination. Michael is AA Chefs' Chef 2007-2008 (see pages 10-11).

Chef: Michael Caines
Owners: Andrew and Christina Brownsword
Times: 12-2/7-9.45
Prices: Fixed L £27-£33, Fixed D £75, Service optional
Wine: 750 bottles over £20, 6 by the glass
Notes: Tasting menu £85, Vegetarian menu, Dress Restrictions, No jeans, trainers or T-shirts
Seats: 60
Children: Min 8 yrs, Menu, Portions
Rooms: 24 (24 en suite)★★★★ CHH
Directions: From Chagford Sq turn right at Lloyds TSB Bank into Mill St, after 150yds right fork, across x-rds into Holy St. Restaurant 1.5m

CHAGFORD   MAP 03 SX78

◎◎◎◎ **Gidleigh Park**

see opposite

◎◎ **Mill End**

Modern French V

A watermill with terrific food in a quiet Dartmoor location

☎ 01647 432282   TQ13 8JN

e-mail: info@millendhotel.com

web: www.millendhotel.com

This 18th-century former flour mill - once the home of Sir Frank Whittle, inventor of the jet engine - comes complete with a working water wheel that churns away delightfully just outside the dining room. The olive green walls, large comfortable chairs, subdued lighting and candles create an air of understated elegance, while service is relaxed and attentive without being obtrusive. The cooking style is modern French, the menu featuring many classic dishes that make good use of saucing and pay attention to detail with presentation. Typical starters might include saffron, leek and mussel soup or carpaccio of Devon Red beef with shavings of poacher cheese, while for mains you could tuck into roast fillet of turbot with brandade cod and orange-braised fennel.

Chef: Christophe Ferraro **Owners:** Keith Green **Times:** 12-2/7-9, Closed L by appoint only (open Sun L) **Prices:** Fixed D £38, Service optional, Group min 8 service 10% **Wine:** 61 bottles over £20, 24 bottles under £20, 7 by the glass **Notes:** Vegetarian menu, Dress Restrictions, No jeans, trainers **Seats:** 42 **Children:** Min 12 yrs **Rooms:** 14 (14 en suite)★★ HL **Directions:** From A30 turn on to A382. Establishment on right before Chagford turning **Parking:** 20

◎◎◎ **22 Mill Street**

see page 121

COLYFORD   MAP 04 SY29

◎ **Swallows Eaves**

Traditional

Classical cuisine in a traditional environment

☎ 01297 553184 Swan Hill Rd EX24 6QJ

e-mail: swallows_eaves@hotmail.com

web: www.lymeregis.com/swallowseaveshotel

Swallows Eaves is an Edwardian hotel located a short distance from the coast. Traditional values are upheld in the genuinely warm welcome, the immaculate presentation of the property and the

homely décor, with china ornaments, oil paintings and prints inside and lovingly tended gardens outside. Similarly, the daily menu has a traditional feel with dishes like chicken liver and sherry pâté; fresh halibut with lemon parsley butter, and whisky and raspberry posset with honey and oatmeal. The cooking has flair and quality local ingredients are allowed to take centre stage.

Chef: Jane Beck **Owners:** Mr & Mrs J Beck **Times:** 7-8, Closed Nov-Feb, Closed L Mon-Sun **Prices:** Fixed D £27.50, Service included **Wine:** 1 by the glass **Notes:** Fixed D 4 courses **Seats:** 16 **Children:** Min 14 yrs **Rooms:** 8 (8 en suite) ★★ HL **Directions:** In village centre on A3052 opposite village shop **Parking:** 10

DARTMOUTH   MAP 03 SX85

◎ **The Dart Marina Hotel**

Modern British V NEW 🖥

Riverside restaurant serving up fine fresh produce

☎ 01803 832580 Sandquay TQ6 9PH

e-mail: info@dartmarinahotel.com

web: www.dartmarina.com

The River Restaurant offers diners superb views across the river and the chance to dine alfresco in summer. Substantial investment in recent years has seen the hotel become a mini resort. With an alternative eating option, the Wildfire Bistro, the main River Restaurant menu draws inspiration from top-quality produce like hand-dived scallops and really fresh fish and meat. Confident cooking is demonstrated in dishes like a main course of brill with potato purée, oxtail, parmesan and beetroot foam. Desserts like the assiette of chocolate prove irresistible.

Chef: Mark Streeter **Owners:** Richard Seton **Times:** 12.30-2/6.30-9.30, Closed L Mon-Fri **Prices:** Fixed L £10-£25, Fixed D £12-£30, Starter £5.50-£10, Main £9.50-£30, Dessert £5.50-£7.50, Service optional **Wine:** 45 bottles over £20, 23 bottles under £20, 8 by the glass **Notes:** Vegetarian menu, Dress Restrictions, Smart casual, Civ Wed 100, Air con **Seats:** 64 **Children:** Menu, Portions **Rooms:** 49 (49 en suite) ★★★ HL

◎ **Jan and Freddies Brasserie**

Modern British NEW

Enjoyable food in a relaxed atmosphere

☎ 01803 832491 10 Fairfax Place TQ6 9AD

e-mail: info@janandfreddiesbrasserie.co.uk

web: www.janandfreddiesbrasserie.co.uk

This relaxed and friendly brasserie is located in the heart of Dartmouth, a stone's throw from the River Dart. With a lively bar area at the rear, the stylish yet comfortable décor helps create an informal atmosphere. The new head chef prepares unfussy, modern British dishes, with an emphasis on top-quality local ingredients and a focus on flavour. Try seared local scallops on a bed of cauliflower purée to start, or maybe salmon and prawn fishcakes with a soft herb salad and mustard mayonnaise, followed by pan-fried sea bass with a spiced root purée, and ginger and lemongrass sauce. Finish with a delicious caramel pannacotta.

Chef: Richard Hilson **Owners:** Jan & Freddie Clarke **Times:** 12.30-2/6.30-9, Closed Xmas, Sun, Closed L Sun-Mon **Prices:** Starter £4.95-£7.95, Main £14.95-£18.95, Dessert £4.95-£6.95, Service optional **Wine:** 8 bottles over £20, 22 bottles under £20, 10 by the glass **Seats:** 40 **Children:** Min 5 yrs **Directions:** Fairfax Place runs parallel to S Embankment. Restaurant faces Hawley Rd **Parking:** On street

ENGLAND

The New Angel

DARTMOUTH MAP 03 SX85

Modern French V ▮ NOTABLE WINE LIST

Revitalised harbour-side eatery from one of England's master chefs

☎ 01803 839425 2 South Embankment TQ6 9BH
e-mail: reservations@thenewangel.co.uk
web: www.thenewangel.co.uk

The TV serialisation of John Burton Race's exploits in setting up this place (and his *French Leave* series) have helped draw the crowds to this wonderful, half-timbered Tudor building on the waterfront. It's incredibly busy peak season, a testament to its success and the quality of the cuisine, while menus outside attract throngs of interest from passers-by. There are two floors, both simply but stylishly decorated and both with fabulous views over the busy river Dart estuary and harbour. Pale grey floorboards, darkwood tables, comfortable wicker chairs and antique chandeliers set a relaxed modern edge. The lively ground-floor room has an open kitchen with all the theatre of the chefs on show, which bumps up the atmosphere and volume, while upstairs provides a quieter, more intimate option. Service is relaxed and friendly but appropriately professional.

Burton Race's kitchen shows polished skill and self assurance, with great respect paid to the simple treatment of the very best and freshest local Devon produce; take roasted rump of Blackawton lamb with a herb crust, dauphinoise potato and tomato minestrone, or perhaps roasted fillet of John Dory with crab brandade, Parmentier potatoes and a light chicken juice. The cooking's modern approach is French-orientated with daily specials supporting the repertoire and reacting to availability, and there's no obligation to have more than one course - a further nod to the restaurant's philosophy for easy and relaxed dining.

Chef: John Burton Race & Robert Spencer
Owners: Kim & John Burton Race
Times: 12-2.30/6.30-10, Closed Jan, Mon, Closed D Sun
Prices: Fixed L £19.50, Starter £6.50-£13, Main £18-£25, Dessert £8.50, Service optional, Group min 8 service 10%
Wine: 90 bottles over £20, 20 bottles under £20, 20 by the glass
Notes: Vegetarian menu, Air con
Seats: 70, Pr/dining room 50
Children: Menu, Portions
Directions: Dartmouth centre, on the water's edge
Parking: Mayor's Avenue, centre of Dartmouth

DARTMOUTH CONTINUED

◎◎◎ The New Angel

see opposite

EXETER   MAP 03 SX99

◎ Alias Hotel Barcelona

Modern European

Bright, lively restaurant with a relaxed atmosphere

☎ 01392 281000 Magdalen St EX2 4HY
e-mail: barcelona@aliashotels.com
web: www.aliasbarcelona.com

Set in a converted Victorian eye hospital just outside Exeter city centre, Hotel Barcelona is part of the Alias group of boutique hotels. Located in a light, modern marquee-style conservatory, Café Paradiso is a buzzing, stylish restaurant with a distinct lack of pretension. Produce is locally-sourced whenever possible, and good use is made of the wood-fired oven for pizzas and oven-baked dishes, while the bistro-style fare is largely Mediterranean in inspiration, as in bucatini and sardines with tomato, saffron, sultanas, pinenuts, chilli and pangratatto. In the summer, head for the sun terrace in the walled garden.

Chef: Chris Archambault **Owners:** Alias Hotels plc **Times:** 12-2/7-10
Prices: Fixed L £10.95, Starter £4.95-£7.95, Main £9.50-£19.95, Dessert £4.50-£6.50, Service optional, Group min 10 service 10% **Wine:** 27 bottles over £20, 30 bottles under £20, 16 by the glass **Notes:** Vegetarian available, Air con **Seats:** 60, Pr/dining room 20 **Children:** Menu, Portions **Rooms:** 46 (46 en suite) ★★★★ TH **Directions:** M5 junct 30 onto A379 to Exeter. At Countess Wear rdbt take 3rd exit to city centre and follow Topsham Rd for 2m. At main junct follow into right lane into Magdalen St. Hotel on right **Parking:** 32

◎ Barton Cross Hotel

British, French V

Quality cooking in engaging 17th-century thatched property

☎ 01392 841245 Huxham, Stoke Canon EX5 4EJ
e-mail: bartonxhuxham@aol.com

Converted 17th-century thatched longhouse in a pretty rural setting just five miles from Exeter. The restaurant is an impressive room with a huge inglenook fireplace and a minstrels' gallery, and looks fabulous by candlelight. Cob walls and low beams remind guests of the building's age, while the food is more modern: expect assured cuisine from a kitchen that makes good use of local produce and well deserves its loyal local following. Begin with lobster risotto perhaps, and then tuck into pheasant with a tarte Tatin of root vegetable and watercress sauce, followed by warm pear and almond tart with honey and ginger ice cream.

Chef: Paul Bending **Owners:** Brian Hamilton **Times:** 6.30-mdnt, Closed Sun, Closed L Mon **Prices:** Fixed D £23.50, Starter £4.50-£6.50, Main £13-£18.50, Dessert £5, Service optional **Wine:** 49 bottles over £20, 42 bottles under £20, 6 by the glass **Notes:** Vegetarian menu, Dress Restrictions, Smart casual **Seats:** 50, Pr/dining room 15 **Children:** Menu, Portions **Rooms:** 9 (9 en suite) ★★★ HL **Directions:** 0.5 mile off A396 at Stoke Canon, 3m N of Exeter **Parking:** 50

EXETER CONTINUED

◎◎ Best Western Lord Haldon Country House Hotel

Modern European

Stylish country-house dining near Exeter

☎ 01392 832483 Dunchideock EX6 7YF
e-mail: enquiries@lordhaldonhotel.co.uk
web: www.lordhaldonhotel.co.uk

Former country seat of the Lords of Haldon hidden away amidst rural tranquillity four miles from Exeter. A popular dining venue for locals and guests, the historic country house affords glorious views over the Exe, while the elegant Courtyard Restaurant makes full use of the views of the 'Capability' Brown landscape. Cooking combines classics with European influences, the daily-changing menus featuring skilfully conceived and executed dishes using locally-sourced produce. A typical meal may take in warm asparagus salad with a raspberry dressing and quail's egg to start, followed by crispy skin sea bass with orange and fennel risotto. Knowledgeable service from uniformed staff.

Times: 12-2.30/7.15-9.30, Closed L Mon-Sat **Rooms:** 23 (23 en suite) ★★★ **HL Directions:** From M5 junct 31 or A30 follow signs to Ide, continue through village for 2.5m, left after red phone box, 0.5m, pass under stone bridge, left

◎ Galley Fish & Seafood Restaurant with Rooms

Seafood 🖥

Contemporary seafood in rustic restaurant

☎ 01392 876078 41 Fore St, Topsham EX3 0HU
e-mail: fish@galleyrestaurant.co.uk
web: www.galleyrestaurant.co.uk

An old brick and beamed building on Topsham's high street provides the setting for this untypical seafood restaurant. The informal welcome is part of the philosophy here, embracing Zen styling and 'balancing the Yin and Yang' in some exotic dishes. Fresh local fish and seafood is transformed on the premises into innovative, healthy dishes. Thai, Indian and Caribbean influences feature on a lively menu including the likes of line-caught sea bass on pesto and lavender-crushed potatoes, fillets of John Dory with Bombay potatoes, coriander, spiced mango and cream, and grilled fillets of halibut on seaweed mash.

Chef: P Da-Costa Greaves **Owners:** Mark Wright/Paul Da-Costa Greaves **Times:** 12-1.30/7-9.30, Closed Sun **Prices:** Fixed L £28.50-£31.50, Starter £7.50-£9.95, Main £22-£25, Dessert £6.95-£9.95, Service optional, Group min 7 service 10% **Wine:** 14 bottles over £20, 20 bottles under £20, 10 by the glass **Seats:** 48 **Children:** Min 12 yrs **Rooms:** 2 (2 en suite) ★★★★★ RR **Directions:** M5 junct 30, follow signs for Topsham. Come through High St see Globe Hotel on left, continue for 250yds **Parking:** 3

◎◎ Michael Caines at Abode Exeter

Modern European V

Classy modern cooking overlooking the cathedral

☎ 01392 223638 Cathedral Yard EX1 1HD
e-mail: tablesexeter@michaelcaines.com
web: www.michaelcaines.com

Stylish refurbishment turned this Exeter veteran into the first of a chain of boutique hotels that were rolled out in historic towns and key city centres across the UK. Fashionable art decks the walls in the bright modern dining room, with its darkwood floor and crisp white linen setting the scene for some tempting contemporary, polished cuisine. The kitchen shows a strong commitment to local produce and seasonality, backed by highly accomplished cooking. Perhaps roasted Cornish sea bass served with a cauliflower purée and tempura, braised chard and a truffle sauce, or Gressingham duckling with braised button onions, caramelised gnocchi, Savoy cabbage and a light spiced jus. A small champagne bar for aperitifs rounds off an upbeat, cosmopolitan package.

Chef: Ross Melling **Owners:** Michael Caines & Andrew Brownsword **Times:** 12-2.30/7-10, Closed Sun, Closed D Xmas **Prices:** Fixed L £13, Starter £7.50-£13.95, Main £18.50-£24.50, Dessert £8.50, Service optional, Group min 10 service 12.5% **Wine:** 158 bottles over £20, 8 bottles under £20, 8 by the glass **Notes:** Tasting menu £64, Vegetarian menu, Dress Restrictions, Smart casual, Civ Wed 50, Air con **Seats:** 70, Pr/dining room 80 **Children:** Menu, Portions **Rooms:** 53 (53 en suite) ★★★★ HL **Directions:** Town centre, opposite Cathedral **Parking:** Mary Arches St car park

◉ No 21

Modern European NEW

Relaxed, contemporary bistro dining overlooking the cathedral

☎ 01392 210303 21a Cathedral Yard EX1 1HB
e-mail: restaurant@21cathedralyard-exeter.co.uk
web: www.21cathedralyard-exeter.co.uk

Set amongst a row of attractive shops, restaurants and bars overlooking the cathedral, this relaxed bistro (formerly the Carved Angel) reopened in 2006 after refurbishment and rebranding. Inside, chunky oak tables, chairs and floor deliver traditional bistro styling, while the décor and artwork lend a more contemporary edge to proceedings. There's a servery that's used during the day when menus offer a quick-snack café format, while in the evenings it is a more formal affair with full table service. The accomplished modern European approach uses good-quality local produce; take a dinner carte duo of lamb (pine nut and herb encrusted best end) with confit shoulder, celeriac fondant, sweet potato purée and basil sauce.

Chef: Andrew Shortman **Owners:** Andrew Shortman **Times:** 9.30-5/6-9.30, Closed 25 Dec, Closed D Sun **Prices:** Fixed D £21.95, Starter £5-£7.50, Main £15-£21, Dessert £4.95-£6.50, Service optional **Wine:** 6 bottles over £20, 20 bottles under £20, 4 by the glass **Seats:** 56, Pr/dining room 18 **Children:** Portions **Directions:** Opposite Exeter Cathedral

---

GULWORTHY   MAP 03 SX47

◉◉◉ The Horn of Plenty

see page 128

HAYTOR VALE   MAP 03 SX77

◉ Rock Inn

British

Beautifully located country inn serving accomplished British food

☎ 01364 661305 TQ13 9XP
e-mail: reservations@rockinn.co.uk
web: www.rock-inn.co.uk

Old-world country inn with beams and flagstone floors, dating from the 1750s and set below the Haytor Rocks just inside the Dartmoor National Park. It's a family-run establishment, traditional in style, with classic fare such as Devon lamb rump served with buttered wilted spinach, béarnaise sauce and dauphinoise potatoes, or fillet of sea bass on stir-fried vegetables with sweet chilli sauce on the dinner menu. Dishes are based on best-quality local ingredients, with vegetables, fish, poultry and meat delivered fresh daily. Devon cheeses

are a special feature and wines include the county's own Dart Valley Reserve from the Sharpham vineyard.

Chef: Sue Beaumont Graves **Owners:** Mr C Graves **Times:** 12-2.15/6.30-9, Closed 25-26 Dec **Prices:** Food prices not confirmed for 2008. Please telephone for details, Service optional **Notes:** Dress Restrictions, No jeans **Seats:** 75 **Children:** Menu, Portions **Rooms:** 9 (9 en suite) ★★ HL **Directions:** From A38 at Drum Bridges, join the A382 to Bovey Tracey. After 2m join B3387 towards Haytor and continue for 3.5m, follow brown signs **Parking:** 25

HOLBETON   MAP 03 SX65

◉ The Dartmoor Union Inn

International

Stylish restaurant in a village setting

☎ 01752 830288 Fore St PL8 1NE
e-mail: sue.constantine@dartmoorunion.co.uk
web: www.dartmoorunion.co.uk

There's plenty of style at this lively establishment. The interior is all clean lines with lots of wood and a log fire surrounded by deep sofas and comfortable seating. The long bar has shelves at the back displaying a large selection of wines, and the small restaurant area has separate tables and good quality high-backed leather chairs. Bar snacks are served in addition to a comprehensive carte and daily specials. Modern dishes include proscuitto ham salad with red pepper dressing, oven-roasted monkfish wrapped in Parma ham and sage, with caramelised banana Tatin with Devon clotted cream to finish.

Times: 12-2.30/5.30-11

The Horn of Plenty

GULWORTHY   MAP 03 SX47

International

Country-house setting with focus on fine cuisine

☎ 01822 832528   PL19 8JD
e-mail: enquiries@thehornofplenty.co.uk
web: www.thehornofplenty.co.uk

Originally built in 1870 for the Mine Captain of the Great Devon Consol, this creeper-clad, archetypal country-house hotel is well established in five acres of wonderful gardens with mature trees, walled gardens and wild orchards. The chic, light and airy restaurant is simply decorated and all eyes are drawn to the windows, where magnificent views can be enjoyed across the Tamar Valley. The mood is romantic at night, when the room is lit by table lanterns.

In the kitchen, a well-established team led by Peter Gorton produces modern British cuisine with international influences, drawing on fine seasonal ingredients. Clever combinations produce complementary flavours and textures; sample a starter like tortellini of braised lamb shank with mushroom beurre blanc. A simple but perfectly executed main course choice would be pan-fried brill with creamy jasmine rice and coriander broth. Round off with an exemplary warm chocolate tart with coconut sorbet, pineapple and caramel sauce. The wine list is equally well constructed, offering an extensive selection plus a good range of ports and digestifs.

Chef: Peter Gorton
Owners: Mr & Mrs P Roston, Peter Gorton
Times: 12-4/7-12, Closed 24-26 Dec, Closed L Mon
Prices: Fixed L £26.50, Fixed D £45, Service included, Group min 10 service 10%
Wine: 115 bottles over £20, 20 bottles under £20, 11 by the glass
Notes: Fixed L 3 courses, Dress Restrictions, Smart casual, Civ Wed 150, Air con
Seats: 60, Pr/dining room 20
Children: Menu, Portions
Rooms: 10 (10 en suite) ★★★ HL
Directions: 3m from Tavistock on A390. Turn right at Gulworthy Cross, follow signpost
Parking: 20

HOLSWORTHY · MAP 03 SS30

🏵 Rydon Inn & Restaurant
Modern British NEW
Traditional pub-atmosphere dining but with accomplished, careful cooking

☎ 01409 259444   EX22 7HU

The Rydon Inn may call itself a gastro-pub but it offers a far more modern dining experience than the usual traditional pub grub. This Devon longhouse - internally heavily beamed and decked out with pine-topped tables, benches and chairs - comes with a modern extension and a conservatory that overlooks the 2-acre grounds. The accomplished kitchen makes the best use of local seasonal produce in carefully cooked, simple, tried-and-tested dishes, intelligently delivered without unnecessary garnish. Take slow-roasted belly pork stuffed with sage and garlic and served with rösti potatoes, followed perhaps by a 'Francis Coulson' inspired sticky toffee pudding. A children's menu is also available.

Times: 12-2/6.15-8.45, Closed 2 weeks in Nov, Mon (exc Winter)

HONITON · MAP 04 ST10

🏵🏵 Combe House Hotel and Restaurant, Gittisham
Modern British V ⚡NOTABLE WINE LIST 🍴
Fine-dining experience in stunning Elizabethan mansion

☎ 01404 540400   Gittisham EX14 3AD
e-mail: stay@thishotel.com
web: www.thishotel.com

An Elizabethan mansion at the end of a winding mile-long drive provides a grand setting for this country-house hotel. The interior is hugely atmospheric, with ornate ceilings, ancestral portraits, fine antiques, fresh flowers and blazing log fires throughout the panelled public rooms. Dining is equally impressive, with a skilled kitchen using the best of local, seasonal and home-grown produce to underpin contemporary British dishes with French influences. There's a good choice for vegetarians (open cep raviollo with braised baby vegetables and Madeira cream), and vegans are willingly catered for. Brixham fish, bought daily at auction, might include roast monkfish medallions and fresh lobster tail with a foaming bisque sauce, followed by dark Valrhona chocolate tart with lime ice cream.

Chef: Hadleigh Barrett, Stuart Brown **Owners:** Ken & Ruth Hunt
Times: 12-2/7-9.30, Closed 2 wks end Jan **Prices:** Fixed L £20, Fixed D £39.50, Service optional **Wine:** 78 bottles over £20, 11 bottles under £20, 8 by the glass **Notes:** Tasting menu Sun-Thu £49, Sun L 3 courses £29, Vegetarian menu, Dress Restrictions, Smart casual, Civ Wed 100 **Seats:** 60,

Pr/dining room 48 **Children:** Menu, Portions **Rooms:** 16 (16 en suite)★★★ HL **Directions:** M5 junct 28/29, A373 to Honiton. Right in High St and follow signs for Sidmouth A375, then brown tourist signs for Combe **Parking:** 35

🏵 Home Farm Restaurant & Hotel
British NEW
Former farmhouse hotel offering refined cuisine

☎ 01404 831278   Wilmington EX14 9JR
e-mail: info@thatchedhotel.co.uk
web: www.thatchedhotel.co.uk

Set in well-tended gardens, this thatched former farmhouse has been transformed into a comfortable hotel. The refurbished restaurant has a contemporary style and in keeping with the hotel's name, diners are made to feel really at home. The chef makes good use of herbs, delicate flavours and fine ingredients, offering a balanced choice of dishes. Starters might include fresh pan-seared scallops in clarified butter with frisée and sherry vinegar syrup. Main courses feature the likes of pan-seared fillet of sea bass with celeriac and butternut squash, whisky and horseradish cream sauce.

Times: 12-2/7-9 **Rooms:** 12 (12 en suite) ★★ SHL

HORNS CROSS · MAP 03 SS32

🏵 The Hoops Inn & Country Hotel
Modern British
Gastro-pub fare at an ancient inn

☎ 01237 451222   EX39 5DL
e-mail: sales@hoopsinn.co.uk
web: www.hoopsinn.co.uk

Dating back to the 13th century, this thatched Devon longhouse makes a pretty dinner destination. The oak-panelled dining room has an open fire, red-tiled floor, excellent prints on the wall and an eclectic mixture of tables and chairs. In warmer months you can eat outside in the courtyard. The modern British menu has some French and occasional Asian influences, and favourite dishes include a starter of warm smoked salmon with crème fraîche and capers, followed by line-caught local wild sea bass with wilted spinach and saffron and dill beurre blanc, and sticky toffee pudding with butterscotch sauce to finish.

Chef: M Somerville & Jo Winter **Owners:** Gerry & Dee Goodwin
Times: 12-3.30/6-10.30 **Prices:** Food prices not confirmed for 2008. Please telephone for details **Wine:** 91 bottles over £20, 90 bottles under £20, 20 by the glass **Notes:** Vegetarian available, Dress Restrictions, Smart casual **Seats:** 90, Pr/dining room 16 **Children:** Menu, Portions **Rooms:** 13 (13 en suite) ★★★ HL **Directions:** Follow A39 from Bideford towards Clovelly/Bude, through Fairy Cross and Horns Cross, restaurant on the right **Parking:** 100

ILFRACOMBE
MAP 03 SS54

◎◎ The Quay

Modern British

Exciting food in an 'upturned boat'

☎ 01271 868090 & 868091 11 The Quay EX34 9EQ
e-mail: info@11thequay.com
web: www.11thequay.com

Owned by artist Damien Hirst and adorned with his work, you wouldn't expect a traditional restaurant and you won't be disappointed - it's a first-floor dining room in the shape of a fish, but with the appearance of an upturned boat! The white-painted boards, clothed tables, banquette seating and chairs are all pretty straightforward however, as is the traditional British cooking, with a modern emphasis. The Taste Menu also comes with the option of selected wines. If you prefer to get a bit more involved, choose the likes of crab and tarragon risotto to start, followed by Gressingham duck breast with red cabbage, vanilla mash and five-spice jus from the Dining Menu, or maybe salmon Wellington with red onion confit and cauliflower purée.

Chef: Lawrence Hill-Wickham **Owners:** Simon Browne & Damien Hirst **Times:** 10-3/6-9.30, Closed 25-26 Dec, 2-25 Jan **Prices:** Starter £6.25-£10.95, Main £15.95-£22.95, Dessert £4.50-£7.95, Service optional **Wine:** 50 bottles over £20, 30 bottles under £20, 29 by the glass **Notes:** Tasting menu 6 courses, Sun L menu available **Seats:** 32, Pr/dining room 28 **Children:** Menu, Portions **Directions:** Follow signs for harbour and pier car park. Restaurant on left before car park **Parking:** Pier car park 100yds

ILSINGTON
MAP 03 SX77

◎◎ Best Western Ilsington Country House Hotel

International

Traditional dining in Dartmoor country-house hotel

☎ 01364 661452 Ilsington Village TQ13 9RR
e-mail: hotel@ilsington.co.uk
web: www.ilsington.co.uk

This family-owned country-house hotel enjoys a secluded, elevated position on the edge of Dartmoor. The newly built restaurant has been specifically designed to capture the impressive views across the moor and the Haytor Rocks, and the walls are hung with moor views by local painters. The kitchen takes care in its sourcing of top-quality ingredients and skilful preparation produces mostly French dishes full of flavour. Try a starter of seared sea scallops with crab and langoustine ravioli and a chive butter sauce, followed perhaps by a main course of pan-fried saddle of venison with seared wild mushrooms and a juniper and thyme jus. Desserts include a marbled chocolate marquise with pistachio anglaise.

Best Western Ilsington Country House Hotel

Chef: Mike O'Donnell **Owners:** Tim & Maura Hassell **Times:** 12-2/6.30-9 **Prices:** Fixed L £13.95, Fixed D £32.50, Starter £5.50-£8.50, Main £12.50-£19.50, Dessert £5.50-£6.95, Service optional **Wine:** 24 bottles over £20, 39 bottles under £20, 9 by the glass **Notes:** Dress Restrictions, Shirt with a collar (smart casual), Air con **Seats:** 75, Pr/dining room 75 **Children:** Portions **Rooms:** 25 (25 en suite) ★★★ HL **Directions:** A38 to Plymouth, exit at Bovey Tracey turn, then 3rd exit from rdbt to Ilsington, then 1st right and hotel 5m after Post Office **Parking:** 60

INSTOW
MAP 03 SS43

◎ Decks Restaurant

Modern British

Hearty modern cooking at a renowned Devon seafront restaurant

☎ 01271 860671 Hatton Croft House, Marine Pde EX39 4JJ
e-mail: decks@instow.net
web: www.decksrestaurant.co.uk

Set smack on the seafront, this two-floored beachside restaurant comes with fantastic views. Eat alfresco or at a window table on the first floor to make the most of the stunning estuary views, and expect hearty, contemporary cuisine. Think pan-fried fillet of sea bass served with pak choi and a warm couscous salad, or fillet of West Country beef with béarnaise sauce, roast potatoes, mushrooms and French fries, and to finish, perhaps a chocolate tart with whipped vanilla cream. Lighter fare is available at lunchtime, there's also a fixed-price option running alongside the carte, plus there's a downstairs bar.

Chef: Lee Timmins **Owners:** Lee Timmins **Times:** 12-2.30/7-9.30, Closed 25-26 Dec, 1 Jan, Sun-Mon **Prices:** Fixed D £21.45-£25, Starter £5-£9, Main £12-£21, Dessert £5-£7, Service optional **Notes:** Vegetarian available, Air con **Seats:** 50 **Children:** Menu, Portions **Directions:** From Barnstaple follow A38 to Bideford. Following signs for Instow, restaurant situated at far end of sea front **Parking:** On street; beach car park

KINGSBRIDGE   MAP 03 SX74

◉◉ *Buckland-Tout-Saints*

British, French

Quality cooking in an elegant William and Mary manor house

☎ 01548 853055 Goveton TQ7 2DS
e-mail: buckland@tout-saints.co.uk
web: www.tout-saints.co.uk

Nestling in its own valley in Devon's stunning South Hams, this elegant classic country-house hotel is a conversion of a manor house dating back some 300 years, set in extensive, beautifully tended gardens and woodland. Striking Russian pine panelling, antiques and open fires are features of the luxurious interior, with the restaurant, bar and lounge lovingly restored back to their original grandeur. The restaurant has quality table appointments and comfortable high-backed suede chairs and showcases the best of the county's abundant produce from a concise, seasonal, modern-focused French menu. Fresh fish, Devon lamb and beef appear, with dishes such as baked cod with rösti potatoes and saffron butter sauce, or pan-fried fillet steak with fondant potatoes and wild mushroom casserole. A young and friendly team attentively deliver service.

Buckland-Tout-Saints

Times: 12-1.30/7-9, Closed 3 wks end Jan **Rooms:** 16 (16 en suite) ★★★ CHH **Directions:** 3m NE of Kingsbridge off A381. Through hamlet to Goveton, 500 yds past church

◉◉◉

The Masons Arms Inn

KNOWSTONE   MAP 03 SS82

Modern British, French

Stunning food in the relaxed setting of a charming inn

☎ 01398 341231 EX36 4RY
e-mail: dodsonmasonsarms@aol.com
web: www.masonsarmsdevon.co.uk

This 13th-century thatched village inn oozes character and charm, and has been welcoming people for generations. The beamed bar has a very low doorway, with steps towards the restaurant in its more modern rear extension with stunning views of the Exmoor countryside. Hand-painted murals adorn the apex ceiling here, and it offers a complete contrast to the bar areas of the original inn. Mark Dodson's cooking has fine pedigree (for many years he was head chef at The Waterside Inn in Bray - see entry), his style here oozes maturity and confidence in refreshingly uncluttered, clean-cut dishes that use top-notch ingredients. And his modern take on British and French classics has justifiably been creating a real stir; take a fillet of halibut served with a potato crust and cider sauce, or perhaps Devon beef fillet and rich oxtail with parsnip purée and a red wine jus. Finish with a stunning iced Amaretto parfait teamed with vanilla plums and pistachio biscuit. It's deservedly busy so book well in advance, especially for weekends.

Chef: Mark Dodson **Owners:** Mark & Sarah Dodson **Times:** 12-2/7-9, Closed First two wks Jan, Mon, Closed D Sun **Prices:** Starter £7.50-£12.50, Main £12.50-£17.50, Dessert £6.50-£8, Service optional **Wine:** 21 bottles over £20, 8 bottles under £20, 8 by the glass **Notes:** Sun L 3 courses £29.50, Vegetarian available **Seats:** 24 **Children:** Portions **Directions:** Signed from A361, turn right once in Knowstone **Parking:** 10

Lewtrenchard Manor

LEWDOWN MAP 03 SX48

Modern British V

Fine food in Jacobean splendour in a secret valley

☎ 01566 783222   EX20 4PN
e-mail: info@lewtrenchard.co.uk
web: www.lewtrenchard.co.uk

Chef: Jason Hornbuckle
Owners: von Essen Hotels
Times: 12-1.30/7-9, Closed
L Mon
Prices: Fixed L £15, Fixed
D £40, Service optional
Notes: Fixed D 4 courses,
Vegetarian menu, Dress
Restrictions, L smart casual,
D no jeans or T-shirts, Civ
Wed 100
Seats: 45, Pr/dining room
22
Children: Min 8 yrs,
Menu, Portions
Rooms: 14 (14 en
suite)★★★ HL
Directions: Take A30
signed Okehampton from
M5 junct 31. Continue for
25m and exit at Sourton
Cross. Follow signs to
Lewdown, then
Lewtrenchard
Parking: 40

Once the home of the celebrated hymn writer and novelist Reverend Sabine Baring-Gould of 'Onward Christian Soldiers' fame, this magnificent Jacobean manor house is secreted away in a quiet valley on the fringe of Dartmoor, surrounded by idyllic gardens and peaceful parkland. Seemingly untouched by time, the interior oozes understated charm and wonderful period detail, complete with oak panelling, beautifully ornate ceilings, stained-glass windows, large fireplaces, period furnishings and family portraits. The candlelit, panelled dining room continues the theme - it's a relatively intimate affair overlooking the pretty colonnaded courtyard, bedecked with flowers in summer and providing the perfect setting for alfresco dining. The kitchen takes a modern approach with the focus on top-quality fresh local produce and seasonality, including Devonshire game (you can pre-book a specially prepared Gastro Game Menu), fish from the quayside at Looe, and herbs and vegetables from the hotel's own walled garden. Deceptively and intelligently simple-themed dishes conceal a flair and confidence to allow clear, clean flavours to shine, as in seared scallops with sweet pickled vegetables and mackerel jelly, or perhaps pan-fried pollack with split green pea purée, sautéed scallops, roast salsify and beurre noisette jus with rosemary, while a delightful crème brûlée served with passionfruit and banana sorbet and coconut and butterscotch sauce might prove a fitting dessert. Service is expectedly formal, but with a friendly yet professional approach, while a good-value wine list bolsters the package.

KNOWSTONE MAP 03 SS82

⊚⊚⊚ The Masons Arms Inn

see page 131

LEWDOWN MAP 03 SX48

⊚⊚⊚ Lewtrenchard Manor

see opposite

LIFTON MAP 03 SX38

⊚⊚ Arundell Arms

Modern British V

Luxurious coaching inn focusing on local produce

☎ 01566 784666 PL16 0AA
e-mail: reservations@arundellarms.com
web: www.arundellarms.com

This delightfully located 18th-century coaching inn stands near the River Tamar on the edge of Dartmoor and has been in the same hands since 1961. It has been lovingly renovated to create stylish rooms, including a well-lit, classical-styled restaurant with a tasteful yellow and cream décor. Fresh flowers bring additional appeal to tables, while the cooking is a celebration of seasonal produce from the abundant local larder - major suppliers are individually identified on the menu. The confident kitchen takes an accomplished, straightforward modern approach. Think a fillet of line-caught sea bass with a ragout of Falmouth Bay scallops, lobster and saffron, or perhaps pan-fried fillet of English new season lamb served with a compôte of slightly sweetened Tamar Valley rhubarb and a white wine sauce.

Chef: Steven Pidgeon **Owners:** Anne Voss-Bark **Times:** 12.30-2.30/7.30-10, Closed 24 Dec, Closed D 25-26 Dec **Prices:** Fixed L £23, Fixed D £36, Service optional **Wine:** 51 bottles over £20, 30 bottles under £20, 7 by the glass **Notes:** Fixed D 5 courses, Vegetarian menu, Smart casual, no shorts or T-shirts, Civ Wed 80 **Seats:** 70, Pr/dining room 24 **Children:** Menu, Portions **Rooms:** 21 (21 en suite) ★★★ HL **Directions:** Just off A30 in village of Lifton, 3m E of Launceston **Parking:** 70

⊚ Tinhay Mill Guest House and Restaurant

British, French V

Cottage-style restaurant serving food of uncompromising quality

☎ 01566 784201 Tinhay PL16 0AJ
e-mail: tinhay.mill@talk21.com
web: www.tinhaymillrestaurant.co.uk

Two former mill cottages, dating from the 15th century, were converted to provide this delightful restaurant with rooms. The interior is traditional with thick whitewashed walls, low beams, fires and ticking clocks. Chef proprietor Margaret Wilson has long been a champion of local produce - she has decades of experience behind her and is the author of three cookbooks. Her food is honest, simple and effective with excellent saucing. There's also a great selection of single malt whiskies that Mr Wilson will happily guide you through.

Chef: Margaret Wilson **Owners:** Mr P & Mrs M Wilson **Times:** 7-9.30, Closed 2 wks Nov, 2 wks Apr, Sun & Mon (ex residents), Closed L all week **Prices:** Fixed D £23.50-£28.50, Starter £4.50-£8.50, Main £13.95-£21.50, Dessert £4.50-£7.50, Service optional **Wine:** 14 bottles over £20, 16 bottles under £20, 4 by the glass **Notes:** Vegetarian menu, Dress Restrictions, No jeans or trainers **Seats:** 24, Pr/dining room 24 **Children:** Min 12 yrs **Rooms:** 5 (5 en suite) ★★★★ RR **Directions:** From M5 take A30 towards Okehampton/Launceston. Lifton off A30 on left. Follow brown tourist signs. Restaurant at bottom of village near river **Parking:** 20

LYDFORD MAP 03 SX58

⊚⊚ Dartmoor Inn

Modern British V

Stylish, rural gastro-pub

☎ 01822 820221 EX20 4AY
e-mail: info@dartmoorinn.co.uk
web: www.dartmoorinn.com

Old-fashioned charm at this smart country inn is successfully balanced by modern interior décor, with influences from Sweden and New England. There's a tiny bar, with a log fire and real ales, while the restaurant comprises a series of small dining rooms with well-spaced tables and upholstered chairs. Cooking is consistent and menus are tightly aligned to seasonal produce. A set menu is offered alongside a simpler carte of perennial favourites (fish and chips, or oxtail and Madeira). Impressive dishes include potted pork rillettes, or fillet of organically farmed salmon with crayfish and saffron butter. The organic credentials evident in both the superb colour and flavour of the fish.

CONTINUED

LYDFORD CONTINUED

Chef: Philip Burgess & Andrew Honey **Owners:** Karen & Phillip Burgess
Times: 12-2.15/6.30-9.30, Closed Mon, Closed D Sun **Prices:** Starter
£4.50-£7.75, Main £12.75-£22.50, Dessert £5.95-£6.50, Service optional,
Group min 10 service 10% **Wine:** 25 bottles over £20, 19 bottles under
£20, 6 by the glass **Notes:** Sun L menu available, Vegetarian menu
Seats: 65, Pr/dining room 20 **Children:** Min 5 yrs, Menu, Portions
Directions: On A386, Tavistock to Okehampton road **Parking:** 35

LYNMOUTH   MAP 03 SS74

◎◎ *Rising Sun Hotel*

British, French

Former smugglers' inn with literary connections

☎ 01598 753223 Harbourside EX35 6EG
e-mail: risingsunlynmouth@easynet.co.uk
web: www.risingsunlynmouth.co.uk

Classic thatched inn dating from the 14th century in a fine location
overlooking the harbour and Lynmouth Bay. Once the haunt of
smugglers, the inn has a fascinating history; R D Blackmore wrote
several chapters of *Lorna Doone* here, and Shelley purportedly chose
the place as his honeymoon tryst. The building is full of character,
outside and in, and has been refurbished. The oak-panelled dining
room is candlelit at night. Quality local produce, cooked with care,
appears in dishes of hare and pearl barley terrine encased in pancetta
and leek; and fillet of Devon Red Ruby beef in a sun-blushed tomato
and parsley paste.

Times: 7-9, Closed L all week **Rooms:** 16 (16 en suite) ★★ HL
Directions: M5 junct 23 (Minehead). Take A39 to Lynmouth. Opposite the
harbour

◎ **Tors Hotel**

Modern European

*Enjoyable dining in relaxed surroundings overlooking
the sea*

☎ 01598 753236 EX35 6NA
e-mail: torshotel@torslynmouth.co.uk
web: www.torslynmouth.co.uk

Friendly hotel set high up on a hill amid 5 acres of woodland, with
superb views of the harbour and out to sea. The smartly decorated
restaurant has a colonial feel and makes a spacious and welcoming
venue for some accomplished modern European cuisine. A daily-
changing menu plunders the Devon larder to offer the best of local
seafood, game and meat, and delivers its finds to the table without

over-working them, allowing the flavour of ingredients to come
through. Mains might include West Country loin lamb chops with
minted pea purée and rosemary jus, or whole sea bream baked in
Thai spices and served with crushed new potatoes. Lighter fare is
available in the bar.

Chef: Andy Collier **Owners:** Mrs Braunton, Mrs Dalgarno **Times:** 7-9,
Closed 3 Jan - 4 Feb (wknds only in Feb), Closed L all week **Prices:** Fixed
D £30-£50, Service included **Wine:** 11 bottles over £20, 39 bottles under
£20, 3 by the glass **Notes:** Civ Wed 80 **Seats:** 50 **Children:** Menu,
Portions **Rooms:** 31 (31 en suite) ★★★ HL **Directions:** M5 junct 23
(Bridgwater). Continue 40m on A39 through Minehead. Hotel at base of
Countisbury Hill on left **Parking:** 40

LYNTON   MAP 03 SS74

◎◎ **Lynton Cottage Hotel**

Modern British V

Stunning views and carefully cooked food

☎ 01598 752342 North Walk EX35 6ED
e-mail: enquiries@lynton-cottage.co.uk
web: www.lynton-cottage.co.uk

With the sea pounding 500 feet below, this country house hotel,
perched on the hillside, offers understandably marvellous views. The
restaurant has a fresh and vibrant feel with colourful artworks and
makes the best of the magnificent outlook, while friendly, caring staff
encourage relaxation. The short carte is well balanced, with local,
organic and seasonal produce making their own positive statement.
Expect modern presentations and careful cooking that shows maturity
and a deft touch. Start with timbale of crab, crayfish and chorizo with
avocado purée, follow with roast rump of lamb with confit of winter
greens and a red wine sauce, and round off with hot chocolate
fondant with vanilla ice cream and date purée.

Chef: Allan Earl **Owners:** Allan Earl, Heather Biancardi **Times:** 12-2.30/
7-9.30, Closed Dec & Jan **Prices:** Fixed D £24.95-£29.95, Service included
Wine: 8 bottles under £20, 4 by the glass **Notes:** Fixed D 4 courses,
Vegetarian menu **Seats:** 40 **Children:** Portions **Rooms:** 16 (16 en suite)
★★★ HL **Directions:** M5 junct 27, follow A361 towards Barnstaple.
Follow signs to Lynton A39. In Lynton turn right at church. Hotel on right
Parking: 18

MORETONHAMPSTEAD   MAP 03 SX78

◎◎◎ **Bovey Castle**

see opposite

Bovey Castle

MORETONHAMPSTEAD

MAP 03 SX78

French, British NEW

Elegant dining in opulent surroundings

☎ 01647 445000   TQ13 8RE

e-mail: pnh@boveycastle.com

web: www.boveycastle.com

Built in 1907, this magnificent house turned five-star hotel has been restored to its former glory, with architecture typical of the extravagance of the era. Delightfully located in immaculately maintained grounds, the entrance is set with smart shrubs, while a liveried doorman greets and ushers you inside. Beautiful public rooms include the Cathedral Room (with wood panelling and a minstrels' gallery), the snooker room and the library. Artwork - in keeping with the 20's theme - is also a feature, while lounges offer deep comfort. The main Palm Court restaurant is a spacious and luxurious setting, its style continuing the theme, with restful hand-painted silk wallpaper, and, most evenings, a pianist plays. Service is appropriately skilled and friendly. The talented kitchen delivers exciting, well-considered and well-constructed modern dishes, with great emphasis placed on quality produce and the successful combinations of flavour and texture. Expect a fillet of Devon spring lamb served with wild garlic, morels and a thyme jus, and perhaps a Valrhona chocolate and hazelnut fondant with mandarin sorbet. (A smaller, fine-dining restaurant is planned for late 2007, while there's also an informal bistro here, too.)

Times: 12-2/7-9.30 **Rooms:** 65 (65 en suite) ★★★★★ HL

Directions: 2 miles from Moretonhampstead towards Princetown on B3212

NEWTON ABBOT

MAP 03 SX87

⊛ Sampsons Farm Hotel & Restaurant

British 🖥

Fresh local produce in a charming farmhouse hotel

☎ 01626 354913 Preston TQ12 3PP

e-mail: info@sampsonsfarm.com

web: www.sampsonsfarm.com

A centuries-old thatched farmhouse, the hotel has been in the same family for over 30 years. The cosy interior with low beams, subdued lighting and crackling log fires is all very reassuring and romantic. The place is Devon through and through, the food has impeccable local credentials and service is genuine under the proprietor's enthusiastic leadership. The menu is bang up to date, offering superb scallops from Dartmouth, with pea purée and port reduction, or stuffed saddle of Littlehempstead rabbit wrapped in Parma ham with cinnamon and lemon cream.

Times: 12-2/7-9, Closed 25-26 Dec **Rooms:** 11 (8 en suite) ★★★★ GA

Directions: M5/A380/B3195 signed Kingsteignton. Pass Ten Tors Inn on left & take 2nd rd signed B3193 to Chudleigh. At rdbt 3rd exit, left after 1m

---

NEWTON POPPLEFORD

MAP 03 SY08

⊛⊛ Moores Restaurant & Rooms

Modern British

Stylish village restaurant serving imaginative dishes

☎ 01395 568100 6 Greenbank, High St EX10 0EB

e-mail: mooresrestaurant@aol.com

web: www.mooresrestaurant.co.uk

Formerly two cottages, one of which doubled as a grocer's store, this attractive building now houses an elegant restaurant. The intimate dining room is classically furnished in neutral colours, with tables dressed with crisp white linen and fresh flowers, and two wide windows overlooking the village. The husband-and-wife team offers warm hospitality and Mr Moore catches much of the fish himself. Starters might include warm confit of mackerel with sweet lavender dressing, followed by a mains of grilled John Dory fillet with braised red rice, asparagus and a pink peppercorn cream. For dessert try Tia Maria and kiwi fruit crème brûlée or Poire William pear poached in cinnamon-scented red wine, served with stem ginger ice cream.

Chef: Jonathan Moore **Owners:** Jonathan & Kate Moore **Times:** 12-1.30/7-9.30, Closed 25 & 26 Dec, first 2 wks in Jan, Mon **Prices:** Fixed L £10-£14, Fixed D £19.50-£24.50, Service optional **Wine:** 19 bottles over £20, 12 bottles under £20, 6 by the glass **Notes:** Sun L 3 courses £10.95, Vegetarian available **Seats:** 32, Pr/dining room 12 **Children:** Portions **Rooms:** 3 (1 en suite) ★★★ RR **Directions:** Located on A3052, close to M5 junct 30 **Parking:** 2

PARKHAM   MAP 03 SS32

◉ Penhaven Country Hotel

Traditional British

Country-house cooking in an orangery restaurant

☎ 01237 451711   Rectory Ln EX39 5PL
e-mail: reception@penhaven.co.uk
web: www.penhaven.co.uk

The countryside is very much at the heart of this Victorian
establishment - with a bit of luck guests can even spot the tame
badgers that roam the ten acres of gorgeous grounds. The restaurant
is found in a beautiful orangery with well-spaced tables. Popular with
both guests and locals alike, the seasonal menu features locally
sourced organic meats and fresh fish. There's a comforting feel to the
British menu very much in keeping with the relaxed, unpretentious air
of the hotel. Starters might include local mackerel fillets with honey
and mustard dressing, followed by skate wing with lemon, caper and
herb butter; the home-made desserts are always worth making room
for.

Chef: Richard Copp, Scott Amos **Owners:** Penhaven Leisure Resorts Ltd
Times: 12-2/7-9.00, Closed L Mon-Sat **Prices:** Fixed L £13.95, Starter
£3.95-£4.95, Main £10.95-£16.50, Dessert £4.50, Service optional **Wine:** 18
bottles over £20, 21 bottles under £20, 3 by the glass **Notes:** Fixed L 3
courses, Vegetarian available, Dress Restrictions, Smart casual, no jeans
Seats: 45, Pr/dining room 10 **Children:** Menu, Portions **Rooms:** 12 (12
en suite) ★★★ CHH **Directions:** From Bideford A39 to Horns Cross, left
opposite pub, follow signs to Parkham; turn 2nd left with church on right
Parking: 50

PLYMOUTH   MAP 03 SX45

◉ Artillery Tower Restaurant

British

*Accomplished cooking in a unique setting at Plymouth's
waterside*

☎ 01752 257610   Firestone Bay PL1 3QR
web: www.artillerytower.co.uk

This circular 16th-century stone-built tower looks out across Plymouth
Sound towards Drakes Island and was once part of the strategic sea
defences in Plymouth. The restaurant is simply furnished with wooden
tables set against stone walls in a round room. As a champion of local
produce, the kitchen offers unfussy dishes prepared with respect for
the excellent quality of the ingredients. An impressive starter of roast
monkfish with provençale tomatoes and salsa verde might be
followed by a tender, accurately cooked loin of venison with celeriac
mash and pepper sauce, and crème brûlée with mulled pears for
dessert.

Chef: Peter Constable **Owners:** Peter Constable **Times:** 12-2.15/7-9.30,
Closed Xmas & New Year, Sun-Mon, Closed L Sat **Prices:** Fixed L £23.50,
Fixed D £25.50-£35 **Wine:** 60 bottles over £20, 30 bottles under £20, 6 by
the glass **Seats:** 40, Pr/dining room 16 **Children:** Portions
Directions: 1m from city centre and train station **Parking:** 20

◉ Barbican Kitchen

Modern British NEW

*The Tanner Brothers' latest venture is a stylish brasserie
serving contemporary food*

☎ 01752 604448   Plymouth Gin Distillery,
60 Southside St PL1 2LQ
e-mail: info@barbicankitchen.com
web: www.barbicankitchen.com

Housed in the Plymouth Gin distillery, the oldest surviving industrial
building in Plymouth, the Barbican Kitchen might be a new restaurant
but it was in this building that the Pilgrim Fathers ate their last meal
before setting sail on the *Mayflower*. The open-plan kitchen and
vibrant brasserie fuse old and new with grey and pink colour schemes
and clever use of light and space. Come for lunch, a pre-theatre meal,
dinner or a Sunday roast. Dishes are simple and well-executed and
the menu offers a flexible feast with main courses like seared calves'
liver with confit garlic mash and crispy pancetta or try 'create your own
steak' - the cut, sauce and starch.

Chef: Lee Holland **Owners:** Christopher & James Tanner **Times:** 12-3/5-
10, Closed 25-26 & 31Dec, Closed D Sun eve **Prices:** Starter £3.95-£6.95,
Main £6.95-£14.95, Dessert £4.95-£5.25, Service included **Wine:** 16 bottles
over £20, 22 bottles under £20, 13 by the glass **Notes:** Sun L £8.95,
Vegetarian available, Air con **Seats:** 80 **Children:** Menu, Portions
Directions: On Barbican, 5 mins walk from Bretonside bus station
Parking: Drakes Circus, Guildhall Hall

◉ Best Western Duke of Cornwall Hotel

British, European

Contemporary dishes in elegant hotel surroundings

☎ 01752 275850   Millbay Rd PL1 3LG
e-mail: info@thedukeofcornwallhotel.com
web: www.thedukeofcornwallhotel.com

A grand hotel, much refurbished, with a stunning restaurant. A huge
domed ceiling and enormous chandelier attract the eye and there are
also some impressive paintings of marine scenes. Service is friendly,
attentive and efficient, with some staff here on a foreign exchange
scheme through the local catering college. Cooking is some of the
best in Plymouth, with attractively presented dishes like mussel and
crab chowder or salmon and tarragon fishcakes, followed by pork fillet
with wild mushroom confit, pomme purée and Madeira jus. Desserts
might include Tia Maria delice with coffee anglaise.

Times: 7-10, Closed 26-31 Dec, Closed L all week **Rooms:** 71 (71 en suite)
★★★ HL **Directions:** City centre, follow signs 'Pavilions', hotel road is
opposite

⚜ Bistro Bene

Modern British NEW

Relaxed, friendly harbourside bistro

☎ 01752 254879 Dolphin House, Sutton Harbour,
The Barbican PL4 0DW
e-mail: enquiries@bistrobene.co.uk
web: www.bistrobene.co.uk

Enjoying a fantastic setting overlooking the harbour, this established
restaurant is ideally situated to offer the catch of the day. The
unpretentious interior has stripped wooden flooring, clothed tables
and chalkboards dotted around the place to highlight the specials. The
menu is similarly unpretentious, offering some novel combinations in
successful dishes like a starter of chargrilled ox tongue with piccalilli
and slow-roast tomatoes. Main courses make excellent use of local
produce in simple treatments like fillet of Devon beef with caramelised
onion and peppercorn sauce, or free-range Devon duck breast with
confit leg.

Times: 12-2/7-9.30 (Last Orders 9.30), Closed 25 Dec, 1 Jan, Sun, Mon,
Closed L Sat **Directions:** From A38 follow signs at Marsh Mill to City
Centre, then to Barbican. Left to Sutton Wharf and Barbican

⚜ Langdon Court Hotel

Modern British

Wonderful produce and creative cuisine

☎ 01752 862358 Down Thomas PL9 0DY
e-mail: enquiries@langdoncourt.com
web: www.langdoncourt.com

A magnificent Grade II listed Tudor manor, set in 7 acres of lush
countryside with direct access to the beach and coastal footpaths. A
simple menu is on offer in the bar, while the restaurant serves up fine
cooking, producing lots of interesting flavours and making good use of
spices. Fresh local seafood is a speciality; you will also find organically-
reared meat, game and local produce. Try seared scallops with
butternut squash, baby leaves and red onions, followed by a grilled
fillet of sea bass with a prawn and lemon reduction, and lemon
meringue with lemon curd and citrus syrup to finish.

Chef: Mark Jones **Owners:** Mark and Ruth Jones **Times:** 12-2.30/6.30-
9.30, Closed 25-26 Dec (exceptions in the event of wedding parties)
Prices: Fixed L £10.95, Fixed D £25, Starter £6.25-£7.25, Main £16.95-
£22.50, Service optional **Wine:** 10 bottles over £20, 36 bottles under £20,
20 by the glass **Notes:** Civ Wed 80 **Seats:** 60, Pr/dining room 60
Children: Portions **Rooms:** 18 (18 en suite) ★★★ CHH
Directions: From A379 at Elburton, follow brown tourist signs
Parking: 80

⚜⚜ Tanners Restaurant

Modern British V ✍

AA Restaurant of the Year for England

☎ 01752 252001 Prysten House, Finewell St PL1 2AE
e-mail: tannerbros@aol.com
web: www.tannersrestaurant.co.uk

Housed in Plymouth's oldest building, this restaurant offers modern
style in an impressive 15th-century setting that blends flagstones,
beams, vaults and an ancient well with contemporary art. The Pilgrim
Fathers may have eaten their last meal in England in the courtyard
here, but it's a forgone conclusion it wouldn't have included modern
dishes cooked with such flair. Think roast partridge served with
bubble-and-squeak and a thyme sauce, or perhaps seared fillet of brill
teamed with smoked salmon croquettes and a horseradish velouté.
This is still a popular venue thanks to consistent standards and the
owners' TV appearances: the Tanner brothers have also now opened a
sibling contemporary brasserie - the Barbican Kitchen (see entry).

Chef: Christopher & James Tanner **Owners:** Christopher & James Tanner
Times: 12-2.30/7-9.30, Closed 25, 31 Dec, 1st wk Jan, Sun & Mon
Prices: Fixed L £13.50, Fixed D £30, Service optional **Wine:** 40 bottles over
£20, 20 bottles under £20, 8 by the glass **Notes:** Tasting menu available,
Vegetarian menu, Dress Restrictions, Smart casual preferred **Seats:** 45,
Pr/dining room 26 **Children:** Portions **Directions:** Town centre. Behind St
Andrews Church on Royal Parade **Parking:** On street, Car parks

---

ROCKBEARE   **MAP 03 SY09**

⚜⚜ The Jack In The Green

Modern British ✍

An informal setting for some serious cooking

☎ 01404 822240 EX5 2EE
e-mail: info@jackinthegreen.uk.com
web: www.jackinthegreen.uk.com

CONTINUED

ROCKBEARE *Continued*

A popular dining pub with a great atmosphere, the restaurant at The Jack In the Green Inn is contemporary and relaxed, happily accommodating all comers, whether in jeans or suits. There is great emphasis on using fresh local produce wherever possible and menus change every six weeks to make best use of seasonal fare. Dishes are traditional using French principles of cooking, as in a starter of crispy Crottin Chavignol with beetroot fondant and saffron shallots, a main course of pan-fried fillet of brill with provençale vegetables and pistou and a dessert of apple and Calvados brûlée. There is also a tasting menu and an impressive choice of bar meals.

Chef: Matthew Mason, Craig Sampson **Owners:** Paul Parnell **Times:** 12-2/6-9.30, Closed 25 Dec-5 Jan **Prices:** Fixed L £18.45, Fixed D £25, Starter £4.75-£8.50, Main £10.50-£19.50, Dessert £5.50, Service optional **Wine:** 40 bottles over £20, 60 bottles under £20, 12 by the glass **Notes:** Tasting menu available Mon-Sat (pm), Vegetarian available, Dress Restrictions, Smart casual, Air con **Seats:** 80, Pr/dining room 60 **Children:** Menu, Portions **Directions:** 3m E of M5 junct 29 on old A30 **Parking:** 120

ROUSDON	MAP 04 SY29

✿✿ Dower House Hotel

Modern British

Imaginative cuisine in country house

☎ 01297 21047 Rousdon DT7 3RB
e-mail: info@dhhotel.com
web: www.dhhotel.com

The Dower House is a late Victorian country property located three miles west of Lyme Regis on the main road to Seaton, set back in its own grounds. There's an attractive contemporary-style bar and two eating options: the traditional fine dining restaurant, Peeks, or the more light-hearted Bistro 3. Cooking offers an impressive level of creative flair and innovation, using local produce to good effect in dishes such as crab and mussels with carrot Sauternes and chervil, and free-range pork tenderloin with Savoy cabbage, black pudding, apple and walnut. Vegetarian dishes are available from the longer bistro menu. Service is relaxed and friendly.

Times: 12-2/6.30-9 **Rooms:** 10 (10 en suite) ★★ HL **Directions:** 3m W of Lyme Regis on A3052 coast road

SALCOMBE	MAP 03 SX73

✿✿ Restaurant 42

Modern British

Classy cooking in an idyllic setting

☎ 01548 843408 Fore St TQ8 8JG
e-mail: jane@restaurant42.demon.co.uk
web: www.restaurant42.co.uk

Restaurant 42 takes its name from Douglas Adams' answer to 'Life, the Universe and Everything'. Ten metres from the sea, it enjoys spectacular views of the beaches and estuary from its lovely terrace. You can also relax in the lounge on great squashy leather sofas. The restaurant capitalises on its splendid location by offering sensible, serious food with ingenious touches. The format has recently been extended to offer a wine bar, brasserie and restaurant, and not-to-be-missed dishes include Salcombe crab, Bigbury Bay oysters, and chargrilled fillet of Aune Valley Aberdeen Angus beef, served with slow-roasted plum tomato, field mushroom and balsamic onions.

Chef: Thomas & David Bunn **Owners:** Jane & Neil Storkey **Times:** 7-12, Closed Sun (Sep-May), Mon (except Jul-Aug), Closed L winter **Prices:** Starter

£5.25-£7.95, Main £12.50-£19.95, Dessert £5.95, Service optional **Wine:** 33 bottles over £20, 10 bottles under £20, 18 by the glass **Notes:** Vegetarian available **Seats:** 42 **Children:** Portions **Directions:** 15m from A38 Exeter to Plymouth **Parking:** Whitestrands Car Park

✿✿ Soar Mill Cove Hotel

Modern British V

Stunning coastal views and superb local ingredients

☎ 01548 561566 Soar Mill Cove, Marlborough TQ7 3DS
e-mail: info@soarmillcove.co.uk
web: www.soarmillcove.co.uk

Set amid spectacular Devon countryside with dramatic sea views, this family-owned hotel's elegant restaurant and lounge make the most of their location in an enviable position above the lovely tranquil cove. Glorious sunsets are just one of the benefits, and the comfortable restaurant has a relaxing neutral-themed décor with polished wood tables, and local artists' paintings on display. The outside terrace is also perfect for alfresco dining. The cooking is ingredient-led, with an emphasis on quality produce from the abundant West Country larder. The accomplished kitchen's approach is via a fixed-price menu and tasting option, and not surprisingly fresh fish and seafood is a speciality on the seasonal menus. Watch the lobster pots being emptied in the bay, and then enjoy the catch served with queen scallops and a saffron reduction, or simply grilled with garlic butter.

Chef: I Macdonald **Owners:** Mr & Mrs K Makepeace & family **Times:** 7.15-9, Closed Jan, Closed L all week **Prices:** Fixed D £38, Starter £5-£12, Main £10-£20, Dessert £5-£8, Service optional **Wine:** 40 bottles over £20, 6 bottles under £20, 4 by the glass **Notes:** Tasting menu £50, Vegetarian menu **Seats:** 60 **Children:** Menu, Portions **Rooms:** 22 (22 en suite) ★★★★ HL **Directions:** A381 to Salcombe, through village follow signs to sea **Parking:** 25

◉ Tides Reach Hotel

Modern British

Holiday hotel dining in splendid beach location

☎ 01548 843466   South Sands TQ8 8LJ
e-mail: enquire@tidesreach.com
web: www.tidesreach.com

Snugly situated in the valley immediately behind South Sands beach, with beautiful views over Salcombe estuary, this personally-run holiday hotel has a modern yet timeless feel throughout elegant public areas. Competition for the window tables is brisk in the conservatory-style Garden Room restaurant. Cooking breathes a contemporary feel into a traditional British menu, which specialises in local fish and seafood. Daily fixed-price menus may list tian of Salcombe crabmeat, tomato and avocado to start, followed by pan-fried sea bass with aubergine caviar and chorizo, with blueberry frangipane tart for dessert.

Chef: Finn Ibsen **Owners:** Edwards Family **Times:** 7-9, Closed Dec-Jan, Closed L all week **Prices:** Fixed D £36.50, Service included **Wine:** 90 bottles over £20, 14 bottles under £20, 6 by the glass **Notes:** Dress Restrictions, Smart casual, no jeans or T-shirts **Seats:** 80 **Children:** Min 8 yrs **Rooms:** 35 (35 en suite) ★★★ HL **Directions:** Take cliff road towards sea and Bolt Head **Parking:** 80

SAUNTON   MAP 03 SS43

◉ Saunton Sands Hotel

Modern British V NEW

Seaside hotel with a wide-ranging menu

☎ 01271 890212   EX33 1LQ
e-mail: reservations@sauntonsands.com
web: www.sauntonsands.com

Smart art deco hotel with stunning sea views and direct access to five miles of sandy beach. Dine in the restaurant, an airy room decorated

in traditional style, or at the new café/bar, which serves light lunches and imaginative evening meals. An extensive menu includes a grill selection for those in the mood for straightforward fare such as fresh lobster, lamb cutlets, or tender steak, as well as more involved dishes: fillet of beef in pancetta perhaps, served with a potato and mustard soufflé cake, shallot confit, black pudding and foie gras ravioli. Crisp-fried fillet of turbot is another typical main, accompanied by Champagne-poached oysters, asparagus, buttered spinach and Champagne sauce.

Chef: Graham Brundle **Owners:** Brend Hotels **Times:** 12.30-2/7.30-9.30 **Prices:** Fixed L £15.50, Fixed D £30-£48, Starter £8.95, Main £17, Dessert £8.95, Service optional **Wine:** 120 bottles over £20, 30 bottles under £20, 20 by the glass **Notes:** Fixed D 4 courses, Vegetarian menu, Dress Restrictions, Jacket and tie preferred, Civ Wed 200, Air con **Seats:** 250, Pr/dining room 100 **Children:** Menu, Portions **Rooms:** 92 (92 en suite) ★★★★ HL **Directions:** M5 junct 27 onto A361 towards Braunton, left onto B3231 Saunton rd. **Parking:** 100

SIDMOUTH   MAP 03 SY18

◉◉ Riviera Hotel

Modern British

Fine Regency hotel dining with sea views

☎ 01395 515201   The Esplanade EX10 8AY
e-mail: enquiries@hotelriviera.co.uk
web: www.hotelriviera.co.uk

This smart, bow-windowed Regency building at the centre of the Esplanade is true to its name - a classic English Riviera hotel with fine views over Lyme Bay. The chintzy-styled restaurant epitomises traditional standards, comfort and elegance, with windows offering sea views and a terrace perfect for alfresco summer dining. The kitchen's intelligent combination of innovative and more traditional dishes admirably plays to the gallery, with fixed-priced menus bolstered by carte and dedicated vegetarian options. Expect seared spiced salmon with pepper couscous, rösti potatoes, spring onion crème fraîche and caviar, perhaps followed by sautéed apricots served with pistachio nuts, clotted cream and vanilla syrup, or plump for one of the 'sweets from the trolley'.

Chef: Matthew Weaver **Owners:** Peter Wharton **Times:** 12.30-2/7-9 **Prices:** Fixed L £25, Fixed D £36, Starter £8.50-£12, Main £20.50-£29, Dessert £6-£6.95 **Wine:** 45 bottles over £20, 30 bottles under £20, 4 by the glass **Notes:** Fixed L 5 courses, Fixed D 6 courses, Vegetarian available, Smart casual, Air con **Seats:** 85, Pr/dining room 65 **Children:** Menu, Portions **Rooms:** 26 (26 en suite) ★★★★ HL **Directions:** From M5 junct 30 take A3052 to Sidmouth. Situated in centre of Esplanade **Parking:** 26

SIDMOUTH CONTINUED

◎◎ The Salty Monk

Modern British

Talented and stylish cooking in an old ecclesiastical building

☎ 01395 513174 Church St, Sidford EX10 9QP
e-mail: saltymonk@btconnect.com
web: www.saltymonk.co.uk

Originally a salt house used by Benedictine monks, this roadside building dates from the 16th century and is kept in immaculate condition. The lounge and bar are full of original character, while the L-shaped restaurant at the rear has a more contemporary feel with rich opulent colours; light and airy with views over the award-winning gardens. Tables are well spaced and West Country artists' work adorns the walls. Good use is made of local produce, especially fresh fish with dishes changing regularly to make the best of market availability. Take pan-fried fillets of line-caught sea bass on leek rösti with a casserole of mussels, while alternatives might include a filo parcel of braised ruby red brisket with honeyed root vegetables garnished with sirloin on a red wine and beef jus. Alfresco summer dining proves an added bonus.

Chef: Annette & Andy Witheridge **Owners:** Annette & Andy Witheridge
Times: 12-1.30/7-9, Closed 3 wks Jan, 2 wks Nov, Closed L Sun-Wed
Prices: Fixed L £18.50-£22, Fixed D £32.50, Service optional, Group min 15 service 10% **Wine:** 24 bottles over £20, 56 bottles under £20, 6 by the glass **Notes:** Mineral water complimentary, Smart casual **Seats:** 55, Pr/dining room 14 **Children:** Portions **Rooms:** 5 (5 en suite) ★★★★★ RR **Directions:** From M5 junct 30 take A3052 to Sidmouth, or from Honiton take A375 to Sidmouth, left at lights in Sidford, 200yds on right **Parking:** 18

◎ Victoria Hotel

Traditional

Victorian splendour, friendly service and appetising dishes

☎ 01395 512651 The Esplanade EX10 8RY
e-mail: info@victoriahotel.co.uk
web: www.victoriahotel.co.uk

The Victoria is a smart hotel in an elevated position at the end of the promenade, set in well tended gardens overlooking the bay. The interior retains its period character and the restaurant is a large room with high ceilings and ornate plaster moulding. The décor is restful and dividers with plantings break up the well-spaced tables. The menu offers traditional-style dishes with modern influences - grilled salmon

fillet with mustard sauce, roast loin of pork with apple sauce, Exmoor venison casserole or grilled lobster with lemon butter, prawns and saffron rice - notable for quality, freshness and flavour.

Times: 1-2/7-9 **Rooms:** 61 (61 en suite) ★★★★ HL **Directions:** At the western end of The Esplanade

---

SOUTH BRENT   MAP 03 SX66

◎ Glazebrook House Hotel & Restaurant

British

Flavourful cooking in a tranquil setting

☎ 01364 73322 TQ10 9JE
e-mail: enquiries@glazebrookhouse.com
web: www.glazebrookhouse.com

An 18th-century former gentleman's residence, this intimate country-house hotel is set in pretty gardens on the edge of Dartmoor National Park. Beautifully maintained and classic in style, it's a relaxing place to eat, with a log fire you won't want to move away from in winter. Local produce is selected for quality, and dishes are cooked to order and quite simply presented - your choice might include Dover sole poached in white wine with a tomato and tarragon sauce, or Gressingham duck roasted with honey and crushed peppercorns. Save room for dessert: chilled praline and Armagnac parfait perhaps, or fresh pineapple flamed in rum with coconut ice cream.

Chef: David Merriman **Owners:** Dave & Caroline Cashmore, Rob Walker
Times: 7-9, Closed 1 wk Jan, 1 wk Aug, Sun, Closed L all week
Prices: Fixed D £19.50-£26, Starter £4.50-£6.50, Main £16.50-£20.50, Dessert £4.50, Service optional **Wine:** 19 bottles over £20, 16 bottles under £20, 6 by the glass **Notes:** Civ Wed 80 **Seats:** 60, Pr/dining room 12 **Children:** Portions **Rooms:** 10 (10 en suite) ★★ HL
Directions: From A38, between Ivybridge and Buckfastleigh turn off at South Brent and follow hotel signs **Parking:** 40

TAVISTOCK   MAP 03 SX47

◎◎◎ Hotel Endsleigh

see opposite

THURLESTONE   MAP 03 SX64

◎ Thurlestone Hotel

Modern British V

Simple enjoyable food in long-established seaside hotel

☎ 01548 560382 TQ7 3NN
e-mail: enquiries@thurlestone.co.uk
web: www.thurlestone.co.uk

In the same family ownership since 1896, this elegant seaside hotel doesn't rest on its laurels, with an extensive selection of leisure facilities added over the years, including indoor and outdoor pools, a beauty salon and golf course. The restaurant benefits from floor-to-ceiling windows overlooking the bay. The menu changes daily and acknowledges its seaside location with plenty of local fish and seafood taking starring roles in dishes like tian of Salcombe crab, with mango, chilli, coriander and limes, or Brixham skate wing with spring onion mash, chargrilled courgettes and sauce vièrge. Banana bavarois with passionfruit syrup and English toffee ice cream won't disappoint at dessert.

CONTINUED ON PAGE 143

Hotel Endsleigh

TAVISTOCK   **MAP 03 SX47**

Modern European V 🖳

Memorable setting, stunning surroundings, accomplished cooking

☎ 01822 870000   Milton Abbot PL19 0PQ
e-mail: mail@hotelendsleigh.com
web: www.hotelendsleigh.com

Transformed into a boutique-style hotel by Olga Polizzi (see entry for Hotel Tresanton, St Mawes), this former shooting lodge was built in 1812 for the Duke of Bedford. Perched on a hillside in 108 acres of beautifully kept gardens and woodlands along a lovely stretch of the Tamar River, the location is quite stunning. The house is a grand, design-led place with many facets; some could be likened to French, some to traditional English and others really cottagey and quaint. Uniformed staff are professional, though with a friendly air, while the panelled dining room itself splits into two, and on fine sunny days the terrace overlooking the valley offers alfresco opportunities. In the evening, this magnificent room is entirely lit by candlelight. The accomplished kitchen shows pedigree, too, with Shay Cooper (ex Talland Bay Hotel, Talland Bay) at the helm, and focuses on high-quality local ingredients, the accurate cooking running on clean lines without too many unnecessary complexities. Its modern approach delivers accuracy and clear flavours - take a dinner offering of slow-cooked suckling pig with spring cabbage, butternut squash tortellini and shallot and thyme dressing, while mascarpone mousse with gingerbread lemon curd and rhubarb ice cream might head-up desserts.

Chef: Shay Cooper   **Owners:** Olga Polizzi   **Times:** 12.30-2.30/7-10   **Prices:** Fixed L £23, Fixed D £39, Service optional   **Wine:** 108 bottles over £20, 27 bottles under £20, 15 by the glass   **Notes:** Tasting menu available, Vegetarian menu, Civ Wed 100   **Seats:** 50, Pr/dining room 40   **Children:** Menu, Portions   **Directions:** Follow Tavistock signs for B3362, continue through Milton Abbot. On brow of hill, next to school, turn right for hotel. At top of drive turn right at lodge

---

The Elephant Bar & Restaurant

TORQUAY   **MAP 03 SX96**

Modern British 🍃

Contemporary harbourside restaurant with fresh vibrant food

☎ 01803 200044   3/4 Beacon Ter TQ1 2BH
e-mail: info@elephantrestaurant.co.uk
web: www.elephantrestaurant.co.uk

Housed in two stylishly converted Georgian houses overlooking the bustling harbour, the Elephant is a smart, contemporary restaurant that continues to impress. There are plans afoot to open a new first-floor fine-dining restaurant - The Room - which will showcase the award-winning cuisine of Simon Hulstone and his accomplished team, set against the backdrop of spectacular bay views. Downstairs, the more informal Elephant Brasserie has also been refurbished, open for lunch and dinner and serving good quality, simple brasserie dishes at affordable prices.
At the stove is a chef with a strong culinary pedigree, whose growing reputation for precise, confident and accomplished cooking sees the popularity of this establishment continue to blossom. Quality West Country ingredients and vibrant flavours shine through well-constructed dishes, and a six-course tasting menu is available alongside the carte; perhaps pan-roasted John Dory on parsnip purée with a verjus and spring onion butter sauce, or loin of Haldon Estate venison with vanilla-roasted butternut and baby beetroot jus, might jostle for your attention. To finish, perhaps dark chocolate truffle with passionfruit coulis and hibiscus jelly.

Chef: Simon Hulstone   **Owners:** Peter Morgan   **Times:** 11.30-2.30/6.30-9.30, Closed 1st 2 wks Jan, Sun (Wed in Feb-Mar)   **Prices:** Fixed L £15.95, Fixed D £22.50, Starter £6-£12, Main £13-£22, Dessert £6-£8, Service optional, Group min 8 service 10%   **Wine:** 36 bottles over £20, 15 bottles under £20, 9 by the glass   **Notes:** Vegetarian available, Air con   **Seats:** 65, Pr/dining room 25   **Children:** Portions   **Directions:** Follow signs for Living Coast, restaurant opposite   **Parking:** Opposite restaurant

Corbyn Head Hotel & Orchid Restaurant

TORQUAY MAP 03 SX96

Modern British

Superb views combine with superlative cooking

☎ 01803 296366 & 213611   Sea Front TQ2 6RH
e-mail: dine@orchidrestaurant.net
web: www.orchidrestaurant.net

Renowned fine-dining restaurant in a luxurious resort hotel overlooking Torbay. Smartly refurbished in simple style, the Orchid has an upmarket ambience and treats its guests to well-spaced, elegantly clothed tables and stunning views across the bay. Service is similarly formal and mainly French, while the food is refreshingly simple and modern.
There's a confidence to the cooking that impresses, with dishes notable for both imagination and top-notch local produce: you might start with marinated salmon, oyster beignet, pickled cucumber and horseradish cream, and then tuck into a pavé of halibut with vanilla, peas à la française, pomme dauphinoise and a red wine reduction, or South Devon beef fillet with fried organic egg, pomme Pont-Neuf and Dijon foam. Desserts are similarly divine and include the likes of kaffir limeleaf crème brûlée, served with coconut sorbet, or white chocolate Bailey's parfait with praline biscuits and caramelised banana. Ancillaries like canapés, bread and petits fours maintain the form through to the end.

Chef: Daniel Kay / Marc Evans
Owners: Rew Hotels Ltd
Times: 12.30-2.30/7-9.30, Closed 2 wks Jan, 2 wks Nov, 1wk Apr, Sun-Mon, Closed L Tue
Prices: Fixed L £20.95, Fixed D £35.95, Service optional
Wine: 47 bottles over £20, 65 bottles under £20, 11 by the glass
Notes: Dress Restrictions, Formal dress/smart casual, no trainers, Air con
Seats: 26
Children: Min 6 yrs, Menu, Portions
Rooms: 45 (45 en suite) ★★★ HL
Directions: Follow signs to Torquay seafront, turn right, hotel on right on the edge of Cockington Valley, on seafront
Parking: 50

THURLESTONE *Continued*

Chef: H Miller **Owners:** Grose family **Times:** 12.30-2.30/7.30-9, Closed L Mon-Sat **Prices:** Fixed L £18-£19, Fixed D £35-£37.50, Service optional **Wine:** 113 bottles over £20, 40 bottles under £20, 8 by the glass **Notes:** Fixed L 3 courses, Fixed D 4 courses, Fish tasting menu, Vegetarian menu, Dress Restrictions, Jacket, Civ Wed 150, Air con **Seats:** 150, Pr/dining room 150 **Children:** Menu, Portions **Rooms:** 64 (64 en suite) ★★★★ HL **Directions:** At Buckfastleigh on A38, take A384 into Totnes and then A381 (Kingsbridge). Continue for 10m then turn right at mini rdbt onto A379 towards Churchstow, turn left at rdbt onto B3197, then turn right into lane signed Thurlestone **Parking:** 120

TORQUAY   MAP 03 SX96

◉◉◉ Corbyn Head Hotel & Orchid Restaurant

see opposite

◉◉◉ The Elephant Bar & Restaurant

see page 141

◉ Orestone Manor Hotel & Restaurant

Modern
Beguiling country house serving West Country produce

☎ 01803 328098 Rock House Lane, Maidencombe TQ1 4SX
e-mail: enquiries@orestonemanor.com
web: www.orestonemanor.com

There has been a change of hands and a change of chef at this colonial-style manor house. It's located away from Torquay town centre in wooded seclusion with views of the coast and Lyme Bay. The elegant restaurant, decorated in bold colours, offers an imaginative menu that takes full advantage of wonderful seasonal, local produce, including South Devon beef and Lathy Farm ham, plus herbs, fruits and vegetables from the kitchen garden. Butter-poached fillet of South Devon beef with confit onion and horseradish emulsion or halibut steak with white bean cassoulet and ham hock beignet are fine examples of the fare. A Terrace menu is available in the summer months.

Times: 12-2.30/7-9 **Rooms:** 12 (12 en suite) ★★★ **Directions:** From Teignmouth take A379 through Shaldon towards Torquay. 3m take sharp left into Rockhouse Lane. Hotel signed **Parking:** 40

TOTNES   MAP 03 SX86

◉ The Normandy Arms

Modern European NEW
Revitalised village local serving seriously good food

☎ 01803 712884 Chapel St TQ9 7BN
e-mail: peter.alcroft@btconnect.com
web: www.thenormandyarms.co.uk

Taking a serious approach to food, this recently refurbished village local comes with a rapidly expanding fan base, while successfully managing to stay true to its pubby roots by retaining a small bar. Inside is open-plan with a simple, uncluttered feel; think tiled floors

and solid-wood tables, while the delightful service comes without airs and graces. The accomplished kitchen's sensibly compact menus fit the bill perfectly, with careful but unfussy presentation and bold flavours that allow the quality produce centre stage; take pan-fried fillet of brill served with sautéed wild mushrooms, cod fritters and a balsamic reduction.

Chef: Peter Alcroft **Owners:** Peter Alcroft, Sharon Murdoch **Times:** 12-2/7-11, Closed 25 Dec, last wk Jan, 2nd wk Sep, Mon, Closed L Tue, D Sun **Prices:** Fixed L £12.95, Starter £4-£7.95, Main £9.95-£16.95, Dessert £4.95, Service optional **Wine:** 6 bottles over £20, 14 bottles under £20, 6 by the glass **Seats:** 40 **Children:** Menu, Portions **Directions:** From Totnes follow A3188 for 9m and continue onto the A3122 (Dartmouth Rd) and turn right into the village of Blackawton **Parking:** 3

TWO BRIDGES   MAP 03 SX67

◉ Prince Hall Hotel

Modern British V
Carefully sourced food at a Dartmoor hotel

☎ 01822 890403 PL20 6SA
e-mail: info@princehall.co.uk
web: www.princehall.co.uk

The hotel was built as a private residence and dates back some 200 years. The restaurant, stylishly combining the historical and the contemporary, has exposed granite walls hung with modern paintings and offers stunning moor and river views. Dishes are based on local produce, and thought is given to flavour, texture and visual excitement. Starters might include seared Copplestone pigeon with crispy Denhay air-dried ham and white grape and walnut jus, with roast West Country monkfish fillet with mussels and tarragon-scented tagliatelle to follow, and treacle and quince compôte tart with duo of mango sorbet and coulis for dessert.

Chef: Marc Slater, Anne Grove **Owners:** John & Anne Grove **Times:** 7-8.30, Closed Jan-early Feb, Closed L Mon-Sun **Prices:** Fixed D £35-£40, Service optional, Group min 8 service 10% **Wine:** 17 bottles over £20, 22 bottles under £20, 4 by the glass **Notes:** Vegetarian menu, Dress Restrictions, Smart casual preferred **Seats:** 24 **Children:** Min 10 yrs **Rooms:** 8 (8 en suite) ★★ CHH **Directions:** Located on B3357 (Ashburton to Tavistock road), 1m E of Two Bridges junct with B3212 **Parking:** 12

WOODBURY   MAP 03 SY08

® Woodbury Park Hotel, Golf & Country Club

Modern European

Modern hotel with straightforward cooking and lavish leisure facilities

☎ 01395 233382   Woodbury Castle EX5 1JJ
e-mail: enquiries@woodburypark.co.uk
web: www.woodburypark.co.uk

Owned by Grand Prix champion Nigel Mansell and set in 500 acres of grounds, this hotel has good leisure facilities including golf and The World of Racing Museum. The Atrium Restaurant is modern in style and has a welcoming atmosphere, with staff striking just the right balance between formality and friendliness. Menus comprise simple, modern British dishes with the occasional Mediterranean accent. Typical examples include goat's cheese and tapenade parcel on rocket salad, followed by pan-fried lamb rump, accurately cooked just as requested. Lemon tart for dessert has good depth of flavour, or maybe try brioche and butter pudding with apricot and white chocolate.

Chef: Marion Dorricott **Times:** 12-2.30/6-9.30, Closed L Mon-Sat **Prices:** Fixed L £12.50-£22.50, Fixed D £15-£30, Starter £4.50-£9.95, Main £10-£20.95, Dessert £4.50-£9.95, Service optional **Wine:** 12 bottles over £20, 20 bottles under £20 **Notes:** Sun L carvery available, Vegetarian available, Dress Restrictions, Smart casual, no jeans or T-shirts, Civ Wed 150, Air con **Seats:** 100, Pr/dining room 180 **Children:** Menu, Portions **Rooms:** 60 (60 en suite) ★★★★ HL **Directions:** M5 junct 30, take A376/A3052 towards Sidmouth, turn right opposite Halfway Inn onto B3180 towards Budleigh Salterton to Woodbury Common, hotel signed on right **Parking:** 400

WOOLACOMBE   MAP 03 SS44

® Watersmeet Hotel

European

Edwardian property in a stunning seaside location

☎ 01271 870333   Mortehoe EX34 7EB
e-mail: info@watersmeethotel.co.uk
web: www.watersmeethotel.co.uk

Dinner at the Watersmeet has a dramatic backdrop - sunset over the rugged north Atlantic coast and Woolacombe Bay to Lundy Island. Wide windows and a tiered Pavilion restaurant ensure that most tables take advantage of the panoramic views, which no doubt contributes to the relaxed and friendly atmosphere. The kitchen draws on quality local produce, particularly fresh fish, to deliver dishes such as seared king scallops with a carrot and coriander rösti and yoghurt dressing, or

mains along the lines of veal loin steak with a Madeira sauce and sweet potato and apple dauphinoise. Save room for desserts like Bramley apple crumble with blackberry ice cream.

Chef: John Prince **Owners:** Mr & Mrs James **Times:** 12-2/7-8.30, Closed L all week **Prices:** Fixed L £13.95, Fixed D £44.95, Service optional **Notes:** Fixed D 5 courses, Dress Restrictions, Jacket & tie preferred **Seats:** 50 **Children:** Min 8 yrs, Portions **Rooms:** 25 (25 en suite) ★★★ HL **Directions:** M5 junct 27. Follow A361 to Woolacombe, right at beach car park, 300yds on right **Parking:** 40

YEALMPTON   MAP 03 SX55

® The Rose & Crown

Modern British, Pacific Rim

Village gastro-pub

☎ 01752 880223   Market St PL8 2EB
e-mail: info@theroseandcrown.co.uk
web: www.theroseandcrown.co.uk

Part of owner John Steven's burgeoning empire of gastro-pubs (which includes the Dartmoor Union at Holbeton), this ordinary village local has been transformed into a stylish modern eatery with large, comfortable sofas, an enticing log fire and an open plan bar. While there's an international bistro feel to this informal menu, local produce is very much in evidence in dishes such as hand-picked Newlyn crab with sweet pepper coulis and pesto to start or rib-eye of Ugborough beef with béarnaise sauce.

Chef: Laur Gales **Owners:** Wykeham Inns Ltd **Times:** 12-2/6.30-9.30 **Prices:** Fixed L £9.95, Fixed D £12.95, Starter £3.95-£5.50, Main £8.95-£17.50, Dessert £3.95-£5.50, Service optional **Wine:** 3 bottles over £20, 15 bottles under £20, 12 by the glass **Notes:** Tasting menu £35.00 **Seats:** 38, Pr/dining room 8 **Children:** Min 12 yrs, Portions **Directions:** A379 8m from Plymouth. A38 from Exeter, take A3121 through Ermington, turn right onto A379 towards Plymouth **Parking:** 70

®® The Seafood Restaurant

Seafood

Quality dining in contemporary setting

☎ 01752 880502   Market St PL8 2EB
e-mail: info@theroseandcrown.co.uk
web: www.theroseandcrown.co.uk

Opposite The Rose & Crown, at first sight, oak floorboards and whitewashed wood-panelled walls may give the impression of a fisherman's shanty, but the atmosphere is thoroughly modern and minimal, with well-spaced white-clothed tables and an open kitchen giving diners a feeling of involvement. Photographs of local fishing boats and fisherman complete the décor, while the formal table service delivers accomplished modern British seafood dishes, using the freshest local produce. Kick off with a starter of succulent seared scallops served with a warm Jerusalem artichoke mousse, beignets and truffle sauce. Main courses may include pan-fried brill with bubble-and-squeak, scallops and sauce gribiche, followed by steamed ginger sponge with caramel sauce, or warm mango and lime rice pudding with passionfruit sorbet.

Chef: Daniel Gillard **Owners:** Wykeham Inns Ltd **Times:** 12-2/6.30-9.30, Closed Mon, Closed D Sun **Prices:** Fixed L £9.95, Fixed D £12.95, Starter £3.95-£5.50, Main £8.95-£17.50, Dessert £3.95-£5.50, Service optional **Wine:** 3 bottles over £20, 15 bottles under £20, 12 by the glass **Notes:** Tasting menu £35 **Seats:** 40 **Children:** Min 12 yrs, Portions **Directions:** A379 8m from Plymouth. A38 from Exeter, take A3121 through Ermington, turn right onto A379 towards Plymouth **Parking:** 70

YELVERTON   MAP 03 SX56

⊛ Moorland Links Hotel

Traditional British

Classic cooking in hotel with views

☎ 01822 852245   PL20 6DA
e-mail: moorland.links@forestdale.com
web: www.forestdale.com

Set in 9 acres of well-tended grounds in Dartmoor National Park, this long-established hotel overlooks spectacular moorland scenery and the Tamar Valley. Understandably, it's a popular venue for weddings. The restaurant is formal but relaxed and friendly, and has a good local following. The classical décor of the room is matched by British cuisine with French influences (think coquilles St Jacques, or suprême of chicken with mushrooms, shallots, and bacon in red wine sauce). Light meals are served in the Gun Room Bar and afternoon tea can be enjoyed in the lounge.

Chef: Steven Holmes **Owners:** Forestdale Hotels Ltd **Times:** 12.30-2/7.30-10 **Prices:** Starter £4.50-£7.50, Main £14-£22, Dessert £4.50-£6.50 **Wine:** 12 bottles over £20, 23 bottles under £20, 6 by the glass **Notes:** Sun L £13.50, Vegetarian available, Civ Wed 150 **Seats:** 90, Pr/dining room 150 **Children:** Menu, Portions **Rooms:** 44 (44 en suite) ★★★ HL **Directions:** Please telephone for directions **Parking:** 100

DORSET

BEAMINSTER   MAP 04 ST40

⊛ Bridge House Hotel

British

Good food, locally sourced, in Beaminster's oldest building

☎ 01308 862200   3 Prout Bridge DT8 3AY
e-mail: enquiries@bridge-house.co.uk
web: www.bridge-house.co.uk

A lovely period property with immense character, dating from the 13th century and with plenty of original features, including mullioned windows, inglenook fireplaces and even a priest's hole. There's nothing covert about the restaurant, however, a striking Georgian panelled room with a subtle modish tone and small conservatory to one side. The kitchen makes good use of local produce on an appealing modern menu, the fixed-price repertoire offering a versatile choice that might include pan-roasted monkfish tail on a bed of buttered spinach, served with chargrilled new potatoes and curried mussel sauce, and perhaps a baked egg custard tart with date and pecan compôte to finish.

Chef: Mrs Linda Paget **Owners:** Mark and Joanna Donovan **Times:** 12-2/7-9 **Prices:** Fixed L £10, Fixed D £31.50, Service optional, Group min 10 service 10% **Wine:** 36 bottles over £20, 35 bottles under £20, 11 by the glass **Notes:** Sun L 2 courses £13, Vegetarian available, Civ Wed 50 **Seats:** 36, Pr/dining room 30 **Children:** Portions **Rooms:** 14 (14 en suite) ★★★ HL **Directions:** From A303 take A356 towards Dorchester. Turn right onto A3066, 200mtrs down hill from town centre **Parking:** 20

BLANDFORD FORUM   MAP 04 ST80

⊛ Castleman Hotel

British, French

Pleasant country hotel with good-value food

☎ 01258 830096   Chettle DT11 8DB
e-mail: enquiry@castlemanhotel.co.uk
web: www.castlemanhotel.co.uk

The former dower house to the Chettle Estate dates back 400 years and exudes historic atmosphere, from the Regency-style drawing room and ornate plasterwork ceilings in the dining room, to Jacobean fireplaces and a fine galleried hall. The restaurant is a long airy room with soft yellow walls and indigo curtains, where the British-based menu makes good use of local seasonal produce. The dinner party-style menu offers the likes of chicken liver parfait with spiced apricot chutney, or grilled whole turbot with red pepper, anchovy and caper butter. Appealing desserts includes the likes of dark chocolate and morello cherry torte, or rhubarb frangipane tart with honey ice cream.

Chef: Barbara Garnsworthy, R Morris **Owners:** Edward Bourke, Barbara Garnsworthy **Times:** 12/7, Closed Feb, 25, 26 & 31 Dec, Closed L Mon-Sat **Prices:** Fixed L £21, Starter £4-£6, Main £9-£18, Dessert £5, Service optional **Wine:** 6 by the glass **Notes:** Fixed L 3 courses **Seats:** 40 **Children:** Portions **Directions:** 1m from A354. Hotel is signed in village **Parking:** 20

BOURNEMOUTH   MAP 05 SZ09

⊛ Best Western the Connaught Hotel

Modern British NEW

Friendly, relaxed hotel restaurant serving unpretentious cuisine

☎ 01202 298020   West Hill Rd, West Cliff BH2 5PH
e-mail: sales@the connaught.co.uk
web: www.theconnaught.co.uk

Conveniently located on the West Cliff close to the beaches and town centre, this privately-owned hotel has a relaxed and friendly atmosphere, though staff are appropriately professional. The unpretentious-styled restaurant comes decked out in white table linen donned with fresh flowers, while the kitchen delivers simply cooked and presented dishes from quality local produce. Take blackened cod accompanied by mushrooms, garlic-scented mash and chive oil, or perhaps rump of Bridport lamb served with tomato jam, thyme and a red wine jus. Finish with lemon tart or bread-and-butter pudding with apricot compôte.

Times: 6.30-9, Closed L all week **Rooms:** 89 (89 en suite) ★★★ HL

BOURNEMOUTH CONTINUED

Bistro on the Beach

Rosettes not confirmed at time of going to press

Modern British

Popular, thoroughly unpretentious seaside café-bistro

☎ 01202 431473 Solent Promenade,
Southbourne Coast Rd, Southbourne BH6 4BE
e-mail: bistroonthebeach@yahoo.co.uk
web: www.bistroonthebeach.co.uk

The name says it all, sat smack on the seafront promenade with superb sea views through floor-to-ceiling windows and aqua-coloured walls that bring the seaside theme indoors - the steep walk down the slope from the road is worth the effort. Totally unpretentious, relaxed and informal (blue plastic tables and chairs), this is strictly no-frills dining; by day a popular beachfront café, by night, cranking up a gear as a casual bistro. The food is as straightforward and unfussy as the surroundings and takes a modern approach, including the likes of half crispy aromatic chicken with cocotte potatoes, mushrooms and salad.

Times: Café from 9am Jun-Sept, Bistro from 6.30pm Jun-Sept. Please telephone for further details **Directions:** From Bournemouth take coast road to East Cliff, at lights right, then right again. Join overcliff. 1m to mini rdbt, take 2nd turn. 400yds to car park

⊛ Chine Hotel

Modern European

Seaside hotel with views from spacious restaurant

☎ 01202 396234 Boscombe Spa Rd BH5 1AX
e-mail: reservations@chinehotel.co.uk
web: www.fjbhotels.co.uk

Benefiting from superb views over the treetops and out to sea across Poole Bay, this popular hotel and former 19th-century school stands in delightful gardens with private access to the seafront and beach. Open for both lunch and dinner, the Seaview Restaurant makes the most of its location with huge picture windows and classic décor. The cooking style is modern British with Mediterranean influences, the set three-course menus making good use of quality ingredients. For starters, why not take salmon fishcakes with home-made tartare sauce, followed perhaps by a well cooked breast of duck, or fillet of bass with seafood sauce and ribbon vegetables.

Chef: Jesse Uzzell **Owners:** Brownsea Haven Properties Ltd
Times: 12.30-2/7-9, Closed L Sat **Prices:** Fixed L £12.50, Fixed D £25.95, Service optional **Wine:** 43 bottles over £20, 19 bottles under £20, 13 by the glass **Notes:** Sun L 3 courses £13.50 incl coffee, Vegetarian available, Dress Restrictions, No jeans, T-shirts or trainers at D, Civ Wed 130, Air con **Seats:** 160, Pr/dining room 130 **Children:** Menu, Portions **Rooms:** 87 (87 en suite) ★★★ HL **Directions:** From M27, A31 and A338 follow signs to Boscombe Pier, Boscombe Spa Rd is off Christchurch Rd near Boscombe Gardens **Parking:** 67

⊛ Langtry Restaurant

Modern V

Contemporary cuisine in an Edwardian setting

☎ 01202 553887 Langtry Manor, 26 Derby Rd, East Cliff
BH1 3QB
e-mail: lillie@langtrymanor.com
web: www.langtrymanor.com

This splendid Edwardian manor was built by Edward VII in 1877 for Lillie Langtry as a 'love nest' for their illicit affair. The restaurant, where Edwardian banquets were once held, is in keeping with the house's origins, complete with minstrels' gallery, rich décor and elegant tableware. The fixed-price menu offers a good range of dishes and features some local and seasonal produce such as poached fillet of beef with root vegetables and horseradish dumplings. An open omelette of goat's cheese and baby spinach with rocket salad can be found on the separate vegetarian menu.

Chef: Matthew Clements **Owners:** Mrs P Hamilton-Howard **Times:** 12-2/7-9, Closed L all week **Prices:** Fixed D £29.50, Service optional **Notes:** Fixed D 2 courses, Sun L menu available monthly, Vegetarian menu, Dress Restrictions, Smart casual, Civ Wed 100 **Seats:** 60, Pr/dining room 16 **Children:** Menu, Portions **Rooms:** 20 (20 en suite) ★★★ HL **Directions:** On the East Cliff, at corner of Derby & Knyveton Roads **Parking:** 20

⊛ 'Oscars' at the De Vere Royal Bath Hotel

Modern British

City-centre hotel restaurant with a fine reputation

☎ 01202 555555 Bath Rd BH1 2EW
web: www.devere.co.uk

Once a haunt of Oscar Wilde, this historic Victorian hotel with panoramic views across Bournemouth sea front, has lent his name to the house restaurant. The attentive staff at Oscar's add to the formal yet friendly atmosphere that pervades the stylishly retro-themed dining rooms. The menu consists largely of classic British dishes with an imaginative twist, using the freshest, locally-sourced ingredients. Start with seared king scallops with saffron, then, after sampling a refreshing pink gin and grapefruit sorbet, progress onto pan-fried fillet of Hampshire pork with carrot mash, caramelised apple, braised Savoy cabbage and bacon cider cream.

Chef: Andrew Crowley **Owners:** De Vere - AHG **Times:** 12.30-1.45/7-9.45 **Prices:** Fixed L £15, Fixed D £25, Starter £6.50-£9.50, Main £13-£24, Dessert £6.50-£7.50, Service optional **Wine:** 29 bottles over £20, 13 bottles under £20, 10 by the glass **Notes:** Fixed L 3 courses, Vegetarian available, Dress Restrictions, Smart dress, Civ Wed 400 **Seats:** 80, Pr/dining room 240 **Children:** Menu, Portions **Rooms:** 140 (140 en suite) ★★★★ HL **Directions:** A338 follow signs for pier and beaches. Hotel is in Bath Rd, just before the Bournemouth International Centre **Parking:** 70

West Beach

Modern

Buzzy, modern, relaxed beachfront restaurant

☎ 01202 587785 Pier Approach BH2 5AA
e-mail: info@west-beach.co.uk
web: www.west-beach.co.uk

This contemporary, relaxed brasserie is ideally situated on the prom overlooking the pier and beach, and enjoys uninterrupted sea views through floor-to-ceiling windows, which open in summer. Light colours and pale wood create a light and airy modern vibe, and there's a decked terrace for alfresco dining in summer. The open kitchen (with chefs on show) uses the freshest of ingredients, delivering a simple, modern menu with a focus on seafood. You might start with scallops and sunblushed tomato risotto with rocket pesto, followed by monkfish medallions with Parma ham, pesto spaghetti and sauce vièrge, and crème brûlée with raspberry and Bacardi compôte to finish. Tempting children's menu available.

Chef: Lee Bishop, Neil Mooney **Owners:** Andrew Price **Times:** 12-3.30/6-10, Closed 25 Dec, Closed D 26 Jan, 1 Jan **Prices:** Fixed L £25-£50, Fixed D £25-£50, Starter £4.50-£8, Main £7.50-£50, Dessert £5.50-£6, Service optional, Group min 10 service 10% **Wine:** 41 bottles over £20, 16 bottles under £20 **Notes:** Fixed L 3 courses, Dress Restrictions, No bare feet or bikinis, Air con **Seats:** 90 **Children:** Menu, Portions **Directions:** 100yds W of the pier **Parking:** NCP 2 mins

Riverside Restaurant

Seafood, International

Seaside location for celebrated 1970s architecture and local seafood

☎ 01308 422011 West Bay DT6 4EZ
e-mail: artwatfish@hotmail.com
web: thefishrestaurant-westbay.co.uk

This 'island' restaurant - overlooking the busy West Bay fishing port - was designed in the late 1970s by the well-known architect Piers Gough, and has been widely acclaimed for its use of natural materials. The business has been in the same family for some 44 years, with the emphasis today unsurprisingly based around fresh fish and shellfish - mostly from local waters - alongside an intelligent, simply-cooked approach. Take Lyme Bay dressed crab, Devon rock oysters, or perhaps a fillet of brill served with crispy spinach and a sorrel sauce. Meat and vegetarian options are offered on the daily specials list.

Chef: N Larcombe, G Marsh, G Blogg **Owners:** Mr & Mrs A Watson **Times:** 12-2.30/6.30-9.00, Closed 26 Nov-mid Feb/Valentines Day, Mon (ex BHs), Closed D Sun **Prices:** Fixed L £16, Starter £4.75-£8.95, Main £11.95-£19.50, Dessert £4.50-£6.25, Service optional, Group min 6 service 10% **Wine:** 23 bottles over £20, 35 bottles under £20, 10 by the glass **Notes:** Vegetarian available **Seats:** 70, Pr/dining room 30 **Children:** Menu, Portions **Directions:** A35 Bridport ring road, turn to West Bay at Crown rdbt **Parking:** Public car park closeby

ENGLAND

CHRISTCHURCH   MAP 05 SZ19

⚫ The Avonmouth Hotel and Restaurant

Modern British

Hotel restaurant offering innovative cuisine

☎ 01202 483434 95 Mudeford BH23 3NT
e-mail: info@theavonmouth.co.uk
web: www.theavonmouth.co.uk

Built in the 1830s as a gentleman's residence, this elegant hotel offers lovely views of Mudeford Quay and Christchurch Harbour. The elegant Quays restaurant is tastefully decorated in muted shades of green and blue. Local produce features on an interesting menu with dishes like Dorset air-dried ham with melon and parmesan salad to start, while main courses might include red mullet fillet with a saffron risotto and grilled red onions.

Times: 12-2/7-9.30 **Rooms:** 40 (40 en suite) ★★★ HL **Directions:** 1m from A35, outside Christchurch

Best Western Waterford Lodge Hotel

Rosettes not confirmed at time of going to press

Modern

Informal restaurant with knowledgeable staff

☎ 01425 272948 87 Bure Ln, Friars Cliff, Mudeford BH23 4DN
e-mail: waterford@bestwestern.co.uk
web: www.waterfordlodge.com

It used to be the lodge to Highcliffe Castle, but this old building has been extended and modernised to become a hotel popular with business and holiday users. The intimate restaurant is relaxed and friendly, and overlooks the pretty gardens complete with fish pond. The carefully prepared food is brought by attentive staff who make everyone feel at home. Modern creations like millefeuille of oak-smoked salmon and crisp wafer potatoes might appear on the fixed-price menus, with perhaps slow-braised haunch of New Forest venison cooked with juniper, red wine and thyme, and dark chocolate torte with Kirsch-soaked cherries, coffee sauce and hazelnut crisp. At the time of going to press a new chef had been appointed.

Chef: Daniel Foy **Owners:** Michael & Vicki Harrison **Times:** 12-1.30/7-9 **Prices:** Fixed L £12.50-£16.50, Fixed D £27.50-£29.50, Starter £4.50-£7.50, Main £12.50-£17.50, Dessert £4.50-£7.50, Service optional **Wine:** 4 by the glass **Notes:** Dress Restrictions, No jeans, trainers or T-shirts **Seats:** 40, Pr/dining room 70 **Children:** Min 7 yrs, Menu, Portions **Rooms:** 18 (18 en suite) ★★★ HL **Directions:** A35 through Lyndhurst to Christchurch. Turn left onto A337. Follow signs to rdbt to hotel **Parking:** 36

⚫⚫ Captain's Club Hotel

International NEW

Contemporary riverside restaurant focusing on locally-sourced ingredients

☎ 01202 475111 Wick Ferry, Wick Ln BH23 1HU
e-mail: enquiries@captainsclubhotel.com
web: www.captainsclubhotel.com

This modern hotel beside the River Stour has a luxurious, contemporary interior. The appropriately-named Tides restaurant comes decked out with wooden tables, fabric-covered chairs and carpeted floors, while large patio windows overlook the river along one side. Service is professional and friendly, with waiting staff in long black aprons. The kitchen deals in quality fresh local ingredients, the uncomplicated, attractively presented, modern dishes delivering their promised flavours. Menu favourites might include roasted monkfish wrapped in Parma ham and served with saffron potatoes and a shellfish broth, perhaps rib-eye steak with thick-cut chips, grilled tomatoes and béarnaise, or, from the shellfish options, local Mudeford crab with lemon and herb mayonnaise. Finish with a Granny Smith apple tart and cinnamon ice cream.

Chef: Andrew Gault **Owners:** Platinum One Hotels Ltd **Times:** 12-2.30/7-10 **Prices:** Starter £6-£12, Main £13-£35, Dessert £6-£8, Service optional **Wine:** 90 bottles over £20, 35 bottles under £20, 14 by the glass **Notes:** Civ Wed 100, Air con **Seats:** 72, Pr/dining room 44 **Children:** Menu, Portions **Rooms:** 29 (29 en suite) ★★★★ HL **Directions:** Hotel just off Christchurch High St, towards Christchurch Quay **Parking:** 41

⚫⚫ The Lord Bute Hotel & Restaurant

British, European

Fine dining in sumptuous surroundings

☎ 01425 278884 170-181 Lymington Rd, Highcliffe-on-Sea BH23 4JS
e-mail: mail@lordbute.co.uk
web: www.lordbute.co.uk

The historic setting for this hotel and restaurant is in grounds just behind the original entrance lodges of Highcliffe Castle. The entrance hall displays pictures of former resident and Prime Minister Lord Bute, as well as famous visitors to the castle. Diners can relax in the orangery or patio area for pre-dinner drinks, before taking a seat in the elegantly furnished restaurant. Well-prepared modern British food is on offer here, making good use of quality produce, sourced locally where possible. Take a duo of pork (roasted tenderloin filled with apricot and dusted with herbs, served with pepper-crusted pork belly, champ potato and an apple and cider glaze), or perhaps grilled Dover sole with a fresh lime crown and parsley butter.

The Lord Bute Hotel & Restaurant

Times: 12-2/7-9.30, Closed Mon, Closed L Sat, D Sun **Rooms:** 13 (13 en suite) ★★★★★ GA **Directions:** Follow A337 to Lymington, opposite St Mark's churchyard in Highcliffe

◉ The Ship In Distress

Seafood NEW

Buzzing local pub restaurant serving plenty of fresh seafood

☎ 01202 485123 66 Stanpit BH23 3NA

This lively, popular pub has cosy sofas and bar seating. The restaurant is at the rear and has a blue, fish theme reflecting a menu based firmly around seafood. Young, local staff are very friendly and serve a loyal following from the area and further afield. Bar meals and snacks supplement a full carte and daily specials like langoustine and tomato linguine or whole rainbow trout. Starters might include pan-fried foie gras and quail's eggs en croûte with watercress salad, while desserts feature a fantastic lemon tart with clotted cream. Alfresco dining is available during warmer weather.

Times: 12/6.30

◉◉ Splinters Restaurant

British, International

Family-run restaurant in listed building

☎ 01202 483454 12 Church St BH23 1BW
e-mail: eating@splinters.uk.com
web: www.splinters.uk.com

The prettiest of a row of quaint buildings leading up to the old priory, this Christchurch institution oozes character with its winding corridor, old wooden staircase, cosy booths and various nooks and crannies. The main focus is the bar-lounge from which five private dining areas lead. Begin with a tasty chicken liver parfait perhaps, served with Cumberland sauce and toasted brioche, and then move on to Barbary duck breast served on roasted butternut squash with orange and peach sauce. Desserts should also delight: try poached pear with Grand Marnier parfait and chocolate sauce, or fig, lemon and walnut pudding served warm with lemon syrup and honey yogurt. The cooking, like the service and setting, is consistently appealing.

Chef: Paul Putt **Owners:** Paul & Agnes Putt **Times:** 11-2/7-10, Closed 26 Dec, 1-10 Jan, Sun-Mon **Prices:** Fixed L £10.95, Fixed D £25.95-£37.50, Main £30.50-£37.50, Service included, Group min 8 service 10% **Wine:** 91 bottles over £20, 28 bottles under £20, 4 by the glass **Notes:** ALC 2-3 courses, Vegetarian available **Seats:** 42, Pr/dining room 30 **Children:** Portions **Directions:** Directly in front of Priory gates

---

CORFE CASTLE   MAP 04 SY98

◉◉ Mortons House Hotel

Traditional British

Notable dining in Elizabethan surroundings

☎ 01929 480988 East St BH20 5EE
e-mail: stay@mortonshouse.co.uk
web: www.mortonshouse.co.uk

With the ruins of Corfe Castle as a backdrop and set in delightful gardens and grounds, this impressive Tudor house was built in an 'E' shape to honour Queen Elizabeth I. Beautifully updated and stylishly furnished, it retains a timeless feel. The serene oak-panelled dining room may have formal table settings, but service is friendly and knowledgeable. Classical in style, the British and international cooking is skilful and accomplished, with well-executed dishes utilising produce of high quality, sourced locally wherever possible. Seared scallops with Jerusalem artichoke risotto and hazelnut sauce, or braised shin of beef with parsnip purée, cep boudin and baby beetroot are fine examples of the fare. For dessert, why not try Grand Marnier soufflé, served with a mandarin granité.

Chef: Ed Firth **Owners:** Mr & Mrs Hageman, Mr & Mrs Clayton **Times:** 12-1.45/7-9 **Prices:** Starter £5-£10, Main £15-£25, Dessert £5-£10, Service optional, Group min 20 service 10% **Wine:** 55 bottles over £20, 8 bottles under £20, 4 by the glass **Notes:** Sun L 3 courses £19.50 incl coffee, Vegetarian available, Dress Restrictions, Smart casual, Civ Wed 60 **Seats:** 50, Pr/dining room 22 **Children:** Min 5 yrs, Menu, Portions **Rooms:** 21 (21 en suite) ★★★ HL **Directions:** In centre of village on A351 **Parking:** 40

CORFE MULLEN   MAP 04 SY99

◉ The Coventry Arms

Modern British

Local delicacies in popular country pub

☎ 01258 857284 Mill St BH21 3RH

Ideally situated by the river, this converted 15th-century watermill oozes rustic, old-world charm with its original flagstone floors, large open fireplace, low ceilings and exposed beams. The fishing paraphernalia reflects the interests of the proprietor, who supplies the menu with local rod-caught trout. Local produce also includes a variety of game when in season and venison, pigeon and pheasant are sourced from local estates. The modern British menu includes the likes of terrine of crab and lobster with langoustines, followed by fillet of John Dory with mussels, clams and saffron chowder.

Chef: Ian Gibbs **Owners:** John Hugo & David Armstrong Reed **Times:** 12-2.30/6-9.30 **Prices:** Starter £5-£8.50, Main £10-£19, Dessert £5.25-£6, Service optional **Wine:** 10 bottles over £20, 10 bottles under £20, 10 by the glass **Seats:** 70 **Children:** Menu, Portions **Directions:** A31 2m from Wimborne **Parking:** 50

CRANBORNE   MAP 05 SU01

◉ La Fosse at Cranborne

Modern British

Accomplished cuisine in long-established friendly village restaurant

☎ 01725 517604 London House, The Square BH21 5PR
e-mail: mac@la-fosse.com
web: www.la-fosse.com

This large Victorian house was developed from a 16th-century farmhouse, complete with low ceilings, beams and an inglenook fireplace. Mac La Fosse and his wife Sue have run this charming restaurant with rooms for over 20 years now, and have a well-earned local reputation for hospitality and fine food. They deliver a varied and interesting menu of dishes, ranging from old favourites such as half lobster and scallop thermidor or slow-roast rare breeds pork with apple sauce, to more imaginative fare: New Forest game soup, for example, or suprême of salmon with a ginger crumb and champagne sauce.

Times: 12-2/7-9.30, Closed Mon-Tue, Closed D Sun **Rooms:** 3 (3 en suite) ★★★★ RR **Directions:** M3, M27 W to A31 to Ringwood. Turn left to B3081 to Verwood, then Cranborne (5 m)

Sienna

DORCHESTER   MAP 04 SY69

Modern British

Small but beautifully formed restaurant of real class

☎ 01305 250022 36 High West St DT1 1UP
e-mail: browns@siennarestaurant.co.uk
web: www.siennarestaurant.co.uk

This unassuming, shop-fronted restaurant at the top of the high street - run by delightful husband-and-wife team, Russell and Elena Brown - may come on an endearingly bijou scale, but the cooking is beautifully formed. With just 15 covers (booking is essential) there's an obvious intimacy, the décor suitably understated, with a restful 'sienna' colour scheme, unclothed wooden-topped tables and modern artwork all lending a contemporary feel. Elena delivers a charming front-of-house presence, ensuring diners experience a real treat, with graceful, unhurried and professional service.

Russell struts his stuff behind the scenes at the stove with equal aplomb; his elegant and well-conceived cooking parades with deft touches, beautifully balanced combinations, clear flavours and accurate seasoning. Underpinned by high-quality produce, the confident cooking intelligently flourishes without over embellishment or empty bravado. Take a truffle-crusted medallion of Limousin veal served with potato purée, sautéed girolle mushrooms and a summer

truffle sauce, while Russell's pastry is sublime too, so don't miss the likes of a glazed coffee tart with espresso ice cream, maple syrup and walnut sauce. Sit back and enjoy a highly personal and memorable experience.

Chef: Russell Brown **Owners:** Russell & Elena Brown **Times:** 12-2/7-9.30, Closed 2 wks Feb/Mar, 2 wks Sep/Oct, Sun-Mon **Prices:** Fixed L £16.50, Fixed D £33.50, Service optional **Wine:** 24 bottles over £20, 14 bottles under £20, 7 by the glass **Seats:** 15 **Children:** Min 10 yrs **Directions:** Near top of town rdbt in Dorchester **Parking:** Top of town car park, on street

DORCHESTER — MAP 04 SY69

◎◎◎ Sienna

see opposite

◎◎ Yalbury Cottage

Modern British

A quintessentially English country cottage with an idyllic, tranquil feel and great British fare

☎ 01305 262382 Lower Bockhampton DT2 8PZ
e-mail: yalburyemails@aol.com
web: www.yalburycottage.com

This small hamlet was the inspiration for the village of Mellstock in Thomas Hardy's *Under The Greenwood Tree*. The 300-year-old thatched cottage (in its time home to both the keeper of the water meadow and a local shepherd) that houses the restaurant stands in beautiful gardens. Steeped in tradition, the dining room comes replete with wood burner, oak beams and wooden floors - yet it's in no sense old-fashioned. The food itself puts an inventive twist on all things Great and British, using fresh, quality local ingredients, including produce grown in the hotel's garden. Take slow-roasted best end of Dorset Horn lamb served with gratin potatoes, young spinach and a light coriander jus, and perhaps a summer pudding finish, simply accompanied by vanilla ice cream.

Times: 7-9, Closed 2 wks Jan, Closed L all week **Rooms:** 8 (8 en suite)
★★★★★ GH **Directions:** 2m E of Dorchester, off A35

EVERSHOT — MAP 04 ST50

◎ The Acorn Inn

Modern, Traditional

Village inn of literary legend and local fare

☎ 01935 83228   DT2 0JW
e-mail: stay@acorn-inn.co.uk
web: www.acorn-inn.co.uk

Called 'The Sow and Acorn' from *Tess of the D'Urbervilles* by Thomas Hardy, this 16th-century stone-built inn has a lovely village setting in the heart of Thomas Hardy country. Historic features include beams, flagstone floors, oak panelling and open fires. A good choice of food

CONTINUED

◎◎◎

Summer Lodge Country House Hotel

EVERSHOT — MAP 04 ST50

Modern British NOTABLE WINE LIST

Idyllic, intimate retreat meets refined cooking

☎ 01935 482000   DT2 0JR
e-mail: summer@relaischateaux.com
web: www.summerlodgehotel.com

This former dower house turned intimate, quintessential country-house hotel can be found nestling in a fold of the Dorset Downs in lovely grounds (designed in part by local architect and celebrated chronicler, Thomas Hardy no less). It is a true hideaway, blessed with a picture-postcard village setting. There's an air of luxury and high quality about the interior, decked out in classic, chintzy country-house style. Service is predictably on the formal side (with cheese trolley, dessert wine trolley and roast trolleys for Sunday lunch), but appropriately friendly too, while the sommelier brings serious expertise to the classy wine list. The spacious, split-level dining room follows the theme, and is elegant and classically traditional with fabric-covered walls, fine table appointments and views over the gardens while the gazebo offers an enchanting alfresco summer option. The accomplished kitchen's modern focus, underpinned by a classical theme, suits the surroundings to a tee, focusing on prime local produce, its refined treatment displaying high skill, clean, clear

flavours, balance and modern presentation. Think Cornish turbot served with confit pork belly and herb-crushed potatoes.

Chef: Steven Titman **Owners:** Red Carnation Hotels **Times:** 12-2.30/7-9.30 **Prices:** Starter £11.50-£16.95, Main £19.95-£26.95, Dessert £8.95-£12.50, Service included, Group min 12 service 12.5% **Wine:** 1,100 bottles over £20, 10 bottles under £20, 9 by the glass **Notes:** Tasting menu available £60, Dress Restrictions, No shorts, T-shirts or sandals, jackets pref, Civ Wed 30, Air con **Seats:** 48, Pr/dining room 12 **Children:** Min 7 yrs D, Menu, Portions **Rooms:** 24 (24 en suite)★★★★ CHH
Directions: 1.5m off A37 between Yeovil and Dorchester **Parking:** 60

ENGLAND

EVERSHOT CONTINUED

ranges from a popular bar menu to more formal fare in the cosy restaurant. Quality local produce figures strongly in well-presented dishes, bolstered by blackboard specials. Take pan-fried plaice served with mussels and a white wine and chive sauce, or perhaps roasted loin of Dorset lamb teamed with braised leeks, twice-baked mushroom and cheddar soufflé, and a Madeira sauce.

Chef: Justin Mackenzie **Owners:** Red Carnation Hotels **Times:** 12-2/6.45-9.30 **Prices:** Starter £4.25-£8.95, Main £11.25-£21.95, Dessert £4.75-£7.95, Service optional **Wine:** 13 bottles over £20, 13 bottles under £20, 8 by the glass **Notes:** Sun L 2 courses £16, 3 courses £20.50, Dress Restrictions, Smart casual **Seats:** 45, Pr/dining room 65 **Children:** Portions **Rooms:** 10 (10 en suite) ★★★★ INN **Directions:** 2m off A37, between Dorchester and Yeovil. In village centre **Parking:** 40

◉◉◉ Summer Lodge Country House Hotel

see page 151

FARNHAM   MAP 04 ST91

◉◉ The Museum Inn

Modern British

Great gastro-pub with accomplished cooking and contemporary spin

☎ 01725 516261   DT11 8DE
e-mail: enquiries@museuminn.co.uk
web: www.museuminn.co.uk

This red-brick and thatched inn stands in an idyllic village setting and makes a charming statement. Sympathetic refurbishment has retained original flagstones and fireplaces, but pastel tones, a light-and-airy feel and stylish country furnishings add a modern, upmarket vibe, albeit with a relaxed, friendly atmosphere. Eat from the same menu in a variety of comfortable bar rooms, or in the more formal Shed restaurant at weekends. Driven by judiciously sourced quality produce (meats are fully traceable and traditionally reared, many other ingredients are organic or free range, while fish is delivered daily from the south coast), the accomplished kitchen takes a modern British line; think slow-roast belly pork with cider apple sauce, spinach and colcannon potatoes. There's also a sunny terrace.

Chef: Daniel Turner **Owners:** Mark Stephenson, Vicky Elliot **Times:** 12-2/7-9.30, Closed 25 & 31 Dec **Prices:** Starter £6-£8, Main £14-£17, Dessert £5-£6.50, Service optional **Wine:** 120 bottles over £20, 28 bottles under £20, 12 by the glass **Seats:** 80, Pr/dining room 30 **Children:** Min 10 yrs, Portions **Directions:** 12m S of Salisbury, 7m N of Blandford Forum on A354 **Parking:** 20

FONTMELL MAGNA   MAP 04 ST81

◉ The Crown Inn

British

All change at a cosy village inn

☎ 01747 811441   SP1 0PA
e-mail: crowninnfm@hotmail.com
web: www.crowninn.me.uk

Once part of the defunct Flowers Brewery of Fontmell, this traditional Georgian-style country inn has a farmhouse feel to it, with a cosy bar and a popular restaurant area. As we went to press we understand there was a change of ownership taking place. Please visit www.theAA.com for further information.

Times: 12-2.45/6.45-9, Closed 25 Dec **Rooms:** 5 (3 en suite) ★★ INN **Directions:** On A350 towards Blandford S, pass through Cann & Compton Abbas villages - restaurant on x-rds, centre of Fontmell Magna on right

GILLINGHAM   MAP 04 ST82

◉◉◉ Stock Hill Country House Hotel & Restaurant

see opposite

LYME REGIS   MAP 04 SY39

◉ Hotel Alexandra & Restaurant

Modern British V

Attractively presented food in an elegant setting

☎ 01297 442010 Pound St DT7 3HZ
e-mail: enquiries@hotelalexandra.co.uk
web: www.hotelalexandra.co.uk

The plethora of model sailing ships, and marine and local pictures around this Grade II listed hotel leave you in no doubt that this elegant restaurant is by the sea, even if you miss the amazing view over Lyme Bay. The good-value menu also leans towards the sea, though you'll find meaty choices too among the accomplished repertoire. Take grilled whole lemon sole served with a fennel risotto and courgette ribbons, while meat-lovers might opt for roasted rack of lamb with dauphinoise potatoes and a panaché of green vegetables.

Chef: Ian Grant **Owners:** Kathryn Richards **Times:** 12-2/7-8.30, Closed last Sun before Xmas-end Jan **Prices:** Fixed L £17.95, Fixed D £29.95, Service optional **Wine:** 29 bottles over £20, 29 bottles under £20, 5 by the glass **Notes:** Fixed L 3 courses, Fixed D 4 courses, Vegetarian menu, Dress Restrictions, Smart casual, Air con **Seats:** 60, Pr/dining room 24 **Children:** Min 10 yrs, Menu, Portions **Rooms:** 26 (26 en suite) ★★★ HL **Directions:** From Bridport take A35 to Lyme Regis, through Chideock, Marcombe Lake, past Charmouth, turn left at Charmouth rdbt, follow for 2m **Parking:** 26

Stock Hill Country House Hotel & Restaurant

GILLINGHAM MAP 04 ST82

Austrian, European V

Classic cuisine with an Austrian twist in elegant country house

☎ 01747 823626 & 822741 Stock Hill SP8 5NR
e-mail: reception@stockhillhouse.co.uk
web: www.stockhillhouse.co.uk

This elegant, lovingly restored Victorian country house is situated at the end of a beech-lined drive, set in 11 acres of attractive gardens and parkland. Luxurious décor in the period style with fine antique furnishings, rich fabrics, oil paintings and deep sofas grace public rooms, while the elegant dining room continues the theme with views over the manicured lawns from comfortable chairs and white-clothed tables. Service is friendly but efficient, and sets the scene for chef-patron Peter Hauser's fine classical cuisine with its Austrian accent.

Quality, fresh seasonal ingredients appear on Stock Hill's daily-changing menus, with meat sourced locally and fish fresh from Brixham, while herbs, fruit and vegetables come direct from the hotel's walled potager. Highly skilled technique, flair, balanced combinations and full-on flavours really deliver, and the Austrian flag denotes specialities. Take pan-cooked medallion of veal served with garden sorrel, white wine cream and a beetroot gâteau, and for dessert, perhaps a Baiser meringue filled with exotic fruits and served with a mango sorbet and vanilla cream.

Chef: Peter Hauser, Lorna Connor
Owners: Peter & Nita Hauser
Times: 12.30-1.45/7.30-8.45, Closed L Sat & Mon
Prices: Fixed L £18, Fixed D £40, Group min 10 service 10%
Wine: 6 bottles under £20, 6 by the glass
Notes: Fixed D 4 courses, Vegetarian menu, Dress Restrictions, No jeans or T-shirts
Seats: 24, Pr/dining room 12
Children: Min 7 yrs, Portions
Rooms: 9 (9 en suite)★★★ CHH
Directions: 3m E on B3081, off A303
Parking: 20

ENGLAND

◉ Mariners Hotel

Modern British

Enjoyable dining in hotel with character and sea views

☎ 01297 442753 Silver St DT7 3HS
e-mail: enquiries@hotellymeregis.co.uk
web: www.hotellymeregis.co.uk

Located in the heart of town, this small, friendly hotel has plenty of period character and charm. A conversion from a 17th-century coaching inn, the property was immortalised by Beatrix Potter in her *Tale of Little Pig Robinson*. From the garden there are views of Lyme Bay and the surrounding countryside. Locally-caught fish is a highlight on the menu; take roast monkfish wrapped in Parma ham and served with onion jam, otherwise, expect a roast rack of lamb with honey and rosemary sauce, and a finish of mango crème brûlée with home-made apricot sorbet.

Chef: Nick Larby **Owners:** Nick & Claire Larby **Times:** 12-2/7-9, Closed 27 Dec-28 Jan, Closed L Mon-Sat, D Sun **Prices:** Fixed L £10.50, Fixed D £21.50, Service optional **Wine:** 4 bottles over £20, 27 bottles under £20, 3 by the glass **Seats:** 40 **Children:** Min 10 yrs **Rooms:** 12 (12 en suite) ★★ HL **Directions:** Please telephone for directions **Parking:** 20

◉ Rumours

Modern

Friendly, seaside restaurant featuring fresh local fish

☎ 01297 444740 14-15 Monmouth St DT7 3PX
e-mail: fish@rumoursrestaurant.eclipse.co.uk
web: www.lyme-regis-charmouth.co.uk

A husband-and-wife-run restaurant, Rumours is located in the old part of town just a few minutes from the seafront. The dining room is contemporary in style with an original black-and-white tiled floor. The repertoire is awash with the fruits of the sea, locally-caught where possible. Try Lyme Bay king scallops seared with crispy Parma ham, home-cured gravad lax with horseradish cream, or West Bay Dover sole grilled with tarragon butter. There are plenty of non-fish options too - perhaps chargrilled Dorset steak with straw potatoes and garlic butter, and all the desserts are home made.

Chef: Lynda Skelton **Owners:** Lynda & Ron Skelton **Times:** 7-10, Closed Dec-Feb, Sun & Wed (open Sun Bank Hols), Closed L all week **Prices:** Starter £4.25-£7.25, Main £9.95-£17.95, Dessert £4.50-£4.95, Service optional **Wine:** 1 bottle over £20, 21 bottles under £20, 4 by the glass **Notes:** Vegetarian available **Seats:** 26 **Children:** Min 14 yrs **Directions:** Please telephone for directions **Parking:** On street 25 yds

---

MAIDEN NEWTON   MAP 04 SY59

◉ Le Petit Canard

Modern British

Pretty village restaurant, delicious dining

☎ 01300 320536 Dorchester Rd DT2 0BE
e-mail: craigs@le-petit-canard.co.uk
web: www.le-petit-canard.co.uk

Set in a conservation area, this pretty 350-year-old building contains a small but charming dining room with exposed brickwork and old beams highlighted by sensitive décor and lighting and crisp white linen. Service is professional and attentive with a good knowledge of

ingredients and the wine list. Fixed-priced menus are modern focused, the repertoire bolstered by daily specials. Expect a loin of local lamb served with pea purée and a lemon garlic reduction, or perhaps pan-fried sea bass with fennel mash and a red wine dressing, while a blueberry crème brûlée might head-up desserts.

Le Petit Canard

Chef: Gerry Craig **Owners:** Mr & Mrs G Craig **Times:** 12-2/7-9, Closed Mon, Closed L all week (ex 1st & 3rd Sun in month), D Sun **Prices:** Fixed L £21, Fixed D £29-£33, Service optional **Wine:** 17 bottles over £20, 13 bottles under £20, 6 by the glass **Notes:** Sun L only 3 courses, Vegetarian available, Dress Restrictions, Smart casual preferred **Seats:** 28 **Children:** Min 12 yrs **Directions:** In centre of Maiden Newton, 8m W of Dorchester **Parking:** On street/village car park

---

POOLE   MAP 04 SZ09

◉◉ Harbour Heights Hotel

Modern British, French

Contemporary bistro commanding the best views across Poole Harbour

☎ 01202 707272 73 Haven Rd, Sandbanks BH13 7LW
e-mail: enquiries@harbourheights.net
web: www.fjbhotels.co.uk

The name gives a clue to this modern, stylish seaside hotel's main drawcard; a contemporary Harbar bistro with floor-to-ceiling picture windows and a sun terrace (for alfresco summer dining) that offers panoramic views across Poole Harbour. It's a smart, open-planned affair of lounge, bar and restaurant, the latter decked out with modern polished-wood tables and matching chairs with brown leather upholstery. Service is relaxed, efficient and friendly, while the kitchen's modern brasserie approach suits the surroundings, with skilfully prepared, well-presented and conceived dishes that utilise quality local ingredients. Think a baked fillet of sea bass with crushed saffron potatoes, fennel, mussels and chervil in a rich butter sauce, and perhaps a prune and Armagnac tart finish, served with caramel and yogurt sauce.

Chef: Stephanie Jouan **Owners:** FJB Hotels **Times:** 12-2.30/7-9.30 **Prices:** Fixed L £15.50-£19.50, Starter £5.95-£16.60, Main £15.10-£20.10, Dessert £5.85, Service optional **Wine:** 235 bottles over £20, 5 bottles under £20, 13 by the glass **Notes:** Dress Restrictions, Smart casual, Civ Wed 120, Air con **Seats:** 90, Pr/dining room 120 **Children:** Menu, Portions **Rooms:** 38 (38 en suite) ★★★★ HL **Directions:** From A338 follow signs to Sandbanks, restaurant on left past Canford Cliffs **Parking:** 80

◎◎ Haven Hotel

Modern British V

Fine dining with stunning sea views

☎ 01202 707333 Banks Rd, Sandbanks BH13 7QL
e-mail: reservations@havenhotel.co.uk
web: www.fjbhotels.co.uk

Overlooking the mouth of Poole Harbour, this well established hotel was once home to the Victorian radio pioneer Marconi. La Roche restaurant - with its chic modern décor, formal table service, and relaxed atmosphere - enjoys stunning views across the bay, while the lounge terrace is the perfect venue for alfresco dining in summer. The menu offers locally-sourced seasonal produce in British dishes with an emphasis on fish and seafood, including fresh lobster or catch of the day. Starters may include Cornish diver-caught scallops with Pierre Robert pannacotta and beetroot relish, while for mains you might tuck into slow-braised Twelve Green Acres organic pork shoulder, served with truffle, celeriac and apple and golden sultana dressing. Dessert might take in an unusual hot lavender doughnut with blackberry compôte, or perhaps a classic autumn apple and pear tarte Tatin with mascarpone and cinnamon ice cream.

Chef: Carl France **Owners:** Mr J Butterworth **Times:** 12-2/7-9, Closed Xmas, Mon (winter), Closed D Sun (winter) **Prices:** Starter £5.50-£9.95, Main £13.50-£19.50, Dessert £5.50-£8.50, Service optional **Wine:** 46 bottles over £20, 21 bottles under £20 **Notes:** Vegetarian menu, Dress Restrictions, No shorts or beach wear, Civ Wed 180, Air con **Seats:** 59, Pr/dining room 160 **Children:** Menu, Portions **Rooms:** 78 (78 en suite) ★★★★ HL **Directions:** Follow signs to Sandbanks Peninsula; hotel next to Swanage ferry departure point **Parking:** 90

Hotel du Vin Poole

Rosettes not confirmed at time of going to press

Modern British

Modern cooking in an exclusive townhouse setting

☎ 01202 685666 Thames St BH15 1JN

Situated in a picturesque cobbled mews, a short stroll from Poole's lively quayside, this elegant Georgian townhouse is now a luxury hotel. The smart restaurant has a formal style but the ambience is friendly and relaxed. Expect straightforward modern British cooking with an emphasis on first-rate local ingredients, including fish from the nearby quay, meat and game from Dorset and West Country cheeses. Twice-baked Dorset cheddar cheese soufflé in a cheese and chive sauce is a typical starter, while mains range from grilled fillet of beef in a ginger and red wine sauce, to fillet of black bream with sun-blushed tomato risotto, crispy pancetta and basil dressing. As we went to press we understand that this hotel had been taken over by Hotel du Vin and will be refurbished over the coming months.

Times: 12-2/7-9.30, Closed L Sat, D Sun (ex BHs) **Directions:** A350 into town centre follow signs to Channel Ferry/Poole Quay, left at bridge, 1st left is Thames St **Parking:** 46

ENGLAND

⊛ H V Restaurant

Modern, Pacific Rim NEW

Modern hotel restaurant with harbour views and fresh fish

☎ 01202 666800 & 0870 333 9143 Thistle Hotel Poole,
The Quay BH15 1HD
e-mail: poole@thistle.co.uk
web: www.thistlehotels.com/poole

Situated on the quayside overlooking Poole harbour, this modern hotel's refurbished, first-floor HV Restaurant (a fashionable abbreviated take on 'harbour view') delivers stunning views. Dream away your lottery millions at the yachts and speedboats moored alongside, or watch the day's catches being landed from the windows. A smart, modern affair, the room comes decked out with formally laid tables, and there's a small fish counter where you can choose your fish for chef to cook. Otherwise, the menu's straightforward modern approach (including some meat options) might take in grilled fillet of local sea bass served with green pea purée, chorizo crisps, and a brûlée of mango and chorizo oil.

Chef: Gary Newman **Times:** 12-2/7-9.45 **Prices:** Fixed L £10-£15, Starter £5-£8.50, Main £14-£20, Dessert £4.50-£5.50, Service optional **Wine:** 14 bottles over £20, 24 bottles under £20, 12 by the glass **Notes:** Dress Restrictions, Smart casual, Civ Wed 80 **Seats:** 120, Pr/dining room 40 **Children:** Menu, Portions **Directions:** Follow signs to Poole port (A350) & Poole Pottery signs. Hotel on waterfront **Parking:** 120

⊛ Sandbanks Hotel

Traditional European V

Beachside, contemporary brasserie with exciting menu

☎ 01202 707377 15 Banks Rd, Sandbanks BH13 7PS
e-mail: reservations@sandbankshotel.co.uk
web: www.fjbhotels.co.uk

Set on the delightful Sandbanks peninsula, this popular hotel enjoys stunning views across Poole Harbour and has direct access to the blue flag beach. There's a choice of dining venues, the aptly-named Seaview restaurant for fair-weather dining, and the more formal Sands brasserie - its octagonal shape taking full advantage of 180° views over the bay. The brasserie's style is modern and minimalist, with glass walls and well-appointed tables. The carte is equally contemporary, offering variations of classical dishes with European influences, using the freshest local ingredients. Start with local crab accompanied by tomato, beetroot and avocado tian, followed by baked Atlantic cod with goat's cheese mash, and for dessert chocolate pannacotta with red wine and cinnamon ice cream.

Chef: Paul Harper **Owners:** Mr J Butterworth **Times:** 12-3/6-10, Closed Mon-Tue, Closed D Sun-Tue **Prices:** Fixed L £15, Fixed D £19.50, Starter £6.50-£10.50, Main £13.50-£20, Dessert £6.50-£6.90, Service optional **Wine:** 60 bottles over £20, 23 bottles under £20, 6 by the glass **Notes:** Sun L menu available, Vegetarian menu, *Dress Restrictions, No jeans, smart casual, Civ Wed 40, Air con **Seats:** 65, Pr/dining room 40 **Children:** Menu, Portions **Rooms:** 110 (110 en suite) ★★★★ HL **Directions:** From Poole or Bournemouth, follow signs to Sandbanks Peninsula. Hotel on left **Parking:** 130

PORTLAND   MAP 04 SY67

⊛ The Bluefish Restaurant

Modern European

Relaxed dining in simple surroundings

☎ 01305 822991 15-17a Chiswell DT5 1AN
e-mail: thebluefish@tesco.net
web: www.thebluefishcafe.co.uk

This simple yet stylish restaurant is housed at the top of a 400-year-old Portland stone building. You can dine alfresco in fine weather or sit in one of the two interconnecting dining rooms under starry lights. You'll find meat and vegetarian choices as well as fish on the modern European menu. Starters include crayfish tart au gratin with baby soya beans and grain mustard, followed by mains like wild halibut with citrus-braised endive, pea purée, tapenade and red wine jus. For dessert, take orange financier with crème anglaise and Grand Marnier chantilly.

Chef: Luciano Da Silva **Owners:** Jo & Luciano Da Silva **Times:** 12-3/6.30-10, Closed L Times seasonal, D Times seasonal **Prices:** Fixed D £19.95, Starter £4.50-£8.50, Main £10.50-£14.95, Dessert £4.50, Group min 8 service 10% **Wine:** 3 bottles over £20, 15 bottles under £20, 6 by the glass **Notes:** Vegetarian available **Seats:** 35 **Children:** Portions **Directions:** Take A354 by Chesil Bank, off Victoria Square in Portland, over rdbt towards Chesil Beach **Parking:** 72-hr free car park, on street

SHAFTESBURY   MAP 04 ST82

⊛ Best Western Royal Chase Hotel

Modern British

Imaginative cooking in friendly surroundings

☎ 01747 853355   Royal Chase Roundabout SP7 8DB
e-mail: royalchasehotel@btinternet.com
web: www.theroyalchasehotel.co.uk

This one-time monastery in pretty Shaftesbury is now a friendly hotel, but still plays home to a former resident, said to walk the halls in ghostly form. It's located not far from Gold Hill, a picture-perfect street that featured in Ridley Scott's celebrated adverts for Hovis bread, and has graced the cover of countless chocolate boxes. The dining room is an intimate affair, presided over by a team who strike just the right note of friendliness and formality. Expect modern British cooking that might take in the likes of caramelised Barbary duck with potato dauphinoise, or lamb glazed with redcurrant sauce with a smoked garlic and basil mousse.

Chef: Stuart Robbins **Owners:** Travel West Inns **Times:** 12-2/7-9.30 **Prices:** Fixed L £10.95-£11.95, Starter £3.95-£5.95, Main £12.95-£18.95, Dessert £4.50-£5.25, Service optional **Wine:** 11 bottles over £20, 39 bottles under £20, 5 by the glass **Notes:** Sun L available £8.95, Vegetarian available, Civ Wed 78 **Seats:** 65, Pr/dining room 120 **Children:** Menu, Portions **Rooms:** 33 (33 en suite) ★★★ HL **Directions:** On rdbt at A350 & A30 junction (avoid town centre) **Parking:** 100

⊛⊛ La Fleur de Lys Restaurant with Rooms

French, European

Smart restaurant with rooms to suit all tastes

☎ 01747 853717   Bleke St SP7 8AW
e-mail: info@fleurdelys.co.uk
web: www.lafleurdelys.co.uk

Located just a few minutes' walk from the famous Gold Hill, this light and airy restaurant with rooms combines efficient service within a relaxed and friendly atmosphere. The elegant L-shaped dining room, with conservatory extension, comes decked out in beige carpet, white cloths and Queen Anne-style upholstered chairs. A comfortable lounge for pre-dinner drinks rounds off the package. The kitchen's approach is modern, underpinned by classical French techniques. Straightforward, accomplished dishes, with some interesting combinations, use quality seasonal ingredients and confident delivery and presentation. Expect pan-fried fillet of Aberdeen Angus beef with spinach and creamy stilton and truffle sauces, or grilled fillets of Dover sole served with a dill sauce.

Chef: D Shepherd & M Preston **Owners:** D Shepherd, M Preston & M Griffin **Times:** 12-2.30/7-10.30, Closed 3 wks Jan, Closed L Mon & Tue, D Sun **Prices:** Fixed L £23.50, Fixed D £28.50, Starter £6-£11, Main £18-£22, Dessert £6, Service optional **Wine:** 180 bottles over £20, 20 bottles under £20, 8 by the glass **Notes:** Dress Restrictions, Smart casual, No T-shirts or dirty clothes **Seats:** 45, Pr/dining room 12 **Children:** Portions **Rooms:** 7 (7 en suite) ★★★★ RR **Directions:** Junct A350/A30 **Parking:** 10

SHERBORNE   MAP 04 ST61

⊛⊛ Eastbury Hotel

Modern British

Handsome Georgian property serving modern British cuisine

☎ 01935 813131   Long St DT9 3BY
e-mail: enquiries@theeastburyhotel.com
web: www.theeastburyhotel.co.uk

Located in the heart of historic Sherborne, a short walk from the abbey, this elegant Georgian townhouse is set in extensive grounds. Peruse the menu over a drink in the choice of lounges, before going through to the restaurant - a split-level conservatory with great character and views over the walled garden. The large tables are well spaced, the chairs comfortably upholstered, and there's a terrace for summer dining. Local produce is used where possible, with fruit and herbs arriving courtesy of the kitchen garden when in season. Expect a modern British menu plus a few retro classics to please the crowd: steamed mutton pudding with mint and caper jelly perhaps, or roast scallops with pea shoots and cauliflower.

Chef: Brett Sutton **Owners:** Mr & Mrs P King **Times:** 12-2/7-9.30 **Prices:** Fixed D £30, Service optional **Wine:** 40 bottles over £20, 20 bottles under £20, 12 by the glass **Notes:** Civ Wed 80 **Seats:** 40, Pr/dining room 12 **Children:** Menu, Portions **Rooms:** 21 (21 en suite) ★★★ HL **Directions:** 5m E of Yeovil, follow brown signs for The Eastbury Hotel **Parking:** 20

⊛⊛ The Green

Modern British

Modern cooking in a popular West Country location

☎ 01935 813821   3 The Green DT9 3HY
web: www.thegreensherborne.co.uk

The smart green-painted woodwork makes this attractive old stone Grade II listed property easy to spot. Inside, the character of the old building is retained in the exposed beams, wooden floor and antique wooden tables and chairs. Relaxed, friendly service and atmosphere - there's a real buzz - establishes this as a popular venue. Cooking is modern in style with simple but stylish presentation from a talented team. You might try monkfish tails with salsify, buttered leeks, asparagus, fir apple potatoes, shrimps and basil, and perhaps an iced mascarpone parfait finish, served with honey, toasted almonds and apricots.

Chef: Michael Rust **Owners:** Michael & Judith Rust **Times:** 12-2/7-9, Closed 2 wks Jan,1 wk Jun,1 wk Sept,BHs,Xmas, Sun-Mon **Prices:** Fixed L £15-£22.50, Fixed D £28.95, Service optional **Wine:** 19 bottles over £20, 31 bottles under £20, 12 by the glass **Seats:** 40, Pr/dining room 25 **Parking:** On street, car park

ENGLAND

TARRANT MONKTON   MAP 04 ST90

⊛ The Langton Arms

Modern European

Refurbished country inn serving modern food

☎ 01258 830225   DT11 8RX
e-mail: info@thelangtonarms.co.uk
web: www.thelangtonarms.co.uk

This 17th-century thatched pub oozes character, tucked away in a village reached via a shallow ford. Popular with local people, parties and weddings, the Stables restaurant is housed in a converted stable and new conservatory, and is open Wednesday to Saturday evenings and Sunday lunchtimes. Cooking focuses on the use of top-notch local ingredients, including game from local farms and estates. Typical dishes might include scallop, roasted pepper and avocado gâteau to start, followed by roast peppered sirloin of beef with braised sweet red cabbage, château potato and port and thyme jus.

Chef: Andrew Parker   **Owners:** Barbara & James Cossins   **Times:** 12-2.30/7-12 (last orders 9), Closed Mon & Tue, Closed L Wed to Sat, D Sun **Prices:** Starter £4.95-£8.95, Main £12.25-£19.95, Dessert £5.95-£6.95, Service optional   **Wine:** 10 bottles over £20, 15 bottles under £20, 7 by the glass   **Notes:** Vegetarian available, Civ Wed 60   **Seats:** 40, Pr/dining room 24   **Children:** Menu, Portions   **Rooms:** 6 (6 en suite) ★ ★ ★ ★ INN **Directions:** A354 turn off for Tarrant Hinton towards Tarrant Monkton, continue through a ford and pub is directly ahead   **Parking:** 100

WEYMOUTH   MAP 04 SY67

⊛⊛ Moonfleet Manor

Modern British

Top-notch cooking in an enchanting hideaway

☎ 01305 786948   Fleet DT3 4ED
e-mail: info@moonfleetmanor.com
web: www.moonfleetmanor.com

Popular with young families, this enchanting Georgian house is tucked away in the village of Fleet, overlooking Chesil Bay and the sea. Its airy restaurant is a relaxed and informal venue staffed by a friendly and attentive waiting team, who deliver tempting dishes of acclaimed modern British cuisine. Tease your taste buds with a starter of cream of butternut soup with curry oil and mint, before tucking into pan-fried breast of corn-fed chicken with creamed leeks and braised lentils, and desserts such as hot gingerbread pudding with lemon curd ice cream and caramel sauce.

Times: 12.30-2/7-9.30   **Rooms:** 39 (39 en suite) ★ ★ ★ HL **Directions:** A354 from Dorchester, right into Weymouth at Manor Rdbt, right at next rdbt, left at next rdbt, up hill (B3157) then left, 2m towards sea

---

⊛ Perry's Restaurant

Modern British 🍷 NOTABLE WINE LIST

Satisfying food in a pleasant harbourside location

☎ 01305 785799   4 Trinity Rd, The Old Harbour DT4 8TJ
e-mail: enquiries@perrysrestaurant.co.uk
web: www.perrysrestaurant.co.uk

Set on the charming quayside and occupying a former merchant's house, this long-established and unpretentious eatery specialises in local fish and seafood. Book a window table to watch the maritime manoeuvres in the harbour and tuck into starters like pan-fried scallops with Jerusalem artichoke purée, or Portland crab ravioli with saffron mussel sauce, spring onion and chilli. Follow with baked brill, served with warm smoked haddock and potato mousse and dill cream, or perhaps grilled fillet of wild sea bass with crab and potato cake, stir-fried greens with ginger, and lime butter sauce. If you still have room, round off with passionfruit brûlée.

Chef: Andy Pike   **Owners:** Matt & Liz Whishaw   **Times:** 12-2/7-9.30, Closed 25-27 Dec, Jan, Mon (winter), Closed L Mon (summer), D Sun (winter)   **Prices:** Fixed L £14.95, Starter £4.95-£8.50, Main £11.50-£18.95, Dessert £5.50-£6.50, Service optional, Group min 8 service 10% **Wine:** 124 bottles over £20, 30 bottles under £20, 10 by the glass **Seats:** 60, Pr/dining room 36   **Children:** Portions   **Directions:** On western side of old harbour - follow signs for Brewers Quay   **Parking:** On street or Brewers Quay car park (200yds)

Vaughan's

☎ 01305 769004   7 Custom House Quay DT4 8BE
web: www.vaughansbistro.co.uk

Situated on the harbour, this restaurant offers plenty of local produce, fish and shellfish.

WIMBORNE MINSTER   MAP 05 SZ09

⊛⊛ Les Bouviers Restaurant with Rooms

French V

Well-established restaurant in converted residential house outside town

☎ 01202 889555   Arrowsmith Rd, Canford Magna BH21 3BD
e-mail: info@lesbouviers.co.uk
web: www.lesbouviers.co.uk

Smart and welcoming, Les Bouviers is set in tranquil grounds, complete with lake and stream. The fresh, modern, country-house dining room has a cosy, intimate feel and comes with solid-wood tables and custom-designed upholstered chairs along with art and pieces of furniture creating an eclectic style. Service is relaxed, but professional. The kitchen's French-influenced, imaginative selection of modern dishes parade alongside fresh, local ingredients on a repertoire of fixed-price menus, including carte, seven-course surprise and gourmand offerings. Expect dishes like pan-fried fillets of wild cod on sautéed noodles and spring onion with baby aubergine and balsamic reduction, and perhaps an acacia honey and lime parfait with a compôte of strawberry and mango to close. Alfresco dining in warmer weather is an added bonus.

Chef: James Coward **Owners:** James & Kate Coward **Times:** 12-2.15/7-9.30, Closed D Sun **Prices:** Fixed L £16.95-£18.95, Fixed D £29.95-£31.95, Starter £10-£18, Main £18-£25, Dessert £6-£8, Group min 7 service 10% **Wine:** 100+ bottles over £20, 100+ bottles under £20, 24 by the glass **Notes:** Fixed D 4 courses, Tasting menu 7 courses £65, Vegetarian menu, Dress Restrictions, No jeans or shorts, Civ Wed 100, Air con **Seats:** 50, Pr/dining room 150 **Children:** Menu, Portions **Rooms:** 6 (6 en suite) ★★★★★ RR **Directions:** 1.5m S of Wimborne on A349, turn left onto A341, after 1m turn right into Arrowsmith Rd. Continue for 300 yds, 2nd property on right **Parking:** 40

see advert opposite

CO DURHAM

BEAMISH   MAP 19 NZ25

◉◉ Beamish Park Hotel

Modern, International

International bistro dining in modern surroundings

☎ 01207 230666 Beamish Burn Rd NE16 5EG
e-mail: reception@beamish-park-hotel.co.uk
web: www.beamish-park-hotel.co.uk

Located within a stylish split-level hotel set amid beautiful open countryside, the Conservatory bistro is modern and chic with contemporary colours, imaginative lighting, unusual fabrics and a host of individual design features. The lounge bar has been recently refurbished and you can take coffee on the small terrace. The restaurant's varied monthly-changing menu is modern British in style and includes a selection of traditional dishes with some international influences, using local, seasonal produce. Try a main course of line-caught sea bass with fresh crab gnocchi and shellfish bisque dressing, or perhaps an individual steamed leek suet pudding with creamed woodland mushrooms, before finishing with a dessert of lemon polenta cake and poached soft fruits.

Chef: Christopher Walker **Owners:** William Walker **Times:** 12-2.30/7-10.30 **Prices:** Fixed L £12.50, Starter £4.25-£8, Main £12-£16, Dessert £4.75-£6, Service optional **Wine:** 6 bottles over £20, 11 bottles under £20, 7 by the glass **Notes:** Vegetarian available, Dress Restrictions, Smart casual preferred, Air con **Seats:** 70, Pr/dining room 150 **Children:** Portions **Rooms:** 42 (42 en suite) ★★★ HL **Directions:** A1(M) turn off onto A692, continue for 2m into Sunniside. At traffic lights take A6076 signposted Beamish Museum & Tanfield Railway. Hotel is situated behind Causey Arch Inn **Parking:** 100

DARLINGTON   MAP 19 NZ21

◉ Headlam Hall

British, French

Interesting modern dishes served in a Jacobean hall

☎ 01325 730238 Headlam, Gainford DL2 3HA
e-mail: admin@headlamhall.co.uk
web: www.headlamhall.co.uk

Set in beautiful walled gardens, this grand Jacobean mansion has its own 9-hole golf course surrounded by rolling countryside. The main house retains many original features, including flagstone floors and a pillared hall. The restaurant is divided into four areas, with distinctive and contrasting styles, from the airy patio room to the splendour of the panelled dining room. A menu of modern dishes is based on locally-supplied fresh ingredients wherever possible, and includes seared black bream with braised spring onions, king prawns and prawn bisque, followed by warm chocolate fondant with vanilla ice cream.

Chef: Austen Shaw **Owners:** JH Robinson **Times:** 12-2.30/7-9.30, Closed 25-26 Dec **Prices:** Fixed L £11-£15, Fixed D £25-£35, Starter £5-£10, Main £14-£20, Dessert £5-£8, Service optional **Wine:** 25 bottles over £20, 30 bottles under £20, 10 by the glass **Notes:** Dress Restrictions, No sportswear or shorts, Civ Wed 150 **Seats:** 70, Pr/dining room 30 **Children:** Menu, Portions **Rooms:** 40 (40 en suite) ★★★ HL **Directions:** 8m W of Darlington off A67 **Parking:** 70

DARLINGTON Continued

◉ Hugo's Restaurant

Modern International

16th-century manor with a short modern menu

☎ 01325 300400 Hall Garth Golf & Country Club, Coatham Mundeville DL1 3LU
e-mail: hallgarth@foliohotels.com
web: www.foliohotels.com

Originally a manor house, dating from the 16th century, the hotel is located just off the A1(M), and offers golf, leisure and conference facilities. Country-house style lounges are warmed by log fires, and the relaxed atmosphere is enhanced by soft music. Hugo's, the intimate candlelit restaurant, has good views over the grounds and offers a welcoming and friendly dining experience for all occasions. Cooking is straightforward and modern, using good-quality ingredients. Try cedar plank-cooked Chilean sea bass, followed by a main course of Italian Caprese salad with prosciutto ham, finishing with classic crêpes Suzette.

Chef: Robert Hendrix **Owners:** Folio Hotels **Times:** 7-9.30 **Prices:** Fixed D £23.95, Starter £4.50-£10, Main £12.50-£30, Dessert £4.50-£7, Service optional **Wine:** 10 bottles over £20, 35 bottles under £20, 9 by the glass **Notes:** Vegetarian available, Dress Restrictions, Smart casual, No T-shirts or trainers, Civ Wed 160 **Seats:** 60, Pr/dining room 18 **Children:** Menu, Portions **Rooms:** 51 (51 en suite) ★★★ HL **Directions:** A1(M) junct 59 (A167) (Darlington), top of hill turn left signed Brafferton, hotel 200yds on right **Parking:** 100

DURHAM   MAP 19 NZ24

◉ Bistro 21

British, European 💻

Stylish bistro offering popular cuisine

☎ 0191 384 4354 Aykley Heads House, Aykley Heads DH1 5TS

A modern business park has sprung up around this 18th-century former farmhouse. Original features include white-painted stone walls, wooden and stone floors, an inner courtyard and a vaulted bar. These, combined with the rustic chic décor, create the feel of a French country bistro. The bistro-style dishes are simple and effective with clean, clear flavours, demonstrated in pear, chicory and dolcelatte salad with lovely fresh walnuts, or perhaps grilled tiger prawns with chilli and garlic, followed by seared sea bream with Puy lentils and ratatouille, and cinder toffee parfait with diced Cox apple and vanilla syrup for dessert.

◉◉◉
Seaham Hall Hotel - The White Room Restaurant

SEAHAM   MAP 19 NZ44

Modern, Traditional British, European V 🍷 NOTABLE WINE LIST

Exciting dining in contemporary, luxury spa hotel

☎ 0191 516 1400 Lord Byron's Walk SR7 7AG
e-mail: reservations@seaham-hall.com
web: www.seaham-hall.com

In 1815 Lord Byron married Annabella Milbanke here, and stayed on for their honeymoon, no doubt, benefiting from the bracing North Sea coastal ozone. This imposing, listed hotel with its 19th-century façade, stylish, modern interiors and lavish spa facilities continues to attract visitors from far and wide. The contemporary theme continues in the dining room with wooden floors, neutral colours and quality furnishings creating a calm and comfortable ambience. Fully draped tables have expensive settings, and service is formal and discreet. Adventurous and skilfully executed combinations characterise unashamedly modern dishes that make full use of best quality ingredients. In between the numerous appetisers, amuses and extras, fit a crab salad with confit salmon, avocado ice cream passionfruit vinaigrette and caviar or a main course of Balmoral Estate venison loin with pumpkin purée, chestnuts and crosnes, bitter chocolate sauce and scallop. Cheese and desserts come with wine pairings.

Chef: Stephen Smith **Owners:** Tom & Jocelyn Maxfield **Times:** 12-2.30/7-10 **Prices:** Fixed L £17.50, Fixed D £30-£45, Main £45, Service optional **Wine:** 100% bottles over £20, 9 by the glass **Notes:** ALC L&D 3 courses, Sun L 3 courses £22.50, Vegetarian menu, Dress Restrictions, Smart casual, Civ Wed 112, Air con **Seats:** 55, Pr/dining room 20 **Children:** Portions **Rooms:** 19 (19 en suite)★★★★★ HL **Directions:** A19 at 1st exit signed B1404 Seaham and follow signs to Seaham Hall **Parking:** 150

Times: 12-2/7-10.25, Closed 25 Dec, 1Jan, BHs, Sun **Directions:** Off B6532 from Durham centre, pass County Hall on right and Dryburn Hospital on left. Turn right at double rdbt into Aykley Heads

ROMALDKIRK   MAP 19 NY92

◉◉ Rose & Crown Hotel

Traditional British

Cosy country inn in a quintessential English setting

☎ 01833 650213   DL12 9EB
e-mail: hotel@rose-and-crown.co.uk
web: www.rose-and-crown.co.uk

Oozing warmth and character, this sophisticated but relaxed 18th-century coaching inn is secreted away in a picture-postcard Teesdale village. Situated on the village green opposite the old stocks and water pump, next to the Saxon church, its traditionally styled oak-panelled restaurant is replete with starched white linen and evening candlelight; you can also dine in the cosy bar, complete with crackling fire, carriage lamps, old settle and prints. The kitchen showcases well-executed, clear-flavoured classic British fare with modern and regional influences; think pan-fried pink wood pigeon with wilted spinach and chestnuts, in a juniper berry sauce, or halibut with local Cotherstone cheese and red onion marmalade. Desserts might include hot sticky walnut and syrup tart with vanilla ice cream, and there's a good selection of local cheeses.

Chef: Chris Davy, Andrew Lee **Owners:** Mr & Mrs C Davy **Times:** 12-1.30/7.30-9, Closed Xmas, Closed L Mon-Sat **Prices:** Fixed L £17.75-£19.50, Fixed D £28-£32, Service optional **Wine:** 46 bottles over £20, 20 bottles under £20, 14 by the glass **Notes:** Fixed L 3 courses, Fixed D 4 courses **Seats:** 24 **Children:** Min 6 yrs, Portions **Rooms:** 12 (12 en suite)★★ HL **Directions:** 6m NW of Barnard Castle on B6277 **Parking:** 24

SEAHAM   MAP 19 NZ44

◉◉◉ Seaham Hall Hotel - The White Room Restaurant

see opposite

BRAINTREE   MAP 07 TL72

◉ The Cock Inn

British, Italian NEW

Vibrant, gastro-pub of TV fame serving Italian-influenced dishes

☎ 01371 850 566 Beazley End CM7 5JH
e-mail: info@thecock-inn.com
web: www.thecock-inn.com

Many TV viewers will have seen chef-patron Aaron Craze's exploits (a graduate of Jamie Oliver's Fifteen restaurant, see entry) cutting the apron strings to set up shop here in this venture initially funded by the celebrity chef's charity, The Fifteen Foundation. Now a vibrant gastro-pub, it's aptly named Graduate restaurant serves an appealing range of imaginative dishes with an authentic Italian buzz, driven by quality local and Italian produce. The talented team's lunch menu offer a lighter touch (perhaps pappardelle carbonara with guancial and grated parmigiano), while dinner cranks up the ante; think roast baby chicken with Italian greens, beetroots and mascarpone, and perhaps an apricot frangipane dessert.

Chef: Aaron Craze **Owners:** Aaron Craze, Nicci Williams **Times:** 12.30-3.30/6.30-9.30, Closed Mon **Prices:** Fixed L £10, Fixed D £28, Starter £7.50-£10, Main £12-£21, Dessert £5, Service optional **Wine:** 18 bottles over £20, 12 bottles under £20, 11 by the glass **Notes:** Vegetarian available **Seats:** 90 **Children:** Portions **Directions:** From M11 take A120 towards Colchester/Stansted **Parking:** 30

BRENTWOOD   MAP 06 TQ59

◉◉ Marygreen Manor

Modern European

Exciting dining in baronial setting

☎ 01277 225252 London Rd CM14 4NR
e-mail: info@marygreenmanor.co.uk
web: www.marygreenmanor.co.uk

Located in this striking 16th-century manor house, the dining room is the original baronial hall decorated in grand style complete with barley-twist columns, high beamed ceiling and crests of arms. Clothed tables with formal settings and helpful staff create a pleasant dining ambience. The modern European dishes on the carte and tasting menu are based on seasonal produce. To start, try the diver scallops with cauliflower, hazelnuts and Xérès vinegar dressing. Main courses include pan-fried fillet of halibut with pumpkin, shiitake mushrooms and bok choy. Finish with apple and cinnamon crêpes with Calvados sabayon or one of the fine cheeses from the trolley. There is also a six-course tasting menu.

CONTINUED

BRENTWOOD Continued

Marygreen Manor

Chef: Paul Peters **Owners:** Mr S Bhattessa **Times:** 12.30-2.30/7.15-10.15, Closed D Sun **Prices:** Fixed L £19.50, Fixed D £42.50, Service included
Wine: 80 bottles over £20, 21 bottles under £20, 7 by the glass
Notes: Tasting menu £45.50 6 courses, Dress Restrictions, No jeans or trainers, Civ Wed 60, Air con **Seats:** 80, Pr/dining room 85
Children: Portions **Rooms:** 56 (56 en suite) ★★★★ HL **Directions:** 1m from Brentwood town centre, 0.5m from M25 junct 28 **Parking:** 100

CHELMSFORD   MAP 06 TL70

⑳ New Street Brasserie

Modern, International

Brasserie dining in modern town-centre hotel

☎ 01245 268179 Best Western Atlantic Hotel, New St CM1 1PP
e-mail: info@atlantichotel.co.uk
web: www.newstreetbrasserie.com

There's a stylish new look to the contemporary brasserie of this purpose-built modern hotel. White leather and rich dark woods are complemented by aubergine and fuchsia colours and set the relaxing scene for some accomplished modern cooking. Using good-quality produce, the kitchen delivers well-executed dishes, perhaps crab, chilli and lime fettucine to start, followed by baked cod with black olive sauce, or calves' liver and black pudding with sage jus. To finish, try the chocolate and praline truffle torte. White-linen dressed tables and professional, yet relaxed service from uniformed staff fit the bill, too.

Times: 12-3/6-10.30, Closed 27-30 Dec, Closed L Sat-Sun **Rooms:** 59 (59 en suite) ★★★ HL **Directions:** 5-minute walk from High Street

⑳ Russells

Modern English, French

Innovative cuisine in an ancient barn

☎ 01245 478484 Bell St, Great Baddow CM2 7JR
e-mail: russellsrestaurant@hotmail.com
web: www.russellsrest.co.uk

A Grade II listed conversion of a 14th-century barn, Russells comprises a lounge, bar and restaurant divided into four areas. The place is traditionally decorated and very smart with formal service, and the cooking has both French and English influences. Recommended dishes include a seared trio of scallops with oven-dried plum tomatoes and bacon vinaigrette to start, and a main course of roast rack of lamb with soft herb crust, minted leeks and rosemary jus. Finish with a rich

chocolate fondant, served with equally rich chocolate sauce and vanilla ice cream.

Russells

Chef: Barry Warren-Watson **Owners:** Mr B J Warren-Watson **Times:** 12-2.30/7-11.30, Closed 2 wks from 2 Jan, Mon, Closed L Sat, D Sun
Prices: Fixed L £10.95-£16, Fixed D £14.95-£21.95, Starter £5.95-£10.95, Main £12.95-£21.95, Dessert £4.50-£7.95, Service optional, Group min 10 service 15% **Wine:** 42 bottles over £20, 30 bottles under £20, 8 by the glass
Notes: Dress Restrictions, No jeans, Air con **Seats:** 70, Pr/dining room 36
Children: Portions **Directions:** Please telephone for directions **Parking:** 40

COGGESHALL   MAP 07 TL82

⑳ Baumann's Brasserie

British, French 🖥

Serious food in a light-hearted atmosphere

☎ 01376 561453 4-6 Stoneham St CO6 1TT
e-mail: food@baumannsbrasserie.co.uk
web: www.baumannsbrasserie.co.uk

Celebrating its 21st anniversary, this busy brasserie occupies a historic hall house in the heart of town. Clothed tables and antique chairs contrast with stripped floors and whitewashed walls hung with colourful artwork. The seasonally-changing menu is gutsy and interesting, offering an eclectic mix of well-executed dishes. Try the crispy duck salad with Japanese coleslaw and a bariyaki shooter, followed by tandoori rolled loin of lamb with minty haricot beans. Check out 'The Billingsgate Best' for daily fresh fish, and the light lunch for great value. Jazz nights feature.

Chef: Mark Baumann, C Jeanneau **Owners:** Baumann's Brasserie Ltd
Times: 12-2/7-9.30, Closed 2 wks Jan, Mon-Tue **Prices:** Fixed L £12.95, Fixed D £22, Starter £5.50-£8.95, Main £16-£19.50, Dessert £6.50, Service optional **Wine:** 20 bottles over £20, 24 bottles under £20, 11 by the glass
Seats: 80 **Children:** Portions **Directions:** A12 from Chelmsford, turn off at Kelvedon into Coggeshall, restaurant is in centre opposite the Clock Tower **Parking:** Opposite

ENGLAND

COLCHESTER MAP 13 TL92

◎◎ Best Western Rose & Crown Hotel

Traditional, International V

Casual, contemporary dining in a traditional Tudor building

☎ 01206 866677 East St CO1 2TZ
e-mail: info@rose-and-crown.com
web: www.rose-and-crown.com

Said to be the oldest hotel in the oldest recorded town in England, this black and white 14th-century posting inn retains much of its original character, with a wealth of exposed beams and timbered walls. Inside, furnishings and colours surprise with a contemporary look that blends well with the historic setting, the smart, stylish and relaxed brasserie - the East Street Grill - echoing the theme. The menu also moves with the times, fusing global flavours with fresh local produce. Think baked sea bass served with purple potato mash, tossed peppers and a yellow lentil sauce, while desserts might feature ginger melon mousse with pistachio biscotti.

Chef: Venu Mahankali **Times:** 12-2/7-9.45, Closed 27-30 Dec, Closed D Sun **Prices:** Fixed L £10-£16, Fixed D £13-£23, Starter £3.75-£6.75, Main £8.25-£16.95, Dessert £3.95-£4.50, Service added but optional 10%, Group min 5 service 10% **Wine:** 12 bottles over £20, 19 bottles under £20, 6 by the glass **Notes:** Vegetarian menu, Civ Wed 150 **Seats:** 80, Pr/dining room 50 **Children:** Portions **Rooms:** 38 (38 en suite) ★★★ HL **Directions:** From A12 take exit to Colchester North onto the A1232 **Parking:** 60

◎ Clarice House

Modern British NEW

Accomplished cooking at a health spa

☎ 01206 734301 Kingsford Park, Layer Rd CO2 0HS
e-mail: colchester@claricehouse.co.
web: www.claricehouse.co.uk

At first glance, this imposing building appears to be a hotel, but in fact, it's a health spa offering an extensive range of treatments and an array of leisure facilities. Snacks are available in the trendy bar and lounge, but those in need of serious culinary pampering should treat themselves to some accomplished and eclectic cuisine in the restaurant, where bamboo chairs, a magnolia colour scheme and conservatory roof create the feel of an orangery. Ham hock terrine is a typical starter, wrapped in dark green Savoy cabbage and served with home-made piccalilli, while mains might include slow-roast pork belly with bacon, bubble-and-squeak, and a Calvados and Bramley drizzle.

Chef: Paul Boorman **Owners:** Clarke House (Colchester) Ltd **Times:** 12-2.30/7-9, Closed 25-26 Dec, 1 Jan, Closed D Sun-Wed **Prices:** Fixed L £16, Fixed D £24-£26 **Wine:** 15 bottles over £20, 20 bottles under £20, 8 by the glass **Notes:** Vegetarian available, Dress Restrictions, Smart casual, Civ Wed 75, Air con **Seats:** 60 **Directions:** SW of town centre on B1026 towards Layer **Parking:** 100

DEDHAM MAP 13 TM03

◎◎ Le Talbooth Restaurant

Modern British ⚑NOTABLE WINE LIST

Traditional quality in a picture-postcard setting

☎ 01206 323150 CO7 6HP
e-mail: talbooth@milsomhotels.com
web: www.milsomhotels.com

A riverside setting, immaculate lawns, a picturesque bridge, leaded windows and a timber frame - no wonder Constable painted this magnificent property. Inside it boasts old beams, leather chairs, striking artwork and smart table settings, and you'd need a vivid imagination to picture it as the weaver's cottage and toll booth it once was. There's a terrace for all-weather alfresco dining, complete with sail canopy and heaters. The food matches the setting, with its emphasis on superior ingredients, local wherever possible, revealed on a balanced carte with modern undertones. You might choose bourride of shellfish to start, or perhaps potato and goat's cheese roulade with beetroot and gherkin salad, and move on to Dover sole meunière, with an apple tarte Tatin finish.

Chef: Ian Rhodes **Owners:** Paul Milsom **Times:** 12-2/7-9, Closed D Sun (Oct-Apr) **Prices:** Fixed L £19.50, Starter £6.25-£14.95, Main £16.50-£28, Dessert £6.50-£8.25, Service included **Wine:** 560 bottles over £20, 38 bottles under £20, 10 by the glass **Notes:** Vegetarian available, Dress Restrictions, Smart casual, No jeans, Civ Wed 50 **Seats:** 75, Pr/dining room 34 **Children:** Portions **Directions:** 6m from Colchester: follow signs from A12 to Stratford St Mary, restaurant on left before village **Parking:** 50

DEDHAM CONTINUED

milsoms

International

Fun and informal dining experience in the Dedham Vale

☎ 01206 322795 Stratford Rd CO7 6HN
e-mail: milsoms@milsomhotels.com
web: www.milsomhotels.com

This split-level bar/restaurant has a relaxed contemporary look achieved with natural fabrics, stone, wood and leather. The redesigned terrace with new lighting and heating enables diners to enjoy eating outside for most of the year. There is a no-booking policy and diners write up their own orders on the notepads provided. There's no dress code and no predominant age group, and the customers love it. The chef's travels have brought a variety of influences to bear on the lengthy, crowd-pleasing, brasserie-style menu, which includes the likes of Asian, Greek and British favourites. Take the chef's meze to start, or perhaps Gloucestershire Old Spot sausages with leek mash and shallot gravy or a Malay chicken satay to follow.

Chef: Stas Anastasiades **Owners:** Paul Milsom **Times:** 12/9.30
Prices: Starter £4.25-£9.25, Main £9.75-£18.50, Dessert £5.50, Service optional **Wine:** 11 by the glass **Seats:** 80, Pr/dining room 16
Children: Menu, Portions **Rooms:** 15 (15 en suite) ★★★ SHL
Directions: 7m N of Colchester, just off A12 **Parking:** 60

FELSTED   MAP 06 TL62

Reeves Restaurant

Modern British

Seasonal produce in charming setting

☎ 01371 820996 Rumbles Cottage, Braintree Rd CM6 3DJ
e-mail: reevesrestaurant@tiscali.co.uk
web: www.reeves-restaurant.co.uk

Housed in a 16th-century cottage, this intimate oak-beamed restaurant is full of character with large windows, starched linen and plenty of fresh flowers. The cosy lounge is a lovely place for after-dinner drinks. The menus offer a range of interesting dishes inspired by the head chef's worldwide travel with the McLaren racing team. Starters might feature griddled summer quail, tarragon dressing and fried celery leaves, while main courses include the likes of rump of new season lamb with gratin potatoes, Puy lentils and Cumberland sauce. The elderflower crème brûlée might be a good choice to finish on.

Times: 12-2/7, Closed Mon-Wed **Directions:** A120 E from Braintree, B1417 to Felsted

GREAT CHESTERFORD   MAP 12 TL54

The Crown House

British

Refreshing cooking in a peaceful village setting

☎ 01799 530515 CB10 1NY
e-mail: stay@thecrownhouseonetel.net
web: www.thecrownhousehotel.com

Much of the original character has been retained at this sympathetically restored Georgian coaching inn. Public rooms include an attractive lounge bar, oak-panelled restaurant and a conservatory.

Terrace dining is an option in the summer months, between the main house and the walled garden. Sound cooking from good-quality produce delivers simple dishes with excellent flavours. Expect the likes of Crown House fishcake (crab and salmon) with mixed salad and sweet chilli sauce, followed by tender noisette of new season lamb, with minted caramelised pears, dauphinoise potatoes and thyme and port gravy. Finish with a chocolate brownie with a quenelle of Chantilly cream.

The Crown House

Times: 12-2/7-9.15 **Rooms:** 22 (22 en suite) ★★★ HL

GREAT DUNMOW   MAP 06 TL62

◉◉ **Starr Restaurant**

Modern British V

Skilful English cooking with a French accent

☎ 01371 874321 Market Place CM6 1AX
e-mail: starrrestaurant@btinternet.com
web: www.the-starr.co.uk

The Starr is a timber-framed, 15th-century coaching inn overlooking the village market place. Billed as a restaurant with rooms, it has built

up a loyal following for its smart décor, good food and friendly service. The restaurant occupies a converted stable block to the rear of the main building and, together with the conservatory, makes an excellent venue for serious dining. A skilful kitchen team produces modern British dishes with some French influences. House favourites include pan-seared Lyme Bay scallops with parsnip purée and parsnip crisps, and Suffolk pork belly 'four ways' with caramelised endive, fondant potato and apple velouté. Another multi-faceted dish is a pudding of lemon 'three ways'.

Chef: Mark Pearson **Owners:** Terence & Louise George **Times:** 12-1.30/7-9.30, Closed 27 Dec-6 Jan, Closed D Sun **Prices:** Fixed L £17.50-£27.50, Fixed D £45, Service added but optional 10% **Wine:** 76 bottles over £20, 3 bottles under £20, 8 by the glass **Notes:** Tasting menu 7 courses £59.50 Mon-Fri, Vegetarian menu, Dress Restrictions, No jeans, trainers or shorts **Seats:** 70, Pr/dining room 36 **Children:** Portions **Rooms:** 8 (8 en suite) ★★★ HL **Directions:** M11 junct 8, A120 7m E towards Colchester. In town centre **Parking:** 16

GREAT YELDHAM   MAP 13 TL73

◉ **White Hart**

British, European V

Historic inn with an extensive menu

☎ 01787 237250 CO9 4HJ
web: www.whitehartyeldham.com

This ancient inn has recently celebrated its 500th birthday and boasts a number of historic curiosities, from a tiny prison that was used to hold highwaymen, to a private dining room that served as a communications centre in World War II. Heavily timbered and brimful of character, it stands on the banks of the River Colne in landscaped grounds and offers an extensive selection of crowd-pleasers (beef Wellington with Parmentier potatoes and cep jus), alongside more adventurous fare, such as monkfish fillets wrapped in Parma ham with an oriental potato cake and Thai froth. More informal brasserie dining is also available.

Chef: Stuart Barber/Kevin White **Owners:** Matthew Mason **Times:** 12-3/6-9.30, Closed D 25-26 Dec **Prices:** Fixed L £12.95, Fixed D £18.95, Starter £4.95-£10.95, Main £12.95-£21.95, Dessert £4.95-£5.95, Service optional, Group min 7 service 10% **Wine:** 46 bottles over £20, 32 bottles under £20, 7 by the glass **Notes:** Sun L/D 3 courses £21.95, Vegetarian menu, Dress Restrictions, Smart casual, Civ Wed 80 **Seats:** 60, Pr/dining room 36 **Children:** Menu, Portions **Directions:** On A1017, between Halstead and Haverhill **Parking:** 40

HARWICH   MAP 13 TM23

◉◉ **The Pier at Harwich**

Seafood, European

Modish seafood restaurant in quayside hotel

☎ 01255 241212 The Quay CO12 3HH
e-mail: pier@milsomhotels.com
web: www.milsomhotels.co.uk

Perfect for seafood lovers, The Pier is situated smack on the quay overlooking the ports of Harwich and Felixstowe. Converted into a small contemporary hotel, its first-floor Harbourside restaurant is a stylish affair, replete with chrome cocktail bar and leather armchairs. The open-plan dining space comes decked out with neatly-clothed, well-spaced tables, fantastic clear-weather views and relaxed but

CONTINUED

ENGLAND

HARWICH CONTINUED

professional service. The lengthy menu (offering a good choice of dishes that can be taken as starter or mains) unsurprisingly comes awash with the fruits of the sea, its wide selection of fish and shellfish featuring fresh, locally-caught and locally-smoked produce. Expect lobster thermidor, moules marinière, or perhaps grilled fillet of wild sea bass with lime and chive butter. (Downstairs, the Ha'penny offers informal bistro-style fare.)

The Pier at Harwich

Chef: Chris Oakley **Owners:** Paul Milsom **Times:** 12-2/6.30-9.30, Closed 25 Dec evening **Prices:** Food prices not confirmed for 2008. Please telephone for details **Notes:** Vegetarian available, Dress Restrictions, Smart casual, Civ Wed 50, Air con **Seats:** 80, Pr/dining room 16 **Children:** Menu, Portions **Rooms:** 14 (14 en suite) ★★★ HL **Directions:** A12 to Colchester then A120 to Harwich harbour front **Parking:** 20

INGATESTONE   MAP 06 TQ69

◎◎ The Woolpack

Modern British

Modern dining in traditional inn

☎ 01277 352189 Mill Green Rd CM4 0HS
e-mail: info@thewoolpack-fryerning.co.uk
web: www.thewoolpack-fryerning.co.uk

There has been a Woolpack Inn since the 1100s, but the current building is 19th century. A contemporary interior features polished oak floors, oak beams, ivory-coloured half panelling and luxurious leather seating. Smoked glass, wooden blinds and 1950s fashion photographs complete the look. The kitchen brigade delivers accomplished modern British cooking offering clean, clear flavours from excellent produce. Hand-dived scallops, nicely caramelised, are served on a full-flavoured pea purée with mixed leaves drizzled with truffle oil, followed by braised shin of beef with stilton dumpling and port jus. Finish with freshly baked rich chocolate fondant and home-made vanilla ice cream.

Chef: Ben Horle **Owners:** John & Lisa Hood **Times:** 12-4/7-12.30, Closed 2 wks in Aug, 2 wks after Xmas, Mon, Closed L Tue & Sat, D Sun **Prices:** Fixed L £11.95-£13.95, Fixed D £20.95-£29.95, Starter £4.95-£8.95, Main £12.95-£16.95, Dessert £5.95-£6.95, Service optional **Wine:** 36 bottles over £20, 12 bottles under £20, 5 by the glass **Notes:** Sun L 3 courses £19.95, Dress Restrictions, Smart casual, no headgear, Air con **Seats:** 45 **Children:** Min 12 yrs **Directions:** M25 junct A12, between Brentwood & Chelmsford **Parking:** 20

MANNINGTREE   MAP 13 TM13

◎ The Mistley Thorn

International

Delightful inn serving quality, locally-sourced produce

☎ 01206 392821 High St, Mistley CO11 1HE
e-mail: info@mistleythorn.co.uk
web: www.mistleythorn.co.uk

A setting beside the River Stour is part of the appeal of this bustling Georgian inn, built on what was once the site of some of Matthew Hopkins' infamous Witchfinder trials. Inside the bistro-style restaurant has an air of American New England about it - light and airy with terracotta-tiled floors, high-quality furnishings, exposed beams and tongue-and-groove walls. Seating is high-backed wicker chairs or banquettes. The simple approach to cooking suits the venue, with the abundant local, seasonal produce ensuring good, clean flavours. Think seared wild sea bass served with sauce vierge, new potatoes and spinach, and perhaps a plum and almond tart with vanilla ice cream to finish. Cookery lessons are available.

Chef: Sherri Singleton **Owners:** Sherri Singleton, David McKay **Times:** 12-2.30/6.30-9.30, Closed 25 Dec **Prices:** Fixed L £10.95, Fixed D £14.95, Starter £3.95-£7.95, Main £7.95-£16.95, Dessert £4.50-£4.95, Service optional, Group min 8 service 10% **Seats:** 75, Pr/dining room 28 **Children:** Menu, Portions **Directions:** From A12 take A137 for Manningtree and Mistley **Parking:** 7

SAFFRON WALDEN   MAP 12 TL53

◎ The Cricketers' Arms

Modern European NEW

Remodelled village inn with accomplished modern cooking

☎ 01799 543210 Rickling Green CB11 3YG
e-mail: reservations@cricketers.demon.co.uk
web: www.thecricketersarms.com

Overlooking the village cricket green - as the name suggests - this 18th-century red-brick inn is a focal point of attractive Rickling Green. The interior retains many original features, including exposed beams and fireplaces, while contemporary restyling takes on a fashionable minimalist approach to highlight quality furnishings; take wooden floors and tables, leather sofas, a traditional bar and Japanese-style terrace garden. The kitchen's equally modern approach comes dotted with a taste of Italy, alongside good seasonal produce and flavour combinations. Take an Italian stew of seared Loganica sausage with white bean cassoulet, or perhaps a veal cutlet served with soft fried egg, anchovies and a butter and caper sauce.

Chef: Hitchem Lazri **Owners:** Barry Hilton **Times:** 12-2.30/6-9.30
Prices: Fixed D £27.75-£32.75, Starter £4.95-£9.25, Main £10.50-£17.95, Dessert £5.75, Service optional **Wine:** 15 bottles over £20, 12 bottles under £20, 8 by the glass **Seats:** 60, Pr/dining room 12 **Children:** Menu **Rooms:** 9 (9 en suite) ★★★★ INN **Directions:** M11 junct 8, A120 to Bishops Stortford then B1383 and follow signs to Rickling **Parking:** 40

SOUTHEND-ON-SEA MAP 07 TQ88

◉ Fleur de Provence

French
Modern French cooking in resort restaurant

☎ 01702 352987 52-54 Alexander St SS1 1BJ
e-mail: mancel@fleurdeprovence.co.uk
web: www.fleurdeprovence.co.uk

A stone's throw from the town centre, the frosted glass, high-street frontage of this French restaurant may look unassuming, but inside the stylish, intimate and cosy restaurant has soft colours and lighting to create a genuinely romantic setting, while service is friendly but discreet. Modern meets classical in the menu; take rib-eye of beef with a bourguignon sauce, or lamb cannon coated in minted breadcrumbs with a garlic-scented jus, and to finish, perhaps an assiette of chocolate or trio of crème brûlees.

Chef: Marcel Bouchenga **Owners:** Marcel Bouchenga **Times:** 12-2/7-10, Closed 1st 2 wks Jan, BHs, Sun, Closed L Sat **Prices:** Fixed L £15, Fixed D £15, Starter £7.95-£12.95, Main £16.95-£18.95, Dessert £7.95-£10.95, Service optional, Group min 6 service 10% **Wine:** 44 bottles over £20, 18 bottles under £20, 8 by the glass **Notes:** Fixed L 3 courses, Dress Restrictions, Smart casual, Air con **Seats:** 50, Pr/dining room 20 **Children:** Portions **Parking:** On street parking, public car parks

STOCK MAP 06 TQ69

◉ Bear Restaurant & Bar

European
Innovative cuisine in historic surroundings

☎ 01277 829100 The Square CM4 9LH
e-mail: info@thebearinn.biz
web: www.thebearinn.biz

This restaurant and bar occupies a listed 16th-century coaching inn on the village square. It offers a flexible approach with a light lounge menu, fine-dining restaurant, Sunday breakfast and a champagne brunch. Children are also made welcome with their own menu. Typical dishes include a feuillette of warm asparagus with oyster mushrooms, leek purée and chive butter sauce, or perhaps confit shoulder of lamb with anchovies, rosemary, dauphinoise potatoes, braised green lentils and a simple jus. The four-course, mid-week menu is good value with a bottle of wine thrown in per couple.

Chef: Nourreddine Hofri **Owners:** Lee & Kathryn Anderson-Frogley **Times:** 12-3/5-12.30, Closed 25-26 Dec, Mon, Closed D Sun **Prices:** Fixed L £18, Fixed D £18, Starter £4.95-£10.95, Main £11.95-£23.95, Dessert £5.95-£8.95, Service optional **Wine:** 30 bottles over £20, 14 bottles under £20, 12 by the glass **Notes:** Fixed L 3 courses, Sun L 3 courses £18.95, Vegetarian available **Seats:** 90, Pr/dining room 26 **Children:** Menu, Portions **Directions:** M25 junct 28, onto A12, turn off for Billericay, into village, restaurant just off High St **Parking:** 30

TOLLESHUNT KNIGHTS MAP 07 TL91

◉◉ Camelot

Modern British
Fine-dining restaurant in a resort hotel

☎ 01621 868888 Five Lakes Hotel, Colchester Rd CM9 8HX
e-mail: enquiries@fivelakes.co.uk
web: www.fivelakes.co.uk

Set in 320 acres of Essex countryside, this resort hotel boasts extensive health, leisure and sporting facilities. The split-level Camelot restaurant

CONTINUED

Five Lakes Hotel, Golf, Country Club & Spa
Fine dining restaurant in a resort hotel
Colchester Rd, Essex CM9 8HX Tel: 01621 868888
e-mail: enquiries@fivelakes.co.uk
web: www.fivelakes.co.uk

This well-equipped resort hotel sits in 320 acres of open countryside where guests can use the extensive country club and other health and leisure facilities. The split-level Camelot restaurant, themed around the romantic myth of King Arthur, is serenaded by live piano music from the lobby. Close attention to detail keeps the modern British and European food to a high standard, with a short Indulgence Menu offering what it promises in two or three courses, and a longer carte finishing with a good choice of cheeses. Seared scallop and tiger prawns in a light nage of saffron and lemon thyme, to the robust braised venison and oyster pie with winter vegetables show the spread on a seasonal offering.

ENGLAND

TOLLESHUNT KNIGHTS CONTINUED

is themed around the legend of King Arthur. Close attention to detail keeps the modern British and European food to a high standard, with a short Indulgence Menu delivering what it promises in two or three courses, and a longer carte finishing with a good choice of cheeses. Start with warm Maldon oyster beignet and pancetta salad with a lemon and coconut dressing, followed perhaps by grilled fillet of sea bass with a spaghetti of vegetables and aubergine caviar, or meat-eaters might opt for fillet of beef topped with blue cheese gratin, rösti potato and thyme sauce. Finish with key lime pie with citrus and vanilla syrup, or choose from a selection of home-made ice creams and sorbets.

Camelot

Chef: Mark Joyce **Owners:** Mr A Bejerano **Times:** 7-10, Closed 26, 31 Dec, 1 Jan, Mon & Sun **Prices:** Fixed D £27, Starter £5.50-£7.25, Main £11.25-£20.50, Dessert £5.50-£6.95, Service optional **Wine:** 63 bottles over £20, 18 bottles under £20, 7 by the glass **Notes:** Vegetarian available, Dress Restrictions, Smart casual, No trainers, T-shirts or jeans, Civ Wed 300, Air con **Seats:** 80 **Children:** Menu, Portions **Rooms:** 194 (194 en suite) ★★★★ HL **Directions:** M25 junct 28, then on A12. At Kelvedon take B1024 then B1023 to Tolleshunt Knights, clearly marked by brown tourist signs **Parking:** 550
see advert on page 167

GLOUCESTERSHIRE

ALMONDSBURY   MAP 04 ST68

⊛ *Quarterjacks Restaurant*

Modern British
Relaxed, brasserie-style dining in modern business hotel

☎ 01454 201090 Aztec Hotel & Spa, Aztec West Business Park BS32 4TS
e-mail: aztec@shirehotels.co.uk
web: www.aztechotelbristol.com

This stylish, modern hotel - located to the north of Bristol - is built in the Nordic style, its timber beams, vaulted ceilings and log fires blending with contemporary artwork and stone-flagged floors. The Quarterjacks Restaurant looks out across the terrace - perfect for alfresco summer dining - and gardens at the rear, and oozes a relaxed, informal brasserie vibe. The kitchen offers simply-prepared dishes from high-quality ingredients - perhaps chargrilled halibut with Thatchers cider, buttered cabbage, bacon and herb cream, or roasted pumpkin risotto with walnut dressing, crispy sage and garlic ciabatta. Save room for an excellent white chocolate pannacotta dessert. A bar menu offers lighter options.

Times: 12.30-2/7-10, Closed 26 Dec, Closed L Sat & Sun **Rooms:** 128 (128 en suite) ★★★★ HL **Directions:** Telephone for directions

ARLINGHAM   MAP 04 SO71

⊛⊛ The Old Passage Inn

Seafood
Seafood restaurant with river and forest views

☎ 01452 740547 Passage Rd GL2 7JR
e-mail: oldpassage@ukonline.co.uk
web: www.fishattheoldpassageinn.co.uk

The aptly-named Old Passage is a charming early 19th-century inn on the banks of the tidal River Severn - formerly a ferry station for services crossing the river. The large dining room has a fresh and airy look in mint and cream, and in summer there's a garden terrace for meals outside with river views. For private parties there's a second intimate dining room. The food is almost exclusively fish and shellfish, with two seawater tanks to store the latter. Dishes are imaginatively presented, with intelligently simple treatment of sea-fresh produce. Take roast tranche of turbot served with parsley new potatoes and hollandaise, perhaps a whole lobster thermidor or amoricaine, or fruits de mer.

Chef: Mark Redwood, Raoul Moore **Owners:** The Moore Family **Times:** 12-2/6.30-9, Closed 24-30 Dec, Mon, Closed D Sun **Prices:** Starter £5.50-£13.50, Main £11.90-£20.50, Dessert £4.30-£6.50, Service optional **Wine:** 53 bottles over £20, 36 bottles under £20, 15 by the glass **Seats:** 60, Pr/dining room 14 **Children:** Portions **Rooms:** 3 (3 en suite) ★★★★ RR **Directions:** Telephone for directions **Parking:** 40

BARNSLEY   MAP 05 SP00

⊛⊛ The Village Pub

Modern British 🖥
An inn for all seasons

☎ 01285 740421 GL7 5EF
e-mail: info@thevillagepub.co.uk
web: www.thevillagepub.co.uk

As the name might suggest, you can still expect a warm welcome, flagstones and floorboards, beams and open winter fires at this revamped, weathered-stone Cotswold inn. But this is no average village pub. Here five interconnecting dining areas radiate round a central bar, decked out with eclectic wooden furniture and contemporary décor. There's a garden patio for summer eating, too. Modern thinking shows its hand in the cooking, with dishes intelligently not overcomplicated and showing a strong reliance on quality local produce. Take roast duck breast served with Savoy cabbage and parsnips, perhaps roast pollack with mussels, clams, aubergine and coriander, or crowd-pleasing beer-battered fish and chips with tartare sauce. Desserts follow the theme, from a chocolate St Emilion and crème fraîche, to warm beer cake with thick cream.

Chef: Rory Duncan **Owners:** Tim Haigh & Rupert Penered **Times:** 11-2.30/7-9.30 **Prices:** Starter £4-£7.50, Main £10.50-£15.50, Dessert £6, Service optional **Wine:** 29 bottles over £20, 19 bottles under £20, 11 by the glass **Notes:** Vegetarian available **Seats:** 100, Pr/dining room 16 **Children:** Portions **Directions:** 4m from Cirencester, on B4425 to Bibury **Parking:** 40

BIBURY
MAP 05 SP10

◎◎ Bibury Court

British V ◭ NOTABLE WINE LIST

Comfortable and relaxing formal dining in Tudor manor

☎ 01285 740337 & 740324   GL7 5NT

e-mail: info@biburycourt.com

web: www.biburycourt.com

Grand country mansion tucked away behind a beautiful Cotswold village in a picture-postcard spot with six acres of grounds on the River Coln. Dating back to 1633, it offers an oasis of calm in gracious rooms that ooze historic charm and character, with traditional wood-panelling, log fires, comfy sofas and antique furniture, but the atmosphere is warm, relaxed and informal. For such a grand and elegant setting the cooking is refreshingly unfussy, unpretentious and understated. A confident kitchen uses fine, seasonal ingredients to create quality, modern dishes with a classical base; take a breast of free-range Cotswold guinea fowl served with truffled mash, braised leek and morels. Dine in the more informal conservatory at lunch and the formal, newly refurbished restaurant over dinner.

Chef: Antony Ely **Owners:** Robert Johnston **Times:** 12-2/7-9
Prices: Fixed L £12.50-£19.50, Fixed D £35-£39, Service optional, Group min 6 service 10% **Wine:** 117 bottles over £20, 24 bottles under £20, 8 by the glass **Notes:** Tasting menu available, Vegetarian menu, Civ Wed 32
Seats: 65, Pr/dining room 30 **Children:** Menu, Portions **Rooms:** 18 (16 en suite) ★★★ CHH **Directions:** On B4425 between Cirencester & Burford; hotel behind church **Parking:** 100

BUCKLAND
MAP 10 SP03

◎◎ Buckland Manor

Traditional French ◭ NOTABLE WINE LIST

Contemporary cooking in medieval manor

☎ 01386 852626   WR12 7LY

e-mail: info@bucklandmanor.com

web: www.bucklandmanor.com

There's quite the feeling of quintessential Englishness about this grand 13th-century, mellow-stone Cotswold manor house set in immaculate grounds. Inside has more a feeling of traditional country home than luxury country-house hotel, with roaring open fires, stone floors, tapestries and comfortable sitting rooms, while the atmosphere is one of calm and tranquility. The equally traditional restaurant has unusual white-painted wood panelling, portraits and lovely views, backed by skilled, attentive service. The kitchen's accomplished modern approach is underpinned by a classical theme and showcases quality fresh local

produce. Take caramelised breast of Gressingham duck served with spiced red cabbage and a black fig tart Tatin, and to finish, raspberry soufflé with whisky anglaise and honey ice cream.

Buckland Manor

Chef: Matt Hodgkinson **Owners:** Buckland Manor Country House Hotel Ltd **Times:** 12.30-1.45/7.30-9 **Prices:** Fixed L £19.50, Starter £7.95-£19.95, Main £22.50-£32.50, Dessert £9.25-£10.50, Service optional **Wine:** 543 bottles over £20, 11 bottles under £20, 17 by the glass **Notes:** Sun L 3 courses £25.50, 4 courses £27.50, Vegetarian available, Dress Restrictions, Jacket & tie **Seats:** 40 **Children:** Min 8 yrs **Rooms:** 13 (13 en suite) ★★★ HL **Directions:** 2m SW of Broadway. Take B4632 signed Cheltenham, then take turn for Buckland. Hotel through village on right **Parking:** 30

CHARINGWORTH
MAP 10 SP13

◎◎ The John Greville Restaurant

Modern International

Modern cuisine in an ancient manor

☎ 01386 593555 Charingworth Manor GL55 6NS

e-mail: charingworthmanor@classiclodges.co.uk

web: www.classiclodges.co.uk

The ancient manor of Charingworth lies in beautiful Cotswold countryside within a 54-acre estate. The present building dates back to the early 14th century, with beams showing original medieval decoration. The small, traditional restaurant has beamed ceilings and a warm décor of red rag-rolled walls with tables divided into separate areas. Service is informal and relaxed, although there is a dress code for men. Food is modern in style - underpinned by a classic French base - with clear flavours. Daily-changing menus are sensibly compact and might feature pan-seared loin of blue fin tuna served with lightly spiced Moroccan couscous, wilted spinach and tapenade, or perhaps honey-glazed breast of Gressingham duckling with braised red cabbage, confit leg spring roll, coriander and chilli.

CONTINUED

CHARINGWORTH CONTINUED

Chef: Andrew Lipp **Owners:** Classic Lodges **Times:** 12-2/7-9.30
Prices: Fixed D £37.95-£42.95 **Wine:** 45 bottles over £20, 5 bottles
under £20, 10 by the glass **Notes:** Fixed D 4 courses, Tasting menu
available, Dress Restrictions, Smart dress, Civ Wed 50 **Seats:** 44,
Pr/dining room 30 **Children:** Menu, Portions **Rooms:** 26 (26 en suite)
Directions: M40 exit at signs for A429 Stow. Follow signs for Moreton in
the Marsh. From Chipping Camden follow signs for Charingworth Manor
Parking: 100

CHELTENHAM   MAP 10 SO92

◉ Café Paradiso at Alias Hotel Kandinsky

Modern Mediterranean

*Funky townhouse with a cool vibe and warm
Mediterranean menu*

☎ 01242 527788 Bayshill Rd, Montpellier GL50 3AS
e-mail: kandinsky@aliashotels.com
web: www.aliashotels.com

Regency villa with a quirky decorative style that is welcoming and
bright, with a touch of mid-20th century furniture, art and
paraphernalia - expect the odd puppet and discarded top hat. The
overall effect is pretty cool, especially when you throw in the
soundtrack. Staffing is contemporary with an informally dressed young
team, but there's nothing casual about the service. An interesting
modern menu for a refreshingly different hotel is offered in the Café
Paradiso, including authentic pizzas from the wood-fired oven.
Otherwise try confit Blythburgh pork belly and Lincolnshire fillet
served with flageolet beans and spring onion sauce.

Chef: Adam Murray **Owners:** Alias Hotels **Times:** 12-2/6.30-10
Prices: Fixed L £15, Starter £8-£12, Main £10-£25, Dessert £6-£12, Service
optional **Wine:** 15 bottles over £20, 15 bottles under £20, 20 by the glass
Notes: Vegetarian available **Seats:** 40, Pr/dining room 24
Children: Menu, Portions **Rooms:** 48 (48 en suite) ★★★★ TH
Directions: From M5 junct 11 follow A40 towards town centre. Right at
rdbt, 2nd exit at next rdbt into Bayshill Rd **Parking:** 25

◉◉◉◉ Le Champignon Sauvage

see opposite

◉ George Hotel - Monty's Bar & Brasserie

Modern International

Confident cooking in stylish, contemporary setting

☎ 01242 235751 St Georges Rd GL50 3DZ
e-mail: hotel@stayatthegeorge.co.uk
web: www.montysbraz.co.uk

One of Cheltenham's finest Regency hotels, just a few minutes walk
from the tree-lined promenades and elegant terraces in the town
centre, the George is home to two dining venues: the modern, lively
Monty's Brasserie with luxurious leather seating and warm,
contemporary décor, and the stylish Monty's Dining Room, a quieter
venue offering the same menu but in a more intimate environment.
The chic designer cocktail bar in the basement is also popular, with
live entertainment at weekends. The confident, innovative, elegant
modern cooking fits the bill, and reflects skilled treatment of quality
ingredients. Take a starter of warm fresh crab and crispy squid nero

spaghetti, or perhaps a fillet of John Dory with crayfish risotto,
steamed asparagus and shellfish foam.

Times: 6.30-10, Closed Xmas, Sun-Mon, Closed L all week **Rooms:** 30 (30
en suite) ★★★ HL

◉◉ The Greenway

British, European V ◗ NOTABLE WINE LIST

Creative modern cooking in an Elizabethan manor

☎ 01242 862352 Shurdington GL51 4UG
e-mail: info@thegreenway.co.uk
web: www.the-greenway.co.uk

Classic country house in style - albeit on the outskirts of Cheltenham
rather than in the depths of the countryside - this mellow Elizabethan
manor house offers plenty of period features and a timeless quality of
understated relaxed charm and elegance. Think deep sofas and
crackling fire in the cosy lounge and a bright, elegant conservatory
restaurant furnished in appropriate style with views over the sunken
garden. The accomplished kitchen demonstrates creative flair and
passion with interesting combinations driven by the finest local
produce. Classical principles come coupled by modern innovative
twists; take a cannon of pork with pumpkin purée, langoustine
cannelloni, roast button onions and lentil jus, for instance, or how
about a honey-roast parsnip and thyme soufflé dessert, served with
sweet cardamom ice cream, bitter chocolate and olive oil.

Chef: Marc Hardiman **Owners:** von Essen Hotels **Times:** 12-2.30/7-10
Prices: Fixed L £16.50, Fixed D £45, Service optional **Wine:** All bottles
over £20, 10 by the glass **Notes:** ALC 3 courses £45,Tasting menu 6
courses £55, Vegetarian menu, Dress Restrictions, Smart casual, No jeans,
T-shirts or trainers, Civ Wed 45 **Seats:** 50, Pr/dining room 30
Children: Portions **Rooms:** 21 (21 en suite) ★★★ HL **Directions:** 3m
S of Cheltenham on A46 (Stroud), pass through the village of Shurdington
Parking: 50

◉◉ Lumière

Modern ◗ NOTABLE WINE LIST

Bold modern cooking at a chic town-centre haunt

☎ 01242 222200 Clarence Pde GL50 3PA
e-mail: dinner@lumiere.cc
web: www.lumiere.cc

It's all in the name, perhaps. This 'light' and thoroughly stylish,
intimate, clean-lined dining room comes secreted away behind an
unassuming etched-glass frontage that conceals one of the town
centre's shining culinary lights. Modern abstract artworks, white
tablecloths, elegant chairs and mirror-lined banquette seating all add

CONTINUED ON PAGE 172

Le Champignon Sauvage

CHELTENHAM   MAP 10 SO92

Modern

Serious French cooking, attentive service and modern, stylish environment

☎ 01242 573449   24 Suffolk Rd GL50 2AQ
e-mail: mail@lechampignonsauvage.co.uk
web: www.lechampignonsauvage.com

Chef: David Everitt-Matthias
Owners: Mr & Mrs D Everitt-Matthias
Times: 12.30-1.30/7.30-9, Closed 10 days Xmas, 3 wks Jun, Sun-Mon
Prices: Fixed L £23-£39, Fixed D £28-£48, Service optional
Wine: 97 bottles over £20, 45 bottles under £20, 6 by the glass
Seats: 40
Directions: S of the town centre, on A40, near Cheltenham College
Parking: Public car park (Bath Rd)

Expanded and refurbished, this culinary big-hitter has a long-standing, much-deserved reputation for culinary excellence. With chef-patron David Everitt-Matthias' innovative and polished skills combining with some surprisingly reasonable prices, it's set to continue as a national favourite with regulars, foodies and professionals alike, all beating a path to its doors for memorable dining and inspiration. Unassumingly tucked away in a terrace of shops on a busy main road in the quieter Montpellier district of town, this smart French restaurant provides few clues from outside of its premier-league status and enduring charm. Inside, however, the new spaciousness is immediately apparent to all but first-timers, though there's an instant warmth and vitality here that can be appreciated by all. Bright and spacious, it makes the most of its shop-front windows, and there's a small lounge area with comfortable leather chairs. Decorated with lovely white ash panelling, its light blue walls are hung with striking modern art. Carpet and darkwood upholstered chairs continue the blue theme, alongside simply but elegantly dressed tables, while service, headed-up by wife Helen, is friendly, attentive and knowledgeable.
There's no shortage of flair and imagination from David's kitchen - technical skill seems to abound here, the highly accomplished style delivering some classic combinations alongside more contemporary flashes, and always pleases. His peerless reputation for hard work and dedication to his craft is evident in the matching and balancing of flavours, which is exemplary, combined with the use of some interesting ingredients. Think a chump of Cotswold lamb paired with Jerusalem artichoke cream, globe artichokes and liquorice and almonds, or perhaps seared zander served with a casserole of ceps and a red wine emulsion. Peripherals like breads, amuse-bouche, pre-desserts and petits fours are equally impressive. This is inspirational cooking from start to finish!

CHELTENHAM CONTINUED

to the warm contemporary edge, while service is run with oodles of charm and vitality by Lin Chapman, who's equally informed and passionate about husband Geoff's cooking and the well-chosen wine list. His dishes are bold, generous, clean-cut and highly personal, with the sensibly compact, fixed-price menus certainly standing out from the crowd. Expect cashew-dusted rack of lamb with mustard tarragon sauce and curried leek potatoes, or perhaps chargrilled spring bok fillet served with a baby mushroom soufflé and roast potato cake from this dinner-only affair.

Chef: Geoff Chapman **Owners:** Lin & Geoff Chapman **Times:** 7-8.30, Closed 2 wks Jan, 2 wks summer, Sun-Mon, Closed L all week, D 25 Dec **Prices:** Fixed D £38-£41, Service optional, Group min 6 service 10% **Wine:** 75 bottles over £20, 2 bottles under £20, 4 by the glass **Seats:** 30 **Children:** Min 8 yrs **Directions:** Town centre, near bus station **Parking:** On street, nearby car parks

® Mercure Queen's Hotel

International NEW

Fashionable Regency hotel with assured cooking

☎ 01242 514754 The Promenade GL50 1NN
e-mail: H6632@accor.com
web: www.mercure-uk.com

The recently refurbished, conservatory-style Napier dining room at the Queen's an elegant, fashionable Regency hotel in the heart of the city comes with a real contemporary, neo-colonial edge. Think sleek wooden floors, high ceilings, unclothed tables, high-backed chairs, eye-catching planters and superb natural light, while staff here are friendly and attentive. The kitchen's well-balanced, well-executed modern approach blends classics alongside more contemporary combinations using quality seasonal produce. Take a confit of pork belly with roasted root vegetables and dauphinoise potatoes, or grilled Scottish rib-eye steak with béarnaise sauce, and perhaps a classic crème brûlée to finish.

Times: 12.30-2/7-9.30 **Rooms:** 79 (79 en suite) ★★★★ HL

®® *Parkers*

Modern British

Brasserie food in contemporary surroundings in period building

☎ 01242 518898 The Hotel on the Park, 38 Evesham Rd GL52 2AH
e-mail: stay@hotelonthepark.co.uk
web: www.hotelonthepark.com

This Grade II listed building dating from 1830 has been given a modern lease of life as a contemporary brasserie. The polished oak floors, American black walnut tables and stylish cutlery make this a place to be seen. Carefully cooked seasonal produce features on a menu offering some old favourites as well as more modern dishes. Try the likes of hot and sour seafood soup or pan-fried foie gras with warm fig salad for starters. Main courses might include roasted belly of Gloucestershire Old Spot pork with chorizo risotto and pea foam, or seared line-caught sea bass.

Times: 12-2/6.30-9.30, Closed D 25 Dec **Rooms:** 12 (12 en suite)★★★ SHL **Directions:** 4m from M5 junct 10. 0.75m from Cheltenham racecourse

Mayflower

☎ 01242 522426 32-34 Clarence St GL50 3NX

Chinese with an extensive menu that includes plenty of the familiar as well as more unusual dishes.

Off the Square Restaurant

☎ 01242 227757 8 The Courtyard, Montpellier St GL50 1SR

web: www.offthesquarerestaurant.co.uk

Friendly restaurant, with modern cuisine including good vegetarian options.

CHIPPING CAMPDEN MAP 10 SP13

®®® Cotswold House

see opposite

® Hicks' Brasserie and Bar

British NEW 💻

Relaxed, modern brasserie-style dining in contemporary surroundings

☎ 01386 840330 The Cotswold House Hotel, The Square GL55 6AN
e-mail: reception@cotswold.com
web: www.cotswoldhouse.com

The more relaxed dining option at this contemporarily designed hotel hits all the right notes. The décor's typically stylish and modern like everything else here, with its warm colours and modern furnishings, artwork and lighting. Think marble-topped bar, ivory or burgundy-coloured walls, banquettes or cool chairs and polished-wood tables, all colour-coordinated and suitably fashionable. The youthful service is unstuffy and friendly, while the kitchen's modern approach to brasserie fare takes a straightforward but highly accomplished line, playing to the gallery by offering something for everyone. Expect braised pork belly served with seared scallops and herb lasagne, and a passionfruit brûlée with pistachio biscotti finish.

Times: 12-3/5:00-9:30

® Three Ways House

Modern British

Cotswold home of the famous Pudding Club

☎ 01386 438429 Mickleton GL55 6SB
e-mail: reception@puddingclub.com
web: www.puddingclub.com

A Cotswold country-house hotel offering traditional comforts, though the restaurant is more contemporary in style, with a light and simple décor, and plenty of fresh flowers. This is the home of the famous Pudding Club, founded in 1985 to promote the great British dessert, where you will also find pudding-themed bedrooms. The menu offers contemporary to traditional British fare using quality, local seasonal produce. Try braised Gloucestershire Old Spot pork belly with an

Cotswold House

CHIPPING CAMPDEN   **MAP 10 SP13**

Modern British V ⚑NOTABLE WINE LIST 🖥

Vibrant and stylish cooking and interior design

☎ 01386 840330 The Square GL55 6AN
e-mail: reception@cotswoldhouse.com
web: www.cotswoldhouse.com

Appearances can be deceptive, and there are certainly surprises in store beyond the front door of this otherwise archetypal, Cotswold-stone former Regency wool merchant's house at the heart of this delightful town. An amazing staircase and bold, design-led decorative style cuts an unexpectedly stylish, contemporary edge inside; the artwork and design as exciting as the food on the plate. But this is contemporary elegance without pomposity, the service professional but nicely relaxed. Juliana's restaurant continues the theme, while the kitchen's appropriately modern approach comes underpinned by a classical theme on enticing and intelligently compact fixed-price menus that bring high skill, flair and clean, clear flavours to top-notch produce. Think tian of Cornish crab with tomato fondue, fennel and cress salad, or perhaps Buccleuch beef fillet with foie gras, and, heading up dessert, maybe a caramelised fig gratin with spiced port wine sorbet. An extensive wine list, decent range of cheeses and ancillaries like excellent breads, canapés and petits fours all hold form

through to the end, while bedrooms offer the same pampering, with a beguiling blend of style, quality and comfort at this much-talked-about hotel.

Chef: Jamie Forman **Owners:** Christa & Ian Taylor **Times:** 12-2.30/7-10, Closed L Mon-Sat **Prices:** Fixed D £49.50-£55, Service optional, Group min 8 service 10% **Wine:** 150 bottles over £20, 10 by the glass **Notes:** Sun L 3 courses £27.50, Vegetarian menu, Smart casual, Civ Wed 80, Air con **Seats:** 40, Pr/dining room 96 **Children:** Portions **Rooms:** 29 (29 en suite)★★★★ HL **Directions:** 1m N of A44 between Moreton-in-Marsh & Broadway on B4081 **Parking:** 25

English mustard jus, and finish with one of those scrumptious custard-enhanced English puddings; rhubarb crumble, syrup sponge or sticky toffee.

Three Ways House

Chef: Mark Rowlandson **Owners:** Simon Coombe & Peter Henderson **Times:** 12-2.30/7-9.30, Closed L Mon-Sat **Prices:** Fixed L £18.50-£21, Fixed D £34-£40, Service optional **Notes:** Vegetarian available, Civ Wed 80, Air con **Seats:** 80, Pr/dining room 70 **Children:** Menu, Portions **Rooms:** 48 (48 en suite) ★★★ HL **Directions:** On B4632, in village centre **Parking:** 37

CIRENCESTER   **MAP 05 SP00**

⚙ **Hare & Hounds**

Traditional, International V

Satisfying food in a charming Cotswold inn

☎ 01285 720288 Fosse-Cross GL54 4NN
e-mail: stay@thehareandhoundsinn.com
web: www.hareandhoundsinn.com

This typical Cotswold inn, parts of which date back to the 14th century, is bursting with character with open fires, stone and wood floors and cosy, candlelit nooks and crannies for intimate dining. Expect a mix of traditional and international cooking, which shows great efforts to incorporate local produce. You could expect a starter of North Cerney goat's cheese soufflé, or seared scallops with whisky cream sauce followed by medallions of pork fillet on braised fennel with lemon and sage jus. The dessert list is heavy on robust favourites such as sticky toffee pudding. There is alfresco dining available in the warmer months.

Chef: G Ragosa, M Howe **Owners:** Geraldo Ragosa & Angela Howe **Times:** 12-3/6-10, Closed Xmas, New Yr, BHs **Prices:** Starter £4.95-£8.95, Main £7.95-£18.50, Dessert £4.50-£5.50, Group min 7 service 10% **Wine:** 7 bottles over £20, 4 bottles under £20, 8 by the glass **Notes:** Sun L £9.95, Vegetarian menu **Seats:** 97, Pr/dining room 18 **Children:** Menu, Portions **Rooms:** 10 (10 en suite) ★★★★ INN **Directions:** On A429 Stow road 6m from Cirencester **Parking:** 80

CLEARWELL   MAP 04 SO50

◉◉ Tudor Farmhouse Hotel

Traditional British ☺

Hearty fare at romantic converted farm

☎ 01594 833046   GL16 8JS

e-mail: info@tudorfarmhousehotel.co.uk

web: www.tudorfarmhousehotel.co.uk

Situated within walking distance of Clearwell Castle in the heart of the Forest of Dean, Tudor Farmhouse is an ideal place to stay over. The architectural style is heavily hinted at in the name: this 13th-century, Grade II listed converted farm has the requisite oak beams, exposed stone and, more unusually, wooden spiral staircases. With a growing reputation in the area, the cooking is accomplished and demonstrates clear technical ability. Seasonality and local ingredients are duly celebrated in British dishes such as a duo of beef fillet and oxtail suet pudding served with puréed root vegetables and thyme fondants, or perhaps wild sea bass with wilted sea spinach, olive oil mash and a herb beurre blanc. Portions are generous and full-flavoured.

Chef: Peter Teague **Owners:** Owen & Eirwen Evans **Times:** 12-5.30/7-9, Closed 24-27 Dec **Prices:** Fixed L £10-£13.50, Fixed D £27.50-£30, Service optional **Wine:** 8 bottles over £20, 27 bottles under £20, 7 by the glass **Seats:** 30, Pr/dining room 22 **Children:** Menu, Portions **Rooms:** 22 (22 en suite) ★★★ HL **Directions:** Leave Monmouth to Chepstow road at Redbrook, follow signs Clearwell, turn left at village cross. Hotel on left **Parking:** 24

◉ The Wyndham Arms Hotel

Modern British NEW

Ancient hostelry serving up modern gastro-pub fare

☎ 01594 833666   GL16 8JT

e-mail: stay@thewyndhamhotel.co.uk

web: www.thewyndhamhotel.co.uk

The history of this charming village inn can be traced back over 600 years. Exposed stone walls, original beams and an impressive inglenook fireplace all add to the cosy, relaxed atmosphere. An extensive bar menu serves modern British fare in hearty portions, while à la carte is available in the Old Spot Country restaurant. Produce is locally sourced and free-range where possible. For mains, try succulent Gloucester Old Spot pork fillet medallions served with apple, date and cider cream sauce, with chocolate fudge tart with a dark chocolate milkshake for dessert. Ice creams are home-made.

Chef: Mark Belford **Owners:** Nigel Stanley **Times:** 12-2/6.30-9, Closed 1st wk Jan **Prices:** Starter £4.50-£7.50, Main £9.50-£16.50, Dessert £4.50-£7.50, Service optional **Wine:** 6 bottles over £20, 24 bottles under £20, 12 by the glass **Notes:** Vegetarian available, Civ Wed 80 **Seats:** 50, Pr/dining room 24 **Children:** Menu, Portions **Rooms:** 18 (18 en suite) ★★★ HL **Parking:** 30

CORSE LAWN   MAP 10 SO83

◉◉ Corse Lawn House Hotel

British, French V ⚑ NOTABLE WINE LIST

Attractive Queen Anne house with dining of long-standing reputation

☎ 01452 780771   GL19 4LZ

e-mail: enquiries@corselawn.com

web: www.corselawn.com

An elegant property, Grade II listed, Corse Lawn House was originally a coaching inn. Set back from the village green and surrounded by 12 acres of gardens and fields, it is fronted by an unusual ornamental pond - the last remaining coach wash in England. The hotel has been home to the Hine family since 1978 and maintains high standards of service and cuisine. Classic and modern, French and English culinary influences blend seamlessly on an extensive menu that features plenty of fish and game in season. Cooking is precise delivering clarity of flavours, and produces respectfully treated in dishes of potted crab with mango and cucumber, best end of lamb with chargrilled vegetables, and lemon tart with lemon ice cream.

Chef: Andrew Poole **Owners:** Hine Family **Times:** 12-2/7-9.30, Closed 24-26 Dec **Prices:** Fixed L £20.50, Fixed D £30.50, Starter £4.95-£9.95, Main £14.95-£19.95, Dessert £5.95-£7.95, Service optional **Wine:** 400 bottles over £20, 39 bottles under £20 **Notes:** Vegetarian menu, Dress Restrictions, Smart casual, no jeans or T-shirts, Civ Wed 80 **Seats:** 50, Pr/dining room 28 **Children:** Portions **Rooms:** 19 (19 en suite) ★★★ HL **Directions:** 5m SW of Tewkesbury on B4211, in village centre **Parking:** 60

FRAMPTON MANSELL   MAP 04 SO90

◉ The White Horse

Modern British

Colourful foodie pub

☎ 01285 760960   Cirencester Rd GL6 8HZ

e-mail: emmawhitehorse@aol.com

web: www.cotswoldwhitehorse.com

This outwardly unassuming roadside pub on the A419 has a remodelled interior and relaxed dining-pub vibe. Pastel-coloured walls, seagrass carpeting, high-backed chairs and colourful artwork create that restaurant edge, while a large bow window overlooks the garden with its alfresco dining opportunities - there's a separate bar area too. The modern British menu makes sound use of quality produce presented in a simple, unpretentious style. Take pan-fried calves' liver served with roasted pears, chestnuts and bacon jus, or perhaps grilled sea bass with lemon and thyme risotto and a watercress sauce. Crowd-pleasing desserts - like steamed marmalade pudding and crème anglaise - provide the finale.

Chef: Howard Matthews **Owners:** Emma & Shaun Davis **Times:** 11-3/6-11, Closed 24-26 Dec, 1 Jan, Closed D Sun **Prices:** Fixed L £15.25, Fixed D £16.95, Starter £3.95-£8.50, Main £10.95-£15.95, Dessert £3.50-£4.95, Service optional **Wine:** 22 bottles over £20, 21 bottles under £20, 9 by the glass **Notes:** Fixed L/D menu only available Mon-Thu, Vegetarian available **Seats:** 45 **Children:** Portions **Directions:** 6m from Cirencester on the A419 towards Stroud **Parking:** 30

GLOUCESTER　　　MAP 10 SO81

◉ Carrington's Restaurant

Modern European
European cuisine in a country-house hotel

☎ 01452 617412　Hatton Court Hotel, Upton Hill, Upton St Leonards GL4 8DE
e-mail: res@hatton-court.co.uk
web: www.hatton-court.co.uk

Carrington's Restaurant is part of Hatton Court Hotel, where there's an emphasis on traditional style and service and waiting staff delight diners with a daily dish flambéed at the table. That continental touch continues throughout the attractive à la carte menu with dishes such as confit duck leg with braised red cabbage and fondant potato, or seared sea bass with spaghetti and mixed bean and herb cassoulet, with perhaps an Amaretto and white chocolate-filled chocolate cup with coffee cream for dessert. Delightful views over the surrounding countryside and the thoughtful arrangement of outdoor seating make this a wonderful place to enjoy in summer.

Chef: Glyn Crosthwaite **Owners:** Hatton Hotels **Times:** 12.30-2/7-9.30 **Prices:** Fixed L £16.95, Fixed D £26.95, Starter £5.95-£6.95, Main £13.95-£22.95, Dessert £6.50-£7.50, Service optional **Wine:** 35 bottles over £20, 20 bottles under £20, 10 by the glass **Notes:** Dress Restrictions, Smart casual, Civ Wed 80, Air con **Seats:** 90, Pr/dining room 45 **Children:** Portions **Rooms:** 45 (45 en suite) ★★★ HL **Directions:** On B4017 between Gloucester and Painswick **Parking:** 70

LOWER SLAUGHTER　　　MAP 10 SP12

◉◉ Lower Slaughter Manor

Modern
Historic manor house offering elegant country-house dining

☎ 01451 820456　GL54 2HP
e-mail: info@lowerslaughter.co.uk
web: www.lowerslaughter.co.uk

A manor house has stood on this site since AD 1004. Used as a convent in the 15th century, it was rebuilt as a house in 1658 and is today an elegant country house oozing style and sophistication.

Recently refurbished throughout, the restaurant is decked out with chocolate brown silk walls, Murano crystal and ocean blue chandeliers which conspire to create a stylish, intimate atmosphere. The original chapel is used for private dining parties. Accomplished and flavourful cuisine includes the likes of home-smoked and cured salmon, or pan-fried king scallops with shellfish risotto and crisp shallots. Main courses make use of wonderful produce and might include sea bass with buttered red chard, Brixham crab and red pepper polenta cake.

Lower Slaughter Manor

Chef: David Kelman **Owners:** von Essen Collection **Times:** 12-2.30/7-9.30 **Prices:** Fixed L £17.50, Fixed D £45, Service optional **Wine:** All bottles over £20, 6 by the glass **Notes:** Dress Restrictions, Smart, no jeans or trainers, Civ Wed 75 **Seats:** 55, Pr/dining room 20 **Children:** Portions **Rooms:** 19 (19 en suite)★★★ HL **Directions:** Off A429, signposted The Slaughters. 0.5m into village on right **Parking:** 30

◉◉ Washbourne Court Hotel

Modern British, French
Fine dining in a riverside setting

☎ 01451 822143　GL54 2HS
e-mail: info@washbournecourt.co.uk
web: www.washbournecourt.co.uk

CONTINUED

LOWER SLAUGHTER CONTINUED

Set in riverside gardens in the quintessential Cotswold village of Lower Slaughter, this charming old building dates back to the 17th century and has beamed ceilings, log fires and flagstone floors to prove it. An elegant dining room, replete with chandeliers and gold wall lights, provides a fairly formal setting, but friendly staff stop things from getting stuffy. The modern cooking draws on quality seasonal ingredients, displaying clear flavours and some interesting combinations. Start with seared scallops with a fricassée of asparagus and morels, and then tuck into the likes of sea bass with crab cake and avocado salad, or Cotswold lamb with provençale vegetables and mint jus. A sunny terrace proves an added bonus for summer drinks and light lunches.

Owners: von Essen Hotels **Times:** 12.30-3/7-9, Closed L Mon-Sat **Prices:** Fixed D £40, Starter £7-£12, Main £18-£26, Dessert £7.50-£9, Service optional, Group min 10 service 10% **Wine:** 40 bottles over £20, 12 bottles under £20, 8 by the glass **Notes:** Dress Restrictions, Smart casual, no jeans, trainers or T-shirts, Civ Wed 60 **Seats:** 60, Pr/dining room 20 **Children:** Min 12 yrs, Menu, Portions **Rooms:** 30 (30 en suite) ★★★ HL **Directions:** Off A429, village centre by river **Parking:** 40

MORETON-IN-MARSH MAP 10 SP23

◎◎ Mulberry Restaurant

Modern British V

Contemporary dining in ancient Cotswold manor house

☎ 01608 650501 Manor House Hotel, High St GL56 0LJ
e-mail: bookings@cotswold-inns-hotels.co.uk
web: www.cotswold-inns-hotels.co.uk

The Cotswold stone frontage of this 16th-century manor-house hotel hides an endearing mélange of ancient and modern. Old beams, stone walls and fireplaces are still evident, but the dining room has been given a stylish modern makeover, with high-backed chairs, leather banquettes, wall-length mirrors, bold patterned carpet and modern artwork. The cooking is equally stylish, with an ambitious kitchen delivering light, accurate, clear-flavoured, elegantly presented dishes. Its modern British approach comes with French influences; take slow-cooked Blythburgh free-range pork belly served with seared scallops, cocao jelly, girolles and caramelised cauliflower purée, and to finish, a dark chocolate fondant with warm chocolate and banana milkshake and peanut butter ice cream. (There's an alfresco patio and walled garden too.)

Chef: Eric Worger **Owners:** Michael & Pamela Horton **Times:** 12-2.30/7-9.30 **Prices:** Food prices not confirmed for 2008. Please telephone for details **Wine:** 53 bottles over £20, 26 bottles under £20, 8 by the glass **Notes:** Vegetarian menu, Dress Restrictions, Smart casual, no jeans, shorts or trainers, Civ Wed 120 **Seats:** 76, Pr/dining room 120 **Children:** Min 8 yrs, Portions **Rooms:** 38 (38 en suite) ★★★ HL **Directions:** Off A429 at south end of town **Parking:** 32

NAILSWORTH MAP 04 ST89

◎ Egypt Mill Hotel

British

Pleasant waterside inn with rewarding food

☎ 01453 833449 GL6 0AE
e-mail: reception@egyptmill.com
web: www.egyptmill.com

A former corn mill with its origins in the 16th century, this attractive hotel is situated on the edge of the River Frome in a pretty Cotswold village and still has the original millstones and working waterwheels. The cellar bar and atmospheric restaurant are decorated in an up-to-date style and quirky objets d'art. The lengthy menu ranges from simple, familiar classics to rather bolder, more complex dishes. Try pan-fried calamari salad with sautéed pancetta, mushrooms and lemon chive butter followed by Guinness-glazed breast of duck with onion confit sauce on boulangère potatoes. Desserts should not be overlooked.

Times: 12-2/6.30-9.30 **Rooms:** 28 (28 en suite) ★★ HL **Directions:** Centre of Nailsworth, on A46

◎ The Mad Hatters Restaurant

British, French

Wholesome cooking at an engaging restaurant with rooms

☎ 01453 832615 3 Cossack Square GL6 0DB
e-mail: mafindlay@waitrose.com

The interior of this old Cotswold farmhouse is a riot of stained glass in oak frames, paintings from local artists and locally handcrafted furniture. Big bay windows look out on to a picturesque square in this delightful old mill town. Genuine hospitality, attentive service and organic food are just some of the highlights. Hand-written menus reflect mainly French with some Arab, Asian and Mediterranean influences. Try velvety fish soup with rouille, or tender lamb with a full-flavoured red wine sauce, followed by apple crumble tart with proper custard demonstrating excellent cooking skills.

Times: 12.30-2/7.30-9, Closed end Jan-early Feb, 1st wk Jun, 1st 2wk Aug, Mon-Tue, Closed D Sun-Tue **Rooms:** 3 (1 en suite) ★★★★ RR **Directions:** M5 junct 13. A419 to Stroud and then A46 to Nailsworth. Take a right at rdbt and then an immediate left, restaurant is located opposite Britannia Pub

NEWENT　　　　　　　　　MAP 10 SO72

◎◎ Three Choirs Vineyards

Modern British

Tuscan-style vineyard views and summer terrace dining

☎ 01531 890223　GL18 1LS
e-mail: ts@threechoirs.com
web: www.threechoirs.com

Three Choirs Vineyards is a special place, not least for its idyllic setting. The full output from the vineyard is available in this thriving restaurant with rooms, which provides a wonderfully different place to stay for wine lovers. Spacious, high-quality bedrooms have their own private patio and, like the modern Vineyard restaurant with its leather-backed chairs and large picture windows, look out across the 100-acre estate. Well executed dishes make good use of local produce, and clarity of flavour is demonstrated in dishes of prawn boche (like a vol-au-vent) in a lobster bisque, and roast fillet of cod with a rocket salad and balsamic reduction, served with buttered new potatoes. For dessert, why not try iced white rum and sultana parfait with a pineapple shot and coconut foam.

Chef: Darren Leonard　**Owners:** Three Choirs Vineyards Ltd　**Times:** 12-2/7-9　**Prices:** Fixed L £15, Fixed D £24.95-£35.95, Starter £3.95-£9.50, Main £9.50-£19.50, Dessert £3.50-£5.50, Service optional, Group min 10 service 10%　**Wine:** 20 bottles over £20, 34 bottles under £20, 12 by the glass　**Notes:** Sun L 3 courses £21.50, Smart casual　**Seats:** 50, Pr/dining room 20　**Children:** Menu, Portions　**Rooms:** 8 (8 en suite) ★★★★ RR
Directions: 2m N of Newent on B4215, follow brown tourist signs
Parking: 50

NORTHLEACH　　　　　　　MAP 10 SP11

◎◎ The Puesdown Inn

Modern British

Stylishly refurbished coaching inn offering quality local produce cooked with skill and flair

☎ 01451 860262　Compton Abdale GL54 4DN
e-mail: inn4food@btopenworld.com
web: www.puesdown.cotswoldinns.com

This traditional Cotswold coaching inn, said to date back to 1236, has been lovingly and stylishly refurbished by its hands-on owners. The warm colours, cosy sofas and log fires create a welcoming, relaxed atmosphere, while chic Italian chairs and a personal collection of paintings and photographs add additional style. The daily-changing menu reflects market and seasonal variations, with quality produce

carefully sourced from local producers. While wife Maggie is found front of house, chef-proprietor John Armstrong - with a classical training starting out at The Savoy - is passionate about attention to detail. Typical dishes might include a suprême of duck with beetroot risotto, honey-soused vegetables and a green peppercorn sauce, and perhaps a bread-and-butter pudding finish, served with marmalade ice cream.

The Puesdown Inn

Chef: John Armstrong　**Owners:** John & Maggie Armstrong　**Times:** 11-3/6.30-11, Closed 1-2 wks Jan, Closed D Sun　**Prices:** Fixed L £14.50-£18.75, Fixed D £19.95-£35, Starter £5.95-£9.50, Main £12.75-£20, Dessert £6.25, Service optional　**Wine:** 13 bottles over £20, 22 bottles under £20, 15 by the glass　**Seats:** 48, Pr/dining room 30　**Children:** Portions　**Rooms:** 3 (3 en suite) ★★★★ INN　**Directions:** On A40 (Cheltenham-Oxford), 7m from Cheltenham, 3m from Northleach　**Parking:** 80

PAXFORD　　　　　　　　MAP 10 SP13

◎ Churchill Arms

Modern British

Confident cooking in charming Cotswold pub

☎ 01386 594000　GL55 6XH
e-mail: mail@thechurchillarms.com
web: www.thechurchillarms.com

An inglenook fireplace, beams, flagstones and oak flooring are what you might expect to find at this endearingly unpretentious, mellow Cotswold stone pub. However, the Churchill's clean-cut, modern-focused cooking will surprise all but the well informed. And, though the space may have been opened up, it still retains bags of rustic charm and informality, from the assortment of wood furniture to yellow walls hung with prints and wine and menu chalkboards. Food is ordered at the bar in the traditional fashion. Think attractively presented, light, modern dishes with a nod to quality and seasonality, perhaps steamed fillet of brill with grapes and white wine or a lamb pasty with onion gravy.

Chef: D Toon & S Brooke-Little　**Owners:** Sonya & Leo Brooke-Little
Times: 12-2/7-9, Closed 25 Dec　**Prices:** Starter £4-£8.50, Main £9-£18, Dessert £4-£5, Service optional　**Wine:** 12 bottles over £20, 24 bottles under £20, 8 by the glass　**Seats:** 60　**Children:** Portions
Directions: Situated 2m E of Chipping Campden　**Parking:** On street

SOUTHROP   MAP 05 SP10

◎◎ *The Swan at Southrop*

British, European NEW

Accomplished modern cooking in peaceful, gastro-pub style surroundings

☎ 01367 850205   GL7 3NU
web: www.theswanatsouthrop.co.uk

Set on the edge of the green in a sleepy Cotswold village, the Swan still maintains its pub roots with a public bar and skittle alley, though the real focus these days is on its accomplished cuisine. The dining room retains a rustic vibe, with ceiling beams and low-beamed doorways, while walls are hung with artwork and old pub photographs. Solid-wood tables (some desks), fresh flowers and efficient yet relaxed and friendly service suit the surroundings too. The kitchen's modern approach makes use of fresh local produce, with dishes pleasingly not overworked. Flavours come clean cut in well-presented, brasserie-style dishes like escargots de Bourgogne, or grilled entrecote with béarnaise sauce, pommes frites and green salad, and a pumpkin tarte Tatin with star anise ice cream.

Times: 12-2.30/Mon-Sat 7-9.30, Sun 12-2/7-9

STOW-ON-THE-WOLD   MAP 11 SP12

◎ *The Conservatory Restaurant*

British, French

Venerable Cotswold hotel with punchy cooking

☎ 01451 830344   Best Western Grapevine Hotel, Sheep St GL54 1AU
e-mail: enquiries@vines.co.uk
web: www.vines.co.uk

A typically beautiful Cotswold-stone building, this long-established watering and lodging venue has its roots in the 17th century. The restaurant's canopy is the ancient Black Hamburg vine, making an enchanting setting for candlelit dining in the evenings. A youthful team ensures service is unstuffy and there's just enough formality to make it special. Good flavours abound on this competently cooked, ambitious menu - try smoked salmon and sole terrine with chive and horseradish sauce, followed by Gloucestershire Old Spot pork cutlet with champ potato and cider jus. A second restaurant, La Vigna, is a Mediterranean brasserie.

Times: 12-2.30/7-9.30   **Rooms:** 22 (22 en suite) ★★★ HL
Directions: Take A436 towards Chipping Norton; 150yds on right facing green

◎◎ *Fosse Manor*

Modern British

Modern cuisine in country-house setting

☎ 01451 830354   GL54 1JX
e-mail: enquiries@fossemanor.co.uk
web: www.fossemanor.co.uk

Built in the style of a Cotswold manor house, this stylish and comfortable country-house hotel stands in its ivy coat in tranquil grounds set back from the A429 (originally the Fosse Way). Modern British cuisine is very much rooted in classical techniques here, using lots of interesting ingredients. Try a starter of marinated tuna loin for example, served with wasabi, soy, pickled cucumber and chilli jam. You could choose breast of Gressingham duck served with cocotte potatoes, butternut squash purée and plum sauce for mains, while delicious desserts include rhubarb crumble tart with crème anglaise and nutmeg ice cream. More informal dining is available in the brasserie.

Times: 12.30-2/7-9   **Rooms:** 19 (19 en suite) ★★★ HL
Directions: From Stow-on-the-Wold take A429 S for 1m

◎ Kings Head Inn & Restaurant

British NEW

Charming village-green inn serving accomplished traditional food

☎ 01608 658365   The Green, Bledington OX7 6XQ
e-mail: kingshead@orr-ewing.com
web: www.kingsheadinn.net

Set on the delightful village green near the river, this 16th-century inn with rooms has spacious public areas, pleasingly featuring the expected archetypal open fires, wobbly floors, beams and wood furniture. Its comfortable restaurant offers excellent dining and friendly and professional service. Simply presented, homely and traditional dishes are the kitchen's forte, driven by quality local seasonal produce. Think smoked haddock and crayfish pie served with mashed potato and peas, while a chocolate caramel brownie served with butterscotch sauce might rock your boat - and the bathroom scales - at dessert.

Times: 12-2/7-9.30   **Rooms:** 12 (12 en suite) ★★★★ INN

◎ The Old Butcher's

Modern NEW

Relaxed, contemporary dining in attractive Cotswold town

☎ 01451 831700   Park St GL54 1AQ
e-mail: info@theoldbutchers.com
web: www.theoldbutchers.com

One-time butcher's shop now contemporary, brasserie-styled eatery, the Old Butcher's stands out from the crowd in attractive, bustling Stow, with its modern glass frontage, awnings, signboard and sprinkling of terrace tables at the front. Inside continues the modern theme, with polished wood tables, comfortable chairs or banquette seating, white linen napkins, a stylish bar area and friendly, relaxed but professional service. The kitchen follows the modern approach too, utilising fresh, quality local produce - some home-grown - in refreshingly uncomplicated, clean-cut, well-presented modern dishes on regularly-changing menus. Think calves' liver with Italian bacon, mashed potato and spinach, and perhaps pannacotta served with raspberries and grappa to finish.

Times: 12-2.30/Mon-Thu 6-9.30, Fri-Sat 6-8, Sun 7-9

⊛⊛ The Royalist Hotel

Modern European

Assured cooking in a historic hostelry

☎ 01451 830670 Digbeth St GL54 1BN
e-mail: info@theroyalisthotel.co.uk
web: www.theroyalisthotel.co.uk

Dating from 947AD, this delightful Jacobean building is the oldest inn in Britain. Historical curiosities include 1,000-year-old timbers, a leper hole and, in the contemporary-styled restaurant, a grand fireplace featuring the markings of a witch. Cooking is accomplished, with well-judged combinations and quality ingredients. Expect good flavours from a starter of silky wild mushroom velouté, topped with garlic foam and served in a cup for a cappuccino effect. Mains take in Cornish mackerel with pomme gratin, oxtail tortellini and pea dressing, or breast of guinea fowl with creamed Savoy cabbage and mustard-scented Puy lentils. Desserts are a highlight, notably sticky toffee soufflé with butterscotch milkshake and vanilla ice cream.

Times: 12-2.30/7-9.30, Closed Sun-Mon **Rooms:** 14 (14 en suite) ★★★ HL **Directions:** Please telephone for directions

⊛ The Unicorn Hotel

Modern British NEW

Clean, vibrant cooking in a relaxed atmosphere

☎ 01451 830257 Sheep St GL54 1HQ
e-mail: reception@birchhotels.co.uk
web: www.birchhotels.co.uk

Set on the edge of this popular Cotswold village, the Unicorn Hotel may have traditional darkwood furnishings in the cosy bar, but the restaurant is light, airy and furnished with maple furniture and leather upholstered seating. Tables are unclothed to offer a more informal style of dining and matched by the relaxed service. The food is honest and straightforward, using top-quality produce, and vibrant flavours can be found in pancetta and duck terrine with balsamic pickled onions and grilled fillet of sea bass with a warm salad of asparagus, slow-roasted cherry tomatoes and olives.

Times: 12-2/7-9, Closed Please ring for details **Rooms:** 20 (20 en suite) ★★★ HL

STROUD MAP 04 SO80

⊛ The Bear of Rodborough

Traditional British

A welcoming inn offering traditional British cuisine

☎ 01453 878522 Rodborough Common GL5 5DE
e-mail: info@bearofrodborough.info
web: www.cotswold-inns-hotels.co.uk/index.aspx

This historic hostelry is set in 300 acres of National Trust land and enjoys lovely views. A stone archway separates the brightly decorated dining areas, softened by luxurious drapes and paintings of the local area. The British cuisine is inspired by the best local produce and good ingredients. Typical starters might include salad of local smoked Bibury trout and eel with avocado and a lime vinaigrette, with main courses such as medallions of Herefordshire beef bourguignon. There is a grill menu and extensive bar menu offering sandwiches, selected starters and mains, pasta dishes and salads.

Times: 12-2.30/7-9.30, Closed L Mon & Sat **Rooms:** 46 (46 en suite) ★★★ HL **Directions:** 2.5m S from Stroud

⊛ Burleigh Court Hotel

British, European

Classical country-house style

☎ 01453 883804 Burleigh, Minchinhampton GL5 2PF
e-mail: info@burleighcourthotel.co.uk
web: www.burleighcourthotel.co.uk

This Grade II listed, 18th-century Cotswold-stone manor house is set in 3.5 acres of gardens. The restaurant is true to these classical country-house roots, providing a formal setting for enjoyable modern British cuisine. The freshest local produce is used and many herbs and vegetables are home grown. The menu is extensive with the likes of twice-baked Cerney goat's cheese and hazelnut soufflé to start, followed by glazed loin of Gloucester Old Spot pork with a celeriac purée as a main course, and caramelised dark cherry brûlée with shortbread to finish. The Sunday lunch menu has a range of traditional options.

Chef: Adrian Jarrad **Owners:** Louise Noble **Times:** 12-2/7-9, Closed 24-26 Dec **Prices:** Fixed L £20.95, Fixed D £32.50-£42.50 **Wine:** 50 bottles over £20, 15 bottles under £20, 7 by the glass **Notes:** Vegetarian available, Smart casual, no jeans, Civ Wed 50 **Seats:** 34, Pr/dining room 18 **Children:** Menu, Portions **Rooms:** 18 (18 en suite) ★★★ HL **Directions:** 2.5m SE of Stroud, off A419 **Parking:** 28

TETBURY

MAP 04 ST89

◉◉ Calcot Manor

Modern British 🍷 NOTABLE WINE LIST

Perfect Cotswold retreat with enjoyable dining

☎ 01666 890391 Calcot GL8 8YJ

e-mail: reception@calcotmanor.co.uk

web: www.calcotmanor.co.uk

Built in the 14th century by Cistercian monks, this sprawling farmhouse-hotel-restaurant nevertheless has a very 21st-century feel with beautifully designed bedrooms, a stunning health spa and outstanding facilities for children. The light-and-airy Conservatory restaurant, with its understated elegance, makes a delightful dinner venue with white linen-clad tables and good-quality settings; it's a classy venue in an area with some really good dining establishments. Service is both professional and friendly. Modern British dishes include liberal splashes of the Mediterranean as in starters like slow-braised rabbit with sage and black olive pappardelle followed by honey-roasted Gloucester Old Spot pork belly with chestnut gnocchi and seared scallops, or wood-roasted rump of organic Highgrove beef. Desserts are similarly adventurous - how about liquorice crème brûlée with blackberry sorbet?

Chef: Michael Croft **Owners:** Richard Ball (MD) **Times:** 12-2/7-9.30 **Prices:** Fixed L £19, Starter £8-£12.95, Main £16.95-£19.25, Dessert £7.50, Service included **Wine:** 11 bottles under £20, 10 by the glass **Notes:** Vegetarian available, Civ Wed 100, Air con **Seats:** 100, Pr/dining room 100 **Children:** Menu, Portions **Rooms:** 35 (35 en suite)★★★★ HL **Directions:** M4 junct 18, take A46 towards Stroud and at x-roads with A4135 turn right and then 1st left **Parking:** 150

◉◉ The Trouble House

Traditional French

Exquisite, innovative food with a relaxed atmosphere that favours drinkers as well as diners

☎ 01666 502206 Cirencester Rd GL8 8SG

e-mail: enquiries@troublehouse.co.uk

web: www.troublehouse.co.uk

At first glance, this unassuming roadside inn looks no different from any of the other Cotswold stone pub. Step inside and it's a different matter - it's usually bustling with both drinkers and diners who flock here for this next-generation gastro-pub food. Interiors have been sensitively upgraded to a contemporary style with white walls, bare wood unclothed tables and wood floors. On the menu, simple, rustic and honest dishes (shin of beef braised in red wine with spicy couscous or jugged hare in Yorkshire puddings) rub shoulders with more adventurous offerings (roast squid stuffed with sun-dried tomatoes and mozzarella with chilli lentils) that betray the chef's background at high-end establishments such as Le Manoir and City Rhodes.

Chef: Michael Bedford **Owners:** Michael & Sarah Bedford **Times:** 12-2/7-9.30, Closed Xmas to New Year & BHs, Mon, Closed D Sun **Prices:** Starter £6.50-£12, Main £15-£20, Dessert £6.50-£11, Service optional, Group min 8 service 10% **Wine:** 41 bottles over £20, 32 bottles under £20, 12 by the glass **Seats:** 50 **Children:** Min 10 yrs D, Portions **Directions:** 1.5m outside Tetbury on A433 towards Cirencester **Parking:** 25

THORNBURY

MAP 04 ST69

◉◉ Thornbury Castle

Modern British 🍷 NOTABLE WINE LIST

Modern cuisine in a fairytale castle setting

☎ 01454 281182 Castle St BS35 1HH

e-mail: info@thornburycastle.co.uk

web: www.thornburycastle.co.uk

A grand Tudor castle that combines atmosphere and history with modern comforts. Baronial public rooms are impressive, featuring magnificent fireplaces, high mullioned windows, tapestries, grand portraits and suits of armour. Elegant, wood-panelled dining rooms are candlelit at night and make a memorable setting for a leisurely meal. Sensibly compact and straightforward British based menus are enhanced with international influences. A competent kitchen demonstrates good technical skills and makes good use of quality seasonal ingredients, including home-grown herbs and vegetables. Choices include the likes of seared scallops with cauliflower purée and squid ink beurre blanc, John Dory with braised ox cheeks and sautéed girolles, and hot coconut soufflé with tropical fruit salsa.

CONTINUED ON PAGE 182

Lords of the Manor

UPPER SLAUGHTER MAP 10 SP12

Modern British V 🖳

Relaxed and welcoming country-house dining

☎ 01451 820243   GL54 2JD
e-mail: enquiries@lordsofthemanor.com
web: www.lordsofthemanor.com

A 17th-century former rectory of mellow Cotswold stone, this welcoming hotel - with Victorian-era additions - sits in 8 acres of gardens and parkland that deliver an idyllic, picture-postcard setting. There's a feeling of home from home, its traditional interiors decked out in true country-house style with open winter fires, deep sofas and period pieces - and there's just the ticking of a hallway clock or the scrunch of gravel on the drive to disturb the peace. The smart, classic dining room continues the theme, with cream walls, heavy tapestry drapes, comfortable high-backed chairs and tables set with eye-catching flower displays, while service is professional, discreet and informed.

The kitchen's modern approach comes underpinned by a classical theme and uses well-sourced, high-quality local ingredients. Attention to detail and consistency characterise the style, with plentiful skill and passion parading alongside some innovative elements on a repertoire of crisply scripted, fixed-price menus that includes a tasting option. Think pan-fried foie gras with tamarind ice cream and aged balsamic vinegar to start, perhaps followed by roast Old Spot tenderloin of pork served with pasta garganelli, crosnes and vanilla, and to finish, perhaps a warm carrot cake with orange pannacotta and buttermilk sorbet. Alfresco summer dining completes the accomplished package.

Chef: Les Rennie
Owners: Empire Ventures
Times: 12-2.30/7-8
Prices: Fixed L £19.50, Fixed D £40-£49, Service added but optional 10%
Wine: 246 bottles over £20, 4 bottles under £20, 12 by the glass
Notes: Tasting menu 7 courses £59, Sun L 4 courses £25.50, Vegetarian menu, Dress Restrictions, Smart casual, no trainers or jeans, Civ Wed 50
Seats: 50, Pr/dining room 30
Children: Min 7 yrs, Menu, Portions
Rooms: 27 (27 en suite)★★★ CHH
Directions: Follow signs towards The Slaughters 2m W of A429. Hotel on right in centre of Upper Slaughter
Parking: 40

ENGLAND

THORNBURY CONTINUED

Chef: Paul Mottram **Owners:** von Essen **Times:** 12-2/7-9.30
Prices: Food prices not confirmed for 2008. Please telephone for details
Wine: 278 bottles over £20, 2 bottles under £20, 7 by the glass
Notes: Vegetarian available, Dress Restrictions, Smart casual, no jeans, trainers, T-shirts, Civ Wed 50 **Seats:** 72, Pr/dining room 22 **Children:** Min 12 yrs, Menu, Portions **Rooms:** 25 (25 en suite)★★★ HL
Directions: M5 junct 16. N on A38. Continue for 4m to lights and turn left. Following brown Historic Castle signs **Parking:** 50

UPPER SLAUGHTER   MAP 10 SP12

◉◉◉ Lords of the Manor

see page 181

WICK   MAP 04 ST77

◉◉ Oakwood

British NEW

Resort hotel dining with quality produce and straightforward approach

☎ 0117 9372251 The Park, Bath Rd BS30 5RN
web: www.theparkresort.com

Part of The Park hotel resort, surrounded by two championship golf courses, Oakwood is set in an old Masonic lodge at this magnificent Georgian mansion. Its fascinating stone carvings remain a feature today, as does the modern open-plan kitchen with its large woodstone

oven, where seasonal fresh meat, fish and game are roasted. The cooking's straightforward approach is driven by high-quality, seasonal produce, simply presented allowing the main ingredient to shine without over-complication. Take grilled loin of pork served with lentils and horseradish, or perhaps the 'fish of the day' option (maybe cod with 12-year-old aged balsamic), and to finish, a chocolate and pistachio sponge with thick cream.
Times: 7-9, Closed Sun-Mon

WINCHCOMBE   MAP 10 SP02

◉◉◉ 5 North Street

see below

◉◉ Wesley House

Modern Mediterranean

Popular Cotswold restaurant noted for quality

☎ 01242 602366 High St GL54 5LJ
e-mail: enquiries@wesleyhouse.co.uk
web: www.wesleyhouse.co.uk

Named after John Wesley who stayed here in the 18th century, this black and white timbered former merchant's house dates from the 15th century and has all the proper credentials to prove it. Beamed ceilings and open stone fireplaces sit comfortably with modern aspects like a glass atrium over the terrace, and effective modern lighting. Seasonal variations ring the changes on the modern British menus with Mediterranean influences, and look out for special offers at lunch.

---

5 North Street

WINCHCOMBE   MAP 10 SP02

Modern European V

Unpretentious, stunning cooking in Cotswolds

☎ 01242 604566 5 North St GL54 5LH
e-mail: marcusashenford@yahoo.co.uk

This understated little eatery in the heart of Winchcombe is one of the Cotswolds' gourmet gems. Tucked away behind a mellow-stone shopfront, there is an intimate, split-level interior, simple and pared back, with wooden beams and bare tables, and oozing with rustic charm. The friendly service creates a relaxed atmosphere.
Marcus Ashenford's cooking is clean-cut in style and delightfully simple, but delivering wonderful flavours without pretension. Focusing on quality ingredients and high skill, combinations are interesting, seasonality is well respected and flavours are prominent. Expect a modern approach underpinned by a classical French foundation, the sensibly compact, fixed-price menus bolstered by a ten-course taste option or seven-course gourmet menu (wife Kate, who heads-up front-of-house, is always at hand to explain individual courses). Begin with pan-fried mackerel perhaps, served with warm piccalilli, aubergine purée, salt cod beignet and watercress, before moving on to line-caught sea bass with ceps, leeks, grapes, razor clams and vanilla sauce. Round things off with warm plum frangipane tart with

bay leaf ice cream and caramel sauce, or the intriguing presentation of caramel.

Chef: Marcus Ashenford **Owners:** Marcus & Kate Ashenford
Times: 12.30-1.30/7-9, Closed 1st 2 wks Jan, 1wk Aug, Mon, Closed L Tue, D Sun **Prices:** Fixed L £19.50, Fixed D £28-£40, Starter £7-£12, Main £14-£20, Dessert £6-£10, Service optional **Wine:** 60 bottles over £20, 12 bottles under £20, 6 by the glass **Notes:** Gourmet menu 7 courses £45, Tasting menu 10 courses £55, Vegetarian menu **Seats:** 26 **Children:** Menu, Portions **Directions:** 7m from Cheltenham **Parking:** On street, pay & display

A sample menu starts with Isle of Lewis smoked salmon, pickled thyme cucumber and quail's eggs, followed by roast partridge with pearl barley risotto, thyme jus, stuffed cabbage and a confit of partridge leg.

Wesley House

Chef: Martin Dunn **Owners:** Matthew Brown **Times:** 12-2/7-9, Closed Xmas, Closed D Sun **Prices:** Fixed L £15, Fixed D £35-£38, Service optional **Wine:** 80 bottles over £20, 20 bottles under £20, 20 by the glass **Notes:** Vegetarian available, Civ Wed 60, Air con **Seats:** 70, Pr/dining room 24 **Children:** Portions **Rooms:** 5 (5 en suite) ★★★★ RR **Directions:** In centre of Winchcombe **Parking:** In the square

GREATER MANCHESTER

ALTRINCHAM   MAP 15 SJ78

◉◉◉◉ **Juniper**

see page 184

HORWICH   MAP 15 SD61

◉◉ *De Vere Whites*

Modern British, French
Football fans' dream restaurant

☎ 01204 667788 De Havilland Way BL6 6SF
e-mail: whites@devere-hotels.com
web: www.devereonline.co.uk

This classy restaurant is part of the Reebok stadium, home to Bolton Wanderers. Situated on the second floor, Reflections restaurant is accessed via a wooden illuminated walkway and offers a bird's eye view of the football pitch. Booths in front of a plate glass window that overhangs the pitch offer the best seats in the house. The restaurant has its own cocktail-style bar, well-spaced tables, classic white linen and fresh flowers. Service is relatively formal with cloched dishes,

reflecting the classical feel of the French-influenced menu which offers the likes of John Dory on potato rösti, with an etuve of leek and sauce lie de vin. You can dine here Wednesday to Saturday evenings, although on a match night it might be difficult to keep your eye on the ball and enjoy the fine cuisine at the same time.

De Vere Whites

Times: 7-10, Closed 25 Dec, Sun-Tues, Closed L all week **Rooms:** 125 (125 en suite) ★★★★ HL **Directions:** Off M61 junct 6

MANCHESTER   MAP 16 SJ89

◉ **Brasserie Blanc**

Traditional French
Authentic French cooking at a slick, modern city-centre brasserie

☎ 0161 832 1000 55 Kings St M2 4LQ
e-mail: manchester@brasserieblanc.co.uk
web: www.brasserieblanc.co.uk

Despite a modern, minimalist décor, this funky brasserie (part of the established small chain) oozes comfort and crowd appeal. Think black leather booth seating or upholstered chairs, wooden tables, feature artworks and a bar for aperitifs. Staff are relaxed and knowledgeable. The menu is imaginative; expect classical French dishes with a modern twist, conjured from quality, fresh seasonal British produce. The confident kitchen avoids fuss in favour of clear and vibrant flavours; take Cornish lamb rack served with pistachio couscous or perhaps coq au vin, with a classic lemon tart finish.

Chef: Anshul Dhayani **Owners:** Raymond Blanc, Loch Fyne Restaurants **Times:** 12-2.45/5.30-10.45, Closed 25-26 Dec **Prices:** Fixed L £11.50, Fixed D £17.50, Starter £4.95-£6.95, Main £10.50-£18, Dessert £4.50, Service optional, Group min 6 service 10% **Wine:** 20 bottles over £20, 6 bottles under £20, 12 by the glass **Notes:** Vegetarian available, Smart casual, Air con **Seats:** 110, Pr/dining room 30 **Children:** Menu, Portions **Directions:** King St, City centre **Parking:** NCP Deansgate

ENGLAND

Juniper

ALTRINCHAM MAP 15 SJ78

Modern French

Dazzling culinary fun

☎ 0161 929 4008 21 The Downs WA14 2QD
e-mail: reservations@juniper-restaurant.co.uk
web: www.juniper-restaurant.co.uk

Chef: Paul Kitching
Owners: P & D Keeling,
P Kitching, K O'Brien
Times: 12-2/7-10, Closed 1
wk Feb, 2 wks summer,
Sun-Mon, Closed L Tue-
Thur
Prices: Fixed L £20, Fixed
D £40-£45, Service
included
Wine: 5 bottles under £20,
10 by the glass
Notes: Fixed L 3 courses,
Gourmet menu 8 courses
£60, Air con
Seats: 36
Directions: A556, Chester-
Manchester road.
Altrincham town centre
Parking: On street

With its classic shop-front conversion, there's little to distinguish Juniper from the average mild-mannered suburban restaurant, but don't be fooled, this is the culinary playground of an expressionist chef and one of the country's most renowned and talked about restaurants. The interior, decked out on two levels, is equally discreet and unpretentious, yet cool, the dining room decorated in shades of green, with quirky artwork, subdued lighting and tables dressed in crisp white linen resplendent with highly polished glassware and cutlery. Service is equally polished and nothing less than flawless, while a swish basement bar kicks off the Juniper adventure over cocktails while perusing the flamboyant menu.

But, there's little to prepare the uninitiated for chef-patron Paul Kitching's highly individual style - reading the menu is an eye-opening experience that challenges conventional thinking. No one else comes close to his expressional and aspirational cooking style - it's a one-off, idiosyncratic, bold, improvisational and breathtaking, delivered with masterful technique and underpinned by a classical French theme. Expect exquisite, full flavours of freshness and vitality on a repertoire of predominantly fixed-price menus that include gourmet surprise offerings that deliver an impromptu medley unique to each table, where one simply sits back and enjoys the ride. Main menu dishes sometimes come with witty subtitles or the odd supplement, but whatever, be prepared to be wowed. Take a threesome: warm scallops with Scotch broth, apricot egg pancake, garlic beignet and broccoli cream; slow-cooked fillet of pork assiette served with wild rice, sweetcorn and blueberry cookie, and Earl Grey, brazil nut and crab mayonnaise; and to finish, a treacle sponge soufflé with Horlicks and praline ice cream.

MANCHESTER Continued

◉ Choice Bar & Restaurant

Modern British 💻

Friendly waterside

☎ 0161 833 3400 Castle Quay, Castlefield M15 4NT
e-mail: book@choicebarandrestaurant.co.uk
web: www.choicebarandrestaurant.co.uk

This 1830s spice warehouse overlooking the canal has been converted into a chic, modern restaurant with exposed brickwork, low ceilings and cream furnishings. In the evening candlelight creates an intimate ambience, as does the romantic piano bar, whilst there's live music on Saturday nights and alfresco dining in fine weather. The menu's roots are in the north west, focusing on local produce and regional recipes with a contemporary twist. Take a starter of tempura battered haddock, sweet potato chips and wasabi mushy peas, then move on to beef fillet three ways (steak and chips with béarnaise sauce, steak-and-kidney pie on smashed peas, and mini cottage pie), and round off with peach and pomegranate crumble and custard.

Chef: Mark Urry **Owners:** Jon Grieves **Times:** 11/11, Closed 25-30 Dec **Prices:** Fixed L £12.95-£24.95, Fixed D £15.95-£29.95, Starter £4.95-£7.50, Main £12.95-£18.95, Dessert £5.50-£6.50, Service added but optional 10% **Wine:** 14 bottles over £20, 19 bottles under £20, 33 by the glass **Notes:** Sun L £12.95 2 courses, £15.95 3 courses, Vegetarian available, Air con **Seats:** 60 **Children:** Portions **Directions:** A5067 & A56 x-rds, off Bridgewater viaduct **Parking:** Limited day 25 spaces after 6pm, NCP 50yds

◉ Copthorne Hotel Manchester

International 💻

Stylish waterfront dining

☎ 0161 873 7321 Clippers Quay, Salford Quays M50 3SN
e-mail: roomsales.manchester@mill-cop.com
web: www.copthorne.com

This smart modern red-brick hotel enjoys an enviable location next to the quays in the redeveloped Salford Docks, close to Old Trafford and the Lowry Centre. The crescent-shaped Chandler's restaurant makes the most of waterfront views with a new minimalist look featuring stripped pine flooring and clean lines. A couple of Lowry prints adorn the walls alongside changing artwork by a local artist. The chef serves up an interesting mix of classical dishes with modern twists and some fusion elements using oils and spices. Typical starters might include pan-fried foie gras with home-made gingerbread and olive and fig chutney. Classically-inspired mains include a cannon of lamb slow-poached in red wine on mint pea velouté.

Times: 7-9.30, Closed Xmas, 1 Jan, Sun, Closed L Tue-Sat **Rooms:** 166 (166 en suite) ★★★★ HL **Directions:** From M602 follow signs to Salford Quays/Trafford Park. Hotel is 0.75m along A5063 (Trafford Rd)

◉◉ The French

French

Imposing Edwardian hotel for an opulent dining experience

☎ 0161 236 3333 The Midland Hotel, Peter St M60 2DS
e-mail: midlandsales@qhotels.co.uk
web: www.qhotels.co.uk

Grade II listed property, purpose-built for the Midland Railway in 1903 to accommodate the discerning traveller. Still one of Manchester's most popular hotels, it attracts plenty of VIPs. The restaurant is magnificent, with high ceilings, chandeliers, and a colour scheme of pale pinks and golds. Staff are superb and a long-standing crowd of regulars flock here to enjoy the excellent service as well as the food. The menu is more modern these days (poached turbot with pea and tarragon risotto, confit vine tomatoes and asparagus), with traditional elements (Chateaubriand for two from the flambé trolley). Finish, perhaps, with the raspberry soufflé and milk chocolate ice cream.

Chef: Paul Beckley **Owners:** QHotels **Times:** 7-11, Closed BHs, Sun-Mon, Closed L all week **Prices:** Fixed D £31, Starter £7.50-£14.50, Main £19.95-£32.95, Dessert £7.95, Service added but optional 10% **Wine:** 56 bottles over £20, 6 bottles under £20, 18 by the glass **Notes:** Dress Restrictions, Smart casual, no sportswear, Civ Wed 500, Air con **Seats:** 55 **Children:** Portions **Rooms:** 312 (312 en suite) ★★★★ HL **Directions:** Telephone for directions **Parking:** NCP behind hotel

◉ Greens

Modern Vegetarian V

Well-established vegetarian restaurant

☎ 0161 434 4259 43 Lapwing Ln, Didsbury M20 2NT
e-mail: greensrestaurant@tiscali.co.uk
web: www.greensrestaurant.net

Serving up classy vegetarian food for over ten years, Greens is something of an institution, which goes some way to explaining the permanently bustling atmosphere. Rather peculiarly for a vegetarian restaurant, the chef-owner is actually a meat-eater - a fact that can only be impacting on the food in a good way, as the menu here is a both eclectic and exciting. Try deep-fried oyster mushrooms with Chinese pancakes and plum sauce to start, for example, then continue with a main such as filo pastry strudel with leeks, mushrooms, tomatoes, ricotta and a port wine sauce.

Chef: Simon Connolly & Simon Rimmer **Owners:** Simon Connolly & Simon Rimmer **Times:** 12-2/5.30-10.30, Closed BHs, Closed L Mon & Sat **Prices:** Fixed D £12.95, Starter £3.95-£6.50, Main £10.95, Dessert £5.50, Service optional, Group min 6 service 10% **Wine:** 6 bottles over £20, 10 bottles under £20, 8 by the glass **Notes:** Fixed D 2 courses, Vegetarian menu **Seats:** 48 **Children:** Menu, Portions **Directions:** Telephone for directions, or see website **Parking:** On street

ENGLAND

MANCHESTER CONTINUED

Harvey Nichols Second Floor Restaurant

Modern European NOTABLE WINE LIST

Trendy dining for designer shoppers, overlooking Exchange Square

☎ 0161 828 8898 21 New Cathedral St M1 1AD
e-mail: secondfloor.reservations@harveynichols.com
web: www.harveynichols.com

A place to meet as well as eat, this stylish restaurant shares the trendy department store's second floor with an upmarket food hall and a more informal brasserie and bar. The black and white colour scheme makes a bold statement and the floor-to-ceiling windows offer expansive views over the Manchester skyline. Lunch, afternoon tea and dinner are served. The fresh modern menu is constantly evolving, with classic dishes combined with French influences, such as ballotine of cured salmon with oyster beignet and dill potatoes, followed by halibut, cassoulet of white bean, cockles and clams with cep dressing. As an added benefit, anything that catches your eye on the global wine list can be purchased from the food hall.

Chef: Alison Seagrave **Owners:** Harvey Nichols **Times:** 10-3/6-10.30, Closed 25-26 Dec, 1 Jan, Easter Sun, Closed D Sun-Mon **Prices:** Starter £7-£11, Main £14-£22, Dessert £7-£8, Service added but optional 10% **Wine:** 100+ bottles over £20, 30 bottles under £20, 20 by the glass **Seats:** 50 **Children:** Menu, Portions **Directions:** Just off Deansgate, town centre. 5 min walk from Victoria Station, on Exchange Sq **Parking:** Under store, across road

Lowry Hotel, The River Restaurant

Modern British

A designer setting for contemporary cuisine

☎ 0161 827 4000 & 827 4041 50 Dearmans Place, Chapel Wharf, Salford M3 5LH
e-mail: hostess@roccofortehotels.com
web: www.roccofortehotels.com

A chic hotel on the edge of the city centre with a modish restaurant to match. Overlooking the River Irwell, it's a bright and airy space decked out in brown and cream, with leather banquettes, designer chairs and tables dressed in crisp white linen. Chef Eyck Zimmer's pedigree shines through in an accomplished, skilled kitchen delivering an appealing brasserie menu of modern fare. Take oyster ravioli with leeks and a smoked bacon foam, or olive oil poached lamb with white bean purée, and to finish, perhaps pear and cranberry bread-and-butter pudding. There's also a daily pie menu (Lancashire mutton and black pudding pie for instance) and a fixed-price offering with a choice of three dishes at each turn.

Chef: Eyck Zimmer **Owners:** Sir Rocco Forte & family **Times:** 12-2.30/6-10.30 **Prices:** Fixed L £20, Fixed D £25, Starter £7.50-£12, Main £15.50-£30, Dessert £7.50-£9, Service added but optional 10% **Wine:** 100 bottles over £20, 10 bottles under £20, 8 by the glass **Notes:** Sun L £20 2 courses, £30 3 courses, Vegetarian available, Smart casual preferred, Civ Wed 108, Air con **Seats:** 108, Pr/dining room 20 **Children:** Menu, Portions **Rooms:** 165 (165 en suite) ★★★★★ HL **Directions:** Telephone for directions **Parking:** 100

Malmaison Brasserie

British, French NEW

Contemporary dining in buzzing yet relaxed atmosphere

☎ 0161 278 1000 1-3 Piccadilly M1 1LZ
e-mail: manchester@malmaison.com
web: www.malmaison.com

Situated in a striking converted warehouse, this city-centre offering from the Malmaison boutique hotel group has bags of style. Outside there's an old Renault van which sets the French tone, while echoing the blend of old and new here. Take the restaurant, which marries art deco with booth-style seating, for instance, while the bar-lounge comes with an impressive cocktail range and there's an on-display wine cellar. The accomplished brasserie-style cooking suits the surroundings, majoring on flavour rather than flouncy presentation, its seasonally-changing carte offering a grill selection as well as vegetarian options while providing a helping of good humour in dishes like spam fritters. Otherwise enjoy the likes of grilled halibut with warm mussels and chorizo salad, or braised lamb shepherd's pie, and a classic crème brûlée to finish.

Chef: Kevin Whiteford **Owners:** Malmaison **Times:** 12-2.30/6-11 **Prices:** Fixed L £13.50, Fixed D £15.50, Starter £4.95-£8, Main £12.50-£25, Dessert £6.25-£6.50, Service added but optional 10% **Wine:** 173 bottles over £20, 19 bottles under £20, 21 by the glass **Notes:** Vegetarian available **Seats:** 78, Pr/dining room 10 **Children:** Portions **Rooms:** 167 (167 en suite) ★★★ HL **Directions:** From M56 follow signs to Manchester, then to Piccadilly **Parking:** NCP

⊚ Marriott Worsley Park Hotel & Country Club

British NEW

Modern European food in a popular setting

☎ 0161 975 2000 Walkdeb Road, Worsley M28 2QT
e-mail: anna.colloer@marriotthotels.com
web: www.marriott.co.uk

Once the Duke of Bridgwater's estate, this hotel and country club is set in over 200 acres of delightful parkland. Brindley's is the hotel's fine-dining option. Light and airy, with contemporary décor and well-spaced tables, it offers good views of the courtyard and surrounding area. The menu is modern with a European twist, with dishes simply yet attractively presented. Friendly and efficient staff serve starters such as twice-baked parmesan soufflé with beef carpaccio and coriander oil, with wild sea trout, asparagus and chanterelle ragout, shallot and parsley cream to follow, rounding off with a melting chocolate fondant with Amaretto ice cream.

Chef: Sean Kelly **Owners:** Marriott Hotels **Times:** 12-3/5-10 **Prices:** Fixed L £15-£18.95, Fixed D £21-£32, Starter £5.75-£11.25, Main £14.25-£22.25, Dessert £5.75-£8.75, Service optional **Wine:** 40 bottles over £20, 27 bottles under £20, 15 by the glass **Notes:** Fixed L 3 courses, Tasting menu 6 courses £45, Vegetarian available, Dress Restrictions, Smart casual, Civ Wed 200, Air con **Seats:** 140, Pr/dining room 14 **Children:** Menu, Portions **Rooms:** 158 (158 en suite) ★★★★ HL **Directions:** Just off M60 junct 13, take A575. Hotel is signposted **Parking:** 500

Michael Caines at Abode Manchester

Rosettes not confirmed at time of going to press

Modern, Classic

Funky Abode restaurant in the heart of the city

☎ 0161 247 7744 & 200 5665 107 Piccadilly M1 2DB
e-mail: reservationsmanchester@abodehotels.co.uk
web: www.abodehotels.com

Formerly Alias Hotel Rossetti, this landmark city-centre hotel close to Manchester's Piccadilly station, major shops and the business district has recently been acquired by the Abode Chain. Currently undergoing complete refurbishment, the new incarnation is due to open in autumn 2007 and will feature a Michael Caines restaurant and champagne bar, with the funky Abode styling in place throughout the hotel. Please visit www.theAA.com for further details.

Chef: Ian Matfin **Owners:** Andrew Brownsword, Michael Caines **Times:** 12-2.30/7-10, Closed 1 Jan, Sun **Prices:** Fixed L £12.50, Fixed D £25, Starter £7.50-£13.95, Main £17.50-£22, Dessert £8.50, Service added but optional 11% **Wine:** 150 bottles over £20, 10 bottles under £20, 15 by the glass **Notes:** Tasting menu £55, Pre theatre D opens at 6pm, Dress Restrictions, Smart casual, Air con **Seats:** 56, Pr/dining room 24 **Children:** Portions **Rooms:** 61 (61 en suite) **Directions:** Located in city centre 2min walk from Piccadilly station **Parking:** Opposite hotel 20% discount

⊚ Moss Nook

Modern British, French

Classical food in formal setting

☎ 0161 437 4778 Ringway Rd, Moss Nook M22 5WD

This spacious open-plan restaurant is decorated in traditional style with well-spaced tables laid with crisp linen and quality tableware, befitting the formal but friendly cloche service. Cuisine is classical French with some modern interpretations of traditional dishes. Choose between fresh fish of the day, or a traditional main course like herb-crusted best end of local lamb with parsnip mousse or pan-fried escalope of veal with chive sauce. If you're undecided, why not let the chef select a surprise menu for the whole table and guide you through several tasting courses from canapés to petits fours. There is a stunning outside terrace for the summer months.

Chef: Kevin Lofthouse **Owners:** P & D Harrison **Times:** 12-1.30/7-10, Closed 2 wks Xmas, Sun & Mon, Closed L Sat **Prices:** Fixed L £19.50, Fixed D £37, Starter £8-£14, Main £19.50-£23, Dessert £4.50-£7.50, Service included **Wine:** 100 bottles over £20, 18 bottles under £20, 5 by the glass **Notes:** Fixed L 5 courses, Fixed D 7 courses, Vegetarian available, Dress Restrictions, No jeans, trainers, Air con **Seats:** 65 **Children:** Min 12 yrs **Directions:** 1m from airport at junction of Ringway with B5166 **Parking:** 30

⊚ *Palmiro*

Modern Italian

Contemporary Italian dining in up-and-coming area of Manchester

☎ 0161 860 7330 197 Upper Chorlton Rd M16 0BH
e-mail: bookings@palmiro.net
web: www.palmiro.net

Behind a frosted-glass frontage in a small row of shops in Manchester's Chorlton district, you'll find this atypical, modern Italian restaurant. Recently extended including a bar area, distressed wooden floors and grey walls with splashes of red from chairs and pictures all contribute to a cheerful interior, whilst a new walled terrace and decking area are ideal for pre-meal drinks or dining if weather permits. Expect simple, well-executed rustic Italian combinations based on well-sourced fresh ingredients, some direct from Italy. Begin with brown shrimp and bay leaf tagliatelle perhaps, followed by main courses such as grilled monkfish with sage mash and salsa verde. Finish with hazelnut cake with moscato ice cream.

Times: 12-5/4-10.30, Closed 25-30 Dec, 1-4 Jan, Closed L Mon-Fri **Directions:** Please telephone for directions

MANCHESTER CONTINUED

⊛ Simply Heathcotes

British 🖥

Stylish metropolitan dining with extensive menu

☎ 0161 835 3536 Jacksons Row, Deansgate M2 5WD
e-mail: manchester@heathcotes.co.uk
web: www.heathcotes.co.uk/simply/index.php

Tucked away in Manchester's old registry office, this buzzy, spacious, first-floor restaurant - accessed via a sweeping staircase - has a cool designer interior. Modern and minimalist, with high ceilings, big mirrors, natural surfaces, Philippe Starck bucket chairs and smiley, knowledgeable staff, its lengthy menu plays to the gallery and deals in modern brasserie staples that embrace regional British cooking. Take a deep-fried black pudding hash brown to start, perhaps roast cutlet of lamb and navarin of mutton to follow, and to close, maybe a trifle with rosewater and strawberry jelly and elderflower custard.

Chef: Eve Worsick **Owners:** Mr P Heathcote **Times:** 12-2.30/5.30-10, Closed 25-26 Dec, 1-3 Jan, BHs **Prices:** Starter £5.50, Main £15.50-£24.50, Dessert £4.95, Service added but optional 10%, Group service 10% **Wine:** 49 bottles over £20, 19 bottles under £20, 10 by the glass **Notes:** Sun L 2 courses £14.50, 3 courses £17, Vegetarian available, Civ Wed 60, Air con **Seats:** 170, Pr/dining room 60 **Children:** Menu, Portions **Directions:** M62 junct 17. Restaurant at top end of Deansgate **Parking:** On street

◉⊛ Watersreach

Modern European

Popular contemporary eatery at Man U's official hotel

☎ 0161 873 8899 Golden Tulip, Trafford Park M17 1WS
e-mail: info@goldentulipmanchester.co.uk
web: www.goldentulipmanchester.co.uk

The official hotel of Manchester United FC, the Golden Tulip, is situated opposite Old Trafford football stadium, within easy reach of the airport and motorway. The interiors are spacious and comfortable, designed to contemporary standards, and the recently refurbished Watersreach restaurant offers a lounge bar area with sofas, American diner booths, and open windows into the kitchen. Menus offer consistently good, interesting modern food including British classics and international dishes. Favourites include crispy duck salad with Japanese noodles, braised blade of beef and creamy mash, or Lancashire cheese and pepper quiche. Finish with rum pannacotta served with chocolate and banana beignets and rum-and-raisin ice cream. Service is informal yet professional, and if there's a home win you can be sure of a good atmosphere.

Chef: Stuart Plant **Owners:** Golden Tulip UK **Times:** 12-2.30/6-10, Closed L Sat-Sun **Prices:** Fixed L £15.95-£16.95, Fixed D £19.95-£21.95, Starter £3.95-£7.50, Main £9.95-£19.95, Dessert £3.95-£5.45, Service added but optional 10% **Wine:** 12 bottles over £20, 20 bottles under £20, 8 by the glass **Notes:** Vegetarian available, Civ Wed 160, Air con **Seats:** 86, Pr/dining room 160 **Children:** Menu, Portions **Rooms:** 160 (160 en suite) ★★★★ HL **Directions:** Telephone for directions. **Parking:** 180

⊛ Yang Sing Restaurant

Chinese V 🖥

Famous Chinese restaurant and banqueting rooms

☎ 0161 236 2200 34 Princess St M1 4JY
e-mail: info@yang-sing.com
web: www.yang-sing.com

A regular fixture of Manchester's China Town since 1977, this venerable institution is as popular today as when it opened. Redesigned in 2006 by renowned architect Roberta Fulford, the restaurant is set over several floors and pretty much rammed to the rafters day and night. The stylish décor is described as 'contemporary, classic oriental with a touch of 1930s Shanghai' - dark aubergine, ginger and ivory colours with huge mirrors, strategic lighting and leather seating. The famous banquets or dim sum are the best way to experience the food here - try steamed beef dumpling with ginger and spring onion, roast pork bun or steamed chopped ribs in garlic.

Chef: Harry Yeung **Owners:** Harry & Gerry Yeung **Times:** 12/11.30, Closed 25 Dec **Prices:** Food prices not confirmed for 2008. Please telephone for details **Wine:** 91 bottles over £20, 15 bottles under £20, 3 by the glass **Notes:** Vegetarian menu, Air con **Seats:** 260, Pr/dining room 220 **Children:** Portions **Directions:** Located in city centre on Princes St, which runs from Albert Square **Parking:** Public car park adjacent

🖥 Label

☎ 0161 833 1878 78 Deansgate M3 2FW
web: www.theaa.com/travel/index.jsp

In a prime spot on Manchester's Deansgate. The British/Med menu is a happy-go-lucky mix of nibbles, sharing plates, salads, mains, sandwiches and great desserts.

Market Restaurant

☎ 0161 834 3743 104 High St, Northern Quarter M4 1HQ

Quirky, well-established restaurant focusing on freshly-prepared dishes and organic ingredients.

Restaurant Bar and Grill

☎ 0161 839 1999 14 John Dalton St M2 6JR

Trendy, fusion oriented bar and restaurant.

🍴 Royal Orchid Thai Restaurant

☎ 0161 236 5183 36 Charlotte St M1 4FD

web: www.theaa.com/travel/index.jsp

Excellent food and a chatty menu to guide you through the whole ordering procedure and direct you to the range of flavours of classic Thai cuisine. The food is authentic, the ambience friendly and relaxed.

🍴 Samsi

☎ 0161 279 0022 36-38 Whitworth St M1 3NR

web: www.theaa.com/travel/index.jsp

The basement is home to Samsi Express (casual eating in a modern space) and a colourful Japanese supermarket. Upstairs, things are slightly more formal. The exciting menu lists a huge range of dishes from every corner of Japan.

Shere Khan

☎ 0161 256 2624 52 Wilmslow Rd, Rusholme M14 5TQ

Something of a local legend, justly popular and a haunt of celebrities.

🍴 Shimla Pinks Manchester

☎ 0161 831 7099 Dolefield, Crown Square M3 3HA

web: www.theaa.com/travel/index.jsp

One of a chain of very funky, modern Indian eateries. Traditional and lesser known dishes on offer.

🍴 Stock

☎ 0161 839 6644 The Stock Exchange, 4 Norfolk St M2 1DW

web: www.theaa.com/travel/index.jsp

Stunning location in the old Stock Exchange building. Hearty and inventive Southern Italian dishes.

Wagamama

☎ 0161 839 5916 1 The Printworks, Corporation St M4 4DG

Informal noodle bar with no booking required.

🍴 Zinc Bar and Grill

☎ 0161 827 4200 The Triangle, Hanging Ditch M4 3ES

web: www.theaa.com/travel/index.jsp

Contemporary Conran-owned eatery.

MANCHESTER AIRPORT   MAP 15 SJ88

◉ Etrop Grange Hotel

Modern British, International

Country-house elegance handy for the airport

☎ 0161 499 0500 Thorley Ln M90 4EG

e-mail: etropgrange@foliohotels.com

web: www.foliohotels.com

Given its proximity to the airport, it might be surprising that the Georgian Etrop Grange still manages to attain an ambience more akin to a rural country house than a heaving international thoroughfare. (It is currently undergoing a complete refurbishment.) The stylish Coach House restaurant is a modern affair with a classical twist and oozes style and sophistication, while the fixed-priced menus follow the décor's theme. Take roast loin of venison teamed with red cabbage, fondant potato and a bitter chocolate sauce, or perhaps seared dourade served with a ragout of white beans and rouille.

Chef: Marc Mattocks, Patrick Mansel **Owners:** Folio Hotels Ltd
Times: 12-2/6.30-10, Closed L Sat **Prices:** Fixed D £35.95 **Wine:** 5 bottles under £20, 14 by the glass **Notes:** Civ Wed 80, Air con **Seats:** 60, Pr/dining room 90 **Children:** Portions **Rooms:** 64 (64 en suite) ★★★ HL **Directions:** Off M56 junct 5. Follow signs to Terminal 2, take 1st left (Thornley Ln), 200yds on right **Parking:** 80

◉ Radisson SAS Hotel Manchester Airport

Modern International

Sophisticated restaurant overlooking the runway

☎ 0161 490 5000 Chicago Av M90 3RA

e-mail: sales.manchester.airport@radisson.com

web: www.radissonsas.com

Perfect for plane spotters, the vibrant-coloured crescent-shaped Phileas Fogg restaurant has plate-glass windows down one side that look out on to the airport and runway. Quick access to the terminals, and smart tables with comfortable seating, make this a must for travellers too. Given the setting, the creative international cuisine goes down a treat with well-heeled guests and locals, though it's only

CONTINUED

ENGLAND

MANCHESTER AIRPORT CONTINUED

available in the evenings (buffet available at lunch). On the imaginative seasonal menu you might find roasted loin of rabbit, Spanish ham, rillette of leg with garlic pomme purée.

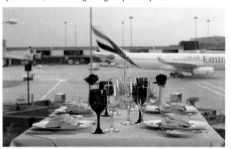

Radisson SAS Hotel Manchester Airport

Chef: Adam Tracey **Owners:** Rezidar Hotel Group **Times:** 12-2.30/7-10.30, Closed L Sat-Sun **Prices:** Fixed D £30.50, Starter £7.50-£10, Main £15-£22, Dessert £6, Service optional **Wine:** 43 bottles over £20, 2 bottles under £20, 9 by the glass **Notes:** Vegetarian available, Civ Wed 220, Air con **Seats:** 180, Pr/dining room **Children:** Menu, Portions **Rooms:** 360 (360 en suite) ★★★★ HL **Directions:** M56 junct 5, follow signs for Terminal 2, take 1st exit at rdbt for railway station, hotel opposite station **Parking:** 220

OLDHAM   MAP 16 SD90

◎◎ White Hart Inn

Modern British, European

Great food in a restored inn with bags of character

☎ 01457 872566 51 Stockport Rd, Lydgate OL4 4JJ
e-mail: bookings@thewhitehart.co.uk
web: www.thewhitehart.co.uk

A destination dining venue set on the rugged moors above Oldham, this 200-year-old inn has much to offer, with a brasserie, restaurant, private dining room, function room and civil wedding licence. The rustic brasserie, with its beams, brickwork and open fire, provides a sharp contrast to the stylish appeal of the contemporary restaurant, but the bold and imaginative cooking is the same in each. A good choice of dishes includes spiced sweet potato risotto cake with excellent saffron, sultana and coriander mayonnaise, followed by pan-roasted fillet of line-caught sea bass with dauphinoise potato and oyster bourguignon, or perhaps Welsh Black beef with boneless oxtail, thyme carrots and waxed potatoes. Finish with an excellent chocolate and cherry iced parfait with cherry compôte and vanilla ice cream.

Chef: John Rudden **Owners:** Mr C Brierley & J Rudden **Times:** 12-2.30/6-9.30, Closed Mon-Tue (brasserie open Mon-Sun), Closed L Wed-Sat, D Sun **Prices:** Fixed D £39.50, Service optional **Wine:** 150 bottles over £20, 40 bottles under £20, 18 by the glass **Notes:** Civ Wed 85, Air con **Seats:** 50, Pr/dining room 38 **Children:** Portions **Directions:** M62 junct 20, take A627 and continue to the end of bypass, then take the A669 to Saddleworth. Enter Lydgate turn right onto Stockport road, White Hart Inn is 50yds on left **Parking:** 75

ROCHDALE   MAP 16 SD81

◎◎ Nutters

Modern British V ⚱ NOTABLE WINE LIST

'Not just a meal but an adventure'

☎ 01706 650167 Edenfield Rd (A680), Norden OL12 7TT
e-mail: enquiries@nuttersrestaurant.com
web: www.nuttersrestaurant.com

Built in 1888 as Wolstonholme Manor, with superb gothic arches, it was bought by Lord Shawcross and donated to Rochdale Council in 1929 for use as a hospital. It was transformed into a restaurant in 1988, becoming Nutters in 1994. The interior is no less impressive than the exterior, and a cosy bar and relaxed but formal dining rooms overlook Ashworth Moor. Expect modern British cuisine using the finest of local and regional produce, sometimes in a rather quirky fashion. Try shellfish bisque with ginger and coriander to start; then perhaps seared Tatton venison with lime, spring onion and toasted sesame. For dessert, feast on tiramisù cheesecake with espresso ice cream.

Chef: Andrew Nutter **Owners:** Mr A Nutter, Mr R Nutter, Mrs K J Nutter **Times:** 12-2/6.30-9.30, Closed 1-2 days after Xmas and New Year, Mon **Prices:** Fixed L £12.95, Starter £4.80-£9.50, Main £16.50-£18.90, Dessert £3.95-£6.50, Service optional, Group min 10 service 10% **Wine:** 108 bottles over £20, 28 bottles under £20, 9 by the glass **Notes:** Gourmet menu 6 courses £34, Sun L 3 courses £22, Vegetarian menu, Dress Restrictions, Smart casual, Civ Wed 120, Air con **Seats:** 154, Pr/dining room 30 **Children:** Menu, Portions **Directions:** From Rochdale take A680 signed Blackburn. Nutters is situated on Edenfield Rd and is on right when leaving Norden **Parking:** 100

WIGAN   MAP 15 SD50

🏵 Simply Heathcotes Wrightington

Modern British

Simple British cooking at its best in contemporary surroundings

☎ 01257 478244 & 424500 Wrightington Hotel, Moss Ln, Wrightington WN6 9PB
e-mail: wrightington@heathcotes.co.uk
web: www.heathcotes.co.uk

This modern hotel eatery belongs to the Heathcote chain. The split-level dining room is a bright, minimalist affair with bold artwork, polished wooden tables and pretty views; take your seat and peruse the brasserie-style menu as the chefs cook up a storm in the open-plan kitchen. Expect modern British dishes conjured from the best of seasonal local produce: black pudding and ham hock salad, for example, or citrus-seared sea bass with braised fennel, spinach and garlic butter. Children are well catered for with their own separate menu, plus there are one-day cookery courses for those hoping to take a little of the Heathcote magic home.

Chef: Michael Noonan **Owners:** Heathcotes Restaurants Ltd **Times:** 12-2.30/6-10 **Prices:** Fixed L £15, Starter £5.50, Main £15.50, Dessert £4.95-£7.45, Service optional, Group min 8 service 10% **Wine:** 71 bottles over £20, 20 bottles under £20, 16 by the glass **Notes:** Sun L 2 courses £14.50, 3 courses £17, Vegetarian available, Dress Restrictions, Smart casual, Air con **Seats:** 75, Pr/dining room 25 **Children:** Menu, Portions **Directions:** From M6 junct 27, at rdbt onto Crow Orchard Rd, then right onto Moss Ln, hotel on right **Parking:** 100

HAMPSHIRE

ALTON   MAP 05 SU73

🏵🏵 Alton Grange Hotel

Modern European

Contemporary cuisine in a country hotel

☎ 01420 86565 London Rd GU34 4EG
e-mail: info@altongrange.co.uk
web: www.altongrange.co.uk

Alton Grange is a family-run hotel on the outskirts of town, set in lovely landscaped gardens. Public areas incorporate a cocktail bar and lounge and a choice of dining venues. The intimate atmosphere in Truffles restaurant is created by a host of Tiffany lamps, oriental objets d'art and lush green plants. Outside there is seating on the fragrant sun terrace, and lighter meals are served in Muffins brasserie. Modern European dishes draw on best quality seasonal ingredients to offer the likes of risotto of organic mushrooms with chives and white truffle oil, followed by roast loin of venison on braised red cabbage and fondant potato, with Amaretto pannacotta with marinated prunes in Armagnac and pear sorbet to finish.

Alton Grange Hotel

Chef: David Heath **Owners:** Andrea & David Levene **Times:** 12-2.30/7-9.30, Closed 24 Dec-3 Jan, ex 31 Dec **Prices:** Fixed D £32.50, Service added but optional 10% **Wine:** 122 bottles over £20, 18 bottles under £20, 12 by the glass **Notes:** 7 course Gourmet menu also available, Dress Restrictions, No shorts or jeans, Civ Wed 100 **Seats:** 45, Pr/dining room 18 **Children:** Min 5 yrs, Portions **Rooms:** 30 (30 en suite) ★★★ HL **Directions:** 300yds from A31 on A339 **Parking:** 40

ANDOVER   MAP 05 SU34

🏵🏵 Esseborne Manor

Modern British

Contemporary cooking in timeless country-house setting

☎ 01264 736444 Hurstbourne Tarrant SP11 0ER
e-mail: esseborne@aol.com
web: www.esseborne-manor.co.UK

Set in rolling countryside high on the North Wessex Downs, this attractive Victorian country house enjoys superb views over the well-tended gardens and fields beyond from its smart restaurant's windows. Elegant fabric-lined walls, floor-to-ceiling curtains and an open log fire feature in the coral red dining room, while canapés are taken in the adjoining bar and coffees in the comfortable lounge. The kitchen's modern approach is reflected in a range of menus, with the carte a typically more ambitious, innovative experience, displaying high technique, quality produce and clear flavours. Choose a starter of lobster and salmon ravioli with spinach au gratin perhaps, followed by fillet of Angus beef with Madeira truffle sauce, dauphinoise potatoes, and a fricassée of mushrooms.

Chef: Steven Ratic **Owners:** Ian Hamilton **Times:** 12-2/7-9.30 **Prices:** Fixed L £13, Fixed D £22, Starter £5-£9, Main £16.50-£26, Dessert £7.50, Service optional **Wine:** 81 bottles over £20, 38 bottles under £20, 10 by the glass **Notes:** Fixed D inc wine 2-4 courses £21-£34, Vegetarian available, Dress Restrictions, Smart dress, Civ Wed 100 **Seats:** 35, Pr/dining room 80 **Children:** Portions **Rooms:** 20 (20 en suite) ★★★ HL **Directions:** On A343, halfway between Andover and Newbury **Parking:** 40

BARTON-ON-SEA MAP 05 SZ29

◉ Pebble Beach

French, Mediterranean

Clifftop restaurant specialising in seafood

☎ 01425 627777 Marine Dr BH25 7DZ
e-mail: mail@pebblebeach-uk.com
web: www.pebblebeach-uk.com

Full-length windows make the most of the superb views over The Needles, Hurst Castle and the Isle of Wight coast, and in summer a terrace is available for alfresco dining. An open kitchen provides good entertainment for diners, delivering a versatile menu with French influences. Plenty of fresh local seafood (monkfish, turbot and sea bass) is available, along with meaty options like braised lamb shank with dauphinoise potatoes, and gammon hock with a morel mushroom jus. Breton-style fish soup, chargrilled squid and gambas sautéed in garlic and brandy butter feature among the starters.

Chef: Pierre Chevillard **Owners:** Mike Caddy **Times:** 11-2.30/6-11, Closed D 25 Dec & 1 Jan **Prices:** Starter £4.25-£17.80, Main £10.50-£19.50, Dessert £6, Service optional, Group min 10 service 10% **Wine:** 52 bottles over £20, 26 bottles under £20, 11 by the glass **Notes:** Vegetarian available, Smart casual, no beachwear, Air con **Seats:** 70
Children: Portions **Directions:** Follow A35 from Southampton on to A337 to New Milton, turn left down Barton Court Ave to clifftop **Parking:** 20

BASINGSTOKE MAP 05 SU65

◉ Apollo Hotel

International 🖥

Elegant hotel dining

☎ 01256 796700 Aldermaston Roundabout RG24 9NU
e-mail: admin@apollo-hotels.co.uk
web: www.apollohotels.com

This well-appointed hotel boasts a business centre and leisure club, as well as a choice of two eateries. A brasserie serves more informal fare, while the fine-dining restaurant, Vespers, is an intimate room where the tables are dressed with crisp white napery, unusual glassware and fresh flowers. It's only open for dinner and serves a modern menu of well-balanced dishes; your choice might include salmon tournedos with a smoked salmon and leek risotto, or breast of duck with pear chutney and vanilla parsnip purée, followed by steamed orange pudding with marmalade ice cream, or deep-fried rice pudding with raspberry coulis. Book in advance.

Chef: Jo Booth **Owners:** Huggler Hotel **Times:** 12-2/7-10, Closed Xmas, New Year, Sun, Closed L Sat **Prices:** Fixed L £12.95, Fixed D £22, Starter £5.95-£6.95, Main £15.50-£21, Dessert £5.95, Service included **Wine:** 13 bottles over £20, 20 bottles under £20, 14 by the glass **Notes:** Fixed D carvery, Sun L 2 courses £10.95, 3 courses £13.95, Vegetarian available, Dress Restrictions, Smart casual, Civ Wed 200, Air con **Seats:** 28, Pr/dining room 200 **Children:** Portions **Rooms:** 125 (125 en suite) ★★★★ HL
Directions: From M3 junct 6 follow ring road N & signs for Aldermaston/Newbury. Follow signs for A340 (Aldermaston) & on rdbt take 5th exit onto Popley Way. Hotel entrance 1st left **Parking:** 120

◉ The Hampshire Court Hotel

Modern British NEW

Imaginative cooking in a smart, modern hotel restaurant

☎ 01256 319700 Centre Dr, Chineham RG24 8FY
e-mail: hampshirecourt@qhotels.co.uk
web: www.qhotels.co.uk/hotels/the-hampshire-court-basingstoke-hampshire/

This impressive modern hotel is conveniently located for business and leisure guests. Overlooking a terrace and the centrecourt, the smart, contemporary restaurant has traditional white linen dressed tables and friendly service. An extensive monthly-changing menu offers traditional British dishes with a contemporary twist. Ambitious cooking sees starters like carpaccio of beef with rocket, dressed with olive oil and dolcelatte cream, while mains might feature delicious combinations like slow-roast Gloucester Old Spot pork belly with fondant potato, apple purée, pancetta and sage jus. The bittersweet marquise of chocolate clotted cream and salt caramel sugar-dipped almonds might prove irresistible for dessert.

Chef: James Parsons, Neil Dance **Owners:** QHotels **Times:** 12-2/7-9.30, Closed L Sat **Prices:** Fixed L £10.95-£25.95, Fixed D £29.95-£36.95, Starter £5.50-£8, Main £16.95-£19.95, Dessert £5.50, Service optional **Wine:** 39 bottles over £20, 22 bottles under £20, 9 by the glass **Notes:** Dress Restrictions, Smart casual, no shorts or swimwear, Civ Wed 200, Air con **Seats:** 200, Pr/dining room 170 **Children:** Menu, Portions **Rooms:** 90 (90 en suite) ★★★★ HL **Directions:** M3 junct 6 take A33 towards Reading. Right at Chineham centre rdbt onto Great Binfields Rd. Hotel 400m on left **Parking:** 200

BEAULIEU MAP 05 SU30

◉ Beaulieu Hotel

Modern British, European V

Classic country-house cuisine

☎ 023 8029 3344 Beaulieu Rd SO42 7YQ
e-mail: beaulieu@newforesthotels.co.uk
web: www.newforesthotels.co.uk

A lovely country-house hotel set in open heathland with stunning panoramic views of the New Forest. Traditional country-house cooking is popular with locals and guests alike. Starters might feature cream of mushroom and sherry soup or roasted chicken ballotine with apricot relish, followed by the likes of roasted duck breast with garlic mashed potato and griottine cherry jus, or red onion marmalade and goat's cheese tartlet. Irresistible desserts include Sicilian lemon pannacotta, and iced mocha and mandarin parfait.

Chef: Michael Mckell **Owners:** New Forest Hotels plc **Times:** 7-9 **Prices:** Fixed D £21.50, Service optional **Wine:** 32 bottles over £20, 29 bottles under £20, 2 by the glass **Notes:** Sun L £12.95, Vegetarian menu, Civ Wed 60 **Seats:** 40, Pr/dining room 60 **Children:** Menu, Portions **Rooms:** 23 (23 en suite) ★★★ HL **Directions:** On B3056 between Lyndhurst & Beaulieu. Near Beaulieu Rd railway station

◎◎ The Montagu Arms Hotel

British, European

Old-world charm meets modern cuisine

☎ 01590 612324 Palace Ln SO42 7ZL
e-mail: reservations@montaguarmshotel.co.uk
web: www.montaguarmshotel.co.uk

Nestling at the heart of this famous, picturesque village, in sight of the river and palace, this traditional country-house hotel is brimful of original features. The oak-panelled Terrace restaurant overlooks a rear courtyard with well-kept gardens, while high-backed seating, smartly dressed tables and knowledgeable, formally turned-out staff complete the fine-dining experience. The accomplished cooking takes on a surprisingly modern, simple and unfussy approach, letting local, seasonal and organic ingredients do the talking. A wild mushroom risotto starter, followed by roast loin of pork with pistachio crust and celeriac purée, or turbot with braised fennel and Montpellier butter, and puddings like plum and vanilla crumble tart are fine examples of the fare.

Chef: Scott Foy **Owners:** Greenclose Ltd, Mr Deach **Times:** 12-2.30/7-9.30 **Prices:** Fixed L £19 (2 courses), Fixed D £42, Service optional **Wine:** 200+ bottles over £20, 9 bottles under £20, 12 by the glass **Notes:** Dress Restrictions, Smart casual, Civ Wed 60 **Seats:** 60, Pr/dining room 32 **Children:** Min 8 yrs, Portions **Rooms:** 22 (22 en suite)★★★ HL **Directions:** From M27 junct 2 take A326 & B3054 for Beaulieu **Parking:** 45

see advert opposite

BROCKENHURST　　　　　　　**MAP 05 SU30**

◎ Balmer Lawn Hotel

Modern British V

Fine dining at a grand New Forest hotel

☎ 01590 623116 Lyndhurst Rd SO42 7ZB
e-mail: info@balmerlawnhotel.com
web: www.balmerlawnhotel.com

This imposing hotel in a gorgeous New Forest setting, just outside Brockenhurst, was once a hunting lodge. The Beresfords restaurant is the last word in luxury, with its leather seating, rich decorations and understated contemporary style. Service is professional yet friendly, creating a relaxed atmosphere. The menu is modern British and makes good use of local ingredients. Follow Lymington crab and avocado tian with twice-braised galantine of Dorset lamb with cauliflower purée, braised red cabbage and fondant potato, or grilled turbot with béarnaise. To finish, try the white chocolate fondant pudding or a plate of interesting local cheeses.

Balmer Lawn Hotel

Chef: John Underhill, Richard Walsh **Owners:** Mr C Wilson **Times:** 12.30-2.30/6.30-9.30 **Prices:** Fixed L £13.95, Fixed D £27.95-£42.95, Starter £5.25-£8.50, Main £15.95-£25.95, Dessert £5.95-£7.95, Service optional, Group min 10 service 12.5% **Wine:** 24 bottles over £20, 19 bottles under £20, 8 by the glass **Notes:** Fixed D 4 courses, Sun L 3 courses £15.95, Vegetarian menu, Dress Restrictions, Smart casual, no jeans or trainers, Civ Wed 120, Air con **Seats:** 90, Pr/dining room 100 **Children:** Menu, Portions **Rooms:** 55 (55 en suite) ★★★ HL **Directions:** Take A337 towards Brockenhurst, hotel on left after 'Welcome to Brockenhurst' sign **Parking:** 100

BROCKENHURST CONTINUED

Brookleys

Modern British V

Contemporary bistro in popular New Forest village

☎ 01590 624625 58 Brookley Rd SO42 7RA
e-mail: info@brookleysbistro.co.uk
web: www.brookleysbistro.co.uk

Fronted by a terrace with seating and parasols, this relaxed, contemporary restaurant - remodelled from a former shop - cuts a clean, minimalist edge. Suede tub chairs and banquettes in the small bar give way to the dining room decked out with darkwood Venetian blinds or modern wall-lighting panels, while unclothed tables are broken up by screens to create intimacy. The concise carte plays to the gallery, offering simple, crowd-pleasing, bistro-style dishes bolstered by a few daily blackboard specials. Perhaps roasted cod with Bombay potatoes, tiger prawns and a curry bisque, or chargrilled calves' liver and herb sausage with a sherry vinegar sauce, mash, smoked cherry tomato chutney and bacon crisps.

Chef: Gareth Bowen & Matt Gingell **Owners:** Gareth Bowen & Matthew Cromie **Times:** 12-2.30/6.30-9.30, Closed Mon **Prices:** Fixed L £10-£12.95, Fixed D £15, Starter £4.50-£9.50, Main £12-£16.95, Dessert £4.50-£6.50, Service optional, Group min 8 service 10% **Wine:** 20 bottles over £20, 15 bottles under £20, 6 by the glass **Notes:** Vegetarian menu, Air con **Seats:** 60 **Children:** Portions **Directions:** M27 junct 1, follow signs for Lyndhurst then signposted Brockenhurst **Parking:** 50

Carey's Manor Hotel

Modern British

Great local produce in elegant manor house surroundings

☎ 01590 623551 SO42 7RH
e-mail: stay@careysmanor.com
web: www.careysmanor.com

Carey's Manor provides quite a range of eating and relaxation options. Blaireau's French bistro and bar is found in the grounds, and the fabulous Thai-style Sen Spa has its own Zen Garden restaurant. The Manor restaurant in the main hotel offers traditional hotel dining in formal surroundings. The cooking style is British, with French and European influences, and service is attentive, professional and friendly. The chef takes care to source quality products, and as far as possible these are local, free-range and organic. A house favourite to start is deep-fried local goat's cheese. Follow this with New Forest venison, Romsey pork or steamed organic salmon.

Chef: Chris Wheeldon **Owners:** Greenclose Ltd **Times:** 12-2/7-10, Closed L Mon-Sat **Prices:** Fixed D £34-£50, Starter £8.50-£13.50, Main £18-£27.50,

Dessert £6-£11, Service optional **Wine:** 70 bottles over £20, 24 bottles under £20, 8 by the glass **Notes:** Dress Restrictions, No jeans, T-shirts, trainers, shorts, sandals, Civ Wed 100 **Seats:** 80, Pr/dining room 100 **Children:** Min 7 yrs, Portions **Rooms:** 80 (80 en suite) ★★★★ HL **Directions:** M27 junct 2, follow signs for Fawley A326. Continue over 3 rdbts, at 4th rdbt take right lane signposted Lyndhurst A35. Follow A337 Lymington/Brockenhurst **Parking:** 100

New Park Manor Hotel & Spa

Modern International V

Honest cuisine in historic country setting

☎ 01590 623467 Lyndhurst Rd SO42 7QH
e-mail: info@newparkmanorhotel.co.uk
web: www.newparkmanorhotel.co.uk

Once the favoured hunting lodge of King Charles II, this well-presented hotel enjoys a peaceful setting in the New Forest and comes complete with its own equestrian centre, croquet lawn and spa. Stylish and contemporary with sofas and log fires in winter, the public areas are very comfortable. Dinner is served in an oak-panelled room adorned with oil paintings, while large windows provide views of the parkland and forest, but it's refreshingly informal and friendly, with lighter meals served in the Polo Bar. The kitchen's modern approach is based on fresh, quality seasonal produce - especially game - and an intelligently simple style. Take New Forest venison served with poached pear and a juniper and blackberry jus, or perhaps South Coast brill with braised oxtail, creamed cabbage and a pommery mustard croquette.

Chef: Mark Speller **Owners:** von Essen Hotels **Times:** 12-2/7-9 **Prices:** Fixed D £38.50 **Wine:** 70 bottles over £20, 10 bottles under £20, 16 by the glass **Notes:** Fixed D 2 courses, Sun L from £18, Vegetarian menu, Dress Restrictions, Smart casual, no jeans or trainers, Civ Wed 80 **Seats:** 65, Pr/dining room 16 **Children:** Menu, Portions **Rooms:** 24 (24 en suite) ★★★ HL **Directions:** On A337, 8m S of M27 junct 1 **Parking:** 70

Le Poussin at Whitley Ridge Hotel

see opposite

Rhinefield House

Modern British V NOTABLE WINE LIST

Impressive dining in magnificent surroundings

☎ 01590 622922 Rhinefield Rd SO42 7QB
e-mail: info@rhinefieldhousehotel.co.uk
web: www.rhinefieldhousehotel.co.uk

The Italianate ponds and ornamental gardens are nearly as stunning as the Alhambra and Parliament inspired décor at this impressive

Le Poussin at Whitley Ridge Hotel

BROCKENHURST   MAP 05 SU30

Modern British, French

Fine dining, a tranquil setting and some of the best food in the New Forest

☎ 01590 622354   Beaulieu Rd SO42 7QL
e-mail: info@whitleyridge.co.uk
web: www.whitleyridge.com

Set in secluded grounds in the heart of the New Forest, this Georgian former royal hunting lodge plays host to Alex Aitken's renowned restaurant. The Aitkens haven't abandoned their original Parkhill hotel at nearby Lyndhurst though, rather using this as a staging post while Parkhill undergoes major refurbishment to create a luxury spa hotel and restaurant. But they don't stand still wherever they are, with plans to revamp the endearing fading grandeur at Whitley Ridge. The small but elegant, off-white themed dining room has large linen-donned tables, a high ceiling, beautiful mirrors and chandelier to give that luxury feel, while large bay windows offer views over the grounds. Alex has always been at the forefront of New Forest gastronomy, and continues to go from strength to strength. His modern approach is underpinned by a classical theme, enhanced by the New Forest larder. Quality reigns supreme throughout, from breads to petits fours or tasting menu, with dishes displaying accomplished skill and fine professionalism. So expect the carte to deliver the likes of oak-smoked saffron and pearl barley risotto with soft poached egg and herb salad to start, followed by slow-roast brill with root vegetable essence and stuffed cabbage, with an interesting Valrhona chocolate fondant, tiramisù, sweet potato bark and espresso ice cream for dessert.

Chef: Alex Aitken, Neil Duffet   **Owners:** A & C Aitken   **Times:** 12-2/6.30-9.30   **Prices:** Fixed L £15-£20, Fixed D £45, Service added but optional 10%   **Wine:** 200 bottles over £20, 30 bottles under £20, 30 by the glass   **Notes:** Tasting menu 8 courses £55, Vegetarian available, Dress Restrictions, Smart casual, Civ Wed 45   **Seats:** 50, Pr/dining room 24   **Children:** Min 10 yrs   **Rooms:** 20 (20 en suite) ★★★ HL   **Directions:** 1m along Beaulieu Rd   **Parking:** 30

---

baronial-style hotel. The elegant Armada restaurant is richly furnished and features a huge Elizabethan-style carved fireplace, which took several years to complete. Imaginative modern British and European dishes range from New Forest fur and feather game pie to Poole scallops with warm smoked salmon, artichoke stew and sweet curry emulsion, to start. Main courses include a tasting of free-range local lamb with thyme galette, or pan-fried John Dory with clam bubble-and-squeak. Earl Grey tea ravioli with frozen whisky mousse and almond cake makes an intriguing dessert. There is a delightful terrace for alfresco dining.

Rhinefield House

Chef: Kevin Hartley   **Owners:** Hand Picked Hotels Ltd   **Times:** 12.30-2/7-9.30   **Prices:** Fixed L £19.95, Fixed D £37.45, Service optional   **Wine:** 100+ bottles over £20, 4 bottles under £20, 10 by the glass   **Notes:** Fixed L 3 courses, Vegetarian menu, Dress Restrictions, Smart casual preferred, Civ Wed 130   **Seats:** 58   **Children:** Menu, Portions   **Rooms:** 50 (50 en suite)★★★★ HL   **Directions:** From M27 junct 1 take A337 to Lyndhurst, follow A35 W towards Christchurch. 3.5m from Lyndhurst, turn left into the Forest at sign for Rhinefield House. Hotel 1.5m on right   **Parking:** 150

⊛⊛ Simply Poussin

Modern

Pretty village dining destination

☎ 01590 623063   The Courtyard, Brookley Rd SO42 7RB
e-mail: info@simplypoussin.co.uk
web: www.simplypoussin.com

Tucked away behind Brockenhurst's high street, this courtyard eatery specialises in local and wild produce. The former stable block has been sympathetically converted and features a conservatory dining area with York stone flooring and Lloyd Loom furniture. Tables and chairs are also provided outdoors in summer. Simply Poussin is the sister restaurant to Le Poussin at Whitley Ridge Hotel (see above), and the original Le Poussin cheese soufflé is a good choice of starter. Follow with a posh version of chicken and chips: stuffed breast and breaded leg of poussin served with pea purée and chunky chips. Soufflés are a strength for dessert, too, alongside crème brûlée or a classic tiramisù.

CONTINUED

BROCKENHURST CONTINUED

Chef: Martin Dawkins **Owners:** Alex Aitken **Times:** 12-2/6.30-9.45, Closed Sun-Mon **Prices:** Fixed L £10.50, Fixed D £15, Starter £3.50-£8.50, Main £10.50-£17.50, Dessert £5-£8.50, Service added but optional 10% **Wine:** 14 bottles over £20, 6 bottles under £20, 10 by the glass **Seats:** 36 **Children:** Portions **Directions:** Village centre through an archway between two shops on the High St **Parking:** 4

BROOK   MAP 05 SU21

◉ Briscoe's
Modern English
Friendly golfing hotel near the New Forest

☎ 023 8081 2214   Bell Inn SO43 7HE
e-mail: bell@bramshaw.co.uk
web: www.bellinnbramshaw.co.uk

Part of the Bramshaw Golf Club, the hotel is tailored to suit this market with golf breaks a popular option. Public areas have recently undergone complete refurbishment and the restaurant has been re-launched as Briscoe's. Whether you eat in the cosy bar or restaurant, the produce is sourced as much as possible from local producers. The menu takes a modern approach to traditional dishes, including the likes of seared fillet of salmon with fondant potato and pea salsa, or breast of chicken stuffed with ricotta and spinach, served with sauté potatoes. Desserts might include Bailey's bread-and-butter pudding with crème anglaise, or sticky toffee pudding with honeycomb sauce.

Chef: Anthony Sturge **Owners:** Crosthwaite Eyre Family **Times:** 12-2.30/7-9.30, Closed L Mon-Sat **Prices:** Fixed D £28-£35, Service optional **Wine:** 33 bottles over £20, 29 bottles under £20, 10 by the glass **Notes:** Vegetarian available, Dress Restrictions, No jeans, T-shirts, trainers or shorts **Seats:** 50, Pr/dining room 40 **Children:** Menu, Portions **Rooms:** 25 (25 en suite) ★★★ HL **Directions:** M27 junct 1 (Cadnam) 3rd exit onto B3079, signed Brook, follow for 1m on right **Parking:** 40

BUCKLERS HARD   MAP 05 SU40

◉◉ Master Builders House Hotel
British, French
Contemporary cooking in historic maritime setting

☎ 01590 616253   SO42 7XB
e-mail: res@themasterbuilders.co.uk
web: www.themasterbuilders.co.uk

Originally the home of master shipbuilder Henry Adams, who oversaw construction of the navy's fleet during the great age of sail, this 18th-century building stands in a famous shipbuilding village and the grounds run down to the Beaulieu River. Heavy beams and maritime memorabilia set the scene in the Yachtsman's Bar, and the brasserie-style Riverside restaurant, with its wood flooring and light modern décor, enjoys tranquil river views. A light modern menu combines excellent local ingredients, innovative ideas and sound cooking skills to produce honest and uncomplicated dishes. Typical examples include smoked haddock and spinach risotto to start, followed by a main course of steamed free-range chicken filled with wild mushrooms. Desserts include the likes of hazelnut chocolate terrine with kumquat compôte.

Chef: Denis Rhoden **Owners:** Jeremy Willcock, John Illsley **Times:** 12-3/7-10 **Prices:** Fixed L £16.50, Fixed D £29.95, Starter £5.95-£7.25, Main £16.75-£21.95, Dessert £6.50, Service included **Wine:** 37 bottles over £20, 27 bottles under £20, 64 by the glass **Notes:** Dress Restrictions, Smart casual, Civ Wed 60 **Seats:** 80, Pr/dining room 40 **Children:** Menu, Portions **Rooms:** 25 (25 en suite) ★★★ HL **Directions:** From M27 junct 2 follow signs to Beaulieu. Turn left onto B3056, then 1st left, hotel in 2m **Parking:** 60

BURLEY   MAP 05 SU20

◉ Moorhill House
Modern British
New Forest hotel dining

☎ 01425 403285   BH24 4AG
e-mail: moorhill@newforesthotels.co.uk
web: www.newforesthotels.co.uk

Built as a gentleman's residence, this grand house with extensive grounds is located deep in the New Forest on the edge of a pretty village. The hotel's Burley restaurant overlooks the attractive gardens and opens on to a patio area. Here the fixed-price, three-course dinner menu is available to non-residents, comprising modern British dishes with some European influences. The emphasis is on local produce in dishes of cream of cauliflower and parsley soup, followed by baked pork tenderloin coated in grain mustard café crème and served with fondant potato. Rich lemon pannacotta with raspberry sauce to finish perhaps.

Times: 12-2/7-9, Closed L Mon-Sat **Rooms:** 31 (31 en suite) ★★★ HL

CADNAM   MAP 05 SZ21

◉ Bartley Lodge
British
Former hunting lodge with food that hits the spot

☎ 023 8081 2248   Lyndhurst Rd SO40 2NR
e-mail: reservations@newforesthotels.co.uk
web: www.newforesthotels.co.uk

Built in 1759 as a hunting lodge for the founder of the New Forest hounds, this friendly hotel is quietly situated in picturesque grounds despite being only minutes from the M27. A host of charming period features include hand-crafted oak panelling, a minstrels' gallery and a magnificent fireplace. The Crystal restaurant has wonderful views over the garden and offers a British based menu with influences from France, the Mediterranean and Asia. Start with spinach, leek and tarragon risotto, followed perhaps by seared fillets of John Dory with vanilla cream and saffron potatoes, and an iced strawberry parfait.

Chef: John Lightfoot **Owners:** New Forest Hotels plc **Times:** 12.30-2.30/7-9, Closed L Mon-Sat **Prices:** Fixed D £21.50-£30, Service optional **Notes:** Civ Wed 80 **Seats:** 60 **Children:** Menu, Portions **Rooms:** 31 (31 en suite) ★★★ HL **Directions:** M27 junct 1, A337 and follow signs for Lyndhurst. Hotel on left **Parking:** 60

DENMEAD   MAP 05 SU61

◉ Barnard's Restaurant

Modern

Accomplished cooking in friendly neighbourhood restaurant

☎ 023 9225 7788 Hambledon Rd PO7 6NU
e-mail: mail@barnardsrestaurant.co.uk
web: www.barnardsrestaurant.co.uk

Exposed brick walls, a warm yellow décor and bright prints enliven this small, homely, family-run country restaurant tucked away in a row of shops in sleepy Denmead. Expect relaxed and informal service, an upbeat atmosphere and consistent modern cooking using fresh local produce. Accomplished, straightforward dishes are well presented and deliver distinct flavours. Take a sea bass fillet served with sun-blushed tomatoes, garlic and a coriander sauce, or perhaps an English lamb cutlet with tartlette of minted pea purée. Leave room for a dessert like banoffee fool, or lemon posset with shortbread.

Chef: David & Sandie Barnard **Owners:** Mr & Mrs D Barnard, Mrs S Barnard **Times:** 12-1.30/7-9.30, Closed 25-26 Dec, New Year, Closed L Sat **Prices:** Fixed L £8.50-£25, Fixed D £18.50, Starter £5.20-£7.95, Main £11.50-£19.95, Dessert £5.20-£6.95, Service optional **Wine:** 8 bottles over £20, 20 bottles under £20, 8 by the glass **Seats:** 40, Pr/dining room 34 **Children:** Portions **Directions:** A3M junct 3, B1250 into Denmead. Opposite church **Parking:** 3

EAST TYTHERLEY   MAP 05 SU22

◉◉ The Star Inn Tytherley

Modern British

Typically English inn with modern, heart-warming food

☎ 01794 340225 & 340678 SO51 0LW
e-mail: info@starinn-uk.com
web: www.starinn-uk.com

This 16th-century coaching inn has a quintessentially English feel with views of the village cricket green, a pretty courtyard garden and a traditional theme to the décor. The atmosphere is cosy, with warm colours, exposed beams and open log fires, while the restaurant occupies a separate wing and is a light-and-airy space with smartly dressed tables and subdued lighting. Modern and imaginative menus come underpinned by traditional and classic dishes, delivered in refined mode with plenty of care taken over presentation. Fresh local produce with a strong emphasis on fish and game is the style; take poached halibut fillet with red rice, braised fennel and sauce gribiche, or suprême of guinea fowl and confit leg with

bubble-and-squeak, while desserts could deliver glazed lemon tart with raspberry coulis.

The Star Inn Tytherley

Owners: Allan & Lesley Newitt **Times:** 11-2.30/6-11, Closed Mon winter, Closed D Sun **Prices:** Fixed L £12, Starter £3.95-£7.95, Main £13.50-£17.95, Dessert £5.50, Service optional **Wine:** 6 by the glass **Notes:** Sun L 2 courses £15.95, 3 courses £18.95, Vegetarian available, Dress Restrictions, Smart casual **Seats:** 30, Pr/dining room 15 **Children:** Menu, Portions **Rooms:** 3 (3 en suite) ★★★★ INN **Directions:** Romsey A3057 N, left to Awbridge, Kents Oak, through Lockerley on right **Parking:** 60

EMSWORTH   MAP 05 SU70

◉◉ Fat Olives

Modern British, Mediterranean

Friendly brasserie by the sea

☎ 01243 377914 30 South St PO10 7EH
e-mail: info@fatolives.co.uk
web: www.fatolives.co.uk

You can almost smell the sea air from this cosy, traditional fisherman's cottage just up from the quayside. A bowl of the eponymous fat olives sits on every table, and the stripped floorboards and plain wooden tables strike a pleasing contemporary note. 'Fresh' is the kitchen's keyword, with the punchy, exciting and reassuringly simple menu making good use of the adjacent sea as well as local game and meats, and producing wonderful honest flavours. Cooking is modern British with Mediterranean influences and dishes may include seared scallops with pea shoot and pancetta cream, halibut with garlic polenta and lemon butter sauce, or partridge with Puy lentil velouté, with baked chocolate mousse among the desserts.

Chef: Lawrence Murphy **Owners:** Lawrence & Julia Murphy **Times:** 12-1.45/7-9.15, Closed 2 wks Xmas, 2 wks Jun, Sun-Mon & Tue after a BH **Prices:** Fixed L £15.25-£15.50, Starter £5.25-£8.50, Main £13.50-£20, Dessert £5.25-£6.50, Service optional, Group min 10 service 10% **Wine:** 35 bottles over £20, 15 bottles under £20, 7 by the glass **Seats:** 28 **Children:** Min 8 yrs **Directions:** In town centre, 1st right after Emsworth Square, 100yds towards the Quay. Restaurant on left with public car park opposite **Parking:** Opposite restaurant

EMSWORTH *Continued*

⬡ Spencers Restaurant & Brasserie
Modern British
A popular venue in restaurant-rich Emsworth

☎ 01243 372744 & 379017 36 North St PO10 7DG
web: www.spencersrestaurant.co.uk

A smart refurbishment has left both the downstairs brasserie and the restaurant upstairs looking fresh and inviting. Opt for a more casual style of dining in the brasserie, where tables are closer together and the bar is handily close, or climb the rustic staircase to dine in one of the booths or alcoves, where the tables are crisply white and further apart. Wherever you choose, the excellent menu is the same, with the early bird choice giving great value for money. Fish in imaginative guises always dominates the menu, typically Indian spiced baked cod fillet.

Chef: Denis Spencer **Owners:** Denis & Lesley Spencer **Times:** 12-2/6-10, Closed 25-26 Dec, BHs, Sun, Mon (Brasserie Mon-Sat 12-2, 6-10) **Prices:** Fixed L £10.25, Fixed D £14, Starter £3.50-£6, Main £13-£16.95, Dessert £5, Service optional **Wine:** 14 bottles over £20, 18 bottles under £20, 6 by the glass **Notes:** Fixed price menu only avail 6-7pm, Vegetarian available, Air con **Seats:** 64, Pr/dining room 8 **Children:** Portions **Directions:** Off A259, in town centre

⬡⬡⬡ 36 on the Quay
see below

EVERSLEY   MAP 05 SU76

⬡ New Mill
Modern British
Waterside dining in an old mill setting

☎ 0118 973 2277 New Mill Rd RG27 0RA
e-mail: info@thenewmill.co.uk
web: www.thenewmill.co.uk

Complete with a working waterwheel, this 400-year-old converted mill perched on the River Blackwater positively oozes character. Under new ownership since November 2006, a sympathetic renovation is under way and its traditional country interior includes exposed beams, open fires and flagstone floors. The resident chef remains and is developing new menus with an emphasis on simplicity and the use of fresh local ingredients - organic where possible, creating innovative modern English dishes with Mediterranean and Asian influences. Expect starters such as carpaccio of Aberdeen Angus beef, with pan-seared flounder served with buttered wild mushrooms, prawns and purple sprouting broccoli to follow.

Chef: Colin Robson-Wright **Owners:** Sean Valentine & John Duffield **Times:** 12-2/7-10, Closed 26-29 Dec, Closed L Sat **Prices:** Fixed L £15, Fixed D £25, Starter £7-£11.50, Main £17-£24, Dessert £5.50-£7.50, Service optional **Wine:** 125 bottles over £20, 15 bottles under £20, 10 by the glass **Notes:** Fixed L 3 courses, Sun L £22, Vegetarian available, Dress Restrictions, Smart casual, Civ Wed 180, Air con **Seats:** 80, Pr/dining room 40 **Children:** Portions **Directions:** Off A327 2m S of Arborfield Cross. N of village and follow brown signs. Approach from New Mill Rd **Parking:** 40

⬡⬡⬡
36 on the Quay

EMSWORTH   MAP 05 SU70
Modern French ⬥NOTABLE WINE LIST
Exciting modern food by the waterfront

☎ 01243 375592 & 372257 47 South St PO10 7EG
e-mail: info@36onthequay.com
web: www.36onthequay.co.uk

As the name suggests, this pristine 17th-century house is located right on the quayside of this picturesque fishing village, taking in all the sights and sounds of the sea and enjoying lovely views over the estuary.
The elegant restaurant occupies centre stage, its peaceful neutral shades punctuated with brightly coloured artwork creating a contemporary vibe. Tables are well spaced, service is polished and friendly, and the mood relaxed. There's a cosy bar for aperitifs and canapés, while the small terrace comes into its own in summer.
Home to some of the best cuisine on the South Coast, the kitchen's modern approach is delivered via a fixed-price repertoire that includes a good-value lunch, impressive carte and eleven-course tasting option. Quality ingredients, flawless execution and memorable flavours distinguish the complex cooking style: expect mains such as fillet of brill, roasted on caramelised fennel and confit tomato, with a fresh mussel, white onion and parsley chowder, followed perhaps by iced peanut parfait with mini butterscotch doughnuts and coffee and white chocolate foam. An impressive wine list and four en-suite bedrooms complete the comprehensive package.

Chef: Ramon Farthing **Owners:** Ramon & Karen Farthing **Times:** 12-2/7-10, Closed 23-30 Oct, 1-22 Jan, Sun, Mon **Prices:** Fixed L £18.95-£36, Fixed D £45, Service optional **Wine:** 15 bottles over £20, 10 bottles under £20, 7 by the glass **Notes:** Dress Restrictions, Smart casual, no shorts **Seats:** 45, Pr/dining room 12 **Children:** Portions **Rooms:** 5 (5 en suite) ★★★★ RR **Parking:** 6

FAREHAM   MAP 05 SU50

⊛ The Richmond Restaurant

Modern European

Elegant surroundings for fine European-style cuisine

☎ 01329 822622   Lysses House Hotel, 51 High St PO16 7BQ

e-mail: lysses@lysses.co.uk

web: www.lysses.co.uk

The Richmond Restaurant is housed in a later addition to the main building of the elegant Lysses House Hotel. It offers a calm, relaxing atmosphere with soft décor in shades of green, pale pink and cream. Cooking is mainly modern European in style, using fresh ingredients cooked to order, and the menu features a range of dishes from the grill. Other options are smoked duck breast salad with mango and vinaigrette, followed by pan-fried scallops with fennel, shallots and mushrooms on chive mash, with banoffee Pavlova and dark chocolate sauce to finish.

Chef: Clive Wright **Owners:** Dr Colin Mercer **Times:** 12-1.45/7.30-9.45, Closed 24 Dec-2 Jan, BHs, Sun, Closed L Sat **Prices:** Fixed L £10-£21.95, Fixed D £21.95-£25.95, Service optional **Wine:** 8 bottles over £20, 19 bottles under £20, 8 by the glass **Notes:** Civ Wed 95, Air con **Seats:** 60, Pr/dining room 10 **Children:** Portions **Rooms:** 21 (21 en suite) ★★★ HL **Directions:** M27 junct 11, follow signs for Fareham. Stay in left lane to rdbt, 3rd exit into East St - road veers to right onto High St. Hotel on left opposite junction with Civic Way **Parking:** 30

⊛ Solent Hotel

British, International

Modern cuisine in revamped setting

☎ 01489 880000   Rookery Av, Whiteley PO15 7AJ

e-mail: solent@shirehotels.com

web: www.shirehotels.com

Close to the M27 and not far from the Solent, this smart, purpose-built hotel enjoys a peaceful location, set in landscaped gardens surrounded by meadowland. The Woodlands Restaurant has a fresh feel, though it still retains its signature log fires, while the informal Nightingales Bar and the extended alfresco terrace adds another dimension in summer. The kitchen delivers simple, well-executed, colourful dishes using quality local produce (suppliers listed on the menu); tiger prawn tempura with dipping sauce, tagine style rump of lamb with butter couscous and warm chocolate tart with espresso ice cream are fine examples of the fare.

Chef: Peter Williams **Owners:** Shire Hotels Ltd **Times:** 12.15-2/7-9.30, Closed 26 Dec, Closed L Sat-Sun **Prices:** Fixed L £17, Starter £6.50-£9, Main £14-£18.50, Dessert £2.50-£6.50, Service optional **Wine:** 44 bottles over £20, 17 bottles under £20, 15 by the glass **Notes:** Vegetarian available, Dress Restrictions, No jeans, T-shirts, Civ Wed 160, Air con **Seats:** 130, Pr/dining room 40 **Children:** Menu, Portions **Rooms:** 111 (111 en suite) ★★★★ HL **Directions:** From M27 junct 9 follow signs to Solent Business Park & Whiteley. At rdbt take 1st left, then right at mini rdbt **Parking:** 200

FLEET   MAP 05 SU85

⊛ The Gurkha Square

Nepalese

Subtle Nepalese specialities in traditional surroundings

☎ 01252 810286 & 811588   327 Fleet Rd GU51 3BU

e-mail: gurkhasquare@hotmail.com

web: www.gurkhasquare.com

Authentic pictures, woodcarvings and artefacts transport diners to the Himalayan Kingdom at this intimate little restaurant in a parade of shops. The interior is highly traditional, with its white textured walls lined with wooden roof awnings, red carpet, clothed tables and cane chairs. Friendly uniformed waiters guide you through the extensive menu of Nepalese specialities, which include some clay oven dishes. Methi chicken, charcoal cooked, with ginger, garlic and dry coriander sauce, is a favourite along with phewa machha - pan-fried monkfish with chilli, garlic and fresh onion sauce. For dessert, try pistachio kulfi.

Chef: Pradip Basnet **Owners:** Bishnu & Imansingh Ghale **Times:** 12-2.30/6-11, Closed 25-26 Dec, Nepalese festivals **Prices:** Fixed L £10-£16.99, Fixed D £15-£16.99, Starter £3.25-£9, Main £6-£10.90, Dessert £1.95-£3.50 **Wine:** All bottles under £20, 2 by the glass **Notes:** Fixed L 3 courses, Fixed D 4 courses, Vegetarian available, Air con **Seats:** 44 **Directions:** Telephone for directions **Parking:** Gurkha Square public car park

FORDINGBRIDGE   MAP 05 SU11

⊛ Hour Glass 💻

Modern British

Rustic charm blended with modern designs

☎ 01425 652348 07788 132114   Burgate SP6 1LX

e-mail: hglassrestaurant@aol.com

web: thehourglassrestaurant.co.uk

From the outside it epitomises rural England, with its low walls and thatched roof. Inside, though, it's a surprising mixture of styles: a modern bar area, with smart black leather sofas and informal tables attracting casual diners, leads into a warren of beamed alcoves that show the building's 16th-century origins. A huge inglenook fireplace dominates, and tables set in nooks and crannies ensure privacy. Tantalising dishes from every corner of the globe appear on menus that are full of interest. Despite the wide scope of the dishes, most ingredients are firmly local, with traditional vegetable paella a typical cosmopolitan offering.

Chef: Daniel Towell **Owners:** Hannah & Charlotte Wiggins **Times:** 12-2/7-10, Closed 25 Dec, 1 Jan, Mon (incl BHs), Closed D Sun **Prices:** Starter £5.95-£8.50, Main £14.95-£20.95, Dessert £5.50-£6.95, Service optional, Group min 6 service 10% **Wine:** 22 bottles over £20, 23 bottles under £20, 10 by the glass **Notes:** ALC Sun L, Vegetarian available **Seats:** 45 **Children:** Portions **Directions:** 1m from Fordingbridge on A338 towards Salisbury **Parking:** 30

HIGHCLERE   MAP 05 SU45

🏵🏵 Marco Pierre White's Yew Tree Inn

British, French

Stylish dining pub close to Highclere Castle

☎ 01635 253360   Hollington Cross, Andover Rd RG20 9SE

e-mail: info@theyewtree.net
web: www.theyewtree.net

This sympathetically remodelled white-washed, 17th-century inn - owned, as the name suggests, by one of the industry's big hitters - retains bags of character, its low-beamed ceilings and log fires blending harmoniously with a more contemporary dining-pub edge. While the bar area has dining tables, there's a more formal restaurant laid with white linen off to one side. The Anglo-French cooking takes a brasserie approach that's steeped in the classics and stamped with Marco's influence. The menu - split into sections like hors d'oeuvre, soups and potages, egg dishes, fish and seafood, and roasts and grills - delivers accomplished, well-presented, intelligently straightforward dishes driven by quality ingredients; think eggs Arnold Bennett with sauce mornay or rib-eye with sauce béarnaise, plus less glitzy offerings like Yew Tree shepherd's pie.

Chef: Neil Thornley **Owners:** Marco Pierre White **Times:** 12-3/6-10 **Prices:** Fixed L £14-£16, Starter £5-£12, Main £11-£27, Dessert £5-£8, Service included **Wine:** 10 bottles over £20, 10 bottles under £20, 10 by the glass **Seats:** 90 **Children:** Portions **Directions:** M4 junct 13, A34 S, 4th junct on left signed Highclere/Wash Common, turn right towards Andover A343, Yew Tree Inn on right **Parking:** 40

LIPHOOK   MAP 05 SU83

Nippon-Kan

Rosettes not confirmed at time of going to press

Japanese

Refined Japanese cooking in country-club location

☎ 01428 724555   Old Thorns Hotel, Golf & Country Club, Griggs Green GU30 7PE

e-mail: info@oldthorns.com
web: www.oldthorns.com

This Japanese restaurant is situated in the grounds of the Old Thorns Hotel and has only five normal tables and two teppan-yaki tables so there's an air of exclusivity and intimacy that sits well with the traditional décor. Gold wallpaper, wood panelling and bare wood tables laid with chopsticks ensure a thoroughly oriental experience with courteous and professional staff on hand to explain the menu. The presentation is simple with food speaking for itself and the interactive thrills of teppan-

yaki on offer for many of the dishes on the menu. Artful sushi dishes are presented on large trays with wasabi and good quality soy sauce. The comprehensive menu includes a selection of wanmono (soup), sushi, noodle dishes, rice dishes, and sashimi. As we went to press, we understand that there was a change of ownership taking place.

Times: 12-2/6.30-10, Closed Mon **Rooms:** 33 (32 en suite) **Directions:** Telephone for directions

LYMINGTON   MAP 05 SZ39

🏵 Stanwell House

Modern

Hearty cooking in a stylish setting

☎ 01590 677123   High St SO41 9AA

e-mail: sales@stanwellhousehotel.co.uk
web: www.stanwellhousehotel.co.uk

Located on the high street, this former Georgian coaching inn offers a carte menu in both the restaurant and bistro. Both rooms are decorated with luxurious purple fabrics and dark-stained wood. The restaurant tables have large candles creating a romantic feel, and there's a bistro adjoining the bar. Robust dishes are attractively presented and hearty appetites are well catered for. Diners might choose a starter of seared tuna sashimi with glass noodles and soy, followed by a pan-fried fillet of beef with dolcelatte and brandy sauce, with honey ice cream and bee pollen to finish, washed down with a recommended dessert wine. Jazz fans might want to visit on a Tuesday night, when there's live jazz in the restaurant.

Chef: Colin Nash **Owners:** Mrs J McIntyre **Times:** 12-2/7-9.30 **Prices:** Fixed L £9.95, Starter £4.95-£7.95, Main £12.95-£18.95, Dessert £5.95, Service included **Wine:** 10 by the glass **Notes:** Vegetarian available, Civ Wed 90 **Seats:** 70 **Children:** Portions **Rooms:** 29 (29 en suite) ★★★ HL **Directions:** M27 junct 1, follow signs for Lyndhurst/Brockenhurst, A337 and Lymington. Head into the main high street for hotel **Parking:** Public car park or on street

MILFORD ON SEA   MAP 05 SZ29

🏵 Rouille Restaurant

Modern British

Competent cooking with plenty of choice near the sea

☎ 01590 642340   69-71 High St SO41 0QG

e-mail: rouille2003@aol.com

A civilised spot not far from the coast, with well-dressed tables that take on a warm glow in the evening once the candles are lit. There's a small bar area where guests are greeted on arrival, and presented with the choice of daily dishes. At lunchtime you'll find a short set menu offering the likes of fillet of peppered smoked mackerel with horseradish mayonnaise, and crispy confit of duck leg. Dinner brings a wider choice that might include oven-baked rack of lamb or pepper-crusted monkfish, and the well presented desserts are always worth savouring.

Times: From 7, Closed D Sun-Mon **Directions:** From A337 take B3058 to Milford, 150yds on L in village centre

◉◉ Westover Hall

Modern French

Fine dining in magnificent Victorian mansion with stunning sea views

☎ 01590 643044 Park Ln SO41 0PT
e-mail: info@westoverhallhotel.com
web: www.westoverhallhotel.com

A Grade II listed Victorian mansion with superb sea views overlooking the Needles and the Isle of Wight, this family-run hotel is packed with stained-glass windows, oak panelling and decorative ceiling friezes. Service is friendly and professional, and the intimate, stylish restaurant also boasts contemporary photography and direct sea views. The kitchen delivers modern interpretations of classics alongside some dishes with innovative twists. Expect eye-catching presentation and quality seasonal produce - sourced from small New Forest suppliers - in dishes like grilled fillet of sea bass served with cockles and mussels, a winter vegetable broth and pommes dauphinoise, and to finish, perhaps a show-stealing tower of griottine tiramisù with mocha ice cream. Try for a window seat.

Chef: Andrew Jacob **Owners:** David & Christine Smith **Times:** 12-2/7-9 **Prices:** Fixed L £15-£19.50, Fixed D £40-£49, Starter £10.50-£14.50, Main £21-£26, Dessert £8.50, Service optional **Notes:** Tasting menu available, Civ Wed 50 **Seats:** 40, Pr/dining room 10 **Children:** Min 12 yrs, Portions **Rooms:** 12 (12 en suite) **Directions:** From M27 junct 1 take A337 then B3058. Hotel just outside centre of Milford, towards clifftop **Parking:** 60

NEW MILTON   **MAP 05 SZ29**

◉◉◉ Chewton Glen Hotel

see page 202

OLD BURGHCLERE   **MAP 05 SU45**

◉ The Dew Pond Restaurant

Modern British, French

Country-house cooking with fine views

☎ 01635 278408   RG20 9LH
web: www.dewpond.co.uk

This 16th-century country-house restaurant enjoys fine views over rural Hampshire, including the famous Watership Down, Beacon Hill and Highclere Castle. Inside there are two beautiful dining rooms with original oak beams, and pleasant staff provide unassuming service. The food is British in style, taking its cue from local seasonal produce, with simple yet flavourful dishes - as in a starter of wild mushroom, rocket and parmesan risotto, followed by pan-fried fillet of line-caught sea bass with a shellfish bisque, buttered spinach, baby fennel and crushed potatoes. Finish with bourbon vanilla crème brûlée. There's a delightful terrace and garden for pre-prandial drinks.

Chef: Keith Marshall **Owners:** Keith Marshall **Times:** 7-9.30, Closed 2 wks Xmas & New Year, 2 wks Aug, Sun-Mon, Closed L by appointment only **Prices:** Fixed D £32-£40, Service optional **Wine:** 70 bottles over £20, 35 bottles under £20, 12 by the glass **Seats:** 45, Pr/dining room 30 **Children:** Portions **Directions:** Telephone for details **Parking:** 20

PETERSFIELD   **MAP 05 SU72**

◉ Annie Jones Restaurant

Modern European NEW

Intimate dining in a rustic setting

☎ 01730 262728   10 Lavant St GU32 3EW
e-mail: stevenranson@hotmail.com
web: www.anniejones.co.uk

Conveniently situated close to the centre of Petersfield, the Annie Jones Restaurant has a distinctly rustic feel, with chunky wooden tables and comfy cushioned pews, large church candles on the tables and gentle music all adding to the warm and friendly atmosphere. Good use is made of seasonal produce which is used simply and imaginatively. For starters, try the five-spiced duck consommé with confit of duck, wild mushrooms and vermicelli noodles, followed by pavé of wild sea bass with crème of seafood linguine and chilli garlic, and a hot chocolate fondant dessert with white chocolate ice cream.

Chef: Steven Ranson **Owners:** Steven Ranson, Jon Blake **Times:** 12-2/7-late, Closed Mon, Closed L Tue, D Sun **Prices:** Fixed L £14.95, Fixed D £14.95, Starter £5.95-£8.95, Main £12.95-£19.95, Dessert £5.95, Service added but optional 10% **Wine:** 6 bottles over £20, 26 bottles under £20, 4 by the glass **Notes:** Sun L 2-3 courses £17.95-£21.95, Tasting menu 7 courses £30 **Seats:** 30 **Children:** Portions **Directions:** A3 town centre, head towards Winchester. Restaurant situated in Lavant St (road which leads to railway station)

Chewton Glen Hotel

NEW MILTON MAP 05 SZ29

Modern British V ✪

Fine dining in impeccable, Palladian-style country-house hotel

☎ 01425 275341 Christchurch Rd BH25 6QS
e-mail: reservations@chewtonglen.com
web: www.chewtonglen.com

Set in landscaped grounds, this outstanding, internationally renowned country-house hotel is a haven of luxury and tranquillity. From the moment you drive through the iron entrance gates you know you've arrived at a very special place indeed, with impeccable service that endures throughout any visit. Warming log fires, afternoon teas and traditional country-house furnishings cosset, alongside views from lounges and bar over the sweeping, picture-postcard croquet lawn. The equally renowned and stylish restaurant, also focused around garden views, has a refreshed styling and a more contemporary feel, while the chic, mainstay conservatory impresses with a tented ceiling.

Like the surroundings, plenty of luxury graces the menus, and carefully sourced, fresh, top-quality produce is the key to success here; the kitchen's suppliers are laudably chronicled at the back of the menu. Classical dishes form the backbone, with the accomplished, refined cooking delivering clear, clean and well-balanced flavours on an appealing repertoire of fixed-priced options and five-course Menu Gourmand. Kick off with a terrine of local game and follow with turbot fillet served with horseradish mashed potato, baby onions, white wine jus and truffle cream or Quantock duck breast with parsnip purée, salsify, butternut squash and blueberry sauce. The dazzling wine list has more than 500 bins.

Chef: Luke Matthews
Owners: Chewton Glen Hotels Ltd
Times: 12.30-1.45/7.30-9.30
Prices: Fixed L £19.50, Fixed D £62.50, Starter £6.50-£85, Main £24.50-£32.50, Dessert £9.50, Service included
Wine: 750 bottles over £20, 13 bottles under £20, 18 by the glass
Notes: Sun L 3 courses £37.50, Tasting menu 5 courses £77.50, Vegetarian menu, Dress Restrictions, Jackets preferred, no denim, Civ Wed 60, Air con
Seats: 120, Pr/dining room 120
Children: Min 5 yrs, Menu, Portions
Rooms: 58 (58 en suite)★★★★★ HL
Directions: Off A35 (Lyndhurst) turn right through Walkford, 4th left into Chewton Farm Rd
Parking: 150

PETERSFIELD *Continued*

Frederick's - Langrish House

British, French

Historic setting for accomplished cooking

☎ 01730 266941 Langrish House, Langrish GU32 1RN
e-mail: frontdesk@langrishhouse.co.uk
web: www.langrishhouse.co.uk

Set amid rolling countryside just outside Petersfield, this 17th-century manor house is brimming with history. Prisoners taken by Cromwell in the Battle of Chewton dug the vaults, where there is now a bar. The intimate restaurant, Frederick's, has garden views and a cosy log fire in winter. Good use is made of quality, seasonal ingredients in a French-influenced, classic British menu, offering the likes of duck and green peppercorn parfait with pickled plums and charred brioche, or roast haddock set on crab ravioli and green asparagus with shellfish bisque.

Chef: Graham Smith **Owners:** Mr & Mrs Talbot-Ponsonby **Times:** 12-2/7-9.30 **Prices:** Fixed L £15.50, Fixed D £29.95, Service optional **Wine:** 19 bottles over £20, 16 bottles under £20, 2 by the glass **Notes:** Dress Restrictions, Smart casual, Civ Wed 60 **Seats:** 24, Pr/dining room 20 **Children:** Min 8 yrs, Menu, Portions **Rooms:** 13 (13 en suite) ★★★ HL **Directions:** From Petersfield A272 towards Winchester, turn left into Langrish & follow hotel signs **Parking:** 100

❀❀❀ JSW

see below

see page 204

❀❀❀
JSW

PETERSFIELD MAP 05 SU72

Modern British V

Quality and élan are the bywords of this restaurant with exceptional food and wines

☎ 01730 262030 20 Dragon St GU31 4JJ

Some may have heard that Jake Watkins relocated his town-centre JSW restaurant to new, larger premises just a couple of hundred yards round the corner at the back-end of 2006, but not all will appreciate that it just got better! The new premises - a former pub - underwent a total makeover, the interior offering a much more spacious version of the previous incarnation. There's a relaxed contemporary vibe, with light-oak beams, cream walls - still featuring those thoughtful line drawings of nudes (by the chef-proprietor's sister) - and well-spaced tables. Service is skilled and attentive with a young, knowledgeable team on hand to recommend dishes and relay information on the outstanding wines from the chef himself.
Remarkable quality ingredients and superb flavours are at work throughout, with Jake's deceptively simple, sophisticated modern approach well thought out. There's bags of self-assured confidence and great balance of flavour, delivered by set menu, carte and eight-course tasting option. Take scallops with pea purée and bacon to start, perhaps followed by turbot with asparagus, wild garlic pesto and

tagliatelle, or loin of lamb with root vegetable and Hampshire hot pot, while salted caramel mousse with hazelnut praline might head-up desserts. One to watch, with an inspired kitchen at work in their new surroundings.

Chef: Jake Watkins **Owners:** Jake Watkins **Times:** 12-1.30/7-9.30, Closed 2 wks Jan & summer, Sun-Mon **Prices:** Fixed L £19.50-£25, Fixed D £32.50-£42.50, Service optional, Group min 10 service 10% **Wine:** 454 bottles over £20, 14 bottles under £20, 10 by the glass **Notes:** Tasting menu 8 courses L £35, D £45, Vegetarian menu **Seats:** 40, Pr/dining room 20 **Children:** Min 7 yrs **Directions:** A3 to town centre, follow signs to Festival Hall car park. Restaurant 80yds from car park **Parking:** 19

ROMSEY   MAP 05 SU32

◉ Berties Restaurant

Modern British

Lively converted inn with French atmosphere

☎ 01794 830708 80 The Hundred SO51 8BX

e-mail: sales@berties.co.uk

web: www.berties.co.uk

This converted, one-time coaching inn continues to offer a relaxed, bistro-style experience, with its friendly and attentive front-of-house team proving a real bonus. There's a warm, cosy character to the original building, while a conservatory extension at the back adds a contemporary edge. Original artworks and mirrors decorate light walls, while polished-wood furniture and blue carpet add to the comforts. The kitchen's modern British cooking ideally suits the surroundings, with clear-flavoured, cleanly presented, straightforward dishes. The choice might include a braised blade of beef with roasted onion mash and braised chicory, and perhaps a fig and almond tart with clotted cream and red wine syrup to finish.

Chef: David Heyward **Owners:** David Birmingham **Times:** 12-2.30/6.30-10, Closed 26-30 Dec, BHs, Sun **Prices:** Fixed D £15.95, Starter £4.95-£7.95, Main £11.95-£18.95, Dessert £5.75, Group min 6 service 10% **Wine:** 23 bottles over £20, 30 bottles under £20, 9 by the glass **Seats:** 100, Pr/dining room 36 **Children:** Portions **Directions:** 200yds from Broadlands' gate in town centre **Parking:** 10

see advert on page 203

The Three Tuns

☎ 01794 512639 58 Middlebridge St SO51 8HL

Smart modern character pub serving quality food.

ROTHERWICK   MAP 05 SU75

◉◉ Tylney Hall

Modern British 🖥️

Smart formal dining in opulent country-house surroundings

☎ 01256 764881   RG27 9AZ

e-mail: sales@tylneyhall.com

web: www.tylneyhall.com

An imposing, 19th-century, red-brick mansion set in 66 acres of grounds, with fine Gertrude Jekyll gardens that include cascading waterfalls, ornamental lakes and woodland walks. Within, expect oak

panelling, ornate ceilings, log fires, an old-fashioned style of service and a sense of grandeur, with the glass-domed Oak Room restaurant overlooking the garden. The modern cooking focuses on quality (and often luxurious) British produce, dishes have a refreshing simplicity, based on classical roots with an innovative modern twist. Think porcini ravioli on creamed Savoy cabbage, followed by breast of chicken with truffle mousse. Finish with pomegranate pannacotta. Daily dish from the carving trolley is a must.

Tylney Hall

Chef: Stephen Hine **Owners:** Elite Hotels **Times:** 12.30-2/7-10 **Prices:** Fixed L £16, Fixed D £35, Starter £8.50-£12.50, Main £23-£27, Dessert £7.50, Service included **Wine:** 350 bottles over £20, 2 bottles under £20, 10 by the glass **Notes:** Vegetarian available, Dress Restrictions, Jacket & tie at D, no jeans, Civ Wed 100 **Seats:** 80, Pr/dining room 100 **Children:** Menu, Portions **Rooms:** 112 (112 en suite)★★★★ HL **Directions:** M3 junct 5 take A287 (Newnham). From M4 junct 11 take B3349 (Hook), at sharp bend left (Rotherwick), left again & left in village (Newnham) 1m on right **Parking:** 150

SHEDFIELD   MAP 05 SU51

◉ Marriott Meon Valley Hotel & Country Club

Modern International NEW

Conveniently located resort and country club for relaxing break

☎ 01329 833455 Sandy Ln SO32 2HQ

e-mail: david.creighton@marriotthotels.co.uk

This classy south-coast hotel boasts its own golfing academy as well as two championship courses, so if your swing's a little rusty it's the perfect place to brush up your skills. An array of other facilities includes tennis courts, a health and beauty spa, and two eateries: the aptly named 'Long Weekend' for casual meals, and the split-level Treetops Restaurant for fine dining. The latter offers a modern

ENGLAND

International menu of straightforward fare, distinguished by quality ingredients and well-balanced combinations with good technical skills. Duck liver parfait is a typical starter, served with orange plum chutney and toasted sultana bread, while mains might include grilled sea bass with crushed new potatoes, wilted spinach and salsa verde.

Times: 1-2/7-9.45, Closed L Mon-Sat **Rooms:** 113 (113 en suite) ★★★★ HL **Directions:** Telephone for directions

SOUTHAMPTON   MAP 05 SU41

◎◎ Best Western Botleigh Grange

Modern European

Country-house hotel offering a formal dining experience

☎ 01489 787700 Hedge End, Grange Rd SO30 2GA
e-mail: enquiries@botleighgrangehotel.co.uk
web: www.botleighgrangehotel.co.uk

This impressive mansion is set in extensive grounds with two lakes. The restaurant is a spacious affair, flooded with sunlight from a domed glass ceiling and wide windows that overlook the terrace and well-tended garden. Popular with locals and residents alike, it delivers a tempting menu of modern European dishes conjured from the freshest ingredients. Start with a timbale of smoked salmon and smoked trout mousse with prawn, or grilled goat's cheese with a roast walnut salad and poached raisins, and for mains dither between salmon with creamed potatoes and a shellfish sauce, or rib-eye steak with roasted root vegetables, red wine jus and watercress purée.

Chef: Peter Patchett **Owners:** David K Plumpton **Times:** 12.30-2.30/7-9.45, Closed L Sat **Prices:** Fixed L £19.95, Fixed D £27.95, Service optional **Wine:** 19 bottles over £20, 31 bottles under £20, 14 by the glass **Notes:** Vegetarian available, Dress Restrictions, No jeans, Civ Wed 200 **Seats:** 80, Pr/dining room 180 **Children:** Menu, Portions **Rooms:** 56 (56 en suite) ★★★★ HL **Directions:** On A334, 1m from M27 junct 7 **Parking:** 300

◎◎ De Vere Grand Harbour Hotel

European

Eclectic fine dining at Southampton's premier hotel

☎ 023 8063 3033 West Quay Rd SO15 1AG
e-mail: grandharbour@devere-hotels.com
web: www.devereonline.co.uk

You can't help but feel inspired by the bold modern architecture of this soaring glass structure on Southampton's waterfront. It is the city's only five-star hotel and with fabulous leisure facilities and a choice of three dining options it certainly exerts a pull on the local affluent set. Through large windows, Allertons looks across at the old fortified walls of the town and almost has the feel of a luxury ocean liner. Take your seat and tuck into a dish of seared scallops with cauliflower purée, pancetta and balsamic, followed by an eye-catching concoction of curried monkfish, couscous, and mussels in a leek and tomato ragout, and a zesty lemon tart with raspberry sorbet.

Chef: Clifford McCrea **Owners:** Alternative Hotel Group **Times:** 7-10, Closed Mon, Closed L Private parties for L only **Prices:** Fixed L £18.50-£21, Fixed D £42.50-£59.50, Starter £8.50-£13.50, Main £22.50-£37.50, Dessert £7.50-£12.50, Service optional **Wine:** 77 bottles over £20, 2 bottles under £20, 10 by the glass **Notes:** Vegetarian available, Dress Restrictions, Smart - jacket & tie not required, Civ Wed 300, Air con **Seats:** 50 **Children:** Min 8 yrs **Rooms:** 173 (173 en suite) ★★★★★ HL **Directions:** M3 junct 13/M27 junct 3, follow Waterfront signs to West Quay Rd **Parking:** 190

◎ Dockgate 4 Bar & Grill

British, European V NEW

Contemporary dining to a backdrop of the cruise-liner heyday

☎ 023 8033 9303 1 South Western House SO14 3AS
e-mail: info@dockgate4.com
web: www.dockgate4.com

Set in the former ballroom of South Western House - once a hotel and restaurant for those sailing to the USA - and located close to the city's popular Oxford Street. The fine period building has been stylishly remodelled, its contemporary image aptly offering a nod to the grand cruise-liner era. Open-plan with an island bar, it comes decked out with wooden tables, starched linen napkins and comfortable seating. Attentive service is delivered by an immaculately presented team, while the kitchen's modern approach features well-executed, balanced dishes. Take pan-seared sea bass fillets served with locally picked wild mushrooms, or steak and kidney pudding with purée of winter vegetables.

Chef: Andrew Hollinby **Owners:** Jenny & Ted Wood, Steve Hughes, Patrick Trant **Times:** 12-2.30/6-mdnt **Prices:** Fixed L £13.50, Fixed D £25-£30, Starter £4.50-£8.95, Main £11.95-£32, Dessert £6, Service optional, Group min 10 service 10% **Wine:** 83 bottles over £20, 17 bottles under £20, 10 by the glass **Notes:** Vegetarian menu, Dress Restrictions, Smart casual, Civ Wed 80, Air con **Seats:** 130, Pr/dining room 12 **Children:** Portions **Directions:** A33/M3, follow signs for The Docks & West Quay shopping centre. Restaurant located on Terminus Terrace, between Oxford St and Ocean Village. Car park voucher available from reception **Parking:** 20

White Star Tavern & Dining Rooms

☎ 023 8082 1990 28 Oxford St SO14 3DJ

A stylish bar and restaurant, with a relaxed, informal atmosphere combined with a menu of modern British dishes.

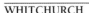

STOCKBRIDGE · MAP 05 SU33

◉◉ *The Greyhound*
Modern British

Popular gastro-pub on the River Test

☎ 01264 810833 · High St SO20 6EY

A smart gastro-pub remodelling of an 18th-century high street inn, set in the charming market village of Stockbridge, famous as a fly-fishing centre, the Greyhound makes good use of its back garden setting on the River Test. Inside it has a relaxed, informal character but with a modern edge. Old beams and timbers, floorboards and inglenook fireplaces meet with stripped wooden tables and high-backed leather chairs. The kitchen's modern approach sits well, delivering high-quality 'city' food without pretension, based around fresh, high-quality seasonal produce. Expect the likes of pan-fried halibut served with boulangère potatoes, wild mushrooms and sauce lie de vin, and perhaps a warm chocolate fondant with roast hazelnut ice cream to finish.

Times: 12-2.30/7-9.30, Closed 25-26 Dec, 1 Jan, Closed D Sun
Directions: 9m NW of Winchester, 8m S of Andover

WHITCHURCH · MAP 05 SU44

◉ *Red House Inn*
Modern European

Busy roadside inn popular with locals

☎ 01256 895558 · London St RG28 7LH

The Red House is in fact a white-painted inn situated on the main road of this busy town famous for its one-time silk industry. Informal meals are served in the bar, while stripped pine flooring, polished wooden tables, exposed red brickwork and blackened beams welcome diners in the restaurant. An honest approach is taken to food with clear menu descriptions and well defined flavours. Seared scallops with crispy pancetta and tomato essence might feature as a starter, followed by slow-cooked poussin with baby roast potatoes. A good selection of steaks is also available.

Times: 12-2/6.30-9.30 **Directions:** Between Andover and Basingstoke, off the A34

WICKHAM · MAP 05 SU51

◉◉ **Old House Hotel & Restaurant**
Modern International

Georgian splendour and impressive cuisine

☎ 01329 833049 · The Square PO17 5JG
e-mail: oldhousehotel@aol.com
web: www.oldhousehotel.co.uk

You can't help admiring this handsome, creeper-clad Grade II listed early Georgian townhouse on the village square. Its three separate dining areas - with one room set at the front - have a contemporary look and can easily be adapted for private dining. Staff are dressed smartly in black and white with long black aprons adding to the European brasserie-type vibe. This fits with the modern menu that features British and International dishes using local produce. Take a starter of seared diver scallops with a light tomato butter, followed perhaps by best end of lamb served with boulangère potatoes, buttered young vegetables and a light coriander jus, and to finish, an indulgent dark chocolate fondant with vanilla cream and pineapple confit.

Old House Hotel & Restaurant

Chef: Ben Streak **Owners:** Mr & Mrs P Scott **Times:** 12-2.30/7-9.30, Closed 26-30 Dec, Closed D Sun **Prices:** Fixed L £14.95, Fixed D £27.95, Starter £5.95-£8.95, Main £11.95-£20.95, Dessert £5.95-£7.95, Service optional, Group min 8 service 10% **Wine:** 40 bottles over £20, 20 bottles under £20, 9 by the glass **Notes:** Vegetarian available, Civ Wed 70 **Seats:** 85, Pr/dining room 45 **Children:** Portions **Rooms:** 12 (12 en suite) ★★★ HL **Directions:** In centre of Wickham, 2m N of Fareham at junct of A32 & B2177 **Parking:** 12

WINCHESTER · MAP 05 SU42

◉◉◉ **Avenue Restaurant**
see opposite

◉◉ **The Chesil Rectory**
Modern French

Modern fine dining in an ancient building

☎ 01962 851555 · 1 Chesil St SO23 0HU
e-mail: info@chesilrectory.co.uk
web: www.chesilrectory.co.uk

Reputed to be Winchester's oldest house, dating from 1425, this oak-framed building exudes historic character. It stands at the foot of town beyond King Alfred's statue and the River Itchen. Original beams and timbers, low ceilings, white walls and an inglenook fireplace create a warm, uncluttered setting for dining. Everything from bread to petits fours is made in-house, and the accomplished kitchen's modern French output is studded with luxury items and boosted by quality local produce, including superbly fresh fish. To start, try confit of organic salmon with warm cep and sun-dried cherry tomatoes, Cornish cock crab and Oscietra caviar, followed by line-caught Solent sea bass with creamy parsnip purée and oyster and vanilla sauce.

CONTINUED ON PAGE 208

Avenue Restaurant

WINCHESTER MAP 05 SU42

Modern British ♦ NOTABLE WINE LIST

An elegant country-house restaurant serving creative food

☎ 01962 776088 Lainston House Hotel, Sparsholt SO21 2LT
e-mail: enquiries@lainstonhouse.com
web: www.exclusivehotels.co.uk

At the end of a long winding drive, surrounded by 50 acres of beautifully kept grounds, you will find this charming William and Mary country house. Inside is just as majestic where historic charm and contemporary elegance blend seamlessly, with expansive lounges looking out over a magnificent avenue of lime trees, and a clubby bar made entirely from a single cedar that fell in the grounds in the 1930s. The elegant panelled restaurant (one of two rooms) is reminiscent of an English manor house dining room and is complemented by a terrace for alfresco dining or to enjoy one of the house speciality cocktails.

The cooking in these fine surroundings more than lives up to the billing, offering a classical menu with some tried-and-tested combinations. Locally-sourced produce, flair, imagination and clean flavours all come together in dishes like wild sea bass served with Portland crab sausage, globe artichoke and saffron infusion, or corn-fed Aberdeen Angus beef three ways (roasted fillet, braised feather blade and oxtail faggot). A blackberry and apple soufflé served with black pepper ice cream might feature at dessert.

Chef: Andre Mackenzie
Owners: Exclusive Hotels
Times: 12-2/7-10
Prices: Fixed L £22.50, Fixed D £41, Starter £9.50-£13.90, Main £17.50-£26.90, Dessert £9.50, Service optional
Wine: 200 bottles over £20, 200 by the glass
Notes: Tasting menu £65, Sun L £32.50, Vegetarian available, Dress Restrictions, Smart dress, Civ Wed 200
Seats: 60, Pr/dining room 120
Children: Menu, Portions
Rooms: 50 (50 en suite)★★★★ HL
Directions: 2.5m NW off A272, road to Stockbridge, signed
Parking: 200

WINCHESTER CONTINUED

Chef: Mr R Quehan **Owners:** Mr & Mrs Carl Reeve **Times:** 12-2/7-9.30, Closed 2 wks Xmas-New Year, 2 wks Aug, Sun-Mon, Closed L Tue **Prices:** Fixed L £19, Fixed D £49, Service optional, Group min 7 service 12.5% **Wine:** 90 bottles over £20, 4 bottles under £20, 6 by the glass **Notes:** Tasting menu £59, Vegetarian menu, Civ Wed 30 **Seats:** 42, Pr/dining room 15 **Directions:** S from King Alfred's statue at bottom of The Broadway, cross small bridge, turn right, restaurant on left, just off mini rdbt **Parking:** 600

⑧⑧ Hotel du Vin & Bistro

Traditional, International

Busy bistro in popular, city-centre, boutique-chain hotel

☎ 01962 841414 14 Southgate St SO23 9EF
e-mail: info@winchester.hotelduvin.co.uk
web: www.hotelduvin.com

The hotel occupies an early 18th-century townhouse in a city-centre location and, as its name suggests, wine is the dominant theme. The charming interior has a relaxed elegance, shown to best effect in the bustling, French-style bistro and bar. Here bare boards, an eclectic mix of polished tables and chairs, and wine memorabilia crowding the walls, form the backdrop for an International-influenced menu. Expect simple, light, clean-cut, well-presented classics with imaginative twists: mackerel escabèche and olive tapenade perhaps, or pheasant breast with bread pudding, watercress and pomme gaufrette. Finish with tarte Tatin and yogurt ice cream, or warm chocolate brownie with espresso ice cream. Knowledgeable staff apply Gallic commitment, and the wine list is a delight.

Chef: Matthew Sussex **Owners:** MWB **Times:** 12-1.45/7-9.45 **Prices:** Starter £6.50-£8.50, Main £14.95-£19.95, Dessert £6.50-£6.95, Service optional, Group service 10% **Wine:** 90% bottles over £20, 10% bottles under £20, 10 by the glass **Notes:** Vegetarian available, Civ Wed 60 **Seats:** 65, Pr/dining room 48 **Children:** Menu, Portions **Rooms:** 24 (24 en suite) ★★★★ TH **Directions:** M3 junct 11, follow signs to Winchester town centre **Parking:** 40

⑧⑧ The Running Horse

Modern International

Seasonal fare in an up-market pub restaurant

☎ 01962 880218 88 Main Rd, Littleton SO22 6QS
e-mail: runninghorse@btconnect.com
web: www.therunninghorsepubrestaurant.co.uk

A refurbished rural gastro-pub, The Running Horse is set in the pretty, rural village of Littleton on the western outskirts of Winchester. Local atmosphere combines with high quality cuisine in a setting of warm colours, clean lines, tiled floors, leather sofas and a marble-topped bar. Choose from the restaurant, bar or blackboard menus, and in fine weather dine out on the terraces. Service is friendly and the cooking accomplished, from an enthusiastic kitchen. A typical selection begins with Thai fishcakes with Asian dressing and salad leaves, followed by pan-fried lamb's liver with wilted spinach, mash, port and pancetta jus. Locally brewed beers and a comprehensive wine list complete the package.

Owners: Light Post Ltd **Times:** 11-3/5.30-11, Closed 25 Dec **Prices:** Starter £4.95-£7.95, Main £10.95-£19.95, Dessert £4.95-£6.95, Service optional, Group min 8 service 10% **Wine:** 9 bottles over £20, 17 bottles under £20, 10 by the glass **Notes:** Vegetarian available **Seats:** 48 **Children:** Menu, Portions **Rooms:** 9 (9 en suite) **Directions:** 3m from Winchester city centre, 2m off A34 **Parking:** 42

⑧ The Winchester Royal

Traditional NEW

Well-designed menu offering something for everyone in Winchester's historic centre

☎ 01962 840840 St Peter St SO23 8BS
e-mail: winchester.royal@forestdale.com
web: www.thewinchesterroyalhotel.co.uk

This historic town-centre hotel provides a delightful backdrop for the Conservatory restaurant, which is set in a bright room overlooking the garden. The food is stylishly presented and makes good use of quality produce, providing some interesting food combinations. A starter of pressed beetroot and goat's cheese gâteau with walnut and parsley pesto, or a roasted vine tomato tartlet with buffalo mozzarella and basil oil show the style. For mains, expect the likes of pan-fried fillet of sea bass on a bed of steamed pak choi, served with a liquorice and garlic dressing.

Times: 12/7 **Rooms:** 75 (75 en suite) ★★★ HL **Directions:** Take one-way system through Winchester, turn right off St George's Street into St Peter Street. Hotel on right.

Loch Fyne Restaurant & Oyster Bar

☎ 01962 872930 18 Jewry St SO23 8RZ
Quality seafood chain.

HEREFORDSHIRE

HEREFORD   MAP 10 SO53

⑧⑧⑧ Castle House

see opposite

KINGTON   MAP 09 SO25

⑧⑧ The Stagg Inn and Restaurant

Modern British ☺

Friendly, quality-driven gastro-pub

☎ 01544 230221 Titley HR5 3RL
e-mail: reservations@thestagg.co.uk
web: www.thestagg.co.uk

The Stagg provides a country restaurant with a pub atmosphere, including large farmhouse tables and open fires. There are three dining rooms on different levels, the largest in a medieval barn. All the dining rooms connect to the bar where the locals enjoy a drink and a chat. The kitchen's classy but unpretentious modern approach makes admirable use of quality seasonal and local produce. Recommended dishes include seared scallops on parsnip purée to start, followed by a main course of Herefordshire beef fillet served with horseradish cream, and for dessert three crème brûlées of vanilla, elderflower and lime, or maybe bread-and-butter-pudding with vanilla custard. An extensive range of regional cheeses bolsters the repertoire.

Chef: S Reynolds, G Powell, M Handley **Owners:** Steve & Nicola Reynolds **Times:** 12-3/6.30-9.30, Closed 1st wk Nov, 25-26 Dec, 1 Jan, 1 wk Feb, BHs, Mon, Closed D Sun **Prices:** Starter £3.90-£8.50, Main £13.90-£18, Dessert fr £5.40, Service included **Wine:** 8 by the glass **Notes:** Sun L £15.50 **Seats:** 70, Pr/dining room 30 **Children:** Portions **Directions:** Between Kington and Presteigne on B4335 **Parking:** 22

Castle House

HEREFORD   MAP 10 SO53

Modern British

Adventurous cooking in contemporary luxury

☎ 01432 356321   Castle St HR1 2NW
e-mail: info@castlehse.co.uk
web: www.castlehse.co.uk

Tucked away in a residential street, this Grade II listed property is now a modern, stylish and elegant Georgian town-house hotel. The bar is sumptuously furnished and decorated with bold lamps, silver-framed pictures and coats of arms, while the chic Castle House restaurant has a topiary theme and aptly extends out on to the terrace on warm summer days, with its views over the old castle moat and gardens. Tables are clothed in their best whites with good-quality settings of silver and crystal. Staff are impeccably trained, well informed and knowledgeable.
The kitchen's fresh, contemporary interpretations - underpinned by classical roots - are driven by well-sourced, tip-top ingredients and come delivered on a repertoire that includes a seven-course tasting option. Expect pan-fried fillet of halibut with spring onion polenta, truffled peas and an oyster beignet, or perhaps a fillet of Herefordshire beef served with creamed greens, a tian of liver and morel jus, while a rhubarb and vanilla soufflé might catch the eye at dessert.

Chef: Claire Nicholls
Owners: David Watkins
Times: 12.30-2/7-10
Prices: L from £12 (2 courses), D from £25 (3 courses), Service optional
Wine: 6 by the glass
Notes: Tasting menu 7 courses £49, Air con
Seats: 30
Children: Portions
Rooms: 15 (15 en suite)
★★★ HL
Directions: City centre, follow signs to Castle House Hotel
Parking: 12

ENGLAND

LEDBURY

MAP 10 SO73

◎ Feathers Hotel

Modern British

Popular and well-established inn serving modern food

☎ 01531 635266 High St HR8 1DS
e-mail: mary@feathers-ledbury.co.uk
web: www.feathers-ledbury.co.uk

This impressive black and white coaching inn has dominated historic Ledbury's main street since Elizabethan times. Oozing charm and character, it combines all the characteristics of a town-centre hostelry with the comforts of a modern hotel. Dinner is served in the elegant Quills restaurant or the bustling Fuggles brasserie with adjoining bar. The cooking style is modern British and features local beef and lamb, and a good range of fresh fish dishes. For starters, take chicken liver parfait with home-made chutney, followed by a main course of fillet of Herefordshire beef with fondant potato.

Chef: Steve Rimmer **Owners:** David Elliston **Times:** 12-2/7-9.30
Prices: Starter £5.25-£7.50, Main £11.50-£17.50, Dessert £6.50, Service added but optional 10% **Wine:** 45 bottles over £20, 57 bottles under £20, 10 by the glass **Notes:** Vegetarian available, Civ Wed 100, Air con
Seats: 55, Pr/dining room 60 **Children:** Portions **Rooms:** 19 (19 en suite) ★★★ HL **Directions:** M50 junct 2, Ledbury is on A449/A438/A417, hotel is on main street **Parking:** 30

◎ Seven Ledbury

Modern British, Mediterranean

Bistro menu at a restaurant with rooms

☎ 01531 631317 11 The Homend HR8 1BN
e-mail: jasonkay@btconnect.com

Behind the ancient timbered exterior dating back to the 16th century, the tasteful modern interior of this relaxed bistro comes as something of a surprise. A popular eatery, it's open all day and serves everything from coffee and pastries, all-day breakfast to a three-course meal. The menus emphasise local beef, lamb and chicken, all traceable to nearby farms, and include dishes such as Hereford beef fillet on creamed potato and beetroot salsa, gnocchi in roquefort cream sauce with rocket and crumbled walnuts, or smoked haddock and saffron risotto with baby spinach and a poached egg. There's a strong Mediterranean influence to the cooking, with a choice of tapas dishes available as starters.

Times: 11-10 **Rooms:** 3 (3 en suite) **Directions:** Telephone for directions

◎◎ The Verzon Bar, Brasserie & Hotel

British, European

Quality local produce in a modern brasserie environment

☎ 01531 670381 Hereford Rd, Trumpet HR8 2PZ
e-mail: info@theverzon.co.uk
web: www.theverzon.co.uk

This large Georgian country house - with far-reaching views of the Malvern Hills from its extensive grounds - has now been refurbished throughout. Modern and stylish interiors abound, with a selection of dining areas - from main restaurant to bar/brasserie option - sharing the same menu and relaxed but attentive service. The accomplished kitchen deals in high-quality, locally-sourced and carefully prepared ingredients; maybe Gloucestershire Old Spot pork with a cider jus and potato rösti, or perhaps Hereford beef, pan-fried rib-eye with sautéed potatoes and sauce au poivre, all treated with due care and respect. Classics bolster the repertoire, too, as in poached salmon with a chive hollandaise, while careful balance and flavour combinations prove a strength of the intelligently uncomplicated style.

Times: 12-2/7-9.30 **Rooms:** 8 (8 en suite) **Directions:** M5 junct 8, M50 junct 2 (signposted Ledbury A417). Follow signs for Hereford (A438)

MUCH MARCLE

MAP 10 SO63

◎ The Scrumpy House Restaurant & Bar

British

Quality local produce in an authentic scrumpy house

☎ 01531 660626 The Bounds HR8 2NQ
e-mail: matt@scrumpyhouse.co.uk
web: www.scrumpyhouse.co.uk

This cosy rustic restaurant is situated in a former scrumpy house, and is decorated with lots of cider memorabilia. Part of the Weston's cider estate, it's independently owned and many guests go for a tour of the cider-making process before enjoying lunch. The light lunch menu includes simple but good quality basics such as cider-braised ham, free-range eggs and home-made chunky chips, while from the main daily menu pan-fried rib-eye of Much Marcle beef comes highly recommended, served with champ potato and a thyme and red onion sauce. Traditional desserts include the likes of sticky toffee pudding. Alfresco dining is available in summer.

Chef: Matthew & Annalisa Slocombe **Owners:** Matthew & Annalisa Slocombe **Times:** 12-3/6.30-11, Closed D Sun-Tue **Prices:** Fixed L £22, Fixed D £22, Starter £4-£8, Main £8-£18, Dessert £4-£6, Service optional, Group min 10 service 10% **Wine:** 8 bottles over £20, 13 bottles under £20, 5 by the glass **Notes:** Fixed L 3 courses, Sun L 2 courses £15.95, 3 courses £19.95, Vegetarian available, Dress Restrictions, Smart casual preferred, Air con **Seats:** 45 **Children:** Portions **Directions:** On A417 between Ross-on-Wye & Ledbury. At village shop follow signs to Cider Mill **Parking:** 100

ROSS-ON-WYE   MAP 10 SO52

◉◉ The Bridge at Wilton
British, French V
Accomplished cooking on the banks of the Wye

☎ 01989 562655 Wilton HR9 6AA
e-mail: info@bridge-house-hotel.com
web: www.bridge-house-hotel.com

A boutique-style hotel, located by a medieval bridge over the River Wye and the ancient remains of Wilton Castle. It is a period property with a partially walled garden running down to the water's edge - the perfect spot for drinks in summer. From its gnarled oak floorboards to the display of contemporary paintings by a local artist, the restaurant offers both comfort and style. Quality ingredients proudly sourced in Herefordshire include vegetables and herbs from the hotel's own garden. Captivating combinations include assiette of suckling pig (roast cutlet, slow-roasted belly and blanquette of leg), followed by bitter chocolate delice with pear compôte and toasted barley ice cream.

Chef: James Arbourne **Owners:** Mike & Jane Pritchard **Times:** 12-2/7-9 **Prices:** Fixed L £16.50, Starter £6-£9.50, Main £15-£20, Dessert £5.50-£7.50, Service optional **Wine:** 29 bottles over £20, 18 bottles under £20, 4 by the glass **Notes:** Vegetarian menu, Dress Restrictions, Smart casual **Seats:** 30, Pr/dining room 18 **Children:** Min 14 yrs **Rooms:** 9 (9 en suite) ★★★★ RR **Directions:** A49 3rd rdbt and left into Ross. 150yds on left before river bridge **Parking:** 40

◉ Glewstone Court
Modern British, French
Local produce lovingly prepared in fine surroundings

☎ 01989 770367 Glewstone HR9 6AW
e-mail: glewstone@aol.com
web: www.glewstonecourt.com

Three miles from Ross-on-Wye, this Georgian and late Regency house is set amid orchards in an Area of Outstanding Natural Beauty overlooking the Wye Valley. Original features include a carved oak staircase spiralling up to a galleried and porticoed landing. The Georgian dining room is decorated in contemporary style, while the cooking is traditionally based using the best local supplies. The wide-ranging menu features Herefordshire beef fillet and rib-eye, and grilled chump fillet of local lamb with roasted red onion stuffed with Tintern cheese, herb breadcrumbs and red wine gravy.

Chef: C Reeve-Tucker, P Meek, M Price **Owners:** C & W Reeve-Tucker **Times:** 12-2/7-10, Closed 25-27 Dec **Prices:** Starter £4.95-£8.25, Main £12.95-£18.90, Dessert £5.50-£5.75, Service optional, Group min 8 service 10% **Wine:** 20 bottles over £20, 22 bottles under £20, 6 by the glass **Notes:** Dress Restrictions, No baseball caps or mobile phones **Seats:** 36, Pr/dining room 36 **Children:** Menu, Portions **Rooms:** 8 (8 en suite) ★★ CHH **Directions:** From Ross Market Place take A40/A49 (Monmouth/Hereford) over Wilton Bridge. At rdbt left onto A40 (Monmouth/S Wales), after 1m turn right for Glewstone. Hotel 0.5m on left **Parking:** 28

ROSS-ON-WYE Continued

◉ Harry's

Modern European
Ambitious cuisine in an elegant Georgian hotel

☎ 01989 763161 Chase Hotel, Gloucester Rd
HR9 5LH
e-mail: res@chasehotel.co.uk
web: www.chasehotel.co.uk

Harry's at The Chase Hotel has a contemporary feel with clean, crisp décor enhanced by a flood of natural daylight and subtle lighting. The colour scheme is warm and inviting and the ambience relaxed and informal. A starter of shellfish risotto with spiced lobster broth and saffron butter is particularly impressive, maybe followed by venison loin with vanilla glaze, rosemary-poached pears and garlic-roasted sweet potato hash. For a classic finale try vanilla crème brûlée with hazelnut shortbread and cappuccino froth.

Chef: Russell Martin **Owners:** Camanoe Estates Ltd **Times:** 12-2/7-10, Closed 24-30 Dec **Prices:** Fixed L £10-£15, Fixed D £17.50-£25, Starter £5.25-£9.75, Main £12.95-£24, Dessert £5.50-£7.95 **Wine:** 19 bottles over £20, 23 bottles under £20, 11 by the glass **Notes:** Sun L £16.50, Vegetarian available, Civ Wed 300 **Seats:** 70, Pr/dining room 300 **Children:** Portions **Rooms:** 36 (36 en suite) ★★★ HL **Directions:** M50 junct 4 A449, A440 towards Ross-on-Wye **Parking:** 150

◉ The Lough Pool Inn at Sellack

British, Mediterranean
Popular inn of great charm serving rustic fare

☎ 01989 730236 Sellack HR9 6LX
e-mail: jon@loughpool.co.uk
web: www.loughpoolinn.co.uk

Set in a peaceful valley just outside Ross-on-Wye, this pub is full of character, with inglenook fireplaces, beams, flagstone floors and granite-topped bar. Food can be taken in the bar or the bistro-style restaurant, with its pine tables and ochre-painted walls hung with paintings by local artists. Robust dishes prepared from seasonal local ingredients include Herefordshire Ragstone goat's cheese brûlée with tomato and chive salad, or a trio of Welsh lamb cutlets with herb roast new potatoes, and port wine jus. Finish with pear and ginger pudding with cinnamon ice cream.

The Lough Pool Inn at Sellack

Owners: David & Janice Birch **Times:** 12-2.30/6.30-9.30, Closed Mon (Nov, Jan-Feb), Closed D Sun (Nov, Jan-Feb) **Prices:** Starter £5.50-£8.95, Main £11.95-£16.50, Dessert £6.75, Service optional, Group min 12 service 5% **Wine:** 5 bottles over £20, 28 bottles under £20, 10 by the glass **Notes:** Sun L available, Dress Restrictions, Smart casual **Seats:** 40 **Children:** Portions **Directions:** 4m NW of Ross-on-Wye. A49, take Sellack exit **Parking:** 50

◉◉ Mulberry Restaurant

British, German ✋
Charming period property with great food

☎ 01989 562569 Wilton Court Hotel, Wilton Ln
HR9 6AQ
e-mail: info@wiltoncourthotel.com
web: www.wiltoncourthotel.com

Dating back to the 16th century, this country-house hotel set in a walled garden has great charm and a wealth of character. Situated on the banks of the River Wye, a relaxed and unhurried atmosphere pervades the light-and-airy Mulberry Restaurant, with its mullion windows, original oak beams, Lloyd Loom furniture and delightful views over the terrace and gardens. Service is attentive and unobtrusive, and the carefully prepared, modern British cooking with European twists includes locally-sourced products which are listed on the weekly-changing menu. You might kick off with Ragstone goat's cheese baked over a pepperonata, followed by fillet of Hereford beef set on bacon potato rösti, glazed with Madeira sauce.

Chef: Hans-Peter Hilsmann **Owners:** Roger and Helen Wynn **Times:** 12-2.30/7-9.30, Closed L Mon-Sat, D Sun **Prices:** Fixed L £10, Starter £4.50-£6.50, Main £12.95-£17.95, Dessert £3.95-£5.25, Service optional **Wine:** 11 bottles over £20, 23 bottles under £20, 7 by the glass **Notes:** Dress Restrictions, Smart casual preferred, Civ Wed 50 **Seats:** 40, Pr/dining room 12 **Children:** Menu, Portions **Rooms:** 10 (10 en suite) ★★★ HL **Directions:** M50 junct 4 follow signs to Ross, turn into Ross at rdbt at junct of A40 and A49. Take 1st right after 100yds, hotel opposite river **Parking:** 25

ULLINGSWICK
MAP 10 SO54

Three Crowns Inn

British, French

Traditional English village inn with a gastro-pub menu

☎ 01432 820279 HR1 3JQ
e-mail: info@threecrownsinn.com
web: www.threecrownsinn.com

This half-timbered village inn is a converted 16th-century farmhouse and erstwhile cider house. Log fires, brick fireplaces, quarry tiled floors and dark oak beams set the scene for an eclectic collection of wooden tables and chairs, creating a warm, welcoming and relaxed atmosphere. A straightforward menu of mainly modern British dishes includes classic sauces and the odd Asian influence. The finest seasonal produce from local, trusted suppliers features heavily in starters such as Little Hereford cheddar cheese and spinach soufflé, followed by frilled rump cap of Rob Thomas' Risbury Court beef, with bone marrow, thyme butter and bordelaise sauce. Round off with a classic crème caramel served with Armagnac prunes, or fine local cheeses.

Chef: Brent Castle **Owners:** Brent Castle & Rachel Baker **Times:** 12-3/7-10, Closed 2 wks from 24 Dec, Mon **Prices:** Fixed L £12.95, Starter £6.50, Main £14.50, Dessert £5, Service optional **Wine:** 14 bottles over £20, 12 bottles under £20, 7 by the glass **Notes:** Sun L roast, Vegetarian menu **Seats:** 75, Pr/dining room 36 **Children:** Portions **Directions:** Telephone for directions **Parking:** 30

WEOBLEY
MAP 09 SO45

The Salutation Inn

Traditional British

Popular country inn serving good local produce

☎ 01544 318443 Market Pitch HR4 8SJ

Combining a former ale and cider house and an adjoining timbered cottage, this 500-year-old inn stands in the heart of medieval Weobley. Beams, sloping floors and low doors abound, and there's a fine inglenook fireplace in the cosy Oak Room restaurant. French influence is evident in the cuisine, and the emphasis is on local produce with traditional sauces. Dishes may include wild mushroom, caramelised onion and goat's cheese tartlet, steak and ale pie with scented new potatoes and roast root vegetables, or rack of Welsh lamb with herb and mustard crust and honey and mint jus. Good bar meals are also offered.

Times: 12-2/7-9.30, Closed 25 Dec, Closed D Sun (bar meals served all week) **Rooms:** 4 (4 en suite) INN **Directions:** On A4112, just off Leominster-Hereford road

BISHOP'S STORTFORD
MAP 06 TL42

Ibbetson's Restaurant

Modern French

Stylish dining in imposing country-house hotel

☎ 01279 731441 Down Hall Country House Hotel, Hatfield Heath CM22 7AS
e-mail: reservations@downhall.co.uk
web: www.downhall.co.uk

Built by Sir Henry Selwin Ibbetson, the imposing Victorian country house of Down Hall is surrounded by 100 acres of grounds. The beautifully presented public areas, including the Ibbetson's dining room, are impressive - full of Victorian design excess and open fires. Seasonal availability of local ingredients dictates a menu of accomplished modern French dishes of exacting flavours, which come underpinned by a classical theme. Take roasted fillet of pork wrapped in Parma ham and served with Savoy and pancetta, turnip Anna and a gratin mustard jus, or perhaps pan-seared scallops with chorizo, herb salad, apple purée and a lime dressing. Finish with a glazed lemon tart and raspberry sorbet, or crème brûlée.

Chef: Mark Jones **Owners:** Mr Gulhati, Veladail Hotels Ltd **Times:** 7-9.45, Closed Xmas, Sun-Mon, Closed L all week **Prices:** Fixed L £19.50, Fixed D £32, Starter £5-£15, Main £15-£32, Dessert £7-£10, Service added but optional 10% **Wine:** 100+ bottles over £20, 2 bottles under £20, 12 by the glass **Notes:** Vegetarian available, Dress Restrictions, No denim or trainers, Civ Wed 120, Air con **Seats:** 36 **Children:** Min 12 yrs **Rooms:** 99 (99 en suite) ★★★★ HL **Directions:** Take A414 towards Harlow. At 4th rdbt follow B183 towards Hatfield Heath, keep left and follow hotel sign **Parking:** 150

ENGLAND

ELSTREE   MAP 06 TQ19

⊛ Corus hotel Elstree

Traditional British

Stylish dining in Tudor-style grandeur with views of the city

☎ 0870 6096151 Barnet Ln WD6 3RE
e-mail: elstree@corushotels.com
web: www.corushotels.com/elstree

Oozing character with a magnificent Tudor-style exterior and rich carvings, this impressive hotel is set in beautiful landscaped gardens surrounded by 10 acres of woodland. Panoramic views over London can be enjoyed from the relaxed Edgwarebury bar, while the stately Cavendish restaurant makes a romantic and stylish dinner destination, delivering a tempting seasonally-changing menu. Kick off with a salad of ham, asparagus and oven-dried tomatoes perhaps, before tucking into lamb chops with a redcurrant glaze, or fish-lovers may opt for grilled sea bass. Sticky toffee pudding is a typical dessert.

Chef: Miklos Takacs **Owners:** Corus Hotels **Times:** 12.30-2.30/7-9.30
Prices: Fixed L £19-£26.45, Fixed D £23-£31.95, Starter £4-£7.50, Main £15-
£18.95, Dessert £4-£5.50, Service optional **Wine:** 7 bottles over £20,
21 bottles under £20, 2 by the glass **Notes:** Dress Restrictions, Smart
casual, Civ Wed 90 **Seats:** 60, Pr/dining room 40 **Children:** Menu,
Portions **Rooms:** 47 (47 en suite) ★★★ HL **Directions:** From A1 take
A411 from Stirling Corner **Parking:** 100

HARPENDEN   MAP 06 TL11

⊛ *A Touch of Novelli at the White Horse*

British, French

Glamorous gastro-pub

☎ 01582 713428 Hatching Green AL5 2JP
e-mail: info@atouchofnovelli.com
web: www.atouchofnovelli.co.uk

A swanky gastro-pub with stripped beams, sparkling chandeliers and a modish pink and aubergine colour scheme. Those in need of liquid refreshment can head through to the bar, but the restaurant is the real draw with its bold, flavourful food. Tuck into chargrilled tuna with mango and chilli, leg of lamb marinated in yoghurt, or chicken breast stuffed with sweet mincemeat served on a bed of sweetcorn, ham and concasse tomato. Save room for top-notch desserts such as champagne jelly with summer berries and elderflower or carpaccio of pineapple topped with coconut and tarragon ice cream. The Terrace is an alfresco eating area, open from May to September weather permitting, complete with its own menu.

Times: 12.30-3/6-10, Closed 25 & 26 Dec **Directions:** Telephone for directions

⊛ The Silver Cup

Modern British NEW

Traditional inn serving local produce in exciting combinations

☎ 01582 713095 5 St Albans Rd AL5 2JF
e-mail: info@silvercup.co.uk
web: www.silvercup.co.uk

This cosy traditional inn, overlooking Harpenden Common, comes attractively decorated to retain much of its original character. The kitchen serves a lengthy, crowd-pleasing repertoire of modern dishes - with a nod to the Mediterranean - driven by fine local produce. Take mushroom, chorizo and roasted-shallot tagliatelle, perhaps chicken stuffed with sun-blushed tomatoes and mozzarella and served with garlic-sautéed potatoes and rich tomato sauce, or grilled tuna with saffron rice and roasted peppers, and to finish, a brioche and rum pudding with passionfruit clotted cream. (Bar/snack/lights-meal menu also served.)

Times: 12-3/6-9.30

▭ The Bean Tree

☎ 01582 460901 20a Leyton Rd AL5 2HU
web: www.theaa.com/travel/index.jsp

A cosy converted cottage with a relaxed atmosphere. The seasonally-changing menu is French and the chef is passionate about the quality and freshness of his ingredients.

HATFIELD   MAP 06 TL20

⊛⊛ Bush Hall

Modern British ▭

Accomplished modern cooking at an elegant hotel

☎ 01707 271251 Mill Green AL9 5NT
e-mail: enquiries@bush-hall.com
web: www.bush-hall.com

A popular wedding and conference venue, Bush Hall stands amid 120 acres of attractive parkland. Riverside terraces and a lake garden make the most of the Lea as it meanders through the grounds, while a host of outdoor activities are available for those who feel like more than a post- or pre-meal stroll. Dinner is served in the Kiplings restaurant, a cosy room with green and gold décor and oak panelling, and there's a comfortable lounge for aperitifs or late-night tipples. Expect an accomplished modern British approach; grilled bream fillet served with a smoked mussel chowder perhaps, or lightly spiced pork belly with sweet black cabbage and fondant potatoes.

Bush Hall

Chef: Scott McKenzie **Owners:** Kiplings **Times:** 12-2/7-10, Closed D 25 Dec-early Jan, Closed L Sat-Sun **Prices:** Fixed L £21.95-£50, Fixed D £25-£50, Service added but optional 12.5% **Wine:** 60 bottles over £20, 60 bottles under £20, 8 by the glass **Notes:** Dress Restrictions, Smart casual, Civ Wed 150, Air con **Seats:** 38, Pr/dining room 22 **Children:** Min 8 yrs, Portions **Rooms:** 25 (25 en suite) ★★★ HL **Directions:** From A1 (M) follow signs for A414 (Hereford/Welwyn Garden City). Take slip road onto A1000 (signs for Hatfield Hse). Left at lights, immediately left into hotel drive **Parking:** 100

HITCHIN   MAP 12 TL12

◉ Redcoats Farmhouse Hotel

Traditional European

Family-run hotel with a busy restaurant

☎ 01438 729500 Redcoats Green SG4 7JR

e-mail: sales@redcoats.co.uk

web: www.redcoats.co.uk

Set in 4 acres of landscaped grounds a short drive from the A1, this delightful 14th-century farmhouse has many original features (exposed brickwork, oak beams and open fireplaces). The building has been restored over the years and now has an attractive Victorian red-brick frontage. The menu at the thriving, busy restaurant - the main dining area is a conservatory - consists of enduring classics cooked with precision using quality local produce. Expect roast breast of local pheasant wrapped in bacon and served with a bread sauce, game chips and game gravy, and perhaps a pistachio crème brûlée to finish.

Chef: Scott Liversedge **Owners:** Mr P Butterfield & Mrs J Gainsford **Times:** 12/6.30, Closed 1 wk after Xmas, BH Mons, Closed L Sat, D Sun **Prices:** Fixed L £15.25, Fixed D £25, Starter £3.50-£8.50, Main £15-£26, dessert £5-£8.50, Service optional, Group min 8 service 10% **Wine:** 114 bottles over £20, 45 bottles under £20, 11 by the glass **Notes:** Sun L £9.50, Dress Restrictions, Smart casual, No jeans or T-shirts, Civ Wed 70 **Seats:** 70, Pr/dining room 24 **Children:** Portions **Rooms:** 13 (13 en suite) ★★★ SHL **Directions:** Telephone for directions **Parking:** 30

POTTERS BAR   MAP 06 TL20

◉ Ponsbourne Park Hotel

Modern International 🖳

Stately manor with a contemporary flavour

☎ 01707 876191 & 879277   SG13 8QT

e-mail: reservations@ponsbournepark.co.uk

web: www.ponsbournepark.co.uk

Dating back to the 17th century, this grand old house set amid a 200-acre estate in peaceful countryside makes an imposing first impression. Inside, by contrast, it's a restrained contemporary affair - all bold colours and clean lines - and the restaurant offers food to match, delivering a comprehensive menu of modern dishes firmly rooted in classic French cuisine, complemented by formal yet relaxed service. Expect the likes of a fillet of halibut with a soft herb crust, stir-fried winter greens and a Gewürztraminer velouté, or perhaps a

CONTINUED

ENGLAND

POTTERS BAR CONTINUED

chocolate chip and morello cherry cheesecake with chocolate cookie base to close.

Chef: Sushmito Roy **Owners:** Tesco **Times:** 12-4/6.30-11, Closed 1 Jan **Prices:** Fixed L £22.95, Fixed D £32.95, Service included **Wine:** 8 bottles over £20, 21 bottles under £20, 3 by the glass **Notes:** Fixed L 3 courses, Sun L £22.95, Vegetarian available, Dress Restrictions, Smart casual, Civ Wed 86, Air con **Seats:** 70, Pr/dining room 90 **Children:** Menu, Portions **Rooms:** 51 (51 en suite) ★★★★ HL **Directions:** Telephone or see website for directions **Parking:** 80

see advert on page 215

RICKMANSWORTH   MAP 06 TQ09

◉◉◉ **The Grove**

see below

ROYSTON   MAP 12 TL34

◉ **The Cabinet at Reed**

Modern British, European

Impressive food in a cosy village inn

☎ 01763 848366 High St, Reed SG8 8AH
e-mail: thecabinet@btconnect.com
web: www.thecabinetatreed.co.uk

With its low ceilings, original beams and open fire, this charming, 16th-century inn has a fresh and contemporary style under new

owners. The restaurant promises a relaxed dining experience and seasonal menus that utilise plenty of local produce. Mediterranean and more exotic influences can be found in a starter of Chinese five-spice Suffolk duck and plum spring rolls and main courses such as pan-fried monkfish tail with tarragon-crushed new potatoes and chilli-infused coconut sauce. Desserts take in the more traditional baked lemon cheesecake and crème caramel with rum-infused sultanas.

The Cabinet at Reed

Chef: Richard King **Owners:** Simon Smith **Times:** 12-2.30/7-9, Closed 1 Jan, Mon (some in winter), Closed D Sun **Prices:** Fixed L £14.50, Fixed D £24.50, Starter £5.50-£5.95, Main £12.50-£24.50, Dessert £4.80-£6.25, Service added but optional 10% **Wine:** 30 bottles over £20, 3 bottles under £20, 8 by the glass **Notes:** Sun L 3 courses £25.50, Vegetarian available, Dress Restrictions, Smart casual, Civ Wed 50 **Seats:** 50, Pr/dining room 12 **Children:** Portions **Directions:** Just off A10 between Buntingford and Royston **Parking:** 40

◉◉◉

The Grove

RICKMANSWORTH   MAP 06 TQ09

Modern British 🍷 NOTABLE WINE LIST

Fine dining in smart, contemporary, relaxed setting of 'London's country estate'

☎ 01923 296015 Chandler's Cross WD3 4TG
e-mail: restaurants@thegrove.co.uk
web: www.thegrove.co.uk

An 18th-century stately home transformed into a world-class, contemporary hotel, The Grove successfully combines historic character with cutting-edge modern design. It stands in 300 acres of rolling grounds, replete with championship golf course, impressive formal gardens and beautiful views over Charlotte's Vale. This sophisticated and stylish hotel houses a fabulous spa, stunning suites, a relaxing bar and lounge, and three dining choices. Colette's is the fine-dining operation, the two high-ceilinged dining rooms blending Georgian features with stripped-wood floors, cream leather chairs and modern art.

Cooking is classically based with a great level of refinement, the bold, ambitious, technically accomplished approach showcasing British dishes with modern and European twists. Luxury ingredients are successfully combined using classic techniques, resulting in excellent clarity of flavour and some exciting dishes with stunning presentation.

Typically, a salad of Cornish crab with lemongrass pannacotta, crab beignet and sesame, perhaps followed by poached turbot served with hot smoked oyster, lentil and Savoy cabbage purée and a parsnip emulsion, and to finish, caramelised apple, walnut frangipane and cinnamon ice cream.

Chef: Chris Harrod **Owners:** Ralph Trustees Ltd **Times:** 7-10.30, Closed Sun-Mon (except Sun before BHs), BH Mon, 2 wks Jan & Aug, Closed L all week **Prices:** Fixed D £54, Service optional **Wine:** 250 bottles over £20, 15 by the glass **Notes:** Tasting menu 5 courses £58, 7 courses £65, Civ Wed 450, Air con **Seats:** 45 **Children:** Portions **Rooms:** 227 (227 en suite) ★★★★★ HL **Directions:** M25 junct 19, follow signs to Watford. At first large rdbt take 3rd exit. Continue on 0.5m entrance on right **Parking:** 500

ST ALBANS   MAP 06 TL10

◉◉ St Michael's Manor

Modern British

Accomplished cooking in a luxury hotel

☎ 01727 864444 Fishpool St AL3 4RY
e-mail: reservations@stmichaelsmanor.com
web: www.stmichaelsmanor.com

Set by a lake in attractive landscaped gardens, this luxurious country-house hotel has an airy dining room within an elegant conservatory. Simply decorated with fresh flowers, mirrors and sparkling glassware, it also boasts a sun terrace - perfect for that fair-weather pre-dinner glass of champagne. Tables are covered in linen cloths and smart, uniformed staff provide friendly, professional service. The menu - driven by fresh local produce - offer a broad choice of accomplished modern British dishes displaying technical skill and deceptive simplicity, with good flavours, textures and balance. Take pan-fried John Dory served with pak choi, razor clams and sauce Genevoise, and to finish, perhaps a rhubarb crème brûlée with berry compôte and shortbread biscuit.

Chef: Paul Hayson **Owners:** David & Sheila Newling-Ward **Times:** 12-2.30/7-9.30, Closed L 31 Dec **Prices:** Fixed L £19.95, Fixed D £24.95, Starter £4.50-£8, Main £11.95-£19.95, Dessert £5.90-£6.50, Service added but optional 10% **Wine:** 30 bottles over £20, 20 bottles under £20, 15 by the glass **Notes:** Fixed L 3 courses, Vegetarian available, Dress Restrictions, Smart casual, Civ Wed 90 **Seats:** 95, Pr/dining room 24 **Children:** Menu, Portions **Rooms:** 30 (30 en suite) ★★★★ HL **Directions:** At the Tudor Tavern in High St turn into George St. After abbey & school on left, road continues onto Fishpool St. Hotel is 1m on left **Parking:** 75

The **RESTAURANT**
at **SOPWELL HOUSE**
St. Albans

With its stylish interiors and fresh new menu, The Restaurant at Sopwell House is in a class of its own. The setting is modern but elegant – wooden floors, mirrors and New England shutters. To complement this look, the menu focuses on modern British cuisine with emphasis on seasonal and simple dishes that are made fresh from local ingredients. Potted Dorset crab, brown shrimps, and mixed cress is a typical starter, followed by Lasagne of Haugley farm chicken, salsify, broad beans and morels with sticky toffee pudding and fromage frais for dessert. The restaurant also prides itself on its superb wine wall, featuring an outstanding collection from some of the world's best wine regions.

The Restaurant at
Sopwell House
Cottonmill Lane,
St Albans AL1 2HQ

Tel: 01727 864477
Web: www.sopwellhouse.co.uk

◉ Sopwell House

Modern British 🖥

Sophisticated dining in an elegant country-house hotel

☎ 01727 864477 Cottonmill Ln, Sopwell AL1 2HQ
e-mail: enquiries@sopwellhouse.co.uk
web: www.sopwellhouse.co.uk

The former home of Lord Mountbatten houses this modernised hotel with impressive spa, leisure and conference facilities. The stunning centrepiece of the Georgian country house is the modern but elegant restaurant, with its wooden floors, mirrors and New England shutters, and great service by a professional team. The modern British menu makes excellent use of local produce; think Telmara Farm duck with Anna potatoes, salsify and morels, or perhaps wild sea trout, deep-fried sprats, crushed new potatoes and samphire.

CONTINUED

ST ALBANS CONTINUED

Chef: Leigh Diggins **Owners:** Abraham Bejerano **Times:** 12-2.30/7-10, Closed L Sat, Mon **Prices:** Fixed L £15, Fixed D £29.50, Starter £6-£10.50, Main £12.50-£18, Dessert £7, Service optional **Wine:** 74 bottles over £20, 18 bottles under £20, 6 by the glass **Notes:** Dress Restrictions, No jeans or trainers, Civ Wed 250, Air con **Seats:** 100, Pr/dining room 12 **Children:** Menu, Portions **Rooms:** 129 (129 en suite) ★★★★ HL **Directions:** On London road from St Albans follow signs to Sopwell, under railway bridge, over mini-rdbt, hotel 0.25m on left **Parking:** 350

see advert on page 217

◉ Thistle St Albans

Modern NEW

Interesting menus in a popular hotel restaurant

☎ 0870 333 9144 Watford Rd AL2 3DS
e-mail: Reservations.StAlbans@Thistle.co.uk
web: www.thistlehotels.com/stalbans

Conveniently located close to St Albans, this Thistle Hotel - set in its own grounds - has fed and watered travellers since Victorian times. The hotel offers two dining experiences - the Oak and Avocado restaurant and bar and the bright and airy, conservatory-style Noke restaurant with its attractive traditional décor. The Mediterranean-influenced menus offer lots of local and seasonal produce, with flambé dishes being a main attraction. Pigeon en croûte could be followed by Cornish monkfish wrapped in Parma ham with brown butter sauce and tangy celeriac remoulade. For a spectacular finish, try fresh fig and orange crêpes prepared at the table.

Times: 12-1.45/7-9.45, Closed Mon, Closed L Sat, D Sun **Rooms:** 111 (111 en suite) ★★★★ HL

Carluccio's Caffè

☎ 01727 837681 Christopher Place AL3 5DQ

Quality Italian chain.

Sukiyaki

☎ 01727 865009 6 Spencer St AL3 5EG

Neat and authentic Japanese offering a range of good value dishes.

Wagamama

☎ 01727 865 122 Unit 6, Christopher Place AL3 5DQ

Informal noodle bar with no booking required.

TRING   MAP 06 SP91

◉ Pendley Manor

Modern British

Fine dining in a historic old manor house

☎ 01442 891891 Cow Ln HP23 5QY
e-mail: admin.pmanor@btconnect.com
web: www.pendley-manor.co.uk

Dating back to the Domesday Book, this historic Grade II listed manor house is set in 35 acres of wooded parkland. Its public rooms include a

cosy bar and conservatory lounge, as well as The Oak Room, a panelled restaurant with high ceilings, large bay windows and heavy drapes. Traditional napery and well-spaced tables give an opulent feel. The chef favours modern English cooking but includes the occasional Asian twist, making good use of local and seasonal produce. Your choice of dishes might include venison with a vanilla and white chocolate jus, or sea bass with crab ravioli, crab bisque and parsnip mash.

Pendley Manor

Chef: Simon Green **Owners:** Craydawn Pendley Manor **Times:** 12.30-2.30/7-9.30 **Prices:** Fixed L £17.95, Fixed D £31, Starter £6-£8, Main £18-£21, Dessert £5.75-£7.50, Service optional **Wine:** 34 bottles over £20, 22 bottles under £20, 1 by the glass **Notes:** Dress Restrictions, Smart casual, Civ Wed 225 **Seats:** 75, Pr/dining room 200 **Children:** Portions **Rooms:** 73 (73 en suite) ★★★★ HL **Directions:** M25 junct 20. Take A41 and Tring exit, follow signs for Berkhamsted. 1st left, right after rugby club **Parking:** 250

WARE   MAP 06 TL31

◉◉ *Marriott Hanbury Manor Hotel*

French, European

Exciting dining in chain hotel restaurant

☎ 01920 487722 SG12 0SD
e-mail: gisele.clark@marriotthotels.co.uk
web: www.hanbury-manor.com

Built in 1890, this Jacobean-style mansion is surrounded by 200 acres of grounds and has wonderful views across the lake. Once the house's summer dining room, the restaurant is now decorated in opulent style with richly coloured drapery. Lit by huge chandeliers, the painted ceiling depicts the signs of the Zodiac. Crisply clothed tables are given the final touch with expensive crockery and glassware. Classic dishes are presented with modern and exotic twists. Start with the truffle sandwich and lobster burger with tuna sushi and Caesar salad, followed by main courses of grilled John Dory on aubergine and orange purée, or duck flauta and cardamom yogurt. Finish with warm Austrian topfenknoedel with quince compôte perhaps.

Times: 12-2/7.30-9.30, Closed BHs, 1-9 Jan, Mon, Closed L Sat, D Sun
Rooms: 161 (161 en suite) ★★★★★ HL **Directions:** From M25 junct 25, take A10 towards Cambridge. Follow A10 for 12m. Leave A10 Wadesmill/Thundridge/Ware. Right at roundabout, hotel on left

---

WELWYN   MAP 06 TL21

◎◎ Auberge du Lac

Modern European 🍷 NOTABLE WINE LIST 💻

Classy restaurant in fabulous location

☎ 01707 368888 Brocket Hall AL8 7XG
e-mail: auberge@brocket-hall.co.uk
web: www.brocket-hall.co.uk

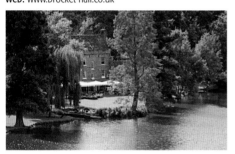

This beautifully restored, former 18th-century hunting lodge sits - as its name suggests - beside a tranquil lake overlooking stately Brocket Hall, whose estate also encompasses a swish golf complex. The airy, elegant restaurant boasts large windows and fabulous flower arrangements, and is presided over by an attentive serving team. Cheese and Armagnac trolleys should provoke some pleasurable dithering, while the kitchen's focus is on a modern approach, delivering well-presented dishes distinguished by some unusual combinations. High-quality produce and impressive skills shine throughout; think poached beef fillet with oxtail croustillante and salsify, or coconut parfait with pineapple sorbet and coconut foam. And, if the sun is shining, try for a table on the terrace.

Chef: Phil Thompson **Owners:** CCA International **Times:** 12-2.30/7-10, Closed 27 Dec-6 Jan, Mon, Closed D Sun **Prices:** Fixed L £29.50, Fixed D £55, Service added but optional 10% **Wine:** 750 bottles over £20, 20 by the glass **Notes:** Fixed L 3 courses, Tasting menu £65, Sun L £35, Vegetarian menu, Dress Restrictions, Smart casual preferred, no jeans or trainers, Civ Wed 65, Air con **Seats:** 70, Pr/dining room 24
Children: Menu, Portions **Directions:** A1(M) junct 4, B653 to Wheathampstead. In Brocket Ln take 2nd gate entry to Brocket Hall **Parking:** 50

see advert below

ENGLAND

WILLIAN
MAP 12 TL23

🏵 The Fox

Modern British
Relaxed gastro-pub in a peaceful village setting

☎ 01462 480233 Baldock Ln SG6 2AE
e-mail: info@foxatwillian.co.uk
web: www.foxatwillian.co.uk

Sister restaurant to the widely acclaimed White Horse at Brancaster Staithe in Norfolk (see entry), this popular gastro-pub is well presented with oak floors, soft grey walls, sage-painted woodwork and fashionable furniture and table settings. The cooking is simple, unpretentious and well executed, using quality ingredients, and offers plenty of choice. There's also an attractive bar menu. For starters, take tempura of tiger prawns with dressed leaves and chilli, followed by delicious pan-fried calves' liver with creamed mash potato, black pudding and shallot and red wine jus. Honey and peach mousse is a must for dessert. Advance booking is advised at weekends.

Chef: Hari Kodagoda **Owners:** Cliff Nye **Times:** 12-2/6.45-9.15, Closed D Sun (winter only) **Prices:** Starter £3.95-£8.95, Main £9.95-£16.95, Dessert £4.95-£5.95, Service optional **Wine:** 31 bottles over £20, 29 bottles under £20, 12 by the glass **Notes:** Sun L, Vegetarian available, Dress Restrictions, Smart casual, no shorts or sleeveless shirts, Air con **Seats:** 70 **Children:** Portions **Directions:** A1M junct 9 towards Letchworth, 1st left to Willian village, The Fox is 0.5m on left **Parking:** 40

KENT

ASHFORD
MAP 07 TR04

🏵🏵 Eastwell Manor

English, French
Grand country-house hotel with classical cooking

☎ 01233 213000 Eastwell Park, Boughton Lees TN25 4HR
e-mail: enquiries@eastwellmanor.co.uk
web: www.eastwellmanor.co.uk

Magnificently set in 62 acres of manicured grounds, this historic hotel exudes grandeur, with its carved wood-panelled rooms, rich fabrics and huge baronial fireplaces. The restaurant is breathtaking too - a long room replete with Italianate chairs and contemporary artwork, high ceilings and oak panelling, laid out with elegant table appointments - while the polished, formal service suits this dress-for-dinner affair. The menus reflect a modern interpretation of classical cooking, based on well-sourced local fresh produce. Culinary skill,

refined presentation and clean, precise flavours deliver in dishes like pan-fried Scottish West Coast scallops with vièrge dressing, followed by fillet of line-caught halibut in a mussel, salad onion and marjoram cream, and perhaps a warm chocolate fondant with vanilla ice cream for dessert.

Eastwell Manor

Chef: Neil Wiggins **Owners:** Turrloo Parrett **Times:** 12-2.30/7-10 **Prices:** Fixed L £10, Fixed D £37.50, Service optional **Wine:** 16 bottles under £20, 22 by the glass **Notes:** Tasting menu available, Traditional Sun L, Dress Restrictions, Jacket and tie at D, no jeans, Civ Wed 250 **Seats:** 80, Pr/dining room 80 **Children:** Menu, Portions **Rooms:** 62 (62 en suite)★★★★ HL **Directions:** From M20 junct 9 take 1st left (Trinity Rd). Through 4 rdbts to lights. Take left filter onto A251 signed Faversham. 1.5m to sign for Boughton Aluph, then 200yds to hotel **Parking:** 120

🏵🏵 The Wife of Bath

Modern French 💻
Eclectic French cooking in a charming village

☎ 01233 812540 & 812232 4 Upper Bridge St, Wye TN25 5AF
e-mail: reservations@wifeofbath.com
web: www.wifeofbath.com

Taking its name from the pilgrims that used to stop in the village, this charming 18th-century coaching house was sensitively converted from the village doctor's into a delightful restaurant with rooms 30 years ago. With oodles of contemporary elegance, the dining room shouts out laid-back refinement, while knowledgeable and attentive staff ensure both residents and local diners are well cared for. With a distinct leaning toward Gallic cooking styles, there are some great ideas successfully delivered on this pleasing menu, underpinned by simple, fresh flavours in unpretentious, imaginatively presented dishes. Start with panaché of freshwater crayfish, shellfish and summer vegetables followed by fillet of wild local sea bass with home-made linguine, chive velouté and pea purée.

Chef: Robert Hymers **Owners:** Nicola & Andrew Fraser **Times:** 12-1.30/7-9.30, Closed 2 wks Aug, 2 wks Xmas/New Year, Sun-Mon **Prices:** Fixed L £12.50, Fixed D £24.50, Starter £6-£11.50, Main £18.50-£24, Dessert £7, Group min 8 service 10% **Wine:** 85 bottles over £20, 10 bottles under £20, 2 by the glass **Seats:** 52 **Children:** Portions **Rooms:** 5 (5 en suite) ★★★★★ RR **Parking:** 20

AYLESFORD MAP 06 TQ75

◎◎ Hengist Restaurant

Modern French V 🖥

Fine dining with design impact and culinary success

☎ 01622 719273   7 - 9 High St ME20 7AX
e-mail: the.hengist@btconnect.com
web: www.thackeraysrestaurant.co.uk

Hengist and his brother Horsa led the invasion that landed in
Aylesford in 449AD and named themselves the first kings of Kent.
Here the lavish interior design is worthy of royalty, set in a building
dating back to the 1560s. (There is also private dining available in the
dramatic Japanese Room and romantic Crystal Room.) The cooking
takes an accomplished modern French approach and makes fine use
of excellent local produce. Take pan-fried fillet of sea bream served
with tomato fondue, baby fennel, roasted courgettes and sauce vièrge,
and to finish, perhaps a Seville orange soufflé with blood orange
sorbet and Suzette sauce. Try a 'Perfect Hengist' champagne cocktail in
the bar before dinner.

Chef: R Phillips & Jean-Marc Zanetti **Owners:** Richard Phillips, Paul Smith
& Kevin James **Times:** 12-2.30/6.30-10.30, Closed 26 Dec & 1 Jan, Mon,
Closed D Sun **Prices:** Fixed L £6.95-£10.50, Fixed D £19.95, Starter £4.50-
£11.50, Main £8.50-£16.50, Dessert £5.95, Service added but optional 11%
Wine: 24 bottles over £20, 12 bottles under £20, 11 by the glass
Notes: Fixed L Tue-Sun, Fixed D Tue-Thu, Vegetarian menu, Dress
Restrictions, Smart casual, Air con **Seats:** 70, Pr/dining room 18
Children: Portions **Directions:** M20 junct 5 & 6, follow signs to Aylesford
village **Parking:** Free car park nearby

BEARSTED MAP 07 TQ85

◎ Soufflé Restaurant

Modern European

Understated, cosy and relaxed village dining

☎ 01622 737065   31 The Green ME14 4DN
web: www.soufflerestaurant.co.uk

Once the village bakery, this charming 16th-century cottage overlooks
the historic village green. Cricket aficionados will note that the cricket
ground is thought to be the oldest in Kent where overarm bowling
was pioneered. The front terrace is perfect for alfresco dining, while
inside exposed brickwork, low beams, timbers and an inglenook add
traditional character, set off by high-backed chairs and white-clothed
tables. The accomplished kitchen takes an appealing modern
approach, underpinned by a classical theme; think pan-fried scallops
with black pudding, creamed potatoes and an olive oil hollandaise,
followed by suprême of salmon with a lobster and coriander bisque.

An eponymous soufflé might head-up desserts, perhaps hot prune
and Armagnac with vanilla ice cream.

Soufflé Restaurant

Chef: Nick Evenden **Owners:** Nick & Karen Evenden **Times:** 12-2.30/7-
10, Closed Mon, Closed L Sat, D Sun **Prices:** Fixed L £13.50, Fixed D £25,
Starter £7.50-£10, Main £16-£19.50, Dessert £7.50, Service added but
optional 10% **Wine:** 38 bottles over £20, 25 bottles under £20, 6 by the
glass **Notes:** Sun L 3 courses £18.50 **Seats:** 40, Pr/dining room 23
Children: Portions **Directions:** Please telephone for directions
Parking: 15

BIDDENDEN MAP 07 TQ83

◎◎ The West House

Modern European

Assured modern cooking in picturesque village setting

☎ 01580 291341   28 High St TN27 8AH
e-mail: thewesthouse@btconnect.com
web: www.westhouserestaurant.com

At the heart of the tiny Wealden village with its charming ancient
houses and shops, The West House oozes character, charm and
confidence. Grade II listed and once weavers' cottages, think old
beams, white walls and an inglenook with log-burning stove, teamed
with high-backed cream leather chairs, polished-wood tables, colourful
artwork and modern floorboards. A relaxed, friendly atmosphere
completes the smart but unstuffy setting. The kitchen's modern
approach - underpinned by a classical theme - fits the bill, delivering
accomplished, clear-flavoured dishes on appealing fixed-price, daily-
changing menus using top-notch, local seasonal ingredients with
accomplished skill. Think a grilled fillet of hake with white bean,
cabbage and chestnut casserole, followed by rhubarb and ginger
pannacotta with ginger madeleine.

Chef: Graham Garrett **Owners:** Jackie Hewitt & Graham Garrett
Times: 12-2/7-9.30, Closed 25 Dec-1 Jan, Mon, Closed L Sat, D Sun
Prices: Fixed L £21, Fixed D £29.50, Service added but optional 12.5%
Wine: 46 bottles over £20, 20 bottles under £20, 6 by the glass **Seats:** 32
Children: Portions **Directions:** Junct of A262 & A274. 14m S of
Maidstone **Parking:** 7

BRANDS HATCH   MAP 06 TQ56

◉◉ *Brandshatch Place Hotel*

Modern British

Elegant Georgian country house near the racing circuit

☎ 01474 875000   Brands Hatch Rd, Fawkham DA3 8NQ
e-mail: brandshatchplace@handpicked.co.uk
web: www.handpicked.co.uk

Close to the entrance to Brands Hatch racing circuit, this red-brick Georgian manor dates back to 1806 and stands in 12 acres of tranquil gardens. Elegant public rooms, a charming country-house feel and smart leisure and spa facilities make the hotel a peaceful place to unwind after a day at the track. The dining room is tastefully decked out in cream with mirrors, objets d'art, and gleaming glassware on linen-clothed tables. Expect a good range of well-presented, modern dishes with European influences. The kitchen uses first-rate ingredients to produce glazed goat's cheese and fig tart fine with port syrup, seared cod supreme, pea and cockle risotto, and pineapple tart Tatin with Malibu and coconut ice ream.

Times: 12-2/7-9.30, Closed L Sat   **Rooms:** 38 (38 en suite) ★★★★ HL
Directions: From M25/M20 follow signs for Brands Hatch Circuit onto A20. Follow signs to Paddock entrance, hotel is located on Brands Hatch Rd

◉ Thistle Brands Hatch

Modern British NEW

Trackside hotel serving accomplished cuisine

☎ 0870 333 9128   DA3 8PE
e-mail: BrandsHatch@Thistle.co.uk
web: www.thistlehotels.com/brandshatch

Right on the edge of the Brands Hatch racing track, this purpose-built hotel has a large open-plan restaurant with neatly laid, well-spaced tables and professional service. The menu is influenced by French and Italian cooking with a good selection of imaginative dishes. Starters might include spring lobster ravioli or foie gras terrine. Main courses range from classics like grilled rack of lamb to more adventurous dishes like fillet of black eye sea bream served with couscous, piquillas and tomato tagine. Desserts include traditional British favourites like summer pudding.

Chef: George Opendo   **Owners:** Thistle Hotels Ltd   **Times:** 12.30-2.30/7-9.45   **Prices:** Starter £6.50-£9.50, Main £14-£18, Dessert £6.50-£7, Service optional   **Wine:** 16 bottles over £20, 22 bottles under £20, 12 by the glass   **Notes:** Sun L £19.95, Vegetarian available, Dress Restrictions, Civ Wed 120, Air con   **Seats:** 80, Pr/dining room 40   **Children:** Menu, Portions   **Rooms:** 121 (121 en suite) ★★★★ HL   **Directions:** M25 junct 3 follow signs for A20 Brands Hatch. At Brands Hatch main gates turn left off slip road   **Parking:** 250

CANTERBURY   MAP 07 TR15

◉◉ **Michael Caines at Abode Canterbury**

Modern British NEW

Classy modern cooking in the heart of the city

☎ 01227 766266   High St CT1 2RX
e-mail: reservationscanterbury@abodehotels.co.uk
web: www.abodehotels.co.uk

Dating back to the 12th century, this hotel has undergone a total makeover to bring it under the Abode banner - a blossoming boutique hotel chain that delivers smart, modern and comfortable styling alongside classy food. The Michael Caines Restaurant follows the theme, its cream walls hung with modern art and smart black-and-white photos, while tables are white-linen clad and leather chairs come in cream or dark-brown leather. The kitchen delivers some exciting, sophisticated modern food, assured and well timed, impressing with its presentation, balanced flavours and focus on high-quality ingredients. Take line-caught sea bass with braised fennel, fennel cream and a red wine sauce, and perhaps a passionfruit soufflé finish, served with banana ice cream. There's a chef's table overlooking the kitchen, as well as a champagne bar and informal Tavern.

Times: 12-2.30/7-10, Closed D Sun   **Rooms:** 72 (72 en suite) ★★★★ HL

◉ Augustine's Restaurant

Modern European

Impressive food in popular modern restaurant

☎ 01227 453063   1 & 2 Longport CT1 1PE
e-mail: info@augustinesrestaurant.co.uk
web: www.augustinesrestaurant.co.uk

This double-fronted, period townhouse is the stylish setting for an intimate dining experience. Large sash windows overlook the street, while darkwood tables, high-backed chairs and ambient lighting complete the scene. The chef delivers a combination of traditional French and British dishes with European flair, using good quality primarily organic produce. Take ravioli of St Ives Bay lobster with poached baby leeks, followed by an exquisitely flavoured pan-fried brill fillet with caper and red wine sauce. A new first-floor function room seats up to 18. Booking is recommended for dinner.

Chef: Ben Williams, Simon Corke   **Owners:** Nigel Willis & Lesley Stephens   **Times:** 12-2/6.30-9.30, Closed 2 wks Xmas, Mon, Closed D Sun   **Prices:** Fixed D £17, Starter £6.50-£9.50, Main £14-£20, Dessert £6.50, Service optional   **Wine:** 4 by the glass   **Seats:** 38, Pr/dining room 18   **Directions:** Follow signs to St Augustine's Abbey, facing entrance to Abbey turn left, restaurant is ahead   **Parking:** On street

◉ *The Dove Inn*

French

French flavours visit deepest Kent

☎ 01227 751360   Plumpudding Ln, Dargate ME13 9HB
e-mail: nigel@thedoveinn.fsnet.co.uk

This attractive converted pub makes a great venue for enjoyable dining. The ivy-clad, brick exterior hides a plain and simple interior with wooden floors, wooden tables and bags of character. It's a popular place so booking is advisable at weekends. Menus comprise mainly British and French dishes and there's a blackboard advertising the daily specials. Start with Bayonne ham and oyster mushroom tart and follow with either fresh fish from nearby Whitstable or perhaps braised lamb shank with a tomato and basil jus flavoured with local beetroot. Finish with tarte Tatin and vanilla ice cream.

Times: 12-2/7-9, Closed Mon, Closed D Sun, Tue **Directions:** 5m NW of Canterbury. Telephone for directions

◉ The White Horse Inn
Traditional British
Sophisticated dining in country inn setting

☎ 01227 832814 High St, Bridge CT4 5LA

Historic inn turned upmarket gastro-pub within easy reach of Canterbury. The smart restaurant is one half traditionally styled, the other modern and bright with doors into the garden. The list of local suppliers on the menu suggests a passion for quality, a passion reflected in seasonal English traditional cooking with modern flair. Starters may include spiced fishcakes with carrot, onion and cucumber salad, with main courses taking in beer-battered fillet of cod, or a deliciously creamy and full-flavoured wild mushroom risotto. Round off with rhubarb and apple crumble served with ice cream and vanilla custard, or a good choice of cheeses.

Times: 12-3/7-11, Closed 25 Dec, 1 Jan **Directions:** 3m S of Canterbury on Dover road, A2 signed for Bridge

---

CHATHAM   MAP 07 TQ76
◉◉ Bridgewood Manor
Modern British
Modern, purpose-built hotel with informal or fine dining

☎ 01634 201333 Bridgewood Roundabout, Walderslade Woods ME5 9AX
e-mail: bridgewoodmanor@qhotels.co.uk
web: www.qhotels.co.uk/hotels/bridgewood-manor-chatham-kent/

There's a subtle gothic theme to the décor at this modern, purpose-built hotel on the outskirts of Rochester, with warm, deep colours creating an inviting ambience in the dining areas. Dine in the more informal Terrace Bistro, or - if you're in a celebratory mood - choose the more formal Squires restaurant. Staff are smartly dressed, friendly and attentive, while the food on the reasonably-priced modern British menu - with its international influences - relies on classical principles, an emphasis on quality produce, and is accurately cooked and well presented. Expect roasted salmon with an aubergine caviar and crayfish bisque, pressed confit belly of pork with apple fondant and a cider and thyme jus, and perhaps a chocolate buttercream slice with burnt orange ice cream.

Chef: Nigel Stringer **Owners:** QHotels **Times:** 12.30-2.30/7-9.45, Closed 24-27 Dec (ex residents), Closed L Sat **Prices:** Fixed L £13.95, Fixed D £25-£34, Starter £5-£7, Main £15-£20, Dessert £5-£7, Service optional **Wine:** 30 bottles over £20, 25 bottles under £20, 10 by the glass **Notes:** Sun L 4 course carvery, Vegetarian available, Dress Restrictions, Smart casual, no denim or trainers, Civ Wed 150, Air con **Seats:** 120, Pr/dining room 30 **Children:** Menu, Portions **Rooms:** 100 (100 en suite) ★★★★ HL **Directions:** From M2 junct 3 or M20 junct 6 follow A229 towards Chatham. At Bridgewood rdbt take 3rd exit (Walderslade). Hotel 50yds on left **Parking:** 170

CRANBROOK   MAP 07 TQ73
◉◉◉ Apicius
see page 224

◉ The George Hotel and Brasserie
Modern British ❀
Charming restaurant with great local reputation

☎ 01580 713348 Stone St TN17 3HE
e-mail: reservations@thegeorgehotelkent.co.uk
web: www.thegeorgehotelkent.co.uk

This Cranbrook landmark combines period and contemporary style, and has a long tradition of hospitality dating back to the 14th century and lists Queen Elizabeth I among its former guests. the tempting menu can be taken either in a vibrant new brasserie overlooking the local church, or in the more formal restaurant, a striking contemporary room with opulent chandeliers, an imposing inglenook fireplace and comfortable leather chairs. Ingredients come courtesy of the Kent and Sussex coast and countryside wherever possible, and arrive at the table in dishes such as pot-roasted Park Farm lamb with braised couscous, Mediterranean vegetables and yogurt.

Chef: Paolo Fernandes **Owners:** Mark & Sara Colley **Times:** 12-3/6-9.30, Closed 25-26 Dec **Prices:** Starter £5.50-£7, Main £9.50-£14, Dessert £6-£7.50, Service optional **Wine:** 16 bottles over £20, 14 bottles under £20, 18 by the glass **Notes:** Vegetarian available **Seats:** 60 **Children:** Menu, Portions **Rooms:** 12 (12 en suite) ★★ HL **Directions:** A229 into Cranbrook and Stone St, on left. **Parking:** 12

DARTFORD   MAP 06 TQ57
◉◉ Rowhill Grange
Modern European
Classy country setting for a formal conservatory restaurant

☎ 01322 615136 DA2 7QH
e-mail: admin@rowhillgrange.com
web: www.rowhillgrange.co.uk

Set amid 9 acres of mature woodland, complete with a lake and Victorian walled garden, this part-thatched 19th-century country house enjoys a tranquil setting, while being within easy reach of the motorway network. There are two dining options: a relaxed brasserie for lighter meals, or the main culinary attraction, the recently refurbished Truffles restaurant, which boasts its own Victorian conservatory with views across the gardens. Alternatively, make the most of the idyllic setting and dine out on the terrace when weather permits. Truffles is stylishly furnished, complete with high-backed leather chairs, crisp linen and heavy drapes, and is especially romantic at night with subdued lighting and candles. An extensive and varied menu of international and modern European cuisine takes in the likes of pan-fried herb-crusted sardines with tomato vièrge and kalamata tapenade dressing, or roast fillet of brill with parsley mousseline, crisp fennel and sauce bouillabaisse.

Chef: Richard Cameron **Owners:** Utopia Leisure **Times:** 12-2.30/7-9.30, Closed L Sat **Prices:** Fixed L £16.50-£21.50, Fixed D £35-£44, Starter £8-£10, Main £19-£24, Dessert £8, Service added but optional 12.5% **Wine:** 38 bottles over £20, 11 bottles under £20, 12 by the glass **Notes:** Tasting menu £50, Sun L from £16.50, Vegetarian available, Dress Restrictions, No shorts, T-shirts, trainers, Civ Wed 120, Air con **Seats:** 90, Pr/dining room 160 **Children:** Min 16 yrs D **Rooms:** 38 (38 en suite) ★★★★ HL **Directions:** M25 junct 3, take B2173 towards Swanley, then B258 towards Hextable. Straight on at 3 rdbts. Hotel 1.5m on left **Parking:** 200

❀❀❀

Apicius

CRANBROOK   MAP 07 TQ73

Modern European

Serious cuisine in pretty town setting

☎ 01580 714666 23 Stone St TN17 3HF

Named after a famous Roman gastronome and tucked away in the narrow streets of this pretty Kent town of Cranbrook, Apicius delivers some stand out cuisine that's designed to wow. The setting is a glass-fronted, timber-clad building that dates back to 1530 and was once used by Flemish weavers to ply their trade. Low-beamed ceilings and old timbers are teamed with high-backed chairs, lightwood floorboards and crisp white tablecloths to make an intimate and relaxed setting for some truly accomplished cuisine. Service, led by Faith Hawkins, is personal, friendly and attentive, while the kitchen is Tim Johnson's domain, his sensibly compact, fixed-price menus taking a modern approach to classic combinations at unexpectedly reasonable prices. Quality seasonal ingredients shine in clear-flavoured, refined and well-presented dishes that reflect high skill, meticulous workmanship and plenty of creativity: slow-roast shoulder of venison arrives with red cabbage marmalade and caramelised apple, for example, while a poached fillet of brill is accompanied by cockle, sweetcorn and saffron chowder. Vanilla roast pineapple with coconut pannacotta and Malibu cream might catch the eye for dessert.

Chef: Timothy Johnson **Owners:** Timothy Johnson, Faith Hawkins **Times:** 12-2/7-9, Closed 2 wks summer, 2 wks Xmas/New Year, Etr, Mon, Closed L Tue, Sat, D Sun **Prices:** Fixed L £20, Fixed D £28, Service added but optional 10% **Wine:** 26 bottles over £20, 5 bottles under £20, 7 by the glass **Seats:** 22 **Children:** Min 8 yrs **Directions:** In town centre, opposite Barclays Bank, 50yds from church **Parking:** Public car park at rear premises

---

DEAL   MAP 07 TR35

❀❀ Dunkerleys Hotel

Modern British

Fresh seafood on the seafront

☎ 01304 375016 19 Beach St CT14 7AH
e-mail: ddunkerley@btconnect.com
web: www.dunkerleys.co.uk

Situated opposite the pier, this friendly bistro-style restaurant is run by the chef-proprietor. Pre-dinner drinks are served in the small bar where you can relax on a comfy sofa. Seafood is definitely the draw here, with some of the freshest produce around given simple but skilful treatment in the kitchen. The carte is complemented by a set menu, popular with guests staying over for dinner, bed and breakfast. Start with crab and lobster bisque, or perhaps caramelised scallops with smoked bacon and a light velouté, and follow with sautéed

turbot with a lightly cooked omelette and dill sauce, or duck breast duet with braised cabbage and red wine sauce. Indulge in a bitter dark chocolate tart with caramelised orange for dessert.

Chef: Ian Dunkerley **Owners:** Ian Dunkerley & Linda Dunkerley **Times:** 12-2.30/7-9.30, Closed L Mon **Prices:** Fixed L £11.95, Fixed D £22.95, Starter £6.95-£10.95, Main £14.95-£24.95, Dessert £5.95-£8.95, Service optional **Wine:** 29 bottles over £20, 47 bottles under £20, 11 by the glass **Notes:** Vegetarian available, Dress Restrictions, Smart casual preferred, Air con **Seats:** 50 **Children:** Portions **Rooms:** 16 (16 en suite) ★★★ HL **Directions:** Turn off A2 onto A258 to Deal - situated 100yds before Deal Pier **Parking:** Public car park

---

DOVER   MAP 07 TR34

❀❀ Oakley & Harvey at Wallett's Court

Modern British

Historic manor not far from the white cliffs

☎ 01304 852424 Wallett's Court, West Cliffe,
St Margarets-at-Cliffe CT15 6EW
e-mail: dine@wallettscourt.com
web: www.wallettscourt.com

Set in pretty gardens in a peaceful location on the outskirts of town, this country-house hotel is based around a lovely Jacobean manor. The cosy lounge bar has a buzzy atmosphere, while the restaurant - a dinner-only affair - is formally laid with white linen and high-backed chairs, set to a backdrop of oak beams, inglenook fireplaces and evening candlelight. Walls are hung with original art, and there are carved pillars dating back to 1627. But there's nothing remotely historic about the cooking, the accomplished modern British repertoire -

driven by a commitment to quality local seasonal produce, including ingredients from the hotel's kitchen garden - comes fashionably dotted with European influences. Take locally-landed cod with aubergine caviar, chorizo and sautéed potatoes, or perhaps a rack of Kentish lamb served with ratatouille, rosemary and fondant potatoes.

Chef: Stephen Harvey **Owners:** Gavin Oakley **Times:** 12-2/7-9, Closed 25-26 Dec, Closed L Mon-Sat **Prices:** Fixed L £23, Fixed D £40, Service added but optional 10% **Wine:** 60 bottles over £20, 20 bottles under £20, 17 by the glass **Notes:** Fixed L 3 courses **Seats:** 60, Pr/dining room 40 **Children:** Menu, Portions **Rooms:** 16 (16 en suite) ★★★ HL **Directions:** M2/A2 or M20/A20, follow signs for Deal (A258), 1st right for St Margaret's at Cliffe. Restaurant 1m on right **Parking:** 50

Cullin's Yard
☎ 01304 211666 11 Cambridge Rd CT17 9BY
Bistro-style restaurant in yachting marina.

EDENBRIDGE   MAP 06 TQ44
◉ Haxted Mill & Riverside Brasserie
Modern French 🖳
Quality ingredients and classic-inspired cooking in riverside setting

☎ 01732 862914 Haxted Rd TN8 6PU
e-mail: david@haxtedmill.co.uk
web: www.haxtedmill.co.uk

A roadside working watermill in a tranquil setting with a restaurant in adjacent converted stables. Enter via the ground-floor bar, up a steep staircase to the beamed restaurant, featuring photos and angling memorabilia. Service is professional but quite informal, while a terrace overlooks the millpond, ideal for summer dining. An evolving list of dishes is offered from a carte of classically-inspired cooking dotted with international influences; the emphasis is on quality, fresh seasonal ingredients, sympathetic handling and unfussy presentation. Take fillet steak served with a bordelaise sauce, or a tagine of lamb, and to finish, crème brûlée or chocolate fondant.

Chef: David Peek, Olivier Betremieux **Owners:** David & Linda Peek **Times:** 12-2/7-9, Closed 23 Dec-6 Jan, Mon (Winter), Closed D Sun (Winter) **Prices:** Fixed L £16.95, Fixed D £26, Starter £5.95-£13.95, Main £13.95-£19.95, Dessert £5, Service added but optional 12.5% **Wine:** 45 bottles over £20, 9 bottles under £20, 6 by the glass **Notes:** Sun L 4 courses £21.95, Dress Restrictions, Smart casual **Seats:** 52 **Directions:** M25 junct 6, A22 towards East Grinstead. Through Blindley Heath and after Texaco garage left at lights, 1m take 1st left after Red Barn PH. 2m to Haxted Mill **Parking:** 100

EYNSFORD   MAP 06 TQ56
The Watermark Restaurant
☎ 01322 860300 2 Riverside DA4 0AE
web: www.thewatermarkrestaurant.co.uk
Seasonal fresh produce, specialising in seafood and game, is the hallmark of this attractive restaurant.

FAVERSHAM   MAP 07 TR06
◉◉◉ Read's Restaurant
see page 226

HYTHE   MAP 07 TR13
◉ The Hythe Imperial Hotel
Modern British
Smart restaurant in elegant Victorian surroundings

☎ 01303 267441 The Mews, Prince's Pde CT21 6AE
e-mail: hytheimperial@qhotels.co.uk
web: www.qhotels.co.uk/hotels/the-hythe-imperial-hythe-kent/

There's much to recommend this smart seafront hotel, with its elegant Victorian splendour and 50-acre golf course. Superb indoor and outdoor leisure facilities are complemented by treatment rooms and, not least, a plush restaurant with views over the Channel. The sense of luxury extends to the compact modern menu; think pan-fried, wild local sea bass served with confit carrot and spring onion and olive, and lime crème fraîche, while a chocolate fondant with confit cherries might provide the finish. Seasonal herbs come straight from the garden, while the modern, airy Terrace bar offers lighter fare.

Chef: Richard Duckworth **Owners:** QHotels **Times:** 12.30-2.30/7-9.30, Closed L Sat **Prices:** Fixed L £14.50-£19.95, Fixed D £26.50-£38, Starter £6.75-£9, Main £15-£21, Dessert £5.75-£6.75, Service optional **Wine:** 40 bottles over £20, 23 bottles under £20, 12 by the glass **Notes:** Vegetarian available, Dress Restrictions, Smart casual, no jeans or trainers, Civ Wed 100 **Seats:** 200, Pr/dining room 60 **Children:** Menu, Portions **Rooms:** 100 (100 en suite) ★★★★ HL **Directions:** M20 junct 11/A261 to Hythe signs to Folkestone, right into the Twiss Road to hotel **Parking:** 200

LENHAM   MAP 07 TQ85
◉◉ Chilston Park Hotel
Modern British
Stylish cooking in splendid Georgian mansion

☎ 01622 859803 Sandway ME17 2BE
e-mail: chilstonpark@handpicked.co.uk
web: www.handpicked.co.uk

A Georgian country house with impeccable credentials, Chilston Park is set in beautiful parkland and dates back to at least 1100. The sunken Venetian-style restaurant has a grand fireplace and elegant crystal chandeliers. The British menu with French influences offers thoughtful wine recommendations by the glass or bottle for many of the dishes. Using the best of ingredients, accurate cooking and clarity of flavour is the key to success here with many interesting and unusual

CONTINUED

Read's Restaurant

◉◉◉

FAVERSHAM   MAP 07 TR06

Modern British 🍷 NOTABLE WINE LIST

Distinctive cuisine in an elegant Georgian manor house

☎ 01795 535344 Macknade Manor, Canterbury Rd
ME13 8XE

e-mail: enquiries@reads.com

web: www.reads.com

Read's Restaurant can be found in a beautiful Georgian manor house
built in 1778, set in 4 acres of mature gardens, including a walled
kitchen garden. Six individually designed bedrooms are tastefully
furnished in period style, complemented by an elegant drawing room
and the grand, spacious restaurant. Here you will find distinctive
cooking of passion and simplicity using home-grown herbs and
vegetables in dishes that make fine use of local game and fish fresh
from the quayside at nearby Whitstable and Hythe. Modern British
cuisine is the order of the day, with dinner a grander affair than lunch.
The menu offers an impressive choice of dishes with detailed
descriptions and little gems of quotations to accompany them, like the
immortal words of Miss Piggy ... 'Never eat more than you can lift'.
With that in mind, you could try the seven-course tasting menu, or
order from the appealing carte. Expect the likes of roasted cannon of
Kentish lamb served with a hazelnut crust, braised button onions,

dauphinoise potatoes and a thyme jus, while a roasted pineapple tart
with a peppered coulis, vanilla caramel and pineapple sorbet might
catch the eye at dessert. The equally accomplished wine list has an
extensive choice (over 250 wines) with many heavyweights and a
good selection by the glass, too.

Chef: David Pitchford & Ricky Martin **Owners:** David & Rona Pitchford
Times: 12-2.30/7-10, Closed BHs, Sun, Mon **Prices:** Fixed L £23, Fixed D
£48, Service optional **Wine:** 250 bottles over £20, 12 bottles under £20
Notes: Fixed L 3 courses, D 4 courses Tasting menu 7 courses £48,
Vegetarian available, Dress Restrictions, Smart casual, Civ Wed 60
Seats: 40, Pr/dining room 30 **Children:** Portions **Directions:** From M2
junct 6 follow A251 towards Faversham. At T-junct with A2 (Canterbury
road) turn right. Hotel 0.5m on right **Parking:** 30

LENHAM CONTINUED

combinations to choose from. Take roast pigeon breast with sweetcorn
fritter and game jus or assiette of Kentish pork with apple and sage jus
for example; alternatively, choose something more traditional like
Chateaubriand to share. Alfresco dining available during the warmer
months.

Chef: Gareth Brown **Owners:** Hand Picked Hotels **Times:** 12-1.30/7-9.30,
Closed L Sat **Prices:** Fixed L £13-£30, Starter £7-£7.50, Main £15.50-£22,
Dessert £6-£9, Service optional **Wine:** 90 bottles over £20, 1 bottle under
£20, 6 by the glass **Notes:** Sun L £22.50, Civ Wed 90 **Seats:** 35, Pr/dining
room 8 **Children:** Menu, Portions **Rooms:** 53 (53 en suite)★★★★ HL
Directions: Telephone for directions. **Parking:** 100

SEVENOAKS   MAP 06 TQ55

◉ Brasserie St Nicholas

French 🖥

Sophisticated dining in relaxed French brasserie

☎ 01732 456974 61 London Rd TN13 1AU

e-mail: info@brasseriestnicholas.com

web: www.brasseriestnicholas.com

Once a schoolhouse, this chic French brasserie is set back off a busy
town-centre street. The smart 1930s-style décor of pale walls, dark
wood, lots of black and gold, mirrors and modern lighting creates a
relaxed, inviting ambience. A la carte lunch, prix fixe and dinner
menus offer a wide selection of traditional French dishes with modern
influences. Ideal for a business lunch or a special evening meal, the
stylish fare features seasonal, local produce and includes the likes of

fresh mussels and saffron velouté, or confit belly of pork with grilled
endive and butter bean purée.

Brasserie St Nicholas

Chef: Christian Cilia **Owners:** Jane Armstrong & Louise O'Sullivan
Times: 12-3/6-10.30, Closed Mon, Closed D Sun **Prices:** Fixed L £14-
£17.50, Fixed D £16.95-£20.50, Starter £6.75-£9.75, Main £10.95-£27,
Dessert £6.75-£9.50, Service optional, Group min 6 service 12.5%
Wine: 38 bottles over £20, 20 bottles under £20, 10 by the glass
Notes: Vegetarian available, Air con **Seats:** 75 **Children:** Menu, Portions
Directions: M25 junct 5 follow signs to town centre **Parking:** Car park
opposite

◎◎ Greggs Restaurant

Modern British, European

Popular high street restaurant with hands-on owners

☎ 01732 456373 28-30 High St TN13 1HX
web: www.greggsrestaurant.com

With its triple-bay window frontage and black-and-white paintwork, Greggs is a distinctive listed property, located at the top of town near the entrance to the National Trust's Knole House. Inside, the original features of the 16th-century building - dark wood beams and timbers - set off light floors, high-backed black leather chairs and white tablecloths. The atmosphere is relaxed and friendly. The kitchen takes a modern line, with imaginative dishes creatively presented. The supremely fresh fish impresses in a dish of pan-fried brill fillet served with pak choi and lyonnaise potatoes. Finish with ginger crème brûlée with raspberry sorbet. There is a weekly-changing market menu available.

Chef: Gavin Gregg **Owners:** Gavin & Lucinda Gregg **Times:** 12-2/6.30-9.30, Closed 25-26 Dec, Mon, Closed D Sun **Prices:** Fixed L £10.95-£13.95, Fixed D £21-£25, Service added but optional 10% **Wine:** 34 bottles over £20, 16 bottles under £20, 8 by the glass **Notes:** Sun L 2 courses £16.95, 3 courses £19.95 (incl coffee), Vegetarian menu, Air con **Seats:** 50, Pr/dining room 32 **Children:** Portions **Directions:** 1m from Sevenoaks train station. 500yds from top of town centre towards Tonbridge on left **Parking:** Town centre

---

SISSINGHURST   MAP 07 TQ73

◎ Rankins

Modern British

Bistro-style cuisine in rustic surroundings

☎ 01580 713964 The Street TN17 2JH
e-mail: rankins@btconnect.com
web: www.rankinsrestaurant.com

A one-time saddler's and general store, this timber-framed building dates from 1898 and found a new lease of life as a restaurant in 1971. The beamed interior has the intimate feel of a cottage, with well-spaced tables offering a certain privacy, while the cooking is bistro-style with an emphasis on quality ingredients and simple but attractive presentation. Specialities of the house include seared scallops with buttered leeks and mustard sauce, and roast confit of duck with cassoulet sauce. A masterful dessert is chocolate nemesis, a rich chocolate cake lightened with a compôte of raspberries, blackberries and redcurrants.

Chef: Hugh Rankin **Owners:** Hugh & Leonora Rankin **Times:** 12.30-2/7.30-9, Closed BHs, Mon, Tue, Closed L Wed-Sat, D Sun **Prices:** Fixed L

£22.50, Fixed D £32.50, Service optional **Wine:** 11 bottles over £20, 17 bottles under £20, 2 by the glass **Notes:** Dress Restrictions, Smart casual minimum **Seats:** 25 **Children:** Portions **Directions:** Village centre, on A262 **Parking:** On street

---

SITTINGBOURNE   MAP 07 TQ96

◎ Lakes Restaurant

British, French 🖳

Conservatory restaurant serving imaginative cuisine

☎ 01795 428020 Hempstead House Country Hotel, London Rd, Bapchild ME9 9PP
e-mail: lakes@hempsteadhouse.co.uk
web: www.hempsteadhouse.co.uk

Hempstead House, now a country hotel, was built in 1850 by Robert Lake. Lakes Restaurant is named in his honour and various portraits commemorate his life. Fine dining is offered in the relaxed atmosphere of an elegant conservatory extension. Cooking is ambitious, with interesting ideas skilfully executed on a British menu with French influences. The quality produce is full of flavour in dishes such as hot crab brûlée finished with parmesan cheese and melba toast, followed by flash-roasted duck breast, succulent and cooked to perfection, served with seasoned glass noodles, lightly braised cabbage roll and plentiful plum and ginger sauce.

Chef: John Cosgrove, Darren Hatcher **Owners:** Mr & Mrs A J Holdstock **Times:** 12-2.30/7-10 **Prices:** Fixed L £12.50, Fixed D £24.50, Service optional **Wine:** 30 bottles over £20, 25 bottles under £20, 4 by the glass **Notes:** Sun L £19.50, Vegetarian available, Dress Restrictions, Smart casual, Civ Wed 150 **Seats:** 70, Pr/dining room 30 **Children:** Portions **Rooms:** 27 (27 en suite) ★★★ HL **Directions:** On A2 1.5m E of Sittingbourne **Parking:** 100

SMARDEN   MAP 07 TQ84

The Chequers Inn

☎ 01233 770217 The Street TN27 8QA
web: www.thechequerssmarden.com

Good pub food at picturesque Kentish inn.

ENGLAND

Thackeray's

TUNBRIDGE WELLS (ROYAL) MAP 06 TQ53

Modern French V 🖳

Inventive, contemporary cuisine in chic surroundings

☎ 01892 511921   TN1 1EA
e-mail: reservations@thackeraysrestaurant.co.uk
web: www.thackerays-restaurant.co.uk

This fashionable restaurant occupies celebrated novelist William Makepeace Thackeray's former home, a wide-fronted property that has the distinction of being the oldest building in Tunbridge Wells and comes covered in original, whitewashed Kent Peg tiles. The stylish interior combines period architecture with modish modern touches such as chocolate suede banquettes, cream tub chairs, wooden floors, and glass panels. There's also a Japanese terrace for alfresco dining, and a choice of chic candlelit bars, as well as a private dining area with deep red leather textured walls and a table decorated with old-fashioned fish bowls (complete with goldfish). Service is formal and attentive but delivered in a friendly and relaxed style.

The kitchen's modern approach - underpinned by a classical theme - sits perfectly with its sleek surroundings and oozes confidence and ambition. High-quality luxury ingredients, modern presentation, flair, style and high technical skill all deliver on a repertoire of value fixed-price lunch and dinner menus, plus tasting option and enticing carte. Try pan-fried escalope of foie gras from Landes with roasted polenta cake, caramelised apples and sweet wine and wild chive sauce with perhaps roast loin of wild venison to follow, served with cep purée, caramelised onions and chestnuts, foie gras ravioli and sauce au poivre. Desserts are frothy, flamboyant concoctions such as passionfruit and mango mousse, with Piña Colada sorbet, or mandarin, saffron and Grand Marnier soufflé.

Chef: Richard Phillips
Owners: Richard Phillips
Times: 12-2.30/6.30-10.30, Closed Mon, Closed D Sun
Prices: Fixed L £14.95, Fixed D £28.50-£45.50, Starter £8.95-£13.95, Main £17.95-£28.50, Dessert £9.95, Service added but optional 12.5%
Notes: Tasting menu £58 (£88 inc wine), Sun L 3 courses £28.50, Vegetarian menu, Air con
Seats: 54, Pr/dining room 16
Children: Portions
Directions: A21/A26, towards Tunbridge Wells. On left 500yds after the Kent & Sussex Hospital
Parking: NCP, on street in evening

TUNBRIDGE WELLS (ROYAL) MAP 06 TQ53

◎◎ Hotel du Vin & Bistro

European

Elegant bistro in stylish townhouse

☎ 01892 526455 Crescent Rd TN1 2LY
e-mail: info@tunbridgewells.hotelduvin.com
web: www.hotelduvin.com

One of this spa town's architectural landmarks, this imposing 18th-century building often welcomed the young Princess Victoria as a guest in the days before she took the throne. Today it has been transformed into a contemporary boutique hotel by the hugely respected Hotel du Vin chain, with stylish accommodation and a tastefully designed bar and bistro. The latter draws discerning diners with its inspired modern menu, which successfully balances modern dishes with simple classics. You might begin with duck eggs Benedict with honey-roast ham, and then move on to venison with pearl barley mash and vegetable ragout, or calves' liver with bacon, sweet red onions and jus. Exceptional wine list.

Chef: James O'Connor **Owners:** Hotel du Vin Ltd **Times:** 12-1.45/7-9.45, Closed L 31 Dec **Prices:** Fixed L £15.50, Starter £6.75-£9.50, Main £10.75-£18.50, Dessert £6.75, Service optional, Group min 14 service 10% **Wine:** 700 bottles over £20, 50 bottles under £20, 5 by the glass **Notes:** Vegetarian available, Civ Wed 60 **Seats:** 80, Pr/dining room 84 **Children:** Menu, Portions **Rooms:** 34 (34 en suite) ★★★★ TH **Directions:** Please telephone for directions **Parking:** 30

◎ Right on the Green

Modern British

Pleasant, intimate bistro-style dining with stylish cooking

☎ 01892 513161 15A Church Rd, Southborough TN4 0RX
e-mail: info@rightonthegreen.co.uk
web: www.rightonthegreen.co.uk

Originally an antiques warehouse, this comfortable, cosy restaurant has an intimate feel - especially when tables are candlelit in the evening. The décor in the main dining area is pleasantly eccentric with striking ceiling beams and large windows overlooking the green. The food puts an interesting twist on upmarket bistro-style cooking with an appealing selection of modern dishes that are cooked with aplomb. Take seared loin of blue fin tuna served with pak choi and lentil salsa, or roast rump of lamb with gratin potatoes and mint jus. As we went to press, we understand that there was a change of ownership taking place.

Times: 12-2.30/7-12, Closed 25-26 Dec, 4 Jan, Mon, Sun, Closed L Sat **Directions:** A26 towards Tunbridge Wells next to Henry Baines antique shop and Southborough cricket green

◎ The Spa Hotel

Modern British

Serious cuisine in fine-dining environment

☎ 01892 520331 Mount Ephraim TN4 8XJ
e-mail: info@spahotel.co.uk
web: www.spahotel.co.uk

The restaurant at this imposing Georgian country house - set in 14 acres of landscaped grounds - provides a grand, spacious backdrop for elegant dining. Sparkling chandeliers, high ceilings, freshly cut flowers and quality tableware set the scene, complemented by suitably formal table service. The menu offers a range of modern British dishes featuring seasonal local produce and traditional techniques. Think guinea fowl 'en crepinette' with Mediterranean vegetables and rosemary polenta, or perhaps medallion of pancetta monkfish served with braised oxtail, vegetables and crispy brisket, and to finish, a caramelised apple sponge with sauce anglaise and sweet basil syrup.

The Spa Hotel

Chef: Steve Cole **Owners:** Goring Family **Times:** 12.30-2/7-10, Closed L Sat **Prices:** Fixed L £13-£15, Fixed D £29.50, Service included **Wine:** 69 bottles over £20, 29 bottles under £20, 8 by the glass **Notes:** Vegetarian available, Dress Restrictions, Smart casual, No jeans or T-shirts, Civ Wed 200 **Seats:** 80, Pr/dining room 250 **Children:** Menu, Portions **Rooms:** 69 (69 en suite) ★★★★ HL **Directions:** On A264 leaving Tunbridge Wells towards East Grinstead **Parking:** 140

◎◎◎ Thackeray's

see opposite

WEST MALLING   MAP 06 TQ65

◎ The Swan

British 🖥

Brasserie cooking in lively, modern setting of a transformed pub

☎ 01732 521910 35 Swan St ME19 6JU
e-mail: info@theswanwestmalling.co.uk
web: www.theswanwestmalling.co.uk

A radical conversion of a 15th-century coaching inn brings a contemporary, brasserie-style vibe to this pretty Kent village. Wood, granite and stainless steel are softened by fashionable neutral tones, banquette seating and modern artwork and mirrors. It's lively and vibrant, with two sleek bars, dining on two levels, a smart lounge and a paved and shaded terrace for alfresco dining. Youthful, black-clad staff provide attentive service, while the accomplished kitchen's simple, modern, clean-cut, brasserie-inspired dishes hit all the right notes, too. Expect a menu offering fish pie with crab mash and greens, or confit belly pork with celeriac mash and apple sauce.

Chef: A Clarke, S Goss **Owners:** Fishbone Ltd **Times:** 12-2.45/6-10.45, Closed 26 Dec, 1 Jan, Closed L 27 Dec, 2 Jan **Prices:** Fixed L £13, Fixed D £16, Starter £5-£10, Main £10-£20, Dessert £5-£6, Service added but optional 12.5% **Wine:** 62 bottles over £20, 19 bottles under £20, 12 by the glass **Notes:** Dress Restrictions, Smart dress, Civ Wed 100, Air con **Seats:** 90, Pr/dining room 20 **Children:** Menu, Portions **Directions:** M20 junct 4 follow signs for West Malling **Parking:** Long-stay car park

ENGLAND

WESTERHAM
MAP 06 TQ45

⊛ Rendezvous Café

French, Mediterranean NEW

Popular modern brasserie serving French cuisine

☎ 01959 561408 & 561387 26 Market Square TN16 1AR
e-mail: info@rendezvous-brasserie.co.uk
web: www.rendezvous-brasserie.co.uk

Situated on the high street, the restaurant's huge front windows offer diners a perfect view of this charming village. The décor is modern with muted colours, while service is attentive and knowledgeable. The cuisine is purely French and uses a combination of freshly imported French and local produce. Take white crab meat and avocado millefeuille served with brown crab meat aïoli and tomato chutney, followed perhaps by roast wild halibut with a chestnut purée and glazed salsify served with a white truffle emulsion. Finish off with warm chocolate pudding served with tea mousse and chocolate ice cream.

Chef: A Mourdi **Owners:** A Mourdi, Mr Chaib-Doukkali **Times:** 8.30/10 **Prices:** Fixed L £15-£18, Fixed D £22-£25, Starter £7-£8.75, Main £15-£18.75, Dessert £4.75-£5.75, Service added but optional 10% **Wine:** 20 bottles over £20, 20 bottles under £20, 13 by the glass **Notes:** Vegetarian available, Dress Restrictions, Smart casual, Air con **Seats:** 50 **Children:** Menu, Portions **Directions:** M25 junct 5 towards Westerham. M25 junct 6 take A22, then A25 towards Oxted/Westerham **Parking:** 25

WHITSTABLE
MAP 07 TR16

⊛ Crab & Winkle Seafood Restaurant

Seafood

Buzzy, weather-boarded harbour restaurant with the freshest of fish

☎ 01227 779377 South Quay, The Harbour CT5 1AB
web: www.seafood-restaurant-uk.com

Located above the town's fish market on the quay overlooking the harbour, this recently refurbished, modern, buzzing restaurant has a light-and-airy feel, appropriately decked out with maritime art and polished lightwood tables and chairs. The decked balcony is a great place for alfresco dining in summer and, on less clement days, the views of the harbour and fishing fleet more than compensates. Given its location, it's no surprise that the modern menus come awash with fish and seafood, straight from the boats and simply cooked. Take steamed fillet of wild sea bass with herb-crushed new potatoes, spring onions and a smoked salmon and chive velouté, or perhaps poached Loch Duart salmon with buttered cabbage and fennel sour cream.

Chef: Ben Walton **Owners:** Andrew & Victoria Bennett **Times:** 11.30/9.30, Closed 25 Dec, Closed D 26 Dec, 1 Jan **Prices:** Fixed L £11-£25, Fixed D £25-£32.50, Starter £4.50-£9.25, Main £12.50-£20.50, Dessert £4.50-£7.50, Service added but optional 12.5%, Group min 8 service 12.5% **Wine:** 12 bottles over £20, 25 bottles under £20, 10 by the glass **Notes:** Vegetarian available, Air con **Seats:** 72 **Children:** Portions **Directions:** Please telephone for directions **Parking:** Gorrel Tank Car Park

⊛⊛ The Sportsman

Modern British ⦿

Superb fresh fish in unpretentious surroundings

☎ 01227 273370 Faversham Rd, Seasalter CT5 4BP
web: www.thesportsmanseasalter.co.uk

Relaxed and cheery gastro-pub with a modern colonial cum shaker style - stripped wooden floorboards, half wood-clad walls, reclaimed timber tables, local art on the walls and a couple of open fireplaces. The daily-changing modern menu offers a good choice of mainly fish, but also plenty of other local produce, much of it from the surrounding countryside. Presentation is simple - almost rustic - letting the quality and freshness of the ingredients speak for themselves. A good example would be a starter of half a dozen Whitstable native oysters, followed by roast leg and braised shoulder of Monkshill Farm lamb with mint sauce and warm chocolate mousse with salted caramel and milk sorbet.

Chef: Stephen Harris **Owners:** Stephen & Philip Harris **Times:** 12-3/6-11, Closed 25-26 Dec, Mon, Closed D Sun **Prices:** Starter £4.95-£7.95, Main £13.95-£19.95, Dessert £5.50, Service optional, Group min 6 service 10% **Wine:** 21 bottles over £20, 30 bottles under £20, 7 by the glass **Seats:** 60 **Children:** Portions **Directions:** 3.5m W of Whitstable **Parking:** 20

LANCASHIRE

BARTON
MAP 18 SD53

⊛ Healey's @ Barton Grange Hotel

Modern NEW

Stylish hotel restaurant offering innovative modern British and European menu

☎ 01772 862551 Garstang Rd PR3 5AA
e-mail: stay@bartongrangehotel.com
web: www.bartongrangehotel.com

This modern, stylish hotel has much to offer, including an award-winning garden centre and leisure facilities. Healey's restaurant is open on week nights only, offering a seasonally-changing menu based firmly on local produce. Dishes like rack of local suckling pig, or Lakeland chicken breast and melting mustard brie, deliver flair and creativity, with high-quality accompaniments. It's hard to choose just one dish from such an imaginative menu and those lucky enough to live within reach, or with an excuse to stray from the M6, will want to come back for more, time and time again.

Chef: Andrew Nash, John Riding **Owners:** The Topping Family **Times:** 7-9, Closed 25 Dec- 2 Jan, Sun, Closed L all week **Prices:** Starter £5.95-£9.95, Main £14.50-£22, Dessert £5.95-£8.95, Service optional **Wine:** 12 bottles over £20, 19 bottles under £20 **Notes:** Dress Restrictions, No jeans or T-shirts, Civ Wed 300, Air con **Seats:** 35, Pr/dining room 20 **Children:** Min 11 yrs **Rooms:** 51 (51 en suite) ★★★★ HL **Directions:** M6 junct 32, travel N A6 Garstang. Barton Grange is 2.5m on right **Parking:** 240

BLACKBURN   MAP 18 SD62

◎◎ The Millstone at Mellor

Modern British 🕭

Cosy, traditional restaurant, a firm favourite with locals and residents

☎ 01254 813333   Church Ln, Mellor BB2 7JR
e-mail: info@millstonehotel.co.uk
web: www.shirehotels.com

The Millstone has a traditional bar and an elegant, refurbished restaurant, both immaculately presented. The restaurant is wood-panelled with a beamed ceiling, grandfather clock and framed prints of countryside images. These set the scene for tables clothed in white linen adorned with fresh flowers and laid with quality glassware. A flexible approach is taken to food, with the bar and restaurant menu available in either venue. Simple, straightforward classic dishes are offered, cooked from the best local, seasonal ingredients. Think braised and glazed Pendle lamb shank served with spring onion champ, buttered green beans and rosemary jus, or perhaps a fresh fillet of haddock in Bomber beer batter with mushy peas, thick-cut chips and tartare sauce. Equally crowd-pleasing desserts follow the egg custard tart, baked ginger parking and sticky toffee pudding route.

Chef: Anson Bolton   **Owners:** Shire Hotels Ltd   **Times:** 12-2.15/6.30-9.30
Prices: Fixed D £28.95, Starter £3.50-£7.50, Main £14.50-£21.50, Dessert £5.50-£6.50   **Wine:** 55 bottles over £20, 30 bottles under £20, 8 by the glass   **Notes:** Sun L available between 12-9, Vegetarian available, Dress Restrictions, Smart casual, Civ Wed 60   **Seats:** 62, Pr/dining room 20
Children: Menu, Portions   **Rooms:** 23 (23 en suite) ★★ HL
Directions: 4m from M6 junct 31 follow signs for Blackburn. Mellor is on right 1m after 1st set of lights   **Parking:** 45

BLACKPOOL   MAP 18 SD33

◎ Kwizeen

Modern European

Serious cooking in an area normally renowned for its fast food

☎ 01253 290045   47-49 Kings St FY1 3EJ
e-mail: info@kwizeen.co.uk
web: www.kwizeen.co.uk

The oriental façade of this chic modern restaurant looks right at home amid the joke shops, pubs, nightclubs and kitsch close to the famous Tower, but the exterior belies the cool, contemporary, minimalist décor of the interior with its wood floors, chrome furniture and subtle lighting. The appealing, good-value menus take an equally modern

Kwizeen Restaurant is set behind Blackpool town centre and a three-minute walk from the front of the winter gardens. Kwizeen sources its dishes with fresh local produce and is recognised by "Made in Lancashire". The style of food is simply cooked, seasonal and clean in taste. In 2006 "Restaurant Magazine" voted Kwizeen third in the country for "Best Dishes 2006 Tapa's". This small boutique restaurant holds the "Taste Lancashire Highest Quality Assured" from Lancashire Tourism and in February 2007 was voted "Taste of Blackpool".

Kwizeen Restaurant
47-49 King Street
Blackpool, FY1 3EJ
01253 290045
Email: info@kwizeen.co.uk
Web: www.kwizeen.co.uk

approach; think a fillet of sea bass partnered by dauphinoise potatoes and a ginger and lime beurre blanc, or perhaps Staining pheasant breasts served with parsnip purée and a liquorice sauce.

Chef: Marco Calle-Calatayud   **Owners:** Marco Calle-Calatayud, Antony Beswick   **Times:** 12-1.45/6, Closed 21 Feb-10 Mar, last wk Aug, Sun, Closed L Sat   **Prices:** Fixed L £6.50, Fixed D £22.50-£34.45, Starter £5.50-£8.95, Main £12.50-£21, Dessert £4.50-£10, Service included   **Wine:** 6 by the glass
Notes: Dress Restrictions, Smart casual   **Seats:** 40   **Directions:** From front of Blackpool Winter Gardens, 100yds to King St, and as road forks restaurant 30yds on left   **Parking:** On street
see advert above

CARNFORTH   MAP 18 SD47

◎ Essence

Modern British NEW

Modern bistro-style cuisine in relaxed surroundings

☎ 01524 735093   2 Scotland Rd LA5 9JY
e-mail: info@essence-dining.co.uk
web: www.essence-dining.co.uk

A Victorian terraced house with shop-window style frontage, giving way to high-ceilinged rooms with original cornicing and an open-plan kitchen. Contemporary furnishings and neutral brown and cream décor give a warm, stylish feel, enhanced by mood lighting and jazz music. The menu offers an impressive range of dishes based on local produce, like salt marsh lamb, venison and local cheeses. A few more unusual ingredients appear, like purple Moroccan potatoes, while extras like truffle essence and saffron oil add a touch of luxury. Desserts might feature fig and frangipane tart with honey ice cream.

CONTINUED ON PAGE 234

Northcote Manor

LANGHO MAP 18 SD73

Modern British V 🎵 NOTABLE WINE LIST 🍷

A powerhouse of regional British gastronomy

☎ 01254 240555 Northcote Rd BB6 8BE
e-mail: sales@northcotemanor.com
web: www.northcotemanor.com

A gastronomic haven, its famous kitchen twice producing the Young Chef of the Year, Northcote and chef-patron Nigel Haworth celebrated their 21st year in business back in 2005.

The restaurant itself is a spacious affair with contemporary styling, minimalist and softly lit with displays of eye-catching, local modern art. Light and airy with a conservatory front, it has views over Nigel's organic garden where many of the herbs, salads and vegetables are used in season. Crisp white linen, a wine list of some 450 bins and service with a formal air of professionalism all play their part at this foodie destination.

Nigel creates an enticing repertoire (carte, seasonal lunch, tasting and gourmet options), which have their roots firmly in Lancashire, making the most of the North West's abundant local larder to create dishes of true terroir. The cooking is intelligently simple, with an emphasis on freshness and the quality of prime seasonal ingredients, and exudes high technique. Think fillet of Bowland beef with smoked foie gras and crispy black pudding, or perhaps a melting ginger pudding served with Simpson's iced double cream and caramel custard to finish.

Chef: Nigel Haworth/ Lisa Allen
Owners: Nigel Haworth, Craig Bancroft
Times: 12-2/7-9.30, Closed 25 Dec, 1-2 Jan
Prices: Fixed L £17, Starter £7-£11.95, Main £21.50-£27.50, Dessert £8.25-£10.50, Service optional
Wine: 285 bottles over £20, 22 bottles under £20, 6 by the glass
Notes: Tasting menu 8 courses £70, 10 courses £85, Vegetarian menu, Dress Restrictions, No jeans, Civ Wed 40
Seats: 80, Pr/dining room 40
Children: Menu, Portions
Rooms: 14 (14 en suite)
Directions: M6 junct 31 take A59, follow signs for Clitheroe. Left at 1st traffic light, onto Skipton/Clitheroe Rd for 9m. Left into Northcote Rd, hotel on right
Parking: 60

The Longridge Restaurant

LONGRIDGE MAP 18 SD63

Modern British v

Chic contemporary setting for first-rate British cuisine

☎ 01772 784969 104-106 Higher Rd PR3 3SY
e-mail: longridge@heathcotes.co.uk
web: www.heathcotes.co.uk/collection/longridge/

This chic eatery started life as a series of working men's cottages, and moonlighted as a pub, a cyclists' café and an Indian restaurant before assuming its current incarnation as the flagship of Paul Heathcote's culinary empire. A lounge - with comfortable sofas and brown leather chairs - leads the way to the interconnected dining areas, with their suede seating, lightwood floors and elegantly clothed tables, while upstairs discreet windows on to the kitchen let diners in on all the culinary action. Its brigade consistently impresses, handling high-quality ingredients with confident simplicity to deliver an appealing, seasonal-influenced, bistro-style carte - complemented by daily specials - of straightforward modern British fare.

Take roast fillet of Bowland beef and braised cheek served with crushed Jersey Royals, baby carrots, garden peas and tarragon, or pan-fried skate wing with a herb salad, capers, lemon pickle and new potatoes, while a classic Heathcote bread-and-butter pudding (with clotted cream and apricots), or more adventurous iced-almond parfait with honey-roasted white peach, marzipan and fresh raspberries might catch the eye at dessert. Treat yourself to the seven-course tasting menu to really do the place justice, or a day course at the cookery school, many of which are hosted by Paul Heathcote himself.

Chef: James Holah, Paul Heathcote
Owners: Paul Heathcote
Times: 12-2.30/6-10, Closed 1 Jan, Mon, Closed L Sat
Prices: Fixed L £19.50, Fixed D £35, Starter £8.50, Main £20, Dessert £6.50, Service optional, Group min 8 service 10%
Wine: 22 bottles under £20, 10 by the glass
Notes: Fixed D 5 courses £45, Tasting menu £65, Vegetarian menu
Seats: 70, Pr/dining room 18
Children: Portions
Directions: Follow signs for Golf Club & Jeffrey Hill. Higher Rd is beside White Bull Pub in Longridge
Parking: 10

CARNFORTH CONTINUED

Chef: John Adler-Connor **Owners:** John & Donna Adler-Connor
Times: 11.30-2/7, Closed 24-27 Dec, Sun-Mon, Closed L Tue-Wed
Prices: Starter £4.50-£8.50, Main £13.95-£18.95, Dessert £5.50-£7.50, Service optional **Wine:** 6 bottles over £20, 16 bottles under £20, 2 by the glass
Seats: 26 **Directions:** From M6 follow Carnforth signs (A6). On main crossroads in town centre, on left **Parking:** On street, pay & display at station

---

LANCASTER   MAP 18 SD46

🏵 Lancaster House Hotel

Modern, Traditional British

Modern hotel dining offering local produce

☎ 01524 844822 Green Ln, Ellel LA1 4GJ
e-mail: lancaster@elhmail.co.uk
web: www.elh.co.uk/hotels/lancaster

This modern country-house hotel enjoys a rural setting south of the city and close to the university. Leading from the minstrels' gallery, the Gressingham Restaurant is a split-level dining room where modern British cooking makes good use of interesting local ingredients. Start off with Glosson Dock peppered mackerel fillet with grain mustard mayonnaise, then try the lemon- and parsley-crusted sea bass with wilted spinach and crushed new potatoes. The sweet-toothed might like to order the strawberry Eton Mess.

Times: 12.30-2/7-9.30, Closed L Sun **Rooms:** 99 (99 en suite) ★★★★ HL **Directions:** 3m from Lancaster city centre. From S M6 junct 33, head towards Lancaster. Continue through Galgate village, and turn left up Green Ln just before Lancaster University

---

LANGHO   MAP 18 SD73

🏵🏵🏵 Northcote Manor

see page 232

LONGRIDGE   MAP 18 SD63

🏵🏵🏵 The Longridge Restaurant

see page 233

LYTHAM ST ANNES   MAP 18 SD32

🏵 Chicory

Modern International

Generous, eclectic menus in a lively ambience

☎ 01253 737111 5 Henry St FY8 5LE
web: www.chicorygroup.co.uk

The ochre façade of this contemporary restaurant, with the stylish Flambé cocktail bar above, makes it an unmissable landmark. The look extends throughout the comfortable and cosy interior, with a huge double-sided banquette which neatly divides it in two. Well-drilled staff serve dishes from a generous, eclectic menu, where Mediterranean meze sit alongside sashimi of horseradish-marinated salmon with sautéed tiger prawns. Among the main courses, a trinity of aged Bowland beef vies for attention with sea bass fried in Chinese five spice, served on soba noodles and Asian vegetables. Cleanse the palate with passionfruit crème brûlée.

Chicory

Chef: F Santoni & R Martin **Owners:** B Middleton, G Cartwright, F Santoni & R Martin **Times:** 12-2/6-9.30, Closed 25 Dec, 1 Jan **Prices:** Fixed D £18.95, Starter £4.25-£14.50, Main £14.95-£22.95, Dessert £5.95, Service optional **Wine:** 20 bottles over £20, 19 bottles under £20, 17 by the glass **Notes:** L ALC only, Dress Restrictions, Smart Casual, Air con **Seats:** 70 **Children:** Menu, Portions **Directions:** In town centre, behind Clifton Arms Hotel **Parking:** On street

---

🏵 Greens Bistro

Modern British

Imaginative modern cooking in an intimate atmosphere

☎ 01253 789990 3-9 St Andrews Rd South,
St Annes On Sea FY8 1SX
e-mail: info@greensbistro.co.uk
web: www.greensbistro.co.uk

Hidden among the shops and residences in the heart of town, the stairs down to this romantic cellar restaurant create an immediate sense of expectation, even, perhaps, a little theatre. Inside, the subtle décor and lighting - with tables discreetly hidden in nooks and crannies and smart uniformed staff - all conspire to create an ideal atmosphere for a special night out. The food is modern British and punches above its weight with great ingredients ticking the requisite local and seasonal boxes. Expect roast tenderloin of pork with a Brussels sprout bubble-and-squeak, Bury black pudding and sage and onion gravy, and perhaps a warm Bakewell tart served with Amaretto ice cream to finish.

Chef: Paul Webster **Owners:** Paul Webster **Times:** 6-10, Closed 25 Dec, BHs, 2 wks Jan, 1 wk summer, Sun-Mon, Closed L all week **Prices:** Fixed D £15.95, Starter £3.95-£5.95, Main £12.95-£15.95, Dessert £4.50, Service optional, Group min 8 service 10% **Wine:** 7 bottles over £20, 15 bottles under £20, 7 by the glass **Seats:** 38 **Children:** Portions **Directions:** Just off St Annes Sq **Parking:** On street

⊛ The West Beach Restaurant

Modern British V

Stylish hotel restaurant offering fine dining

☎ 01253 739898 Clifton Arms Hotel, West Beach
FY8 5QJ
e-mail: welcome@cliftonarms-lytham.com
web: www.cliftonarms-lytham.com

The Clifton Arms Hotel is an impressive, modern seafront hotel overlooking Lytham Green and the Ribble estuary, and the elegant West Beach Restaurant offers a unique setting and an intimate ambience. Enjoy candlelit dining from an imaginative menu, complemented by fine wines. Modern British cuisine is exemplified by dishes like pan-seared sea bass with tomato vinaigrette, or roast leg of lamb with rosemary and berry jus. No surprise then to find sticky toffee pudding on the menu, with a lovely butterscotch sauce, or vanilla pannacotta with red fruit coulis.

Chef: Jamie Sankey **Owners:** Paul Caddy **Times:** 12-2.30/7-9.30
Prices: Fixed L £15-£20, Fixed D £25-£30, Starter £5.95-£9, Main £9.95-£22, Dessert £4.50-£6, Service optional **Wine:** 55 bottles over £20, 19 bottles under £20, 10 by the glass **Notes:** Fixed L 3 courses, Vegetarian menu, Civ Wed 100 **Seats:** 60, Pr/dining room 140 **Children:** Portions **Rooms:** 48 (48 en suite) ★★★★ HL **Directions:** M55 junct 4, first left onto A583 (Preston), take right hand lane. At lights turn right onto Peel Rd. Turn right at t-junct into Ballam Rd. Continue onto Lytham town centre. Turn right and then left into Queen St **Parking:** 50

see advert on this page

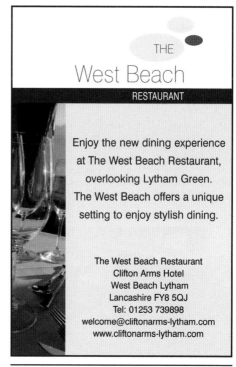

PRESTON   MAP 18 SD52

⊛ Pines Hotel

Traditional British

Traditional fare in comfortable surroundings

☎ 01772 338551 570 Preston Rd, Clayton Le-Woods
PR6 7ED
e-mail: mail@thepineshotel.co.uk
web: www.thepineshotel.co.uk

Originally a cotton mill owner's house, set in 4 acres of mature grounds, the hotel has been extended over the years and the function suite is a renowned cabaret venue. Haworths Bar and Grill serves quality local produce in traditional style, on a seasonally-changing menu. Kick off with a starter of home-made soup or classic Caesar salad. For mains, traditional British dishes such as roast beef and Yorkshire pudding, or pot-roast English lamb, sit alongside king scallops with Bury black pudding, or perhaps Chateaubriand to share. Finish with baked rice pudding and raspberry jam, or marmalade glazed bread-and-butter pudding.

Pines Hotel

Chef: Michael Slater, Ryan Greene, Sarah Love **Owners:** Betty Duffin
Times: 12-2.30/6-9.30 **Prices:** Fixed L £12.50, Starter £4.25-£6.95, Main £10.25-£21, Dessert £4.75-£5.95, Service optional **Wine:** 20 bottles over £20, 22 bottles under £20 **Notes:** Vegetarian available, Dress Restrictions, No jeans, T-shirts or trainers, Civ Wed 200 **Seats:** 95, Pr/dining room 46 **Children:** Portions **Rooms:** 37 (37 en suite) ★★★ HL **Directions:** M6 junct 29 heading S 1m towards Chorley. M6 junct 29 heading N 1m towards Blackburn **Parking:** 150

PRESTON CONTINUED

⊕ Winckley Square Chop House and Bar

Modern British

Classic town-centre brasserie dining

☎ 01772 252732 23 Winckley Square PR1 3JJ
e-mail: preston@heathcotes.co.uk
web: www.heathcotes.co.uk

Right in the town centre, this former convent school has been converted into one of celebrity chef, Paul Heathcote's chain of brasseries. The interior boasts an impressive bar space and eclectic décor, with lots of marble and hardwood surfaces and a mixture of contemporary and antique furniture. The menu is a crowd-pleaser, mixing classic hand-made dishes like steak and chips with local produce such as honey and ginger-spiced pork belly with spring vegetable broth and pak choi. Puddings include a melting chocolate tart with lime sorbet, or try the delicious home-made ice creams.

Times: 12-2.30/6-10, Closed 1-2 Jan, BHs, Closed L 3 Jan **Directions:** City centre, on Winckley Sq, near train station

THORNTON   MAP 18 SD34

⊕ Twelve Restaurant and Lounge Bar

Modern British

Modern food in an intriguing architectural setting

☎ 01253 821212 Marsh Mill Village, Marsh Mill-in-Wyre FY5 4JZ
e-mail: info@twelve-restaurant.co.uk
web: www.twelve-restaurant.co.uk

Twelve is a converted dance studio with the stylish new addition of a lounge bar; the bar's glazed roof and wall offering stunning views of the 60-ft Marsh Mill windmill that stands just feet away. The restaurant is contemporary in design with a sculptural feel and an industrial theme: exposed brickwork, steel girders and aluminium fencing on the mezzanine floor. Local ingredients shine in dishes of potted Southport shrimps with seared scallops and peppered gazpacho, or best end of Bowland Forest lamb with baby vegetables, creamed potatoes and parsnip crisps.

Chef: Paul Moss **Owners:** Paul Moss & Caroline Upton **Times:** 12-3/6.30-12, Closed 1st 2wks Jan, Mon, Closed L Tue-Sat **Prices:** Fixed D £18.95-£23.50, Starter £5.50-£8.50, Main £14.50-£24, Dessert £4.95-£6.95, Service optional **Wine:** 47 bottles over £20, 39 bottles under £20, 12 by the glass **Notes:** Vegetarian available, Air con **Seats:** 90 **Children:** Portions **Directions:** A585 follow signs for Marsh Mill Complex. Turn right into Victoria Rd East, entrance 0.5m on left **Parking:** 150

WHITEWELL   MAP 18 SD64

⊕ The Inn at Whitewell

Modern British

Historic inn with imaginative cooking in an area of outstanding natural beauty

☎ 01200 448222 Forest of Bowland, Clitheroe BB7 3AT
e-mail: reception@innatwhitewell.com
web: www.inn@whitewell.com

Within the Forest of Bowland, beside the River Hodder, this period inn (parts of which date back to the 1300s) has immense charm with rustic furniture, antiques and memorabilia throughout adding to its character. The informative menu is written with a sense of humour and dishes are modern British in style with an obvious Mediterranean influence - rillette of pork belly with a cider apple compôte and caraway seed toast, for example, or roast breast of Goosnargh corn-fed chicken with home-made sausage, pistachio nuts, parsnip purée and a light jus.

Chef: Jamie Cadman **Owners:** The Inn at Whitewell Ltd **Times:** 12-2/7.30-9.30, Closed L all week **Prices:** Starter £4-£9, Main £14-£23, Dessert £4-£4.50, Service optional **Wine:** 120 bottles over £20, 60 bottles under £20, 16 by the glass **Notes:** Civ Wed 80 **Seats:** 60, Pr/dining room 20 **Children:** Portions **Rooms:** 17 (17 en suite) ★★★★★ INN **Directions:** Telephone for directions **Parking:** 70

WRIGHTINGTON   MAP 15 SD51

⊕⊕ The Mulberry Tree

Modern British V

Ambitious cooking in Lancashire village gastro-pub

☎ 01257 451400 Wrightington Bar WN6 9SE

Just two miles off the M6, this family-run gastro-pub in a tranquil Lancashire village setting is popular with the locals for its generously-sized, imaginative dishes in a bright, modern setting. Simple table settings and personable service make this a favoured venue, with its bar and restaurant menu for more refined items. Cooking is accomplished modern British with European influences, so expect the likes of pan-fried sea bass served with an aubergine and smoked mackerel potato cake, lobster and crayfish bisque, griddled Mediterranean vegetables and garlic-buttered tiger shrimps, or perhaps a fillet of beef teamed with Anna potatoes, creamy mushroom Stroganoff and a red wine and sun-blushed tomato jus.

Chef: Mark Prescott **Owners:** Mr M Prescott & Mr J Moore **Times:** 12-2.30/6-9.30, Closed 26 Dec, 1 Jan **Prices:** Fixed L £16.95-£30, Fixed D £17.95-£36, Starter £4.50-£10.95, Main £7.50-£19.95, Dessert £5.95, Service added but optional 10% **Wine:** 45 bottles over £20, 15 bottles under £20, 8 by the glass **Notes:** Vegetarian menu, Air con **Seats:** 60
Children: Portions **Directions:** 4m from Wigan. From M6 junct 27 towards Parbold, right after motorway exit, by BP garage into Mossy Lea Rd. On right after 2m **Parking:** 80

LEICESTERSHIRE

BELTON   MAP 11 SK42

◎◎ The Queen's Head

Modern European NEW

Modern gastro-pub operation with food to match

☎ 01530 222359 2 Long St LE12 9TP
e-mail: enquiries@thequeenshead.org
web: www.thequeenshead.org

A former coaching inn, the Queen's Head is now a gastro-pub vogue affair, with contemporary styling and décor. The large open-plan bar, once the local alehouse, comes with blondwood flooring that continues into its two dining rooms. Here cream walls, modern pictures and quality table appointments maintain the theme, while service is appropriately relaxed, friendly and helpful. The fashionable, modern European cooking fits the bill too, dealing in quality local produce, good flavours and balance. Take a fillet of beef served with cep ravioli, perhaps accompanied by turned carrots and shallots and a red wine froth, while desserts may feature a strawberry and Cointreau soufflé.

Chef: Mark Billings **Owners:** Henry & Ali Weldon **Times:** 12-2.30/7-9.30, Closed 25-26 Dec, 1 Jan, Closed D Sun **Prices:** Fixed L £13, Fixed D £17, Starter £5.50-£9.50, Main £11.50-£19.50, Dessert £5.75-£7, Service added 10% **Wine:** 49 bottles over £20, 25 bottles under £20, 13 by the glass **Notes:** Sun L 2 courses £13, 3 courses £17 **Seats:** 70, Pr/dining room 40
Children: Menu, Portions **Rooms:** 6 (6 en suite) ★★★★ RR
Directions: Located just off B5324 between Loughborough and Ashby de la Zouch **Parking:** 20

BUCKMINSTER   MAP 11 SK82

◎◎ The Tollemache Arms

Modern British

Vibrant restaurant at the cutting edge of modern cooking

☎ 01476 860007 48 Main St NG33 5SA
e-mail: enquiries@thetollemachearms.com
web: www.thetollemachearms.com

This 18th-century village inn on the Tollemache estate has been given a new focus as a restaurant with rooms, though locals can still prop up the bar and chat to visitors. The grey stone roadside inn now has a smart minimalist interior too, decked out with leather chairs, oak floors and fresh flowers. Lovers of fine food appreciate the modern approach of Mark Gough, whose classical training and love of fresh produce continue to make this venture a hit. Expect a saddle of local venison served with a potato gratin and port sauce, or perhaps pan-fried sea bream teamed with basil mash and baby chorizo sausages, while a classic apple tart Tatin with vanilla ice cream might catch the eye at dessert.

Chef: Mark Gough **Owners:** Mark Gough **Times:** 12-3.30/5.30-12, Closed Mon, Closed D Sun **Prices:** Fixed L £10, Fixed D £14, Starter £4.50-£10, Main £9.50-£16, Dessert £5-£7.50, Service optional **Wine:** 15 bottles over £20, 10 bottles under £20, 6 by the glass **Notes:** Sun L 1-3 courses £10-£18.50, Vegetarian available **Seats:** 50, Pr/dining room 20
Children: Menu, Portions **Rooms:** 5 (5 en suite) ★★★★ GA
Parking: 15

CASTLE DONINGTON   MAP 11 SK42
FOR RESTAURANT DETAILS SEE EAST MIDLANDS AIRPORT

EAST MIDLANDS AIRPORT   MAP 11 SK42

◎ Best Western Premier Yew Lodge Hotel

Traditional

Imaginative cooking in relaxed surroundings

☎ 01509 672518 Packington Hill, Kegworth DE74 2DF
e-mail: info@yewlodgehotel.co.uk
web: www.yewlodgehotel.co.uk

Handy for both the motorway and East Midlands Aiport, this smart hotel has extensive leisure facilities and is a popular venue for conferences and weddings. Take a drink in the library bar overlooking the Orchard restaurant, before moving downstairs for some tempting modern cuisine. Large windows let in lots of natural light, and diners are seated at smartly appointed tables, presided over by friendly and attentive staff. Chicken and bacon terrine starter, comforting old favourites like steak and kidney pud to more exotic fare: Cajun-spiced salmon with citrus sauce and garlic mash, or fillet steak with sweet potato and blue cheese muffin and sultana jus, are fine examples of the fare.

Times: 12-2.30/6.30-10, Closed L Sat **Rooms:** 87 (87 en suite) ★★★★ HL **Directions:** M1 junct 24, follow signs for Loughborough & Kegworth on A6. At bottom of hill take 1st right onto Packington Hill. Hotel 400yds on right

EAST MIDLANDS AIRPORT CONTINUED

◉ Donington Manor Hotel

Modern British NEW

Accomplished modern cooking in traditional surroundings

☎ 01332 810253 High St, Castle Donington DE74 2PP
e-mail: enquiries@doningtonmanorhotel.co.uk
web: www.doningtonmanorhotel.co.uk

Many original features have been pleasingly preserved at this refined Georgian hotel near the village centre, now undergoing a modern transformation. Its elegant Adam-styled dining room is particularly appealing, with its traditional feel and attentive and helpful service. The kitchen's modern approach comes aptly underpinned by classical influences, driven by the intelligently sympathetic handling of quality ingredients and flavour. Think seared salmon served with spicy chorizo and a potato and chive salad, while to finish, perhaps a vanilla and crème fraîche pannacotta with rhubarb and ginger compôte might catch the eye.

Times: 12-2.30/7-9.30, Closed Xmas **Rooms:** 32 (32 en suite) ★★★ HL

◉◉ The Priest House on the River

Modern British

Unique location for fine dining

☎ 01332 810649 Kings Mills, Castle Donington DE74 2RR
e-mail: thepriesthouse@handpicked.co.uk
web: www.handpicked.co.uk

Perched on the banks of the River Trent amid 54 acres of mature woodland, the original watermills on the site of the Priest House were mentioned in the Domesday Book. Nowadays modern comforts are found throughout the hotel, which includes conference rooms, a modern brasserie and a fine-dining restaurant. The cooking style is modern, and menus are both seasonal and regional, focusing on local speciality ingredients and dishes. Everything is home-made, including the olive oil from the hotel's villa in Italy. Starters may include goat's cheese, black olive and courgette tortellini with burnt sage butter, while for mains you could expect organic Yorkshire pork cooked two ways with confit belly, fondant potatoes, glazed salsify and rosemary jus. Finish with a Bakewell tart and vanilla custard.

Chef: Fritz Ronnenberg **Owners:** Hand Picked Hotels **Times:** 12-3/7-10, Closed L Mon-Sat **Prices:** Fixed D £29.50, Starter £7.95-£9.95, Main £17.95-£22.50, Dessert £7.95, Service included **Wine:** 75 bottles over £20, 2 bottles under £20, 8 by the glass **Notes:** Dress Restrictions, No shorts, Civ Wed 90, Air con **Seats:** 45, Pr/dining room 100 **Children:** Portions **Rooms:** 42 (42 en suite) ★★★★ HL **Directions:** Northbound: M1 junct 23A to airport. After 1.5m turn right to Castle Donington. Left at 1st lights, 2m. Southbound: M1 junct 24A onto A50. Take 1st sliproad signed Long Eaton/Castle Donington. Turn right at lights in Castle Donington **Parking:** 200

HINCKLEY MAP 11 SP49

◉◉ *Best Western Sketchley Grange Hotel*

British, European

Modern hotel with its finger on the culinary pulse

☎ 01455 251133 Sketchley Ln, Burbage LE10 3HU
e-mail: reservations@sketchleygrange.co.uk
web: www.sketchleygrange.co.uk

This modern hotel boasts an impressive line up of facilities including a health and leisure complex, choice of bars, and two eateries. A brasserie serves light meals, but the real draw is the Willow Restaurant, a spacious venue that overlooks pretty gardens and is candlelit by night. It's staffed by a well-trained and enthusiastic kitchen brigade who incorporate the best of culinary fashion in their food and offer an ambitious modern menu of dishes. Start with langoustine tempura du Puy lentil cappuccino, pear purée and shellfish dust, followed by mains such as loin of local venison with parsnip purée, Savoy spiced fig chutney and a port wine dressing.

Times: 7-9.30, Closed Mon, Closed L Tues-Sat, D Sun **Rooms:** 52 (52 en suite) ★★★★ HL **Directions:** From M69 junct 1 take B4109 (Hinckley). Straight on 1st rdbt, left at 2nd rdbt & immediately right into Sketchley Lane. Hotel at end of lane

KEGWORTH MAP 11 SK42
FOR RESTAURANT DETAILS SEE EAST MIDLANDS AIRPORT

KNIPTON MAP 11 SK83

◉ The Manners Arms

Modern British NEW

Local inn serving imaginative food

☎ 01476 879222 Croxton Rd NG32 1RH
e-mail: info@mannersarms.com
web: www.mannersarms.com

Part of the Rutland Estate, this former hunting lodge built for the 6th Duke of Rutland has been redesigned by the current 11th Duchess. Period features abound, and the restaurant boasts high corniced ceilings, wooden floors, polished wooden furniture, and heavy drapes matching the banquette seating. A tian of Cornish crabmeat and Whitby prawns has fresh flavours with just enough spice to add interest, while sea bass with crisp skin - meaty, moist and nicely seasoned - comes stacked with tomato salsa, lobster cream sauce and crushed new potatoes. Finish with a raspberry brûlée.

Chef: Paul Hoad **Owners:** Duke of Rutland **Times:** 12.30-3/7-9, Closed D Sun (after 8pm), 25 Dec **Prices:** Fixed L £9.99-£12.50, Starter £5-£15, Main £15-£22, Dessert £5-£6, Service optional **Wine:** 15 bottles over £20, 15 bottles under £20, 8 by the glass **Notes:** Civ Wed 50 **Seats:** 50, Pr/dining room 20 **Children:** Menu, Portions **Rooms:** 10 (10 en suite) ★★★★ GA **Directions:** From Grantham take A607 (Melton road), after approx. 4m turn right at Croxton Kerrial **Parking:** 80

LEICESTER   MAP 11 SK50

◉ Best Western Belmont House Hotel

British

Calm dining in a busy city

☎ 0116 254 4773 De Montfort St LE1 7GR
e-mail: info@belmonthotel.co.uk
web: www.belmonthotel.co.uk

Built in the 1860s, this graceful building stands in New Walk, a leafy pedestrianised street that dates back to the late 18th century and connects the town with nearby Victoria Park. Now an elegant hotel, it offers a choice of three eateries, with Jamies Bar and Bowies Brasserie offering informal fare as an alternative to Cherry's, the main restaurant, which serves a tempting range of British and international dishes. Start with roast quail, braised Puy lentils and crispy bacon perhaps, before tucking into mains like sautéed sirloin of beef with wild mushroom brandy sauce, stilton mash and French beans, or lobster thermidor with basmati rice and butter beans.

Chef: Stewart Westwater **Owners:** The Bowie Family **Times:** 12.30-2/7-9, Closed BH Mon, 26-28 Dec, Closed L Sat, D Sun **Prices:** Fixed L £11.95-£25.95, Starter £4.95-£7.95, Main £9.95-£21.95, Dessert £5.95, Service added but optional 10% **Wine:** 40 bottles over £20, 34 bottles under £20, 11 by the glass **Notes:** Dress Restrictions, Smart casual, Civ Wed 100, Air con **Seats:** 65, Pr/dining room 30 **Children:** Portions **Rooms:** 77 (77 en suite) ★★★ HL **Directions:** M1 junct 21/A6 S onto A6 rdbt follow signs for railway station **Parking:** 70

◉◉ Watsons Restaurant & Bar

Modern International

Modern brasserie-style cooking in one of Leicester's most popular eateries

☎ 0116 222 7770 5-9 Upper Brown St LE1 5TE
e-mail: watsons.restaurant@virgin.net

Set in an 18th-century former cotton mill, this well-established restaurant has a strong regular clientele - booking is advisable even at lunchtime. There's a compelling contemporary feel to the décor - polished-wood floors, subtle halogen lighting and generously spaced

tables. Service is relaxed, friendly and professional and as for the food - classic French and Mediterranean influences run throughout the menu and there's a high level of skill and obvious attention to detail in the cooking, alongside quality ingredients. Open with the likes of a Parma ham, rocket and pea risotto, and, to follow, perhaps Tuscan-style braised lamb shank, with chocolate Grand Marnier fondue with fruits and marshmallows to finish.

Chef: Graeme Watson, Scott Mills **Owners:** Graeme Watson **Times:** 12-2.30/7-10.30, Closed BHs, 10 days at Xmas, Sun **Prices:** Fixed L £9.95, Fixed D £15, Starter £5-£7.50, Main £9.95-£16.50, Dessert £5.50-£6, Service added but optional 10% **Wine:** 12 bottles over £20, 18+ bottles under £20, 10 by the glass **Notes:** Fixed D available Mon-Fri, Vegetarian available, Air con **Seats:** 80 **Children:** Portions **Directions:** City centre, next to Phoenix Arts Theatre

San Carlo

☎ 0116 251 9332 Granby St LE1 1DE

Extremely busy Italian with open kitchen and wood-burning oven.

MEDBOURNE   MAP 11 SP89

◉◉ The Horse & Trumpet

Modern British

Culinary adventures in a sleepy village

☎ 01858 565000 Old Green LE16 8DX
e-mail: info@horseandtrumpet.com
web: www.horseandtrumpet.com

Tucked away behind the village bowling green, this carefully restored, thatched former farmhouse offers fine dining in three intimate dining areas, or alfresco in summer. The imaginative food comes courtesy of an accomplished kitchen team, who deliver a creative menu of modern dishes distinguished by quality ingredients, fresh flavours, and clever combinations - all washed down with a bottle from the carefully selected wine list. Start with Cornish crab with fennel biscuit and avocado cream and then tuck into loin of venison with celeriac, sweet potato and mustard fruits, followed by hazelnut polenta cake served with chocolate mousse, or - better still - treat yourself to the imaginative tasting menu.

Chef: G Magnani **Owners:** Horse & Trumpet Ltd **Times:** 12-1.45/7-9.30, Closed 1st week Jan, Mon, Closed D Sun **Prices:** Fixed L £18, Starter £6.75-£15, Main £16-£25, Dessert £6.75, Service optional, Group min 16 service 10% **Wine:** 40 bottles over £20, 6 bottles under £20, 8 by the glass **Notes:** Tasting menu available Tue-Sat L+D, Dress Restrictions, Smart casual, no trainers or baseball caps **Seats:** 50, Pr/dining room 32 **Children:** Min 12 yrs **Rooms:** 4 (4 en suite) ★★★★ RR **Directions:** Between Market Harborough and Uppingham on B664 **Parking:** On street parking

ENGLAND

MELTON MOWBRAY   MAP 11 SK71

◎◎ Stapleford Park

Modern French

Fine dining amid the splendour of Capability Brown parkland

☎ 01572 787000 Stapleford LE14 2EF
e-mail: reservations@stapleford.co.uk
web: www.staplefordpark.com

Set in 500 acres of Capability Brown-designed parkland, this stunning former stately home dates back to the 14th century. There are two dining rooms: the main room boasts Grinling Gibbons carvings inspired by the Spanish Riding School in Vienna, while The Old Kitchen - a cosier room with an impressive vaulted ceiling - has a more medieval feel. Starters might include seared scallops with creamed leeks, Oscietra caviar and vichyssoise sauce, or maybe a warm salad of John Dory with roast salsify and walnut dressing, while for mains you might try beautifully fresh sea bass, served with crab risotto and fennel purée. Hazelnut pannacotta with mocha ice cream rounds things off in style. Try the tasting menu for a complete overview.

Chef: Wayne Vickerage **Times:** 12.30-2.30/7-9.30, Closed L Mon-Sat **Prices:** Fixed D £37, Starter £12.50-£16, Main £22.50-£28.50, Dessert £9.50-£12.50, Service added but optional 5% **Wine:** 164 bottles over £20, 6 by the glass **Notes:** Sun L 3 courses £27.50, Tasting menu 7 courses £65, Dress Restrictions, Jacket required, no denim, Civ Wed 120 **Seats:** 60, Pr/dining room 180 **Children:** Min 9 yrs **Rooms:** 55 (55 en suite)★★★★ HL **Directions:** A1 to Colsterworth rdbt. left onto B676, signed Melton Mowbray.In approx 9m turn left to Stapleford **Parking:** 120

NORTH KILWORTH   MAP 11 SP68

◎◎ Kilworth House Hotel

Modern British

Country-house hotel offering comfortable elegance and opulent fine dining

☎ 01858 880058 Lutterworth Rd LE17 6JE
e-mail: info@kilworthhouse.co.uk
web: www.kilworthhouse.co.uk

This splendid country-house hotel is set amid 38 acres of parkland and gardens. Gracious public rooms feature period pieces and original artworks, and dining options include the opulent Wordsworth restaurant, with its ornate vaulted ceiling and glittering chandeliers, the restored Victorian Orangery for fine views and a lighter menu, and private dining rooms for special occasions. The Wordsworth's fine-

dining menu reads almost lyrically with dishes like suprême of guinea fowl with foie gras farce, duck-fat potatoes and stuffed ripe fig, or sautéed turbot with seared king scallops, baby greens, poached oyster, and caviar and champagne cream. Desserts are particularly artistic, as in passionfruit Chiboust with strawberry salsa, kumquat ragout and home-made Bounty balls.

Chef: Carl Dovey **Owners:** Mr & Mrs Mackay **Times:** 12-3/7-9.30 **Prices:** Fixed L £20-£30, Fixed D £34-£45, Starter £8-£15, Main £15-£25, Dessert £7-£12, Service optional **Notes:** Dress Restrictions, No jeans or trainers, Civ Wed 130 **Seats:** 70, Pr/dining room 130 **Children:** Menu, Portions **Rooms:** 44 (44 en suite) ★★★★ HL **Directions:** Located on A4304, 4m E of M1 junct 20 towards Market Harborough **Parking:** 140

QUORN   MAP 11 SK51

◎◎ Quorn Country Hotel

Modern, International V

Country-house dining by the river

☎ 01509 415050 Charnwood House, 66 Leicester Rd LE12 8BB
e-mail: sales@quorncountryhotel.co.uk
web: www.quorncountryhotel.co.uk

A riverside setting in 4 acres of landscaped gardens just begins to describe the appeal of this 17th-century manor house hotel. Shires Restaurant is an intimate room with low-beamed ceilings, candlelight and close-set tables, while the informal alternative is the Orangery bistro. The cooking style is traditional country-house with some modern forays, backed by silver service and a comprehensive wine list. Accurately cooked dishes are prepared from high-quality produce, locally supplied. A separate vegetarian menu is offered - taking in the likes of mushroom ravioli and roast parsnip galette - while from the main menu come redwood smoked salmon with blinis and lemon, and roast rump of lamb with red Leicester dauphinoise, rosemary, and redcurrant reduction.

Chef: David Wilkinson **Owners:** Mr Walshe **Times:** 12-2/7-9, Closed L Sat **Prices:** Fixed L £18, Fixed D £25, Starter £6-£10, Main £17.50-£24, Dessert £6, Service optional **Wine:** 60 bottles over £20, 11 bottles under £20, 5 by the glass **Notes:** Sun L 3 courses available, Vegetarian menu, Civ Wed 120 **Seats:** 112, Pr/dining room 240 **Children:** Menu, Portions **Rooms:** 30 (30 en suite) ★★★★ HL **Directions:** M1 junct 23/A6 towards Leicester, follow signs for Quorn **Parking:** 120

Ferrari's Trattoria

☎ 01509 412191 4 High St LE12 8DT
Family-run Italian in an old cottage in the main street.

STATHERN   MAP 11 SK73

◉ Red Lion Inn

Modern British V

Modern bistro food in a friendly village inn

☎ 01949 860868   Red Lion St LE14 4HS
e-mail: info@theredlioninn.co.uk
web: www.theredlioninn.co.uk

Set in a lovely village nestling under Belvoir Scarp, this country inn has a traditional feel without being overbearingly old world. It's a comfortable British pub in the best possible sense, with furniture and fittings that create a homely atmosphere. The modern-focused food is rustic and well done, using local produce throughout. The daily-changing menu might include pan-fried sea bream with potato and chorizo Parmentier, or braised shoulder of lamb with a herb crust, fondant potato and ratatouille, and to finish, perhaps and apple and plum crumble with vanilla ice cream. Also on site is Red Lion Foods, offering everything from takeaway bread, dressings and marinades, to hampers for a day out.

Chef: Sean Hope **Owners:** Ben Jones, Sean Hope **Times:** 12-2/7-9.30, Closed 1 Jan, Closed D Sun **Prices:** Fixed L £13, Starter £4.50-£6.25, Main £8.50-£16.50, Dessert £5.75-£6.25, Service optional, Group min 11 service 10% **Wine:** 9 bottles over £20, 21 bottles under £20, 6 by the glass **Notes:** Sun L 3 courses £16.50, Vegetarian menu **Seats:** 50 **Children:** Menu, Portions **Directions:** From A1 take A52 towards Nottingham signed Belvoir Castle, take turn to Stathern on left **Parking:** 20

LINCOLNSHIRE

CLEETHORPES   MAP 17 TA30

◉ Kingsway Hotel

Traditional British

Traditional dining by the sea

☎ 01472 601122   Kingsway DN35 0AE
e-mail: reception@kingsway-hotel.com
web: www.kingsway-hotel.com

Four generations of the Harris family have run this veteran seaside hotel and their care has been rewarded by the loyalty of staff and guests alike. Decorated in traditional style, the dining room is a popular venue for business lunches and family gatherings, delivering a tempting menu of straightforward dishes, not to mention some commanding views of the Humber estuary. The extensive selection might include starters such as chicken liver and brandy pâté, or chicken and bacon salad Niçoise, while mains are along the lines of Gressingham duck with a port and black cherry sauce, or crumbed pork with apple, poached celery and melted Applewood cheese.

Chef: Guy Stevens **Owners:** Mr J Harris **Times:** 12.30-1.45/7-9, Closed 26-27 Dec, Closed D 25 Dec **Prices:** Fixed L £16, Fixed D £25.95, Starter £4.95-£8.95, Main £12.95-£22.95, Dessert £5.95, Service optional **Wine:** 31 bottles over £20, 40 bottles under £20, 6 by the glass **Notes:** Sun L £18.75 **Seats:** 85, Pr/dining room 24 **Children:** Min 5 yrs, Portions **Rooms:** 49 (49 en suite) ★★★ HL **Directions:** At junction of A1098 and seafront **Parking:** 50

GRANTHAM   MAP 11 SK93

◉ Angel & Royal Hotel

Traditional British

Dining in the historic haunt of kings

☎ 01476 565816   High St NG31 6PN
e-mail: enquiries@angelandroyal.co.uk
web: www.angelandroyal.co.uk

Dating back to the 14th century, this is reputedly one of the oldest coaching inns in Britain. A host of original features remain, including fine plaster ceilings, elaborate stone oriel windows and a huge log fire. A high standard of cooking is offered in both the modern ground-floor bistro bar Simply Berties, and in the baronial first-floor King's Room which is open for lunch and dinner at weekends. Fixed-price menus include baked poached pear studded with Lincolnshire blue, braised shank of lamb with creamed potatoes, braised red cabbage and rosemary and red wine jelly, and lemon bavaroise with winter berry compôte.

Chef: Jean Francois Pozzetto **Owners:** Ashdale UK Ltd **Times:** 12-2.30/7-9.30, Closed L Mon-Sat, D Sun-Thu **Prices:** Fixed L £12-£15, Fixed D £25.95-£27.95, Starter £4.95-£6.95, Main £8.50-£14.50, Dessert £4.25-£6.95, Service optional **Wine:** 13 bottles over £20, 32 bottles under £20, 14 by the glass **Notes:** Sun L 2 courses £11.95, 3 courses £15, Dress Restrictions, Smart casual, Civ Wed 70, Air con **Seats:** 55, Pr/dining room 16 **Children:** Menu, Portions **Rooms:** 29 (29 en suite) ★★★ HL **Directions:** Grantham exit off A1 and follow signs to the town centre **Parking:** 55

◉◉◉ Harry's Place

see page 242

GRIMSBY   MAP 17 TA21

◉ Beeches Hotel

French

Airy brasserie-style surroundings for international cuisine

☎ 01472 278830 & 752883   42 Waltham Rd, Scartho DN33 2LX
e-mail: themanager@thebeecheshotel.com
web: www.thebeecheshotel.com

This contemporary hotel in a remodelled Victorian building has a cool contemporary look to the bar and conservatory restaurant. The low leather sofas and oriental rugs on hardwood floors are conducive to relaxation. The brasserie restaurant has a good local following and the menu offers an interesting range of dishes such as crab risotto with spring onions and parmesan cheese, followed by roast Lincolnshire partridge wrapped in pancetta with juniper berry sauce. Finish with cheese, plum bread and biscuits, or a tempting dessert like pear tart Bourdaloue with mocha ice cream, or chocolate and Amaretto torte with tutti-frutti ice cream.

Chef: David Ramackers **Owners:** Ramsden Family **Times:** 12-2/7-9, Closed Xmas & New Year, Closed L Mon-Tue **Prices:** Starter £4.50-£9, Main £16-£25, Dessert £5-£6.50, Service optional **Wine:** 19 bottles over £20, 24 bottles under £20, 3 by the glass **Seats:** 50 **Children:** Portions **Rooms:** 18 (18 en suite) ★★★ HL **Directions:** On A1203, off A16 from Louth **Parking:** 30

ENGLAND

◉◉◉

Harry's Place

GRANTHAM   MAP 11 SK93

Modern French

Tiny restaurant with exquisite food

☎ 01476 561780   17 High St, Great Gonerby NG31 8JS

A former farmhouse and wheelwrights, Harry's Place is set in a splendid listed Georgian building. The intimacy of the dining room, complete with antique furniture lots of fresh flowers and a relaxing ambience, and the fact your meal is guaranteed to have been lovingly cooked by chef-owner Harry Hallam are major factors in the restaurant's appeal. With only three tables and an international reputation for fine food, you can expect a fairly serious wait for a table at this intimate restaurant. Add into this a passion for quality ingredients that borders on the obsessive and imaginative, technically impressive cooking with real panache and you have a winning formula for one of the North East's best restaurants. With only two choices for each course, deliberating over the menu needn't be the trial faced in some restaurants - everything is exceptional. Start with lightly-seared Orkney king scallops served with a spicy marinade with chives, spring onion and a julienne of red pepper and orange, then continue with a main of Lincolnshire salt marsh teal with blueberries and a sauce of red wine, Madeira, sage, thyme and rosemary, then finish with cherry brandy jelly with black pepper and yogurt.

Chef: Harry Hallam **Owners:** Harry & Caroline Hallam **Times:** 12.30-2/7-9, Closed 1 wk from 25 Dec, Sun & Mon **Prices:** Starter £6.50-£17.50, Main £32-£35, Dessert £7, Service optional **Wine:** All bottles over £20, 4 by the glass **Seats:** 10 **Children:** Min 5 yrs, Portions **Directions:** 1.5m NW of Grantham on B1174 **Parking:** 4

HORNCASTLE   MAP 17 TF26

◉◉ Magpies Restaurant

British, European NEW

Innovative cooking in an intimate setting

☎ 01507 527004   71-75 East St LN9 6AA
web: www.eatatthemagpies.co.uk

Set in a delightful row of 200-year-old black and white cottages, a short stroll from the town centre, this small, family-run restaurant certainly punches above its weight. Enjoy pre-dinner drinks in the honey and russet-coloured lounge, or the small alfresco patio in warmer months, before moving through to the L-shaped dining room with its smart table appointments, linen cloths and fresh flowers. The principally British cuisine has some global influences, but everything is driven by the seasons and the best produce possible. With an emphasis on good presentation, a starter of seared scallops wrapped in pancetta and thyme on celeriac purée could be followed by oven-baked halibut with baby spinach and courgette fritters. Finish with warm blueberry tart with blueberry ripple cream cheese ice cream.

Chef: Andrew Gilbert **Owners:** Caroline Ingall **Times:** 12-2.30/7-9.30, Closed 27-30 Dec, Mon-Tues, Closed L Sat **Prices:** Fixed L £21, Fixed D £32, Service optional, Group **Wine:** 62 bottles over £20, 50 bottles under £20, 4 by the glass **Notes:** Fixed D 4 courses, Gourmet menu £39.50 last Thu monthly, Dress Restrictions, Smart casual, Air con **Seats:** 34 **Children:** Portions **Directions:** 0.5 miles from town centre on A158 toward Skegness **Parking:** On street

HOUGH-ON-THE-HILL   MAP 11 SK94

◉ The Brownlow Arms

British NEW

Popular village inn with something to suit everyone

☎ 01400 250234   High Rd NG32 2AZ
e-mail: paulandlorraine@thebrownlowarms.com
web: www.thebrownlowarms.com

Tucked away in a pretty Lincolnshire village, this cosy inn dates back to the 17th century and boasts a number of original features. Its popular restaurant is often booked up weeks in advance, so call ahead to be sure of a table. Once there, you're in for a treat - a tempting selection from an experienced chef who makes good use of local produce, including game from nearby estates and fish from Brixham. Daily specials supplement a fairly traditional menu: your choice might include a starter of baked cheese soufflé with natural smoked haddock, leeks and cream, followed by roast rib-eye of lamb, with parmesan mash, preserved tomatoes and rosemary jus.

Chef: Paul Vidic **Owners:** Paul & Lorraine Willoughby **Times:** 12-3/6.30-9.30, Closed 25-26 Dec, 1-23 Jan, 1 wk Sep, Mon, Closed L Tues-Sat, D Sun **Prices:** Fixed L £15.95, Starter £4.50-£7.95, Main £12.95-£21, Dessert £5.25-£5.95, Service optional **Wine:** 23 bottles over £20, 22 bottles under £20, 5 by the glass **Seats:** 80, Pr/dining room 26 **Children:** Min 14 yrs **Rooms:** 4 (4 en suite) ★★★★★ INN **Parking:** 26

LINCOLN MAP 17 SK97

⚜ Lakeside Restaurant

Modern International

Contemporary food in Victorian country-house splendour

☎ 01522 793305 Branston Hall Hotel, Branston Park, Branston LN4 1PD
e-mail: jon@branstonhall.com
web: www.branstonhall.com

Dating back to 1885, this imposing country-house hotel is set in 88 acres of wooded parkland and lakes. The elegant Lakeside Restaurant comes suitably decked out with chandeliers, paintings, Italian-style chairs and plenty of original features. The ambitious carte and fixed-price menus take a distinctly modern approach, with fine regional produce, imagination, culinary skill and careful service all coming together with style. Expect pan-fried calves' liver with braised faggots and split peas, or crisp-skinned sea bass with Bantry Bay mussels and a poached celery and watercress sauce. To finish, perhaps take a warm apple tart Tatin served with cinnamon ice cream.

Chef: Miles Collins **Owners:** Southsprings Ltd **Times:** 12-2/7-9.30, Closed 1 Jan **Prices:** Fixed L £13.50, Fixed D £25.75, Starter £5.25-£9.50, Main £15.25-£20.95, Dessert £5.25-£7.50, Service optional **Wine:** 17 bottles over £20, 36 bottles under £20, 14 by the glass **Notes:** Dress Restrictions, Smart casual, no jeans or T-shirts, Civ Wed 120 **Seats:** 75, Pr/dining room 28 **Children:** Min 12 yrs, Portions **Rooms:** 50 (50 en suite) ★★★ CHH **Directions:** On B1188, 3m S of Lincoln. In village, hotel drive opposite village hall **Parking:** 75

The award winning 4 star and 2 AA Rosette Old Bakery Restaurant with Rooms is ideally located in the Uphill area of Lincoln, close to the castle and cathedral. In addition to receiving the Lincolnshire Life Best Restaurant of the Year Award 2006, winning the Tastes of Lincolnshire Restaurant Category in February 2006 and highly commended in 2007, The Old Bakery are winners in the Lincolnshire Star Awards 2007 under the heading "Profit through Passion".

26/28 Burton Road,
Lincoln LN1 3LB
Tel: 01522 576057
 (outside UK +44 1522 576057)
Text: 07949 035554 or
 07795 604996

Email: enquiries@theold-bakery.co.uk
Web address: www.theold-bakery.co.uk

⚜⚜ The Old Bakery

International NEW

Accomplished, flavour-driven cooking using quality local produce in former bakery

☎ 01522 576057 26/28 Burton Rd LN1 3LB
e-mail: enquiries@theold-bakery.co.uk
web: www.theold-bakery.co.uk

As the name suggests, this restaurant with rooms was once a bakery (1837-1945) and still retains many of the original features, including the quarry-tiled floor and ovens still in the walls. Consisting of two well-furnished rooms, the restaurant's atmosphere is rustic, homely and full of character, a theme not lost on the attentive staff either, who are fittingly friendly and polite. The skilled Italian chef-patron is passionate about the food, clear flavours and use of local, seasonal Lincolnshire produce. The approach is modern underpinned by a

CONTINUED

LINCOLN Continued

classical base; think chargrilled entrecote of Lincolnshire Red beef with creamed Savoy cabbage and smoked crispy streaky bacon or hay slow-roasted pig, and do save room for the home-made breads and impressive cheese selection.

Chef: Ivano de Serio **Owners:** Alan & Lynn Ritson, Tracey & Ivano de Serio **Times:** 12-2.30/7-9.30, Closed Mon **Prices:** Fixed L £12-£14.50, Fixed D £30-£34, Starter £4.50-£9.75, Main £14.50-£21, Dessert £5.25-£6.75, Service optional, Group min 5 service 5% **Wine:** 37 bottles over £20, 38 bottles under £20, 9 by the glass **Notes:** Sun L £14.50 adults, £12.50 children, Dress Restrictions, Smart casual **Seats:** 45, Pr/dining room 15 **Children:** Portions **Rooms:** 4 (2 en suite) ★★★★ RR **Directions:** From A46 follow directions for Lincoln North & follow brown signs for The Historic Centre **Parking:** On street, public car park 20mtrs

see advert on page 243

⊛ Wig & Mitre

British, International

A shrine to good eating on the old pilgrim trail

☎ 01522 535190 30/32 Steep Hill LN2 1TL
e-mail: email@wigandmitre.com
web: www.wigandmitre.com

Located at the top of the well-named Steep Hill, this old inn is open from early to late, offering comfort and good food throughout the day. From the upstairs dining room there are striking views of the floodlit cathedral. The food is an unfussy but imaginative blend of modern ideas, listed on a carte and blackboard, with the likes of creamed celeriac and potato soup, followed by braised blade of beef on mustard mash with caramelised onions and, for dessert, a cherry Bakewell tart with clotted cream. Wines are suggested for each dish.

Chef: Valerie Hope **Owners:** Hope family **Times:** 8/11 **Prices:** Fixed L £11, Starter fr £4.75, Main £10.95-£22.95, Dessert £4.95, Service optional **Wine:** 43 bottles over £20, 33 bottles under £20, 25 by the glass **Notes:** Vegetarian available **Seats:** 65, Pr/dining room 20 **Children:** Portions **Directions:** At the top of Steep Hill, adjacent to Lincoln Cathedral and Lincoln Castle car parks **Parking:** Public car park adjacent

The Cheese Society

☎ 01522 511003 1 St Martin's Ln LN2 1HY
Wide range of cheese dishes served in modern café attached to specialist cheese outlet.

SCUNTHORPE   MAP 17 SE81

⊛ Forest Pines Golf and Country Club Hotel

International, Seafood

Well-equipped hotel with an elegant restaurant

☎ 01652 650770 Ermine St, Broughton DN20 0AQ
e-mail: forestpines@qhotels.co.uk
web: www.qhotels.co.uk

This luxury golf and country-club hotel has recently undergone a £12m refurbishment and boasts an array of facilities including a gym, beauty spa, and 27-hole championship course. There are three eateries to choose from including a formal restaurant complete with Mediterranean feel, where diners are seated at well-spaced, marble-

topped tables, laid with quality settings. The food is well regarded locally and based on the freshest possible ingredients with fish and seafood from nearby Grimsby a particular draw. Take your seat in the comfortable dining room or on the alfresco terrace in summer and choose from a tempting menu of international and more traditional dishes.

Chef: Paul Montgomery **Owners:** Q Hotels Group Ltd **Times:** 6.30-10, Closed 23 Dec-8 Jan, Sun-Mon, Closed L Tue-Sat **Prices:** Starter £6-£20, Main £12-£35, Dessert £6-£12, Service optional **Wine:** 38 bottles over £20, 12 bottles under £20, 10 by the glass **Notes:** Vegetarian available, Dress Restrictions, Smart, no jeans or trainers, Civ Wed 300, Air con **Seats:** 90 **Children:** Min 14 yrs **Rooms:** 188 (188 en suite) ★★★★ HL **Directions:** From M180 junct 4, travel towards Scunthorpe on A18. Continue straight over rdbt, hotel is situated on left **Parking:** 300

SPALDING   MAP 12 TF22

⊛ Cley Hall Hotel

British, International

Overlooking the River Welland, a fine Georgian hotel

☎ 01775 725157 22 High St PE11 1TX
e-mail: cleyhall@enterprise.net
web: www.cleyhallhotel.com

Grade II listed after being rescued from near dereliction in the 1960s, this fine Georgian property has again undergone a refurbishment. The restaurant is divided in two, but forms an integral part of the ground floor area, and has a pleasant atmosphere. The straightforward use of quality ingredients results in a consistently good menu, with plenty to interest even the most jaded palates. Confit of pork wrapped in Parma ham, roast rack of lamb with stuffed vegetables, and a superb rib-eye steak with mustard butter and hand-cut chips are some of the reasons for its popularity.

Times: 12-2.00/6.30-9.30, Closed D 25-26 Dec **Rooms:** 15 (15 en suite) ★★ SHL **Directions:** Telephone for directions

STAMFORD   MAP 11 TF00

⊛ The George of Stamford

Traditional British 🍷 NOTABLE WINE LIST

Coaching inn popular for its old-fashioned charm

☎ 01780 750750 71 St Martins PE9 2LB
e-mail: reservations@georgehotelofstamford.com
web: www.georgehotelofstamford.com/

Dating back over 900 years, this splendid building's open stonework and architectural features stand testimony to its colourful history as a

hostelry to the great and the good as they travelled the length of England. Meals are served in the magnificent oak-panelled restaurant, the Garden Lounge or in the ivy-clad courtyard. Cooking is careful and accurate with much traditionally based fare on offer - think dessert, cheese and carving trolleys. For mains, expect the likes of roasted breast of partridge with a suet pudding of braised pheasant and rich port gravy, or perhaps more adventurous roasted monkfish with a mussel chowder risotto.

Chef: Chris Pitman, Paul Reseigh **Owners:** Lawrence Hoskins **Times:** 12.30-2.30/7.30-10.30 **Prices:** Fixed L £18.95, Starter £5.75-£14.25, Main £16.45-£31, Dessert £5.95, Service optional **Wine:** 107 bottles over £20, 56 bottles under £20, 17 by the glass **Notes:** Vegetarian available, Dress Restrictions, Jacket & tie, Civ Wed 50 **Seats:** 90, Pr/dining room 40 **Children:** Min 10 yrs, Portions **Rooms:** 47 (47 en suite) ★★★ HL **Directions:** From A1(N of Peterborough) take rdbt signed B1081. Follow road to 1st set of lights, hotel on left **Parking:** 120

Fratelli's

☎ 01780 754333   PE9 2DP

Very popular Italian serving a good selection of reliable dishes.

SUTTON ON SEA   MAP 17 TF58

◉ Grange & Links Hotel

European, International

A beautiful setting for really good fresh food

☎ 01507 441334 Sea Ln, Sandilands LN12 2RA
e-mail: grangeandlinkshotel@btconnect.com
web: www.grangeandlinkshotel.co.uk

A friendly family-run hotel in 5 acres of grounds close to the beach, with its own 18-hole links golf course. Superb fresh food, simply cooked and presented are what this place is all about. Fish from Grimsby, Lincolnshire Red beef and local vegetables are examples of some of the fine produce on the menu. Try duck and orange terrine, followed by fillet of halibut with roasted peppers. There's also a selection of lobster dishes, including américaine with tomato, garlic, fresh herbs, white wine and brandy. Finish with a dessert from the trolley, or take a selection of cheeses.

Chef: Tina Harrison **Owners:** Ann Askew **Times:** 7-10, Closed L all week **Prices:** Starter £4-£6.80, Main £11.50-£15.50, Dessert £4.50, Service optional **Wine:** 6 bottles over £20, 20 bottles under £20, 6 by the glass **Notes:** Sun L, Carvery, Cold buffet, Vegetarian available, Dress Restrictions, Jacket & tie, Civ Wed 150 **Seats:** 60 **Children:** Menu, Portions **Rooms:** 23 (23 en suite) ★★★ HL **Directions:** Please telephone for directions **Parking:** 60

WINTERINGHAM   MAP 17 SE92

◉◉◉◉ Winteringham Fields

see page 246

WOOLSTHORPE   MAP 11 SK83

◉ The Chequers Inn

Modern British

Coaching inn turned gastro-pub

☎ 01476 870701 Main St NG32 1LU
e-mail: justinnabar@yahoo.co.uk
web: www.chequers-inn.net

A cosy warren of dining rooms furnished with darkwood tables and high-backed leather chairs, the interior of the 17th-century inn looks quite contemporary set against the beams and exposed brickwork. The Chequers is set in the lee of Belvoir Castle, by the village cricket pitch, and has its own petanque lawn. Recommendations include crab and saffron tart to start, followed by breast of corn-fed chicken with confit of tomatoes, melted taleggio and Parmentier potatoes, with warm chocolate brownie served with Jersey cream to finish. There's also a good choice of real beers and lagers.

Chef: Steve Durham **Owners:** Justin & Joanne Chad **Times:** 12-3/5.30-11, Closed D 25-26 Dec, 1 Jan **Prices:** Fixed L £11.50, Fixed D £15, Starter £4.50-£7.50, Main £9.50-£19, Dessert £5.50, Service optional **Wine:** 25 bottles over £20, 29 bottles under £20, 29 by the glass **Notes:** Sun L 2 courses £10.95 **Seats:** 70, Pr/dining room 14 **Children:** Menu, Portions **Rooms:** 4 (4 en suite) ★★★★ INN **Directions:** From A1 exit A607 towards Melton Mowbray follow heritage signs for Belvoir Castle **Parking:** 35

ENGLAND

Winteringham Fields

WINTERINGHAM MAP 17 SE92

Modern French, European

Famous haunt lives on in new hands

☎ 01724 733096   DN15 9PF
e-mail: wintfields@aol.com
web: www.winteringhamfields.com

Though Germain and Annie Schwab may have sold up and left in 2005 after something like two decades here, the new owner continues to run Winteringham in the same fashion, and, with highly-talented young Germain protégé Robert Thompson at the helm in the kitchen (he'd been heading up the kitchen brigade for a couple of years under Germain), continuity at this much-loved venue is in safe hands. The endearing 16th-century former manor house remains much the same: original beams, log fires, sloping floors and period features. Victorian style predominates here with chintz, antiques, pictures and collectables, while quality and comfort prevail alongside a warm, inviting and relaxed atmosphere. There's a choice of sitting rooms and a conservatory for aperitifs, while in summer the rose garden comes into play. The restaurant is a long, slim room with a tiled floor and country feel, decked out with flowing tablecloths, and there's plenty of showmanship with cheese and bread trolleys. Staff are French, knowledgeable and attentive but not at all stuffy, while the sommelier is very sharp - do use his skills.

Robert Thompson's cooking takes a modern French approach underpinned by a classical theme and focuses on top-quality seasonal ingredients (including vegetables, fruit and herbs from Winteringham's own potager when available), delivered via an appealing repertoire that includes a tasting menu surprise. Expect refined, precision cooking, with clean, clear flavours, interesting combinations and supreme technical skill. Think quenelles of crab and chicken with a sweetcorn soup and kafia lime, followed by line-caught turbot with courgette and tomato, shellfish tortellini and a scallop roe sauce, and to finish, aumoniére of pear and plum with an almond pannacotta and pear crisps. Ancillaries (amuse-bouche, breads, pre-desserts, a superb cheeseboard and petits fours) all hit top form, while the wine list is considerable and expectedly classy.

Chef: R Thompson
Owners: Colin McGurran
Times: 12-2/7-10, Closed 2 wks Xmas, last wk Apr, last 2 wks Aug, Sun-Mon
Prices: Fixed L £30, Starter £18.50-£24.50, Main £22-£36.50, Dessert £11-£20, Service optional
Wine: 200 bottles over £20, 18 by the glass
Notes: Menu Surprise £79, Vegetarian available, Dress Restrictions, Smart dress preferred
Seats: 42, Pr/dining room 10
Children: Portions
Rooms: 10 (10 en suite)
★★★★★ RR
Directions: Village centre, off A1077, 4m S of Humber Bridge
Parking: 20

London

Index of London Restaurants

This index shows rosetted restaurants in London in aphabetical order, followed by their map references and postcodes. Page numbers precede each entry

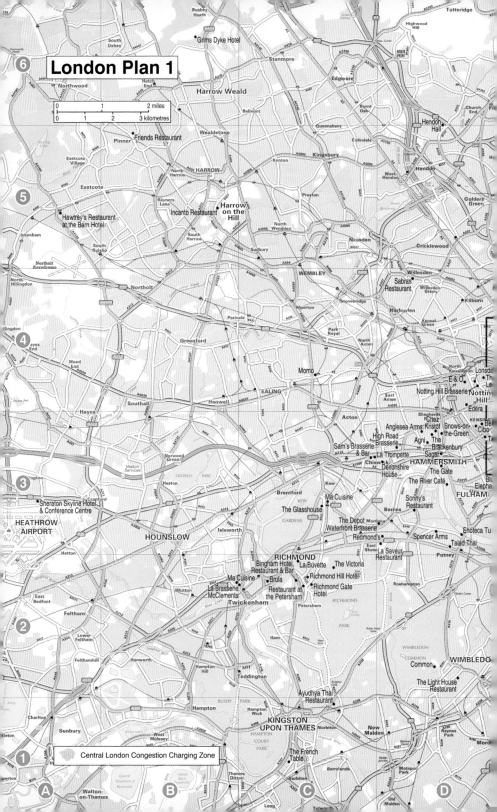

London Plan 1

6

Totteridge
Bushey Heath
Grims Dyke Hotel
Highwood Hill
Mill Hill
South Oxhey
Stanmore
Edgware
Church End
Northwood
Hatch End
Harrow Weald
Belmont
Burnt Oak
Hendon Hall

0   1   2 miles
0   1   2   3 kilometres

Pinner
Friends Restaurant
Wealdstone
Queensbury
Colindale
Hendon
Eastcote Village
North Harrow
HARROW
Kenton
West Hendon
Golders Green

5

Rayners Lane
Incanto Restaurant
Hawtrey's Restaurant at the Barn Hotel
Harrow on the Hill
North Wembley
Preston
Cricklewood
Ickenham
South Harrow
Sudbury
Neasden
Willesden
Kilburn
Northolt Aerodrome
South Ruislip
WEMBLEY
Sabras Restaurant
Willesden Green
North Hillingdon
Northolt
Alperton
Stonebridge
Harlesden
Kensal Green

4

Hayes End
Perivale
Park Royal
Greenford
North Acton
Momo
North Kensington
Lonsda
E & O
The
Wood End
Notting Hill Brasserie
Notting Hill
Edéra
Hayes
Southall
Hanwell
EALING
East Acton
Chez
Snows-on-the-Green
Bé
Cibo
Acton
Kristo
Agni
The Brackenbury
Sagar
Anglesea Arms
High Road Brasserie
Sam's Brasserie & Bar
La Trompette
Devonshire House
HAMMERSMITH
The Gate

3

Kew
Ma Cuisine
Chiswick
The River Café
Sheraton Skyline Hotel & Conference Centre
Cranford
Brentford
KEW GARDENS
The Glasshouse
Sonny's Restaurant
FULHAM
Blu
Elepha
HEATHROW AIRPORT
Heston Services
OSTERLEY PARK
Heston
Barnes
The Depot
Waterfront Brasserie
Redmond's
Mortlake
Spencer Arms
Enoteca Tu
Talad Thai
Hatton
Isleworth
HOUNSLOW
East Sheen
La Saveur Restaurant
Putney
Roehampton

2

East Bedfont
Whitton
RICHMOND
Bingham Hotel, Restaurant & Bar
La Buvette
The Victoria
Richmond Hill Hotel
Ma Cuisine
Brula
Richmond Gate Hotel
RICHMOND PARK
WIMBLEDON COMMON
WIMBLEDO
Feltham
La Brasserie McClements
Restaurant at the Petersham
Petersham
Common
Lower Feltham
Twickenham
Ham
Felthamhill
Hampton Hill
Teddington
Ayudhya Thai Restaurant
The Light House Restaurant

1

Charlton
Sunbury
West Molesey
Hampton
BUSHY PARK
Hampton Wick
KINGSTON UPON THAMES
Norbiton
New Malden
Raynes Park
Mor
HAMPTON COURT PARK
Central London Congestion Charging Zone
The French Table
Motspur Park
Walton-on-Thames
Thames Ditton
Surbiton
Berrylands
Old Malden
Queen Elizabeth II Reservoir

A   **B**   **C**   **D**

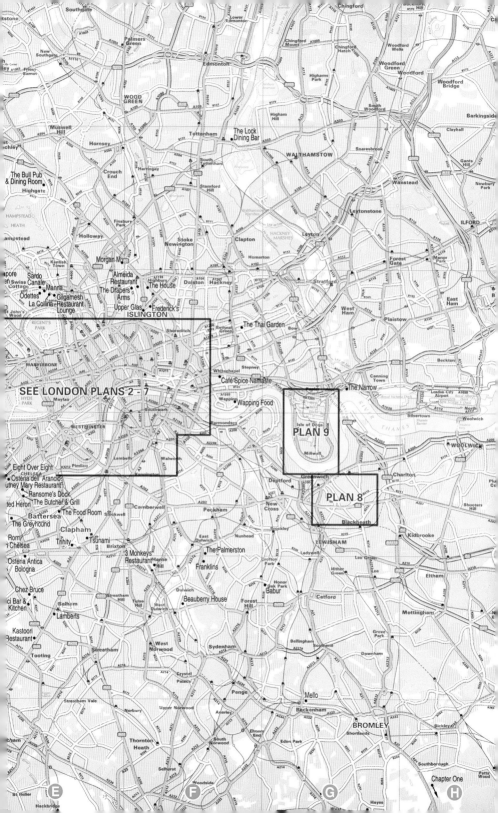

SEE LONDON PLANS 2 - 7

PLAN 9

PLAN 8

Chapter One

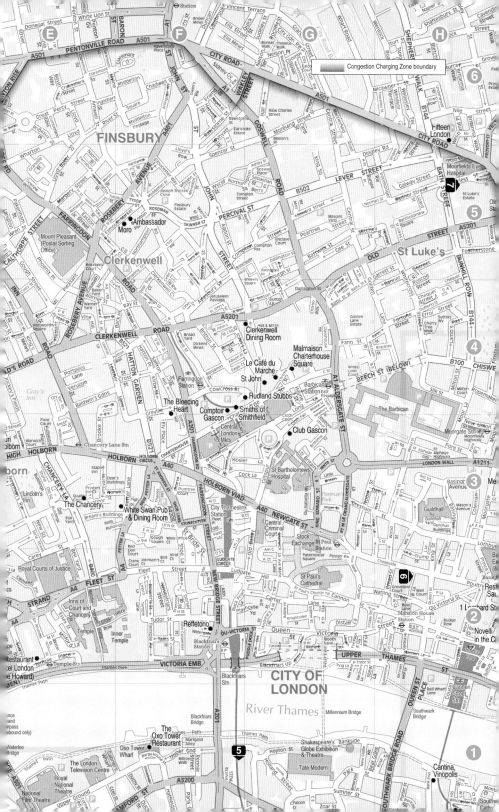

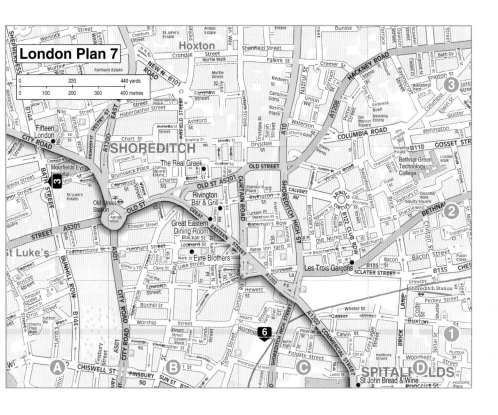

London Plan 7

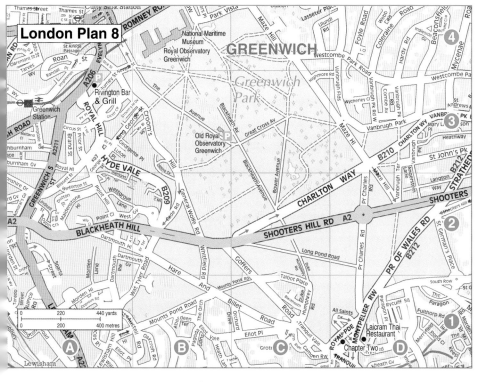

London Plan 8

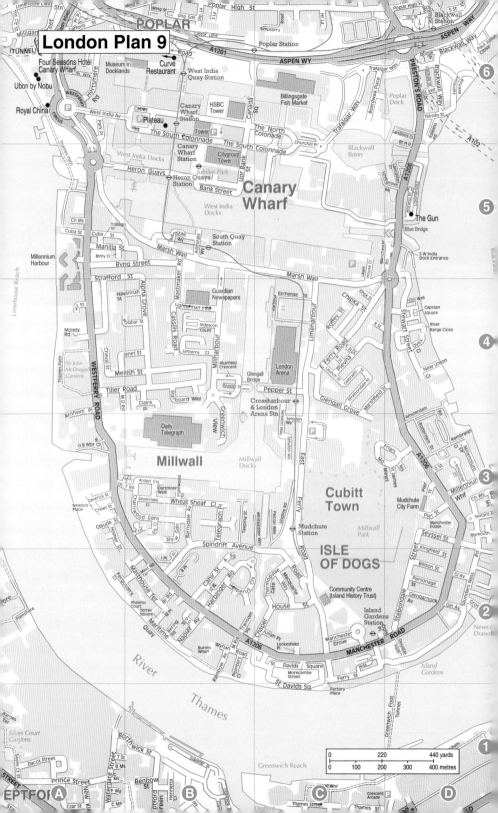

LONDON

Greater London Plans 1-9, pages 252-264. (Small-scale maps 6 & 7 at back of Guide.) Restaurants are listed below in postal district order, commencing East, then North, South and West, with a brief indication of the area covered. Detailed plans 2-9 show the locations of restaurants with AA Rosette Awards within the Central London postal districts. If you do not know the postal district of the restaurant you want, please refer to the index preceding the street plans for the entry and map pages. The Plan reference for each restaurant also appears within its directory entry.

LONDON E1

Café Spice Namasté

Indian
Authentic Indian café dining

☎ 020 7488 9242 16 Prescot St E1 8AZ   Plan 1-F4
e-mail: binay@cafespice.co.uk
web: www.cafespice.co.uk

East London eatery occupying a listed building that began life in the 18th century as a magistrate's court. These days it offers an altogether warmer welcome - 'namasté' means 'gracious hello', and you'll certainly be received like an old friend here. The speciality menu changes every fortnight, and this together with an extensive and well-annotated carte provides a choice of unusual dishes from all over Asia, conjured from the very best of British produce. Classic dishes jostle for attention with more modern fare: tuck into Goan lobster curry perhaps, or one of the most intricate of all Indian curries, galinha xacutti, which requires more than 21 different ingredients, each pan-roasted individually.

Chef: Angelo Collaco, Cyrus Todiwala **Owners:** Cafe Spice Ltd **Times:** 12-3/6.15-10.30, Closed Xmas, BHs, Sun, Closed L Sat **Prices:** Fixed L £30, Fixed D £30, Starter £4.75-£7.25, Main £14.25-£19, Service added but optional 12.5% **Wine:** 20 bottles over £20, 20 bottles under £20, 10 by the glass **Notes:** Fixed L 3 courses, Tasting menu available, Vegetarian available, Dress Restrictions, Smart casual, Air con **Seats:** 120 **Children:** Portions **Directions:** Nearest station: Tower Gateway (DLR), Aldgate East, Tower Hill Walking distance from Tower Hill **Parking:** On street; NCP

Canteen

Modern British
All-day eatery in Spitalfields

☎ 0845 686 1122 2 Crispin Place, Spitalfields E1 6DW
Plan 6-D6
e-mail: info@canteen.co.uk
web: www.canteen.co.uk

This unpretentious eatery in Spitalfields Market opened in 2006 to rave reviews and has heaved with an eclectic mix of foodies, locals

and city types ever since. Glass-walled on three sides, it teams retro booth seating with long shared tables and prides itself on offering high-quality cuisine at reasonable prices. A lengthy all-day menu includes breakfast items and designated 'fast service' dishes, as well as a daily roast, home-made pies and fish options. Expect British classics conjured from the freshest of ingredients - macaroni cheese, for example, or pie, mash, greens and gravy - plus a diet-busting array of homely desserts such as steamed syrup pudding and custard, or orange jelly with ice cream and shortbread.

Chef: Cass Titcombe, Patrick Clayton-Malone, Dom Lake **Owners:** Patrick Clayton-Malone, Dom Lake **Times:** 8/11, Closed 25-26 Dec **Prices:** Starter £4.50-£8, Main £4.50-£13.50, Dessert £5, Service added but optional 12.5% **Wine:** 16 bottles over £20, 12 bottles under £20, 17 by the glass **Notes:** Vegetarian available, Air con **Seats:** 150 **Children:** Portions **Directions:** Nearest station: Liverpool Street Overlooking Spitalfields Market

Lanes Restaurant & Bar

British, European
Modern city brasserie with cooking to match

☎ 020 7247 5050 109-117 Middlesex St E1 7JF
Plan 6-C5
e-mail: info@lanesrestaurant.co.uk
web: www.lanesrestaurant.co.uk

This modern but relaxed, informal basement restaurant and bar comes conveniently tucked away off Bishopsgate, just a short stroll from Liverpool Street station. Decked out with polished-wood floors, the split-level space is laid out with burgundy leather banquettes and chairs, while mirrors or large contemporary artworks top part-clad walls and pillars. Leather tub chairs and matching bar stools populate the bar area, while service is suitably youthful and attentive. The cooking fits with the contemporary styling, its modern-European brasserie repertoire driven by quality ingredients and a carefully presented, clean-cut, accomplished approach. Expect a fillet of halibut wrapped in pancetta and served with braised fennel and vine tomato, or classic seared rib-eye with chips and herb butter.

Chef: Liam Cooper **Owners:** James Robertson & Hamish Smith **Times:** 12-3/5.30-10, Closed BHs, 25 Dec, 1 Jan, Sun, Closed L Sat **Prices:** Fixed D £21.50, Starter £7.50-£12.95, Main £13.50-£24.95, Dessert £6.50, Service added but optional 12.5% **Wine:** 60 bottles over £20, 6 bottles under £20, 14 by the glass **Seats:** 70, Pr/dining room 28 **Children:** Min 7 yrs L, Portions **Parking:** On street after 6.30 pm

ENGLAND

ENGLAND

LONDON E1 CONTINUED

◉ St John Bread & Wine

British

Unpretentious restaurant, bakery and wine shop in old Clerkenwell

☎ 020 7251 0848 94-96 Commercial St E1 6LZ
Plan 6-D6
e-mail: reservations@stjohnbreadandwine.com
web: www.stjohnbreadandwine.com

Tucked behind the old Spitalfields Market, this no-frills sibling to big brother St John (see entry) is a resolutely British affair. Whitewashed walls, parquet flooring and simple wooden tables and chairs set a wholly unpretentious, utilitarian edge. The British food is flavour-driven and unfussy, using quality produce while delivering some earthy dishes using humble ingredients. Ox faggot and mash, brawn and pickled cucumber, Blackface lamb and fennel, or sea bass, ruby chard and green sauce set the style. Service is attentive, friendly and informed, while wines, like the wonderful breads, are on sale to take out.

Chef: James Lowe **Owners:** Trevor Gulliver & Fergus Henderson **Times:** 9/11, Closed 24 Dec-2 Jan, BHs, Closed D Sun **Prices:** Starter £5.40-£10.20, Main £11-£15, Dessert £5.90-£6.20, Service optional, Group min 6 service 12.5% **Wine:** 30 bottles over £20, 30 bottles under £20, 25 by the glass **Seats:** 60 **Parking:** on street

◉ Les Trois Garçons

Modern French 🖥

Quirky ex-pub with authentic French menus

☎ 020 7613 1924 1 Club Row E1 6JX   Plan 7-C2
e-mail: info@lestroisgarcons.com
web: www.lestroisgarcons.com

The cooking is classically French, though you might wonder at the setting, a cross between an exotic Eastern bazaar and a Victorian antique shop. Colourful objets d'art fill every conceivable space, a surreal background to the serious dining and an amusing conversation piece. There's nothing funny about the set lunch and dinner (Monday to Wednesday pm only) menus or the evening carte, where duck rillettes, carrot velouté and tempura frogs' legs served with asparagus translate into authentic French starters. Seared sweetbread with braised shin, petit artichoke, salsify and sherry jus is a typical main dish, with tarte Tatin a suitably Gallic dessert.

Times: 12-4/7-12, Closed Sun **Directions:** Nearest station: Liverpool Street. 10mins walk from station, at the end of Brick Ln

◉ Wapping Food

Modern International

Inspired cooking meets industrial heritage at the Wapping Project

☎ 020 7680 2080 Wapping Hydraulic, Power Station, Wapping Wall E1W 3ST   Plan 1-F4
web: www.thewappingproject.com

An hydraulic pumping station in the East End may not sound like a conventional place to dine, but then Wapping Food isn't a conventional eatery. Part restaurant, part art gallery, it teams old machinery, tiles and girders from its industrial days with dangling chandeliers, designer furniture and flickering candles to create a chic urban décor. Expect a menu of inspired international dishes distinguished by high-quality ingredients and imaginative combinations. Smoked eel is a typical starter, served with beetroot, horseradish and mixed herbs, while mains might include roast middle white pork with braised cavolo nero and butternut squash.

Wapping Food

Chef: Cameron Emirali **Owners:** Womens Playhouse Trust **Times:** 12-3/6.30-11, Closed 24 Dec-3 Jan, BHs, Closed D Sun **Prices:** Fixed L £45, Fixed D £45, Starter £6-£12, Main £12.50-£20, Dessert £6-£10, Service added but optional 12.5% **Wine:** 118 bottles over £20, 8 bottles under £20, 20 by the glass **Notes:** Fixed L 3 courses, Brunch at wknds, Vegetarian available **Seats:** 150 **Children:** Portions **Directions:** Nearest station: Wapping Turn right from tube, walk east & parallel to the river (approx 4 mins) **Parking:** 20

Café Naz

☎ 020 7247 0234 46-48 Brick Ln E1 6RF
Smart Bangladeshi with a touch of sophistication.

🖥 Lilly's

☎ 020 7702 2040 75 Wapping High St E1W 2YN
web: www.theaa.com/travel/index.jsp

A real local crowd-pleaser, this neighbourhood restaurant offers classic American brasserie-style dishes; a selection of starters, dishes from the grill, platters to share, mains from the kitchen, sandwiches and salads, and daily-changing lunch specials.

🖥 One Blossom Street

☎ 020 7247 6532 1 Blossom St E1 6BX
web: www.theaa.com/travel/index.jsp

Stylish restaurant with simple but effective Italian food and a good wine list.

LONDON E2

◉ The Thai Garden

Thai V

Authentic vegetarian Thai restaurant

☎ 020 8981 5748 249 Globe Rd E2 0JD   Plan 1-F4
e-mail: thaigarden@hotmail.com
web: www.thethaigarden.co.uk

The authentic vegetarian and seafood Thai cuisine here is the real deal, despite its unlikely setting in Bethnal Green. The unpretentious shop-front bistro gives way to a small dining room with 20 seats. The cooking is fragrant with some serious chillies, so be prepared - or go for dishes with fragrant herb flavours as a gentler option on the palate. The menu is in Thai and English and sticks to vegetarian and seafood dishes with a wide choice and unique, flavoursome options. Think water chestnuts fried with dry chilli and vegetables, or perhaps prawns in red curry with coconut cream.

Chef: Napathorn Duff **Owners:** S & J Hufton **Times:** 12-2.30/6-11, Closed BHs, Closed L Sat & Sun **Prices:** Food prices not confirmed for 2008. Please telephone for details **Seats:** 32, Pr/dining room 12 **Children:** Portions **Directions:** Nearest station: Bethnal Green 2nd left off Roman Rd (one-way street). Near London Buddhist Centre **Parking:** on street

Hanoi Café

☎ 020 7729 5610 98 Kingsland Rd E2 8DP
web: www.theaa.com/travel/index.jsp

Choose from over 100 freshly home-made Vietnamese dishes in a buzzy atmosphere.

LONDON E8

Shanghai

☎ 020 7254 2878 41 Kingsland High St E8 2JS
web: www.theaa.com/travel/index.jsp

A former Victorian pie and mash shop with marble counter and tiled walls. Classic Chinese favourites and westernised versions.

LONDON E14

◉ Curve Restaurant & Bar

Fish & Seafood

Relaxed docklands dining

☎ 020 7517 2808 & 7517 2806 London Marriott West India Quay, 22 Hertsmere Rd, Canary Wharf E14 4ED
Plan 9-B6
e-mail: mhrs.loncw.restaurant.supervisor@marriotthotels.com
web: www.marriott.co.uk

Located in a spectacular skyscraper, this new-build hotel overlooks West India Quay in the heart of Docklands. The Curve restaurant is an upmarket choice for a relaxed bite. It takes its name from the imposing glass sweep of the building's façade, and the full-length windows afford unrestricted views over the quay. The emphasis is on fresh fish from nearby Billingsgate, plus a number of grills. Dishes are modern, fresh and simple in presentation and typical options include New England clam chowder, lobster tortelloni, and glazed Alaskan black cod, followed by an interesting Thai crème brûlée with coconut sago, lime and pandan leaf.

Curve Restaurant & Bar

Chef: Surjan Singh **Owners:** Marriott Hotels **Times:** 12-2.30/5-10.30 **Prices:** Fixed L £17, Fixed D £30-£35, Starter £5.50-£14.75, Main £11.50-£22.75, Dessert £5.50-£6.50, Service added but optional 12.5% **Wine:** 65 bottles over £20, 17 bottles under £20, 22 by the glass **Notes:** Business L 2 courses £17, Vegetarian menu, Civ Wed 250, Air con **Seats:** 86, Pr/dining room 40 **Children:** Menu, Portions **Rooms:** 301 (301 en suite) ★★★★★ HL **Directions:** Nearest station: Canary Wharf/West India Quay DLR Telephone for directions **Parking:** On street

◉ Four Seasons Hotel Canary Wharf

Italian

Simple Italian fare in chic surroundings

☎ 020 7510 1999 Westferry Circus, Canary Wharf E14 8RS   Plan 9-A6
web: www.fourseasons.com/canarywharf

Expect Italian sophistication at Quadrato, a sleek and chic Thames-side eatery set in this stylishly modern Docklands hotel. With superb views over the London skyline, you can tuck into a versatile range of modern Italian dishes or some classic regional specialities, all prepared with contemporary flair from first-class ingredients in the impressive open-to-view theatre kitchen. Simple, flavoursome combinations might include risotto mantecato with porcini and mascarpone, or perhaps oven-baked herb-crusted rack of lamb served with roasted artichokes and potato tortino. The predominantly Italian staff are friendly, enthusiastic and passionate about food and wine.

Chef: Marco Bax **Owners:** Four Seasons Hotels **Times:** 12-3/6-10.30 **Prices:** Fixed L £34-£40, Fixed D £34-£40, Starter £9-£24, Main £14.50-£29, Dessert £9-£12, Service optional, Group min 6 service 12.5% **Wine:** 29 by the glass **Notes:** Sun brunch buffet £37.50, Dress Restrictions, Smart casual preferred, Civ Wed 200, Air con **Seats:** 90 **Children:** Menu, Portions **Rooms:** 142 (142 en suite) ★★★★★ HL **Directions:** Nearest station: Canary Wharf Just off Westbury Circus rdbt **Parking:** 26

◉ The Gun

British

Smart docklands gastro-pub serving modern British food

☎ 020 7515 5222 27 Coldharbour, Docklands E14 9NS
Plan 9-D5
e-mail: info@thegundocklands.com
web: www.thegundocklands.com

A fabulous Thames-side location with a stunning terrace affording great views of the Millennium Dome and the river are among the attractions at this beautifully restored 18th-century dockers' pub. No longer spit-and-sawdust, expect oak timber floors, Georgian-style

CONTINUED

ENGLAND

LONDON E14 CONTINUED

fireplaces, crisp linen-clothed tables in smart dining rooms, and an inviting bar. Competent modern British cooking results in versatile menus that include the likes of mussel, fennel and saffron broth, or sirloin steak with garlic butter and fat chips, alongside pan-fried John Dory with shellfish velouté. The Gun is also a great spot for Sunday brunch and summer barbecues.

Chef: Mickey O'Connor **Owners:** Tom & Ed Martin **Times:** 12-3/6-10.30, Closed 25-26 Dec **Prices:** Starter £7-£11, Main £12-£19, Dessert £6-£8, Service added but optional 12.5% **Wine:** 97 bottles over £20, 27 bottles under £20, 21 by the glass **Seats:** 40, Pr/dining room 24
Children: Portions **Directions:** Nearest station: South Quay DLR, Canary Wharf From South Quay DLR, E down Marsh Wall to mini rdbt, turn left, over bridge then take 1st right **Parking:** On street

The Narrow

British NEW

Gordon Ramsay's inaugural waterside pub serving classic British dishes

☎ 020 7592 7950 44 Narrow St E14 8DP   Plan 1-G4
e-mail: thenarrow@gordonramsay.com
web: www.gordonramsay.com/thenarrow

Gordon Ramsay's first excursion into the pub market saw him open The Narrow on London's Limehouse back in April 2007. Set on the edge of the Thames, this Grade II listed building - formerly the dockmaster's house - commands wonderful river views. The ground floor is divided into a bar area, a relaxed section for eating, and a dining room. Sympathetic renovation has retained bags of character, with half-wall panelling, fireplaces and black-and-white vintage photography and prints. ('The Captain's Table' private dining room is on the first floor.) The food focuses on classic British dishes based around quality seasonal produce; take cock-a-leekie pie and mash, or perhaps braised Gloucestershire pig cheeks with mashed neeps.

Times: 11.30am-10.30pm

Plateau

Modern French 🖵

Sophisticated, contemporary fine-dining in futuristic landscape

☎ 020 7715 7100 Canada Place, Canada Square, Canary Wharf E14 5ER   Plan 9-B6
e-mail: plateau@conran-restaurants.co.uk
web: www.conran.com

This modern glass-and-steel restaurant is the epitome of contemporary style, overlooking Canada Square and its Manhattan-style skyline. A stunning complex with floor-to-ceiling glass frontage and two dining areas divided by a semi-open kitchen, each side with its own outside terrace and bar. The bustling Bar & Grill (offering a simpler menu) is first up, while the restaurant beyond offers a calmer atmosphere. The design mixes classic 1950s with warm, restrained colours and contemporary spin. Think white tulip-style swiveling chairs, marble-topped tables, swirling banquettes and huge floor-standing arching lamps. The menu follows the theme, with highly accomplished, clean-cut modern dishes driven by high-quality

ingredients and delivered dress to thrill. Expect dishes like monkfish wrapped in Parma ham with a fennel and tomato terrine. Service is slick and professional. (The restaurant is accessed via a lift from Canada Place shopping mall.)

Chef: Tim Tolley **Times:** 12-3/6-10.15, Closed 25-26 Dec, 1 Jan, BHs, Sun, Closed L Sat **Prices:** Fixed D £27, Starter £9.50-£15, Main £22-£30, Dessert £8, Service added but optional 12.5% **Wine:** All bottles over £20, 13 by the glass **Notes:** Tasting menu 5 courses £52 (£83 inc wine), Vegetarian menu, Dress Restrictions, Smart casual, Civ Wed 180, Air con **Seats:** 124, Pr/dining room 24 **Children:** Portions **Directions:** Nearest station: Canary Wharf Facing Canary Wharf Tower and Canada Square Park **Parking:** 200

Royal China

Traditional Chinese

Accomplished Chinese food with wonderful views of the river

☎ 020 7719 0888 Canary Wharf Riverside, 30 Westferry Circus E14 8RR Plan 9-A6
e-mail: info@royalchinagroup.co.uk
web: www.royalchinagroup.co.uk

An impressive glass-fronted building on the river's edge at Canary Wharf is the setting for this popular Chinese restaurant. The interior features lots of black and gold lacquering and crisp white linen. Head outside in summer for fantastic views and savour the wholesome, traditional Cantonese cooking, which makes the most of good ingredients. Dishes range from set meals and gourmet seafood including lobster to dim sum, cold appetisers, plenty of seafood, meat dishes, vegetables and bean curd. There's also a good selection of rice and noodle dishes.

Chef: Man Chau **Times:** Noon/11, Closed 23-25 Dec **Prices:** Fixed L £11, Fixed D £30, Starter £5.20-£6.20, Main £6.50-£30, Dessert £2.30-£4.20, Service added but optional 13% **Wine:** 85 bottles over £20, 7 bottles under £20, 2 by the glass **Notes:** Fixed D 2 courses, Vegetarian available, Air con **Seats:** 155, Pr/dining room 40 **Parking:** 2 mins away

Ubon by Nobu

Japanese, American 🖵

Swish celebrity hangout with an impeccable dining experience

☎ 020 7719 7800 34 Westferry Circus, Canary Wharf E14 8RR Plan 9-A6
e-mail: ubon@noburestaurants.com
web: www.noburestaurants.com

One of London's most fashionable restaurants, Ubon continues the exceptional fusion of stylish design, flawless service and innovative food that has made Nobu one of the hottest names in restaurant dining in the world. This chic Docklands restaurant, with an exceptional Thames-side location, has a panoramic view with floor-to-ceiling glass walls on three sides of the dining room. You can sample some truly cutting-edge cuisine that takes classic Japanese and adds a liberal sprinkling of South American tastes and textures with oodles of contemporary panache. Indulge your palate with dishes such as lobster with wasabi pepper sauce, perhaps sea urchin tempura, Chilean sea bass with moro miso, beef toban-yaki or anti-cucho Peruvian-style spicy rib-eye steak.

Chef: Nobuyuki Matsuhisa **Owners:** Nobuyuki Matsuhisa **Times:** 12-2/6-10, Closed BHs, Sun, Closed L Sat **Prices:** Fixed L £45-£50, Fixed D £80, Starter £5.50-£15, Main £12.50-£29, Dessert £7.50-£9, Service added 15% **Wine:** 60 bottles over £20, 7 by the glass **Notes:** Fixed L 5 courses, Fixed D 8 courses, Vegetarian available, Air con **Seats:** 120 **Directions:** Nearest station: Westferry, Canary Wharf Follow signs to Canary Wharf, then Canary Riverside. Restaurant behind Four Seasons Hotel **Parking:** Riverside car park

Carluccio's Caffè

☎ 020 7719 1749 2 Nash Court, Canary Wharf E14 5AG
Quality Italian chain.

Corney & Barrow at Canary Wharf

☎ 020 7512 0397 9 Cabot Square E14 4QF
City wine bar chain offering contemporary dishes.

LONDON E16

🖥 Yi-Ban

☎ 020 7473 6699 London Regatta Centre, Dockside Rd, Royal Albert Dock E16 2QT
web: www.theaa.com/travel/index.jsp
A large open Chinese restaurant with great river views. Gigantic menu of traditional dishes - emphasis on seafood.

LONDON EC1

◉◉ Ambassador

European NEW
Relaxed, super-friendly Clerkenwell dining

☎ 020 7837 0009 55 Exmouth Market EC1R 4QL
Plan 3-F5
e-mail: clive@theambassadorcafe.co.uk
web: www.theambassadorcafe.co.uk

This unassuming Exmouth Market newcomer on its trendy, bustling street proves a jewel in the Clerkenwell crown, with a focus on the friendliest of service and enjoyable cuisine at reasonable prices. Plainly decorated in magnolia, offset by the odd print or mirror, the long room comes decked out with dark green tables, simple wooden seating and crimson banquettes. A long bar struts its stuff along one wall, while glass doors open out on to the street with the bonus of outside, fair-weather seating. The kitchen's modern approach is assured and accomplished, and suits the surroundings; take chicken breast served with ceps, leeks and macaroni, or a warm chocolate pudding with almond ice cream to finish.

Chef: Tobias Jilsmark **Owners:** Clive & Stella Greenhalgh **Times:** 12-/6.30-12, Closed 1 wk Xmas, Closed D Sun **Prices:** Fixed L £12.50, Starter £4.50-£12, Main £5.50-£17, Dessert £5-£6, Service optional **Wine:** 49 bottles over £20, 29 bottles under £20, 14 by the glass **Notes:** Brunch served 11-4 Sat-Sun, Vegetarian available, Air con **Seats:** 65 **Children:** Menu, Portions **Directions:** Nearest station: Farringdon Take 1st right off Roseberry Av, heading N from Farringdon Rd junct. Turn right into Exmouth Market

◉ The Bleeding Heart

Modern French 🍷 NOTABLE WINE LIST
Discreet and hospitable Hatton Garden French restaurant

☎ 020 7242 2056 Bleeding Heart Yard, off Greville St EC1N 8SJ Plan 3-F4
e-mail: bookings@bleedingheart.co.uk
web: www.bleedingheart.co.uk

Behind the unusual name is a gruesome story: the Dickensian building stands on a cobbled courtyard where Lady Elizabeth Hatton was found murdered in the 17th century. The establishment comprises a tavern, bistro and restaurant, exuding atmosphere, with wooden floors and beams. The place buzzes with gallic charm, slick service and modern French cuisine. Outstanding fresh fish impresses in the form of herb-crusted John Dory, served with roasted salsify and watercress sauce, offered alongside classics like pan-fried foie gras with beetroot and herb salad, and Chateaubriand with sauce béarnaise. Desserts take in the likes of brochette of exotic fruit on French rice pudding, or warm chocolate pudding with vanilla ice cream.

Chef: Christophe Fabre **Owners:** Robert & Robyn Wilson **Times:** 12-3.15/6-11, Closed Xmas & New Year (10 days), Sat-Sun **Prices:** Fixed L £29.50, Fixed D £29.50, Starter £5.95-£9.95, Main £12.45-£22.95, Dessert £6.45, Service added but optional 12.5% **Wine:** 270 bottles over £20, 8 bottles under £20, 20 by the glass **Notes:** Fixed L 3 courses, Vegetarian available, Air con **Seats:** 110, Pr/dining room 40 **Children:** Min 7 yrs **Directions:** Nearest station: Farringdon Turn right out of Farringdon Station onto Cowcross St, continue down Greville St for 50mtrs. Turn left into Bleeding Heart Yard **Parking:** 20 evening only, NCP nearby

◉ Le Café du Marché

French
Welcoming French brasserie near the markets

☎ 020 7608 1609 Charterhouse Mews, Charterhouse Square EC1M 6AH Plan 3-G4
web: www.cafedumarche.co.uk

Tucked away down a cobbled mews, a short hop from several major markets, is this truly welcoming little brasserie. Friendly French staff add their bit to the authentic atmosphere, which comes undiluted from provincial France. Exposed bricks and beams, and closely packed tables, lend a cosy touch, and though it's usually packed with business people it doesn't feel overcrowded. The pick of the markets finds its way on to the fixed-price menus, where the freshest of fish, perhaps pan-fried marlin, and the hottest cuts of meat (rib of veal with morels maybe), are well matched by the day's soups, starters and desserts.

Chef: Simon Cottard **Owners:** Anna Graham-Wood **Times:** 12-2.30/6-10, Closed Xmas, New Year, Easter, BHs, Sun, Closed L Sat **Prices:** Fixed L £29.95, Fixed D £29.95, Service added but optional 15% **Notes:** Fixed L 3 courses, Air con **Seats:** 120, Pr/dining room 65 **Children:** Portions **Directions:** Nearest station: Barbican Telephone for directions (or see website) **Parking:** Next door (small charge)

ENGLAND

LONDON EC1 CONTINUED

◎◎ Clerkenwell Dining Room & Bar

Modern European

Relaxed fine dining in trendy Clerkenwell

☎ 020 7253 9000 69-73 St. John St EC1 4AN Plan 3-G4
e-mail: restaurant@theclerkenwell.com
web: www.theclerkenwell.com

Behind a blue and terracotta-red frontage, The Clerkenwell's interior surprises with its clean, warm tones and contemporary lines. White-clothed tables, black leather chairs and cream leather banquettes provide the comforts, while parquet floors, modern artwork and flamboyant flower displays catch the eye, combining with slick and professional service to create an upbeat mood and style. The ambition of the kitchen echoes the surroundings, its creatively presented, cultured and confident modern approach driven by quality produce; take lamb saddle served with tagliolini, mint, sweet pea emulsion and pea shoots, or perhaps halibut accompanied by baby squid with lemon and parsley, white coco bean purée and tomato and light curry sauce. (Also see sister restaurant, The Chancery, EC4.)

Chef: Andrew Thompson **Owners:** Zak Jones & Andrew Thompson **Times:** 12-3/6-11, Closed Xmas, BHs, Sun, Closed L Sat **Prices:** Fixed L £14.50, Fixed D £19.50, Starter £7-£10, Main £14.50-£17, Dessert £7-£8.50, Service added but optional 12.5% **Wine:** 13 bottles over £20, 5 bottles under £20, 6 by the glass **Notes:** Dress Restrictions, Smart casual, Air con **Seats:** 100, Pr/dining room 40 **Children:** Portions **Directions:** Nearest station: Farringdon, Barbican From Farringdon station, continue 60mtrs up Farringdon Rd, left into Cowcross St, left into Peters Ln, left into St John St **Parking:** On street (free after 6.30pm)

◎◎◎ Club Gascon

see below

◎ Le Comptoir Gascon

Traditional French

Bistro/deli serving classic French dishes

☎ 020 7608 0851 61-63 Charterhouse St EC1M 6HJ Plan 3-F4
e-mail: comptoirgascon@btconnect.com
web: www.comptoirgascon.com

Part of the Club Gascon collection, this small establishment opposite Smithfield Market comprises a bistro-style restaurant with around a dozen small tables and a deli serving quality takeaway items in the same room. The aim is to provide generous portions of traditional French food inspired by the South West of France in a setting that recreates easy-going country chic in the city. Many items are sourced directly from France. Don't miss the cassoulet, or try the Toulouse sausages and French fries cooked in duck fat. Prunes in Armagnac and nougat might feature at dessert. Booking is highly advisable.

Chef: Laurent Sanchis **Owners:** Vincent Labeyrie, Pascal Aussignac **Times:** 12-2/7-11, Closed 25 Dec, 1 Jan, Sun & Mon **Prices:** Starter £3.50-£9.50, Main £9.50-£16, Dessert £3.50-£5.50, Service added but optional 12.5% **Wine:** 14 bottles over £20, 3 bottles under £20, 8 by the glass **Seats:** 32 **Directions:** Nearest station: Farringdon, Barbican, St Paul's, Chancery Ln Telephone for directions, or see website

---

◎◎◎

Club Gascon

LONDON EC1

Modern French NOTABLE WINE LIST

With the cuisine of Gascony as its bedrock, this Smithfield stalwart has a huge following

☎ 020 7796 0600 57 West Smithfield EC1A 9DS Plan 3-G3
e-mail: info@clubgascon.com
web: www.clubgascon.com

With a location overlooking St Bart's hospital and the main entrance to Smithfield's market, this chic London restaurant is endowed with a rich sense of history in both its surroundings and the building it occupies - formerly a Lyons teahouse. A favourite spot for the fabled 'long lunch' of the City, you can expect to be greeted on arrival by stunning flower arrangements created by the chef himself, then drink in the marble-clad walls and old oak flooring in this small bustling dining room. Advance booking is imperative - as is confirming the booking; service from the smart, black-tied waiting staff can be unhurried so leave plenty of time to indulge.

The cuisine here has its roots in the French provincial cooking of Gascony - foie gras is a speciality with six versions of the venerable ingredient on the carte alone - and comes with a contemporary twist. All the ingredients are of the very best quality, painstakingly sourced from South West France; so expect the likes of Charolais beef fillet with pickled trompettes, oyster and crosnes, and to finish, perhaps 'Gold Sensation' - sweet foie gras, vanilla, candied chestnuts and gold martini. The extensive French wine list specialises in the South and South West of France.

Chef: Pascal Aussignac **Owners:** P Aussignac & V Labeyrie **Times:** 12-2/7-10, Closed Xmas, New Year, BHs, Sun, Closed L Sat **Prices:** Fixed D £35-£60, Starter £7.50-£55, Main £17-£23, Dessert £7.50-£17, Service added but optional 12.5% **Wine:** 101 bottles over £20, 3 bottles under £20, 9 by the glass **Notes:** Monthly 5 course tasting menu, Vegetarian available, Air con **Seats:** 45 **Children:** Portions **Directions:** Nearest station: Barbican or Farringdon Telephone for directions **Parking:** NCP opposite restaurant

⊛ *Malmaison Charterhouse Square*

Modern British, French

Boutique hotel with accessible, easy-going brasserie

☎ 020 7012 3700 18-21 Charterhouse Square, Clerkenwell EC1M 6AH Plan 3-G4
e-mail: london@malmaison.com
web: www.malmaison.com

An attractive red-brick Victorian building, once a nurses' residence for St Bart's, the hotel is set in a cobbled courtyard just off Charterhouse Square and shares the same high production values upheld by the other establishments in the Malmaison chain. In the buzzing brasserie-style restaurant tables are set on two levels, some in brick-backed alcoves. The menu offers mainly French cuisine delivered with simplicity, skill and fresh flavours throughout: a warm salad of chicken livers and pancetta, followed by sautéed monkfish cheeks and braised oxtail with herb risotto, and vanilla crème brûlée show the style.

Times: 12-2.30/6-10.30 **Rooms:** 97 (97 en suite) ★★★ HL

⊛⊛ Moro

Islamic, Mediterranean

Exotic fare from an open kitchen in the City

☎ 020 7833 8336 34/36 Exmouth Market EC1R 4QE Plan 3-F5
e-mail: info@moro.co.uk
web: www.moro.co.uk

High ceilings, round pillars and a simple understated style - think unclothed tables and polished wooden floor - make the long zinc bar all the more striking at this expansive Clerkenwell restaurant, with its open-view kitchen and lively, relaxed atmosphere. Tapas is served all day at the bar, and the kitchen's unpretentious approach suits the surroundings, with food cooked on the charcoal grill or wood-burning oven. Dishes generally explore something less familiar, with the robust flavours of Spain and the exotic spices of North Africa and the Middle East. So expect the likes of charcoal grilled lamb served with tomato bulgar, grilled peppers, yogurt and allspice, and perhaps Malaga raisin ice cream with Pedro Ximenez to finish.

Chef: Samuel & Samantha Clark **Owners:** Mr & Mrs S Clark & Mark Sainsbury **Times:** 12.30-2.30/7-10.30, Closed Xmas, New Year, BHs, Sun **Prices:** Starter £6-£7.50, Main £14.50-£17.50, Dessert £5-£5.50, Group min 6 service 12.5% **Wine:** 45 bottles over £20, 11 bottles under £20, 11 by the glass **Seats:** 90, Pr/dining room 14 **Children:** Portions
Directions: Nearest station: Farringdon or Angel 5 mins walk from Sadler's Wells theatre, between Farringdon Road and Rosebery Ave **Parking:** NCP Farringdon Rd

⊛⊛ Rudland & Stubbs

Fish NEW

City-based fish and seafood restaurant

☎ 020 7253 0148 35-37 Green Hill Rants, Cowcross St EC1M 6BN Plan 3-G4
e-mail: reservations@rudlandstubbs.co.uk
web: www.rudlandstubbs.co.uk

After a refit, new owners relaunched this long-established Clerkenwell fish restaurant and bar back in 2006, set in a one-time sausage factory a stone's throw from Smithfield Market. Cream tile work, wooden floors and high ceilings are among original features retained, while marble-topped tables, wooden chairs, retro lighting and friendly, relaxed service add to its appeal as a welcoming neighbourhood eatery. The menu is almost exclusively fish, delivering colourful and well-presented dishes that combine the traditional alongside the more adventurous. Take miso-glazed tuna with bean sprouts, gai lang and pickle, or pan-fried baby turbot, braised oxtail, summer greens and saffron.

Chef: Konrad Ingelrahm **Owners:** Raymond De Fazio **Times:** 12-3/6-10.30, Closed Xmas 1 week, BHs, Sat, Sun **Prices:** Starter £4.50-£7.50, Main £9.50-£14.95, Dessert £5.50, Service added but optional 12.5%
Wine: 90 bottles over £20, 12 bottles under £20, 16 by the glass **Seats:** 70
Directions: Nearest station: Farringdon Next to Smithfield Market
Parking: Smithfield NCP & on street

⊛⊛ St John

British

The best of British nose-to-tail cooking

☎ 020 7251 0848 26 St John St EC1M 4AY Plan 3-G4
e-mail: reservations@stjohnrestaurant.com
web: www.stjohnrestaurant.com

Fergus Henderson's stark, utilitarian-styled former smokehouse sits across the road from Smithfield Market and continues to draw the crowds. Upstairs, above the bustling bar and bakery, the high-ceilinged dining room is an equally pared-down affair of coat-hook-lined white walls, white-painted floorboards, white paper-clothed tables and wooden café-style chairs, set in serried ranks that echo the rows of industrial-style lights above. The kitchen's open to view, staff are knowledgeable, friendly and relaxed, in tune with the robust, honest, simplistic, bold-flavoured British food that utilises the whole animal. Menus change twice daily and there's plenty of humble ingredients; think roast bone marrow and parsley salad, perhaps tripe and chips or beef and squash, or bread pudding and butterscotch sauce. (See also Spitalfields spin-off, St John Food & Wine.)

Chef: Christopher Gillard **Owners:** T Gulliver & F Henderson **Times:** 12-3/6-11, Closed Xmas, New Year, Easter BH, Sun, Closed L Sat
Prices: Starter £5.80-£12.80, Main £12.80-£28, Dessert £6.20-£7.40, Service optional, Group min 6 service 12.5% **Wine:** 30 bottles over £20, 30 bottles under £20, 25 by the glass **Seats:** 100, Pr/dining room 18
Directions: Nearest station: Farringdon 100yds from Smithfield Market, northside **Parking:** Meters in street

ENGLAND

LONDON EC1 CONTINUED

◉◉ Smiths of Smithfield

Modern British
Impressive warehouse conversion in Smithfield Meat Market

☎ 020 7251 7950 (Top Floor), 67-77 Charterhouse St EC1M 6HJ Plan 3-F4
e-mail: reservations@smithsofsmithfield.co.uk
web: www.smithsofsmithfield.co.uk

Boasting views over the City and St Paul's Cathedral, this Grade II listed four-floor restaurant is situated in London's Smithfield Meat Market. The building was empty for over 40 years before being converted by the Smiths team and is now a popular and stylish dining venue. Original brick walls, reclaimed timber and steel all add to the ambience, with each floor having its own individual style. This also extends to the food, which offers something to suit every pocket and occasion. The menu in the Top Floor restaurant includes luxury ingredients like Irish rock oysters and caviar, as well as the best aged steaks. For mains, try venison Wellington with spinach and juniper sauce.

Times: 12-3.30/6.30-12, Closed 25-26 Dec, 1 Jan, Closed L Sat
Directions: Nearest station: Farringdon, Barbican, Chancery Lane Opposite Smithfield Meat Market

Alba

☎ 020 7588 1798 107 Whitecross St EC1Y 8JD

Contemporary Italian within a short walk of the Barbican. The generous carte is supplemented by daily specials.

Carluccio's Caffè

☎ 020 7329 5904 12 West Smithfield EC1A 9JR

Quality Italian chain.

💻 Cicada

☎ 020 7608 1550 132-136 St John St, Farringdon EC1V 4JT
web: www.theaa.com/travel/index.jsp

A trendy bar-restaurant in fashionable Clerkenwell, serving great Pan Asian dishes from an open-plan kitchen.

💻 Fish Shop on St John Street

☎ 020 7837 1199 360-362 St John St EC1V 4NR
web: www.theaa.com/travel/index.jsp

A modern, minimalist take on that old British favourite, the chippy. Try the deep-fried fish of the day (in batter, egg or matzo meal) and chips, or something more adventurous. The menu consists solely of fish and shellfish fresh from Billingsgate Market, and changes daily.

💻 The Peasant

☎ 020 7336 7726 240 St John St, Clerkenwell EC1V 4PH
web: www.theaa.com/travel/index.jsp

One of the original gastro-pubs, The Peasant has a beautiful first-floor restaurant, with soaring ceilings and huge windows looking out over Clerkenwell and the City University. Terrific vegetarian options.

💻 Sofra - Exmouth Market

☎ 020 7833 1111 19-21 Exmouth Market EC1R 4QD
web: www.theaa.com/travel/index.jsp

A sister restaurant to Ozer in Langham Place, offering a similar mix of modern and traditional Turkish dishes.

💻 Strada

☎ 020 7278 0800 8-10 Exmouth Market EC1R 4QA
web: www.theaa.com/travel/index.jsp

Superior pizza from quality ingredients cooked in wood-fired ovens.

Yo! Sushi

☎ 020 7841 0785 95 Farringdon Rd EC1R 3BT

Sushi, sashimi, noodles and more delivered by conveyor belt and priced according to colour-coded plates.

LONDON EC2

◉◉◉ Aurora at Great Eastern Hotel
see opposite

◉ Boisdale of Bishopsgate

Traditional 💻
A great taste of Scotland in the heart of the City

☎ 020 7283 1763 Swedeland Court, 202 Bishopsgate EC2M 4NR Plan 7-C5
e-mail: katie@boisdale-city.co.uk
web: www.boisdale.co.uk

Set down a narrow Dickensian alley off Bishopsgate, Boisdale oozes character. Like its Belgravia sister venture, it comes decked out in patriotic Scottish style with a buzzy, clubby atmosphere. The ground floor is a traditional champagne and oyster bar, while the restaurant and piano bar are in the cellar downstairs. Vibrant red-painted brick walls laden with pictures and mirrors, tartan carpet or dark floorboards, leather banquettes and tartan or leather chairs all create a moody, upbeat atmosphere. The Caledonian menu supports the theme, the kitchen's approach driven by traditional, high-quality north-of-the-border produce. Think Speyside Angus beef steaks, Macsween haggis, Lochcarnan hot-smoked salmon or Shetland Isle scallops.

Chef: Neil Churchill **Owners:** Ranald Macdonald **Times:** 11-3/6-12, Closed Xmas, 31 Dec, BHs, Sat & Sun **Prices:** Fixed L £17.80, Fixed D £29.50-£37.50, Starter £5.65-£16.50, Main £12.15-£26.50, Dessert £6, Service added but optional 12.5% **Wine:** 106 bottles over £20, 21 bottles under £20, 16 by the glass **Notes:** Dress Restrictions, Smart casual, Air con **Seats:** 100 **Directions:** Nearest station: Liverpool Street Opposite Liverpool St station **Parking:** Middlesex St

---

Aurora at Great Eastern Hotel

LONDON EC2

Modern European 📖

Modern cooking with flair in a dramatic setting

☎ 020 7618 7000 Liverpool St EC2M 7QN Plan 6-C5
e-mail: aurorareception.longe@hyattintl.com
web: www.aurora-restaurant.com

Set within the chic, designer City hotel adjacent to Liverpool Street station, Aurora is a stunning, palatial Victorian dining room dominated by a majestic stained-glass dome, while ceilings also reach lofty cathedral height and there are pillars and high-arched windows. Billowing voiles in deep red and grey and enormous, striking funky chandeliers keep things contemporary while making the most of the original architecture. A stylish, brushed-steel bar lines one side of the room, while service is knowledgeable, slick and professional. The kitchen's modern European approach - underpinned by a classical theme - is delivered via an appealing range of menus that make the best of tip-top seasonal produce. Exciting dishes of flair, imagination and flavour fit the fine-dining City bill; take poached pork loin and confit belly with carrot and cumin and roasting juices, and to finish, perhaps a pistachio soufflé with pistachio ice cream and chocolate sauce. There's the addition of a daily lunchtime carving trolley - of imposing dimensions - serving more traditional roasts, plus a seven-course dégustation option, excellent breakfasts for early-morning business meetings, and big-hitting wine list to complete the slick package.

Chef: Dominic Teague **Owners:** Hyatt **Times:** 12-2.30/6.45-10, Closed Xmas, New Year, BHs, Sat-Sun **Prices:** Fixed L £23.50, Starter £10-£14, Main £18-£32, Dessert £6.50-£11.50, Service added but optional 12.5%
Wine: 11 bottles under £20, 12 by the glass **Notes:** Civ Wed 160, Air con
Seats: 100 **Rooms:** 267 (267 en suite) ★★★★★ HL
Directions: Nearest station: Liverpool Street Telephone for directions
Parking: NCP

◉◉ Bonds

Modern French ◉ NOTABLE WINE LIST 📖

A grand setting for some slick modern cooking

☎ 020 7657 8088 & 7657 8090 Threadneedles,
5 Threadneedle St EC2R 8AY Plan 6-B4
e-mail: bonds@theetongroup.com
web: www.bonds-restaurant.com

Built to imperious Victorian specifications, this grand dining room retains many features recognisable from its days as a financial institution. The client base is strictly city business folk with generous expense accounts, and the menu is succinctly scripted, studded with luxury produce and shows clear aspiration from a talented kitchen. A good-value lighter lunch is offered, while the carte lifts quality, technique and pricing accordingly. Try ravioli of lobster with Armagnac bisque, or Dorset crab with smoked salmon, crème fraîche and Oscietra caviar, followed by roast duck with caramelised red onion tart Tatin, fondue of gem lettuce and Madeira jus, or roast cod, scallops and octopus daube, confit celeriac and potato purée, with banana and caramel parfait and passionfruit sorbet to finish.

Chef: Barry Tonks **Owners:** The Eton Collection **Times:** 12-2.30/6-10, Closed 2 wks Xmas, 4 days Etr & BHs, Sat, Sun **Prices:** Fixed L £19.50, Starter £7.50-£15.50, Main £15.50-£23, Dessert £5.50-£6.50, Service added but optional 12.5% **Wine:** 137 bottles over £20, 11 bottles under £20, 18 by the glass **Notes:** Vegetarian available, Dress Restrictions, Smart casual, Air con **Seats:** 80, Pr/dining room 16 **Parking:** London Wall NCP

◉◉ Eyre Brothers

Spanish, Portuguese 📖

Lively Iberian dining in trendy Shoreditch

☎ 020 7613 5346 70 Leonard St EC2A 4QX Plan 7-B2
e-mail: eyrebros@btconnect.com
web: www.eyrebrothers.co.uk

Tucked away down a long street of reclaimed Shoreditch loft buildings, this gem is just a short hike from Old Street and Liverpool Street stations. The plate glass windows and smart sign offer a hint of what is inside, but the sharp metropolitan blend of dark wood, cool leather and long trendy bar are still a welcome surprise. It's a place for relaxed business lunches, for groups of friends to spread out and feel at home, and there are quiet spots for more discreet get-togethers. Authentic Portuguese regional cooking and classic Spanish cuisine combine effortlessly to achieve bold rustic dishes with big flavours and lively colours: grilled Mozambique tiger prawn piri-piri with pilaf rice fits the bill nicely. Attentive staff encourage the mood.

Chef: Dave Eyre, Joao Cleto **Owners:** Eyre Bros Restaurants Ltd
Times: 12-3/6.30-11, Closed Xmas-New Year, BHs, Sun, Closed L Sat
Prices: Starter £6-£16, Main £12-£24, Dessert £6-£7, Service optional
Wine: 40 bottles over £20, 13 bottles under £20, 6 by the glass **Seats:** 100
Parking: On street, 2 car parks on Leonard St

ENGLAND

LONDON EC2 CONTINUED

◎◎ Fishmarket

Modern European, Seafood 🖥️

Enjoyable seafood dining in a city hotel

☎ 020 7618 7200 Great Eastern Hotel, Liverpool St EC2M 7QN Plan 6-C5

e-mail: restaurantres.longe@hyattintl.com

web: london.greateastern.hyatt.com

This trendy seafood restaurant is located in an elegant marble-clad corner of the Great Eastern Hotel. A wide selection of fresh and saltwater fish is offered plus an award-winning wine list. The centrepiece is the attractive display of fish and the 'altar' where chefs prepare crustacea in front of diners. The Champagne Bar, dominated by a mosaic-covered horseshoe bar, has an extensive list of Champagnes, including some rare vintages, and serves favourite dishes from the restaurant menu. These might include crab and pickled mackerel spring roll or escabèche of Cornish sardines, followed by black bass with olive mash, aubergine and snakebean cannelloni and sauce vièrge, or crisp fried sea bream with globe artichokes, girolles, truffle and cauliflower purée, and pesto sauce.

Chef: Stuart Lyall **Owners:** Hyatt **Times:** 12-2.30/6-10.30, Closed Xmas, New Year, BHs, Sun, Closed L Sat **Prices:** Starter £6.75-£14.75, Main £12.75-£32, Dessert £6-£7.50, Service added but optional 12.5% **Wine:** 95% bottles over £20, 5% bottles under £20, 8 by the glass **Seats:** 96 **Directions:** Nearest station: Liverpool Street Please telephone for directions **Parking:** NCP

◎ Great Eastern Dining Room

Pan Asian 🖥️

High-octane Asian-style eatery

☎ 020 7613 4545 54 Great Eastern St EC2A 3QR Plan 7-B2

e-mail: martyn@thediningrooms.com

web: www.greateasterndining.co.uk

A trendy, buzzy, contemporary bar-restaurant in the vibrant, gritty, up-and-coming City extremities. It gets packed even on mid-week evenings, so don't expect much space at your paper-clad table. Service is relaxed with knowledgeable staff, while darkwood walls and floors, leather seating and funky chandeliers reign alongside high decibels. A well-executed Pan-Asian menu - based on the grazing concept and ideal for sharing - delivers on presentation and flavour. From dim sum to sashimi, curries to barbecues and roasts or house specials; think black cod with sweet miso, perhaps an aubergine and lychee green curry, or coconut and pandon pannacotta dessert.

Times: 12-3/6-10.30, Closed Xmas & Etr, Sun, Closed L Sat

◎ Mehek

Indian 🖥️

Modern Indian dining with innovative and classic dishes in stylish surroundings

☎ 020 7588 5043 & 7588 5044 45 London Wall, Moorgate EC2M 5TE Plan 7-B5

e-mail: info@mehek.co.uk

web: www.mehek.co.uk

Tardis-like, Mehek opens out from an inconspicuous entrance in a row of shops into several stylish eating areas. A long, glamorous bar draws in the local office crowd post work, while discreet lighting, smartly dressed tables and genuinely interested waiters make it easy to linger over a meal. The food is a modern take on Northern Indian traditional dishes, though the creative kitchen team bring in classics from other parts of the subcontinent as well. You'll find biryanis, kormas and pasandas, but also the likes of duck in a coconut and peanut sauce, and lots of novel seafood choices.

Chef: A Matlib **Owners:** Salim B Rashid **Times:** 11.30-3/5.30-11, Closed Xmas, New Year, BHs, Sat-Sun **Prices:** Fixed L £12.50-£17.90, Fixed D £24.50-£28.50, Starter £3.20-£10.90, Main £6.90-£18.90, Dessert £2.95-£4.95, Service added but optional 10% **Wine:** 19 bottles over £20, 11 bottles under £20, 9 by the glass **Notes:** Fixed L 5 courses, Fixed D 8 courses, Vegetarian available, Dress Restrictions, Smart casual, Air con **Seats:** 120 **Directions:** Nearest station: Moorgate/Liverpool St Nearby Moorgate Station, close to junct of Moorgate and London Wall **Parking:** On street, NCP

◎◎◎ Rhodes Twenty Four

see opposite

◎ Rivington Bar & Grill

British V 🖥️

Straightforward, best of British classics in buzzy setting

☎ 020 7729 7053 28-30 Rivington St EC2A 3DZ Plan 7-B2

e-mail: shoreditch@rivingtongrill.co.uk

web: www.rivingtongrill.co.uk

A combined restaurant, bar and deli, this buzzy place is tucked away down a narrow side street in fashionable Hoxton. White walls and wooden floors make for a suitably relaxed backdrop to a parade of simple, confident, seasonal, no-frills modern British cooking using top-notch produce. Think roast Lancashire suckling pig with greens and quince sauce, or fish fingers and chips with mushy peas, while comforting desserts might feature Bakewell tart with vanilla ice cream. Nice touches include chips served in little buckets and your own small loaf of bread. (Also sibling establishment in Greenwich, see entry.)

Chef: Damian Clisby **Owners:** Caprice-Holdings Ltd **Times:** 12-3/6.30-11, Closed Xmas & New Year, Closed L Sat **Prices:** Starter £5.25-£12.75, Main £9.25-£25.50, Dessert £4.50-£10.50, Service added but optional 12.5% **Wine:** 40 bottles over £20, 8 bottles under £20, 8 by the glass **Notes:** Sun L 3 courses £22.50, Vegetarian menu, Air con **Seats:** 85, Pr/dining room 27 **Directions:** Nearest station: Old St/Liverpool St Telephone for directions **Parking:** On street

⊛ *Tatsuso Restaurant*

Japanese
Authentic City oriental

☎ 020 7638 5863 32 Broadgate Circle EC2M 2QS
Plan 6-C5

This slick, glass-fronted, atmospheric, two-tier City Japanese - on the lower level of Broadgate Circle - comes brimming with corporate suits, professional service and clean modern lines. Lightwood furniture and screens set the scene with waitresses in traditional Japanese dress. On the ground floor there's the theatre of the teppan-yaki grill to enjoy, where lobster, Dover sole and sirloin with foie gras tempt, while in the basement, a lengthy, authentic carte and sushi menu reign in a more relaxed atmosphere. You will find quality ingredients, plentiful set-menu options and City prices.

Times: 11.45-2.45/6.30-10.15, Closed Xmas, New Year, BHs, Sat-Sun
Directions: Nearest station: Liverpool Street. Ground floor of Broadgate Circle

Corney & Barrow at Broadgate Circle
☎ 020 7628 1251 19 Broadgate Circle EC2M 2QS
Wine bar offshoot from famous wine merchants.

Corney & Barrow at Citypoint
☎ 020 7382 0606 1 Ropemaker St EC2Y 9AW
Wine bar offshoot from famous wine merchants.

Corney & Barrow at Exchange Square
☎ 020 7628 4367 5 Exchange Square EC2A 2EH
Wine bar offshoot from famous wine merchants.

Corney & Barrow at Mason's Avenue
☎ 020 7726 6030 12 Mason's Av EC2V 5BT
City wine bar chain offering contemporary dishes.

Corney & Barrow at Old Broad Street
☎ 020 7638 9308 111 Old Broad St EC2N 1AP
Wine bar offshoot from famous wine merchants.

The Fox Dining Room
☎ 020 7729 5708 28 Paul St EC2A 4LB
Rustic, unfussy food in a restaurant designed to create the impression of a 1950s municipal library.

Wagamama
☎ 020 7256 9992 22 Old Broad St EC2N 1HQ
Informal noodle bar with no booking required.

Wagamama
☎ 020 7588 2688 1a Ropemaker St EC2V 9AW
Informal noodle bar with no booking required.

⊛⊛⊛

Rhodes Twenty Four

LONDON EC2

Modern British 🖼
Truly classic Rhodes cuisine overlooking the City

☎ 020 7877 7703 Tower 42, Old Broad St EC2N 1HQ
Plan 6-C5
web: www.rhodes24.co.uk

This ear-poppingly high restaurant is set on the 24th floor of the tallest building in the Square Mile, with stunning take-your-breath-away views over London by day or night. The sophisticated operation has its own bar (with seats naturally facing away from it to take in those views), while the dining room comes dressed in its best white linen armed with stylish appointments, where all tables enjoy the spectacular panoramas.
Service is slick and friendly, with good attention paid to wine, while the cuisine is Gary's hallmark modern British with a twist, as you'd expect. Impeccable ingredients, crystal-clear flavours, perfect balance and sharp presentation parade on exciting dishes. Clearly defined menus might feature roast beef fillet with red wine onions, oxtail hash and poached egg béarnaise, or perhaps steamed fillet of brill served with crayfish tails and buttered leeks, and to finish, it has to be the bread-and-butter pudding.
And do leave time for security check-in at this important tower block.

(Rhodes W1 Restaurant - and sister Rhodes W1 Brasserie - are new Gary Rhodes ventures at the Cumberland Hotel, Marble Arch.)

Chef: Gary Rhodes, Adam Gray **Owners:** Restaurant Associates
Times: 12-2.30/6-9, Closed BHs, Xmas, Sat-Sun **Prices:** Starter £8.20-£16.50, Main £17.50-£24, Dessert £8.50-£10.50, Service added but optional
Wine: 10 by the glass **Notes:** Vegetarian available, Dress Restrictions, No ripped jeans or dirty trainers, Air con **Seats:** 75 **Children:** Portions
Directions: Nearest station: Bank/Liverpool Street Telephone for directions, see website **Parking:** On street

ENGLAND

LONDON EC3

◎◎ Addendum

Modern European NEW 💻

Skilled modern cooking in slick, boutique hotel

☎ 020 7977 9500 & 7702 2020 Apex City of London Hotel, No 1 Seething Ln EC3N 4AX Plan 6-C4
e-mail: reservations@addendumrestaurant.co.uk
web: www.addendumrestaurant.co.uk

The modern, yet elegant restaurant, Addendum, contributes to the overall cutting-edge design at this new City hotel. Think dark chocolate-coloured fixtures and fittings, amber lighting, clever use of mirrors, leather seats and booths, and tables turned out in their best whites, while service is slick from a friendly team of equally impeccably presented staff. Skilled, passionate cooking focusing on stunning ingredients, seasonality and crisp, clear flavours is the kitchen's style. Menus offer real value and quality, with classic dishes benefiting from modern twists, and there's plenty of luxury too.

Chef: Darren Thomas **Owners:** Norman Springford **Times:** 12-2.30/6-9.30, Closed 23 Dec-3 Jan, BHs, Sat-Sun **Prices:** Fixed L £21.95, Starter £7.75-£12.50, Main £16.75-£21.50, Dessert £7.50, Service added but optional 12.5% **Wine:** 78 bottles over £20, 2 bottles under £20, 11 by the glass **Notes:** Dress Restrictions, Smart casual, Air con **Seats:** 65, Pr/dining room 50 **Rooms:** 130 (130 en suite) ★★★★ HL **Directions:** Nearest station: Tower Hill, Fenchurch Street Follow Lower Thames St, left onto Trinity Square, left onto Muscovy St, right onto Seething Ln, opposite Seething Ln gardens **Parking:** Car park in Lower Thames St

◎◎ Chamberlains Restaurant

Modern British, Seafood 💻

Market-fresh fish beloved of city slickers

☎ 020 7648 8690 23/25 Leadenhall Market EC3V 1LR
Plan 6-C4
e-mail: info@chamberlains.org

Colourful Leadenhall Market, thronging with City workers at midday and early evening, makes a relaxed setting for this seafood restaurant. It sits beneath the restored Victorian glass roof of the old market, alongside the cobbled walkway, with excellent views of the exquisite architecture from the first floor and mezzanine dining areas. You can also eat more casually in the basement wine bar, or bag a table outside on warmer days. Fish from owners Chamberlain and Thelwell (suppliers to the trade) is delivered right up to opening times, with freshness guaranteed. Try a starter of lobster bisque with collops of lobster and chopped dill, followed by sesame-seared tuna with caponata and grilled Mediterranean vegetables. There's plenty of meat too, though the speciality fish and chips remains popular.

Chef: Glen Watson **Owners:** Chamberlain & Thelwell **Times:** 12/9.30, Closed Xmas, New Year & BHs, Sat & Sun **Prices:** Fixed D £19.95, Starter £6.50-£15, Main £19-£35, Dessert £7.50, Service optional **Wine:** 60 bottles over £20, 10 bottles under £20, 8 by the glass **Notes:** Vegetarian available, Air con **Seats:** 150, Pr/dining room 65 **Children:** Portions
Directions: Nearest station: Bank and Monument Telephone for directions

◎◎ 1 Lombard Street - Fine Dining Restaurant

Modern 💻

Bank on sophisticated dining at luxurious prices

☎ 020 7929 6611 1 Lombard St EC3V 9AA Plan 6-B4
e-mail: hb@1lombardstreet.com
web: www.1lombardstreet.com

In the shadow of the Bank of England, 1 Lombard Street is a sleek City operation. A former City banking hall, it combines a neo-classical interior with contemporary design and neutral colours. There's a buzzy, informal brasserie with circular bar and domed skylight up front, while the intimate, discreet, fine-dining restaurant at the rear is the luxury focus of the enterprise. Here a classical backdrop - think Titian's Rape of Europa - sets the stage for the elegant décor and furnishings. Like the restaurant's surroundings, the food is unashamedly expensive, the appealing repertoire dotted with luxury and sophistication, with the kitchen's modern approach - underpinned by a classical French theme - delivering high quality in refined, well-presented, clear-flavoured dishes of precision and flair. A mignon of veal served with a green pea compôte à la Française, autumn truffles, girolles and a Chablis velouté shows the style.

Chef: Herbet Berger **Owners:** Jessen & Co **Times:** 12-2.30/6-10, Closed Xmas, New Year, BHs, Sat-Sun, Closed D 24 Dec **Prices:** Food prices not confirmed for 2008. Please telephone for details **Wine:** 186 bottles over £20, 3 bottles under £20, 13 by the glass **Notes:** Air con **Seats:** 40, Pr/dining room 40 **Directions:** Nearest station: Bank Opposite Bank of England **Parking:** NCP Cannon Street

◎◎ Prism Restaurant and Bar

Modern International 🏆NOTABLE WINE LIST 💻

Eclectic dining opposite Leadenhall Market

☎ 020 7256 3888 147 Leadenhall St EC3V 4QT
Plan 6-C4
web: www.harveynichols.com

The Square Mile houses several restaurants, but few as impressive as this one. Once the Bank of New York, its lofty ceiling and vast spaces make a palatial backdrop for fine dining. For a more discreet experience there is the Conservatory, separated from the main restaurant and ideal for meals à deux. The menu offers a lively choice of dishes inspired from around the globe, with the accent on detail and flavour. Starters like ballontine of rabbit, date and Parma ham, with a rabbit velouté and celeriac remoulade make a punchy prelude to chargrilled swordfish, borlotti bean and sweet pepper ragout, with chorizo-stuffed baby squid. Harvey Nichols quality is stamped throughout.

ENGLAND

Chef: Jonathan Warner **Owners:** Harvey Nichols **Times:** 11.30-3/6-10, Closed 25 Dec, BHs, Sat & Sun **Prices:** Starter £8-£14, Main £18-£24, Dessert £7.45, Service added but optional 12.5% **Wine:** 412 bottles over £20, 4 bottles under £20, 20 by the glass **Seats:** 120, Pr/dining room 40 **Children:** Portions **Directions:** Nearest station: Bank and Monument Please telephone for directions **Parking:** On street & NCP

◎◎ Restaurant Sauterelle

French

Stylish French cuisine inside the Royal Exchange building

☎ 020 7618 2483 The Royal Exchange EC3V 3LR
Plan 6-B4
e-mail: alessandrop@danddlondon.com
web: www.danddlondon.com/restaurants/sauterelle/home

Set on the first-floor mezzanine of the Royal Exchange, Restaurant Sauterelle overlooks the bustling courtyard interior, where the Grand Café and many world-famous jewellers and retailers ply their trade. The atmosphere is fittingly chic, while service is correspondingly efficient, welcoming and professional. The carefully prepared, straightforward but classy, classic regional French cuisine uses the freshest produce from the markets and sits well with the surroundings. Typically, start with rock oysters with champagne velouté, follow with suprême of halibut with a fricassée of wild mushrooms, sauce verte and fresh truffles, or perhaps Chateaubriand steak with roast field mushroom and béarnaise sauce, and finish with pear tart Tatin with crème fraîche.

Chef: Darren Kerley **Owners:** D & D London **Times:** 12-2.30/6-10, Closed BHs, Sat & Sun **Prices:** Fixed L £35-£50, Starter £5-£12, Main £16.50-£21.50, Dessert £5.50, Service added but optional 12.5% **Wine:** 50 bottles over £20, 9 bottles under £20, 8 by the glass **Notes:** Vegetarian available, Air con **Seats:** 66, Pr/dining room 20 **Children:** Portions **Directions:** Nearest station: Bank In heart of business centre. Bank tube station exit 4

Corney & Barrow at Jewry Street

☎ 020 7680 8550 37A Jewry St EC3N 2EX

City wine bar chain offering contemporary dishes.

Corney & Barrow at Monument

☎ 020 7929 3220 2B Eastcheap EC3M 1AB

Wine bar offshoot from famous wine merchants.

🖳 Just Gladwins

☎ 020 7444 0004 Minster Court, Mark Ln, Tower Hill EC3R 7AA
web: www.theaa.com/travel/index.jsp

A stylish basement dining room, with plenty of space between the tables. The menu is internationally inspired and the ice cream home made.

🖳 Kasturi

☎ 020 7480 7402 57 Aldgate High St EC3N 1AL
web: www.theaa.com/travel/index.jsp

One of a chain of Indian restaurants offering Pakhtoon cuisine - a healthier variety of Indian dishes.

🖳 Ruskin's

☎ 020 7680 1234 60 Mark Ln, Tower Hill EC3R 7NE
web: www.theaa.com/travel/index.jsp

City bar and restaurant housed in an old rum importer's, built in 1864. A friendly, professional atmosphere, it's busy with City boys at lunchtime.

LONDON EC4

◎◎ *The Chancery*

Modern European 🖳

Enjoyable brasserie-style dining in legal land

☎ 020 7831 4000 9 Cursitor St EC4A 1LL Plan 3-E3
e-mail: reservations@thechancery.co.uk
web: www.thechancery.co.uk

This aptly named, intimate, modern, glass-fronted restaurant (sibling to the Clerkenwell Dining Room, see entry) comes secreted away close to Lincoln's Inn and Chancery Lane, set among the narrow streets and historic buildings of the law community. Contemporary black leather chairs and white linen blend seamlessly with polished mahogany floors, black woodwork and white walls hung with mirrors and modern abstract art. There's a bar downstairs, while the dining space - split into two sections with arched openings - is as modern, crisp, confident and clean-cut as the well-executed cooking. Expect the likes of roast monkfish with chorizo, razor clams and saffron emulsion, or perhaps fillet of beef served with oxtail tortellini, Savoy cabbage and Madeira jus to feature on the value, fixed-price menus.

Times: 12-2.30/6-10.30, Closed Xmas, Sat-Sun **Directions:** Nearest station: Chancery Lane Situated between High Holborn and Fleet St

LONDON EC4 CONTINUED

◎◎ Refettorio

Italian 🖥

Authentic Italian concept in chic surroundings

☎ 020 7438 8052 Crowne Plaza Hotel, 19 New Bridge St EC4V 6DB Plan 3-F2

e-mail: loncy.refettorio@ichotelsgroup.com

web: www.refettorio.com

Sleek, stylish and contemporary, Refettorio blends comfortably with the swish modernism of the Crowne Plaza Hotel. The L-shaped room has a long bar, high windows hung with Venetian blinds and polished-wood floors and tables. Smart, brown leather booth-style seating provides discreet dining along one wall, while young black-clad staff are suitably attentive. Authentic Italian food; excellent breads, a superb array of impeccably-sourced regional cheeses, hams and salamis, home-made pasta and an all-Italian wine list provide the impressive backdrop to an appealing menu of straightforward but accomplished and well-presented dishes. Start with selection of cured meats and cheeses followed by steamed sea bass with fennel salad and lemon perhaps.

Chef: Mattia Camorani **Owners:** Parallel/Crowne Plaza **Times:** 12-2.30/6-10.30, Closed Xmas, New Year & BHs, Sun, Closed L Sat **Prices:** Fixed L £45-£65, Fixed D £45-£65, Starter £7.50-£10, Main £8.50-£22, Dessert £6.50-£7, Service added but optional 12.5% **Wine:** 7 bottles under £20, 10 by the glass **Notes:** Fixed L 3 courses, Pre Theatre D 3 courses £20, Vegetarian available, Dress Restrictions, Smart casual, Civ Wed 100, Air con **Seats:** 70, Pr/dining room 30 **Children:** Portions **Directions:** Nearest station: Blackfriars Situated on New Bridge St, opposite Blackfriars underground (exit 8) **Parking:** NCP - Queen Victoria St

◎ The White Swan Pub & Dining Room

Modern, Traditional British 🖥

Busy, upmarket gastro-pub with a smart dining room

☎ 020 7242 9696 108 Fetter Ln EC4A 1ES Plan 3-F3

e-mail: info@thewhiteswanlondon.com

web: www.thewhiteswanlondon.com

Beyond the bar of this tastefully restored pub is a mezzanine area, available for drinks parties, and a formal first-floor dining room. Decked out with white-clothed tables, its handsome wooden floors, contemporary chairs, banquettes and mirrored ceiling cut an upmarket edge. Friendly, attentive and relaxed French service adds to the experience. The menu combines classics alongside more esoteric dishes; think braised rabbit tortellini with cep foam and vichy carrots, or red wine braised monkfish cheeks with gremolata mash and deep-fried leeks. Desserts might feature chocolate sponge with hot fudge and white chocolate sorbet, while daily specials provide additional interest.

Owners: Tom & Ed Martin **Times:** 12-3/6-10, Closed 25 Dec, 1 Jan and BHs, Sat-Sun (except private parties) **Prices:** Fixed L £23, Starter £6-£9, Main £15-£18.50, Dessert £5, Service added but optional 12.5%, Group service 12.5% **Notes:** Vegetarian available, City dress, Air con **Seats:** 48, Pr/dining room 48 **Children:** Portions **Directions:** Nearest station: Chancery Lane Tube Station Fetter Lane runs parallel with Chancery Lane in the City of London and it joins Fleet St with Holborn **Parking:** On Street and NCP (Hatton Garden)

Corney & Barrow at Fleet Place

☎ 020 7329 3141 3 Fleet Place EC4M 7RD

City wine bar chain offering contemporary dishes.

The Don

☎ 020 7626 2606 The Courtyard, 20 St Swithins Ln EC4 8AD

Modern European menu, in vibrant city restaurant.

🖥 Paternoster Chop House

☎ 020 7029 9400 Warwick Court EC4M 7DX

web: www.theaa.com/travel/index.jsp

A modern, white-walled restaurant in a new development in Paternoster Square, offering simple, excellently sourced British produce.

🖥 Vivat Bacchus

☎ 020 7353 2648 47 Farringdon St, Holborn EC4A 4LL

web: www.theaa.com/travel/index.jsp

Classic French and international dishes and three wine cellars to choose wine from, plus a cheese cellar.

LONDON N1

◎◎ Almeida Restaurant

French 🍷 NOTABLE WINE LIST

Conran eatery serving rustic French food

☎ 020 7354 4777 30 Almeida St, Islington N1 1TD
Plan 1-F4

e-mail: almeida-reservations@conran-restaurants.co.uk
web: www.almeida-restaurants.co.uk

Just down from Highbury Corner on the way to Islington, the Almeida
is one of the cosiest eateries in the Conran empire, combining rustic
French cooking with a fashionably muted décor. Relax over a drink in
the intimate bar, and then move through to the expansive dining area,
where a theatre kitchen puts all the culinary action on show - you'll
find an extensive menu on offer, with dishes distinguished by a pared-
down approach - including a tapas-style menu - that lets top-notch
ingredients shine through. Straightforward starters and mains show
the style; choose crayfish and coriander salad with saffron dressing, or
perhaps seared scallops with endive marmalade, cucumber and olive
salad, with blackcurrant delice and apple compôte to finish.

Chef: Ian Wood **Owners:** Sir Terence Conran **Times:** 12-2.30/5.30-11,
Closed 25-26 Dec, 1 Jan, Good Fri, 17 Apr **Prices:** Fixed L £14.50-£20,
Fixed D £17.50-£27, Service added but optional 12.5% **Wine:** 350 bottles
over £20, 18 bottles under £20, 18 by the glass **Seats:** 100, Pr/dining room
20 **Children:** Portions **Directions:** Nearest station:
Angel/Islington/Highbury Turn right from station, along Upper St, past
church **Parking:** Parking around building

◎ The Drapers Arms

Modern European

Convivial gastro-pub in trendy Islington

☎ 020 7619 0348 44 Barnsbury St N1 1ER Plan 1-F4
e-mail: info@thedrapersarms.co.uk
web: www.thedrapersarms.co.uk

Gastro-pub in a smart residential area of Islington; a lovely building
with wooden floors and comfy sofas. A central door opens into the
bar area with long wide spaces on either side for tables. The place is
packed Sunday lunchtime with young families, older couples and
groups of friends. The restaurant upstairs occupies the same large
space with a fireplace at either end. Cooking is modern and seasonal
with influences from around the world. Try twice-cooked pork belly
with Thai spiced salad, followed by maize-fed chicken with roast
tomato couscous and tzataki. Desserts include the likes of apple and
walnut Bakewell with crème fraîche.

Chef: Mark Emberton **Owners:** Paul McElhinney, Mark Emberton
Times: 12-3/7-10.30, Closed 24-27 Dec, 1-2 Jan, Closed L Mon-Sat, D Sun

Prices: Starter £5-£8, Main £12-£16.50, Dessert £5.50, Service added but
optional 12.5% **Wine:** 33 bottles over £20, 16 bottles under £20, 14 by the
glass **Seats:** 50, Pr/dining room 45 **Children:** Menu, Portions
Directions: Nearest station: Highbury & Islington/Angel Situated between
Angel/Highbury & Islington tube stations, opposite town hall

◎ Fifteen London

Italian, Mediterranean V 🍷 NOTABLE WINE LIST 💻

Funky, informal, unpretentious not-for-profit outfit

☎ 0871 330 1515 13 Westland Place N1 7LP Plan 3-H6
web: www.fifteen.net

Jamie Oliver's pioneering culinary venture into youth training - as seen
on TV - is still going strong, with current offshoots in Cornwall (see
entry), Amsterdam and Melbourne. Tucked away in a cobbled side
street in the fashionably down-at-heels margins of the Old Street area,
this unpretentious, funky warehouse-style joint still pulls in the crowds
and tourists. On the ground floor there's a laid-back, buzzy trattoria for
lighter meals, while the restaurant is in the basement. Here there's an
open kitchen, graffiti-esque murals and brown leather banquettes or
chairs. The cooking's approach is Italian-Mediterranean, driven by
quality fresh, seasonal ingredients and straightforward simplicity on a
daily-changing repertoire (six-course tasting affair only at dinner); take
chargrilled Welsh lamb with marinated aubergine, Italian spinach and
an anchovy-rosemary dressing.

Chef: Jamie Oliver, Andrew Parkinson **Owners:** Fifteen Foundation
Times: 12-2.45/6.30-9.30, Closed Xmas, New Year **Prices:** Fixed L £22,
Starter £9.50-£12.50, Main £20-£25, Dessert £6.50, Service added but
optional 12.5% **Wine:** 200+ bottles over £20, 12 by the glass
Notes: Tasting menu 6 courses £60, Vegetarian £50, Vegetarian menu, Dress
Restrictions, Smart casual, Air con **Seats:** 68 **Children:** Portions
Directions: Nearest station: Old Street Exit 1 from Old St tube station, walk
up City road, opposite Moorfields Eye Hospital **Parking:** On street & NCP

◎ Frederick's Restaurant

Modern European 💻

Fashionable food in contemporary setting

☎ 020 7359 2888 Camden Passage, Islington N1 8EG
Plan 1-F4

e-mail: eat@fredericks.co.uk
web: www.fredericks.co.uk

Tucked away in Islington's antiques quarter, the Victorian façade of this
well-established restaurant opens up into a smart and stylish bar and
restaurant. A large conservatory and al fresco dining area are
complemented by painted and plain brick walls, clothed tables and
suede chairs, while modern art and clever lighting all add to the
ambience. The equally modern menu offers plenty of choice and
includes some traditional dishes with a modern twist, as well as some
vegetarian options. For mains, try fillet of beef with roquefort, roasted
tomatoes and crushed new potatoes, and double chocolate pudding
soufflé to finish.

Chef: Adam Hilliard **Owners:** Louis Segal **Times:** 12-2.30/5.45-11.30,
Closed Xmas, New Year, BHs, Sun (ex functions) **Prices:** Fixed L £14, Fixed
D £17, Starter £6.50-£12, Main £12-£19.50, Dessert £5.50, Service added but
optional 12.5% **Wine:** 100 bottles over £20, 40 bottles under £20, 35 by
the glass **Notes:** Vegetarian available, Civ Wed 200, Air con **Seats:** 150,
Pr/dining room 30 **Children:** Menu, Portions **Directions:** Nearest station:
Angel From underground 2 mins walk to Camden Passage. Restaurant
among the antique shops **Parking:** NCP Business Design Centre

ENGLAND

LONDON N1 CONTINUED

⊛ The House

Modern British 🖳

Enjoyable, simple cooking in a relaxed and comfortable environment

☎ 020 7704 7410 63-69 Canonbury Rd N1 2DG Plan 1-F4
e-mail: info@inthehouse.biz
web: www.inthehouse.biz

Behind a maroon-awninged, red-brick façade lies this cosy neighbourhood restaurant which has quite a local following. Wooden floors, whitewashed walls and simple artwork give the dining room a light-and-airy feel during the day. In the evening, locals gather around the comfortable bar sofas and well-spaced dining tables. Simple dishes prove very satisfying in this setting, using organic produce wherever possible. Try Loch Fyne smoked salmon with buckwheat blinis to start, then maybe sea bass with a ragout of borlotti beans and baby onions with braised fennel, and finish with warm Valrhona chocolate pudding served with espresso ice cream. Everything from the breads to ice creams and sorbets is home made.

Chef: Jeremy Hollingsworth **Owners:** Barnaby & Grace Meredith/Jeremy Hollingsworth **Times:** 12-2.30/6-10.30, Closed L Mon **Prices:** Starter £5.95-£10.50, Main £12.95-£22.50, Dessert £5.50-£6, Service added but optional 12.5% **Wine:** 6 bottles over £20, 7 bottles under £20, 12 by the glass **Notes:** Vegetarian available **Seats:** 80 **Children:** Menu, Portions **Directions:** Nearest station: Highbury & Islington tube Behind town hall on Upper St Islington. Between Highbury Corner and Essex Rd **Parking:** Meter parking on street

⊛ The Real Greek

Greek 🖳

Popular, bustling, earthy, authentic Hoxton Greek

☎ 020 7739 8212 15 Hoxton Market N1 6HG Plan 7-B2
e-mail: admin@therealgreek.demon.co.uk

The name sums it up; a fashionable, authentic, unpretentious Greek outfit located on the market square between two old buildings. While retaining some of this old charm, stripped-wood floors, closely packed plain wooden tables, an open kitchen and youthful, friendly service fit the bill, while the adjoining Mezedopolis (a wine and mezedes bar) cranks up the volume. The lengthy menu (in English and Greek) draws on the plentiful Greek larder, delivering simple, robust and colourful authentic dishes, packed with mezedes (appetisers) and partnered by Greek wines. A typical meal might begin with crevettes saganaki with Ismir-style meat dumplings served with trahana to follow.

Times: 12 noon-11pm, Closed 24-26 Dec, BHs, Sun **Directions:** Nearest station: Old Street Situated in square behind Holiday Inn on Old St. From tube station walk down Old St past fire station then 1st left 1st right to the back of inn

⊛ Upper Glas

Swedish

Swedish restaurant in a new location

☎ 020 7359 1932 359 Upper St N1 0PD Plan 1-F4
e-mail: glas@glasrestaurant.com
web: www.glasrestaurant.co.uk

This Scandinavian restaurant was formerly known as Glas and was located in SE1. Now housed in a listed Victorian tram shed building, and much bigger than before, the interior could be described as authentic Swedish, with antique paintings and modern chandeliers. On offer are a traditional three-course menu and a grazing menu, both using much high quality produce. Of course you can expect herring on the menu - perhaps spiced Matjes herring with sour cream, chives and onion, and there could be smoked venison with beetroot salad and horseradish, or West Coast seafood cappucino with warm langoustine salad.

Chef: Rafael Nabulon **Owners:** Anna Mosesson **Times:** 12-3/5.30-11, Closed Xmas, Etr, Sun **Prices:** Fixed L £12, Starter £4.50-£9.50, Main £9-£16.50, Dessert £4.50-£5, Service added but optional 12.5% **Wine:** 20 bottles over £20, 14 bottles under £20, 12 by the glass **Notes:** Vegetarian available, Air con **Seats:** 80 **Children:** Portions **Directions:** Nearest station: Angel Please telephone for directions **Parking:** On street

🖳 Canal 125

☎ 020 7837 1924 125 Caledonian Rd N1 9RG
web: www.theaa.com/travel/index.jsp

A real find, unassumingly tucked away, with three floors, including a restaurant, bar and two terraces and a Modern European menu.

🖳 Cru

☎ 020 7729 5252 2-4 Rufus St, Hoxton N1 6PE
web: www.theaa.com/travel/index.jsp

European dishes with some global additions, served in a relaxing friendly environment.

Masala Zones

☎ 020 7359 3399 80 Upper St N1 0NP

Modern Indian with a balanced approach.

🖳 Strada

☎ 020 7226 9742 105-106 Upper St N1 1QN
web: www.theaa.com/travel/index.jsp

Superior pizza from quality ingredients cooked in wood-fired ovens.

Wagamama

☎ 020 7226 2664 The N1 Centre, Parkfield St, Islington N1

Informal noodle bar with no booking required.

🖥 Zigni House

☎ 020 7226 7418 330 Essex Rd N1 3PB

web: www.theaa.com/travel/index.jsp

A vibrant East African restaurant and bar that is a place of pilgrimage for those who love this cuisine. As well as the à la carte menu there's a superb buffet - very popular.

LONDON N5

🖥 Iznik

☎ 020 7354 5697 19 Highbury Park N5 1QJ

web: www.theaa.com/travel/index.jsp

Turkish restaurant with bright walls and darkwood fittings. Authentic, freshly prepared Ottoman dishes.

LONDON N6

◉◉ The Bull Pub & Dining Room

British, French 🖥

Lively modern gastro-pub offering confident cooking

☎ 0845 456 5033 13 North Hill N6 4AB Plan 1-E5

e-mail: info@inthebull.biz

web: www.inthebull.biz

This contemporary, informal gastro-pub (sister to The House at Islington), situated in a two-storey Grade II listed building, has a buzzy central bar and smart dining area with an open hatch to the kitchen.

(Upstairs are private function facilities and a games room.) Polished-wood floors, leather banquettes and modern art create a relaxed, upbeat vibe, while at the front there's a terrace for fair-weather dining. Confident modern British cuisine is the thing here, with the emphasis on simplicity, freshness and quality produce. The carte comes supplemented by blackboard specials and includes an express lunch option, so theres something for everyone; take roast sea bass served with chorizo, new potato, baby spinach and saffron caramel, or perhaps a cherry clafoutis and chocolate sauce finish.

Chef: Jeremy Hollingsworth, Andres Alemany **Owners:** J E Barnaby Meredith **Times:** 12-3.30/6-10.30, Closed L Mon, D 25 Dec **Prices:** Starter £5.50-£12.50, Main £12-£25, Dessert £6, Service optional **Wine:** 65 bottles over £20, 16 bottles under £20, 11 by the glass **Seats:** 100, Pr/dining room 20 **Children:** Portions **Directions:** Nearest station: Highgate 5 min walk from Highgate tube station **Parking:** 3

LONDON N7

◉◉◉ Morgan M

see below

Morgan M

LONDON N7

Modern French V 🍷NOTABLE WINE LIST 🖥

Authentic, top-notch French cooking in intimate surroundings

☎ 020 7609 3560 489 Liverpool Rd, Islington N7 8NS Plan 1-F5

web: www.morganm.com

The small, unassuming, frosted-glass frontage seems perfectly in keeping with the restrained elegance of chef-patron Morgan Meunier's highly intimate, neighbourhood eatery. The square room sports a richer new look, with walls decorated in plush burgundy and wood panels, while white linen cloths and simple, but elegant table appointments complete the upbeat tone.

Service is predictably very French, polished and attentive, while Morgan circulates tables at the end of service with style and good humour. His is real French cooking, technically highly adept while using superb-quality seasonal ingredients, with lots of produce brought in fresh from France and cooked with true passion. Think roasted fillet of turbot with petit farci of crab, carrot and ginger risotto and a light carrot jus, or perhaps roasted Anjou squab pigeon, with parsnip purée, braised pear and crispy pepper potato in a red wine jus, while a signature dark chocolate fondant with mandarin sorbet,

orange and olive oil sauce and a Grand Marnier drink might catch the eye at dessert. Morgan's intelligently compact carte comes bolstered by his signature six-course tasting option (including a superb vegetarian alternative), while the wine list takes an unsurprisingly, predominantly patriotically French line. Lunch may be a quieter affair but offers super value.

Chef: M Meunier & S Soulard **Owners:** Morgan Meunier **Times:** 12-2.30/7-10.30, Closed 24 Dec-30 Dec, Mon, Closed L Tues, Sat, D Sun **Prices:** Fixed L £19.50, Fixed D £34, Service added but optional 12.5% **Notes:** Tasting menu £43 (vegetarian £38), Vegetarian menu, Dress Restrictions, Smart casual, Air con **Seats:** 48, Pr/dining room 12 **Children:** Portions **Parking:** On Liverpool Rd

ENGLAND

LONDON N8

⌨ Les Associes

☎ 020 8348 8944 172 Park Rd, Crouch End N8 8JY
web: www.theaa.com/travel/index.jsp

French through and through, from décor to menu and wine list. Intimate atmosphere. Some tables outside too.

LONDON N17

◉◉ The Lock Dining Bar

Modern British ⌨

Great value destination

☎ 020 8885 2829 Heron House, Hale Wharf, Ferry Ln N17 9NF Plan 1-F5
e-mail: thelock06@btconnect.com
web: thelock-diningbar.com

Just a few minutes walk from Tottenham Hale station, this chic eatery has the feel of a New York loft house, its North African furnishings teamed with pine flooring, chocolate leather sofas and works of art by local painters. An open-plan kitchen delivers a menu of modern British dishes with a focus on seasonal produce. Starters might include the likes of baked polenta fritter and Crottin goat's cheese dressed with truffle emulsion, or pan-fried scallops with plantain, and garlic froth, followed by pan-fried fillet of dorade with sautéed potatoes and slow caramelised onions. Finish with deep-fried rice pudding beignets with mixed berry sauce. It's all reasonably priced, particularly at lunchtime, and great value for money.

Chef: Adebola Adeshina **Owners:** Adebola Adeshina, Fabrizio Russo **Times:** 12-2.30/6.30-10, Closed L Sat (except match days), D Mon, Sun **Prices:** Fixed L £10-£15, Fixed D £19.50-£25, Starter £4-£10, Main £10.50-£22, Dessert £5-£6, Service optional **Wine:** 10 bottles over £20, 15 bottles under £20, 12 by the glass **Notes:** Vegetarian available, Dress Restrictions, Smart casual, no hats/caps, Air con **Seats:** 60, Pr/dining room 18 **Children:** Menu, Portions **Directions:** Nearest station: Tottenham Hale, Black Horse Station Telephone for directions **Parking:** 20

LONDON NW1

◉ La Collina

Italian NEW

Authentic, vibrant Italian cooking in swanky Primrose Hill

☎ 020 7483 0192 17 Princess Rd, Chalk Farm NW1 8JR Plan 1-E4

It's a rare London eatery that manages to capture all the flavour and authenticity of Italian cooking back home. La Collina is a period-style building close to picturesque Primrose Hill, with white-washed walls, linen-clothed tables, wooden chairs and stripped wooden floorboards. Dine upstairs and watch the well-heeled passers-by, or downstairs, where an open kitchen lets you in on the culinary action. Friendly, attentive staff create a warm informal environment. The kitchen delivers fresh, vibrant mainly Northern dishes with Piedmontese influences that are homely and full of flavour. Tuck into the likes of chestnut noodles with wild boar ragu, or grilled tuna with stewed peppers.

Times: 12-2.30/6-11, Closed Xmas wk, Closed L Mon-Fri

◉ Dorset Square Hotel

Modern British

Relaxed bar-restaurant with cricketing roots

☎ 020 7723 7874 39-40 Dorset Square NW1 6QN Plan 2-F4
e-mail: info@dorsetsquare.co.uk
web: www.dorsetsquare.co.uk

Standing on the original site of Lords cricket ground, this smart Regency townhouse hotel is home to the popular lower-ground floor Potting Shed restaurant and bar - a split-level affair with skylights and a warm, sunny feel. The gardening theme is developed with an array of terracotta pots and seed boxes across one wall, while a cricketing mural adorns another wall. The cooking is predominantly British with contemporary twists. The seasonal menu is kept simple and wholesome, focusing on accurate flavours. Tuck into a tender rump of lamb with garlic cream potatoes, or a Dorset blue cheese and leek tart with grape chutney, followed by a tangy glazed lemon tart with fresh raspberries.

Chef: Martin Halls **Owners:** LHP **Times:** 12-3/6-10.30, Closed 25 Dec, BHs, Closed L Sat, D Sun **Prices:** Fixed L £13.50-£15, Fixed D £22.50-£25, Starter £4.50-£9.50, Main £11.50-£19.50, Dessert £5, Service added but optional 12.5% **Wine:** 22 bottles over £20, 6 bottles under £20, 11 by the glass **Notes:** Dress Restrictions, Smart casual, Air con **Seats:** 45, Pr/dining room 10 **Children:** Portions **Rooms:** 37 (37 en suite) ★★★★ TH **Directions:** Nearest station: Baker St/Marylebone Telephone for directions **Parking:** NCP Marylebone Rd

◉ Gilgamesh

Pan-Asian NEW ⌨

Eclectic range of dishes in mega-lavish surroundings

☎ 020 7482 5757 Camden Stables Market, Chalk Farm Rd NW1 8AH Plan 1-E4

This £12m, Babylonian-inspired, mega-lavish, elaborately decorated, restaurant/bar/tearoom/private lounge offers more of a 'food theatre' experience than out-and-out restaurant with its fantastic atmosphere and all this in Camden! Think a huge bar of lapis stone, constantly-changing lighting and a vast retractable roof, while seating is a mix of high bar stools, banquettes and foot stalls that come paired with matching-height, solid-wood tables. The menu is classic Ian Pengelley and so fits the bill, with Pan-Asian cuisine swiftly served by knowledgeable and friendly staff. The eclectic mix takes in the likes of sashimi, tempura, dim sum and Gilgamesh signature dishes like hoba miso Chilean sea bass.

Times: 12-2.30/6, Closed L Mon-Thu, D Fri-Sun

◉ Novotel London Euston

Modern European 🖵

Sleek modern hotel restaurant with a wide-ranging carte

☎ 020 7666 9080 100-110 Euston Rd NW1 2AJ
Plan 3-C5
e-mail: h5309-fb@accor.com
web: www.novotel.com

Centrally located, this popular purpose-built hotel offers a wide range of facilities, including Mirrors restaurant and bar. The restaurant's décor is stylish and contemporary with lots of glass, neutral woods, large potted fig trees and colourful upholstery combining to create a sense of space set around a carvery and open kitchen area. The atmosphere is vibrant and service good. Featuring modern European cooking, and combining the classics with global influences, the menu includes a terrine of Iberico ham, gammon and lobster with Bramley apple purée and golden raisins, and dry aged Scottish rump with salt beef hash and fried quail's egg.

Chef: Denzil Newton **Owners:** Accor UK Business & Leisure **Times:** 12-2.30/6-10.30, Closed L Sat, Sun, BHs **Prices:** Fixed L £16.95-£17.95, Fixed D £21.95, Starter £5.25-£8, Main £12.50-£19.95, Dessert £5.50-£6.50, Service added but optional 10% **Wine:** 9 bottles over £20, 10 bottles under £20, 17 by the glass **Seats:** 89, Pr/dining room 250 **Children:** Menu, Portions **Rooms:** 312 (312 en suite) ★★★★ HL **Directions:** Nearest station: King's Cross/Euston 5 mins walk between King's Cross and Euston station, opposite British Library. 1m from Regent's Park **Parking:** Ibis Euston

◉◉◉ Odette's

see below

◉◉ Sardo Canale

Italian 🖵

Authentic Italian cuisine in a surprising setting

☎ 020 7722 2800 42 Gloucester Av NW1 8JD Plan 1-E4
e-mail: info@sardocanale.com
web: www.sardocanale.com

This unusual restaurant is located in a new building, designed around an old tunnel and tower dating back to 1850. The original brick tunnel with cobbled stones was used by horses pulling barges in the nearby Grand Union Canal. It's certainly a novel place to find a modern Italian restaurant, serving up regional Italian cooking using fresh ingredients and authentic Sardinian recipes. Service is formal, but the atmosphere is relaxed and friendly, so take some time to peruse the extensive Italian menu, complete with English subtitles. Signature dishes include linguine al granchio - a pasta sauce made of fresh crab meat with extra virgin olive oil, parsley and fresh chillies, and for dessert try frozen coffee cream with mascarpone.

CONTINUED

Odette's

LONDON NW1

British, European V

Intimate neighbourhood restaurant with loyal local clientele under new ownership

☎ 020 7586 8569 130 Regent's Park Rd NW1 8XL
Plan 1-E4
e-mail: odettes@vpmg.net
web: www.odettesprimrosehill.com

This revitalised Primrose Hill favourite has changed hands - now owned by music promoter and nightclub owner Vince Power - but continues to pull in an adoring crowd. Though completely refurbished by designer Shaun Clarkson, it still retains its intimate neighbourhood vibe with a modern 'boudoir'-style interior in a strong yellow theme; think orangey-yellow leather chairs, harmonising floral wallpaper, green light shades, exposed brick and modern carpeting. Service is attentive but relaxed, while the kitchen shows pedigree in the capable hands of chef Bryn Williams (ex Le Gavroche and the Orrery, see entries). His technically assured, light, well-balanced modern approach delivers with clean, unfussy presentation, clear flavours and a focus on quality seasonal ingredients - including produce from his native Wales where possible. The appealing repertoire of fixed-price menus - including a six-course tasting option and vegetarian offering - might deliver the likes of roasted rack and braised shoulder of Elwy Valley lamb served with its own jus, pine nuts and courgette, or perhaps pan-fried turbot with cockles and oxtail, while a warm Valrhona chocolate fondant served with milk ice cream, or poached rhubarb crumble accompanied by a rhubarb sorbet and ginger custard might catch the eye at dessert.

Chef: Bryn Williams **Owners:** Vince Power **Times:** 12-2.30/6.30-10.30, Closed 25 Dec, Mon (incl BHs), Closed D Sun **Prices:** Fixed L £14.45-£17.95, Fixed D £21.95-£25, Starter £6-£12.50, Main £15-£25, Dessert £4.50-£8.50, Service added but optional 12.5% **Wine:** 134 bottles over £20, 3 bottles under £20, 20 by the glass **Notes:** Tasting menu 7 courses £60, Sun L 2-3 courses £25-£30, Vegetarian menu, Air con **Seats:** 75, Pr/dining room 25 **Children:** Portions **Directions:** Nearest station: Chalk Farm. By Primrose Hill. Telephone for directions **Parking:** On street

ENGLAND

LONDON NW1 *CONTINUED*

Chef: Claudio Covino **Owners:** Romolo & Bianca Mudu **Times:** 12-3/6-11, Closed 25-26 Dec, BHs, Closed L Mon **Prices:** Fixed L £13, Fixed D £30, Starter £6.90-£8.90, Main £12-£17.50, Dessert £5.50-£6, Service added but optional 12.5% **Wine:** 22 bottles under £20, 13 by the glass **Notes:** Sun L 3 courses £23, Vegetarian available, Air con **Seats:** 100, Pr/dining room 40 **Children:** Portions **Directions:** Nearest station: Chalk Farm/Camden Town Please telephone for directions **Parking:** On street

◎◎ The Winter Garden

Modern British 🖳

Stunning atrium restaurant

☎ 020 7631 8000 The Landmark London, 222 Marylebone Rd NW1 6JQ Plan 2-F4
e-mail: restaurants.reservation@thelandmark.co.uk
web: www.landmarklondon.co.uk

Former headquarters of British Rail and one of the last great railway hotels, the building is over 100 years old. The Winter Garden is a stunning open-plan, naturally lit restaurant situated at the base of an eight-storey atrium complete with palm trees, which also features the sophisticated Mirror Bar. At night, the restaurant turns into a more intimate affair. A selection of modern British dishes is offered on a menu featuring fresh quality produce. Typical starters might include shellfish bisque with vodka crème fraîche, while a main course of pine nut-crusted rack of lamb is accompanied with basil mash, Provençal vegetables and shallot jus. Desserts might include rhubarb and vanilla baked Alaska with rhubarb compôte.

Chef: Gary Klaner **Owners:** Jatuporn Sihanatkathakul **Times:** 11.30-3/6-11.30 **Prices:** Starter £6-£12, Main £15-£40, Dessert £6-£10, Service optional **Wine:** 38 bottles over £20, 15 by the glass **Notes:** Civ Wed 280, Air con **Seats:** 80, Pr/dining room 360 **Children:** Menu, Portions **Rooms:** 299 (299 en suite)★★★★★ HL **Directions:** Nearest station: Marylebone M25 turn on to the A40 and continue 16m following signs for West End. Continue along Marylebone Rd for 300 mtrs. Restaurant on left **Parking:** 75

🖳 Belgo

☎ 020 7267 0718 72 Chalk Farm Rd NW1 8AN
web: www.theaa.com/travel/index.jsp

Belgian style, with strong beer, good seafood (mussels of course) and staff in habits.

Wagamama

☎ 020 7428 0800 11 Jamestown Rd, Camden NW1 7BW

Informal noodle bar with no booking required.

LONDON NW2

🖳 King Sitric

☎ 020 8452 4175 142-152 Cricklewood Broadway NW2 3ED

web: www.theaa.com/travel/index.jsp

A fusion of modern Irish and international dishes in modern, art deco influenced surroundings.

🖳 Philpotts Mezzaluna

☎ 020 7794 0455 424 Finchley Rd NW2 2HY
web: www.theaa.com/travel/index.jsp

Italian restaurant with modern interior. Clothed tables, red walls and modern art set the scene for enjoying inventive dishes.

🖳 Spice of Hampstead

☎ 020 7794 5922 448 Finchley Rd, Child's Hill NW2 2HY

web: www.theaa.com/travel/index.jsp

Bright white walls, wooden floors and modern art at this friendly Indian restaurant.

LONDON NW3

⊛ Manna

International Vegetarian V 🖵

Charming, fun and informal vegetarian restaurant

☎ 020 7722 8028 4 Erskine Rd, Primrose Hill NW3 3AJ
Plan 1-E4
e-mail: yourhost@manna-veg.com
web: www.manna-veg.com

Believed to be the oldest vegetarian dinner restaurant in England, Manna was founded in the 1960s to bring a gourmet experience to vegetarians and vegans. Top-quality organic ingredients are used in uncomplicated but imaginative dishes that take their inspiration from around the world. Think a kashmiri curry of potato, okra, cauliflower and yogurt topped with almonds and served with rice, aubergine chutney and poppadoms, or perhaps a black bean taco - a corn tortilla filled with spicy black beans and served with grilled sweet potato, chilli corn rice, blackened tomato sauce, leaf salad, guacamole and sour cream. A takeaway service is also available.

Chef: Matthew Kay **Owners:** S Hague, R Swallow, M Kay **Times:** 12.30-3/6.30-11, Closed 25 Dec-1 Jan (open New Year's Eve), Closed L Mon-Sat **Prices:** Starter £4.50-£7.25, Main £9.50-£13.25, Dessert £4.50-£7.25 Service added but optional 12.5% **Wine:** 20 bottles under £20, 10 bottles over £20, 4 by the glass **Notes:** Vegetarian menu, Air con **Seats:** 50 **Children:** Menu, Portions **Directions:** Nearest station: Chalk Farm Telephone for directions **Parking:** On street

Artigiano

☎ 020 7794 4288 12a Belsize Ter NW3 4AX

web: www.etruscarestaurants.com

Mix of contemporary Italian cuisine.

🖵 Hellenic

☎ 020 7431 1001 291 Finchley Rd NW3 6ND

web: www.theaa.com/travel/index.jsp

Home-made Greek cooking - Mezedes a speciality (ten cold starters and ten hot main dishes). Fantastic value.

The Wells

☎ 020 7794 3785 30 Well Walk NW3 1BX

web: www.thewellshampstead.co.uk

Relaxed, but stylish dining in a delightful former coaching inn.

Yo! Sushi

☎ 020 7431 4499 02 Centre, 255 Finchley Rd
NW3 6LH

Sushi, sashimi, noodles and more delivered by conveyor belt and priced according to colour-coded plates.

LONDON NW4 *See* LONDON SECTION
Plan 1 D5

⊛⊛ Hendon Hall Hotel

Modern European NEW

Dramatic setting for modern bistro fare

☎ 020 8203 3341 & 020 8457 2500 Ashley Ln, Hendon
NW4 1HF
e-mail: info@hendonhall.com
web: www.hendonhall.com

In more recent times, this historic mansion has been a girls' school and an RAF convalescent home, but became a hotel again after World War II. A dramatic, theatrical, Gothic dining room awaits, complete with a rich décor of deep reds, grand columns, high-back seating, polished-wood tables and crisp white napery. Service is delightful, while the crowd-pleasing menu offers a cosmopolitan bistro-style that's driven by quality, local-sourced produce. Here chicken and mushroom pie or a Caesar salad might shimmy up alongside the likes of calves' liver served with caramelised onions and sage, or perhaps eight-hour lamb with roasted garlic potatoes, while desserts could feature a pineapple tart Tatin or millefeuille of white and dark chocolate.

Chef: Paul Sage **Times:** 12-2.30/7-10 **Prices:** Fixed L £15.50, Starter £6-£7.50, Main £13-£20, Dessert £6.50-£7.50, Service optional **Wine:** 32 bottles over £20, 15 bottles under £20, 11 by the glass **Notes:** Vegetarian available, Dress Restrictions, Smart casual, Civ Wed 120, Air con **Children:** Portions **Rooms:** 57 (57 en suite)★★★★ HL **Directions:** Nearest station: Hendon M1 junct 2. A406. Right at lights onto Parson St. Next right into Ashley Lane, Hendon Hall is on right **Parking:** 70

🖵 The Gallery

☎ 020 8202 4000 407-411 Hendon Way NW4 3LH

web: www.theaa.com/travel/index.jsp

Art gallery highlighting the talents of young British and French artists. English cuisine with French influences.

ENGLAND

LONDON NW6

◉ Singapore Garden Restaurant

Singaporean, Malaysian 💻

Well established Oriental with a mixture of Chinese and Singaporean dishes

☎ 020 7328 5314 & 7624 8233 83-83a Fairfax Rd, West Hampstead NW6 4DY Plan 1-E4
web: www.singaporegarden.co.uk

Situated in a parade of upmarket shops close to Finchley Road tube, this modern restaurant has contemporary décor and a sophisticated feel. The Lim family has built up a loyal clientele, drawn by the animated ambience and by the menu which includes a variety of authentic dishes inspired by Chinese, Malay and Singaporean cuisine. Typical dishes include starters like kuay pie tee - crispy pastry cups with bamboo shoots, chicken and prawns - followed by the likes of black pepper and butter crab, or beef rendang - slow-cooked beef in thick coconut sauce. Outside decked area for dining in warmer weather.

Chef: Kok Sum Toh **Owners:** Hibiscus Restaurants Ltd **Times:** 12-2.45/6-10.45, Closed 4 days at Xmas **Prices:** Fixed L £20, Fixed D £23.50-£38.50, Starter £5-£12, Main £7.20-£29, Dessert £4.50-£6.50, Service added but optional 12.5% **Wine:** 39 bottles over £20, 4 bottles under £20, 6 by the glass **Notes:** Fixed L 3 courses, Fixed D 4 courses, Vegetarian available, Air con **Seats:** 85, Pr/dining room 6 **Directions:** Nearest station: Swiss Cottage, Finchley Road Off Finchley Rd, on right before Belsize Rd rdbt **Parking:** Meters on street

Gourmet Burger Kitchen

☎ 020 7794 5455 331 West End Ln, West Hampstead NW6 1RS

New Zealand inspired burger joint using top notch beef.

LONDON NW8

💻 Sofra - St John's Wood

☎ 020 7240 4411 11 Circus Rd NW8 6NX
web: www.theaa.com/travel/index.jsp

Traditional Turkish restaurant with modern approach. Menu includes healthy eating choices.

LONDON NW10

◉ Sabras Restaurant

Indian vegetarian V

Surati regional restaurant serving exclusively vegetarian Indian cooking

☎ 020 8459 0340 263 High Rd, Willesden Green NW10 2RX Plan 1-D4

In a high street location with glass shop front looking onto the street, the interior of this restaurant is well-lit with light white and cream decor. For over 30 years it has served exclusively vegetarian cuisine from the Surati region of India, cooked with enthusiasm and skill. With a well-established reputation, the specialist cuisine draws a wide following to enjoy dishes like Ragda patish (spiced potato cake with a

mild yellow pea sauce) and Makai Kaju (sweetcorn, sweet peppers and cashew nuts in a tomato sauce). If you enjoy Indian cuisine and fancy trying something a bit different this would be an excellent choice.

Times: 6.00-10.00, Closed 25 & 26 Dec, BH Mon, Mon, Closed L all week
Directions: Nearest station: Dollis Hill. Telephone for directions

LONDON SE1

◉◉ The Anchor & Hope

Traditional European 🕲

Lively gastro-pub with attitude

☎ 020 7928 9898 36 The Cut SE1 8LP Plan 5-F5
e-mail: anchorandhope@btconnect.com

This popular gastro-pub is packed as soon as the doors open and, as there's no booking, it's a case of turning up early and waiting for a table. Wooden floors, bare walls, an open kitchen and a buzzy, lively, yet relaxed, atmosphere set the scene. A heavy curtain separates the bar from the restaurant area, though it's a similarly sociable affair with close-set tables that you may have to share. The menus show an equally rustic simplicity with their fresh quality ingredients and uncompromising flavours. Perhaps cabbage, white bean and preserved pork soup, or rare roast venison, duck fat potato cake, bacon and chestnuts, with a pear and almond tart or pannacotta and rhubarb to follow.

Times: 12-2.30/6-10.30, Closed BHs, 25 Dec-1 Jan, Sun, Closed L Mon
Directions: Nearest station: Southwark/Waterloo. Telephone for directions

◉ Baltic

Eastern European 💻

Authentic Eastern European cooking served to a trendy crowd in stylish surroundings

☎ 020 7928 1111 74 Blackfriars Rd SE1 8HA Plan 5-F5
e-mail: info@balticrestaurant.co.uk
web: www.balticrestaurant.co.uk

A striking chandelier made of shards of amber dominates this otherwise minimalist open-plan restaurant. Light pours in through the roof windows, while beams give a rustic feel to the stylish space. Vodka cocktails, jazz and an extensive Eastern European menu appeal to a trendy, friendly crowd. Start with blini and caviar, smoked eel and bacon salad, or Polish black sausage with pickled cabbage. Mains take in roast saddle of wild boar and cranberries, wiener schnitzel with beetroot and shallot salad, and pan-fried sea bass with fennel and tomatoes. Nalesniki (crêpes stuffed with sweet cheese, almonds and raisins) is an appealingly authentic way to finish.

Chef: Peter Resinski **Owners:** Jan Woroniecki **Times:** 12-3.30/6-11, Closed Xmas, 1 Jan, BHs **Prices:** Fixed L £12.50, Fixed D £28.50, Starter £5.50-£14.50, Main £13.50-£18.50, Dessert £6-£8, Service added but optional 12.5% **Wine:** 23 bottles over £20, 8 bottles under £20, 6 by the glass **Notes:** Civ Wed 300, Aircon **Seats:** 100, Pr/dining room 35 **Children:** Menu, Portions **Directions:** Nearest station: Southwark Opposite Southwark station, 5 mins walk from Waterloo **Parking:** Meters on The Cut

⊛ *Cantina del Ponte*

Italian 💻

Trendy riverside Italian

☎ 020 7403 5403 The Butlers Wharf Building, 36c Shad Thames SE1 2YE Plan 6-D2
e-mail: cantina@conran-restaurants.co.uk
web: www.conran.com

A heated terrace overlooking the river Thames affords plenty of opportunities for people and boat-watching alike. Inside a large mural of a Mediterranean marketplace gives an indication of the gastronomic experience in store. The lengthy, seasonally-changing menu comprises a good range of rustic Italian dishes with strong, robust flavours. Tuck into the likes of pumpkin and prosciutto gnocchi, grilled grey mullet or veal osso buco. A decadent chocolate and pistachio tart with pistachio ice cream could be washed down with a glass of Vín Santo. Factor in the sunset over Tower Bridge and you have the recipe for a very romantic evening.

Times: 12-3/6-11, Closed 24-26 Dec **Directions:** Nearest station: Tower Hill, London Bridge. SE side of Tower Bridge, on riverfront

⊛⊛ **Cantina Vinopolis**

Mediterranean 💻

Delightful dishes to complement the wine cellar tours

☎ 020 7940 8333 1 Bank End SE1 9BU Plan 6-A3
e-mail: info@cantinavinopolis.com
web: www.cantinavinopolis.com

The wine-related attraction Vinopolis is located in the cavernous old railway vaults on Bankside by the Thames, with a large glass entrance and cocktail lounge. The restaurant is set against a backdrop of vaulted arches with an open-plan kitchen at the far end. Produce comes fresh from Borough Market next door and is carefully prepared, accurately cooked and served in traditional style with influences that embrace French, Italian and North African cuisine. A tian of grilled Mediterranean vegetables and mozzarella cheese with herb and balsamic vinaigrette, or Spanish black pudding with chorizo and potato salad and shallot vinaigrette deliver simple and true flavours, while desserts take in the likes of upside-down apple and polenta cake with vanilla ice cream. The wine list reflects Vinopolis expertise and offers great value.

Chef: Moges A Wolde **Owners:** Claudio Pulge, Trevor Guppier
Times: 12-3/6-10.30, Closed BHs, Closed D Sun **Prices:** Starter £4.95-£8.25, Main £10.50-£18.50, Dessert £4.65-£6.25, Service added but optional **Wine:** 278 bottles over £20, 46 bottles under £20, 63 by the glass **Notes:** Vegetarian available, Dress Restrictions, Smart casual, Air con **Seats:** 200 **Children:** Portions **Directions:** Nearest station: London Bridge 5 min walk from London Bridge on Bankside between Southwark Cathedral & Shakespeare's Globe Theatre

⊛ **Champor Champor**

Modern Pacific Rim 💻

Creative modern Malaysian cooking in atmospheric, ethnic surroundings

☎ 020 7403 4600 62-64 Weston St SE1 3QJ Plan 6-B2
e-mail: mail@champor-champor.com
web: www.champor-champor.com

Champor-Champor means 'mix-and-match' in Malay, and this applies to the bohemian décor as well as the food of this intimate and atmospheric restaurant. Forgive the side street location behind London Bridge Station as, once through the door, vivid colours, tribal artefacts and Buddhist statues mingle with modern art and the whiff of incense in the busily decorated space. The creative cooking follows the theme, with its mix of Asian cuisines grafted on to Malay roots; think cream of Cantonese roast duck soup and roast fillet of ostrich with black pepper sauce and sweet potato mash.

Chef: Adu Amran Hassan **Owners:** Champor-Champor Ltd
Times: 6.15-10.15, Closed Xmas-N Year (7 days), Etr (5 days), BHs, Closed L Times may vary - please check **Prices:** Fixed L £24, Fixed D £26-£30, Service added but optional 12.5% **Wine:** 19 bottles over £20, 22 bottles under £20, 4 by the glass **Notes:** Fixed L 3 courses, Tasting menu 7 courses £44, Air con **Seats:** 38, Pr/dining room 8 **Directions:** Nearest station: London Bridge, Joiner St exit. Left onto Saint Thomas St & 1st right into Weston St, restaurant 100yds on left **Parking:** On street, Snowsfields multi-storey

⊛ **The County Hall Restaurant**

Modern British NEW 💻

Stunning Thames-side setting in the heart of Westminster

☎ 020 7902 8000 London Marriott Hotel, Westminster Bridge Rd SE1 7PB Plan 5-D5
web: www.marriotthotels.com/marriott/lonch

Formerly the members' reading room of County Hall, the restaurant here is a high-ceilinged, oak-panelled room facing the Palace of Westminster and Big Ben, looking out across the River Thames. It's a wonderful setting by day or by night and the formal feel is reflected in high levels of staffing and classical, but friendly and informative, service. The dishes on the fixed-price menu and carte are modern British with European influences. Main courses might include fillets of John Dory with brown shrimp risotto, broad beans and basil sauce, or pumpkin gnocchi, wilted spinach, goat's cheese and walnut sauce.

Chef: Craig Carew-Wootton **Owners:** Marriott International **Times:** 12-2.30/6-10.30, Closed D 26 Dec **Prices:** Fixed L £19-£21, Fixed D £23-£25, Starter £6-£13.50, Main £16-£25.50, Dessert £6-£7.50, Service optional **Wine:** 104 bottles over £20, 14 by the glass **Notes:** Sun L jazz menu £25, Vegetarian available, Dress Restrictions, Smart casual, Civ Wed 100, Air con **Seats:** 90, Pr/dining room 80 **Children:** Menu, Portions **Rooms:** 200 (200 en suite) ★★★★★ HL **Directions:** Nearest station: Waterloo, Westminster Situated next to Westminster Bridge on the South Bank. Opposite Houses of Parliament. **Parking:** Valet parking for 25

ENGLAND

◉ Fire Station

Modern European

Bustling gastro-pub in a former fire station close to Waterloo station

☎ 020 7620 2226 150 Waterloo Rd SE1 8SB
Plan 5-E5
e-mail: firestation.waterloo@pathfinderpubs.co.uk
web: www.pathfinderpubs.co.uk

Converted brick-built fire station with a bar area at the front and particularly large windows - once the drive-in doors for the fire engines - with a spacious dining area and open-plan kitchen to the rear. Rough red-brick walls are adorned with fire service paraphernalia. It's an unpretentious pub setting offering speedy service of fresh, seasonal, quality food, mostly cooked to order - Fire Station fish platter (to share as a main course), roast pork belly, crème brûlée - to a crowd of regulars. Food is served from midday, and bar snacks are also available. There's an extensive list of easy-drinking, good-value wines.

Times: 12-3/5.30-11 **Directions:** Nearest station: Waterloo Adjacent to Waterloo station

◉◉ Magdalen

European NEW

Classy, new restaurant offering dishes with French influence

☎ 020 7403 1342 & 7403 9950 152 Tooley St SE1 2TU
Plan 6-C2
e-mail: info@magdalenrestaurant.co.uk
web: www.magdalenrestaurant.co.uk

With its burgundy décor, bentwood chairs, mirrors and enormous sprays of fresh flowers, there is a deceptively French feel to this popular two-storey restaurant. The food, however, has a more British foundation with European influences and the daily-changing menu is fiercely seasonal, with much of the produce sourced from nearby Borough Market. There are Mediterranean flourishes in a starter of hot foie gras with caramelised blood oranges or a main course of roast cod with white beans and garlic leaves, while pork and pigeon terrine, venison and trotter pie and treacle tart and cream are gutsy dishes with a strong British accent. A notable, French-heavy wine list includes many by the carafe.

Chef: James Faulks, Emma Faulks, David Abbott **Owners:** Roger Faulks & James Faulks **Times:** 12-2.30/6.30-10.30, Closed Xmas, BHs, 2wks Aug, Sun, Closed L Mon **Prices:** Food prices not confirmed for 2008. Please telephone for details **Wine:** 66 bottles over £20, 12 bottles under £20, 22 by the glass **Seats:** 90 **Directions:** Nearest station: London Bridge 5 min walk from London Bridge end of Tooley Street. Restaurant opposite Unicorn Theatre **Parking:** On street

◉◉ The Oxo Tower Restaurant

Modern European V

Stylish venue with a 'top of the world' feel and innovative food

☎ 020 7803 3888 8th Floor, Oxo Tower Wharf, Barge House St SE1 9PH Plan 3-F1
e-mail: oxo.reservations@harveynichols.co.uk
web: www.harveynichols.com

Echoing the design of a 1930s ocean liner, this stylish modern restaurant is beautiful in its simplicity. Situated on the eighth floor with glass down both sides, it features a unique louvred ceiling with blue neon lights which creates a beautiful moonlit effect in the evenings. There's also a long open terrace enabling diners to take full advantage of the stunning views over the Thames and St Paul's, and leather-clad bars, slate tables and original art all add to the luxurious feel. The innovative modern European menu features a series of classics with a twist, as well as a sprinkling of dishes combining Mediterranean/Pacific Rim and French/Asian ingredients. Tempting descriptions highlight each dish's many component parts, as in a starter of salt-and-pepper cuttlefish with watermelon, mint and coconut salad and chilli caramel, or sea bass with confit garlic-braised haricot beans, roasted cherry tomatoes and truffle oil mascarpone.

Chef: Jeremy Bloor **Owners:** Harvey Nichols & Co Ltd **Times:** 12-2.30/6-11, Closed 25-26 Dec, Closed D 24 Dec **Prices:** Fixed L £31.50, Starter £9.50-£18, Main £16.50-£26, Dessert £7.25-£8, Service added but optional 12.5% **Wine:** 660 bottles over £20, 19 bottles under £20, 23 by the glass **Notes:** Vegetarian menu, Civ Wed 120, Air con **Seats:** 250 **Children:** Menu, Portions **Directions:** Nearest station: Blackfriars/Waterloo Between Blackfriars & Waterloo Bridge **Parking:** On street, NCP

◎◎ Le Pont de la Tour

Traditional French 💻

Wharfside restaurant, stylish destination dining and unbeatable views

☎ 020 7403 8403 The Butlers Wharf Building, 36d Shad Thames SE1 2YE Plan 6-D2

web: www.lepontdelatour.co.uk

A popular waterfront wharf location with stunning views of Tower Bridge, especially at night when it's floodlit. The terrace is busy in summer as diners flock to watch the world go by on the river, while inside this elegant restaurant you step into the luxury world of a cruise liner. Smart table settings, clean lines and well-dressed staff set the tone for some serious cooking. The French menu offers an extensive choice of dishes, drawing on traditional ingredients like a terrine of foie gras maison with Armagnac jelly to start. There's lots of fresh fish, crustacea or caviars, while meat options might feature a rump of lamb with spiced aubergine caviar and sauce vièrge. There's an impressive and extensive wine list, too.

Chef: James Walker **Owners:** Conran Restaurants **Times:** 12-3/6-11 **Prices:** Fixed L £30, Starter £7.50-£16.50, Main £13.50-£35.50, Dessert £7.50, Service added but optional 12.5% **Wine:** 100 bottles over £20, 100 bottles under £20, 20 by the glass **Notes:** Fixed L 3 courses, Vegetarian available, Dress Restrictions, Smart casual, Air con **Seats:** 160, Pr/dining room 20 **Children:** Menu, Portions **Directions:** Nearest station: Tower Hill, London Bridge SE of Tower Bridge **Parking:** On street & car park

◎ *RSJ, The Restaurant on the South Bank*

Modern British

Perfect pre-theatre dining

☎ 020 7928 4554 33 Coin St SE1 9NR Plan 5-F6

e-mail: sally.webber@rsj.uk.com

web: www.rsj.uk.com

Long-established, simple, modern restaurant, popular with media types and theatre- or concert-goers from the adjacent South Bank. Friendly staff keep everything moving efficiently with an eye on performance times. The menu changes monthly or more frequently, reflecting a passion for fresh seasonal produce. With Loire Valley wines a speciality, there are wine events from time to time. The cuisine makes good use of fine quality ingredients to deliver carefully prepared, attractively presented dishes, like wild halibut served with truffled wild mushroom coquiette, and perhaps a raspberry crème brûlée to finish.

Times: 12-2/5.30-11, Closed Xmas, 1 Jan, Sun, Closed L Sat **Directions:** Nearest station: Waterloo Telephone for directions

◎ Roast

British 🍷 NOTABLE WINE LIST 💻

Airy modern restaurant perched above Borough Market

☎ 020 7940 1300 The Floral Hall, Borough Market, Stoney St SE1 1TL Plan 6-B3

e-mail: info@roast-restaurant.com

web: www.roast-restaurant.com

Borough Market provides the atmospheric setting for this first-floor establishment, with views of the hubbub below from the bar and over to St Paul's Cathedral from its glass-fronted dining room. The floral portico featured in the dining room was bought from Covent Garden for £1 by Borough Market trustees. Menus make good use of quality produce in classic British dishes. Think roast Banham chicken with bread sauce and Ayshire bacon, Inverawe smoked Loch Etive trout with watercress and lemon, or roast Welsh black sirloin. Breakfast and afternoon tea are served, and there's a superb cocktail list.

Chef: Lawrence Keogh **Owners:** Iqbal Wahhab **Times:** 12-3/5.30-11, Closed D Sun **Prices:** Fixed L £19.50, Starter £5-£10, Main £12.95-£25, Dessert £4-£7, Service included **Wine:** 6 bottles under £20 **Seats:** 110 **Children:** Menu, Portions **Directions:** Nearest station: London Bridge Please telephone for directions

💻 La Cave Restaurant

☎ 020 7378 0788 Bank Chambers, Montague Close, 6-10 Borough High St SE1 9QQ

web: www.theaa.com/travel/index.jsp

French food, French wine and attentive French service in this rustic café close to Southwark Cathedral.

💻 Georgetown

☎ 020 7357 7359 10 London Bridge St SE1 9SG

web: www.theaa.com/travel/index.jsp

Authentic Malay plus Indian Malaysian and Chinese Malaysian dishes. Décor is colonial with wicker chairs and lots of plants.

ENGLAND

Yo! Sushi

☎ 020 7928 8871 County Hall, Belvedere Rd SE1 7GP

Sushi, sashimi, noodles and more delivered by conveyor belt and priced according to colour-coded plates.

LONDON SE3

◉◉◉ *Chapter Two*

see below

◉ Laicram Thai Restaurant

Thai V

Authentic Thai in a cosy setting

☎ 020 8852 4710 1 Blackheath Grove, Blackheath SE3 0DD Plan 8-D1

This Thai restaurant of long-standing is in the centre of Blackheath village, enjoying a fine reputation in the area for good food and being easy on the wallet. The décor has a homely feel, with understated Thai touches such as prints of the Thai royal family on the walls and typically welcoming and friendly service from the staff. The menu consists largely of mainstream Thai dishes such as green curry, prawn satay, fishcakes, phat Thai noodles goong pau (grilled prawns in a spicy sauce), and pla neung (steamed sea bass with lime sauce and fresh chilli).

Chef: Mrs S Dhirabutra **Owners:** Mr D Dhirabutra **Times:** 12-2.30/6-11, Closed Xmas & BHs, Mon **Prices:** Starter £3-£6.50, Main £5.80-£13.90, Dessert £2.50-£4, Service added but optional 10% **Notes:** Vegetarian menu, Air con **Seats:** 50 **Directions:** Nearest station: Blackheath Off main shopping street, in a side road near the Post Office. Opposite station, near library

LONDON SE5

🖥 Mozarella e Pomodoro

☎ 020 7277 2020 21-22 Camberwell Green SE5 7AA

web: www.theaa.com/travel/index.jsp

Chic, modern Italian restaurant with discreet service and wide-ranging menu.

LONDON SE10

◉ *Rivington Bar & Grill - Greenwich*

British, European NEW V 🖥

Buzzy surroundings for simple British food

☎ 020 8293 9270 178 Greenwich High Rd, Greenwich SE10 8NN Plan 8-A3

e-mail: greenwich@rivingtongrill.co.uk
web: www.rivingtongrill.co.uk

Right next to the Greenwich Picture House, this converted pub - sibling to the sister establishment of the same name in Shoreditch (see entry) - delivers the blueprint buzzy, informal brasserie act.

Chapter Two

LONDON SE3

Modern European 🖥

Prominent and stylish heathside restaurant with imaginative cuisine

☎ 020 8333 2666 43-45 Montpelier Vale, Blackheath Village SE3 0TJ Plan 8-D1

e-mail: richard@chaptersrestaurants.co.uk
web: www.chapterrestaurants.co.uk

This little gem - sibling to big brother Chapter One (see entry) - is a place you'll want to return to again and again. Chic, modern and split-level, the glass-fronted restaurant's small ground-floor dining room is visible from the street, while a spiral staircase connects it to a larger basement space and bar. Decked out with slashes of vibrant colours (blues, reds and dark browns), lightwood floors and chrome, the clever use of mirrors adds to the feeling of lightness and space, while a combination of banquette seating and high-backed chairs (set around white-linen dressed tables) bears out the modern styling. Service is equally slick, but friendly and well informed, with regulars greeted like old friends.

The kitchen's modern European approach is thoroughly imaginative, with accurate, skilful cooking displaying culinary pedigree, utilising

produce of high quality and delivering fresh, clean flavours - and all this at affordable prices. Expect the likes of wild halibut with coco beans and a fumet of fennel and shellfish, and desserts such as a hot chocolate fondant served with blackberry coulis and stout and currant ice cream.

Times: 12-2.30/6.30-10.30, Closed 2-4 Jan **Directions:** Nearest station: Blackheath 5 mins from Blackheath Village train station

It's decked out in informal style, with dark wooden floors, white-washed walls and white paper-clothed tables, which offer the perfect backdrop for the kitchen's simple, seasonal, modern British cooking. With a separate vegetarian menu available, quality raw materials shine in dishes like Wetherall's Blackface mutton and turnip pie, or perhaps Glen Fyne steak and chips, and a Bakewell tart finish. There's a small alfresco terrace and a mezzanine level above the ground floor.

Times: 12-3/6:30-11

🍽 North Pole Piano Restaurant

☎ 020 8853 3020 131 Greenwich High Rd, Greenwich SE10 8JA

web: www.theaa.com/travel/index.jsp

Elegant restaurant serving European dishes. Roast Sunday lunch a good deal and live jazz Sunday evenings.

LONDON SE11

🍽 The Lobster Pot

☎ 020 7582 5556 3 Kennington Ln, Kennington SE11 4RG

web: www.theaa.com/travel/index.jsp

Small eatery with nautical theme and French cooking - mainly seafood.

LONDON SE21

◉◉ Beauberry House

French, Japanese V 🍽

Contemporary French meets oriental fusion food in Georgian splendour

☎ 020 8299 9788 Gallery Rd SE21 7AB Plan 1-F2

web: www.circagroupltd.co.uk

Pure white décor - with tables all turned out in their best whites and set against a juicy orange floor and chairs - provides the stylish setting for this French meets East Asian fusion restaurant. The beautiful Georgian mansion (formerly Belair House) is set in leafy parkland near Dulwich village, its revamped interiors respecting the classical features while adding bags of contemporary pizzazz. Outdoor terraces abound for alfresco dining with views over gardens and lawns, while service is attentive and informed. The kitchen's fittingly contemporary approach delivers French cuisine with oriental influences using top-quality ingredients; take lobster tempura served with ponzu and wasabi mayonnaise, or flash-fried wagyu beef fillet with black truffles.

Chef: Jerome Tauvron **Owners:** Ibi Issolah **Times:** 12-3/6-11, Closed Xmas, 1 Jan, Mon, Closed D Sun **Prices:** Fixed L £14.50, Fixed D £17.50, Starter £6.50-£9.50, Main £13.50-£22, Dessert £5-£7.50, Service added 12.5% **Wine:** 490 bottles over £20, 30 bottles under £20, 22 by the glass **Notes:** Tasting menu 5 courses £45, Brunch 2-3 courses £18.50-£21, Vegetarian menu, Civ Wed 60 **Seats:** 60, Pr/dining room 50 **Children:** Menu, Portions **Directions:** Nearest station: West Dulwich Telephone for directions **Parking:** 40

LONDON SE22

◉ Franklins

British

Smart restaurant and popular pub operation

☎ 020 8299 9598 157 Lordship Ln SE22 8HX Plan 1-F2

e-mail: info@franklinsrestaurant.com

web: www.franklinsrestaurant.com

A traditional pub on the outside, Franklins opens off Lordship Lane into a well-frequented locals' bar where the open-all-day policy attracts a posse of regulars. A few paces beyond this atmospheric space can be found the bright bistro-style restaurant where diners glimpse the kitchen operation through a wide hatch. Seasonal produce from in and around the UK dominates the carte, with its daily-changing set lunch menu offering excellent value for money. Traditional English favourites like Old Spot belly with fennel and black pudding, Glamorgan sausages, and mutton faggots with pease pudding will be found alongside guinea fowl with butter beans and chorizo.

Chef: Tim Sheehan **Owners:** Tim Sheehan & Rodney Franklin **Times:** 12/12, Closed 25-26, 31 Dec, 1 Jan **Prices:** Fixed L £9.50, Starter £5-£9, Main £10.50-£18, Dessert £5, Service optional, Group min 6 service 10% **Wine:** 7 bottles over £20, 5 bottles under £20, 6 by the glass **Notes:** Vegetarian available, Air con **Seats:** 42, Pr/dining room 24 **Children:** Portions **Directions:** Nearest station: East Dulwich Please telephone for directions **Parking:** Bawdale Road

◉ The Palmerston

Modern British

Popular gastro-pub close to Dulwich village

☎ 020 8693 1629 91 Lordship Ln, East Dulwich SE22 8EP Plan 1-F3

e-mail: thepalmerston@tiscali.co.uk

web: www.thepalmerston.co.uk

There are pubs aplenty down trendy Lordship Lane, but few have reinvented themselves as successfully as this one. Behind the pastel-painted exterior, the long bar and separate dining area - each warmed by a real fire in winter - are wood-panelled, brightly coloured and welcoming. But the real delight is the food, a homage to fresh, carefully sourced ingredients deftly handled without a hint of artifice. Expect to find potted beef with pickled beetroot, grilled veal chop with celeriac remoulade and sauce charcuterie, and perhaps a homely rhubarb and custard tart with rhubarb compôte to finish. The set lunch is a real bargain.

Chef: Jamie Younger **Owners:** Jamie Younger, Paul Rigby, Remi Olajoyegbe **Times:** 12-2.30/7-midnight, Closed 25-26 Dec, 1 Jan **Prices:** Fixed L £10, Starter £5-£8, Main £11-£16.50, Dessert £4-£6.50, Service added but optional 10% **Wine:** 34 bottles over £20, 22 bottles under £20, 17 by the glass **Seats:** 70 **Children:** Portions **Directions:** Nearest station: East Dulwich 2m from Clapham, 0.5m from Dulwich Village, 10min walk from East Dulwich station **Parking:** On street

ENGLAND

LONDON SE23

◉◉ Babur

Indian

Contemporary Indian restaurant

☎ 020 8291 2400 & 8291 4881   119 Brockley Rise, Forest Hill SE23 1JP   Plan 1-G2
e-mail: mail@babur.info
web: www.babur.info

This popular brasserie has been serving southeast London for over 20 years. Easily identified by the life-size, prowling Bengal tiger on its roof, inside the restaurant has been fully renovated and expanded. The décor is stylish and modern with a contemporary ethnic feel, eye-catching artwork and exposed Victorian brickwork adding to the ambience. The menu includes unusual options such as ostrich and kangaroo and is dotted with tiger heads to indicate the intensity of the chilli heat expected. One head equals hot and two means roaring hot! Start perhaps with ostrich infused with sandlewood and fenugreek, then follow with medallions of monkfish in a spicy tomato masala, or whole lobster with tomato and onion Madeira sauce. The selection of home-made chutneys is exquisite.

Chef: Enam Rahman & Jiwan Lal **Owners:** Babur 1998 Ltd **Times:** 12.30-2.30/6-11.30, Closed 25-26 Dec **Prices:** Starter £4.95-£6.95, Main £8.95-£16.95, Dessert £3.95-£5.95, Service optional **Wine:** 13 bottles over £20, 26 bottles under £20, 13 by the glass **Notes:** Sun buffet L £10.95, Children 7-12yrs £6.95, under 7yrs free, Vegetarian available, Air con **Seats:** 72
Directions: Nearest station: Honor Oak 5 mins walk from Honor Oak station, where parking is available **Parking:** On street

LONDON SE24

◉ 3 Monkeys Restaurant

Indian 🖥

Contemporary neighbourhood Indian

☎ 020 7738 5500   136-140 Herne Hill SE24 9QH
Plan 1-F2
e-mail: info@3monkeysrestaurant.com
web: www.3monkeysrestaurant.com

Arranged over two levels with stripped wooden floors, white walls - replete with attractive modern artwork - and furniture draped in white cotton, this is certainly not your run-of-the-mill curry house, but a cool, calm, elegant restaurant. Staff are knowledgeable and happy to make recommendations to those less au fait with the cuisine of the sub-continent, with menus offering a delightful cross-section of authentic regional Indian cuisine. With a state-of-the-art open grill as the centre of attraction, think methi murgh (chicken sautéed with fresh fenugreek in dry ginger powder flavoured with tomato and onion), or macher malabar (fish stewed in coconut milk with curry leaves and tamarind). Takeaways are also available.

Chef: Raminder Malhotra **Owners:** Kuldeep Singh, Raminder Malhotra **Times:** 12-2.30/6-11, Closed Xmas **Prices:** Fixed L £4.95-£7.95, Fixed D £15.95-£22, Starter £3.95-£7, Main £7.25-£14.95, Dessert £3.25-£4.50, Service added but optional 12.5% **Notes:** Sun buffet, executive L, Vegetarian available, Air con **Seats:** 90 **Children:** Menu, Portions
Directions: Nearest station: Herne Hill, Brixton Adjacent to Herne Hill Station **Parking:** On street

LONDON SW1

◉ Al Duca

Modern Italian

Straightforward Italian cooking just off Piccadilly

☎ 020 7839 3090   4-5 Duke of York St SW1Y 6LA
Plan 5-B6
e-mail: info@alduca-restaurant.co.uk
web: www.alduca-restaurant.co.uk

This smart, modern Italian, conveniently situated in St James's, draws the crowds with its affordable pricing, contemporary good looks and buzzy atmosphere. Etched glass, neutral tones and leather banquettes cut a stylish but relaxed edge, while feature wine racks set into the wall catch the eye, and patio-style windows fold back for an alfresco look in summer. Straightforward, unpretentious and enjoyable Italian cooking is the kitchen's style, skilfully combining the freshest ingredients to bring out the best of the wide range of traditional dishes, some with a modern twist. Think braised osso buco with Sardinian couscous and leeks, or perhaps pan-fried fillet of wild sea bass with basil-scented courgettes and grilled radicchio, while pre- and post-theatre menus and an all-Italian wine list bolster the fixed-price carte.

Chef: Aron Johnson **Owners:** Cuisine Collection **Times:** 12-2.30/6-11, Closed Christmas, New Year, BHs, Sun **Prices:** Fixed L £21, Fixed D £26.50, Service added but optional 12.5% **Wine:** 84 bottles over £20, 5 bottles under £20, 16 by the glass **Notes:** Vegetarian available, Dress Restrictions, Smart casual, no shorts, Air con **Seats:** 56 **Children:** Portions
Directions: Nearest station: Piccadilly 5 mins walk from station towards Piccadilly. Right into St James, left into Jermyn St. Duke of York St halfway along on right **Parking:** Jermyn St, Duke St

◉◉ Amaya

Indian V 💻

Entertaining kitchen theatre with enticing South Asian food

☎ 020 7823 1166 Halkin Arcade, Motcomb St SW1X 8JT
Plan 4-G4
e-mail: amaya@realindianfood.com
web: www.realindianfood.com

The pink sandstone panels, hardwood floors and rosewood furniture of this smart contemporary Indian grill are flooded with light from its glass atrium. Indian statuary and glass plates add to the vibrant ambience created by the open-plan theatre kitchen where chefs marinate meats or labour over tandoors or sigris - charcoal grills. Dishes are mostly North Western in style but regional dishes also figure, with the emphasis on clean, clear flavours and combinations and modern presentation. Many dishes are offered in small or mains sizes, so you might start with griddled diver-caught king scallops in a light green herb sauce, and to follow, perhaps tandoori monkfish tikka served with fenugreek leaf and turmeric, or grilled lamb chops with ginger, lime and coriander. Finish with a coconut crème brûlée with tamarind sauce.

Chef: Karunesh Khanna **Owners:** R Mathrani, C Panjabi, N Panjabi
Times: 12-2.30/6-11.15, Closed 25 Dec **Prices:** Fixed L £15.50-£25, Fixed D £37.50-£55, Starter £6.50-£20, Main £6.50-£20, Dessert £7.50, Service added but optional 12.5% **Wine:** 70 bottles over £20, 2 bottles under £20, 26 by the glass **Notes:** Fixed D 2 courses, Tasting menus £55, Vegetarian tasting menu £35.50, Air con **Seats:** 90, Pr/dining room 14
Directions: Nearest station: Knightsbridge Please telephone for directions
Parking: NCP

◉ Aslan

Modern British NEW

Modern food in an elevated dining room overlooking Jermyn Street

☎ 020 7930 2111 Cavendish London, 81 Jermyn St
SW1Y 6JF Plan 5-B6
e-mail: info@thecavendishlondon.com
web: www.thecavendishlondon.com

Located in the stylish Cavendish London Hotel, the restaurant enjoys an enviable location in the prestigious St James's area of central London. The restaurant itself is situated on the first floor, with large plate-glass windows that take full advantage of the views, while the dark woods, beige and caramel colour scheme create a relaxed atmosphere. The menu is contemporary modern British with European

influences. You might start with pan-fried Scottish sea scallops with Jerusalem artichoke purée, before moving on to the likes of grilled sea bass fillet with crushed potatoes, spinach and saffron dressing.

Chef: David Britton, Gretano Monteriso **Owners:** De Vere Hotels & Leisure Ltd **Times:** 12-2.30/5.30-10.30, Closed 25-26 Dec, 1 Jan, Closed L Sat-Sun **Prices:** Fixed L £14.95, Starter £5-£9.50, Main £14.50-£21.50, Dessert £6.50, Service added but optional 12.5% **Wine:** 10 bottles over £20, 10 bottles under £20, 10 by the glass **Notes:** Pre-theatre menu available, Dress Restrictions, Smart casual, Air con **Seats:** 80, Pr/dining room 80
Children: Menu, Portions **Rooms:** 230 (230 en suite) ★★★★ HL
Directions: Nearest station: Green Park, Piccadilly Circus **Parking:** 60

◉ The Avenue

European 💻

Buzzy, contemporary bar and restaurant

☎ 020 7321 2111 7-9 St James's St SW1A 1EE Plan 5-B5
e-mail: avenue@egami.co.uk
web: www.egami.co.uk

This large, cavernous, starkly minimalist brasserie makes an ever-popular St James's destination, and reverberates with a buzzy atmosphere. High ceilings come decked out with recessed spots, plain white walls donned with large colourful modern art and floors clad in limestone. There's a long bar up front, while trendy dining chairs come in white or grey and tables clothed in white linen. The lengthy brasserie-format menu offers a straightforward, uncomplicated modern approach, blending the more contemporary alongside classics. Take halibut served with crayfish mash and leek frittata, or goujons of cod with tartare sauce.

Chef: Richard Bannister **Owners:** Image Restaurants **Times:** 12-3/5.45-11.30, Closed 25-26 Dec, 1 Jan, Sun, Closed L Sat **Prices:** Fixed L £19.95, Fixed D £20.95, Service added but optional 12.5% **Notes:** Civ Wed 150, Air con **Seats:** 180 **Children:** Portions **Directions:** Nearest station: Green Park Turn right past The Ritz, 2nd turning into St James's St. Telephone for further details **Parking:** Parking meters on streets

◉ Bistro 51

English, French NEW

Modern, stylish hotel dining, brasserie style

☎ 020 7834 6655 Crowne Plaza London St James,
Buckingham Gate SW1E 6AF Plan 5-B4
e-mail: dine@bistro51.co.uk
web: www.bistro51.co.uk

Set in the heart of Westminster and the prestigious St James's area - only a few minutes' walk from Buckingham Palace - the Crowne Plaza is a fittingly elegant Victorian hotel. Its Bank restaurant is accessed via the street or hotel lobby, while the adjacent and stylish Zander cocktail bar boasts the longest bar in town. Bank is ultra modern too, and shaped in semi-circular format, with glass windows and one side overlooking a delightful courtyard. The kitchen deals in fresh, vibrant modern-European brasserie-style fare; take roast monkfish with Serrano ham, served with squid, asparagus and tomato salsa.

Chef: Brian Henry **Owners:** Taj Hotels **Times:** 12-3/6-11 **Prices:** Fixed L £12, Fixed D £18.50, Starter £6.15-£7.75, Main £9.75-£25.50, Dessert £5.65-£6.50, Service added but optional 12.5% **Wine:** 42 bottles over £20, 4 bottles under £20, 26 by the glass **Notes:** Sun L £14.50, Air con
Seats: 74 **Children:** Menu, Portions **Rooms:** 342 (342 en suite) ★★★★ HL **Parking:** NCP

ENGLAND

LONDON SW1 CONTINUED

⊛ Boisdale of Belgravia

British 📖

Traditional, clubby but fun Scottish restaurant

☎ 020 7730 6922 15 Eccleston St SW1W 9LX Plan 4-H3
e-mail: info@boisdale.co.uk
web: www.boisdale.co.uk

A determinedly Scottish experience is delivered at this Belgravia restaurant-cum-whisky and cigar bar, with its deep reds and greens, tartan, dark floorboards and panelled, picture-laden walls. There is an endearingly clubby atmosphere to its labyrinth of dining areas and bars, and live jazz adds to the atmosphere in the evenings. The Caledonian menu supports the theme with Dunkeld oak-smoked salmon, ravioli of Western Isles king scallops, a daily game dish, and 28-day matured Scottish beef served with a wide choice of sauces and accompaniments. Desserts tempt with the likes of warm pear and fig tart served with prune and Armagnac ice cream, or hot chocolate cake with Banyuls syrup.

Chef: Colin Wint **Owners:** Mr R Macdonald **Times:** 12-2.30/7-11.15, Closed Xmas, New Year, Easter, BHs, Sun, Closed L Sat **Prices:** Fixed L £14-£17.80, Fixed D £17.80, Starter £7.50-£17.50, Main £14.50-£28.50, Dessert £6.50, Service added but optional 12.5% **Wine:** 125 bottles over £20, 11 bottles under £20, 22 by the glass **Notes:** Fixed D 2 courses, Air con **Seats:** 100, Pr/dining room 22 **Directions:** Nearest station: Victoria Turn left along Buckingham Palace Rd heading W, Eccleston St is 1st on right **Parking:** On street, Belgrave Sq

⊛⊛ Boxwood Café

British V ♦ NOTABLE WINE LIST 📖

Upmarket brasserie in high-class hotel

☎ 020 7235 1010 The Berkeley Hotel, Wilton Place, Knightsbridge SW1X 7RL Plan 4-G4
e-mail: boxwoodcafe@gordonramsay.com
web: www.gordonramsay.com

From the Gordon Ramsay stable, this upmarket interpretation of a New York-style café predictably oozes class, located on one corner of The Berkeley Hotel with its own street entrance on Knightsbridge. The elegant dining room is a stylish, split-level basement affair, with a bar and smart table settings. Natural earthy tones parade alongside golds and bronzes and lashings of darkwood and leather, while service is youthful, slick but relaxed, and there's a vibrant metropolitan buzz. The accomplished kitchen's upmarket brasserie repertoire hits the spot, utilising high-quality seasonal ingredients with the emphasis on flavour, innovative combination and stylish presentation; think braised fillet of wild halibut served with baked potato gnocchi, peas, broad beans and courgette flower.

Chef: Stuart Gillies **Owners:** Gordon Ramsay Holdings Ltd **Times:** 12-3/6-11 **Prices:** Fixed L £21, Starter £7.50-£16, Main £16-£28, Dessert £6-£10, Service added but optional 12.5% **Wine:** 700 bottles over £20, 40 bottles under £20, 27 by the glass **Notes:** Fixed L 3 courses, Taste of Boxwood £55, Vegetarian menu, Air con **Seats:** 140, Pr/dining room 16 **Children:** Menu, Portions **Directions:** Nearest station: Knightsbridge Please telephone for directions **Parking:** On street

⊛⊛ Brasserie Roux

French

Stylish brasserie serving rustic French cuisine

☎ 020 7968 2900 & 747 2200 Sofitel St James London, 6 Waterloo Place SW1Y 4AN Plan 5-B6
e-mail: h3144-fb8@accor.com
web: www.sofitelstjames.com

This vibrant, elegant, high-ceilinged brasserie set within the Sofitel St James hotel comes with stylish Pierre Yves Rochon design. Its main decorative theme, the cockerel, is the logo of this former banking hall's owners (Cox's & King's) and also, of course, the symbol of France. Bright red leather chairs, pale yellow walls, huge lampshades and bare-wood tables embody the modern, chic but relaxed styling, backed by friendly and knowledgeable service. The traditional, wholesome, unfussy French regional cuisine fits the authentic brasserie style, offering classics that utilise quality produce with flavour at their heart - as in mussels with a light curry sauce, duck cassoulet, lemon sole with hollandaise and clafoutis with prunes and Armagnac.

Chef: Paul Danabie **Owners:** Accor UK **Times:** 12-3/5.30-11 **Prices:** Fixed L £15-£24.50, Fixed D £15-£24.50, Starter £6.50-£14, Main £9-£22, Dessert £6.50, Service added but optional 12.5% **Wine:** 21 by the glass **Notes:** Fixed L 3 courses, Pre-theatre menu 5.30-7pm, Vegetarian available, Civ Wed 150, Air con **Seats:** 100, Pr/dining room 130 **Children:** Menu, Portions **Rooms:** 186 (186 en suite) ★★★★★ HL **Directions:** Nearest station: Piccadilly Circus Telephone for directions **Parking:** NCP at Piccadilly

⊛⊛ Le Caprice Restaurant

Modern European V

Quality cooking in a restaurant that brings out the stars

☎ 020 7629 2239 Arlington House, Arlington St SW1A 1RT Plan 5-A6
web: www.le-caprice.co.uk

This classy restaurant has been a darling of the celebrity circuit for many years. The interior is predominantly black and white, with David Bailey photographs, large mirrors and comfortable seating at fairly closely set tables. There are no airs and graces here, and friendly waiting staff treat all guests with the same even-handed respect. Cooking is based on excellent produce and the comprehensive European menu offers comfort eating to appeal to every taste: aubergine and mozzarella ravioli; griddled tiger prawns with wild garlic; pan-fried gilt-head sea bream with lemon and herb butter; chargrilled quails with butternut squash, pancetta and oregano. Sunday brunch is a popular option with pitchers of Bloody Mary or Buck's fizz. Separate vegetarian menu available.

Times: 12-3/5.30-12, Closed 25-26 Dec, 1 Jan, Aug BH, Closed D 24 Dec
Directions: Nearest station: Green Park Arlington St runs beside The Ritz. Restaurant is at end

◎ Caraffini

Traditional Italian

Busy, lively traditional Italian

☎ 020 7259 0235 61-63 Lower Sloane St SW1W 8DH
Plan 4-G2
e-mail: info@caraffini.co.uk
web: www.caraffini.co.uk

Close to fashionable Sloane Square, a large white awning picks out this smart and welcoming Chelsea Italian. Frequented by a sophisticated clientele of locals and visitors, its pastel yellow walls are hung with contemporary watercolours and mirrors, and blond-wood floorboards, blue banquettes and upholstered rattan-style chairs help cut a sunny, relaxed atmosphere. The eclectic carte is bolstered by daily specials and all-Italian wines, presented in Italian with English subtitles. Modern overtones are evident in classic regional dishes, with an emphasis on simplicity, freshness and flavour. Take a starter of tiger prawns in hot chilli and olive oil, followed by fresh scallops flavoured with spinach and mushrooms.

Chef: John Patino, S Ramalhoto **Owners:** F di Rienzo & Paolo Caraffini
Times: 12.15-2.30/6.30-11.30, Closed BHs, Xmas, Sun **Prices:** Starter £4.95-£13.25, Main £8.75-£20.95, Dessert £4.25-£7.50, Service optional, Group min 6 service 12.5% **Wine:** 43 bottles over £20, 10 bottles under £20, 3 by the glass **Notes:** Vegetarian available, Air con **Seats:** 70
Directions: Nearest station: Sloane Square Please telephone for directions **Parking:** Meters on street

◎◎ Le Cercle

Modern French

Discreet basement restaurant offering modern French grazing food

☎ 020 7901 9999 1 Wilbraham Place SW1X 9AE
Plan 4-F3
e-mail: info@lecercle.co.uk

Close to Sloane Square, this discreet basement restaurant continues to pull in the punters. The dining areas combine a sense of refined intimacy with a surprising spaciousness, accentuated by the high ceilings, neutral colour scheme and artful lighting. The glass-fronted wine cave and cheese room provide suitable stages to highlight two French passions celebrated here, while the menu offers a good overview of the rest of Gallic gastronomy. Dishes such as haddock fillet, smoked carrot emulsion and pickled carrot, or squid ink

tagliatelle with shellfish and spinach velouté are cooked with aplomb, with small but perfectly-formed portions and refined presentation. An extensive wine list and the menu have many recommendations for wines by the glass to accompany each course.

Chef: Thierry Beyris **Owners:** Vincent Labeyrie & Pascal Aussignac
Times: 12-3/6-11, Closed Xmas & New Year, Sun, Mon **Prices:** Fixed L £15.50, Fixed D £17.50, Starter £4.50-£6, Main £5.50-£7.50, Dessert £5.50-£6, Service added 12.5% **Wine:** 200 bottles over £20, 15 by the glass
Notes: Fixed D 5 courses, Vegetarian available, Air con **Seats:** 60, Pr/dining room 10 **Directions:** Nearest station: Sloane Square Just off Sloane St **Parking:** Outside after 6pm, NCP in Cadogan Sq

◎◎ The Cinnamon Club

Indian 💻

Sophisticated Indian dining in former library

☎ 020 7222 2555 The Old Westminster Library,
Great Smith St SW1P 3BU Plan 5-C4
e-mail: info@cinnamonclub.com
web: www.cinnamonclub.com

The former Westminster library makes an unusual setting for a contemporary Indian restaurant. Polished parquet floors, dark wood, high ceilings, domed skylights and a gallery of books retain the building's heritage and old English charm. The restaurant has a clubby feel with high-backed suede chairs and crisp white tablecloths, all very simple and elegant. Traditional Indian cuisine is based around fine ingredients and well-judged spicing. Breakfast, lunch, pre- and post-theatre and carte menus offer a wide selection of dishes. Try dishes such as chargrilled duck breast with cloves and star anise with apple chutney, or wild African prawns baked with 'kasundi' mustard with lemon rice. A good choice of desserts features date pancake with vanilla and toasted coconut ice cream.

Times: 12-3/6-11, Closed Xmas, Etr, BHs, Sun, Closed L Sat
Directions: Nearest station: Westminster Take exit 6, across Parliament Sq, then pass Westminster Abbey on left. Take 1st left into Great Smith St

ENGLAND

ENGLAND

LONDON SW1 CONTINUED

◉◉ Il Convivio

Italian 💻

Stylish Italian dining in upmarket Belgravia

☎ 020 7730 4099 143 Ebury St SW1W 9QN Plan 4-H2
e-mail: comments@etruscarestaurants.com
web: www.etruscarestaurants.com

Set in a quiet residential street in trendy Belgravia, this chic split-level restaurant has a few sought-after tables at street level, with the main restaurant and conservatory-style room on the lower level. Deep red walls hung with stone slabs inscribed with quotes from Dante's *Il Convivio* are set off by modern wooden-backed chairs and cream leather cushions. The upmarket Italian cuisine includes a few unconventional touches that show the kitchen knows its stuff: a Parma ham starter arrives with home-made sweet pickled vegetables, while mains include Arctic black cod caramelised with balsamic and served with asparagus and Muscat grapes, or salt marsh lamb with black olive sauce and glazed baby turnips. A wide-ranging choice is supplemented by daily specials and an extensive wine list.

Chef: Lukas Pfaff **Owners:** Piero & Enzo Quaradeghini **Times:** 12-2.45/7-10.45, Closed Xmas, New Year, BHs, Sun **Prices:** Food prices not confirmed for 2008. Please telephone for details **Notes:** Dress Restrictions, Smart casual, Air con **Seats:** 65, Pr/dining room 14
Directions: Nearest station: Victoria 7 min walk from Victoria Station - corner of Ebury St and Elizabeth St. **Parking:** On street

◉◉ Drones

Traditional French 💻

Classy Belgravia venue with experience factor

☎ 020 7235 9555 1 Pont St SW1X 9EJ Plan 4-G3
e-mail: sales@whitestarline.org.uk
web: www.whitestarline.org.uk

This classic from the Marco Pierre White stable oozes style, glamour and confidence. Walls are lined with black and white photographs of show-biz legends - think David Niven and Audrey Hepburn - while floors are polished parquet, there's leather banquette seating, tables are white clothed and service is slick and attentive. The discreet glass frontage is hung with Venetian blinds, while there's an eye-catching bar and art-deco style wall lighting. The crisply scripted, lengthy menu parades a repertoire of classic French dishes using quality ingredients and an assured, intelligent, straightforward style. Expect Dover sole à la meunière or perhaps a grilled veal chop with sage and butter. Desserts like a Harvey's lemon tart or crème brûlée catch the eye too, while the fixed-price lunch is great value.

Drones

Chef: Joseph Croan **Owners:** Marco Pierre White, Jimmy Lahoud
Times: 12-2.30/6-11, Closed 26 Dec, 1 Jan, Closed L Sat, D Sun
Prices: Fixed L £15.95, Starter £7.50-£19.50, Main £14.50-£24.50, Service added but optional 12.5%, Group service 15% **Wine:** 70 bottles over £20, 1 bottle under £20, 12 by the glass **Notes:** Sun L 3 courses £22.50, Vegetarian available, Dress Restrictions, Smart casual, Air con **Seats:** 90, Pr/dining room 40 **Children:** Portions **Parking:** Cadogan Place

◉◉ Ebury

British, French 💻

Fashionable, buzzy Pimlico eatery serving highly accomplished modern cuisine

☎ 020 7730 6784 11 Pimlico Rd SW1W 8NA Plan 4-G2
e-mail: info@theebury.co.uk
web: www.theebury.co.uk

This large, smart, contemporary bar-brasserie-restaurant certainly stands out from the crowd. On the ground floor there's a lively bar, crustacea counter and stylish, low-slung brown leather seating for more relaxed dining, while the upstairs restaurant has a more formal, romantic edge. An equally modern confection, it comes decked out in white linen with cream leather seating, stunning chandeliers and photographs of jazz legends. A glass window allows glimpses into the kitchen, while service is slick, professional and friendly. The refined, modern brasserie-style repertoire is underpinned by a classical French theme, driven by quality ingredients, clear flavours and creative presentation. Take roast rump of lamb served with boulangère potatoes and caramelised onion purée, or hot chocolate fondant with peanut ice cream and honeycomb.

Times: 12-3.30/6-10.30, Closed 24-30 Dec **Directions:** Nearest station: Sloane Sq/Victoria From Sloane Sq Tube left into Holbein Place, then left at intersection with Pimlico Rd. The Ebury is on right on corner of Pimlico Rd & Ranelagh Grove. From Victoria, left down Buckingham Palace Rd, then right onto Pimlico Rd

Foliage

LONDON SW1

Modern European ♦ NOTABLE WINE LIST 🖥

One of the capital's finest

☎ 020 7235 2000 Mandarin Oriental Hyde Park,
66 Knightsbridge SW1X 7LA Plan 4-F4
e-mail: molon-reservations@mohg.com
web: www.mandarinoriental.com/london

Backing on to Hyde Park, this imposing luxury Knightsbridge hotel fairly bristles with class. To the uninitiated, its liveried doorman and fluttering flags outside might give the impression of a grand Edwardian edifice in the old tradition, yet it's anything but. Smiling greeting staff are contemporarily dressed, as are the equally fashionable bar and glass-fronted wine-store entrance to Foliage, the fine-dining restaurant. Chic, stylish and intimate, the restaurant's theme is all in the name, with giant glass wall panels enclosing thousands of white silk leaves that come alive with lighting and change colour to echo the seasons. A split-level floor ensures all have a view of park life, and striking flower displays and luxury fabrics and furnishings add to the sophisticated modern tone. These fine details support the dining room's reputation as one of London's finest under chefs David Nicholls' and Chris Staines' sublime cooking. Their approach is via an enticing repertoire of fixed-price menu options that take in a terrific-value lunch jour, carte and tasting offering. Luxury ingredients grace the intricate cooking showcasing the kitchen's silky technical skills, with well-conceived, well-presented dishes of clean, clear, balanced flavours that set the tastebuds alight. Think a fillet of Buccleuch beef with 24-hour braised wagyu, oysters, smoked potato purée and pickled Thai shallots, or perhaps pan-fried fillets of John Dory with crushed ratte potatoes, red pepper, tomato and clam vinaigrette.

Chef: David Nicholls, Chris Staines
Owners: Mandarin Oriental Hyde Park
Times: 12-2.30/7-10.30
Prices: Fixed L £27, Fixed D £52, Service added but optional 12.5%
Wine: 400 bottles over £20, 2 bottles under £20, 15 by the glass
Notes: Fixed L 4 courses, Tasting menu 5 courses £72, Vegetarian available, Dress Restrictions, Smart casual, Civ Wed 250, Air con
Seats: 46
Rooms: 198 (198 en suite)★★★★★ HL
Directions: Nearest station: Knightsbridge In Knightsbridge with Harrods on right, hotel is 0.5m on left, opposite Harvey Nichols
Parking: Valet parking, NCP

ENGLAND

ENGLAND

LONDON SW1 *Continued*

✿✿ Fifth Floor Restaurant

French, European 🍷 NOTABLE WINE LIST 🖥️

Star-studded dining at top London store

☎ 020 7235 5250 & 7235 5000 Harvey Nichols, 109-125 Knightsbridge SW1X 7RJ Plan 4-F4
e-mail: reception@harveynichols.com
web: www.harveynichols.com

Dine in style on the fifth floor of one of London's most fashionable stores. This contemporary space high above the Knightsbridge traffic is as chic as it is comfortable, with designer white leather chairs and feature lighting creating a relaxed, intimate ambience. The new Swedish-born head chef brings Scandinavian flair to the menus, making the most of seasonal flavoursome ingredients. Lunch, dinner, tasting and weekend brunch menus are available, as well as a new market menu that utilises produce from the food market. Kick off with Bassett stilton with toasted walnuts, wild rocket and olive oil, followed by Shetland organic cod with marinated white anchovies, mange tout, hazelnut salad and Janson's temptation. Round things off in style with pineapple cannelloni, served with passionfruit mousse, French meringue and mascarpone.

Chef: Jonas Karlsson **Owners:** Harvey Nichols Ltd **Times:** 12-3/6-11, Closed Xmas, Closed D Sun **Prices:** Fixed L £19.50, Fixed D £24.50-£39.50, Starter £7.50-£13.50, Main £14-£25, Dessert £6.50-£9.50, Service added but optional 12.5% **Wine:** 700 bottles over £20, 30 bottles under £20, 30 by the glass **Notes:** Tasting menu £48, Air con **Seats:** 120 **Children:** Menu, Portions **Directions:** Nearest station: Knightsbridge, Hyde Park Corner Entrance on Sloane Street **Parking:** On street, NCP opposite

✿✿✿✿✿ Foliage

see page 297

✿ Franco's Restaurant

Italian

A classy reincarnation of an Italian institution

☎ 020 7499 2211 61 Jermyn St SW1Y 6LX Plan 5-A6
e-mail: reserve@francoslondon.com
web: www.francoslondon.com

Situated in the heart of St James's, this long-established restaurant has returned to Jermyn Street refreshed and revitalised. The perfect location in which to enjoy classically-based Italian food in sumptuous surroundings, a dark green awning overhangs the part-frosted windows and some popular outside tables, while inside there are two interconnecting rooms, the 1940s-style interior complementing the Edwardian façade. You might start with Aberdeen Angus beef tartare, with raw quail's egg and baby asparagus, and for mains try pan-fried mackerel with barba di frate and porcini sauce, or maybe organic salmon, sea bass, or sirloin steak from the grill.

Chef: Paulo Parlanti **Owners:** Jason Philips **Times:** 12-2.30/5.30-12, Closed last wk Dec, Sun, BHs **Prices:** Fixed L £25-£30, Fixed D £30-£35, Starter £7.50-£15, Main £10-£24, Dessert £6-£10, Service added but optional 12.5% **Wine:** 98% bottles over £20, 2% bottles under £20, 16 by the glass **Notes:** Fixed D 2 courses, Pre/Post-theatre 2-3 courses £15-£20, Vegetarian available, Air con **Seats:** 100, Pr/dining room 50 **Directions:** Nearest station: Green Park, Piccadilly Circus Telephone for directions
Parking: On street

✿✿ The Goring

Traditional British 🍷 NOTABLE WINE LIST

Carefully prepared food in grand hotel setting

☎ 020 7396 9000 Beeston Place SW1W 0JW Plan 4-H4
e-mail: reception@goringhotel.co.uk
web: www.goringhotel.co.uk

A sumptuous and elaborate hotel done out in the grand style, as befits a traditional property in its central London location just behind Buckingham Palace. This family-owned property may be traditional in style but it's anything but stuffy with staff providing friendly and efficient service. David Linley's redesign has created a lighter, modern touch to the grand Victorian dining room, with its sumptuous silks and contemporary centrepiece 'Blossom' chandeliers. Menus are a celebration of all things British, accomplished classics using prime-quality, fresh produce. Think Dover sole (grilled or pan fried) served with new potatoes and spinach, or perhaps steak and kidney pie with cream potatoes, while there are British cheeses from the trolley and puddings like a classic custard tart.

Chef: Derek Quelch **Owners:** Goring Family **Times:** 12.30-2.30/6-10, Closed L Sat **Prices:** Fixed L £32.50, Fixed D £44, Service added but optional 12.5% **Wine:** 100+ bottles over £20, 10 by the glass **Notes:** Fixed L 3 courses, Dress Restrictions, Smart dress, Civ Wed 50, Air con **Seats:** 70, Pr/dining room 50 **Children:** Menu, Portions **Rooms:** 71 (71 en suite)★★★★★ HL **Directions:** Nearest station: Victoria From Victoria St turn left into Grosvenor Gdns, cross Buckingham Palace Rd, 75yds turn right into Beeston Place **Parking:** 5

◉ Inn the Park

British
All-day eatery in park setting

☎ 020 7451 9999 St James's Park SW1A 1AA Plan 5-C5
e-mail: info@innthepark.co.uk
web: www.innthepark.co.uk

The long, grass-roofed, Scandinavian-style building blends invisibly into the rolling landscape of St James's Park. The cleverly named all-day eatery looks out across the lake to Duck Island and beyond to the London Eye. A café by day, with a counter for quick snacks, it becomes a restaurant at night offering simple, full-flavoured, brasserie-style dishes using quality produce from small suppliers. Expect the likes of ham hock terrine, broad beans, pea shoots and spring onion followed by roasted belly of pork, quince jam and parsnip purée. There is a super decked area for summer alfresco dining.

Times: 12-3/6-10.45, Closed D Sun-Mon (winter) **Directions:** Nearest station: St James, Charing Cross 200 metres down The Mall towards Buckingham Palace

◉ Just St James

Modern British 💻
Dining in high style in old St James's

☎ 020 7976 2222 12 St James's St SW1A 1ER Plan 5-B5
e-mail: bookings@juststjames.com
web: www.juststjames.com

The lavish, impressive, Edwardian Baroque interior with its marble columns, arched windows and corniced ceilings has been cleverly softened with contemporary styling (think suede banquette seating, modern artwork and a glass lift to a mezzanine gallery) to provide a striking setting for some accomplished modern dining. It used to be a private bank, so don't be shocked at some of the St James's prices, but then the menu comes dotted with luxury. The cooking is self-assured and stylishly presented, so open your account with a ballotine of foie gras, duck salad and toasted brioche, and perhaps baked wild halibut with a herb crust, boulangère potatoes and green beans to follow. A large, glass-topped bar and leather seating completes a class act.

Chef: Peter Gladwin **Owners:** Peter Gladwin **Times:** 12-3/6-11, Closed 25-26 Dec, 1 Jan, Sun, Closed L Sat **Prices:** Food prices not confirmed for 2008. Please telephone for details **Wine:** 14 by the glass **Seats:** 120, Pr/dining room 140 **Children:** Portions **Directions:** Nearest station: Green Park Turn right on Piccadilly towards Piccadilly Circus, then right into St James's St. Restaurant on corner of St James St & King St **Parking:** St James's Square - meters

◉◉ Ken Lo's Memories of China

Chinese
Refined Chinese cooking close to Victoria

☎ 020 7730 7734 65-69 Ebury St SW1W 0NZ
Plan 4-H3
e-mail: memoriesofchina@btconnect.com
web: www.memories-of-china.co.uk

A well-established and popular Pimlico restaurant with a refined, upmarket feel that owes much to the very stylish table settings. Quality abounds from the starched linen to the chopsticks, and the subtle Chinese décor has a contemporary edge. A lengthy carte showcases the classic Chinese food, backed up by a set menu that offers excellent value for money from the same quality produce and refined presentations. Accurate flavours reflect the skilful handling of good raw ingredients, yielding the likes of fresh scallops steamed in shells with black bean sauce, stir-fried fresh lobster with ginger and spring onion noodles and black pepper, or maybe pan-fried medallions of beef. Service is speedy and efficient.

Chef: Kam Po But **Owners:** A-Z Restaurants **Times:** 12-2.30/7-11, Closed BHs, Closed L Sun **Prices:** Fixed L £18.50-£21.50, Fixed D £30, Starter £3-£12.95, Main £11.50-£34, Service added but optional 12.5%, Group min 15 service 15% **Wine:** 129 bottles over £20, 4 bottles under £20, 6 by the glass **Notes:** Fixed L 3 courses, Vegetarian available, Dress Restrictions, Smart casual, Air con **Seats:** 120, Pr/dining room 20 **Children:** Portions **Directions:** Nearest station: Victoria At junction of Ebury Street & Eccleston St. Near Victoria Station **Parking:** On street

◉◉ The Lanesborough

International 💻
Park Lane grandee with a leafy conservatory

☎ 020 7259 5599 Hyde Park Corner SW1X 7TA
Plan 4-G5
e-mail: info@lanesborough.com
web: www.lanesborough.com

You can expect world-class luxury, stunning service and crisply-cooked traditional British food at this grand hotel on Hyde Park Corner. Sip an aperitif in the swanky cocktail bar, and then move through to the glass-roofed conservatory restaurant, where a pianist plays softly as you take a seat among exotic palms and trickling fountains, at a table set with the finest crystal and china. Quality ingredients are to the fore on the wide-ranging modern menu, and there's no shortage of skill. Kick off with lobster ravioli with provençale dressing perhaps, followed by Scottish beef fillet with shallot purée and Barolo jus, or braised halibut with rosemary truffle broth. Vegetarian dishes are a speciality - try wild herb couscous with chickpea and spinach beignets, or maybe shallot Tatin with roasted squash, porcini and almonds.

Times: 12-2.30/6-11.30 **Rooms:** 95 (95 en suite)★★★★★ HL **Directions:** Nearest station: Hyde Park Corner On Hyde Park corner

ENGLAND

LONDON SW1 CONTINUED

◉◉ Luciano

Italian

Classy St James's Italian with a touch of 'Marco' magic

☎ 020 7408 1440 72-73 St James's St SW1A 1PH
Plan 5-B5
e-mail: info@lucianorestaurant.co.uk
web: www.lucianorestaurant.co.uk

The St James's collaboration between Marco Pierre White and Sir Rocco Forte, Luciano's comes brimful of class and glamour. There's a large chic bar at the front with a mosaic-tiled floor and large windows overlooking St James's Street - just the place for a pre-meal Bellini. The atmospheric restaurant - down a few steps beyond the bar - oozes style and glamour. Think provocative photograph-lined walls, slate pillars, polished-wood floors, burgundy leather banquettes and matching chairs, and eye-catching mood lighting; there's oodles of experience with an art-deco nudge in true Marco style. Smartly attired mainly Italian staff, and an Italian-dominated wine list is impressive too. Cooking is classic Italian using top-notch produce delivering straightforward, full-flavoured dishes; take ravioli of leeks and scamorza, or perhaps roast John Dory with Jerusalem artichoke and tomato.

Times: Closed 25-28 Dec **Directions:** Please telephone for directions

◉ Mango Tree

Thai NEW

Contemporary authentic Thai food in a stylish setting

☎ 020 7823 1888 46 Grosvenor Place, Belgravia SW1X 7EQ Plan 4-G4
e-mail: reservations@mangotree.org.uk
web: www.mangotree.org.uk

This fine-dining Thai restaurant is located in Belgravia and is the sister restaurant to Awana in Chelsea (see entry). The dining room is large and spacious with a sleek, modern feel, with materials sourced direct from Thailand to create a beautiful and authentic setting. The authentic Thai food takes in starters like por pia hang hong (shrimp spring rolls served with a sweet and spicy sauce), or perhaps tod mun pla (spicy fishcakes seasoned with curry and kaffir lime leaf), followed by talay pad med mamuang (stir-fried mixed seafood with cashew nuts), or pla pow (sea bass fillet wrapped in banana leaves on a cress salad with spicy lime and tamarind).

Times: 12.30-3/6-11, Closed Sat **Prices:** Food prices not confirmed for 2008. Please telephone for details

◉ Mint Leaf

Modern Indian

Trendy Indian restaurant offering authentic modern cuisine

☎ 020 7930 9020 Suffolk Place, Haymarket SW1Y 4HX
Plan 5-C3
e-mail: reservations@mintleafrestaurant.com
web: www.mintleafrestaurant.com

Located in the basement of a recently converted bank, this modern Indian restaurant makes clever use of wire mesh screens, wooden slats, and ambient lighting. Darkwood walls, leather seating and polished stone floors continue the style, and staff are friendly and attentive. The

kitchen's focus is on quality produce and vibrant spicing, using modern presentation. For mains, try minced lamb kofta cooked in cardamom-scented sauce, and for a real treat tuck into some tasty peshwari naan which is really up to the mark. Tempting desserts include apple tart with mango sorbet. The trendy cocktail bar serves snacks until midnight.

Mint Leaf

Chef: K K Anand **Owners:** Out of Africa Investments **Times:** 12-3/5.30-11, Closed 25 & 26 Dec, 1 Jan, BHs, Etr Sun, Closed L Sat, Sun **Prices:** Fixed L £15-£45, Fixed D £40-£65, Starter £6.50-£12, Main £8-£32, Dessert £5.50-£7.50, Service added but optional 12.5% **Wine:** 140 bottles over £20, 4 bottles under £20, 12 by the glass **Notes:** Vegetarian available, Dress Restrictions, Smart casual, no scruffy jeans or trainers, Civ Wed 100, Air con **Seats:** 144, Pr/dining room 66 **Children:** Portions **Directions:** Nearest station: Piccadilly/Charing Cross At end of Haymarket, on corner of Pall Mall and Suffolk Place. Opposite Her Majesty's Theatre, 100m from Trafalgar Square **Parking:** NCP, on street

◉ Mitsukoshi

Japanese

Authentic Japanese cooking in a department store restaurant

☎ 020 7930 0317 Dorland House,
14-20 Lower Regent St SW1Y 4PH Plan 3-B1
e-mail: lonrest@mitsukoshi.co.jp
web: www.mitsukoshi-restaurant.co.uk

Set in the basement of its namesake Japanese department store just off Piccadilly Circus, Mitsukoshi is very much a traditional-styled Japanese. Descend the stairs to the popular sushi bar, or down a further tier to the main dining room, decked out in simple, light, neutral tones with booth-style areas set with dark lacquered tables. The kitchen deals in fresh, quality ingredients and a broad selection of authentic Japanese cuisine. Sushi, sukiyaki and shabu-shabu are the main specialities, with plenty of set-meal options on offer too. Otherwise expect grilled beef fillet with teriyaki sauce or perhaps deep-fried prawns with tempura sauce.

Times: 12-2/6-10, Closed 25, 26 Dec, 1 Jan, Etr

◎◎ Mocoto

Brazilian NEW

South American food in striking setting

☎ 020 7838 1044 145 Knightsbridge SW1X 7PA Plan 4-F4
web: www.mocoto.co.uk

This ambitious new Knightsbridge Brazilian - on the site of the one-time Isola restaurant - comes with a bar on the ground floor and beautifully designed basement restaurant. Calm and neutral, there's plenty of wood, hessian and crisp white linen, while chairs are simple 1960s design covered in soft cowhide. A huge wooden-screen wall runs down one side, while a bar takes up the entire length of the other wall and adds a tropical buzz. The accomplished Brazilian-inspired food suits the surrounds, and is fun, vibrant and well executed, driven by first-rate ingredients and well-considered, distinctive flavours. Take roast king prawns with vapapa sauce, peanut sprouts, okra and coriander, or perhaps pork loin with smoked ribs, sausages, sun-dried beef, braised black beans, kale and farofa.

Times: 12-2.30/6-10.30, Closed Sun

◎ MU at Millennium Knightsbridge

French, Pacific Rim

Reliable dining in the heart of Knightsbridge

☎ 020 7201 6330 17 Sloane St, Knightsbridge
SW1X 9NU Plan 4-F4
e-mail: mju@mill-cop.com
web: www.millenniumhotels.com/knightsbridge

Occupying a curvaceous space on the first floor of the fashionable Millennium Hotel in the prestigious shopping area of Knightsbridge, MU combines contemporary design and urban chic with classic colours, imaginative lighting and artwork to dramatic effect without losing a sense of warmth and intimacy. The kitchen concentrates on hearty dishes with a modern edge, focussing on interesting combinations of ingredients. Start perhaps with warm Jerusalem artichoke and sun-dried tomato tart with rocket coulis, followed by confit duck leg with parsnip purée and sweet and sour sauce.

Times: 12-2.30/6-10.30, Closed Sun, Closed L Sat **Rooms:** 222 (222 en suite) ★★★★ HL **Directions:** Nearest station: Knightsbridge/Victoria 200yds from Knightsbridge Stn/near Harrods

◎◎◎ Nahm *see below*

◎◎◎ La Noisette
see page 302

◎◎◎ One-O-One
see page 302

◎◎◎

Nahm

LONDON SW1

Thai V

Top-notch traditional Thai in chic hotel

☎ 020 7333 1234 The Halkin Hotel, Halkin St, Belgravia
SW1X 7DJ Plan 4-G4
e-mail: res@nahm.como.bz
web: www.halkin.como.bz

Located in Belgravia, the Halkin is a discreet and luxurious bolthole for the well heeled. It's perhaps a surprising choice for an internationally renowned chef to set up home but it works - particularly in the evening when Nahm resounds with the cooing of diners enjoying the unforgettable flavours of what many consider the world's best Thai food. Slatted wooden panelling creates intimate spaces within a large, bright room, while gold, reds and teak add to the minimalist furnishings. This unassuming décor allows the food to do the talking - backed up by assured and knowledgeable service. The Arharn Thai tasting menu offers the best overview of this sophisticated and very often extraordinary cuisine. Tickle the palate with a hor mok hoi shell appetiser - red curry of scallops with Thai basil and kaffir lime leaves; then sample dishes such as a salad of crispy pork with squid and chilli jam, gen gari gai (an aromatic chicken curry with cucumber relish) or dtom hang wua (oxtail braised with coriander seeds and spring onions).

If the prices leave you a little breathless you can content yourself with the knowledge that it's cheaper than flying to Bangkok.

Chef: David Thompson, Matthew Albert **Owners:** Halkin Hotel Ltd
Times: 12-2.30/7-11, Closed 25 Dec & BHs, Closed L Sat-Sun **Prices:** Fixed L £20, Fixed D £49.50-£75, Starter £14.50, Main £8.50-£16, Dessert £9.50, Service added but optional 12.5% **Wine:** 190 bottles over £20, 12 by the glass **Notes:** Fixed D 4 courses, Vegetarian menu, Dress Restrictions, No jeans, Air con **Seats:** 78, Pr/dining room 36 **Children:** Portions
Rooms: 41 (41 en suite) ★★★★★ TH **Directions:** Nearest station: Hyde Park Corner Halkin Street just off Hyde Park Corner **Parking:** On street

ENGLAND

◉◉◉

La Noisette

LONDON SW1

Modern French 🍷 NOTABLE WINE LIST NEW 🖥️

A class act with cooking that embraces the seasons

☎ 020 7750 5000 164 Sloane St SW1X 9QB Plan 4-F4
e-mail: lanoisette@gordonramsay.com
web: www.gordonramsay.com/lanoisette/

A serious addition to the London restaurant scene from its opening in 2006 (formerly Pengelley's), this Gordon Ramsay backed venture - set among the fashionable, top-end boutiques of Knightsbridge - has the acclaimed, ex-Greenhouse chef, Bjorn van der Horst at the helm. Inside exudes style and quality, with service predominantly French, highly professional and appropriately understated. The brown and beige colour scheme uses natural materials to good effect, with an abundant use of wood panelling and slate-effect tiles on walls. Tables are well spaced, with leather banquette booths at both ends and contemporary artwork to break up the somewhat 1960s styling and ambience.

The kitchen's modern approach is assured, innovative and classy, with great emphasis placed on sourcing top-quality, seasonal ingredients. Presentation is equally stylish, in places even guéridon in style, with waiting staff decanting items cooked and served au feu, for instance. Appealing to the eye and living up to expectation on the palate, dishes exude clean flavours, balance, texture and colour interest, and are delivered via an exceptional range of fixed-price menus that truly explore the seasons. Take black bream en papillote with chestnuts, fig and salsify, and a guanaja chocolate marquise with toasted brioche and praline shake on an autumn repertoire.

Chef: Bjorn van der Horst **Owners:** Gordon Ramsay **Times:** 12-3/6-10.30, Closed BHs, 2 wks Xmas & New Year, Sun, Closed L Sat **Prices:** Fixed L £21, Fixed D £60-£75, Service added 12.5% **Wine:** 350 bottles over £20, 1 bottle under £20, 10 by the glass **Notes:** Fixed L 3 courses, Fixed D 7 courses, Vegetarian available, Air con **Seats:** 80 **Children:** Portions **Directions:** Nearest station: Knightsbridge, Sloane Sq Sloane St, between Knightsbridge and Sloane Sq, attached to Carlton Tower Hotel **Parking:** NCP Cadogan Place

◉◉◉

One-O-One

LONDON SW1

French, Seafood 🖥️

First-rate seafood restaurant

☎ 020 7290 7101 Sheraton Park Tower,
101 Knightsbridge SW1X 7RN Plan 4-F4
e-mail: darren.neilan@luxurycollection.com
web: www.luxurycollection.com/parktowerlondon

There's more than a hint of goldfish bowl to the curvaceous windows of this chic hotel dining room in the Sheraton Park Tower, and deliberately so, perhaps, since it's one of the finest seafood restaurants in London. Discreet frosted glass puts paid to pedestrian ogling, but a snatched glimpse would reveal an aquatic-inspired blue-and-white interior, with aquamarine leather chairs, a swirling blue carpet and a stainless steel sculpture of a fish.

Service is slick and delightfully friendly, and the kitchen never misses a beat; chef Pascal Proyart insists on superb quality ingredients and lets their freshness shine through. Fabulous seafood is the driving force, but there are a few meaty options too, and dishes are all distinguished by classic combinations, clean flavours and moments of inspiration. You can choose from an extensive carte, but with cooking this good, it's worth taking a look at the Menu Gormandise. Try soupe de poisson to start, followed, perhaps, by John Dory and baby squid à la plancha with cassoulet bean purée and braised pork belly, or roast lobster with curry leaf tamarind sauce and lemon coriander rice. When someone fancies fish in London, this is the place that first springs to mind.

As we went to press we understand a complete renovation had just taken place, together with a new menu.

Chef: Pascal Proyart **Times:** 12-2.30/7-10.30 **Rooms:** 280 (280 en suite) ★★★★★ HL **Directions:** Nearest station: Knightsbridge E from station, just after Harvey Nichols **Parking:** 60

Pétrus

LONDON SW1

Modern European V 🖥️

Top-of-the-range dining in an opulent Knightsbridge hotel

☎ 020 7235 1200 The Berkeley, Wilton Place, Knightsbridge
SW1X 7RL Plan 4-G4
e-mail: petrus@marcuswareing.com
web: www.marcuswareing.com

Chef: Marcus Wareing
Owners: Marcus Wareing at the Berkeley Ltd
Times: 12-2.30/6-11, Closed 1 week Xmas, Sun, Closed L Sat
Prices: Fixed L £30-£80, Fixed D £60, Service added but optional 12.5%
Wine: 1000 bottles over £20, 4 bottles under £20, 10 by the glass
Notes: Fixed L 3 courses, Vegetarian menu, Dress Restrictions, Smart-jacket preferred, no jeans/trainers, Air con
Seats: 70, Pr/dining room 16
Children: Portions
Rooms: 214 (214 en suite)★★★★★ HL
Parking: NCP and on street

Oozing sophistication and opulence, Pétrus comes discreetly located off the foyer and beyond the stylish Caramel Room lounge-bar at the luxury Berkeley Hotel - the unobtrusive name on the handles of its tinted-glass doors lets you know you've arrived. As soon as you enter you're cosseted by slick and attentive staff, consummate professionals, though not at all stuffy. Rich, vivid and sexy, the interior is the work of design guru David Collins, the sensual claret colours and textures reflecting that of the world-renowned wine that lends the restaurant its name. Eye-catching features grab the attention - two giant abacuses complete with blown-glass beads act as a screen for the wine chillers, fantastic chandeliers, stunning French blinds, chairs of soft burgundy leather and red velvety walls all seduce. Trolleys for cheeses, liqueurs and, most importantly, the bonbons, with its wonderful selection of sweetmeats, all circle the floor in style and add a sense of theatre to the occasion. There's also a small lounge area for aperitifs and a chef's table in the kitchen for up to eight guests. It's all a bold and striking complement to the impeccable cooking that makes Pétrus a dining magnet on the international culinary map.

Marcus Wareing's modern approach is classically based, has great integrity and owes much to the insistence on the absolute best in raw ingredients. The elegant, richly detailed cuisine oozes technical wizardry, precision, balance, clear flavours and wow factor ... this is skill of the highest order! Think grilled Dorset halibut teamed with new season leeks, confit potato, Oscietra caviar and parsley, while dessert might showcase a peanut parfait with rice crisp crunch and Valrhona chocolate mousse. A serious wine list, with a good selection by glass, naturally includes offerings from that namesake château, while set-price lunch continues to offer great value at this level.

ENGLAND

LONDON SW1 *CONTINUED*

◉ One Twenty One Two

Modern NEW

Hotel fine dining in the heart of Whitehall

☎ 0870 3339 1222 Royal Horseguards Hotel,
2 Whitehall Court SW1A 2EJ Plan 5-D5
e-mail: royalhorseguards@thistle.co.uk
web: www.royalhorseguards.com

This majestic hotel in the heart of Whitehall sits beside the Thames
and enjoys unrivalled views of the city skyline. The interior is
impressive, with modern refinement seamlessly woven into the
architectural elegance. Paying tribute to its once former neighbour,
Scotland Yard, the restaurant is named after the Yard's once universally
famous telephone number, Whitehall 1212. 'One Twenty One Two'
offers contemporary dining in sophisticated but relaxed surroundings,
with views over the outdoor terrace. The kitchen shows skill and
imagination in a repertoire blending modern with traditional, and a
focus on fresh quality produce. Take Dover sole served with new
potatoes, baby spinach and a lime butter sauce, or perhaps a classic
Chateaubriand for two.

Chef: Michael Birmingham **Owners:** Thistle Hotels **Times:** 12-2/6-9.45,
Closed L Sat, Sun **Prices:** Fixed L £19.95, Fixed D £27.95, Starter £5.50-
£13.50, Main £17.50-£32, Dessert £6-£7.95, Service added but optional
12.5% **Wine:** All bottles over £20, 12 by the glass **Notes:** Vegetarian
available, Dress Restrictions, Smart casual, Civ Wed 200, Air con **Seats:** 40,
Pr/dining room 40 **Children:** Menu, Portions **Rooms:** 280 (280 en suite)
★★★★ HL **Directions:** Nearest station: Embankment, Charing Cross
From Trafalgar Sq take exit to Whitehall. Turn into Whitehall Place then into
Whitehall Court

◉◉ L'Oranger

French

*Classic French cuisine at one of London's most beautiful
restaurants*

☎ 020 7839 3774 5 St James's St SW1A 1EF Plan 5-B5
e-mail: oranger.restaurant@googlemail.com
web: www.loranger.co.uk

In keeping with its classy St James's address, L'Oranger is an
impeccably elegant dinner destination. The long panelled room is
adorned with flower displays and antique mirrors, with a domed glass
ceiling to let in the light, and there's a pretty courtyard for alfresco
dining in summer. Fish is a speciality, but the wide-ranging French
menu covers all the bases, featuring a selection of classics brought back
to life by the odd modern twist and the food is rich and flavours robust

and bold. Roasted scallops and smoked duck magret is a typical starter,
served with truffle mousse and raspberry vinaigrette dressing, while
mains might include cod poached in saffron broth with fennel and
aïoli.

Chef: Laurent Michel **Owners:** A to Z Restaurants Ltd **Times:** 12-2.30/6-
11, Closed BHs, Sun, Closed D Sat **Prices:** Fixed L £27, Fixed D £32, Starter
£14-£26, Main £26-£32, Dessert £8-£9, Service added but optional 12.5%
Wine: 290 bottles over £20, 4 bottles under £20, 6 by the glass
Notes: Menu Degustation £75, Dress Restrictions, Smart casual, Air con
Seats: 55, Pr/dining room 24 **Children:** Portions **Directions:** Nearest
station: Green Park Access by car via Pall Mall **Parking:** On street or NCP

◉◉◉◉ Pétrus

see page 303

◉ Quaglino's

Modern European 🖥

Vast basement St James's brasserie

☎ 020 7930 6767 16 Bury St, St James's SW1Y 6AJ
Plan 5-B6
e-mail: saschak@conran-restaurants.co.uk
web: www.quaglinos.co.uk

Built on the site of the original society restaurant, there's no shortage
of glamour and style in this well-established contemporary incarnation.
A dramatic marble staircase sweeps down into a cavernous space
supported by colourful columns, and there's a bar, live music and
ranks of white-clothed tables. The restaurant attracts an animated
crowd, which adds to the atmosphere and sense of theatre. Simple
seasonal dishes are the staple of the extensive brasserie-style menu:
think Chateaubriand with sauce béarnaise, or perhaps a lobster and
crab cake with spinach and beurre blanc. A fixed-price lunch and pre-
theatre menu are also available.

Chef: Craig James **Owners:** Conran Restaurants **Times:** 12-3/5.30-mdnt,
Closed 24-25 Dec, 1 Jan, Closed L 26, 31 Dec, 2 Jan **Prices:** Fixed L
£16.50, Starter £6.50-£14.50, Main £11.50-£32, Dessert £6-£12.50, Service
added but optional 12.5% **Wine:** 85 bottles over £20, 15 bottles under
£20, 14 by the glass **Notes:** Vegetarian available, Dress Restrictions, Smart
casual, Air con **Seats:** 267, Pr/dining room 44 **Children:** Menu, Portions
Directions: Nearest station: Green Park/Piccadilly Circus Bury St is off
Jermyn St **Parking:** Arlington Street NCP

◉ The Quilon

Indian V NEW

☎ 020 7821 1899 41 Buckingham Gate SW1E 6AF
Plan 5-B4
e-mail: info@quilonrestaurant.co.uk

This smart Indian rubs shoulders with the best address in town, set
just behind Buckingham Palace and decked out with curry powder
yellow seating and a modern décor with oil paintings adding that extra
pizzazz. There is also a separate waiting and bar area. The menu has
an English-style format (laid out as starters, mains and desserts), while
the kitchen specializes in the cooking from the south west coast, with
key spices, chillies, peppers and vinegars imported direct from the
southern region. Expect the likes of duck breast, pot-roasted with red
chilli paste, onion, aniseed and tomato, or marinated tilapia fish fillet
wrapped in banana leaves and pan fried.

Chef: Sriram Aylur **Owners:** Taj International Hotels Limited **Times:** 12-

2.30/6-11, Closed 25-26 Dec, Closed L Sat **Prices:** Fixed D £32-£42.50, Starter £6.50-£9.50, Main £17.50-£25, Dessert £5-£5.25, Service added but optional 12.5% **Wine:** 80 bottles over £20, 1 bottle under £20, 13 by the glass **Notes:** Fixed D 4 courses, Vegetarian menu, Dress Restrictions, Smart casual **Seats:** 90 **Children:** Portions **Directions:** Nearest station: St James's Park Next to Crowne Plaza Hotel St James **Parking:** On street, NCP

◎◎ Quirinale

Modern Italian 🖳
High-end Italian a stone's throw from Parliament

☎ 020 7222 7080 North Court, 1 Great Peter St SW1P 3LL Plan 5-C3
e-mail: info@quirnale.co.uk
web: www.quirnale.co.uk

A smart, modern interior from design guru David Collins sets the scene at this intimate, upmarket, basement Italian, discreetly tucked away on a pleasant street in the lee of the Houses of Parliament. Mirrors, limed floorboards, pastel shades and cleverly dressed pavement windows create a light, airy space, while white tablecloths, elegant chairs and central banquette seating provide the comforts. The cooking is unashamedly Italian, a mixture of classic and modern, the presentation and flavours as clean-cut and stylish as the surroundings or quality ingredients. The carte comes bolstered by daily specials, while there's an impressive selection of Italian breads, cheeses and wines. Expect home-made tagliolini with celeriac and black truffles, or perhaps baked fillet of John Dory served with a vegetable tagliatelle and basil pesto.

Chef: Stefano Savio **Owners:** Nadine Gourgey **Times:** 12-3/6-12, Closed Xmas & New Year, 2 wks Aug, Sat & Sun **Prices:** Starter £7.50-£10.50, Main £12.50-£17.50, Dessert £6.50, Service added but optional 12.5% **Wine:** 98 bottles over £20, 4 bottles under £20, 13 by the glass **Notes:** Vegetarian available, Air con **Seats:** 50 **Children:** Portions **Directions:** Nearest station: Westminster From Parliament Sq to Lambeth Bridge take 2nd left into Great Peter St, restaurant on left **Parking:** Street parking available, NCP

◎◎ The Rib Room

British V 🖳
Robust British cooking in the heart of Knightsbridge

☎ 020 7858 7250 Jumeirah Carlton Tower Hotel, Cadogan Place SW1X 9PY Plan 4-F4
e-mail: JCTinfo@jumeirah.com
web: www.jumeirah.com

Housed on the ground floor of the towering Jumeirah Carlton Tower Hotel, this buzzy restaurant has a sophisticated and moody club-like atmosphere and comes richly furnished with acres of wood panelling, awesome floral displays, seductive lighting, artwork by Feliks Topolski and crisp napery. The service gently balances British etiquette with friendliness. Tantalising aromas waft from the large open 'theatre' kitchen, its repertoire pure British gastronomy driven by the best home-reared produce and the successful blend of traditional and more contemporary style. Enjoy classic signature dishes like calves' liver with spring onion mash and fricassée of lentils, bacon and mushrooms, hard to resist Aberdeen Angus rib of beef with Yorkshire pudding or Rib Room seafood platter. A pianist entertains in the evenings.

Chef: Simon Young **Times:** 12.30-2.45/7-10.45 **Prices:** Fixed L £32, Starter £8-£18, Main £24-£64, Dessert £8.50-£9.50, Service added but optional 12.5% **Notes:** Sun L £45, Vegetarian menu, Dress Restrictions, Smart casual, Civ Wed 400, Air con **Seats:** 84, Pr/dining room 16 **Children:** Menu, Portions **Rooms:** 220 (220 en suite)★★★★★ HL

Directions: Nearest station: Knightsbridge From major roads follow signs for City Centre, towards Knightsbridge/Hyde Park/Sloane Sq, then into Sloane St/Cadogan Place **Parking:** 70

◎◎ Roussillon

Modern French 🖳
Discreet French restaurant focused on the seasons

☎ 020 7730 5550 16 St Barnabas St SW1W 8PE Plan 4-G2
e-mail: michael@roussillon.co.uk
web: www.roussillon.co.uk

There is no doubting the serious aspirations of this Pimlico restaurant with its large curved bay window: a formal and professional French team complete with sommelier matches the fine-dining menus and sophisticated modern ambience. With cream and brown décor and low lighting, the generously-sized, spacious tables are ideal for business lunches or evening get-togethers. A short lunch menu, carte and several specialist menus present classical French dishes based on luxury seasonal ingredients. The cooking is accurate and very imaginative, and there's a rustic style to the presentation. Typical dishes include classic foie gras terrine with walnut and artichoke salad to start, followed by lobster and sautéed girolle, oven-roasted pigeon with creamed morels, or Highland venison chasseur, with perhaps pineapple delice with caramel ice cream and white chocolate to finish.

Chef: A Gauthier **Owners:** J & A Palmer, A Gauthier **Times:** 12-2.30/6.30-11, Closed 24 Dec-5 Jan, Sun, Closed L Sat **Prices:** Fixed L £35, Fixed D £48, Service added 12.5% **Wine:** 350 bottles over £20, 20 bottles under £20, 20 by the glass **Notes:** Fixed L 3 courses, Tasting menu 6 courses £60, Air con **Seats:** 46, Pr/dining room 28 **Children:** Min 8 yrs, Portions **Directions:** Nearest station: Sloane Square Telephone for directions **Parking:** NCP

◎ The Rubens at the Palace

British, European 🖳
Quintessentially British hotel overlooking Buckingham Palace

☎ 020 7834 6600 39 Buckingham Palace Rd SW1W 0PS Plan 5-A4
e-mail: bookrb@rchmail.com
web: www.redcarnationhotels.com

Just opposite Buckingham Palace, this tourist favourite was the headquarters of the commander in chief of the Polish forces in World War II. The Library restaurant's décor follows its name's theme, and has the intimate feel of a Gentleman's club, with rich embroidered fabrics and large comfortable armchairs. There's an unobtrusive formality to the service, with traditional flourishes, such as smoked salmon being carved at the table. Simple presentation, good-sized portions and quality ingredients are evident throughout the menu, epitomised by dishes like roasted Gressingham duck breast served with fondant potato, glazed apples and an organic cider jus.

Chef: Daniel Collins **Owners:** Red Carnation Hotels **Times:** 7-10.30, Closed Xmas week, Closed L all week **Prices:** Starter £7-£12.50, Main £19.50-£46, Dessert £6.50-£8.50, Service added but optional 12.5% **Wine:** 4 bottles over £20, 8 bottles under £20, 12 by the glass **Notes:** Vegetarian available, Dress Restrictions, No shorts or track suits, Air con **Seats:** 30, Pr/dining room 50 **Children:** Menu **Rooms:** 161 (161 en suite) ★★★★ HL **Directions:** Nearest station: Victoria From station head towards Buckingham Palace **Parking:** NCP at Victoria Coach Station

ENGLAND

LONDON SW1 CONTINUED

ⓢ St Alban

Modern Mediterranean NEW

Hot new opening serving Mediterranean-inspired food where booking ahead is essential

☎ 020 7499 8558 4-12 Lower Regent St SW1Y 4PE
Plan 5-B6
web: www.stalban.net

This hungrily awaited opening from Wolseley duo Chris Corbin and Jeremy King (the pair originally behind The Ivy, Le Caprice and J. Sheekey, see entries) has hit the ground running. It's a smart modern affair, from the bright seating to the contemporary graphic murals of household objects lining the frosted glass windows and grey walls. Service is spot on, while the kitchen's modern, simply presented approach (under chef Francesco Mazzei) is inspired by the flavours of his native Italy as well as Spain and Portugal; think tagliata of beef with bone marrow mash potato, or a seafood fregola, and perhaps a vanilla pannacotta ristretto finish. One of the hottest openings of winter 2006, and under such fine parentage, there's already a high celebrity count.

Chef: Francesco Mazzei **Owners:** Chris Corban & Jeremy King
Times: 12-3/5.30-mdnt, Closed 25-26 Dec, 1 Jan, Aug BH, Closed D 24 & 31 Dec **Prices:** Starter £5.75-£18, Main 9.25-£26, Dessert £5-£8.50, Service added 12.5% **Wine:** 141 bottles over £20, 17 bottles under £20, 33 by the glass **Notes:** Vegetarian available, Air con **Seats:** 140
Children: Portions **Directions:** Nearest station: Piccadilly Circus From Piccadilly Circus tube station into Regent Street. Carlton Street 2nd left

ⓢ Salloos Restaurant

Pakistani 🖳

Romantic mews restaurant with a Pakistani menu

☎ 020 7235 4444 62-64 Kinnerton St SW1X 8ER
Plan 4-G4

Long established, professional and well run, Salloos deserves its undeniable status. It's a real family business, with a touch of luxury and glamour to the interior. Chicken shish kebab is an excellent all-round dish, delivered to the table on a large skewer with peppers and onions, the meat having a great tandoor flavour. Nargisi kofta is another masterful offering: egg coated in minced meat, halved and presented like a narcissus flower with a rich subtlety-spiced sauce. Warm carrot pudding, covered with real silver leaf and sprinkled almonds, makes an interesting dessert. Service is friendly with formal touches.

Chef: Abdul Aziz **Owners:** Mr & Mrs M Salahuddin **Times:** 12-3/7-11.45, Closed Xmas, Sun **Prices:** Food prices not confirmed for 2008. Please telephone for details **Wine:** 2 by the glass **Seats:** 65 **Children:** Min 6 yrs **Directions:** Nearest station: Knightsbridge Kinnerton St is opposite Berkeley Hotel on Wilton Place **Parking:** Meters & car park Kinnerton St

ⓢⓢ Santini

Italian 🖳

Sophisticated, family-run Italian restaurant

☎ 020 7730 4094 & 7730 8275 29 Ebury St SW1W 0NZ
Plan 4-H3
e-mail: info@santini-restaurant.com
web: www.santini-restaurant.com

A long-established, refined Belgravia Italian restaurant with alfresco terrace dining in summer. Inside, large windows, slatted blinds, light marble floors, pastel walls and suede banquettes and tub-style chairs cut an elegant, modern edge. The carte offers a typically lengthy choice of authentic, seasonally inspired, regional Italian dishes with a strong Venetian accent and emphasis on simplicity, flavour and quality ingredients. Expect home-made tagliolini with fresh hand-picked Cornish crab, and classics like veal chop in breadcrumbs (crisply fried), with tiramisù to finish. Attentive, professional service and good wines ooze Italian appeal too.

Chef: Luca Lamari **Owners:** Mr G Santin **Times:** 12-3/6-11.30, Closed Xmas, 1 Jan, Etr Sun, Closed L Sat & Sun **Prices:** Starter £8-£16, Main £13-£31, Dessert £6.50-£9, Service added optional 12.5% **Notes:** Pre-theatre menu £25, Vegetarian available, Dress Restrictions, Smart casual, Air con **Seats:** 65, Pr/dining room 30 **Children:** Portions
Directions: Nearest station: Victoria Take Lower Belgrave St off Buckingham Palace Rd. Restaurant on 1st corner on left opposite Grosvenor Hotel **Parking:** Meters (no charge after 6.30pm)

ⓢⓢ The Stafford Hotel

British 🍷 NOTABLE WINE LIST 🖳

Luxurious hotel dining in an exclusive location

☎ 020 7493 0111 16-18 St James's Place SW1A 1NJ
Plan 5-A5
e-mail: information@thestaffordhotel.co.uk
web: www.thestaffordhotel.co.uk

Tucked away behind Green Park, this genteel hotel has the feel of a luxurious country house in the heart of St James's. Public areas are comfortable with an understated opulence. The world-famous American bar, known for mixing a mean martini, displays an eccentric collection of club ties, sporting momentoes and signed celebrity photographs. A simpler menu is offered at lunchtime with a daily special from the trolley Sunday to Friday, generally a roast, and fish on Friday. Luxury ingredients are to the fore on the extensive carte: starters might include a soufflé of lobster and sole with caviar and champagne sauce, or steak tartare, while mains range from roast wild duck with apple and foie gras, to Chateaubriand.

Chef: Mark Budd **Owners:** Shire Hotels **Times:** 12.30-2.30/6-10.30, Closed L Sat **Prices:** Fixed L £29.50, Starter £9.50-£20.50, Main £14.50-£35, Dessert £9.50, Service included **Wine:** 340 bottles over £20, 6 by the glass **Notes:** Fixed L 3 courses, Vegetarian available, Dress Restrictions, Jacket, Civ Wed 44, Air con **Seats:** 52, Pr/dining room 44 **Rooms:** 105 (105 en suite)★★★★ HL **Directions:** Nearest station: Green Park 5 mins St James's Palace **Parking:** NCP on Arlington Street

⊛⊛ Volt

Modern European 🖳

Trendy modern restaurant with Mediterranean-influenced cuisine

☎ 020 7235 9696 17 Hobart Place SW1W 0HH Plan 4-H4
e-mail: info@voltlounge.com
web: www.voltlounge.com

There's a nightclub-like vibe about this cool Belgravia newcomer. An elegantly curved dining room radiates around a funky central bar seating area decked out in vivid red, with eye-catching soft purple strip light inset into walls and framing the bar. Contemporary chairs, leather banquettes and smartly dressed tables shout style, while three equally chic, intimate dining areas, fringing the main room, can be booked for private dining. The cooking complements the surroundings, its modern Mediterranean approach oozing Italian influence, while excellent home-made breads and petits fours add further appeal. Dishes are clean-cut, clear-flavoured and elegantly presented and use top-quality produce; think home-made rabbit ravioli with wild mushrooms, or perhaps pan-fried veal served with baby fennel, potato galette and a white aubergine sauce.

Chef: Santino Busciglio **Owners:** Bou Antoun **Times:** 12-3/6-11, Closed Xmas, last 2 wks Aug, BHs, Sun, Closed L Sat **Prices:** Fixed L £14, Fixed D £24.50, Service optional, Group service 12.5% **Wine:** 90 bottles over £20, 7 bottles under £20, 8 by the glass **Notes:** Vegetarian available, Dress Restrictions, Smart casual, Air con **Seats:** 120, Pr/dining room 45 **Children:** Portions **Directions:** Nearest station: Victoria Behind Buckingham Palace **Parking:** On street

⊛⊛ W'Sens by La Compagnie des Comptoirs

Modern French V 🖳

Chic Waterloo dining choice

☎ 020 7484 1355 12 Waterloo Place, St James SW1Y 4AU Plan 5-B6
e-mail: reservation@wsens.co.uk
web: www.wsens.co.uk

Inside this Grade II listed building you'll find a long retro-lit marble bar designed by an ex-student of Philippe Starck. This is one of the highlights of the warm, contemporary chic design, featuring a mix of fireplaces, black leather tables and a library. The menu offers French- and Mediterranean-style cooking with influences from North Africa and Asia. Look out for dishes like cured carpaccio and tartare of red salmon, then fillet of beef Rossini, pan-fried foie gras, spinach, potato purée with mixed wild mushrooms and truffle jus. A tasting menu and a vegetarian tasting menu for a whole table are also on offer. At the time of going to press we understand that this restaurant was undergoing a major refurbishment.

Times: 12-2.30/6.30-11, Closed 2 wks before Xmas, Sun, Closed L Sat
Directions: Nearest station: Piccadilly Telephone for directions

---

⊛⊛⊛
Zafferano

LONDON SW1

Traditional Italian 🏆 NOTABLE WINE LIST

Chic and popular Knightsbridge Italian

☎ 020 7235 5800 15 Lowndes St SW1X 9EY Plan 4-F4
e-mail: info@zafferanorestaurant.com
web: www.zafferanorestaurant.com

This stylish, deservedly popular Italian may look somewhat understated from the outside, but when judged by the difficulty in securing a table, it's clear that this is somewhere special. Drawing an adoring crowd, the suave, upmarket surroundings include a chic cocktail bar/lounge and private dining room and there's a relaxed, friendly vibe and vibrant see-and-be-seen atmosphere throughout. Dark wood, glass, exposed brick and tiled floors deliver a sophisticated modern edge to the recently refurbished main dining room, punctuated by flower displays, crisp white linen, elegant chairs and banquettes, and friendly, professional service. Andrew Needham's drawcard cooking makes certain this Italian is packed for all the right reasons. Intelligently simple, accomplished dishes allow the freshest, top-notch seasonal ingredients to shine. Flawless execution, clear flavours and clean, colourful presentation feature on the appealing fixed-price menus (with a few supplements), while a well-constructed, patriotic Italian wine list and fabulous bread selection rounds things off in style. Expect to be seduced by the likes of linguine with lobster and tomato, perhaps grilled monkfish with courgettes and sweet chilli, or a fillet of beef with celeriac and baby leeks, and maybe a bread-and-butter panettone pudding finish. By popular demand, Zafferano Delicatessen has opened adjacent to the restaurant.

Chef: Andrew Needham **Owners:** A-Z Restaurants **Times:** 12-2.30/7-11, Closed 1 wk Xmas & New Year, BHs **Prices:** Fixed L £25.50, Fixed D £39.50, Service added 13.5%, Group min 8 service 15% **Wine:** 400 bottles over £20, 15 bottles under £20, 6 by the glass **Notes:** Seasonal truffle menu available, Vegetarian available, Dress Restrictions, Smart casual, Air con **Seats:** 85, Pr/dining room 22 **Children:** No Children **Directions:** Nearest station: Knightsbridge Located off Sloane St, behind Carlton Tower Hotel **Parking:** NCP behind Restaurant

ENGLAND

LONDON SW1 *Continued*

◉◉◉ Zafferano

see page 307

💻 Aura Kitchen and Bar

☎ 020 7499 9999 48-49 St James St SW1A 1JT

web: www.theaa.com/travel/index.jsp

Pan-Asian menu under Caviar House in St James's. Silent movies flicker over the bar and there's live DJ music.

💻 The Contented Vine

☎ 020 7834 0044 17 Sussex St SW1V 4RR

web: www.theaa.com/travel/index.jsp

Chefs are on view at this popular brasserie. English/European menu of freshly prepared dishes.

💻 The Footstool

☎ 020 7222 2779 St John's, Smith Square SW1P 3HA

web: www.theaa.com/travel/index.jsp

Modern, atmospheric restaurant in St John's crypt with modern European menu. Open at concert times.

💻 Greens Restaurant and Oyster Bar

☎ 020 7930 4566 36 Duke St, St James' SW1Y 6DF

web: www.theaa.com/travel/index.jsp

Clubby atmosphere and an emphasis on fish, which is perfectly cooked. Classic nursery puddings round things off.

Wagamama

☎ 020 7321 2755 8 Norris St SW1Y 4RJ

Informal noodle bar with no booking required.

Yo! Sushi

☎ 020 7235 5000 5th Floor, Harvey Nichols Food Hall, 109-125 Knightsbridge SW1X 7RJ

Sushi, sashimi, noodles and more delivered by conveyor belt and priced according to colour-coded plates.

LONDON SW3

◉ Awana

Traditional Malaysian 💻

Authentic Malaysian restaurant and satay bar

☎ 020 7584 8880 85 Sloane Av SW3 3DX Plan 4-E2

e-mail: info@awana.co.uk

web: www.awana.co.uk

The name means 'in the clouds' in Malay and this restaurant is the newest venture of Eddie Lim, owner of The Mango Tree in Belgravia (see entry). The dining room is inspired by traditional Malaysian teak houses; think lush silk panels, delicate glass screens and burgundy leather seating to highlight the darkwood interior. Modern style is given to authentic Malaysian cuisine too, featuring satay, skewered dishes, starters, soups, curry, grills and stir-fries. Typical dishes include assorted seafood from the satay bar (where you can watch the chefs at work) like diver-caught scallops or maybe corn-fed chicken served with home-made spicy peanut sauce, while bestsellers like beef rendang or butterfish wrapped in banana leaf might catch the eye.

Chef: Mark Read **Owners:** Eddie Lim **Times:** 11-3/6-11, Closed 25-26 Dec, 1 Jan, Closed D 24 Dec **Prices:** Fixed L £12.50, Starter £3.50-£10.50, Main £9.50-£25, Dessert £5.50-£7.50, Service added 12.5% **Wine:** All bottles over £20, 12 by the glass **Notes:** Tasting menu £26, Vegetarian available, Dress Restrictions, Smart casual, Air con **Seats:** 110 **Children:** Portions **Directions:** Nearest station: South Kensington Left out of South Kensington station onto Penam Rd. Continue past Fulham Rd and this will lead onto Sloane Av

◉◉ Bibendum

European 💻

Classic and contemporary dishes with Conran style

☎ 020 7581 5817 Michelin House, 81 Fulham Rd SW3 6RD Plan 4-E3

e-mail: manager@bibendum.co.uk

web: www.bibendum.co.uk

Light, airy and elegant restaurant occupying the first floor of the art deco Michelin building, with its fabulous stained-glass windows portraying Bibendum, the Michelin man, in various poses. It's accessed via the ground-floor oyster bar, which serves all manner of crustacea, and the complex also includes a coffee bar. French and British brasserie dishes are brought up to date, Bibendum-style, at this slick operation, using fresh ingredients and accurate execution: rabbit and chorizo rillettes; braised pork cheeks in Sauternes with apricots and herbs; and blackcurrant, pear and almond tart served with amaretto ice cream. There's a great atmosphere, too, perfect for celebrity spotting, plus attentive, knowledgeable service and a notable wine list.

Times: 12-2.30/7-11.30, Closed Dec 25-26, 1 Jan, Closed D Dec 24

◉◉◉◉ The Capital

see opposite

The Capital

LONDON SW3

French 🍷 NOTABLE WINE LIST

Inspired cooking and impeccable service at Knightsbridge landmark

☎ 020 7589 5171 Basil St, Knightsbridge SW3 1AT Plan 4-F4
e-mail: reservations@capitalhotel.co.uk
web: www.capitalhotel.co.uk

Chef: Eric Chavot
Owners: Mr D Levin & Mr J Levin
Times: 12-2.30/7-11, Closed 25 Dec D
Prices: Fixed L £29.50, Fixed D £55, Service added but optional 12.5%
Wine: All bottles over £20, 15 by the glass
Notes: Fixed L 3 courses, Dégustation menu L £48, D £68, Dress Restrictions, Smart casual, Air con
Seats: 35, Pr/dining room 24
Children: Min 12 yrs, Portions
Rooms: 49 (49 en suite)★★★★★ TH
Directions: Nearest station: Knightsbridge Off Sloane St, beside Harrods
Parking: 10

Secreted away in the heart of Knightsbridge - on a quiet street just around the corner from Harrods and Harvey Nichols - this discreet, luxury boutique hotel thoroughly lives up to its name. Its stylish, new-look restaurant is a sophisticated, light-and-airy affair, delivering a suave but understated look inspired by the 1940s, while the adjoining cocktail bar has a Harry's Bar vibe. Lightwood panelling is partnered by cool, pale-blue velvet upholstered chairs, drapes and blinds in the intimate dining room, while contemporary styled chandeliers hang from high ceilings. Artwork by Dalí and sculpture by Henry Moore further enhance the elegance and chic, but add crisp white napery, highly professional table service, a serious wine list and inspired cooking from a formidably talented kitchen, and you have premier-league status. Chef Eric Chavot's cuisine comes close to perfection, sophisticated and utilising the finest-quality ingredients and plenty of luxury.

Though his roots are firmly entrenched in the French classical style (inspired by France's South West region), there's nothing staid or straight-laced here, instead a wonderful light, modern approach that comes dotted with some surprise elements. Refinement, balance and high skill reign supreme, with dishes delivered dressed to thrill and flavours clear and pronounced. Take a fillet of sea bass with crushed potatoes and aïoli dressing, followed by a chestnut sponge with matcha tea foam and passionfruit cream. Superbly made in-house breads, amuse-bouche, pre-dessert and petits fours hold style through to the end, while an excellent-value lunch bolsters the enticing carte and Menu Dégustation.

ENGLAND

LONDON SW3 CONTINUED

Le Colombier

French 💻

Popular French brasserie in the middle of Chelsea

☎ 020 7351 1155 145 Dovehouse St SW3 6LB
Plan 4-D2

e-mail: lecolombier1998@aol.com

web: www.lecolombier-sw3.co.uk

Tucked away just off the Fulham Road in the lee of the Royal Marsden Hospital, this popular, buzzy, traditional French-style brasserie comes brimful of Gallic charm and atmosphere. A blue and cream colour scheme, polished floorboards, white linen and smartly turned-out staff hit all the right notes, while a glass-covered terrace up front offers that all-year-round alfresco touch. The straightforward, well-presented brasserie fare uses quality ingredients and a light touch; expect classics like a fillet of beef with béarnaise sauce or poached brill with hollandaise and perhaps a tarte Tatin or crème brûlée finish.

Chef: Nigel Smith **Owners:** Didier Garnier **Times:** 12-3/6.30-10.30
Prices: Fixed L £16-£19, Starter £5.80-£12.50, Main £13.50-£22.80, Dessert £5.80, Service added but optional 12.5% **Wine:** 150 bottles over £20, 12 bottles under £20, 10 by the glass **Notes:** Dress Restrictions, Smart casual **Seats:** 70, Pr/dining room 30 **Children:** Min 10 yrs **Directions:** Nearest station: South Kensington Please telephone for directions
Parking: Metered parking

Eight Over Eight

Pan-Asian 💻

Pan-Asian cooking with real attitude

☎ 020 7349 9934 392 King's Rd SW5 5UZ Plan 1-E3
e-mail: richard@eightovereight.nu

web: www.eightovereight.nu

The bright red Eight Over Eight logo (it means 'lucky forever' in China) stands out over the pale grey walls of this corner bar/restaurant, divided inside by Japanese-style mock ironwork. The contemporary brown-and-beige look is spare and stylish, with beautiful low-hanging oriental lampshades. The menu takes in the standard Pan-Asian cooking styles, with sushi/sashimi, curries, dim sum, salads, tempura, roasts and specials, but there is nothing bland about the cooking. Expect black cod with sweet miso, perhaps chicken teriyaki with oba sake, or a roast monkfish Thai green curry.

Chef: Alex Ziverts **Owners:** Will Ricker **Times:** 12-3/6-11, Closed 24-29 Dec, Closed L Sun **Prices:** Fixed L £15, Starter £6-£10, Main £10.50-£21.50, Dessert £5-£6.50, Service added but optional 12.5% **Wine:** 68 bottles over £20, 6 bottles under £20, 12 by the glass **Seats:** 95, Pr/dining room 12 **Directions:** Nearest station: Sloane Sq Telephone for directions

Frankie's Italian Bar & Grill

Italian 💻

Glitzy basement restaurant serving simple Italian food

☎ 020 7590 9999 3 Yeoman's Row, Brompton Rd SW3 2AL Plan 4-E3
e-mail: infofrankies@btconnect.com

web: www.frankiesitalianbarandgrill.com

Tucked away in a Knightsbridge side street, the ground-level entrance hardly prepares you for the shimmering basement interior. A collaboration between Marco Pierre White and jockey Frankie Dettori, the glitzy décor oozes Marco class, from mirror-lined walls and huge revolving disco balls to good-sized tables, leather seating and attentive, informed staff. A chequered mosaic-style floor and small bar complete a sparkling line up, served up to a 1950s backing track and buzzy atmosphere. No fuss, simple Italian food, accurately cooked from fresh ingredients on a straightforward menu of one-price antipasti, pasta, burgers and grills - like escalope of veal Milanese - hits just the right note.

Times: 12-3/6-11, Closed 26 Dec, Closed D 25 Dec **Directions:** Nearest station: South Kensington/Knightsbridge Near The Oratory on Brompton Rd, close to Harrods

Manicomio

Italian

Regional Italian cuisine in stylish surroundings

☎ 020 7730 3366 85 Duke of York Square, Chelsea SW3 4LY Plan 4-F2
e-mail: manicomio@btconnect.com

web: www.manicomio.co.uk

The name means madhouse, but that's not a reflection on the current restaurant, rather on its history as a military asylum! Today you'll find rustic chic with exposed brickwork, oak tables and flooring and leather seating. The huge terrace is complemented by a private conservatory-style dining room and courtyard. Authentic regional Italian dishes are prepared simply using fresh ingredients. Home-made pastas and grills are the cornerstones of an interesting and wide-ranging menu. Try tuna tartare with capers, rocket, shallots and lemon, or broad bean and ricotta tortelli, followed by chargrilled tiger prawns with fregola, tomato, chilli and garlic.

Chef: Bobby Cabral & Tom Salt **Owners:** Ninai & Andrew Zarach
Times: noon-3/6.30-10.30, Closed Xmas & New Year **Prices:** Starter £7.50-£10.50, Main £9.50-£23.50, Dessert £6.75-£7.75, Service added but optional 12.5% **Wine:** 63 bottles over £20, 8 bottles under £20, 17 by the glass **Notes:** Vegetarian available, Air con **Seats:** 70, Pr/dining room 30 **Children:** Portions **Directions:** Nearest station: Sloane Square Duke of York Sq 100mtrs along King's Rd from Sloane Sq **Parking:** on street

Nozomi

Japanese

Luxury Japanese cuisine in chic Knightsbridge

☎ 020 7838 1500 7838 0181 14 - 15 Beauchamp Place, Knightsbridge SW3 1NQ Plan 4-E4
e-mail: info@nozomi.co.uk

web: www.nozomi.co.uk

The impressive entrance with its stylish black canopy, two sets of marble steps, and uniformed doorman set an ambitious tone which a visit to this high-class restaurant does nothing to dispel. A cocktail bar furnished with silvery grey leather seating is the first port of call, and then there's the understated elegance of the restaurant with its white silk-lined walls, subtle beige banquettes and crisp white tablecloths. The food, too, leads off in a new and independent direction, though the modern interpretations are underpinned by traditional Japanese themes. Thus the menu is divided into the usual sushi and sashimi, yakitori, tempura, fish, meat and poultry, with luxury items like wagyu beef with mushrooms, shallots and white truffles.

Owners: Marius George **Times:** 12-3/6.30-11.30 **Prices:** Food prices not confirmed for 2008. Please telephone for details **Notes:** Vegetarian available, Dress Restrictions, Smart casual **Seats:** 110, Pr/dining room 35 **Directions:** Nearest station: Knightsbridge Telephone fo directions

◉◉ Racine

French

Popular French brasserie upholding the bourgeois culinary tradition

☎ 020 7584 4477 239 Brompton Rd SW3 2EP
Plan 4-E3

A neighbourhood restaurant, located across the road from the Brompton Oratory, this establishment is dedicated to French bourgeois cooking. Popular with Knightsbridge shoppers and foodies alike, Racine's success is in the detail. Formally-attired waiters provide correct, unfussy service while the curtained entrance, darkwood floors and leather banquette seating add nostalgic allure to a menu of French culinary classics. Typical dishes are hot foie gras on toast with red wine sauce and a warm duck egg yolk, or grilled rabbit with

mustard sauce and smoked bacon. Finish with pear poached in spiced red wine with cinnamon custard or enjoy La Fromagerie French farmhouse cheeses. Booking is essential.

Chef: Henry Harris **Owners:** Eric Garnier, Henry Harris **Times:** 12-3/6-10.30, Closed 25 Dec **Prices:** Fixed L £16.50, Fixed D £18.50, Starter £6-£13.25, Main £13.25-£21.50, Dessert £6-£7.50, Service added but optional 14.5% **Wine:** 55 bottles over £20, 13 bottles under £20, 16 by the glass **Notes:** Fixed D up to 7.30 only, Vegetarian available, Air con **Seats:** 75, Pr/dining room 16 **Children:** Portions **Directions:** Nearest station: Knightsbridge, South Kensington Restaurant opposite Brompton Oratory

◉◉◉ Rasoi Restaurant

see below

◉◉◉◉◉ Restaurant Gordon Ramsay

see page 312

◉◉◉◉◉ Tom Aikens

see page 313

◉◉◉

Rasoi Restaurant

LONDON SW3

Modern Indian V

Elegant townhouse Indian restaurant - simply the best

☎ 020 7225 1881 10 Lincoln St SW3 2TS Plan 4-F2
e-mail: rasoi.vineet@btconnect.com
web: www.vineetbhatia.com

Discreetly tucked away down a side street off the King's Road close to Sloane Square, this elegant Chelsea townhouse (where you have to ring the doorbell to gain entry) is home to the much-lauded Vineet Bhatia's rasoi (kitchen). Bhatia's modern, progressive attitude to Indian cuisine is echoed in the décor, rich in vibrant Eastern styling that sets the scene for an intimate, relaxed but sophisticated experience. Sandy-beige and chocolate-brown tones, silk cushions, woodcarvings and a bewitching array of tribal masks create an exotic atmosphere, alongside specially-sourced, contemporary cutlery and crockery, crisp white linen and a pleasant marriage of slick and professional Western and Indian front-of-house service. There's a snug front room overlooking the street, while the back room is bathed in daylight from conservatory-style skylight.

Vineet Bhatia's contemporary, thoroughly evolved cuisine redefines the concept of Indian food and dining, and makes a visit here a real experience. There's an elegance to the kitchen's technical skill, with

fine clarity and balance to vibrant flavours, textures and colours, while presentation is refined, cultured and eye-catching. Luxury ingredients parade on an enticing range of menu options that includes a stunning seven- or nine-course Rasoi Gourmand menu (with or without wine selection). Expect the likes of pan-fried sea bass topped with aubergines cooked in Hyderabadi coconut and peanut masala with steamed rice, or a mango mousse with lemon jelly and strawberry sorbet to finish. This is a must visit for lovers of modern Indian cuisine!

Chef: Vineet Bhatia **Owners:** Vineet & Rashima Bhatia **Times:** 12-2.30/6.30-10.30, Closed Xmas, New Year, BHs, Sun, Closed L Sat **Prices:** Fixed L £21-£35, Fixed D £40-£84, Starter £12-£20, Main £14-£39, Dessert £9-£14, Service added but optional 12.5% **Wine:** 250 bottles over £20, 4 bottles under £20, 10 by the glass **Notes:** Tasting menu 7 courses £81, Vegetarian menu, Dress Restrictions, Smart casual, Air con **Seats:** 35, Pr/dining room 24 **Directions:** Nearest station: Sloane Square Near Peter Jones and Duke of York Sq **Parking:** on street

ENGLAND

Restaurant Gordon Ramsay

LONDON SW3

French 🖥

London's finest and Britain's most celebrated chef

☎ 020 7352 4441 68 Royal Hospital Rd SW3 4HP Plan 4-F1
web: www.gordonramsay.com

While his face is rarely off our TV screens and the Ramsay restaurant empire may have gone global, this Chelsea temple of gastronomy - opened back in 1998 - still remains the mothership of his London operations, delivering the best cooking in the capital. A slick black frontage discreetly marks out the restaurant's entrance, while the extensive refurbishment of the intimate dining room by design guru David Collins is wonderfully stylish and sophisticated, the clean lines cleverly allowing the food centre stage. The cream interior also delivers the contemporarily elegant platform for unparalleled front-of-house service - this is as good as it gets. Slick, professional and polished, charmingly orchestrated by maître d' Jean-Claude Breton, whose unique, magical management style makes you feel like you're the only diners in the room. Enthusiastic explanations of dishes increase anticipation, while there's plenty of help navigating the fabulous wine list, too.

Classical dishes with contemporary spin grace the kitchen's tantalising fixed-price repertoire of lunch, carte and seven-course Menu Prestige, which come studded with luxury. Simplicity, integrity and lightness of touch are hallmarks of the approach, coupled with innovation, flair, stunning ingredients, precision and depth of flavour. The superlatives may roll on, but the skills on display are exceptional, with consistency and execution nigh faultless. So expect to be wowed by the likes of roasted fillet of halibut with carrot and coriander pappardelle, baby navet, salsify and a passionfruit butter sauce, or best end of Cornish lamb served with confit shoulder, provençale vegetables, baby spinach, black olives and a basil lamb jus, while a Granny Smith parfait with honeycomb, bitter chocolate and champagne foam might catch the eye at dessert. Royal Hospital Road remains as popular as ever, thus bookings can only be made a month in advance, so be ready to hang on the end of the telephone to secure that table. You certainly won't be disappointed, this is one of life's musts!

Chef: Gordon Ramsay, Mark Askew
Owners: Gordon Ramsay
Times: 12-2.30/6.30-11, Closed Sat, Sun
Prices: Fixed L £40, Fixed D £70, Main £85, Service added but optional 12.5%
Wine: 100+ bottles over £20, 2 bottles under £20, 18 by the glass
Notes: ALC 3 courses, Menu prestige £110, Vegetarian available, Dress Restrictions, Smart dress, Air con
Seats: 70
Children: Portions
Directions: Nearest station: Sloane Square At junct of Royal Hospital Road & Swan Walk

Tom Aikens

LONDON SW3

Modern French V 🍷NOTABLE WINE LIST 🖥

Gastronomic big-hitter of supreme class and distinction

☎ 020 7584 2003 43 Elystan St SW3 3NT Plan 4-E2
e-mail: info@tomaikens.co.uk
web: www.tomaikens.co.uk

Chef: Tom Aikens
Owners: T & L Ltd
Times: 12-2.30/6.45-11,
Closed 2 wks Xmas & N
Year, lst 2 wks Aug & BHs,
Sat & Sun
Prices: Fixed L £29, Fixed
D £65, Service added but
optional 12.5%
Wine: 590 bottles over
£20, 10 bottles under £20,
12 by the glass
Notes: Fixed L 3 courses,
Tasting menu 7-8 courses
£80-£100, Vegetarian
menu, Dress Restrictions,
Smart dress, no jeans/T-
shirts, jacket pref, Air con
Seats: 60, Pr/dining
room 10
Children: Portions
Directions: Nearest
station: South Kensington
Off Fulham Rd (Brompton
Rd end)
Parking: Parking meters
outside

This eponymous, much-heralded Chelsea temple to the serious foodie has deservedly put Tom Aikens up there among the pinnacle of top London kitchens. It's an understated, discreet setting for a premier leaguer, a one-time pub transformed by Anouska Hempel's design into a dining room dedicated to the theatre of fine dining. Dark wooden floors and window shutters, black leather chairs and white walls dotted with modern artwork set the interior's minimalist, self-confident lines. Bamboo screens, table lamps set high into window frames and sumptuous flower displays further distinguish the room, alongside the crockery, cutlery and slate serving plates and well-directed, professional and knowledgeable service. The presentation of Aikens' fixed-priced menu repertoire (lunch, dinner and tasting option) follows the theme of the clean-lined surroundings, with dishes eye-catchingly laid out under their main ingredient; take 'Oyster', which translates as poached oysters with lemongrass, avocado purée and Gewürztraminer jelly. But it's the successful marriage of classical roots, modern interpretation, first-class ingredients and flamboyant presentation that makes Aikens' food sexy and stand out from the crowd. Attention to detail dominates every aspect with its sheer quality, with ancillaries like breads, amuse-bouche, pre-dessert and breathtaking petits fours (of afternoon-tea proportions) hitting top form. Technical skill and intricate design and presentation pepper inventive, generous-portioned, vibrant dishes, their innovative combinations showering the senses with visual and flavour sensations. Expect the likes of steamed pigeon teamed with chestnut cannelloni, turnip fondant and chestnut sauce to wow the taste buds, while a suitably extensive, French-themed wine list befits the cuisine. This is zenith-class cooking from one of the country's greatest culinary talents - so do make this Chelsea pilgrimage.

ENGLAND

LONDON SW3 CONTINUED

◎◎ Tom's Kitchen

British, French NEW

Posh comfort food served in a trendy Chelsea diner

☎ 020 7349 0202 27 Cale St SW3 3QP Plan 4-E2
e-mail: info@tomskitchen.co.uk
web: www.tomskitchen.co.uk

This trendy see-and-be-seen brasserie-style diner near the King's Road is the latest addition to the Tom Aikens empire, located in a quiet area of Chelsea. Housed in a period-style building with large windows, the brasserie has an informal, upbeat vibe, with light wooden tables and coloured and black-and-white canvasses on whitewashed walls adding to the atmosphere. You can relax with a cocktail in the first-floor bar and games room, and there's also a private dining room with its own lounge. The cooking style is based on English and French brasserie dishes, delivered in style from an accomplished team. You might start with butternut squash, sage and honey soup, or maybe wild mushroom risotto with sage and pine kernels, and follow with baked fillet of sea bass with red pepper relish, wilted spinach and olive oil mash. Open every day for dinner, and for breakfast and lunch from 7am Monday to Friday, there's also a brunch menu at weekends.

Chef: Guy Bossom **Owners:** Tom Aikens **Times:** 12-3/6-12, Closed 24-27 Dec, Closed L 28 Dec **Prices:** Starter £5.50-£12.50, Main £10.50-£25, Dessert £6, Service added but optional 12.5% **Wine:** 70 bottles over £20, 10 bottles under £20, 16 by the glass **Notes:** Vegetarian available, Air con **Seats:** 75, Pr/dining room 22 **Children:** Portions **Directions:** Nearest station: South Kensington W from Sloane Sq along Kings Rd. Right onto Markham St and then left into Cale St **Parking:** On street

◎ Toto's

Traditional Italian

Popular, friendly Italian restaurant

☎ 0871 332 7293 020 7589 0075 Walton House, Walton St SW3 2JH Plan 4-F3

Tucked away at the back of Knightsbridge, this lovely white-painted corner property has a patio/courtyard area where you can lunch alfresco. Inside a mezzanine overlooks the main dining room, taking in the sunny yellow walls, petrol blue chairs and fresh flowers, while a Venetian chandelier makes a striking centrepiece. The friendly service and great Italian cooking make this a very popular destination, packed with locals and those lucky enough to get a table by chance. The extensive menu offers modern Italian cuisine with classical undertones. Carpaccio of milk lamb with basil and white celery hearts sits comfortably alongside gratinated home-made veal cannelloni.

Chef: Paolo Simioni **Owners:** Antonio Trapani **Times:** 12.15-3/7-11.30, Closed 25-27 Dec **Prices:** Fixed L £21, Starter £9-£14, Main £12-£25, Dessert £7 **Wine:** 7 by the glass **Notes:** Vegetarian available, Dress Restrictions, Smart casual **Seats:** 90 **Children:** Portions

▭ Brasserie St Quentin

☎ 020 7589 8005 243 Brompton Rd SW3 2EP
web: www.theaa.com/travel/index.jsp

Good value French inspired dishes (and wines) in stylish brasserie dining room.

▭ Ciro's Pizza Pomodoro

☎ 020 7589 1278 51 Beauchamp Place SW3 1NY
web: www.theaa.com/travel/index.jsp

Longstanding and popular pizzeria with live music every evening and plenty of atmosphere.

▭ The Collection

☎ 020 7225 1212 264 Brompton Rd SW3 2AS
web: www.theaa.com/travel/index.jsp

Buzzy, vibrant and fashion conscious bar-restaurant.

▭ Cross Keys

☎ 020 7349 9111 1 Lawrence St, Chelsea SW3 5NB
web: www.theaa.com/travel/index.jsp

Gastro-pub with a very popular conservatory eating area. Modern Mediterranean menu.

▭ Haandi

☎ 020 7823 7373 136 Brompton Rd SW3 1HY
web: www.theaa.com/travel/index.jsp

Northern Frontier Indian cuisine often served in haandis (narrow necked cooking pots). The chefs can be seen hard at work.

Riccardos

☎ 020 7370 6656 126 Fulham Rd SW3 6HU
Elegant Italian food with a modern twist.

🖵 Shikara

☎ 020 7581 6555 87 Sloane Av SW3 3DX

web: www.theaa.com/travel/index.jsp

Wholesome Indian fare and earthly dishes of the tandoor.

Spiga Chelsea

☎ 020 7351 0101 312 Kings Rd SW3 5UH

Contemporary but classic Italian with superior pasta and pizza. Sister of Spiga W1.

LONDON SW4

❀❀❀ Trinity Restaurant

see below

❀ Tsunami

Japanese

Contemporary neighbourhood Japanese restaurant

☎ 020 7978 1610 5-7 Voltaire Rd SW4 6DQ Plan 1-E3
web: www.tsunamijapaneserestaurant.co.uk

Tucked away down a side street near Clapham Station, this buzzy, stylish neighbourhood Japanese restaurant is a honey pot for a cool crowd. Contemporary seating and lighting, colourful flower displays, an open kitchen and black-clad staff create a vibrant platform for the modern Japanese fusion cuisine. Tempura, sashimi, sushi and oysters each have their own section on the lengthy menu, with the quality

ingredients and imaginative presentation also showing in specials like black cod in sweet miso, chargrilled lamb with wasabi pepper sauce, and beef fillet with balsamic teriyaki sauce.

Chef: Ken Sam **Owners:** Ken Sam **Times:** 12.30-4/6-11, Closed 25 Dec-4 Jan, Closed L Mon-Fri **Prices:** Fixed L £10.50, Starter £2.50-£12.95, Main £6.50-£20.95, Dessert £3.95-£10.95, Service added but optional 12.5% **Wine:** 25 bottles over £20, 15 bottles under £20, 10 by the glass **Notes:** Fixed L 3 courses, Air con **Seats:** 90 **Children:** Portions **Directions:** Nearest station: Clapham North Off Clapham High Street **Parking:** On street

🖵 Morel Restaurant

☎ 020 7627 2468 14 Clapham Park Rd, Clapham SW4 7BB

web: www.theaa.com/travel/index.jsp

Trendy modern décor, modern French food, and a relaxed atmosphere.

San Marco

☎ 020 7622 0452 126 Clapham High St SW4 7UH

Attractively simple pizzeria with checked tablecloths and house wine drunk out of tumblers.

🖵 Strada

☎ 020 7627 4847 102-104 Clapham High St, Clapham SW4 7UL

web: www.theaa.com/travel/index.jsp

Superior pizza from quality ingredients cooked in wood-fired ovens.

Trinity Restaurant

LONDON SW4

British, French NEW
AA Restaurant of the Year for London

☎ 020 7622 1199 4 The Polygon, Clapham Old Town SW4 0JG Plan 1-E3

Trinity sees chef-restaurateur Adam Byatt return to his Clapham roots after a sojourn among the bright lights of WC2 - ex Thyme and Origin at Covent Garden's Hospital media complex, and originally of the much-acclaimed Thyme in Clapham Park Road. Here he's landing back in the Old Town area on the edge of leafy Clapham Common, and has created an exciting, buzzy, neighbourhood venture. Set well back from the road, it catches the eye and the light with its smart exterior and large window frontage. Inside there's a sophisticated, friendly atmosphere, the room decked out with white-clothed tables, elegant cream and chocolate-coloured walls, comfortable cane-backed chairs and soft lighting, all providing a contemporary backdrop to the polished, modern French cooking. There are also distant glimpses of the kitchen, plus a large private-dining 'kitchen table' that offers a closer window on all the action. Service is relaxed and friendly, yet suitably professional and knowledgeable. Adam's appealing menus feature interesting and adventurous combinations alongside some simpler dishes (including a Joint of the Day) on a repertoire that

includes his hallmark tasting options. High technique, clear flavours, creative presentation and tip-top produce add to the wow-factor; take 'sea bass - crosnes - artichoke' (which translates to slow-cooked fillet of sea bass served with a ragout of ceps, hazelnuts, crosnes and Jerusalem artichoke soup).

Chef: Adam Byatt **Owners:** Angus Jones **Times:** 12.30-2.30/6.30-10.30, Closed 24-26 Dec, Closed L Mon **Prices:** Fixed L £12, Starter £6-£10, Main £15-£20, Dessert £4-£8, Service added but optional 12.5% **Wine:** 80 bottles over £20, 9 bottles under £20, 10 by the glass **Notes:** Sun L/D 3 courses £20, Air con **Children:** Menu **Parking:** On street

ENGLAND

LONDON SW5

⊚ Cambio De Tercio

Spanish

Authentic Spanish cuisine in a lively atmosphere

☎ 020 7244 8970 163 Old Brompton Rd SW5 0LJ
Plan 4-C2

web: www.cambiodetercio.co.uk

Just round the corner from Earl's Park in Old Brompton Road, what appears at first sight to be a small restaurant is actually fairly large inside, with tables stretching back and a bar on one side. Wooden flooring and red cotton-covered chairs set off the white tablecloths, while lively Spanish music adds to the buzzy atmosphere. Authentic Spanish cuisine is the order of the day, with deep-fried squid with ink and garlic mayonnaise, roast suckling pig Segovian style, and monkfish with smoked pancetta, pine nuts and creamy spinach on a menu written in both Spanish and English.

Chef: Alberto Criado **Owners:** Abel Lusa **Times:** 12-2.30/7-11.30, Closed 2 wks at Xmas, New Year **Prices:** Starter £6-£15.75, Main £14.50-£18, Dessert £5.50-£6.50, Service added but optional 12.5% **Wine:** 250 bottles over £20, 10 bottles under £20, 6 by the glass **Notes:** Vegetarian available, Air con **Seats:** 45, Pr/dining room 22 **Directions:** Nearest station: Gloucester Road Close to junction with Drayton Gardens **Parking:** 10

🖥 Kare Kare

☎ 020 7373 0024 152 Old Brompton Rd SW5 0BE

web: www.theaa.com/travel/index.jsp

Modern, romantic, atmospheric location for a contemporary, healthy Indian. Special children's menu.

🖥 Strada

☎ 020 7835 1180 237 Earls Court Rd SW5 9AH

web: www.theaa.com/travel/index.jsp

Superior pizza from quality ingredients cooked in wood-fired ovens.

Tendido Cero

☎ 020 7370 3685 174 Old Brompton Rd SW5 0BA

Simpler sister of Cambio de Tercio with good tapas.

LONDON SW6

⊚ Blue Elephant

Traditional Thai 🖥

Truly extravagant Fulham Thai

☎ 020 7385 6595 4-6 Fulham Rd SW6 1AA Plan 1-D3
e-mail: london@blueelephant.com
web: www.blueelephant.com

From bustling Fulham Broadway, this extravagant Thai restaurant instantly transports you to another world - the experience is almost like dining in a tropical rainforest. Think lush plants, trickling fountains, bridges spanning koi carp-filled ponds, and truly welcoming Thai staff. Candles twinkle, while the scent of tropical flowers mingles with the heady aroma of exotic herbs and spices flown in fresh to service an equally flamboyant, lengthy menu. 'Pearls of the Blue Elephant' is a selection of starters enabling you sample a number of classic dishes, including a wonderful filo-wrapped prawn with peanut stuffing. For mains, expect homok talay (a spicy fish stew), or perhaps chiang rai (a very spicy stir-fried pork with chillies, garlic and green peppercorns). Vegetarian dishes are plentiful.

Times: 12-2.30/7-12, Closed Xmas, Closed L Sat **Directions:** Nearest station: Fulham Broadway Please telephone for directions

⊚⊚ Deep

Seafood

A real treat for fish and shellfish enthusiasts in contemporary surroundings

☎ 020 7736 3337 The Boulevard, Imperial Wharf SW6 2UB Plan 1-E3
e-mail: info@deeplondon.co.uk
web: www.deeplondon.co.uk

Stunning waterside location in Imperial Wharf, the luxurious dining room has floor-to-ceiling windows to make the most of the view and cream upholstery, while alfresco dining can be enjoyed on two terraces complete with café-style chrome tables and chairs. The friendly, switched-on team give attentive service. An interesting combination of mainly French, with Baltic and Scandinavian cooking features on a menu dominated by fish and shellfish. Carefully sourced produce is demonstrated in the amazing range of starters that include mussels steamed in wine and shallots, and ballotine of gravad lax with a fennel salad. Main courses might be a warm smoked trout with horseradish and braised beetroots, or paella 'Deep' style.

Chef: Mr C Sandefeldt & Mr F Bolin **Owners:** Christian & Kerstin Sandefeldt **Times:** 12-3/7-11, Closed Mon, Closed L Sat, D Sun **Prices:** Fixed L £15.50, Starter £6.50-£12, Main £13-£26, Dessert £5-£5.50, Service added but optional 12.5% **Wine:** 60 bottles over £20, 9 bottles under £20, 7 by the glass **Notes:** Tasting menu 6 courses £65, Dress Restrictions, Smart casual, Air con **Seats:** 120 **Directions:** Nearest station: Fulham Broadway From Fulham Broadway Underground Station take Harwood Rd then Imperial Rd **Parking:** Public car park, street parking after 5.30pm

⊚⊚ Saran Rom

Thai V 🖥

Luxury riverside Thai restaurant specialising in authentic cuisine

☎ 020 7751 3111 & 7751 3110 Imperial Wharf, The Boulevard, Townmead Rd SW6 2UB Plan 1-E3
e-mail: info@saranrom.com
web: www.imperialwharf.com/saranrom

This chic eatery brings a touch of eastern glamour to west London, its sumptuous décor paying homage to Thailand's royal palaces. No expense was spared in its creation and visitors dine amid a luxurious hotch-potch of silk hangings, 19th-century antiques and teak carvings. Add a ground floor bar, an outside terrace and riverside views, and it all adds up to a fantastic location to enjoy some traditional Thai hospitality. Main courses might include meaty fare such as panang beef or smoked duck curry, while vegetarians are well catered for too: a separate menu features the likes of sweet-and-sour tofu, tom yam hed - the famous hot and spicy Thai soup - and som tom je - papaya salad with carrots and peanuts flavoured with lemon and chilli.

Chef: Yupa Sontisup **Owners:** Mr Kobchok Negoypaiboon **Times:** 12-3/5-midnight, Closed 25 Dec, 1-4 Jan **Prices:** Service added but optional 12.5%, Group service 12.5% **Wine:** 40 bottles over £20, 9 bottles under £20, 22 by the glass **Notes:** Vegetarian menu, Air con **Seats:** 200, Pr/dining room 100 **Children:** Portions **Directions:** Nearest station: Fulham Broadway 1.5m from Stamford Bridge/Fulham Broadway tube station **Parking:** 100

Yi-Ban Chelsea

Japanese, Chinese

Stylish modern oriental dining at Chelsea Wharf-side location

☎ 020 7731 6606 No 5 The Boulevard, Imperial Wharf, Imperial Rd SW6 2UB Plan 1-E3
e-mail: michael@yi-ban.co.uk
web: www.yi-ban.co.uk

A stylish, contemporary restaurant at Chelsea's Imperial Wharf. The dining area is located beyond a funky bar and teppan-yaki counter, where voile curtains, dark wood and red pendant lights give a moody, modern feel. The contemporary oriental cuisine here encompasses teppan-yaki and Chinese food, the former cooked at a counter where diners can watch the chef in action. For an oriental restaurant there is a good selection of desserts.

Times: 6-11, Closed 1 wk from 22 Dec, Sun, Closed L all week
Directions: Nearest station: Fulham Broadway Please telephone for directions

The Farm

☎ 020 7381 3331 18 Farm Ln SW6 1PP
web: www.theaa.com/travel/index.jsp

Possibly the UK's first cash-free restaurant. European food with a spicy ethnic twist.

1492 Latin Fusion

☎ 020 7381 3810 404 North End Rd, Fulham Broadway SW6 1LU

web: www.theaa.com/travel/index.jsp

Wide-ranging Latin American cuisine, orange walls and dark wood set the scene.

Strada

☎ 020 7731 6404 175 New Kings Rd, Parsons Green SW6 4SW

web: www.theaa.com/travel/index.jsp

Superior pizza from quality ingredients cooked in wood-fired ovens.

LONDON SW7

◉◉ The Bentley Kempinski Hotel

French, European

Fine-dining experience in ornate restaurant

☎ 020 7244 5555 27-33 Harrington Gardens SW7 4JX
Plan 4-C2
e-mail: info@thebentley-hotel.com
web: www.thebentley-hotel.com

No expense has been spared on this luxury townhouse hotel, discreetly set in the heart of residential Kensington. Originally four grand private residences, it has been tastefully and sympathetically restored behind the original façades and positively oozes lavish opulence, the yellows and golds and wall-to-wall marble adding an almost Louis XV edge to proceedings. The setting for the fine-dining dinner-only 1880 restaurant (named after the date of the building) is an equally palatial affair that offers a real sense of occasion. Think elaborate ceilings, crystal chandeliers, silk wall panels and richly-coloured carpets and furnishings. The 1880s sophisticated and contemporary cooking is notable for its grazing-concept menus, with six-, seven-, eight- and nine-course options all miniature versions of dishes on the substantial, fixed-price carte, while service - from an international team - is appropriately slick and professional. Expect sautéed scallops with artichoke purée, grapefruit and vanilla, or marinated octopus carpaccio with piperade and balsamic syrup.

Chef: Paolo Saba **Times:** 12-2.30/6-10, Closed Easter & Xmas, BHs, Sun-Mon **Rooms:** 64 (64 en suite) ★★★★★ HL **Directions:** Nearest station: Gloucester Road Off A4 Cromwell Rd, opposite Gloucester Hotel

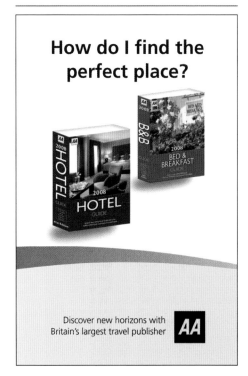

ENGLAND

LONDON SW7 CONTINUED

⊛⊛ Brunello

Italian 🍷 NOTABLE WINE LIST 💻

An opulent setting for classy Italian cuisine

☎ 020 7368 5700 Baglioni Hotel, 60 Hyde Park Gate, Kensington Rd SW7 5BB Plan 4-C4
e-mail: l.virgilio@baglionihotels.com
web: www.baglionihotels.com

Situated in the Baglioni, a sophisticated Italian hotel overlooking Hyde Park, the Brunello has a truly chic and opulent feel. Oozing luxury and style, the restaurant's huge mirrors, black silk curtains and ornate black Murano glass chandeliers - together with burnished gold velvet seating and large gilded napkin rings - create an almost regal setting for intimate candlelit dining. The restaurant's extensive carte is divided into antipasti, soups, pasta and risotto, and the fish and meat dishes include seafood and meat from the grill. Innovative interpretations of classic regional Italian dishes include 'modern' style veal chop Milanese, alongside artfully constructed salads like lobster, ceps and watercress with black truffle. Superb ingredients - many coming direct from Italy - accompanied by an outstanding wine list and enthusiastic service, keep foodies coming back for more, especially the Italian Sunday lunch.

Chef: Stefano Stecca **Owners:** Baglioni Hotels **Times:** 12-2.30/7-10.45
Prices: Fixed L £20, Fixed D £48, Starter £8-£18, Main £10-£40, Dessert £7-£15, Service added but optional 12.5% **Notes:** Vegetarian available, Air con
Seats: 70, Pr/dining room 60 **Children:** Portions **Rooms:** 68 (68 en suite)★★★★★ HL **Directions:** Nearest station: Kensington High Street Hotel entrance on Hyde Park Gate facing park & Kensington Palace
Parking: NCP (Young St)

⊛ L'Etranger

French, Japanese V 💻

Stylish, contemporary setting for classy fusion cuisine

☎ 020 7584 1118 36 Gloucester Rd SW7 4QT Plan 4-C4
e-mail: axelle@etranger.co.uk
web: www.circagroupltd.co.uk

Part of a complex with an adjacent wine shop and basement cocktail bar, L'Etranger is chic, sophisticated and elegant. Rich colours, fresh orchid displays, leather chairs and white linen add to the upmarket atmosphere of the restaurant, where service is attentive, professional and Gallic. A strong French influence also dictates the Asian fusion menu, which utilises high-quality core ingredients in innovative, well-presented dishes with a particular nod to Japan; take scallop, beef and prawn shabu shabu with lime leaves, or signature caramelised black cod with miso. There's a serious wine list too.

Chef: Jerome Tauvron **Owners:** Ibi Issolah **Times:** 12-3/6-11, Closed 25 Dec, 1 Jan, Closed L Sat **Prices:** Fixed L fr £14.50, Fixed D £16.50, Starter £7.50-£15, Main £15.50-£49, Dessert £6.50-£9.50, Service added but optional 12.5% **Wine:** 10 bottles under £20, 21 by the glass
Notes: Dégustation menu Sun brunch 2-3 courses £16.50-£19.50, Vegetarian menu, Air con **Seats:** 55, Pr/dining room 20
Children: Portions **Directions:** Nearest station: Gloucester Rd 5 mins walk from Gloucester Rd tube station at junct of Queens Gate Terrace and Gloucester Rd **Parking:** NCP

⊛ Swag and Tails

Modern International

Upmarket Knightsbridge village gastro-pub

☎ 020 7584 6926 10-11 Fairholt St SW7 1EG
Plan 4-E4
e-mail: theswag@swagandtails.com
web: www.swagandtails.com

Discreetly hidden away just across the road from Harrods, this convivial, well-heeled, flower-festooned Knightsbridge mews pub is predictably well groomed. There's stripped floorboards, winter fire, honeyed-wood furniture, swagged-and-tailed curtains and newspapers to peruse in the bustling bar, while the small, quieter restaurant behind parades a lighter, more contemporary edge. Here cream walls come adorned with attractive prints, while service is attentive and friendly. The same crowd-pleasing, bistro-style menu is served throughout; expect herb-crusted fillet of sea trout with chive mash, buttered spinach and parsley and caper oil, or perhaps date sponge served with caramel sauce and vanilla ice cream to finish.

Chef: Alan Jenkins **Owners:** Annemaria & Stuart Boomer-Davies
Times: 12-3/6-10, Closed Xmas, New Year, BHs, Sat-Sun **Prices:** Starter £4.95-£10.95, Main £9.95-£16.50, Dessert £5.25-£6, Service added but optional 10% **Wine:** 17 bottles over £20, 16 bottles under £20, 11 by the glass **Notes:** Vegetarian available **Seats:** 34 **Directions:** Nearest station: Knightsbridge Close to Harrods **Parking:** On street

◉◉ *Zuma*

Modern Japanese

Stylish, cutting-edge Japanese cuisine

☎ 020 7584 1010 5 Raphael St SW7 1DL Plan 4-F4
e-mail: info@zumarestaurant.com
web: www.zumarestaurant.com

A stone's throw from Harrods and Harvey Nichols in the heart of Knightsbridge, Zuma's cutting-edge modernity and stylish design is matched by its fashionable, glamorous clientele. The innovative Japanese cuisine is conjured from ultra fresh produce to create vibrant flavours in an extensive repertoire of beautifully-presented dishes served from the main kitchen, the sushi bar or the robata grill as they are cooked. This parade of dishes is ideal for sharing: thinly sliced sea bass with yuzu, truffle oil and salmon roe, or perhaps rib-eye steak with daikon ponzu sauce and garlic crisps. Desserts include Zuma sorbet with king lychee and coconut biscuit.

Times: 12-2.30/6-10, Closed 25-26 Dec, 1 Jan, Closed D 24 Dec
Directions: Nearest station: Knightsbridge Telephone for directions

🖥 The Delhi Brasserie

☎ 020 7370 7617 134 Cromwell Rd SW7 4HA
web: www.theaa.com/travel/index.jsp

Elegant, authentic Indian restaurant. The menu includes slightly more unusual dishes as well as old favourites.

🖥 FireHouse

☎ 020 7584 7258 3 Cromwell Rd SW7 2HR
web: www.theaa.com/travel/index.jsp

Stylish, three-storey restaurant opposite Natural History Museum serving British and European dishes.

LONDON SW8

◉◉ The Food Room

French 🖥

Stylish contemporary Battersea dining

☎ 020 7622 0555 123 Queenstown Rd SW8 3RH
Plan 1-E3
web: www.thefoodroom.com

Popular, modern, minimalist French eatery in Battersea (sibling to The French Table in Surbiton), decorated in warm, soft muted colours with stylish mirrors, metal and abstract art. This spacious, airy venue - with large windows facing onto the street - comes with relaxed, friendly service and a warm atmosphere. Classic French and Mediterranean dishes vie for selection alongside others with more imaginative flair, all produced using fresh seasonal produce and an emphasis on clear, subtle flavours. Take black tiger prawns, pineapple and sage risotto and curry sauce, or pork fillet in Parma ham with potato and blue cheese timbale and rosemary, and perhaps a rhubarb clafoutis finish with mascarpone ice cream.

Chef: Mr E Guignard **Owners:** Eric & Sarah Guignard **Times:** 7-10.30, Closed 25-26 Dec, BHs, Sun & Mon, Closed L all week **Prices:** Starter £5.50-£9.80, Main £10.50-£16.80, Dessert £5.50-£6.50, Service added but optional 12.5% **Wine:** 38 bottles over £20, 12 bottles under £20, 9 by the glass **Notes:** Smart casual, Air con **Seats:** 60 **Children:** Portions
Directions: Nearest station: Queenstown Road 10 min from Clapham Junction **Parking:** On street

LONDON SW10

◉◉◉◉ Aubergine

see page 320

◉◉ Chutney Mary Restaurant

Indian 🖥

Seductive Indian restaurant offering refined Indian cuisine

☎ 020 7351 3113 535 King's Rd, Chelsea SW10 0SZ
Plan 1-E3
e-mail: chutneymary@realindianfood.com
web: www.realindianfood.com

This highly acclaimed Chelsea eatery has been luring lovers of Indian cooking to the King's Road for almost 20 years now and has a well-deserved reputation for refined and creative cuisine. Antique etchings of India are teamed with mirrors and moody lighting to

CONTINUED ON PAGE 321

ENGLAND

Aubergine

LONDON SW10

Modern French

Accomplished and refined cooking from eminent Chelsea eatery

☎ 020 7352 3449 11 Park Walk, Chelsea SW10 0AJ Plan 4-C1
e-mail: info@auberginerestaurant.co.uk
web: www.auberginerestaurant.co.uk

Chef: William Drabble
Owners: A-Z Restaurants
Times: 12-2.30/7-11,
Closed Xmas, Etr, BHs, Sun,
Closed L Sat
Prices: Fixed D £64,
Service added but optional
12.5%
Wine: 500 bottles over
£20, 1 bottle under £20
Notes: Menu gourmand
£77, Fixed L 3 courses incl
wine & water £34, Dress
Restrictions, Smart casual
preferred, Air con
Seats: 60
Directions: Nearest
station: South Kensington,
Fulham Broadway W
along Fulham Rd, close to
Chelsea and Westminster
Hospital
Parking: Local parking
available

The namesake-coloured aubergine canopy and front door make this renowned, well-heeled Chelsea fixture easy to spot on its side street just off the Fulham Road's hustle and bustle, where William Drabble's modern French cuisine continues to shine. Aubergine cruets, dress plates and menus continue the theming inside at generous-sized, white-clothed tables with chocolate undercloths, where the room's muted, subtle tones create a relaxed, understated, stylish mood. Floors are light wood, walls beige ragged-effect hung with abstract artworks, and comfortable high-backed chairs come in cream, apricot and dark red. There's a stunning floral display at the entrance and a small seating area to enjoy aperitifs.

The predominantly Gallic service is professional, attentive and friendly, providing the perfect support act for Drabble's refined modern cooking that comes underpinned by a classical theme. Intelligently simple, stylish and self-confident, it focuses around the use of the highest-quality ingredients (including luxury items), with dishes impressively uncomplicated by unnecessary embellishment. It's accurate, delicate, perfectly timed and balanced and oozes clean, clear flavours. Think roasted John Dory with creamed yellow-leg chanterelles, or perhaps an assiette of pork (braised cheek, roast belly and black pudding) served with a mustard jus, and to finish, a tart Tatin with vanilla ice cream. The repertoire's delivered via a fixed-price menu format of lunch (this three-courses affair - with half-bottle of wine and half-bottle of mineral water - is considered a bargain), plus an enticing carte and seven-course gourmand option, while peripherals like bread, amuse-bouche and petits fours all hit form, too.

LONDON SW10 CONTINUED

create a romantic modern setting, while service comes courtesy of a friendly and knowledgeable team. The menu draws inspiration from diverse regions, remaining true to classic recipes as well as introducing the best of modern Indian trends to the UK. Malabar scallop is a typical starter (scallops with a creamy coconut and ginger sauce), while mains might include lamb osso buco, or chicken with blood orange and turmeric. Tasting menu available.

Chutney Mary Restaurant

Chef: Nagarajan Rubinath **Owners:** Masala World, R Mathrani, N Panjabi **Times:** 12.30-3/6.30-11.30, Closed D Xmas **Prices:** Fixed L £20, Starter £6.75-£14.25, Main £14.50-£21, Dessert £5.75-£7, Service added but optional 12.5% **Wine:** 100 bottles over £20, 4 bottles under £20, 30 by the glass **Notes:** Fixed L 3 courses, Sun L 3 courses £20, Civ Wed 100, Air con **Seats:** 110, Pr/dining room 24 **Directions:** Nearest station: Fulham Broadway On corner of King's Rd and Lots Rd; 2 mins from Chelsea Harbour. **Parking:** Parking meters outside

Osteria dell'Arancio

Modern Italian 🖥

Great Italian regional food and wine in a lively Chelsea setting

☎ 020 7349 8111 383 King's Rd SW10 0LP Plan 1-E3
e-mail: info@osteriadellarancio.co.uk
web: www.osteriadellarancio.co.uk

Smack on the corner of Milman's Street, a green-and-white striped awning and a few fair-weather pavement tables pick out this vibrant, unpretentious, authentic little Italian osteria from the King's Road crowd. Colourful, eye-catching artwork and lighting, and an eclectic medley of unclothed wooden tables catch the sunny Mediterranean mood, while service is equally relaxed and friendly. The rustic, home cooking of the Marche region comes driven by quality ingredients and simplicity. Look out for rigatoni all'amatriciana (with Italian bacon and pecorino cheese), or tagliata con rucola (beef with rocket). An excellent all-Italian wine list completes the package.

Chef: Giuseppe De Gregorio **Owners:** Rachel & Harry Hampson **Times:** 12-3/6.30-11 **Prices:** Food prices not confirmed for 2008. Please telephone for details **Notes:** Vegetarian available, Air con **Seats:** 75, Pr/dining room 30 **Children:** Menu, Portions **Directions:** Nearest station: Sloane Square Situated next to Moravian Church in Chelsea's World's End **Parking:** On street

The Painted Heron

Modern Indian 🖥

Stylish, upmarket and impressive modern Indian venue and cuisine

☎ 020 7351 5232 112 Cheyne Walk SW10 0DJ Plan 1-E3
e-mail: thepaintedheron@btinternet.com
web: www.thepaintedheron.com

A blue awning and glass frontage picks out this modern Chelsea Indian close to Battersea Bridge. Minimalist décor with black lacquered leather-upholstered chairs, dark slatted blinds and plain white walls adorned with striking modern art deliver a stylish, contemporary edge to this deceptively roomy, split-level restaurant. There's just a hint of the nautical reflecting its Thames-side location, with blond-wood floors and black metal handrails lining steps, together with a small bar, and an alfresco courtyard at the back. High-quality modern Indian cooking, with traditional dishes given contemporary spin and presentation, focuses on fresh ingredients and intelligently subtle spicing. Take black tiger prawns and queen scallops in a hot-and-sour Goan curry, and perhaps a honey and cinnamon pudding with cardamom ice cream to finish.

Times: 12-3/6.30-11, Closed Xmas & Etr, Closed L Sat **Directions:** Nearest station: South Kensington Telephone for directions

Vama

Indian 🖥

Upmarket Indian restaurant on the King's Road

☎ 020 565 8500 & 7565 8500 438 King's Rd SW10 0LJ Plan 1-E3
e-mail: manager@vama.co.uk
web: www.vama.co.uk

There's a separate party room, bar and waiting area here at Vama, with the restaurant stylishly decorated in warm colours. Large floor tiles, carved teak chairs with cushioned seats, rich ochre walls and large wooden-framed pictures give a fresh, comfortable, modern feel. Classical North West Indian food, mainly Punjabi, is showcased using traditional dishes cooked in a clay oven with authentic marinades. Typical dishes include the likes of bhunna zeera murg (roasted cumin and black salt-coated chicken combined with ginger and garlic), while a typical dessert might feature kishmish samosa (a soft cheese and raisin samosa served with Earl Grey tea ice cream and chocolate sauce).

Chef: Andy Varma **Owners:** Andy Varma, Arjun Varma **Times:** 12-4/6.30-12, Closed 25-26 Dec, 1 Jan **Prices:** Starter £4.50-£13, Main £4.50-£16, Dessert £5.50-£7.50, Service added 12.5%, Group min 6 service 12.5% **Wine:** 26 bottles over £20, 9 bottles under £20, 12 by the glass **Notes:** Vegetarian available, Dress Restrictions, Smart casual, Air con **Seats:** 120, Pr/dining room 35 **Directions:** Nearest station: Sloane Square About 20 mins walk down King's Rd **Parking:** 25

LONDON SW11

⊛ The Butcher & Grill

Modern, Traditional NEW

A carnivore's delight in warehouse-style surroundings

☎ 020 7924 3999 39-41 Parkgate Rd, Battersea
SW11 4NP Plan 1-E3
e-mail: info@thebutcherandgrill.com
web: www.thebutcherandgrill.com

With its bustling atmosphere, this Battersea newcomer has quickly made a mark on the south-of-the-river dining scene. As the name suggests, entry to the Grill restaurant is via an impressive, stylish butchery shop and deli/food emporium. Décor is warehouse style, with bare red-brick walls, whitewashed ceilings and wooden tables, chairs and floors, while service is friendly and informative. The food fits the surroundings, with top-notch raw materials prepared with skill and passion. A carnivore's delight, the menu offers a wide range of meat cuts (from T-bone or rib to Barnsley chop) simply delivered with a sauce of your choice (perhaps hollandaise or onion gravy).

Chef: David Massey **Owners:** Paul Grout, Dominic Ford, Simon Tindall **Times:** 12-3.30/6-11, Closed 25-26 Dec, 1 Jan, Closed D Sun **Prices:** Starter £4.95-£12.50, Main £6-£17, Dessert £5, Service added but optional 12.5% **Wine:** 52 bottles over £20, 16 bottles under £20, 13 by the glass **Notes:** Sun L 13.50, Air con **Seats:** 131 **Children:** Menu, Portions **Parking:** On street

⊛⊛ The Greyhound at Battersea

Modern European ⬛NOTABLE WINE LIST ⬛

Trendy, stylish gastro-pub with top-notch cuisine and wines

☎ 020 7978 7021 136 Battersea High St SW11 3JR
Plan 1-D3
e-mail: eat@thegreyhoundatbattersea.co.uk
web: www.thegreyhoundatbattersea.co.uk

The transformation of an old down-at-heels pub on bustling Battersea High Street to chic, trendy local and dining room presses all the right quality buttons. Large flash bar, leather seating, polished-wood floors, with crystal glasses and expensive table appointments place it a cut above your average gastro-pub. Service is attentive, friendly and relaxed, and product knowledge is excellent. Great quality, serious skill and some innovative dishes show the kitchen's fine pedigree and prove a match for the fabulous wine list. Clear flavours, fine presentation, seasoning and balance all hit a high note. Expect a starter of grilled octopus, carrot salad, ginger and white wine sauce and main dishes such as slow-roasted pork belly, Savoy cabbage and potato purée.

Chef: Alessio Brusadin **Owners:** Mark & Sharlyn Van der Goot **Times:** 12-3/7-10, Closed 23 Dec-3 Jan, Mon, Closed D Sun **Prices:** Fixed L £15, Fixed D £31, Starter £4.50-£6, Main £9.50-£16, Dessert £4.50-£6, Service added but optional 12.5% **Wine:** 20 by the glass **Notes:** ALC L wkdays only, Dress Restrictions, Smart casual **Seats:** 55, Pr/dining room 25 **Children:** Until 6pm, Portions **Directions:** Nearest station: Clapham Junct Located near Battersea Bridge and Clapham Junction **Parking:** On street

⊛⊛ Ransome's Dock

Modern British ⬛NOTABLE WINE LIST

Simple seasonal cooking in waterside setting

☎ 020 7223 1611 & 7924 2462 35-37 Parkgate Rd,
Battersea SW11 4NP Plan 1-E3
e-mail: chef@ransomesdock.co.uk
web: www.ransomesdock.co.uk

This popular waterside restaurant is located in a former ice cream factory close to Albert Bridge. With its cornflower blue walls and modern food-and-wine related artwork, this friendly, relaxed venue is unpretentious and informal, with snacks and coffees available in the bar area, while outside dining proves an added summer bonus. The sourcing of quality, seasonal produce - much of it organic - is paramount to the kitchen's success; take Creedy Carver free-range duck breast served with minted peas, carrots, Jersey potatoes and a red wine and orange jus, or slow-roast pork belly with raisin and Pedro Ximenez sherry, Pardina lentils and green beans. A notable wine list completes the upbeat package.

Chef: Martin Lam, Vanessa Lam **Owners:** Mr & Mrs M Lam **Times:** 12/6-11, Closed Xmas, Closed D Sun **Prices:** Fixed L £15, Starter £5-£12.50, Main £10.50-£23, Dessert £5-£7.75, Service added but optional 12.5% **Wine:** 360 bottles over £20, 22 bottles under £20, 10 by the glass **Notes:** Brunch menu Sat & Sun **Seats:** 55 **Children:** Portions **Directions:** Nearest station: Sloane Square/Clapham Junction Between Albert Bridge & Battersea Bridge **Parking:** 20

⬛ Chez Manny

☎ 020 7223 4040 145 Battersea High St SW11 3JS
web: www.theaa.com/travel/index.jsp

Extremely friendly restaurant with a genuine welcome. Very relaxed atmosphere for enjoying French dishes.

Gourmet Burger Kitchen

☎ 020 7228 3309 44 Northcote Rd SW11 1NZ

New Zealand inspired burger joint using top-notch beef.

Osteria Antica Bologna

☎ 020 7978 4771 23 Northcote Rd SW11 1NG

Rustic Italian restaurant serving authentic food with an emphasis on fresh and seasonal produce.

⬛ Strada

☎ 020 7801 0794 11-13 Battersea Rise SW11 1HG
web: www.theaa.com/travel/index.jsp

Superior pizza from quality ingredients cooked in wood-fired ovens.

LONDON SW12

◉◉ Lamberts

Modern British NEW

Relaxed, modern fine dining with impressive cooking

☎ 020 8675 2233 2 Station Pde, Balham High Rd SW12 9AZ Plan 1-E2

e-mail: bookings@lambertsrestaurant.com

web: www.lambertsrestaurant.com

Balham's Lamberts is a cool, minimalist-vogue, modern venue and, whilst styling itself as a fine-dining restaurant, offers a relaxed and comfortable atmosphere. It is a deservedly popular venue, with a growing reputation, where the food is fresh and vibrant. No surprise then that the kitchen prides itself on using the freshest seasonal British ingredients, including organic produce, with the majority of meat sourced direct from farms while fish comes straight from day boats. The impressive, well-presented cooking takes a modern approach that suits the surroundings, with old favourites sitting comfortably alongside contemporary interpretations of classics; think Farmer Sharp's Herdwick mutton, wether and lamb, and don't miss the blueberry cheesecake and white chocolate ganache.

Chef: Chas Tapaneyasastr **Owners:** Mr Joe Lambert **Times:** 12/7-10.30, Closed 25 Dec, 1 Jan, Mon, Closed L Tues, Wed, Thur, Fri **Prices:** Fixed L £12-£18, Fixed D £20-£25, Starter £6-£9, Main £14-£18, Dessert £6, Service added but optional 12.5% **Wine:** 60 bottles over £20, 20 bottles under £20, 8 by the glass **Seats:** 50 **Children:** Menu, Portions **Directions:** Nearest station: Balham Just S of Balham station on Balham High Rd **Parking:** On street

LONDON SW13

◉◉ Sonny's Restaurant

Modern 🖥

Imaginative cooking in modern surroundings

☎ 020 8748 0393 94 Church Rd, Barnes SW13 0DQ Plan 1-D3

e-mail: barnes@sonnys.co.uk

web: www.sonnys.co.uk

Tucked away in a parade of shops behind a glass frontage, this smart, long-standing neighbourhood favourite is bigger than it looks from outside. Bright and contemporary, its pale blue and white décor comes dotted with opaque glass bricks and peppered with striking modern artwork. White tablecloths, a black floor and modern chairs hit the spot too, while the atmosphere's buzzy and upbeat and service breezy, friendly and relaxed. The accomplished kitchen's modern European brasserie approach is a skilful, clean-cut affair that delivers quality ingredients, clear flavours and colourful presentation; think braised short rib of beef with parsnip purée, or roast fillet of cod with piperade and thyme, with bitter chocolate fondant and coconut sorbet to finish, accompanied by a delicious pudding wine. Sonny's shop is next door and the café opens at 10.30am.

Chef: Ed Wilson **Owners:** Rebecca Mascarenhas, James Harris **Times:** 12.30-2.30/7.30-11, Closed BHs, Closed D Sun **Prices:** Fixed L £15.50, Fixed D £21.50, Starter £6.25-£9.50, Main £10.25-£18, Dessert £5.50-£6.75, Service added but optional 12.5% **Wine:** 44 bottles over £20, 17 bottles under £20, 23 by the glass **Seats:** 100, Pr/dining room 26 **Children:** Menu, Portions **Directions:** Nearest station: Barnes/Hammersmith From Castelnau end of Church Rd on left by shops **Parking:** On street

🖥 Strada

☎ 020 8392 9216 375 Lonsdale Rd SW13 9PY

web: www.theaa.com/travel/index.jsp

Good value traditional Italian food in a grand, airy old brick building overlooking the Thames.

LONDON SW14

◉ The Depot Waterfront Brasserie

Modern British 🖥

Popular riverside brasserie

☎ 020 8878 9462 Tideway Yard, Mortlake High St SW14 8SN Plan 1-D3

e-mail: info@depotbrasserie.co.uk

web: www.depotbrasserie.co.uk

With a Thames-side location, situated in what used to be a stable block, this waterfront brasserie blends rusticity with contemporary styling (think banquette seating around the walls) to give the place both style and character. Simple bare tables, neutral shades and high ceilings complement the look. The menu consists of a good selection of simply constructed modern brasserie-style dishes; a fishcake with baby leaf salad and wasabi dressing, or Parma ham and sage wrapped chicken breast with roasted pumpkin and cherry vine tomatoes, and puddings like baked Alaska or Eton Mess (served with exotic fruits and crème Chantilly).

Times: 12-3.30/6-12, Closed 24-26 Dec **Directions:** Nearest station: Barnes Bridge Between Barnes Bridge & Mortlake stations

◉◉ Redmond's

Modern British 🖥

Well-executed cooking in a sophisticated setting

☎ 020 8878 1922 170 Upper Richmond Rd West SW14 8AW Plan 1-D3

e-mail: pippa@redmonds.org.uk

web: www.redmonds.org.uk

A big blue awning and white-painted frontage distinguish this high-street restaurant in Sheen. It's a fitting setting for chef-patron Redmond Hayward, and wife Pippa leading front of house. The chic, understated dining room is hung with modern artwork, while simple glassware gleams in the mood lighting, and tables are clad in crisp white linen. Top-notch raw materials are competently handled; cooking is sound, and presentation stylish. There are some classic combinations like roast partridge with roast root vegetables, pommes Anna and game port jus, and dishes with a more modern twist like fillets of plaice wrapped in smoked salmon with braised leeks and basil sauce.

Times: 12-2.30/7-10, Closed 4 days Xmas, BH Mons, Closed L Mon-Sat, D Sun **Directions:** Nearest station: Mortlake located halfway between Putney and Richmond. On the South Circular Road at the Barnes end of Sheen

ENGLAND

LONDON SW14 CONTINUED

⬧ La Saveur Restaurant

French NEW

Classic French bistro cooking

☎ 020 8876 0644 201 Upper Richmond Rd West SW14 8QT Plan 1-D3
e-mail: info@brula.co.uk
web: www.brula.co.uk

Set in a parade of shops, this long, narrow restaurant has mirrored walls to create a spacious feel to the room which has all the hallmarks of classic neighbourhood French bistros. The tightly-packed tables are clad in white linen cloths and the walls are plastered with French art nouveau paintings. With windows that fold back to open up the frontage in good weather, there is also a small decked terrace allowing limited alfresco dining. Using quality ingredients, the food is classic bistro fare in the shape of foie gras de canard with brioche and Madeira and Armagnac jelly, steak frites, halibut à la grenobloise and le petit pot au chocolat.

Chef: Bruce Duckett, Steve Gupta **Owners:** Bruce Duckett, Lawrence Hartley **Times:** 12-3/6-10.30, Closed 25-26 Dec, 1 Jan **Prices:** Fixed L £12, Starter £4.50-£9, Main £10-£23, Dessert £4.50-£4.75, Service added but optional 12.5% **Wine:** 14 bottles over £20, 6 bottles under £20, 12 by the glass **Notes:** Sun L 3 courses £17, Vegetarian available **Seats:** 60 **Children:** Menu, Portions **Directions:** Nearest station: Mortlake Br A205, turn right at Mortlake Bridge, continue 160 yds, at lights turn left, restaurant is 300 yds on right **Parking:** On street

⬧⬧ The Victoria

British, European 🖳

Good simple food in a friendly gastro-pub

☎ 020 8876 4238 10 West Temple Sheen SW14 7RT Plan 1-C2
e-mail: bookings@thevictoria.net
web: www.thevictoria.net

This stylish gastro-pub is a firm favourite with locals and has seven comfortable bedrooms for foodies from further afield. The pub is bright and airy with white walls, white painted floorboards and leather armchairs. The conservatory restaurant, with well-spaced tables and a wood-burning stove, has French doors opening out on to the patio and the newly made-over garden for summer dining. The menu, with an emphasis on seasonality and quality produce, serves traditional British, French, Spanish, Italian and Mediterranean dishes in a contemporary style, such as purple sprouting broccoli with gorgonzola polenta and romesco sauce, or Charolais rib-eye or sirloin steaks with chips and salad. Heart-warming desserts offer up the likes of steamed orange pudding with treacle and Cornish clotted cream.

Chef: Darren Archer, Stephen Paskins **Owners:** Mark Chester & Darren Archer **Times:** 12-2.30/7-10, Closed 4 days Xmas **Prices:** Starter £4.95-£9.95, Main £9.95-£21.95, Dessert £3.95-£6.95, Service added but optional 12.5% **Wine:** 30 bottles over £20, 17 bottles under £20, 14 by the glass **Seats:** 70, Pr/dining room 45 **Children:** Menu, Portions **Rooms:** 7 (7 en suite) ★★★★ RR **Directions:** Nearest station: Mortlake Between Upper Richmond Road and Richmond Park, halfway between Putney and Richmond **Parking:** 18

LONDON SW15

⬧⬧ Enoteca Turi

Italian ⬧ NOTABLE WINE LIST 🖳

Seasonal, regional Italian cooking in Putney

☎ 020 8785 4449 28 Putney High St SW15 1SQ Plan 1-D3
e-mail: enoteca@tiscali.co.uk
web: www.enotecaturi.com

A stone's throw from the river, this family-run restaurant brings a genuine taste of Italy to Putney, with its stylish interior, warm rustic Tuscan colours, and wooden floors and wine racks. Inspired by regional Italian cuisine, high-quality seasonal ingredients form the backbone of the cooking. Well-presented dishes are executed with confidence and flair. There's a great set lunch menu with choices like pan-fried mackerel wrapped in pancetta with balsamic dressing to start. For mains, choose between hearty risottos and tasty pasta dishes, like corn-fed chicken breast with parcels of aubergine filled with smoked mozzarella, parmesan and fresh basil, plus fresh San Marzano sauce. The wine list is impressive and suggested wines for each dish are available by the glass.

Chef: Mr B Fantoni **Owners:** Mr G & Mrs P Turi **Times:** 12-2.30/7-11, Closed 25-26 Dec, 1 Jan, Sun, Closed L BHs **Prices:** Fixed L £14.50, Starter £6.50-£10.50, Main £10.50-£19.50, Dessert £5.50-£5.75, Service added but optional 12.5% **Wine:** 300 bottles over £20, 16 bottles under £20, 9 by the glass **Notes:** Vegetarian available, Dress Restrictions, Smart casual, Air con **Seats:** 85, Pr/dining room 28 **Children:** Portions **Directions:** Nearest station: Putney Bridge Opposite Odeon Cinema near bridge **Parking:** Putney Exchange car park

⬧ The Spencer Arms

British 🖳

Putney gastro-pub serving food with flair

☎ 020 8788 0640 237 Lower Richmond Rd SW15 1HJ Plan 1-D3
e-mail: info@thespencerarms.co.uk
web: www.thespencerarms.co.uk

Shabby chic sums up the style of this cosy gastro-pub on the edge of Putney Common, with sofas around the fireside, tongue-and-groove panelling, oak tables, church chairs and ox blood banquette seating. Great British food is freshly prepared and the menu offers honest pub grub dishes of macaroni cheese, English salad, and rib-eye steak on the bone with herb butter. Take leek and potato broth with Welsh rarebit, or perhaps grilled scallops with crayfish and radish and celery leaf, and for dessert tuck into chocolate brownie and rhubarb, or Dundee cake with egg custard. House-made chutneys and pickles are also available to buy.

Chef: Adrian Jones, Adam Highley **Owners:** Jamie Sherriff **Times:** 12-2.30/6.30-10, Closed 25-26 Dec **Prices:** Fixed L £10-£15, Fixed D £20-£27.50, Starter £4.95-£8.50, Main £7.50-£17.50, Dessert £4.50, Service added but optional 12.5%, Group min 12 service 12.5% **Wine:** 32 bottles over £20, 19 bottles under £20, 13 by the glass **Notes:** Vegetarian available, Air con **Seats:** 70 **Children:** Portions **Directions:** Nearest station: Putney S over Putney Bridge, take 1st right. The Spencer Arms is last building on left on Lower Richmond Rd. Opposite Putney hospital **Parking:** On street

ENGLAND

⊛ Talad Thai

Thai

Hearty cooking at a popular Thai restaurant

☎ 020 8789 8084 320 Upper Richmond Rd, Putney SW15 6TL Plan 1-D3
e-mail: info@taladthai.co.uk
web: www.taladthai.co.uk

A relaxed and friendly Thai restaurant in a quiet part of Putney, with its own Thai supermarket a few doors away. The modern set-up includes wooden tables packed closely together, so this is not somewhere to share intimate secrets. The lengthy traditional menu offers a journey through Thai cuisine, with food listed by type, such as stir fries, curry dishes, noodle dishes etc, and authentic ingredients arrive fresh from Thailand. Expect the likes of gaeng phed - red curry with pork, prawns, beef, chicken or vegetable - and numerous seafood dishes such as ta-lay hot (mixed seafood with hot chilli).

Chef: Suthasinee Pramwew **Owners:** Mr Sa-ard Kriangsak **Times:** 11.30-3/5.30-11, Closed 25 Dec, 1 Jan **Prices:** Starter £4.55-£4.75, Main £5.50-£7.75, Dessert £2.50-£5, Service optional **Wine:** 1 by the glass **Notes:** Vegetarian available, Air con **Seats:** 40, Pr/dining room 40 **Directions:** Nearest station: Putney/East Putney Please telephone for directions **Parking:** On street opposite

⌂ Emiles

☎ 020 8789 3323 96 Felsham Rd, East Putney SW15 1DQ
web: www.theaa.com/travel/index.jsp

Unpretentious and friendly restaurant, very popular with locals serving modern British dishes.

Gourmet Burger Kitchen

☎ 020 8789 1199 333 Putney Bridge Rd, Putney SW15 2PG
New Zealand inspired burger joint using top-notch beef.

⌂ Isola del Sole

☎ 020 8785 9962 16 Lacy Rd SW15 1NL
web: www.theaa.com/travel/index.jsp

Delicious, healthy and genuine Italian food, with a bias for Sardinian regional dishes; excellent service and terrific value for money.

⌂ Louhannah

☎ 020 8780 5252 30 Putney High St, Putney SW15 1SQ
web: www.theaa.com/travel/index.jsp
Popular with shoppers and cinema goers this eatery has a modern continental menu and a laid-back atmosphere.

LONDON SW17

⊛ Amici Bar & Italian Kitchen

Italian NEW

Authentic Italian dining in a relaxed setting

☎ 020 8672 5888 35 Bellevue Rd, Wandsworth Common SW17 7EF Plan 1-E3
e-mail: info@amiciitalian.co.uk
web: www.amiciitalian.co.uk

Overlooking Wandsworth Common, this stylish eatery is already a local favourite. Behind the commanding frontage, a contemporary bar replete with comfy sofas leads seamlessly into the dining area, where the chefs serve up classic, unfussy dishes from the busy open kitchen. Wood panelling inset with coloured glass, Venetian blinds and a stone bath doubling as a bread station all add to the informal atmosphere. Try fritto misto con verdure (fried shrimp, calamari, sea bass and red mullet), followed by risotto with radicchio, gorgonzola and Chianti, and make sure you try the excellent fresh bread. Carte, lunch, Sunday brunch and children's menus are all on offer and in summer you can dine alfresco on the shady terrace.

Chef: Paolo Zara **Owners:** Christopher Gilmore **Times:** 12-3/6-10.30, Closed 24-26 Dec **Prices:** Starter £4.50-£7.50, Main £8.50-£15, Dessert £4-£4.75, Service added but optional 12.5% **Wine:** 24 bottles over £20, 10 bottles under £20, 11 by the glass **Notes:** Vegetarian available, Dress Restrictions, Smart casual, Air con **Seats:** 90 **Children:** Menu, Portions **Directions:** Nearest station: Wandsworth A214, situated on corner of Bellevue Rd **Parking:** On street

⊛⊛⊛ Chez Bruce

see page 326

⊛ Kastoori

Indian V

Fresh vegetarian dishes made daily from scratch

☎ 020 8767 7027 188 Upper Tooting Rd SW17 7EJ
Plan 1-E2

Worth the trek from further into London or the suburbs if you're not a local, this welcoming vegetarian Indian presents an assuming face with its bright, closely-packed tables and relaxing colour scheme of yellow, white, grey and blue. A delightful choice of Gujarati dishes is threaded with East African flavours in main dishes like spring onion curry, or Methiringan (fennu and aubergine cooked with coriander and garlic sauce). Remember to ask for the chef's choices and daily specials.

Chef: Manoj Thanki **Owners:** Mr D Thanki **Times:** 12.30-2.30/6-10.30, Closed 25-26 Dec, Closed L Mon & Tue **Prices:** Food prices not confirmed for 2008. Please telephone for details **Wine:** 1 bottle over £20, 19 bottles under £20, 2 by the glass **Notes:** Vegetarian menu **Seats:** 82 **Children:** Portions **Directions:** Nearest station: Tooting Bec & Tooting Broadway. Situated between two stations. **Parking:** On street

ENGLAND

Chez Bruce

LONDON SW17

Modern French 🍷 NOTABLE WINE LIST 💻

Memorable dining at Wandsworth big-hitter

☎ 020 8672 0114 2 Bellevue Rd, Wandsworth Common SW17 7EG Plan 1-E2

e-mail: enquiries@chezbruce.co.uk

web: www.chezbruce.co.uk

This small, unassuming place - that looks more like a bistro from outside rather than Wandsworth's culinary star - is set in a parade of shops overlooking the common, and is heaving most of the time. First-timers should look out for the large maroon-coloured planters bursting with flowers outside, or just follow the savvy crowd who are full of admiration for Bruce Poole's memorable cuisine. Inside cuts a relaxed, modern edge, with wooden floors, muted restful beiges and caramels, soft lighting and a collection of prints. The effect is simple but pleasing, though space is at a premium, and, with no drinks area, diners are shown straight to white-linen clad tables, where service proves friendly, eager, attentive and knowledgeable.

The kitchen's accomplished modern approach pays due respect to classical and regional France, alongside wider Mediterranean influences, but remains pleasingly unfussy while focusing on the highest quality ingredients with an eye for seasonality. Noteworthy flavours, perfect balance and impeccable skill make for a memorable experience. Expect the likes of a fillet of sea bream served with a mushroom duxelle, potato pancake, oyster beignet and dill, while a classic crème brûlée or perhaps a cherry and almond croustade with cinnamon ice cream might head-up desserts. Regularly-changing menus, affordable prices (particularly at lunch) and an impressive wine list complete a consistently classy act.

Chef: Bruce Poole, Matt Christmas **Owners:** Bruce Poole, Nigel Platts-Martin **Times:** 12-2/6.30-10.30, Closed 24-26 Dec, 1 Jan, Closed L 27, 31 Dec & 2nd Jan **Prices:** Fixed L £19.50-£26.50, Fixed D £37.50, Service added but optional 12.5% **Wine:** 9 bottles under £20, 20 by the glass **Notes:** Dress Restrictions, Smart casual, Air con **Seats:** 75, Pr/dining room 16 **Children:** L only, Menu, Portions **Directions:** Nearest station: Wandsworth Common/Balham Near Wandsworth Common station **Parking:** On street, station car park

---

LONDON SW18

◉ Ditto Bar & Restaurant

Modern European NEW

Popular, informal local offering bags of choice

☎ 020 8877 0110 55-57 East Hill SW18 2QE Plan 1-D3

e-mail: info@doditto.co.uk

web: www.doditto.co.uk

This relaxed, informal bar-restaurant comes conveniently set on the high street just off Wandsworth Common and proves a populist local. Front windows open on to the street - great on hot days or to watch the world go by - while inside comes with well-trodden wooden floors and grey walls enlivened with paintings by a local artist. There's rugged wooden and leather furniture in the bar area, while the restaurant section is decked out with polished wooden tables and suede and leather chairs. The kitchen's simple, well-presented modern approach fits the bill, with a lengthy, crowd-pleasing repertoire offering something for everyone; think pan-fried loin of pork with butter beans, red wine, thyme and chorizo.

Times: 12/11, Closed 25 Dec, 1 Jan, Closed L Mon-Fri, D Sun

LONDON SW19

◉◉ Common

Modern European NEW

Country-house hotel dining with views and imaginative cooking

☎ 020 8879 1464 Cannizaro House, West Side, Wimbledon Common SW19 4UE Plan 1-D2

e-mail: info@cannizarohouse.com

web: www.cannizarohouse.com

This elegant, 18th-century house has a long tradition of hosting the rich and famous of London society, and comes peacefully set overlooking Cannizaro Park, its former grounds. Inside theres a country-house vibe, which extends to the Common dining room, save its dark walls and modern artworks that is. Carpeting, upholstered chairs and clothed tables offer the comforts, while efficient service and stunning views over the grounds lend added bonus. The accomplished kitchen's modern European approach fits the bill, delivering quality fresh produce with skill and plenty of flair; take a fillet of turbot poached in red wine and served with pommes mousseline and ceps, and perhaps an apple parfait with Granny Smith apple sorbet.

Chef: Christian George **Owners:** Bridgehouse Hotels **Times:** 12-3/7-10 **Prices:** Fixed L £16.50, Fixed D £26.95-£41, Starter £6.95-£12.95, Main £14-£22.50, Dessert £6, Service optional **Wine:** 110 bottles over £20, 20 bottles under £20, 14 by the glass **Notes:** Sun L 3 courses £29.50, Vegetarian available, Dress Restrictions, No shorts, Civ Wed 60 **Seats:** 46, Pr/dining room 120 **Children:** Menu, Portions **Rooms:** 45 (45 en suite) ★★★★ CHH **Directions:** Nearest station: Wimbledon From A3 (London Rd) Tibbets Corner, take A219 (Parkside) R into Cannizaro Rd, then R into West Side **Parking:** 55

◉◉ The Light House Restaurant

Modern International 💻

Simple modern cooking in upmarket Wimbledon

☎ 020 8944 6338 75-77 Ridgway, Wimbledon SW19 4ST Plan 1-D2

e-mail: info@lighthousewimbledon.com

web: www.lighthousewimbledon.com

Set in a small row of shops in Wimbledon's upmarket village, this relaxed eatery does a brisk trade, particularly at weekends, so reservations are advised. A minimalist modern décor of wooden floors and sand-coloured walls provides a low-key background for some great food. Dishes are simple, rustic creations rooted in Italian cuisine, with influences from further afield, particularly Asia. Mains might include pan-fried cod with saffron and tomato paella, or braised lamb shank with herb tabouleh and pomegranate and mint relish, while puddings are contemporary concoctions such as mango semi-freddo with raspberry pannacotta.

Chef: Chris Casey **Owners:** Mr Finch & Mr Taylor **Times:** 12-2.30/6.30-10.30, Closed 24-26 Dec, 1 Jan, Etr Sun & Mon, Closed D Sun **Prices:** Fixed L £14, Fixed D £18.50, Starter £5-£10, Main £10.50-£16.50, Dessert £5.50, Service added but optional 12.5% **Wine:** 56 bottles over £20, 14 bottles under £20, 12 by the glass **Notes:** Sun L 2 courses £18, 3 courses £23, Vegetarian available **Seats:** 80 **Children:** Menu, Portions **Directions:** Nearest station: Wimbledon From station turn right up Wimbledon Hill then left at mini-rdbt onto Ridgway, restaurant on left

San Lorenzo

☎ 020 8946 8463 Worple Rd Mews, Wimbledon SW19

Reliable neighbourhood restaurant.

Strada

☎ 020 8946 4363 91 High St SW19 5EG

Superior pizza from quality ingredients cooked in wood-fired ovens.

LONDON W1

◉ Alastair Little Restaurant

European

Harmonious flavours and vibrant colours in Soho

☎ 020 7734 5183 49 Frith St W1V 5TE Plan 3-B2

It's well worth seeking out this unassuming shop-fronted restaurant in the heart of bustling Soho. The interior reflects the admirably uncomplicated style of the cuisine, with wooden floors, simple chairs and smartly set tables. Bold pictures add a splash of colour and the unusual ceiling lights are quite a feature. It's a popular place with a warm atmosphere and friendly service. Straightforward modern cooking delivers clear, well-balanced flavours in dishes like lamb chump, pork belly and chorizo with fennel and white beans, and pannacotta with rhubarb and pistachio praline.

Chef: Juliet Peston **Owners:** K Pedersen, M Andre-Vega **Times:** 12-3/5.30-11.30, Closed Xmas, BHs, Sun, Closed L Sat **Prices:** Fixed L £38, Fixed D £40, Service optional, Group min 8 service 12.5% **Wine:** 55 bottles over £20, 2 bottles under £20, 4 by the glass **Notes:** Fixed L 3 courses, Air con **Seats:** 42, Pr/dining room **Children:** Portions **Directions:** Nearest station: Tottenham Court Rd/Leicester Square Near Ronnie Scott's Jazz Club **Parking:** Brewer St, Poland St

◉ Alloro

Italian

A taste of Italy in the heart of Mayfair

☎ 020 7495 4768 20 Dover St W1S 4LU Plan 3-A1

e-mail: alloro@hotmail.co.uk

A blue awning and glass frontage picks out this smart, discreet, contemporary Italian just off Piccadilly close to the Ritz. Banquettes and leather chairs, polished dark and lightwood flooring, pastel tones, sculptured laurel leaf-themed artwork ('alloro' means 'laurel') and smartly attired staff all set a classy tone at this popular restaurant with an interconnecting small bar. The modern Italian cooking delivers simplicity, quality ingredients and a light touch on its fixed-price repertoire and separate bar menu. Think braised veal osso buco with home-made tagliatelle and fresh thyme, and a peach and amaretti biscuit tart finish.

Chef: Daniele Camera **Owners:** A-Z Restaurant Ltd **Times:** 12-2.30/7-10.30, Closed Xmas, 4 days Etr & BHs, Sun, Closed L Sat **Prices:** Fixed L £26, Fixed D £33, Starter £8, Main £20, Dessert £6, Service added but optional 12.5% **Wine:** 2 bottles under £20 **Notes:** Vegetarian available, Dress Restrictions, No shorts or sandals, Air con **Seats:** 60, Pr/dining room 16 **Children:** Portions **Directions:** Nearest station: Green Park From Green Park stn continue towards Piccadilly, Dover St is 2nd on left

◉◉◉ Angela Hartnett at The Connaught

see page 328

◉◉◉ Arbutus Restaurant

see page 328

◉◉ Archipelago

International 💻

Unique, romantic and adventurous dining experience

☎ 020 7383 3346 110 Whitfield St W1T 5ED Plan 3-B3

e-mail: info@archipelago-restaurant.co.uk

web: www.archipelago-restaurant.co.uk

There's nothing to prepare you on the outside - set on an unremarkable side street not far from the Telecom Tower - for the unique journey of exploration within this tiny, offbeat restaurant. A treasure trove of peacock feathers, golden Buddhas, primitive carvings, bird cages and colourful fabrics and seating are among the riot of exotic memorabilia that fill every inch of the green and red walls; it's dark, romantic and atmospheric. Even the menu is unusual, a ribbon-bound scroll with an ancient map on the back reveals the

CONTINUED ON PAGE 329

ENGLAND

Angela Hartnett at The Connaught

LONDON W1

Italian, Mediterranean 🖳

Mayfair opulence meets refined, contemporary cooking

☎ 020 7592 1222 Carlos Place W1K 2AL Plan 2-G1
e-mail: reservations@angelahartnett.com
web: www.angelahartnett.com

Magnificent, rich, modern and swish all rolled into one, the beautifully refurbished, Nina Campbell designed, Menu dining room integrates the Connaught's grandeur and classicism with a feeling of welcome, warmth, light and intimacy. Darkwood panelling, blinds, bold modern oil paintings and classic napery give a nod to the contemporary cooking of Angela Hartnett - now a household name. And, if you want to get close to the action, there's a chef's table in the kitchen seating up to ten. Service at the Menu is sharp, prompt and well informed, but approachable and friendly, too.

Hartnett's highly refined, Ramsay-influenced cuisine delivers much more excitement and oomph than the normal hotel restaurant. The modern approach draws on her Italian background to create enticing combinations on a fixed-price repertoire that includes a tasting option. High skill, tip-top quality produce, bold, clear flavours, clean-cut presentation and intelligent simplicity score on the plate. Take confit halibut with a thyme and raisin crust, pepperonta and braised treviso, and perhaps a vanilla semi-fredo with a carrot and courgette muffin and coconut and lime sorbet to finish. A tome of a wine list rounds off a class act, with a strong by-the-glass selection, while an elegant terrace provides the opportunity for alfresco dining.

Chef: Angela Hartnett **Owners:** Gordon Ramsay Holdings Ltd **Times:** 12-2.45/5.45-11 **Prices:** Fixed L £30-£70, Fixed D £60, Service added but optional 12.5% **Wine:** 700 bottles over £20, 40 bottles under £20, 27 by the glass **Notes:** Fixed L 3 courses, Menu Prestige 8 courses £70, Dress Restrictions, No jeans or trainers, smart, jacket preferred, Air con **Seats:** 70, Pr/dining room 50 **Children:** Menu, Portions **Rooms:** 92 (92 en suite)★★★★★ HL **Directions:** Nearest station: Bond Street/Green Park Please telephone for directions **Parking:** Adams Row

Arbutus Restaurant

LONDON W1

Modern European NEW 🖳

Stunning but simple, affordable food and wine from Soho gem

☎ 020 7734 4545 63-64 Frith St W1D 3JW Plan 3-B2
e-mail: info@arbutusrestaurant.co.uk
web: www.arbutusrestaurant.co.uk

The ex-Putney Bridge restaurant duo of Anthony Demetre and Will Smith have certainly hit the ground running with their universally acclaimed Soho newcomer ever since its opening back in 2006. An unassuming dark-grey frontage with plenty of glass picks this high-achiever out from the crowd at the Soho Square end of bustling Frith Street. Inside is understated; cool, calm and neutral, with colours dominated by creams and dark browns, while the atmosphere is relaxed and informal and white-tablecloth free in the style of the bistro moderne. The U-shaped dining room has bar-seating too, while service (with Will Smith out front) is friendly but slick and polished, yet not overbearing in anyway.

Anthony Demetre's modern bistro cooking has obvious pedigree, the style intelligently simple, highly skilled, imaginative and innovative, with a shopping-list of more humble ingredients also helping to elevate it above the crowd. Flavours are clear and confident, combinations well judged; take a saddle of rabbit with shoulder cottage pie, golden carrots and mustard sauce, or perhaps a vanilla cheesecake served with blueberries. Top-drawer breads, a sensible pricing structure and a cleverly constructed wine list - with wines also available by 250ml carafe - bolster a class act.

Chef: Anthony Demetre **Owners:** Anthony Demetre, Will Smith **Times:** 12-2.30/5-10.30, Closed 25-26 Dec, 1 Jan **Prices:** Fixed L £13.50, Starter £4.95-£9.95, Main £11.50-£15.95, Dessert £5.95, Service added but optional 12.5% **Wine:** 40 bottles over £20, 10 bottles under £20, 50 by the glass **Notes:** Pre-theatre D 5-7pm 2 courses £15.50, 3 courses £17.50, Air con **Seats:** 75 **Children:** Portions **Directions:** Nearest station: Tottenham Court Road Exit Tottenham Court Road tube station, turn left into Oxford St. Left onto Soho St, cross over or continue around Soho Sq, restaurant is on Frith St 25m on right

LONDON W1 CONTINUED

treasures in store; an equally idiosyncratic safari of accomplished, exotic-named dishes that might include crocodile, peacock, wildebeest or marsupial - perhaps zhug-marinated kangaroo fillet with water spinach, choi and crushed chilli potatoes. Service is knowledgeable, relaxed and friendly.

Chef: Daniel Creedon **Owners:** Bruce Alexander **Times:** 12-2.30/6-11, Closed Xmas, BHs, Sun, Closed L Sat **Prices:** Fixed L £12.50, Fixed D £31.50-£38.50, Starter £6.50-£10.50, Main £13.50-£19.50, Dessert £6-£7, Service added but optional 12.5% **Wine:** 44 bottles over £20, 4 bottles under £20, 4 by the glass **Notes:** Vegetarian available, Air con **Seats:** 32 **Directions:** Nearest station: Warren Street From underground south along Tottenham Court Rd. 1st right into Grafton Way. 1st left into Whitfield St **Parking:** NCP, on street

◉ The Athenaeum, Damask

Traditional British 🖾

Out with the old and in with the new at this famous hotel

☎ 020 7499 3464 116 Piccadilly W1J 7BJ Plan 4-H5
e-mail: info@athenaeumhotel.com
web: www.athenaeumhotel.com

The sumptuous Athenaeum is discreet in every way but the interior of the building, despite limited space, oozes contemporary style after a designer make-over. It's all change with the food options too, by way of the introduction of 'The Elevenses' menu offered from 11am to 11pm (flexible all-day dining with something for everyone) to complement the set lunch and dinner menus and the retro-chic daily-changing carving trolley. The new Damask restaurant is a glamorous yet relaxed space, where the likes of risotto of New Forest mushrooms and truffles, grilled new season Dorset lamb with buttered spinach and glazed onions followed by a double-baked chocolate pudding might tempt the palate. Service is of the highest level, superbly hosted and supervised and smartly attired.

Chef: David Marshall **Owners:** Ralph Trustees Ltd **Times:** 12.30-2.30/5.30-10.30 **Prices:** Fixed L £15, Fixed D £25, Starter £7-£12.50, Main £15-£28.50, Dessert £8, Service optional **Wine:** 41 bottles over £20, 4 bottles under £20, 14 by the glass **Notes:** All-day dining menu 11am-11pm, Pre-theatre D available, Vegetarian available, Civ Wed 55, Air con **Seats:** 46, Pr/dining room 44 **Children:** Menu, Portions **Rooms:** 157 (157 en suite)★★★★★ HL **Directions:** Nearest station: Hyde Park Corner, Green Park Telephone for directions **Parking:** Close car park

◉ Automat

American

Stylish dining in American-style brasserie

☎ 020 7499 3033 33 Dover St W1S 4NF Plan 3-A1
e-mail: info@automat-london.com
web: www.automat-london.com

This elegant diner-themed restaurant delivers American-style comfort food to Mayfair. Up front there's a café edge, in the middle an upmarket diner vibe with leather banquette-style booth seating, subdued lighting and lots of wood veneer, while at the back there's a brighter, buzzier space with an open kitchen, white-tiled walls and tables set on different levels. The food is uncomplicated but accomplished, featuring some stereotypical Stateside diner favourites, though dishes benefit from modern interpretation and presentation,

and quality ingredients. Take a Manhattan clam chowder, perhaps an Automat burger or New York strip-loin steak, and a Mississippi mud pie finish.

Chef: Shaun Gilmore **Owners:** Carlos Almada **Times:** 12-3/6-11, Closed Xmas, New Year, Closed L Sun **Prices:** Fixed L £19-£40, Fixed D £26-£50, Starter £7-£11, Main £7-£25, Dessert £6, Service added but optional 12.5% **Wine:** 78 bottles over £20, 8 bottles under £20, 20 by the glass **Notes:** Brunch available Sat & Sun, Vegetarian available, Air con **Seats:** 110 **Directions:** Nearest station: Green Park Dover St is off Piccadilly **Parking:** On street

◉ Bam-Bou

French, Vietnamese, Pan-Asian 🖾

Lively restaurant inspired by Indo-China

☎ 020 7323 9130 1 Percy St W1T 1DB Plan 3-B3
e-mail: sthompson@bam-bou.co.uk
web: www.bam-bou.co.uk

Located in a Georgian townhouse smack bang in the middle of Fitzrovia, Bam-Bou is a discreet Asian-style restaurant with a French colonial feel. Intimate rooms, replete with authentic artefacts, wood floors, retro lighting and jazzy music, provide the setting for sampling a vibrant ethnic menu that draws on Thai, Vietnamese and Chinese cuisine with a strong Western influence. Menu choice is not over elaborate and sound cooking results in full-flavoured dishes. Service is informal and friendly, with good suggestions on how to enjoy the food. Herb-baked Chilean sea bass with hot-and-sour greens, or crackling roast belly pork with watercress and spiced jambu are typical mains.

Times: 12-3/6-11, Closed 25-26 Dec, BH Mons, Sun, Closed L Sat **Directions:** Nearest station: Tottenham Court Rd/Goodge St 1 min from Oxford St

◉ Barrafina

Spanish NEW

Barcelona-style tapas in the heart of Soho

☎ 020 7813 8016 54 Frith St, Soho W1D 4SL Plan 3-B2
web: www.barrafina.co.uk

Tucked away in the middle of Soho, Sam and Eddie Hart have used the iconic Cal Pep tapas bar in Barcelona for inspiration. With no booking policy, prepare to queue in this long, narrow room for the high stools that run around the L-shaped, marble-topped counter. Sip on a glass of fino or manzanilla as you wait for plates of charcuterie or well-cooked authentic hot and cold tapas such as mussels à la plancha, lamb's sweetbreads with capers, tuna tartare, morcilla with piquillo peppers and jamon and spinach tortilla. Staff are lively and friendly.

Times: 12-3/5-11, Closed BHs, Sun

ENGLAND

LONDON W1 CONTINUED

◉ Bar Shu

Sichuanese NEW

One of the Capital's 'hottest' Chinese restaurants dedicated to the glories of Sichuanese cuisine

☎ 020 7287 6688 28 Frith St W1D 5LF Plan 3-C2

web: www.bar-shu.co.uk

Just over the road from Chinatown, this contemporary looking, glass-fronted Soho Chinese is dedicated to the food of the Sichuan province of Southwest China, famous for the fiery spiciness that comes from its liberal use of chillies and lip-tingling Sichuan peppercorns. The décor is clean-lined and modern, dotted with more traditional touches like red lanterns, authentic wood furniture and objets d'art. Staff are both knowledgeable and helpful, while the kitchen delivers dishes like fire-exploding kidney flowers, Dongpo pork knuckle and a dessert of stewed exotic frog jelly in papaya. But heat's not the whole story here, it's also about the layers of flavour, so look out for the so-called 'fish-fragrant' or 'lychee-flavoured' sauces as well as the 'numbing-and-hot'.

Times: 12 noon-11.30pm

◉ Bellamy's

French

Classy brasserie in quiet Mayfair mews

☎ 020 7491 2727 18-18a Bruton Place W1J 6LY
Plan 2-H2

e-mail: gavin@bellamysrestaurant.co.uk

web: www.bellamysrestaurant.co.uk

There's a buzz to this French brasserie that's very appealing - come at lunchtime or for dinner and it's perennially popular. Tightly packed tables foster a sense of occasion, and the staff keep the conversation and service flowing despite the pressure. The food is classic French brasserie fare, simply but competently prepared from top-notch ingredients and delivered with all due ceremony. Expect mains such as turbot rôti served with sauce champagne, or sliced entrecote of beef with pommes frites to feature alongside oysters, lobster, caviar and whatever other delights the appealing carte has on offer.

Chef: Stephane Pacoud **Owners:** Gavin Rankin and Syndicate **Times:** 12-3/7-10.30, Closed BHs, Sun, Closed L Sat **Prices:** Fixed L £24, Fixed D £28.50, Starter £7.50-£18, Main £18.50-£28.50, Dessert £6.50, Service added but optional 12.5% **Wine:** 50 bottles over £20, 15 by the glass **Seats:** 70 **Children:** Portions **Directions:** Nearest station: Green Park/Bond St Off Berkeley Sq, parallel with Bruton St **Parking:** On street, NCP

◉◉ Benares

Indian ▣

Fine-dining Indian with striking design and cutting-edge cooking

☎ 020 7629 8886 12 Berkeley Square W1J 6BS
Plan 2-H1

e-mail: reservations@benaresrestaurant.com

web: www.benaresrestaurant.com

Discreetly set on Berkeley Square, Benares puts on a classy Mayfair performance with its striking contemporary design. A wide staircase sweeps up to a cool, funky bar with a series of water-filled ponds decorated with brightly coloured floating flowers. The slick dining room is decked out with limestone flooring, dark leather banquettes and ebony-coloured chairs with creamy white upholstery. The modern Indian cuisine is as sophisticated as the surroundings. Highly lauded chef-patron Atul Kochhar (previously at Tamarind) produces eye-catching food, utilising tip-top, luxury European-style produce. Vibrant cooking, subtle spicing and authenticity triumphantly fuse East and West. Expect dishes such as sea bass poached in a coconut and tamarind sauce and served with coconut rice, or perhaps grilled lamb chops marinated with cardamom and fennel and served with pomegranate, dates, green beans, feta cheese and mint salad.

Chef: Atul Kochhar **Owners:** Atul Kochhar **Times:** 12-2.30/5.30-11, Closed 23-26 Dec, Closed L 27-31 Dec, Sat **Prices:** Fixed L £29.95, Fixed D £25-£45, Starter £9.50-£16.95, Main £16.95-£38, Dessert £6.50, Service included **Wine:** All bottles over £20, 11 by the glass **Notes:** Fixed L 3 courses, Air con **Directions:** Nearest station: Green Park E along Piccadilly towards Regent St. Turn left into Berkeley St and continue straight to Berkeley Square

◉◉ Bentley's Oyster Bar & Grill

British, European ▣

Classic seafood powerhouse

☎ 020 7734 4756 11/15 Swallow St W1B 4DG Plan 3-B1

e-mail: cyril.lommaert@bentleys.org

web: www.bentleysoysterbarandgrill.co.uk

When this legendary seafood restaurant came up for sale in 2005, TV chef Richard Corrigan decided to restore it to its former glory. Sensitively refurbished with an eye to its Arts and Crafts heritage, there are green leather booths downstairs in the relaxed oyster bar and more formal tables in the Grill restaurant and private dining rooms, both providing the perfect setting for grazing on native or rock oysters in the shell. Corrigan draws on his Irish roots to deliver a menu of accomplished cuisine, firmly focusing on the freshness of Bentley's fish, meat and game, and allowing the main ingredients to shine through. Typical dishes might include wild sea bass with soft fennel and herbs or steamed Elwy Valley lamb pudding. Black-clad staff provide professional service.

Times: 12/11.30 **Directions:** Nearest station: Piccadilly Circus 2nd right after Piccadilly Circus

◉◉ *The Berkeley Square*
Modern European 🖥
Mayfair fine dining without the pomp

☎ 020 7629 6993 7 Davies St, Berkeley Square W1K 3DD Plan 2-H1
e-mail: info@theberkeleysquare.com
web: www.theberkeleysquare.com

Intimate two-floor restaurant in famous Berkeley Square with a colourful, contemporary décor. Aubergine curtains are teamed with brown leather chairs and lime banquettes, while the walls are hung with bright abstract artworks. Take your seat and choose from a repertoire of fixed-price menus, including a seven-course surprise selection. Whatever you plump for, you're in for some accomplished cuisine - tip-top produce is treated with confident deftness and presented with great elegance, and there's an impressive list of tipples on offer to wash it down. Kick off with seared scallops served with foie gras, parsnip purée and a salsify ragout, and then move on to fillet of Aberdeen Angus beef with Sarladaise potatoes, parsley root purée and baby carrots.

Times: 12-2.30/6-10, Closed Xmas, New Year, BHs, last 2 wks Aug, Sun, Sat **Directions:** Nearest station: Bond Street, Green Park NW end of Berkeley Sq

◉ Blandford Street
Modern British, European 🍷NOTABLE WINE LIST 🖥
Discreet little restaurant in stylish Marylebone

☎ 020 7486 9696 5-7 Blandford St, Marylebone W1U 3DB Plan 2-G3
e-mail: info@blandford-street.co.uk
web: www.blandford-street.co.uk

An intimate restaurant in upmarket Marylebone, with a smart terrace on the front pavement for summer dining. Customers can linger at the bar just inside the door before heading for their table, where seating is on comfy maroon banquettes or brown leather chairs. The service is as discreet as the setting, and the menus simply executed around the day's catch at Poole, well-hung beef, and other market-fresh quality ingredients. From the set lunch menu you might find an authentic cassoulet of Toulouse sausage, confit duck and salted rare breed pork belly, or a simple mushroom risotto. The evening carte offers a broader range but still delivers good value.

Chef: Martin Moore **Owners:** Nicholas Lambert **Times:** 12-2.30/6.30-10.30, Closed Xmas, New Year, Etr, BHs, Sun, Closed L Sat **Prices:** Fixed L £12.95-£21.95, Starter £5.95-£12.95, Main £10.95-£21.95, Dessert £5.95, Service added but optional 12.5% **Wine:** 8 by the glass **Seats:** 55, Pr/dining room 18 **Children:** Portions **Directions:** Nearest station: Bond Street Turn right out of Oxford St exit, cross road and down Marylebone Ln to Marylebone High St. Onto Blandford St, restaurant on left **Parking:** NCP: Weymouth Street

◉ Brian Turner Mayfair
Modern British 🖥
Back-to-basics British cooking in upmarket hotel

☎ 020 7596 3444 Millennium Hotel, 44 Grosvenor Square, Mayfair W1K 2HN Plan 2-G1
e-mail: annie.mckale@mill-cop.com
web: www.brianturneronline.co.uk/mayfair.asp

In contrast to the other smart eateries in this swanky Mayfair hotel, Brian Turner's split-level restaurant - which makes the most of the views across Grosvenor Square - boasts understated retro-chic, decked out in contemporary shades and natural materials. Famed for his interest in traditional British comfort food, cooking is based on simple, wholesome and satisfying British classics, yet dishes are given a light and modern touch. Think spit-roast duck on butternut purée with crisp potato, broad beans and bacon, or Finnebrogue venison loin with potato and parsnip terrine, while a soft-centred chocolate pudding with Jaffa Cake ice cream might catch the eye at dessert.

Chef: Brian Turner & Paul Bates **Owners:** Millennium Hotels **Times:** 12.30-2.30/6.30-10.30, Closed BHs, Sun, Closed L Sat **Prices:** Fixed L £24.50, Starter £7.50-£15.50, Main £15-£42, Dessert £7.50, Service added but optional 12.5% **Wine:** 60 bottles over £20, 7 by the glass **Notes:** Civ Wed 100, Air con **Seats:** 86, Pr/dining room 60 **Children:** Portions **Rooms:** 348 (348 en suite) ★★★★ HL **Directions:** Nearest station: Bond Street, Green Park Close to Oxford St, Bond St and Park Ln **Parking:** NCP next door

◉ Butler's
Traditional British 🖥
Traditional dining in elegant Mayfair retreat

☎ 020 7491 2622 Chesterfield Mayfair Hotel, 35 Charles St, Mayfair W1J 5EB Plan 4-H6
e-mail: fandbch@rchmail.com
web: www.chesterfieldmayfair.com

Step through the door of this exclusive hotel and you'll find a luxurious Georgian interior appropriate to its prestigious Mayfair address. A clubby feel pervades the public spaces thanks to high-

CONTINUED

ENGLAND

LONDON W1 CONTINUED

quality antiques, leather chairs, and heavy fabrics, and the elegance continues into Butlers restaurant, a sumptuous room with a strong red and brown décor and a subtle African theme. Dine here or in the light and airy Conservatory, where a traditional British menu offers a good range of straightforward dishes based on high-quality ingredients. Kick things off with a pear, gorgonzola and pecan salad, before tucking into the likes of rump of lamb with herb mash and red wine and bay leaf sauce, or choose from the carving trolley, followed by Eton Mess or sticky toffee pudding.

Chef: Andrew Fraser **Owners:** Red Carnation Hotels **Times:** 12.30-2.30/5.30-10.30 **Prices:** Fixed L £18.50, Fixed D £26, Starter £8-£13.50, Main £17.50-£23, Dessert £8, Service added but optional 12% **Wine:** 88 bottles over £20, 30 by the glass **Notes:** Vegetarian available, Civ Wed 100, Air con **Seats:** 65, Pr/dining room 24 **Children:** Menu, Portions **Rooms:** 110 (110 en suite) ★★★★ HL **Directions:** Nearest station: Green Park From N side exit tube station turn left and then first left into Berkeley St. Continue down to Berkeley Sq and then left heading towards Charles St **Parking:** NCP - 5 minutes

◉ Camerino

Traditional Italian 💻

Friendly Italian restaurant stamped with originality

☎ 020 7637 9900 16 Percy St W1T 1DT Plan 3-B3
e-mail: info@camerinorestaurant.com
web: www.camerinorestaurant.com

Theatrical from the glamorous fuschia-coloured wall drapes to the Italian welcome and service, Camerino (the name means 'theatre changing room') is well worth the short trek up Tottenham Court Road. You can eat modestly from the set menus or pre-theatre choice, or more extravagantly from the carte, but the market-fresh produce is the same, and so is the expert handling from a forward-looking kitchen team. Modern presentation make the likes of deep-fried eel with black truffle risotto, and roasted pheasant with porcini mushrooms and pheasant look as good as they taste, and desserts are another strength.

Chef: Valerio Daros **Owners:** Paolo Boschi **Times:** 12-3/6-11, Closed 1 wk Xmas, 1st Jan, Etr Day, most BHs, Sun, Closed L Sat **Prices:** Fixed L £19.50, Fixed D £23.50, Starter £6-£9.50, Main £16-£19.50, Dessert £5.50, Service added but optional 12.5%, Group min 8 service 12.5% **Wine:** 95 bottles over £20, 6 bottles under £20, 8 by the glass **Notes:** Vegetarian available, Dress Restrictions, Smart casual preferred, Air con **Seats:** 70 **Directions:** Nearest station: Tottenham Court Rd, Goodge St Please telephone for directions **Parking:** Goodge St

◉◉ Cecconi's

Traditional Italian

All-day Italian cuisine and cutting-edge design

☎ 020 7434 1500 5a Burlington Gardens W1X 1LE
Plan 3-A1
web: www.cecconis.co.uk

In keeping with its swish location, opposite Burlington Arcade, Cecconi's is a chic, stylish modern restaurant that attracts a trendy crowd. An extensive all-day menu means you can come in at any time and enjoy a great range of simple, well-presented dishes offering good value for money, including Italian tapas dishes like octopus with lemon and green olives. Start from 7am with breakfast, or brunch at weekends from 12 until 5. Pop in for a light lunch with choices like crab ravioli, lobster spaghetti, or fettucini with wild boar ragout, or indulge in a leisurely dinner. Main courses include new variations on Italian classics - try wild sea bass with clams, tomato and basil.

Times: 12/midnight, Closed Xmas, New Year **Directions:** Nearest station: Piccadilly Circus/Oxford Circus Burlington Gdns between New Bond St and Savile Row

◉◉ China Tang

Chinese

Sophisticated Chinese set in luxurious surroundings

☎ 020 7629 9988 The Dorchester, Park Ln W1A 2HJ
Plan 4-G6
e-mail: reservations@chinatanglondon.co.uk

Lavish, opulent and stunning are just a few words to describe this ultra-deluxe Chinese setting in the basement of The Dorchester, where no expense has been spared. There's a lavish cocktail bar and spacious dining room, the décor a mix of art deco and traditional Chinese. Interior design is mirrored pillars, stunning glass-fronted artworks, tables with marble inset tops laid with heavy silver chopsticks, hand-carved chairs and deep banquette seating. The classic Cantonese cooking, utilising top-quality produce, parades on dim sum and carte menus that come dotted with luxuries. Try stir-fry lobster in black bean sauce, or deep-fried crab claws stuffed with shrimp mousse.

Chef: Ringo Chow **Owners:** David Tang **Times:** 11/midnight, Closed 25 Dec **Prices:** Fixed L £15, Starter £4, Main £42, Dessert £8, Service added but optional 12.5% **Wine:** 512 bottles over £20, 5 bottles under £20, 12 by the glass **Notes:** Vegetarian available, Dress Restrictions, Smart casual, Air con **Seats:** 120, Pr/dining room 80 **Children:** Portions **Directions:** Nearest station: Hyde Park Corner Please telephone for directions

◉◉ *Cipriani*

Italian

A dazzling piece of Venice in Mayfair

☎ 020 7399 0500 25 Davies St W1E 3DE Plan 2-H2
web: www.cipriani.com

Arrigo Cipriani's first venture outside Venice - haunt of the fashionable, rich and famous - is ideally located just off Berkeley Square. The modern glass-fronted exterior leads to a large, stylish dining room, where impeccable art deco style meets beautiful Murano chandeliers, and white-jacketed staff offer slick and attentive service. Low, leather-upholstered seating and magnolia tablecloths provide added comfort. Classic, accurate, straightforward Italian cooking - with lots of Cipriani touches, authentic, top-quality ingredients and unfussy presentation - hits the mark in dishes such as tagliatelle with fresh peas starter, followed by beef medallions alla Rossini. Do save room for the dessert selection of cakes and fine breads.

Times: 12-3/6-11.45, Closed 25 Dec **Directions:** Nearest station: Bond Street Please telephone for directions

◉ *Cocoon*

Pan-Asian 🖥

Happening Pan-Asian restaurant

☎ 020 7494 7600 65 Regents St W1B 4EA Plan 3-B1
e-mail: reservations@cocoon-restaurants.com
web: www.cocoon-restaurants.com

Booking is essential at this unreservedly popular restaurant, even on a weekday. The loud clamour of after-work conversation is minimised by the careful placing of tables in hidden nooks and crannies, with the clever use of net curtains effectively screening groups away from each other. You can dine at the sushi bar and watch the chefs at work, or pick and choose from a comprehensive menu that takes in the best of the Asian culinary world. Dim sum, sashimi, teriyaki, tempura, green miso soup are all there, along with some interesting fusion dishes.

Times: 12-2.45/5.30-11.30, Closed 25-26 Dec, 1 Jan **Directions:** Nearest station: Piccadilly Circus 1 min walk from Piccadilly Circus

◉ *The Cumberland - Rhodes*

Modern British 🖥

Exciting concept at Rhodes W1

☎ 0870 333 9280 Great Cumberland Place W1A 4RF
Plan 2-F2
e-mail: enquiries@thecumberland.co.uk
web: www.guoman.com

A high-ceilinged restaurant split into two dining areas either side of a bar creates a modern and impressive backdrop for some exciting cuisine. Expect British dishes with Gary's influence, simply and well prepared, and easy to eat. The menu offers crowd-pleasing classics and new dishes, taking in the likes of crayfish tails with spring onion and bucatini pasta in tomato and chilli sauce, perhaps followed by braised oxtail with mashed potatoes. And what better than finishing off with a much loved British classic - bread-and-butter pudding.

Times: 12-2.30/6-10.15 **Rooms:** 1015 (1001 en suite) ★★★★ HL
Directions: Telephone for directions

◉◉ *Deya at Best Western Mostyn Hotel*

Indian 🖥

Hip restaurant with contemporary Indian food

☎ 020 7224 0028 34 Portman Square W1H 7BY
Plan 2-F2
e-mail: info@deya-restaurant.co.uk
web: www.deya-restaurant.co.uk

Located just behind Oxford Street, the Mostyn Hotel was originally built as a residence for Lady Black, a lady-in-waiting at the court of George II. A bangers-and-mash joint in the basement belies these lofty origins and offers plenty to tempt, but the real draw is the hotel's chic Indian eatery, Deya. It offers innovative Indian cooking that's full of flavour and arranged in eye-popping style on the plate. The décor is discreet and modern with a subtle Indian theme most evident in the murals on the wall divisions - there's also a trendy bar, which attracts a sophisticated crowd for cocktails and chatter. Highlights from the menu include smoked salmon kebabs, chilli and coconut prawn curry, and butter chicken.

Chef: Virappan Muragappan **Owners:** Claudio Pulze/Raj Sharma
Times: 12-2.45/6.30-10.45, Closed 24-25 Dec, 31 Dec, Sun, Closed L Sat
Prices: Fixed L £14.95, Starter £6.50-£9.95, Main £12.50-£15.95, Dessert £4.50-£9.50, Service added but optional 12.5% **Wine:** 110 bottles over £20, 4 bottles under £20, 10 by the glass **Notes:** 3 tasting menus available 5 courses, Vegetarian available, Dress Restrictions, Smart casual, Air con
Seats: 80 **Children:** Portions **Rooms:** 121 (121 en suite) ★★★ HL
Directions: Nearest station: Marble Arch/Bond St On the corner of Seymour St and Portman St **Parking:** NCP Bryanston St

◉◉ *Embassy London*

Modern European 🖥

Modern, sophisticated Mayfair restaurant and club

☎ 020 7851 0956 29 Old Burlington St W1S 3AN
Plan 3-A1
e-mail: embassy@embassylondon.com
web: www.embassylondon.com

Set behind a modern glass frontage in the heart of the West End, this Mayfair restaurant is as stylish and sophisticated as its address. The ground-floor dining room is a contemporary, split-level affair, with chic bar, floor-to-ceiling windows and small alfresco terrace at the front. Soothing creams and browns, white linen, mirrored surfaces and stunning flower displays cut an understated, upmarket edge. Attentive black-clad staff, a vibrant atmosphere and enticing modern European cooking all fit the bill, too. Expect clear, clean-cut flavours and presentation, balanced combinations and tip-top produce to deliver the likes of tuna and wild oyster tartare with sweet pickled cucumber, followed by roast curried lobster, apple and ginger, with sauce Jacqueline. Dine before descending to the nightclub below.

Times: 12-3/6-11.30, Closed 25-26 Dec, 1 Jan, Good Fri, Sun-Mon, Closed L Oct-Apr & Sat **Directions:** Nearest station: Green Park, Piccadilly Circus Just off Burlington Gardens, running between Bond and Regent St

ENGLAND

◉◉ L'Escargot - The Ground Floor Restaurant

French 🍷 NOTABLE WINE LIST ▢

Soho institution that teams a winning menu with breathtaking artwork

☎ 020 7439 7474 48 Greek St W1D 4EF Plan 3-C2
e-mail: sales@whitestarline.org.uk
web: www.lescargotrestaurant.co.uk

L'Escargot's art collection alone makes it worth a visit - Chagall, Miró, Warhol, Hockney and Matisse are all represented - and with accomplished French cuisine also on offer, its reputation as a Soho grandee is easy to understand. Classic bistro fare is the order of the day, whisked up from quality seasonal produce and delivered to the table by an obliging serving team who handle the crowds with aplomb. Start with smoked haddock ravioli perhaps, served with creamed leeks and mustard beurre blanc, and then plump for pan-fried calves' liver with pomme mousseline and sauce diable, or sea bream with aubergine caviar and olive jus. There's a full carte at lunch and dinner, and a good-value menu du jour for lunch and pre-theatre dinner.

Chef: Simon Jones **Owners:** Jimmy Lahoud & Marco Pierre White
Times: 12-2.30/6-11.30, Closed 25-26 Dec, 1 Jan, Sun, Closed L Sat
Prices: Fixed L £15, Starter £8.50, Main £12.95-£14.95, Dessert £6.50-£8.95, Service added but optional 12.5%, Group min 13 service 15% **Wine:** 289 bottles over £20, 6 bottles under £20, 8 by the glass **Notes:** Pre-theatre menu available, Vegetarian available, Smart casual, Air con **Seats:** 70, Pr/dining room 60 **Children:** Portions **Directions:** Nearest station: Tottenham Court Rd, Leicester Square Telephone for directions
Parking: NCP Chinatown, on street parking

◉◉◉ L'Escargot - The Picasso Room

see opposite

◉◉ Fino

Spanish 🍷 NOTABLE WINE LIST ▢

Fashionable tapas with an authentic range and good service

☎ 020 7813 8010 33 Charlotte St W1T 1RR Plan 3-B3
e-mail: info@finorestaurant.com
web: www.finorestaurant.com

An upmarket and lively Spanish restaurant hidden away in a surprisingly bright and airy basement off chic Charlotte Street. High ceilings, pale wood floors, red leather chairs and a contemporary mezzanine bar set the stylish scene for sampling some skilfully cooked tapas. Great for grazing and groups' dining from a daily menu that lists both classic and contemporary offerings, and watch them being prepared in the open-to-view kitchen. Expect robust, gutsy dishes and flavours, such as snails with garlic purée, crispy pork belly, or foie gras with chilli jam. Extremely helpful, well-drilled service.

Chef: Jean Philippe Patruno **Owners:** Sam & Eddie Hart **Times:** 12-2.30/6-10.30, Closed Xmas & BH, Sun, Closed L Sat **Prices:** Starter £1.80-£16.50, Main £8-£20, Dessert £3.50-£7.50, Service added but optional 12.5% **Wine:** 9 by the glass **Notes:** Vegetarian available, Air con **Seats:** 90 **Directions:** Nearest station: Goodge St/Tottenham Court Rd Entrance on Rathbone St

◉ Four Seasons Hotel London

Modern European, Asian ▢

Relaxed, contemporary dining with views of Hyde Park and Park Lane

☎ 020 7499 0888 Hamilton Place, Park Ln W1A 1AZ Plan 4-G5
e-mail: fsh.london@fourseasons.com
web: www.fourseasons.com

This is sophisticated dining just a stone's throw from Hyde Park. The well-known Lanes restaurant is a lovely dark, clubby-feel dining room oozing understated luxury - think stained glass, wood panelling and marble. Spotlights illuminate each table and the wall-to-ceiling shelves showcase some beautiful glassware. Service here is seamless yet unpretentious, with obvious attention to detail. The cosmopolitan menu has Asian influences from the chef's time in the Far East, seen in dishes like lamb nasi goreng and lamb satay with fried egg and spicy peanut sauce. It also includes traditional British favourites like bread-and-butter pudding or cherry crumble. A buzzy bar and regular jazz dinners are a feature, too.

Chef: Bernhard Mayer **Owners:** Four Seasons Hotels & Resorts
Times: 12-3/6-11 **Prices:** Fixed L £30, Fixed D £38, Starter £9-£19, Main £22-£35, Dessert £10, Service included **Wine:** 14 by the glass
Notes: Fixed L 3 courses, Civ Wed 300, Air con **Seats:** 90, Pr/dining room 300 **Children:** Menu, Portions **Rooms:** 219 (219 en suite)★★★★★ HL
Directions: Nearest station: Green Park/Hyde Park Corner Hamilton Place, just off Hyde Park Corner end of Park Lane **Parking:** 50

ENGLAND

L'Escargot - The Picasso Room

LONDON W1

Modern French V 🍷NOTABLE WINE LIST 🖥

Accomplished French cuisine in an intimate dining room

☎ 020 7439 7474 48 Greek St W1D 4EF Plan 3-C2
e-mail: sales@whitestarline.org.uk
web: www.lescargotrestaurant.co.uk

Dedicated to Picasso, this dining room above the famous Ground Floor restaurant boasts a collection of original ceramics by the artist as well as a number of prints. Comfortable leather seating and quality table settings are provided, with service both formal and discreet.
Starters featuring snails, frogs' legs and smoked foie gras set the tone for a predominantly French dining experience, but if that doesn't appeal you might kick off with seared Cornish scallops with lemon and parsley, or red mullet with cauliflower mayonnaise and roasted langoustines. Mains showcase lots of top British produce and might include roasted Dorset lobster with Jerusalem artichoke purée, served with a fricassée of girolles and chanterelles, or fillet of John Dory with braised oxtail, and potato and chive risotto. Desserts stick to the Gallic theme with the likes of parfait of bananas with warm chocolate fondant and chocolate sauce. An extensive wine list, dominated by the main French regions, echoes the quality of the food.

Chef: Warren Geraghty
Owners: Jimmy Lahoud & Marco Pierre White
Times: 12-2.15/7-11, Closed 2 wks from 24 Dec (excluding New Year), 4 wks Aug, Sun-Mon, Closed L Sat
Prices: Fixed L £20.50, Fixed D £42, Service added but optional 15%
Wine: 289 bottles over £20, 6 bottles under £20, 8 by the glass
Notes: Tasting menu available, Vegetarian menu, Air con
Seats: 30
Children: Min 8 yrs
Directions: Nearest station: Tottenham Court Rd, Leicester Square Telephone for directions
Parking: NCP or street parking

LONDON W1 CONTINUED

◉◉ *Galvin at Windows*

Modern French 🖥

Exciting destination restaurant in the heart of Mayfair with magnificent views

☎ 020 7208 4021 London Hilton on Park Ln, 22 Park Ln W1K 1BE Plan 4-G5
e-mail: galvinatwindows@hilton.com
web: www.hilton.co.uk/londonparklane

Unrivalled 360-degree views over the capital's skyline prove an irresistible feature of this 28th-floor restaurant perched atop of the London Hilton on Park Lane. Chef-patron Chris Galvin (see also Galvin - Bistrot de Luxe) oversees André Garrett (ex Orrery) in the kitchens of this slick modern French affair. It's glamorous, swish and contemporary, with leather seating, crisp linen and an eye-catching golden-ribbon feature suspended from the ceiling, while the raised central area allows all a view. The spacious bar enjoys the panorama, too, while the confident, skilful modern-French approach is driven by tip-top seasonal ingredients and clean-cut flavours and presentation; take a fillet of Speyside beef served with braised cheek, foie gras and ceps. (Also open for breakfast.)

Times: 12-2.30/7-10.30, Closed L Sat, D Sun **Directions:** Nearest station: Green Park, Hyde Park Corner On Park Lane, opposite Hyde Park

◉◉ Galvin - Bistrot de Luxe

French 🍷 NOTABLE WINE LIST

Top-notch cuisine at a classy bistro

☎ 020 7935 4007 66 Baker St W1U 7DH Plan 2-G3
e-mail: info@galvinuk.co.uk
web: www.galvinuk.co.uk

The brothers Galvin worked in some of London's top kitchens before going it alone in order to create this classy bistro with a Parisian feel. Their name above a grey awning and glass frontage is the only clue as to the pedigree of the place halfway along Baker Street. Panelled walls, black leather banquettes and crisp white linen set the tone, while fans whirl overhead, mirrors adorn the walls, and tantalising glimpses are offered of the kitchen. Fittingly, the highly accomplished cooking is unmistakeably Gallic, with great ingredients and superb flavours at value-for-money prices. Duck liver parfait is a typical starter, served with shallot confit, while mains are rooted in traditional cuisine: daube of Denham Estate venison for example, with poached quince and chestnuts, or côte de porc noir with pommes mousseline and pruneaux d'Agen.

Chef: Chris & Jeff Galvin **Owners:** Chris & Jeff Galvin **Times:** 12-2.30/6-11, Closed 25 & 26 Dec, 1 Jan, Closed D 24 Dec **Prices:** Fixed L £15.50, Fixed D £17.50, Starter £6-£15, Main £11.50-£18.50, Dessert £5-£6.50, Service added but optional 12.5% **Wine:** 102 bottles over £20, 15 bottles under £20, 14 by the glass **Notes:** Fixed L 3 courses, Vegetarian available, Air con **Seats:** 95 **Children:** Portions **Directions:** Nearest station: Baker Street Please telephone for directions **Parking:** On street & NCP

◉◉◉ Le Gavroche Restaurant

see opposite

◉◉◉ Gordon Ramsay at Claridge's

see opposite

◉◉◉ The Greenhouse

see page 338

◉◉ The Grill

Traditional English, Continental 🍷 NOTABLE WINE LIST 🖥

Elegant, traditional-vogue dining in famous, remodelled London hotel

☎ 020 7518 4060 Brown's Hotel, Albemarle St W1S 4BP Plan 3-A1
e-mail: reservations.brownshotel@roccofortehotels.com
web: www.roccofortehotels.com

This landmark Mayfair hotel has emerged from complete refurbishment and retains an air of its original charm with the successful marriage of traditional and contemporary styling. The Grill (the oldest hotel restaurant in London - previously called Restaurant 1837) follows the theme and, whilst modern and stylish in appearance, hasn't lost its Victorian-era elegance. Think oak panelling, moss green leather banquette booths, hanging lanterns and specially commissioned wall lights, linen tablecloths and traditional, highly professional service. The kitchen continues the theme, its modern continental approach likewise tempered by a traditional English note, with a focus on old favourites; think English lamb cutlets from the grill selection, to seared Crinnan scallops with cauliflower purée and braised fennel. Brown's renowned afternoon teas are served in the lounge, while there's a modernised, clubby bar for aperitifs.

Chef: Laurence Glayzer **Owners:** Rocco Forte Hotels **Times:** 12.30-2.30/7-10.30 **Prices:** Fixed L £25, Fixed D £30, Starter £8-£19.50, Main £14.50-£26, Dessert £8.50, Service optional **Wine:** 350 bottles over £20, 20 by the glass **Notes:** Pre-theatre D 2 courses £25, 3 courses £30, Dress Restrictions, Jacket required, Civ Wed 70, Air con **Seats:** 85, Pr/dining room 70 **Rooms:** 117 (117 en suite) ★★★★★ HL **Directions:** Nearest station: Green Park Off Piccadilly between Green Park tube station and Bond Street **Parking:** Valet/Burlington St

ENGLAND

Le Gavroche Restaurant

LONDON W1

French NOTABLE WINE LIST

Mayfair's bastion of French tradition

☎ 020 7408 0881 & 7499 1826 43 Upper Brook St
W1K 7QR Plan 2-G1
e-mail: bookings@le-gavroche.com
web: www.le-gavroche.co.uk

Entering this famous and unique Mayfair basement restaurant is like being transported into a timeless hospitable world, epitomising a style of classic French cooking and service that is close to unique on this side of the Channel. The crown of Britain's best cooking may long have been relinquished to innovation across town or up river at Bray's Fat Duck, but the exacting standards of its kitchen and service - in the safe hands of Michel Roux Jr - remain impeccable, while this gilt-edged venue never fails to let you know you're somewhere very special indeed.

The Roux brothers' first British venture, Le Gavroche may be 40 years old, but its packed tables testify to its enduring appeal and popularity. Cosseting and opulent, the dining room comes awash with legions of dedicated staff and decorated with rich fittings and furnishings, while tables are set with crisp linen and lavish crystal and silver, all setting the tone for a truly classical French experience. Like the décor, Michel

Jr's superb, skilful cooking drips with luxuries (you'll have to dig deep into your pockets), while blending classical dishes with others that show a lighter touch and more contemporary taste. Beef fillet and foie gras with port sauce and truffled macaroni cheese, or steamed lobster with pasta and a light cream brandy sauce, are rounded off perfectly with a warm bitter chocolate tart with sorbet, trifle and spiced milk chocolate mousse. A tasting Menu Exceptional and a serious, French-dominated wine list wraps up this classy Gallic act.

Chef: Michel Roux Jr **Owners:** Le Gavroche Ltd **Times:** 12-2/6.30-11, Closed Xmas, New Year, BHs, Sun, Closed L Sat **Prices:** Fixed L £46, Starter £19.80-£52.80, Main £26.80-£46.60, Dessert £12.80-£30.60, Service added but optional 12.5% **Wine:** 2,000 bottles over £20, 20 bottles under £20, 4 by the glass **Notes:** Fixed L 3 courses, Tasting menu 8 courses, Dress Restrictions, Jacket required, No jeans, Air con **Seats:** 60
Children: Portions **Directions:** Nearest station: Marble Arch From Park Lane into Upper Brook St, restaurant on right **Parking:** NCP - Park Lane

Gordon Ramsay at Claridge's

LONDON W1

European V

Elegant dining and gastronomic flair

☎ 020 7499 0099 Brook St W1K 4HR Plan 2-H2
e-mail: gordonramsay@claridges.com
web: www.gordonramsay.com

Once renowned as the resort of kings and princes, Claridge's today continues to set the standards by which other hotels are judged, while its marriage with Gordon Ramsay has elevated it to one of London's most popular dining venues. The restaurant exudes 1930s sophistication, from its dramatic three-tiered light shades to its delicate etched-glass panels. The elegant, high-ceilinged room - restored to its former art deco glory by designer and architect Thierry Despont - is all very grand. Service is expectedly slick and professional and tables elegantly appointed, while there's an intimate bar area, and, for the ultimate experience, a 'chef's table' in the heart of the kitchen.

Chef Mark Sargeant's highly accomplished, modern haute-European cuisine focuses around top-class seasonal ingredients, the fixed-price repertoire of lunch, carte and six-course tasting option dotted with luxury, the cooking fitting perfectly under the Ramsay stable umbrella. There's an intelligent simplicity and integrity that allows main ingredients to shine in clean-flavoured dishes; perhaps roasted John

Dory and sautéed langoustines served with baby artichokes, pink fir potatoes, carrot purée and a light fennel sauce, and maybe a buttermilk pannacotta with vanilla biscuit and rhubarb jus to close. Save room for all the extra touches (tasters, inter-courses, petits fours), while a galaxy of stars populate the serious wine list.

Chef: Mark Sargeant **Owners:** Gordon Ramsay Holdings Ltd **Times:** 12-2.45/5.45-11 **Prices:** Fixed L £30-£75, Fixed D £65, Service added but optional 12.5% **Wine:** 800 bottles over £20, 3 bottles under £20, 10 by the glass **Notes:** Fixed L 3 courses, Prestige menu 6 courses £75, Vegetarian menu, Dress Restrictions, Smart, jacket preferred, no jeans/trainers, Air con **Seats:** 100, Pr/dining room 60 **Children:** Portions **Rooms:** 203 (203 en suite)★★★★★ HL **Directions:** Nearest station: Bond Street At the corner of Brook & Davies St **Parking:** On street

ENGLAND

The Greenhouse

LONDON W1

Modern European 🖵

Fine dining at a discreet Mayfair address

☎ 020 7499 3331 27a Hay's Mews W1J 5NY Plan 4-H6
e-mail: reservations@greenhouserestaurant.co.uk
web: www.greenhouserestaurant.co.uk

A chic, modern Mayfair-mews restaurant, with a subtle botanical theme - in keeping with its name - comes stylishly kitted out in neutral tones and natural textures, and dotted with a classy collection of art nouveau decorative glass. The entrance is via a smartly furnished terrace garden with wooden decking and pot plants, while inside it's smart, calm and softly lit. Celebrated chef Bjorn van der Horst may have moved on to join the Gordon Ramsay stable at La Noisette on Sloane Street, but talented chef Antonin Bonnet (formerly of Morton's, London) heads-up the highly accomplished kitchen at The Greenhouse in fine style. His modern approach is inspired by the highest-quality produce from the markets, putting a creative spin on French and Mediterranean classics on a fixed-price repertoire of lunch, carte and a brace of tasting options. Expect crab and daikon ravioli with spicy Korean red chilli pepper, perhaps followed by seared grey mullet with swede purée and Alenois watercress, and to finish, a choice of millefeuille: vanilla bavaroise and prune ice cream, or clementine and jasmine tea ice cream. A fabulous wine list and various tasters, inter-courses and ancillaries hold interest right through to the end.

Chef: Antonin Bonnet **Owners:** Marlon Abela Restaurant Corporation
Times: 12-2.30/6.45-11, Closed 25-26 Dec, 1 Jan, BHs, Sun, Closed L Sat
Prices: Fixed L £28, Fixed D £60, Service added but optional 12.5%
Wine: 3,005 bottles over £20, 19 bottles under £20, 23 by the glass
Notes: Tasting menu £75, Air con **Seats:** 65, Pr/dining room 10
Children: Portions **Directions:** Nearest station: Green Park, Hyde Park, Bond St Behind Dorchester Hotel just off Hill St **Parking:** NCP, Meter Parking

---

The Grill (Dorchester Hotel)

LONDON W1

Modern British 🖵

Splendid food in opulent surroundings

☎ 020 7629 8888 The Dorchester, Park Ln W1K 1QA
Plan 4-G6
e-mail: restaurants@thedorchester.com
web: www.thedorchester.com

Now redecorated, this grand, world-renowned hotel's Grill Room has a whimsical, flamboyantly Scottish feel, the work of famous designer Thierry Despont. Large murals of heroic Highlanders gaze down from burnished gold walls, oversized lampshades and colourful tartan chairs all deliver a striking statement, while formal settings and a luxurious ambience also help make this a wonderful venue to sample some equally striking cooking. The menu may still feature a few classic grills, such as roast beef from the trolley (with Yorkshire pudding and roast potatoes) or perhaps grilled Dover sole (with béarnaise sauce), but the main thrust takes a modern British approach in the hands of young head chef, Aiden Byrne - a protégé of Tom Aikens, and previously at Danesfield House Hotel in Marlow. Highly accomplished dishes are multi-faceted but deliver well-balanced combinations, driven by tip-top quality ingredients and fresh, clean flavours that are presented with real panache. Think roasted scallops with white chocolate and truffle risotto, pan-fried John Dory served with celeriac, apple and horseradish, or perhaps squab pigeon with pickled cabbage and a sweet garlic-butter sauce.

Chef: Aiden Byrne **Owners:** The Dorchester Collection **Times:** 12.30-2.30/6-11 **Prices:** Fixed L £25, Starter £10-£19.50, Main £19.50-£30, Dessert £10.50, Service added but optional 12.5% **Wine:** 400 bottles over £20, 5 bottles under £20, 18 by the glass **Notes:** Sun L 3 courses £35, Vegetarian available, Dress Restrictions, Smart casual, Civ Wed 450, Air con
Seats: 81 **Children:** Menu, Portions **Rooms:** 250 (250 en suite)★★★★★ HL **Directions:** Nearest station: Hyde Park Corner On Park Ln, overlooking Hyde Park **Parking:** South Audley St

ENGLAND

@@@

Hakkasan

LONDON W1

Chinese

Exotic Chinese dining in central London

☎ 020 7927 7000 No 8 Hanway Place W1T 1HD
Plan 3-B3
e-mail: reservation@hakkasan.com

Fashionably secreted away in a back street off Tottenham Court Road, Hakkasan is housed in a dramatic basement at the bottom of an Indian slate stairwell presided over by a doorman. Dark and with a club-like atmosphere, it is an incredibly popular restaurant and bar that attracts an adoring crowd. The dazzling modern interior reflects the wealth of Chinese culture: think black lacquer and red calligraphy, with delicate Balinese latticework used to divide up seating areas lit by low-slung spotlights. Add close-set, darkwood-polished tables and leather banquette seating, club-style music, a long bar and attentive, knowledgeable staff and the backdrop's set for some exceptional Chinese cuisine. The lengthy menu is built on Cantonese foundations, with influences from other regions, and includes a dim sum selection (available lunchtime only) as well as a range of 'small eat' snacks, and a handful of specials requiring 24-hour notice, such as Peking duck with Royal Beluga caviar, or double-boiled shark's fin soup with abalone, dried scallop and sea cucumber. There are old favourites too,

often with a twist, and distinguished by first-class ingredients, dazzling technique and plenty of flair. And if all that weren't enough, the cocktail list is great too: a frothy collection of tipples that includes a Purple Emperor, Rose Petal Martini and the intriguingly named, Walking Buddha. Not to be missed.

Chef: C Tong Chee Hwee **Owners:** Alan Yau **Times:** 12-2.45/6-12.30, Closed 25 Dec, Closed L 26 Dec, 1 Jan, D 24 Dec **Prices:** Fixed L £50-£100, Fixed D £50-£100, Starter £5.50-£18.50, Main £9.50-£52, Dessert £6-£13.50, Service added but optional 13% **Wine:** 301 bottles over £20, 10 by the glass **Notes:** Fixed L 3 courses, Vegetarian available, Dress Restrictions, No jeans, shorts, trainers, caps or vests, Air con **Seats:** 225
Directions: Nearest station: Tottenham Court Rd From station take exit 2, then 1st left, 1st right, restaurant straight ahead **Parking:** Valet parking (dinner only), NCP

LONDON W1 CONTINUED

@@@ **The Grill (Dorchester Hotel)**
see opposite

@ **Kai Mayfair**

Chinese 🖥

Luxurious venue for authentic Chinese cooking

☎ 020 7493 8988 65 South Audley St W1K 2QU Plan 4-G6
e-mail: kai@kaimayfair.co.uk
web: www.kaimayfair.co.uk

A setting of oriental opulence is provided at this upmarket restaurant, with a décor of rich reds and muted gold and silver. Staff are dressed in military-style jackets finished with a Swarovski crystal emblem of the restaurant's name in Chinese characters. The kitchen prides itself on authenticity with some fairly traditional dishes, but new flavours are

created and the repertoire adapted by including non-traditional ingredients. Maybe opt for the enticing 'Mermaids in the Mist' - Chilean sea bass in a light miso-type broth, followed by 'The Drunken Phoenix on the Scented Tree' - a whole spring chicken marinated in a fragrant infusion of cinnamon bark and Chinese wine.

Chef: Alex Chow **Owners:** Bernard Yeoh **Times:** 12-2.15/6.30-11, Closed 25-26 Dec, New Year **Prices:** Fixed L £30, Fixed D £75, Starter £11-£108, Main £16-£53, Dessert £7-£10, Service added but optional 12.5%
Wine: 115 bottles over £20, 8 by the glass **Notes:** Vegetarian available, Air con **Seats:** 110, Pr/dining room 12 **Directions:** Nearest station: Marble Arch Telephone for directions, or see website **Parking:** Directly outside
see advert on page 340

@@ **The Langham Hotel**

Modern International 🖥

Modern international cuisine in a new look restaurant

☎ 020 7973 7544 1c Portland Place W1B 1JA Plan 2-H4
e-mail: lonmemories@langhamhotels.com
web: www.langhamhotels.com

At the time of going to press this restaurant was undergoing a major refurbishment. Designed by the renowned David Collins, this chic new operation will seat approximately 100 people and include two private dining rooms, a cocktail room and a wine corridor. Colour schemes will incorporate powder blues with lime green leather, gold wood and mosaic flooring. The cuisine will be modern international with classical French roots. A new feature will be the off-street entrance that will give the restaurant its own identity and render it extremely accessible for both hotel guests and non-residents.

Kai Mayfair
foods of china

Best Chinese Restaurant in London
Zagat Guide 2005, 2004 & 2003
Harden's London Restaurant Guide 2002

Best Oriental Restaurant in Britain
Carlsberg Best in Britain Awards 2005

Best Kitchen Finalist
Tatler Magazine Restaurant Awards 2006

Best Chinese Chef
Westminster Chinese Masterchef Awards 2005

65 South Audley Street, London W1K 2QU   Tel:020 74938988   www.kaimayfair.co.uk

LONDON W1 CONTINUED

Owners: Langham Hotels **Times:** 12-2.30/6-10.30 **Prices:** Food prices not confirmed for 2008. Please telephone for details **Notes:** Dress Restrictions, Smart casual, Civ Wed 220, Air con **Seats:** 100, Pr/dining room 14 **Children:** Menu, Portions **Rooms:** 427 (427 en suite) ★★★★★ HL **Directions:** Nearest station: Oxford Circus On north end of Regent St, by Oxford Circus **Parking:** On street & NCP

 Latium

Italian 🖥

Fresh, authentic Italian cooking with service to match

☎ 020 7323 9123 21 Berners St W1T 3LP Plan 3-B3

e-mail: info@latiumrestaurant.com

web: www.latiumrestaurant.com

Given the Latin name for the chef-patron's home town (Latina), this smart, intimate restaurant (one of the Capital's best kept secrets) provides such authentic tastes and atmosphere, you'll feel as though you were in Italy. Maurizio Morelli's unique passion for Italian cuisine has created a great seasonal menu with a strong commitment to sourcing fine Italian produce and delivering authentic flavours with flair and panache. Ravioli is a particular speciality, with a separate menu offering a choice of five fresh filled pasta dishes as starters and mains. Try oxtail ravioli with celery sauce or, alternatively, get that Latin fix via dishes like roasted saddle of lamb with baby artichokes, roast potato and asparagus, or an almond and chocolate tart with Amaretto sauce.

Chef: Maurizio Morelli **Owners:** Maurizio Morelli, Claudio Pulze **Times:** 12-2.45/6-10.30, Closed BHs, Sun, Closed L Sat **Prices:** Fixed L £15.50, Fixed D £28.50, Service added but optional 12.5% **Wine:** 97 bottles over £20, 5 bottles under £20, 7 by the glass **Notes:** Vegetarian available, Dress Restrictions, Air con **Seats:** 50 **Children:** Portions

◎ **Levant**

Lebanese, Middle Eastern

Vivid colours, scents and flavours in an atmospheric basement restaurant

☎ 020 7224 1111 Jason Court, 76 Wigmore St W1H 9DQ Plan 2-G3

e-mail: info@levant.co.uk

web: www.levant.co.uk

Leave the sobriety of Wigmore Street behind when you descend the stone stairs of Levant into a scene from the *Arabian Nights*. Lanterns light the way into an exotic basement where colours are rich, fabrics sumptuous, and the atmosphere seductive and beguiling. A long banquette and separate tables dominate the centre of the room, while cosy private areas offer floor cushions for lounging over the Lebanese cooking. The Middle Eastern spices bring an authentic flavour to hot and cold mezzes, and special treats like slow-roasted whole shoulder of lamb served with a nut pilaf.

Times: 12/midnight, Closed 25-26 Dec **Directions:** Nearest station: Bond Street From Bond St station, walk through St Christopher's Place, reach Wigmore St, restaurant across road

◎◎◎◎ **Locanda Locatelli**

see page 342

◎◎◎ **Maze**

see page 343

◎◎◎

Lindsay House Restaurant

LONDON W1

Modern European V 🖥

Vibrant flavours and top-notch ingredients in a Soho townhouse

☎ 020 7439 0450 21 Romilly St W1D 5AF Plan 3-C2

e-mail: richardcorrigan@lindsayhouse.co.uk

web: www.lindsayhouse.co.uk

This well-known Soho restaurant is discreetly tucked away behind the doors of an elegant townhouse. The four-storey building dates back to 1740 and instead of the restaurant frontage you might expect in Soho, it's all very low key with a doorbell to be rung on arrival. Inside you'll find elegant traditional-style dining rooms on the ground and first floors, plus a private dining room called the Chef's Library on the second floor.

Diners can choose from an array of menus, including a seasonal lunchtime market menu, garden (vegetarian), tasting option and carte to suit the occasion, waistband or wallet. The cooking style relies on carefully sourced top-quality ingredients and robust simple flavours, hallmarks of Richard Corrigan's Irish roots. It's hard to choose from all the delights, but clever combinations and excellent presentation might deliver the likes of pan-roasted brill with wild mushroom linguine, or a loin of West Cork beef served with spinach purée, gratin potatoes and

caramelised ceps, while desserts could feature a quince tart with golden raisin and Sauternes ice cream.

Chef: Richard Corrigan **Owners:** Searcy Corrigan **Times:** 12-2.30/6-11, Closed 1 wk Etr, BHs & Xmas, Sun, Closed L Sat-Sun, D Sun **Prices:** Fixed D £56, Starter £8-£16, Main £14-£22, Dessert £8, Service added but optional 12.5%, Group min 8 service 15% **Wine:** 19 by the glass **Notes:** ALC L only, Tasting menu 6 courses £68, Vegetarian menu, Dress Restrictions, Smart casual, Air con **Seats:** 50, Pr/dining room 40 **Children:** Portions **Directions:** Nearest station: Leicester Square Just off Shaftesbury Avenue, off Dean Street **Parking:** NCP

ENGLAND

Locanda Locatelli

LONDON W1

Italian NOTABLE WINE LIST

Inspired Italian cuisine in chic contemporary setting that attracts a celebrity crowd

☎ 020 7935 9088 Hyatt Regency London, The Churchill, 8 Seymour St W1H 7JZ Plan 2-F2
e-mail: info@locandalocatelli.com
web: www.locandalocatelli.com

This slick, sophisticated and much-vaunted Italian - about the best in the country - is tucked away off Portman Square in the back of the Hyatt Regency Churchill Hotel, and is the haunt of a well-heeled, celebrity crowd. Cream leather banquette seating, concave mirrors and subdued lighting (in the evenings) set the scene at this buzzy, classy David Collins designed restaurant. Its retro yet stylish interior features parquet flooring, grained-wood walls, glass dividers and modern artworks, including pieces by Paul Simonan (of the Clash pop band) and Damien Hirst. The service is as sleek and notable as the décor, Italian staff court customers with flair and passion and have a real appreciation of the food, while chef Giorgio Locatelli glides between tables surveying his clientele and ensuring his delicious food is being enjoyed with the passion shown in its creation.
The ingredients are the absolute best and lovingly sourced, and the breads (some nine items, like foccacia, pane carasau, grissini, etc) and pasta are phenomenal. The style is modern northern Italian, and there's a real freshness about the cooking, enhanced by great combinations while nothing is over-worked or too complicated, so flavours sing out. The traditionally laid-out menu offers plenty of choice, so do come hungry and set to go four rounds - antipasta, pasta, main and dessert - to do the ultimate justice to Giorgio's inspired cooking ... it doesn't come better in the Italian format! Think home-made chestnut tagliatelle with wild mushrooms, perhaps pan-fried calves' kidney served with potato purée and ceps, and to finish, maybe a panettone bread-and-butter pudding with panettone ice cream. A sommelier is on hand to help navigate the impressive regionally-focused, all-Italian wine list with its superb vintages from Tuscany and Piemonte. But do book well in advance as it's always busy. This is one not to be missed!

Chef: Giorgio Locatelli
Owners: Plaxy & Giorgio Locatelli
Times: 12-3/7-11, Closed Xmas, BHs
Prices: Starter £8-£14.50, Main £12-£28, Dessert £6-£8, Service optional
Wine: 2 bottles under £20, 24 by the glass
Notes: Vegetarian available, Air con
Seats: 70
Children: Portions
Rooms: 445 (445 en suite) ★★★★★ HL
Directions: Nearest station: Marble Arch Please telephone for directions
Parking: NCP adjacent, parking meters

Maze

LONDON W1

French, Asian

Grazing in elegance at the heart of Mayfair

☎ 020 7107 0000 10-13 Grosvenor Square W1K 6JP
Plan 2-G2
e-mail: maze@gordonramsay.com
web: www.gordonramsay.com

This exciting addition to the Gordon Ramsay stable isn't difficult to find, with entrances from the imposing London Marriott Hotel Grosvenor Square or directly off Grosvenor Square itself. Contemporary and bright, the extensive dining area follows the maze theme, decked out in split levels with the lowest at the centre, surrounded by a glass screen featuring the restaurant's maze motif. Tables are simply laid, while service exudes style and panache, from its professional demeanour to its knowledge. There is also a chef's table overlooking the main pass.
Executive chef Jason Atherton - formerly of Ramsay's Dubai venture, Verre - delivers a modern French approach with Asian influences, via a fashionable, grazing-style menu featuring an impressive and appealing array of innovative, complex and highly accomplished tapas-style dishes that come dressed to thrill and showcase the best seasonal ingredients (with six to eight dishes recommended per head). There's

also a traditional carte, essentially based on larger portions of the grazing options, plus a Sunday roast offering. Expect the likes of Orkney scallops roasted with spices, peppered golden raisin purée and cauliflower, followed by roasted brill with provençale cockle vinaigrette, pistou and baby spinach, and to finish, pain au chocolat (chocolate ganache with caffè latte sorbet, vanilla bread-and-milk mousse). The 'flights of wines' innovation epitomises the attention to detail throughout, offering three glasses based on a country or grape variety, which ideally suits the grazing concept.

Chef: Jason Atherton **Owners:** Gordon Ramsay Holdings Ltd **Times:** 12-2.30/6-10.30 **Prices:** Fixed L £28.50, Fixed D £50, Starter £7-£9.50, Main £7.50-£10.50, Dessert £6-£8, Service added but optional 12.5% **Wine:** 600 bottles over £20, 2 bottles under £20, 21 by the glass **Notes:** Fixed L 4 courses, Fixed D 6 courses, Sun L 4 courses £24.50, Dress Restrictions, Smart casual, Air con **Seats:** 90, Pr/dining room 10 **Children:** Portions **Rooms:** 236 (236 en suite) ★★★★ HL **Directions:** Nearest station: Bond Street Entrance off Grosvenor Sq **Parking:** Grosvenor Sq

---

LONDON W1 CONTINUED

⊚⊚ Mews of Mayfair

Modern NEW

Chic place to see and be seen with cooking to match

☎ 020 7518 9395 & 7518 9388 10-11 Lancashire Court W1S 1EY Plan 2-H2
e-mail: info@mewsofmayfair.com
web: www.mewsofmayfair.com

As its name suggests, this lively and contemporary restaurant, set amid Mayfair's premier-league shops, stands in a lovely mews just off Bond Street. There's a bar and terraced tables on the ground floor, while upstairs the main restaurant offers a more sophisticated edge. Smart and modern is the style, set off with a striking black-and-white theme; think white walls and white embossed leather upholstery. Service is friendly but professional. The kitchen's experienced international team delivers refined dishes with a wealth of interesting combinations based around tip-top produce. Expect clear flavours and sound balance in dishes like roast sea bass with artichoke purée and pickled chanterelles, and perhaps vanilla roast figs and pistachio ice cream to close.

Chef: David Selex **Owners:** James Robson & Robert Nearn **Times:** 12-3/6-11, Closed 25-26 Dec, New Year, Etr Mon, Closed D Sun **Prices:** Fixed L £19.50, Starter £6.50-£14.50, Main £14.50-£29.50, Dessert £6.50-£8, Service added but optional 12.5% **Wine:** 30+ bottles over £20, 8 bottles under £20, 16 by the glass **Notes:** Tasting menu £45, Sun L £22.50, Vegetarian available, Dress Restrictions, Smart casual, Air con **Seats:** 70, Pr/dining room 30 **Children:** Portions **Directions:** Nearest station: Bond Street Between Brook St & Maddox St. Opposite Dolce & Gabbana **Parking:** On street

⊚⊚ Mirabelle

Traditional French 🖳

Classic French cuisine with Mayfair glamour

☎ 020 7499 4636 56 Curzon St W1J 8PA Plan 4-H6
e-mail: sales@whitestarline.org.uk
web: www.whitestarline.org.uk

Step through the low-key lobby of this Mayfair grandee and you'll find a glamorous bar and restaurant, complete with art deco mirrors, bold artworks and a resident pianist. Part of the Marco Pierre White empire, it lures a well-heeled crowd with its easy cosmopolitan ambience and classic French dishes. Expect unfussy, flavourful cooking that belies the grand surroundings and has an authentic Gallic feel: sole à la provençale, for example, or braised pig's trotters with morels, pomme purée and sauce Périgueux. Desserts might include prune and Armagnac soufflé or lemon tart, and there's an extensive wine list.

Continued

ENGLAND

LONDON W1 CONTINUED

Private dining rooms are available with a separate menu and there are great-value set lunches.

Mirabelle

Chef: Igor Timchishin **Owners:** Marco Pierre White, Jimmy Lahoud
Times: 12-2.30/6-11.30, Closed 26 Dec & 1 Jan **Prices:** Fixed L £19.50, Starter £7.50-£18.95, Main £16.50-£25.50, Dessert £8.50, Service added but optional 12.5% **Wine:** 270 bottles over £20, 4 bottles under £20, 6 by the glass **Notes:** Sun L 3 courses £23, Vegetarian available, Dress Restrictions, Smart casual, Air con **Seats:** 120, Pr/dining room 48 **Children:** Portions
Directions: Nearest station: Green Park Telephone for directions.
Parking: Berkeley Sq

◎◎ *Mosaico*

Italian 🖥

Slick, stylish and modern Mayfair Italian

☎ 020 7409 1011 13 Albemarle St W1S 4HJ
Plan 3-A1
e-mail: mosaico-restaurant.co.uk

Set beneath the DKNY store opposite Brown's Hotel and just round the corner from The Ritz, this Mayfair Italian couldn't be anything else but sophisticated and upmarket. Think red-leather banquettes or stylish chairs, tables dressed in their best whites and limestone floors. Cream walls, prints of Italian scenes and a mirrored frieze above the seating keeps things light, while staff are slick, attentive and Latin. The kitchen takes an equally stylish, modish approach with a northern Italian slant, using quality ingredients, including textbook pastas and cracking breads and grissini. Expect light, well-presented, clear-flavoured dishes like ravioli filled with artichokes in a light vegetable sauce, or perhaps grilled calves' liver and kidneys with truffle-scented olive oil.

Times: 12-2.30/6.30-10.45, Closed Sun, Closed L Sat, Sun, Xmas, Etr, BHs
Directions: Telephone for further details

◎ Nicole's

Mediterranean 🖥

Fashionable lunchtime retreat for the chic and well-heeled

☎ 020 7499 8408 158 New Bond St W1S 2UB
Plan 3-A1
e-mail: nicoles@nicolefarhi.com
web: www.nicolefarhi.com

A wide stone staircase leads down to the bright, split-level restaurant below Nicole Farhi's fashion store on exclusive Bond Street. And, as you'd expect of a haute-couture eatery, there's a stylish, contemporary edge to match that designer label. A small upper level has a steel and glass bar with more informal tables, while oak floors, brown leather and white linen distinguish the main dining area a few steps down. The cooking takes an assured modern approach, based around simplicity and quality seasonal ingredients. For mains expect the likes of grilled halibut with roasted leeks, crispy potatoes and chanterelles, or perhaps baked garlic- and lemon-crusted cod with crab mash and red chard, followed by a chocolate pot and espresso cookie to finish. The bread selection is excellent. A separate bar menu is also available.

Chef: Annie Wayte **Owners:** Stephen Marks **Times:** 12-3.30, Closed BHs, Sun, Closed D all week **Prices:** Starter £6.50-£11.25, Main £18-£24.75, Dessert £7, Service added but optional 15% **Wine:** 4 bottles over £20, 4 bottles under £20, 16 by the glass **Seats:** 65, Pr/dining room 80
Directions: Nearest station: Green Park, Bond St Between Hermès & Asprey

◎◎◎ *Nobu*

see opposite

◎◎ *Nobu Berkeley Street*

Japanese

Fun modern restaurant with a serious approach to food

☎ 020 7290 9222 15 Berkeley St W1J 8DY Plan 5-A6
e-mail: ecb@ecbpr.co.uk
web: www.noburestaurants.com

The sister of the famous Nobu restaurant off Park Lane (see entry), this Mayfair newcomer has already established itself as a place to see and be seen. Downstairs a spacious bar serves drinks till the early hours, while the upstairs restaurant is open for dinner only and features a sushi bar with an open kitchen, a wood-burning oven and a 12-seater hibachi table where guests can cook their own food with a chef's assistance. The waiters know their stuff and are happy to guide you through the menu or even choose a surprise selection; alternatively plump for the six-course tasting menu to really do the place justice. Crispy Gloucestershire Old Spot pork with spicy miso is a hit, as is chocolate harumaki (spring rolls) with passionfruit dipping sauce.

Times: 6-1am, Closed 25 & 26 Dec, Closed L all week
Directions: Nearest station: Green Park Telephone for directions

Orrery

see opposite

ENGLAND

Nobu

LONDON W1

Japanese

Stylish, minimalist, upmarket Japanese with outstanding cuisine

☎ 020 7447 4747 The Metropolitan, Old Park Ln
W1Y 4LB Plan 4-G5
e-mail: ecb@ecbpr.co.uk
web: www.noburestaurants.com

Attracting a hip clientele of celebrities and foodies alike, Nobuyuki Matsuhisa's first UK restaurant - he has other restaurants in London (see entry for Nobu Berkeley Street, also in W1, and Ubon by Nobu, E14), LA and New York - has acquired international standing. Taking up the whole of the first floor of the trendy Metropolitan Hotel, Nobu's interior is ultra sleek and minimalist, its clean lines accentuated by stylish neutral colours, stark tiled floors, leather banquettes and chairs, while huge windows deliver superb views over Park Lane and Hyde Park. It's still one of London's most fashionable venues, so tables are fairly close together and you need to book in advance. Service is swift, with friendly and unassuming black-clad staff ready to guide the uninitiated through the lengthy, flexible-styled menu, predominantly aimed at grazing and sharing. The accomplished kitchen's style is clearly Japanese but with the occasional South

American twist, in dishes like anti-cucho Peruvian-style spicy rib-eye steak, or Chilean sea bass with moro miso. The focus is on exceptionally fresh produce, with defined and vibrant flavours and impressive presentation, as in the must-have black cod with miso. Finish off with an indulgent chocolate bento box - perfect for sharing. There's also a sushi bar to round up a class act.

Times: 12-2.15/6, Closed L Sat-Sun **Rooms:** 150 (150 en suite)
★★★★★ HL

Rosettes not confirmed at time of going to press

Orrery

LONDON W1

Modern European 🖥

Stunning food and service in equal measures in prestigious dining venue

☎ 020 7616 8000 55-57 Marylebone High St W1U 5RB
Plan 2-G4
e-mail: oliviere@conran-restaurants.co.uk
web: www.orrery.co.uk

Perched above the Conran shop, this first-floor restaurant is all cool, clean lines and sophisticated simplicity, with an etched glass screen at the far end depicting the namesake orrery - a mechanical model of the solar system. One of London's most prestigious dining venues, it's set on the High Street in Marylebone village in what was once the site of Henry VIII's hunting lodge. The pedigree of Terence Conran design is unmistakable; contemporary, streamline and typically understated, it comes flooded by light from large arched windows and skylights. Two long rows of tables lined with banquettes and chairs fill the narrow, bright room, where service is as stylish as the surroundings, while there's a small, intimate lounge bar for pre-meal drinks.
The cooking style is suitably innovative and creative, intricate, light and contemporary, its roots firmly in the classics. Meticulous presentation, highly accomplished technical skills and top-notch produce pepper the

repertoire; think best end of new season lamb with slow-braised shoulder, aubergine purée and olive jus, or perhaps steamed monkfish wrapped in prosciutto with braised oxtail and truffle macaroni.
As we went to press we understand that there was a change of chef taking place.

Times: 12-2.30/6.30-10.30, Closed 25-26 Dec, New Year, Good Friday, Closed D 24 Dec **Directions:** Nearest station: Baker St, Regent's Park At north end of Marylebone High St

ENGLAND

LONDON W1 CONTINUED

ⓐⓐ Ozer

Turkish, Middle Eastern 💻

A bustling Turkish delight just a stone's throw from Oxford Circus

☎ 020 7323 0505 5 Langham Place, Regent St W1B 3DG Plan 3-A3
e-mail: info@sofra.co.uk
web: www.sofra.co.uk

Modern and upmarket, Ozer breaks all the old Turkish restaurant clichés. Deep red, curvy, marble-effect walls, a tiled floor and contemporary ceiling lighting kick things off in style. Up front there's a buzzy bar area, while at the back the restaurant comes decked out in white tablecloths and black or red leather chairs. The atmosphere's vibrant, bustling and loud, with hard working staff. The array of menu options offer a wide, affordable range of traditional dishes, including excellent meze, as well as some more unusual offerings, and all kicked off by complimentary houmous, olives and bread. It's straightforward but accomplished and well-presented; try a meze platter followed up by lamb kulbasti (tender fillet with oregano).

Chef: Mustafa Guzen **Owners:** Huseyin Ozer **Times:** Noon/mdnt
Prices: Fixed L £8.95-£10.95, Fixed D £20.95, Starter £3.45-£6.95, Main £6.95-£19.95, Dessert £3.45-£4.25, Service added but optional 12.5%
Wine: 22 bottles over £20, 20 bottles under £20, 7 by the glass
Notes: Vegetarian available, Air con **Seats:** 115 **Children:** Portions
Directions: Nearest station: Oxford Circus 2 min walk towards Upper Regent Street **Parking:** On street

ⓐⓐ Passione

Italian

Wonderful flavours from an intimate, lively Italian

☎ 020 7636 2833 10 Charlotte St W1T 2LT Plan 3-B3
web: www.passione.co.uk

Its pinkish-terracotta and glass frontage seem somewhat unremarkable for a widely esteemed Italian, though the name on the awning perfectly sums up this small but big-hearted restaurant, epitomising chef-patron Gennaro Contaldo's love affair with great food. Green walls are hung with food photographs, while blond-wood floors and chairs add a modern edge to close-set tables and a lively, informal atmosphere; there's an endearing neighbourhood local vibe here. It's not difficult to see why Gennaro is a Jamie Oliver mentor, his regional Italian cooking driven by fresh, high-quality seasonal produce, herbs and simple, clean-flavoured style. Perhaps try tagliatelle with summer truffle sauce, or wild sea bass served with sauté peas and broad beans and marinated samphire.

Times: 12.30-2.15/7-10.15, Closed 1 wk Xmas, BHs, Sun, Closed L Sat
Directions: Nearest station: Goodge Street 5 min walk from underground station

ⓐⓐ Patterson's

Modern European 💻

Inventive cuisine in an elegant, stylish setting

☎ 020 7499 1308 4 Mill St, Mayfair W1S 2AX Plan 3-A2
e-mail: pattersonmayfair@btconnect.com
web: www.pattersonsrestaurant.com

Tucked away in a tiny Mayfair street at the top end of Savile Row, Patterson's provides an elegant setting for fine dining, complemented by slick, professional service. The bar area, complete with lobster and tropical fish tanks, leads to a spacious, long, narrow dining room with oak flooring, high-backed leather chairs and white walls enlivened by colourful artwork. You can relax here and peruse the menu's modern approach - underpinned by a classical French theme and founded on carefully-sourced, tip-top local and organic produce. Father-and-son team Raymond and Tom produce dishes that surprise and delight with their flavour and presentation. Expect loin of lamb in filo pastry with green spring vegetables and curried crab mousseline, and perhaps a pineapple and crème fraîche sorbet millefeuille with fruit salad to finish.

Chef: Raymond & Thomas Patterson **Owners:** Raymond & Thomas Patterson **Times:** 12-3/6-11, Closed 25-26 Dec, 1 Jan, Good Fri & Etr Mon, Sun, Closed L Sat **Prices:** Fixed L £15, Fixed D £40, Starter £13, Main £17, Dessert £10, Service added but optional 12.5% **Wine:** 92 bottles over £20, 4 bottles under £20, 9 by the glass **Seats:** 70, Pr/dining room 20
Children: Menu, Portions **Directions:** Nearest station: Oxford Circus Located off Conduit St opposite Savile Row entrance **Parking:** Savile Row

ⓐⓐⓐⓐ Pied à Terre

see opposite

ⓐⓐ The Providores

Fusion 🏆 NOTABLE WINE LIST

Complex-flavoured fusion food in contemporary surroundings

☎ 020 7935 6175 109 Marylebone High St W1U 4RX Plan 2-G3
e-mail: anyone@theprovidores.co.uk
web: www.theprovidores.co.uk

Once a Victorian pub, The Providores - smack at the heart of Marylebone High Street - now delivers a buzzy, contemporary, all-day café, wine/ tapas bar operation downstairs and a fine-dining restaurant upstairs. Enjoy breakfast, brunch, coffee and a fascinating menu of tapas-inspired fare below, and an extensive choice of fusion food in the dining room above. Both menus change frequently according to produce and inspiration, but chef-patron Peter Gordon's New Zealand

CONTINUED

Pied à Terre

LONDON W1

Modern French V 🍷NOTABLE WINE LIST 🖥

Outstanding, highly refined, modern cooking in contemporary, understated luxury surroundings

☎ 020 7636 1178 & 7419 9788 34 Charlotte St W1T 2NH
Plan 3-B3
e-mail: info@pied-a-terre.co.uk **web:** www.pied-a-terre.co.uk

Chef: Shane Osborn
Owners: David Moore & Shane Osborn
Times: 12-2.45/6.15-11, Closed 2 wks Xmas & New Year, Sun, Closed L Sat
Prices: Fixed L £24.50-£49.50, Fixed D £30-£62, Service added but optional 12.5%
Wine: 620 bottles over £20, 11 bottles under £20, 15 by the glass
Notes: Tasting menu 9 courses £80 available all wk, Vegetarian menu, Air con
Seats: 40, Pr/dining room 12
Directions: Nearest station: Goodge Street S of BT Tower and Goodge St
Parking: Cleveland St

Having risen from the ashes of a fire back in 2005, this class act continues to run on top form with some superlative and exciting cooking. The frontage is intimate and unassuming, while the sleek interior is fittingly stylish and glamorous. The décor is contemporary and oozes understated luxury, with cream suede and rosewood furniture and architectural glass combining harmoniously. There's also a bar upstairs to relax both pre- and post-meal, featuring leather seats and art by Hamilton, Blake and Hodgkin. Service is as impeccable as ever, led by excellent host David Moore. Oz-born chef Shane Osborn continues to deliver his brand of stylish and creative modern French cuisine; it is sophisticated, refined and brimful of class and emphatic flavours, using top-notch luxury ingredients and innovation - technically superb, it ticks all the boxes. The tantalising fixed-price repertoire of lunch, carte and tasting menu (with the option of accompanying wines) promotes an agony of choice, delivering top-drawer dishes. Maybe roasted and poached loin of mid-Devon venison served with a quince purée, pommes soufflé and a sauté of bacon, Savoy cabbage and fresh chestnuts, or perhaps roasted halibut with courgette and basil cream, courgette and truffle fondue, razor clams and a lemon oil emulsion, while dessert might feature a bitter-sweet chocolate tart with stout ice cream and Macadamia nut cream. A stunning range of ancillaries (canapés, amuse-bouche, breads, pre-desserts and petits fours) burst with flavour and attention to detail like everything else here, while an impressive wine list rounds off this highflyer in style.

ENGLAND

LONDON W1 CONTINUED

roots shine through with his use of unfamiliar ingredients and combinations in innovative, exciting, well-executed and presented dishes. Take seared kangaroo loin on a five-spice celeriac fritter with Kalamansi tomato chutney and Greek yogurt to start, and perhaps slow-braised duck with Spanish black bean, feta and chipotle chilli spring rolls with tamarind to follow.

Chef: Peter Gordon **Owners:** P Gordon, M McGrath, J Leeming
Times: 12-10.30, Closed 24 Dec-3 Jan **Prices:** Starter £8-£15, Main £19-£25, Dessert £9, Service added but optional 12.5% **Wine:** 89 bottles over £20, 5 bottles under £20, 31 by the glass **Notes:** Vegetarian available, Air con **Seats:** 38 **Children:** Portions **Directions:** Nearest station: Bond St, Baker St, Regent's Park From Bond St station cross Oxford St, down James St, into Thayer St then Marylebone High St

⊛⊛ Quo Vadis

Modern Italian 🖥

Showcase for authentic Italian cuisine and modern art

☎ 020 7437 9585 26-29 Dean St W1D 3LL Plan 3-B2
e-mail: sales@whitestarline.org.uk
web: www.whitestarline.org.uk

Although Karl Marx once lived in this building, one of the oldest in Soho, its real claim to fame has been as 'Leo Quo Vadis' - one of London's most respected Italian restaurants, founded in the 1930s by Peppino Leoni. The ground-floor restaurant has stained glass windows and a simply restored interior displaying striking works of art by artists like Damien Hirst, Andy Warhol and Modigliani. The modern Italian cuisine is just as impressive, serving up antipasti, pasta, risottos, fish, meat and salad dishes on an authentic and varied Italian menu. Try smoked aubergine 'cannelone', tuna and crispy parmesan, broth of chicken with chicken tortelloni, ekony mushroom and baby leeks, and to follow peach and pistachio tarte feuillete with pistachio and red wine sauce.

Chef: Fernando Corradazzi **Owners:** Jimmy Lahoud, Marco Pierre White
Times: 12-2.30/5.30-11.30, Closed 24-25 Dec, 1 Jan, Sun, Closed L Sat
Prices: Fixed L £14.95, Fixed D £17.95-£19.95, Starter £7-£11, Main £11-£19, Dessert £5, Service added but optional 12.5% **Wine:** 90+ bottles over £20, 4 bottles under £20, 6 by the glass **Notes:** Pre-theatre and tasting menu available, Air con **Seats:** 80, Pr/dining room 90 **Parking:** On street or NCP

⊛⊛ The Red Fort

Traditional Indian 🖥

Stylish, elegant and contemporary Soho Indian

☎ 020 7437 2525 & 7437 2115 77 Dean St W1D 3SH Plan 3-B2
e-mail: info@redfort.co.uk
web: www.redfort.co.uk

This Soho stalwart may have been around for 20 years, but this stylish, upmarket Indian certainly isn't stuck in a time warp. The entrance leads to either its subterranean Akbar Bar or ground-floor dining room, where restful, neutral tones set the scene alongside walls adorned with authentic artefacts. Banquettes line walls, tables are laid with white linen and the staff are smartly attired. The menu continues the theme, with dishes being primarily Mughal Court/North Western in style, utilising top-notch ingredients. Think monkfish tikka to start, followed by anaari champ - Scottish lamb chops from the grill, in star anise and pomegranate jus - or perhaps zaafrani lobster with saffron and garlic, with raspberry shrikhand (yogurt) to finish. There are also good-value fixed-price lunch and pre-theatre menus.

Chef: Iqbal Ahamad **Owners:** Amin Ali **Times:** 12-2.15/5.45-11.15, Closed 25 Dec, Closed L Sat & Sun **Prices:** Fixed L £12, Fixed D £16, Starter £6.50-£9.95, Main £14-£33, Dessert £7-£8, Service added but optional 12.5% **Wine:** 70 bottles over £20, 15 bottles under £20, 7 by the glass **Notes:** Vegetarian available, Air con **Seats:** 84 **Directions:** Nearest station: Leicester Square Walk north on Charing Cross Rd. At Cambridge Circus turn left into Shaftesbury Ave. Dean St is 2nd rd on right

⊛⊛ Ristorante Semplice

Italian NEW

Classy Italian with a passion for authenticity

☎ 0207 4951509 10 Blenheim St W1S 1LJ Plan 2-H2

'Semplice' means 'simple' in Italian and that's the mantra of this chic Mayfair eatery, formerly two small restaurants. Highly polished ebony walls with gold carvings, accompanied by leather seating in brown and cream, and an impressive Murano chandelier, set the scene. Top-notch ingredients form the foundation, either garnered from the best British producers, or flown in from home (mozzarella arrives daily). A variety of regional Italian dishes are delivered with an emphasis on flavour. Free-range Italian meat also wows, and arrives at the table in dishes like roasted and pan-fried rabbit with baby carrots, broad beans and artichoke sauce or free-range chicken cooked 'sous-vide' with grilled vegetables and parmesan shavings. Service is slick and very Italian.

Times: 12-2.30/7-10.30, Closed BHs, Sun

⊛⊛ The Ritz

Modern British, French 🍷 NOTABLE WINE LIST 🖥

Sumptuous cuisine from a Piccadilly grandee

☎ 020 7493 8181 150 Piccadilly W1J 9BR Plan 5-A6
e-mail: enquire@theritzlondon.com
web: www.theritzlondon.com

Renowned as one of the most beautiful dining rooms in Europe, the Ritz restaurant is an opulent confection of Louis XVI furnishings, gold chandeliers, and trompe d'oeil frescos. Dressing up is de rigueur, so break out the glad rags and make the most of the occasion by booking ahead for a table overlooking the patio and park. The menu is as grand as the setting; rooted in classical French cuisine with the odd nod to modern trends, it's crammed with luxury ingredients and big flavours, and offers an array of choice that's sure to cause pleasurable dithering. Take a fillet of beef with truffle and ox-tongue gratin, seared duck livers and hermitage jus, or perhaps rosemary-braised turbot with white asparagus and a chicken and ginger emulsion.

The Ritz

Chef: John T Williams **Owners:** The Ritz Hotel (London) Ltd **Times:** 12-2.30/6-10.30 **Prices:** Fixed L £38, Fixed D £65-£85, Starter £14-£28, Main £19-£47, Dessert £13-£28, Service included **Wine:** 725 bottles over £20, 11 by the glass **Notes:** Fixed L 3 courses, Fixed D 4 courses, Vegetarian available, Dress Restrictions, Jacket & tie requested, No jeans or trainers, Civ Wed 50, Air con **Seats:** 90, Pr/dining room 14 **Children:** Menu, Portions **Rooms:** 135 (135 en suite)★★★★★ HL **Directions:** Nearest station: Green Park 10-minute walk from Piccadilly Circus or Hyde Park Corner **Parking:** NCP on Arlington Street

◉◉◉ Roka

see below

◉◉ Salt Yard

Italian, Spanish

Tapas restaurant offering vibrant little dishes for sharing

☎ 020 7637 0657 54 Goodge St W1T 4NA Plan 3-B4
e-mail: info@saltyard.co.uk
web: www.saltyard.co.uk

A very popular tapas restaurant (booking is essential most nights) where you can dine in the relative calm of the basement restaurant or join the hip and noisy crowd eating and drinking in the bar. Downstairs the tables are neatly laid between high-backed leather chairs, and you can watch the kitchen buzz as you sample the fare. It's the same food wherever you sit, and the carefully-sourced ingredients are handled simply and with inspiration by a committed team. Try a hearty octopus and lentil stew in red wine, or a delicate tuna carpaccio with baby broad beans and salsa verde, but don't miss the soft chocolate cake.

Chef: Benjamin Tish **Owners:** Sanja Morris & Simon Mullins **Times:** 12-3/6-11, Closed BHs, 25 Dec & 1 Jan, Sun, Closed L Sat **Prices:** Main £3-£17, Dessert £4.50-£6.50, Service added but optional 10% **Wine:** 40 bottles over £20, 11 bottles under £20, 10 by the glass **Notes:** Vegetarian available, Air con **Seats:** 60 **Directions:** Nearest station: Goodge St Near Tottenham Court Rd **Parking:** NCP Cleveland St, meter parking Goodge Place

---

◉◉◉
Roka

LONDON W1

Japanese

Stylish, friendly, funky Japanese grill

☎ 020 7580 6464 37 Charlotte St W1T 1RR Plan 3-B3
e-mail: info@rokarestaurant.com
web: www.rokarestaurant.com

Catching the eye on bustling Charlotte Street with its floor-to-ceiling glass frontage and trendy blend of wood, stainless steel and glass, Roka is an ultra-hip, contemporary Japanese - and sibling to Rainer Becker's other restaurant Zuma, across town in Knightsbridge (see entry). Its robata grill (traditional Japanese barbecue grill) takes centre stage, with bar seating all around allowing diners to watch the chefs in the open theatre kitchen, while traditional-style table settings fill the rest of the room. Downstairs, there's a more informal, cool, club-like vibe, with a central bar again, but this time, followed up by sofa-style seating and occasional tables. Service is friendly, upbeat and knowledgeable.

The new-wave Japanese cooking - ideal for grazing - is delivered via an extensive menu (backed by a couple of tasting options) designed around the robatayaki grill cuisine, together with an impressive selection of fresh, vibrant sashimi and sushi, all based on tip-top quality produce. Take sea bream fillet with ryotei miso and red onion,

or perhaps beef fillet with chilli, ginger and spring onion from the robata. There's no waiting for courses, food just comes when it is cooked, so sit back and enjoy the ride - it's great for sharing.

Chef: Rainer Becker, Nic Watt **Owners:** Rainer Becker, Arjun Waney **Times:** 12-3.30/5.30-11.30, Closed 25 Dec, 1 Jan **Prices:** Fixed L £25, Fixed D £50-£75, Starter £3.60-£15.60, Main £7.90-£55, Service added but optional 13.5% **Wine:** 9 by the glass **Notes:** Fixed D 2 courses, Vegetarian available, Smart casual, Air con **Seats:** 90 **Children:** Portions **Directions:** Nearest station: Goodge St/Tottenham Court Rd 5 min walk from Goodge St **Parking:** on street

ENGLAND

LONDON W1 CONTINUED

Sartoria

Italian 🖥

Modern Italian at the heart of Savile Row

☎ 020 7534 7000 & 7534 7030   20 Savile Row W1S 3PR Plan 3-A2

e-mail: sartoriareservations@conran-restaurants.co.uk
web: www.conran.com

Its location on Savile Row has inspired a subtle tailoring theme to this sophisticated, contemporary Conran Italian. Think suited mannequins in the window, crockery with a button logo and a pinking scissor image fronting the menu. Plain white walls come softened by standard lamps, taupe carpeting and modern sofas and chairs upholstered in grey. It's all as sleek and professional as the service and as accomplished and clean cut as the seasonal Italian cooking driven by high-quality ingredients - breaded veal cutlet with a fennel salad, for example. An extensive regional Italian wine list, separate bar area and fixed-price lunch/pre-theatre menu all catch the eye too.

Times: 12-3/6-11, Closed 25-26 Dec, Sun, Closed L Sat
Directions: Nearest station: Oxford Circus/Green Park Tube to Oxford Circus, take exit 3, turn left down Regent St towards Piccadilly Circus, take 5th right into New Burlington St, end of street on left

Scott's Restaurant

British V NEW

Fashionable, glamorous seafood bar and restaurant in the heart of Mayfair

☎ 020 7495 7309   20 Mount St W1K 2HE Plan 2-G2
web: www.scotts-restaurant.com

This legendary fish restaurant - relaunched by Caprice Holdings (the people behind The Ivy, Le Caprice and J. Sheekey, see entries) - sees it return to its past glories in great style. The contemporary, fashionable remix of this classic oak-panelled restaurant comes inspired by its heyday, with rich burgundy-leather seating, an exquisite chandelier, specially commissioned modern art and a central crustacea bar in the style of a turn-of-the-century cruise liner. There's a doorman to greet, while table service is slick, attentive and polished. The kitchen uses top-notch ingredients in well-presented dishes, with the likes of oysters, caviar, crustacea, smoked fish, whole fish and meat on the bone finding a place. Think classics like Dover sole (grilled or meunière), lobster (américaine, grilled or thermidor), or maybe pan-fried skate with periwinkles, nut-brown butter and capers.

Chef: Kevin Gratton **Owners:** ICD Ltd **Times:** 12-3/5.30-11, Closed Xmas, Jan 1, Aug BH **Prices:** Starter £6.20-£35, Main £18.50-£26.50, Dessert £5.75-£15, Service added 12.5% **Notes:** Vegetarian menu, Air con **Seats:** 125, Pr/dining room 38 **Children:** Portions **Directions:** Nearest station: Bond Street Just off Grosvenor Sq, between Berkeley Sq and Park Ln **Parking:** Park Ln

Sherlock's Bar & Grill

Modern French 🖥

Traditional methods for inspirational cuisine

☎ 020 7486 6161   Sherlock Holmes Hotel, 108 Baker St W1U 6LJ Plan 2-F4
e-mail: shh.fb@parkplazahotels.co.uk
web: www.sherlockholmeshoteluk.com

Situated in a chic boutique hotel, there's no mistaking the links to the famous fictional detective, with paintings and a bronze cast to remind diners of his Baker Street roots. The décor is chic and unfussy with warm colours and modern styling. Interestingly, a mesquite wood-burning stove and a charcoal grill are the main methods of cooking here. The emphasis is on quality ingredients with modern inspiration; think Parma ham rolled monkfish tail served with a potato galette and red pepper caponata, and perhaps a tiramisù or apple tart Tatin finish.

Chef: Rachid Hammoum **Owners:** Park Plaza Hotels **Times:** 12-2.30/6-10.30 **Prices:** Fixed L £12.50, Starter £7.25-£12.50, Main £14.50-£18.25, Dessert £6.50, Service added 12.5% **Wine:** 16 bottles over £20, 10 bottles under £20, 10 by the glass **Notes:** Civ Wed 60, Air con **Seats:** 50, Pr/dining room 50 **Children:** Menu, Portions **Rooms:** 119 (119 en suite) ★★★★ HL **Directions:** Nearest station: Baker Street Located on Baker St, close to the tube station **Parking:** Chiltern St

Shogun, Millennium Hotel Mayfair

Japanese

Authentic Japanese food in the heart of Mayfair

☎ 020 7629 9400   Grosvenor Square W1A 3AN Plan 2-G1

This well-established Japanese restaurant is located in the lavishly decorated basement of the Millennium Hotel Mayfair, an impressive Georgian fronted building overlooking Grosvenor Square. Features of its interior décor are kyudo archery arrows, palms and a large statue of a Samurai warrior, and the simple wooden tables are set with bamboo place mats. Discreet service is provided by friendly staff in traditional Japanese attire, and the strength of the Japanese clientele is testimony to the authenticity of the cooking. Shogun produces some of the best Japanese food in the capital including a number of good-value set dinner menus, hand-rolled sushi, zenzai, dobin-mushi, sashimi, tempura, teriyaki and dessert options.

Times: 6-11, Closed Mon

◉◉◉◉ Sketch (Lecture Room & Library)

see page 353

◉ So Restaurant

Japanese NEW

Modern Japanese with hints of European cuisine

☎ 020 7292 0767 & 7292 0760 3-4 Warwick St W1B 5LS Plan 3-B2
e-mail: info@sorestaurant.com
web: www.sorestaurant.com

Contemporary styling - with minimalist use of dark wood, clean lines and artwork - picks this Japanese out from the crowd. The ground floor has a more informal lunchtime, café-style atmosphere, while the basement restaurant comes with dark lacquered tables, high-backed leather chairs and plain walls hung with French wine posters and modern artwork, and is dominated by a glass-wall open-to-view kitchen. The cooking is contemporary - classical Japanese with some European twists - using top-notch ingredients and simple, attractive presentation. Think French foie gras with sautéed Japanese ∗ mushrooms, or perhaps Spanish Iberico grilled pork marinated in white miso and served with steamed broccoli.

Chef: Kaoru Yamamoto **Owners:** Tetsuro Hama **Times:** 12-3/5.30-10.30, Closed Xmas-New Year, Sun **Prices:** Fixed L £7-£14, Fixed D £20-£50, Starter £3.50-£9, Main £9-£36, Dessert £4, Service added but optional 12.5% **Wine:** 33 bottles over £20, 15 bottles under £20, 4 by the glass **Notes:** Vegetarian available, Air con **Seats:** 70, Pr/dining room 6 **Children:** Portions **Directions:** Nearest station: Piccadilly Circus Exit Piccadilly tube station via exit 1. Turn left along Glasshouse St, restaurant is situated next to The Warwick **Parking:** On street

◉◉◉◉ The Square

see page 354

◉◉ Sumosan Restaurant

Japanese

Authentic Japanese cooking at an upmarket Mayfair address

☎ 020 7495 5999 26 Albermarle St, Mayfair W1S 4HY Plan 3-A1
e-mail: info@sumosan.com
web: www.sumosan.com

This cosmopolitan Japanese restaurant is located in the heart of Mayfair, surrounded by exclusive jewellers, designer clothes shops and fine art vendors. It's a popular venue both with the local business community and those looking for authentic cuisine, and has a pared down modern décor of cool clean lines, parquet flooring, and polished darkwood tables. All the bases are covered, from teppan-yaki and tempura to sushi and sashimi; you can choose from an extensive carte, or plump for the seven-course lunch selection. Kick off with beef tartare with nashi pear and sesame before tucking into the likes of spicy somen noodles with lobster and baby asparagus or lamb chops furikaki.

Sumosan Restaurant

Chef: Bubker Belkhit **Owners:** Janina Wolken **Times:** 12-3/6-11.30, Closed Xmas, New Year, BHs, Closed L Sat-Sun **Prices:** Fixed L £22.50, Fixed D £45-£79, Starter £3.50-£12, Main £11-£55, Dessert £6.50-£12, Service added but optional 15% **Wine:** All bottles over £20, 5 by the glass **Notes:** Tasting menu L £50, D 90 (max 8 persons), Vegetarian available, Air con **Seats:** 115, Pr/dining room 32 **Children:** Portions **Directions:** Nearest station: Green Park Please telephone for directions **Parking:** On street

◉◉ *Taman Gang*

South East Asian 🖥

Vivacious, upmarket basement venue with late opening and elegant cuisine

☎ 020 7518 3160 141 Park Ln W1K 7AA Plan 2-F2
e-mail: info@tamangang.com
web: www.tamangang.com

Leave the chaos of Marble Arch behind and descend to this exotic, dimly lit, split-level basement bar and dining room packed with Eastern promise. Hand-carved limestone walls, mahogany furniture, lanterns and low banquettes evoke the look and feel of ancient Indonesia. Flickering candles, white orchids, contemporary music and youthful, knowledgeable and attentive black-clad staff add to the trendy, atmospheric vibe. The cuisine fits the surroundings, a fashionable, modern, sophisticated Pan-Asian mix, kind of Chinese by way of Japan and Thailand. Stunning presentation, tip-top ingredients, vibrant flavours and skilful handling form a repertoire that promotes sharing. Expect dishes like wok-flashed salt and pepper prawns with green pepper and spring onion, and Merlot black pepper beef with crispy noodles. Don't miss the oriental-inspired cocktail list.

Times: 12-3.30/6-1, Closed L Mon-Sat

England

Wine Award Winner
and Overall Winner

Sketch (Lecture Room & Library)

Page 353

Sketch (Lecture Room & Library)

LONDON W1

Modern European V 🍷 NOTABLE WINE LIST 🖥

AA Wine Award Winner for England & Overall Winner

☎ 0870 777 4488 9 Conduit St W1S 2XG Plan 3-A2
web: www.sketch.uk.com

This one-time HQ of Christian Dior comes brimful of surprises, outrageous flamboyancy and refinement. A collaboration between Mourad Mazouz and Parisian super-chef Pierre Gagnaire that offers a multi-level food-based extravaganza, which includes the vibrant, ground-floor Gallery brasserie (opulent, exciting and bursting with signature art deco), plus the cool Parlour tea room by day, hyper-trendy bar by night. The fine-dining Lecture Room and Library upstairs - two parts of the same space - is elegantly decorated in shades of orange, with ivory walls of studded leather and high ceilings, while thick-piled, brightly coloured carpets and long dangling lampshades cut a somewhat Middle Eastern edge. Dishes bear the unmistakable creative genius of consultant Pierre Gagnaire's distinctive culinary style (delivered here by head chef and Gagnaire protégé, Pascal Sanchez); it's stunning, exciting, innovative and technically superb. The very best quality fresh produce is transformed into an enormous range of textures and flavours, ensuring a surprise at each turn. It's complex and deeply French, with dishes combining many elements, like a signature starter 'Langoustines Addressed in Five Ways', perhaps poached fillet of Simmenthal beef in a port bouillon, braised lettuce with beef marrow and pochas beans, condiment, vinegar and sea salt wild mushrooms, while to finish, perhaps another signature offering 'Pierre Gagnaire Grand Desserts' which could arrive as five miniatures.

Chef: P Gagnaire, P Sanchez
Owners: Pierre Gagnaire, Mourad Mazouz
Times: 12-2.30/7-11, Closed 21 Aug-4 Sep, 25-29 Dec, Sun-Mon, Closed L Sat
Prices: Fixed L £35, Starter £14-£48, Main £39-£48, Dessert £14-£18, Service added but optional 12.5%
Wine: 518 bottles over £20, 11 bottles under £20, 23 by the glass
Notes: Fixed L 3 courses, Tasting menu 7 courses £90, Vegetarian menu, Civ Wed 50, Air con
Seats: 50, Pr/dining room 24
Children: Portions
Directions: Nearest station: Oxford Circus 4 mins walk from Oxford Circus tube station, take exit 3, down Regent St, Conduit St is 4th on right
Parking: Cavendish Sq, NCP Soho

ENGLAND

The Square

LONDON W1

Modern French V ♦ NOTABLE WINE LIST 🖥

A class culinary act in the heart of Mayfair

☎ 020 7495 7100 6-10 Bruton St W1J 6PU Plan 3-A1
e-mail: info@squarerestaurant.com
web: www.squarerestaurant.com

Style and sophistication lie beyond the glass frontage of this discreet, chic, premier-league restaurant in a sought-after address just off fashionable Bond Street and its designer boutiques. The expansive dining room - accessed via a small bar - is furnished in slick contemporary style, with terracottas, rich browns, steely blues and creams all harmonising. Parquet floors are set out with clothed tables, their rich brown, floor-length undercloths topped-off with crisp white linen, while striking, vibrant abstract artworks add a splash of colour to the neutral tones.

A superb wine list and Philip Howard's bright, intense, memorable cooking prove more than a match for the elegant surroundings and impeccable, professional service. His refreshingly modern approach comes underpinned by a classical French theme; the fixed-priced repertoire, which includes an eight-course tasting option, dotted with luxury items, set to impress any business diner. Cultured dishes impress all, though, displaying an emphasis on well-sourced, top-notch ingredients, interesting combinations and strong, clear flavours, and come dressed to thrill. Consistency, timings, freshness and textures all help the cooking stand out from the crowd too. Take a stunning starter of sea-fresh sauté of langoustine tails and potato gnocchi with field mushroom purée, trompettes de la mort and truffle butter, or perhaps succulent slow-cooked fillet of cod with velvety creamed potato, cauliflower, leek hearts and truffle to follow. Poached pineapple, served with tropical jellies and lime ice cream, might catch the eye at dessert and deliver simplicity at its finest, while peripherals - like a fantastic selection of canapés, breads and petits fours - wrap things up in supreme style.

Chef: Philip Howard
Owners: Mr N Platts-Martin & Philip Howard
Times: 12-3/6.30-10.45, Closed 24-26 Dec, 1 Jan, Closed L Sat & Sun, BHs
Prices: Fixed L £25, Fixed D £65, Service added but optional 12.5%
Wine: 1,400 bottles over £20, 3 bottles under £20, 14 by the glass
Notes: Tasting menu £80 (£130 inc wine), Vegetarian menu, Air con
Seats: 70, Pr/dining room 18
Children: Portions
Directions: Nearest station: Bond Street, Green Park Telephone for directions

LONDON W1 Continued

◉◉ Tamarind

Indian 🖥

Contemporary, classy novelle Indian in Mayfair

☎ 020 7629 3561 20 Queen St, Mayfair W1J 5PR Plan 4-H6

e-mail: manager@tamarindrestaurant.com

web: www.tamarindrestaurant.com

The entrance may be a simple door leading on to a staircase, but it delivers you to this sophisticated and glamorous, designer-styled, buzzy basement Indian in the heart of Mayfair, decked out in contemporary, minimalist style and graced by elegantly attired, attentive and friendly staff. Muted metallic colours, low lighting, wooden floors and a glass theatre kitchen add to the sense of style, with the kitchen delivering a medley of traditional and contemporary cuisine - focused around the tandoor oven - and cooked in authentic North-West Indian style. Expect neatly presented, subtle-flavoured dishes to grace an appealing menu; perhaps ajwaini macchi (grilled monkfish in a marinade of ginger, yogurt and saffron), or classic rogan josh.

Chef: Alfred Prasad **Owners:** Indian Cuisine Ltd **Times:** 12-2.45/6-11.15, Closed 25-26 Dec, 1 Jan, Closed L Sat, BHs **Prices:** Fixed L £16.95, Fixed D £49.50-£68, Starter £7-£12.50, Main £16.50-£23, Dessert £4.95-£7, Service added but optional 12.5% **Wine:** 100 bottles over £20, 4 bottles under £20 **Notes:** Vegetarian available, Dress Restrictions, No jeans or shorts, Air con **Seats:** 90 **Directions:** Nearest station: Green Park Towards Hyde Park, take 4th right into Half Moon St to end (Curzon St). Turn left, Queen St is 1st right **Parking:** NCP

◉◉◉ Theo Randall, InterContinental London

see page 356

◉◉ La Trouvaille

French 🖥

French cooking with a modern twist in intimate surroundings

☎ 020 7287 8488 12a Newburgh St W1F 7RR Plan 3-A2

e-mail: contact@latrouvaille.co.uk

web: www.latrouvaille.co.uk

Set among the cobbled pedestrian lanes and boutiques off Carnaby Street, the small, two-floored La Trouvaille proves quite the Soho find, as its name implies. On the ground floor there's a buzzy, chic wine bar, while on the first floor the more formal yet relaxed restaurant. Bijou comes decked out in white linen, modern perspex chairs, striking mirrors, stripped floorboards and tall windows. Attentive but relaxed French service and a patriotic wine list add to the upbeat mood. Unconventional French cooking - thoughtful and with easygoing invention and well-sourced ingredients - fits the bill. Think a fillet of Galloway beef cooked in broth and served with seasonal vegetables, parsley jus and wasabi gratiné, or a classic hot chocolate fondant with ginger ice cream finish.

Chef: Mr Pierre Renaudeau **Owners:** T Bouteloup **Times:** 12-3/6-11, Closed Xmas, BHs, Sun **Prices:** Fixed L £15, Fixed D £33, Service added but optional 12.5% **Wine:** 32 bottles over £20, 8 bottles under £20, 12 by the glass **Seats:** 45, Pr/dining room 30 **Children:** Portions **Directions:** Nearest station: Oxford Circus Off Carnaby St by Liberty **Parking:** NCP (off Broadwick St)

◉◉◉ Umu

see page 356

◉◉ Vasco & Piero's Pavilion Restaurant

Italian 🖥

Genuine taste of Umbria in intimate, family-run restaurant

☎ 020 7437 8774 15 Poland St W1F 8QE Plan 3-B2

e-mail: vascosfood@hotmail.com

web: www.vascosfood.com

Conveniently tucked away close to the London Palladium and Liberty, this cosy corner restaurant looks somewhat unassuming from outside, but don't be deceived. Once inside the bijou, family-run eatery, the wonders of real Umbrian food and warm hospitality come to life. Closely packed tables, subtle lighting, a warm terracotta colour scheme and attentive, helpful Italian service add to the authenticity. The chef-patron hails from Umbria and continues to import many speciality products direct from the region, while the kitchen's intelligently simple treatment of high-quality ingredients is key. Menus may change daily and pasta is hand made, but clear, vivid flavours reign supreme in dishes like grilled fillet of wild sea bass with spinach, or hand-made agnolotti (Umbrian-style meat ravioli) with rosemary.

Chef: Vasco Matteucci **Owners:** Tony Lopez, Paul Matteucci & Vasco Matteucci **Times:** 12-3/6-11, Closed BHs, Sun, Closed L Sat **Prices:** Fixed D £27-£33, Starter £5-£8.50, Main £12.50-£19.50, Dessert £6.75, Service added but optional 12.5% **Wine:** 4 by the glass **Notes:** Vegetarian available, Dress Restrictions, No shorts, Air con **Seats:** 50, Pr/dining room 36 **Children:** Min 5 yrs, Portions **Directions:** Nearest station: Oxford Circus From Oxford Circus turn right towards Tottenham Court Rd, continue for 5min and turn right into Poland St. On corner of Great Marlborough St & Noel St **Parking:** NCP car park opposite

ENGLAND

Theo Randall, InterContinental London

LONDON W1

Italian **NEW**

Fresh, vibrant rustic-suave Italian cooking in a sophisticated modern setting

☎ 020 7318 8747 1 Hamilton Place, Hyde Park Corner W1J 7QY Plan 4-G5

e-mail: reservations@theorandall.com

web: www.theorandall.com

Overlooking Hyde Park and the London skyline, this deluxe landmark hotel has undergone a multi-million pound refurbishment and now features former River Café head chef Theo Randall's new eponymous restaurant - which replaces the hotel's previous Le Soufflé venue. Clean lined, modern, sophisticated and relaxed, the long beige and grey dining room uses lots of natural materials like wood and leather as a backdrop to the traditional regional Italian cooking. There's also a long gleaming bar (at which diners can eat) and a visible kitchen too. Inspired by his passion for top-quality and seasonal produce, the cooking takes on a rustic-suave theme. Ingredients are cooked with great care and skill, but without unnecessary fuss in well-conceived, well-presented, balanced and clear-flavoured dishes on daily-changing menus. Take the likes of perfectly cooked pan-fried Scottish scallops to start, with parsley and Castelluccio lentils, perhaps a main course of wood-roasted turbot on the bone, with parsley, anchovy and new season asparagus, and to finish, maybe a Meyer lemon tart, or a soft chocolate cake with crema di mascarpone. Unique Theo Randall wicker picnic hampers available, filled with freshly-prepared Italian goodies.

Chef: Theo Randall **Owners:** Intercontinental Hotels Ltd & Theo Randall **Times:** 12-3/6.30-11, Closed Xmas, New Year, 1st wk Jan, BHs, Closed D Sun **Prices:** Fixed L £18, Starter £8-£10, Main £9-£10, Dessert £6-£7, Service added but optional 12.5% **Wine:** 250 bottles over £20, 3 bottles under £20, 11 by the glass **Notes:** Vegetarian available, Dress Restrictions, Smart casual, Air con **Seats:** 124, Pr/dining room **Children:** Portions **Rooms:** 451 (451 en suite) ★★★★★ HL **Directions:** Nearest station: Hyde Park Corner Hyde Park Corner rdbt **Parking:** Car park

Umu

LONDON W1

Japanese, Kyoto 💻

Sophisticated Japanese offering high-quality Kyoto cuisine

☎ 020 7499 8881 14-16 Bruton Place W1J 6LX Plan 2-H2

web: www.umurestaurant.com

London's first Kyoto restaurant is a classy affair, tucked away just off Mayfair's Berkeley Square. Award-winning designer Tony Chi has created his vision of opulent Kyoto styling, with an unobtrusive touch button sliding open the wooden front door on to a sophisticated modern interior - high-quality wood and mirrors, banquette seating and a chef's central sushi table. The staff are welcoming and attentive, necessarily knowledgeable and helpful in guiding diners through the intricacies of the menu.

The cooking - from chef Ichiro Kubota - offers innovative classic and contemporary interpretations of Kyoto cuisine, delivered via a fixed-price lunch option, extensive carte, a separate sushi menu and six tasting options. The sheer quality of ingredients and the freshness, clarity, vibrancy and combinations of flavours strike through in every dish and combine with great attention to detail in superb presentation. So dig deep into your pockets and prepare to be wowed by omakase (chef's choice) or sashimi, grilled toro teriyaki or melt-in-the-mouth Wagyu beef with wasabi, finished off with a stylish dessert of green tea soup and pumpkin ice cream.

Chef: Ichiro Kubota **Owners:** Marlon Abela Restaurants Corporation **Times:** 12-2.30/6-11, Closed between Xmas & New Year, BHs, Sun, Closed L Sat **Prices:** Fixed L £20-£48, Fixed D £60-£135, Starter £6-£22, Main £8-£55, Dessert £6-£10, Service added but optional 12.5% **Wine:** 585 bottles over £20, 14 by the glass **Notes:** Fixed L 3 courses, Fixed D 4 courses, Tasting menu available, Vegetarian available, Air con **Seats:** 60, Pr/dining room 12 **Directions:** Nearest station: Green Park/Bond St Off Bruton St & Berkeley Sq

ENGLAND

LONDON W1 CONTINUED

⊛ Veeraswamy Restaurant

Indian 🖥

Sophisticated Indian with refined traditional cooking

☎ 020 7734 1401 Mezzanine Floor, Victory House,
99 Regent St W1B 4RS Plan 3-B1
e-mail: veeraswamy@realindianfood.com
web: www.realindianfood.com

Expect a sophisticated, chic atmosphere at London's oldest Indian restaurant that continues to maintain all the glamour dating from its creation in 1926. Plush, Mogul-style carpets sit on gleaming black Indian granite or darkwood floors, shimmering chandeliers and vibrant coloured lanterns hang from ceilings, adding to the latticed silver screens, silver banquettes or upholstered chairs, and large tables alongside views over Regent Street. Classic Indian dishes from all its regions grace the menu, authentically and freshly prepared with quality ingredients. Take a Kashmiri rogan josh, lobster Malabar curry, or Kerala recipe sea bass fillets with red spices cooked in a banana leaf.

Chef: Uday Salunkhe **Owners:** R Mathrani, C Panjabi & N Panjabi
Times: 12-2.30/5.30-11.30, Closed D Xmas **Prices:** Fixed L £16.50-£20,
Fixed D £33, Starter £5.25-£9.50, Main £11.50-£25, Service added 12.5%
Wine: 50 bottles over £20, 4 bottles under £20, 14 by the glass
Notes: Fixed D 2 courses, Pre/Post-theatre L/D 2 courses £16.50, Air con
Seats: 114, Pr/dining room 36 **Directions:** Nearest station: Piccadilly
Circus Entrance near junct of Swallow St and Regent St, in Victory House

⊛⊛ Via Condotti

Italian NEW

Stylish Italian with classical-based dishes and impeccable service

☎ 020 7493 7050 23 Conduit St W1S 2XS Plan 3-A2
e-mail: info@viacondotti.co.uk
web: www.viacondotti.co.uk

Tucked away among the fashionable boutiques of Mayfair's Conduit Street (just off Bond Street), this attractive, stylish, friendly Italian comes aptly named after one of Rome's most prestigious shopping streets. Its lilac frontage, awning and planters pick it out from the crowd, while inside there's peach décor, lightwood floors, tasteful posters, expensive leather chairs and dazzling white tablecloths. Service is charming and very Italian, unobtrusive and unpretentious, while the cooking comes based on classical roots with some southern influences - chef Pasquale Amico hails from Campania. There is a pleasant, refreshing simplicity about the food, which showcases quality

ingredients, some sourced direct from Italy. Think ravioli filled with scamorza cheese, sun-dried tomato and basil sauce, or roasted rabbit with cacciatore sauce.

Chef: Pasquale Amico **Owners:** Claudio Pulze, Richard Martinez, Pasquale Amico **Times:** 12-3/6.30-11, Closed BHs, Sun **Prices:** Fixed L £24.50, Fixed D £24.50, Service added but optional 12.5% **Wine:** 70 bottles over £20, 8 bottles under £20, 15 by the glass **Notes:** Vegetarian available, Air con **Seats:** 90, Pr/dining room 18 **Children:** Portions

⊛ Villandry

French, European 🖥

Impressive restaurant, quality foodstore and bar

☎ 020 7631 3131 170 Great Portland St W1W 5QB
Plan 3-A4
e-mail: contactus@villandry.com
web: www.villandry.com

This buzzy and lively bar, restaurant, shop and lunchtime takeout has undergone a stylish refurbishment and re-launch. And, as it prizes the quality of its ingredients, entering the restaurant through its upmarket foodstore really whets the appetite. The glass-fronted, high-ceilinged dining room is chic and modern, with tables dressed in their best whites and friendly yet professional service. The modern approach and accurate cooking makes the most of quality, seasonal produce via classic, brasserie-focused menus; take moules marinière with crusty bread, or pan-fried Scottish beef fillet with béarnaise. A child-friendly attitude and separate bar menu add to the upbeat package.

Chef: David Rood **Owners:** Jamie Barber **Times:** 12-3/6-10.30, Closed 25 Dec, Closed D Sun & BHs **Prices:** Starter £5.50-£12.50, Main £11.50-£32.50, Dessert £5.75, Service added but optional 12.5% **Wine:** 79 bottles over £20, 8 bottles under £20, 16 by the glass **Notes:** Sat & Sun brunch menu, Vegetarian available, Air con **Seats:** 100, Pr/dining room 24
Children: Menu, Portions **Directions:** Nearest station: Great Portland Street/Oxford Circus Entrance at 91 Bolsover St, between Great Portland St tube station & Oxford Circus

LONDON W1 CONTINUED

◉ Westbury Hotel

Modern European 🖥️
Accomplished cooking at an exclusive Mayfair hotel

☎ 020 7629 7755 & 8382 5450 Bond St W1S 2YF
Plan 3-A2
e-mail: artisan@westburymayfair.com
web: www.westburymayfair.com

Built in 1955, this chic hotel - set in the heart of Mayfair just off Bond Street - is styled on the Westbury in New York and is home to the renowned Polo Bar. The large, airy Artisan restaurant overlooks Conduit Street, with its own street entrance, and has a classy contemporary look resplendent in creams and browns, with beautiful inlaid wooden floors, wood-panelled walls with frosted glass sheets, stunning chandeliers, crisp white linen and cream leather banquettes and chairs. The menus take an equally stylish and appealing modern approach; take confit shoulder of rabbit with pommery mousseline or roast Scottish scallops with squid ink polenta and chorizo.

Chef: Daniel Hillier **Owners:** Cola Holdings Ltd **Times:** 12-2.30/6.30-10.30, Closed L Sat, D Sun **Prices:** Fixed L £24.95, Starter £8-£13.50, Main £16-£33.50, Dessert £6-£7, Service added 12.5% **Wine:** 207 bottles over £20, 13 by the glass **Notes:** Vegetarian available, Dress Restrictions, Smart casual, Air con **Seats:** 80, Pr/dining room 20 **Children:** Menu, Portions **Rooms:** 249 (249 en suite) ★★★★ HL **Directions:** Nearest station: Oxford Circus, Piccadilly Circus, Green Park Telephone for directions **Parking:** Burlington St

◉ The Wolseley

European
Bustling domed brasserie offering stylish all-day dining

☎ 020 7499 6996 160 Piccadilly W1J 9EB Plan 5-A6
web: www.thewolseley.com

This European café-style phenomenon continues to be a crowd-pleaser. The former Wolseley car showroom has been reinvented as a buzzing restaurant with a glass-domed roof. The show never stops from 7am to midnight - the menus range from breakfasts to all-day snacks and afternoon tea packages, right through to a full carte including soups, starters, crustacea and caviar, salads, eggs and pasta, fish, entrées and grills, desserts and cakes. The daily-changing plats du jour are of particular note, whether it's wild boar casserole, coq au vin or Lancashire hotpot.

Chef: Julian O'Neill **Owners:** Chris Corbin & Jeremy King **Times:** 7am-mdnt, Closed 25 Dec,1 Jan, Aug BHs, 25 Dec, 1 Jan, Closed D 24 Dec, 31 Dec **Prices:** Starter £5.75-£17.25, Main £9.50-£33, Dessert £4-£7, Service added but optional 12.5% **Wine:** 38 bottles over £20, 7 bottles under £20, 28 by the glass **Notes:** Vegetarian available, Air con **Seats:** 150 **Children:** Portions **Directions:** Nearest station: Green Park 500mtrs from Green Park Underground station

◉◉ Yauatcha

Chinese
Oriental cuisine with formal service

☎ 020 7494 8888 15 Broadwick St W1F 0DL
Plan 3-B2
e-mail: reservations@yauatcha.com

This Soho restaurant is found in 'The Igeni' building, designed by Richard Rogers, with the interior by Christian Liagre. Features include fish tanks embedded in several walls and one that creates the bar. Two distinct spaces mean a tranquil upstairs tea house serving over 150 teas and various pastries, and a more atmospheric basement Dim Sum restaurant with low seating. Traditional Cantonese cooking, some Japanese and other oriental specialities are on offer. Relaxed and friendly formal Asian service means well-informed waiters who can create a bespoke menu for you from the lengthy repertoire. Expect 'steamed' dishes like lotus leaf wrapped turbot, 'baked and fried' options like baked venison puff or grilled Wagyu beef, and 'stir-fries' like black pepper ostrich.

Chef: Mr Soon **Owners:** Alan Yau **Times:** 12/11.30, Closed 24-25 Dec, Closed L 26 Dec, 1 Jan **Prices:** Fixed L £40-£100, Fixed D £40-£60, Starter £3.50-£7.50, Main £9.50-£38, Dessert £4-£13.50, Service added but optional 13% **Wine:** 80 bottles over £20, 2 bottles under £20, 11 by the glass **Notes:** Fixed L 3 courses, Vegetarian available, Air con **Seats:** 109 **Directions:** Nearest station: Tottenham Ct Rd, Piccadilly Circus, Oxford Circus On the corner of Broadwick and Berwick St **Parking:** Poland Street - 100 yds

◉ YMing

Chinese V
Chinese regional specialities in Theatreland

☎ 020 7734 2721 35-36 Greek St W1D 5DL
Plan 3-C2
e-mail: cyming2000@blueyonder.co.uk
web: www.yming.co.uk

Situated in the heart of Soho, this stylish Chinese is less frenetic than its Chinatown neighbours. Duck-egg blue walls with jade carvings surround well-spaced and crisply-clothed tables in the intimate setting of a series of small rooms. Helpful, polite, friendly and polished service makes a good impression, while the uninitiated are guided through the extensive carte and fixed-price menus of Cantonese and regional dishes. Think sizzling lamb with ginger and spring onion, or Gansu duck (a Northwest dish cooked with garlic and a subtle, distinctive flavour of anise), or perhaps salmon steamed with black bean sauce.

Chef: Aaron Wong **Owners:** Christine Yau **Times:** Noon-11.45, Closed 25-26 Dec, 1 Jan, Sun (ex Chinese New Year) **Prices:** Fixed L £10-£20, Fixed D £10-£20, Starter £3.50-£8, Main £5-£26, Dessert £2.50-£5, Service added 10% **Wine:** 15 bottles over £20, 19 bottles under £20, 7 by the glass **Notes:** Vegetarian menu, Dress Restrictions Clean and presentable, Air con **Seats:** 60, Pr/dining room 25 **Parking:** Chinatown car park

⊚ *Yumi Restaurant*

Japanese

Authentic Japanese restaurant

☎ 020 7935 8320 110 George St W1H 5RL Plan 2-G3

Staff are friendly and helpful here and one of the menus is in picture form so guests have an idea of what to order. The rest of the menu is in Japanese and English. Service is formal Japanese with kimono-clothed staff keeping vigil over the predominantly Japanese customers. The main dining area is in the basement with a few private dining areas off the main room. With an array of sushi, sashimi, tempura and terriyaki dishes to choose from, typical main dishes include grilled king fish marinated in miso paste or chicken yakitori.

Times: 5.30-10.30 **Directions:** Telephone for further details

Carluccio's Caffè

☎ 020 7935 5927 St Christopher's Place W1U 1AY

Quality Italian chain.

Carluccio's Caffè

☎ 020 7636 2228 8 Market Place, Oxford Circus W1N 7AG

Quality Italian chain.

Carluccio's Caffè

☎ 020 7629 0699 Fenwick, New Bond St W1A 3BS

Quality Italian chain.

🖵 Chor Bizarre

☎ 020 7629 9802 & 7692 8542 16 Albermarle St, Mayfair W1S 4HW

web: www.theaa.com/travel/index.jsp

Regional Indian cuisine with emphasis on lighter Kashmiri dishes.

🖵 The Delhi Brasserie

☎ 020 7437 8261 44 Frith St W1D 4SB

web: www.theaa.com/travel/index.jsp

Handy location off Soho Square. Traditional, elegant décor, and lots of old favourites on the menu.

🖵 Eat & Two Veg

☎ 020 7258 8595 50 Marylebone High St W1U 5HN

web: www.theaa.com/travel/index.jsp

A super modern diner straight from a cosmopolitan vegetarian's dining dream. Open for breakfast, lunch and dinner seven days a week, serving delicious meat-free food in a lively, light-hearted atmosphere.

🖵 Elena's L'Etoile

☎ 020 7636 1496 30 Charlotte St W1T 2NG

web: www.theaa.com/travel/index.jsp

Immerse yourself in old-fashioned bistro style and bistro cooking. Elena herself makes the rounds to be sure you're being cared for. The menu includes the classics as well as more contemporary dishes.

🖵 The Gay Hussar

☎ 020 7437 0973 2 Greek St, Soho W1D 4NB

web: www.theaa.com/travel/index.jsp

A mainstay of Soho for decades, the menu is original, authentic and unlike any other you will find in the capital. Favourite dishes include chilled wild cherry soup and Kolozsvari Toltott Kaposzta, or Transylvanian stuffed cabbage with sauerkraut and smoked bacon and sausage.

ENGLAND

Marsala Zones
☎ 020 7287 9966 9 Marshall St W1F 7ER
Modern Indian with a balanced approach.

Michael Moore Restaurant
☎ 020 7224 1898 19 Blandford St, Marylebone W1U 3DH
web: www.theaa.com/travel/index.jsp
Fine global cuisine in a warm, intimate restaurant, filled with natural light.

New World Chinese Restaurant
☎ 020 7434 2508 1 Gerrard Place W1D 5PA
In the heart of London's Chinatown, dim sum is a favourite here.

Patara
☎ 020 7437 1071 15 Greek St W1D 4DP
web: www.theaa.com/travel/index.jsp
The fourth London branch of this popular modern Thai concept chain.

La Porte des Indes
☎ 020 7224 0055 32 Bryanston St W1H 7EG
web: www.theaa.com/travel/index.jsp
Indian eatery with eclectic menu in former Edwardian ballroom.

Sardo
☎ 020 7387 2521 45 Grafton Way W1P 5LA
Authentic and satisfying Sardinian specials in a relaxed setting.

Signor Zilli
☎ 020 7734 3924 40 & 41 Dean St W1D 4PR
Fashionable Italian at the heart of medialand. Specialising in good fish.

Strada
☎ 020 7287 5967 15-16 New Burlington St W1S 3BJ
web: www.theaa.com/travel/index.jsp
Superior pizza from quality ingredients cooked in wood-fired ovens.

Strada
☎ 020 7580 4644 9-10 Market Place W1W 8AQ
web: www.theaa.com/travel/index.jsp
Superior pizza from quality ingredients cooked in wood-fired ovens.

Wagamama
☎ 020 7292 0990 10a Lexington St W1R 3HS
Informal noodle bar with no booking required.

Wagamama
☎ 020 7409 0111 101a Wigmore St W1H 9AB
Informal noodle bar with no booking required.

Yo! Sushi
☎ 020 7287 0443 52 Poland St W1V 3DF
Sushi, sashimi, noodles and more.

Yo! Sushi
☎ 020 7318 3944 Selfridges Food Hall, 400 Oxford St W1A 1AB
Sushi, sashimi, noodles and more.

Zilli Fish
☎ 020 7734 8649 36-40 Brewer St W1F 9TA
Fish with an Italian accent from the ebullient Aldo Zilli.

LONDON W2

◎◎ Assaggi
Italian
Imaginative and authentic Italian

☎ 020 7792 5501 39 Chepstow Place W2 4TS
Plan 2-A2
e-mail: nipi@assaggi.demon.co.uk

You'll find this small, colourful restaurant above the fashionable Chepstow Pub in trendy Notting Hill. Large windows give the dining room a fresh, airy feel and its unpretentious décor makes diners feel right at home. Friendly staff offer a warm welcome and invaluable help with translating the menu. It's a great place for people-watching and the Italian food - leaning towards regional Sardinian cooking - is inventive, with the emphasis on flavour and the use of authentic ingredients. Try starters like caposante con salsa allo zafferano (scallops with capers served on a bed of mushroom, courgette and pepper couscous), followed by halibut on a bed of carrots, onion and courgettes, with white chocolate mousse, caramelised orange zest and orange caramel to finish. Simple classics, done extremely well.

Chef: Nino Sassu **Owners:** Nino Sassu, Pietro Fraccari **Times:** 12.30-2.30/7.30-11, Closed 2 wks Xmas, BHs, Sun **Prices:** Starter £9.95-£14.90, Main £18.50-£23.90, Dessert £7.50, Service optional **Wine:** All bottles over £20, 6 by the glass **Seats:** 35 **Children:** Portions **Directions:** Nearest station: Notting Hill Gate Telephone for directions

⊛ Island Restaurant & Bar
Modern British 💻
Designer hotel restaurant with seasonal fare

☎ 020 7551 6070 Royal Lancaster Hotel, Lancaster Ter W2 2TY Plan 2-D2
e-mail: eat@islandrestaurant.co.uk
web: www.islandrestaurant.co.uk

Enter this contemporary hotel restaurant via the salubrious reception area or directly from the street. Huge plate-glass windows overlook the park opposite and there is a sleek bar (with great cocktails) and open-plan kitchen in the split-level dining area. In the evening, crisp white tablecloths and dramatic lighting bring an extra touch of glamour. Quality ingredients are handled with skill to produce a daily-changing choice of dishes, presented in a pleasingly minimalist style. Sourcing from British suppliers, popular dishes sit alongside more sophisticated fare - potted crab and brown shrimps with shellfish mayonnaise, and roast rump of lamb with creamed garlic mash and rosemary jus.

Owners: Lancaster Hotel Co Ltd **Times:** 12/10.30, Closed Xmas, BHs, between Xmas and New Year **Prices:** Starter £4.95-£12.50, Main £9.95-£28, Dessert £4.50-£7.50, Service added but optional 12.5% **Wine:** 23 bottles over £20, 8 bottles under £20, 17 by the glass **Notes:** Vegetarian available, Dress Restrictions, Smart casual, Air con **Seats:** 90 **Children:** Menu, Portions **Parking:** 50

⊛⊛ Jamuna Restaurant
Indian NEW 💻
Quality Indian in quiet part of town

☎ 020 7723 5056 020 7723 5055 38A Southwick St W2 1JQ Plan 2-E3
e-mail: info@jamuna.co.uk
web: www.jamuna.co.uk

Set rather off the beaten track in a small leafy parade of shops, this neighbourhood Indian is located in what was once a private house. A stylish, minimalist affair, it comes with wooden floors, suede chairs and painted walls decorated with traditional and modern art (all for sale). The lengthy carte (with chilli symbols illustrating medium and hot dishes) shows off the kitchen's skilfully prepared and well-presented food, with its infusion of clean, subtle flavours and combination of traditional and less-common North Indian and regional dishes. Expect the likes of adraki chaampen (lamb cutlets from the tandoor, marinated in ginger, peppercorn, mint and yogurt), or more familiar lamb rogan josh (diced leg of lamb with spices, ginger, yogurt and Kashmiri chilli).

Chef: Suresh Manandhar **Times:** 12-2.30/6-11, Closed 25 Dec-1 Jan, 2 weeks in Aug, Sun, Closed L Sat **Prices:** Starter £5.50-£16, Main £12-£36, Dessert £5.50-£7.50, Service added 12.5% **Wine:** 58 bottles over £20, 2 bottles under £20, 6 by the glass **Notes:** Vegetarian available, Dress Restrictions, Smart dress, no jeans or T-shirts, Air con **Seats:** 60 **Children:** Min 12

⊛ Nipa Thai Restaurant
Thai 💻
Authentic Thai cuisine overlooking Hyde Park

☎ 020 7551 6039 The Royal Lancaster Hotel, Lancaster Ter W2 2TY Plan 2-D2
e-mail: nipa@royallancaster.com
web: www.niparestaurant.co.uk

This Thai restaurant on the first floor of the large Royal Lancaster Hotel is surprisingly intimate. Decorated in authentic style with teak panelling and original artefacts, its picture windows overlook Hyde Park. Quality dishes, including regional specialities, are offered from an extensive menu, where chilli symbols helpfully indicate spicing levels. Chef's recommendations include a mild Thai omelette with salty turnips, basil leaves and chilli, crispy soft-shelled crab served with spicy mango salad, or a more fiery steamed fish in a spicy lemon sauce. Desserts include a range of ice creams, and tab tim krob - water chestnuts coated with tapioca in coconut milk and syrup.

Chef: Nongyao Thoopchoi **Owners:** Lancaster Landmark Hotel Co Ltd **Times:** 12-2.30/6.30-10.30, Closed week between Xmas and New Year, BHs, Sun, Closed L Sat **Prices:** Fixed D £27-£32, Starter £6-£18, Main £8.50-£14.50, Dessert £6-£6.50, Service added but optional 12.5% **Wine:** 9 by the glass **Notes:** Fixed D 4 courses, Vegetarian available, Dress Restrictions, Smart casual, Air con **Seats:** 55 **Children:** Portions **Rooms:** 416 (416 en suite) ★★★★ HL **Directions:** Nearest station: Lancaster Gate Opposite Hyde Park on Bayswater Rd. On 1st floor of hotel **Parking:** 50

⊛ *Royal China*
Chinese
Ever-popular, traditional Bayswater Chinese

☎ 020 7221 2535 13 Queensway W2 4QJ Plan 2-B1
e-mail: royalchina@btconnect.com
web: www.royalchinagroup.co.uk

Don't be deceived by the smallish shop front, the spacious dining room extends way back, opulently decked out in black-and-gold lacquered walls, mirrors, and etched glass, or teak screens that create more intimate areas. The large number of Chinese diners is a testimony to its success. Classic Chinese food with quality ingredients (especially seafood) comes together to produce clean-cut dishes and flavours. The extensive menu is bolstered by several set options, with dim sum a favourite and available daily. Expect the likes of Szechuan prawns, crispy aromatic duck with chilli and black beans, or yeung chow rice with pork and shrimps.

Times: 12/11, Closed 25-26 Dec **Directions:** Nearest station: Bayswater, Queensway Stn Please telephone for directions

💻 Levantine
☎ 020 7262 1111 26 London St, Paddington W2 1HH
web: www.theaa.com/travel/index.jsp
Authentic Lebanese restaurant in the heart of Paddington.

Yo! Sushi
☎ 020 7727 9392 Unit 218, Whiteleys Shopping Centre W2 6LY
Sushi, sashimi, noodles and more.

Yo! Sushi
☎ 020 7706 9550 Unit R07, The Lawn, Paddington Station W2 1HB
Sushi, sashimi, noodles and more.

LONDON W4

⊛ High Road Brasserie

European NEW

Cool, bustling west London brasserie

☎ 020 8742 7474   162-164 Chiswick High Rd W4 1PR
Plan 1-D3
web: www.highroadbrasserie.co.uk

French windows and canopied pavement seats pick out this urban-chic High Road brasserie, the latest addition to Nick Jones's blossoming empire. Pillars and mirrors, pewter-topped tables, leather banquettes, patchwork-coloured floor tiles and a marble bar make this a light, modern, stylish venue with a very New York air. The food fits the surroundings - informal, modern European brasserie fare on an all-day menu. From breakfast or food to run through the day, to more substantial dishes - like halibut with clams, mussels and saffron, perhaps a seafood platter, or Pyrenean Black Pig chop. (There's also a private members' club and boutique hotel on site.)

Times: 7/12

⊛⊛ Sam's Brasserie & Bar

European

Modern, informal brasserie with friendly service and quality food

☎ 020 8987 0555   11 Barley Mow Passage W4 4PH
Plan 1-C3
e-mail: info@samsbrasserie.co.uk
web: www.samsbrasserie.co.uk

Secreted away down a narrow walkway just off the Chiswick High Road, this converted, one-time paper factory has a cosmopolitan, New York loft-style edge. Patron Sam (Harrison) previously worked as general manager to Rick Stein's Padstow empire, while chef Rufus Wickham has an impressive track record, too. High ceilings, girders, pillars, industrial piping and cream-painted or bare-brick walls lend that timeless, relaxed urban vibe, while giant oval lampshades, banquettes or black-lacquered chairs and small blond-wood tables fill the vibrant space. There's a smaller mezzanine dining level at the front and a semi-open kitchen to the back, while off to one side, the buzzy bar continues the theme. The cooking delivers simple, clean-cut dishes and flavours driven by top-quality ingredients; take crisp sea bass with sautéed potatoes and horseradish cream.

Times: 12-3/6.30-10.30 **Directions:** Nearest station: Chiswick Park/Turnham Green Behind Chiswick High Rd, next to the Green

⊛⊛⊛ La Trompette

see opposite

⊛ Le Vacherin

French 🖥

Smart Parisian-style bistro serving classic French cuisine

☎ 020 8742 2121 & 8742 0799   76-77 South Pde W4 5LF
Plan 1-C3
e-mail: malcolm.john4@btinternet.com
web: www.levacherin.co.uk

Green awnings and full-length windows pick out this slice of leafy Chiswick that's forever France. Blond-wood floors, a mirror-frieze above banquette-lined cream walls, foodie pictures and posters, attentive French staff clad in long white aprons and a backing track of Gallic music, evoke the atmosphere of a smart Parisian bistro. The cooking follows the script, with simple, classic French brasserie fare and an all-French wine list to match. The namesake soft mountain cow's milk cheese, Vacherin (in season November to February) makes a regular appearance on the menu, and organic produce is used wherever possible, with everything from bread to ice cream being made inhouse. Tuck into the likes of Chateaubriand with French beans and béarnaise sauce, or shallow-fried John Dory fillet with caper butter, finished off with a thin fig tart with Vacherin ice cream.

Chef: Malcolm John **Owners:** Malcolm & Donna John **Times:** 12-3/6-11, Closed 25 Dec, BHs, Closed L Mon **Prices:** Fixed L £12.50-£16, Starter £5.50-£10.50, Main £11.50-£18, Dessert £5.50-£6, Service added but optional 12.5% **Wine:** 20 bottles over £20, 17 bottles under £20, 8 by the glass **Notes:** Vegetarian available, Air con **Seats:** 72, Pr/dining room 30 **Children:** Portions **Directions:** Nearest station: Chiswick Park Turn left and restaurant, 400mtrs on left

🖥 Gravy

☎ 020 8998 6816   142 Chiswick High Rd W4 1PU
web: www.theaa.com/travel/index.jsp

Cosy family owned restaurant and bar where emphasis is on friendly atmosphere.

LONDON W5

⊛ Momo

Japanese

Popular restaurant serving traditional Japanese cuisine

☎ 020 8997 0206   14 Queens Pde, Ealing W5 3HU
Plan 1-C4

CONTINUED

La Trompette

LONDON W4

European

French-inspired cuisine at fashionable and chic restaurant

☎ 020 8747 1836 5-7 Devonshire Rd, Chiswick W4 2EU
Plan 1-C3
e-mail: reception@latrompette.co.uk
web: www.latrompette.co.uk

Set on a quiet side street in fashionable Chiswick, La Trompette sings its own praises, with a more flamboyant frontage than its neighbours that singles it out from the crowd. Potted box trees and an awning cordon off the small outside dining area with a certain style, replete with heaters and white cloths. The tinted-glass, sliding-door frontage adds a further classy, self-assured note, and, with Nigel Platts-Martin and Bruce Poole as its owners (of Chez Bruce fame, see entry), there's no doubting this brasserie-style outfit's pedigree. A muted colour scheme prevails over a sophisticated, relaxing interior, decked out in chocolate leather banquettes, smartly dressed tables and light-oak floors. Efficient, knowledgeable and friendly French service adds a reassuring note, while an award-winning wine list provides a star turn alongside a bustling but unpretentious atmosphere. The accomplished modern European cooking continues the evolved take on French cooking under the assured wing of James Bennington, delivered via appealing, daily-changing, fixed-price menus. Simple, brasserie-style dishes, with fresh, quality ingredients take centre stage, showcasing clean, clear flavours, balance, flair and flawless technique. Superb breads (in at least three flavours) accompany a class act. Expect the likes of an inspired dish of baked quail Pithiviers served with a shallot purée and port sauce to open, perhaps a fillet of red mullet with a shellfish and herb risotto, steamed samphire and grilled fennel to follow, and, to finish, blueberry and almond tart with whipped cream.

Chef: James Bennington **Owners:** Nigel Platts-Martin, Bruce Poole **Times:** 12-2.30/6.30-10.30, Closed 25-26 Dec, 1 Jan **Prices:** Fixed L £18.50-£23.50, Fixed D £35-£45, Starter £8-£13, Main £19-£24, Dessert £8, Service added but optional 12.5% **Wine:** 500 bottles over £20, 30 bottles under £20, 15 by the glass **Seats:** 72 **Children:** Portions **Directions:** Nearest station: Turnham Green From station follow Turnham Green Tce to junct with Chiswick High Rd. Cross road & bear right. Devonshire Rd 2nd left **Parking:** On street

---

This Japanese restaurant is worth seeking out - it enjoys an excellent reputation with locals for its traditional cooking. Hidden away in a quiet residential area of North Ealing, you'll find it in an urban precinct. The restaurant has exotic décor and you can have a traditional Japanese cooking pot (nabemono) at your table if you wish. The menu, in Japanese and English, is divided into sections covering set meals; sushi; sashimi; various appetisers; seafood including king prawns, squid and mackerel dishes; meat and poultry dishes featuring pork, chicken and beef; vegetable or soybean dishes; and an extensive choice of rice and noodle dishes, all at very reasonable prices.

Chef: Shigeru Kondo **Owners:** Mr Kondo **Times:** 12-3/6-11, Closed 2 wk Xmas, 1 wk Aug, BHs, Sun **Prices:** Fixed L £9-£13.50, Fixed D £19.50-£27, Starter £4.20-£6.50, Main £8.50-£25, Dessert £2.30-£4.50, Service added 12% **Wine:** 4 bottles over £20, 4 bottles under £20, 2 by the glass **Notes:** Vegetarian available, Air con **Seats:** 30 **Children:** Menu **Directions:** Nearest station: North Ealing 0.2m from North Ealing station **Parking:** On street

Carluccio's Caffè

☎ 020 8566 4458 5-6 The Green, Ealing W5 5DA
Quality Italian chain.

Charlotte's Place

☎ 020 8567 7541 16 St Matthews Rd, Ealing Common W5 3JT
web: www.theaa.com/travel/index.jsp

Minimalist interior, tempting menu of British and French classics. Extra buzzy at weekends with live jazz.

LONDON W6

Agni

Traditional Indian

Regional Indian cuisine in stylish surroundings

☎ 020 8846 9191 & 8748 6611 160 King St W6 0QU
Plan 1-D3
e-mail: info@agnirestaurant.com
web: www.agnirestaurant.com

Set over two floors, with a relaxed, unfussy bistro style, Agni comes decked out in yellow and gold with a clear Indian theme. This relatively new-kid-on-the-block has pedigree too, with Gowtham Karingi (ex head chef at Zaika and Veeraswamy) and Neeraj Mittra (ex manager at Chutney Mary) at the helm, and service is professional and very friendly. The traditional Indian cuisine is well presented, reflecting the progression of regional Indian food from its ancient roots, with emphasis on quality ingredients, clever spicing and clear flavours. Bags of choice, from a tiger prawn biryani to seafood moilee or chicken tikka tiranga, and to finish, try the beetroot halwa.

Chef: Gowtham Karingi **Owners:** Neeraj Mittra & Gowtham Karingi **Times:** 12-2.30/5.30-11, Closed 25 Dec to 1 Jan, Closed D Mon-Thu **Prices:** Fixed L £6.95-£14.95, Fixed D £12.95-£14.95, Starter £3.25-£6.95, Main £6.50-£12.95, Dessert £3-£4.50, Service added 10% **Wine:** 6 bottles over £20, 14 bottles under £20 **Notes:** Fixed D 2 courses, Tasting menu £40, Vegetarian available, Air con **Seats:** 50, Pr/dining room 45 **Children:** Portions **Directions:** Nearest station: Hammersmith Broadway, Ravenscourt Park Telephone for directions **Parking:** On street, car park

LONDON W6 *Continued*

◉ Anglesea Arms

British, French

Trendy gastro-pub offering simple, robust food

☎ 020 8749 1291 35 Wingate Rd W6 0UR Plan 1-D3

e-mail: anglesea.events@gmail.com

Plenty of hustle and bustle is always guaranteed at this shabby-chic Hammersmith gastro-pub, popular with trendy locals and students alike. A log fire, wooden floors, Victorian décor and an open-plan - sometimes boisterous - kitchen all add to its laid-back charm. Seasonal produce is evident on the daily-changing blackboard menu, which serves up good, hearty and robust food that hits the mark every time. Perhaps smoked eel and potato pancake, quail's egg and egg beignet or sautéed squid, butterbean purée chorizo and rocket.

Chef: Henrik Ritzen **Owners:** Michael Mann, Jill S Sullivan **Times:** 12.30-2.45/7-10.30, Closed 24-31 Dec **Prices:** Starter £4.50-£9.95, Main £9.50-£17.50, Dessert £4.50-£5.50, Service optional, Group min 8 service 12.5% **Wine:** 86 bottles over £20, 14 bottles under £20, 20 by the glass **Seats:** 70 **Children:** Portions **Directions:** Nearest station: Goldhawk Road, Ravenscourt Park. Off Goldhawk Road. **Parking:** On street, pay & display (free at wknds)

◉ The Brackenbury

Modern European

Accomplished cooking in a friendly neighbourhood environment

☎ 020 8748 0107 129-131 Brackenbury Rd W6 0BQ Plan 1-D3

e-mail: lisa@thebrackenbury.fsnet.co.uk

Tucked away on a quiet residential street, The Brackenbury is the epitome of the neighbourhood restaurant genre, with its relaxed, friendly approach. A front terrace proves a fair-weather bonus, while inside this pair of one-time shops, it's a split-level affair decked-out with olive green walls, varnished wooden tables and modern chairs or banquette seating. The kitchen's modern European cooking is delivered with a nod to the Mediterranean on regularly-changing menus driven by quality ingredients, colourful presentation and clear flavours. Think roast lamb rump with fondant potato, slow-roast tomato, baby artichoke and an olive jus.

Chef: Matt Cranston **Owners:** Lisa Inglis **Times:** 12.30-2.45/7-10.45, Closed 24-26 Dec, 1 Jan, Easter Mon, Aug BH Mon, Closed L Sat, D Sun **Prices:** Food prices not confirmed for 2008. Please telephone for details **Seats:** 60 **Children:** Portions **Directions:** Nearest station: Goldhawk Road, Hammersmith Telephone for directions **Parking:** On street

◉ Chez Kristof

French 🖥

Rustic French cooking in neighbourhood bistro

☎ 020 8741 1177 111 Hammersmith Grove W6 0NQ Plan 1-D4

e-mail: info@chezkristof.co.uk

web: www.chezkristof.co.uk

This popular neighbourhood restaurant occupies a corner site in a quiet part of Shepherd's Bush. Squeeze on to one of the closely

packed tables and tuck into some well executed rustic French dishes. Gallic classics include snails with garlic butter, spatchcock coquelet with olives and lemon, and pot au chocolat. A good choice of crustacea also features, including duchess rock oysters, razor clams, and ragout of cockles and mussels. If you want to eat great French food at home, a visit to the restaurant's delicatessen next door is a must.

Chef: Richard McLellan **Owners:** Jan Woroniecki **Times:** 12-3/6-11.15, Closed 24-26 Dec, 1 Jan **Prices:** Starter £6-£9, Main £12.50-£17.50, Dessert £5, Service added 12.5% **Wine:** 9 by the glass, Pr/dining room 45 **Children:** Menu, Portions **Directions:** Nearest station: Hammersmith. Please telephone for directions **Parking:** On street

◉ The Gate

Modern Vegetarian V

Vegetarian restaurant offering inventive cuisine

☎ 020 8748 6932 51 Queen Caroline St W6 9QL Plan 1-D3

e-mail: hammersmith@gateveg.co.uk

web: www.thegate.tv

This is a vegetarian restaurant in an unusual listed building, approached via a church entrance hall. Once inside the room - formerly an artist's studio - it is bright and airy with high ceilings, large windows and dramatic art. The cooking is an inspired alternative to the usual vegetarian choices. It seeks out bold flavours, inventive combinations and fresh ingredients to produce simple but ingenious dishes, with wild mushrooms a speciality. Worldwide influences and modern techniques make this a great choice for vegetarians, vegans and those in search of new tastes. Typical is a root vegetable and chickpea tagine, or wild mushroom fricassee or butternut squash risotto.

Chef: Adrian Daniel, Mariusz Wegrodski **Owners:** Adrian Daniel, Michael Daniel **Times:** 12-3/6-11, Closed 23 Dec-3 Jan, Easter Mon, Sun, Closed L Sat **Prices:** Starter £5.50-£6, Main £8.50-£13.50, Dessert £5.50-£6, Service added but optional 12.5% **Wine:** 2 bottles over £20, 8 bottles under £20, 10 by the glass **Notes:** Vegetarian menu, Air con **Seats:** 60 **Children:** Portions **Directions:** Nearest station: Hammersmith Hammersmith Apollo Theatre, continue down right side for approx 40 yds **Parking:** On street

◉◉◉ The River Café

see opposite

◉◉ Sagar

Vegetarian, Indian V

Authentic south Indian vegetarian cooking in the heart of Hammersmith

☎ 020 8741 8563 157 King St, Hammersmith W6 9JT Plan 1-D3

This unpretentious restaurant with a modern glass frontage is set among shops on a busy Hammersmith street. It's a popular place with a lively atmosphere, close-set tables, blood-wood floorboards and walls dotted with Indian artefacts. The kitchen's lengthy vegetarian repertoire offers a good range majoring on dishes from the Udipi region, including starters such as idli (steamed rice cakes) with sambar and coconut chutney, samosas, vegetable kebabs, and main meals

⊚⊚⊚

The River Café

LONDON W6

Italian

Famous Italian Thames-side trendsetter

☎ 020 7386 4200 Thames Wharf, Rainville Rd W6 9HA
Plan 1-D3
e-mail: info@rivercafe.co.uk
web: www.rivercafe.co.uk

Though celebrating its twenty-first year, people still flock to Rose Gray and Ruth Rogers' famous Hammersmith Italian at the edge of the Thames. The place almost needs no description; a spacious, modern, minimalist white room (converted from an 18th-century warehouse) comes with plenty of steel and glass and an urban vibe that successfully mixes a bustling, informal atmosphere with a fine-dining experience. Light floods in through floor-to-ceiling windows (opening up to the terrace in summer), and there's a long stainless-steel open kitchen with wood-burning oven, lively cocktail bar and close-set tables to add to the buzz.

Menus change twice daily, so there's a sense of spontaneity to the flavour-driven cooking. The authentic, unfussy Italian cuisine - mainly Tuscan and Lombardian influenced - doesn't come cheap, but uses only the very best, freshest produce (with many ingredients specifically sourced for their rarity, locality and seasonality) simply treated with

skill and panache. Take seared calves' liver served with Swiss chard and their stalks, castelluccio lentils with spring herbs and crème fraîche, and perhaps an almond and nespoli tart to finish.

Chef: R Gray, R Rogers, Sian Owen **Owners:** Rose Gray, Ruth Rogers **Times:** 12.30-3/7-11, Closed 24 Dec-1 Jan, Easter, BHs, Closed D Sun **Prices:** Starter £11-£18, Main £25-£32, Dessert £7-£8.50, Service added but optional 12.5% **Wine:** 123 bottles over £20, 12 bottles under £20, 17 by the glass **Seats:** 108 **Children:** Portions **Directions:** Nearest station: Hammersmith Restaurant in converted warehouse. Entrance on S side of Rainville Rd at junct with Bowfell Rd **Parking:** 29

---

incorporating dosas (a must try), uthappams (lentil pizzas), and thalis (a selection of different dishes), plus fresh home-made breads. For dessert, why not try payasam - a hot pudding made with fine vermicelli in milk, cashew nuts and raisins. Dishes are skilfully crafted with clean-cut presentation and distinct flavours and prices are incredibly low for the quality delivered.

Chef: Ramadas **Owners:** S. Shurmielan **Times:** 12-2.45/5.30-10.45, Closed 25-26 Dec **Prices:** Fixed L £5-£8, Fixed D £8.50-£11.50, Starter £2.50-£4, Main £3.50-£5.75, Dessert £5, Service optional **Wine:** 8 by the glass **Notes:** Vegetarian menu, Air con **Seats:** 60 **Directions:** Nearest station: Hammersmith 10min from Hammersmith Tube **Parking:** On street

⊚ **Snows-on-the-Green Restaurant**

Modern 🖥

Friendly, vibrant local restaurant with accomplished Mediterranean cuisine

☎ 020 7603 2142 166 Shepherd's Bush Rd, Brook Green, Hammersmith W6 7PB Plan 1-D3
e-mail: sebastian@snowsonthegreenfreeserve.co.uk
web: www.snowsonthegreen.co.uk

A green awning and glass frontage picks out this popular, long-established neighbourhood restaurant, set in an arcade of shops opposite Brook Green on the busy road between Hammersmith and Shepherd's Bush. Dark-stained floorboards and sage green paintwork sit comfortably alongside white-clothed tables, while black and white photographs, candles, and friendly and attentive service crank up the atmosphere. The kitchen's modern approach takes on a sunny

Mediterranean slant too, cooking with passion, the style robust rather than refined with colourful, clear-flavoured dishes. Think celeriac soup with wild mushrooms to start, followed by pan-fried wild sea trout in a horseradish crust with golden beetroot and pancetta, and espresso crème caramel to finish.

Chef: Sebastian Snow **Owners:** Sebastian Snow **Times:** 12-3/6-11, Closed BH Mon only, Sun, Closed L Sat **Prices:** Fixed L £12-£13, Fixed D £16-£17, Starter £6-£9, Main £13-£17, Dessert £5-£7, Service added but optional 12.5%, Group min 6 service 12.5% **Wine:** 20 bottles over £20, 17 bottles under £20, 12 by the glass **Notes:** Vegetarian available, Air con **Seats:** 80, Pr/dining room 30 **Children:** Menu, Portions **Directions:** Nearest station: Hammersmith Broadway 300yds from station **Parking:** On street

🖥 **Azou**

☎ 020 8563 7266 375 King St, Hammersmith W6 9NJ
web: www.theaa.com/travel/index.jsp

Small, family-run restaurant serving Moroccan, Tunisian and Algerian dishes.

Los Molinos

☎ 020 7603 2229 127 Shepherd's Bush Rd W6 7LP

Tapas and raciones in authentic, bustling surroundings.

LONDON W8

◉ Babylon

Modern International 💻

Minimalist chic, rooftop gardens and extraordinary views

☎ 020 7368 3993 The Roof Gardens, 99 Kensington High St W8 5SA Plan 4-B4
e-mail: babylon@roofgardens.virgin.co.uk
web: www.virgin.com/limitededition

Cracking views over the London skyline from the seventh-floor decked terrace and sleek, glass-sided dining room - framed by the lush greenery from the Roof Gardens below - prove a winning Kensington formula at Richard Branson's Babylon. Contemporary styling, booths, white linen and a small bar with fish-tank walls, provides the stylish backcloth for slick, friendly service and those capital views. The menu's modern approach suits the surroundings and deals in quality produce; think red wine-braised halibut served with parsnip mash, baby onions and red wine jus, and to finish, perhaps organic lemon tart with raspberry crackle sorbet.

Times: 12-3/7-11, Closed 25 Dec & selected dates in Dec-Jan, Closed D Sun
Directions: Nearest station: High Street Kensington From High St Kensington tube station, turn right, then right into Derby St

◉◉ Belvedere

French, European 💻

Jewel in Holland Park, with stunning interior and garden views

☎ 020 7602 1238 Abbotsbury Rd, Holland House, Holland Park W8 6LU Plan 1-D3
e-mail: sales@whitestarline.org.uk
web: www.belvedererestaurant.co.uk

Belvedere

The orangery in pretty Holland Park is the setting for this achingly elegant restaurant, a destination in its own right even without the added attraction of top-notch cuisine. Inspired interior design evokes a 1920s feel; think sparkling mirrors, ornate wallpaper and huge oyster-shell lights. Leafy green plants, brown leather seating, and parquet flooring complete the picture and serve as the perfect backdrop to the kitchen's understated brasserie cooking. You'll find something to suit most tastes, from old favourites such as eggs Benedict, sausage and mash, and rice pudding, to more sophisticated fare - pheasant with chestnuts, bacon lardons and morel jus for example, or pork belly with Puy lentils and potato purée, with pear Tatin and cinnamon ice cream to finish.

Chef: Billy Reid **Owners:** Jimmy Lahoud **Times:** 12-2.30/6-10.30, Closed 26 Dec, 1 Jan, Closed D Sun **Prices:** Fixed L £15, Fixed D £18, Starter £6.50-£12.50, Main £11.50-£22, Dessert £6.50, Service added but optional 12.5%, Group min 13 service 15% **Wine:** 90 bottles over £20, 10 by the glass **Notes:** Wknd L 3 courses £24.95, Vegetarian available, Air con **Seats:** 90 **Directions:** Nearest station: Holland Park On the Kensington High St side of Holland Park **Parking:** 50

◉◉ Cheneston's Restaurant

Modern British 🍴NOTABLE WINE LIST 💻

Intimate restaurant in elegant townhouse hotel

☎ 020 7917 1000 Milestone Hotel, 1 Kensington Court W8 5DL Plan 4-B4
e-mail: bookms@rchmail.com
web: www.milestonehotel.com

Located opposite Kensington Palace and Gardens, this Victorian mansion has been transformed into a hotel of style and class, with many restored original features. Expect stunning bedrooms, luxurious lounges and a sumptuous dining room with leaded Victorian windows and shining crystal and silverware. As befits the surroundings and the clientele, food is classically based and both cooking style and presentation are simple and unfussy. Typical dishes include an open ravioli of Cornish crab and lobster with lobster ginger broth, pot-roast suprême of guinea fowl with celeriac and parsley mash and morel mushroom sauce, and to finish a warm chocolate tart with white chocolate ice cream. Service is formal and professional from an international team.

Times: 12-3/5.30-11 **Rooms:** 57 (57 en suite)★★★★★ HL
Directions: Nearest station: High St Kensington M4/Hammersmith flyover, take 2nd left into Gloucester Rd, left into High St Kensington, 500mtrs on left

⊛⊛ *Clarke's*

Modern Mediterranean

The freshest food simply treated with reverence

☎ 020 7221 9225 124 Kensington Church St W8 4BH
Plan 4-A5
e-mail: restaurant@sallyclarke.com
web: www.sallyclarke.com

Set amongst the well-known antique shops of Kensington Church Street and Notting Hill, you'll find the neat shop front for the restaurant, adjacent to Sally Clarke's famous bread shop. Minimalist décor is chic and modern with crisply starched table linen, and staff are professional and diligent. The restaurant now offers a choice at dinner (three at each turn) and it's no longer necessary to have all four courses (once a set four-course affair), plus there's also a brunch offering on Saturdays from 11am until 2pm. Menus change weekly and are posted on their website each Monday. Ingredients, skill and artistry take priority here, and it is this that makes the cooking so successful and enduring. Modern European-style dishes might include Cornish day-boat monkfish roasted on the bone and served with a relish of Niçoise olives, lovage and young leeks.

Times: 12.30-2/7-10, Closed 8 days Xmas & New Year, Sun, Closed D Mon
Directions: Nearest station: Notting Hill Gate Telephone for directions

⊛⊛ **Eleven Abingdon Road**

European

Cool neighbourhood venue off High Street Kensington

☎ 020 7937 0120 11 Abingdon Rd, Kensington W8 6AH
Plan 4-A4
e-mail: eleven@abingdonroad.co.uk

This light, modern, glass-fronted restaurant is tucked away in a little road just off High Street Ken and proves quite a find; it shares ownership with Sonny's in Barnes. The stylish, restrained, clean-cut interior - with a small chic bar area up front decked out with leopard- and tiger-skin chairs - comes dominated by an eye-catching art collection set to a backdrop of sage-green walls, contemporary lighting, modern darkwood chairs and a friendly, upbeat vibe. Staff dressed in jeans and long black aprons deliver modern, Mediterranean-slant dishes using quality seasonal ingredients; think chargrilled halibut served with slow-cooked fennel, Swiss chard and salsa verde, or perhaps slow-cooked veal shin with risotto Milanese and gremolata.

Chef: David Stafford **Owners:** Rebecca Mascarenhas **Times:** 12.30-2.30/6.30-11, Closed 25 Dec, BHs **Prices:** Fixed L £13.50, Fixed D £19.50, Starter £5.95-£8, Main £10-£17.50, Dessert £4.95-£5.95, Service added but optional 12.5% **Wine:** 35 bottles over £20, 18 bottles under £20, 20 by the glass **Notes:** Fixed D 2 courses, Air con **Seats:** 80 **Children:** Menu, Portions **Directions:** Nearest station: Kensington High St Telephone for directions

⊛⊛ **Kensington Place**

Modern British 🖥

Busy brasserie-style restaurant with vibrant colour and atmosphere

☎ 020 7727 3184 201-9 Kensington Church St W8 7LX
Plan 4-A6
e-mail: kpparty@egami.co.uk
web: www.egami.co.uk

Watch the world go by at this prominently located and ever-popular Notting Hill haunt. Passers-by also get a good look in through the long plate-glass fascia, while a revolving door leads into a bustling, energetic bar, and the main restaurant decorated with a striking mural depicting nearby Kensington Gardens. Closely-set tables and colourful wooden chairs are reminiscent of the schoolroom. Well-executed brasserie food, simple and precise, uses top-quality seasonal produce, with old favourites offered alongside more imaginative creations. Fish is a speciality, with dishes like red mullet, potato and olive pancake, followed by steamed sea bass with cauliflower and skate tempura, and chocolate and mascarpone torte served with coffee sauce to finish. The restaurant has its own uniquely elegant fish shop next door to cater for your every need, and includes goodies from the restaurant.

Chef: Sam Mahoney **Owners:** Place Restaurants Ltd **Times:** 12-3.30/6.30-11.15, Closed 24-26 Dec, 1 Jan **Prices:** Fixed L £19.50-£24.50, Fixed D £24.50, Starter £6.50-£14.50, Main £17-£30, Dessert £6.50-£12.50, Service added but optional 12.5% **Wine:** 168 bottles over £20, 12 bottles under £20, 15 by the glass **Notes:** Fixed L 3 courses, Fixed D Mon-Fri 3 courses £24.50, Air con **Seats:** 140, Pr/dining room 45 **Children:** Menu, Portions **Directions:** Nearest station: Notting Hill Gate Telephone for directions **Parking:** On street

⊛⊛ **Launceston Place Restaurant**

Modern European 🖥

Uncomplicated cuisine in a genteel setting

☎ 020 7937 6912 1a Launceston Place W8 5RL
Plan 4-C4
e-mail: lpr@egami.co.uk
web: www.egami.co.uk

An upmarket eatery in a leafy part of Kensington, the restaurant is 21 years old and still going strong. It occupies a series of small townhouse rooms, quintessentially English in presentation but with a modern twist. It caters to well-heeled locals, suits and lunching ladies. An accomplished kitchen adopts a modern line - with a nod to the Mediterranean - and delivers a menu of straightforward contemporary dishes. Kick off with sweetcorn and tarragon risotto with excellent bite and consistency, and follow with chicken ravioli, full of flavour, served with wild mushroom cream, with a subtly-flavoured pannacotta given a great kick by red berry compôte for dessert. Book early for lunch, it really buzzes around 1-1.30pm.

Chef: Iain Inman **Owners:** Christopher Bodker **Times:** 12.30-2.30/6-11, Closed Xmas, New Year, Etr, Closed L Sat **Prices:** Fixed L £16.50, Fixed D £18.50, Starter £6.50-£13.50, Main £16.50-£24.50, Dessert £6.50-£7.50, Service added but optional 12.5% **Wine:** 87 bottles over £20, 5 bottles under £20, 13 by the glass **Notes:** Sun L 3 courses £24.50, Air con **Seats:** 85, Pr/dining room 14 **Children:** Portions **Directions:** Nearest station: Gloucester Road Just south of Kensington Palace

Royal Garden Hotel

LONDON W8

Modern European V 🖥

Fantastic views and imaginative cuisine

☎ 020 7361 1910 2-24 Kensington High St W8 4PT Plan 4-B5
e-mail: tenthrestaurant@royalgardenhotel.co.uk
web: www.royalgardenhotel.co.uk

Situated in fashionable Kensington just a short walk from the Albert Hall, the hotel is built on the site of the former Kensington Palace vegetable plot, hence its name. Norman Farquharson's gastronomic cooking at The Tenth Floor restaurant is matched only by the stunning views across Kensington Gardens and Hyde Park towards the capital's tallest landmarks. Its huge windows exploit those views, allowing light to flood in. The elegant dining room is a fresh, contemporary space with its own bar and cabaret area; tables are well spaced, and the atmosphere intimate. By day, it feels like a chic insider's haunt; by night it's one of London's most romantic destination restaurants. Modern European cuisine brings together a fusion of traditional cooking techniques and modern twists, with a generous sprinkling of quality ingredients and Asian imports, including lobster, truffles, saffron and oysters, cast across an interesting menu. A separate vegetarian and six-course tasting menu is available. Baked roquefort and leek soufflé with a ruby port reduction might be followed by a main course of pan-fried fillet of John Dory with langoustine and orange sauce, or perhaps saltimbocca of monkfish with Puy lentils, roasted baby onions and red wine jus. Tempting desserts take in the likes of caramel brûlée with pear foam and cranberry muesli cookies. There are gastronomic events with guest chefs throughout the year.

Chef: Norman Farquharson
Owners: Goodwood Group
Times: 12-2.30/5.30-11, Closed Etr wknd, 2 wks Aug, 2 wks Jan, BHs, Sun, Closed L Sat
Prices: Fixed L £17.25, Starter £7.50-£13.50, Main £18.50-£28, Dessert £7, Service optional, Group min 8 service 10%
Wine: 110 bottles over £20, 7 bottles under £20, 9 by the glass
Notes: Tasting menu £65 (£85 inc wine), Vegetarian menu, Dress Restrictions, Smart casual, Civ Wed 100, Air con
Seats: 110
Children: Portions
Rooms: 396 (396 en suite)★★★★★ HL
Directions: Nearest station: Kensington High Street Next to Kensington Palace, Royal Albert Hall
Parking: 200

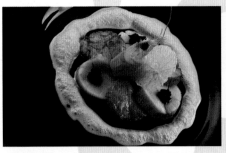

LONDON W8 CONTINUED

◉ Timo

Italian V

Chic, authentic Italian dining

☎ 020 7603 3888 343 Kensington High St W8 6NW
Plan 1-D3

e-mail: timorestaurant@tiscali.co.uk

Located in a quiet stretch of fashionable Kensington High Street, this friendly Italian restaurant is worth seeking out for its authentic regional cuisine at reasonable prices. The neutral décor is modern but relaxed, with tan suede chairs and crisply dressed tables, while huge prints add a splash of colour. The traditional Italian menu aims for flexibility, with side orders to supplement the dishes if you've got a big appetite. Go for a starter of buffalo mozzarella with slow-baked tomato and rocket, followed by tagliatelle with prawns, asparagus and cherry tomatoes and, if you have room, a delicious chocolate and hazelnut fondant.

Chef: Franco Gatto **Owners:** Piero Amodio **Times:** 12-2.30/7-11, Closed Xmas, New Year, BHs, Closed L Sat, D Sun **Prices:** Fixed L £12.50, Fixed D £27-£35, Starter £6.50-£12.50, Main £8.50-£21.50, Dessert £5.50-£7.25, Service optional, Group min 10 service 15% **Wine:** 3 bottles over £20, 3 bottles under £20, 8 by the glass **Notes:** Vegetarian menu, Air con **Seats:** 55, Pr/dining room 18 **Children:** Portions **Directions:** Nearest station: Kensington High St 5 mins walk towards Hammersmith, after Odeon Cinema, on left of street **Parking:** 3

◉◉ Zaika

Modern Indian V 🖳

Lively restaurant serving carefully prepared modern Indian cuisine

☎ 020 7795 6533 1 Kensington High St W8 5NP
Plan 4-B4

e-mail: info@zaika-restaurant.co.uk
web: www.zaika-restaurant.co.uk

High ceilings, double-height stone windows and carved arches grace the panelled interior of this former bank, located opposite Kensington Palace. The restaurant is decorated in a rich palette of colours, including the contemporary chairs and banquettes. Blonde-wood floorboards, Indian artefacts, modern lighting and a bar at the front add to the sophisticated styling, while professional, informed service and an impressive wine list complete the upbeat vibe. The kitchen's innovative menu of modern Indian cuisine delivers well-executed, vibrantly-flavoured and creatively presented dishes from quality ingredients, as in tandoori chicken tikki, tandoori monkfish with curry leaf risotto, and chocolate samosas for dessert. The emphasis is on a lighter approach without the use of clarified butter.

Chef: Sandjay Dwivedi **Owners:** Claudio Pulze, Sandjay Dwivedi **Times:** 12-2.45/6-10.45, Closed BHs, Xmas, New Year, Closed L Sat **Prices:** Fixed L £19.50, Fixed D £40, Starter £7-£12.50, Main £13.50-£19, Dessert £6-£6.50, Service added but optional 12.5% **Wine:** 100+ bottles over £20, 8 bottles under £20, 17 by the glass **Notes:** Fixed L 4 courses, Fixed D 4 courses, Menu gourmand £58, Vegetarian menu, Dress Restrictions, Smart casual preferred, Air con **Seats:** 84 **Children:** Portions **Directions:** Nearest station: Kensington High Street Opposite Kensington Palace

🖳 The Ark

☎ 020 7229 4024 122 Palace Gardens Ter W8 4RT

web: www.theaa.com/travel/index.jsp

Small Italian restaurant where clever design has made the dining area seem a lot bigger - there's also a decked area for alfresco eating.

Wagamama

☎ 020 7376 1717 26a High St Kensington W8 4PW

Informal noodle bars with no booking required.

LONDON W9

🖳 The Waterway

☎ 020 7266 3557 54-56 Formosa St, Little Venice W9 2JU

web: www.theaa.com/travel/index.jsp

Great views with waterfront terrace. Relaxed atmosphere and British-French menu.

LONDON W11

◉ E&O

Pan Asian

Buzzy, fashionable oriental-style eatery and bar

☎ 020 7229 5454 14 Blenheim Crescent W11 1NN
Plan 1-D4

e-mail: eando@rickerrestaurants.com
web: www.rickerrestaurants.com

A red neon sign and dark exterior picks out this corner-set, trendy bar-restaurant (part of the Will Ricker group - see also Eight Over Eight and Great Eastern Dining Room) close to Notting Hill and Portobello Road, which blends oriental style with modern minimalist décor. Think slatted darkwood, plain white walls, giant oval lampshades, brown-leather banquettes or black-lacquer chairs and polished floorboards. Upfront there's a bustling red-walled bar and, to the side, a few alfresco pavement tables, while everywhere the atmosphere's vibrant and upbeat. The modern pan-Asian fusion menu is divided into sections for grazing and sharing from dim sum to tempura, curries or sashimi, and specials like beef yaki-niku.

Chef: Simon Treadway **Owners:** Will Ricker **Times:** 12-3/6-11, Closed Xmas, New Year, Aug BH **Prices:** Food prices not confirmed for 2008. Please telephone for details **Wine:** 80 bottles over £20, 8 bottles under £20, 12 by the glass **Notes:** Vegetarian available, Air con **Seats:** 84, Pr/dining room 18 **Children:** Menu, Portions **Directions:** Nearest station: Notting Hill Gate, Ladbrook Grove At Notting Hill Gate tube station turn right, at mini rdbt turn into Kensington Park Rd, restaurant 10min down hill **Parking:** On street

LONDON W11 *Continued*

⊛⊛ Edera

Modern Italian

Good-value, modern and stylish neighbourhood Italian

☎ 020 7221 6090 148 Holland Park Av W11 4UE
Plan 1-D4
e-mail: edera@btconnect.com

This clean-lined, minimally styled Holland Park Italian - with glass frontage, awning and a few pavement tables to catch the eye - proves a stylish yet friendly venue. Decked out on tiered levels, it comes with blond-wood floors, light walls and terracotta pillars, while banquette seating, coordinated upholstered chairs and white linen provide the upmarket comforts, backed by attentive Latin staff clad in long black aprons. The kitchen, like the patriotic wine list, draws inspiration from the Italian regions, with the occasional nod to Sardinia. Take home-made veal ravioli with a cherry tomato sauce, or perhaps pan-fried monkfish accompanied by an olive mash and mullet roe. The style is straightforward, clean cut and creatively accomplished, driven by high-quality seasonal ingredients.

Chef: Carlo Usai **Owners:** A-Z Ltd/Mr Pisano **Times:** 12-2.30/6.30-11, Closed 25-26 & 31 Dec **Prices:** Starter £8-£12, Main £7-£20, Dessert £6-£8, Service added but optional 12.5% **Wine:** 140 bottles over £20, 3 bottles under £20, 11 by the glass **Notes:** Vegetarian available, Smart casual appreciated, Air con **Seats:** 70, Pr/dining room 20 **Children:** Portions **Directions:** Nearest station: Holland Park Please telephone for directions **Parking:** On street

⊛⊛⊛ The Ledbury

see below

⊛ Lonsdale

Fusion, Modern Asian 🖥

Trendy lounge-style eatery with a cool, youthful clientele

☎ 020 7727 4080 48 Lonsdale Rd W11 2DE Plan 1-D4
e-mail: reception@thelonsdale.co.uk
web: www.thelonsdale.co.uk

A white frontage and doorman make this evening-only, clubby bar-restaurant stand out from the crowd in residential Notting Hill. There's something of a basement vibe, with bold retro styling, a buzzy, trendy atmosphere and black-clad, youthful service. From its brightly lit cocktail bar to the restaurant area at the back, the Lonsdale strips away conventional fine-dining formalities, its close-set, darkwood tables teamed with burgundy leather banquettes or large stools, while mirror-lined lilac walls, matching low-level lights above table and contemporary music hit all the right notes. In tune with the contemporary surroundings, the kitchen takes an equally fashionable approach, its menu laced with Asian influence; think steamed sea bass served with ginger, spring onions and pak choi.

Times: 6-12, Closed 25-26 Dec, 1 Jan, Closed L all week
Directions: Nearest station: Notting Hill/Ladbroke Grove One street parallel N Westbourne Grove between Portobello Rd and Ledbury Rd

⊛⊛⊛ Notting Hill Brasserie

see opposite

⊛⊛⊛

The Ledbury

LONDON W11

Modern French 🍶 NOTABLE WINE LIST

Highly accomplished French cooking in fashionable, residential Notting Hill

☎ 020 7792 9090 127 Ledbury Rd W11 2AQ Plan 1-D4
e-mail: info@theledbury.com
web: www.theledbury.com

This latest offering from Nigel Platts-Martin and Philip Howard (who together also own The Square in Mayfair, see entry) has a smart, refined vibe, and is set in the heart of residential Notting Hill. The interior is contemporary, sophisticated and luxurious, with cream leather chairs alongside long dark curtains and polished parquet floors. Tables are relatively closely set, but the room doesn't feel cramped, helped by a clever use of mirrors, floor-to-ceiling windows and a terrace with additional tables covered by parasols and a canopy. Service is professional and attentive without being stuffy or overbearing.

The accomplished, sophisticated cooking from Philip Howard's protégé, Oz-born Brett Graham, delivers high technical skill through modern dishes underpinned by a classical French theme, with fine visual presentation, interesting combinations and textures. Peripherals like breads, amuse-bouche, pre-desserts and petits fours all hold form, while the fixed-price repertoire of lunch (great value), carte and eight-course tasting option are partnered by a high-class wine list. Expect a loin of cod poached in liquorice and served with creamed potato, razor clams and fennel, or perhaps braised veal cheeks zingara with a gratin of macaroni and black truffle, while a pineapple tart Tatin with fromage blanc and a black pepper and lime sorbet might head-up desserts.

Chef: Brett Graham **Owners:** Nigel Platts-Martin & Philip Howard **Times:** 12-2/6.30-11, Closed 24-26 Dec, 1 Jan, Aug BH wk end **Prices:** Food prices not confirmed for 2008. Please telephone for details **Wine:** 14 by the glass **Seats:** 95 **Directions:** Nearest station: Westbourne Park & Notting Hill Gate 5 min walk along Talbot Rd from Portobello Rd, on corner of Talbot Rd and Ledbury Rd **Parking:** Talbot Rd, metered

Notting Hill Brasserie

LONDON W11

Modern European 🖥

Chic food, chic décor, chic location

☎ 020 7229 4481 92 Kensington Park Rd W11 2PN Plan 4-D4
e-mail: enquiries@nottinghillbrasserie.com

Converted from three Edwardian townhouses, this brasserie oozes quality with its mix of stylish good looks and period features. The swish minimalist, beige-themed décor, modern African art, stunning flower arrangements and confident, friendly service are further enhanced by a separate cocktail bar with lashings of live jazz.

The accomplished kitchen impresses with execution and professionalism with both classic and original twists, while keeping things deceptively simple on crisply-scripted menus driven by quality seasonal ingredients. Expect roasted fillet of cod served with parsnip purée and a lightly curried ragout of mussels, or maybe roast loin of venison with sweet potato purée and braised red cabbage, and perhaps a cinnamon crème brûlée with molasses ice cream, or hot chocolate fondant accompanied by hazelnut ice cream to round things off in style. Excellent breads and the likes of amuse-bouche match the upbeat performance, while Sunday lunch is served up with live jazz.

Chef: Mark Jankel
Owners: Carlo Spetale
Times: 12-4/7-1, Closed D Sun
Prices: Fixed L £17.50, Starter £7-£14.50, Main £19-£25, Dessert £6.50, Service added but optional 12.5%
Seats: 110, Pr/dining room 44
Children: Portions
Directions: Nearest station: Notting Hill Gate 3 mins walk from Notting Hill station
Parking: On street

ENGLAND

LONDON W11 CONTINUED

⊛ Ribbands Restaurant

Modern British, French NEW

Relaxed, assured modern dining in Notting Hill

☎ 020 7034 0301 147-149 Notting Hill Gate W11 3LF
Plan 2-A1

email: eat@ribbandsrestaurants.com
web: www.ribbandsrestaurants.com

This corner-sited Notting Hill Gate venue draws a moneyed neighbourhood crowd. A split-level affair, it comes decked out in fashionable distressed-wood flooring and modern lighting, with walls a mix of brickwork or pale and deep pink panelling. The restaurant is accessed via the bar and reception area, and staff are suitably friendly and attentive. The accomplished kitchen's modern approach deals in quality produce and flavour on a fixed-price repertoire; take roasted duck breast served with Savoy cabbage and a Cassis sauce, while lemon tart with raspberry sorbet might head-up desserts.

💻 Essenza

☎ 020 7792 1066 210 Kensington Park Rd W11 1NR
web: www.theaa.com/travel/index.jsp

Smart and intimate trattoria, serving fresh, seasonal Italian dishes.

💻 Notting Grill

☎ 020 7229 1500 123a Clarendon Rd, Holland Park W11 4JG
web: www.theaa.com/travel/index.jsp

Antony Worrall Thompson's eatery featuring quality meat dishes and produce from his own garden.

LONDON W14

⊛⊛ *Cibo*

Italian 💻

Authentic Italian cooking to linger over

☎ 020 7371 2085 3 Russell Gardens W14 8EZ
Plan 1-D3

e-mail: ciborestaurant@aol.com
web: www.ciborestaurant.co.uk

Colourful, offbeat, abstract Renaissance-style nude paintings immediately catch the eye at this small, long-established

neighbourhood restaurant close to Olympia. White walls and tablecloths come paired with modern blond-wood chairs and colourful crockery and in summer, the full-length glass-front windows fold back so dining feels almost alfresco. Friendly waiting staff bring plenty of extras, from well-ladened bread baskets to large olives and mini pizzas and petits fours. Menus are in Italian with English subtitles, with fish and shellfish a speciality and home-made filled pasta excellent. The cooking focuses on a straightforward but imaginative style driven by quality ingredients; think duck ravioli with a mushroom sauce, grilled swordfish served with roast baby tomatoes, capers and olives, and a zabaglione or tiramisù finish. As you'd expect, wines are exclusively Italian.

Cibo

Times: 12.15-2.30/7-11, Closed Xmas, Etr BHs, Closed L Sat, D Sun
Directions: Nearest station: Olympia/Shepherd's Bush Russell Gardens is a residential area off Holland Road, Kensington (Olympia) Shepherd's Bush

LONDON WC1

⊛ Jurys Great Russell Street

Modern European

Elegant 1930s setting for relaxed dining

☎ 020 7347 1000 16-22 Great Russell St WC1B 3NN
Plan 3-C3

e-mail: restaurant_grs@jurysdoyle.com
web: www.jurysdoyle.com

Designed by the renowned architect Sir Edwin Lutyens in the 1930s, this impressive Neo-Georgian listed building retains many of its original features and houses a smart, spacious restaurant (named after Lutyens) tucked away in the basement. Its clean, traditional lines in keeping with the surroundings, as is the adjacent small, classic cocktail bar for aperitifs. The crowd-pleasing menu fits the bill, too, with the likes of braised wild sea bass served with baby fennel, pan-fried gnocchi, pepper confit and chorizo oil, or perhaps a British game plate (wild guinea fowl confit, stuffed quail, Yorkshire venison and port wine sauce). Desserts might include coconut crème brûlée.

Chef: Paul O'Brien **Owners:** Jurys Doyle Hotel Group Ltd **Times:** 6-10, Closed L all week **Prices:** Starter £5.95-£13.95, Main £11-£22.95, Dessert £6.95-£9.50, Service included **Wine:** 19 bottles over £20, 31 bottles under £20, 11 by the glass **Seats:** 120, Pr/dining room 26 **Children:** Portions **Rooms:** 170 (170 en suite) ★★★★ HL **Directions:** Nearest station: Tottenham Court Road Short walk from Tottenham Court Rd and tube station **Parking:** NCP opposite the hotel

ENGLAND

⊛ Matsuri High Holborn

Japanese 💻

Traditional Japanese in contemporary setting

☎ 020 7430 1970 Mid City Place, 71 High Holborn
WC1V 6EA Plan 3-E3
e-mail: eat@matsuri-restaurant.com
web: www.matsuri-restaurant.com

Futuristic Japanese restaurant occupying a corner site on bustling High Holborn. You'll find a choice of three dining areas that showcase the various styles of cuisine - the sushi counter, the teppan-yaki room and the main dining room with open-plan kitchen. The Japanese ex-pats frequenting this restaurant are a clue to the quality and authenticity of the cooking. Menus are lengthy, yet good ingredients are simply prepared and well presented, with lots of memorable fresh fish. The teppan-yaki set menus provide an overall flavour of Japanese cuisine. The highly acclaimed Wagyu beef has now been added to the menus, and there's a set price Twilight menu available between 6 and 7pm.

Chef: H Sudoh, T Aso, S Mabalot **Owners:** Matsuri Restaurant Group
Times: 12-2.30/6-10, Closed 25-26 Dec, 1 Jan, BHs, Sun **Prices:** Fixed L £8.50,
Fixed D £35-£75, Starter £5-£15, Main £15-£35, Dessert £3.50-£6.50, Service
added but optional 12.5% **Wine:** 93 bottles over £20, 2 bottles under £20,
5 by the glass **Notes:** Fixed D 5 courses, Air con **Seats:** 120, Pr/dining room 10
Directions: Nearest station: Holborn On the corner of Red Lion St. Opposite
the Renaissance Chancery Court Hotel **Parking:** On street (pay & display)

⊛ The Montague on the Gardens

Modern British 💻

Stylish hotel restaurant with modern cuisine

☎ 020 7637 1001 15 Montague St, Bloomsbury
WC1B 5BJ Plan 3-C4
e-mail: bookmt@rchmail.com
web: www.montaguehotel.com

A swish boutique hotel in the heart of Bloomsbury, the Montague has two dining options - the Blue Door bistro or the fine-dining restaurant, the Chef's Table. The latter is a light, airy space with panoramic views over London on three sides and an outside terrace for alfresco dining and summer barbecues. Attentive staff are on hand to make guests feel at ease and the cooking is modern British with some French influences. Expect dishes such as lobster risotto with mascarpone and parmesan crisp, followed by pan-fried sea bream with confit tomato and caviar beurre blanc.

The Montague on the Gardens

Chef: Neil Ramsey **Owners:** Red Carnation Hotels **Times:** 12.30-
2.30/5.30-10.30 **Prices:** Fixed L £20-£30, Fixed D £25-£50, Starter £6.95-
£9.95, Main £13.95-£24.50, Dessert £5.95, Service added but optional
12.5% **Wine:** 61 bottles over £20, 7 bottles under £20, 19 by the glass
Notes: Business and Sun L menu available, Vegetarian available, Civ Wed
90, Air con **Seats:** 45, Pr/dining room 100 **Children:** Menu, Portions
Rooms: 99 (99 en suite) ★★★★ HL **Directions:** Nearest station:
Russell Square 10 minutes from Covent Garden, adjacent to the British
Museum **Parking:** On street, Bloomsbury Square

⊛⊛⊛ Pearl Restaurant & Bar

see page 374

💻 Cigala

☎ 020 7405 1717 54 Lamb's Conduit St WC1N 3LW
web: www.theaa.com/travel/index.jsp

Appealing Spanish restaurant with tapas bar.

Konstam at the Prince Albert

☎ 020 7833 5040 2 Acton St WC1X 9NR

European cuisine using seasonal food locally sourced.

Wagamama

☎ 020 7930 7587 14a Irving St WC1H 7AF

Informal noodle bars with no booking required.

Wagamama

☎ 020 7323 9223 4a Streatham St WC1A 1JB

Informal noodle bars with no booking required.

Yo! Sushi

☎ 020 7636 0076 Myhotel, 11-13 Bayley St WC1B 3HD

Sushi, sashimi, noodles and more.

Pearl Restaurant & Bar

LONDON WC1

Modern French V 💻

Stylish, city-orientated, destination restaurant with highly accomplished modern cooking

☎ 020 7829 7000 Renaissance Chancery Court, 252 High Holborn WC1V 7EN Plan 3-D3
e-mail: info@pearl-restaurant.com
web: www.pearl-restaurant.com

The old Pearl Assurance Building has been transformed into a glamorous, metropolitan, destination restaurant. The achingly chic interior includes original marble pillars, while walnut, hand-spun pearls (what else), cream leather chairs, well-spaced tables with expensive settings and a huge wooden wine cave catch the eye, too. Staff - including a sommelier - provide attentive, professional service, while the appealing medley of lunch, dinner, tasting option and vegetarian menu all come at fixed prices.

The skilful kitchen takes a fresh, modern-French approach, delivering exciting combinations with clear flavours driven by high-quality produce - sprinkled with luxury - in dishes dressed to thrill. Take a terrine of foie gras, smoked pigeon and ham hock served with baby beetroot, walnuts and pickled shallots to start, perhaps turbot poached in red wine and served with creamed black cabbage and crispy oysters to follow, and to finish, maybe Valrhona chocolate shortbread with tonka bean ice cream. Peripherals like canapés, amuse-bouche, breads, pre-dessert and petits fours all hit form, too.

Chef: Jun Tanaka
Owners: Hotel Property Investors
Times: 12-2.30/6-10, Closed Dec, BHs, 2 wks Aug, Sun, Closed L Sat
Prices: Fixed L £25, Fixed D £49, Service added but optional 12.5%
Notes: Vegetarian menu, Tasting menu available, Dress Restrictions, Smart casual, Air con
Seats: 74, Pr/dining room 12
Rooms: 356 (356 en suite) ★★★★★ HL
Directions: Nearest station: Holborn 200 mtrs from Holborn tube station
Parking: NCP

LONDON WC2

◉ The Admiralty Restaurant

Modern French 💻

Contemporary restaurant in Somerset House

☎ 020 7845 4646 Somerset House, The Strand WC2R 1LA Plan 3-D2

e-mail: info@theadmiralityrestaurant.com
web: www.theadmiralityrestaurant.com

Its Thames-side setting, off the courtyard at Somerset House, proves a grand prelude to lunch or dinner in the two high-ceilinged dining rooms that once played host to the Naval Headquarters. This unique venue has recently been refurbished to create a smart and contemporary dining experience. The cooking is French regional with modern twists. Expect duck confit with Puy lentils, or rump of Cornish lamb with dauphinoise potato, flageolet beans and herb jus.

Chef: Chris Wayland **Owners:** Leiths **Times:** 12-2.30/5.30-10.30, Closed 24-27 Dec, Closed D Sun **Prices:** Fixed L £15.50, Starter £6.50-£10, Main £12.50-£16, Dessert £5.75, Service added but optional 12.5% **Wine:** 25 bottles over £20, 3 bottles under £20, 8 by the glass **Notes:** Pre-theatre D until 7pm, Vegetarian available **Seats:** 90, Pr/dining room 60 **Children:** Portions **Directions:** Nearest station: Temple, Covent Garden Telephone for directions, see website

◉◉ *Albannach*

Modern Scottish 🍷 NOTABLE WINE LIST 💻

Highland chic meets city bustle with contemporary twists on Scottish favourites

☎ 020 7930 0066 66 Trafalgar Square WC2N 5DS Plan 5-C6

e-mail: info@albannach.co.uk
web: www.albannach.co.uk

Purple sprouting heather in the windows, kilted staff and, of course, the name provides major clues that you're in a Scottish-themed restaurant. Overlooking Trafalgar Square, the walls of this fabulous mezzanine restaurant are adorned with beautiful Scottish photographs. The darkwood, open-plan dining areas are perhaps more like a bar or a nightclub than a fine-dining restaurant but it's a style that works, creating an atmospheric destination to imbibe generous amounts of whisky or enjoy a full-on foray into eclectic, modern Scottish cuisine with Caledonian produce championed by William Wallace-style fervour. Try the haggis, neeps and tatties with Hermitage sauce, followed by seared West Coast salmon or the rib-eye Buccleuch beef.

Times: 12-3/5-10, Closed 25-26 Dec, 1 Jan, Sun **Directions:** Nearest station: Charing Cross SW corner of Trafalgar Sq, opposite Canada House

◉◉◉ L'Atelier de Joël Robuchon

see page 376

◉ Bank Aldwych

Modern European 💻

Welcoming brasserie close to Covent Garden

☎ 0845 658 7878 020 7379 9012 1 Kingsway WC2B 6XF Plan 3-D2

e-mail: aldres@bankrestaurants.com
web: www.bankrestaurants.com

Despite its enormous size, this former bank is welcoming and cosy. The Aldwych entrance leads into a spacious bar area and through to the vibrant restaurant, where a ceiling of hanging green glass panels creates an intimate effect, and colourful murals show old-fashioned seaside scenes. The brasserie food is well thought-out, carefully cooked and immaculately presented from breakfast through brunch and lunch to dinner. Wild mushroom risotto and truffle oil, grilled calves' liver with onion gravy, grilled venison with poached pear, and monkfish tail with Laksa broth are among an appealing choice that includes good-value set meals, and even a children's menu.

Chef: Damien Pondevie **Owners:** Individual Restaurant Company plc **Times:** 12-2.45/5.30-11.30, Closed 25-26 Dec, 1-2 Jan, BHs, Closed D Sun **Prices:** Fixed L £15, Fixed D £17.50, Starter £5.50-£8.95, Main £6.50-£21.95, Dessert £5.25-£6.50, Service added but optional 12.5% **Wine:** 68 bottles over £20, 17 bottles under £20, 22 by the glass **Notes:** Vegetarian available, Dress Restrictions, Smart casual, Air con **Seats:** 230, Pr/dining room 40 **Children:** Menu, Portions **Directions:** Nearest station: Holborn, Charing Cross, Temple From Holborn Tube station turn left onto Kingsway, continue to end and cross the road, restaurant is on corner of Aldwych & Kingsway **Parking:** NCP Drury Lane

◉ *Christopher's*

Contemporary American 💻

Victorian grandeur meets contemporary American cooking

☎ 020 7240 4222 18 Wellington St, Covent Garden WC2E 7DD Plan 3-D2

e-mail: coventgarden@christophersgrill.com
web: www.christophersgrill.com

Situated smack bang in the middle of Covent Garden and theatreland, Christopher's is an American-themed establishment with a Martini bar downstairs, private dining and a large restaurant upstairs. The fascinating Victorian building, once London's first licensed casino, features a sweeping stone staircase, high, decorative ceilings and tall windows. Contemporary décor adds bold colours, polished wood floors and striking accessories. The huge menu offers lots of steak, fish and fresh seasonal fare, with starters like Caesar salad, followed by Midwestern veal meatloaf, and New York cheesecake to finish. Theatre and weekend brunch menus are popular options.

Times: 12-3/5-11, Closed 24 Dec-2 Jan, 25-26 Dec, 1 Jan, Closed D Sun **Directions:** Nearest station: Embankment/Covent Garden Just by Strand, overlooking Waterloo Bridge

ENGLAND

◉◉◉
L'Atelier de Joël Robuchon

LONDON WC2

French V NEW

Slick, sexy sophistication from French super-chef

☎ 020 7010 8600 13-15 West St WC2H 9HE Plan 3-C2
e-mail: info@joelrobuchon.co.uk

This hotly anticipated West End opening from legendary French super-chef Joël Robuchon is his first foray in the UK. Spread over three floors, the ground-floor L'Atelier serves small signature dishes at the kitchen counter. A flashily designed space, intimate and low-lit, it's illuminated by bright spots of colour; lights trained on chrome birdcages of lemons or tomatoes, produce-filled jars and vibrant-coloured cast-iron pots. Seating is on high stools around the kitchen counter or at high tables. The first-floor dining room, La Cuisine, also has an open kitchen but is lighter and brighter with conventional tables and carte-menu format. The intimate second-floor Le Bar has a nightclub vibe and completes the trio. Staff are smartly clad in black, attentive, friendly and informed, while menus in both restaurants offer many similar dishes, but the focus downstairs is strictly on small grazing plates.
Consistently imaginative, innovative and displaying great finesse, the cooking is fun too, particularly with all the theatre of the open kitchens. Fine ingredients, clear flavours and a lightness of touch

parade in dishes like pan-fried sea bass served with a lemongrass foam and stewed leeks, or steak tartare with hand-made French fries. (Note there's a limited booking policy downstairs - only early tables can be reserved.)

Chef: Frederic Sironin, Olivier Limousin **Owners:** Bahia UK Ltd
Times: 12-3/5.30-11, Closed 25-26 Dec **Prices:** Fixed L £35, Fixed D £35, Starter £9-£60, Main £15-£45, Dessert £9, Service added but optional 12.5%
Wine: 350 bottles over £20, 2 bottles under £20, 16 by the glass
Notes: Fixed L & D 4 courses £35, Tasting menu 9 courses £85, Vegetarian menu, Air con **Seats:** 58 **Children:** Portions **Directions:** Nearest station: Leicester Square Telephone for directions **Parking:** Valet parking service

◉◉◉
Clos Maggiore

LONDON WC2

Modern French

Modern French fine dining in a romantic Covent Garden setting

☎ 020 7379 9696 33 King St, Covent Garden WC2E 8JD
Plan 3-C2
e-mail: enquiries@closmaggiore.com
web: www.closmaggiore.com

A discreet mulberry-coloured awning and frontage picks out this re-launched restaurant (formerly Maggiore's) in the heart of Covent Garden. Inside it oozes romance, reminiscent of a stylish country inn in Provence or Tuscany. Think warm colours, a roaring winter fire in a blossom-adorned conservatory-style courtyard with fully opening glass roof that offers 'internal alfresco dining' in the warmer months, or under the stars at night. Real box hedging and flowers add to the garden feel, with wooden floors, elegantly laid tables and smoked mirrors. Talented chef Marcellin Marc, previously at the two Michelin starred Le Clos de la Violette in Aix-en-Provence, heads-up the kitchen, his cooking modern-focused and underpinned by a classical theme. Classy, sophisticated and driven by high-quality ingredients, this is French cooking at its best. Presentation is simple, portions generous and flavours bold, all accompanied by a superb wine list. Expect roast

rack of Elwy Valley lamb served with smoked pomme purée, glazed Chantenay carrots with confit of lemon, and to finish, perhaps an orange and caramel ile flottante.

Chef: Marcellin Marc **Owners:** Tyfoon Restaurants Ltd **Times:** 12-2.30/5-11, Closed 24-26 Dec & 1 Jan, Sun, Closed L Sat **Prices:** Fixed L £19.50, Fixed D £24.50-£45, Starter £6.90-£13.90, Main £15.50-£44.50, Dessert £6.50-£13.90, Service added but optional 12.5% **Wine:** 1900 bottles over £20, 50 bottles under £20, 15 by the glass **Notes:** Fixed L 3 courses, Tasting menu 6 courses £55, Civ Wed 150, Air con **Seats:** 70, Pr/dining room 30
Children: Portions **Directions:** Nearest station: Covent Garden 1 min walk from The Piazza and Royal Opera House **Parking:** NCP, on street

LONDON WC2 CONTINUED

◉◉◉ Clos Maggiore

see opposite

◉ Imperial China

Chinese

Sophisticated Cantonese cooking meets contemporary décor in Chinatown

☎ 020 7734 3388 White Bear Yard, 25a Lisle St WC2H 7BA Plan 3-B2
e-mail: mail@imperial-china.co.uk
web: www.imperial-china.co.uk

Its glass doors fronting Lisle Street lead through an inner courtyard complete with waterfall, bridge and pond to the contemporary Chinese-designed, glass-fronted dining room set on two floors. Think modern wood panelling, lighting and artwork to slate, lightwood or blue-carpeted floors. White table linen, upholstered chairs in gold and smartly attired, friendly Chinese staff epitomise the upmarket vibe. The light, sophisticated Cantonese cooking fits the bill, drawing the crowds of Chinese Londoners, with its comprehensive dim sum menu and typically lengthy carte dotted with a few unfamiliar choices. Expect grilled black cod or perhaps stir-fried chicken with cashew nuts.

Times: 12/11.30, Closed Xmas **Directions:** Nearest station: Leicester Sq From station into Little Newport St, straight ahead into Lisle St and right into White Bear Yard

◉◉ Incognico

French, Italian 💻

Franco-Italian food in the heart of theatreland

☎ 020 7836 8866 117 Shaftesbury Av, Cambridge Circus WC2H 8AD Plan 3-C2
e-mail: incognicorestaurant@gmail.com
web: www.incognico.com

There's an authentic French brasserie feel to this Shaftesbury Avenue restaurant, a favourite among theatre-goers. The interior is stylishly good looking with leather banquettes, oak panelling, stripped wooden floors and light spilling in from large windows. There's also a spacious bar, and an intimate private dining room in the basement. The food is all about quality raw materials cooked with great assurance. Classic French dishes with an Italian slant are simply presented, including an impressive chicken liver parfait with a rich buttery flavour served with toasted Poulaine bread. Wild salmon fillet with cauliflower purée and red wine sauce proves a good combination for the main course, the fish translucent and supremely fresh. And for dessert, take chocolate pannacotta with griottine cherries.

Times: 12-3/5.30-11, Closed 10 days Xmas, 4 days Etr, BHs, Sun **Directions:** Nearest station: Leicester Sq Behind Cambridge Circus

◉ The Ivy

British, International

Theatreland legend with an accessible menu

☎ 020 7836 4751 1 West St, Covent Garden WC2H 9NQ Plan 3-C2

The Ivy's reputation guarantees a following of celebrities and star-gazers, ably supported by agents, West End producers and various

media types. The result is surprisingly calm and low key, helped by the clublike atmosphere of oak panelling, wooden floors and stained-glass windows. Dedicated staff make a similar fuss of the famous and the anonymous, and the lengthy menu offers everything from old school comforts (double pork sausages, shepherd's pie, corned beef hash with double fried egg, steamed treacle sponge pudding with custard) to the sophisticated (Sévruga caviar, sautéed foie gras with caramelised apples, and fillet of red deer). Booking absolutely essential.

Times: 12-3/5.30-12, Closed 25-26 Dec, 1 Jan, Aug BH, Closed L 27 Dec, D 24 Dec **Directions:** Nearest station: Leicester Square Telephone for directions

◉◉◉ JAAN Restaurant

see page 378

◉ J. Sheekey

Fish, Seafood V

Much loved seafood restaurant in Theatreland

☎ 020 7240 2565 St Martin's Court WC2N 4AL Plan 3-C2
e-mail: reservations@j-sheekey.co.uk
web: www.j-sheekey.co.uk

This London stalwart began life as a seafood stall in the late 19th century, until its owner, J Sheekey, was invited to open a little oyster bar by Lord Salisbury on the condition that he supplied food for his lordship's post-theatre dinner parties. Over time it expanded into the adjoining properties, but today you'll still often see a queue outside the door. Step inside and you'll find a warren of interconnected rooms with closely-set tables, photographs of the celebrities who have dined here and an intimate, buzzy feel. Expect a bistro menu of fish and seafood fare, including the likes of smoked haddock with poached egg and colcannon or lemon sole with shrimps and soft roes. Vegetarian menu also available.

Times: 12-3/5.30-12, Closed 25-26 Dec, 1 Jan, Aug BH, Closed D 24 Dec **Directions:** Nearest station: Leicester Square Telephone for directions

◉ Mon Plaisir

French 💻

A Francophile's delight in central London

☎ 020 7836 7243 21 Monmouth St WC2H 9DD Plan 3-C2
e-mail: eatafrog@mail.com
web: www.monplaisir.co.uk

Charles de Gaulle often held meetings here in the 1940s, and this restaurant remains about as French as you can get this side of the Channel; the cosy network of rooms is decked out with modern abstracts and interesting artefacts. The atmosphere buzzes with pre- and post-theatre diners, muffling the conversation from closely packed neighbours. Everything on the classic and modern French menus is freshly cooked, including very traditional rustic dishes like snails in garlic or pork terrine, French onion soup, coq au vin and ile flottante. All desserts are hand made by the chef patissier. Friendly professional Gallic waiters glide smoothly between the tables.

Chef: Frank Raymond **Owners:** Alain Lhermitte **Times:** 12-2.15/5.45-11.15, Closed Xmas, New Year, BHs, Sun, Closed L Sat **Prices:** Fixed L £12.95, Fixed D £14.50, Starter £5.95-£13.90, Main £14.50-£22.50, Dessert £4.95-£7.50, Service added but optional 12.5% **Notes:** Dress Restrictions, Smart casual, Air con **Seats:** 100, Pr/dining room 28 **Children:** Portions **Directions:** Nearest station: Covent Garden, Leicester Square Off Seven Dials

ENGLAND

JAAN Restaurant

LONDON WC2

Modern French, Asian V 💻

Impressive cuisine in smart Thames-side hotel

☎ 020 7836 3555 & 7300 1700 Swissôtel The Howard, London, Temple Place WC2R 2PR Plan 3-E2
e-mail: jann.london@swissotel.com
web: www.london.swissotel.com

Enjoying superb views across the London skyline from its Thames-side location, this smart hotel's restaurant and bar opens out on to a delightful courtyard garden for alfresco dining in fair weather, which in winter is covered by a marquee. Inside, there's a modern, contemporary edge to the spacious, stylish, clean lines. Wooden floors, luxurious silks, antique Asian artwork and friendly, yet formal service create the ambience.

The kitchen's approach is inspired by modern French cuisine and enhanced by the delicate flavours and scents of Asia, which blend perfectly with the surroundings. The enticing repertoire is delivered via a fixed-price medley, which includes a good-value lunch, tasting options and carte (including a separate vegetarian offering). Top-class ingredients, consistency, sparkling technical artistry and presentation, vision, balance and clarity, and intensity of flavours all find their place. Expect a stylish opener like wild pigeon and foie gras (served with lentils, chanterelles and a liquorice foam), perhaps a rabbit and lobster roulade to follow (with vanilla bean mash, tomato confit and sauce américaine), while a composite dessert - emphasis on apple - might deliver a Bramley crème brûlée, French apple parfait, apple and Calvados confit, meringue shortbread and apple coulis.

Chef: Simon Duff
Owners: New Ray Ltd
Times: 12-2.30/5.45-10.30, Closed 1st wk Jan, BHs, Sun, Closed L Sat
Prices: Fixed L £19.75, Fixed D £38, Starter £15, Main £21, Dessert £9, Service added 12.5%
Wine: 120 bottles over £20, 18 by the glass
Notes: Tasting menu 4 & 6 courses available, Vegetarian menu, Dress Restrictions, Smart, casual, Civ Wed 100, Air con
Seats: 56
Rooms: 189 (189 en suite)
★★★★★ HL
Directions: Nearest station: Temple Telephone for directions (Opposite Temple Tube station)
Parking: 30

ENGLAND

LONDON WC2 CONTINUED

◎◎ One Aldwych - Axis

Modern European 🖥 ⬥ NOTABLE WINE LIST

Dramatic, contemporary dining in the heart of theatreland

☎ 020 7300 0300 & 7300 1000 1 Aldwych WC2B 4RH
Plan 3-D2
e-mail: axis@onealdwych.com
web: www.onealdwych.com

A double-height ceiling and dramatic abstract cityscape mural - the 'Amber City' by Richard Walker - give this hip and trendy metropolitan basement restaurant its wow-factor. It has amazing muted colours and black leather upholstery, plus a balcony bar with views over the dining room and a sweeping staircase entrance. Staff make dining here far from an impersonal experience, with helpful yet professional table service. Quality ingredients are skilfully prepared with an English and seasonal slant. There are sections on the menu that include catch of the day, grills and roast for two. Take potted crab to begin, followed by poached haddock with clams, baby carrots and spinach, while a lemon meringue tart might catch the eye at dessert. (The Axis, one of two dining options at One Aldwych hotel, has a stand-alone vibe with its own street entrance - see also Indigo restaurant below.)

Chef: Jens Folkel **Owners:** Gordon Campbell Gray **Times:** 12-2.45/5.45-10.45, Closed Xmas, New Year, Sun, Closed L Sat **Prices:** Fixed L £17.50, Starter £5.75-£11.50, Main £14.95-£21.95, Dessert £5.50-£6.95, Service added but optional 12.5% **Wine:** 16 by the glass **Notes:** Pre/Post-theatre 2 courses £17.50, 3 courses £20.50, Vegetarian available, Civ Wed 60, Air con **Seats:** 120, Pr/dining room 40 **Children:** Menu, Portions **Directions:** Nearest station: Covent Garden At point where Aldwych meets the Strand opposite Waterloo Bridge. On corner of Aldwych & Wellington St, opposite Lyceum Theatre **Parking:** NCP - Wellington St

◎◎ One Aldwych - Indigo

Modern European V 🖥

Trendy mezzanine dining with a buzzy atmosphere

☎ 020 7300 0400 1 Aldwych WC2B 4RH Plan 3-D2
e-mail: indigo@onealdwych.com
web: www.onealdwych.com

The epitome of modern chic and contemporary styling, this sophisticated restaurant is set on a mezzanine balcony overlooking the buzzy hotel Lobby Bar below, making it the perfect spot for people-watching. Spotlights zoom down on to tables, seats are comfortable, service is focused and the atmosphere fashionable and relaxed. The kitchen follows the theme, with cosmopolitan, flavour-driven, clean-cut dishes delivered on creatively flexible menus that play to the gallery. There's the option to create your own salad dish, others can be taken as a starter or main course, while the more structured fine-dining options might deliver pan-fried monkfish, red mullet and sea bass with a lime and coriander risotto, or perhaps chargrilled Scottish beef fillet and slow-cooked rump steak served with spinach and parsnip purée.

One Aldwych - Indigo

Chef: Alex Wood **Owners:** Gordon Campbell-Gray **Times:** 12-3/6-11.15 **Prices:** Fixed L £21.70-£33.25, Fixed D £29.65-£46.20, Starter £5.75-£10.50, Main £15.95-£22.75, Dessert £6.75, Service added but optional 12.5% **Wine:** 79 bottles over £20, 2 bottles under £20, 17 by the glass **Notes:** Sat & Sun brunch menu, Pre & Post-Theatre D available, Vegetarian menu, Civ Wed 60, Air con **Seats:** 62 **Children:** Menu, Portions **Rooms:** 105 (105 en suite)★★★★★ HL **Directions:** Nearest station: Covent Garden, Charing Cross Located where Aldwych meets The Strand opposite Waterloo Bridge **Parking:** Valet parking

◎ Orso Restaurant

Modern Italian 🖥

Italian food in a buzzing basement

☎ 020 7240 5269 27 Wellington St WC2E 7DB
Plan 3-D2
e-mail: info@orsorestaurant.co.uk
web: www.orsorestaurant.co.uk

A discreet, street-level entrance leads downstairs to the cavernous basement dining room (once an orchid warehouse) at this long-established, all-day Covent Garden Italian that reverberates with energy, conversation and the clinking of glasses and cutlery. Smart staff, constantly flitting about, add to the lively, informal atmosphere. The busy bilingual menu showcases regional Italian cooking and offers bags of choice, from pizza and pasta dishes (perhaps tagliatelle with roasted aubergines, tomato, basil and pecorino) to roast saddle of hare with pomegranate and wet polenta. A pre-theatre menu and weekend brunch offer excellent value.

Chef: Martin Wilson **Owners:** Orso Restaurants Ltd **Times:** Noon/midnight, Closed 24 & 25 Dec, Closed L Sat-Sun (Jul-Aug) **Prices:** Fixed D £18, Starter £5-£10, Main £9-£17.50, Dessert £6, Service optional, Group min 8 service 12.5% **Wine:** 39 bottles over £20, 5 bottles under £20, 15 by the glass **Notes:** Vegetarian available, Air con **Seats:** 100 **Directions:** Nearest station: Covent Garden Telephone for directions **Parking:** On street

LONDON WC2 CONTINUED

⊛ The Portrait Restaurant

Modern British

Stylish, contemporary dining with rooftop views

☎ 020 7312 2490 National Portrait Gallery, St Martins Place WC2H 0HE Plan 3-C1
e-mail: portrait.restaurant@searcys.co.uk
web: www.searcys.co.uk

Offering a stunning London landscape from the rooftop restaurant of Nelson's Column, the Houses of Parliament and the London Eye, this light, sleek and contemporary affair is decked out in grey with a wall of glass windows that lets those views do the talking. Light, colourful, clean-cut, bistro-styled dishes - with the occasional Mediterranean slant - provide a stylish accompaniment to the London skyline. Begin with garden pea and leek tart, glazed asparagus, herb salad and lemon dressing, and follow with pan-fried fillet of sea bass with truffle-crushed baby potatoes, buttered leeks and lobster sauce. A caramelised citrus tart with kumquat syrup and Valrhona chocolate sorbet might round things off. Note that there's a 10 per cent discount for Members of the Gallery.

Chef: Katarina Todosijevic **Owners:** Searcys **Times:** 11.45-2.45/5.30-8.30, Closed 24-26 Dec, 1 Jan, Closed D Sat-Wed **Prices:** Fixed L £14.95-£19.95, Fixed D £29.95-£34.95, Starter £5.95-£8.75, Main £11.95-£28.95, Dessert £5-£6.50, Service added but optional 12.5% **Wine:** 35 bottles over £20, 9 bottles under £20, 14 by the glass **Notes:** Air con **Seats:** 100 **Children:** Menu, Portions **Directions:** Nearest station: Leicester Square, Charing Cross Just behind Trafalgar Square **Parking:** NCP - Orange St

The Savoy Grill

see below

Belgo

☎ 020 7813 2233 50 Earlham St WC2H 9HP

Belgian style, extending to strong beer, good seafood (mussels of course) and staff in habits.

💻 Café du Jardin

☎ 020 7836 8769 28 Wellington St WC2E 7BD
web: www.theaa.com/travel/index.jsp

Mediterranean-style dishes at this bustling split-level restaurant.

💻 Loch Fyne Restaurant, Covent Garden

☎ 020 7240 4999 2-4 Catherine St WC2B 5JS
web: www.theaa.com/travel/index.jsp

Quality seafood chain.

💻 Strada

☎ 020 7405 6293 6 Great Queen St WC2B 5DH
web: www.theaa.com/travel/index.jsp

Superior pizza from quality ingredients cooked in wood-fired ovens.

Rosettes not confirmed at time of going to press

The Savoy Grill

LONDON WC2

Modern British V 💻

Look forward to flawless cooking at this legendary restaurant when the hotel reopens

☎ 020 7592 1600 The Savoy, Strand WC2R 0EU
Plan 3-D1
e-mail: savoygrill@marcuswareing.com
web: www.marcuswareing.com

The Savoy Hotel is due to close to facilitate a stunning refurbishment, but Marcus Wareing will continue to operate this restaurant of great historical importance when the hotel relaunches in 2009 after the major face-lift. Thankfully there will be little, if any, change to Barbara Barry's successful design of this much loved institution, which brought a successful balance between the traditional and the more contemporary. Its historical art deco character incorporates semi-circular banquette seating in sleek tobacco, nougat and black stripe with more traditional chairs, while the shimmering gold-leaf effect ceiling and crisp white linen combine to create understated richness. Marcus Wareing's menu retains some of the restaurant's past tradition (Scottish smoked salmon carved at the trolley) but has ushered proceedings into the present day. The kitchen adopts a modern approach - underpinned by classical French roots - that is based around superb-quality ingredients, precise technical skills and great attention to detail. Clear, clean flavours, seasonality and fine balance parade on a repertoire of fixed-price menus (oozing luxury) that includes a tasting option. Service fits the bill too, and is professional and slick without being overbearing. A serious wine list and a chef's table in the heart of the kitchen wrap up a class package. Whilst the restaurant is closed, diners can enjoy Marcus Wareing's food at Pétrus in The Berkeley in SW1 (see entry).

Chef: Lee Bennett **Owners:** Marcus Wareing at the Savoy Grill Ltd **Times:** 12-3/5.45-11 **Prices:** Fixed L £30-£65, Fixed D £55-£65, Service added but optional 12.5% **Wine:** 550 bottles over £20, 1 bottle under £20, 12 by the glass **Notes:** Fixed L 3 courses, Tasting menu 6 courses £65, Vegetarian menu, Dress Restrictions, No jeans, jackets preferred, Air con **Seats:** 70, Pr/dining room 60 **Children:** Menu, Portions **Rooms:** 263 (263 en suite) **Directions:** Nearest station: Charing Cross/Covent Garden Please telephone for directions **Parking:** On street

🖥 Tuttons Brasserie

☎ 020 7836 4141   11-12 Russell St, Covent Garden WC2B 5HZ

web: www.theaa.com/travel/index.jsp

British and European menus at a relaxed, friendly, child-friendly, watch-the-world-go-by location.

Wagamama

☎ 020 7836 3330   1 Tavistock St, Covent Garden WC2E 7PG

Informal noodle bars with no booking required.

LONDON, GREATER

BARNET   MAP 06 TQ29

◉ Dylan's

Modern European

Modern surroundings for cutting-edge global cuisine

☎ 020 8275 1551 & 8275 1651   21 Station Pde, Cockfosters EN4 0DW

e-mail: dylan@dylansrestaurant.com

web: www.dylansrestaurant.com

Dylan's is a glass-fronted high-street restaurant in the heart of Cockfosters. The décor is fresh and contemporary and a cocktail menu is served in the comfortable lounge bar. Fresh produce is employed to recreate classic dishes in an uncomplicated modern style, accompanied by service which is relaxed and informal, yet efficient and friendly. Cooking is deft and confident, producing the likes of salmon ballotine with lime and leek salad, beetroot and mustard mascarpone, or slow-roasted belly pork with swede mash, red cabbage and blood orange jus. Desserts range from chocolate fondant to orange and ginger pudding.

Chef: Richard O'Connell **Owners:** Dylan Murray, Richard O'Connell **Times:** 12-2.30/6-10, Closed 26 Dec, 1 Jan **Prices:** Fixed L £12.95, Starter £5.50-£9.95, Main £12.50-£19.95, Dessert £5.50-£7.50, Service added but optional 12.5% **Wine:** 16 bottles over £20, 8 bottles under £20, 10 by the glass **Notes:** Vegetarian available, Dress Restrictions, Smart casual, Air con **Seats:** 90, Pr/dining room 8 **Children:** Menu, Portions **Directions:** M25 junct 24, follow A111 towards Cockfosters for 3m, Dylan's on left-hand side of Cockfosters Rd **Parking:** On street

BECKENHAM
See LONDON SECTION   Plan 1-G1

◉◉ Mello

Modern European

Fashionable dining near suburban high street

☎ 020 8663 0994   2 Southend Rd BR3 1SD

e-mail: info@mello.uk.com

web: www.mello.uk.com

Not quite where you might expect to find somewhere delivering such imaginative, clear-flavoured cuisine, but this ambitious modern restaurant - located in a Victorian listed building - is well worth uncovering. High-backed leather and suede chairs, contemporary art

on deep red and warm sand coloured walls, white table linen and a deep red carpet cut a simple but effective style. The kitchen clearly has skill, potential and confidence, with presentation elegant and sophisticated, and ingredients of high quality. The appealing repertoire cuts a modern European line underpinned by classical roots; take roast cannon of Cornish lamb with confit shoulder, aubergine caviar, asparagus and roasting juices, and perhaps a hot chocolate fondant with pistachio ice cream to finish. One to watch.

Mello

Chef: Anton Babarovic **Owners:** A Demirtas **Times:** 12-2.30/6-10, Closed D Sun **Prices:** Fixed L £10, Fixed D £15, Starter £6-£8.50, Main £11.50-£19.50, Dessert £5.50-£8, Service added but optional 12.5% **Notes:** Sun L 3 courses £17, Dress Restrictions, Smart casual, Air con **Seats:** 90, Pr/dining room 36 **Children:** Portions **Directions:** 0.5m from Beckenham town centre, directly opposite Beckenham train station **Parking:** 26

see advert on page 382

BROMLEY
See LONDON SECTION   Plan 1-G1

◉◉◉◉ Chapter One

see page 383

🖥 Tamasha

☎ 020 8460 3240   131 Widmore Rd BR1 3AX

web: www.theaa.com/travel/index.jsp

Indian restaurant with Raj-inspired décor and a comprehensive collection of cricketing memorabilia. Live entertainment early in the week.

Mello

Tel: 020 8663 0994
E-mail: info@mello.uk.com
Web: www.mello.uk.com

This modern European restaurant - just by Beckenham Junction -
is easy to reach either by rail or tram link.

Having its own private car park makes it even more popular
among its customers.

The decoration is classic, but still creative: modern oil paintings,
leather and suede chairs and relaxing colours are making any meal
even more enjoyable.

All the modern European dishes are cooked with quality
ingredients and high skill.

The restaurant offers fantastic lunch and dinner set menus.

Chapter One

BROMLEY

Modern European 🍷 NOTABLE WINE LIST 💻

Sophisticated cooking at unbeatable prices

☎ 01689 854848 Farnborough Common, Locksbottom
BR6 8NF
e-mail: info@chaptersrestaurants.com
web: www.chaptersrestaurants.co.uk

Chef: Andrew McLeish
Owners: Selective Restaurants Group
Times: 12-2.30/6.30-10.30, Closed 1-4 Jan
Prices: Fixed L £16.50, Starter £6.50, Main £16, Dessert £6.50, Service added but optional 12.5%
Wine: 109 bottles over £20, 25 bottles under £20, 14 by the glass
Notes: Sun L 3 courses £17.95, Dress Restrictions, No shorts, jeans or trainers, Air con **Seats:** 120, Pr/dining room 55
Children: Portions
Directions: Situated on A21, 3m from Bromley. From M25 junct 4 onto A21 for 5m
Parking: 90

With its mock-Tudor appearance, Chapter One is home to Andrew McLeish's much-acclaimed cooking. The front door opens into a world of refinement, from the spacious dining room with its new metropolitan styling and serene pastel tones, to the suave, professional and welcoming service. Dark wooden floors, elegant tan-coloured seating, stylish food-related photographs, bevelled-mirror wall and crisp white linen continue the sophisticated theme, while a separate brasserie and stylish bar - also refurbished and with a more informal edge - attracts a wised-up crowd looking for culinary thrills at cheaper prices. McLeish's confident and accomplished cooking aptly suits the surroundings and takes a modern European approach based on classical techniques, with dishes displaying plenty of innovation alongside distinct flavours, balanced combinations and high skill. Tip-top seasonal ingredients are handled with consummate integrity here, and perfectly illustrate the maxim 'less is more'. Take pot-roast belly of Berkshire free-range pork served with caramelised apple, potato fondant and pork jus, or perhaps baked halibut with a comté crust accompanied by sautéed pak choi, braised onion purée and smoked red wine sauce, and to finish, perhaps a hot chocolate fondant with Tahitian vanilla ice cream. The appealing repertoire is a fixed-price affair and reads like central London luxury with suburban prices - lunch offering fantastic value at this level. The wine list shows admirable pedigree, too, while its sister restaurant over in Blackheath is perhaps predictably called Chapter Two (see entry) and is well worth checking out.

ENFIELD
MAP 06 TQ39

◉ Royal Chace Hotel

Traditional British

Attractive hotel brasserie

☎ 020 8884 8181 The Ridgeway EN2 8AR
e-mail: reservations@royalchacehotel.co.uk
web: www.royal-chace.com

Not far from Enfield, the Royal Chace is set in 6 acres of grounds with woodland views just 3 miles from junction 24 of the M25. The refurbished public rooms are smartly appointed and the fine-dining option is the first-floor Chace Brasserie, a spacious restaurant with a warm colour scheme and great views of the surrounding countryside. Traditional English dishes, including scallops and steaks, are prepared from hand-picked ingredients and presented with imaginative flair. Less formal meals and snacks are served in the King's Bar and lounge.

Owners: R Nicholas **Times:** 7-10, Closed Xmas, BH Mon, Closed L Mon-Sat, D Sun **Prices:** Fixed D £25-£28, Starter £5-£8.95, Main £9.95-£18, Dessert £5, Service added but optional 10% **Wine:** 23 bottles over £20, 30 bottles under £20, 6 by the glass **Notes:** Dress Restrictions, No jeans or trainers, Civ Wed 220, Air con **Seats:** 120, Pr/dining room 50
Children: Menu, Portions **Rooms:** 92 (92 en suite) ★★★ HL
Directions: 3m from M25 junct 24, 1.5m to Enfield **Parking:** 220

HADLEY WOOD
MAP 06 TQ29

◉◉ West Lodge Park Hotel, The Cedar Restaurant

Modern British

Solid cooking in a splendid hotel

☎ 020 8216 3900 Cockfosters Rd EN4 0PY
e-mail: westlodgepark@bealeshotels.co.uk
web: www.bealeshotel.co.uk

Located just inside the M25, this stunning country house was converted into a hotel in 1921 and is now decorated with a luxurious balance of modern and traditional themes. There are 35 acres of magnificent grounds, including an arboretum, to explore. The Cedar Restaurant is fairly traditional both in its formal style of service and in the cuisine, which looks to British classics for inspiration, with contemporary flourishes adding zest. You might start with foie gras terrine served with red onion marmalade, then continue with steamed brill with tomato risotto and spinach pâté. Quirky dishes such as iced peanut butter parfait with raspberry jelly for dessert really liven things up.

Chef: Wayne Turner **Owners:** Beales Ltd **Times:** 12.30-2/7-10, Closed L Sat **Prices:** Fixed L £15, Fixed D £25, Starter £6.50-£10.50, Main £17.50-£24.50, Dessert £7.50, Service optional **Wine:** 51 bottles over £20, 24 bottles under £20, 7 by the glass **Notes:** Dress Restrictions, Smart casual, Jacket & tie recommended, Civ Wed 72, Air con **Seats:** 70, Pr/dining room 54 **Children:** Portions **Rooms:** 59 (59 en suite) ★★★★ HL **Directions:** On the A111, 1m S of M25 junct 24 **Parking:** 75

HARROW ON THE HILL

See LONDON SECTION Plan 1-B5

◉ Incanto

Italian NEW

Stylish, relaxed modern Italian restaurant with deli and café

☎ 020 8426 6767 HA1 3HT
e-mail: info@incanto.co.uk
web: www.incanto.co.uk

Originally the old post office, this stylish Italian sits at the heart of Harrow on the Hill, opposite the village green. Clean modern lines grace the long dining room, decked out with wooden floors, banquette seating and upholstered chairs, polished-wood tables, ivory-cream walls hung with modern art and a beautiful crystal chandelier. Original features include a full-length conservatory-style glass roof and sweeping spiral staircase. The simple, authentic Italian cooking takes a modern approach too, utilising fresh, seasonal produce with some items imported directly from Italy. Expect oven-baked halibut wrapped in a potato crust with a red wine and balsamic reduction, or dark chocolate tartlet with espresso sauce and mascarpone to finish.

Chef: Franco Montone **Owners:** David Taylor & Catherine Chiu
Times: 12-2.30/6.30-11, Closed 26 Dec, 1 Jan, Mon, Closed D Sun
Prices: Starter £4.25-£7.20, Main £12.95-£16.50, Dessert £4.50-£5.95, Service added but optional 10% **Wine:** 12 bottles over £20, 11 bottles under £20, 4 by the glass **Notes:** Sun L £14.95 inc glass of house wine, Tasting menu available, Air con **Seats:** 64, Pr/dining room 30
Children: Menu, Portions

HARROW WEALD

See LONDON SECTION Plan 1-B6

◉ Grim's Dyke Hotel

Modern European NEW

Country-house hotel peacefully close to London

☎ 020 8385 3100 Old Redding HA3 6SH
e-mail: enquiries@grimsdyke.com
web: www.grimsdyke.com

The metropolis seems a long way from this quintessential country-house hotel set in wonderful grounds. Once home to the Gilbert half of Gilbert and Sullivan, it is filled with memorabilia from their productions. The traditional dining room - accessed separately from the main hotel - comes with a sumptuous décor to match the ambience and offers views over the gardens. Its good-value set menu and carte take a modern approach using quality ingredients and good cooking skill, plus the kitchen garden's yield; take Scottish Highland venison served with spiced pear and fennel and chocolate oil.

Chef: Daren Mason **Owners:** Sheriffs of Nottingham Holdings
Times: 12.30-2/7-9.30, Closed L Sat **Prices:** Fixed L £14.95-£16.95, Fixed D £22-£23, Starter £6.50-£9.50, Main £15-£26.50, Dessert £5.50, Service optional **Wine:** 69 bottles over £20, 22 bottles under £20, 10 by the glass **Notes:** Dress Restrictions, No jeans or trainers (Fri-Sat), Civ Wed 90 **Seats:** 45, Pr/dining room 40 **Children:** Menu, Portions **Rooms:** 46 (46 en suite) ★★★ HL **Directions:** 3m from M1 between Harrow and Watford **Parking:** 100

HEATHROW AIRPORT
See LONDON SECTION   Plan 1-A3

◉ Sheraton Skyline Hotel & Conference Centre

Italian NEW 🖥

Modern Italian cooking in a stylish hotel restaurant

☎ 020 8759 2535 Bath Rd UB3 5BP
e-mail: res268_skyline@sheraton.com
web: www.sheraton.com/skyline

The Al Dente Ristorante is the principal restaurant at this luxury hotel. The interior is spacious and open with warm-coloured décor, rustic place mats and authentic Italian touches, like Parma ham on the bone and a wheel of parmesan, served as appetisers. Modern Italian cuisine is the order of the day, the innovative menu offering new interpretations of classical dishes. Seared blue fin tuna with saffron risotto and ricola salad is a great example of a main course. Desserts include a dish comprising three versions of tiramisù - strawberry, ice cream and classic.

Chef: Marco di Tullio **Owners:** Starwood Hotels and Resorts **Times:** 12-3/6-10.45 **Prices:** Fixed L £20-£40, Fixed D £35-£65, Starter £6-£11, Main £18-£25, Dessert £6-£8, Service optional **Wine:** 30+ bottles over £20, 15 by the glass **Notes:** Vegetarian available, Civ Wed 300, Air con **Seats:** 80, Pr/dining room 10 **Children:** Menu **Rooms:** 350 (350 en suite) ★★★★ HL **Parking:** 300

KEW
See LONDON SECTION   Plan 1-C3

◉◉◉ The Glasshouse

see below

KINGSTON UPON THAMES
See LONDON SECTION   Plan 1-C1

◉ *Ayudhya Thai Restaurant*

Thai

Authentic, neighbourhood Thai in the heart of suburbia

☎ 020 8546 5878 0208 5495984 14 Kingston Hill KT2 7NH

Set unassumingly in a small parade of shops, this charmingly authentic, long-established Thai transports you to another world with its pitched roof lines and traditional, darkwood-panelled interior. Wood carvings, original artefacts and Thai royal family pictures continue the illusion, complemented by oriental music and authentically costumed staff. The extremely extensive menu offers nearly 100 dishes including desserts, so be prepared to spend some time making your choice. Try gai phat bai kaprow (chicken with chilli and Thai speciality holy basil leaves). Order by dish number unless your Thai language skills are up to scratch.

Times: 12-2.30/6.30-11, Closed Xmas, BHs, Closed L Mon
Directions: 0.5m from Kingston town centre on A308, and 2.5m from Robin Hood rdbt at junction of A3

◉◉◉

The Glasshouse

KEW
See LONDON SECTION   Plan 1-C3

Modern European 🍷 NOTABLE WINE LIST 🖥

Local favourite with sophisticated cooking

☎ 020 8940 6777 14 Station Rd TW9 3PZ
e-mail: info@glasshouserestaurant.co.uk
web: www.glasshouserestaurant.co.uk

This sophisticated, smart and buzzy local restaurant - set in a parade of Kew Village shops close to Kew Bridge tube station - is a class act and sister to the venerable Wandsworth restaurant Chez Bruce (see entry). Glass-fronted in keeping with its name (and probably inspired by its neighbour, the Royal Botanic Gardens), its sleek, contemporary décor has a light-and-airy appeal, drawing a loyal crowd of devotees with its vibrant atmosphere and bustling mix of diners. An eclectic mix of furniture, antiques, cushions and drapes blends with well-spaced tables and the appropriately relaxed and friendly yet professional service. The precision cooking is impressive, too, taking an unfussy modern and seasonal approach, distinguished by a light touch and clean, clear flavours. Think rump of veal with calf's sweetbreads, salsify, broad beans and crispy trompettes, or perhaps poached sea bream with scallops, crab, lettuce and samphire, and to finish, a warm ginger cake with banana and pecan ice cream and sauce anglaise. The appealing menu repertoire comes at fixed prices (and includes a seven-course tasting option), while the wine list is a notable affair, with many available by the glass.

Chef: Anthony Boyd **Owners:** Larkbrace Ltd **Times:** 12-2.30/7-10.30, Closed Xmas, New Year **Prices:** Fixed L £18.50-£24.50, Fixed D £35, Service added but optional 12.5% **Wine:** 376 bottles over £20, 5 bottles under £20, 13 by the glass **Notes:** Tasting menu available Mon-Fri £55, Air con **Seats:** 60 **Children:** Menu, Portions **Directions:** Telephone for directions **Parking:** On street; metered

KINGSTON UPON THAMES Continued

Carluccio's Caffè

☎ 020 8549 5898 Charter Quay KT1 1HT

Quality Italian chain.

Frère Jacques

☎ 020 8546 1332 10-12 Riverside Walk, Bishops Hall KT1 1QN

web: www.frerejacques.co.uk

Simple French fare in a relaxed riverside bistro.

🖳 Strada

☎ 020 8974 8555 1 The Griffin Centre, Market Place KT1 1JT

web: www.theaa.com/travel/index.jsp

One of the newest additions to this perennially popular chain of modern Italian restaurants, occupying two floors of a grand listed building near the Thames.

Wagamama

☎ 020 8546 1117 16-18 High St KT1 1EY

Informal noodle bar with no booking required.

PINNER
See LONDON SECTION Plan 1-B5

◉ Friends Restaurant

Modern British

Tudor property offering suburban brasserie dining

☎ 020 8866 0286 11 High St HA5 5PJ

e-mail: info@friendsrestaurant.co.uk

web: www.friendsrestaurant.co.uk

This high-street restaurant with its black-and-white timber frontage entices impulse diners into the comfortably appointed, two-floor interior. The chef proprietor has been here for 15 years and has a wealth of experience from his early years at the Savoy and the Connaught. Smartly dressed staff move between the leather-clad seating and equally smartly dressed tables dispensing classic dishes, often with a lighter finish. Start with soft poached egg on champ with smoked haddock and gruyère, followed by a more robust jugged hare. A favourite finish is orange bread-and-butter pudding.

Friends Restaurant

Chef: Terry Farr **Owners:** Mr Farr **Times:** 12-3/6.30-10.30, Closed 25 Dec, BHs, Mon in summer, Closed D Sun **Prices:** Fixed L £16-£18, Fixed D £29.50-£30, Starter £6-£10, Main £16-£30, Dessert £6-£8, Service added but optional 10% **Notes:** Vegetarian available, Air con **Seats:** 40 **Children:** Portions **Directions:** In centre of Pinner, 2 mins walk from underground station **Parking:** Nearby car parks x3

RICHMOND UPON THAMES
See LONDON SECTION Plan 1 C2

◉ Bingham Hotel, Restaurant & Bar

Modern British 🖳

Romantic Thames-side dining

☎ 020 8940 0902 61-63 Petersham Rd TW10 6UT

e-mail: reservations@thebingham.co.uk

web: www.thebingham.co.uk

Enjoying a wonderful riverside location, this Georgian townhouse now houses a boutique hotel and its romantic riverside restaurant. Classic contemporary chic décor, glass droplet lighting and art deco mirrors provide a sophisticated atmosphere. For summer evenings, there are balcony tables. Simple, attractively-presented modern British dishes use lots of local ingredients such as buttered medallions of Cornish monkfish, and main courses of cannon of lamb from Dales Farm (Henley-on-Thames) or tenderloin of pork from Mount Gale Farm (Yorkshire) with apple chutney and warm bean salad. Vegetarians might like to order the likes of Ragstone goat's cheese and pumpkin tart. Excellent table service.

Times: 12.30-4/7-10, Closed 26 Dec-early Jan, Closed D Sun **Seats:** 40 **Rooms:** 15 (15 en suite) ★★★ HL **Directions:** Please telephone for directions

⊛ La Buvette

French

Stylish traditional French bistro

☎ 020 8940 6264 6 Church Walk TW9 1SN
e-mail: info@brula.com
web: www.brula.co.uk

Sister restaurant to Brula in Twickenham (see entry), this is a unique property, built in York stone within an old church refectory. The beautiful courtyard seats 40 in summer and is protected from the elements by brick walls, a canopied entrance and an enormous umbrella. The classical French bistrot-style menu features the likes of fish soup with rouille or foie gras with pear chutney as starters, while mains might include beef fillet with celeriac purée, confit garlic and green peppercorn sauce, with petit pot au chocolat to finish. The formula is popular with discerning locals who return to savour the taste of France.

Chef: Buck Carter **Owners:** Lawrence Hartley & Bruce Duckett **Times:** 12-3/6-11, Closed 25-26 Dec, 1 Jan, Good Fri **Prices:** Fixed L £12, Starter £4.50-£9.50, Main £10-£21, Dessert £4.50-£5.25, Service added but optional 12.5% **Wine:** 15 bottles over £20, 6 bottles under £20, 10 by the glass **Notes:** Sun L 3 courses £15.75, Vegetarian available **Seats:** 50 **Children:** Menu, Portions **Directions:** 3 mins from train station, opposite St Mary Magdalene church

⊛ Ma Cuisine Le Petit Bistrot

French

Rustic French cooking in an atmospheric neighbourhood-style bistro

☎ 020 8332 1923 The Old Post Office,
9 Station Approach, Kew TW9 3QB
e-mail: info@macuisinekew.co.uk
web: www.macuisinekew.co.uk

Sister restaurant to the Twickenham eatery of the same name, Ma Cuisine is set in a bank of shops next to Kew station, not far from the famous gardens. Checked tablecloths, posters and a black-and-white tiled floor give it a French bistro feel, while a large picture window lets in plenty of light. The lunch menu is good value and teams a short range of formal choices with sandwich and breakfast selections, but dinner is the main event. Expect unfussy classic French dishes driven by quality ingredients, like fillet steak au poivre with pomme dauphinoise, or perhaps John Dory Mediterranean - served with provençale vegetables, chorizo and tomato.

Chef: Tim Francis **Owners:** John McClements/Dominique Sejourne **Times:** 12-2.30/6.30-11 **Prices:** Fixed L £13-£16, Starter £4.95-£7, Main £12-£15.50, Dessert £4-£4.50, Service added but optional 10% **Wine:** 12 bottles over £20, 18 bottles under £20, 8 by the glass **Notes:** Vegetarian available **Seats:** 45 **Children:** Menu, Portions **Directions:** From Kew Garden Station follow signs to Royal Botanical Gardens. At fork in road keep to the right. Restaurant is 50 mtrs on right **Parking:** On street

⊛⊛ Restaurant at The Petersham

Modern British

Sophisticated dining and breathtaking Thames views

☎ 020 8940 7471 The Petersham, Nightingale Ln
TW10 6UZ
e-mail: enq@petershamhotel.co.uk
web: www.petershamhotel.co.uk

Perched on affluent Richmond Hill, this elegant hotel offers magnificent views over a curving stretch of the Thames. The restaurant matches the classic-meets-contemporary style, with walnut panelling, mirrors and well-spaced tables, while the bright room's full-length windows make the best of those river views - and the planes making their way into nearby Heathrow. A modern British approach, underpinned by French influences and plenty of luxury, graces the appealing, sensibly compact and clearly constructed carte. The sophisticated, accomplished cooking shows a commitment to high-quality produce, and perfectly suits the setting and ambience. Take steamed fillet of halibut served with crab ravioli and white beans with horseradish and soft herbs, or perhaps pot-roasted venison loin with chestnut rissole, braised red cabbage and a bitter chocolate sauce.

Chef: Alex Bentley **Owners:** The Petersham Hotel Ltd **Times:** 12.15-2.15/7-9.45, Closed 25-26 Dec, 1 Jan, Closed D 24 Dec **Prices:** Fixed L £18.50, Starter £8-£12.50, Main £13-£26.50, Dessert £6.50, Service added but optional 10% **Notes:** Dress Restrictions, Smart casual, Civ Wed 40, Air con **Seats:** 70, Pr/dining room 26 **Children:** Menu, Portions **Rooms:** 60 (60 en suite) ★★★★ HL **Directions:** Telephone for directions **Parking:** 60

⊛⊛ Richmond Gate Hotel

Traditional, International

Elegant restaurant in a prestigious hotel

☎ 020 8940 0061 Richmond Hill TW10 6RP
e-mail: richmondgate@foliohotels.com
web: www.foliohotels.com/richmondgate

This elegant 18th-century property is, as its name suggests, situated at the top of Richmond Hill at the gates of the royal park with views over the Thames Valley. The intimate Gates on the Park Restaurant mixes an air of Georgian formality with contemporary style, while the service is epitomised by a relaxed attentiveness. The menu is characterised by modern interpretations of classically-based ideas and the kitchen makes sound use of quality ingredients in unpretentious though not unadventurous dishes that deliver satisfying, clear flavours. Try a starter of pan-roasted scallops on caramelised cauliflower purée and caper dressing, followed by roasted mallard duck with lemon thyme chicory and winter fruit sauce.

Chef: Nenad Bibic **Owners:** Folio Hotels **Times:** 12.30-2/7-9.30, Closed L Sat, BHs **Prices:** Fixed L £15.95-£22.50, Fixed D £28, Starter £5.50-£12.50, Main £12.50-£32, Dessert £5-£7.50, Service optional, Group min 6 service 10% **Wine:** 37 bottles over £20, 17 bottles under £20, 8 by the glass **Notes:** Civ Wed 70, Air con **Seats:** 30, Pr/dining room 70 **Children:** Menu, Portions **Rooms:** 68 (68 en suite) ★★★★ HL **Directions:** At top of Richmond Hill, opposite Star and Garter, just opposite Richmond Park **Parking:** 50

ENGLAND

RICHMOND UPON THAMES CONTINUED

⊛ Richmond Hill Hotel

Modern European NEW 🖳

Sophisticated setting for accomplished cuisine

☎ 020 8939 0265 144-150 Richmond Hill TW10 6RW
e-mail: restaurant.richmondhill@foliohotels.com
web: www.pembrokesrestaurant.com

Conveniently situated for Twickenham Rugby Ground, you might be lucky enough to see some of the teams in residence here. An impressive refurbishment has transformed the restaurant and bar with stylish, contemporary décor. Floors and tables are in dark wood, set off by large-shaded lamps and smart table appointments. The small carte changes seasonally and is supplemented by additional snacks and lighter choices. Cooking is accomplished with tried-and-tested dishes like a main course of braised lamb shank, served with white bean blanquette and truffle mash.

Chef: Mickey Athwain **Times:** 10.30am/10.30pm **Prices:** Fixed L £18-£19.50, Starter £4.95-£6.95, Main £13.50-£19.50, Dessert £4.25, Service added but optional 10% **Notes:** Fixed L 3 courses, Vegetarian available, Dress Restrictions, Smart casual, Civ Wed 80 **Seats:** 85, Pr/dining room 30 **Children:** Menu, Portions **Rooms:** 138 (138 en suite) ★★★★ HL **Directions:** 1m town centre **Parking:** 150

Chez Lindsay

☎ 020 8948 7473 11 Hill Rise TW10 6UQ
Popular neighbourhood restaurant known for its crêpes.

Strada

☎ 020 8940 3141 26 Hill St TW1 1TW

Superior pizza from quality ingredients cooked in wood-fired ovens.

RUISLIP

See LONDON SECTION Plan 1-A5

⊛⊛ Hawtrey's Restaurant at the Barn Hotel

Modern French 🖳

Imaginative, sophisticated cuisine in a smart hotel

☎ 01895 636057 & 679999 The Barn Hotel,
West End Rd HA4 6JB
e-mail: info@thebarnhotel.co.uk
web: www.thebarnhotel.co.uk

In recent years this former farm, set in 3 acres of grounds, has expanded to include a whole complex of buildings with the restaurant styled as a Jacobean baronial hall, complete with tasteful mahogany panelling, chandeliers and gilt-framed oil paintings. Skilful cooking and attention to detail characterise the modern French menu with the five-course prestige tasting menu undoubtedly being the best way to sample the talents of this Gordon Ramsay alumnus. Begin with ravioli of Scottish lobster and salmon poached in a lobster bisque with lemongrass and ginger velouté, then proceed with a fillet of sea bream served with truffle mousseline, roasted crônes, artichoke and wild mushrooms in a civet sauce, or meat-eaters might go for roast beef choucroute with caramelised pancetta and truffle and Madeira sauce.

Chef: Jean Luc Sainlo **Owners:** Pantheon Hotels & Leisure **Times:** 12-2.30/7-10.30, Closed L Sat, D Sun **Prices:** Fixed L £16.50, Fixed D £29-£42.50, Service added but optional 10% **Wine:** 68 bottles over £20, 52 bottles under £20, 9 by the glass **Notes:** Tasting menu £49.50, Vegetarian available, Dress Restrictions, Smart casual, Civ Wed 74, Air con **Seats:** 44, Pr/dining room 20 **Children:** Menu, Portions **Rooms:** 59 (59 en suite) ★★★ HL **Directions:** From M40/A40 - exit at Polish War Memorial junct and follow A4180 towards Ruislip. After 2m turn right at mini rdbt into hotel entrance **Parking:** 50

SURBITON

See LONDON SECTION Plan 1-C1

⊛ The French Table

French 🖳

Modern cuisine in warm, friendly local restaurant

☎ 020 8399 2365 85 Maple Rd KT6 4AW
web: www.thefrenchtable.co.uk

As you would expect from the name, this pretty-looking restaurant with stained-glass windows does a nice trade in Gallic cuisine and is deservedly popular with locals. Interiors are bold, with slate-tiled floor, banquette seating or simple wooden chairs, and modern art adorning the plum-coloured walls. The enjoyable, good-value and creative French/Mediterranean cooking hits just the right note, too, focusing on using fresh seasonal produce. The monthly-changing menu might feature Puy lentil velouté with chorizo and apple ravioli to start or a main of baked cod with boulangère potatoes and a wild mushroom and thyme jus.

Chef: Eric Guignard **Owners:** Eric & Sarah Guignard **Times:** 12-2.30/7-10.30, Closed 25-26 Dec, 10 days Jan, Mon, Closed D Sun **Prices:** Fixed L £16.50, Starter £5.80-£9.80, Main £10.50-£16.80, Dessert £5.50-£7, Service added but optional 12.5% **Wine:** 50 bottles over £20, 11 bottles under £20, 9 by the glass **Notes:** Sun L 3 courses £22.50, Dress Restrictions, Smart casual, Air con **Seats:** 48 **Children:** Portions **Directions:** 5 min walk from Surbiton station, 1m from Kingston **Parking:** On street

TWICKENHAM
See LONDON SECTION   Plan 1-C2

◎◎ La Brasserie Mcclements

French
Brasserie classics in suburban Twickenham

☎ 020 8744 9598   2 Whitton Rd TW1 1BJ
e-mail: info@labrasserietw1.co.uk
web: www.lebrasserietw1.co.uk

A discreetly located establishment in a modest parade of shops, this brasserie maintains its reputation for good French food. The interior is simply presented with dark polished tables set on plain wooden floorboards, though the fully stocked cheese table catches the eye. Choose between the carte or seven-course menu dégustation - with helpful staff on hand to assist. Simple dishes, carefully prepared and well executed, include grilled scallops with chicory tarte Tatin to start, or a mousseline of lobster with shellfish jus. Mains take in turbot with scallops, noodles and chickpea purée, or fresh truffle and cep mushroom risotto. Finish with a classic crème brûlée or chocolate fondant with pistachio ice cream, or why not choose from those appealing cheeses.

Chef: John McClements **Owners:** John McClements/Dominique Sejourne
Times: 12-2.30/7-11, Closed Sun **Prices:** Fixed L £25, Starter £8.50-£9.50, Main £18-£20, Dessert £6-£8.50, Service added but optional 10%
Wine: 30 bottles over £20, 20 bottles under £20, 12 by the glass
Notes: Tasting menu £55, Air con **Seats:** 40 **Children:** Min 9 yrs
Directions: Close to Twickenham station **Parking:** On street/train station

◎ Brula

French
Traditional French bistrot in deepest Twickenham

☎ 020 8892 0602   43 Crown Rd TW1 3EJ
e-mail: info@brula.co.uk
web: www.brula.co.uk

This Victorian former shop became a neighbourhood bistro in the 1970s, although the parquet floor, canopied entrance and stained glass retain a 1920s feel. *Poirot* has been filmed here to strengthen its jazz age credentials. Polite staff deliver keenly-priced French regional dishes to eager diners seated at plain wooden tables. Grandmère would have approved of starters such as salmon terrine with tartare sauce or salad of poached chicken, leeks and aïoli and delightfully simple main courses like steak frites with garlic butter or roast brill with spinach and hollandaise sauce.

Chef: Toby Williams **Owners:** Lawrence Hartley, Bruce Duckett
Times: 12-3/6-10.30, Closed Xmas, 1 Jan, Aug **Prices:** Fixed L £11.50, Starter £4.50-£10, Main £10-£23, Dessert £4.75-£5.50, Service optional
Notes: Sun L 3 courses £15.75, Vegetarian available **Seats:** 40, Pr/dining room 21 **Children:** Menu, Portions **Directions:** Join A305, go straight at lights over the A3004, turn left onto Baronsfield Rd. Restaurant is at the end of T-junct, immediately on the right **Parking:** On street & parking meters

◎ Ma Cuisine Le Petit Bistrot

French
French bistro cuisine

☎ 020 8607 9849   6 Whitton Rd TW1 1BJ
e-mail: info@macuisinetw1.co.uk
web: www.macuisinetw1.co.uk

Very much in the French bistro tradition, with its trademark checked tableclothes, black-and-white tiled floors and posters on the walls, the restaurant is part of a growing group in the area. The food is reassuringly simple - classical French served with style and attention to detail. A real flavour-packed starter is terrine de campagne, made with pork, rough textured and perfectly seasoned, served with properly dressed leaves. Follow with salmon fillet complemented by a light Pernod beurre blanc, and maybe finish with a classic crème brûlée of generous proportions, or chocolate pithivier served with a hot chocolate pastry parcel.

Chef: John McClements **Owners:** John McClements/Dominique Sejourne
Times: 12-2.30/6.30-11 **Prices:** Fixed L £13-£16, Starter £4.95-£7, Main £12-£15.50, Dessert £4-£4.50, Service added but optional 10% **Wine:** 12 bottles over £20, 18 bottles under £20, 8 by the glass **Notes:** Vegetarian available **Seats:** 70 **Children:** Menu, Portions **Directions:** 2 min walk from Twickenham station

💻 Loch Fyne Restaurant & Oyster Bar

☎ 020 8255 6222   175 Hampton Rd TW2 5NG
web: www.theaa.com/travel/index.jsp

Quality seafood chain.

UXBRIDGE   MAP 06 TQ08

💻 Masala

☎ 01895 252925   61 Belmont Rd UB8 1QT
web: www.theaa.com/travel/index.jsp

Dining here is more than an experience, it's an education. Learn first-hand about the different cooking styles of India's various regions.

WEST DRAYTON For restaurant details
See Heathrow Airport (London)

MERSEYSIDE

BIRKENHEAD   MAP 15 SJ38

◉◉◉ Fraiche

see below

FRANKBY   MAP 15 SJ28

◉◉ Hillbark

British, Continental NEW

Country-house setting for accomplished, elegant cuisine

☎ 0151 625 2400   Royden Park CH48 1NP
e-mail: enquiries@hillbarkhotel.co.uk
web: www.hillbarkhotel.co.uk

Who would ever have guessed that this Elizabethan-style mansion majestically set in its 250-acre woodland estate enjoying delightful views towards the River Dee and the hills of North Wales was originally built on Bidston Hill on the Wirral in 1891 and moved here brick by brick in 1931. Today's visitors are certainly none the wiser, but enjoy Hillbark's inviting lounges and choice of two restaurant concepts, though it's the Yellow Room where the real culinary action takes place. Rather formal in style, with its hushed tones and traditional table settings, and service friendly and attentive. The kitchen's modern approach comes underpinned by a classical French theme, delivering intelligently simple, accurate and well-presented dishes; take lobster served with a lobster beurre blanc, broad beans and herb gnocchi.

Rooms: 19 (19 en suite) ★★★★ HL

LIVERPOOL   MAP 15 SJ39

◉ Radisson SAS Hotel Liverpool - Filini

Italian, Sardinian

Stylish modern setting for authentic Italian cuisine

☎ 0151 966 1500   107 Old Hall St L3 9BD
e-mail: info.liverpool@radissonsas.com
web: www.radissonsas.com

Formerly St Paul's Eye Hospital, this smart new hotel has the city's largest suite, The River Suite, and boasts ocean- and urban-themed bedrooms. The restaurant here, named Filini, was created by restaurateur and commentator Roy Ackerman, and offers imaginative, accomplished modern Italian cuisine in stylish surroundings with panoramic views over the bustling River Mersey. Good use is made of the best local and Italian produce; think roasted halibut served with flageolet beans and tarragon, or perhaps ham ravioli accompanied by

---

◉◉◉

Fraiche

BIRKENHEAD   MAP 15 SJ38

Modern French V

Intimate and elaborate fine dining in Merseyside

☎ 0151 652 2914   11 Rose Mount CH43 5SG
e-mail: contact@restaurantfraiche.com
web: www.restaurantfraiche.com

Designed by chef-patron Marc Wilkinson himself and inspired by the views of the shore from his home, this intimate, modern and relaxing little restaurant (of some dozen or so tables) is well worth tracking down. With a new outside eating area in the same seaside theme, inside soft muted beiges in linen and suede create warmth and subtlety. There's a seating area at the front for aperitifs and striking original artwork on the walls, which all create a simple backdrop for the well-trained, friendly service and elaborate, highly skilled cooking. Expect the concise, crisply-scripted, sensibly compact repertoire of fixed-priced menus to excite and surprise the palate and senses, with plenty of twists of flavours, colour, texture and temperature.

The stimulating compositions feature tip-top produce, sourced locally or from the markets of France; a fillet of turbot could be paired with slow-cooked pork belly and herb-scented quinoa, or perhaps organic Cumbrian chicken with broad beans and peas and a light stock infused with morel and lemon balm, while 'textures of chocolate and

cherry' might head-up desserts. And for those dining alone, or the out-and-out foodie, there's a 'culinary box' brimful of the latest cookery books, articles, magazines, menus from great restaurants etc, to peruse.

Chef: Marc Wilkinson   **Owners:** Marc Wilkinson   **Times:** 12-1.30/7-9.30, Closed 25 Dec, 1 Jan, Sun-Mon, Closed L Tue-Thur   **Prices:** Fixed L £22-£24, Fixed D £38-£40, Service optional   **Wine:** 200 bottles over £20, 18 bottles under £20, 6 by the glass   **Notes:** Fixed L 3 courses, Tasting menu £48, ALC £36-£38, Vegetarian menu   **Seats:** 20, Pr/dining room 20   **Children:** Min 8 yrs, Portions   **Directions:** M53 junct 3 towards Prenton. Follow for 2m then take left towards Oxton, Fraiche on right   **Parking:** On street a creamy pea sauce, and to finish, tiramisù or pear zabaglione. The trendy White Bar provides an alternative eating option.

Chef: Chris Marshall **Owners:** Beetham Organisation Ltd **Times:** 12-2.30/6-10.30, Closed Sun **Prices:** Fixed L £10, Fixed D £25-£35, Starter £5.95-£8.50, Main £11.95-£17.95, Dessert £5.95, Service optional, Group min 10 service 10% **Wine:** 17 bottles over £20, 14 bottles under £20, 11 by the glass **Notes:** Fixed D 2 courses, Civ Wed 100, Air con **Seats:** 90, Pr/dining room 140 **Children:** Menu, Portions **Rooms:** 194 (194 en suite)
★★★★ HL **Directions:** Telephone for directions **Parking:** 25
see advert below

◉ Simply Heathcotes

Modern British

Modern eatery with extensive brasserie menu

☎ 0151 236 3536 Beetham Plaza, 25 The Strand L2 0XL
e-mail: liverpool@heathcotes.co.uk
web: www.heathcotes.co.uk

Paul Heathcote's culinary outposts market themselves as laid-back destinations for a quick lunch, classic Sunday roast, or lazy dinner on nights when even making a ready meal feels like hard work. The Liverpool branch is a contemporary concoction of granite, glass, cherry wood and Philippe Starck bucket chairs with a modern British menu to suit - think roast cutlet of lamb and navarin of mutton with haricot beans and rosemary, or roasted haddock fillet with celeriac purée, smoked bacon, baby onions, mushrooms and red wine. Ingredients are fresh and seasonal, and come courtesy of the local area wherever possible, and the result is accomplished brasserie fare that should keep you popping in for more. Children's menu available.

Chef: Steven Urquhart **Owners:** Heathcotes Restaurants **Times:** 12-2.30/6-10, Closed Xmas, BHs **Prices:** Fixed L £15, Fixed D £15, Starter £5.50, Main £15.50, Dessert £4.95, Service optional, Group min 8 service 10% **Notes:** Fixed D 2 courses, Sun L 2 courses £14.50, 3 courses £17, Vegetarian available, Air con **Seats:** 75, Pr/dining room 30 **Children:** Menu, Portions **Directions:** Opposite pier head, located on The Strand, near Princes Dock **Parking:** On street

◉ 60 Hope Street Restaurant

British V

Minimalist setting for smart modern dining

☎ 0151 707 6060 60 Hope St L1 9BZ
e-mail: info@60hopestreet.com
web: www.60hopestreet.com

At the heart of the creative quarter, 60 Hope Street is a Grade II listed building in an avenue between Liverpool's two cathedrals. The townhouse comprises the main restaurant, a basement bistro and a private dining room for special occasions. Simple interior design provides the ideal gallery space for regular art shows. The diverse menu with influences from around the world might include a starter of Garstang blue cheese and pear tart, followed by grilled fillet of Welsh black beef, and a signature dessert of deep-fried jam sandwich with Carnation milk ice cream.

60 Hope Street Restaurant

Chef: Sarah Kershaw **Owners:** Colin & Gary Manning **Times:** 12-2.30/6-10.30, Closed BHs, Sun, Closed L Sat **Prices:** Fixed L £13.95, Starter £6.95-£14.95, Main £10.50-£40, Dessert £5.95-£8.95, Service optional, Group min 8 service 10% **Wine:** 70 bottles over £20, 18 bottles under £20, 6 by the glass **Notes:** Vegetarian menu, Civ Wed 120, Air con **Seats:** 90, Pr/dining room 30 **Children:** Portions **Directions:** From M62 follow city-centre signs, then brown tourist signs for cathedral. Hope St near cathedral **Parking:** On street

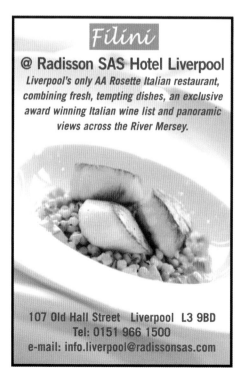

LIVERPOOL Continued

🖥 The Lower Place

☎ 0151 210 1955 Philharmonic Hall, Hope St L1 9BP
web: www.theaa.com/travel/index.jsp

Modern international cuisine in a relaxing atmosphere - all in the midst of the art deco splendour of the Philharmonic Hall. Early evenings are busy with the post-work, pre-concert crowd, then things slow down to a more relaxing pace.

SOUTHPORT   MAP 15 SD31

◉◉ Warehouse Brasserie

International

Chic destination sprinkled with global flavours

☎ 01704 544662 30 West St PR8 1QN
e-mail: info@warehousebrasserie.co.uk
web: www.warehousebrasserie.co.uk

This stylish, buzzy and eye-catching glass-and-chrome restaurant moulded from a former warehouse - complete with theatre kitchen and chefs on show - hits a contemporary note and draws a fashionable crowd of fun seekers and well-heeled business types. The cooking follows the modern theme, with a global repertoire of refreshingly unpretentious, well-presented dishes that might deliver crispy duck roll with mango and coriander salsa, or Thai spiced prawn risotto. Home-grown dishes like rump of Bowland lamb with Jerusalem artichoke purée and minted butter, and great fish and chips, find a place, too, as do well-presented desserts like chocolate jaffa tart. The fixed-price, Early Doors menu bolsters the crowd-pleasing carte.

Chef: Marc Verite, Darren Smith **Owners:** Paul Adams **Times:** 12-2.15/5.30-10.45, Closed 25-26 Dec, 1 Jan, Sun **Prices:** Fixed L £9-£29.90, Fixed D £14.40-£42.85, Starter £3.95-£9.95, Main £9.95-£18.95, Dessert £4.50-£13.95, Service optional, Group min 8 service 10% **Wine:** 57 bottles over £20, 15 bottles under £20, 5 by the glass **Seats:** 110, Pr/dining room 18 **Children:** Portions **Directions:** Telephone for directions **Parking:** NCP - Promenade

---

THORNTON HOUGH   MAP 15 SJ38

◉ The Italian Room Restaurant

Modern British

Sound British cooking at a charming country hotel

☎ 0151 336 3938 Thornton Hall Hotel, Neston Rd CH63 1JF
e-mail: reservations@thorntonhallhotel.com
web: www.thorntonhallhotel.com

The Italian Room at this Victorian former manor house is so named because of its magnificent Italian leather ceiling, hand-tooled and inlaid with mother of pearl. In all other respects it's a traditional country house-style restaurant, with crisp linen and sparkling tableware, overlooking the stunning gardens. Modern British cooking is produced from the freshest ingredients sourced from local suppliers. Try pressed goat's cheese, with aubergine caviar and basil crème fraîche, followed by braised shin of beef with carrot purée and buttery mash, or perhaps roast wild sea bass with parsnip purée, pain d'épice and apple.

Chef: Brian Heron **Owners:** The Thompson Family **Times:** 12-2/7-9.30, Closed 1 Jan, Closed L Sat **Prices:** Fixed L £12.50, Fixed D £29, Main £10-£20, Dessert £6, Service included **Wine:** 44 bottles over £20, 32 bottles under £20, 9 by the glass **Notes:** Sun D 3 courses £35 for 2 people incl bottle house wine, Vegetarian available, Dress Restrictions, Smart casual, no T-shirts or jeans, Civ Wed 400 **Seats:** 45, Pr/dining room 24 **Children:** Menu, Portions **Rooms:** 63 (63 en suite) ★★★★ HL **Directions:** M53 junct 4 onto B5151 & B5136 and follow brown tourist signs (approx 2.5m) to Thornton Hall Hotel **Parking:** 250

NORFOLK

ALBURGH   MAP 13 TM28

◉ The Dove Restaurant with Rooms

French, European

Family-run restaurant with a classic menu

☎ 01986 788315 Holbrook IP20 0EP
e-mail: thedovenorfolk@freeola.com

This former inn turned smart restaurant with rooms is run by a husband-and-wife team who pride themselves on making the most of fresh, quality local and home-grown ingredients, with dishes straightforward and not overworked in 'country French style'. You might start with a seafood chowder in a creamy Pernod sauce, move on to a baked fillet of Scottish salmon on a ratatouille of Mediterranean vegetables with garlic butter and a balsamic reduction, and finish up with white chocolate and coconut torte with rum syrup. Service is relaxed but professional, and there's a cosy lounge for pre- or post-dinner drinks and a terrace for alfresco dining.

Chef: Robert Oberhoffer **Owners:** Robert & Conny Oberhoffer **Times:** 12-2/7-9, Closed Mon-Tue, Closed L Wed-Sat, D Sun **Prices:** Fixed L £12.45-£14.40, Starter £4.95-£5.95, Main £12.95-£17.95, Dessert £4.95, Service optional **Wine:** 6 bottles over £20, 25 bottles under £20 **Notes:** Sun L 2 courses £12.45-£14.40, 3 courses £14.45-£16.40, Dress Restrictions, Smart casual **Seats:** 50 **Children:** Portions **Rooms:** 2 (1 en suite) ★★★★ RR **Directions:** On South Norfolk border between Harleston and Bungay, by A143, at junct of B1062 **Parking:** 20

ENGLAND

ATTLEBOROUGH MAP 13 TM09

◉ The Mulberry Tree

Modern International NEW

Trendy eatery with relaxed atmosphere and superb bedrooms

☎ 01953 452124 NR17 2AS
e-mail: relax@the-mulberry-tree.co.uk
web: www.the-mulberry-tree.co.uk

Former 'The Royal' pub on the main road into Attleborough, recently transformed into a new wave gastro-pub with rooms following extensive refurbishment. Expect a contemporary, brasserie feel with darkwood floors, chunky wooden tables, smart, high-backed wicker chairs and quality table settings. Service is relaxed, friendly and professional from smartly dressed staff. Cooking is competent modern and the sensibly short menu may list pan-fried sea bass with smoked fish bisque and gruyère potato cake, or roast duck breast with braised red cabbage and fondant potato for a main course. Puddings may take in a rich chocolate panettone with caramel sauce.

Chef: Haydn Buxton **Owners:** Philip & Victoria Milligan **Times:** 12-2/6.30-9, Closed 25-26 Dec, Closed D Sun **Prices:** Starter £4.95-£7.95, Main £10.95-£19.95, Dessert £5.95, Service optional **Wine:** 6 bottles over £20, 19 bottles under £20, 7 by the glass **Seats:** 50 **Children:** Portions **Directions:** Turn off A11 to Attleborough town centre. Continue around the one-way system, restaurant is on corner of Station Rd **Parking:** 25

BARNHAM BROOM MAP 13 TG00

◉◉ Flints Restaurant

Modern British, European NEW

Country-club hotel with traditional-style restaurant and creative cooking

☎ 01603 759393 & 759522 Barnham Broom Hotel, Golf & Country Club, Honingham Rd NR9 4DD
e-mail: enquiry@barnhambroomhotel.co.uk
web: www.barnham-broom.co.uk

As the name suggests, this hotel and country club is predictably set amid landscaped grounds and features a golf course and leisure facilities. Flints, the main restaurant, is where the fine-dining action takes place. Traditionally styled, it features white walls that form arches and individual seating areas, while a wall of glass windows looks out on to the golf-course action. Tables come laid with crisp white linen and staff are equally well turned out, while the kitchen deals in quality produce and some assured and creative cooking. Take roast rump of local Shropham lamb with champ mash, tomato fondue and a garlic-scented jus, while a Sweet Shop dessert assiette provides a clever take on those long-gone penny sweets.

Chef: Shane Lloyd **Owners:** Barnham Broom Hotel **Times:** 12-3/7-9.30 **Prices:** Fixed L £14.50, Fixed D £27.50, Starter £7.50-£8.50, Main £15.95-£19.95, Dessert £6.50-£9.95, Service optional **Wine:** 14 bottles over £20, 16 bottles under £20, 9 by the glass **Notes:** Dress Restrictions, Smart casual, no jeans or trainers, Civ Wed 120 **Children:** Menu, Portions **Rooms:** 52 (52 en suite) ★★★ HL **Directions:** A47 towards Swaffham, turn left onto Honingham Rd, hotel 1m on left **Parking:** 500

BLAKENEY MAP 13 TG04

◉ The Blakeney Hotel

Traditional British

Quayside hotel with a wide-ranging menu

☎ 01263 740797 The Quay NR25 7NE
e-mail: reception@blakeney-hotel.co.uk
web: www.blakeney-hotel.co.uk

Situated on the quayside, this attractive brick-and-flint hotel offers panoramic views across the estuary and salt marshes to Blakeney Point. It has two comfortable lounges for pre-dinner drinks, one with a log fire for the winter months and the other a sun room that makes the most of the beauty of the north Norfolk coast. The elegant restaurant offers a lengthy menu firmly rooted in British cuisine, and features old favourites (home-made local fish pie topped with mashed potato and cheese), as well as more sophisticated fare such as a marinated saddle of venison with fondant potato, spiced plum compôte and port sauce.

Chef: Martin Sewell **Owners:** Michael Stannard **Times:** 12-2/6.30-8.45, Closed 24-27 Dec, Closed D 31 Dec **Prices:** Fixed L £11-£16, Fixed D £25-£34.50, Service optional **Wine:** 28 bottles over £20, 25 bottles under £20, 7 by the glass **Notes:** Dress Restrictions, Smart casual for D **Seats:** 100, Pr/dining room 100 **Children:** Min 8 yrs D, Portions **Rooms:** 64 (64 en suite) ★★★ HL **Directions:** From the A148 between Fakenham and Holt, take the B1156 to Langham & Blakeney **Parking:** 60

◉ The Moorings

Modern British

Small, relaxed predominantly fish-based bistro

☎ 01263 740054 01328 878938 High St NR25 7NA
e-mail: reservations@blakeney-moorings.co.uk
web: www.blakeney-moorings.co.uk

Aptly named, relaxed, seaside-style bistro, situated on a busy side road adjacent to the quayside. Yellow walls, oiled wooden boards, closely-packed clothed tables and relaxed service all hit the mark. Unsurprisingly, the menu comes awash with the fruits of the sea, with fish (much of it sourced locally) dominating the fixed-price menu. Cooking is straightforward and accurate, with simple dishes and presentation that don't stint on flavour. Think grilled halibut fillet with wilted spinach and a rich fennel purée, or perhaps roast local partridge with honey and thyme roasted root vegetables and a port jus. Homely puddings, like treacle sponge and custard, provide the finish.

Chef: Richard & Angela Long **Owners:** Richard & Angela Long **Times:** 10.30-5/7-9.30, Closed 2 wks Jan, Mon-Thu (Nov-Mar), Closed D Sun **Prices:** Starter £4.75-£7.95, Main £10.95-£17.50, Dessert £4.50, Service optional **Wine:** 8 bottles over £20, 18 bottles under £20, 7 by the glass **Notes:** Sun L 2 courses £10.95, 3 courses £13.95, Air con **Seats:** 50 **Children:** Menu, Portions **Directions:** Off A149 where High St runs N to the quay **Parking:** On street, car park 50mtrs

◉◉◉ Morston Hall

see page 394

◎◎◎

Morston Hall

BLAKENEY   MAP 13 TG04

Modern British, French ▮NOTABLE WINE LIST V

Inspired cooking in small country house

☎ 01263 741041 Morston, Holt NR25 7AA
e-mail: reception@morstonhall.com
web: www.morstonhall.com

Tucked away on the north Norfolk coast - just across the road from the sea - this small, flint-and-brick Jacobean country-house hotel is set in attractive gardens and offers a tasting menu repertoire that will delight at every course. Morston's not just well known for its chef-patron, Galton Blackiston, it's something of a food lover's paradise, too, with a whole range of cookery demonstrations, courses and wine tastings on offer. Inviting lounges - with roaring log fire on winter days - lead through to the airy, elegant restaurant, resplendent with its bright new conservatory.

Galton's inspired cooking suits the surroundings and is delivered via a daily-changing six-course tasting dinner menu (with a choice at dessert) that includes some classics alongside new ideas. The style aims for skilful and intelligent simplicity, with the focus on fresh, high-quality local seasonal produce and clean, clear flavours. Think diver-caught scallops with oxtail and celeriac, or a cannon of young lamb with spring vegetables and wild garlic, and perhaps a warm chocolate

fondant with chocolate chip ice cream or warm panettone bread-and-butter pudding with real custard to finish. Lovely home-made rolls and petits fours add to the class act.

Chef: Galton Blackiston **Owners:** T & G Blackiston **Times:** 12.30/7.30, Closed 2 wks Jan, Closed L Mon-Sat (ex party booking) **Prices:** Fixed L £32-£34, Fixed D £46-£48, Service optional **Wine:** 160 bottles over £20, 8 bottles under £20, 15 by the glass **Notes:** Fixed L 3 courses, Fixed D 4 courses, coffee incl, Vegetarian menu, Dress Restrictions, Smart casual, no jeans or trainers **Seats:** 35, Pr/dining room 20 **Children:** Menu, Portions **Rooms:** 13 (13 en suite)★★★ HL **Directions:** On A149 coast road **Parking:** 40

BRANCASTER STAITHE   MAP 13 TF74

◎◎ The White Horse

Modern, Traditional British ▮NOTABLE WINE LIST 🌶

Seafood beside the tidal marsh

☎ 01485 210262 PE31 8BY
e-mail: reception@whitehorsebrancaster.co.uk
web: www.whitehorsebrancaster.co.uk

Its location on the edge of the tidal marshes could not be improved, and the views from the conservatory restaurant with adjoining dining area and decked terrace are truly memorable. Tourists and locals alike flock here throughout the year, and relax in informal comfort. If you want a window seat, it would be wise to book very early. Locally-sourced fish and shellfish are the lure here, and their simple handling allows the impeccably fresh flavours full expression - pan-fried sea bass with minted pea purée and a white wine butter sauce, for example. The menus change frequently to take maximum advantage of what's available, and that always includes meat - perhaps slow-braised navarin of English lamb with glazed root vegetables and a thyme jus - as well as seafood.

Chef: Nicholas Parker **Owners:** Cliff Nye **Times:** 12-2/6.30-9 **Prices:** Starter £4.25-£7.25, Main £9.95-£17, Dessert £3.95-£4.95, Service optional **Wine:** 23 bottles over £20, 31 bottles under £20, 12 by the glass **Notes:** Vegetarian available **Seats:** 100 **Children:** Menu, Portions **Rooms:** 15 (15 en suite) ★★★ HL **Directions:** On A149 coast road, midway between Hunstanton & Wells-next-the-Sea **Parking:** 85

BRUNDALL   MAP 13 TG30

◎◎ The Lavender House

Modern British V

Quintessentially English thatched cottage offering a gourmet experience

☎ 01603 712215 39 The Street NR13 5AA
web: www.thelavenderhouse.co.uk

This thatched cottage with heavy oak beams dates from around 1540. Sympathetically restored and extended, it now offers a light modern interior. There are comfortable sofas in the bar and high-backed wicker dining chairs and crisp white table settings in the restaurant areas. The modern British cooking takes advantage of products from artisan local suppliers. An appetiser to start and taster dishes between courses give you a chance to try an enormous selection of wonderful delicacies. Starters like sea-salt grilled mackerel with blinis, tomato, broad bean and olive might be followed by local skate wing with a fricassée of mussels, lettuce and peas, with Calvados-poached apple served with butter cake and candied apple ice cream to finish. The selection of English farmhouse cheeses is extensive.

The Lavender House

Chef: Richard Hughes, Richard Knights **Owners:** Richard Hughes
Times: 6.30-12, Closed 24 Dec-30 Dec, Sun & Mon, Closed L all week
Prices: Fixed D £38, Service optional **Wine:** 50 bottles over £20,
16 bottles under £20, 8 by the glass **Notes:** Fixed D 6 courses, Tasting
menu 10 courses £55, Vegetarian menu **Seats:** 50, Pr/dining room 36
Children: Portions **Directions:** 4m from Norwich city centre
Parking: 16

BURNHAM MARKET MAP 13 TF84

◉ Fishes Restaurant & Rooms

Modern European

A fish-lover's paradise

☎ 01328 738588 Market Place PE31 8HE
e-mail: info@fishesrestaurant.co.uk
web: www.fishesrestaurant.co.uk

As the name suggests, this is the place to come for the catch of the day. Superb quality locally-sourced fish and shellfish are intelligently simply cooked to allow flavours to speak for themselves. The kitchen's classical underpinning is matched with an occasional nod to India and Asia; think butterfish kebab served with pilau rice, raita, mango chutney and onion-seed naan bread, or perhaps a more classic offering like roasted halibut with caramelised fennel, oranges and hollandaise. All this can be enjoyed in the relaxed, contemporary, brasserie-style surroundings of a Georgian double-fronted building on the village green, next door to the Hoste Arms Hotel (see entry).

Chef: M Owsley-Brown & K Hales **Owners:** Matthew & Caroline Owsley-
Brown **Times:** 12-2.15/6.45-10, Closed Xmas for 4 days, Mon (except BHs),
Closed D Sun **Prices:** Fixed L £19, Fixed D £37, Starter £7.50, Main £14.50,
Dessert £5.75, Service optional, Group min 8 service 10% **Wine:** 150
bottles over £20, 8 bottles under £20, 23 by the glass **Seats:** 42, Pr/dining
room 12 **Children:** Min after 8, Portions **Directions:** From Fakenham
take B1065. 8m to Burnham Market, restaurant on the green **Parking:** On
street

◉◉ Hoste Arms Hotel

Modern European, Pacific Rim 🍷 NOTABLE WINE LIST

Stylish inn with wide-ranging impressive menu

☎ 01328 738777 The Green PE31 8HD
e-mail: reception@hostearms.co.uk
web: www.hostearms.co.uk

Choose between the gallery and the garden room at this very relaxed inn close to the north Norfolk coast, and you'll get the same easygoing but professional service. There is also further private dining and an orangery. Local man Lord Nelson was once a regular visitor, but he'd hardly recognise this stylish place now. The walled garden is designed with Indian and Moroccan touches, with all-year-round alfresco dining a bonus. The modern European menu with Pacific Rim influences includes quality snacks and fine dining. Start with seared scallops with Jerusalem artichoke and truffled risotto, followed by seared fillet of sea bass with oriental vegetables, rice noodles and tom yam dressing.

Chef: Rory Whelan **Owners:** Paul Whittome **Times:** 12-2/7-9, Closed L
31 Dec, D 25 Dec **Prices:** Starter £4.50-£11.95, Main £9.75-£23.50, Dessert
£5.95-£10, Service optional **Wine:** 153 bottles over £20, 14 bottles under
£20, 21 by the glass **Notes:** Vegetarian available, Air con **Seats:** 140,
Pr/dining room 24 **Children:** Menu **Rooms:** 35 (35 en suite) ★★★ HL
Directions: 2m from A149 between Burnham & Wells **Parking:** 45

CROMER MAP 13 TG24
See also SHERINGHAM

◉ Elderton Lodge Hotel & Langtry Restaurant

Modern British

Romantic retreat serving the best Norfolk produce

☎ 01263 833547 Gunton Park NR11 8TZ
e-mail: enquiries@eldertonlodge.co.uk
web: www.eldertonlodge.co.uk

CONTINUED

ENGLAND

CROMER CONTINUED

This delightful former shooting lodge set in 6 acres of gardens was once a retreat of Lillie Langtry, hence the name of the hotel's elegant dining room. Here warm Tuscan terracotta walls, high-backed chairs and complementing carpet provide the comforts, while aperitifs are taken in the cosy hotel bar as a prelude to a candlelit dinner. The kitchen's uncomplicated, modern interpretations make intelligent use of quality produce from the abundant local larder, so expect the likes of a local Gunton venison stroganoff with shortcrust pastry, new potatoes and vegetables, and perhaps an elderflower and gooseberry compôte to finish.

Chef: Daniel Savage **Owners:** Rachel Lusher & Patrick Roofe **Times:** 12-2/7-9 **Prices:** Fixed L £11.50, Fixed D £16.50-£29, Service optional **Wine:** 11 bottles over £20, 25 bottles under £20, 6 by the glass **Notes:** Vegetarian available, Civ Wed 55 **Seats:** 50, Pr/dining room 25 **Children:** Portions **Rooms:** 11 (11 en suite) ★★★ HL **Directions:** On A149 (Cromer/North Walsham road), 1m S of village **Parking:** 100

⊚ Sea Marge Hotel

Modern British NEW
Sea views with modern restaurant and cuisine

☎ 01263 579579 16 High St NR27 0AB
e-mail: info@mackenziehotels.com
web: www.mackenziehotels.com

This country-style hotel sits in the village of Overstrand on the outskirts of Cromer and, as the name suggests, has views of the sea beyond the gardens from its smart, conservatory-feel restaurant. Relaxed, with a modern vibe, the dining room comes with leather high-backed chairs and crisply-clothed tables, while the professional staff are smartly turned out in long aprons. The accomplished kitchen's lengthy menu takes an equally modern approach, offering plenty of choice and dishes like free-range belly pork served with smoked ham hock, pease pudding, caramelised apple in brandy and a red wine jus.

Chef: Greg Kaye **Owners:** Mr & Mrs MacKenzie **Times:** 12-2/6.30-9.30 **Prices:** Starter £5-£7, Main £9.50-£19.50, Dessert £5, Service optional **Wine:** 6 bottles over £20, 25 bottles under £20, 5 by the glass **Notes:** Vegetarian available, Dress Restrictions, Smart casual **Children:** Menu, Portions **Rooms:** 23 (23 en suite) ★★★ HL **Parking:** 50

Jacque's Restaurant
☎ 01263 512149 9 Garden St NR27 9HN

Contemporary-style restaurant with a focus on local, seasonal produce.

GREAT BIRCHAM MAP 13 TF73
⊚ The Kings Head Hotel

Modern British
Great food in stylish village hotel

☎ 01485 578265 PE31 6RJ
e-mail: welcome@the-kings-head-bircham.co.uk
web: www.the-kings-head-bircham.co.uk

Situated in a peaceful little village close to Sandringham and the north Norfolk coastline, The Kings Head may look like a very well kept inn, but this stylish hotel and restaurant is one of the new gems of Norfolk.

The contemporary restaurant overlooks a sheltered courtyard which is perfect for alfresco dining in summer. Lots of local, seasonal produce appears on the simple menu of British and Mediterranean dishes. Try slow-cooked free-range belly pork with Puy lentil purée, apple and cinnamon purée, followed by roast fillet of sea bass with marinated vegetable salad, Parmentier potatoes and rocket pesto.

Chef: Neil Rutland **Owners:** William Poole **Times:** 12-2/7-9 **Prices:** Starter £5.25-£7.95, Main £12.95-£18.95, Dessert £5.25, Service optional **Wine:** 25 bottles over £20, 25 bottles under £20, 10 by the glass **Notes:** Vegetarian available, Civ Wed 200, Air con **Seats:** 80, Pr/dining room 20 **Children:** Menu, Portions **Rooms:** 12 (12 en suite) ★★★ HL **Directions:** Telephone for directions **Parking:** 30

GREAT YARMOUTH MAP 13 TG50
⊚ Imperial Hotel

Modern British
Family-run seaside hotel serving quality cuisine

☎ 01493 842000 North Dr NR30 1EQ
e-mail: reception@imperialhotel.co.uk
web: www.imperialhotel.co.uk

The Rambouillet restaurant of this imposing seafront hotel has recently been refurbished in brasserie style with good lighting and a contemporary feel. Prime ingredients are cooked well and simply, and the seasonally-changing menu with daily specials includes steaks from the chargrill, and whole grilled Lowestoft plaice with lemon and parsley butter. An alternative choice of classic dishes includes fresh Morston mussels marinière, smoked eel, and baked chump of Suffolk lamb served with aubergine caviar and tomato confit. Formal table service is combined with a relaxed, friendly approach from staff.

Chef: Stephen Duffield **Owners:** Mr N L & Mrs A Mobbs **Times:** 12-4.30/6.30-10, Closed 24-28 & 31 Dec, Closed L Mon-Sat, D Sun **Prices:** Starter £4.50-£8, Main £9.95-£25, Dessert £5-£7.50, Service optional **Wine:** 26 bottles over £20, 77 bottles under £20, 6 by the glass **Notes:** Dress Restrictions, Smart-casual; no shorts or trainers, Civ Wed 140, Air con **Seats:** 60, Pr/dining room 140 **Children:** Portions **Rooms:** 39 (39 en suite) ★★★ HL **Directions:** North end of Great Yarmouth seafront **Parking:** 45

GRIMSTON
MAP 12 TF72

◎◎ Congham Hall

Modern British V

Imaginative, seasonal cooking in Georgian setting

☎ 01485 600250 Lynn Rd PE32 1AH

e-mail: info@conghamhallhotel.co.uk

web: www.conghamhallhotel.co.uk

This beautifully proportioned, elegant Georgian manor house is set in 30 acres of mature grounds, including a noteworthy herb garden. Traditional features have been maintained, as has a style of décor throughout the inviting and tastefully furnished public rooms. Imaginative cooking is served in the Orangery restaurant, an intimate, summery room with French windows and views looking out over the garden. Local and seasonal produce feature prominently on classically inspired modern menus, which include a tasting gourmand option. Dishes may feature a breast and ballotined leg of guinea fowl with Saradaise potatoes, carrot Lyonnaise and a thyme jus, and to finish, perhaps a Cassis parfait with nutmeg mascarpone and Agen prunes steeped in Armagnac.

Chef: Jamie Murch **Owners:** von Essen Hotels **Times:** 12-1.45/7-9.15 **Prices:** Fixed L £15.50, Fixed D £46, Starter £12, Main £25, Dessert £7, Service optional **Wine:** 60 bottles over £20, 10 bottles under £20, 10 by the glass **Notes:** Gourmand menu L £31.95, D £57, Vegetarian menu, Dress Restrictions, No jeans, shorts or trainers, Civ Wed 100 **Seats:** 50, Pr/dining room 18 **Children:** Min 7 yrs D, Menu, Portions **Rooms:** 14 (14 en suite)★★★ HL **Directions:** 6m NE of King's Lynn on A148, turn right towards Grimston. Hotel 2.5m on left (do not go to Congham) **Parking:** 50

HEACHAM
MAP 12 TF63

◎ Rushmore's

British

Assured cooking of traditional British food

☎ 01485 579393 14 High St PE31 7ER

web: www.heacham.fsnet.co.uk

Good honest service with a smile is offered at this traditional restaurant, with its proper tablecloths and linen napkins. The eponymous chef-patron hails from Norfolk and his monthly menu is drawn from seasonal local ingredients, including shellfish from the coast and game from Sandringham. Utterly British in style, this is simple, effective cooking with a classic feel. Recommended dishes are William pear with vanilla dressing and stilton mousse, or local pork with apricot stuffing and Fenland leeks. Steamed treacle pudding is just one of the great home-made sweets.

Chef: Colin Rushmore **Owners:** P Barrett, D Askew **Times:** 12-2/6.30-9.30, Closed Mon, Closed L Tue & Sat, D Sun **Prices:** Fixed L £10.75, Fixed D £19.95, Service optional **Wine:** 6 bottles over £20, 15 bottles under £20, 3 by the glass **Notes:** Sun L 2 courses £12.95, 3 courses £13.95 **Seats:** 42, Pr/dining room 6 **Children:** Min 5 yrs, Portions **Directions:** A149 towards Hunstanton. At Heacham, turn left at Lavender Fields. Follow into village, take 1st left into High St **Parking:** 25

HETHERSETT
MAP 13 TG10

◎ Park Farm Hotel

Modern, Traditional

Attractive restaurant serving a relaxed style of food

☎ 01603 810264 NR9 3DL

e-mail: enq@parkfarm-hotel.co.uk

web: www.parkfarm-hotel.co.uk

What was once a farm has now evolved into a substantial hotel. The restaurant, overlooking the garden, has a smart orangery-style roof. Plain white walls are hung with bright, unframed canvases, and tables are neatly clothed and laid with contemporary crockery and cutlery. There's a set-price menu for lunch and dinner, and dishes make good use of local seasonal produce. Enjoyable dishes include seared fillet of mullet on a sweet pepper and ginger risotto with a lemon-infused oil, followed by pan-seared salmon fillet with king scallops and red pepper salsa, or pot-roasted partridge served with root vegetables, and a thyme and red wine sauce.

Chef: David Bell **Owners:** David Gowing **Times:** 12-2/7-9.30 **Prices:** Fixed L £12.95-£13.50, Fixed D £23.95-£24.50, Service optional **Wine:** 26 bottles over £20, 38 bottles under £20, 12 by the glass **Notes:** Sun L 3 courses £19.50, Vegetarian available, Dress Restrictions, Smart casual, Civ Wed 100, Air con **Seats:** 60 **Children:** Menu, Portions **Rooms:** 42 (42 en suite) ★★★ HL **Directions:** 6m S of Norwich on B1172 **Parking:** 150

HOLKHAM
MAP 13 TF84

◎◎ The Victoria at Holkham

British, French

Norfolk hideaway with an interesting colonial feel

☎ 01328 711008 Park Rd NR23 1RG

e-mail: victoria@holkham.co.uk

web: www.victoriaatholkham.co.uk

Part of the Holkham Estate, home to the Earls of Leicester since the 1700s, this converted Victorian property has a colonial feel inspired by a Sikh Maharajah, who visited the estate in the 1800s. It's been updated sensitively into a stylish restaurant with rooms, maintaining the ethnic theme in its current contemporary look. The restaurant has benefited from a new conservatory, which adds plenty of natural light. Simple, classic British food abounds on the menu with dishes that stress the inclusion of local ingredients - Thornham mussels with cider cream and gremolata or their legendary Holkham game platters - simply roasted wild duck, partridge, pheasant or woodcock, with roasted root vegetables, game chips and watercress.

Times: 12-2.30/7-9.30 **Rooms:** 10 (10 en suite) ★★ SHL **Directions:** 3m W of Wells-next-the-Sea on A149. 12m N of Fakenham

HOLT   MAP 13 TG03

◎ Butlers Café

Modern European NEW

Friendly, contemporary café, bar and restaurant offering relaxed bistro dining

☎ 01263 710790 9 Appleyard NR25 6BN
e-mail: eat@butlersofholt.com
web: www.butlersofholt.com

Light floods into this modern bistro-style restaurant through the part glass roof and glazed doors; those preferring a little more shade can enjoy the garden and courtyard beneath the leaves of a 200-year-old tree. The atmosphere is relaxed and customers can take a drink at the large oak bar. Seasonal and local produce features in British dishes with some Italian influences. With everything prepared in the open kitchen, pasta, panini or light dishes and mains like 'No fuss' Norfolk sausages and mash are found on the bistro menu. The supper menu offers the likes of fillet of Weybourne sea bass on basil mash and sautéed butternut squash.

Chef: Sean Creasey **Owners:** Sean & Ruth Creasey **Times:** 12-3/6-9, Closed 25, 26 Dec, Closed D Sun (except BH wknds) **Prices:** Starter £4.50-£6.95, Main £7.95-£16.95, Dessert £3.50-£4.95, Service optional **Wine:** 13 bottles over £20, 20 bottles under £20, 12 by the glass **Notes:** Monthly events with special menu, Vegetarian available, Air con **Seats:** 50 **Children:** Portions **Directions:** Just off High Street, signed Appleyard **Parking:** On street (free after 6pm)

HORNING   MAP 13 TG31

◎ Taps

Modern, Traditional

Consistency and good value from an intimate local restaurant

☎ 01692 630219 25 Lower St NR12 8AA
web: www.tapsrestaurant.com

With a reputation that extends way beyond its immediate surrounds, Taps nevertheless has the warm, welcoming atmosphere of a neighbourhood restaurant. Amber- and ivory-coloured walls and wicker furniture give the place a pleasant, airy feel while crisp table linen and candlelight add an evocative touch of formality. Good quality local produce is high on the agenda on this modern British menu peppered with stylistic borrowings from a range of culinary styles. Try crab fish cake with crayfish salsa to start, then roast breast of chicken with sage and apple cream sauce.

Chef: Terry Westall **Owners:** Terry Westall **Times:** 12-2/7-9.30, Closed Mon, Closed D Sun **Prices:** Fixed L £10.50-£13.50, Fixed D £22-£29.50, Starter £3.95-£6.50, Main £12.50-£17.50, Dessert £4.25-£5.50, Service optional **Wine:** 6 bottles over £20, 10 bottles under £20, 7 by the glass **Notes:** Dress Restrictions, Smart casual **Seats:** 40 **Children:** Portions **Directions:** From Norwich follow signs to The Broads on A1151. Through Wroxham and turn right to Horning & Ludham. After 3m turn right into Horning, Lower St 500yds on left **Parking:** NCP: On street

---

HUNSTANTON   MAP 12 TF64

◎ The Neptune Inn & Restaurant

Modern British

Intimate and stylish inn serving quality local produce

☎ 01485 532122 85 Old Hunstanton Rd PE36 6HZ
e-mail: reservations@theneptune.co.uk
web: www.theneptune.co.uk

This former coaching inn has been given a New England style makeover with stunning results. Imagine yourself in Maine, north Norfolk, while you relax and dine amid Lloyd Loom furniture, white-painted panelling and replica boats. The weekly-changing menu offers seasonal and local fresh produce in dishes with a French/Mediterranean twist. Braised halibut teamed with confit peppers, a fondue of leeks and saffron potato, or perhaps pork fillet served with celeriac mousse and a bacon potato pavé show the style. Take time out for the American-style Sunday brunch too.

Chef: Jon Cleland **Owners:** Paul & Hilary Berriff **Times:** 12-3/7-11, Closed 31 Dec **Prices:** Fixed L £11, Starter £6.50-£7.50, Main £17.50-£22, Dessert £6, Service optional **Wine:** 20 bottles over £20, 20 bottles under £20, 6 by the glass **Notes:** Vegetarian available **Seats:** 28 **Children:** Min 10 yrs **Rooms:** 7 (7 en suite) ★★★★ INN **Directions:** Please telephone for directions **Parking:** 8

KING'S LYNN   MAP 12 TF62

◎ Spread Eagle Inn

British, French NEW

Delightful country pub serving wholesome fare from quality local produce

☎ 01366 347995 Barton Bendish PE33 9GF

This simple country inn has a deserved reputation for good-quality food using the best of local seasonal produce. Inside there's a series of small rooms featuring open fires, low-beamed ceilings and murals of the local area. The bar comes with plain tables and wooden floors, while restaurant tables are neatly clothed and accompanied by high-backed leather chairs and carpeting. Service is typically relaxed and friendly but attentive, while the kitchen's wholesome modern approach might deliver roast monkfish with Black Forest ham, Wissey tomatoes and hollandaise, plus desserts like sticky toffee pudding or apple crumble.

Chef: Derek Byrne **Owners:** Phil & Sue Hirst **Times:** 12.30-2.30/6.30-11, Closed Mon, Closed L Tue-Wed, D Sun **Prices:** Starter £4.50-£6.95, Main £12.50-£16.95, Dessert £4.50, Service optional **Wine:** 7 bottles over £20, 25 bottles under £20, 9 by the glass **Notes:** Dress Restrictions, Shirts to be

worn, No vest-style T-shirts **Seats:** 32 **Children:** Portions
Directions: From A1122 take Barton Bendish turning. 1st left into Church
Rd, continue past church on left and straight ahead into cul-de-sac, Spread
Eagle is on left **Parking:** 30

NORTH WALSHAM   MAP 13 TG23

◎ ◎ *Beechwood Hotel*

British, Mediterranean

A passion for local produce in elegant surroundings

☎ 01692 403231   Cromer Rd NR28 0HD
e-mail: enquiries@beechwood-hotel.co.uk
web: www.beechwood-hotel.co.uk

Agatha Christie was a frequent visitor to this gracious ivy-clad 18th-
century property, and fans can see letters to the family displayed in
the hallway. The Beechwood has a strong focus on food, and the
kitchen makes the best use of the abundant Norfolk larder, notably
shellfish from Cromer, Sheringham, Thornham and Morston as well as
local meat and the freshest of vegetables. Modern British dishes with a
Mediterranean influence are served in the smartly appointed
restaurant; take a loin of Norfolk lamb with dauphinoise potatoes and
a rosemary and red wine sauce, or perhaps pan-fried fillet of sea bass
with a purée of broccoli, asparagus, green peas, prawns and a beurre
blanc. Drinks can be taken in the garden or the clubby lounge bar.

Times: 12-1.45/7-9, Closed L Mon-Sat **Rooms:** 17 (17 en suite)★★★ HL
Directions: From Norwich on B1150, 13m to N Walsham. Turn left at lights
and next right. Hotel 150 mtrs on left

NORWICH   MAP 13 TG20

◎ ◎ **Adlard's Restaurant**

Modern French NOTABLE WINE LIST

*Chic city-centre restaurant with serious approach to food
and wine*

☎ 01603 633522 79 Upper St Giles St NR2 1AB
e-mail: info@adlards.co.uk
web: www.adlards.co.uk

In a quiet street close to the city centre stands one of Norwich's
most enduring restaurants hosted by the affable David Adlard. Inside
it's a chic, modern affair, decked out with pine floors, white-clothed
tables and impressive oil paintings on cream-beige walls. It's intimate
and cheerful, with a light-and-airy feel engendered by the décor and
light from its street windows. The kitchen takes a serious line by
carefully sourcing quality seasonal ingredients and delivering clear,
balanced flavours in well-presented dishes underpinned by a
classical French theme. Think roast monkfish tail with braised oxtail,
roast salsify and shallots, or perhaps a chocolate fondant finish,
served with tonka bean ice cream and chocolate tuile. A classy wine
list accompanies.

Chef: Roger Hickman **Owners:** David Adlard **Times:** 12.30-1.45/7.30-
10.30, Closed 1st wk Jan, Sun, Mon **Prices:** Fixed L £18, Fixed D £23,
Starter £9-£12.50, Main £21-£24, Dessert £9, Service optional **Wine:** 250
bottles over £20, 15 bottles under £20, 4 by the glass **Notes:** Tasting menu
£55, Air con **Seats:** 40 **Children:** Portions **Directions:** City centre,
200yds behind the City Hall **Parking:** On street

◎ **Ah-So Japanese Restaurant**

Japanese V

Authentic taste of the land of the rising sun in Norwich

☎ 01603 618901 16 Prince of Wales Rd NR1 1LB
e-mail: booking@ah-so.co.uk
web: www.ah-so.co.uk

This smart, modern restaurant is popular with business types, and a
friendly and relaxed atmosphere pervades. Specialising in teppan-yaki,
the chefs cook meals in front of you on a large stainless steel griddle,
providing some flamboyant culinary theatrics. The menu is
authentically Japanese, assembling fresh, simple ingredients - miso
soup with tofu, or vegetable tempura for example, followed by fillet
steak cooked in butter and served with Japanese onion soup, seasonal
grilled vegetables and fried rice. The set meals are an economical
option, as well as offering the chance to sample a number of dishes at
one sitting.

Chef: Efren Eddsell **Owners:** Marcus Rose **Times:** 12-9/6-12, Closed
Mon, Closed L Tue-Sat **Prices:** Fixed D £18-£23, Starter £2.50-£5, Main
£9.95-£26, Dessert £2.25-£7, Service optional **Wine:** 10 bottles over £20,
10 bottles under £20 **Notes:** Vegetarian menu, Air con **Seats:** 50,
Pr/dining room 32 **Children:** Menu, Portions **Directions:** From station,
cross bridge, restaurant in 600yds on right, near Anglia TV

ENGLAND

NORWICH CONTINUED

⊛ Arlington Grill & Brasserie

Modern British

Enjoyable dining at historic city-centre venue

☎ 01603 617841 The George Hotel, 10 Arlington Ln,
Newmarket Rd NR2 2DA
e-mail: reservations@georgehotel.co.uk
web: www.arlingtonhotelgroup.co.uk

Behind the frosted-glass frontage of this city-centre hotel brasserie lies
a contemporary dining room with leather banquette seating,
darkwood panelling and mirrors which give a bright but intimate
atmosphere - the open-plan grill adds a touch of theatre. Expect
formal service from friendly, uniformed staff. Simply cooked dishes
make good use of fresh seasonal produce such as starters of warm
pigeon breast, bacon lardons and cherry tomatoes, and main courses
of marinated lamb loin with rosemary-roasted potatoes, root
vegetables and red wine jus. Desserts include sticky toffee pudding
with caramel sauce.

Chef: Paul Branford **Owners:** David Easter/Kingsley Place Hotels Ltd
Times: 12-2/6-10 **Prices:** Fixed L £7.95, Fixed D £19.95, Starter £4.45-
£5.95, Main £9.95-£16.95, Dessert £4.75, Service optional **Wine:** 7 bottles
over £20, 19 bottles under £20, 5 by the glass **Seats:** 44, Pr/dining room
60 **Children:** Menu, Portions **Rooms:** 43 (43 en suite) ★★★ HL
Directions: 1m from Norwich city centre, 1m from Norwich city station,
1m from A140 **Parking:** 40

⊛ Beeches Hotel & Victorian Gardens

Traditional

*Relaxed dining in delightful Victorian premises with idyllic
gardens*

☎ 01603 621167 2-6 Earlham Rd NR2 3DB
e-mail: beeches@mjbhotels.com
web: www.mjbhotels.com

If you have time before dinner at this friendly hotel, take a walk down
to the restored Victorian Plantation Garden, a romantic haven with
plenty to admire, including a gothic fountain, Italianate terrace and
rustic bridge. Admission is free to hotel residents and you can build
up an appetite worthy of the Beeches' tempting cuisine. The hotel
occupies three beautifully-restored listed Victorian houses in a
conservation area next to the Roman Catholic Cathedral, and delivers
a mix of traditional and more contemporary dishes: lamb shank with
champ and Madeira jus, for example, or beetroot, feta and watercress
risotto with pine nuts and a pesto dressing.

Chef: Richard Igel **Owners:** Mrs M Burlingham **Times:** 6.30-9.30, Closed L
all week **Prices:** Starter £17.95, Main £21.95, Dessert £24.95, Service optional
Wine: 1 bottle over £20, 35 bottles under £20, 3 by the glass **Seats:** 32
Children: Min 12 yrs, Portions **Rooms:** 41 (41 en suite) ★★★ HL
Directions: W of City on B1108, behind St Johns R C Cathedral **Parking:** 50

⊛⊛ Best Western Annesley House Hotel

Modern International

Conservatory dining in charming surroundings

☎ 01603 624553 6 Newmarket Rd NR2 2LA
e-mail: annesleyhouse@bestwestern.co.uk
web: www.bw-annesleyhouse.co.uk

You can easily walk into the city centre from this smart Grade II listed
hotel in landscaped grounds. The conservatory restaurant is furnished
with Mediterranean-style décor and ornate white and black cast-iron
chairs (cushioned for comfort), with views over the water garden and
waterfall. The modern food with European influences benefits from
straightforward handling that allows quality ingredients to shine. On
the short fixed-price menu you might find pan-fried chicken wrapped
in Parma ham and served with creamed cabbage and leeks with a
potato galette and horseradish froth, while a white chocolate mousse
with home-made lemon and hazelnut biscotti and a raspberry
milkshake might catch the eye for dessert.

Chef: Philip Woodcock **Owners:** Mr & Mrs D Reynolds **Times:** 12-2/6-10,
Closed Xmas & New Year, Closed D Sun **Prices:** Fixed D £25, Service
optional **Seats:** 40, Pr/dining room 18 **Children:** Portions **Rooms:** 26 (26
en suite) ★★★ HL **Directions:** On A11, close to city centre **Parking:** 25

⊛⊛ Brummells Seafood Restaurant

Traditional International

Quaint restaurant for fresh seafood

☎ 01603 625555 7 Magdalen St NR3 1LE
e-mail: brummell@brummells.co.uk
web: www.brummells.co.uk

A rustic chic restaurant with exposed beams and stonework,
Brummells is housed in a 17th-century building in the oldest part of
Norwich. Service is formal but the atmosphere is relaxed, and quite
romantic in the evening by candlelight. Only the finest and freshest
ingredients are used and accurately-cooked seafood dishes begin with
Brancaster mussels in creamed champagne sauce, or marinated
octopus with taramasalata platter and pitta bread, followed by a
complimentary sorbet. Mains take in lobster with garlic butter, or
grilled monkfish tails with wild mushrooms and basil compôte. Non-
fish alternatives include beef or venison steaks. Finish with coconut
custard brûlée with papaya jam and fine butter biscuit.

Brummells Seafood Restaurant

Chef: A Brummell, J O'Sullivan **Owners:** Mr A Brummell **Times:** 12-Flexible/6-Flexible, Closed L Bookings only **Prices:** Starter £6-£16, Main £16-£35, Dessert £5.50, Service optional, Group min 7 service 10% **Wine:** 56 bottles over £20, 27 bottles under £20, 3 by the glass **Seats:** 30 **Children:** Portions **Directions:** In city centre, 2 mins walk from Norwich Cathedral, 40yds from Colegate

⊛ By Appointment

British, Mediterranean V

Dinner in an Aladdin's cave

☎ 01603 630730 27-29 St George's St NR3 1AB
web: www.byappointmentnorwich.co.uk

Occupying three 15th-century merchants' houses, By Appointment comes with a multitude of nooks and crannies and boasts four intimate dining rooms, all very theatrical, with the added luxury of two comfortable drawing rooms. The whole house is filled with antique furniture, and tables are embellished with Victorian silver-plated cutlery and fine china. Dishes are classically English with continental influences, such as fresh mussels cooked with Pernod, leeks, white wine, garlic and cream, or succulent breast of pheasant with cranberry and orange relish, parsnip shavings and juniper and cranberry sauce.

Chef: Timothy Brown **Owners:** Timothy Brown, R Culver **Times:** 7.30-9.30, Closed 25 Dec, Sun-Mon, Closed L all week **Prices:** Starter £6.75-£7.95, Main £19.95-£21.95, Dessert £6.50, Service optional **Wine:** 40 bottles over £20, 19 bottles under £20, 3 by the glass **Notes:** Vegetarian menu **Seats:** 50, Pr/dining room 36 **Children:** Min 12 yrs **Directions:** City centre. Entrance rear of Merchants House **Parking:** 4

⊛ De Vere Dunston Hall

Modern British

Accomplished cuisine in grand hotel

☎ 01508 470444 Ipswich Rd NR14 8PQ
e-mail: dhreception@devere-hotels.com
web: www.devereonline.co.uk

An imposing Grade II listed building set in 170 acres of landscaped grounds, just a short drive from the city centre. The newly refurbished brasserie restaurant offers an extensive carte showcasing modern interpretations of French classics that utilise quality ingredients, so expect soundly cooked dishes and good flavours. Try a starter of ham hock terrine with dressed leaves and piccalilli, followed perhaps by tender crispy belly pork, served with leek and parmesan risotto and roasted root vegetables. Vegetarians are well catered for. Typical desserts include a trio of chocolate - fondant, tart and sorbet.

Chef: Paul Murfitt **Owners:** De Vere Hotels **Times:** 7-10, Closed Sun, Closed L Mon-Sat **Prices:** Fixed D £26.50-£36.50, Starter £5.80-£6.85, Main £16.50-£23.50, Dessert £5.50-£8.50 **Notes:** Vegetarian available, Dress Restrictions, Smart, No jeans, Air con **Seats:** 45, Pr/dining room **Children:** Menu, Portions **Rooms:** 169 (169 en suite) ★★★★ HL **Directions:** On A140 between Norwich & Ipswich **Parking:** 300

⊛ *Marriott Sprowston Manor Hotel*

International

Fine dining in elegant hotel

☎ 01603 410871 Sprowston Park, Wroxham Rd NR7 8RP
e-mail: debbie.phillips@marriotthotels.com
web: www.marriott.co.uk/nwigs

Surrounded by open parkland, this imposing property is set in attractively landscaped gardens with golf and leisure facilities. The hotel is built around a house that dates back 450 years. Dine in the informal Café Zest or in the elegant Manor Restaurant with its crystal chandeliers and mahogany reeded columns. The menus are traditional with British and French influences. At the time of going to press the hotel was undergoing a major refurbishment. Please visit www.theAA.com for up-to-date details.

Times: 12.30-2/6-10, Closed L Sat, D Sun **Rooms:** 94 (94 en suite) ★★★★ HL **Directions:** From A47 take Postwick exit onto Norwich outer ring road, then take A1151. Hotel approx 3m and signed

⊛⊛ Old Rectory

Modern British

A Georgian haven in the heart of Norwich

☎ 01603 700772 & 750772 103 Yarmouth Rd,
Thorpe St Andrew NR7 0HF
e-mail: enquiries@oldrectorynorwich.com
web: www.oldrectorynorwich.com

This Georgian house sits in pretty grounds overlooking the River Yare just a few minutes drive from the centre of Norwich. Deep sofas and comfortable armchairs beckon in the lounge - enjoy a pre-dinner drink, and then move through to the restaurant, a period room lit by candles, with a sensibly concise, set-price menu that changes daily. Dishes are mostly modern British in style, with a winning emphasis on flavour and good-quality local seasonal ingredients. Think marinated roast Gressingham duck breast served with Savoy cabbage, spring onion mash and a roasted young beetroot sauce, and perhaps a baked pressed dark chocolate soufflé cake with crème fraîche and whisky-soaked jumbo sultanas and raisins to finish. Service is attentive and thoughtfully paced.

Chef: James Perry **Owners:** Chris & Sally Entwistle **Times:** 7-10.30, Closed Xmas & New Year, Sun, Mon, Closed L all week **Prices:** Fixed D £25-£28, Service included **Wine:** 12 bottles over £20, 8 bottles under £20, 5 by the glass **Seats:** 18, Pr/dining room 16 **Children:** Portions **Rooms:** 8 (8 en suite) ★★ SHL **Directions:** From A47 take A1042 to Thorpe, then A1242. Hotel right after 1st lights **Parking:** 16

NORWICH CONTINUED

ENGLAND

◉◉ 1 Up

Modern British

Contemporary restaurant and modern food above a popular pub

☎ 01603 627687 The Mad Moose Arms & 1 Up,
21 Warwick St NR2 3LD
e-mail: madmoose@animalinns.co.uk

Aptly named, '1 Up' is upstairs from this trendy, bustling gastro-pub and provides its fine-dining arm at dinner only (plus Sunday lunch). The recently refurbished, elegant, chic look offers a twist on the classical - where modern wallpaper rubs shoulders with chandeliers and luxurious velvet curtains. The atmosphere is intimate, sophisticated and unpretentious and comes backed by appropriately professional yet relaxed service. The food fits the bill, too, the accomplished cooking is big on clear flavours and balance, and committed to the use of high-quality seasonal ingredients from the abundant local larder. Take a loin of Norfolk venison with duck-fat potatoes, creamed Savoy cabbage, baby onions and a bitter chocolate sauce, or perhaps a free-standing cinnamon crème brûlée with grilled figs and plum ice cream to finish. (In addition, a substantial bar menu is offered downstairs.)

Chef: Eden Derrick **Owners:** Mr Henry Watt **Times:** 12-3/7-9.30, Closed 25-26 Dec, 1 Jan, Closed L Mon-Sat, D Sun **Prices:** Fixed L £15, Fixed D £22.50, Starter £5.50-£8.50, Main £10.50-£14.50, Dessert £4.95, Service optional **Wine:** 19 bottles over £20, 32 bottles under £20, 8 by the glass **Notes:** Sun L available, Vegetarian available **Seats:** 48 **Children:** Portions **Directions:** A11 onto A140. Turn right at lights onto Unthank Rd, then left onto Dover/Warwick St **Parking:** On street

◉ St Benedicts Restaurant

Modern British

Imaginative cuisine in a relaxed, contemporary setting

☎ 01603 765377 9 St Benedicts St NR2 4PE
e-mail: stbens@ukonline.co.uk

This local restaurant's contemporary interior gives it an intimate, relaxed feel. The staff are helpful and efficient but never intrusive. Cooking is imaginative with an emphasis on taste - clean flavours and seasonal, local ingredients. Enjoy some of the more unusual dishes like partridge chartreuse with cocotte potatoes, roasted salsify, bacon and game jus, or slow-cooked crispy duck with braised red cabbage. More traditional fare might include double-baked cheese soufflé, followed by chargrilled peppered beef medallions with dauphinoise potatoes and tomato confit, and for dessert iced praline parfait with crème anglaise and toasted almonds. Don't forget to sample the English fruit liqueurs, made by a husband-and-wife team in Devon.

Chef: Nigel Raffles **Owners:** Nigel & Joyne Raffles **Times:** 12-2/7-10, Closed 25-31 Dec, Sun-Mon **Prices:** Fixed L £9.95, Fixed D £16.95, Starter £4.25-£5.95, Main £9.50-£13.50, Dessert £4.75, Service optional, Group min 10 service 10% **Wine:** 15 bottles over £20, 34 bottles under £20, 8 by the glass **Notes:** Fixed L 3 courses, Vegetarian available, Air con **Seats:** 42, Pr/dining room 24 **Children:** Portions **Directions:** Just off inner ring road. Turn right by Toys-R-Us, 2nd right into St Benedicts St. Restaurant is on left by pedestrian crossing **Parking:** On street, Car parks nearby

◉ Shiki

Modern Japanese

Sushi with style whether you want to eat in or takeaway

☎ 01603 619262 6 Tombland NR3 1HE
e-mail: bookings@shikirestaurant.co.uk

With stripped pine floors and bench seating, the restaurant's modern, uncluttered interior epitomises Japanese minimalism. Freshly prepared sushi is the main attraction, both at the counter and on the menu. The choice of fish includes the usual suspects and extends to eel, turbot and yellow tail tuna. Other Japanese specialities include gyoza dumplings and other classic appetisers, with main courses such as Japanese curries, shoga yaki and salmon teriyaki. Fresh ingredients and clean flavours more than live up to expectations. The tapas-style menu allows you to sample three small portions of the main dishes and the all-in-one bento boxes are great value for money.

Chef: Fransisco Papica **Owners:** Kumi Wiedmann **Times:** 12-2.30/5.30-10.30, Closed Xmas, Sun **Prices:** Fixed L £4.50-£10, Fixed D £15, Starter £2-£7.50, Main £6.50-£30, Dessert £2-£4.50, Service optional, Group min 10 service 10% **Wine:** 2 bottles over £20, 14 bottles under £20, 5 by the glass **Notes:** Vegetarian available **Children:** Portions **Directions:** Norwich city centre. From Castle Meadow onto Upper Kings St continue straight onto Tombland, restaurant on left

◉ Stower Grange

Traditional British

Welcoming surroundings for an enjoyable meal

☎ 01603 860210 School Rd, Drayton NR8 6EF
e-mail: enquiries@stowergrange.co.uk
web: www.stowergrange.co.uk

This 17th-century, ivy-clad property is set in a quiet residential area and the elegant restaurant overlooks the rear gardens, providing a relaxing venue for diners. Cooking is straightforward and reassuring, with just about everything made on the premises. A wide choice of dishes includes a subtly flavoured pancetta and gruyère soufflé, grilled sea bass on a spaghetti of chargrilled vegetables with saffron sauce, or roasted pheasant on rösti potato with black pudding and apple compôte. The well executed chocolate pudding provides a pleasing contrast of textures and comes with a quenelle of creamy mascarpone, or you might try an equally delicious individual bread-and-butter pudding with crème anglaise.

Times: 12-2.30/7-9.30, Closed 26-30 Dec, Closed D Sun **Rooms:** 11 (11 en suite) ★★ HL **Directions:** Telephone for directions

◉◉ Tatlers

Modern British

Relaxed and stylish brasserie dining

☎ 01603 766670 21 Tombland NR3 1RF
e-mail: info@tatlers.com
web: www.tatlers.com

Just around the corner from Norwich's beautiful cathedral, a converted Victorian townhouse is the setting for this chic and vibrant restaurant. Each of its dining rooms is individually decorated in colourful modern shades and furnished with chunky oak tables, while an old leather Chesterfield beckons in the upstairs bar, a striking area that doubles as a gallery for exhibitions of contemporary art. The menu changes daily and features modern British dishes with an international twist: hot crispy fillet of beef Thai salad for example, served with holy basil and crushed peanuts, or roast fillet of local cod with mussels and wild garlic leaf. Round things off with apple crumble and rhubarb swirl ice cream, or moist coconut and orange cake with blood orange sorbet.

Chef: Brendan Ansbro **Owners:** Annelli Clarke **Times:** 12-2/6.30-10, Closed 25-26 Dec, BHs, Sun **Prices:** Fixed L £14, Starter £4.95-£8.50, Main £11.50-£17.50, Dessert £7.50, Service optional, Group min 10 service 10% **Wine:** 28 bottles over £20, 11 bottles under £20, 10 by the glass **Seats:** 75, Pr/dining room 30 **Children:** Portions **Directions:** In city centre in Tombland. Next to Erpingham gate by Norwich Cathedral **Parking:** Law courts, Elm Hill, Colegate

⊛ Thailand Restaurant

Thai NEW

Deservedly popular authentic Thai

☎ 01603 700444 9 Ring Rd, Thorpe St Andrew NR7 0XJ

This Thai eatery's mouthwatering cooking has made it something of a favourite with the Norwich natives, so book ahead to avoid disappointment. It's located just off the ring road in a huge detached, white-painted house. Inside, the tables are neatly clothed with dark bamboo-style chairs, and walls are decorated with pictures of Thailand. The staff are smartly dressed in silks, shirts and bow ties, and attentive no matter how busy it gets. The kitchen delivers superb traditional cuisine using excellent quality produce. A typical main sees beef Musaman (beef slow braised in coconut cream with fresh chillies, cinnamon and shallots), while green curry is vibrant and flavoursome.

Times: Please telephone for details

Loch Fyne Restaurant

☎ 01603 723450 30-32 St Giles St NR2 1LL

Quality seafood chain.

SHERINGHAM   MAP 13 TG14

⊛ Dales Country House Hotel

British, European

Country-house hotel in National Trust parkland

☎ 01263 824555   NR26 8TJ
e-mail: dales@mackenziehotels.com
web: www.mackenziehotels.com

The National Trust grounds of Sheringham Park - and its own extensive gardens - contain this Victorian country-house hotel. The intimate Upchers restaurant, in keeping with the house style, is relaxed and smart, traditionally styled with oak panelling and an inglenook fireplace. The kitchen is well supplied with game from local estates, fish from the north Norfolk coast, and quality meats, all delivered on the contemporary lunch, carte and daily specials. The simple cooking style yields excellent flavours, with typical dinner offerings featuring the likes of fresh sea bass fillet served with courgette ribbons, cocotte potatoes and champagne cream, or perhaps slow-braised lamb shank with a honeyed root vegetable purée.

Chef: Howard Bowen **Owners:** Mr & Mrs Mackenzie **Times:** 12-2/7-9.30 **Prices:** Fixed L £14.95-£24.95, Starter £4.30-£6.95, Main £8.50-£20.95, Dessert £4.55-£6.25, Service optional **Wine:** 16 bottles over £20, 28 bottles under £20, 8 by the glass **Notes:** Fixed L 3 courses, Sun L 4 courses £16.50, Dress Restrictions, No shorts or sportswear **Seats:** 50, Pr/dining room 40 **Children:** Portions **Rooms:** 17 (17 en suite) ★★★★ HL **Directions:** On B1157, 1m S of Sheringham. From A148 Cromer to Holt road, take turn at entrance to Sheringham Park. Restaurant 0.5m on left **Parking:** 50

⊛ No. 10 Restaurant

Modern British NEW

Seasonal dishes served in elegant surroundings

☎ 01263 824400 10 Augusta St NR26 8LA
e-mail: eat@no10sheringham.com
web: www.no10sheringham.com

The appealing frontage of this restaurant is formed from two neatly curved windows. The interior boasts high ceilings and sage green walls, with crisp white table settings and gold mirrors and paintings giving a formal feel, as do the smartly-dressed staff, wearing black and white, with long chocolate brown aprons. Excellent bread is followed by a starter like poached skate with roasted red peppers and coriander salsa. Main courses feature the likes of sea bass fillet with broccoli, potato and anchovy sauce. Tasty brunch options like eggs Benedict or beef hash are also popular.

Times: 12-2/6.30-9.30, Closed Sun-Tue

SNETTISHAM   MAP 12 TF63

⊛ Rose & Crown

Modern British

Bustling local with culinary verve

☎ 01485 541382 Old Church Rd PE31 7LX
e-mail: info@roseandcrownsnettisham.co.uk
web: www.roseandcrownsnettisham.co.uk

Behind the rose-covered façade of this 14th-century inn lies a cosy warren of nooks and crannies, uneven floors and log fires. Colourful contemporary décor extends throughout the range of dining areas, which include a garden room opening on to a walled garden with a children's play area. The menu offers pub favourites prepared to a high standard with quality, locally-sourced ingredients. Try a starter of sautéed chicken livers with pancetta, baby spinach and sherry vinegar dressing, followed by a main course of salmon and butterfish brochettes with chilli vegetables, or prime Holkham beef burger with relish and fries.

Chef: Andrew Bruce **Owners:** Anthony & Jeanette Goodrich **Times:** 12-2/6.30-9 **Prices:** Starter £5-£7.50, Main £7.50-£15, Dessert £5.50-£6.50, Service optional, Group min 10 service 10% **Wine:** 10 bottles over £20, 27 bottles under £20, 10 by the glass **Notes:** Vegetarian available **Seats:** 60, Pr/dining room 30 **Children:** Menu, Portions **Rooms:** 16 (16 en suite) ★★ HL **Directions:** From King's Lynn take A149 N towards Hunstanton. After 10m into Snettisham to village centre, then into Old Church Rd towards church. Hotel is 100yds on left **Parking:** 70

STOKE HOLY CROSS   MAP 13 TG20

The Wildebeest Arms

British, French NOTABLE WINE LIST

Modern take on a traditional pub with enticing menus

☎ 01508 492497 82-86 Norwich Rd, Stoke Holy Cross NR14 8QJ
e-mail: mail@animalinns.co.uk
web: www.thewildebeest.co.uk

A fresh, bright, modern, open-plan pub setting mixes beams, panelling, open fire and bare floorboards with fresh flowers and African motifs and artefacts to add a touch of exoticism. The haunt of Norwich movers and shakers, the accomplished kitchen takes a modern European approach - underpinned by a classical French theme - on appealing carte and menu du jour offerings. Staff are friendly and well informed about the quality, locally-sourced produce on offer; take pan-fried skate wing with saffron risotto, steamed mussels in white wine and fennel and a caper and tomato nage, for instance, or perhaps a prune and almond tart to close, served with rum-and-raisin ice cream and rum-and-raisin purée.

Chef: Daniel Smith **Owners:** Henry Watt **Times:** 12-3.30/6-11.30, Closed 25-26 Dec **Prices:** Fixed L £11.95, Fixed D £18.50, Starter £5.95-£6.50, Main £11.95-£17.25, Dessert £5.25-£5.95, Service optional **Wine:** 51 bottles over £20, 75 bottles under £20, 13 by the glass **Notes:** Sun L 2 courses £14.50, 3 courses £16.95, Vegetarian available, Air con **Seats:** 60 **Children:** Portions **Directions:** From A47, take A140 turn off towards Ipswich. Turn first left signposted byway to Dunston. Continue to end of the road and turn left at the T-junct, restaurant on right **Parking:** 40

THORNHAM   MAP 12 TF74

Lifeboat Inn

Modern, Traditional British

Fish features strongly at this historic alehouse

☎ 01485 512236 Ship Ln PE36 6LT
e-mail: reception@lifeboatinn.co.uk
web: www.lifeboatinn.co.uk

This 16th-century smugglers' alehouse, now more of a gastro-pub with rooms, enjoys superb views across open meadows to Thornham Harbour. Inside is equally characterful, with open fires, exposed brickwork and ancient oak beams. The smart restaurant with white-clothed, candlelit tables offers an interesting daily-changing carte, while a bar snack menu is available for lighter fare. As you might expect, fish is a highlight, with mains featuring the likes of wok-fried tiger prawns and red mullet fillets, finished with bok choy, soft noodles and a red Thai sauce, or a steamed fillet of smoked haddock on a creamy seafood risotto. Meat-eaters are also well catered for, with dishes like fillet of beef served with horseradish mash, caramelised onions and poivre sauce. There's also a children's menu.

Chef: Michael Sherman **Owners:** Maypole Group plc **Times:** 7-9.30, Closed L all week **Prices:** Fixed D £28, Service optional **Wine:** 16 bottles over £20, 19 bottles under £20, 8 by the glass **Notes:** Sun L £9.95, Vegetarian available **Seats:** 70, Pr/dining room 18 **Children:** Menu, Portions **Rooms:** 13 (13 en suite) ★★ HL **Directions:** Take A149 from King's Lynn to Hunstanton follow coast road to Thornham, take 1st left **Parking:** 100

The Orange Tree

British, Pacific Rim

Popular gastro-pub on the north Norfolk coast

☎ 01485 512213 High St PE36 6LY
e-mail: email@theorangetreethornham.co.uk
web: www.theorangetreethornham.co.uk

Located opposite the church in this beautiful coastal village, the Orange Tree is a popular gastro-pub with a relaxed and informal vibe and a contemporary twist to its décor. Diners can choose between the beamed bar with its inglenook fireplace, and one of two restaurant dining areas, each with plush leather chairs and modern table settings. Friendly, professional staff serve dishes from a modern British menu with a hint of the Pacific Rim. Tandoori-style tuna loin with cucumber noodles and ginger and coriander oil might sit alongside rump of lamb with potato purée and lemon and mint cream. Local produce includes Thornham Creek oysters, Brancaster mussels and local crab.

Chef: Philip Milner **Owners:** Chris Hinde, Paul Bishop **Times:** 12-2.30/6-9.30, Closed D Sun **Prices:** Fixed L £16.50, Starter £5.50-£7, Main £10-£15, Dessert £5.50, Service optional **Wine:** 11 bottles over £20, 21 bottles under £20, 13 by the glass **Notes:** Vegetarian available **Seats:** 40, Pr/dining room 16 **Children:** Menu, Portions **Rooms:** 6 (6 en suite) ★★★ INN **Directions:** On A149 between Holme-next-the-Sea and Brancaster Staithe **Parking:** 20

TITCHWELL   MAP 13 TF74

Titchwell Manor Hotel

Modern European

Coastal weekend retreat with good seafood

☎ 01485 210221 PE31 8BB
e-mail: margaret@titchwellmanor.com
web: www.titchwellmanor.com

A former 19th-century farmhouse overlooking wild salt marsh, Titchwell Manor provides a comfortable base for exploring the north Norfolk coast. The light, modern décor of white walls, wooden floors and leather furniture goes well with the seaside atmosphere. Meals can be taken in the bar or in the attractively presented conservatory dining room with its neatly clothed tables and relaxing atmosphere. Local and seasonal ingredients, notably seafood, are skilfully prepared to produce dishes with interesting combinations and clear flavours. Expect Brancaster oysters or glazed belly pork with apple fritters and caramel jus to start, followed by Holkham venison with glazed parsnips and figs, chorizo oil and jus, with dark chocolate and espresso mousse to finish.

Chef: Eric Snaith **Owners:** Margaret and Ian Snaith **Times:** 12-2.30/6-9.30 **Prices:** Starter £5-£10, Main £10-£20, Dessert £3-£6, Service added but optional, Group min 8 service 10% **Wine:** 27 bottles over £20, 25 bottles under £20, 9 by the glass **Notes:** Sun L 3 courses £15, Vegetarian available, Dress Restrictions, Smart casual, Air con **Seats:** 50 **Children:** Min 7 yrs D, Menu, Portions **Rooms:** 26 (26 en suite) ★★★ HL **Directions:** On the A149 coast road between Brancaster and Thornham **Parking:** 25

WELLS-NEXT-THE-SEA   MAP 13 TF94

◉ The Crown Hotel

Pacific Rim V
Great location for modern cooking

☎ 01328 710209   The Buttlands NR23 1EX
e-mail: reception@thecrownhotelwells.co.uk
web: www.thecrownhotelwells.co.uk

Located just a few minutes from the beach, this 16th-century former coaching inn retains many original features, including ancient beams in the bar and a lovely open fireplace. In fine weather you can sit outside and soak up some rays on the sheltered sun deck. Inside, the dining room is decorated in sophisticated contemporary style and delivers a forward-looking menu of modern classics distinguished by plenty of local produce. Try potted salmon with horseradish crème fraîche to start, perhaps followed by rack of lamb with provençale vegetables and fondant potato. Desserts might include chocolate and ginger torte.

Chef: Chris Coubrough **Owners:** Chris Coubrough **Times:** 7-9, Closed L all week **Prices:** Fixed D £24.95, Service optional **Wine:** 25 bottles over £20, 19 bottles under £20, 12 by the glass **Notes:** Fixed D 5 courses, Vegetarian menu **Seats:** 30, Pr/dining room 22 **Children:** Menu, Portions **Directions:** 9m from Fakenham. At the top Buttlands Green

---

WYMONDHAM   MAP 13 TG10

◉◉ Number Twenty Four Restaurant

Modern British
Sound cooking in listed townhouse

☎ 01953 607750   24 Middleton St NR18 0AD
web: www.number24.co.uk

There's nothing pretentious or stuffy about this relaxed, friendly, family-run restaurant located in a row of listed terraced cottages. Low-key style, pale cream walls and well-spaced, neatly clothed tables hit just the right note. The compact menu takes a modern approach, with a nod to international influences. Changing daily to reflect quality market choice, the selection includes a vegetarian option. The cooking

is straightforward with clear flavours. Look out for grilled fillet of smoked haddock on parsnip purée with saffron vanilla sauce and watercress, followed by seared loin of venison on bubble-and-squeak with sautéed winter vegetables and port wine gravy. Finish with white chocolate and lemon mousse Pavlova.

Number Twenty Four Restaurant

Chef: Jonathan Griffin **Owners:** Jonathan Griffin **Times:** 12-2/7-9, Closed 26 Dec, 1 Jan, Mon, Closed L Tue, D Sun **Prices:** Fixed L £14.50, Fixed D £23.95 **Wine:** 6 by the glass **Notes:** Sun L 2 courses £12.95, 3 courses £14.95, Vegetarian available, Dress Restrictions, Smart casual, no shorts **Seats:** 60, Pr/dining room 20 **Children:** Portions **Directions:** Town centre opposite war memorial **Parking:** On street opposite. In town centre car park

Casablanca

☎ 01953 607071   2 Middleton St NR18 0AD

High-street restaurant serving great-value Moroccan food.

NORTHAMPTONSHIRE

CASTLE ASHBY   MAP 11 SP85

◉ *Falcon Hotel*

Modern British
Country hotel with an emphasis on good food

☎ 01604 696200   NN7 1LF
e-mail: falcon.castleashby@oldenglishinns.co.uk
web: www.falcon-castleashby.com

This family-run hotel is located in the heart of the village and occupies a large stone-built property and two neighbouring cottages dating from the 16th century. The pretty restaurant overlooks the garden, and dishes are based on fresh local produce including vegetables from the garden. There's a set-price menu for lunch and dinner plus a carte selection offering the likes of warm salmon and king prawn terrine with fresh garden herb sauce, followed by Cajun-spiced cod with creamed mash and crispy leeks.

Times: 12-2.30/7-9.30, Closed D 24 Dec
Rooms: 16 (16 en suite) ★★ HL

DAVENTRY   MAP 11 SP56

The Knightley Restaurant, Fawsley Hall

Rosettes not confirmed at time of going to press

British, Mediterranean V

A grand Tudor manor with fine dining

☎ 01327 892000   Fawsley NN11 3BA

e-mail: reservations@fawsleyhall.com

web: www.fawsleyhall.com

Majestic country house set in an awe-inspiring 2,000 acres of rolling hills and parkland with a history stretching back more than 700 years. The grand interior teams tasteful period charm with modern luxury, a recent renovation seeing the addition of a spa. Afternoon tea or an aperitif in the Great Hall is a particular treat - as imposing as its name suggests, the room boasts wood panelling and a cavernous ceiling as well as sumptuous sofas and a log fire. Afterwards, take your seat in the restaurant, a comfortably appointed venue with well-spaced tables presided over by a friendly waiting team, who avoid the unnecessary fuss often associated with hotels of this calibre. The kitchen produces artfully simple dishes that let high-quality ingredients speak for themselves both in terms of flavour and presentation. At the time of going to press we understand there was a change at the top of the kitchen and the name of the new chef is still to be announced. Please visit www.theAA.com for further details.

Owners: Fawsley Hall Hotel Ltd **Times:** 12-2.30/7-9.30, Closed L Mon-Fri **Prices:** Fixed D £37.50, Starter £6.50-£12, Main £16-£24.50, Dessert £9.50-£12, Service added but optional 12.5% **Notes:** Tasting menu 6 courses £75, Sun L £26.50, Vegetarian menu, Civ Wed 140 **Seats:** 85, Pr/dining room 140 **Children:** Menu, Portions **Rooms:** 52 (52 en suite)★★★★ HL **Directions:** From M40 junct 11 take A361 (Daventry), follow for 12m. Turn right towards Fawsley Hall **Parking:** 100

EYDON   MAP 11 SP54

◉◉ The Royal Oak @ Eydon

Modern British

Refurbished village pub with style

☎ 01327 263167   6 Lime Av NN11 3PG

Everything here has been done well, yet without losing the original bonhomie and character, from flagstone floors to inglenook and leaded windows. A good choice of hand-pumped ales is matched by quality wines by the glass, including champagne, which sums up that stylish edge. The menu's approach is modern focused, backed by a specials board. Fish plays a key role, though there's plenty for meat eaters, too. The accomplished cooking is intelligently simple, accurate and with depth of flavour, allowing high-quality ingredients to shine. Typical main dishes include pan-fried Cornish monkfish tail with chorizo, oven-roasted rack of lamb with mint and pine nut crust, or a choice of first-class steaks with accompaniments.

Times: 12-2/7-9 **Directions:** Telephone for directions

FOTHERINGHAY   MAP 12 TL09

◉ The Falcon Inn

British, Italian

Vibrant cooking in rural Northamptonshire

☎ 01832 226254   Huntsbridge PE8 5HZ

e-mail: falcon@huntsbridge.co.uk

web: www.huntsbridge.com

The Falcon manages to combine its role as village local with that of renowned pub-restaurant. Located in the mellow stone-built village where Mary, Queen of Scots ended her days, the pub has immense character and a lovely garden with views of the church. British classics are served in the bar, and the restaurant menu is Anglo-Italian, with dishes like bruschetta of Portland crab with green bean and rocket salad and dill aïoli, or chargrilled fillet of beef with olive oil braised leeks, roast red onion, horseradish mash and Chianti sauce.

Chef: Dave Simms, Chris Ripping **Owners:** John Hoskins **Times:** 12-2.15/6.15-9.30 **Prices:** Fixed L £13.50, Starter £4.95-£7.95, Main £12.95-£19.95, Dessert £4.75-£7.95, Service optional, Group min 10 service 10% **Wine:** 60 bottles over £20, 30 bottles under £20, 15 by the glass **Seats:** 45, Pr/dining room 25 **Children:** Menu, Portions **Directions:** Off A605 follow signpost Fotheringhay **Parking:** 50

HELLIDON   MAP 11 SP55

◉ Hellidon Lakes

Contemporary

An impressive setting for imaginative cuisine

☎ 01327 262550   NN11 6GG

e-mail: hellidonlakes@qhotels.co.uk

web: www.qhotels.co.uk/hotels/hellidon-lakes-daventry-northamptonshire/

Set in 220 acres of countryside, including 27 holes of golf and 12 lakes, it would be difficult not to have a great view from the fine dining restaurant, but why not ask for a window seat anyway. The menu is extensive with some supplements for speciality dishes. Modern international cuisine can be enjoyed with the likes of tartlet of poached haddock and smoked salmon cream followed by slow-cooked blade of beef, spinach, red wine and thick shallot gravy. The global wine list offers some more unusual wines and a good selection of half bottles and wines by the glass.

Times: 12-2/7-9.45, Closed L Sat & Sun **Rooms:** 110 (110 en suite) ★★★★ HL **Directions:** M40 junct 11 onto A361 towards Charwelton, turn right, hotel 2m

---

HORTON   MAP 11 SP85

◉◉ The New French Partridge

Modern British, French

Confident cooking in stylish country-house restaurant

☎ 01604 870033   Newport Pagnell Rd NN7 2AP

e-mail: info@newfrenchpartridge.co.uk

web: www.newfrenchpartridge.co.uk

Situated in private grounds in the lovely rural village of Horton, this former coaching inn was extended into a traditional country manor in 1622. The current owners have stylishly restored it to its original splendour, including ten individually designed bedrooms and a bar in the vaulted cellar. A well-balanced menu of modern French and British dishes perfectly suits the surroundings and makes good use of high-quality ingredients. You could start with pan-roasted, lightly home-smoked salmon with potato blinis, crème fraîche and tomato compôte, and perhaps follow up with roast fillet of Scottish beef served with salsify, girolle mushrooms, carrot and foie gras purée and pancetta crisp. To finish, maybe an apple crumble soufflé with cinnamon ice cream and caramelised apple.

The New French Partridge

Chef: W Farmer, I Oakenfull **Owners:** Ian Oakenfull, Tanya Banerjee
Times: 11.30-2.30/6.30-10.30, Closed L Sat, D Sun **Prices:** Fixed L £29.50, Fixed D £41.50, Starter £5.90-£11.50, Main £13.50-£19.50, Dessert £6.95
Wine: 9 bottles under £20, 9 by the glass **Notes:** Fixed L 3 courses, Fixed D 4 courses, Vegetarian available, Dress Restrictions, Smart casual, Civ Wed 70 **Seats:** 70, Pr/dining room 12 **Children:** Portions **Rooms:** 10 (10 en suite) ★★ HL **Directions:** On B526 between Milton Keynes and Northampton, in village of Horton **Parking:** 35

KETTERING   MAP 11 SP87

◉ *Kettering Park Hotel*

Modern British

Impressive cuisine in a smart hotel restaurant

☎ 01536 416666 Kettering Parkway NN15 6XT
e-mail: kpark.reservations@shirehotels.com
web: www.ketteringparkhotel.com

This modern hotel combines old world charm with up-to-date comfort. In the split-level Langberry's restaurant you'll find traditional décor with subtle lighting, a welcoming fire in winter and formal table service from well-trained staff; there's an outdoor terrace for alfresco eating in warmer months. The kitchen works hard to source seasonal, local produce from local suppliers for British dishes that might include pressed ham hock and parsley terrine, and seared rump of Stamford lamb, hot pot potatoes, braised red cabbage and rosemary jus. Desserts might feature an apple and bramble crumble with Calvados ice cream. Heart symbols on the menu indicate lighter and simply prepared dishes.

Times: 12.30-2.30/7-9.30, Closed Xmas & New Year (ex residents), Closed L Sat, Sun **Rooms:** 119 (119 en suite) ★★★★ HL **Directions:** Off A14 junct 9

◉◉ The Tresham Restaurant

Traditional British NEW

Highly accomplished cooking in magnificent surroundings

☎ 01536 713001 Rushton Hall, Rushton NN14 1RR
e-mail: enquiries@rushtonhall.com
web: www.rushtonhall.com

The epitome of elegant country-house hotels, the imposing Rushton - dating back to 1438 - is set in acres of parkland surrounded by beautiful countryside. The interior is kitted out in the grand style, from its large, heavy-timbered entrance doors to huge stone and timber fireplaces, ornate plasterwork and stained glass, plus there's a varied array of deep, comfortable lounge seating. The impressive oak, linenfold panelled dining room continues the theme, its modern British approach - underpinned by classical influences - delivering highly accomplished cuisine with fine depth of flavour, utilising high-quality well-sourced produce. Take John Dory and langoustines served with oxtail cannelloni and roast fish sauce, and to finish, perhaps a passionfruit soufflé with mango sorbet.

Chef: Adrian Coulthard **Times:** 12-2.30/7-9

ROADE   MAP 11 SP75

◉ Roade House Restaurant

Modern British

Popular village restaurant serving simple lunches and more serious evening fare

☎ 01604 863372 16 High St NN7 2NW
e-mail: info@roadehousehotel.co.uk
web: www.roadehousehotel.co.uk

An 18th-century, stone-built pub has been sympathetically extended to provide a large, comfortable lounge bar and restaurant. Menus are seasonally based and ingredients are sourced from all over the country, including Scottish beef, Cornish lamb and local game. A starter of cured venison with fig marmalade and fresh pear could be followed by grilled fillet of halibut with pan-fried new potatoes, fine beans and a warm salad of scallops. Set menus are good value at lunch and dinner, and special dining evenings are held throughout the year.

Chef: Chris Kewley **Owners:** Mr & Mrs C M Kewley **Times:** 12-2/7-9.30, Closed 1 wk Xmas, Sun, Closed L Sat **Prices:** Fixed L £23-£25, Fixed D £35, Service optional **Wine:** 40 bottles over £20, 30 bottles under £20, 4 by the glass **Notes:** Dress Restrictions, No shorts for men, Air con **Seats:** 50 **Children:** Portions **Directions:** M1 junct 15 (A508 Milton Keynes) to Roade, left at mini rdbt, 500yds on left **Parking:** 20

ENGLAND

TOWCESTER
MAP 11 SP64

◎◎ Vine House Hotel & Restaurant
Modern British
Fresh local ingredients in a home-from-home atmosphere

☎ 01327 811267 100 High St, Paulerspury NN12 7NA
e-mail: info@vinehousehotel.com
web: www.vinehousehotel.com

Two 300-year-old limestone cottages were converted to create this homely restaurant with rooms, run by husband-and-wife team Marcus and Julie Springett. The emphasis is on relaxed, informal dining in a friendly atmosphere. Original features have been preserved and guests are made to feel really welcome in the cosy dining room. Outside there's a carefully tended cottage garden. Food is rustic and full bodied, offered from a daily-changing menu using as much local produce as possible. Prime examples are home-smoked organic salmon with roasted black pudding and curry oil, or local belly of Tamworth pork with sage and onion, with rhubarb and honey crumble served with clotted cream to finish.

Chef: Marcus Springett **Owners:** Mr M & Mrs J Springett **Times:** 12-2/6-10, Closed L Sun-Mon **Prices:** Fixed L £26.95, Fixed D £29.95, Service added 12.5% **Wine:** 47 bottles over £20, 26 bottles under £20, 2 by the glass **Seats:** 26, Pr/dining room 10 **Directions:** 2m S of Towcester, just off A5 **Parking:** 20

WHITTLEBURY
MAP 11 SP64

◎◎ Whittlebury Hall Hotel & Spa
British, European
Fine-dining restaurant dedicated to Formula 1 commentator Murray Walker

☎ 01327 857857 0845 400 0001 NN12 8QH
e-mail: sales@whittleburyhall.co.uk
web: www.whittleburyhall.co.uk

Just around the corner from Silverstone, Murrays restaurant is named after Murray Walker and is home to a series of Formula 1 anecdotes from his commentary years, as well as photos from Formula 1 drivers and teams. It provides an intimate, sophisticated dining venue with formal service and smart casual dress code, offering modern British cooking with classical and international influences. Try a starter like roast scallops with pickled fennel salad and lemon emulsion. Main courses might feature aged corn-fed beef fillet with oxtail pudding or sea bass with confit potatoes, wilted spinach, girolles and vanilla froth. Desserts are 'The Finale' on the menu and may include a chocolate confection with tonka bean ice cream.

Chef: Craig Rose **Owners:** Macepark (Whittlebury) Ltd **Times:** 7-10, Closed 24-26, 31 Dec, 1-7 Jan, Sun, Mon, Closed L all wk **Prices:** Starter £8-£14, Main £18-£26, Dessert £7-£15, Service optional **Notes:** Dress Restrictions, Smart casual, no jeans, trainers or shorts **Seats:** 48, Pr/dining room 400 **Children:** Min 12 yrs, Menu, Portions **Rooms:** 211 (211 en suite) ★★★★ HL **Directions:** A43/A413 to Whittlebury, through village, hotel at far end on right **Parking:** 300

NORTHUMBERLAND

CORNHILL-ON-TWEED
MAP 21 NT83

◎◎ Tillmouth Park Country House Hotel
Modern British
Modern cuisine in Victorian elegance

☎ 01890 882255 TD12 4UU
e-mail: reception@tillmouthpark.force9.co.uk
web: www.tillmouthpark.co.uk

Set on the banks of the River Till in secluded woodland, this imposing Victorian manor recalls a leisurely country-house age. Think stone and marble fireplaces, stained glass, oil paintings, chandeliers, antiques and fishing objets d'art, all backed by relaxed but attentive service. The intimate, wood-panelled Library Dining Room with its crisp white linen overlooks the garden, while aperitifs are served in the stunning galleried lounge or elegant drawing room. In such surroundings, the kitchen's modern spin on traditional dishes shows flair and imagination. Expect local Northumberland sirloin steak with peppered swede and leek, roasted shallots and fondant potatoes, or maybe herb polenta with root vegetables, tomato fondue, parmesan wafer and herb essence. Finish with maple and pecan tart with vanilla ice cream, or try the local cheeses.

Chef: Gerard Boylan, Tony McKay **Owners:** Tillmouth Park Partnership **Times:** 12-2/7-8.45, Closed 26-28 Dec, Closed L Mon-Sat **Prices:** Fixed L £9.50, Fixed D £32.50, Starter £5.65-£8.75, Main £10.25-£16.95, Dessert £5.50-£6.50, Service optional **Wine:** 50 bottles over £20, 8 bottles under £20, 8 by the glass **Notes:** Fixed L 3 courses, Fixed D 4 courses, Dress Restrictions, Smart casual, no jeans, Civ Wed 60 **Seats:** 40, Pr/dining room 20 **Children:** Portions **Rooms:** 14 (14 en suite) ★★★ HL **Directions:** A698, 3m E from Cornhill-on-Tweed **Parking:** 50

HEXHAM
MAP 21 NY96

◎ De Vere Slaley Hall
Traditional British
Fresh flavours and quality ingredients at this impressive hotel

☎ 01434 673350 Slaley NE47 0BX
e-mail: slaley.hall@devere-hotels.com
web: www.devere.co.uk

ENGLAND

Equally attractive to leisure or corporate guests and diners, this large hotel - an original hall with lots of modern extensions - has a renowned golf course, spa facilities and 1,000 acres of parkland. Comfortable lounges include the recently refurbished bar and clubhouse and more traditional library lounge, and the restaurant is light and attractive in autumnal shades. Food is offered from a daily market menu and a brasserie-style carte with well-executed dishes like pressed terrine of confit duckling - with foie gras and truffle - wrapped in Bayonne ham and Savoy cabbage and served with toasted brioche and a Madeira redcurrant jelly, or perhaps chargrilled sirloin steak with sauce béarnaise.

De Vere Slaley Hall

Chef: Paul Kirby **Owners:** De Vere Hotels **Times:** 1-2.30/7-9.30, Closed L Mon-Sat **Prices:** Fixed D £24.95, Starter £6.75-£8.95, Main £22.95-£26.95, Dessert £6.95-£7.25, Service included **Wine:** 9 by the glass **Notes:** Sun L 3 courses carvery £17.95, Dress Restrictions, Smart casual, Civ Wed 250, Air con **Seats:** 200, Pr/dining room 250 **Children:** Menu, Portions **Rooms:** 142 (142 en suite) ★★★★ HL **Directions:** A1 from S to A68. Follow signs for Slaley Hall. From N A69 to Corbridge then take A68 S and follow signs to Slaley Hall **Parking:** 500

LONGHORSLEY   MAP 21 NZ19

◉◉ Dobson Restaurant

Modern International V

Grade II listed country property set amid extensive parkland

☎ 01670 500000 Macdonald Linden Hall, Golf & Country Club NE65 8XF
e-mail: general.lindenhall@macdonald-hotels.co.uk
web: www.macdonaldhotels.co.uk

This Georgian mansion is set in 450 acres of park and woodland surrounded by beautiful countryside. Facilities include a golf course, a recently refurbished country pub and conference suites. The hotel's Dobson Restaurant, which offers superb views, observes the civilised formalities in terms of dress code. The menu is priced for two or three courses, and the same format applies for lunch and dinner but with a more extensive choice in the evening. Recommended dishes include carefully-cooked scallops set on an aubergine purée with a crisp ratatouille dice, or a lovely local beef fillet, accurately cooked and served with fondant potato, caramelised onions and carrots. For dessert, take a hot chocolate fondant with chocolate sauce and orange curd ice cream, or 'singin hinnies' with a rhubarb compôte and cardamom ice cream.

Chef: Paul Blakey **Owners:** Macdonald Hotels **Times:** 12-2.30/6.30-9.30, Closed L Mon-Sat **Prices:** Starter £7, Main £7-£8, Dessert £6, Service

optional **Wine:** 75 bottles over £20, 10 bottles under £20, 16 by the glass **Notes:** Sun L 2 courses £15, 3 courses £18, Vegetarian menu, Dress Restrictions, No denims in evenings, Civ Wed 120 **Seats:** 80, Pr/dining room 25 **Children:** Menu, Portions **Rooms:** 50 (50 en suite) ★★★★ HL **Directions:** 7m NW of Morpeth on A697 off A1

MATFEN   MAP 21 NZ07

◉◉ Matfen Hall

Modern, International

Satisfying dining in elegant country-house surroundings

☎ 01661 886500 NE20 0RH
e-mail: info@matfenhall.com
web: www.matfenhall.com

Set in 250 acres of classic parkland, this imposing Regency mansion - still owned by the Blackett family who built it - boasts its own championship golf course as well as high-tech spa and leisure facilities. The elegant, spacious, book-lined Library and adjoining Print Room restaurant ooze atmosphere, especially by candlelight, with floor-length tablecloths, fine glassware and lovely views. The cuisine is modern British - underpinned by French influences - featuring accurate, balanced and intelligently uncomplicated dishes that allow well-sourced, fresh local produce and flavour to shine. Take veal paupiette with wild mushroom risotto and a Madeira sauce, or perhaps a pistachio soufflé served with dark chocolate ice cream to illustrate the style.

Chef: Phil Hall **Owners:** Sir Hugh & Lady Blackett **Times:** 12.15-2.30/7-10, Closed L Mon-Sat **Prices:** Fixed D £35, Service optional **Wine:** 63 bottles over £20, 37 bottles under £20, 6 by the glass **Notes:** Sun L 3 courses £17.95, Dress Restrictions, Smart casual, Civ Wed 160 **Seats:** 90, Pr/dining room 120 **Children:** Portions **Rooms:** 53 (53 en suite) ★★★★ HL **Directions:** A69 signed Hexham, leave at Heddon on the Wall. Then B6318, through Rudchester & Harlow Hill. Follow signs on right for Matfen **Parking:** 120

PONTELAND   MAP 21 NZ17

⚜ *Café Lowrey*

British, French

Good value bistro-style eating

☎ 01661 820357   35 The Broadway, Darras Hall,
Ponteland NE20 9PW
web: www.cafelowrey.co.uk

Situated within a small shopping precinct in a residential area of
Ponteland not far from Newcastle airport, this modern bistro-style
restaurant offers an extensive menu featuring modern British and
French-style dishes. The simple interior includes quarry-tiled floors,
clothed tables and Victorian-style wooden chairs. Using local produce,
the menu may include starters such as cheddar cheese and spinach
soufflé, followed perhaps by herb-crusted pork fillet served with mash
and mushroom cream, with caramelised pineapple and coconut
sorbet for dessert. Early evening specials are on offer Monday to
Friday from 5.30-7pm and Saturday lunchtime.

Times: 12-2/5.30-10, Closed BHs, Sun, Closed L Mon-Fri **Directions:** From
A696, follow signs for Darras Hall. Left at mini rdbt, restaurant in 200yds

NOTTINGHAMSHIRE

GUNTHORPE   MAP 11 SK64

⚜ Tom Browns Brasserie

Modern International NEW

Popular brasserie with splendid river views

☎ 0115 9663642   The Old School House, Trentside
NG14 7FB
e-mail: info@tombrowns.co.uk
web: www.tombrowns.co.uk

This converted Victorian school house, set on the banks of the River
Trent, has several dining areas and a popular outside decking area.
Dark chocolate high-backed leather chairs, wooden floors, white
linen-clad tables, candlelight and lively music set a vibrant
atmosphere. Family-run, the brasserie style of this contemporary
décor extends to the fresh, modern feel of the menu, which takes in
starters like classic Mediterranean fish soup with rouille and gruyère
crostini and main courses such as pan-seared sea bass fillet on pea,
dill and fennel risotto, asparagus and sun-dried tomato oil. For
dessert, try the apple and rhubarb tarte Tatin with pecan caramel
sauce and clotted cream.

Chef: Chris Hooton **Owners:** Adam & Robin Perkins **Times:** 12-2.30/6-
9.30, Closed D 25-26 Dec **Prices:** Fixed L £13.95, Fixed D £15.95, Starter
£5.95-£8.50, Main £9.95-£19.95, Dessert £5.75-£6.50, Service optional
Wine: 30 bottles over £20, 30 bottles under £20, 18 by the glass
Notes: Sun L, Dress Restrictions, Smart casual, Air con **Seats:** 100,
Pr/dining room 20 **Children:** Portions **Directions:** A6097, Gunthorpe
Bridge **Parking:** 9

LANGAR   MAP 11 SK73

⚜⚜ Langar Hall

Traditional British 🖥

Impressive cooking in tranquil country-house setting

☎ 01949 860559   NG13 9HG
e-mail: imogen@langarhall.co.uk
web: www.langarhall.com

This Victorian country house has a secluded setting overlooking
gardens and ancient fishponds to the fields and hamlet beyond. The
lounges, library and elegant dining room are furnished with antiques,
complemented by a warm welcome and helpful service. The
comfortable, candlelit, pillared dining room is the perfect setting for
dinner, which comprises seasonal British dishes. Try steamed fillet of
brill with parmesan gnocchi and a mussel sauce, or perhaps roast
saddle and chargrilled leg of Langar lamb with rösti potato, while a
warm apple Charlotte with toffee cream might catch the eye at
dessert. (The garden conservatory provides a lighter menu.)

Chef: Rick Wolverson, Gary Booth **Owners:** Imogen Skirving **Times:** 12-
2/7-10 **Prices:** Fixed L £10-£16.50, Fixed D £25-£39.50, Starter £5.50-
£16.50, Main £13.50-£20, Dessert £7.50, Service added but optional 10%
Wine: 20 bottles over £20, 30 bottles under £20, 4 by the glass
Notes: Vegetarian available, Dress Restrictions, Smart casual, Civ Wed 50
Seats: 30, Pr/dining room 20 **Children:** Portions **Rooms:** 12 (12 en
suite) ★★★ HL **Directions:** Off A46 & A52 in village centre (behind
church) **Parking:** 40

ENGLAND

NOTTINGHAM   MAP 11 SK53

◉◉ Hart's Restaurant

Modern British V

Skilfully prepared dishes in a modern, urban, brasserie setting

☎ 0115 988 1900   Standard Hill, Park Row NG1 6FN
e-mail: ask@hartsnottingham.co.uk
web: www.hartsnottingham.co.uk

Hart's fits comfortably into what used to be part of Nottingham's old General Hospital building. Situated 30 metres from the hotel itself, the modern restaurant has booths and banquettes, warm colours and a lighting scheme that highlights the contemporary art. There's a lively but comfortable, intimate and sophisticated atmosphere. Skilfully prepared modern British dishes are the norm here with extensive use of local produce wherever possible. Subtle presentation only augments the pleasure; take thyme-roasted pork belly served with bubble-and-squeak, sautéed baby leeks and a cider sauce, or perhaps oven-roast cod with rösti potato, capers and brown shrimp butter. Finish with a lemongrass crème brûlée and bitter chocolate sorbet.

Chef: Tom Earle **Owners:** Tim Hart **Times:** 12-2/7-10.30, Closed 26 Dec & 1 Jan, Closed L 31 Dec, D 25 Dec **Prices:** Fixed L £12.95-£14, Fixed D £22.50, Starter £5.50-£13, Main £13.95-£21.50, Dessert £750-£9.50, Service added but optional 12% **Wine:** 57 bottles over £20, 23 bottles under £20, 6 by the glass **Notes:** Fixed D available Sun-Thu, Vegetarian menu, Civ Wed 110 **Seats:** 80, Pr/dining room 90 **Children:** Portions **Rooms:** 32 (32 en suite) ★★★★ HL **Directions:** M1 junct 24, follow A453 to city centre. Follow signs to the Castle. Once on Maid Marion Way turn left at the Gala Casino, continue to top of the hill and turn left through black gates **Parking:** 17

◉ The Lobster Pot

Seafood

A gem of a seafood restaurant

☎ 0115 947 0707   199 Mansfield Rd NG1 3FS

Although unassuming from the outside, you walk by this friendly, relaxed seafood restaurant at your peril! The simple décor features fish-themed objets d'art and Middle Eastern carvings, alongside chunky wooden tables. A range of different smoked salmons is available, and there's also a daily specials board. Saucing is subtle and takes care not to dominate the main ingredient. Starters include the likes of excellent smoked haddock chowder, while for mains you could expect salmon steamed in oyster sauce with fresh ginger. Early booking is advised.

Chef: Mr & Mrs Pongsawang **Owners:** Mr & Mrs Pongsawang **Times:** 12-2/6-10.30, Closed BHs, Mon, Closed L Sun **Prices:** Starter £3.95-£4.50, Main £7.95-£12.95, Dessert £2.95, Service optional **Wine:** 2 bottles over £20, 30 bottles under £20, 3 by the glass **Seats:** 40 **Children:** Portions **Directions:** From Nottingham city centre N on A60 for 0.5m, restaurant on left at the lights where Huntingdon St joins Mansfield Rd

◉ Merchants Restaurant & Bar

Modern French

Classic French brasserie with chic interior

☎ 0115 958 9898 & 952 3211   Lace Market Hotel, 31 High Pavement NG1 1HE
e-mail: dine@merchantsnottingham.co.uk
web: www.merchantsnottingham.co.uk

Situated in the vibrant Lace Market area of Nottingham, this former Georgian lace factory has found a new lease of life as a classic brasserie restaurant. The stylish yet unstuffy décor was designed by the world-renowned David Collins, interior architect to many of Marco Pierre White's restaurants, and includes a Canadian pressed tin ceiling

CONTINUED

ENGLAND

NOTTINGHAM CONTINUED

and an eye-catching frieze of Nottingham lace panels. The award-winning waiting staff are relaxed but attentive, serving up seasonal, wholesome French cooking with a modern edge. Try a starter of seared Saint Mawes diver scallops and tomato confit salad with parmesan, followed perhaps by a main course of roasted saddle of lamb, potato gratin, cherry tomatoes and frog's legs, accompanied by one of the wines from the superb list.

Chef: Patrick Tweedie **Owners:** Lace Market Hotel Ltd **Times:** 12-2.30/7-10.30, Closed 26 Dec, 1 Jan, Sun-Mon, Closed L Sat **Prices:** Fixed L £12.95, Fixed D £35-£55, Starter £8.50-£13.50, Main £18.50-£23.50, Dessert £6.50-£10.50, Service added but optional 10% **Wine:** 40+ bottles over £20, 40+ bottles under £20, 10 by the glass **Notes:** Fixed D 4 courses, Dégustation menu £55, Civ Wed 60, Air con **Seats:** 50, Pr/dining room 20 **Children:** Menu, Portions **Rooms:** 42 (42 en suite) ★★★★ TH **Directions:** Follow city-centre signs for Galleries of Justice, entrance is opposite **Parking:** On street. NCP adjacent

⊛ The Nottingham Belfry
Modern International NEW
Modern hotel with cool design and interesting food

☎ 0115 973 9393 Mellor's Way, Off Woodhouse Way NG8 6PY

e-mail: nottinghambelfry@qhotels.co.uk
web: www.qhotels.co.uk/hotels/the-nottingham-belfry-nottingham-nottinghamshire/

This smart new hotel oozes stylish good looks and comes set in its own grounds, conveniently close to the motorway yet not far from the city centre. There are two restaurants (one bistro style) and two bars, all in contemporary vogue. The main Lawrence restaurant is decked out in delicate mauve-coloured walls donned with interesting artwork based on the works of DH Lawrence, while tables are dark-stained wood (a design feature throughout the hotel). Service is youthful, enthusiastic and friendly, while the ambitious cooking provides bags of appeal too; take a fillet of halibut accompanied by creamed leeks and blackberry shallots, or perhaps apple and pecan tarte Tatin with lemon sorbet.

Chef: Leigh Lambert **Owners:** QHotels **Times:** 12-3/7-10.30 **Prices:** Fixed D £31.95, Starter £4.25-£6.75, Main £13.50-£16.95, Dessert £5-£6.50, Service optional **Notes:** Sun L 2 courses £10.95, 3 courses £15.95, Vegetarian available, Dress Restrictions, Smart casual, no trainers, no ripped jeans, Civ Wed 210, Air con **Seats:** 140 **Children:** Menu, Portions **Rooms:** 120 (120 en suite) ★★★★ HL **Parking:** 200 **Directions:** A6002 towards Stapleford and Beeston, continue for 0.75m. Hotel on right, approaching rdbt, take last exit into Mellor's Way

⊛⊛⊛⊛ Restaurant Sat Bains with Rooms
see opposite

Loch Fyne Restaurant & Oyster Bar
☎ 0115 988 6840 17 King St NG1 2AY
Quality seafood chain.

MemSaab Restaurant
☎ 0115 957 0009 12-14 Maid Marion Way NG1 6HS
web: contact@mem-saab.co.uk
Authentic Indian cuisine in city-centre restaurant with stylish interior.

⊛⊛ World Service
Modern British ⏹ NOTABLE WINE LIST
Globetrotting décor and food in a Georgian property

☎ 0115 847 5587 Newdigate House, Castle Gate NG1 6AF
e-mail: enquiries@worldservicerestaurant.com
web: www.worldservicerestaurant.com

A Nottingham favourite, this chic, buzzy eatery is designed to look like the home of an eccentric traveller, and teams country-house comfort with exotic artefacts to create a relaxed, contemporary, designer interior. Entry is via an oriental garden to a lounge where gilt armchairs, a roaring fire and coconut shell tables await, plus a decadent list of cocktails. Dining tables are darkwood, seating comes in brown leather and walls are lined with low-level mirrors. The food fits the bill, taking an equally modern approach punctuated by precision and finesse; take baked cod served with a prawn cannelloni, roasted fennel and a bouillabaisse sauce, and to finish, a warm greengage and almond tart with green Chartreuse ice cream.

Chef: Preston Walker **Owners:** Daniel Lindsay, Phillip Morgan, Ashley Walter, Chris Elson **Times:** 12-2.15/7-10, Closed 1-7 Jan **Prices:** Fixed L £12, Fixed D £22, Starter £5-£12, Main £12.50-£19.50, Dessert £5.25-£8, Service added but optional 10% **Wine:** 90 bottles over £20, 15 bottles under £20, 10 by the glass **Notes:** Fixed D Sun only, Vegetarian available **Seats:** 80, Pr/dining room 34 **Children:** Min 12 yrs D, Menu, Portions **Directions:** 200mtrs from city centre, 50mtrs from Nottingham Castle **Parking:** NCP

🖥 Georgetown
☎ 0870 755 7756 Colwick Hall Hotel, Colwick Park, Racecourse Rd NG2 4BH
web: www.theaa.com/travel/index.jsp

Set in beautiful Colwick Hall, Georgetown offers superb choices among Malaysian, Chinese and Indian cuisine in a colonial setting.

Restaurant Sat Bains with Rooms

NOTTINGHAM MAP 11 SK53

Modern European V 🍷 NOTABLE WINE LIST

Molecular cooking that strikes to the heart of the palate

☎ 0115 986 6566 Lenton Ln, Trentside NG7 2SA
e-mail: info@restaurantsatbains.net
web: www.restaurantsatbains.com

Tucked away down a quiet lane (take heed of the directions as it is easily missed), this delightful, sympathetically converted Victorian farmhouse sits on the banks of the Trent. Smartly refurbished and fashionably attired, quality reigns supreme, from the restaurant's high-backed leather seats to the spacious tables and first-class tableware - complete with the chef-patron's monogrammed signature. The lounge offers champagne and oysters, and after-dinner relaxing. Exposed beams, veneered flagstone floors, a jazz backing track and expressionist modern art all conspire to create a smooth, classy and restrained backdrop for some flamboyant cooking. Service is delightfully friendly, with genuine warmth and knowledge and passion about both food and wine, while Sat Bains' culinary odyssey is not to be missed - this is modern cooking on the edge from a highly-skilled pioneer.
Abruptly scripted dish descriptions and combinations stretch the imagination and dazzle with a host of innovative techniques, textures and bright, fresh flavours that explore the palate and sensations, delivering bold, distinctive, precise, delightfully balanced and imaginative cooking of such calibre that the tasting menu or surprise offering (including wine tasting options) are almost a requisite. So expect the carte to deliver the likes of Cornish brill served with parsley root, oxtail, lettuce, capers, cockscomb and red wine jus, or perhaps pigeon with carrot, feta, melon, chocolate and grapefruit, while 'textures of pear' - with almond, caramel and vanilla - might catch the eye at dessert. This is a rare style of cooking, something out-of-the-ordinary, new and exciting, so hang on for the ride, or perhaps stay overnight in one of the attractively presented bedrooms to recover from the culinary sojourn.

Chef: Sat Bains
Owners: Sat Bains, Amanda Bains
Times: 7-9.30, Closed 2 wks Jan & 2wks Aug, Sun, Mon, Closed L all week
Prices: Fixed D £47, Service added 12.5%
Wine: 120 bottles over £20, 30 by the glass
Notes: Tasting menu 10 courses £65, Vegetarian menu, Air con
Seats: 30, Pr/dining room 14
Rooms: 8 (8 en suite)★★★ HL
Directions: From M1 junct 24 take A453 for approx 8 m. Through Clifton, road divides into 3 - take middle lane signed Lenton Lane Industrial Estate, then 1st left and left again - brown signpost Restaurant Sat Bains
Parking: 22

ENGLAND

OXFORDSHIRE

ARDINGTON
MAP 05 SU48

◉◉ The Boar's Head

British, European
Relaxed dining in charming village setting

☎ 01235 833254 Church St OX12 8QA
e-mail: info@boarsheadardington.co.uk
web: www.boarsheadardington.co.uk

Set in the timeless downland village of Ardington, this handsome half-timbered pub-cum-restaurant stands in a lovely spot beside the parish church. It extends a friendly welcome whether you're just relaxing over a quiet drink, enjoying a light bar snack, or taking a meal in the rustic-style restaurant. The straightforward carte menu, based on seasonal and local ingredients, certainly delivers some quality modern British dishes. For starters, take a brochette of Scottish langoustines, followed by grilled Cornish cod with rösti and truffle hollandaise, or maybe fillet of Newlyn sea bass with ratatouille and chorizo. The dark and white chocolate slice with home-made raspberry ripple ice cream makes an excellent finish, or if you have room go for the selection of British cheeses with fruitcake.

Chef: Bruce Buchan **Owners:** Boar's Head (Ardington) Ltd **Times:** 12-2/7-10, Closed 25 Dec **Prices:** Fixed L £14.50, Starter £6.95-£12.95, Main £16.50-£20.50, Dessert £6.95-£8.95, Service optional **Wine:** 70 bottles over £20, 30 bottles under £20, 12 by the glass **Notes:** Sun L 3 courses £22.50, Vegetarian available **Seats:** 40, Pr/dining room 24 **Children:** Portions **Rooms:** 3 (3 en suite) ★★★★ INN **Directions:** 2 m E of Wantage on A417 **Parking:** 20

BICESTER
MAP 11 SP52

◉ Bignell Park Hotel

Modern British V
Creative cooking in country setting

☎ 01869 326550 0870 0421024 Chesterton OX26 1UE
e-mail: enq@bignellparkhotel.co.uk
web: www.bignellparkhotel.co.uk

Sixteenth-century charm and character combine well with modern facilities at this small hotel situated in a peaceful country setting near Bicester Shopping Village. Housed in a converted barn, with a dramatic gallery as a backdrop, the oak-beamed restaurant adorned with paintings is the setting for imaginative fixed-price dinners. Daily menus offer value for money and a varied choice of confidently cooked modern dishes and traditional favourites. Examples include confit belly pork, with prune compôte, lamb rump with roasted root vegetables and lentil and chorizo casserole, and sticky toffee pudding with caramel foam and vanilla bean ice.

Chef: Chris Coates **Owners:** Caparo Hotels **Times:** 12-2/7-9.30, Closed D Sun **Prices:** Fixed L £12.50-£15.50, Fixed D £24.95-£27.95, Service optional **Wine:** 16 bottles over £20, 30 bottles under £20, 4 by the glass **Notes:** Sun L £18.95, Vegetarian menu, Civ Wed 60 **Seats:** 60, Pr/dining room 20 **Children:** Menu, Portions **Rooms:** 23 (23 en suite) ★★★ HL **Directions:** M40 junct 9, follow A41 towards Bicester, turn off at Chesterton and hotel is signed at turning **Parking:** 50

BRITWELL SALOME MAP 05 SU69

◎◎ The Goose

Modern French

18th-century gastro-pub offering accomplished cuisine

☎ 01491 612304 OX49 5LG

e-mail: info_thegoose@btconnect.com

Re-opened in summer 2006 following extensive refurbishment under new owners, this well-established restaurant now sports a simple, modern décor with olive green walls, plain wooden tables and comfortable seating. The bar is now at the rear and the warm, inviting dining room is located at the front. Service is attentive from an enthusiastic young team who contribute to a great overall experience. Serious, high-quality cooking is offered here with simple presentation and tip-top seasonal produce. Cooking skills are accomplished, demonstrated in dishes like honey-roasted quail with pickled wild mushrooms and celeriac and mustard remoulade, slow-cooked breast of lamb with crispy lamb sweetbreads, roasted carrot purée and braising jus, and a dessert of warm chocolate tart with orange cream. Good accompaniments include lovely home-made bread.

Chef: Matthew Tomkinson **Times:** 12-3/7-11, Closed D Sun **Prices:** Fixed L £15, Fixed D £19, Starter £6-£12, Main £14-£22, Dessert £6-£7, Service optional **Wine:** 57 bottles over £20, 28 bottles under £20, 11 by the glass **Notes:** Sun L/D 2 courses £10.95 **Seats:** 40, Pr/dining room 25 **Children:** Menu, Portions **Directions:** M40 junct 6 take B4009 to Watlington, then towards Benson. Restaurant on left 1.5m **Parking:** 35

BURFORD MAP 05 SP21

◎◎ The Angel at Burford

Modern European

Simple, effective brasserie fare in a pretty village

☎ 01993 822714 14 Witney St OX18 4SN

e-mail: jo@theangel-uk.com

web: www.theangel-uk.com

This former 16th-century coaching inn is situated at the edge of a quiet picturesque village, wrapped in a cocoon of stone cottages. The bijou restaurant is a delicious haven of rustic elegance, complete with sunny courtyard and walled garden. Inside, the white-painted walls create a bright and breezy feel, with open stonework, wooden beams and log fires, an old church pew in the bar, and a host of interesting artefacts to let the eye wander over while sampling the excellent brasserie-style food. Modern cuisine using local and seasonal produce offers up good, well-balanced flavours, with varied and appropriate presentation. Take a starter of pan-fried scallops with avocado and tomatoes in prawn jelly, perhaps followed by a main course like breast of guinea fowl with herb ricotta on roasted sweet potato.

Times: 12-2/7-9.30, Closed 18 Jan-11 Feb, Mon, Closed D Sun **Rooms:** 3 (3 en suite) ★★★★ RR **Directions:** From A40, turn off at Burford rdbt, down hill 1st right into Swan Lane, 1st left to Pytts Lane, left at end into Witney St

◎ The Bay Tree Hotel

Traditional British

Historic inn with an appealing modern menu

☎ 01993 822791 Sheep St OX18 4LW

e-mail: bookings@cotswold-inns-hotels.co.uk

web: www.cotswold-inns-hotels.co.uk/baytree

Visitors have been welcomed through the solid oak doors of this stone-built inn since 1565, and you can relax before dinner with a drink in the Woolsack bar, with its open fire and comfy leather armchairs. In the restaurant, tapestry hangings, a flagstone floor and original leaded windows combine to create an elegant country feel, and there are views of the patio and garden. Produce is locally sourced and features in dishes of smoked haddock and salmon fishcakes, pan-fried sirloin of beef, and desserts like dark chocolate torte with mascarpone Chantilly, or baked banana and toffee cheesecake with vanilla ice cream.

Chef: Brian Andrews **Owners:** Cotswold Inns & Hotels **Times:** 12-2/7-9.30 **Prices:** Fixed L £14.95, Fixed D £27.95, Service optional **Notes:** Fixed L 3 courses, Sun L £14.95 3 courses, Dress Restrictions, No jeans or trainers, Civ Wed 60 **Seats:** 70, Pr/dining room 24 **Children:** Portions **Rooms:** 21 (21 en suite) ★★★ HL **Directions:** From Oxford, A40, take right at Burford rdbt. Continue halfway down the hill and turn left into Sheep St. Hotel is 200yds on right **Parking:** 55

◎◎ The Lamb Inn

Traditional British

Traditional coaching inn with an imaginative menu

☎ 01993 823155 Sheep St OX18 4LR

e-mail: info@lambinn-burford.co.uk

web: www.cotswold-inns-hotels.co.uk/lamb

Dating from 1420, the inn was originally built as weavers' cottages. The spacious restaurant overlooks a lovely courtyard with Cotswold stone walls and a sitting area that positively buzzes in the summer. Inside, cream walls, mullioned windows and frosted skylights make for a bright, cheerful room decorated with food-related pictures, wooden tables and chairs and large floral displays. The food is imaginative and the flavours concise and well balanced using the best of local produce, such as Gloucestershire Old Spot pork, Hereford beef, Bibury trout and Cerney goat's cheese. House specialities include fried lamb's sweetbreads with rosemary biscuit, or perhaps a duo of beef, followed by chocolate torte with rum-and-raisin ice cream.

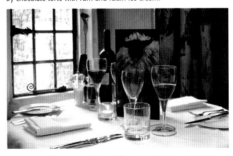

Chef: Sean Ducie **Owners:** Cotswold Inns & Hotels **Times:** 12-2.30/7-9.30 **Prices:** Fixed D £32.50, Service added but optional 10% **Wine:** 9 by the glass **Notes:** Sun D menu, Dress Restrictions, Smart casual, No jeans or T-shirts **Seats:** 55 **Children:** Portions **Rooms:** 17 (17 en suite) ★★★ HL **Directions:** 1st left as you descend on the High St **Parking:** Care of The Bay Tree Hotel

BURFORD CONTINUED

⊛ The Navy Oak

British, European

Traditional surroundings, inventive modern dishes

☎ 01993 878496 Lower End, Leafield OX29 9QQ
e-mail: thenavyoak@aol.com
web: www.thenavyoak.co.uk

The open-plan kitchen in the restaurant of this 400-year-old village pub allows diners to view the chefs at work while enjoying the fruits of their labours. Elsewhere, open fires and cosy lighting contribute to a traditional country inn feel. The cooking style draws on a range of influences to create interesting modern dishes, with the lunch menu taking in baguettes and snacks, while the dinner menu focuses on more complex fare. Starters might include queen scallops with rocket and hazelnut butter, while mains range from spiced Moroccan fish tagine with coriander rice, to pan-fried saddle of Wychwood venison with crushed potatoes, prunes and bacon.

Chef: Alastair Ward & Timothy Pile **Owners:** Alastair & Sarah Ward **Times:** 12.30-2.30/7-9.30, Closed 1-10 Jan, Mon, Closed D Sun **Prices:** Fixed L £10-£15, Starter £5.50-£7.50, Main £8.50-£15.50, Dessert £5-£6.50, Service optional **Wine:** 8 bottles over £20, 7 bottles under £20, 10 by the glass **Notes:** Gastronomic menu 6 courses inc wine £40, Sun L £20 **Seats:** 60, Pr/dining room 30 **Children:** Portions **Directions:** Telephone for directions **Parking:** 25

CHARLBURY   MAP 11 SP31

⊛ The Bell at Charlbury, Hotel & Restaurant

Modern British 🖥

Warm ambience and fine cuisine

☎ 01608 810278 Church St OX7 3PP
e-mail: reservations@bellhotel-charlbury.com
web: www.bellhotel-charlbury.com

This privately-owned 18th-century coaching inn of mellow Cotswold stone is set in over an acre of grounds. The cosy, traditional oak-beamed bar and lounge offer a warm welcome and the dining room has a friendly, informal ambience. Modern British cooking here comes with European influences and makes use of fine local produce on a monthly-changing carte. Typical dishes might include scallop and tiger prawn bruschetta with chilli jam to start, and perhaps pork belly with mashed potato, braised red cabbage and apple, or seared swordfish with champ and a plum and cherry tomato compôte to follow.

Chef: Pete Southey **Owners:** Fergus & Sarah McVey **Times:** 12-2.30/7-9.30 **Prices:** Fixed L £7.50-£9.50, Fixed D £15-£25, Starter £4.95-£8.95, Main £9.95-£19.95, Dessert £4.50-£5.50, Service optional, Group min 8 service 10% **Wine:** 10 bottles over £20, 17 bottles under £20, 8 by the glass **Notes:** Tasting menu available, Vegetarian available **Seats:** 30, Pr/dining room 20 **Children:** Menu, Portions **Rooms:** 12 (12 en suite) ★★ HL **Directions:** Situated 3m off A44 between Oxford and Chipping Norton 5m NW of Woodstock. From London via M40 follow signs for Blenheim Palace, then A44 N. Take 1st left after Woodstock. Hotel is near church **Parking:** 40

CHECKENDON   MAP 05 SU68

⊛⊛ Wheeler's of St James at The Highwayman

British, French

Marco Pierre White transformation of a 17th-century pub

☎ 01491 682020 Exlade St RG8 0UA
e-mail: wheelers@marcopierrewhite.org
web: www.marcopierrewhite.org

A country pub with a sophisticated interior, The Highwayman is tucked away off the main road to Reading on the outskirts of the village. Fixtures and fittings are from the old Wheeler's of St James in London, so expect wood panelling, dark walls, comfortable leather chairs and banquette seating, generous sized tables (some solid marble), and an abundance of black and white photos. It's bigger than you think, with a bar, small dining area, lounge area and main dining room. Food is traditional British with a French twist - soft roes on toast or potage of mussels Billy-By to start, followed by Dover sole meunière or honey-roast belly pork Marco Polo with butter beans - with some dishes revealing their origins - Mirabelle potted salmon and Pierre Koffman au chocolat Amer.

Times: 12-2.30/6-10.30 **Directions:** Telephone for directions

CHINNOR   MAP 05 SP70

⊛⊛ Sir Charles Napier

British, French 🍷 NOTABLE WINE LIST

Country inn of great character filled with beautiful sculptures

☎ 01494 483011 Sprigg's Alley OX39 4BX
e-mail: info@sircharlesnapier.co.uk
web: www.sircharlesnapier.co.uk

Huge fires in winter and comfortable sofas, exposed beams and flagstone floors create a welcoming atmosphere at this popular old country inn. Unusual sculptures dotted around the bar and dining room provide a talking point for visitors, and there's a vine-shaded terrace outside (with more sculptures) for summer dining. The kitchen shows a dedication to quality produce and clean, accurate flavours in some classy cooking underpinned by a classical French theme. Take a double-baked smoked haddock and cheddar soufflé to start, or perhaps scallops with celeriac purée, tortellini and St Jacques velouté, followed up with paupiettes of salmon and sole with linguine and a crab and lemongrass sauce, or maybe wild sea bass with rhubarb, ginger and pommes Anna.

Chef: Sam Hughes **Owners:** Julie Griffiths **Times:** 12-3.30/6.30-10, Closed 25-27 Dec, Mon, Closed D Sun **Prices:** Fixed L £14.50-£15.50, Fixed D

£16.50, Starter £7.50-£13.50, Main £16.50-£20.50, Dessert £6.25-£7.50, Service added but optional 12.5% **Wine:** 200 bottles over £20, 29 bottles under £20, 9 by the glass **Notes:** Fixed D 2 courses, Air con **Seats:** 75, Pr/dining room 45 **Children:** Min 6 yrs D, Menu, Portions **Directions:** M40 junct 6 to Chinnor. Turn right at rdbt, up hill for 2m to Sprigg's Alley **Parking:** 60

CHOLSEY
MAP 05 SU58

⊛ The Sweet Olive

French
French restaurant in charming pub

☎ 01235 851272 Baker St OX11 9DD

Quintessential English pub meets Gallic charm - and what a match! This country restaurant pulls in crowds of diners who enjoy the good honest cooking from a mainly French team. The rustic interior is a combination of simple country inn and French restaurant, with wine cases and bottles decorating the walls. Thankfully, this is one pub where there is still a bar, so you can have a drink and eat in the bar if you choose. Expect starters like French onion soup with croûtons and cheese, followed by a panaché of fish with champagne and saffron sauce served with lemon rice, or Scottish scallops in lime butter sauce.

DEDDINGTON
MAP 11 SP43

⊛ Deddington Arms

Traditional British
Traditional but stylish coaching inn offering fine food

☎ 01869 338364 Horsefair OX15 0SH
e-mail: deddarms@oxfordshire-hotels.co.uk
web: www.deddington-arms-hotel.co.uk

This charming, Cotswold stone coaching inn off the market square has an original oak-beamed bar with flagstone floor and cosy fireplace. Newly refurbished, the smart, air-conditioned restaurant features leather high-backed chairs and carved wood panelling and archways. You'll find traditional British fare on the menu with Mediterranean influences. Typical dishes might include roast pork belly with watercress salad to start, followed by sea bass fillet with seafood cream sauce or rib-eye steak with pepper sauce. For dessert, try lemon and mascarpone cheesecake with orange sorbet, or finish with a plate of English cheeses.

Chef: Nick Porter **Owners:** Oxfordshire Hotels Ltd **Times:** 12-2/6.30-9.45 **Prices:** Fixed L £15.45, Fixed D £20-£30, Starter £4.50-£7.50, Main £10.95-£18.50, Dessert £4.95-£5.95, Service optional **Wine:** 20 bottles over £20, 22 bottles under £20, 9 by the glass **Notes:** Vegetarian available, Air con **Seats:** 60, Pr/dining room 30 **Children:** Menu, Portions **Rooms:** 27 (27 en suite) ★★★ HL **Directions:** Telephone for directions **Parking:** 36

DORCHESTER (ON THAMES) MAP 05 SU59

⊛ George Hotel

Traditional
Classic coaching inn serving traditional food with a twist

☎ 01865 340404 25 High St OX10 7HH
e-mail: thegeorgehotel@fsmail.net
web: www.thegeorgedorchester.co.uk

A centrally located inn, dating from 1495, next door to Dorchester Abbey, the George has plenty of historic character with beams and inglenook fireplaces. The dining room boasts its own secret garden and water feature. Cooking is skilled with an interesting take on some generally traditional fare, such as salad of spiced sausage, black pudding and potato with poached egg, followed by pan-fried fillet of salmon with capers, or lamb shank with mashed potato and minted gravy. Food is also served in the Potboys bar.

Times: 12-2.15/7-9.30, Closed Xmas, New Year, Mon, Closed L Tue-Sat **Rooms:** 17 (17 en suite) **Directions:** In town centre, 8m south of Oxford

⊛⊛ White Hart Hotel

British, French
Historic coaching inn serving fine cuisine

☎ 01865 340074 High St OX10 7HN
e-mail: whitehart@oxfordshire-hotels.co.uk
web: www.oxfordshire-hotels.co.uk

Situated in the heart of a picturesque village, this 17th-century coaching inn retains its original façade with wooden gates, beams and brickwork. Inside, the décor is warm and inviting, complementing the flagstone floors and stone fireplaces with a vaulted timber ceiling in the restaurant. The lunchtime special menu is great value and Sunday lunch is a popular option too. The carte in the recently refurbished restaurant demonstrates a serious approach to cuisine with simple presentation and quality produce. Start with hand-caught scallops served with parsnip purée and bacon and lime dressing before a typical main course of pavé of beef with pesto mash, stuffed tomatoes and red wine reduction. Try iced Drambuie parfait with sweet berries for dessert.

Chef: Stuart Turvey **Owners:** Oxfordshire Hotels Ltd **Times:** 12-2.30/6.30-9.30 **Prices:** Food prices not confirmed for 2008. Please telephone for details **Wine:** 10 bottles over £20, 15 bottles under £20, 6 by the glass **Notes:** Dress Restrictions, Smart casual preferred **Seats:** 40, Pr/dining room 16 **Children:** Portions **Rooms:** 26 (26 en suite) ★★★ HL **Directions:** Village centre. Just off A415/ A4074. 3m from Wallingford, 6m from Abingdon **Parking:** 25

Le Manoir aux Quat' Saisons

GREAT MILTON MAP 05 SP60

Modern French V NOTABLE WINE LIST

An absolute dream of a place

☎ 01844 278881   OX44 7PD
e-mail: lemanoir@blanc.co.uk **web:** www.manoir.com

Whatever the season, a visit to this mellow stone, 15th-century manor-house hotel, set in beautiful grounds, is one of life's not-to-be-missed experiences - it's the epitome of luxury and good taste, where modern style and classic virtues combine with truly memorable cooking and exemplary service. The dining room is in three parts, with the principal rooms a conservatory extension and the Grand Salle which both continue the contemporary theme. But no visit here would be complete without a stroll round the stunning gardens dotted with life-size bronze statues and, among the delights beyond the garden wall, there's a Japanese garden and teahouse and the all-important organic potager. Producing some 90 types of vegetables and over 70 varieties of herbs for the kitchen, it's fundamental to the Blanc cooking philosophy - freshness, quality and seasonality are vital to the ethos here. This extends to the use and sourcing of local produce - organic where possible - reconnecting gastronomy with local producers. So expect classic French dishes in a modern, light, fresh style with clear, precise flavours, balance and subtlety, delivered with breathtaking skill and immaculate presentation. Take braised fillet of turbot with Cornish crab, a bouillon of lemongrass and new season asparagus, and to finish, perhaps a rhubarb and gariguette strawberry crumble with vanilla ice cream. And do save room for the dazzling selection of oven-fresh breads, canapés and petits fours that line up alongside a superb wine list. The number of fine chefs who have learned their trade here is a testament to Raymond's supreme commitment to training and ultimately a tribute to the man and the high esteem in which his kitchen and renowned hotel are held. So don't wait, this is a must-do experience.

Chef: Raymond Blanc & Gary Jones
Owners: Mr R Blanc
Times: 12-2.30/7-10
Prices: Fixed L £45, Starter £32-£34, Main £36-£38, Dessert £19, Service optional
Wine: 1,000 bottles over £20, 5 bottles under £20, 16 by the glass
Notes: Menu Découverte available daily, Fixed L 3 courses, Vegetarian menu, Dress Restrictions, No jeans, trainers or shorts, Civ Wed 50, Air con
Seats: 100, Pr/dining room 50
Children: Menu, Portions
Rooms: 32 (32 en suite)★★★★★ HL
Directions: M40 junct 7 follow A329 towards Wallingford. After 1m turn right, signed Great Milton and Le Manoir aux Quat' Saisons
Parking: 70

GORING
MAP 05 SU68

◎◎ The Leatherne Bottel
British

Unique Thames-side location for enjoyable eating

☎ 01491 872667   RG8 0HS
e-mail: leathernebottel@aol.com
web: www.leathernebottel.co.uk

Right on the Thames, The Leatherne Bottel is the perfect location for alfresco dining when the weather is favourable. Inside the dining room overlooks the river and has striking artwork and fresh flower displays that brighten any mood, and there is a separate bar area. The chef adds Pacific Rim ideas, inspired by her time in New Zealand, to the modern British and European dishes. Perhaps try clear fish soup, poached fish and crab ravioli followed by pan-seared fillet of halibut, samphire seaweed, lemongrass and galangal butter.

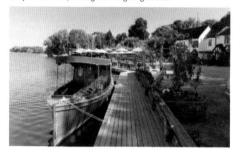

Times: 12-2/7-9, Closed 31 Dec, Closed D Sun   **Directions:** M4 junct 12 or M40 junct 6, signed from B4009 towards Wallingford

HENLEY-ON-THAMES
MAP 05 SU78

◎ The Cherry Tree Inn
Modern British, French

Popular inn with a modern menu

☎ 01491 680430   Stoke Row RG9 5QA
e-mail: info@thecherrytreeinn.com
web: www.thecherrytreeinn.com

Set in the sleepy hamlet of Stoke Row not far from Henley, this 400-year-old inn takes its name from the pretty cherry tree that grows outside. It's a popular local haunt for everything from a quick pint to a special meal and gets busy even on weekdays. Beams and flagstone floors provide an old-world backdrop for contemporary furnishings, while a nearby barn has been converted into four chic bedrooms. Dinner brings hearty portions of value-for-money modern fare: slow-roast belly of Gloucestershire Old Spot pork with creamed mash.

Times: 12-3/7-10, Closed 25-26 Dec   **Rooms:** 4 (4 en suite) ★★★★ RR
Directions: On the A4155 from Henley-on-Thames exit B481 to Sonning Common. Follow signs for Stoke Row, turn right for pub

◎◎ The White Hart Hotel
Modern British

Historic inn with contemporary style and flavour

☎ 01491 641245   28 High St, Nettlebed RG9 5DD
e-mail: info@whitehartnettlebed.com
web: www.whitehartnettlebed.com

Dating back to the 15th century, this historic inn has a modern,

spacious bistro offering high-quality pub food at affordable prices. Both menu du jour and bistro menus offer good value and might feature a starter of marinated scallops and salmon with a lemon and soya dressing, followed by the likes of morel-stuffed rabbit leg with crushed potatoes and mustard cream sauce or braised pork belly with apple purée and cider jus.

Chef: Nick Seckington   **Times:** 12-2.30/6.30-9.30   **Prices:** Fixed L&D £9.95, Starter £4.25/£6.95, Main £9.95/£15.50   **Wine:** 16 bottles over £20, 20 bottles under £20, 8 by the glass (£3.50-£6)   **Seats:** 60   **Rooms:** 12 (12 en suite) ★★★ **Directions:** From Henley take A4130 towards Wallingford. Approx 5m   **Parking:** 50

◎ Hotel du Vin and Bistro
British, French V ⏷ NOTABLE WINE LIST **NEW**

Stylishly converted old brewery with classic bistro fare

☎ 01491 848400   New St RG9 2BP
e-mail: info@henley.hotelduvin.com
web: www.hotelduvin.com

The boutique hotel group have worked their magic again with a stylish conversion of the former Brakspear Brewery, typically retaining much of its architecture and character. Located at the heart of town, not 50 yards from the waterfront, it fosters the chic but relaxed Hotel du Vin stamp, with the hallmark wine theme reigning over the décor. Wooden floors and furniture, hop garlands and wine ephemera combine with a relaxed, lively buzz, and there's an impressive bar and alfresco courtyard. The British and French cooking with European influences delivers light, clean-cut modern bistro fare.

Chef: Matt Green-Armytage   **Owners:** MWB Group   **Times:** 12.30-2.30/7-9.45   **Prices:** Fixed L £18.50, Starter £6.35-£8.25, Main £15.50-£40, Dessert £2-£6.75, Service added 12.5%   **Wine:** 700 bottles over £20, 30 bottles under £20, 16 by the glass   **Notes:** Sun L £23.50, Sun L vegetarian menu £19.50, Vegetarian available, Civ Wed 60, Air con   **Seats:** 90, Pr/dining room 60   **Children:** Menu, Portions   **Rooms:** 43 (43 en suite) ★★★★ TH   **Directions:** M4 junct 8/9, situated in town centre close to river **Parking:** Resident parking only

KINGHAM
MAP 10 SP22

◎◎ Mill House Hotel
Traditional British, European ⌂

Fine country-house dining

☎ 01608 658188   OX7 6UH
e-mail: stay@millhousehotel.co.uk
web: www.millhousehotel.co.uk

CONTINUED

KINGHAM Continued

The Mill House Hotel

The Cotswold-stone mill house dates back to the time of the Domesday Book and was rebuilt in 1770. Set in 10 acres of lawned gardens with a trout stream, it makes a relaxing setting for country-house dining. British dishes make good use of fresh ingredients and the cooking shows skill and imagination. Take a starter of pan-roasted langoustines served with salmon mousse and basil and champagne froth, and move on to pan-roasted sea bass with crushed saffron and dill potatoes in spinach sauce, or perhaps beef fillet with pancetta, wild mushrooms and smoked potato mash. Round things off with glazed lemon tart, or choose from the extensive cheese menu that features some regional favourites.

Chef: Paul Harris **Owners:** John Parslow **Times:** 12-2/6.30-10 **Prices:** Fixed L £12.50, Fixed D £29.50, Service optional **Wine:** 32 bottles over £20, 34 bottles under £20, 9 by the glass **Notes:** Sun L 3 courses £17.50, Vegetarian available, Dress Restrictions, Smart casual, Civ Wed 80 **Seats:** 70, Pr/dining room 50 **Children:** Menu, Portions **Rooms:** 23 (23 en suite) ★★★ HL **Directions:** Just off B4450, between Chipping Norton and Stow-on-the-Wold. On S outskirts of village **Parking:** 60

MURCOTT   MAP 11 SP51

◎◎ The Nut Tree Inn

Modern European NEW

Assured cooking in a characterful country inn

☎ 01865 331253 Main St OX5 2RE

Local foodies have cottoned on to a change of hands at this pretty Oxfordshire inn and shown their support for Michael and Imogen North's efforts to deliver honest, accomplished cooking, based on high-quality ingredients from regional suppliers and artisan producers. Dating back to the 14th century, the thatched stone building sits beside a paddock area complete with the restaurant's own pigs. There are two cosy dining rooms with stripped oak beams and wood-burning stoves, as well as an airy conservatory hung with modern art. Dishes are well executed and uncomplicated, showing plenty of skill and an awareness of seasonality. Kick off with home-smoked organic Orkney salmon, with whipped horseradish cream and salmon skin biscuit, before moving on to slow-roast Oxfordshire pork belly with parsnip purée and apple gravy, and hot chocolate fondant with toffee ice cream.

Chef: Michael North **Owners:** Michael North, Imogen Young **Times:** 12-2.30/6.30-11, Closed Mon, Closed D Sun **Prices:** Fixed L £12, Fixed D £15, Starter £4.50-£9, Main £12-£20, Dessert £5.50-£7, Service optional, Group min 6 service 10% **Wine:** 72 bottles over £20, 27 bottles under £20, 15 by the glass **Notes:** Sun L 1 course £12, 2 courses £15, 3 courses £18 Vegetarian menu **Seats:** 60, Pr/dining room 24 **Children:** Portions **Directions:** M40 junct 9. A34 towards Oxford, take 2nd exit for Islip. At Red Lion pub turn left and then take right towards Murcott **Parking:** 30

OXFORD   MAP 05 SP50

◎ Arezzo Restaurant

Modern Italian NEW

Italian food served in light-and-airy setting

☎ 01865 749988 Hawkwell House Hotel, Church Way, Iffley Village OX4 4DZ
e-mail: info@hawkwellhouse.co.uk
web: www.hawkwellhouse.co.uk

Set in a peaceful residential location, the Arezzo restaurant at Hawkwell House is an Italian bistro-influenced restaurant, with a light-and-airy setting which has an understated Mediterranean feel to it, and friendly, smartly-dressed staff. Deep-fried calamari with garlic and chilli mayonnaise, or bresaola with baby onions, rocket and balsamic reduction might feature as a starter, while for mains you could tuck into chargrilled salmon with wilted spinach, oyster mushrooms and fish velouté, or perhaps choose from one of the pasta and pizza selection - pasta Arrabbiata made with spicy tomato sauce, onion, basil and fresh chilli is a good choice.

Chef: Christopher Kennedy **Owners:** Bespoke Hotels **Times:** 12-2.30/7-9.30 **Prices:** Starter £4.25-£6.95, Main £9.95-£18.95, Dessert £4.50-£6.50, Service optional **Wine:** 6 bottles over £20, 21 bottles under £20, 6 by the glass **Notes:** Civ Wed 120, Air con **Seats:** 55, Pr/dining room 20 **Children:** Menu, Portions **Rooms:** 66 (66 en suite) ★★★ HL **Directions:** A34 follow signs to Cowley, at Littlemore rdbt take A4158 onto Iffley Rd. After lights turn left into Iffley Village **Parking:** 85

◎ Brasserie Blanc

French

Confident French-themed brasserie dining in fashionable suburb

☎ 01865 510999 71-72 Walton St OX2 6AG
e-mail: oxford@brasserieblanc.com
web: www.brasserieblanc.co.uk

A busy yet relaxed French-style brasserie - part of a small chain - is located in the fashionable city quarter of Jericho. Recently refurbished, the spacious, two-roomed restaurant has a smart, contemporary décor, with wooden floors, modern furnishings and colourful prints, while floor-to-ceiling windows allow natural light to flood in. Expect a buzzy atmosphere and brisk but friendly service from black-clothed staff - children are positively welcomed too. As its name suggests, the food is rooted in French culinary excellence, yet utilises the best British ingredients. Expect authentic brasserie dishes like Cornish lamb rack with fondant potatoes, and a classic lemon tart finish.

Chef: Manoj Prasad **Owners:** Blanc Brasseries Ltd **Times:** 12-2.45/6-

10.30, Closed 25 Dec **Prices:** Fixed L £11.50, Fixed D £17.50, Starter £4.95-
£6.95, Main £10.50-£18, Dessert £4.50-£5.50, Group min 6 service 10%
Wine: 23 bottles over £20, 7 bottles under £20, 12 by the glass
Notes: Vegetarian available, Air con **Seats:** 145, Pr/dining room 12
Children: Menu, Portions **Directions:** From city centre. N along St Giles,
left into Little Clarendon St and right at end of Walton St
Parking: Gloucester Green/St Giles

⚜ Cotswold Lodge Hotel

Modern

Elegant dining near city centre

☎ 01865 512121 66a Banbury Rd OX2 6JP
e-mail: aa@cotswoldlodgehotel.co.uk
web: www.cotswoldlodgehotel.co.uk

Situated near the city centre, this family-run Victorian hotel's interior
has an elegant country-house feel and a relaxed, informal ambience.
The refurbished dining room comes with wooden flooring and cerise-
coloured walls hung with pictures, while high-backed chairs and crisp
white linen provide the comforts. Modern British dishes are the focus
of a straightforward, brasserie-style menu; take a fillet of sea bream
with mustard crumble, sage and butter sauce and crushed citrus
butter potatoes, while bread-and-butter pudding, served with apricots
and clotted cream, might prove the finale for dessert.

Chef: Garin Chapman **Owners:** Mrs O Peros **Times:** 12-2.30/6.30-10
Prices: Starter £4.25-£7.25, Main £11.75-£17.50, Dessert £4.25-£6.25, Service
included **Wine:** 15 bottles over £20, 10 bottles under £20, 6 by the glass
Notes: Vegetarian available, Dress Restrictions, Smart casual **Seats:** 48,
Pr/dining room 140 **Children:** Menu, Portions **Rooms:** 49 (49 en suite)
★★★★ HL **Directions:** Take A4165 (Banbury Road) off A40 ring road,
hotel 1.5m on left **Parking:** 50

⚜ The Lemon Tree

Modern, International

Attractive restaurant with a Mediterranean feel

☎ 01865 311936 268 Woodstock Rd OX2 7NW
e-mail: info@thelemontreeoxford.co.uk
web: www.thelemontreeoxford.co.uk

There's a warm, settling ambience to this spacious, bright-and-airy
restaurant - its comfortable bar and the attractive rear walled garden
being as much a part of the experience as the tranquil dining room.
The latter's flagstone flooring, wicker chairs, larger-than-life ferns, big
mirrors and conservatory-style ceiling give an impression of sunnier
Mediterranean climes, influences which also crop up on the modern,
brasserie-style menu, though dishes tend toward home-grown fare.
Take an Aberdeenshire aged rump steak with chips and béarnaise or
fillet of red mullet with lemon oil and crayfish and parmesan risotto,
and perhaps vanilla crème brûlée or sticky toffee pudding for dessert.

Chef: Ross Duncan **Owners:** Clinton Pugh **Times:** 12/11, Closed Xmas, 1
Jan **Prices:** Fixed L £10, Fixed D £25.50-£35, Starter £5.95-£11.95, Main
£10.95-£17.95, Dessert £3.50-£6.95, Service added but optional 12.5%
Wine: 29 bottles over £20, 13 bottles under £20, 15 by the glass
Notes: Sun L available, Vegetarian menu, Civ Wed 90 **Seats:** 90
Children: Portions **Directions:** 1.5m from city centre heading N
Parking: 19

⚜⚜ Macdonald Randolph

Traditional British

Classic Oxford dining experience

☎ 0870 400 8200 Beaumont St OX1 2LN
e-mail: randolph@macdonald-hotels.co.uk
web: www.macdonaldhotels.co.uk

Situated in the heart of Oxford opposite the Ashmolean Museum, this
neo-Gothic hotel was built in 1864 and recently underwent a £6 million
refurbishment. The richly furnished, high-ceilinged restaurant combines
tradition with elegance, while its large picture windows offer diners
wonderful views of the city. British cuisine - underpinned by a classical
base - is on offer using quality seasonal ingredients, simply prepared
and beautifully presented. Take baked fillet of sea bass served with
baby gem lettuce and seared scallops, or seared loin of venison with
spinach and chestnuts, and to finish, perhaps a classic crêpe Suzette or
apple and redcurrant sponge with vanilla ice cream.

Chef: Tom Birks **Owners:** Macdonald Hotels **Times:** 12-2.30/5.30-10
Prices: Fixed L £24, Fixed D £29.50, Starter £6.95-£7.50, Main £18-£24.95,
Dessert £7.95-£9.50, Service optional **Wine:** 12 by the glass **Notes:** Dress
Restrictions, Smart casual, Civ Wed 300 **Seats:** 90, Pr/dining room 30
Children: Menu, Portions **Rooms:** 151 (151 en suite) ★★★★★ HL
Directions: M40 junct 8 onto A40 towards Oxford, follow signs towards
city centre, leads to St Giles, hotel is on right **Parking:** 50

⚜ Malmaison Brasserie Oxford

Modern NEW

Contemporary brasserie dining in former prison

☎ 01865 268400 3 Oxford Castle, New Rd OX1 1AY
e-mail: oxford@malmaison.com
web: www.malmaison.com

This one-time prison is now a city destination, with many of the
hotel's rooms actually old cells. Its popular, relaxed, subterranean
brasserie comes decked out in dark browns and aubergines, while
waiting staff are clad in black. But there's nothing dark about the
bright, clean-cut food that follows the blueprint of other Malmaisons,
with the emphasis on accomplished, modern brasserie-style fare with
a French twist. Take bouillabaisse with rouille and sour dough, or
maybe steak frites, with a baked chocolate tart and pistachio ice cream
finish.

Chef: Russell Heeley **Owners:** MWB **Times:** 12-2.30/6-10.30
Prices: Fixed L £14.50-£16.95, Fixed D £29.95-£31, Starter £4.95-£7.50, Main
£12.50-£22.50, Dessert £5.95-£7, Service added but optional 10%, Group
min 6 service 10% **Wine:** 150 bottles over £20, 50 bottles under £20,
21 by the glass **Notes:** Vegetarian available, Civ Wed 50, Air con
Seats: 100, Pr/dining room 10 **Children:** Menu, Portions **Rooms:** 94 (94
en suite) ★★★ HL **Directions:** M40 junct 9 (signed Oxford A34). Follow
A34 S to Botley Interchange and then take A420 to the city centre

ENGLAND

OXFORD CONTINUED

◉ Quod Brasserie & Bar

Modern Mediterranean

Busy city-centre brasserie

☎ 01865 202505 Old Bank Hotel, 92-94 High St OX1 4BN

e-mail: quod@oldbank-hotel.co.uk
web: www.quod.co.uk

A stylish former banking hall with a collection of contemporary art, stone floors and a huge zinc-topped bar, this bustling brasserie is part of the Old Bank Hotel. Expect the sort of robust food you might find on the Mediterranean coast: wonderful pizza, bread and pasta and a small wine list with most wines by the glass. Not to be missed are the Quod home-made hamburgers, Caesar salad and the crayfish and avocado pizza - all served on wooden boards in a rustic, modern style. The sun deck is an added bonus, plus live jazz every Sunday 5-7pm.

Chef: Michael Wright **Owners:** Mr J Mogford **Times:** 7am/11
Prices: Fixed L £9.95-£10.50, Starter £4.50-£9, Main £6.50-£18.50, Dessert £4.25-£8, Service optional, Group min 5 service 10% **Wine:** 17 bottles over £20, 17 bottles under £20, 17 by the glass **Notes:** Vegetarian available, Air con **Seats:** 164, Pr/dining room 24 **Children:** Menu, Portions
Rooms: 42 (42 en suite) ★★★★ TH **Directions:** Approach city centre via Headington. Over Magdalen Bridge into High St. Hotel 75yds on left
Parking: 50

▭ Cherwell Boathouse Restaurant

☎ 01865 552746 60 Bardwell Rd OX2 6ST
web: www.theaa.com/travel/index.jsp

Enjoy international dishes at this small and intimate restaurant, right on the banks of the Isis in a truly scenic spot.

Edamame

☎ 01865 246 916 15 Holywell St OX1 3SA

Japanese canteen-style dining.

▭ Fishers Seafood Restaurant

☎ 01865 243003 36-37 St Clements OX4 1AB
web: www.theaa.com/travel/index.jsp

Fresh fish is shipped in daily to ensure a wide choice of fresh seasonal shellfish platters, and the atmospheric interior resembles a stylish ship's cabin, with wooden floors, benches and lanterns.

Loch Fyne Restaurant

☎ 01865 292510 55 Walton St OX2 6AE

Quality seafood chain.

STADHAMPTON   MAP 05 SU69

◉◉ The Crazy Bear Hotel

Modern British

Impressive cooking in imaginative surroundings

☎ 01865 890714 Bear Ln OX44 7UR
e-mail: enquiries@crazybear-oxford.co.uk
web: www.crazybeargroup.co.uk

A dramatic restoration of a traditional 16th-century inn that certainly makes an impact, so expect lots of mirrors, leather, atmospheric lighting, and a ceiling of binned wine bottles combined with original features. The bedrooms are decorated in dramatic style, making an overnight stay after dinner an attractive option. It's a relaxing and popular place, with well-informed and friendly staff. Modern British dishes with lots of international influences are prepared using the best ingredients, and dishes are simply but effectively presented. Start with steamed king scallops with ginger and spring onion soy dressing, before a main course of grilled mullet with spinach risotto and iced fennel, or wok-fried Aberdeen Angus beef with sweet basil, chillies and onion. Finish with chocolate tart with vanilla ice cream.

Chef: Stuart Turner **Owners:** Jason Hunt **Times:** 12/10 **Prices:** Fixed L £15, Fixed D £19.50, Starter £7-£18, Main £11.50-£26, Dessert £6.50, Service added but optional 12.5% **Wine:** 106 bottles over £20, 14 bottles under £20, 16 by the glass **Notes:** Fixed L Mon-Fri, Fixed D Mon-Thu, Vegetarian available, Civ Wed 100, Air con **Seats:** 40, Pr/dining room 50
Children: Menu, Portions **Rooms:** 17 (17 en suite) ★★★★★ RR
Directions: From M40 junct 7 turn left onto A329, continue for 4m, left after petrol station & left again into Bear Lane **Parking:** 50

◎◎ Thai Thai

Thai

Truly authentic Thai cuisine in the heart of rural Oxfordshire

☎ 01865 890714 Crazy Bear Hotel, Bear Ln OX44 7UR
e-mail: enquiries@crazybear-oxford.co.uk
web: www.crazybeargroup.co.uk

Expect the unexpected at this hugely individual 16th-century former coaching inn that never fails to surprise. Decked out in the style of a Moroccan Bedouin tent, Thai Thai offers some of the best Thai food in the UK and has become renowned for the authenticity of its cuisine, using only seasonal, organic ingredients, including some flown in from the Far East, to produce the genuine tastes of the country. The long menu includes a dedicated dim sum section, and there are tasting menus for the adventurous. Start with crispy Peking duck roll perhaps, followed by garlic king prawns, wok-fried with black pepper and spring onions. Desserts are decidedly Western Hemisphere - expect the likes of pineapple tarte Tatin.

Chef: Anusak Thepdamrongchaikagul **Owners:** Jason Hunt **Times:** 12-3/6-10, Closed L Sun **Prices:** Starter £6-£9, Main £10.50-£18.50, Dessert £6.50, Service added but optional 12.5% **Wine:** 106 bottles over £20, 14 bottles under £20, 16 by the glass **Notes:** Tasting menu 8 courses £20, 10 courses £25, 12 courses £30, Vegetarian available, Civ Wed 100 **Seats:** 25, Pr/dining room 50 **Children:** Menu, Portions **Directions:** M40 junct 7 turn left onto A329, continue for 4m, left after petrol station and 2nd left again into Bear Lane **Parking:** 50

SWERFORD   MAP 11 SP33

◎ The Mason's Arms

Modern British ✋

Country restaurant with skilfully-produced dishes

☎ 01608 683212 Banbury Rd OX7 4AP
e-mail: themasonschef@hotmail.com
web: www.masons-arms.co.uk

A classic stone-built inn with a dining room extension, The Mason's Arms maintains its traditional identity following complete refurbishment a few years ago. Produce is locally sourced where possible and breads, terrines, pastries and desserts are all home made. Meat is rare breed and traceable, poultry free range, and fish is delivered daily. Fresh, lively and well-presented dishes include home-cured salmon with potato salad and dill dressing, followed by a main course of slow-cooked shoulder of lamb with fondant potato and parsnip and fig purée. Finish with a delightful Belgian chocolate pot served with pistachio ice cream and shortbread.

Chef: Bill Leadbeater **Owners:** B & C Leadbeater, Tom Aldous **Times:** 12-3/7-11, Closed 25-26 Dec, Closed D 24 Dec **Prices:** Fixed L £10.25, Fixed D £15.95, Starter £4.95-£7.95, Main £9.95-£15.95, Dessert £5.50, Service optional, Group min 10 service 10% **Wine:** 13 bottles over £20, 26 bottles under £20, 6 by the glass **Seats:** 75, Pr/dining room 40 **Children:** Menu, Portions **Directions:** Situated between Banbury and Chipping Norton on A361 **Parking:** 60

THAME   MAP 05 SP70

◎ Spread Eagle Hotel

Modern British V

Hotel brasserie in appealing market town

☎ 01844 213661 Cornmarket OX9 2BW
e-mail: enquiries@spreadeaglethame.co.uk
web: www.spreadeaglethame.co.uk

The informal brasserie is part of the Spread Eagle Hotel, a former coaching inn that presides over the main street of this delightful market town. It gets its name, Fothergills, from the diarist and raconteur who owned the hotel in the 1920s. A varied carte is offered in addition to the traditional brasserie menu. Local Oxfordshire beef makes a strong showing on the former, including Chateaubriand, with the likes of calves' liver and bacon, or spicy salmon and crab fishcake from the latter. There's a good-value fixed-price menu on Friday and Saturday.

Chef: Alisdair Dudley **Owners:** Mr D & Mrs S Barrington **Times:** 12.30-2.30/5.30-9 **Prices:** Starter £4.50-£6.75, Main £13.25-£21.95, Dessert £5, Service included **Wine:** 17 bottles over £20, 51 bottles under £20, 9 by the glass **Notes:** Sun L 2 courses £13.95, 3 courses £18.95, Vegetarian available, Civ Wed 200, Air con **Seats:** 65, Pr/dining room 20 **Children:** Menu, Portions **Rooms:** 33 (33 en suite) ★★★ HL **Directions:** M40 - junct 6 from S, junct 8 from N. Town centre on A418 (Oxford to Aylesbury road) **Parking:** 80

◎ The Swan at Tetsworth

Modern British

Elizabethan coaching inn with a timeless atmosphere and accomplished cuisine

☎ 01844 281182 High St, Tetsworth OX9 7AB

Tracing its history back to 1482, The Swan retains all its old-world and rustic charm, and today combines its business as both a restaurant and renowned antiques centre. There's nothing at all dated about the menus however. Whether eating in the garden in the summer or enjoying a cosy candlelit dinner, diners can expect an internationally inspired, seasonal menu underpinned by quality ingredients. Think

CONTINUED

THAME *Continued*

roast crown of poulet noir with roasted foie gras and carrot purée, and to finish, perhaps a sticky toffee pudding - this version delivered with praline ice cream and a miniature apple tart.

Chef: Derek Muircroft **Owners:** Solution Culinaire **Times:** 12-3/7-9.30, Closed D Sun **Prices:** Fixed L £13.50, Starter £7.50-£10, Main £15-£22, Dessert £7-£7.50, Service added but optional 10% **Wine:** 84 bottles over £20, 35 bottles under £20, 11 by the glass **Notes:** Sun L 2 courses £17, 3 courses £20 **Seats:** 55, Pr/dining room 12 **Children:** Portions **Directions:** 3m from M40 junct 6. 5m from M40 junct 8 **Parking:** 120

WALLINGFORD   MAP 05 SU68

◎ Lakeside Restaurant

Modern European V

A popular restaurant in an attractive setting

☎ 01491 836687 The Springs Hotel & Golf Club, Wallingford Rd, North Stoke OX10 6BE

e-mail: info@thespringshotel.com
web: www.thespringshotel.com

Built in 1874 in Victorian mock-Tudor style, the Springs Hotel overlooks a scenic spring-fed lake and delightful grounds - Edward VIII was once a frequent visitor. Inside there is plenty of period detail, including crackling fires in open hearths, comfortable lounges and exposed oak beams. Set in the glass-enclosed Winter Garden, the Lakeside Restaurant offers the attentiveness of formal service with a friendly, unobtrusive feel. The food has a foot in the twin camps of British and European styles - you might expect grilled sea bass with winter greens and lobster butter sauce, or a warm pear and almond tart with vanilla ice cream to finish.

Chef: André Roux **Owners:** Lakeside Restaurant **Times:** 12-2.30/7-9.45 **Prices:** Fixed L £11.50, Fixed D £27.50, Starter £5.50-£8.50, Main £15.50-£19.95, Dessert £6.50, Service optional, Group min 10 service 10% **Wine:** 71 bottles over £20, 15 bottles under £20, 12 by the glass **Notes:** Sun L £25 incl wine and coffee, Vegetarian menu, Dress Restrictions, No denim, trainers or T-shirts, Civ Wed 90 **Seats:** 80, Pr/dining room 30 **Children:** Portions **Rooms:** 32 (32 en suite) ★★★ HL **Directions:** Edge of village of North Stoke **Parking:** 150

WESTON-ON-THE-GREEN   MAP 11 SP51

◎ Weston Manor Hotel

British, European

Modern cuisine in impressive medieval manor-house hotel

☎ 01869 350621   OX25 3QL

e-mail: reception@westonmanor.co.uk
web: www.westonmanor.co.uk

During World War II, Weston Manor served as an officer's mess for American airmen, who must have been impressed by this historic medieval manor. Soon afterwards it was converted into a hotel, maintaining beautiful grounds and many original features. The restaurant is really a baronial dining hall with a high-vaulted ceiling, oak panelling and a minstrels' gallery, and you can easily see why these features make it a popular venue for weddings and functions. A small, regularly-changing menu offers seasonal produce in dishes like pan-fried loin of venison served with juniper-scented braised red cabbage.

Times: 12-2/7-9.30, Closed L Sat-Sun **Rooms:** 35 (35 en suite) ★★★ HL **Directions:** 2 mins from M40 junct 9, via A34 (Oxford) on Weston-on-Green; hotel in village centre

---

WOODCOTE   MAP 05 SU68

◎ Woody Nook at Woodcote

International, Pacific Rim V

Hearty cooking with Australian flair and wines in relaxed, informal atmosphere

☎ 01491 680775   Goring Rd RG8 0SD

e-mail: info@woodynookatwoodcote.co.uk
web: www.woodynookatwoodcote.co.uk

You might spot a game of cricket on the village green from this ivy- and vine-clad restaurant. Wooden beams, low ceilings and leaded windows create a cosy, rustic ambience for informal dining. A recent refurbishment has given the restaurant a fresh, relaxed feel. The international cooking makes good use of quality ingredients in hearty, thoughtfully presented, country-style dishes with Pacific Rim influences. Think pan-fried fillets of barramundi with pesto fettuccini pasta and a shellfish cream sauce, or perhaps chargrilled kangaroo served with a white bean and sweet potato cassoulet and Madeira sauce. The excellent wine list offers the complete range from the owner's Woody Nook boutique winery in Western Australia.

Chef: Stuart Sheperd **Owners:** Jane & Peter Bailey **Times:** 12-2.30/7-

9.30, Closed Aug, Mon & Tue, Closed L Sun **Prices:** Fixed L £12.95-£14.50, Fixed D £17.95-£19.50, Starter £6.50-£7.95, Main £13.75-£19.95, Dessert £4.95-£5.50, Service optional, Group min 6 service 10% **Wine:** 18 bottles over £20, 15 bottles under £20, 6 by the glass **Notes:** Vegetarian menu **Seats:** 50 **Children:** Portions **Parking:** 25

WOODSTOCK   MAP 11 SP41

◉◉ The Feathers

Modern British V 💻

Accomplished modern British cuisine at a sophisticated townhouse hotel

☎ 01993 812291 Market St OX20 1SX
e-mail: enquiries@feathers.co.uk
web: www.feathers.co.uk

Formed from five townhouses dating from the 17th century, this luxurious hotel set in a busy market town not far from Blenheim Palace offers a choice of two eateries. For grazing or light meals, try the bar or bistro, but for most the restaurant is the main draw - a chic, wood-panelled affair made up of three interconnecting rooms decorated in rich plums and creams, with traditional fittings and elegantly appointed tables. Choose from the three-course Market Menu or à la carte, both offering an interesting take on a modern British theme. Start with velouté of white onion, thyme and cider, for example, then progress with confidence to slow-cooked pig's cheeks, kohlrabi and sauce hollandaise, with vanilla pannacotta and spiced quince to finish.

Chef: Simon Garbutt **Owners:** Empire Ventures Ltd **Times:** 12.30-2.30/7-9.30, Closed D Sun **Prices:** Fixed L £19.50, Fixed D £37.50-£46, Service added but optional 10% **Wine:** 140 bottles over £20, 12 bottles under £20, 11 by the glass **Notes:** Sun L 3-4 courses £24.50, Vegetarian menu, Dress restrictions, Smart casual, no trainers **Seats:** 54, Pr/dining room 30 **Children:** Menu, Portions **Rooms:** 20 (20 en suite) ★★★ HL **Directions:** 8m from Oxford on A44, follow signs for Evesham & Blenheim Palace. In Woodstock take 2nd left into the town, hotel 20mtrs on left **Parking:** On street

◉◉ Macdonald Bear Hotel

Modern British 💻

Modern cooking in historic inn

☎ 0870 4008202 Park St OX20 1SZ
e-mail: bear@macdonald-hotels.co.uk
web: www.bearhotelwoodstock.co.uk

Dating back to the 13th century, this ivy-clad hotel on the main street is one of England's oldest coaching inns, brimful of traditional

character and atmosphere. The smart, inviting restaurant, like the rest of the building, oozes character, with oak beams, stone walls, evening candlelight and an open fireplace, while service is warm, relaxed and good humoured. The kitchen takes a modern direction on its seasonal, well-balanced menus, combining skill with quality ingredients. Take seared king scallops with sweet potato purée and lemon dressing to start, with perhaps pan-fried halibut with mustard seed and potato crust, braised chicory and vanilla froth, or Angus beef fillet with pomme Anna and red wine jus for the main course.

Macdonald Bear Hotel

Chef: Adrian Court **Owners:** Macdonald Hotels **Times:** 12.30-2/7-9.30 **Prices:** Service optional **Wine:** 70 bottles over £20, 18 bottles under £20, 12 by the glass **Seats:** 80, Pr/dining room 30 **Children:** Menu, Portions **Rooms:** 54 (54 en suite) ★★★ HL **Directions:** Town centre, facing the market square **Parking:** 45

RUTLAND

CLIPSHAM   MAP 11 SK91

◉◉ The Olive Branch

British, European V ✋

Stone-flagged gastro-pub presenting the best local produce

☎ 01780 410355 Main St LE15 7SH
e-mail: info@theolivebranchpub.com
web: www.theolivebranchpub.com

The Olive Branch is an old village inn furnished with an eclectic mixture of antiques, French monastery pews, pine tables and open fires, extended into a more contemporary barn conversion. The atmosphere throughout is relaxed and informal, with service provided by a knowledgeable young team. The menu offers an innovative modern take on traditional pub fare with some European influences. There's an emphasis on local produce, some fine examples of which are available to buy from the pub each day. Skilfully prepared dishes include a starter of Gloucestershire Old Spot brawn terrine with apple sauce, followed by a main course of poached sea bass fillet with Thai-style noodles, and sticky toffee treacle tart with yogurt ice cream for dessert.

Chef: Sean Hope, Tim Luff **Owners:** Sean Hope, Ben Jones **Times:** 12-2/7-9.30, Closed 26 Dec, 1 Jan, Closed L 31 Dec, D 25 Dec **Prices:** Fixed L £14.50, Starter £4.75-£9.75, Main £11.75-£19.75, Dessert £4.75-£6.75, Service optional, Group min 12 service 10% **Wine:** 20 bottles over £20, 25 bottles under £20, 8 by the glass **Notes:** Sun L 3 courses £19.95, Vegetarian menu **Seats:** 45, Pr/dining room 20 **Children:** Menu, Portions **Directions:** 2m from A1 at Stretton junct, 5m N of Stamford **Parking:** 15

barnsdale lodge
hotel and restaurant

made of seasonal, local ingredients. Start with smoked mackerel pâté and horseradish cream and for mains perhaps pan-fried calves' liver with shallot mash and sweet red cabbage. Puddings include toffee crème brûlée with banana ice cream.

Chef: Richard Carruthers **Owners:** The Hon Thomas Noel **Times:** 12.15-2.15/7-9.30 **Prices:** Fixed L £12.95, Starter £3.95-£7.95, Main £10.95-£16.50, Dessert £4.95-£5.95, Service added but optional 10% **Wine:** 32 bottles over £20, 28 bottles under £20, 10 by the glass **Notes:** Sun L £18.95, Vegetarian available, Civ Wed 100 **Seats:** 120, Pr/dining room 50 **Children:** Menu, Portions **Rooms:** 44 (44 en suite) ★★★ HL **Directions:** Turn off A1 at Stamford onto A606 to Oakham. Hotel 5m on right. (2 miles E of Oakham) **Parking:** 250

see advert on this page

◉◉◉◉ Hambleton Hall Hotel
see opposite

UPPINGHAM   MAP 11 SP89

◉◉ *Lake Isle Hotel & Restaurant*
British, French
Quality food in a sleepy market town

☎ 01572 822951 16 High St East LE15 9PZ
e-mail: info@lakeislehotel.com
web: www.lakeislehotel.com

Formerly a shop, this small hotel in the quiet market town of Uppingham retains many of its original features, including panelled walls and mahogany shop fittings with heavy wooden tables complementing the otherwise chic, up-to-date interiors. Clean, simple and fresh flavours abound, with an emphasis on quality ingredients. The cooking is excellent and all the dishes on the menu invariably live up to their descriptions. Typical dishes might be duck liver parfait with sunflower seed focaccia and spiced apricot compôte or a notably good Cromer crab tartlet to start, or paupiette of salmon and trout with lime crème fraîche dressing for mains. The desserts, like honey and Norfolk lavender pannacotta, are also worthy of note, as is the wine list.

Times: 12-2.30/7-9.30, Closed L Mon, D Sun **Rooms:** 12 (12 en suite) ★★ HL **Directions:** Located on main High St

OAKHAM   MAP 11 SK80

◉ Barnsdale Lodge Hotel
Modern European
Attractively converted farmhouse hotel on the shores of Rutland Water

☎ 01572 724678 The Avenue, Rutland Water, North Shore LE15 8AH
e-mail: enquiries@barnsdalelodge.co.uk
web: www.barnsdalelodge.co.uk

This stylish hotel built around a courtyard was once a 17th-century farmhouse. Original features like bread ovens and stone floors go well with the country-house style furnishings. There's a choice of three dining rooms or the courtyard, and staff are young and helpful. Dishes are modern British in style with European influences and good use is

Hambleton Hall Hotel

OAKHAM MAP 11 SK80

Modern British V NOTABLE WINE LIST

Romantic retreat serving the best of English country-house cuisine

☎ 01572 756991 Hambleton LE15 8TH
e-mail: hotel@hambletonhall.com
web: www.hambletonhall.com

The epitome of the English country-house hotel, Hambleton Hall was established in 1980 by Tim and Stefa Hart. It is set in sweeping landscaped grounds overlooking Rutland Water and as soon as you arrive, Hambleton weaves its spell and bestows an immediate impression of relaxation and confidence that everything will run with absolute aplomb. All the sophisticated, traditional comforts are here. The dining room is intimate and comfortable and comes dressed in warm traditional colours with crisp white linen, fresh flowers, heavy brocade drapes and oil paintings, enhanced by the lovely backdrop of the garden and lake. Service is professional and friendly and the wine list appropriately extensive, while chef Aaron Patterson's inspired cooking delivers a superb, subtly modern take on classic country-house cooking. His style echoes that of his mentor, Raymond Blanc, in its focus on the finest-quality produce, seasonality and clarity of flavour, together with the use of the freshest vegetables, herbs and salads from the hotel's own kitchen garden. Local game is a speciality, while luxury items pepper the sophisticated repertoire of fixed-price menus where technical excellence reigns supreme. The menu might offer roasted loin of venison served with a Szechuan, fig and chocolate-flavoured sauce, perhaps roasted woodcock with a millefeuille of pear and foie gras, or poached fillet of sea bass with Mediterranean vegetables, aubergine fritter and a bouillabaisse sauce. Finish with an assiette of apple and blackberry, or maybe a pavé of white and dark chocolate with raspberries.

Chef: Aaron Patterson
Owners: Mr T Hart
Times: 12-1.30/7-9.30
Prices: Fixed L £19.50, Fixed D £40-£50, Starter £15-£24, Main £32-£39, Dessert £12-£16, Service included
Wine: 375 bottles over £20, 10 bottles under £20, 10 by the glass
Notes: Tasting menu & Sun L menu available, Vegetarian menu, Dress Restrictions, Smart dress, No jeans, T-shirts or trainers, Civ Wed 64
Seats: 60, Pr/dining room 20
Children: Portions
Rooms: 17 (17 en suite)★★★★ CHH
Directions: 8m W of the A1 Stamford junct (A606), 3m E of Oakham
Parking: 36

WING
MAP 11 SK80

◉ Kings Arms
Modern British NEW

Traditional country inn with a modern approach

☎ 01572 737634 13 Top St LE15 8SE
e-mail: info@thekingsarms-wing.co.uk
web: www.thekingsarms-wing.co.uk

This popular, extended 17th-century village pub makes its mark on the local scene. Today it's a modern-style operation, but with all the charm and character of a traditional country inn; think opencast walls, stone flooring, low beams and open fires. The kitchen shows a commitment to fresh, quality produce with everything made in-house, while the lengthy repertoire takes a modern approach and plays to the gallery with something for everyone. Take grilled calves' liver and crispy pancetta with sweet potato mash, sage butter, a sweet sherry vinegar onion sauce and green beans, with Aberdeen Angus fillet steak with celeriac fondant, pomme purée and chanterelle jus catching the eye too. (Bar meals also available.)

Chef: James Goss **Owners:** David, Lisa & James Goss **Times:** 12-2.30/6.30-9, Closed Mon **Prices:** Fixed D £20-£35, Starter £3.50-£10, Main £8.50-£19.50, Dessert £5.50-£8, Service optional, Group min 7 service 10% **Wine:** 20 bottles over £20, 28 bottles under £20, 27 by the glass **Notes:** Fixed D 4 courses **Seats:** 30, Pr/dining room 24 **Children:** Portions **Rooms:** 8 (8 en suite) ★★★★ INN **Directions:** Off A6003, between Oakham and Uppingham **Parking:** 30

SHROPSHIRE

CHURCH STRETTON
MAP 15 SO49

◉ The Studio
British, French

Imaginative food in a former art studio

☎ 01694 722672 59 High St SY6 6BY
e-mail: info@thestudiorestaurant.net
web: www.thestudiorestaurant.net

An interesting collection of art and ceramics reflects the restaurant's former life as an artist's studio. The original paint-palette sign still swings at the front of the building, a small welcoming bar is positioned by the front door and there is a lovely patio garden overlooking the Shropshire hills for alfresco dining. Modern, bistro-style food is the thing here, and all dishes are made in-house using well-sourced, local seasonal produce, underpinned by the classical and traditional skills of the husband-and-wife team. Take loin steak of Walls rare breed pork with confit belly, cassoulet of beans and red wine jus for example.

Chef: Tony Martland **Owners:** Tony & Sheila Martland **Times:** 7-9, Closed 2 wks Jan, 1 wk Apr, 1 wk Nov, Sun & Mon, Closed L all week **Prices:** Fixed D £27.50, Starter £5-£8.25, Main £14.25-£18.25, Dessert £5.50, Service optional **Wine:** 11 bottles over £20, 27 bottles under £20, 6 by the glass **Notes:** Dress Restrictions, Smart casual **Seats:** 34 **Children:** Portions **Directions:** Off A49 to town, left at T-junct onto High Street, 300 yds on left **Parking:** On street parking available

HADNALL
MAP 15 SJ52

◉ Saracens at Hadnall
Modern British NEW

Skilful cooking at an elegant restaurant with rooms

☎ 01939 210877 Shrewsbury Rd SY4 4AG
e-mail: reception@saracensathadnall.co.uk
web: www.saracensathadnall.co.uk

A Grade II listed building, the Saracens was originally a Georgian farmhouse, later a pub and today a smart restaurant with rooms. There are two dining rooms, the Georgian-style front room, with its polished-wood floor, panelled walls and stone fireplace, or the conservatory, which features a capped well. The kitchen deals in skilfully prepared fare, with the emphasis on quality, locally-sourced ingredients. Think pan-fried fillet of Welsh Black beef, with root vegetable mash, sautéed oyster mushrooms and a bacon and horseradish reduction, or pan-fried loin of Attingham Park venison, while an oven-baked apple with pecan and orange crumble and sweet sabayon might tempt at dessert. Children under 12 years not allowed at dinner Fridays and Saturdays.

Owners: Ben & Allison M Christie **Times:** 11.30-2.30/6.30-9.30, Closed Mon, Closed L Tue, D Sun **Prices:** Starter £4.25-£8.50, Main £12.95-£17.95, Dessert £3.95-£7.50, Service optional **Wine:** 11 bottles over £20, 20 bottles under £20, 6 by the glass **Notes:** Sun L starter £4.25, main £7.75, dessert £4.10, Vegetarian available, Dress Restrictions, Smart casual **Seats:** 45 **Children:** Menu **Rooms:** 5 (5 en suite) ★★★★ RR **Directions:** On A49 5m N of Shrewsbury **Parking:** 20

LLANFAIR WATERDINE
MAP 09 SO27

◉◉ The Waterdine
Modern British

Charming countryside dining

☎ 01547 528214 LD7 1TU

The Waterdine is a former drover's inn, dating back over 400 years. Set in wonderful Shropshire countryside, and with the River Teme running at the bottom of the garden, it's full of charm and character. The main restaurant has two different areas, The Garden Room and The Taproom - the oldest part of the building. Friendly, efficient hospitality from the owners puts you at your ease immediately. Here you'll find an experienced chef making great use of quality local produce, including fruit and vegetables from the inn's own garden. The menu is seasonal and changes regularly.

Times: 12-1.45/7-9, Closed 1 wk spring, 1 wk autumn, Closed D Sun, Mon **Rooms:** 3 (3 en suite) ★★★★★ RR

LUDLOW
MAP 10 SO57

◉◉ The Clive Bar and Restaurant with Rooms
British

Bright, modern restaurant in former farmhouse

☎ 01584 856565 & 856665 Bromfield SY8 2JR
e-mail: info@theclive.co.uk
web: www.theclive.co.uk

Once the home of Clive of India, this recently refurbished roadside farmstead has a relaxed and comfortable ambience, with large windows, mirrors, stylish contemporary seating, quality glassware and fresh flowers all adding to the atmosphere. The cooking style is modern British with some Mediterranean influences, using locally-sourced produce wherever possible. Organic locally-smoked salmon with smoked olive oil dressing might be followed by the likes of sirloin of Shropshire beef served with Yorkshire pudding, horseradish sauce and seasonal vegetables, while an appropriate finale might be ginger and pistachio parfait, with hot berry and apple filos, or an excellent 'tulip' of dark chocolate mousse with green tea ice cream. On Sundays, a separate lunchtime menu is available, to include a roast of the day.

The Clive Bar and Restaurant with Rooms

Chef: Adam Ashley **Owners:** Paul & Barbara Brooks **Times:** 12-3/7-9.30, Closed 25-26 Dec **Prices:** Starter £4.95-£7.95, Main £6.95-£15.95, Dessert £4.95-£5.95, Service optional **Wine:** 9 by the glass **Notes:** Sun L available, Vegetarian available **Seats:** 90 **Children:** Portions **Rooms:** 15 (15 en suite) ★★★★★ RR **Directions:** 2m N of Ludlow on A49, near Ludlow Golf Club, racecourse and adjacent to Ludlow food centre **Parking:** 80

◉◉ Dinham Hall Hotel

Traditional British V

Accomplished cuisine in stone-built townhouse in the gastronomic centre

☎ 01584 876464 By the Castle SY8 1EJ
e-mail: info@dinhamhall.co.uk
web: www.dinhamhall.co.uk

Dinham Hall, dating from 1792, is situated just off the main square with lovely gardens and views across the valley beyond. The best outlook can be enjoyed from the Georgian-style restaurant with its large bay window. The pastel-toned décor, original oak floor and good natural light create a welcoming ambience, and a well-deserved reputation for good food ensures a steady stream of local enthusiasts. Quality seasonal produce is handled with confidence and imagination in dishes such as Cornish ling poached gently in red wine with root ginger on a bed of pumpkin seed risotto, seared baby courgettes and fennel with a white wine reduction and hint of star anise. Vegetarian menu available.

Chef: Caitlin Proctor **Owners:** Mr J Mifsud **Times:** 12.30-1.45/7-8.45, Closed D 25 Dec **Prices:** Fixed D £38.50, Starter £4.50-£7.50, Main £14.50-£17.15, Dessert £6.50-£8.50, Service optional **Wine:** 98 bottles over £20, 9 bottles under £20, 8 by the glass **Notes:** Vegetarian menu, Civ Wed 140 **Seats:** 30, Pr/dining room 20 **Children:** Min 8 yrs, Menu, Portions **Rooms:** 13 (13 en suite) ★★★ HL **Directions:** Town centre, off Market Place, opposite Ludlow Castle **Parking:** On street

◉ The Feathers Hotel

British, French

Historic building with up-to-the-minute food

☎ 01584 875261 The Bull Ring SY8 1AA
e-mail: enquiries@feathersatludlow.co.uk
web: www.feathersatludlow.co.uk

Described by Nikolaus Pevsner in *The Buildings of England* as 'that prodigy of timber-frame houses' and more recently in *The New York Times* as 'the most handsome inn in the world', this Jacobean hotel is widely renowned and blessed with old-world charm in spades. The kitchen here balances traditional and innovative concepts in its cooking, with most dishes offering well-conceived flavours with lovely ingredients. Think a fillet of cod served with braised salsify, salsify crisps and trompette mushrooms, or perhaps slow-cooked belly of suckling pig with caramelised cauliflower, swede confit and sherry vinegar.

Chef: Dyllan Bates **Owners:** Ceney Developments **Times:** 12.30-2/6.30-9.30, Closed L Mon-Sat **Prices:** Fixed D £32-£35, Service optional, Group min 12 service 10% **Wine:** 25 bottles over £20, 26 bottles under £20, 10 by the glass **Notes:** Sun L 2 courses £12.95-£14.95, 3 courses £15.95-£17.95, Dress Restrictions, Smart casual, Civ Wed 80 **Seats:** 60, Pr/dining room 30 **Children:** Menu, Portions **Rooms:** 40 (40 en suite) ★★★ HL **Directions:** Town-centre hotel in th middle of Ludlow. Approximately 40 minutes from Hereford **Parking:** 36

La Becasse

Rosettes not confirmed at time of going to press

Modern French NEW

New and exciting addition to Ludlow's gastronomic scene

☎ 01584 872325 17 Corve St SY8 1DA
web: www.labecasse.co.uk

As we went to press we were informed that this restaurant, owned by Alan Murchison of L'Ortolan (Shinfield, Berkshire) fame, would be opening at the premises where Hibiscus used to be. The kitchen will be headed-up by Will Holland who plans to offer modern French cuisine similar in concept to L'Ortolan. Definitely one to watch. Please visit www.theAA.com for further details.

Directions: Town centre, bottom of hill below The Feathers Hotel

◉◉◉ Mr Underhills
see page 430

Overton Grange Country House & Restaurant
see page 430

Mr Underhills

LUDLOW   MAP 10 SO57

Modern International

Unpretentious dining on the riverbank

☎ 01584 874431 Dinham Weir SY8 1EH
web: www.mr-underhills.co.uk

Originally part of the castle corn mill, this attractive restaurant with rooms is set on the banks of the wooded River Teme overlooking the weir. Its small but pretty courtyard garden offers an ideal vantage point, as does the bright-and-airy dining room's large picture windows, allowing views over both garden and the fast-flowing Teme, while the small reception room is the place for aperitifs.

Dinner is a fixed-price tasting affair of six courses plus coffee and petits fours, but there's no choice before dessert. Chef-patron Chris enquires about dietary requirements or dislikes when booking, then on the day you are advised on what the main menu dishes will be. The style keeps things intelligently simple, concentrating on bringing the best out of prime, seasonal ingredients, the emphasis on freshness and natural flavours rather than cutting-edge cuisine. Foie gras custard with sweetcorn cream and sesame glaze, a pavé of halibut on crunchy greens with lemongrass and ginger broth, followed by a main of slow-roasted fillet of Mortimer Forest venison with red wine and thyme and Japanese artichokes and olive potato cake show the style. The choice

of desserts includes the likes of black cherry sponge with cinnamon ice cream. Service, with wife Judy as host, is suitably relaxed and friendly though precise, and there's an endearing feeling of going to a private dinner party with friends about the whole experience. An excellent wine list rounds things off in style.

Chef: Christopher Bradley **Owners:** Christopher & Judy Bradley **Times:** 7.30-8.30, Closed 1 wk Jan, 1 wk Jul, Tue, Closed L all wk, D Mon-Tue **Prices:** Fixed D £45, Service optional **Wine:** 90 bottles over £20, 35 bottles under £20, 8 by the glass **Notes:** Fixed D 7 courses, Tasting menus only, Dress Restrictions, Smart casual **Seats:** 30 **Children:** Portions **Directions:** From Castle Square: with castle in front, turn immediately left, proceed round castle, turn right before bridge, restaurant on left **Parking:** 7

Rosettes not confirmed at time of going to press

Overton Grange Country House & Restaurant

LUDLOW   MAP 10 SO57

Modern French 🍷 NOTABLE WINE LIST

Gourmet paradise on the outskirts of Ludlow

☎ 01584 873500 Old Hereford Rd SY8 4AD
e-mail: info@overtongrangehotel.com
web: www.overtongrangehotel.com

A handsome Edwardian house standing in mature grounds on the outskirts of Ludlow, Overton is popular with both locals and gastro-tourists alike and offers lovely views over the Shropshire countryside. The dining room is in two parts at the rear, with plenty of natural light flooding through large windows dressed with Roman blinds. Aubergine and cream is the modern colour theme, tables are elegantly laid, chairs are high-backed suede and service highly polished, professional and European.

The cooking perfectly matches the surroundings, elegantly blending modern and classical French cuisine with superb technical skill, tip-top produce and bold flavours. Presentation is intricate and appealing to the eye and combinations work in harmony on the palate via a repertoire of crisply-scripted menus, with the eight-course tasting option offering a great introduction to the cuisine. Expect the likes of roast rack of lamb with celeriac mousseline and liquorice sauce, or pan-fried fillet of beef with sautéed potatoes, morel mushrooms and

bourguignon sauce. An extensive, well-chosen wine list offers the perfect accompaniment, as does a pre-meal stroll on the lawns in summer, or sitting beside a blazing fire in one of the two small lounges or bar for aperitifs on colder days. As we went to press we understand that a change of chef was taking place.

Owners: Indigo Hotels Ltd **Times:** 12-2.30/7-10, Closed 27 Dec-7 Jan, Closed L Sun-Wed, D Sun (ex residents) **Prices:** Fixed L £29.50, Fixed D £42.50, Service added 10% **Wine:** 150 bottles over £20, 20 bottles under £20, 12 by the glass **Notes:** Fixed L 3 courses, D 4 courses, Tasting menu £55, Dress Restrictions, Smart casual, Civ Wed 30 **Seats:** 40, Pr/dining room 24 **Children:** Min 6 yrs **Rooms:** 14 (14 en suite) ★★★ HL **Directions:** M5 junct 5. On B4361 approx 1.5m from Ludlow towards Leominster **Parking:** 50

MARKET DRAYTON · MAP 15 SJ63

⊛ The Cottage Restaurant at Ternhill Farm House

Modern International

Local fresh produce served in cottage-style restaurant

☎ 01630 638984 Ternhill TF9 3PX
e-mail: info@ternhillfarm.co.uk
web: www.ternhillfarm.co.uk

A listed Georgian former farmhouse and coaching inn, Ternhill was extended in Victorian times and the farm buildings now provide secure parking. The cottage-style restaurant has well-spaced rustic tables, high-backed leather chairs and a huge inglenook fireplace. Cooking is modern British in style with international influences and lots of fresh seasonal produce. Expect imaginative flavour combinations and contrasts in dishes like thyme- and parmesan-crusted fillet of sea bass accompanied by a warm broccoli and sweet pepper salad with chilli and toasted sesame dressing, and to finish, perhaps a lemon, lime and ginger Pavlova or crème brûlée.

Chef: Michael Abraham **Owners:** Michael & Joanne Abraham **Times:** 7-9, Closed Sun & Mon, Closed L all week **Prices:** Starter £4.25-£5.95, Main £9.25-£16.95, Dessert £4.25-£4.95, Service optional **Wine:** 6 by the glass **Notes:** Midweek warmer menu 3 courses £14.95, Vegetarian available, Dress Restrictions, Smart casual **Seats:** 20, Pr/dining room 16 **Children:** Before 8pm **Rooms:** 5 (5 en suite) ★★★★ RR **Directions:** On x-rds of A41 & A53, 3m W of Market Drayton **Parking:** 16

⊛⊛ Goldstone Hall

Modern British

Modern cooking amidst period charm

☎ 01630 661202 Goldstone TF9 2NA
e-mail: enquiries@goldstonehall.com
web: www.goldstonehall.com

Set in impressive gardens and woodland, Goldstone Hall is a relaxed, comfortable Georgian manor house. Beams, exposed timbers and open fires abound and many rooms, including the elegant dining room, have original panelled walls. The carefully evolving menus are based on seasonal and local produce, notably home-grown herbs and vegetables from the well-stocked walled garden. Fixed-price dinner menus and the light 'Upper Crust' supper choice list simple, contemporary British dishes - wild duck and apricot terrine with damson preserve and toasted brioche, and butterfly fillet of gilt head bream on a warm salad of chickpeas, leeks and sweet potato show the style. Service is relaxed but attentive.

Chef: Andrew Keeling **Owners:** Mr J Cushing & Mrs H Ward **Times:** 12-2.30/7.30-11 **Prices:** Fixed L £17, Fixed D £22.50, Starter £6.50, Main £18, Dessert £6.50, Service included **Wine:** 36 bottles under £20, 9 by the glass **Notes:** Sun L 3 courses £21, Dress Restrictions, Smart casual, Civ Wed 100 **Seats:** 40, Pr/dining room 20 **Children:** Portions **Rooms:** 12 (12 en suite) ★★★ HL **Directions:** From A529, 4m S of Market Drayton, follow signs for Goldstone Hall Hotel **Parking:** 40

⊛ Rosehill Manor

Modern, Traditional

Traditional country-house style restaurant

☎ 01630 638532 & 637000 Rosehill, Ternhill TF9 2JF
web: www.rosehillmanorhotel.co.uk

Privately owned and personally run, this 17th-century manor house is set in 1.5 acres of mature gardens. The bar has lovely exposed beams reflecting the character of the original house, while the restaurant enjoys garden views, an open fire in winter and a relaxing atmosphere. The emphasis is on freshly prepared, traditional cooking complemented by professional service. Dishes from the seasonal menu include celery soup with plenty of flavour, or fried tiger prawns in a Thai sweet chilli sauce. Follow with rack of lamb served in a generous four-chop portion, or maybe vegetarian cannelloni filled with ricotta, with cheese and tomato sauce.

Chef: Jane Eardley **Owners:** Mr & Mrs P Eardley **Times:** 12-2/7-9.30, Closed L Mon-Sat, D Sun **Prices:** Fixed D £16-£20, Starter £4.50-£6, Main £13.50-£17, Dessert £5.25, Service optional **Wine:** 7 bottles over £20, 12 bottles under £20, 4 by the glass **Notes:** Smart Casual, Civ Wed 100 **Seats:** 70, Pr/dining room 30 **Children:** Portions **Rooms:** 8 (8 en suite) ★★ HL **Directions:** On A41 4m from Market Drayton **Parking:** 60

MUCH WENLOCK · MAP 10 SO69

⊛ Raven Hotel

British, Mediterranean

Fresh cooking in historic location

☎ 01952 727251 30 Barrow St TF13 6EN
e-mail: enquiry@ravenhotel.com
web: www.ravenhotel.com

This town-centre hotel brings together several 15th-century almshouses and a medieval great hall, with a coaching inn at its heart. The cosy warren of rooms is dotted with oak beams and open fires, and the airy restaurant looks out over an inner courtyard where you can eat outside on warm summer evenings. Local, seasonal produce and fresh ingredients are key to the cooking here, using herbs from the kitchen garden. Classic dishes are given modern European interpretations along the lines of slow-cooked shank of Stottesdon lamb served with fondant potato, redcurrant sauce and mint oil. A bar menu is also available.

Times: 12-2.30/6.45-9.30, Closed 25 Dec **Rooms:** 15 (15 en suite) ★★★ HL **Directions:** 10m SW from Telford on A4169, 12m SE from Shrewsbury. In town centre

MUNSLOW

MAP 10 SO58

◎◎ Crown Country Inn

Modern British NEW

One-time Tudor inn with highly accomplished cooking

☎ 01584 841205   SY7 9ET

e-mail: info@crowncountryinn.co.uk

web: www.crowncountryinn.co.uk

This three-storey listed Tudor inn, set below the rolling hills of Wenlock Edge, has bags of character with many original features intact - flagstone floors, sturdy oak beams and two inglenook fireplaces. But that's only half of it, as this was once a 'Hundred House' where courts sat and passed judgement on local villains. Today though, the only crime would be not to sample chef-patron Richard Arnold's accomplished cuisine in the Corvedale restaurant. A Master Chef of Great Britain, Richard's cooking oozes pedigree, dealing in quality local produce and clear flavours. Take a breast of Shropshire farm chicken wrapped in pancetta with fondant potato and a chorizo and wild mushroom cream sauce, and do save room for the home-made breads and English cheese selection.

Chef: Richard Arnold   **Owners:** Richard & Jane Arnold   **Times:** 12-2/6.45-9, Closed Xmas, Mon   **Prices:** Fixed L £12, Fixed D £17, Starter £4.75-£7.95, Main £12.50-£16.95, Dessert £4.95, Service optional   **Wine:** 13 bottles over £20, 29 bottles under £20, 5 by the glass   **Notes:** Vegetarian available   **Seats:** 65, Pr/dining room 42   **Children:** Portions   **Rooms:** 3 (3 en suite) ★★★★ INN   **Parking:** 20

NORTON

MAP 10 SJ70

◎◎ Hundred House Hotel

British, European 🍃

Historic backdrop and quirky charm meets modern cuisine

☎ 01952 730353   Bridgnorth Rd TF11 9EE

e-mail: reservation@hundredhouse.co.uk

web: www.hundredhouse.co.uk

Principally Georgian, but with parts dating back to the 14th century, this endearing one-time coaching inn and courthouse is now a friendly, family-run hotel, set in pretty grounds complete with herb and flower gardens. Indoors is rich in original features, with a wealth of exposed beams, open fires, quality rustic furnishings and memorabilia, with aromatic herbs and flowers suspended overhead. With formal or informal rooms for dining, and friendly, well-informed service, dishes are modern British in essence, but with some traditional favourites, too. Fresh, well-sourced produce and clear flavours parade in dishes intelligently not over embellished. Expect grilled fillet steak with rosemary mash, braised beef parcel, wild mushrooms, balsamic sauce and truffle oil.

Chef: Stuart Phillips   **Owners:** Mr H Phillips, Mrs S Phillips, Mr D Phillips, Mr SG Phillips   **Times:** 12-2.30/6-10, Closed D 26 Dec   **Prices:** Starter £6-£9, Main £12.95-£27.50, Dessert £6-£8, Service optional, Group min 7 service 10%   **Wine:** 30 bottles over £20, 15 bottles under £20, 10 by the glass   **Notes:** Vegetarian available, Dress Restrictions, Smart casual, Civ Wed 100   **Seats:** 60, Pr/dining room 30   **Children:** Menu, Portions   **Rooms:** 10 (10 en suite) ★★   HL   **Directions:** Midway between Telford & Bridgnorth on A442. In centre of Norton village   **Parking:** 30

OSWESTRY

MAP 15 SJ22

◎◎ Best Western Wynnstay Hotel

Modern European

Modern cooking in elegant, period-style surroundings

☎ 01691 655261   Church St SY11 2SZ

e-mail: info@wynnstayhotel.com

web: www.wynnstayhotel.com

This listed Georgian property was once a coaching inn and posting house, and surrounds a unique 200-year-old crown bowling green. The hotel's elegant Four Seasons restaurant comes decorated in pastel shades along with hues of yellow and gold, backed by equally smartly turned-out staff who provide suitably attentive, professional and friendly service. A mixture of traditional dishes with modern interpretations incorporating European influences is the kitchen's style, supported by good use of the best available produce, as much as possible locally sourced. Expect Welsh lamb rump served with basil-infused roasted vegetables, or perhaps a lightly grilled fillet of sea bass with wilted spring greens and a citrus butter sauce, and to finish, maybe a lime pannacotta with fresh strawberries.

Chef: Ecky Griffiths   **Owners:** Mr N Woodland   **Times:** 12-2/7-9.30, Closed 25 Dec, Closed D Sun   **Prices:** Fixed L £14.50, Fixed D £21.50-£25, Starter £4.50-£6.50, Main £9.95-£18.50, Dessert £4.50-£6.50, Service optional   **Wine:** 20 bottles over £20, 36 bottles under £20, 7 by the glass   **Notes:** Vegetarian available, Dress Restrictions, Smart casual, Civ Wed 90, Air con   **Seats:** 46, Pr/dining room 200   **Children:** Menu, Portions   **Rooms:** 35 (35 en suite) ★★★   HL   **Directions:** In centre of town, opposite the church   **Parking:** 80

◎◎ Pen-y-Dyffryn Country Hotel

Modern British

Top-notch cooking in hillside haven

☎ 01691 653700   Rhydycroesau SY10 7JD

e-mail: stay@peny.co.uk

web: www.peny.co.uk

Standing amid lush and beautiful grounds in a stunning valley, with glorious rolling country views, this alluring stone building was built as a rectory in 1845. There's a homely feel about the place and the hospitality is warm and welcoming, augmented by the real fires in the comfortable lounges and intimate, refurbished dining room with its huge south-facing sash windows. The dinner menu offers a handful of options at each course and fresh local produce, much of it organic, which underpins the kitchen's philosophy for sourcing quality ingredients. Follow a terrine of Welsh ham hock and piccalilli, with a sirloin of Welsh beef, hand-cut chips and braised oxtail, and round off with a steamed chocolate pudding served with vanilla ice cream.

Chef: David Morris   **Owners:** MJM & AA Hunter   **Times:** 6.45-11, Closed 20 Dec-21 Jan, Closed L all week   **Prices:** Fixed D £28, Service optional   **Wine:** 30 bottles over £20, 40 bottles under £20, 3 by the glass   **Seats:** 25

Children: Min 3 yrs, Menu, Portions **Rooms:** 12 (12 en suite) ★★★ HL
Directions: 3m W of Oswestry on B4580 **Parking:** 18

◉◉ Sebastian's Hotel & Restaurant

French NEW

Relaxed, personally-run outfit with accomplished French fare

☎ 01691 655444 45 Willow St SY11 1AQ
e-mail: sebastian.rest@virgin.net
web: www.sebastians-hotel.co.uk

Parts of this privately-owned and personally-run small hotel date back to 1640. So there's bags of charm and character, with original features like exposed beams and oak panelling defining its comfortable lounge, bar and popular bistro-style restaurant. Here, smart high-backed leather chairs come with linen-clothed tables, while walls are donned with plenty of pictures. Traditional French cooking is the kitchen's stock in trade, delivering skilfully prepared, balanced-flavoured dishes that utilise quality ingredients on a repertoire of sensibly compact, fixed-price, weekly-changing market menus and monthly-changing carte. Expect the likes of loin of lamb with ravioli of braised lamb shank and lavender and honey sauce, followed by a warm apple charlotte finish, served with Calvados crème anglaise.

Chef: Mark Sebastian Fisher, Richard Jones **Owners:** Mark & Michelle Fisher **Times:** 6.30-9.30, Closed 25-26 Dec, 1 Jan, Sun-Mon, Closed L all week **Prices:** Fixed D £17.95, Service optional **Wine:** 11 bottles over £20, 28 bottles under £20, 6 by the glass **Seats:** 35 **Children:** Menu, Portions **Rooms:** 6 (6 en suite) ★★ SHL **Directions:** Telephone for directions **Parking:** 25

SHREWSBURY   MAP 15 SJ41

◉ Albright Hussey Manor Hotel & Restaurant

Modern British

A truly historic setting for fine dining

☎ 01939 290571 & 290523 Ellesmere Rd SY4 3AF
e-mail: info@albrighthussey.co.uk
web: www.albrighthussey.co.uk

Built in 1524, this delightful moated manor house was once garrison to Charles I's Royalist troops during the English Civil War. The village is also mentioned in the Domesday Book. These days the hotel has been modernised and extended in parts, but the restaurant remains full of original character with a wealth of oak beams, panelling and leaded windows, and some of the seating in quirky nooks and crannies providing plenty of privacy. The cooking style is an imaginative blend of traditional and modern with a strong emphasis on quality local ingredients. Expect medallions of Church Stretton beef served with wild mushrooms, Lyonnaise potatoes and a brandy sauce, and to finish, perhaps an Amaretto and honey soufflé.

Chef: Michel Nijsten **Owners:** Franco, Vera & Paul Subbiani **Times:** 12/10 **Prices:** Fixed L £8.50-£16, Starter £5.25-£11.75, Main £12-£19.50, Dessert £6.25, Service optional, Group min 6 service 10% **Wine:** 53 bottles over £20, 43 bottles under £20, 5 by the glass **Notes:** Vegetarian available, Dress Restrictions, No jeans, trainers or T-shirts, Civ Wed 200 **Seats:** 80, Pr/dining room 40 **Children:** Portions **Rooms:** 26 (26 en suite) ★★★★ HL **Directions:** On A528, 2m from centre of Shrewsbury **Parking:** 100

◉◉ Mercure Albrighton Hall

International NEW

Notable food in formal setting

☎ 0870 1942129 Albrighton SY4 3AG

Dating back to 1630, this former ancestral home is set in 15 acres of attractive gardens. An established hotel with a well-equipped health and fitness centre, the elegant public rooms boast rich oak panelling, including the long gallery-style dining room. Well-dressed and well-spaced tables make for a formal setting, although service is friendly. The accomplished cooking is classically based, and contemporary flourishes appear in starters like tomato tarte fine with goat's cheese, tapenade and rocket, or a main course of corn-fed chicken with spinach and morel foam. Desserts are a particular strength and could include blackberry soufflé, or an indulgent dark chocolate moelleux with coffee cappuccino and tonka bean ice cream.

Times: 7-9.45

◉◉ Mytton & Mermaid Hotel

Modern British V

Historic riverside inn serving contemporary cuisine

☎ 01743 761220 Atcham SY5 6QG
e-mail: admin@myttonandmermaid.co.uk
web: www.myttonandmermaid.co.uk

Dating from 1735, this Grade II listed, ivy-clad hotel is within easy reach of Shrewsbury and enjoys spectacular views over the River Severn. During the 1930s it was owned by architect Sir Clough Williams-Ellis, of Portmeirion fame. The restaurant strives for excellence in food and service while maintaining a comfortable, friendly environment, and is furnished with oak floors and antique oak tables adorned with candles and fresh flowers. Local seasonal produce is used wherever possible in dishes such as Attingham Park venison served with fennel mash, creamed leeks, carrot purée and a red wine and juniper jus, and to finish, perhaps a Calvados brûlée with apple tuile, mango compôte and Granny Smiths apple sorbet. There's also a convivial bar with separate menu.

Chef: Adrian Badland **Owners:** Mr & Mrs Ditella **Times:** 11.30-2.30/6.30-10, Closed 25 Dec, Closed D 26 Dec **Prices:** Starter £5.95-£7.25, Main £13.95-£18.50, Dessert £5.95-£6.25, Service optional **Wine:** 26 bottles over £20, 30 bottles under £20, 12 by the glass **Notes:** Vegetarian menu, Civ Wed 90 **Seats:** 100, Pr/dining room 15 **Children:** Menu, Portions **Rooms:** 18 (18 en suite) ★★★ HL **Directions:** Just outside Shrewsbury on the B4380 (old A5). Opposite Attingham Park **Parking:** 80

◉ Rowton Castle Hotel

Modern British

Fine dining in a welcoming hotel

☎ 01743 884044 Halfway House SY5 9EP
e-mail: post@rowtoncastle.com
web: www.rowtoncastle.com

Situated in 17 acres of grounds, this Grade II listed building dates back in parts to 1696. The Cedar restaurant features a 17th-century carved oak fireplace and offers a seasonal menu of two or three courses. Oak panelling adds to the warm and intimate ambience. Dishes might include pan-fried sea bass fillets on chickpea mash scented with

ENGLAND

SHREWSBURY CONTINUED

lemon and garlic, and coriander sauce, or a crisp savoury tartlet of creamed spinach, topped with pan-fried mushrooms and artichokes. Try the interesting seasonal desserts to finish.

Times: 12-2/7-9.30 **Rooms:** 19 (19 en suite) ★★★ HL **Directions:** From Birmingham take M6 west. Follow M54 & A5 to Shrewsbury. Continue on A5 and exit at 6th rdbt. Take A458 to Welshpool. Rowton Castle 4m on right

---

TELFORD   MAP 10 SJ60

◎◎ Best Western Valley Hotel & Chez Maws Restaurant

Modern British

Imaginative menus in historic surroundings

☎ 01952 432247   TF8 7DW
e-mail: info@thevalleyhotel.co.uk
web: www.chezmawsrestaurant.co.uk

This Grade II listed Georgian building on the banks of the River Severn is situated in the World Heritage site of Ironbridge, surrounded by parkland. Once the home of the Maws family who manufactured ceramic tiles, the hotel's bright and contemporary-style restaurant Chez Maws is named after them. Quality local and seasonal ingredients speak for themselves in imaginative daily-changing menus that span the globe. From an eclectic menu, try salmon gravad lax with bean sprouts, chilli and sesame seed salad and a soya glaze, followed by fillet of Welsh black beef with a shallot marmalade and

potato fondant, served with butter spinach, poached egg and béarnaise sauce. Service is friendly and efficient.

Chef: Barry Workman **Owners:** Philip & Leslie Casson **Times:** 12-2/7-9.30, Closed 26 Dec-2 Jan, Closed L Sat & Sun **Prices:** Fixed D £25-£35, Starter £4.50-£6.95, Main £12.95-£19.75, Dessert £4.75-£5.75, Service optional **Wine:** 2 bottles over £20, 27 bottles under £20, 6 by the glass **Notes:** Dress Restrictions, Smart casual, Civ Wed 120 **Seats:** 50, Pr/dining room 30 **Children:** Menu, Portions **Rooms:** 44 (44 en suite) ★★★ HL **Directions:** From M6 on to M54, take junct 6 and follow A5223 to Ironbridge for 4m. At mini island turn right, hotel 80 yds on left **Parking:** 100

◎ Hadley Park House

Modern British

Conservatory restaurant offering modern cuisine

☎ 01952 677269   TF1 6QJ
e-mail: info@hadleypark.co.uk
web: www.hadleypark.co.uk

A Georgian mansion built by Thomas Telford's chief engineer, the hotel has an airy conservatory dining room complemented by a traditional oak-panelled bar. Modern British cooking is reflected in a good choice of dishes prepared from locally-sourced ingredients. Options from the seasonal menu include good quality, fresh seared scallops with saffron and vanilla cream and fennel confit to start, followed by pan-fried fillet of sea bass with roast sweet potato in smoked Thai-spiced coconut sauce, or perhaps Staffordshire beef with slow-roast tomato, black olive mash, balsamic jus and rocket pesto. Tarte Tatin with melt-in-the-mouth pastry is not to be missed for dessert.

Old Vicarage Hotel and Restaurant

WORFIELD   MAP 10 SO79

Modern British

Quality cooking in a one-time vicarage

☎ 01746 716497   WV15 5JZ
e-mail: admin@the-old-vicarage.demon.co.uk
web: www.oldvicarageworfield.com

An Edwardian former vicarage provides an elegant setting for this small family-run hotel, which has its own 2 acres of grounds in a peaceful village location. The interior features fresh flowers and polished wood floors and tables, and the relaxing lounge is perfect for pre-dinner drinks. Lovely views of Shropshire countryside are afforded from the Orangery restaurant, and service is as friendly and unobtrusive as the atmosphere.

The highly accomplished, modern-focused kitchen is firmly driven by flavour and intelligent simplicity, which is entirely appropriate to the surroundings. This refreshing approach allows high-quality produce to shine. The light lunch menu is a useful introduction to the Old Vicarage experience but, for the full effect, try house specialities from the dinner menu, such as a starter of roast chicken and foie gras terrine with golden raisin purée, Muscat jelly and toasted country bread, and a main course of roast Gloucestershire Old Spot pork fillet with truffled haricot beans, chestnut-spiked potato cake and port

sauce. Finish your meal with a dessert of apple and brioche fritter with a sorbet and pannacotta of green apple, a tasting plate of Old Vicarage mini desserts or artisan cheeses from the trolley.

Chef: Simon Diprose **Owners:** Mr & Mrs D Blakstad **Times:** 12-2/7-9, Closed L Mon Tue Sat (by reservation only), D 24-26 Dec **Prices:** Fixed L £23.50, Fixed D £39.50, Service included **Wine:** 50 bottles over £20, 20 bottles under £20, 10 by the glass **Notes:** Tasting menu £52.50 **Seats:** 64, Pr/dining room 20 **Children:** Menu, Portions **Rooms:** 14 (14 en suite)★★★ HL **Directions:** From Wolverhampton take A454 (Bridgnorth road), from M54 junct 4 take A442 towards Kidderminster **Parking:** 30

Chef: Tim Wesley **Owners:** Mark & Geraldine Lewis **Times:** 12-2/7-9.30, Closed L Sat (subject to availability), D Sun (subject to demand) **Prices:** Fixed L £10.75-£22.45, Starter £4.65-£7.95, Main £11.50-£18.95, Dessert £5.25 **Wine:** 18 bottles over £20, 28 bottles under £20, 8 by the glass **Notes:** Vegetarian available, Civ Wed 80, Air con **Seats:** 80, Pr/dining room 12 **Children:** Menu, Portions **Rooms:** 12 (12 en suite) ★★★ HL **Directions:** M54 junct 5 take A5 Rampart Way, at rdbt take A442 towards Hortonwood, over double rdbt, next rdbt take 2nd exit, hotel at end of lane **Parking:** 30

WORFIELD MAP 10 SO79

◉◉◉ **Old Vicarage Hotel and Restaurant**

see opposite

SOMERSET

BATH MAP 04 ST76

◉◉◉ **The Bath Priory Hotel and Restaurant**

see page 436

◉◉◉ **Cavendish Restaurant**

see below

◉ **Combe Grove Manor**

International

Georgian country-house hotel dining

☎ 01225 834644 Brassknocker Hill, Monkton Combe BA2 7HS

e-mail: julianebbutt@combegrovemanor.com
web: www.combegrovemanor.com

Set in over 80 acres of gardens, this delightful hotel has magnificent views and a wealth of leisure and therapy treatments to tempt guests. The Cellars Bistro and Bar (open for lunch and dinner daily) is located in the basement with adjoining terrace and gardens where guests can dine alfresco in summer. The main restaurant, the elegant Georgian Rooms with its high ceiling and large windows and notable countryside views, offers finer dining in a more traditional style. The menu includes the likes of cream of pumpkin and ginger soup, followed by fillet of red mullet with black noodles, orange and basil or slow-cooked rabbit with herb dumplings with strawberry and organic mint crème brûlée and spiced shortcake to finish.

Times: 12-2/7-9.30, Closed Mon-Wed, Closed L Thu-Sat, D Sun
Rooms: 42 (42 en suite) ★★★★ HL **Directions:** Telephone for directions

◉◉◉

Cavendish Restaurant

BATH MAP 04 ST76

Modern British NEW

Georgian splendour meets highly creative cooking

☎ 01225 787960 Dukes Hotel, Great Pulteney St BA2 4DN

e-mail: info@dukesbath.co.uk
web: www.dukesbath.co.uk

An elegant, charming Grade I listed Georgian building, just a few minutes walk from the city's Pulteney Bridge, Dukes Hotel cuts a stylish stance. The elegant Cavendish Restaurant is at its heart - a garden room, light and airy and understated, with white table linen, botanical prints and attentive and friendly staff. It overlooks a secluded walled patio garden, complete with fountain, which offers the option of summer alfresco dining.

The kitchen delivers a highly creative and appealing menu that reflects the seasons, the modern approach underpinned by a classical theme and driven by high-quality West Country produce, with an emphasis on organic and free-range ingredients. Dishes showcase skill, a clean style and light touch, with excellent presentation and flavour combinations that allow the main ingredient to shine. Take confit belly and roast loin of Chew Valley pork served with black-pudding croquette, or perhaps line-caught sea bass with fennel and crab

tortellini, and to finish, a coconut pannacotta with lychee sorbet and roasted banana tart.

Chef: Richard Allen **Owners:** Alan Brookes, Michael Bokenham **Times:** 12-2.30/6.30-10, Closed Mon, Closed D Sun **Prices:** Fixed L £12.95, Starter £7.95-£9.95, Main £14.95-£21.95, Dessert £6.50-£7.50, Service added but optional 10% **Wine:** 26 bottles over £20, 9 bottles under £20, 6 by the glass **Notes:** Vegetarian available **Seats:** 28, Pr/dining room 16 **Children:** Portions **Rooms:** 17 (17 en suite) ★★★ SHL **Directions:** M4 junct18 take A46 to Bath. At lights turn left towards A36, at next lights turn right and right again into Gt Pulteney St **Parking:** On street

The Bath Priory Hotel and Restaurant

BATH MAP 04 ST76

Modern French V 🖥

Intimate country-house restaurant with innovative cooking

☎ 01225 331922 Weston Rd BA1 2XT
e-mail: mail@thebathpriory.co.uk
web: www.thebathpriory.co.uk

Set on a tree-lined residential road behind high walls, you'll find all the trappings of a country-house retreat at this Gothic-style mansion set in 4 acres of impeccably maintained gardens. Although only a few minutes from the city, this tranquil place is enhanced further by the luxurious and sophisticated style. A collection of oil paintings adorns the walls, there are deep sofas and roaring winter fires, and yet the mood is thoroughly relaxed with a friendly but professional approach from staff.

The intimate, formal restaurant continues the theme, with white-clothed tables, deep burgundy and gold soft furnishings, high ceilings and views over the gardens. The kitchen, under chef Chris Horridge, (ex Le Manoir aux Quat' Saisons, see entry) shows pedigree, delivering innovative dishes created and presented with imagination and flair. Tip-top ingredients, interesting combinations, clean flavours and high skill deliver on the contemporary French repertoire. Perhaps slow-poached venison with papaya and celery and young nasturtium leaves, and to finish - Cornish pasta of lemon balm, ginger and lemongrass with kaffir ice. A beautifully presented extensive wine list offers good tasting notes.

Chef: Chris Horridge
Owners: Mr A Brownsword
Times: 12-1.45/7-9.45
Prices: Fixed L £20-£24, Fixed D £55-£59, Service optional
Wine: 180 bottles over £20, 60 bottles under £20, 12 by the glass
Notes: Tasting menu 8 courses £70, Vegetarian menu, Dress Restrictions, No jeans or T-shirts, Civ Wed 64
Seats: 64, Pr/dining room 64
Children: Menu, Portions
Rooms: 31 (31 en suite)★★★★ HL
Directions: Telephone for directions
Parking: 40

BATH Continued

◉ Four Seasons Restaurant

Traditional British NEW

Imaginative cuisine in traditional country-house setting

☎ 01225 723226 Best Western The Cliffe Hotel, Cliffe Dr, Crowe Hill, Limpley Stoke BA2 7FY

e-mail: cliffe@bestwestern.co.uk
web: www.bw-cliffehotel.co.uk

Built as a private gentleman's residence with commanding views across the valley, this country-house hotel is set in peaceful grounds around 3.5 miles south of Bath. The traditional-styled restaurant was once the billiard room and offers a choice of imaginative dishes with international influences on a seasonally-changing menu. With relaxed and friendly service, a meal might begin with a duck confit pancake starter. Main courses feature baked fillets of sea bass wrapped in Parma ham and served with crushed new potatoes and gherkin cream, or fillet of beef with spinach, stilton pâté and red wine jus. Desserts include a pear and prune streusel.

Chef: Adrian Lait **Owners:** Martin & Sheena Seccombe **Times:** 12-2/7-9.30 **Prices:** Fixed L £9.50-£12, Fixed D £22.50-£35, Starter £4.50-£8, Main £12.95-£21, Dessert £4.50-£8, Service optional **Wine:** 12 bottles over £20, 23 bottles under £20, 6 by the glass **Notes:** Sun L £15.95-£18, Vegetarian available, Dress Restrictions, Smart casual **Seats:** 50, Pr/dining room 15 **Children:** Menu, Portions **Rooms:** 11 (11 en suite) ★★★ HL **Directions:** A36 S from Bath for 4m at lights turn left onto B3108 towards Bradford-on-Avon. Before railway bridge turn right into Limpley Stoke, hotel is 0.5m on right **Parking:** 30

◉◉ Macdonald Bath Spa Hotel, Vellore Restaurant

Traditional British

Regency elegance, attentive service, accomplished cuisine

☎ 0870 400 8222 Sydney Rd BA2 6JF

e-mail: sales.bathspa@macdonald-hotels.co.uk
web: www.bathspahotel.com

One of the city's most luxurious hotels, this sumptuously elegant building is rich with neo-classical styling, from the grandiose entrance to the murals that adorn the two restaurants: the conservatory-style Alfresco and the opulent fine-dining venue The Vellore - once a ballroom. Dinner at the latter is the best showcase for the kitchen's culinary skills and for the efficient and entertaining service; there's a sommelier on hand to guide your choice of wine, while bread is

carved from the trolley, for example. Food is both accomplished and appealing with a strong emphasis on quality produce and clean flavours; think braised halibut fillet served with saffron potatoes, leeks and a shellfish and horseradish nage.

Macdonald Bath Spa Hotel, Vellore Restaurant

Chef: Andrew Hamer **Owners:** Macdonald Hotels plc **Times:** 12-2/7-9.45, Closed L Mon-Sat **Prices:** Starter £11.95-£14.50, Main £23.50-£26.95, Dessert £8.50-£9.50, Service optional **Wine:** 140 bottles over £20, 12 by the glass **Notes:** Dress Restrictions, No jeans preferred, Civ Wed 120 **Seats:** 80, Pr/dining room 120 **Children:** Menu, Portions **Rooms:** 129 (129 en suite) ★★★★★ HL **Directions:** A4 and follow city-centre signs for 1m. At lights turn left towards A36. Turn right after pedestrian crossing then left into Sydney Place. Hotel 200yds on right **Parking:** 160

◉◉ The Olive Tree at the Queensberry Hotel

Modern British ♦ NOTABLE WINE LIST ▭

Fresh, vibrant cooking in stylish hotel restaurant

☎ 01225 447928 Russel St BA1 2QF

e-mail: reservations@thequeensberry.co.uk
web: www.thequeensberry.co.uk

CONTINUED

BATH CONTINUED

The Queensberry is a stylish, 18th-century townhouse hotel hidden in the centre of Georgian Bath. Less formal than the hotel, The Olive Tree restaurant combines Georgian opulence with contemporary simplicity, with wooden floors and soft grey walls hung with modern artworks. Brown leather banquettes and unclothed tables add to the relaxed feel. Attentive service from polo-shirted staff is a real strength. Innovative modern British menus are based on quality ingredients and competent cooking with creative flair. Particular attention is paid to seasonality. Expect a starter of pork belly with plum fritters and pickled vegetables, with mains such as partridge casserole with parsnip purée and chorizo dumplings, or Cornish sea bass on crab, leek and basil risotto. Flavours are well managed and clear throughout.

Chef: Marc Salmon **Owners:** Mr & Mrs Beere **Times:** 12-2/7-10, Closed L Mon **Prices:** Fixed L £16, Starter £6-£10.50, Main £16-£27, Dessert £8.50, Service optional, Group min 10 service 10% **Seats:** 60, Pr/dining room 30 **Children:** Portions **Rooms:** 29 (29 en suite)★★★ HL **Directions:** City centre. 100yds N of Assembly Rooms in Lower Lansdown **Parking:** Residents' valet parking; Street pay/display

⑱ **Onefishtwofish**

Modern International NEW

Cellar fish restaurant in city centre

☎ 01225 330236 10 North Pde BA2 4AL
e-mail: katherine@kgreenhead.wanadoo.co.uk
web: www.onefishtwofishbath.co.uk

As the name announces, this popular city restaurant specialises in fresh fish. Unusually set in a cellar, the family enterprise (with Paul

Greenhead at the stove and Katherine front of house) is a friendly, welcoming affair, with exposed stone walls and an intimate, candlelit atmosphere. The emphasis is on fresh fish, but there are some interesting flavour combinations (fresh fish with a twist), including influences from the likes of Europe, the Caribbean and beyond. Expect imaginative dishes such as smoked paprika-marinated red snapper with chorizo mash, warm gazpacho and guacamole ice cream, or perhaps a classic bouillabaisse or lobster thermidor. Blackboard specials bolster the output.

Chef: Paul Greenhead, Ben Whale **Owners:** Paul & Katherine Greenhead **Times:** 6-10, Closed 1st 2 wks Jan, Mon **Prices:** Starter £5.50-£8.50, Main £14-£18, Dessert £6, Service optional **Wine:** 14 bottles over £20, 20 bottles under £20, 6 by the glass **Seats:** 54, Pr/dining room 20 **Children:** Portions **Parking:** Car park nearby, free after 7pm

Royal Crescent Hotel - Pimpernels

see below

⑱ *Woods Restaurant*

British, French

Peaceful setting for relaxed city dining

☎ 01225 314812 9-13 Alfred St BA1 2QX
web: www.woods.co.uk

This well-established restaurant is just a short walk from the historic town centre. A small reception area leads into the large dining room, which has a wooden floor and walls decorated with horse-racing prints. The cooking style is simple and uncluttered, making good use of well-

---

Rosettes not confirmed at time of going to press

Royal Crescent Hotel - Pimpernels

BATH MAP 04 ST76

Modern British

Contemporary fine dining in Georgian splendour

☎ 01225 823333 16 Royal Crescent BA1 2LS
e-mail: info@royalcrescent.co.uk
web: www.royalcrescent.co.uk

The sweeping curve of the city's internationally famous Royal Crescent - John Wood the Younger's masterpiece of Georgian architecture - provides the sublime setting for this elegant hotel. Discreetly secreted away, it's recognisable by the liveried doorman, while inside continues the fanfare of Georgian splendour, with impressive paintings and artefacts. At the time of going to press, we understand that there was a change of chef and also a refurbishment of the entire dower house which houses the fine-dining restaurant. It will also be further enhanced by an elegant, contemporary new bar and drawing room. Please visit www.theAA.com for an update and click the link to Pubs and Restaurants.

Owners: von Essen Hotels **Times:** 12.30-2.30/7-10.30 **Prices:** Fixed L £20, Fixed D £55, Service included **Notes:** Tasting menu £65, Dress Restrictions, Smart casual, No jeans, Civ Wed 60, Air con **Seats:** 70, Pr/dining room 40 **Children:** Menu **Rooms:** 45 (45 en suite) ★★★★★ HL **Directions:** Please telephone for directions **Parking:** 17

sourced produce in dishes like carpaccio of beef with rocket leaves, or grilled Capricorn goat's cheese with a sweet red pepper confit and rocket pesto. Follow with a succulent main course of slow-roasted belly pork with braised cabbage and a subtle cinnamon sauce. Don't miss the iced chocolate mousse, perfectly matched with a wild berry compôte.

Times: 6-10, Closed 26 Dec, 1 Jan, Sun **Directions:** Telephone for directions

Fire House Rotisserie
☎ 01225 482070 2 John St BA1 2JL
Grills, gourmet pizzas and vegetarian dishes in a relaxed setting.

Fishworks
☎ 01225 448707 Green St BA1 2JY
Exciting fish dishes from this café above a fishmonger's.

Loch Fyne Restaurant
☎ 01225 750120 24 Milsom St BA1 1DG
Quality seafood chain.

🖥 No. 5 Bistro
☎ 01225 444499 5 Argyle St BA2 4BA
web: www.theaa.com/travel/index.jsp
Modern British cooking in a relaxed, informal atmosphere. Specials change daily, main menu changes seasonally. There's a great 'bring your own wine' offer - no corkage - on Monday and Tuesday evenings.

Strada
☎ 01225 537753 Beaunash House BA1 1EU
Superior pizza from quality ingredients cooked in wood-fire ovens.

Tilleys Bistro
☎ 01225 484200 North Pde, Passage BA1 1NX
Tremendous variety, including an extensive vegetarian choice.

BRUTON   MAP 04 ST63

◎◎ Bruton House Restaurant
Modern British V
Fine dining and contemporary style in historic village
☎ 01749 813395 High St BA10 0AA
e-mail: info@brutonhouse.co.uk
web: www.brutonhouse.co.uk

The spacious bar and drawing room area are comfortably furnished with sofas and armchairs so you can relax before or after dining. The elegant restaurant retains character features including a large stone fireplace and oak beams, along with more contemporary touches such as bright artwork, wood flooring, and leather chairs. Service is formal and discreet but also friendly. The accomplished and passionate chef-proprietors are making a strong reputation for themselves here, and there is a clear focus on simple, seasonal cuisine with commitment to local produce. Expect a loin of Clarendon Estate venison served with a thyme and juniper sauce, or line-caught sea bass with fennel and orange sauce, and perhaps poached pear with caramelised brioche and fig sorbet to finish.

Chef: Scott Eggleton & James Andrews **Owners:** Christie-Miller Andrews Ltd **Times:** 12-2/7-9, Closed 1-16 Jan, 16 Aug-1 Sep, Sun-Mon **Prices:** Fixed L £20-£25, Fixed D £39-£36.50, Starter £8-£10, Main £23.50-£25, Dessert £7.50-£9, Service optional, Group min 8 service 10% **Wine:** 77 bottles over £20, 12 bottles under £20, 15 by the glass **Notes:** Vegetarian menu **Seats:** 30 **Children:** Portions **Directions:** A303, exit signed Bruton, follow signs to Bruton, restaurant at end of High St, opposite pharmacy **Parking:** on street

◎ Truffles
British
Creeper-clad, intimate restaurant in a charming village
☎ 01749 812255 95 High St BA10 0AR
e-mail: mark@trufflesbruton.co.uk
web: www.trufflesbruton.co.uk

It may have two floors but this pleasant rural restaurant is economical with its tables, no doubt to ensure that guests have a comfortable dining experience and the proprietors have more time to spend giving an extremely friendly service. There's a personal touch to the accomplished cooking too, being intelligently straightforward, and modern British in style that showcases quality local ingredients, seasonality and clear flavours. There could be slow-roasted belly of Bronham pork served with dauphinoise potato and Somerset Pomona sauce, and perhaps a white peach tart Tatin finish, delivered with Somerset dairy cream. Look out for special events.

Chef: Mark Chambers **Owners:** Mr & Mrs Chambers **Times:** 12-2/7-9.30, Closed Mon, Closed L Tue-Wed, D Sun **Prices:** Fixed L £12.95, Fixed D £29.95, Service optional **Wine:** 4 by the glass **Notes:** Sun L 3 courses £18.95, Vegetarian menu, Dress Restrictions, Smart casual preferred, Air con **Seats:** 30, Pr/dining room 10 **Children:** Portions **Directions:** Near A303, in town centre, at start of one-way system, on left **Parking:** On street opposite

CHARD   MAP 04 ST30

◎ Bellplot House Hotel & Thomas's Restaurant
Modern European
Classic Georgian townhouse offering West Country fare
☎ 01460 62600 High St TA20 1QB
e-mail: info@bellplothouse.co.uk
web: www.bellplothouse.co.uk

This Grade II listed property originally stood on a bell-shaped piece of land - hence the name. There's an emphasis on good friendly service in the Georgian-style dining room, where guests enjoy drinking from Royal Brierley cut-glass crystal. The emphasis is on fresh, local and seasonal ingredients, with the suppliers proudly listed on the back of the menu. Modern European dishes with an individual twist include coquilles fruits de mer served in a scallop shell, or maybe tournedos Rossini, followed by Somerset apple dumplings with butterscotch and cider sauce.

Chef: Thomas Jones **Owners:** Dennis Betty, Thomas Jones **Times:** 7-9, Closed Sun, Closed L all week **Prices:** Starter £4.95-£6.95, Main £13.50-£16.50, Dessert £4.50-£6.50, Service optional **Wine:** 2 bottles over £20, 12 bottles under £20, 3 by the glass **Notes:** Vegetarian available **Seats:** 30 **Children:** Menu, Portions **Rooms:** 7 (7 en suite) ★★★★★ GA **Directions:** M5 junct 25/A358 signposted Yeovil. At rdbt take 4th exit A358 from Taunton, follow signs to Chard town centre. 500 mtrs from Guildhall **Parking:** 12

ENGLAND

CREWKERNE   MAP 04 ST40

⊛ *Kempsters Restaurant*

Modern British

Restored Somerset longhouse providing excellent cooking using local produce

☎ 01935 881768   Lower St, West Chinnock TA18 7PT

e-mail: debbie@kempsters.fslife.co.uk

A lovingly restored Somerset longhouse with heavy new oak doors, old beams, pine and slate floors and Somerset country life black-and-white photographs on the walls. Comfortable furnishings and warm décor reflect the high standards and friendly welcome offered here. Cooking is accomplished, making excellent use of predominantly locally and regionally sourced ingredients, right down to local tea and coffee merchants. At dinner, enjoy canapés on arrival, then tuck into a starter of hand-dived seared scallops and a main course of rack of Dorset lamb with mustard grain mash. Vegetarians are well catered for and there is a good selection of cider brandy.

Times: 12-3/7-11.30, Closed 2 wks after 14 Feb, Mon, Closed D Sun **Directions:** From A303 take Crewkerne junct, follow A356 to Chiselborough/West Chinnock, turn left, over hill into West Chinnock

DULVERTON   MAP 03 SS92

⊛ Tarr Farm Inn

Modern Mediterranean

Historic inn with focus on excellent cuisine

☎ 01643 851507   Tarr Steps, Exmoor National Park TA22 9PY

e-mail: enquiries@tarrfarm.co.uk

web: www.tarrfarm.co.uk

Almost hidden away from the outside world, this riverside inn really is the place to escape from it all. Dating back to the 16th century, it sits in a wooded valley at Exmoor's heart by the famed Tarr Steps, and offers relaxed and informal dining in addition to stylish accommodation. Meals - served in a range of dining areas or bar - are accomplished, with the confident modern cooking showcasing quality, locally-sourced ingredients. Expect seared fillet of turbot with a leek and tomato risotto and clam nage, or perhaps a hot chocolate and toffee fondant with vanilla bean ice cream and raspberry coulis to close.

Chef: Jerzy Rozputynski **Owners:** Richard Benn & Judy Carless **Times:** 12-3/6.30-12, Closed 1-10 Feb **Prices:** Starter £4.50-£7.95, Main £11.95-£17.95, Dessert £4.95-£5.95, Service optional **Wine:** 41 bottles over £20, 39 bottles under £20, 8 by the glass **Notes:** Vegetarian available **Seats:** 50, Pr/dining room 20 **Children:** Min 14yrs D, Portions **Rooms:** 9 (9 en suite) ★★★★★ INN **Directions:** Leave M5 junct 27, signed Tiverton. Follow signs to Dulverton, from Dulverton take B3223 signed Tarr Stepps for approx 6.5m **Parking:** 40

⊛⊛ Woods Bar & Dining Room

British 🍷 NOTABLE WINE LIST

Unpretentious setting for accomplished cooking

☎ 01398 324007   4 Banks Square TA22 9BU

Food-lovers are beating a path to this charming pub/restaurant (once an old bakery), where the passion for good food and wine is obvious. Inside, a lovely log fire warms the cosy interior, which is split-level with

a popular bar at the top of the restaurant and a refined barn-style feel, with beams, exposed timbers and hand-made wood furniture. Clean, accurate, straightforward modern British cooking with French influences - using quality West Country produce - is the draw here with a great choice of eating options from simple light lunches to the full carte, which might include roast tenderloin of Somerset pork and slow-cooked belly stuffed with boudin noir. Ask for help in choosing a wine and you won't be disappointed either.

Chef: Olivier Certain, Werner Hartholt **Owners:** Paddy Groves, Sally Harvey **Times:** 11-3/6-11.30, Closed 25 Dec **Prices:** Starter £4.50-£7.50, Main £10-£18.50, Dessert £4.50-£5.50, Service optional **Wine:** 100+ bottles over £20, 150+ bottles under £20, 150 by the glass **Notes:** Vegetarian available **Seats:** 40 **Children:** Portions **Directions:** Telephone for directions **Parking:** On street

DUNSTER   MAP 03 SS94

⊛ The Luttrell Arms Hotel

Traditional British

Historic setting for interesting dishes using fresh local produce

☎ 01643 821555   High St TA24 6SG

e-mail: info@luttrellarms.fsnet.co.uk

web: www.luttrellarms.co.uk/main.htm

The historic setting lends plenty of character to the restaurant within this 15th-century hotel. The split-level restaurant has a contemporary, quality feel with attractive styling and comfortable seating, while the bar area has some lovely old features and interesting nooks and crannies. Friendly local staff offer professional service. The menu changes every few weeks and is supplemented by a special of the day and vegetarian option. Dishes are intelligently straightforward allowing the quality local produce to shine. Take roast loin of Exmoor lamb stuffed with garlic and rosemary and served with boulangère potatoes and a redcurrant and port jus.

Times: 12-3/7-10 **Rooms:** 28 (28 en suite) ★★★ HL **Directions:** A39 to Minehead, Turn S towards Tiverton on the A396. Hotel is in centre of Dunster village

EXFORD   MAP 03 SS83

⊛⊛ Crown Hotel

Modern British

Well-loved country inn

☎ 01643 831554   Park St TA24 7PP

e-mail: info@crownhotelexmoor.co.uk

web: www.crownhotelexmoor.co.uk

The country sports set frequents this famous old hotel situated in lovely gardens in the middle of Exmoor. Others find it irresistible too, and the welcome is warm and genuine. Reputedly the moor's oldest coaching inn, it has a cocktail bar, and romantic candlelit dining room and formal table settings where the traditional menus are perused. With an Exmoor theme to the dishes, local pork belly is sure to be found, perhaps braised with Somerset cider and apples, black pudding and braised red cabbage, along with roast Cornish cod with pea purée, braised celery and saffron potatoes. Starters like foie gras ballontine are a special strength, and old favourites such as cherry clafoutis still have their supporters.

Chef: Paul Webber **Owners:** Mr C Kirkbride & S & D Whittaker **Times:** 7-9, Closed L all week **Prices:** Starter £4.95-£9.50, Main £10.95-£21.50, Dessert £6-£7.25, Service added but optional 10%, Group min 8 service 10% **Wine:** 16 bottles under £20, 19 by the glass **Notes:** Vegetarian available, Dress Restrictions, Smart casual, No jeans, T-shirts, swimwear **Seats:** 30, Pr/dining room 14 **Children:** Min 12 yrs, Portions **Rooms:** 17 (17 en suite) ★★★ HL **Directions:** From Taunton take A38 to A358. Turn left at B3224 & follow signs to Exford **Parking:** 30
see advert on this page

HINTON CHARTERHOUSE MAP 04 ST75

◎◎ Homewood Park

Traditional British 🖥 V

Fine food in a country-house setting

☎ 01225 723731 BA2 7TB
e-mail: info@homewoodpark.co.uk
web: www.homewoodpark.co.uk

All the delights associated with country-house life are experienced to the full at Homewood Park: stunning grounds, comfortable lounges, attentive service and a dining room with garden views. Here, high-backed chairs and fine cutlery, china and glassware enhance the culinary experience. It's clear from the menus that food is a major focus. Take a starter of sautéed scallops and black pudding with chorizo oil, followed by an accomplished grilled fillet of sea bass with home-made pasta and shrimp, mussel and saffron fish cream, and to finish a well-made strawberry soufflé with balsamic ice cream. Dishes are inventive, cooking is precise and the presentation very appealing to the eye. Lighter meals are available in the bar and lounges.

Chef: Jamie Mould **Owners:** von Essen Hotels **Times:** 12-1.45/7-9.30 **Prices:** Fixed L £14.50, Fixed D £44, Starter £12.50, Main £23.50, Dessert £8, Service optional **Wine:** 120 bottles over £20, 10 bottles under £20, 6 by the glass **Notes:** Early bird menu 3 courses £22, Vegetarian menu, Dress Restrictions, Smart casual, No jeans or trainers, Civ Wed 50 **Seats:** 60, Pr/dining room 40 **Children:** Menu, Portions **Rooms:** 19 (19 en suite) ★★★ HL **Directions:** 6m SE of Bath off A36, turn left at second sign for Freshford **Parking:** 50

Crown Hotel

Park St, Somerset TA24 7PP
Tel: 01643 831554
e-mail: info@crownhotelexmoor.co.uk
web: www.crownhotelexmoor.co.uk

The warmest of welcomes awaits everyone who steps over the threshold of this family run 17ᵗʰ Century Coaching Inn, situated in the pretty village of Exford at the heart of the Exmoor National Park. The elegant candle-lit restaurant serves modern English food with a local twist. Pre-dinner drinks and canapés are served in the lounge whilst you peruse the menu. Cornish Scallops and pan fried Foie Gras can be found alongside West Coast fish, Exmoor lamb and organic beef with such delights as aniseed parfait and rhubarb and vanilla soufflé for dessert. Coffee with homemade petit fours finish this lavish meal. All ingredients are locally sourced wherever possible.

Head restaurant chef Darren Edwards with head chef Paul Webber and all the team work hard to produce a well balanced menu and sincerely hope you enjoy your dining experience at the Crown.

HOLFORD MAP 04 ST14

◎ Combe House Hotel

Modern European

Big flavours and fresh local ingredients in a relaxed and comfortable dining room

☎ 01278 741382 TA5 1RZ
e-mail: info@combehouse.co.uk
web: www.combehouse.co.uk

This peaceful Somerset country-house hotel is set in 4 acres of tranquil gardens tucked away in a quiet valley in the Quantock Hills - it could hardly get more idyllic. The beamed restaurant has a huge stone ornamental fireplace and modern Cornish maple and walnut tables. The organic kitchen garden provides the chef with vegetables and soft fruit while other ingredients are sourced locally - meat and game from local farms and shoots, fish from Brixham and, of course, Somerset

CONTINUED

HOLFORD CONTINUED

cheeses. The menu is modern in style with international influences - try chicken liver parfait with red onion marmalade to start, followed by roast filet of brill with cockle and vermouth sauce.

Chef: Lawrence Pratt **Owners:** Andrew Ryan, Ray Fox-Cumming **Times:** 12-2.30/7-9 **Prices:** Starter £4.95-£8.50, Main £15.25-£19.50, Dessert £6.25, Service optional **Wine:** 20 bottles over £20, 20 bottles under £20, 6 by the glass **Notes:** Civ Wed 40 **Seats:** 40, Pr/dining room 8 **Children:** Portions **Rooms:** 18 (18 en suite) ★★ HL **Directions:** Telephone for directions **Parking:** 40

HUNSTRETE   MAP 04 ST66

◎◎ Hunstrete House Hotel

Modern European ☘

Contemporary dining in a country-house setting

☎ 01761 490490   BS39 4NS
e-mail: reception@hunstretehouse.co.uk
web: www.hunstretehouse.co.uk

A deer park on the edge of the Mendips, a Georgian mansion, period paintings and furniture come together to provide the complete country-house experience. The Terrace dining room is decorated in European white and shades of green with sparkling chandeliers. Cooking is contemporary in style and uses the best of local, seasonal ingredients in well-conceived dishes accurately executed. Much of the freshly picked produce comes from the hotel's own Victorian walled garden, and free-range meat from Wiltshire farms. Recommended dishes are escabèche of line-caught mackerel, seared hand-dived scallops with Jerusalem artichoke purée, and fillet of Stokes Marsh Farm beef with braised ox cheek and root vegetables.

Chef: Matthew Lord **Owners:** Culloden Associates **Times:** 12-2/7-9.30 **Prices:** Fixed L £15.95, Fixed D £47.75, Service included **Wine:** 85 bottles over £20, 15 bottles under £20, 7 by the glass **Notes:** Sun L 3 courses £25, Dress Restrictions, No jeans, smart casual, Civ Wed 60 **Seats:** 35, Pr/dining room 50 **Children:** Menu, Portions **Rooms:** 25 (25 en suite) ★★★ CHH **Directions:** On A368 - 8m from Bath **Parking:** 50

MARTOCK   MAP 04 ST41

◎ Ash House Country Hotel

Modern British NEW

A friendly, family-run hotel and restaurant

☎ 01935 822036 823126   41 Main St, Ash TA12 6PB
e-mail: reception@ashhousecountryhotel.co.uk
web: www.ashhousecountryhotel.co.uk

A family-run Georgian country-house hotel where you can dine in the traditional formal restaurant or the relaxed environment of the

---

conservatory overlooking the gardens. All ingredients are carefully sourced from named local suppliers, providing the chef with ample material for dishes like pan-fried fillet of Somerset farm beef with pommes fondant, wild mushroom stuffing, buttered baby pak choi and Marsala jus, or a straightforward home-made steak-and-kidney pie in suet pastry with fresh local vegetables and potatoes. Desserts might feature simple favourites like rhubarb pannacotta.

Chef: David Pegler **Owners:** Nick & Gill McGill **Times:** 12-2/6.30-9, Closed 25-26 Dec, 31 Dec, 1 Jan, Sun-Mon **Prices:** Fixed L £12, Starter £4.50-£6.50, Main £13.95-£20.95, Dessert £4.50-£6.50, Service optional **Wine:** 7 bottles over £20, 16 bottles under £20, 4 by the glass **Notes:** Civ Wed 60 **Seats:** 40, Pr/dining room 20 **Children:** Portions **Rooms:** 9 (9 en suite) ★★★ CHH **Directions:** Leave A303 at Tintinhull Forts junct. After slip road turn left. Continue for approx. 0.75m, hotel on right **Parking:** 35

MIDSOMER NORTON   MAP 04 ST65

◎◎ The Moody Goose At The Old Priory

Modern British

Charming, characterful setting to enjoy innovative flavours and combinations

☎ 01761 416784 & 410846   Church Square BA3 2HX
e-mail: info@theoldpriory.co.uk
web: www.theoldpriory.co.uk

Dating from 1152, The Old Priory is one of the oldest houses in Somerset, complete with inglenook fireplaces, flagstone floors and oak beams. The Moody Goose restaurant is decorated to complement the building's character, period features and contemporary cuisine, with beautiful modern watercolours displayed alongside a 100-year-old cooking range. Menus are designed around fresh seasonal produce, locally sourced where possible, and herbs, fruit and vegetables come from the Priory's own kitchen garden. Dishes are cooked to order with the emphasis on simplicity - maybe pressed terrine of red mullet, aubergine and baby leek with basil vinaigrette, followed by poached rabbit saddle with confit leg, tarragon sauce and herb gnocchi.

Chef: Stephen Shore **Owners:** Stephen Shore **Times:** 12-1.30/7-9.30, Closed 1 Jan, BHs except Good Friday, Sun **Prices:** Fixed L £15, Fixed D £25, Starter £8.50-£12, Main £18.50-£22, Dessert £7.50, Service optional **Wine:** 107 bottles over £20, 14 bottles under £20, 9 by the glass **Seats:** 36, Pr/dining room 16 **Children:** Portions **Rooms:** 7 (7 en suite) ★★★ SHL **Directions:** Down Midsomer Norton High Street, right at lights, right at rdbt in front of church **Parking:** 14

PORLOCK   MAP 03 SS84

◎◎◎ Andrews on the Weir

see opposite

Andrews on the Weir

ENGLAND

PORLOCK MAP 03 SS84

Modern European V ✋

Great local produce in superb bayside location

☎ 01643 863300 Porlock Weir TA24 8PB
e-mail: information@andrewsontheweir.co.uk
web: www.andrewsontheweir.co.uk

Andrews is the epitome of the restaurant-with-rooms genre. Positioned in a delightful setting right on the water's edge, this charming Georgian building overlooks Porlock Bay and the weir. A charming place in classic country-house mode, it has a singular dedication to serving fine food and freshest ingredients that makes the dining experience memorable. The restaurant itself is light and elegant with a relaxed, informal atmosphere and large windows providing splendid views over the harbour.

Service is welcoming, attentive and friendly yet precise, in tune with the atmosphere and kitchen's approach. Chef-patron Andrew Dixon's modern European cooking style is underpinned by classical French roots and inspired by carefully sourced, high-quality local produce that's intelligently simply prepared with flair to let clear, clean flavours shine without unnecessary over-complication. High skill, attention to detail, balanced combinations and spot-on execution all parade on the fixed-price repertoire of lunch, carte and vegetarian menus. Expect Somerset tenderloin pork, slow roasted and perhaps served with mushrooms a la crème, Parmentier potato, pancetta, confit onions and Madeira jus, while lemon pannacotta with carpaccio of pineapple, mango salsa and citrus syrup might prove a suitably impressive finale.

Chef: Andrew Dixon
Owners: Andrew & Sarah Dixon
Times: 12-3/6.30-10, Closed Jan, Mon, Tue
Prices: Fixed L £15.50, Fixed D £38.50, Service optional, Group min 7 service 10%
Wine: 35 bottles over £20, 12 bottles under £20, 8 by the glass
Notes: Sun L 3 courses £24.50, Tasting menu 5 courses £25, Vegetarian menu
Seats: 25
Children: Min 12 yrs, Portions
Rooms: 5 (5 en suite) ★★★★ RR
Directions: From M5 junct 25 follow A358 towards Williton, then A39 through Porlock & onto Porlock Weir. Hotel in 1.5m
Parking: 5

PORLOCK CONTINUED

The Oaks Hotel

British, French

Elegant Edwardian house dining with sea views

☎ 01643 862265   TA24 8ES
e-mail: info@oakshotel.co.uk
web: www.oakshotel.co.uk

A small hotel overlooking Porlock towards the sea, The Oaks is personally run by a husband-and-wife team, Tim and Ann Riley. The restaurant is light with large windows enabling virtually every table to enjoy the splendid view. The daily-changing menu places the emphasis firmly on local produce in simply prepared dishes. A cream of pear and watercress soup starter might be followed by tenderloin of organic Somerset pork with grain mustard and Marsala. Perhaps banana and stem ginger ice cream for dessert.

Times: 7-8, Closed Nov-Mar   **Rooms:** 8 (8 en suite)★★★ HL
Directions: At bottom of Dunstersteepe Road, on left on entering Porlock from Minehead

---

SHEPTON MALLET   MAP 04 ST64

◉◉ Charlton House

Modern British NOTABLE WINE LIST

Innovative cuisine in wonderfully elegant surroundings

☎ 01749 342008   Charlton Rd BA4 4PR
e-mail: enquiries@charltonhouse.com
web: www.charltonhouse.com

It's no surprise that this chic country-house hotel set in delightful grounds exudes style and atmosphere, owned as it is by the founders of the internationally acclaimed design label Mulberry. Decorated with imagination and theatrical panache, exquisite Mulberry fabrics and leather furnishings abound, while the smart and spacious conservatory-style Sharpham Park restaurant comes with quality table settings and overlooks the manicured lawns. The kitchen pays due respect to high-quality local produce, much from the hotel's own organic and rare breed farm (Sharpham Park). Dishes impress with their artistry, flavour and modern stylish presentation; take slow-cooked loin of Sharpham lamb served with braised artichokes and cassoulet of beans, and a fig tart with roasted fig purée and tobacco ice cream finish. A seven-course tasting menu bolsters carte and lunch offerings, while the wine list is extensive and personally chosen by the proprietor. Service is attentive and professional.

Chef: Elisha Carter   **Owners:** Roger Saul   **Times:** 12.30-2.30/7.30-10.15
Prices: Fixed L £22.50, Fixed D £52.50, Service optional, Group min 8 service 10%   **Wine:** 130 bottles over £20, 12 by the glass   **Notes:** Tasting menu £65, Civ Wed 120, Air con   **Seats:** 84, Pr/dining room 70
Children: Menu, Portions   **Rooms:** 26 (26 en suite)★★★★ HL
Directions: On A361. Hotel is located 1m before Shepton Mallet
Parking: 70

◉ Thatched Cottage

British, French, Indian NEW

Modern dining in a traditional-style inn

☎ 01749 342058   63-67 Charlton Rd BA4 5QF
e-mail: david@thatchedcottage.info
web: www.thatchedcottage.info

The main building is 370 years old, thatched and listed Grade II, but the interior is not what you might expect. You'll find oak beams, tiled floors, panelled walls, open stonework and log fires, but through the contemporary approach to design, simple, light-and-airy spaces have been created. Dishes are attractively presented making good use of quality local, seasonal produce. With European influences, and plenty of steaks on offer, rack of salt marsh lamb with tartlet of confit peppers and courgettes, confit of duck with poached pear in red wine and mushroom and potato terrine, and pollack Spanish style are fine examples of the fare.

Chef: Fabrice Belier, Madan Pandley   **Owners:** David Pledger   **Times:** 12-2.30/6.30-9.30   **Prices:** Starter £3.95-£6.95, Main £9.95-£17.95, Dessert £4.95-£6.95   **Wine:** 7 bottles over £20, 27 bottles under £20, 23 by the glass   **Notes:** Sun L 3 courses £11.50-£14.50, Vegetarian available
Seats: 56, Pr/dining room 35   **Children:** Portions   **Rooms:** 8 (8 en suite)
★★★★ INN   **Directions:** 0.6m E of Shepton Mallet, at lights on A361
Parking: 35

◉ The Three Horseshoes Inn

Modern, Traditional NEW

Honest cooking and real ale in 17th-century coaching inn

☎ 01749 850359   Batcombe BA4 6HE
e-mail: bob.wood@zoom.co.uk
web: www.three-horseshoes.co.uk

This honey-stoned 17th-century coaching inn oozes rustic charm with an inglenook fire and wood-burning stove, exposed beams and Somerset stone walls to welcome the diner. The cooking style is modern British and service is relaxed and friendly. Take a warm salad of home-smoked free-range chicken with wild mushrooms and tarragon olive oil, followed by a slow-braised quarter shoulder of local organic lamb served on creamed potatoes served with confit garlic and shallots and red wine gravy. Finish with a trio of treacle sponge, brioche bread-and-butter pudding and spiced apple filo dumpling all served with English custard.

Chef: Mike Jones, Bob Wood **Owners:** Bob Wood & Shirley Greaves **Times:** 12-2/7-9, Closed 25 Dec, Mon **Prices:** Starter £4.25-£6.75, Main £8.25-£18.25, Dessert £5.25, Service optional, Group min 10 service 10% **Wine:** 8 bottles over £20, 28 bottles under £20, 8 by the glass **Notes:** Sun L £10.50, Dress Restrictions, Smart casual **Seats:** 40, Pr/dining room 40 **Children:** D 12yrs+, Portions **Rooms:** 3 (2 en suite) ★★★★ INN **Directions:** Signed from A359 Bruton, Frome **Parking:** 30

SOMERTON   MAP 04 ST42

◉ The Devonshire Arms

Modern British NEW

Former hunting lodge turned gastro-pub with modern brasserie-style cooking

☎ 01458 241271 Long Sutton TA10 9LP
e-mail: mail@thedevonshirearms.com
web: www.thedevonshirearms.com

This Grade II listed former hunting lodge is set on an idyllic village green. Now more in the gastro-pub genre, the restaurant is stylish, light and airy. Modern chunky wood tables and leather chairs or upholstered benches provide the comforts, plus there are a few sofas for relaxing over drinks or coffee. An informal mix of bare or paper-clothed tables completes the relaxed vibe, while staff are suitably unstuffy and efficient. The kitchen follows the modern vogue too, its brasserie-style fare enlivened by a nod to the Mediterranean and beyond; take calves' liver with chargrilled chorizo, creamy mash and calvo nero, with perhaps a rich chocolate parfait with griottine cherries to finish.

Chef: Sasha Matkevich **Owners:** Philip & Sheila Mepham **Times:** 12-2.30/7-9.30, Closed 25 Dec, Closed D Sun (winter) **Prices:** Starter £4.20-£6.50, Main £12.95-£18.50, Dessert £4.50, Service added but optional 10% **Wine:** 6 bottles over £20, 17 bottles under £20, 9 by the glass **Seats:** 40 **Children:** Portions **Rooms:** 9 (8 en suite) ★★★ INN **Directions:** A303 Podimore rdbt. Take A372, continue for 4m and turn left towards Long Sutton **Parking:** 6

STOKE SUB HAMDON   MAP 04 ST41

◉◉ The Priory House Restaurant

Modern British

Enjoyable dining at a smart high-street restaurant

☎ 01935 822826 1 High St TA14 6PP
e-mail: reservations@theprioryhouserestaurant.co.uk
web: www.theprioryhouserestaurant.co.uk

A high-street restaurant decked out in smart contemporary shades of blue and beige. Take a drink in the bar or on the pretty garden terrace in summer, and then move through to the restaurant for some accomplished modern British cuisine, distinguished by technical mastery, attentive sourcing of ingredients, and plenty of flavour. Dishes are gutsy, yet refined, and deliver on both taste and texture: start with pork and herb terrine perhaps, served with beetroot chutney and pickled gooseberries, followed by pink-roasted breast of Devonshire duckling with braised red cabbage and apricot sauce, or Somerset beef fillet with seared foie gras, wild mushrooms, and béarnaise sauce. Wines are supplemented by an interesting selection of Somerset cider brandies.

Chef: Peter Brooks **Owners:** Peter & Sonia Brooks **Times:** 12-2/7-9.30, Closed 25 Dec, BHs, 2 wks May, 2wks Nov, Sun & Mon, Closed L Tue-Fri

Prices: Fixed L £16, Starter £6.50-£9.50, Main £18-£19.50, Dessert £6.50, Service optional **Wine:** 37 bottles over £20, 10 bottles under £20, 7 by the glass **Seats:** 25 **Children:** Min 7 yrs **Directions:** 0.5m from A303 in the centre of Stoke Sub Hamdon **Parking:** Free car park 200yds & street parking

STON EASTON   MAP 04 ST65

◉◉ Ston Easton Park

Modern British

Fine dining in a Palladian mansion

☎ 01761 241631 BA3 4DF
e-mail: info@stoneaston.co.uk
web: www.stoneaston.co.uk

This grand Palladian mansion belongs to one of the West Country's most romantic estates. Designed by the great 18th-century landscape gardener, Humphrey Repton, the grounds reward exploration; take a stroll before dinner and you might stumble upon a ruined grotto, sham castle, or an 18th-century ice house. Inside is as opulent as you'd expect, with dinner served in a number of magnificent dining rooms. The Cedar Tree restaurant serves an imaginative menu of modern dishes, drawing its ingredients from the estate's kitchen garden and the best of local producers. Start with braised beef and foie gras terrine perhaps, and then move on to grilled fillet of sea bass with coriander couscous, poached asparagus and a coconut and lime broth.

Chef: Michael Parke **Owners:** von Essen Hotels **Times:** 12-2/7-9.30 **Prices:** Fixed L £17.50, Starter £12, Main £22.50, Dessert £10, Service optional **Notes:** Dress Restrictions, Smart casual, Civ Wed 100 **Seats:** 40, Pr/dining room 80 **Children:** Min 7 yrs, Menu, Portions **Rooms:** 22 (22 en suite) **Directions:** Follow A39 from Bath for approx. 8m. Turn onto A37 (Shepton Mallet), Ston Easton is next village **Parking:** 100

TAUNTON   MAP 04 ST22

◉ Corner House Hotel

Modern

Enjoyable bistro dining in tastefully updated Victorian surroundings

☎ 01823 284683 Park St TA1 4DQ
e-mail: res@corner-house.co.uk
web: www.corner-house.co.uk

The impressive turrets and stained glass of this Victorian building conceal a contemporary interior. The 4DQ bistro (trendily named after part of its postcode) combines modern comfort with original features to produce a dining venue that has a pleasing, relaxed ambience. The simple, well-executed dishes ride with the surroundings, and come based on fresh Somerset ingredients. Take lamb shank teamed with parsnip mash and thyme-scented carrots, or steak frites (served with garlic butter and string fries and choice of peppercorn, béarnaise or stilton sauce), and to finish, perhaps glazed lemon tart with Chantilly cream, or Bailey's chocolate cheesecake served with chocolate cream.

Owners: Hatton Hotels **Times:** 12-2/6.30-9.30 **Prices:** Fixed L £20.50-£29.50, Fixed D £20.50-£29.50, Starter £3.50-£6.95, Main £7.95-£17.95, Dessert £4.95-£5.50, Service optional **Wine:** 6 bottles over £20, 17 bottles under £20, 9 by the glass **Notes:** Fixed L 3 courses, Sun L 3 courses £11.95 **Seats:** 100, Pr/dining room 55 **Children:** Menu, Portions **Rooms:** 44 (44 en suite) ★★★ HL **Directions:** Telephone for details **Parking:** 40

ENGLAND

TAUNTON CONTINUED

◉◉ The Mount Somerset Hotel

British, French

Elegant Regency property with interesting contemporary food

☎ 01823 442500 Henlade TA3 5NB
e-mail: info@mountsomersethotel.co.uk
web: www.mountsomersethotel.co.uk

An Italian-designed Regency house retaining all of its original grandeur, The Mount Somerset, as its name suggests, is set on top of a hill with magnificent views over the Somerset countryside. The recently refurbished restaurant is splendid, with a magnificent central chandelier and two superb mirrors. Chairs are large and very comfortable and tables are smartly appointed with crisp linen, sparkling silver and contemporary crockery. The likes of a collection of salmon (hot home-smoked salmon, carpaccio and gâteau), a symphony of Quantock duck (tempura of leg, lasagne, breast and a plum jus), and several peripheral courses (canapés, West Country cheeses and petits fours) all add to the sense of occasion.

Chef: Stefan Warwick **Owners:** von Essen Hotels **Times:** 12-2/7-9.30 **Prices:** Fixed L £15, Fixed D £38.50, Starter £9, Main £22.50, Dessert £7, Service optional **Notes:** Dress Restrictions, Smart casual, no jeans or trainers, Civ Wed 60 **Seats:** 40, Pr/dining room 20 **Children:** Menu, Portions **Rooms:** 11 (11 en suite) ★★★ HL **Directions:** From M5 junct 25 take A358 (Chard); turn right in Henlade (Stoke St Mary), then turn left at T-junct. Hotel 400yds on right **Parking:** 50

◉◉ The Willow Tree Restaurant

Modern British

Imaginative regional cooking in a period restaurant

☎ 01823 352835 3 Tower Ln TA1 4AR

Having worked for the Roux brothers for 12 years and run a successful restaurant in London, Darren Sherlock delights in sourcing the finest ingredients from local suppliers. Everything is made in-house - stocks, bread, pasta, pastry and ice cream - and is served in the delightful little restaurant in a Grade II listed building, originally a moat house. Exposed beams and an inglenook fireplace set the scene alongside white-linen dressed tables and bright artwork, while outside there is a charming waterside terrace. The menu makes good reading, the kitchen's modern approach underpinned by a classical French influence; take a navarin of lamb served on Puy lentils with confit shallot and sautéed spinach, or chocolate tart with beetroot ice cream to finish.

Chef: Darren Sherlock **Owners:** Darren Sherlock & Rita Rambellas **Times:** 6.30-10, Closed Jan, Aug, Sun-Mon, Closed L all week **Prices:** Fixed D £22.50-£29.50, Service optional, Group min 7 service 10% **Wine:** 20 bottles over £20, 25 bottles under £20, 4 by the glass **Notes:** Dress Restrictions, Smart casual **Seats:** 25, Pr/dining room 16 **Children:** Min 10 yrs **Directions:** 200 yds from Taunton bus station **Parking:** 20 yds, 300 spaces

WELLINGTON   MAP 03 ST12

◉◉ Bindon Country House Hotel & Restaurant

Traditional British V

Classic cuisine in attractive country retreat

☎ 01823 400070 Langford Budville TA21 0RU
e-mail: stay@bindon.com
web: www.bindon.com

This impressive Grade II listed 17th-century country house is set in 7 acres of stunning formal and woodland gardens, overlooking the Blackdown Hills. Behind its baroque façade lies a Victorian interior that has been renovated to a high standard by the current owners. The elegant Wellesley restaurant is the venue for impressive and accomplished cuisine, accompanied by formal but relaxed service. Good use is made of fresh local ingredients, to create unashamedly traditional British dishes, some with a continental twist. Typical dishes may include seared Brixham scallops with confit shallots and basil potato cake, followed by roast loin of Dartmoor venison with celeriac purée for mains, and a selection of seven different bite-sized chocolate desserts to finish.

Chef: Michael Davies **Owners:** Lynn & Mark Jaffa **Times:** 12-1/7-9.30 **Prices:** Fixed L £12.95, Fixed D £35, Service optional **Wine:** 113 bottles over £20, 27 bottles under £20, 9 by the glass **Notes:** Fixed D 4 courses, Vegetarian menu, Dress Restrictions, Smart casual, no jeans or T-shirts, Civ Wed 50 **Seats:** 50, Pr/dining room 20 **Children:** Min 7 yrs, Menu, Portions **Rooms:** 12 (12 en suite) ★★★ CHH **Directions:** From Wellington B3187 to Langville Budville, through village & right towards Wiveliscombe, right at junct, past Bindon Farm, right after 450yds **Parking:** 25

WELLS   MAP 04 ST54

◉ Best Western Swan Hotel

British

Generous and imaginative dishes in a traditional setting

☎ 01749 836300 Sadler St BA5 2RX
e-mail: swan@bhere.co.uk
web: www.swanhotelwells.co.uk

A former coaching inn with stunning views from the front over Wells Cathedral. The long, narrow dining room, with linen-fold oak panelling and interesting antiques, provides a very traditional setting with a formal but friendly style of service. Imaginative dishes - traditional but with a modern twist - are served in good country portions. Expect the likes of a slow-roast rump of lamb served with a chilli and tarragon jus, or perhaps pan-fried suprême of salmon with a fennel and saffron cream. Cooking is careful with good use made of fresh local produce.

Chef: Paul Mingo-West **Owners:** Christopher Chapman **Times:** 12-2/7-9.30 **Prices:** Fixed L £13.50-£15.50, Fixed D £25.50-£27.50, Starter £4.95-£6.95, Main £12.75-£19.50, Dessert £5.50-£5.95, Service optional **Wine:** 16 bottles over £20, 19 bottles under £20, 7 by the glass **Notes:** Civ Wed 70 **Seats:** 60, Pr/dining room 100 **Children:** Menu, Portions **Rooms:** 49 (49 en suite) ★★★ HL **Directions:** A39, A371, opposite Cathedral **Parking:** 30

◉◉ Goodfellows

Modern European

A contemporary and eclectic combination of restaurant, fishmonger, pâtisserie and deli

☎ 01749 673866 5 Sadler St BA5 2RR
e-mail: goodfellows@btconnect.com
web: www.goodfellowswells.co.uk

The mulberry-coloured shop front of this establishment houses an informal pâtisserie and deli counter. Downstairs provides a modern, bright main restaurant with an open-plan kitchen that shares a cold-fish counter where the chef sells fresh fish and offers cooking tips. There's further restaurant space upstairs with a glass atrium and an adjoining courtyard. Accomplished and versatile cooking can be seen at the open stove. The modern European cuisine offers seafood with Mediterranean influences - a light style with intense flavours from oils and vinaigrettes using the likes of black olives, capers and anchovy or truffle oil. A six-course tasting menu is also available, and typical dishes might include the likes of terrine of skate and shiitake mushrooms with soy and ginger dressing to start, followed by fillet of halibut with a red onion and potato cake, smoked salmon and asparagus and champagne sauce.

Chef: Adam Fellows **Owners:** Adam & Martine Fellows **Times:** 12-2.30/6.30-9.30, Closed 25 Dec, 1 Jan & 1st 2 wks in Jan, Sun & Mon, Closed D Tue & Wed **Prices:** Fixed L £15, Fixed D £33, Starter £6-£14, Main £13-£24, Dessert £4-£7, Service optional, Group min 8 service 8% **Wine:** 45 bottles over £20, 12 bottles under £20, 13 by the glass **Notes:** Tasting menu 6 courses £49, Air con **Seats:** 40, Pr/dining room 10 **Children:** Portions **Directions:** Town centre near Market Place

◉ The Old Spot

European NEW

Contemporary restaurant with friendly, relaxed bistro vibe

☎ 01749 689099 12 Sadlet St BA5 2SE

The large window frontage of this period-style stone building picks out this light-and-airy, contemporary city-centre restaurant. Pale green walls, framed menus and wooden floorboards add fashionable touches to the high ceilings, while a few steps down, an extension overlooks the cathedral. Informal yet professional table service and unclothed tables add to the relaxed, friendly atmosphere. The kitchen takes an intelligently simple approach driven by local seasonal produce, with well-presented, clean-cut, bistro-style dishes. Take a fillet of halibut served with brown shrimps, capers and lemon, and perhaps a pannacotta with praline and coffee syrup to finish.

Chef: Ian Bates **Owners:** Ian & Clare Bates **Times:** 12.30-2.30/6.30-10.30, Closed 1 wk Xmas, Mon, Closed L Tue, D Sun **Prices:** Fixed L £15, Fixed D £26.50, Service optional, Group min 6 service 10% **Wine:** 43 bottles over £20, 15 bottles under £20, 9 by the glass **Seats:** 50 **Children:** Portions **Directions:** On entering village, follow signs for Hotels & Deliveries. Sadler St leads into High St, Old Spot on left opposite Swan Hotel **Parking:** On street, Market Square

---

WEST CAMEL   MAP 04 ST52

◉ The Walnut Tree Hotel

British, French

Fine food in friendly village hotel

☎ 01935 851292 Fore St BA22 7QW
e-mail: info@thewalnuttreehotel.com
web: www.thewalnuttreehotel.com

This small hotel has all the character and atmosphere of a village inn. There is a family-orientated restaurant, with a different kitchen and team to the fine-dining Rosewood restaurant. Here lightwood panelling and white table settings give a clean, airy feel. Accomplished cooking and sound techniques show in a starter of white crabmeat and smoked oysters with avocado and lemon vinaigrette. Main courses like roast English lamb rump with broad bean, pea and mint cassoulet could be followed by brandy snap basket with fresh figs, pecan and honey ice cream.

Chef: Peter Ball, Matthew Burton **Owners:** Mr & Mrs Ball **Times:** 12-2/6-8.45, Closed 25-26 Dec, 1 Jan, Closed L Mon **Prices:** Fixed L £9-£24, Starter £4.95-£6.95, Main £13.95-£18.95, Dessert £3.95-£5.95 **Wine:** 45 bottles over £20, 60 bottles under £20, 8 by the glass **Notes:** Vegetarian available, Dress Restrictions, Smart casual **Seats:** 40 **Children:** Menu, Portions **Rooms:** 13 (13 en suite) ★★ HL **Directions:** Just off A303 between Sparkford & The RNAS Yeovilton Air Base **Parking:** 40

WINCANTON
MAP 04 ST72

◎◎ Holbrook House Hotel & Spa
British, French

Elegant hotel with stylish restaurant

☎ 01963 824466 & 828844 Holbrook BA9 8BS
e-mail: enquiries@holbrookhouse.co.uk
web: www.holbrookhouse.co.uk

A handsome country-house hotel with the feel of a private manor house, standing in 23 acres of parkland and formal gardens, not far from Wincanton. Plush leather sofas in the tastefully decorated lounges, antique furniture and open fires invite diners to linger over drinks before moving into the elegant, traditionally-styled Cedar restaurant, where the warm colour scheme creates a calming atmosphere. The innovative, well-presented food is also worth savouring, with the sensibly compact menu regularly changed to reflect the season's fresh yield, offering dishes like butter-fried Jersey turbot with braised lentils, chorizo and cauliflower beignets, or perhaps roast Devonshire beef fillet served with a layered potato cake and confit Savoy cabbage with pancetta. The hotel's leisure facilities are also worth a visit.

Chef: Kevin Hyde **Owners:** Mr & Mrs J McGinley **Times:** 12.30-2/7-9, Closed L Sat, D Sun **Prices:** Fixed L £10-£20, Fixed D £25.99-£34.50, Starter £5-£11.50, Main £12-£25, Dessert £5-£7.50 **Notes:** Vegetarian available, Dress Restrictions, Smart casual, Civ Wed 120 **Seats:** 49, Pr/dining room 140 **Children:** Portions **Rooms:** 21 (21 en suite) ★★★ CHH **Directions:** From A303 at Wincanton, turn left on A371 towards Castle Cary & Shepton Mallet **Parking:** 100

WINSFORD
MAP 03 SS93

◎ Karslake House
Modern British

Fresh local produce in charming country-house style

☎ 01643 851242 Halse Ln TA24 7JE
e-mail: enquiries@karslakehouse.co.uk
web: www.karslakehouse.co.uk

Situated in a peaceful Exmoor village, this 15th-century former malthouse includes a number of original features and has been sympathetically restored to create a comfortable guest house and restaurant. The restaurant is open to non-residents on Friday and Saturday evenings or by prior arrangement, and the spacious dining room has crisply-set tables with cut glass and fresh flowers. The style of cooking is British with a perhaps unexpected modern twist, and there's a focus on fresh, locally-sourced produce, including fish, meat

and game. For starters, try Parma-wrapped tiger prawns with Exmoor blue cheese and apple dressing, with a fillet of salmon served with a gratin of root vegetables and orange and dill butter sauce for mains.

Karslake House

Chef: Juliette Mountford **Owners:** Mr & Mrs FNG Mountford **Times:** 7.30-8.30, Closed Nov-Apr, Closed D Sun-Thu (ex residents) **Prices:** Fixed D £30, Service optional **Wine:** 16 bottles over £20, 15 bottles under £20, 2 by the glass **Seats:** 18 **Children:** Min 12 yrs **Rooms:** 6 (5 en suite) ★★★★ GH **Directions:** A396 to Winsford, then left up the hill **Parking:** 12

WOOKEY HOLE
MAP 04 ST54

◎ Wookey Hole Inn
Modern International NEW

Carefully prepared seasonal produce in quirky setting

☎ 01749 676677 BA5 1BP

Behind its traditional exterior exists an interesting quirky mix of styles, with a relaxed café ambience, unusual lighting, individual tables and friendly, welcoming service. The kitchen deals in carefully prepared seasonal produce, the menu bolstered by blackboard specials. Take a trio of sea bass, swordfish and salmon (served with noodles, crispy vegetables, a tiger prawn and mussel stirfry, and sashimi soy dressing), followed by warm sticky toffee and pecan pudding with toffee sauce and clotted cream. And, as well as the short wine list, there's a fine selection of Belgian ales to accompany your meal.

Chef: Ashley Rainbow, Mark Rushton **Owners:** Michael & Richard Davey **Times:** 12-2.30/7-9.30, Closed L Sun **Prices:** Starter £5-£8, Main £12-£20, Dessert £4-£6, Service added but optional 10% **Wine:** 6 by the glass **Notes:** Vegetarian available **Seats:** 60, Pr/dining room 12 **Children:** Menu, Portions **Parking:** 12

YEOVIL
MAP 04 ST51

◎ Helyar Arms
British ◐

Accomplished cooking in a Somerset haven

☎ 01935 862332 Moor Ln, East Coker BA22 9JR
e-mail: info@helyar-arms.co.uk
web: www.helyar-arms.co.uk

Made famous by TS Eliot in the poem of the same name, East Coker is one of Somerset's prettiest villages. Its inn dates back to the 15th century and boasts all the character and warm atmosphere one might expect, as well as attractive gardens for alfresco dining. Simple, homely, crowd-pleasing modern cooking is the order of the day, so expect straightforward comfort dishes like pan-seared calves' liver with grilled bacon, caramelised shallots and mash potato, or perhaps chargilled lamb chops with curly kale, rosemary potatoes and a Madeira jus. Ingredients are from local producers wherever possible, while daily blackboard specials bolster the repertoire.

Chef: Mathieu Eke **Owners:** Ian McKerracher **Times:** 12-2.30/6.30-9.30, Closed 25 Dec **Prices:** Starter £5-£8, Main £8-£15, Dessert £5-£6, Service optional **Wine:** 15 bottles over £20, 17 bottles under £20, 31 by the glass **Notes:** Vegetarian available **Seats:** 55, Pr/dining room 40 **Children:** Menu, Portions **Rooms:** 6 (6 en suite) ★★★★ INN **Directions:** 3m from Yeovil. Take A37 or A30. Follow signs for East Coker. Helyar Arms is 50 mtrs from church **Parking:** 30

◉ Lanes

Modern British

Imaginative, modern cooking in contemporary surroundings

☎ 01935 862555 West Coker BA22 9AJ
e-mail: stay@laneshotel.net
web: www.laneshotel.net

Formerly a Victorian rectory, this splendid traditional property has been stunningly restored in contemporary internal style. The brasserie-style restaurant - entered through the Piano Bar - is housed in a stylish modern extension, with floor-to-ceiling windows, wooden floors and modern art on plain white walls. The crowd-pleasing menu evolves with the seasons and offers an imaginative range of dishes, including a few options in smaller or larger portions. Using local produce where

possible, the kitchen might deliver the likes of moules and frites, or perhaps a roasted loin of venison with pumpkin purée, blueberry dauphinoise and soured cabbage.

Lanes

Chef: Jason Eland **Owners:** John & Alison Roehrig **Times:** 12-2.30/7-10, Closed L Sat **Prices:** Starter £4.25-£6.50, Main £8-£16.50, Dessert £3.50-£4.95, Service optional **Wine:** 27 bottles over £20, 21 bottles under £20, 10 by the glass **Notes:** Vegetarian available **Seats:** 85, Pr/dining room 40 **Children:** Portions **Rooms:** 27 (27 en suite) ★★★ HL **Directions:** 2m W of Yeovil, on A30 towards Crewkerne **Parking:** 65

◉◉◉ Little Barwick House

see below

◉◉◉

Little Barwick House

YEOVIL   MAP 04 ST51

Modern European

Delightful house, wonderful grounds, unfussy service and great food

☎ 01935 423902 Barwick Village BA22 9TD
e-mail: reservations@barwick7.fsnet.co.uk
web: www.littlebarwickhouse.co.uk

Set in 3.5 acres of enchanting gardens, this listed Georgian dower house has been tastefully restored by the owners to achieve a balance of period charm and modern interior design sensibilities that shows real discernment. Sumptuous fabrics, Farrow and Ball colours, huge windows overlooking the garden and terrace, and sympathetic modern touches provide an unobtrusive backdrop for fine eating and drinking, which of course, are paramount for this locally renowned restaurant with rooms.

The lack of fuss and gimmickry in the cooking belies the complexity of approach and sophistication of palate that clearly indicate the touch of a highly experienced chef: subtlety and consistency are the watchwords here, backed by the use of prime, fresh seasonal ingredients. Forget undue ceremony, just enjoy the symphony of flavours created throughout this concise menu: perhaps grilled fillet of Cornish red mullet with Portland crab and a lightly infused lemongrass

sauce, or maybe a rhubarb sablé finish, served with poached rhubarb, stem-ginger mousse and rhubarb sorbet.

Chef: Timothy Ford **Owners:** Emma & Timothy Ford **Times:** 12-2/7-9.30, Closed New Year, 2wks Jan, Mon, Closed L Tues, D Sun **Prices:** Fixed L £20.95, Fixed D £36.95, Service optional **Wine:** 179 bottles over £20, 21 bottles under £20, 6 by the glass **Seats:** 40 **Children:** Min 5 yrs, Portions **Rooms:** 6 (6 en suite) ★★★★★ RR **Directions:** Turn off A371 Yeovil to Dorchester opposite Red House rdbt, 0.25m on left **Parking:** 25

YEOVIL Continued

◎◎ Yeovil Court Hotel & Restaurant

Modern European

Enjoyable dining in a modern, family-run hotel

☎ 01935 863746 West Coker Rd BA20 2HE
e-mail: unwind@yeovilhotel.com
web: www.yeovilhotel.com

With its modern décor and convivial bar area, this friendly, family-run hotel has a welcoming ambience. The dining room is also decorated in a modern style with white tablecloths and good-quality settings. After your meal, the helpful staff will lead you to the comfortably furnished lounge. The kitchen takes a modern approach, so expect the likes of seared Scottish scallops with beetroot purée, caviar and coral cream, followed by pan-fried fillet of halibut with herb crust, glass noodles, pak choi and tomato consommé, or maybe baked red onion tart with spinach, tomato compôte, fine beans and red pepper dressing, while a decadent warm dark chocolate squidgy pudding with pistachio ice cream might head-up desserts.

Chef: Simon Walford **Owners:** Brian & Carol Devonport **Times:** 12-1.45/7-9.30, Closed 24 Dec, 26-28 Dec, 1-2 Jan, Closed L Sat **Prices:** Fixed L £12.95-£14.95, Starter £3.95-£6.75, Main £9.95-£17.95, Dessert £4.25-£6.75, Service optional **Wine:** 30 bottles over £20, 28 bottles under £20, 6 by the glass **Seats:** 50, Pr/dining room 80 **Children:** Portions **Rooms:** 30 (30 en suite) ★★★ HL **Directions:** On A30, 2.5m W of town centre **Parking:** 65

STAFFORDSHIRE

BURTON UPON TRENT   MAP 10 SK22

◎ Meynell and Deer Park Restaurant

Modern, International

Traditional inn with a very rural location

☎ 01283 575202 Hoar Cross DE13 8RB
e-mail: info@themeynell.co.uk
web: www.themeynell.co.uk

This handsome brick-built country inn stands at a quiet village crossroads and boasts a traditional pub interior with exposed beams, oak floors and open fires. The Deer Park Restaurant offers a comprehensive à la carte menu featuring locally-sourced produce. Included on the menu are some timeless classics with international influences, such as tempura of king prawns with lemon and fennel salad to begin, followed by Gressingham duck breast served with

confit barrel potatoes and an orange and green peppercorn sauce. Finish off with Bailey's brioche bread-and-butter pudding with vanilla ice cream.

Meynell and Deer Park Restaurant

Chef: Craig Malone **Owners:** Mike and Jane Chappell **Times:** 12-2/6.30-9.30, Closed 25 Dec **Prices:** Starter £4.50-£6.50, Main £12.50-£19.95, Dessert £5.50, Service optional **Wine:** 6 bottles over £20, 10 bottles under £20, 3 by the glass **Notes:** Sun L available, Dress Restrictions, Smart casual **Seats:** 30, Pr/dining room 44 **Children:** Portions **Directions:** 7m W of Burton on Trent, 2 minute drive off the A515 main road between Lichfield on the A50 **Parking:** 50

LEEK   MAP 16 SJ95

◎ Three Horseshoes Inn & Country Hotel

Modern British, Thai

Traditional inn offering an oriental twist to a modern British menu

☎ 01538 300296 Buxton Rd, Blackshaw Moor ST13 8TW
e-mail: enquiries@threeshoesinn.co.uk
web: www.threeshoesinn.co.uk

Run by a friendly family, this ivy-clad inn sits in immaculate grounds and boasts a children's play area. Exposed beams, polished brass and rustic furniture abound throughout, with visitors offered a choice of dining in the bustling brasserie or more formally in the elegant restaurant. Expect a globe-trotting menu that teams hearty British dishes (loin of pork in bacon and sage with bubble-and-squeak and sage jus) with more exotic fare, such as Thai duck curry or wok beef noodles with oyster sauce and greens. Desserts are similarly tempting: melting hot chocolate fondant pudding with roast almond ice cream for example, or nostalgic crêpe Suzette.

Chef: Mark & Stephen Kirk **Owners:** Bill, Jill, Mark & Stephen Kirk **Times:** 12.30-2/6.30-9, Closed 26-30 Dec, Closed L Mon-Sat **Prices:** Starter £5-£7, Main £10-£18, Dessert £4-£7 **Wine:** 30 bottles over £20, 50 bottles under £20, 10 by the glass **Notes:** Tasting menu available, Vegetarian available, Dress Restrictions, Smart casual, Civ Wed 150 **Seats:** 50 **Children:** Menu, Portions **Rooms:** 26 (26 en suite) ★★★ HL **Directions:** M6 junct 15 or 16 onto A500. Exit A53 towards Leek. Turn left onto A50 (Burslem) **Parking:** 100

LICHFIELD
MAP 10 SK10

◎◎ The Four Seasons Restaurant

Modern British

Stunning mansion and impressive cuisine

☎ 01543 481494 Swinfen Hall Hotel, Swinfen
WS14 9RE
e-mail: info@swinfenhallhotel.co.uk
web: www.swinfenhallhotel.co.uk

Set in 100 acres of parkland including a deer park, diners might gasp
when they arrive at the stunning entrance hall to the beautiful 18th-
century Swinfen Hall country-house hotel, but there is more to come.
The lavishly decorated public rooms, including carved ceilings and
impressive oil paintings, soon exhaust all superlatives. Despite the high
style, the place is welcoming and comfortable. A three-course fixed-price
menu showcases the kitchen's modern approach - underpinned by a
classical French theme - in the oak-panelled Four Seasons Restaurant,
with quality, fresh, locally-sourced - often luxury ingredients - taking pride
of place. Expect roast loin of venison served with braised red cabbage,
celeriac, chestnut foam and a bitter chocolate sauce, or perhaps a fillet of
sea bass with boulangère potatoes, roasted salsify and a red wine sauce.

Chef: Neil Peers **Owners:** Helen & Vic Wiser **Times:** 12.30-2.30/7-9.30,
Closed L Sat, D Sun **Prices:** Fixed L £16.95, Fixed D £39.50, Service
optional **Wine:** 108 bottles over £20, 9 bottles under £20, 6 by the glass
Notes: Sun L 2 courses £22.50, 3 courses £29.50, Dress Restrictions, No
trainers or jeans, Civ Wed 120 **Seats:** 50, Pr/dining room 20
Children: Portions **Rooms:** 19 (19 en suite)★★★★ HL
Directions: 2m S of Lichfield on A38 between Weeford rdbt and Swinfen
rdbt. Follow A38 to Lichfield, hotel is 0.5m on right **Parking:** 80

Chandlers
☎ 01543 416688 Corn Exchange Buildings,
Conduit St WS13 6JU

Large brasserie with modern British menu.

RUGELEY
MAP 10 SK01

◎ The Plum Pudding

Modern British

Innovative cooking, canal-side location

☎ 01543 490330 Rugeley Rd, Armitage WS15 4AZ
e-mail: enquiries@theplumpudding.co.uk
web: www.theplumpudding.co.uk

'Plum Pudding' was once a popular name for canal-side pubs but this
is the only one left in the UK. With a large terrace alongside the canal,

the atmosphere in this gastro-pub is relaxed and intimate, with friendly
and attentive service. Fresh, locally-sourced produce, from organic
meats through to local cheeses, is found throughout a modern British
menu that might include a starter of seared tuna with creamed and
roasted corn. Main courses might feature a braised Packington pork
shoulder with roasted stuffed fillet, broad bean and tomato risotto,
while creative desserts are characterised by the likes of mandarin and
cinnamon crème brûlée.

The Plum Pudding

Chef: Carl Jones **Owners:** Mr & Mrs J Takhar **Times:** 12-3.30/6-11.30,
Closed 1 Jan **Prices:** Fixed L £10, Starter £4.50-£6.95, Main £9.95-£15.95,
Dessert £4.50-£7.50, Service optional **Wine:** 15 bottles over £20, 29 bottles
under £20, 9 by the glass **Notes:** Fixed D not available Fri & Sat, Sun L
£8.95, Vegetarian available **Seats:** 70 **Children:** Portions **Rooms:** 4 (4
en suite) ★★★★ INN **Directions:** M6 junct 11 follow signs for Cannock
to Rugeley. Situated on A513 through Rugeley to Lichfield **Parking:** 50

STAFFORD
MAP 10 SJ92

◎◎ Moat House

Modern British

*Cutting-edge menu meets conservatory dining in
canal-side hotel*

☎ 01785 712217 Lower Penkridge Rd, Acton Trussell
ST17 0RJ
e-mail: info@moathouse.co.uk
web: www.moathouse.co.uk

Aptly named, this well restored hotel occupies a moated former
manor house - with a striking canal-side setting. The main building is
full of oak panelling and exposed beams, while the spacious and
stylish conservatory restaurant is a modern, luxurious affair with high-
backed seating and generous-sized tables, set to a backdrop of barges
plying the canal. The enticing menu is dotted with luxury items,
promoting an agony of choice on a classically-based, modern-focused
repertoire. Fresh, high-quality seasonal ingredients combine with a

CONTINUED

ENGLAND

STAFFORD CONTINUED

sense of flair to deliver skilfully crafted, flavour-driven dishes that show the kitchen's pedigree. Take a main course of pan-fried turbot with seared scallops, salsify, garlic confit and Sauternes sauce, or perhaps a rosette of Staffordshire beef with oxtail bon-bon, wilted spinach, girolles, baby onions and red wine and truffle jus.

Chef: Matthew Davies **Owners:** The Lewis Partnership **Times:** 12-2/7-9.30, Closed 25 Dec, 1-2 Jan **Prices:** Food prices not confirmed for 2008. Please telephone for details **Notes:** No jeans, Civ Wed 120, Air con **Seats:** 120, Pr/dining room 150 **Children:** Menu, Portions **Rooms:** 41 (41 en suite) ★★★★ HL **Directions:** M6 junct 13 towards Stafford, 1st right to Acton Trussell, hotel by church **Parking:** 200

⊛ The Swan Hotel

Modern, Traditional

Innovative cooking in town-centre contemporary brasserie

☎ 01785 258142 46 Greengate St ST16 2JA
e-mail: info@theswanstafford.co.uk
web: www.theswanstafford.co.uk

A former coaching inn, this is quite a dining destination locally and an impressive venue. The split-level brasserie with its timber frame and stylish modern décor appeals to discerning locals and residents alike. The restaurant retains a historic feel, with polished wooden and marble tables, crisp napery, candles, and leather banquette and cane seating. The cooking style is precise with clear flavours and smart presentation. Popular dishes might include the likes of confit duck leg with wasabi soy noodles and mixed leaves, followed by pork fillet with sage risotto, apple purée and white wine jus, and Bailey's banana bread-and-butter pudding to finish.

Chef: Mark Williams **Owners:** Chris Lewis **Times:** 12-2.30/5.30-10, Closed 25-26 Dec **Prices:** Fixed L £8, Fixed D £16, Starter £4.25-£5.95, Main £7.95-£18.50, Dessert £4.25-£4.75, Service optional **Wine:** 11 bottles over £20, 30 bottles under £20, 20 by the glass **Notes:** Sun L £16.95 3 courses, Vegetarian available, Air con **Seats:** 80 **Children:** Menu, Portions **Rooms:** 31 (31 en suite) ★★★ HL **Directions:** M6 junct 13 & 14 then to town. Follow signs to rail station, turn right after station at mini rdbt. 1st left into Water St. Hotel on left. (Access via Mill St) **Parking:** 30

STOKE-ON-TRENT   MAP 10 SJ84

⊛ The Elms, Passion of India

Indian

Welcoming Indian restaurant serving healthy dishes

☎ 01782 266360 Snowhill, Shelton ST1 4LY

The building was once home to the pottery owner John Ridgway, becoming a pub during the Victorian era. Today, it's a handsome Indian restaurant, warm and friendly, and richly decorated featuring gold cornices and crisp linen. The regional Indian cooking takes a healthy approach, introducing soft, light flavours with spices and herbs to enhance quality core ingredients, with equal emphasis given to peripherals like breads and rice. Take lamb tawa (cubes of lamb marinated in rare herbs, slowly cooked in tawa and topped with green coriander and ginger), or fish Goanese (boneless fillets tempered with mustard seeds and curry leaves, simmered in a tomato and onion sauce and finished with coconut milk).

Chef: Harish Kumar, Mehboob Hussain **Owners:** Pritpal Singh Nagi **Times:** 6-11.30, Closed 25 Dec, Sun, Closed L Mon-Sat **Prices:** Fixed D £25-£30, Starter £3.95-£8.95, Main £7.90-£14.95, Dessert £3.25-£4.75, Service optional **Wine:** 8 bottles over £20, 2 by the glass **Notes:** Vegetarian available, Dress Restrictions, Smart casual **Seats:** 120, Pr/dining room 30 **Children:** Portions **Directions:** Telephone for directions **Parking:** 80

⊛ Haydon House Hotel

Modern British, European

Family-run hotel with a sound reputation

☎ 01782 711311 Haydon St, Basford ST4 6JD
e-mail: enquiries@haydon-house-hotel.co.uk
web: www.haydon-house-hotel.co.uk

This late Victorian townhouse is set in the Etruria district of Stoke-on-Trent, which was home to the workforce of Josiah Wedgwood's celebrated pottery for 200 years. It retains many original features and is also a popular haunt for locals lured by the gracious décor and reputation for quality cuisine in the Townhouse restaurant. The carte and flambé menus change seasonally, with a weekly-changing fixed-price menu. Expect mains such as braised belly pork with mustard mash, apple compôte and sage and cider gravy, or lemon-roasted chicken with bacon sauce.

Chef: Stacey Stonier **Owners:** Mr J F Machin **Times:** 12-2/7-9.30, Closed 26 Dec, 1 Jan, Closed L Sat **Prices:** Fixed L £8.95, Fixed D £17.95, Starter £3.25-£4.85, Main £9.75-£14.95, Dessert £3-£3.95, Service optional **Wine:** 15 bottles over £20, 22 bottles under £20, 3 by the glass **Notes:** Sun L/D 2 courses £11.95, 3 courses £14.95, Vegetarian available, Dress Restrictions, Smart casual, no jeans, T-shirts, Civ Wed 80 **Seats:** 45, Pr/dining room 76 **Children:** Menu, Portions **Rooms:** 23 (23 en suite) ★★★ HL **Directions:** From M6 take either junct 15 or 16, follow A500 to A53, take A53 signed Newcastle, take 2nd left before lights onto Haydon St **Parking:** 42

ENGLAND

UTTOXETER   MAP 10 SK03

◉◉ **Restaurant Gilmore at Strine's Farm**

Modern British

Friendly, family-run farmhouse restaurant

☎ 01889 507100   Beamhurst ST14 5DZ
e-mail: paul@restaurantgilmore.com
web: www.restaurantgilmore.com

The building is a converted three-storey farmhouse set in acres of open grounds (including cottage gardens, herb and vegetable plots), making it a popular venue for weddings. It's the second incarnation of Restaurant Gilmore, the first was in Birmingham a few years back. This farmhouse version occupies three separate dining rooms, each with its own character. The kitchen takes its role seriously, sourcing the finest produce from all markets, and the cooking incorporates traditional techniques and a modern approach. There's an emphasis on flavours throughout the regularly-changing menu, with dishes like pan-fried fillet of wild sea bass served with piquillo peppers, mange-tout and a bouillabaisse sauce, or Valrhona milk chocolate brûlée, bitter chocolate sorbet and white chocolate foam.

Chef: Paul Gilmore   **Owners:** Paul & Dee Gilmore   **Times:** 12.30-2/7.30-9, Closed 1 wk Jan, 1 wk Etr, 1 wk Jul, 1 wk Oct, Mon & Tue, Closed L Sat & Wed, D Sun   **Prices:** Fixed L £18, Fixed D £35, Service optional, Group min 8 service 10%   **Wine:** 29 bottles over £20, 16 bottles under £20, 4 by the glass   **Notes:** Sun L 3 courses incl coffee £26.50, Dress Restrictions, Smart casual   **Seats:** 24   **Children:** Portions   **Directions:** 1.5m N of Uttoxeter on A522 to Cheadle. Set 400yds back from the road along a fenced farm track   **Parking:** 12

YOXALL   MAP 10 SK11

◉ **Foresters At Yoxall**

Modern British **NEW**

Informal dining with simple flair

☎ 01283 575939   62 Wood Ln DE13 8PH
e-mail: theforesters@hotmail.com
web: www.forestersatyoxall.co.uk

The Foresters is a modern-styled pub-restaurant, set in rural surroundings - as the name indicates - on the main road north of the village. Spread over three rooms - with one decked out with some comfy sofas - it has a mix of wooden and carpeted floors. Tables are plain wood as are chairs, all helping to cultivate a relaxed, informal atmosphere, as does the polite and helpful service. The kitchen shows confident form, with simply prepared, clean-flavoured dishes from quality produce; take lamb fillet with a red wine jus or Barbary duck breast with sweet and sour mango, and a blueberry tart to close.

Chef: Jeff Thomas, Mark Hadfield   **Owners:** Jeff & Lilian Thomas   **Times:** 11.30-3/6.30-11.30, Closed 25-28 Dec, Mon, Closed D Sun   **Prices:** Fixed L £10-£12, Fixed D £20-£22.95, Starter £4.25-£7.50, Main £12.95-£19.50, Dessert £4.95-£6.95, Service optional   **Wine:** 7 bottles over £20, 12 bottles under £20, 19 by the glass   **Notes:** Sun L £18.50-£19.50, Vegetarian available, Dress Restrictions, Smart casual   **Seats:** 50   **Children:** Min 12yrs D, Portions   **Directions:** On A515 Litchfield to Ashbourne road, 1m outside village of Yoxall   **Parking:** 30

SUFFOLK

ALDEBURGH   MAP 13 TM45

◉◉ **152 Aldeburgh**

Modern British, European

Well-tuned cooking in popular resort

☎ 01728 454594   152 High St IP15 5AX
e-mail: info@152aldeburgh.co.uk
web: www.152aldeburgh.co.uk

Located through an archway from the High Street to the beach, this bustling brasserie exactly fits the Aldeburgh bill. Light and clean-cut, the stripped wooden floors, cream panelling, pine tables and chairs, fresh flowers and informal, helpful and cheerful service, create a relaxed, friendly atmosphere that ticks all the right boxes. The innovative, compact seasonal menus make fine use of quality ingredients, with locally-landed fish mingling with game in season and quality meats, and the intelligently straightforward, modern approach delivers clear flavours via accurately cooked dishes. Take John Dory with smoked haddock brandade and rosemary-creamed leeks, or perhaps pot-roasted pheasant with red cabbage and braised roots, and finish with coffee crème brûlée.

Chef: Garry Cook   **Owners:** Garry Cook/Andrew Lister   **Times:** 12-3/6-10   **Prices:** Starter £5.50-£9.50, Main £9.95-£18, Dessert £5.50, Service optional   **Wine:** 13 bottles over £20, 24 bottles under £20, 7 by the glass   **Notes:** Vegetarian available   **Seats:** 56   **Children:** Portions   **Parking:** On street parking on High St & Kings St

◉ **Best Western White Lion Hotel**

Traditional British V

Elegant dining by the sea

☎ 01728 452720   Market Cross Place IP15 5BJ
e-mail: info@whitelion.co.uk
web: www.whitelion.co.uk

Dating in part back to 1563, this popular hotel is situated at the quiet end of town, overlooking the sea. There are two lounges, and an elegant, oak-panelled restaurant where locally-caught fish and seafood feature on the seasonal menu. Service here, from smartly uniformed staff, is professional and friendly. Try dressed Cromer crab salad with wasabi mayonnaise, or a main course of sea bass with parsley mash, braised chicory and lobster bisque sauce. Finish with iced red berry and basil parfait with chocolate crisp. The modern brasserie offers an alternative dining choice.

CONTINUED

ALDEBURGH CONTINUED

Chef: Eleanor Richmond **Owners:** Thorpeness and Aldeburgh Hotels Ltd
Times: 12-2.30/6.30-9.30 **Prices:** Fixed L £10.95-£15.95, Fixed D £23.50-£32.95, Starter £4.95-£7.95, Main £9.95-£19.50, Dessert £4.95-£5.50, Service optional **Wine:** 27 bottles over £20, 26 bottles under £20, 22 by the glass **Notes:** Vegetarian menu, Civ Wed 90 **Seats:** 60, Pr/dining room 50 **Children:** Menu, Portions **Rooms:** 38 (38 en suite) ★★★ HL
Directions: Please telephone for directions **Parking:** 15

◎◎ The Brudenell

Modern

Chic modern brasserie just a few steps from the sea

☎ 01728 452071 The Parade IP15 5BU
e-mail: info@brudenellhotel.co.uk
web: www.brudenellhotel.co.uk

Only a pebble's skim from the beach, this glass-fronted brasserie makes the most of its fabulous location on an unspoiled stretch of Suffolk coast in the beautiful seaside town of Aldeburgh. The split-level restaurant has an informal, contemporary feel thanks to wooden tables, pastel shades and Mediterranean shutters. French, Italian, Asian and British influences sit comfortably on an extensive menu that sidesteps the usual fare to offer clever variations on the bistro theme. Start with pork belly with a tian of crab perhaps, before sampling gourmet fish and chips - a high-comfort mix of haddock fresh from the beach with hand-cut fries and mushy peas. Dine on the terrace in summer.

Chef: Mark Clements **Owners:** Thorpeness & Aldeburgh Hotels Ltd
Times: 12-2.30/6-10 **Prices:** Fixed L £12.95-£18.95, Fixed D £19.15-£32.40, Starter £4.95-£7.95, Main £8.95-£17.95, Dessert £4.95, Service optional
Wine: 37 bottles over £20, 19 bottles under £20, 17 by the glass
Seats: 100 **Children:** Menu, Portions **Rooms:** 42 (42 en suite) ★★★ HL **Parking:** 15

see advert opposite

◎ Regatta Restaurant

Modern British

Busy, bistro-style restaurant featuring locally-caught fish

☎ 01728 452011 171 High St IP15 5AN
e-mail: regatta.restaurant@aldeburgh.sagegost.co.uk
web: www.regattaaldeburgh.com

In harmony with Aldeburgh's maritime tradition, this refurbished, airy bistro-style restaurant features locally-caught fish and seafood as its mainstay. A blackboard gives a daily update on the freshly caught offerings, while the menu lists the alternatives. Staff are stylishly dressed and service is very relaxed. Food comes simply cooked and presented with clear flavours from the wonderful fresh ingredients. Expect starters like a Mediterranean fish soup with rouille and croûtons, then perhaps a hot smoked fillet of organic salmon with chilli, coriander and lime from the smoke house specialities or grilled corn-fed chicken breast with ratatouille, pesto dressing and chips to follow.

Chef: Robert Mabey **Owners:** Mr & Mrs R Mabey **Times:** 12-2/6-10, Closed L 25-26 Dec, D Sun (Nov-Feb) **Prices:** Starter £4-£7, Main £9-£16, Dessert £3.50-£4.50 **Wine:** 6 bottles over £20, 40 bottles under £20, 6 by the glass **Seats:** 90, Pr/dining room 30 **Children:** Menu, Portions
Directions: Middle of High St, town centre **Parking:** On street

◎◎ Wentworth Hotel

Modern British

Traditional values with modern twists in seaside hotel

☎ 01728 452312 Wentworth Rd IP15 5BD
e-mail: stay@wentworth-aldeburgh.co.uk
web: www.wentworth-aldeburgh.com

Overlooking the beach at the quiet end of town, this reassuringly traditional hotel is popular with returning guests and diners, and boasts staff who create a friendly and informal ambience. In this family-friendly atmosphere, the smart dining room, elegantly decorated in Etruscan red, is a beacon of excellence locally, with its mixture of firm favourites and an upbeat modern approach. Seasonal changes and local suppliers keep the food fresh and interesting on daily-changing menus; think roast rump of Suffolk lamb served with rosemary mash and mint sauce, or baked whole sea bream with ratatouille vegetables and sun-dried tomato pesto, and for dessert, perhaps banoffee pie with a rich toffee sauce or a winter strudel with warm vanilla sauce.

Chef: Graham Reid **Owners:** Wentworth Hotel Ltd/Michael Pritt
Times: 12-2/7-9 **Prices:** Fixed L £12.50, Fixed D £16.50-£18.50, Service optional **Wine:** 13 bottles over £20, 41 bottles under £20, 10 by the glass
Notes: Sun D 3 courses £13 **Seats:** 90, Pr/dining room 20
Children: Menu, Portions **Rooms:** 35 (35 en suite) ★★★ HL
Directions: From A12 take A1094 to Aldeburgh. In Aldeburgh straight on at mini rdbt, turn left at x-roads into Wentworth Rd. Hotel on right
Parking: 33

ENGLAND

BARNBY
MAP 13 TM48

◉ *The Swan Inn*

Seafood

Unpretentious pub serving a stunning array of fresh fish

☎ 01502 476646 Swan Ln NR34 7QF

A traditional inn with its distinctive pink walls and village bar, The Swan is also very well known for its fish restaurant called the Fisherman's Cove. In this low-beamed room, the nautical memorabilia includes the bow of a small dinghy mounted on the wall, where blackboards list the day's choice. Owned by a family of Lowestoft fish merchants, it offers a variety of the freshest fish, simply pan fried, grilled or cooked in batter, and served with chips or new potatoes, salads or peas. Expect crab cocktail, jellied eels, home-smoked fish and shellfish among the superb choice.

Times: 12-2/7-9 **Directions:** Telephone for directions

BILDESTON
MAP 13 TL94

◉◉◉ **The Bildeston Crown**

see below

Brudenell Restaurant

Brudenell Hotel The Parade Aldeburgh IP15 5BU
Tel: 01728 452071
Email: info@brudenellhotel.co.uk www.brudenellhotel.co.uk

Situated in a stunning location, with panoramic sea views, the Restaurant at The Brudenell Hotel has been likened by many to dining on a cruise liner. Its contemporary New England décor provides a relaxed ambiance and its emphasis is very much on flexibility and informality. Al fresco dining is available during the summer months on the sea-facing terrace. Menus are constantly changed and feature a wide variety of exciting, yet unpretentious dishes. Fresh seasonal produce is sourced locally whenever possible and specialities include grills, fish and seafood.

◉◉◉

The Bildeston Crown

BILDESTON
MAP 13 TL94

Modern British

Highly accomplished cooking in a stylish country inn

☎ 01449 740510 104 High St IP7 7EB
e-mail: hayley@thebildestoncrown.co.uk
web: www.thebildestoncrown.co.uk

Located in wonderful Suffolk countryside, this charming 15th-century coaching inn has been skilfully renovated to provide comfortable, stylish, modern dining and accommodation. Beams, ancient brickwork, oak floors, leather chairs, imposing artwork and open fires all set the tone, while friendly, helpful staff move between elegantly set tables in the bar, dining room and, in summer, the terrace. Fresh, high-quality local produce, clear flavours and accomplished skills reign on an appealing, crowd-pleasing repertoire of modern and classic dishes. This is innovative, striking and ambitious cooking from a kitchen that really understands flavour. Halibut served with crab, artichoke, iceberg lettuce and a bay leaf foam, shepherd's pie with braised red cabbage or rabbit with tarragon gnocchi, Braeburn purée, caper berries and ceps might be on the menu. The popular Classics repertoire includes steak and kidney pudding and knickerbocker glory. One to watch.

Main £10-£20, Dessert £6, Service optional, Group min 10 service 12.5%
Wine: 60 bottles over £20, 23 bottles under £20, 15 by the glass
Notes: Tasting menu Mon-Sat evenings, Sun L available, Civ Wed 24
Seats: 40, Pr/dining room 16 **Children:** Portions **Rooms:** 10 (10 en suite) ★★★ HL **Directions:** A12 junct 31. B1070 to Hadleigh, B1115 to Bildeston **Parking:** 24

Chef: Chris Lee **Owners:** Mrs G Buckle, Mr J K Buckle **Times:** 12-7/3-10, Closed D 25 Dec, 1 Jan **Prices:** Fixed L £16, Fixed D £20, Starter £6-£10,

ENGLAND

BUNGAY   MAP 13 TM38

◎◎ Earsham Street Café

Modern International

Modern fare in popular café

☎ 01986 893103   11-13 Earsham St NR35 1AE
e-mail: www.earshamstcafe@aol.com

A great hit with locals, this busy, bustling café has an informal and relaxed atmosphere, with a clubby feel. The classic chic décor provides the perfect setting for modern cooking with Mediterranean influences, delivering simple flavours using the freshest ingredients. Dishes are well executed and the daily-changing menus have an emphasis on fresh fish and seafood. Start with sautéed squid with stewed red peppers and white beans, followed by a main course of poached gnocchi dumplings with sautéed chorizo and wild mushrooms, or baked halibut with crab and spring onion risotto. Pear tarte Tatin with maple and walnut ice cream might prove a fitting finale, accompanied by a recommended dessert wine. There's often a queue out the door, so be sure to book a table.

Chef: Stephen David, Christopher Rice **Owners:** Rebecca Mackenzie, Stephen David **Times:** 9.30-4.30/7-9, Closed Xmas, New Year, BHs, Closed D ex last Fri & Sat of month 7-9 **Prices:** Starter £4.50-£9.95, Main £7.95-£19.95, Dessert £5.50, Service optional **Wine:** 27 bottles over £20, 22 bottles under £20, 16 by the glass **Notes:** Vegetarian available **Seats:** 55, Pr/dining room 16 **Children:** Menu, Portions **Directions:** In the centre of Bungay **Parking:** Parking opposite

BURY ST EDMUNDS   MAP 13 TL86

◎◎ Angel Hotel - The Eaterie

Modern British V

Fine dining in an imposing coaching inn

☎ 01284 714000 Angel Hill IP33 1LT
e-mail: sales@theangel.co.uk
web: www.theangel.co.uk

Just a few minutes from the centre of Bury St Edmunds, this imposing coaching inn has a long history of hospitality and boasts Charles Dickens among former guests. It stands in a pretty square looking across to the cathedral, and has a cosy contemporary feel despite its heritage charms. Both the newly refurbished Angel Eaterie, with its stunning artwork and stylish design and the 12th-century stone Vaults restaurant below the ground floor are relaxed in style, and serve accomplished food along modern British lines. Starters might include pan-seared scallops with a pea and mint blini, with slow-roast pork belly a typical main, served with cabbage and an apple and sage jus. Save room for dessert: mango and lime pannacotta perhaps, or lemon tart with red berry coulis.

Angel Hotel - The Eaterie

Chef: Simon Barker **Owners:** Robert Gough **Times:** 7am/10pm **Prices:** Fixed L £11.95, Starter £4.95-£8.50, Main £11.95-£21.50, Dessert £4.95-£7.50, Service optional **Wine:** 45 bottles over £20, 20 bottles under £20, 22 by the glass **Notes:** Vegetarian menu, Dress Restrictions, Smart casual/dress, Civ Wed 85 **Seats:** 85, Pr/dining room 80 **Children:** Portions **Rooms:** 76 (76 en suite) ★★★ HL **Directions:** Town centre, right from Northgate St traffic lights **Parking:** 30

◎◎ Best Western Priory Hotel

Modern British

Accomplished manor-house hotel dining

☎ 01284 766181 Mildenhall Rd IP32 6EH
e-mail: reservations@prioryhotel.co.uk
web: www.prioryhotel.co.uk

Built on the remains of a 13th-century priory, this Grade II listed property is set in a pretty location on the edge of town. The aptly named Garden restaurant lies beyond the landscaped gardens, where modern artwork and contemporary décor create a comfortable environment. After pre-dinner drinks in the lounge, the well-executed cooking incorporating the finest, locally-sourced ingredients ensures an accomplished meal. Try a warm tartlet of celeriac, pear and blue cheese with lime and ginger relish, or seared queen scallops with baby beetroot and apple dressing, followed perhaps by pot-roast guinea fowl breast, served with leg confit, winter vegetable cassoulet and mini dumplings. Still hungry? A richly-flavoured dark chocolate terrine with prune and banana compôte should satisfy the heartiest of appetites.

Times: 12.30-2/7-10, Closed L Sat **Rooms:** 39 (39 en suite) ★★★ HL **Directions:** From Bury St Edmunds follow signs for Mildenhall A1011. 1m out of town centre

◎ Clarice House

Modern European

Upmarket health and beauty spa with modern menu

☎ 01284 705550 Horringer Court, Horringer Rd IP29 5PH
e-mail: enquiry@clarice-bury.fsnet.co.uk
web: www.clarice.co.uk

Healthy options are a feature of the menu at this neo-Jacobean mansion, now a superb country-style hotel, in keeping with its dual role as a health spa. The restaurant is an oak-panelled affair, with well-spaced and neatly clothed tables. Here you can expect lighter options, such as a warm salad of sticky pork, mango, spring onion and cherry tomatoes, as well as more decadent fare: smoked haddock with a cheddar and chive rarebit topping, for example, or beef wrapped in Parma ham, porcini mushrooms and pastry, accompanied by dauphinoise potatoes, French beans and a red wine reduction. There are pretty landscaped grounds for an after-lunch stroll.

Times: 11-3/6-11, Closed Xmas, Boxing Day, New Year's Day **Rooms:** 13 (13 en suite) ★★★★★ GA **Directions:** From Bury St Edmunds on A143 towards Horringer and Haverhill, hotel 1m from town centre on right

⊛⊛ The Leaping Hare Restaurant & Country Store

Modern British
Seasonal and local produce served in a vineyard restaurant

☎ 01359 250287 Stanton IP31 2DW
e-mail: info@wykenvineyards.co.uk
web: www.wykenvineyards.co.uk

This is a vineyard restaurant, part of the Wyken Hall estate, set in a 400-year-old Suffolk barn with high ceilings, wooden flooring, old beams, wood-burning stoves and paintings and tapestries of leaping hares. (The barn is divided between a restaurant and café.) Modern simple cooking - with the emphasis on flavour - makes fine use of quality local produce (usually from within a 5-mile radius). Think braised Wyken hare served with potato gnocchi to start, and perhaps mains like Troston chicken breast with greens, parsley and garlic, or Bardwell Redpoll rib-eye steak with hand-cut chips and green salad. The wine list naturally features the estate-made Wyken wines amongst others, while the adjacent Country Store - and Saturday morning farmers' market - is well worth a visit too.

Chef: Peter Harrison **Owners:** Kenneth & Carla Carlisle **Times:** 12-2.30/7-9, Closed 2 wks Xmas, Closed D Sun-Thu **Prices:** Fixed L £16.95, Starter £4.95-£6.95, Main £11.95-£16.95, Dessert £4.95, Service optional **Wine:** 18 bottles over £20, 34 bottles under £20, 22 by the glass **Notes:** Vegetarian available **Seats:** 55 **Children:** Portions **Directions:** 8m NE of Bury St Edmunds, 1m off A143. Follow brown signs at Ixworth to Wyken Vineyards **Parking:** 50

⊛⊛ Maison Bleue

French
Upbeat French seafood brasserie

☎ 01284 760623 30-31 Churchgate St IP33 1RG
e-mail: info@maisonbleue.co.uk
web: www.maisonbleue.co.uk

This smart French seafood restaurant - set in the centre of town - has had a modern, stylish makeover. With professional and friendly service, an enthusiastic local crowd creates a lively atmosphere. Seafood is treated simply and served as freshly as possible by charming French staff. A bargain 'plat du jour with coffee' lunch is not to be missed, and do book ahead for the plateau de fruits de mer. Otherwise, expect accomplished, well-presented dishes like whole roasted sea bass served with fennel and lemon and olive oil dressing, or perhaps poached fillet of brill topped with a mushroom duxelle and wrapped in wafer-thin zucchini with a beurre blanc. Finish with a crème brûlée flavoured with vanilla.

Chef: Pascal Canevet **Owners:** Regis Crepy **Times:** 12-2.30/7-9.30, Closed Jan, 2 wks in summer, Sun-Mon **Prices:** Fixed L £13.95, Fixed D £25.95, Starter £4.50-£10.95, Main £12.50-£18.95, Dessert £4.95, Service optional **Wine:** 80 bottles over £20, 62 bottles under £20, 7 by the glass **Seats:** 65, Pr/dining room 35 **Children:** Portions **Directions:** Town centre, Churchgate St is opposite cathedral **Parking:** On street

⊛ Nazar

Turkish V NEW
Authentic Turkish cuisine in relaxed, lively surroundings

☎ 01284 704870 19-21 Angel Hill IP33 1UZ
e-mail: info@nazar-bse.co.uk
web: www.nazar-bse.co.uk

Situated on Angel Hill, this traditional-style building with wooden beams and furniture is brought to life with Turkish music and tapestry-style tablecloths, creating a relaxing atmosphere in which to enjoy some authentic cuisine. Home-made houmous and flatbread make a simple, fresh starter, while mains include the likes of Ispannakli kofte - a special hand-prepared lamb mince with onions, mushrooms, spinach and grated mild Turkish cheese, cooked on the charcoal grill and served with fresh vegetables and a timbale of white and brown rice. Try the traditional layered filo pastry, honey and pistachio nut Baklava for dessert.

Times: 12-2.30/6-11 Closed Mon **Notes:** Vegetarian menu

⊛⊛ Ravenwood Hall Hotel

Traditional Mediterranean
Tudor hall with traditional food

☎ 01359 270345 Rougham IP30 9JA
e-mail: enquiries@ravenwoodhall.co.uk
web: www.ravenwoodhall.co.uk

With its origins in the reign of Henry VIII, this historic property comes set in 7 acres of tranquil countryside. The hall itself has been restored over the years but retains an ornate carved oak structure, inglenook fireplaces and rare 15th-century wall paintings. Accommodating staff and accomplished cuisine make dining here a truly relaxed and unpretentious affair, with prime local produce to the fore. The cooking style tends toward more familiar classics with seasonal twists, while home-smoked fish and meats and herbs from the garden add a homely touch. Think aged fillet of beef wrapped in Suffolk Black bacon with wild mushrooms and Café de Paris butter, and perhaps a hot chocolate fondant with poached Kirsch cherries to finish.

Chef: David White **Owners:** Craig Jarvis **Times:** 12-2.30/7.30-9.30 **Prices:** Fixed D £25.75, Starter £5.95-£9.95, Main £15.50-£26.95, Dessert £6.95-£8.25, Service optional **Wine:** 54 bottles over £20, 32 bottles under £20, 11 by the glass **Notes:** Sun L 3 courses £24.75 (inc coffee), Vegetarian available, Civ Wed 130 **Seats:** 50 **Children:** Menu, Portions **Rooms:** 14 (14 en suite) ★★★ HL **Directions:** 3m from Bury St Edmunds, just off A14 junct 45 signed Rougham **Parking:** 150

DEBENHAM
MAP 13 TM16

◉ The Angel Inn

Modern British

Flavourful cooking in rustic restaurant with rooms

☎ 01728 860954 5 High St IP14 6QL
e-mail: dgiven@btconnect.com
web: www.theangelinn-debenham.org

Set in the heart of a peaceful village, this 16th-century inn turned restaurant with rooms has stayed true to its roots with a rustic décor comprised of whitewashed walls, beams, pictures of country scenes and heavy wooden tables and chairs. The cooking though is an altogether more modern affair, conjured from fresh local produce with good depth of flavour. Plump for the seasonal carte or a daily blackboard special: chicken with vegetable mousseline and roast garlic sauce perhaps, or a lamb and mushroom kebab with roast pork loin, roast butternut squash and pesto pasta. Round things off with a Bailey's and pistachio cheesecake. Lighter snacks are served in the bar.

Chef: Jonathan Watson **Owners:** Darren Given **Times:** 12-2.30/6.30-9.30, Closed D Sun **Prices:** Fixed L £9.95-£11.95, Starter £4-£6.50, Main £7-£16, Dessert £4.25-£4.50, Service optional **Wine:** 4 bottles over £20, 16 bottles under £20, 6 by the glass **Notes:** Vegetarian available **Seats:** 32, Pr/dining room 24 **Children:** Portions **Rooms:** 3 (3 en suite) ★★★ RR **Directions:** Telephone for directions **Parking:** 12

FRESSINGFIELD
MAP 13 TM27

◉◉ Fox & Goose Inn

Modern British

Pub turned restaurant in a pretty village setting

☎ 01379 586247 IP21 5PB
e-mail: foxandgoose@uk2.net
web: www.foxandgoose.net

The Fox & Goose is a country inn next door to the church in a classic village location. All the comforting features are here - exposed timbers and open fires - with a handsome bar and two smart dining rooms set off by lovely fabrics, modern art and a background of light jazz. On offer are a good-value lunch, an evening seven-course tasting menu and a great choice from the carte. The modern British dishes - with French influences - read beautifully, their various elements blending harmoniously on the plate. Think a fillet of halibut served with cauliflower purée, dill gnocchi, buttered spinach and a mustard vinaigrette, and to finish, perhaps an apple tarte Tatin with fennel and caramelised almond ice cream.

Chef: P Yaxley, M Wyatt **Owners:** Paul Yaxley **Times:** 12-2/7-9, Closed 27-30 Dec, 2nd wk Jan for 2 weeks, Mon **Prices:** Fixed L £11.95-£13.50, Starter £4.50-£8.25, Main £11.95-£17.95, Dessert £4.50-£5.75, Service optional **Wine:** 25 bottles over £20, 38 bottles under £20, 7 by the glass **Notes:** Tasting menu 6 courses £40 **Seats:** 48, Pr/dining room 25 **Children:** Min 9 yrs D, Portions **Directions:** A140 & B1116 (Stradbroke) left after 6m - in village centre by church **Parking:** 15

HINTLESHAM
MAP 13 TM04

◉◉◉ Hintlesham Hall

see opposite

HORRINGER
MAP 13 TL86

◉ The Beehive

Modern British NEW

Great gastro-pub dining in charming cottage-style surroundings

☎ 01284 735260 The Street IP29 5SN

A traditional-looking brick and flint pub, converted from a Victorian cottage, and full of period features. Embracing the gastro-pub concept, you'll find antique wooden tables and a chalkboard menu, updated during service. Patio seating and a walled beer garden with picnic benches are a popular option in summer. Traditional pub food is given a modern twist with French influences, using excellent fresh ingredients. Try a starter like cream of spinach and crabmeat soup, or a main course like steak and kidney cooked in ale, served on a bed of creamy mashed potatoes with root vegetables.

Chef: Dougie Lindsay **Owners:** Gary & Di Kingshott **Times:** 12-2/7-9.30, Closed 25-26 Dec, Closed D Sun **Prices:** Starter £4.95-£6.95, Main £9.95-£15.95, Dessert £4.95, Service optional **Wine:** 4 bottles over £20, 29 bottles under £20, 6 by the glass **Notes:** Vegetarian available **Seats:** 50 **Directions:** A149 (Bury St Edmunds to Haverhill road). Restaurant towards end of village **Parking:** 30

◉◉ The Ickworth Hotel

International

Modern, eclectic cooking in National Trust-owned hotel

☎ 01284 735350 IP29 5QE
e-mail: ickworth@luxuryfamilyhotels.com
web: www.ickworthhotel.com

Gifted to the National Trust in 1956, this stunning property is part luxurious hotel that combines the glorious design and atmosphere of the past with modern-day facilities including a crèche, children's play area, tennis courts and spa. The hotel boasts eclectic décor and The Inferno - a Mediterranean café concept - is aimed at families, while more formal dining is available in the main restaurant. Here the menu boasts the likes of ballotine of sea trout with tiger prawns as a starter, followed by pan-roasted monkfish with clam risotto and bacon, or sea bass baked in a herb crust with saffron mash. Desserts might feature plum clafoutis and vanilla ice cream, or chocolate-lovers might not be able to resist bitter chocolate marquise with local berries.

Times: 12-2/7-9.30 **Rooms:** 38 (38 en suite) ★★★★ HL **Directions:** From A14 take 1st exit for Bury St Edmunds (junct 42). Follow signs for Westley & Ickworth Estate

IPSWICH
MAP 13 TM14

◉ Il Punto

French

Solid brasserie cooking in full sail!

☎ 01473 289748 Neptune Quay IP4 1AX
e-mail: info@ilpunto.co.uk
web: www.ilpunto.co.uk

Hop aboard this vintage Dutch barge moored at Neptune Quay - a short walk from the town centre - and you'll find a dining room split between two decks. The nautical styling fits the shipboard venue, decked out with a polished-wood interior and bright blue and white

CONTINUED ON PAGE 460

Hintlesham Hall

ENGLAND

HINTLESHAM MAP 13 TM04

Modern European

Fine dining in outstanding country house

☎ 01473 652334   IP8 3NS
e-mail: reservations@hintleshamhall.com
web: www.hintleshamhall.com

Chef: Alan Ford
Times: 12-1.30/7-9.30, Closed L Sat
Rooms: 33 (33 en suite)★★★★ HL
Directions: 5m W of Ipswich on A1071

You'll find plenty of comfortable lounges, open fires and fine pieces of art and china at this magnificent 16th-century country-house hotel set in 175 acres of grounds and landscaped gardens. The fine-dining Salon restaurant is a truly grand and formal affair (a jacket will be readily provided to those unaware of the dress code), with its high domed ceiling decorated with gold leaf, ornate cornices, a huge branched chandelier and large windows that look out onto the grounds. As one would expect, table service is both formal and efficient. The kitchen takes a modern approach, though underpinned by a classical theme. Top-quality ingredients, sound execution and good depth of flavour abound. This is classic country-house cooking, consistent, accomplished and pleasing rather than cutting-edge, and aptly suited to the surroundings. For mains, perhaps choose a suprême of sea bass, simply grilled and served with a fennel mash and citrus beurre blanc, or roast and confit partridge delivered with mixed potato dauphinoise and a white wine sauce, and to finish, a pistachio crème brûlée with crisp tuile biscuit. Weekday lunch offers exceptional value and there's a serious wine list, too, with a good selection by the glass and a great selection of half-bottles.

459

IPSWICH *Continued*

fabrics, though the food navigates more of a French brasserie passage. Well-executed, simple classics - using quality ingredients - come attractively presented; think roast rack of lamb topped with a garlic and herb crust, or perhaps oven-baked halibut fillet and grilled scallops with a red wine and butter sauce. The perfect spot for lunch on a sunny day.

Chef: Frederic Lebrun **Owners:** Mr R Crepy **Times:** 12-2.30/7-9.30, Closed Jan, Sun-Mon **Prices:** Fixed L £12.95, Fixed D £24.95, Starter £4.95-£8.50, Main £11.50-£18.50, Dessert £4.95, Service optional **Notes:** Vegetarian available **Seats:** 80, Pr/dining room 30 **Children:** Menu, Portions **Directions:** Telephone for directions **Parking:** NCP

◉◉ Salthouse Harbour Hotel, Brasserie

Modern Mediterranean
Relaxed contemporary brasserie overlooking the marina

☎ 01473 226789 No 1 Neptune Quay IP4 1AX
e-mail: staying@salthouseharbour.co.uk
web: www.salthouseharbour.co.uk

Overlooking the trendy area of Neptune Marina, this 48-bedroomed hotel is set in a converted early 19th-century warehouse. Combining contemporary minimalism with original features, the busy ground-floor brasserie comes decked out in sleek lines, with a stylish intimate bar, leather banquette seating, modern artwork, huge windows and a relaxed atmosphere. The emphasis is firmly on fresh, locally-sourced produce. Dishes are well executed with clear flavours, as in fillet of British Excellence beef with a wild mushroom tartlet, fondant potatoes and shallot purée, or breast of duck with gratin dauphinoise, baby figs and peppered rum syrup. In summer, dine alfresco in the stylish courtyard and soak in the atmosphere of the marina.

Chef: Robert Gough **Owners:** Robert Gough **Times:** 12-3/6-10 **Prices:** Fixed L £11.95, Starter £4.95-£7.95, Main £9.95-£19.95, Dessert £3.95-£7.95, Service optional **Wine:** 20 bottles over £20, 16 bottles under £20, 24 by the glass **Notes:** Vegetarian available, Civ Wed 80 **Seats:** 60 **Children:** Menu, Portions **Rooms:** 43 (43 en suite) ★★★★ TH **Directions:** A14 junct 53, A1156 to town centre and harbour, off Key St **Parking:** 30

IXWORTH   MAP 13 TL97

◉ Theobalds Restaurant

Modern British
Village restaurant that's stood the test of time

☎ 01359 231707 68 High St IP31 2HJ
web: www.theobaldsrestaurant.co.uk

Simon and Geraldine Theobald turned this oak-beamed cottage into a restaurant more than two decades ago and have built up a loyal following over the years. It's simply decorated with fresh flowers and paintings by local artists, and boasts a comfy lounge with an inglenook fireplace for after-dinner coffee, plus a pretty patio garden for drinks in summer. Expect flavourful cooking conjured from quality ingredients: twice-baked cheddar cheese soufflé is a typical starter, while mains might include lamb with roast garlic and a Madeira and rosemary sauce, or sea bass with spinach purée and a wholegrain mustard sauce.

Chef: Simon Theobald **Owners:** Simon & Geraldine Theobald **Times:** 12.15-1.30/7-9, Closed 10 days in Summer, Mon, Closed L Tues, Thurs, Sat, D Sun **Prices:** Fixed L £20, Fixed D £27, Starter £6.75-£8.95,

Main £14.95-£19.50, Dessert £6.75, Service optional **Wine:** 44 bottles over £20, 19 bottles under £20, 6 by the glass **Seats:** 42, Pr/dining room 16 **Children:** Min 8 yrs D, Portions **Directions:** 7m from Bury St Edmunds on A143 Bury/Diss rd **Parking:** On street

---

LAVENHAM   MAP 13 TL94

◉ The Angel

Modern British
Medieval inn with lip-smacking food

☎ 01787 247388 Market Place CO10 9QZ
e-mail: angellav@aol.com
web: www.theangelhotel.com

First licensed in 1420, The Angel is at the centre of one of England's finest medieval villages and is replete with traditional period décor, including oak beams, inglenook fireplace and sturdy wooden tables and chairs. The cooking style is simple, combining modern British dishes with traditional pub favourites, with careful preparation of quality ingredients. Expect good flavours and well cooked dishes, like haddock, crab and chilli fishcakes with spicy tomato sauce, grilled fillet of arctic char with braised leeks and red pepper sauce, or chargrilled tuna with lemon and thyme risotto. Finish with a classic pear and almond tart, or a comforting steamed syrup pudding.

Chef: Michael Pursell **Owners:** Mr & Mrs R Whitworth & Mr J Barry **Times:** 12-2.15/6.45-9.15, Closed 25-26 Dec **Prices:** Starter £3.95-£6.95, Main £9.95-£19.95, Dessert £4.50, Service optional, Group min 10 service 10% **Wine:** 9 bottles over £20, 34 bottles under £20, 9 by the glass **Notes:** Vegetarian available, Dress Restrictions, Smart casual **Seats:** 100, Pr/dining room 16 **Children:** Portions **Rooms:** 8 (8 en suite) ★★ **Directions:** Between Bury St Edmunds and Sudbury on A1141. In town centre, Market Place just off High St **Parking:** 5

◉◉ Lavenham Great House 5 Star Restaurant with Rooms

Traditional French
Gallic charm in Tudor setting

☎ 01787 247431 Market Place CO10 9QZ
e-mail: info@greathouse.co.uk
web: www.greathouse.co.uk

The Great House is a resolutely French restaurant (with rooms) with French staff in the most English of settings. The 15th-century house with a Georgian façade stands just opposite the historic Guildhall in this well-preserved medieval town. The beamed Tudor dining room boasts a huge inglenook and smell of logs, with oak floors and uneven walls, making a splendid setting for high-quality rural French cuisine. An accomplished kitchen favours well-sourced luxury ingredients and an elaborate style, so expect to find the likes of grilled ink risotto with razor clams and grilled scallops on lobster bisque, turbot with tomato concasse and basil polenta, saddle of venison with Burgundy wine sauce, and dark chocolate terrine on the menu.

Chef: Regis Crepy **Owners:** Mr & Mrs Crepy **Times:** 12-2.30/7-9.30, Closed Jan, Mon, Closed L Tue, D Sun **Prices:** Fixed L £15.95, Fixed D £25.95, Starter £6-£9.50, Main £11-£22.50, Dessert £4.75-£6.75, Service optional, Group min 10 service 10% **Wine:** 65 bottles over £20, 75 bottles under £20, 10 by the glass **Notes:** Sun L £25.95, Vegetarian available **Seats:** 40, Pr/dining room 12 **Children:** Portions **Rooms:** 5 (5 en suite) ★★★★★ RR **Directions:** In Market Place (turn onto Market Lane from High Street). **Parking:** Market Place

◎◎ The Swan Hotel

Modern, Traditional V

Dine surrounded by medieval splendour

☎ 01787 247477 High St CO10 9QA
e-mail: info@theswanatlavenham.co.uk
web: www.theswanatlavenham.co.uk

This 14th-century hotel, which had an important connection to the town's wool trade, stands out even amongst its medieval and Tudor village setting. A collection of delightful listed buildings, the interior is a riot of oak beams, panelled walls and leaded lights. The elegant medieval great hall, complete with a minstrels' gallery, is populated by well-spaced tables, comfortably upholstered chairs, expensive table linen and formal settings. Attentive staff serve accomplished, well-presented modern British and European dishes using prime local produce; think roasted Denham Estate venison with slow-cooked red cabbage, honey and parsnip fondant potato and a thyme jus, and perhaps a warm passionfruit tart finish, served with a mango sorbet. There's also an informal brasserie and rustic bar.

Chef: David Ryan **Owners:** Thorpeness & Aldeburgh Hotels Ltd
Times: 12-2.30/7-9.30 **Prices:** Fixed L £11.95, Fixed D £28.95, Starter £6.50-£9.50, Main £16.45-£20.45, Dessert £5.50-£8, Service optional
Wine: 85 bottles over £20, 40 bottles under £20, 12 by the glass
Notes: Sun L 3 courses £21.95, Vegetarian menu, Dress Restrictions, No jeans or trainers, Civ Wed 80, Air con **Seats:** 90, Pr/dining room 32
Children: Menu, Portions **Rooms:** 51 (51 en suite) ★★★★ HL
Directions: From Bury St Edmunds take A134 for 6m. Lavenham is 6m along B1071 **Parking:** 50
see advert on this page

LONG MELFORD   MAP 13 TL84

◎ The Black Lion Hotel

Traditional, Mediterranean

Stylish hotel dining overlooking the village green

☎ 01787 312356 Church Walk, The Green CO10 9DN
e-mail: enquiries@blacklionhotel.net
web: www.blacklionhotel.net

Guests have enjoyed hospitality at this charming Georgian building since at least 1661. Overlooking the village green, today it combines contemporary furnishings and crisp white linen with exquisite antiques and oil paintings, giving the restaurant a formal, elegant feel. Local, flavoursome produce is used to the full in British dishes that have a Mediterranean twist. Try beef and Adnams suet pudding with bubble-and-squeak, or fritto misto - crispy fried seafood in beer batter served with anchovy mayonnaise. Desserts are a treat too and might include

chocolate bread-and-butter pudding, or lemon and lime tart with raspberry coulis and clotted cream. The same innovative menu is also available in the cosy lounge-bar.

Chef: Annette Beasant **Owners:** Craig Jarvis **Times:** 12-2/7-9.30
Prices: Fixed L £24.75, Fixed D £24.75, Starter £5.25-£9.50, Main £11.95-£18.95, Dessert £5.25-£6.95, Service optional **Wine:** 53 bottles over £20, 31 bottles under £20, 10 by the glass **Notes:** Fixed L 3 courses, Sun L 3 courses £18.95, Vegetarian available, Civ Wed 50 **Seats:** 50, Pr/dining room 20 **Children:** Menu, Portions **Rooms:** 10 (10 en suite) ★★★ HL
Directions: From Bury St Edmunds take A134 to Sudbury. Turn right onto B1064 to Long Melford. Right onto A1092 to Cavendish. Black Lion on the green **Parking:** 10

◎◎ Scutchers Restaurant

Modern

Friendly bistro serving imaginative fare

☎ 01787 310200 Westgate St CO10 9DP
e-mail: eat@scutchers.com
web: www.scutchers.com

Dating from the 16th century, this bright and lively bistro artfully combines the ancient and modern, with coloured fabrics, pine furnishings, artwork and modern lighting sitting happily with the old beams. The smart surroundings belie an easy-going and relaxed atmosphere however, where modern British cooking produces competently cooked dishes, the intelligently simple style allowing the quality and freshness of the ingredients to shine through. Typical choices on the extensive carte include deep-fried tiger prawns in

CONTINUED

LONG MELFORD CONTINUED

tempura batter with sweet chilli mayonnaise, followed by spicy 'Southern fried' Suffolk chicken breast, served with hand-cut chips, home-made slaw and blue cheese dressing, with a trio of home-made sorbets in a tuile basket to finish. A good-value fixed-price weekday menu is also available.

Chef: Nicholas Barrett **Owners:** Nicholas & Diane Barrett **Times:** 12-2/7-9.30, Closed 25 Dec, 2wks Mar, last wk Aug, Sun-Mon **Prices:** Fixed L £15, Fixed D £20, Starter £6-£12, Main £12-£23, Dessert £6, Service optional **Wine:** 90 bottles over £20, 7 bottles under £20, 17 by the glass **Seats:** 70 **Children:** Portions **Directions:** About 1m from Long Melford towards Clare **Parking:** 12

LOWESTOFT   MAP 13 TM59

◉◉ The Crooked Barn

British, European

Characterful dining in restful Broads setting

☎ 01502 501353 Ivy House Country Hotel, Ivy Ln, Oulton Broad NR33 8HY

e-mail: aa@ivyhousecountryhotel.co.uk

web: www.ivyhousecountryhotel.co.uk

This converted 18th-century thatched barn - complete with creaking floorboards and crooked beams - makes a delightful dinner venue with its beautiful garden views and ornamental lily ponds. Local artists' works hang on the wall and tables are clad in pale green with crisp linen napkins. Outside there's a courtyard for summer dining, and uniformed staff are friendly and helpful. Modern British and European dishes - made with fresh, predominantly local ingredients - revel in their simplicity and freshness. Try a starter of pan-fried king scallops with fennel purée and crispy Parma ham, and for mains pan-fried fillet of 21-day aged Suffolk beef with creamed potatoes, roasted garlic and Puy lentils, finishing with hot orange and treacle tart.

Chef: Martin Whitelock **Owners:** Caroline Coe **Times:** 12-1.45/7-9.30, Closed 24 Dec-8 Jan **Prices:** Fixed L £15.95-£18.95, Fixed D £27.50-£29.50, Starter £4.95-£9.95, Main £12.95-£24.95, Dessert £4.95-£8.95, Service included **Wine:** 12 bottles over £20, 23 bottles under £20, 4 by the glass **Notes:** Vegetarian available, Dress Restrictions, Smart casual, no shorts, Civ Wed 100 **Seats:** 45, Pr/dining room 16 **Children:** Portions **Rooms:** 20 (20 en suite) ★★★ HL **Directions:** A146 into Ivy Lane **Parking:** 50

MONKS ELEIGH   MAP 13 TL94

◉◉ The Swan Inn

British, Mediterranean NEW

Attractive pub with culinary clout

☎ 01449 741391 The Street IP7 7AU

e-mail: carol@monkseleigh.com

web: www.monkseleigh.com

This attractive thatched pub comes situated in the heart of this 'chocolate-box' Suffolk village and, while remaining true to its local roots, is driven by culinary aspirations. The refurbished, light modern bar area comes decked out with oak floors, beamed ceilings and an open fire, while blackboard menus confirm the kitchen's serious intent. Driven by quality local seasonal produce, the cooking's modern bistro-style approach is intelligently unfussy, allowing the main ingredient to shine. Take braised lamb knuckle with a Puy lentil sauce, creamy mashed potatoes and buttered broad beans, or perhaps whole roast sea bass with ginger and coriander butter served with a mixed-leaf salad and new potatoes.

Chef: Nigel Ramsbottom **Owners:** Nigel Ramsbottom **Times:** 12-2/7-9.30, Closed 25-26 Dec, 1 Jan, Mon-Tue **Prices:** Starter £4.50-£7.50, Main £10-£20, Dessert £4.75-£6.75, Service optional **Wine:** 10 bottles over £20, 30 bottles under £20, 10 by the glass **Notes:** Sun L ALC, Vegetarian available **Seats:** 30, Pr/dining room 24 **Children:** Portions **Parking:** 12

NAYLAND   MAP 13 TL93

◉◉ The White Hart Inn

French, Italian, Mediterranean

First-rate gastro-pub cuisine with a French twist

☎ 01206 263382 High St CO6 4JF

e-mail: reservations@whitehart-nayland.co.uk

web: www.whitehart-nayland.co.uk

This ancient, smartly turned-out 15th-century coaching inn - set in a charming, quintessentially English village in the heart of Constable country - comes brimful of character. Think heavy wooden beams, tiled floors and feature fireplaces, while the restaurant (formally laid at dinner) is a more elegant affair, and there's a terrace for alfresco summer dining, too. The kitchen's French flair is complemented by polished, friendly and mostly Gallic service, with seasonality and quality local produce distinguishing accomplished, assured dishes on the weekly repertoire. Expect potted rillette of rabbit to open, perhaps a classic coq au vin or warm escabèche of sea bream served with saffron potatoes to follow, and a hot chocolate fondant with Bailey's ice cream to close. (Lunchtimes see a lighter selection.)

Owners: The White Hart (Nayland) plc **Times:** 12-2/7-9 **Prices:** Fixed L £12.90, Starter £5.60-£13.90, Main £11.70-£19.60, Dessert £5.60-£7.90, Service optional, Group min 6 service 10% **Wine:** 31 bottles over £20, 8 bottles under £20, 7 by the glass **Notes:** Civ Wed 70 **Seats:** 40, Pr/dining room 36 **Children:** Portions **Rooms:** 6 (6 en suite) ★★★★ INN **Directions:** 6m N of Colchester on A134 towards Sudbury **Parking:** 10

NEWMARKET   MAP 12 TL66

◎◎ Bedford Lodge Hotel

Modern International V

A perfect place to dine during Newmarket races

☎ 01638 663175 Bury Rd CB8 7BX
e-mail: info@bedfordlodgehotel.co.uk
web: www.bedfordlodgehotel.co.uk

Based around an 18th-century Georgian hunting lodge, Bedford Lodge is a popular destination for the racing crowd who enjoy its combination of period elegance and leisurely informality as well as the proximity to the gallops at Newmarket. Public rooms have been enhanced by the creation of a small lounge area next to the lounge bar. The Orangery restaurant, decorated in sympathy with the original property, offers an inventive and distinguished menu. Dishes to catch the eye are pan-seared scallops with caramelised pork belly, crisp pancetta and St Edmunds russet apple purée, or tempura of yellow fin tuna, with creamy wasabi mash, courgette ribbons, egg noodles and a very good teriyaki sauce.

Chef: Chris Lawrence **Owners:** Barnham Broom Golf Club **Times:** 12-2.30/7-9.30, Closed L Sat **Prices:** Fixed L £15-£16, Fixed D £26.50-£28, Starter £6.50-£10, Main £14.50-£24, Dessert £6-£9, Service optional **Wine:** 41 bottles over £20, 27 bottles under £20, 9 by the glass **Notes:** Sun L 2 courses £17.50, 3 courses £22, Vegetarian menu, Dress Restrictions, No shorts, sandals, vests, Civ Wed 120, Air con **Seats:** 47, Pr/dining room 150 **Children:** Menu, Portions **Rooms:** 55 (55 en suite) ★★★★ HL **Directions:** From town centre follow A1303 towards Bury St Edmunds for 0.5m **Parking:** 100

Star Inn

☎ 01638 500275 The Street, Lidgate CB8 9PP
Catalan-influenced cooking from Mediterranean fish soup to tortillas.

ORFORD   MAP 13 TM45

◎◎ The Crown & Castle

Modern 🐌

Quality fine dining on the Suffolk coast

☎ 01394 450205 IP12 2LJ
e-mail: info@crownandcastle.co.uk
web: www.crownandcastle.co.uk

Proprietor, food writer Ruth Watson, has put this red-brick Victorian inn on the culinary map. It stands on Orford's old market square, next to the castle keep, overlooking the estuary. There is a relaxed style to the Trinity restaurant with its plush bench seating and dark wooden floors and tables. Staff wear long black aprons, and service is professional but laid back. The emphasis is on local produce and many of the dishes are featured in Ruth's cookbooks. The menu divides into raw, cold and hot dishes, including Orford-smoked eel, beetroot and potato salad with horseradish crème fraîche, or braised Suffolk lamb shank with pearl barley and mustard mash. Rosewater and cardamom pannacotta with poached apricots, or blackberry and frangipane tart with custard might catch the eye at dessert.

Chef: Ruth Watson, Max Dougal **Owners:** David & Ruth Watson **Times:** 12.15-2.15/7-9.30, Closed 7-11 Jan **Prices:** Starter £6.95-£9.50, Main £12.50-£16.50, Dessert £5.75-£6.50, Service optional, Group min 8 service 10% **Wine:** 89 bottles over £20, 23 bottles under £20, 14 by the glass **Notes:** Fixed D Sat & BHs only, Vegetarian available **Seats:** 60, Pr/dining room 10 **Children:** Min 8 yrs D, Menu, Portions **Rooms:** 18 (18 en suite) ★★ HL **Directions:** 9m E of Woodbridge, off A12 **Parking:** 20

The Butley-Orford Oysterage

☎ 01394 450277 Market Hill IP12 2LH
Salmon, eels, cod roe, mackerel and kippers smoked on the premises.

SOUTHWOLD   MAP 13 TM57

◎◎ The Crown

Modern British 🍷 NOTABLE WINE LIST

Coaching inn offering modern city-style cuisine

☎ 01502 722275 90 High St IP18 6DP
e-mail: crown.reception@adnams.co.uk
web: www.adnams.co.uk

An original early 19th-century coaching inn with a wonderful panelled, nautical-themed snug back bar, casual front bar and small restaurant. Service is relaxed and friendly throughout. The main front bar is lively with a cosmopolitan feel and offers a more informal dining option, while the restaurant delivers a quieter atmosphere. The same modern city-style cuisine is served throughout, using fresh locally-sourced ingredients. Roasted cod fillet on a crumble of celeriac, leek, potato and spinach, or perhaps seared Suffolk lamb's liver served with red cabbage marmalade and a sage and bacon bread-and-butter pudding show the style. And to finish, perhaps a rhubarb tart with stem ginger sorbet, or warm steamed treacle sponge pudding with custard and clotted cream ice cream.

Chef: Ian Howell **Owners:** Adnams plc **Times:** 12-2/6.30-9.30 **Prices:** Starter £4.95-£6.95, Main £9.95-£19.95, Dessert £5.50-£6.95, Service optional **Wine:** 144 bottles over £20, 73 bottles under £20, 14 by the glass **Notes:** Vegetarian available **Seats:** 65, Pr/dining room 30 **Children:** Menu, Portions **Rooms:** 14 (13 en suite) ★★ HL **Directions:** Take A1095 from A12; hotel in the middle of the High Street **Parking:** 15

SOUTHWOLD CONTINUED

⊛ The Randolph

Modern, Traditional

Chic gastro-pub meets upmarket restaurant

☎ 01502 723603 41 Wangford Rd, Reydon IP18 6PZ
e-mail: reception@randolph.co.uk
web: www.therandolph.co.uk

Situated on the outskirts of Southwold, this welcoming restaurant with rooms makes a great base from which to explore the Suffolk coast. Once a pub, it still retains a traditional bar, but high-backed leather chairs, wood-stripped flooring and comfortable sofas have been added to create a gastro-pub ambience. Expect unfussy, flavourful cooking and a modern British menu of dishes such as goat's cheese and apple cakes served with balsamic dressing, followed by deep-fried cod in a beer batter with hand-cut chips and peas. Round it all off with a chocolate brownie smothered in white chocolate sauce.

Chef: Paul Buck **Owners:** David Smith **Times:** 12-2/6.30-9, Closed D 25 Dec **Prices:** Starter £3.50-£7.50, Main £7.95-£15, Dessert £3.95-£5.95, Service optional **Wine:** 2 bottles over £20, 12 bottles under £20, 6 by the glass **Seats:** 65 **Children:** Menu, Portions **Directions:** 1m from Southwold **Parking:** 40

⊛⊛ Sutherland House

Modern NEW ♨

Trendy eatery in the heart of town

☎ 01502 724544 56 High St IP18 6DN
e-mail: enquiries@sutherlandhouse.co.uk
web: www.sutherlandhouse.co.uk

A smart townhouse in the heart of the bustling town centre plays host to this contemporary-styled restaurant. Its two dining areas are linked by a central fireplace decked out with a couple of plush armchairs and coffee table, while elsewhere, modern darkwood tables, mauve padded chairs and trendy carpeting complete the upbeat picture. Staff are relaxed, casually dressed and friendly, while the kitchen takes an appropriately modern approach driven by local seasonal produce - with daily game and fish specials bolstering menus that highlight 'food miles' against dishes. Expect the likes of belly of Blythburgh pork served with fondant potato, roast parsnip and pork broth.

Chef: Alan Paton **Owners:** Peter & Anna Banks **Times:** Please telephone for details **Rooms:** ☆☆☆☆☆ RR

⊛⊛ Swan Hotel

Modern British

Accomplished cooking in a seaside inn

☎ 01502 722186 Market Place IP18 6EG
e-mail: swan.hotel@adnams.co.uk
web: www.adnamshotels.co.uk

A former 17th-century coaching inn set at the heart of this pretty seaside town it may be, but today's Swan oozes cosy, contemporary styling. There's a comfortable drawing room, bar and lounge, while the elegant, bay-fronted restaurant looks out over the square. The accomplished kitchen's modern approach pays due reverence to quality fresh local produce from the abundant local larder in well-executed dishes; perhaps pan-fried calves' liver served with truffle-

scented mash potatoes, wilted spinach and an oxtail and beetroot sauce, and to finish, maybe a glazed orange and passionfruit tart with passionfruit sauce and Seville orange marmalade jelly and sorbet. There's an excellent wine list and range of Adnams ales, too, and if staying over, the Admiral's Room comes complete with telescope to survey the sea.

Times: 12-2.30/7-9.30 **Rooms:** 42 (42 en suite) ★★★ HL
Directions: Turn right off A12 signed Southwold/Reydon, continue for 4m into Southwold. Follow main street into Market Place, hotel on left

---

STOKE-BY-NAYLAND   MAP 13 TL93

⊛ The Angel Inn

Modern British

Traditional coaching inn with innovative cooking

☎ 01206 263245 Polstead St CO6 4SA
e-mail: theangel@tiscali.co.uk
web: www.horizoninns.co.uk

This romantic 16th-century oak-beamed coaching inn comes complete with an original well in the restaurant. The style of the place is relaxed and you'll find period features set against modern art and leather sofas. The menu draws on locally-sourced produce and some favourite dishes include deep-fried brie with raspberry coulis and green peppercorns, followed by baked cod with tapenade crust, chorizo potato cake and wilted spinach, or mussels steamed in white wine and cream sauce. Vegetarian options include the likes of spinach roulade stuffed with wild mushrooms in a cheese sauce.

Chef: Steve Jessup **Owners:** Horizon Inns **Times:** 12-2/6.30-9.30
Prices: Starter £3.50-£7.25, Main £9.95-£21.95, Dessert £4.50, Service optional **Notes:** Vegetarian available **Seats:** 28 **Children:** Portions
Rooms: 6 (6 en suite) ★★★★ INN **Directions:** From A12, take Colchester right turn, then A135, 5m to Nayland from A125, take B1068
Parking: 20

STOWMARKET   MAP 13 TM05

⊛ The Shepherd and Dog

Modern British NEW

Relaxed gastro-pub atmosphere with cooking to match

☎ 01449 711361 & 710464 Forward Green IP14 5HN
e-mail: marybruce@btinternet.com

Pretty much in the gastro-pub mould, with its stripped-pine tables, plain walls and casually dressed staff, the Shepherd & Dog name seems rather appropriate (the proprietors who once owned the town's Tot Hill House restaurant) having been guided back here after a sojourn in Wales. The place is split into two main areas, the bar (serving snacks) and the restaurant, where the kitchen's modern approach might deliver roast rump of lamb with sweet potato purée and white onion sauce, or a pear and ginger sponge finish, perhaps served with a rich chocolate sauce.

Chef: Christopher Bruce & Daniela Bruce **Owners:** Christopher & Mary Bruce **Times:** 12-3/7-11, Closed mid Jan, Mon, Closed D Sun
Prices: Fixed L £10.50-£15.50, Fixed D £19.50-£21.50, Starter £4.50-£7.50, Main £12.50-£18.50, Dessert £5-£6.50, Service optional **Wine:** 28 bottles over £20, 25 bottles under £20, 15 by the glass **Notes:** Sun L 2 courses £15.50, 3 courses £18.50, Vegetarian available **Seats:** 38, Pr/dining room 24 **Children:** Portions **Directions:** On A1120 between A14 and A140
Parking: 25

WALBERSWICK · MAP 13 TM47

⊛⊛ The Anchor

Modern 🍃

Gastro-pub serving unpretentious modern- and traditional-influenced food

☎ 01502 722112 Main St IP18 6UA
e-mail: info@anchoratwalberswick.com
web: www.anchoratwalberswick.com

Very much in the gastro-pub mould, The Anchor comes with stripped-pine seating, tables and floors and a typically relaxed atmosphere. The food is as unpretentious as the service, but strikes an interesting modern approach, while playing to the gallery with simpler comfort food, too. Rather interestingly, each dish is matched with a beer or wine, while the kitchen works with quality locally-sourced produce - many items admirably home grown on the owners' allotments. Expect the accomplished cooking to take in the likes of sea bass en papillote served with mixed leaves and spiced rice, or a salmon and cod fishcake with creamy leeks and hand-cut chips, while dessert might feature a treacle sponge with vanilla ice cream.

Chef: Sophie Dorber **Owners:** Sophie & Mark Dorber **Times:** 11-4/6-11, Closed 25 Dec **Prices:** Food prices not confirmed for 2008. Please telephone for details **Wine:** 12 by the glass **Seats:** 55 **Children:** Menu, Portions **Directions:** On entering village The Anchor is on the right, immediately after garage **Parking:** 60

WESTLETON · MAP 13 TM46

⊛⊛ The Westleton Crown

Modern British 🍃

Great British food in a great British setting

☎ 01728 648777 The Street IP17 3AD
e-mail: reception@westletoncrown.co.uk
web: www.westletoncrown.co.uk

This traditional 12th-century coaching inn retains the rustic charm of its heritage with the comfort you'd expect of contemporary dining. Diners can choose between the cosy parlour, elegant dining room, or large airy conservatory. In fine weather, the pretty terrace also provides the perfect setting for alfresco dining. An extensive menu includes daily specials and offers classic dishes with a twist. Mains might include 7-hour slow-roast leg of lamb with its own shepherd's pie and beer gravy, or roast loin of venison with griottine cherries and roast vegetable creamed potatoes. For dessert, why not try pear tarte Tatin with blackberry ice cream, accompanied by a suggested dessert wine. And don't forget the excellent range of home-made breads.

The Westleton Crown

Chef: Richard Bargewell **Owners:** Agellus Hotels Ltd **Times:** 12-2.30/7-9.30 **Prices:** Starter £4.25-£7, Main £9.50-£22, Dessert £4.50-£5.50, Service optional **Wine:** 24 bottles over £20, 19 bottles under £20, 8 by the glass **Notes:** Vegetarian available **Seats:** 80, Pr/dining room 40 **Children:** Portions **Rooms:** 25 (25 en suite) ★★★ HL **Directions:** From Ipswich head N on A12, turn right past Yoxford, follow tourist signs for 2m **Parking:** 30

WOODBRIDGE · MAP 13 TM24

⊛ The Captain's Table

Modern European NEW

Busy, friendly, relaxed brasserie

☎ 01394 383145 3 Quay St IP12 1BX
e-mail: eat@captainstable.co.uk
web: www.captainstable.co.uk

Originally three 16th-century cottages, this charming restaurant - situated in a side road just off the main street - comes decorated in pale yellow with blue curtains, wood floors and a wealth of oak beams. Relaxed and friendly, its interconnecting rooms are decked out with darkwood furniture, while there's the bonus of alfresco dining in the garden during the summer. The food fits the surroundings, the straightforward, unfussy but accomplished approach driven by fresh, quality local ingredients (organic where possible). Think slow-roast duck leg confit served with red cabbage and a red wine sauce, and perhaps a hot toffee pudding with hot toffee sauce to finish.

Chef: Pascal Pommier **Owners:** Mr P & Mrs J M Pommier **Times:** 12-2/6.30-9.30, Closed Sun-Mon (except BHs) **Prices:** Starter £3-£6.50, Main £5.95-£13.95, Dessert £4.50, Service included **Wine:** 11 bottles over £20, 22 bottles under £20, 5 by the glass **Notes:** Vegetarian available **Seats:** 50, Pr/dining room 34 **Children:** Menu, Portions **Directions:** From A12. Quay St opposite rail station and theatre. Restaurant 200m on left **Parking:** 6

WOODBRIDGE CONTINUED

◎◎ Seckford Hall Hotel

Modern British

Sound cooking amid Elizabethan splendour

☎ 01394 385678 IP13 6NU
e-mail: reception@seckford.co.uk
web: www.seckford.co.uk

With its imposing red-brick Tudor façade, tall chimneys and huge carved oak entrance door, it's easy to imagine that Queen Elizabeth I once held court here. In the same family for over 500 years, today its stately feel extends to the elegant oak-panelled restaurant - an intimate setting for sumptuous dining, decorated with rich tapestries, wood carvings and fresh flower displays. An extensive menu of modern British cuisine is served, and the accomplished kitchen makes good use of local produce, with lobster dishes and farmed local Suffolk duckling among the specialities. Start with slow-roasted pressing of local pork studded with apricots and pistachio, followed by whole lobster fricassée with fettucine and light ginger sauce. Leave room for a dark chocolate meringue soufflé, with caramel sauce.

Chef: Mark Archer **Owners:** Mr & Mrs Bunn **Times:** 12.30-1.45/7.30-9.30, Closed 25 Dec, Closed L Mon **Prices:** Fixed L £14.50, Service included **Wine:** 40 bottles over £20, 45 bottles under £20, 11 by the glass **Notes:** ALC 3 courses £29.50-£39.50, Vegetarian available, Dress Restrictions, Smart casual, No jeans or trainers, Civ Wed 125, Air con **Seats:** 70, Pr/dining room 100 **Children:** Menu, Portions **Rooms:** 32 (32 en suite) ★★★ CHH **Directions:** Hotel signposted on A12 (Woodbridge bypass). Do not follow signs for town centre **Parking:** 100

YAXLEY   MAP 13 TM17

◎◎ The Bull Auberge

Traditional European 🖳

Great cooking at a restaurant with rooms

☎ 01379 783604 Ipswich Rd IP23 8BZ
e-mail: deestenhouse@fsmail.net
web: www.the-auberge.co.uk

This ancient inn has been lovingly converted by the present owners into a restaurant with rooms. Exposed brickwork and oak beams testify to its age, but there's nothing old-fashioned about the food: expect simple, almost rustic dishes, packed with flavour and created from the best of local ingredients. A starter of chicken liver parfait is served with flavoursome pear chutney, followed perhaps by succulent oxtail braised in red wine, or cod with pea purée and red peppers. For dessert, tuck into rum baba, complemented by coconut and rum ice cream and caramelised pineapple. It's all served in an intimate dining room, where candles create a cosy ambience and the tables are smartly laid with crisp napkins.

Chef: John Stenhouse **Owners:** John & Dee Stenhouse **Times:** 12-2/7-9.30, Closed Xmas, Sun & Mon, Closed L Sat **Prices:** Fixed L £13-£16, Fixed D £20-£24, Starter £5-£9, Main £12.50-£19, Dessert £6, Service optional **Wine:** 35 bottles over £20, 25 bottles under £20, 8 by the glass **Seats:** 30, Pr/dining room 20 **Children:** Portions **Rooms:** 4 (4 en suite) ★★★★★ RR **Directions:** 5m S of Diss on A140 **Parking:** 25

YOXFORD   MAP 05 TM36

◎◎ Satis House Hotel

Malaysian

Listed 18th-century country house serving authentic Malaysian food

☎ 01728 668418 IP17 3EX
e-mail: yblackmore@aol.com

Charming privately-owned hotel set amid landscaped grounds just off the A12. Charles Dickens was once a regular visitor and the property's name features in his book *Great Expectations*. The decent-sized menu of Malaysian cuisine offers a good range of balanced dishes, from mild and spicy to pretty hot, and can be quite inexpensive, according to choice. Take sabah lamb (a succulent lamb dish with spices and yogurt), perhaps rendang daging (spicy coconut beef), or turmeric-chilli mackerel (in a lemon and coconut milk dressing). Desserts might feature a Malaysian black rice pudding, while the fixed-price Satis Kenduri (Malaysian banquet menu) is also offered at weekends.

Chef: Ms D Ferrance, Mrs C Blackmore **Owners:** Mrs Y C Blackmore **Times:** 7-9.30, Closed 25 Dec-3 Jan, Sun, Closed L (by arrangement only) **Prices:** Food prices not confirmed for 2008. Please telephone for details **Wine:** 6 bottles over £20 **Notes:** Dress Restrictions, Smart casual **Seats:** 30, Pr/dining room 16 **Children:** Min 5 yrs, Portions **Rooms:** 8 (8 en suite) ★★ SHL **Directions:** Between Ipswich and Lowestoft on A12, N of village **Parking:** 30

SURREY

ABINGER HAMMER — MAP 06 TQ04

◉◉ Drakes on the Pond

Modern British

Skilful cooking in a classy village restaurant

☎ 01306 731174 Dorking Rd RH5 6SA
web: www.drakesonthepond.com

Personally run by the friendly proprietors, this cottage-style building is situated on the edge of the village with views across the Surrey hills. The décor is kept simple, with primrose yellow walls creating a light-and-airy feel, set off by white-clothed tables, blue glassware and fresh flowers. Good, honest cooking makes the most of quality, fresh ingredients, and service is formal but friendly. The seasonally-changing menu includes the likes of tian of fresh white crab and creamed coconut for starters, followed by a mains of fillet of sea bass with caramelised onion and tomato Tatin. And for dessert, perhaps try almond and treacle tart served with salt caramel ice cream.

Chef: John Morris **Owners:** John Morris & Tracey Honeysett **Times:** 12-2/7-10, Closed 2 wks Aug-Sep, Xmas, New Year, BHs, Sun, Mon, Closed L Sat **Prices:** Fixed L £18.50, Starter £12-£16, Main £21-£24, Dessert £8-£9, Service optional, Group min 8 service 10% **Wine:** 65 bottles over £20, 9 bottles under £20, 9 by the glass **Notes:** Dress Restrictions, Smart casual, Air con **Seats:** 32 **Children:** Min 10 yrs **Directions:** On the A25 between Dorking and Guildford **Parking:** 20

BAGSHOT — MAP 06 SU96

◉◉ The Brasserie

Modern British NEW

Skilful modern cooking in five-star hotel setting

☎ 01276 471774 Pennyhill Park Hotel & Spa, London Rd GU19 5EU
e-mail: enquiries@pennyhillpark.co.uk
web: www.exclusivehotels.co.uk

The more informal option to the smaller, sister fine-dining Latymer restaurant at this renowned five-star hotel (see entry), The Brasserie has a wall of windows overlooking manicured lawns and the grand spa. There's a spacious lounge for pre- or post-meal drinks, while the décor of the restaurant has something of a Mediterranean tone, the large open room decked out with marble floor, big leather armchairs and well-spaced darkwood tables, all set around a central white statue. The dinner carte offers an eye-catching modern approach driven by tip-top produce; think seared fillet of halibut with fennel and apple salad, basquaise and a mussel curry sauce, and perhaps a prune and Armagnac tart finish, served with crème fraîche.

Chef: Andrew Turner, Graham Chatham **Owners:** Exclusive Hotels **Times:** 12-2.30/7-10.30 **Prices:** Fixed L £30, Starter £8.50-£12, Main £15-£32, Dessert £7-£9, Service optional **Wine:** 300+ bottles over £20, 2 bottles under £20, 300 by the glass **Notes:** Fixed L 3 courses, Sun Jazz L £35, Civ Wed 160, Air con **Seats:** 120, Pr/dining room 8 **Children:** Menu **Directions:** M3 junct 3, continue through Bagshot village & turn left onto A30. Hotel is 0.5m past Notcutts on right **Parking:** 500

◉◉◉ The Latymer

see page 468

BANSTEAD — MAP 06 TQ25

◉◉ Post

Modern V NEW

First-class Post arrives in leafy Banstead

☎ 01737 373839 28 High St SM7 2LG
e-mail: enquiries@postrestaurant.co.uk
web: www.postrestaurant.co.uk

Celebrity chef-patron Tony Tobin has created this new cosmopolitan-style brasserie, restaurant and delicatessen operation in the former Post Office in the High Street, and it presses all the right buttons. Contemporary design, accomplished modern food and a buzzy atmosphere is the style. The deli's at the front, to the rear is the airy all-day brasserie, while the first floor is home to the intimate fine-dining restaurant. Here cream leather banquettes, funky swivel leather tub chairs and a small bar complete the upbeat, modern setting. Three fixed-price eight-course tasting menus (plus a vegetarian option) deliver delicate small portions that excite the palate and the eye, using top-quality ingredients and bags of skill; think roasted halibut with braised oxtail and lemon and parsley oil, for instance.

Chef: Tony Tobin **Owners:** Tony Tobin **Times:** 11am-10pm **Notes:** Vegetarian menu

CAMBERLEY — MAP 06 SU86

◉◉ Macdonald Frimley Hall Hotel & Spa

Modern European

Smart country-house dining

☎ 0870 400 8224 Lime Av GU15 2BG
e-mail: gm.frimleyhall@macdonald-hotels.co.uk
web: www.macdonaldhotels.co.uk

This dignified Victorian manor has been refurbished to a high standard, combining modern décor with traditional features. The Linden restaurant has established an excellent local reputation as a fine-dining venue. Decorated in a fresh, contemporary style, it offers pretty views over a woodland garden from well-spaced tables and looks elegant by candlelight in the evening. Quality seasonal ingredients are a feature of the modern European menu, which offers starters such as pan-fried scallops with calamari salad, followed by the likes of confit pork belly with smoked apple mash, and Madeira jus. Desserts don't let the side down: a white chocolate and honeycomb parfait arrives with some of the freshest, plumpest raspberries to be had.

Chef: Max Pettini **Owners:** Macdonald Hotels **Times:** 12.30-2/7-9.45, Closed L Sat **Prices:** Fixed L £21, Fixed D £27.50, Starter £7.50-£10, Main £16-£24, Dessert £6, Service added but optional 12.5% **Notes:** Civ Wed 120, Air con **Seats:** 70 **Children:** Menu, Portions **Rooms:** 98 (98 en suite) ★★★★ HL **Directions:** From M3 junct 3 follow signs for Bagshot. Turn left onto A30 signed Camberley/Basingstoke. At rdbt branch left onto A325, then right into Conifer Dr & Lime Ave to hotel **Parking:** 100

CHARLWOOD — MAP 06 TQ24

For restaurant details *see* under Gatwick Airport (London), (Sussex, West)

The Latymer

BAGSHOT MAP 06 SU96

Modern British 🍷 NOTABLE WINE LIST

Innovative cuisine in peaceful, relaxed surroundings

☎ 01276 471774 Pennyhill Park Hotel & Spa, London Rd GU19 5EU
e-mail: enquiries@pennyhillpark.co.uk
web: www.exclusivehotels.co.uk

Set in 120 acres of grounds, there's a nostalgic grandeur to the exterior of this ivy-clad Victorian manor now delightful country-house hotel, with state-of-the-art spa and fine-dining Latymer restaurant. Set in the original part of the house, the Latymer is classical and classy, small and intimate. Think oak panelling, leaded windows and wooden beams teamed with heavy tapestries, innovative flower displays and beautifully presented tables.

And, while the setting may be traditional, the food's certainly a more contemporary affair. Expect innovative and skilful modern cooking underpinned by a classical theme on a fixed-price repertoire centred around tip-top, seasonal, fresh produce with clean, clear flavours. Mains might comprise loin of venison with pumpkin purée, creamed Savoy cabbage and blackberries, or perhaps line-caught turbot with oxtail ravioli, shallot cream and jus braisage, while vanilla-roasted pineapple with coconut sorbet and marshmallows might catch the eye at dessert. As anticipated, service is formal yet friendly, while a jacket and tie are preferred. The wine list is extensive and offers numerous wines by the glass, with examples to suit each dish on the menu.

Chef: Andrew Turner
Owners: Exclusive Hotels
Times: 12-2.30/7-10, Closed between Xmas & New Year, 1st 2 wks Jan
Prices: Fixed L £22.50, Fixed D £55, Service optional
Wine: 220 bottles over £20, 220 by the glass
Notes: Tasting menu 7 courses £75, Dress Restrictions, Smart casual, Civ Wed 160, Air con
Seats: 36, Pr/dining room 8
Children: Min 12 yrs, Menu
Rooms: 123 (123 en suite)★★★★★ HL
Directions: M3 junct 3, through Bagshot village, take left onto A30. 0.5m on right
Parking: 500

DORKING   MAP 06 TQ14

◉◉ Mercure Burford Bridge Hotel

Modern European

Historic hotel offering contemporary design and accomplished dining

☎ 01306 884561   Burford Bridge, Box Hill RH5 6BX
web: www.mercure.com

Sitting at the foot of beautiful Box Hill, the hotel dates back to the 16th century and is reputedly where Lord Nelson and Lady Hamilton met for the last time before the Battle of Trafalgar. Today, it's a smart, contemporary hotel, with comfortable armchairs and sofas in the bar and an elegant modern restaurant with low ceilings and candlelit tables overlooking the gardens. The modern cooking, underpinned by a classical theme, encompasses quality produce alongside excellent presentation and succinct flavours on crisply-scripted menus. Take roast salmon with spicy chorizo and confit tomatoes, or braised lamb shank served with mashed potato, and perhaps a tonka bean brûlée with white coffee ice cream and coffee sauce to finish.

Chef: Cyril Strub **Times:** 12-2.30/7-9.30 **Prices:** Fixed L £17.95, Fixed D £29.50, Service included **Wine:** 75 bottles over £20, 11 bottles under £20, 13 by the glass **Notes:** Dress Restrictions, No jeans, T-shirts or trainers, Civ Wed 200 **Seats:** 70, Pr/dining room 18 **Children:** Menu, Portions **Rooms:** 57 (57 en suite) ★★★★ HL **Directions:** M25 junct 9. Towards Dorking, the hotel is on the A24 at the Burford Bridge rdbt **Parking:** 140

◉◉ Two To Four

Modern, International

Eclectic dining in chic new town-centre restaurant

☎ 01306 889923   2-4 West St RH4 1BL
e-mail: eliterestaurants@hotmail.com

Dining on three floors is offered at this charming Grade II listed building, tucked away between boutiques and antique shops in the town centre. The interior has a chic minimalist feel, with bare wooden tables, ceramic tiled floors and natural decorations, and there's a friendly, bustling atmosphere with professional service. Dishes from the short carte and chalkboard specials are modern in style with international influences. Examples from the range include a starter of Asian smoked duck and watercress salad with chilli lime dressing, crispy garlic and shallots, followed by roasted fillet of lamb, pumpkin mash, courgette provençal and redcurrant glaze, or perhaps whole Dover sole served with buttered baby vegetables and creamy mashed potatoes. Finish with the cheese selection or a 2to4 knickerbocker glory.

Chef: Rob Gathercole **Owners:** Elite Restaurants **Times:** 12-2.30/6.30-10, Closed Xmas, Easter, BHs, 2wks Aug, Sun-Mon **Prices:** Fixed L £12, Starter £7.50, Main £17.95, Dessert £6.50, Service added but optional 10% **Wine:** 29 bottles over £20, 8 bottles under £20, 4 by the glass **Notes:** Air con **Seats:** 70, Pr/dining room 18 **Children:** Portions **Directions:** M25, exit at Leatherhead junct, follow signs to Dorking town centre **Parking:** West St car park

EGHAM   MAP 06 TQ07

◉◉ The Oak Room at Great Fosters

Modern British   🍷 NOTABLE WINE LIST

Regal Elizabethan setting for accomplished cuisine

☎ 01784 433822   Stroude Rd TW20 9UR
e-mail: enquiries@greatfosters.co.uk
web: www.greatfosters.co.uk

Steeped in history, this former royal retreat and now majestic Elizabethan manor hotel, sits in acres of celebrated landscaped grounds. Dark woods, deep sofas and magnificent tapestries blend with exquisite period features in its stately interior, while the elegant Oak Room restaurant cleverly blends modern design with more traditional features. Think vaulted oak-beamed ceiling, ornate wood-carved fireplace and mullioned windows versus high-backed chairs, large contemporary tapestry and friendly, polished service. The kitchen's modern approach flirts with the classical, delivering accomplished dishes showcasing quality produce. Expect the likes of confit Cornish mackerel with celeriac remoulade, seed mustard potatoes and a purée of autumn roots, followed by pan-seared brill with razor clams and cockles, herb spätzle and shellfish consommé, with hot cherry soufflé and mulled cherry sauce to finish.

Chef: Christopher Basten **Owners:** Great Fosters (1931) Ltd **Times:** 12.30-2/7-9.30, Closed L Sat **Prices:** Fixed L £20, Fixed D £33, Starter £9.50-£13, Main £23-£25, Dessert £8.50, Service added but optional 10% **Wine:** 285 bottles over £20, 2 bottles under £20, 22 by the glass **Notes:** Sun L 3 courses £28, Civ Wed 170 **Seats:** 60, Pr/dining room 20 **Children:** Portions **Directions:** 1m from town centre **Parking:** 200

ENGLAND

EPSOM   MAP 06 TQ26

◎◎ Chalk Lane Hotel

British, French ✋

Accomplished cooking close to Epsom Downs Racecourse

☎ 01372 721179   Chalk Ln, Woodcote End KT18 7BB
e-mail: smcgregor@chalklanehotel.com
web: www.chalklanehotel.com

Tucked down a little lane a short walk from Epsom Downs Racecourse, this endearing hotel is worth seeking out. It's a listed building, dating from 1805 and the restaurant is cosy and comfortable with mood lighting. Food is imaginative and accomplished using great ingredients cooked with obvious technical ability. There's a dine-with-wine lunch Monday to Friday with a free glass of wine thrown in, and a tasting menu of many courses. Interesting options from the regular menu include Carnaroli risotto of roasted ceps, pea tendrils and parmesan with Alba truffle oil, or fillet of strawberry grouper, with a nage of shiitake mushrooms, chervil and radish, and pappardelle of cucumber. Finish with a praline pannacotta, or pear and almond tarte served with crème anglaise.

Chef: Greg Lewis **Owners:** Steven McGregor **Times:** 12.30-2.30/7-10, Closed L Sat **Prices:** Fixed L £10-£19.50, Fixed D £38.50, Starter £6.50-£12, Main £16.50-£25, Dessert £5.50-£8.50, Service added but optional 12.5% **Wine:** 75 bottles over £20, 25 bottles under £20, 10 by the glass **Notes:** Vegetarian available, Dress Restrictions, Smart casual **Seats:** 40, Pr/dining room 20 **Children:** Portions **Rooms:** 22 (22 en suite) ★★★ HL **Directions:** M25 junct 9 then A24 towards Ashtead & Epsom. Just in Epsom turn right at BP garage, then left into Avenue Rd & follow hotel signs **Parking:** 60

FARNHAM   MAP 05 SU84

◎◎ Bishop's Table Hotel

Modern

Friendly formal dining in elegant surroundings

☎ 01252 710222   27 West St GU9 7DR
e-mail: welcome@bishopstable.com
web: www.bishopstable.com

Centrally located in the historic market town of Farnham, the hotel restaurant offers diners a formal setting for lunch or dinner. In previous incarnations the building was owned by the Marquise of Lothian, as well as being a school for clergy, and even has its own resident ghost known as 'William'! The cooking style is a combination of English and French classical cuisine with a modern twist. For starters, try a perfectly cooked wild pigeon breast with tomato

pancetta risotto, followed perhaps by a main course of venison Wellington served with beetroot fondant and bubble-and-squeak, or seafood and white bean cassoulet, chorizo, saffron and baby vegetables with rock oyster beignets. Desserts might include Bailey's pannacotta with Jack Daniel's iced parfait.

Chef: Mark Routledge **Owners:** Mr K Verjee **Times:** 12.30-1.45/7-9.45, Closed 26 Dec-5 Jan **Prices:** Fixed L £15-£15.50, Starter £6.95-£9.95, Main £15.95-£20.50, Dessert £6.95-£7.50, Service optional **Wine:** 32 bottles over £20, 25 bottles under £20 **Notes:** Fixed L 3 courses, Sun £15.50, Dress Restrictions, Smart casual, no jeans or T shirts **Seats:** 55, Pr/dining room 36 **Children:** Portions **Rooms:** 17 (17 en suite) ★★★ HL **Directions:** M3 junct 4 take A331 follow signs to town centre, next to public library **Parking:** Street parking, pay & display (300 yds)

GODALMING   MAP 06 SU94

◎ La Luna

Modern Italian

Stylish two-tone Italian of quality

☎ 01483 414155   10 Wharf St GU7 1NN
e-mail: info@lalunarestaurant.co.uk
web: www.lalunarestaurant.co.uk

This sophisticated, light and airy, contemporary Italian, smack in the centre of town, comes with a striking black and white décor - black high-backed chairs and crisp white-clothed tables set on a wooden floor - and exudes quality. Service is effortless, charming and very Italian, as is the patriotic and impressive wine list. There's a serious approach to the seasonal menus too, combining the classic flavours of Italy. Quality ingredients are handled with flair and imagination, and dishes come stylishly presented; take pan-fried John Dory fillets in Sicilian mixed citrus sauce and fresh herbs, served with sautéed spinach, garlic and mild chilli, while home-made tiramisù might head-up desserts.

Chef: Valentino Gentile, Francesco Viserti **Owners:** Daniele Drago & Orazio Primavera **Times:** 12-2/7-10, Closed early Jan, 2 wks in Aug, Mon, Closed D Sun **Prices:** Fixed L £12.95, Starter £5-£9.50, Main £15.50-£19.50, Dessert £4.75-£5.95 **Wine:** 134 bottles over £20, 12 bottles under £20, 4 by the glass **Notes:** Tasting menu 5 courses £55, Sun L 1-3 courses £14-£22, Vegetarian available, Air con **Seats:** 58, Pr/dining room 24 **Children:** Portions **Directions:** In centre of Godalming, junction of Wharf St & Flambard Way **Parking:** Public car park behind restaurant
see advert opposite

GUILDFORD   MAP 06 SU94

◉ Café de Paris

French

Informal restaurant with an authentic French flavour

☎ 01483 534896 35 Castle St GU1 3UQ

e-mail: cafedeparis35@aol.co.uk

web: www.cafedeparisguildford.co.uk

This much expanded restaurant has the avowed intention of providing an authentic taste of Paris right in the heart of Guildford. It's a large building with a stone-built Georgian frontage located opposite the castle grounds in the back streets along with many other bistro-style eateries. Cooking is very Parisienne, with lots of fish and a blend of traditional and creative dishes. Think bowls of moules marinière, escargots à la bourguignonne, tournedos Rossini, Dover sole meunière and tarte Tatin flambéed with Calvados and served with crème Chantilly or crêpe Suzette served with orange and Grand Marnier sauce.

Chef: Davide Creuzet **Owners:** Frank & Maya Kraus **Times:** 12-2.30/6-10.30, Closed Xmas week, BHs (except Good Fri), Sun (except Mothering Sun) **Prices:** Fixed L £12.50, Starter £5.50-£11.50, Main £12.50-£24.50, Dessert £5.50-£6.50, Service added but optional 10% **Wine:** 38 bottles over £20, 24 bottles under £20, 9 by the glass **Notes:** Fixed D 2 courses, Pre-theatre D £12.50, Smart casual, Air con **Seats:** 80, Pr/dining room 50 **Children:** Portions **Directions:** Guildford town centre, On the corner of Castle & Chapel St (just off lower High St) **Parking:** NCP

HASLEMERE   MAP 06 SU93

◉◉ *Lythe Hill Hotel*

Modern European

Sumptuous hotel dining in Surrey countryside

☎ 01428 651251 Petworth Rd GU27 3BQ

e-mail: lythe@lythehill.co.uk

web: www.lythehill.co.uk

Lythe Hill has been created from a collection of distinctive farm buildings, which include a splendid Elizabethan house, plus stylish, newer additions, each furnished in a style that complements the age of the property, and all set in 30 acres of glorious parkland. The Auberge de France restaurant is located in the timbered farmhouse and oozes historic charm, with mellow oak panelling and ancient beams creating an evocative dining ambience. The French-based menu acknowledges modern-day trends and classic dishes are given a fusion twist. Expect the likes of seared scallops with wild mushrooms, spinach and scallop velouté, roast monkfish with chorizo froth, with a classic lemon tart to finish. The contemporary Italian Garden restaurant offers lighter dishes.

Times: 12.30-2.15/7.15-9.45, Closed 25-26, 31 Dec, Closed L Mon-Sat **Rooms:** 41 (41 en suite) ★★★★ HL **Directions:** 1 mile E of Haslemere on B2131

La Luna

Set in the heart of Surrey with cuisine cooked with passion by our Napolitan Chef Valentino Gentile. He combines regional recipes, from The Valtellina to the Amalfi Coast and Sicily, home of the Sommelier Daniele Drago and Restaurant manager Orazio Primavera. La Luna had selected carefully 150 special wines from the white of Alto Adige and Friuli to the reds of Tuscany and Piemonte. We combine all the classic flavours of Italy for you to enjoy in our modern surroundings.

Godalming Surrey
Tel: 01483 414155   email: laluna@tiscali.co.uk

HORLEY For restaurant details
See Gatwick Airport (London), (Sussex, West)

LIMPSFIELD   MAP 06 TQ45

◉◉ Alexander's at Limpsfield

Modern NEW

Sophisticated food with relaxed and friendly service

☎ 01883 714365 The Old Lodge, High St RH8 0DR

e-mail: info@alexanders-limpsfield.co.uk

web: www.alexanders-limpsfield.co.uk

This 16th-century building has undergone a major refurbishment to offer a modern, contemporary style. Next to the small bar and brasserie area serving its simple bistro fare, the fine-dining restaurant boasts a high vaulted ceiling, dark oak-panelled walls and candlelit tables. Plenty of local and seasonal produce makes an appearance and the cooking is confident and simply presented on both the tasting menu and carte. Take a starter of roasted langoustine, macaroni of pork and langoustine bisque, followed by roast rump of Cornish lamb with root vegetables, Puy lentils and raspberry vinegar, or maybe Scottish halibut with tomato and olive-crushed potatoes, bouillabaisse sauce and anchovy beignet. Finish with a well-made Valrhona chocolate fondant with salted caramel and caramel ice cream.

Chef: Simon Attridge **Owners:** Patricia & James Douglas **Times:** 10am-midnight Closed Mon **Directions:** N of A25 on B269

OCKLEY
MAP 06 TQ14

⊕ Bryce's Seafood Restaurant & Country Pub

Modern Seafood V
Rural fish destination with pub and restaurant options

☎ 01306 627430 The Old School House RH5 5TH
e-mail: bryces.fish@virgin.net
web: www.bryces.co.uk

Former boys' boarding school dating from around 1750, now split into a pub area and more formal restaurant. The place is not on a main road and can be difficult to spot in the dark, but provides a warm, welcoming environment. The main menu is all fish, backed up by a blackboard, offering a modern take on fresh British seafood. Typical dishes are tiger prawn and Portland white crab cocktail with Marie Rose sauce, or South Coast fillet of sea bream on a warm porridge of Shetland mussels, chorizo and Parma ham.

Chef: B Bryce and Richard Attkins **Owners:** Mr B Bryce **Times:** 12-2.30/7-9.30, Closed 25-26 Dec, 1 Jan, Closed D Sun (Nov & Jan-Feb) **Prices:** Fixed L £23-£28, Fixed D £29-£34, Service optional, Group min 8 service 10% **Wine:** 16 by the glass **Notes:** Vegetarian menu **Seats:** 50 **Children:** Portions **Directions:** From M25 junct 9 take A24, then A29. 8m S of Dorking on A29 **Parking:** 35

REDHILL
MAP 06 TQ25

⊕⊕ Nutfield Priory – Cloisters Restaurant

Modern European
A unique setting for some tasty cuisine

☎ 01737 824400 Nutfield RH1 4EL
e-mail: nutfieldpriory@handpicked.co.uk
web: www.handpicked.co.uk

Built in the late 19th century, this stately country mansion retains a host of original features, including elaborate stone carvings, wood panelling and stunning stained glass. With panoramic views across three counties and an imposing cathedral-style arched ceiling, dining in the Cloisters restaurant is a memorable affair. The capable kitchen offers seasonal menus using locally-sourced produce where possible, delivering the likes of warm confit pork belly with pressed apple cake and cider oil, and Scottish beef fillet with summer beans and pea shoots. Finish off with the Egyptian trio of chocolate mousses.

Chef: Roger Gadsden **Owners:** Hand Picked Hotels **Times:** 12-2/7-9.30, Closed L Sat **Prices:** Fixed L £15, Fixed D £36, Starter £7-£12, Main £18-£28, Dessert £7-£9, Service optional **Wine:** 4 bottles under £20, 21 by the glass **Notes:** Sun L 3 courses £25, Vegetarian available, Dress Restrictions, No jeans or trainers, Civ Wed 80 **Seats:** 60, Pr/dining room 100 **Children:** Portions **Rooms:** 60 (60 en suite) ★★★★ HL **Directions:** On A25, 1m E of Redhill, off M25 junct 8 or M25 junct 6, follow A25 through Godstone **Parking:** 130

REIGATE
MAP 06 TQ25

⊕⊕ The Dining Room

Modern British V
Inspirational cooking in contemporary setting

☎ 01737 226650 59a High St RH2 9AE

This modern, stylish restaurant brings a touch of the London scene to Reigate. The bar, with leather sofas and soft lights, is creating a stir as a fabulous location for pre- and post-dinner drinks. In the restaurant, Tony Tobin continues to offer imaginative British dishes using fresh, seasonal ingredients. His cooking draws inspiration from the Mediterranean and further afield Thailand and Australia. So, dishes along the lines of bang-bang chicken salad with celeriac coleslaw followed by caramelised, sweet and spicy brill with a chilli and mango salsa might be on offer. The weekly-changing four-course 'Sunday Roast at the Dining Room' proves popular, and vegetarians have their own interesting selection of dishes.

Chef: Tony Tobin **Times:** 12-2/7-10, Closed Xmas & BHs, Closed L Sat, D Sun **Directions:** First-floor restaurant on Reigate High St

RIPLEY
MAP 06 TQ05

⊕⊕⊕ Drake's Restaurant

see opposite

SHERE
MAP 06 TQ04

⊕⊕ Kinghams

Modern British
Local produce showcased in attractive cottage restaurant surroundings

☎ 01483 202168 Gomshall Ln GU5 9HE
e-mail: paul@kinghams-restaurant.co.uk
web: www.kinghams-restaurant.co.uk

Drake's Restaurant

RIPLEY — MAP 06 TQ05

Modern French

Skilled, artisan cooking in village restaurant

☎ 01483 224777 The Clock House, High St GU23 6AQ
web: www.drakesrestaurant.co.uk

An imposing, red-brick Georgian house, with an old restored clock set above the doorway, picks out this Surrey culinary high-flyer. Home to chef-patron Steve Drake (previously of Drake's on the Pond at Abinger Hammer), the eponymous restaurant has fine pedigree and goes from strength to strength, driven by a committed young team who show clear dedication and passion to their craft. Warm earthy tones are complemented by interesting artwork and the open-plan space has an unstuffy vibe, smart but in an unpretentious and relaxed way. Tables are formally laid and there's a small seating area for aperitifs, plus the bonus of a pretty walled garden for summer drinks. Steve's cooking takes a modern approach (he likes to describe it as 'artisan cooking') and oozes skill, flair and finesse, creating dishes presented with elegant simplicity and clean, clear flavours from the freshest, high-quality seasonal produce. Think roast monkfish with celeriac fondant, braised chicken wings, spinach and an almond milk velouté, while to finish, perhaps a pineapple tarte Tatin served with aniseed ice cream. And do save room for the cracking petits fours, too.

Chef: Steve Drake **Owners:** Steve & Serina Drake **Times:** 12-1.30/7-9, Closed 2 wks Xmas, 2 wks Aug, Sun, Mon, Closed L Sat **Prices:** Fixed L £19.50, Fixed D £42.50, Service optional **Wine:** 166 bottles over £20, 16 bottles under £20, 9 by the glass **Notes:** Tasting menu £58, Smart casual **Seats:** 34, Pr/dining room 10 **Children:** Min 12 yrs **Directions:** M25 junct 10/A3 towards Guildford. Follow Ripley signs off A3, restaurant in centre of village **Parking:** 2

Built in the 1620s, this pretty red-brick cottage enjoys a picturesque Surrey village setting. The interior has a welcoming, relaxed feel with low ceilings and beams, crisp white linen and well-trained staff attending to customers' needs. There is a heated gazebo in the garden for the summer months. Cooking is imaginative with excellent presentation and uses lots of quality local, seasonal farm produce. Fresh fish is delivered daily, so expect the likes of a fillet of wild sea bass with roasted tomatoes, shallots and creamed artichokes on the fish board, or alternatively, try roasted venison served with fig stuffing and a pear and pickled ginger sauce. To finish, perhaps a white chocolate and Bailey's bread-and-butter pudding with a dark chocolate velouté.

Chef: Paul Baker **Owners:** Paul Baker **Times:** 12.15-2.30/7-9.30, Closed 25 Dec-4 Jan, Mon, Closed D Sun **Prices:** Fixed L £16.50, Fixed D £22.45, Starter £8.95-£9.95, Main £12.95-£21.95, Dessert £4.85-£5.95, Service optional, Group min 8 service 10% **Wine:** 12 bottles over £20, 26 bottles under £20, 6 by the glass **Notes:** Sun L 3 courses £22.95 **Seats:** 48, Pr/dining room 24 **Children:** Portions **Directions:** On A25 between Guildford and Dorking. 12 mins from M25 junct 10 **Parking:** 16

STOKE D'ABERNON — MAP 06 TQ15

◉◉ Woodlands Park Hotel

French

Victorian grandeur with contemporary cuisine

☎ 01372 843933 Woodlands Ln KT11 3QB
e-mail: woodlandspark@handpicked.co.uk
web: www.handpicked.co.uk

Originally built for the Bryant family (of matchmaker fame), this elegant Victorian mansion is set in over 10 acres of attractive parkland in the Surrey countryside. The original house retains many period features including a grand hall, minstrels' gallery and impressive staircase. Whether you're eating in the relaxed Quotes brasserie or in the more formal Oak Room, you can enjoy a pre-dinner drink in the cocktail bar while you peruse the menu. There's a nice balance of imagination and classically-rooted technique in dishes like beetroot risotto with horseradish and scallops - a typically imaginative starter - and main courses like rump of lamb with couscous salad or Chateaubriand (for two).

Chef: Peter Wallner **Owners:** Hand Picked Hotels **Times:** 12-2.30/7-10, Closed Mon, Closed L Mon-Sat, D Sun **Prices:** Fixed L £14.50-£22, Starter £6-£9, Main £20-£50, Dessert £6-£9, Service optional **Wine:** 125 bottles over £20, 4 bottles under £20, 10 by the glass **Notes:** Jazz evenings in brasserie, Vegetarian available, Dress Restrictions, No jeans or trainers, Civ Wed 200 **Seats:** 35, Pr/dining room 130 **Children:** Menu, Portions **Rooms:** 57 (57 en suite) ★★★★ HL **Directions:** From M25 junct 10, A3 towards London. Through Cobham centre and Stoke D'Abernon, left at garden centre into Woodlands Lane. Hotel 0.5m on left **Parking:** 150

SUSSEX, EAST

BATTLE
MAP 07 TQ71

◉ Powder Mills Hotel

Modern British V

Modern menu in a well-appointed conservatory dining room

☎ 01424 775511 Powdermill Ln TN33 0SP
e-mail: powdc@aol.com
web: www.powdermillshotel.com

This stunning 18th-century country-house hotel nestles in 150 acres of beautiful parkland - guests and diners can enjoy walks on the many woodland trails. Originally the site of a gunpowder works, Powder Mills has now been skilfully converted into a fascinating hotel. The large conservatory restaurant is sumptuously Georgian and has a colonial style, with marble floors, Greek statues and huge windows looking out on to the terrace and swimming pool. The food, however, is resolutely modern; take a warm risotto of black truffle and smoked haddock with coriander, followed perhaps by pan-fried sea bass with a pine-nut crust, parsnip purée and a red wine and shallot sauce.

Chef: James Penn **Owners:** Mr & Mrs D Cowpland **Times:** 12-2/7-9 **Prices:** Fixed L £19, Fixed D £29.50, Service added but optional 10% **Wine:** 4 by the glass **Notes:** Fixed L 3 courses, ALC 3 courses, Vegetarian menu, Dress Restrictions, Smart casual, no jeans, shorts or T-shirts, Civ Wed 100 **Seats:** 90, Pr/dining room 16 **Children:** Menu, Portions **Rooms:** 40 (40 en suite) ★★★ HL **Directions:** A21/A2100 past Battle Abbey. Turn into Powdermill Lane, first right **Parking:** 100

BRIGHTON
MAP 06 TQ30

◉ Due South

British ✿

Seaside dining, committed to organic and local produce

☎ 01273 821218 139 Kings Rd Arches BN1 2FN
e-mail: eat@duesouth.co.uk
web: www.duesouth.co.uk

Once a fishermen's net-mending shed, this modern glass-fronted restaurant is set in an old archway right on the seafront, with an outside terrace for alfresco dining. Inside, the style is modern with banquette seating and polished pine tables. The restaurant's strong commitment to the environment and renewable resources is reflected in local, seasonal produce from organic and free-range sources, 80% of which is sourced within a 20-mile radius. Take for example Ditchling Court Farm Garden lamb or whole baked sea bass stuffed with lemon and herbs. Wines are also English and European to cut down on import distances.

Chef: Roz Batty **Owners:** Robert Shenton **Times:** 12-4/6-10, Closed 2 wks Xmas & New Year **Prices:** Starter £4.50-£7.50, Main £11.50-£18.95, Dessert £5, Service added but optional 12.5% **Wine:** 36 bottles over £20, 22 bottles under £20, 9 by the glass **Notes:** Vegetarian available, Civ Wed 50 **Seats:** 55, Pr/dining room 12 **Children:** Portions **Directions:** On seafront, beneath cinema **Parking:** NCP Churchill Sq

◉ The Gingerman Restaurant

Modern British

Impressive cuisine at a busy neighbourhood-style eatery

☎ 01273 326688 21A Norfolk Square BN1 2PD
e-mail: info@gingermanrestaurants.com
web: www.gingermanrestaurants.com

This small, popular, relaxed Brighton eatery - with a discreet frontage - has an easy-on-the-eye modern décor of stripped pine floorboards, white walls and smartly dressed tables. Lunch is good value, but dinner brings more complex fare. Expect an appealing modern repertoire created from quality local ingredients - with fresh fish from the boats a daily speciality - delivered with minimum fuss and pretension. Think scallops with crispy pig's cheek, or perhaps roast partridge with cauliflower cheese, Madeira and thyme, while desserts such as a warm chocolate tart and pistachio ice cream make the perfect finale.

Chef: Ben McKellar/David Keates **Owners:** Ben & Pamela McKellar **Times:** 12.30-2/7-10, Closed 1 wk Xmas, Mon **Prices:** Fixed L £13, Fixed D £27, Service optional, Group min 6 service 10% **Wine:** 12 bottles over £20, 7 bottles under £20, 8 by the glass **Notes:** Sun L 3 courses £20, Air con **Seats:** 32 **Children:** Portions **Directions:** A23 to Palace Pier rdbt. Turn right onto Kings Rd. At Art Deco style Embassy building turn right into Norfolk Sq

◉ Hotel du Vin Brighton

French, European ⚑ NOTABLE WINE LIST

Stylish brasserie dining in Metropolitan hotel setting

☎ 01273 718588 Ship St BN1 1AD
e-mail: info@brighton.hotelduvin.com
web: www.hotelduvin.com

Perfectly located between the seafront and The Lanes shopping area, this stylish hotel and bistro occupies a tastefully converted mock-Tudor building. Décor has a strong wine theme, from the individually designed bedrooms through to the buzzy, split-level bar and the relaxed brasserie-style restaurant, with its wooden floors and subtle lighting. Cooking is classic bistro style. The menu has a pronounced French accent, as seen in terrine of confit chicken, garlic and tarragon with pear chutney and sour dough and roast venison with celeriac purée and pommes dauphinoise. Excellent wine list.

Chef: Rob Carr **Times:** 12-2/7-10, Closed D Dec 31 **Prices:** Fixed L £15.50, Starter £5.50-£11, Main £12.50-£22, Dessert £6.75-£6.95, Service added but optional 10% **Wine:** 300 bottles over £20, 50 bottles under £20, 12 by the glass **Notes:** Vegetarian available **Seats:** 85, Pr/dining room 36 **Children:** Menu, Portions **Rooms:** 37 (37 en suite) ★★★★ TH **Directions:** A23 to seafront, at rdbt take right, then right onto Middle St, bear right until Ship St, hotel is at sea end, on the right **Parking:** 10

⚜ Okini

Chinese NEW

Set your taste buds alight with Fusion Chinese cuisine in contemporary surroundings

☎ 01273 779933 70 East St BN1 1HQ
e-mail: info@okini-restaurant.co.uk
web: www.okini-restaurant.co.uk

Situated in the heart of The Lanes in Brighton, this relative newcomer specialises in Pan-Asian cuisine, inspired by Thai, Malaysian, Japanese and Chinese specialities. The setting is super-modern with a plain glass front, polished chrome cocktail bar, slate flooring and bright red perspex along one wall, with floor-to-ceiling red flowers on the opposite wall. Don't let the décor distract you from the food however, you'll find a range of exotic dishes tinged with the fresh flavours of lemongrass, chillies, basil leaves, lime and mint. Dishes might include twice-baked belly of pork with baby fennel and Chinese plum and beetroot sweet and sour sauce, or Sha Cha sea bass served with Thai fish mousse ravioli.

Chef: R J Yang, Marcus Guhren **Owners:** Terry Tan **Times:** 12-late
Prices: Starter £5-£8.50, Main £10-£20, Dessert £5-£5.50, Service added but optional 10% **Wine:** 18 bottles over £20, 29 bottles under £20, 8 by the glass **Notes:** Vegetarian available, Air con **Seats:** 90, Pr/dining room 25 **Directions:** Opposite Palace Pier off A259 **Parking:** On street, NCP

⚜⚜ One Paston Place

Modern Italian

Imaginative, skilful cooking in plush surroundings

☎ 01273 606933 1 Paston Place BN2 1HA
e-mail: info@onepastonplace.co.uk
web: www.onepastonplace.co.uk

The baroque and classical interior comes with wooden floors and walls decked out with mirrors that help lighten the formality of the dining room (as do the friendly and knowledgeable staff). Well-spaced tables and crisp white linen combine with chandeliers and a giant silver ice bucket brimful of champagne and wine. Contemporary European cooking is the style and, with Francesco Furriello at the stove, there's more than a touch of Italian inspiration about the repertoire, too. There are three menus: an everyday menu, a taster option and carte. Think pan-fried veal fillet with crisp sweetbreads, sweet potato, and a mascarpone and summer truffle risotto, or venison with Chianti, glazed shallots and Tuscan kale, with a peach and franciacorta gâteau finish, served with white peach sorbet. Peripherals like amuse-bouche and pre-desserts add interest.

Chef: Francesco Furriello **Owners:** Gusto Ltd **Times:** 12-2.30/7-late, Closed Sun-Mon **Prices:** Fixed L £16, Fixed D £29, Starter £9-£14.50, Main £18-£25, Dessert £8-£9, Service optional, Group min 25 service 12.5% **Wine:** 65 bottles over £20, 2 bottles under £20, 4 by the glass **Notes:** Tasting menu £59, Vegetarian available, Air con **Seats:** 40 **Children:** Min 7 yrs, Portions **Directions:** Between Palace Pier & Marina **Parking:** Street parking available

⚜ Pintxo People

Catalan NEW 🖥 V

Bar, deli and restaurant with a Catalan twist and dishes for sharing

☎ 01273 732323 95-99 Western Rd BN1 2LB
web: www.pintxopeople.co.uk

Situated on the Brighton end of Western Road, this unique concept fuses a style bar (coffee shop, deli and bar) on the ground floor with an intimate first-floor restaurant and cocktail bar, both with a Catalan twist. It's all thoroughly modern with a contemporary vibe, with a wrought-iron spiral staircase leading up to the real dining action upstairs. Here red leather banquettes and black leather chairs provide the seating, while tables come white clothed. Fine Catalan cuisine is the thing, with dishes designed to share, like Bellota acorn-fed Iberico ham with tomato toast, to ox sirloin served with rosemary fries.

Times: 12-4/6-10.30, Closed L Mon-Thu **Directions:** Opposite Waitrose

⚜⚜ Promenade Restaurant at Thistle Brighton

Modern British NEW

Exciting dining with amazing sea views

☎ 0870 3339129 King's Rd BN1 2GS
e-mail: brighton@thistle.co.uk
web: www.thistlehotels.com/brighton

Stunning views from this attractive second-floor restaurant, with its floor-to-ceiling windows, are easily matched by the exciting menu based on regional and seasonal produce. The contemporary décor includes high-backed chairs and smart wooden tables. Classic English and French techniques and skills produce a well-balanced menu. Expect a starter of warm pigeon breast delicately roasted, finely sliced and served with a medley of fresh leaves and French vièrge dressing. Main courses include succulent Sussex rack of lamb, magret duck and mustard-crusted pork fillet. An eye-catching dessert of bitter sweet chocolate parfait with orange sorbet, Grand Marnier cream and a spun minted-sugar decoration makes a splendid finale. Imaginative vegetarian dishes are offered.

Times: 12.30-2.30, 7-9.30 **Prices:** Starter £6-£8, Main £12-£24, Dessert £5-£8 **Rooms:** 208 (208 en suite) ★★★★ HL

BRIGHTON Continued

⚬ The Saint Restaurant

French, Mediterranean NEW

Bistro-style venue using quality local organic produce

☎ 01273 607835 22 St James St BN2 1RF

e-mail: info@thesaintrestaurant.co.uk

web: www.thesaintrestaurant.co.uk

Located in the heart of Kemptown, The Saint is a simple, relaxed, fun local restaurant with a real bustle when full. Darkwood tables, stripped floorboards and mood spotlighting lend a romantic edge, while service from a youthful team is attentive and friendly. The kitchen deals in simple, well-presented, classically-inspired, modern bistro-style fare, delivered by value, daily-changing, fixed-price menus. Passionate about using quality local organic produce, they also use a forager for their wild herbs and mushrooms, while fish comes daily from Newhaven. Expect Dungeness diver-caught scallops with celeriac purée and saffron vinaigrette, or roast loin of local venison with brandied prunes.

Chef: David Phillips, Gianfranco Zitoli **Owners:** Alexander Cadogan
Times: 12-2.30/6-9.30, Closed 25, 26 Dec, 1 Jan, Mon **Prices:** Fixed L £11.95,
Fixed D £18.95-£26.95, Service added but optional 12.5% **Wine:** 34 bottles
over £20, 12 bottles under £20, 4 by the glass **Notes:** Gastronomic nights every
3 months **Seats:** 40 **Children:** Portions **Parking:** On street or nearby NCP

⚬ Sevendials

Modern European

Former bank transformed into a stylish restaurant offering modern cuisine

☎ 01273 885555 1-3 Buckingham Place BN1 3TD

e-mail: info@sevendialsrestaurant.co.uk

web: www.sevendialsrestaurant.co.uk

This former bank is built in a triangular shape dictated by roads running either side of the town's busy Seven Dials junction. It is now a stylish contemporary restaurant with high ceilings featuring deep cornicing and beige walls punctuated by dark-stained wood window surrounds. Darkwood tables, modern art and a buzzy atmosphere contribute to a clubby feel. Its simple, modern brasserie-style European cookery suits the surroundings and deals in top-notch ingredients and flavour-packed, imaginative dishes. Take chargrilled rump of lamb with sunblushed tomato polenta and pot-au-feu of baby vegetables, or perhaps a classic vanilla crème brûlée finish. A fair-weather decked terrace completes the upbeat act.

Chef: Sam Metcalfe **Owners:** Sam Metcalfe **Times:** 12-3/7-10.30, Closed
25-29 Dec, Closed D Sun **Prices:** Fixed L £10-£12.50, Starter £5-£10, Main
£10-£20, Dessert £5-£8, Service added but optional 12% **Wine:** 23 bottles
over £20, 11 bottles under £20, 6 by the glass **Notes:** Civ Wed 80
Seats: 55, Pr/dining room 20 **Children:** Menu, Portions
Directions: From Brighton station turn right 0.5m up hill, restaurant
situated at Seven Dials rdbt **Parking:** 2

⚬⚬ Terre à Terre

Modern Vegetarian V 🖥

Vegetarian cooking with a unique interpretation

☎ 01273 729051 71 East St BN1 1HQ

e-mail: mail@terreaterre.co.uk

web: www.terreaterre.co.uk

An oasis in Brighton's hectic centre, the small, shop-fronted Terre à Terre stands out for its unswerving devotion to vegetarian cooking. The long, slim space is constantly filled, though the rear-covered terrace adds a warm-weather option. Pastel walls, close-knit tables and wooden floors create a modern, clean-cut vibe, while the food almost defies description. Nothing is straightforward, and the kitchen's verve and imagination can be breathtaking, with quirky descriptions and the use of a myriad of interesting ingredients assembled with skill. Take 'miso pretty', a sweet ginger sushi reversed roll in Szechuan chilli flakes served with roasted yellow pepper and white miso dressing, soused enoki mushrooms, lime and tamari ketchup, cashew and coriander salad gazpacho with hot and sour soup and dry miso powder. Slick, knowledgeable service and clever presentation catch the eye too.

Chef: Glen Lester **Owners:** Ms A Powley & Mr P Taylor **Times:** 12/10.30,
Closed 24-26 Dec, 1 Jan, Mon **Prices:** Fixed D £29.95, Starter £5.70-£8,
Main £13.10-£13.95, Dessert £6.75-£7.50, Service optional, Group min 6
service 10% **Wine:** 24 bottles over £20, 14 bottles under £20, 13 by the
glass **Notes:** Vegetarian menu, Air con **Seats:** 110 **Children:** Menu,
Portions **Directions:** Town centre near casino, close to Palace Pier & The
Lanes **Parking:** NCP, on street

see advert opposite

📖 Fringe

☎ 01273 623683   10 Kensington Gardens BN1 4AL

web: www.theaa.com/travel/index.jsp

Café and bar with simple, rustic food, make-your-own cocktails, live DJ music. Breakfasts served too.

📖 Leonardo Restaurant

☎ 01273 328888   55 Church Rd, Hove BN3 2BD

web: www.theaa.com/travel/index.jsp

A welcoming, exuberant place with a great atmosphere. The menu is Italian all the way, with a combination of old favourites and new inventions.

Regency Restaurant

☎ 01273 325014   131 Kings Rd BN1 2HH

Classic seafood restaurant dating back to the 1930s.

EASTBOURNE   MAP 06 TV69

◉◉ Grand Hotel (Mirabelle)

Modern, Classic 📖

Seaside grandee serving sophisticated cuisine

☎ 01323 412345 & 435066   King Edward's Pde BN21 4EQ

e-mail: reservations@grandeastbourne.com

web: www.grandeastbourne.com

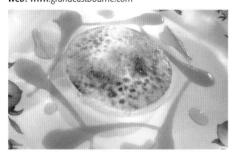

This celebrated Victorian hotel veteran of the Eastbourne seafront successfully integrates late 19th-century charm and grandeur with modern comforts. Tastefully restored to its former glory, it's a suitably palatial venue that comes complete with spacious lounges, a luxurious health club, and a Grand Hall, where afternoon tea is served amid marble-columned splendour. Mirabelle is the light-and-airy fine-dining restaurant, offering a choice of set menus alongside a seven-course tasting selection for those who really want to do the place justice. Dishes are mostly modern European, with British and international influences. A starter of seared scallops with smoked salmon and avocado ice cream, or a main course of fillet steak topped with lobster ravioli and glazed asparagus tips show the style.

Grand Hotel (Mirabelle)

Chef: Keith Mitchell, Gerald Roser   **Owners:** Elite Hotels   **Times:** 12.30-2/7-10, Closed 1-14 Jan, Sun-Mon   **Prices:** Fixed L £17.50, Fixed D £36.50-£44, Starter £7.50-£16, Main £23-£36, Dessert £7.50, Service added but optional 10%   **Wine:** 360 bottles over £20, 35 bottles under £20, 14 by the glass   **Notes:** Tasting menu 6 courses £55 (incl coffee & petits fours), Dress Restrictions, Jacket or tie for D, Civ Wed 200, Air con   **Seats:** 50   **Children:** Min 12 yrs   **Rooms:** 152 (152 en suite) ★★★★★ HL   **Directions:** Western end of the seafront, 1m from Eastbourne station   **Parking:** 50

FOREST ROW　　　　MAP 06 TQ43

◉◉ Anderida Restaurant

Modern, Traditional British, European 🖥

Grand hotel dining in a country-house setting

☎ 01342 824988 Ashdown Park Hotel, Wych Cross RH18 5JR

e-mail: reservations@ashdownpark.com
web: www.ashdownpark.com

This impressive Victorian country house, set amid 180 acres of landscaped gardens and parkland, boasts an extensive range of facilities including a cocktail bar and 18-hole golf course. Reached via a long corridor, the restaurant is a grand and formal affair, enjoying stunning views over the lake and grounds. Professional, friendly staff put their silver service skills to good use, with cloches used for main courses, and soups served from tureens. Traditional dishes like Chateaubriand and Dover sole are carved and filleted respectively at the table. The menu is firmly rooted in classical dishes with traditional accompaniments, with the occasional foray into something more adventurous, such as seared scallops with aubergine ravioli, or quail and foie gras with orange-crushed potatoes and cauliflower purée.

Chef: Graeme Campbell **Owners:** Elite Hotels **Times:** 12-2/7-10
Prices: Fixed L £17, Fixed D £35, Service added 10% **Wine:** 334 bottles over £20, 14 bottles under £20, 16 by the glass **Notes:** ALC 3 courses £47, Sun L £25, Dress Restrictions, Jacket and tie for gentlemen after 7pm, Civ Wed 150 **Seats:** 120, Pr/dining room 160 **Children:** Menu, Portions
Rooms: 106 (106 en suite)★★★★ HL **Directions:** A22 towards Eastbourne, pass through Forest Row, continue on A22 for 2m. At Wych Cross turn left, hotel 0.75m on right **Parking:** 120

HASTINGS & ST LEONARDS MAP 07 TQ80

St Clement's

☎ 01424 200355 3 Mercatoria TN38 0EB

Seasonal produce served in a relaxed atmosphere.

HERSTMONCEUX　　　MAP 06 TQ61

◉ Sundial Restaurant

French

Pretty cottage setting for classic French cuisine

☎ 01323 832217   BN27 4LA
e-mail: sundialrestaurant@hotmail.com
web: www.sundialrestaurant.co.uk

Located on the village high street, this charming red-brick country cottage combines ancient oak beams and Tudor-style windows with a modern décor, well appointed tables, and fine napery, china, silver and glassware. The unreservedly classic French cooking features seasonal delicacies like pheasant, partridge, guinea fowl and venison, as well as fresh fish from nearby Rye and Hastings. Diners can choose between the carte, monthly and seasonal fixed-price menus, and the chef's Menu Dégustation. Take warm lobster with a crispy vegetable roll and light tarragon cream sauce to start, followed by pan-fried fillet of beef with confit shallot Tatin. Chocolate-lovers may not be able to resist the 'all chocolate dégustation' for dessert.

Chef: Vincent Rongier **Owners:** Mr & Mrs V & M Rongier **Times:** 12-2/7-10, Closed Mon, Closed D Sun **Prices:** Fixed L £18.50-£27.50, Fixed D £22-£35, Starter £8.50-£19.75, Main £17.75-£19.95, Dessert £5.55-£10.75, Service added but optional 10% **Wine:** 150 bottles over £20, 12 bottles under £20, 4 by the glass **Notes:** Menu dégustation 5 courses £45, Dress Restrictions, Smart casual preferred **Seats:** 50, Pr/dining room 22 **Children:** Portions
Directions: In village centre, on A271, between Bexhill & Hailsham
Parking: 16

JEVINGTON　　　　　MAP 06 TQ50

◉ Hungry Monk Restaurant

British, French

Charming, long-established 14th-century cottage restaurant

☎ 01323 482178   BN26 5QF
web: www.hungrymonk.co.uk

This 14th-century flint house was once a monastic retreat, and original oak beams and log fires continue to set a traditional tone in antique-furnished lounges and the intimate, candlelit dining room.

Accomplished, classic French country cooking draws on wider European influences to offer quality ingredients - presented without unnecessary fuss - on daily fixed-price menus. Expect a rack of lamb, perhaps served with celeriac and parsnip mash, and redcurrant and rosemary jus, and, as this is reputedly where the ubiquitous banoffee pie was invented, there's only one way to finish.

Hungry Monk Restaurant

Chef: Gary Fisher, Matt Comben **Owners:** Mr & Mrs N Mackenzie
Times: 12-2/6.45-9.45, Closed 24-26 Dec, BHs, Closed L Mon-Sat
Prices: Fixed L £29.95, Fixed D £32.95, Group min 7 service 12.5%
Wine: 101 bottles over £20, 43 bottles under £20, 9 by the glass
Notes: Fixed L 3 courses, Air con **Seats:** 38, Pr/dining room 16
Children: Min 4 yrs, Portions **Directions:** A22, turn towards Wammock at Polegate x-rds. Continue for 2.5m, restaurant on right **Parking:** 14

LEWES   MAP 06 TQ41

◉ Circa

Modern International 🖥

Dazzling dining in contemporary setting

☎ 01273 471333 & 471345 Pelham House,
St Andrews Ln BN7 1UW
e-mail: eat@circacirca.com
web: www.circacirca.com

Situated on the ground floor of the Pelham House Hotel, this trendy restaurant has a light, bright interior decorated in the art deco style. Wooden floors, wicker and leather chairs, bold artwork and simply clothed tables set the scene for some exuberant dining. Clipboard carte menus include a vibrant selection of dishes from around the world, with those highlighted in bold print available as a two-course set-price affair. Presentation lives up to vivacious descriptions; think grilled duck breast with braised mung beans, palm peanut jus and goma honey, and to finish, perhaps baked yogurt cake with fruit mint salad and rosewater syrup.

Chef: Marc Bolger **Owners:** Ashley Renton, Marc Bolger **Times:** 12-2.30/6.30-9, Closed Xmas **Prices:** Fixed L £14.50, Starter £4.50-£9.20, Main £11.95-£17.95, Dessert £6, Service added but optional 10% **Wine:** 23 bottles over £20, 7 bottles under £20, 9 by the glass **Notes:** Fixed L 2 courses, Civ Wed 100 **Seats:** 50, Pr/dining room 180 **Children:** Menu, Portions **Parking:** 16

◉◉ *The Shelleys*

Modern British

Elegant market town hotel dining

☎ 01273 472361 High St BN7 1XS
e-mail: info@shelleys-hotel-lewes.com
web: www.shelleys-hotel.com

The classically proportioned exterior of this elegant 16th-century hotel is echoed within, with public rooms graced by beautiful chandeliers and fine oil paintings. It takes its name from the poet Shelley whose family once lived here. The airy, spacious dining room is romantically candlelit and overlooks a peaceful private garden. A confident kitchen sources quality Sussex ingredients, producing simply-presented yet appealing dishes that are listed on a modern British menu that takes influences from across Europe. Examples are Sussex crab and melon salad with coriander mayonnaise, and roast breast of guinea fowl with chestnuts and pancetta. Service is professional and friendly and not at all stuffy. As we went to press we understand that a change of ownership was taking place. Please visit www.theAA.com for further details.

Times: 12-2.15/7-9.15 **Rooms:** 19 (19 en suite) **Directions:** From Brighton take A27 towards Eastbourne. Follow signs for Lewes town centre

NEWICK

MAP 06 TQ42

◎◎ Newick Park Hotel & Country Estate

Modern European

Accomplished cooking in elegant country house

☎ 01825 723633   BN8 4SB

e-mail: bookings@newickpark.co.uk

web: www.newickpark.co.uk

This delightful Georgian mansion - set in over 200 acres of landscaped gardens and parkland - offers a quintessential country-house experience. Interiors are grand, with tasteful fabrics and genteel colours, while open fires cosset in winter and a terrace beckons in summer. Floor-to-ceiling windows, high ceilings, bright summery colours, striking flower displays and artwork grace the elegant restaurant, while the kitchen makes admirable use of quality fresh local ingredients, including produce from its own organic kitchen garden. The cooking impresses with its highly accomplished execution, modern approach and interpretations of classics. Think roasted turbot teamed with saffron gnocchi, braised pancetta, leeks and a crab bisque, or perhaps roast Newick Park pheasant with pommes fondant, chestnut chartreuse and meat juices.

Chef: Chris Moore **Owners:** Michael & Virginia Childs **Times:** 12-2.30/7-9, Closed New Year **Prices:** Fixed L £16.50, Fixed D £38.50, Service optional **Wine:** 85 bottles over £20, 25 bottles under £20, 6 by the glass **Notes:** Civ Wed 120 **Seats:** 40, Pr/dining room 74 **Children:** Menu, Portions **Rooms:** 16 (16 en suite)★★★ HL **Directions:** From village green on A272, turn right into Church Ln. Continue along lane for 1m, past pubs and garage to T-junct. Turn left and continue to entrance on right **Parking:** 100

◎◎ Two Seven Two

Modern European

Sophisticated cooking in stylish surroundings

☎ 01825 721272   20/22 High St BN8 4LQ

e-mail: twoseventwo@hotmail.co.uk

web: www.272restaurant.co.uk

This former whitewashed village hardware store on the A272 (hence the name) has been transformed into a stylish modern restaurant, with a simple cream and beige colour scheme. Polished light-oak flooring, painted brickwork, pine tables and hand-made, high-backed Italian chairs make a smart impression. Appealing, fixed-price menus offer good value and complement the more serious modern European carte. Top-notch ingredients and stylish presentation showcase the highly-accomplished, sophisticated cooking; take pan-seared brill with vanilla mash, poached baby gems and a red wine and thyme sauce, and perhaps a raspberry and honeycomb parfait finish, served with lemon crisps and raspberry coulis. Service is relaxed, informal and friendly and suits this upbeat act.

Chef: Neil Bennett **Owners:** Simon Maltby **Times:** 12-2.30/7-9.30, Closed 25-26 Dec, 1-2 Jan, Mon, Closed L Tue, D Sun **Prices:** Fixed L £10.50, Fixed D £19.95, Starter £4.95-£7.95, Main £12.95-£21.50, Dessert £4.50-£6.95, Group min 8 service 10% **Wine:** 52 bottles over £20, 35 bottles under £20, 6 by the glass **Notes:** Sun L 3 courses £19.95, Air con **Seats:** 60 **Children:** Portions **Directions:** On A272, 7m E of Haywards Heath and 7m N of Lewes **Parking:** 10

RYE

MAP 07 TQ92

◎ Mermaid Inn

Traditional French V

Local legend with a traditional menu

☎ 01797 223065 & 223788   Mermaid St TN31 7EY

e-mail: info@mermaidinn.com

web: www.mermaidinn.com

Tucked away down a cobbled side street, the Mermaid is one of England's oldest and loveliest inns and numbers everyone from Queen Elizabeth I to Johnny Depp among former guests. Also once a popular haunt for smugglers, uneven floors, creaky staircases and a heavily timbered ceiling are testament to its advanced age, and are teamed with open fires and comfy sofas. The panelled restaurant is an airy room with graciously appointed tables; take your seat for a menu of traditional fare such as smoked chicken and asparagus consommé, followed by grilled Dover sole with parsley and lemon butter, or rack of lamb with aubergine caviar, Lyonnaise potatoes and rosemary jus. Vegetarian menu also available.

Chef: Robert Malyon **Owners:** Mrs J Blincow & Mr R I Pinwill **Times:** 12-2.30/7-9.30 **Prices:** Fixed L £19, Fixed D £38.50, Starter £6.50-£10.50, Main £17.50-£31, Dessert £7, Service added but optional 10% **Wine:** 35 bottles over £20, 21 bottles under £20, 14 by the glass **Notes:** Fixed D 4 courses, Sun L 2 courses £19.50, 3 courses £24, Vegetarian menu, Dress Restrictions, Smart casual, no jeans or T-shirts **Seats:** 64, Pr/dining room 12 **Children:** Menu, Portions **Rooms:** 31 (31 en suite) ★★★ HL **Directions:** Rye is situated on A259 between Ashford and Hastings **Parking:** 26

◉ Webbes at The Fish Café

Modern British

Fish and seafood restaurant in an amiable setting

☎ 01797 222226 & 222210 17 Tower St TN31 7AT
e-mail: info@thefishcafe.com
web: www.thefishcafe.com

This former toy factory has been tastefully restored with modishly minimal interiors while retaining many of the old warehouse-style features of the original building - the exposed brickwork and high ceilings in particular. The restaurant is laid out over three floors: a café-style ground floor, a more formal first floor for dinner, and a private function room on the second floor. The kitchen takes an appealing modern approach using fresh local seafood; steamed flounder served with mussel, cider and mustard sauce, or perhaps pan-fried Rye Bay scallops with caramelised onion, a chive vermouth sauce and pancetta show the style.

Chef: Paul Webbe **Owners:** Paul & Rebecca Webbe **Times:** 6-9.30, Closed 25-26 Dec, 2-11 Jan, Mon, Closed L all week, D Sun **Prices:** Starter £5-£9, Main £11-£20, Dessert £5-£6, Service optional **Wine:** 6 by the glass **Seats:** 52, Pr/dining room 70 **Children:** Menu, Portions **Directions:** 100mtrs before Landgale Arch **Parking:** Cinque Port Street

Landgate Bistro

☎ 01797 222829 5-6 Landgate TN31 7LH
web: www.landgatebistro.co.uk

Bustling bistro with varied menu.

TICEHURST   MAP 06 TQ63

◉ Dale Hill Hotel & Golf Club

Modern European

Formal dining in modern golfing hotel

☎ 01580 200112 TN5 7DQ
e-mail: info@dalehill.co.uk
web: www.dalehill.co.uk

Views from the formal Wealden restaurant at this smart, modern golfing hotel take in the 18th green and the broad expanse of the Kentish Weald. The hotel has two golf courses, a swimming pool and

gym, a conservatory brasserie and the Spike Bar. The kitchen offers an interesting range of modern dishes on an extensive carte or a three-course fixed-price menu. Begin with smoked ham hock terrine, move on to confit duck leg with braised root vegetables, or seared tuna loin with basil broth, and finish with warm plum and almond tart.

Times: 12-2.30/6.30-9, Closed L Mon-Sat **Rooms:** 35 (35 en suite) ★★★★ HL **Directions:** At junction of A21 & B2087 follow signs for Ticehurst & Flimwell; Dale Hill is 1m on left

---

UCKFIELD   MAP 06 TQ42

◉◉ The Dining Room

Modern, Traditional

Masterful cooking in classical surroundings

☎ 01825 733333 Buxted Park Hotel, Buxted Park, Buxted TN22 4AY
e-mail: buxtedpark@handpicked.co.uk
web: www.handpicked.co.uk

A prime ministerial home and a playground for Hollywood stars, in its time, this impressive Palladian mansion is set in 300 acres of beautiful parkland and formal gardens. The restaurant, located in the original Victorian orangery, retains many original features but still feels modern and bright. It's a stylish and relaxing place in which to dine, with views over the gardens. Accomplished modern British and European cuisine blends classic and modern ideas and is based around top-quality ingredients. Examples from the wide range include Sussex crab with cucumber jelly, followed by rack of Sussex lamb with Niçoise vegetables and garlic potatoes, and iced nougatine parfait with apricot coulis and pink grapefruit compôte for dessert.

Chef: Mark Murphy **Owners:** Hand Picked Hotels **Times:** 12-2/7-9.30 **Prices:** Fixed L £12.95, Fixed D £28-£38, Starter £5-£9, Main £19-£28, Dessert £8-£8.50, Service optional **Wine:** 118 bottles over £20, 3 bottles under £20, 10 by the glass **Notes:** Tasting menu £48, Sun L £22.50, Vegetarian available, Dress Restrictions, Smart casual, Civ Wed 130, Air con **Seats:** 40, Pr/dining room 120 **Children:** Menu, Portions **Rooms:** 44 (44 en suite) ★★★★ HL **Directions:** Turn off A22 Uckfield bypass (London-Eastbourne road), then take A272 to Buxted. Cross lights, entrance to hotel 1m on right **Parking:** 100

◉◉ Horsted Place

Modern British

Opulent country-house restaurant, formal but friendly

☎ 01825 750581 Little Horsted TN22 5TS
e-mail: hotel@horstedplace.co.uk
web: www.horstedplace.co.uk

Built in 1850, the house has interiors designed by Augustus Pugin, and is set in its own 1,100-acre estate. It celebrated its 20th anniversary as a country-house hotel in 2006, and the elegant, traditional restaurant was tastefully redesigned to mark the occasion. The kitchen's modern approach produces plenty of interest in generously proportioned dishes; take medallions of local organic veal served with spätzle noodles and girolle mushrooms, or perhaps halibut with a herb and brioche crust and vermouth sauce. A Kirsch and vanilla pannacotta might provide the finish, served on a compôte of English strawberries.

Chef: Allan Garth **Owners:** Perinon Ltd **Times:** 12-2/7-9.30, Closed L Sat **Prices:** Fixed L £15.95, Starter £8.50, Main £19.50, Dessert £8, Service optional **Wine:** 120 bottles over £20, 8 bottles under £20, 8 by the glass **Notes:** Dress Restrictions, No jeans, Civ Wed 100 **Seats:** 40, Pr/dining room 80 **Children:** Min 7 yrs, Portions **Rooms:** 20 (20 en suite) ★★★ HL **Directions:** 2m S on A26 towards Lewes **Parking:** 50

ENGLAND

WESTFIELD   MAP 07 TQ81

◉ The Wild Mushroom Restaurant
Modern British
Cosy dining in a converted farmhouse

☎ 01424 751137   Woodgate House, Westfield Ln
TN35 4SB
e-mail: info@wildmushroom.co.uk
web: www.wildmushroom.co.uk

This converted Victorian farmhouse has a lovely garden - you can enjoy pre-dinner drinks here or in the bar - before moving through to the intimate L-shaped restaurant. White linen-dressed tables, mint green chairs and ornaments on the mushroom theme create a relaxed, homely atmosphere. Service may be formal here, but fittingly relaxed and welcoming. The kitchen's modern approach makes sound use of quality local produce in accomplished, well-presented dishes. Take wood pigeon with bubble-and-squeak, pancetta and a Madeira jus, or perhaps a glazed passionfruit mousse with grenadine sorbet. (Sister to Webbes at The Fish Café, Rye, see entry.)

Chef: Paul Webbe/Matthew Drinkwater   **Owners:** Mr & Mrs P Webbe
Times: 12-2.30/7-10, Closed 25 Dec, 2 wks at New Year, Mon, Closed L Sat, D Sun   **Prices:** Fixed L £15.95, Starter £5.50-£9, Main £12-£20, Dessert £6.50, Service optional   **Notes:** Tasting menu 6 courses £32, Sun L 3 courses £20, Dress Restrictions, Smart casual   **Seats:** 40
Children: Portions   **Directions:** From A21 towards Hastings, turn left onto A28 to Westfield. Restaurant 1.5m on left   **Parking:** 20

WILMINGTON   MAP 06 TQ50

◉◉ Crossways
Modern British
Small country house with a focus on food

☎ 01323 482455   BN26 5SG
e-mail: stay@crosswayshotel.co.uk
web: www.crosswayshotel.co.uk

Set amid well-kept gardens in the heart of the Cuckmere Valley, this Georgian country house was once the home of Elizabeth David's parents. A friendly and relaxed atmosphere is assured by the proprietors and the restaurant is very much the focus of the hotel. Food is prepared with love and affection from fresh ingredients, local where possible. Dishes are offered from a set monthly menu, perhaps red onion and parmesan tart or seafood pancake for starters, and main courses like game pie and crispy pork belly with sesame, soy and ginger sauce. Ice creams, sorbets and petits fours are all home made, as are the puddings.

Chef: David Stott   **Owners:** David Stott, Clive James   **Times:** 7.30-8.30, Closed 24 Dec-24 Jan, Sun-Mon, Closed L all week   **Prices:** Fixed D £35.95, Service optional   **Wine:** 18 bottles over £20, 25 bottles under £20, 10 by the glass   **Notes:** Fixed D 4 courses   **Seats:** 24   **Children:** Min 12 yrs
Rooms: 7 (7 en suite) ★★★★ RR   **Directions:** On A27, 2m W of Polegate   **Parking:** 20

SUSSEX, WEST

AMBERLEY   MAP 06 TQ01

◉◉◉ Queens Room at Amberley Castle
see opposite

ARUNDEL   MAP 06 TQ00

◉ Arundel House Restaurant and Rooms
Modern European NEW
Well-balanced menu and flavours in high street restaurant with rooms

☎ 01903 882136   11 High St BN18 9AD
web: www.arundelhouseonline.co.uk

Behind the handsome Georgian façade of this high-street restaurant with rooms you will find a smart modern interior, subtly lit and tastefully appointed in shades of red and beige. The ground-floor restaurant delivers an assured and varied menu of modern dishes, including old friends such as chicken Caesar salad, as well as more involved mains: venison with sprout and ham hock bubble-and-squeak, for example, or rack of lamb with buttered leeks, champ and nutmeg-scented sauce. Combinations are well judged and the presentation simple, yet stylish, with desserts particularly easy on the eye. Choose an aperitif from the range of champagne cocktails and you're in for a treat.

Chef: Luke Hackman, Claire Small   **Owners:** Billy Lewis-Bowker, Luke Hackman   **Times:** 12.30-2/7-9.30, Closed 2 wks Feb, 2 wks Oct, 24-26 Dec, Sun, Closed L Mon   **Prices:** Fixed L £16, Fixed D £22-£28, Starter £6, Main £10-£16, Dessert £6, Service optional, Group min 9 service 10%   **Wine:** 80 bottles over £20, 23 bottles under £20, 6 by the glass   **Notes:** Fixed L 3 courses, Gourmet D 8 courses £45 3rd Fri each mth, Dress Restrictions, Smart casual   **Seats:** 34   **Children:** Portions   **Directions:** On High St in town centre opposite post office

◉ The Bay Tree
British, Mediterranean NEW
Relaxed bistro-style dining

☎ 01903 883679   21 Tarrant St BN18 9DG

A 16th-century timber-framed building houses this friendly family-run restaurant in the town centre. With a stylish calming cream and pale green décor, diners can relax in the contemporary interior, or on a pretty sun-dappled terrace, while the chefs create modern British dishes with a Mediterranean or Pacific Rim twist. Successful combinations include a starter of toasted coconut-battered tiger prawns with a pineapple and sweet chilli risotto. Seasonal and local produce form the basis of more traditional dishes like chargrilled venison fillet on a parsnip and thyme rösti. Try desserts like wild strawberry and cracked black pepper samosa.

Chef: Jason Wimbleton, David Partridge, Kate Holle, Karen Bowley
Owners: Valerie & Mike Moore   **Times:** 11-3/7-9.30, Closed Mon, Closed D Sun   **Prices:** Starter £4.95-£7.95, Main £12.95-£19.95, Dessert £5.25-£5.95, Service optional   **Wine:** 10 bottles over £20, 16 bottles under £20, 6 by the glass   **Notes:** Dress Restrictions, Smart casual   **Seats:** 30
Children: Min 5yrs, Portions   **Directions:** A27 between Chichester and Worthing. Restaurant is in Tarrant St just off High St   **Parking:** On street & car park nearby - free after 6pm

Queens Room at Amberley Castle

AMBERLEY   MAP 06 TQ01

Modern European V **NEW**

Serious and complex fine dining in fairy-tale castle surroundings

☎ 01798 831992   BN18 9LT

e-mail: info@amberleycastle.co.uk

web: www.amberleycastle.co.uk

This really is the stuff of legends; dating back 900 years, Amberley sits in fabulous grounds in the lee of the South Downs. It became a romantic ruin after the Civil War and in 1893 was bought by the Duke of Norfolk who transformed it into a delightful family home, but since 1988 it has been owned by the Cummings who have turned it into today's luxury hotel.

From the impressive gatehouse and portcullis to antique rooms with high-vaulted ceilings, massive fireplaces and suits of armour, this place oozes character. The magnificent Queens Room is the principle dining room, with its 12th-century barrel-vaulted ceiling and walls adorned with coats of arms and original paintings, while tables come beautifully appointed. Service is appropriately polished and attentive, while chef James Dugan shows his pedigree and passion via a sophisticated, contemporary approach underpinned by classical roots. The classy cooking is driven by seasonal local produce, with well-conceived

dishes dressed to thrill. Take John Dory with roast vine tomatoes, sandwiched creamed potato, tomato risotto and hairy bitter cress, and to finish, perhaps baked spiced fig cake served with a lemon jelly, toasted almond foam and fig ice cream.

Chef: James Dugan **Owners:** Joy & Martin Cummings **Times:** 12-2/7-9.30 **Prices:** Fixed L £43, Fixed D £50, Service optional, Group min 10 service 10% **Wine:** 150 bottles over £20, 4 bottles under £20, 12 by the glass **Notes:** Sun L 3 courses £30, Tasting menu 7 courses, Vegetarian menu, Dress Restrictions, Smart casual, Jacket or tie, Civ Wed 55 **Seats:** 70, Pr/dining room 40 **Children:** Min 12 yrs, Portions **Rooms:** 19 (19 en suite) ★★★★ CHH **Directions:** Off B2139 between Storrington and Houghton **Parking:** 30

The Townhouse

Modern Mediterranean NEW

Precise cooking in a stunning setting

☎ 01903 883847   65 High St BN18 9AJ

e-mail: enquiries@thetownhouse.co.uk

web: www.thetownhouse.co.uk

This elegant Regency property is set across the road from the castle that dominates the town. The crowning glory of the building, the carved and gilded walnut ceiling in the restaurant, is much older, dating from the Italian Renaissance and is reputed to have come from a Medici palace. The menu is up to date and rooted in classical combinations, as in South Coast cod and scallops with cauliflower purée and spinach, or fillet of wild sea bass served with olive oil mash, and fine beans with mussel and chive velouté. Finish with a highly recommended blackcurrant gratin with vanilla ice cream, or maybe try chocolate ice cream with honeycomb and white chocolate sauce, washed down with one of the selected dessert wines.

Chef: Lee Williams **Owners:** Lee & Kate Williams **Times:** 12-2.30/7-9.30, Closed Xmas, 2 wks Jan, 2 wks Oct, Sun-Mon **Prices:** Fixed L £12.50, Fixed D £27.50, Service optional **Wine:** 29 bottles over £20, 15 bottles under £20, 4 by the glass **Notes:** Vegetarian available **Seats:** 24 **Children:** Portions **Directions:** A27 to Arundel. Follow road to High Street

---

BOSHAM   MAP 05 SU80

Millstream Hotel

Modern British

Indulgent dining in a gorgeous village setting

☎ 01243 573234   Bosham Ln PO18 8HL

e-mail: info@millstream-hotel.co.uk

web: www.millstream-hotel.co.uk

Lying in the heavenly little village of Bosham, this popular hotel lures a well-heeled sailing crowd from nearby Chichester, thanks to a picture-perfect location and accomplished cooking. At dinner, the ambitious kitchen pulls out all the stops to deliver a luxurious meal. The chef here clearly has high aspirations - the food is both imaginative and technically accomplished with quality ingredients used with care and sensitivity throughout this large menu. Try Shetland scallops with a hazelnut and coriander crust to start

CONTINUED

BOSHAM CONTINUED

followed by sea trout with almond butter, spinach and shrimp risotto.

Chef: James Fairchild-Dickson **Owners:** The Wild Family **Times:** 12.30-2/6.45-9.15 **Prices:** Fixed D £30-£36, Starter £5-£6.95, Main £10.50-£13.95, Dessert £5.50, Service optional **Wine:** 53 bottles over £20, 28 bottles under £20, 11 by the glass **Notes:** ALC available L only, Dress Restrictions, Smart casual, no jeans in the evenings, Civ Wed 92, Air con **Seats:** 60, Pr/dining room 92 **Children:** Menu, Portions **Rooms:** 35 (35 en suite) ★★★ HL **Directions:** Take A259 exit from Chichester rdbt and in village follow signs for quay **Parking:** 40

BRACKLESHAM   MAP 05 SZ89

◎ Cliffords Cottage Restaurant

French

Cosy cottage restaurant close to the sea

☎ 01243 670250 Bracklesham Ln PO20 8JA

Exposed oak beams, some of them very low, attest to the great age of this whitewashed, thatched cottage near the seafront. The small dining room is cosy and welcoming, and staff know many of the clientele by name. Fish features on the menu as you might expect given the location, but there is ample meat and game too, perhaps in the form of pan-fried breast of guinea fowl with red wine jus, or roast sirloin with Yorkshire pudding. Puddings from the trolley are a much-loved Sunday fixture.

Times: 12.30-5/7-9.30, Closed Jan **Directions:** From A27 follow signs for The Witterings. A286 to Birdham, B2198 to Bracklesham

BURGESS HILL   MAP 06 TQ31

◎ Taylor's Restaurant

Modern French NEW

Popular town-centre restaurant serving simply great food

☎ 01444 233311 2 Church Hill, Burgess Hill RH15 9AE
e-mail: michelle@taylorsrestaurant.uk.com
web: www.taylorsrestaurant.uk.com

Set in a parade of shops near the station, this popular restaurant has simple cream décor, modern artwork and plain pine tables. Good raw ingredients are skilfully and simply prepared with European and some Asian influences. The deli board is a nice idea, you can choose a selection of nibbles, starters or tasters to share, or have a selection chosen for you. Starters and light bites feature soups, salads and dishes like creamy seafood tagliatelle with tarragon. Main courses might include slow-roasted belly of pork with red cabbage and star anise, red wine and juniper berry sauce. Taylor's also provide an outside catering service.

Chef: Frederic Bodeau **Owners:** Michelle Taylor **Times:** 12-3/6.30-10, Closed 1st week Jan, Sun, Closed L Sat, D Mon **Prices:** Fixed L £16.50, Fixed D £20.50, Starter £4.95-£6.50, Main £12-£16 **Dessert:** £4.50-£4.95 Service added 10% **Wine:** 3 bottles over £20, 15 bottles under £20, 7 by the glass **Seats:** 40 **Children:** Portions **Directions:** M3 junct 11, A23 towards Brighton. Left onto A2300 towards Burgess Hill. Take Jane Murray Way (A273) towards town centre, B2113 **Parking:** Car park 200yds

BURPHAM   MAP 06 TQ00

◎ George & Dragon

British, French

Idyllically-located old inn on the South Downs

☎ 01903 883131   BN18 9RR

Perfectly placed at the end of a lane on the South Downs, and ideal for a walk before or after dinner. Old beams, stone floors and bags of atmosphere draw a crowd, particularly at weekends, so come early for a good table. Expect honest pub grub from a kitchen that does the basics well: a salad of smoked chicken, crispy pancetta and mango to start perhaps, followed by pan-seared scallops and tiger prawns with pea and mint risotto and shellfish cream sauce, or slow-cooked lamb shank with a mint and apricot glaze and chive mash. A short carte is supplemented by a lengthy specials board, with an additional bar selection served at lunchtime.

Times: 12-2/7-9, Closed 25 Dec, Closed D Sun **Directions:** 2.5m along no-through road signed Burpham off A27, 1m E of Arundel

CHICHESTER   MAP 05 SU80

◎ Comme Ça

French

Classic French cooking in friendly restaurant

☎ 01243 788724 & 536307 67 Broyle Rd PO19 6BD
e-mail: comme.ca@commeca.co.uk
web: www.commeca.co.uk

A long-established French eatery on the fringe of Chichester. Inside, there's a mix of Victorian and Edwardian prints with objets d'art. The simple, cosy restaurant is decorated in bright, bold colours and there is a garden room with French doors leading on to a patio and sunken garden. A lengthy carte at dinner serves up French classics at every course, mainly true to Normandy roots. The wine list naturally focuses on France, but gives space to other global labels. Expect Pyrénées pan-fried médallions of pork tenderloin with confit of smoked garlic and chive cappuccino, with pomegranate bavarois to finish. Fixed-price, pre- and post-theatre menus also available.

Chef: Michael Navet, Mark Howard **Owners:** Mr & Mrs Navet **Times:** 12-2/6-10.30, Closed Xmas week & New Year week, BHs, Mon, Closed L Tue, D Sun **Prices:** Fixed L £18.95, Starter £6.65-£8.95, Main £15.95-£18.95, Dessert £6.65 **Wine:** 60 bottles over £20, 60 bottles under £20, 7 by the glass **Notes:** Dress Restrictions, Smart casual preferred **Seats:** 100, Pr/dining room 14 **Children:** Menu, Portions **Directions:** On A286 near Festival Theatre **Parking:** 46

◎ Croucher's Country Hotel & Restaurant

Modern V

Modern cooking in bright, characterful surroundings

☎ 01243 784995 Birdham Rd PO20 7EH
e-mail: crouchers@btconnect.com
web: www.crouchersountryhotel.com

The hotel is a former farmhouse incorporating more recently built barn-style public rooms housing the restaurant and bar. Relax on leather sofas in the bar-lounge before dining in the restaurant with its high beamed ceilings. Large windows overlook the courtyard and fields, and pre-dinner drinks can be enjoyed on the terrace in summer. Modern cooking offers imaginative combinations and fresh flavours in an aesthetically pleasing starter of scallops served with asparagus, parsnip purée and shellfish cream, followed by tender rump of lamb with champ potato and rosemary jus. For dessert, take spiced poached pear served with vanilla crème brûlée and red wine sorbet, or perhaps a selection of cheeses.

Chef: G Wilson, N Markey **Owners:** Mr L van Rooyen & Mr G Wilson **Times:** 12.30-2.30/7-11, Closed 26 Dec, 1 Jan **Prices:** Fixed L £14.50, Fixed D £21.50, Starter £5.25-£9.50, Main £12.95-£19.95, Dessert £5.50, Service optional, Group min 12 service 12.5% **Wine:** 29 bottles over £20, 18 bottles under £20, 4 by the glass **Notes:** Sun L menu available, Vegetarian menu, Dress Restrictions, Smart casual **Seats:** 80, Pr/dining room 20 **Children:** Menu, Portions **Rooms:** 18 (18 en suite) ★★★ HL **Directions:** From A27, S of Chichester, take A286 to The Witterings. Hotel 2m on left **Parking:** 60

◉◉ Hallidays

Modern European

A charming traditional village restaurant serving modern cuisine

☎ 01243 575331 Funtington PO18 9LF
web: www.hallidays.info

Three flint and thatched cottages dating from the 14th century have been transformed to create this intimate two-room restaurant with a wealth of original features, and pale green and yellow décor. It is a family business offering friendly service, rewarded by plenty of local custom. Weekly-changing menus based solely on quality seasonal ingredients (locally-sourced where possible) offer a range of modern European dishes with a classical theme. Take roast rump of South Downs lamb with local broad beans and fresh morels, or perhaps a fillet of line-caught sea bass served with cider, Meaux mustard and thyme, while a Seville orange buttermilk mousse with new season's rhubarb might catch the eye at dessert.

Chef: Andrew Stephenson **Owners:** Mr A Stephenson & Mr P Creech **Times:** 12-1.45/7-9.45, Closed 2 wks Mar, 1 wk Sep, Mon-Tue, Closed L Sat, D Sun **Prices:** Fixed L £17.50, Fixed D £32, Starter £6-£8.50, Main £15-£18.50, Dessert £5.25-£6.50, Service optional **Wine:** 65 bottles over £20, 25 bottles under £20, 5 by the glass **Notes:** Sun L 3 courses £22, Dress Restrictions, No shorts **Seats:** 26 **Children:** Portions **Directions:** Telephone for directions **Parking:** 12

◉ Royal Oak Inn

Modern Mediterranean

Traditional food and buzzy atmosphere with a sophisticated twist

☎ 01243 527434 Pook Ln PO18 0AX
e-mail: enquiries@royaloaklavant.co.uk
web: www.thesussexpub.co.uk

Set in a quiet village 2 miles north of the city, this tastefully converted cottage, barn and inn is now a relaxing restaurant bar and place to stay with a smart, sophisticated edge; beams, bare brick walls, fireplaces and an intimate bar area meet leather sofas and armchairs. The restaurant continues the theme, with pine tables and tall, modern leather chairs. The crowd-pleasing menu successfully mixes tradition with Mediterranean touches, bolstered by daily blackboard specials.

Try seared scallops and tiger prawn salad with lime and shallot dressing, continue with confit duck leg with red wine and Puy lentil sauce, and finish with a classic crème brûlée.

Royal Oak Inn

Chef: Samuel Baker **Owners:** Nick & Lisa Sutherland **Times:** 12-2/6.15-9.30 **Prices:** Starter £5.25-£11.50, Main £12.50-£18.95, Dessert £3.75-£5.50, Service optional **Wine:** 19 bottles over £20, 19 bottles under £20, 12 by the glass **Seats:** 47 **Children:** Menu, Portions **Rooms:** 6 (6 en suite) ★★★★★ INN **Directions:** From Chichester take A286 towards Midhurst, 2m to mini rdbt take right, signposted East Lavant. Royal Oak on the left **Parking:** 23

◉◉ West Stoke House

Modern British, French NEW

Sophisticated but relaxed dining for creative modern cuisine

☎ 01243 575226 Downs Rd, West Stoke PO18 9BN
e-mail: info@weststokehouse.co.uk
web: www.weststokehouse.co.uk

Set on the edge of the Sussex Downs, this Georgian mansion surrounded by beautiful countryside offers sophisticated dining in a relaxed atmosphere. The décor is stylish with a classic appeal, with French antiques and contemporary artwork, while tables come turned out in their best whites. Sensibly compact, fixed-price, crisply scripted dinner menus (a tasting option is also available) are explained in detail by the professional yet friendly front-of-house team, while the kitchen's modern approach underpinned by a classical French theme utilises fresh, local and seasonal produce. Dishes come intelligently simply presented but with a wow element; take an assiette of suckling pig (loin, shoulder, faggot, trotter and rib), or roasted loin of new season lamb, fondant potato and flageolet bean purée.

Chef: Darren Brown **Owners:** Rowland & Mary Leach **Times:** 12-2/7.30-9.30, Closed Xmas, Mon-Tue, Closed D Sun **Prices:** Fixed L £12.50-£17.50, Fixed D £39, Service optional, Group min 8 service 12.5% **Wine:** 50 bottles over £20, 14 bottles under £20, 8 by the glass **Notes:** Civ Wed 60 **Seats:** 40, Pr/dining room 28 **Children:** Min 12 yrs, Portions **Rooms:** 6 (6 en suite) ★★★★★ RR **Directions:** N of Chichester leave A286 at Lavant church and continue to West Stoke **Parking:** 20

CHILGROVE MAP 05 SU81

◉◉ The Chilgrove White Horse

Modern, Traditional 🍷 NOTABLE WINE LIST 🍷

Accomplished cooking at a pretty, rural restaurant with rooms

☎ 01243 535219   PO18 9HX

e-mail: info@whitehorsechilgrove.co.uk

web: www.whitehorsechilgrove.co.uk

Located on the edge of the South Downs, this former 18th-century inn makes a pretty destination, its whitewashed walls decked with blooms of lilac wisteria. Inside there's a friendly bar and lounge with leather sofas and a crackling fire, in addition to a more formal dining area where tables are neatly clothed and set with linen napkins. There's certainly no shortage of skill in the kitchen; flavour combinations are deftly judged and organic ingredients used where possible, with mains along the lines of fillet of steamed sea bass with smoked salmon mousse, served with scallop sauce, spinach and creamed potato, or maybe Rother Valley fillet of organic beef with green peppercorn sauce on a galette potato. Tempting desserts might include raspberry soufflé. The international wine list is extensive.

Chef: Chris Richards **Owners:** Charles & Carin Burton **Times:** 12-2/7-10, Closed Mon, Closed D Sun **Prices:** Starter £5.95-£15, Main £14-£22, Dessert £6.95, Service added 10% **Wine:** 70 bottles over £20, 6 bottles under £20, 6 by the glass **Notes:** Sun L available, Dress Restrictions, Smart casual, Air con **Seats:** 60, Pr/dining room 14 **Children:** Portions **Rooms:** 9 (9 en suite) ✦✦✦✦ RR **Directions:** 7m N of Chichester on B2141. W of A286 onto B2141at Lavant restaurant 4m on right **Parking:** 60

CLIMPING MAP 06 SU90

◉◉ Bailiffscourt Hotel & Spa

Modern British

A fascinating architectural folly offering creative modern cooking

☎ 01903 723511   BN17 5RW

e-mail: bailiffscourt@hshotels.co.uk

web: www.hshotels.co.uk

Set in 30 acres of parkland with moats and small streams, this architectural gem was built in 1927 by Lord Moyne in the style of an authentic medieval manor house, using reclaimed stone and woodwork gathered from across England. Gothic-style mullioned windows overlook the rose-clad courtyard, while narrow passageways lead you through a series of intimate lounges and sitting rooms, many of which feature open fires and fine antiques. The restaurant, with its heavy wooden ceiling, stone window frames with leaded lights, and walls adorned with rich tapestries, continues the medieval illusion. The cooking style, however, is definitely in the present, concentrating on simple flavours and straightforward cuisine with French and Italian influences. Starters might include crisply-baked Crottin goat's cheese with tomato and pepper coulis, while main courses range from roasted sea bass with fondant potato, black olive tapenade, bok choy and scallop velouté, to grilled fillet of beef with creamed celeriac, horseradish and red wine and shallot sauce.

Bailiffscourt Hotel & Spa

Chef: Russell Williams **Owners:** Pontus & Miranda Carminger **Times:** 12-1.30/7-9.30 **Prices:** Fixed L £11.50, Fixed D £45.50-£57.50, Service optional **Wine:** 150+ bottles over £20, 6 bottles under £20, 12 by the glass **Notes:** Dress Restrictions, Smart casual, no jeans or T-shirts, Civ Wed 60 **Seats:** 70, Pr/dining room 70 **Children:** Menu, Portions **Rooms:** 39 (39 en suite) ★★★ HL **Directions:** From A27 (Arundel), take A284 towards Littlehampton. Continue to the A259, Bailiffscourt is signed towards Climping Beach **Parking:** 60

COPTHORNE For restaurant details
See Gatwick Airport (London), (Sussex, West)

CRAWLEY For restaurant details
See Gatwick Airport (London), (Sussex, West)

CUCKFIELD MAP 06 TQ32

◉◉◉ Ockenden Manor

see opposite

EAST GRINSTEAD MAP 06 TQ33

◉◉◉ Gravetye Manor Hotel

see opposite

Ockenden Manor

CUCKFIELD MAP 06 TQ32

Modern French V ⚫ NOTABLE WINE LIST

Creative cuisine in an elegant manor

☎ 01444 416111 Ockenden Ln RH17 5LD

e-mail: reservations@ockenden-manor.com

web: www.hshotels.co.uk

You may feel you're stepping back in time when you arrive at this Elizabethan manor house set in a Tudor village. Walking through the magnificent gardens it's easy to imagine what it would have been like to live here in days gone by, and as a guest you're welcomed like an old friend. The wood-panelled restaurant with stained-glass windows and ornate painted ceiling provides a formal setting for dinner. Rich red and yellow décor and a warming log fire create a relaxing and intimate environment. Be prepared for a tempting choice of dishes from the carte, making great use of local produce, or opt for the full gastronomic experience with the seven-course tasting menu, or the vegetarian menu. Whichever menu you choose from, you'll find expertly cooked dishes with a distinct French influence and top-quality ingredients. Try a starter like braised oxtail with truffled polenta, root vegetables and parsnip crisps, followed by a main course of roast brill with Savoy cabbage, smoked salmon and horseradish velouté. Home-made ice cream is a speciality and the wine list is extensive.

Chef: Mr Steve Crane **Owners:** The Goodman & Carminger Family **Times:** 12-2/7-9 **Prices:** Fixed L £13.95-£15.95, Main £47.50, Service optional, Group min 10 service 10% **Wine:** 197 bottles over £20, 17 bottles under £20, 11 by the glass **Notes:** ALC fixed price, Tasting menu £65, Sun L £28.95, Vegetarian menu, Dress Restrictions, No jeans, Civ Wed 74 **Seats:** 40, Pr/dining room 75 **Rooms:** 22 (22 en suite)★★★ HL **Directions:** Village centre **Parking:** 45

Gravetye Manor Hotel

EAST GRINSTEAD MAP 06 TQ33

Modern British

Fabulous country-house hotel with historic gardens and memorable cuisine

☎ 01342 810567   RH19 4LJ

e-mail: info@gravetyemanor.co.uk

web: www.gravetyemanor.co.uk

No visit to Gravetye Manor would be complete without exploring some of the 30 acres of garden created by Victorian William Robinson as the Natural English Garden. Robinson also restored the house, which became a hotel in 1958. The current owners continue the custodianship of house and gardens and the tradition of country-house hospitality with care and affection. The traditional oak-panelled restaurant has a carved white ceiling and winter log fires. Chef Mark Raffan has his culinary roots in classical French cuisine from his time with the Roux brothers, plus a stint as personal chef to the late King Hussein of Jordan. This background and his considerable experience here at Gravetye ensure an interesting and eclectic menu of broadly modern English cuisine delivered with high skill and top-class local ingredients - with fruit and vegetables coming from the hotel's kitchen garden. Typical dishes include roast fillet of West Coast turbot served with braised oxtail, parsnip purée and cockles marinière, or perhaps

braised cheek of veal with roasted sweetbreads, a cassoulet of beans with pancetta, braising juices and sage butter.

Chef: Mark Raffan **Owners:** A Russell & M Raffan **Times:** 12.30-1.45/7-9.30, Closed D 25 Dec (ex residents) **Prices:** Fixed L £19-£22, Fixed D £34, Starter £12, Main £28, Dessert £9, Service added but optional 12.5% **Wine:** 500 bottles over £20, 15 bottles under £20, 25 by the glass **Notes:** Sun L £35, Dress Restrictions, Jacket & tie preferred, Civ Wed 45 **Seats:** 50, Pr/dining room 20 **Children:** Min 7 yrs, Portions **Rooms:** 18 (18 en suite)★★★ HL **Directions:** From M23 junct 10 take A264 towards East Grinstead. After 2m take B2028. After Turners Hill, follow signs **Parking:** 45

ENGLAND

GATWICK AIRPORT (LONDON)
MAP 06 TQ24

⊚⊚ Langshott Manor

Modern British
Fine dining in elegant Elizabethan manor house

☎ 01293 786680 Langshott Ln, Horley RH6 9LN
e-mail: admin@langshottmanor.com
web: www.langshottmanor.com

Ideally located for Gatwick Airport, this charming timber-framed manor house, dating back to 1580, sits in 3 acres of beautiful mature grounds complete with a pond. The Mulberry restaurant retains many original features such as the leaded windows overlooking the gardens, complemented by discreetly modern décor. This is serious, impressive cooking, firmly in the modern British camp with a keen eye on quality, seasonal ingredients and some bold flavour combinations throughout the menu. You might expect sauté rabbit saddle with cured foie gras and roast melon to start, followed by roast hake with hazelnut praline, sour cream and spring onions, and to finish, smoked Valrhona chocolate with tangerine caviar and vanilla ice cream. Alfresco dining available in the warmer months.

Chef: David Lennox **Owners:** Peter & Deborah Hinchcliffe **Times:** 12-2.30/7-9.30 **Prices:** Fixed L £15, Fixed D £40, Service added 12.5%, Group service 12.5% **Wine:** 80 bottles over £20, 4 bottles under £20, 11 by the glass **Notes:** Tasting menu £55, Sun L £25, Vegetarian available, Dress Restrictions, No Jeans, jacket and tie, Civ Wed 60 **Seats:** 55, Pr/dining room 22 **Children:** Min 12 yrs, Portions **Rooms:** 22 (22 en suite)★★★ CHH **Directions:** From A23, Horley, take Ladbroke Rd turning off Chequers Hotel rdbt, 0.75m on right **Parking:** 25

⊚⊚ The Old House Restaurant

Modern British
Fine dining in comfortable, traditional surroundings

☎ 01342 712222 Effingham Rd, Copthorne RH10 3JB
e-mail: info@oldhouserestaurant.co.uk
web: www.oldhouserestaurant.co.uk

A converted 16th-century house is the venue for this homely restaurant, which is bright and sunny with plenty of charm. The décor is Tudor-style, with white walls, black painted beams, diamond-leaded windows and an inglenook fireplace. The dining room is suitably grand, in gold, cream and navy, without being intimidating. There's an emphasis on good quality ingredients, locally sourced wherever possible. The creamy crab and tiger prawn risotto is a good example of the dish, while the main course of poached salmon arrives fresh and tender served with a selection of mini vegetables. An enjoyable

dessert is the chef's own version of bread-and-butter pudding, using chocolate and Bailey's but dispensing with the fruit, served with cookie dough ice cream.

The Old House Restaurant

Chef: Alan Pierce **Owners:** Mr & Mrs C Dormon **Times:** 12.15-2/6.30-9.30, Closed Xmas, New Year, 1 wk spring, BHs, Mon, Closed L Sat, D Sun **Prices:** Fixed L £16, Fixed D £35-£45, Starter £6.50-£10, Main £19-£35, Dessert £6.50-£7, Service optional, Group service 10% **Wine:** 112 bottles over £20, 18 bottles under £20 **Notes:** Dress Restrictions, Smart casual, no jeans or trainers, Air con **Seats:** 80, Pr/dining room 35 **Children:** Min 10 yrs **Directions:** From M23 junct 10 follow A264 to East Grinstead, take 1st left at 2nd rdbt, left at crossroads, restaurant 0.75m on left **Parking:** 45

⊚ Restaurant 1881

Modern French, Mediterranean
Fine dining in elegant surroundings

☎ 01293 862166 Stanhill Court Hotel, Stanhill Rd, Charlwood RH6 0EP
e-mail: enquiries@stanhillcourthotel.co.uk
web: www.stanhillcourthotel.co.uk

Surrounded by 35 acres of ancient woodland including an amphitheatre and Victorian walled garden, this attractive country house was built in 1881 and is within easy reach of Gatwick Airport. The romantic, wood-panelled Restaurant 1881 is elegantly appointed and has cracking views over the grounds. Using quality ingredients, the food is largely classical French in inspiration, with European influences offering well-presented dishes with some innovative ideas. Start with sweet potato soup, or smoked salmon and crayfish risotto, followed by roast striploin of beef with roast potatoes and vegetables, Yorkshire pudding and natural jus, and then round things off with a rhubarb crème brûlée.

Times: 12-3/7-11, Closed L Sat **Rooms:** 34 (34 en suite) ★★★ HL **Directions:** Telephone for directions

GOODWOOD   MAP 06 SU80

⊚⊚ The Richmond Room/The Goodwood Park Hotel

Modern British
Sporting and leisure hotel close to Goodwood

☎ 01243 775537 PO18 0QB
e-mail: reservations@thegoodwoodparkhotel.co.uk
web: www.goodwoodparkhotel.co.uk

Given its location within the 12,000-acre Goodwood Estate, it's perhaps no surprise that this smart, modern hotel and country club has a leaning toward sport and leisure - in fact the facilities are excellent with a golf course, swimming pool and spa and a cocktail bar bedecked with motor sport memorabilia. Set within the entrance arch of the original 17th-century building, The Richmond Room restaurant is the fine-dining option, with a forward-thinking modern British menu offering imaginative dishes using the finest local ingredients. Start with an assiette of salmon (ballotine, smoked cube and gravad lax), followed by darne of monkfish with risotto Milanese, tomato and parsley gremolata. Desserts like white chocolate fondant with Cassis sorbet are always worth leaving room for.

Chef: Nick Funnell **Owners:** The Goodwood Estate Company Ltd **Times:** 12-2/7-10 **Prices:** Starter £6.50-£9.95, Main £15.95-£24.95, Dessert £6-£7.10, Service optional **Wine:** 2 bottles over £20, 9 bottles under £20, 8 by the glass **Notes:** Sun L 3 courses £18.95-£24.95, Vegetarian available, Dress Restrictions, Smart casual, no jeans or T-shirts, Civ Wed 80 **Seats:** 80, Pr/dining room 120 **Children:** Menu, Portions **Rooms:** 94 (94 en suite) ★★★★ HL **Directions:** Just off A285, 3m NE of Chichester. Follow signs for Goodwood, once in Estate follow signs for hotel **Parking:** 350

HAYWARDS HEATH MAP 06 TQ32

◉ Jeremy's at Borde Hill

Modern European

Attractive restaurant with a creative kitchen

☎ 01444 441102 Balcombe Rd RH16 1XP
e-mail: reservations@jeremysrestaurant.com
web: www.jeremysrestaurant.com

Housed in a converted stable block in the grounds of the Borde Hill Estate, Jeremy's overlooks a Victorian walled garden where the kitchen's herbs are grown, and is approached via a cobbled courtyard. The vibrant interior combines wooden floors and high-backed leather chairs with a striking collection of modern art, and the south-facing terrace provides a fair-weather bonus. A menu of modern European cooking is built around fresh seasonal produce, with starters such as seared Rye Bay scallops with vanilla beurre blanc, followed by a main course of slow-roast free-range pork belly with bubble-and-squeak and Calvados-flamed apples, with blood orange parfait, citrus jelly and a brandy snap for dessert.

Chef: J & V Ashpool, Andre Ebert **Owners:** Jeremy & Vera Ashpool **Times:** 12-2.30/7-9.30, Closed 1st wk Jan, Mon, Closed D Sun **Prices:** Fixed L £17.50, Fixed D £17.50, Starter £7-£10, Main £14.50-£22, Dessert £6-£7.50, Service optional, Group min 8 service 10% **Wine:** 70 bottles over £20, 18 bottles under £20, 10 by the glass **Notes:** Fixed D 2 courses, Tasting menu 5 courses £32.50, Civ Wed 55 **Seats:** 55 **Children:** Portions **Directions:** 1.5m N of Haywards Heath. From M23 junct 10a take A23 through Balcombe **Parking:** 20

HORSHAM MAP 06 TQ13

◉ Stan's Way House Restaurant

Modern European NEW ◔

Smart setting for modern European dining with a twist

☎ 01403 255688 3 Stan's Way, East St RH12 1HU
e-mail: sl@stanswayhouse.co.uk
web: www.stanswayhouse.co.uk

This impressive Grade II listed building has oak floors throughout, with a solid oak staircase leading to the first-floor restaurant. Here you will find 600-year-old oak beams, wooden furnishings and crisp white napery set off with fresh flowers. Candlelight in the evening adds to the atmosphere, making it a lovely venue for a special meal. The cooking is generally modern European in style, with an eclectic combination of New World ingredients and spices combined with classical techniques and smart presentation. Try braised smoked gammon shank with sesame honey glaze, and chickpea and coriander daal for example.

Chef: Mr Steven Dray **Owners:** Steven & Stephanie Dray **Times:** 12-3/7-10, Closed BHs, 2 wks summer, 1 wk New Year, Sun, Mon **Prices:** Fixed L £12.95, Fixed D £28.50, Service added but optional 10% **Seats:** 40 **Parking:** Piries Place free after 6pm

---

LICKFOLD MAP 06 SU92

◉ The Lickfold Inn

Modern British

Ancient inn with thoroughly modern food

☎ 01798 861285 Lickfold GU28 9EY
e-mail: thelickfoldinn@aol.com
web: www.thelickfoldinn.co.uk

Dating back to the 15th century, this charming family-run inn oozes style and sophistication. Built in a herringbone brick pattern, it boasts

CONTINUED ON PAGE 491

The Camellia Restaurant at South Lodge Hotel

LOWER BEEDING MAP 06 TQ22

French, Mediterranean

Country-house cuisine overlooking the South Downs

☎ 01403 891711 Brighton Rd RH13 6PS
e-mail: enquiries@southlodgehotel.co.uk
web: www.exclusivehotels.co.uk

A haven of gracious living, this impeccably presented Victorian country-house hotel stands in 90 acres of mature gardens and grounds, and offers stunning views over the South Downs. With its wood panelling, oil paintings, heavy fabrics and sense of space, it was built to impress and it certainly does. The sumptuous, candlelit restaurant - named after the 100-year-old camellia which still grows against the terrace wall - continues the theme, with ornate ceilings, wood panelling and floors and crisp white tablecloths, while large windows offer views over the downs. Service is formal but appropriately friendly.

The kitchen's approach is intelligently simple, with the emphasis on allowing tip-top seasonal produce to shine. The style is modern-focused and underpinned by a classical theme, with the fixed-price menu repertoire refreshingly unpretentious. Dishes are delivered with flair and a lightness of touch and enjoy well-defined flavours and combinations. For mains, take a fillet of halibut served with braised shallots, roast salsify and potato purée, or slow-cooked beef fillet paired with carrot purée and Madeira sauce, and for dessert, perhaps a caramelised apple tartlet with custard ice cream.

Chef: Lewis Hamblet
Owners: Exclusive Hotels
Times: 12-2/7-9.45
Prices: Fixed L £14, Fixed D £46, Starter £12-£14.50, Main £23-£34, Dessert £7.95-£8.75, Service optional
Wine: 280 bottles over £20, 4 bottles under £20, 260 by the glass
Notes: Tasting menu £59, Sun L 3 courses £26, Vegetarian available, Civ Wed 130
Seats: 75
Children: Menu, Portions
Rooms: 46 (46 en suite)★★★★ CHH
Directions: A281 Brighton road out of Horsham, through Monksgate. Hotel is on right past Leonardslee Gardens on left
Parking: 200

an abundance of original features - not least a large inglenook fireplace, flagstone floors and sturdy oak beams. The large terrace is the perfect place for summer dining, and cheerful staff ensure efficient service. There's an emphasis on fish and seafood on the crowd-pleasing menu, which includes the likes of roast rack of herb-coated lamb with a rosemary and redcurrant jus. Portions are generous, so remember to leave room for dessert - rich dark chocolate fondant pot pudding perhaps.

Times: 12-2.30/7-9.30, Closed 25-26 Dec, Mon, Closed D Sun
Directions: Signposted from A272, 6m E of Midhurst. From A285 6m S of Haslemere, follow signs for Lurgashall Winery and continue on to Lickfold village

LOWER BEEDING   MAP 06 TQ22

◉◉◉ The Camellia Restaurant at South Lodge Hotel

see opposite

MANNINGS HEATH   MAP 06 TQ22

◉ Mannings Heath Golf Club

British, Mediterranean
Traditional cuisine at an elegant golf club

☎ 01403 210228 Hammerpond Rd RH13 6PG
e-mail: enquiries@manningsheath.com
web: www.manningsheath.com

Mannings may be a members-only golf course, but its elegant restaurant is open to all and offers superb views across the Waterfall Golf Course. Dine on the terrace if weather permits, or take shelter in the wood-panelled Goldings dining room with its open log fire and beamed ceiling. The menu offers brasserie-style British favourites with Mediterranean and Asian influences. Try poached smoked haddock with curried risotto, or crisp belly pork on spring onion mash, and round things off with a rich treacle tart served with home-made caramel ice cream.

Chef: Robby Pierce **Owners:** Exclusive Hotels **Times:** 12-3/7-9, Closed D Sun-Wed **Prices:** Fixed L £15, Fixed D £21, Starter £5.50-£9.50, Main £8.50-£15.95, Dessert £5.50, Service optional **Wine:** 20 bottles over £20, 15 bottles under £20, 4 by the glass **Notes:** Vegetarian available, Dress Restrictions, Smart casual, collared shirt required, Civ Wed 100 **Seats:** 43, Pr/dining room 12 **Children:** Menu, Portions **Directions:** From Horsham A281, for 2m. Approaching Mannings Heath, left at the Dun Horse. Follow road to T-junct, left then follow road past village green. At T-junct, right then right again **Parking:** 120

MIDHURST   MAP 06 SU82

◉◉ Spread Eagle Hotel and Spa

Modern British
Accomplished classical cooking in a character setting

☎ 01730 816911 South St GU29 9NH
e-mail: reservations@spreadeagle-midhurst.com
web: www.hshotels.co.uk/spread/spreadeagle-main.htm

Dating from 1430, this beautiful old property occupies a prime position at the foot of the town, yet enjoys the seclusion of its own delightful

grounds. The building retains many original features, including ancient beams, sloping floors and oak panelling. Two interconnecting rooms make up the restaurant, separated by a large stone fireplace complete with a copper canopy adorned with old copper pots. The hospitality here is renowned and the food is similarly spot-on, with appealing dishes delivered with good technical skill and clear flavours. Recommendations include Gales beer-battered whiting, or assorted fish casserole with fennel, dill and a white wine sauce. 'Floating islands' with caramel and toasted almonds might feature at dessert.

Times: 12.30-2/7-9.30 **Rooms:** 39 (39 en suite) ★★★ HL
Directions: Town centre

ROWHOOK   MAP 06 TQ13

◉ Neals Restaurant at The Chequers Inn

British, Mediterranean
Enjoyable rural pub dining

☎ 01403 790480 RH12 3PY
e-mail: thechequers1!@aol.com
web: www.nealsrestaurants.biz

Traditionally decorated with open fires, oak beams, flagstone floors and rustic wooden tables, this cosy village pub dates back to the 15th century. There's a separate restaurant area and a terrace for summer dining. Pan-fried scallops set on cauliflower purée with sherry raisins and fresh truffle is a very stylish and well executed starter, followed by an equally masterful pan-fried medallions of venison, pink and juicy, served with bubble-and-squeak rösti and a rich roast chestnut jus. Finish with a light fruit and nut Belgian chocolate mousse with orange sorbet, or perhaps tonka bean pannacotta with bee pollen and honey biscotti.

Times: 12-2/7-9, Closed D Sun **Directions:** From Horsham take A281 towards Guildford. At rdbt take A29 signposted for London. After 200 mtrs turn left, follow signs for Rowhook

RUSPER   MAP 06 TQ23

◉◉ Ghyll Manor

Modern European
Creative and accomplished cooking at peaceful country-house hotel

☎ 0845 345 3426 High St RH12 4PX
e-mail: reception@ghyllmanor.co.uk
web: www.ghyllmanor.co.uk

Set in 45 acres of idyllic grounds, this traditional mansion house turned country-house hotel is situated in the pretty and peaceful village of Rusper. The hotel retains many period features and the restaurant, located in the original part of the house, comes with oak beams and spacious seating, exuding a warm, cosy ambience. Service is efficient and friendly, and the kitchen's modern European style is delivered via fixed-price dinner, carte and six-course tasting menus. Expect pan-fried quail with kohlrabi salad, beetroot jelly and lime crème fraîche dressing to start, followed perhaps by pan-fried diver scallops with celeriac variation and a port balsamic reduction, or seared wild sea bass with baby fennel, lobster ravioli and lobster essence. For dessert, try chocolate, orange and Bailey's kaiserschmarrn with chocolate ice cream, or tuck into a selection of French and English cheeses with fig compôte.

CONTINUED

RUSPER CONTINUED

Chef: Alec Mackins **Owners:** Civil Service Motoring Association
Times: 12-2/7-9.30 **Prices:** Fixed L £19.95, Fixed D £25-£29, Starter £7-£9, Main £16-£22, Dessert £7-£9, Service optional **Wine:** 76 bottles over £20, 16 bottles under £20, 8 by the glass **Notes:** Fixed L 3 courses, Dress Restrictions, Smart casual, Civ Wed 80 **Seats:** 40, Pr/dining room 30
Children: Min 10 yrs, Portions **Rooms:** 29 (29 en suite) ★★★ CHH
Directions: M23 junct 11, join A264 signed Horsham. Continue to third rdbt, take 3rd exit towards Faygate and Rusper **Parking:** 100

STORRINGTON   MAP 06 TQ01

◎ Old Forge

Modern
Fine food and wine in a historic setting

☎ 01903 743402 6 Church St RH20 4LA
e-mail: contact@oldforge.co.uk
web: www.oldforge.co.uk

The restaurant comprises three small dining rooms in what was originally a lead working forge and adjacent cottages, dating from the 16th century. The old-world beams and low ceilings make for a cosy atmosphere, and husband-and-wife team Cathy and Clive Roberts offer a warm welcome. The modern cooking draws on traditional British and international flavours and ideas, with dishes ranging from seared scallops with white wine sauce, butternut squash, garden peas and pesto, to saddle of rabbit with prune and chicken farce and grain mustard mash.

Indigo is a very popular local restaurant overlooking Steyne Gardens right by the sea. Unfussy, smart, cosmopolitan says as much about the style of Indigo as it does the food.
"keep it simple, flavoursome and seasonal" is the mantra of Head Chef Luca Mason.
Locally caught fish and lobsters are available daily (weather permitting!) and some fabulous 28 day hung steaks from the Yorkshire Dales, which people travel from far to enjoy.
There is a fixed menu with additional a la carte dishes available at extremely competitive prices.
Pop along and sup champagne or your favourite tipple in a very chic lounge before and perhaps even after enjoying a sumptuous meal in what remains the highest rated and still the only rosette restaurant in Worthing.

Chef: Cathy Roberts **Owners:** Mr & Mrs N C Roberts **Times:** 12.15-1.30/7.15-9, Closed Xmas-New Year, 2 wks spring, 2 wks autumn, Mon-Wed, Closed L Sat, D Sun **Prices:** Fixed L £14.50, Fixed D £34, Service included **Wine:** 42 bottles over £20, 39 bottles under £20, 10 by the glass
Notes: Fixed L incl glass of wine, Sun L 2 courses £16, 3 courses £20, Dress Restrictions, Smart casual **Seats:** 34, Pr/dining room 12
Children: Portions **Directions:** On side street in village centre
Parking: On street

TURNERS HILL   MAP 06 TQ33

◎◎ Alexander House Hotel & Utopia Spa

Modern European
Country-house grandeur and imaginative cuisine

☎ 01342 714914 East St RH10 4QD
e-mail: info@alexanderhouse.co.uk
web: www.alexanderhouse.co.uk

This imposing country mansion dates back to the 17th century and is set in over 100 acres of parkland and landscaped gardens. It has been transformed in recent years, the latest addition being a sumptuous spa with stunning new rooms. The restaurant is in the oldest part of the hotel and offers country-house grandeur, with luxurious furnishings and splendid works of art. Service is formal, but in a relaxed and friendly atmosphere. The cooking style is French with some European influences. For starters, try chargrilled medallions of tuna with a rillette of crab, avocado and tomato, then opt for roasted fillet of beef with fondant potato, asparagus tips and a caramelised tomato jus, or perhaps herb-crusted halibut with shellfish fricassée, with dark chocolate tart served with black cherry ice cream and pistachio foam to finish.

Chef: Kirk Johnson **Owners:** Alexander Hotels Ltd **Times:** 12-3/7-10, Closed Mon, Closed D Sun **Prices:** Fixed L £22, Fixed D £39.50, Starter £8.50-£12, Main £18.50-£27, Dessert £9.50-£11, Service added but optional

12.5% **Wine:** 130 bottles over £20, 4 bottles under £20, 18 by the glass
Notes: Sun L £26, Vegetarian available, Dress Restrictions, No jeans or
trainers, Civ Wed 90 **Seats:** 40, Pr/dining room 16 **Children:** Min 7 yrs,
Portions **Rooms:** 38 (38 en suite)★★★★ HL **Directions:** On B2110
between Turners Hill & East Grinstead; 6m from M23 junct 10
Parking: 150

WORTHING MAP 06 TQ10

◉ *Ardington Hotel*

International 🖥

Contemporary cuisine by the sea

☎ 01903 230451 Steyne Gardens BN11 3DZ
web: www.ardingtonhotel.co.uk

In contrast to the character and age of the building - set near the
seafront in a pretty garden square - the Indigo restaurant is a bright,
airy, contemporary affair, decked out with vibrant abstract artwork and
high-backed chairs. The kitchen delivers some adventurous dishes
alongside straightforward offerings. Perhaps try a chicken and walnut
terrine with sweet pepper chutney, before main courses of pan-fried
scallops, ginger and fennel cream, or seared wild sea trout, crushed
peas and marjoram. The glazed prune and Armagnac tart, or selection
of Sussex cheeses might round things off nicely.

Times: 12-2/7-8.45, Closed 23 Dec-7 Jan, Closed L Mon-Tue **Rooms:** 45
(45 en suite) ★★★ HL **Directions:** Telephone for directions
see advert opposite

The Fish Factory
☎ 01903 207123 51 Brighton Rd BN11 3EE
A modern British restaurant where there is more to choose from than
fish.

GATESHEAD MAP 21 NZ26

◉ **Eslington Villa Hotel**

Modern British V 🖥
Modern cooking in a charming setting

☎ 0191 487 6017 & 420 0666 8 Station Rd, Low Fell
NE9 6DR
e-mail: home@eslingtonvilla.co.uk
web: www.eslingtonvilla.co.uk

Set in 2 acres of gardens, this smart hotel combines a bright,
contemporary atmosphere with the period style of its Victorian past;
think high ceilings, fireplaces and cornices. Eat in the classical dining
room or conservatory - overlooking the Team Valley - decorated in
more contemporary style, with tartan carpets and thistle drapes.
Modern British and European-influenced cuisine is served in relaxed,
friendly surroundings. Expect fillet steak with horseradish dauphinoise,
parsnip purée and red wine, or perhaps a fillet of halibut served with
parmesan risotto cake, rocket and provençal vegetables. To finish,
maybe choose between a whisky and orange bread-and-butter
pudding or classic treacle tart.

Chef: Andy Moore **Owners:** Mr & Mrs N Tulip **Times:** 12-2/7-9.45, Closed
25-26 Dec, 1 Jan, BHs, Closed L Sat, D Sun **Prices:** Fixed L £14-£16, Fixed D
£20-£22, Starter £5.50-£8.50, Main £15-£19, Dessert £4.95-£6.95, Service
optional **Wine:** 17 bottles over £20, 24 bottles under £20, 8 by the glass
Notes: Vegetarian menu **Seats:** 80, Pr/dining room 30 **Children:** Portions
Rooms: 17 (17 en suite) ★★★ HL **Directions:** From A1 (M) turn off to
Team Valley Trading Estate, up Eastern Avenue. Turn left at PDS car
showroom. Hotel is 100 yds on left **Parking:** 30

🖥 **Riverside Restaurant & Bar - Baltic Mill**
☎ 0191 440 4942 BALTIC Centre for Contemporary Art,
South Shore Rd NE8 3BA
web: www.theaa.com/travel/index.jsp

Making the most of the setting beside the Tyne with floor-to-ceiling
windows across the length of the restaurant, it offers lunches from
light meals to three courses (midday to 4.30pm). The restaurant
reopens two hours later with a full modern British menu.

NEWCASTLE UPON TYNE MAP 21 NZ26

◉◉ **Black Door**

Modern French NEW 🖥
Smart, contemporary venue with innovative cuisine

☎ 0191 260 5411 32 Crayton St West NE1 5DZ
e-mail: justine.ladd@btconnect.com
web: www.blackdoorrestaurant.co.uk

Though hidden away somewhat unobtrusively behind a namesake
black door in a Georgian-style city-centre townhouse, it hasn't stopped
this restaurant making waves in the North East. Inside has a very
modern edge, with brown leather sofas, suede stools, wooden floors
and leather-topped tables. Cream-painted walls are hung with black
and white artwork of famous Newcastle landmarks and tables are
clothed, while the well-stocked bar proves a prominent feature.
Service is friendly and knowledgeable, while the kitchen delivers a

CONTINUED

NEWCASTLE UPON TYNE CONTINUED

repertoire of innovative modern French cuisine that uses the best local ingredients. Technical skill, timings and balance are spot on, and dishes have a certain air of excitement; take herb-crusted Northumberland lamb with red chard, artichokes and tomato vinaigrette, or mango ravioli with mango sorbet and passionfruit. Certainly one to watch.

Chef: David Kennedy **Owners:** David Ladd & David Kennedy **Times:** 12-2/7-10, Closed 1st wk Jan, Sun & Mon **Prices:** Fixed L £15.50, Fixed D £42.50, Service optional, Group min 6 service 10% **Wine:** 50 bottles over £20, 18 bottles under £20, 11 by the glass **Seats:** 34 **Children:** Portions **Directions:** Opposite St Mary's Cathedral, close to Newcastle Central stn

◉ Blackfriars Restaurant

Modern British

Modern dining in ancient surroundings

☎ 0191 261 5945 Friars St NE1 4XN
e-mail: info@blackfriarsrestaurant.co.uk
web: www.blackfriarsrestaurant.co.uk

Once the refectory of an early 13th-century priory, this informal eatery (café, bar and restaurant) may have the oldest dining room in the country. Massive stone walls, ancient beams, wooden floors and inglenooks lit by huge flickering candles set a Gothic tone. But you can escape to the peaceful courtyard for summer dining. Friendly, efficient staff serve modern British dishes based on fresh local ingredients, interesting flavours and simple, contemporary presentation. Take Tamworth pork loin served with mead-roasted apple stuffed with walnuts and a rosemary jus. (Afternoon tea and summer picnic menus are also available.)

Chef: Simon Brown **Owners:** Andy & Sam Hook **Times:** 12-2.30/6-12, Closed BHs except Good Fri, Closed D Sun **Prices:** Fixed L £10.50, Fixed D £15, Starter £4-£8, Main £10.50-£22, Dessert £5-£7, Service optional, Group min 6 service 10% **Wine:** 19 bottles over £20, 14 bottles under £20, 7 by

the glass **Notes:** Vegetarian available, Air con **Seats:** 70, Pr/dining room 50 **Children:** Portions **Directions:** Take the only small cobbled road off Stowel St (China Town). Blackfriars 100yds on left **Parking:** Car park next to restaurant

◉ Café 21 Newcastle

French, International

Busy bistro in Newcastle's trendy Quayside area

☎ 0191 222 0755 Quayside NE1 3UG
e-mail: bh@cafetwentyone.co.uk

City centre bistro with contemporary colour and style. The walls are hung with large mirrors, little pictures and old French recipes. White clothed wooden tables are set on wooden floors, each with a bowl of olives, tea lights, and branded crockery with the Café 21 logo. Well presented and accurately cooked French bistro dishes with British and Asian influences, with regularly changing specials, are based on local produce where possible. Try cheese and spinach soufflé, fishcakes with chips and parsley sauce or peppered saddle of venison with creamed celeriac and blue cheese fritter. There's also a selection of farmhouse cheeses. Service is informal and friendly.

Times: 12-2.30/6-10.30, Closed Xmas, BHs **Directions:** Telephone for directions

◉◉ The Fisherman's Lodge

British, French

Tranquil setting for imaginative cooking

☎ 0191 281 3281 Jesmond Dene, Jesmond NE7 7BQ
e-mail: enquiries@fishermanslodge.co.uk
web: www.fishermanslodge.co.uk

Occupying a wonderfully secluded parkland location, this restaurant is within easy reach of the city centre. Formerly Lord Armstrong's private dwelling, the décor is in the style of a smart, shooting lodge but very modern, tasteful and elegant. Fine linen and glassware add extra sparkle to the dining room. The accomplished kitchen takes a modern focus - underpinned by a classical French theme - to deliver carefully presented, imaginative menus (dotted with luxury ingredients and showcasing a penchant for fish). Take mild curried monkfish with a mussel nage and baby vegetables, or roast loin of Northumberland lamb with crushed peas, fondant potato and breaded sweetbreads, and perhaps a lemon soufflé finish, served with poppy seed meringue and lemon cream and sherbet ice cream.

Times: 12-2/7-10.30, Closed 25 Dec, BHs, Sun, Closed L 31 Dec, D Sun **Directions:** 2.5m from city centre, off A1058 (Tynemouth road). Turn into Jesmond Rd then 2nd right on Jesmond Dene Rd. Follow signs

◎◎ Jesmond Dene House

Modern British

Fashionable hotel restaurant with a keen eye on contemporary food trends

☎ 0191 212 3000 Jesmond Dene Rd NE2 2EY
e-mail: info@jesmonddenehouse.co.uk
web: www.jesmonddenehouse.co.uk

Built in the early 1820s, this Georgian house overlooking the wooded valley of Jesmond Dene has plenty of rural charm yet is only 5 minutes from the centre of town. Recently converted into a trendy contemporary hotel, the décor throughout looks pristine, with comfortable wood-panelled lounges and a restaurant split into two dining areas - a former music room with a dramatic colour scheme and the oak-floored garden room. The cooking is generous and skilful, with a seasonally-inspired menu concentrating on well-matched flavours with dashes of thoughtful innovation. Think sea bass served with a nage of Lindisfarne mussels, root vegetables, Yukon Gold potato gnocchi and fresh herbs, or perhaps suckling pig with Chantenay carrots and parsnips, Bramley apple purée and a sage pork jus.

Chef: Terry Laybourne, Andrew Richardson **Owners:** Terry Laybourne, Peter Candler **Times:** 12-2.30/7-10.30 **Prices:** Fixed L £19.50-£21.50, Starter £8-£15, Main £15-£28, Dessert £4-£11, Service added but optional 10% **Wine:** 180 bottles over £20, 30 bottles under £20, 16 by the glass **Notes:** Dress Restrictions, Smart casual, Civ Wed 100 **Seats:** 60, Pr/dining room 18 **Children:** Menu, Portions **Rooms:** 40 (40 en suite) ★★★★ HL **Directions:** From Newcastle city centre follow A167 to junct with A184. Turn right towards Matthew Bank. Turn right into Jesmond Dene Rd. **Parking:** 64

◎ Malmaison Hotel

French 💻

Good brasserie dining in trendy location

☎ 0191 245 5000 Quayside NE1 3DX
e-mail: newcastle@malmaison.com
web: www.malmaison.com

Former warehouse, now a chic modern hotel on the trendy and popular Newcastle quayside, with stunning views of the Millennium Bridge. Enjoy drinks in the first-floor bar overlooking the River Tyne, with its stripped wood floors, oversized sofas and bustling atmosphere, then move through to the equally contemporary brasserie-style restaurant. Bold colours, moody lighting and giant picture windows set the relaxing scene for sampling some traditional brasserie classics, like eggs Benedict as a starter, or a main of plaice goujons, fat-cut chips and tartare sauce, or maybe the 'Mal' burger. Vegetarians have their own section on the menu and there's a Sunday brunch menu, too.

Times: 12-2.30/6-11 **Rooms:** 120 (120 en suite) ★★★ HL **Directions:** Telephone for directions

◎ Park Restaurant

Traditional British

Formal hotel dining room overlooking Gosforth Park

☎ 0191 236 4111 Newcastle Marriott Hotel, High Gosforth Park, Gosforth NE3 5HN
e-mail: frontdesk.gosforthpark@marriotthotels.co.uk
web: www.marriott.co.uk

What a splendid location for a smart modern hotel: on the outskirts of the city amid 12 acres of woodland, handy for the bypass, airport and racecourse. The Park Restaurant is richly decorated, with marble-tiled and carpeted floors, heavy drapes and upholstered seating. Lunches tend to be geared to conferences and include a buffet offering. At dinner there's a daily fixed-price menu of fairly straightforward dishes and a more ambitious carte studded with luxury items. Representative dishes are smoked haddock chowder served with a lightly poached egg, seared breast of Gressingham duck, and tournedos of sea bass and salmon. Chats Café Bar is the alternative venue for informal meals.

Chef: Simon Devine **Owners:** Marriott International **Times:** 12.30-2/5-10, Closed 31 Dec, Closed L Sat (Mon-Fri for conferences only) **Prices:** Fixed L £16.95, Fixed D £27-£29, Starter £5.50-£8.90, Main £13.50-£25.50, Dessert £5.50, Service optional **Wine:** 41 bottles over £20, 26 bottles under £20, 21 by the glass **Notes:** Vegetarian available, Civ Wed 200, Air con **Seats:** 120, Pr/dining room 30 **Children:** Menu, Portions **Rooms:** 178 (178 en suite) ★★★★ HL **Directions:** From A1 take A1056 (Killingworth/Wideopen) 3rd exit to hotel ahead **Parking:** 300

◎ Vermont Hotel

British, European 💻

Elegant location for quayside dining

☎ 0191 233 1010 Castle Garth NE1 1RQ
e-mail: info@vermont-hotel.co.uk
web: www.vermont-hotel.com

A landmark building dating from the 1930s, the hotel is located next to the castle and close to the bustling quayside. Formerly the County Hall, it is Grade II listed and overlooks the Tyne and Millennium bridges. The aptly-named Bridge restaurant, with spectacular views of the Tyne Bridge, is the fine-dining option and has recently been refurbished. Cooking is Anglo-French with European influences, producing dishes such as rustic smoked chicken salad, or confit of lamb shoulder with redcurrant jus, with vanilla pannacotta, macerated strawberries and champagne sorbet for dessert.

Owners: Lincoln Group **Times:** 12-2.30/6-11 **Prices:** Fixed L £15, Fixed D £24 **Wine:** 123 bottles over £20, 54 bottles under £20, 17 by the glass **Notes:** Sun L 2 courses £14, 3 courses £17, Vegetarian available, Dress Restrictions, Very smart; no casual dress, no jeans, Civ Wed 150, Air con **Seats:** 80, Pr/dining room 80 **Children:** Portions **Rooms:** 101 (101 en suite) ★★★★ HL **Directions:** City centre, by high level bridge and castle keep **Parking:** 70

Barn Under a Wandering Star

☎ 0191 281 7179 21a Leazes Park Rd NE1 4PF

Fun, safari-tinged surroundings with a global menu to match.

TYNEMOUTH — MAP 21 NZ36

◉ Sidney's Restaurant

Modern

Buzzing bistro in Tyneside town centre

☎ 0191 257 8500 & 213 0284 3-5 Percy Park Rd
NE30 4LZ
e-mail: bookings@sidneys.co.uk
web: www.sidneys.co.uk

This cosy, modern bistro was once a Victorian butcher's shop - although given the wooden floors, leather benches, unclothed tables with simple settings and local art adorning the walls, you would never guess its origins. The buzzy atmosphere is helped along by friendly and efficient staff while the modern menu relies on fresh local ingredients (including locally-landed fish). The bistro-style dishes are accurate with clear flavours. Starters might include marinated lamb kebab with tomato and coriander salad, with mains such as parmesan-crusted whiting and braised potatoes with peas.

Chef: A O'Kane **Owners:** A O'Kane **Times:** 12-2.30/6-12, Closed BHs ex Good Friday, Sun **Prices:** Fixed L £12, Fixed D £18, Starter £4.50-£6.95, Main £11.50-£18.50, Dessert £4.50-£7, Service optional, Group min 6 service 10% **Wine:** 4 bottles over £20, 20 bottles under £20, 10 by the glass **Seats:** 50, Pr/dining room 20 **Children:** Menu, Portions **Directions:** From Newcastle take A1058 to Tynemouth. Restaurant on corner of Percy Park Rd & Front St **Parking:** On street

WARWICKSHIRE

ABBOT'S SALFORD — MAP 10 SP05

◉ Best Western Salford Hall Hotel

Modern, Traditional

Modern food in a historic setting

☎ 01386 871300 WR11 5UT
e-mail: reception@salfordhall.co.uk
web: www.salfordhall.co.uk

The hotel has an interesting history, having first been a retreat for the Abbot of Evesham, then a family home in the Tudor period and finally a nunnery before becoming a hotel. The restaurant is very traditional, with oak panelling, a large fireplace and mullioned windows. The modern British menu offers simple dishes - cream and coriander soup, or wilted spinach and ricotta cheese tart to start, followed by pan-fried medallions of monkfish, pancetta and wild mushroom ragout, and sticky stem ginger pudding to close. The best of fresh ingredients, locally sourced, are used where appropriate.

Times: 12.30-2/7-10, Closed Xmas, Closed L Sat **Rooms:** 33 (33 en suite) ★★★ HL **Directions:** Off A46 between Stratford-upon-Avon & Evesham. Take road signed Salford Priors, 1.5m on left

ALDERMINSTER — MAP 10 SP24

◉◉ Ettington Park Hotel

British, French V

Dine in Gothic splendour

☎ 01789 450123 CV37 8BU
web: www.handpicked.co.uk

Set in 40-acre grounds in the Stour Valley, this imposing Victorian-Gothic manor offers the best of both worlds - the peace of the countryside and easy access to the motorway network. Tables clothed in formal white linen, polished glassware and cutlery, and views across the garden to the 12th-century family chapel set a traditional note in the stately oak-panelled dining room. By contrast, there's a sense of adventure about the cooking, though the food remains classically French based, with the skilled kitchen delivering some complex cooking. Maybe langoustine tortellini to start, followed by a trio of beef or beef fillet served with a watercress rouille, gâteau of celeriac and spinach and shallot red wine sauce, with vanilla pannacotta and rhubarb compôte to finish.

Chef: Giles Stonehouse **Owners:** Hand Picked Hotels **Times:** 12-2/7-9.30, Closed L Mon-Fri **Prices:** Fixed L £15-£30, Fixed D £30-£75, Service optional **Wine:** 52 bottles over £20, 6 bottles under £20, 12 by the glass **Notes:** Tasting menu £55, Sun L £19.95, Vegetarian menu, Smart casual, Civ Wed 96 **Seats:** 50, Pr/dining room 80 **Children:** Menu, Portions **Rooms:** 48 (48 en suite)★★★★ HL **Directions:** M40 junct 15/A46 towards Stratford-upon-Avon, then A439 into town centre onto A3400 5m to Shipston. Hotel 1/2m on left **Parking:** 80

ATHERSTONE — MAP 10 SP39

◉ Chapel House Hotel

French, European

Elegant surroundings for imaginative cooking

☎ 01827 718949 Friar's Gate CV9 1EY
e-mail: info@chapelhousehotel.co.uk
web: www.chapelhousehotel.co.uk

Formerly the dower house to Atherstone Hall, Chapel House was built in 1729 as an elegant townhouse, and Florence Nightingale was a frequent visitor here. Extended and upgraded over the years, it retains many period features. The restaurant is a light, elegant Georgian dining room with well-spaced tables, crisp white linen and silver cutlery. The cooking style is mainly classical French but with a modern, lighter touch. The chef uses fresh local produce as much as possible and the menu features the likes of sliced breast of local wild duck with a port, orange and redcurrant sauce, served with confit duck leg and potato rösti.

Chef: Richard Henry Napper **Owners:** Richard & Siobhan Napper **Times:** 7-9, Closed 24 Dec-3 Jan, Etr wk, late Aug-early Sep, Sun, Closed L all week **Prices:** Starter £4.95-£8.95, Main £17.45-£21.95, Dessert £5.95-£8.95, Service optional **Wine:** 61 bottles over £20, 44 bottles under £20, 9 by the glass **Notes:** Dress Restrictions, Smart casual **Seats:** 24, Pr/dining room 12 **Children:** Portions **Rooms:** 12 (12 en suite) ★★ HL **Directions:** Off Market Sq in Atherstone, behind High St **Parking:** On street

BRANDON   MAP 11 SP47

⊛ Mercure Brandon Hall Hotel & Spa

Modern British, French 🖥

Modern restaurant in a large country hotel

☎ 0870 400 8105 Main St CV8 3FW

web: www.mercure.com

A former hunting lodge, this large country hotel is set amid 17 acres of well-tended lawns and woodland and offers excellent leisure facilities. A feature of the contemporary-style restaurant is its host of mirrors. Simplicity is the key to the kitchen's success, with an appealing repertoire that holds the interest through to the end. Dishes to show off the kitchen's accomplishments are crab tian with red pepper ice cream, followed by a main course of blade of Scottish beef with morel jus, with sweet egg brioche, roasted figs and caramelised blueberries for dessert.

Chef: Neil Oates **Times:** 12.30-2.30/7-9.30, Closed L Mon-Sat **Prices:** D £29.95, Service optional **Wine:** 60 bottles over £20, 10 bottles under £20 **Notes:** Vegetarian available, Civ Wed 80 **Seats:** 90, Pr/dining room 280 **Children:** Menu, Portions **Rooms:** 120 (120 en suite) ★★★★ HL **Directions:** From A46 follow signs on A428 towards Binley Woods/Brandon, turn right at village green, hotel 500yds on right **Parking:** 260

FARNBOROUGH   MAP 11 SP44

⊛ The Inn at Farnborough

British, French

Skilful cooking in the heart of a small village

☎ 01295 690615 Main St OX17 1DZ

e-mail: enquiries@innatfarnborough.co.uk

web: www.innatfarnborough.co.uk

Dating from around 1700, this former butcher's shop is now a restaurant and pub all in one. The old and the contemporary sit happily together creating a relaxed atmosphere in which to eat and drink - service comes with a smile! Essentially French, the menu is based on local produce and features some interesting choices. Shellfish bisque with scallops and tiger prawns flamed in Cognac, followed by confit of Cornish lamb with pea and mint purée, dauphinoise potatoes and roast red peppers, then hot chocolate fondant show the style.

Chef: Anthony Robinson **Owners:** Oyster Inns Ltd **Times:** 12-3/6-10, Closed 25 Dec **Prices:** Fixed L £10.95, Fixed D £12.95-£19.95, Starter £5-£12, Main £12-19.95, Dessert £5.50, Service added but optional 10% **Wine:** 15 bottles over £20, 15 bottles under £20, 16 by the glass **Seats:** 80, Pr/dining room 16 **Children:** Portions **Directions:** M40 junct 11 - (Banbury). 3rd rdbt turn right onto A423 to Southam. After 4m turn left down road signed Farnborough. After 1m turn right into the village - The Inn at Farnborough is on right **Parking:** 40

KENILWORTH   MAP 10 SP27

⊛⊛ Simply Simpsons

Modern British V

Stylish bistro serving classically-based modern dishes

☎ 01926 864567 101-103 Warwick Rd CV8 1HL

e-mail: info@simplysimpsons.com

web: www.simplysimpsons.com

A contemporary bistro on the pretty town's main street. The fashionable affair has quarry-tiled floors, polished wooden tables, artwork and painted bricks. Its name says it all, sister restaurant to the fine-dining Simpsons in Edgbaston (see entry), but here you'll find simpler cooking with a good balance of flavours and friendly informal service. Fresh local produce and stylish presentation combine in accomplished dishes like a pavé of cod with curried yellow split peas, belly of pork with black pudding and apple sauce, or grilled calves' liver with onions and smoked bacon. For dessert, perhaps try vanilla pannacotta with an exotic fruit brochette.

Chef: Iain Miller **Owners:** Andreas & Alison Antona **Times:** 12.30-2/6.30-10, Closed Last 2 wks of Aug, BHs, Sun, Mon **Prices:** Fixed L £14.50, Starter £5.25-£6.50, Main £13-£19, Dessert £5.95, Service added but optional 10% **Wine:** 34 bottles over £20, 24 bottles under £20, 5 by the glass **Notes:** Vegetarian menu, Air con **Seats:** 70, Pr/dining room 40 **Children:** Portions **Directions:** A452. In main street in Kenilworth centre **Parking:** 15

🖥 Coconut Lagoon

☎ 01926 864500 149 Warwick Rd CV8 1HY

web: www.theaa.com/travel/index.jsp

Southern Indian cuisine from Goa, Kerala, Karnataka, and Andhra Pradesh.

🖥 Raffles

☎ 01926 864300 57 Warwick Rd CV8 1HN

web: www.theaa.com/travel/index.jsp

Malaysian cuisine, including Indian and Chinese. Colonial atmosphere and Singapore Slings a must.

LEAMINGTON SPA (ROYAL)   MAP 10 SP36

◉ *Episode - Leamington*

Modern British NEW

Modern townhouse hotel and brasserie cooking

☎ 01926 883777 64 Upper Holly Walk CV32 4JL
e-mail: leamington@bestwestern.co.uk
web: www.episodehotels.com

This Victorian townhouse hotel is situated near the town's thriving shopping centre, its once endearing face of yesteryear now swept away in a contemporary new look following major renovation. The atmospheric, informal brasserie takes an equally modern approach to cooking with a fashionable continental nod, driven by quality local seasonal produce. Take a threesome of cod, crab and crayfish fishcake with sweet chilli dressing to start, perhaps slow-cooked Cornish lamb shank served with rosemary jus and red cabbage to follow, and to finish, maybe a sticky toffee fondant with vanilla ice cream.

Times: Please telephone for details **Rooms:** 32 (32 en suite) ★★★ HL **Directions:** Along Newbold Terrace, turn L at lights. Hotel on right-hand corner of Willes Rd and Upper Holly Walk

◉◉◉ **Mallory Court Hotel**

see below

◉◉ **Restaurant 23**

Modern European NEW

Accomplished cooking in a modern restaurant

☎ 01926 422422 23 Dormer Place CV32 5AA
e-mail: info@restaurant23.co.uk
web: www.restaurant23.co.uk

The open-plan kitchen, subtle citrus décor, unaffected artwork and large windows give this tiny pearl of a restaurant a fresh, spacious feel. If you can take your eyes off the food you'll realise that there's a magnificent view of Jefferson Park just over the street. An eclectic European style of cooking is offered; dishes are well balanced and presentation is interesting. Fine slices of smoked duck are presented with tiny wedges of beetroot and slivers of parmesan as a starter, contrasting beautifully with the accompanying rocket leaves, while skate wing, cooked just enough to prevent the flavour turning, comes with capers and a light red pepper sauce. Finish with chocolate fondant served with coconut sorbet and caramelised banana.

Chef: Peter Knibb **Owners:** Peter & Antje Knibb **Times:** 12.15-2.30/6.15-9.45, Closed 2 wks Aug, 1 wk Jan, Sun, Mon **Prices:** Fixed L £12, Fixed D £22, Starter £6-£8, Main £14-£20, Dessert £6.50, Service optional, Group min 6 service 10% **Wine:** 50 bottles over £20, 14 bottles under £20, 9 by the glass **Seats:** 24 **Children:** Min 12 yrs **Directions:** M40 junct 13 onto A452 towards Leamington Spa. Follow signs for town centre **Parking:** On street opposite

---

◉◉◉
Mallory Court Hotel

LEAMINGTON SPA (ROYAL)   MAP 10 SP36

Modern British V 🍷 NOTABLE WINE LIST

Exquisitely prepared dishes in country-house splendour

☎ 01926 330214 Harbury Ln, Bishop's Tachbrook CV33 9QB
e-mail: reception@mallory.co.uk
web: www.mallory.co.uk

This magnificent Lutyens-style country-house hotel is idyllically situated in picturesque countryside, in 10 acres of landscaped grounds and manicured lawns. Its harmonious blend of country-house splendour and contemporary design creates a wonderfully relaxed, homely atmosphere. Relax over drinks or coffee in the sumptuous lounges, or take advantage of the pool and tennis court. There are two dining options: the formal oak-panelled Dining Room, and the contemporary art deco-style Brasserie - a new addition converted from the former groundskeeper's cottage, offering lighter meals. In summer, guests can also dine in the charming walled garden. The accomplished modern British cooking is underpinned by classical French themes, bringing together top-class ingredients in sophisticated and tempting combinations. Flavours are clear, and presentation designed to impress. The fixed-price menu is intelligently compact and enticing; enjoy a bisque of shellfish with crab tortellini and Pernod cream to

start, followed by venison loin with braised pork belly and a peppery port sauce.

Chef: Simon Haigh **Owners:** Sir Peter Rigby **Times:** 12-1.45/6.30-9 **Prices:** Fixed L £23.50, Fixed D £39.50-£55, Service optional **Wine:** 2 bottles under £20, 7 by the glass **Notes:** Vegetarian menu, Dress Restrictions, No jeans or sportswear, Civ Wed 160 **Seats:** 50, Pr/dining room 27 **Children:** Portions **Rooms:** 30 (30 en suite) ★★★ HL **Directions:** M40 junct 13 N-bound. Turn left, and left again towards Bishops Tachbrook. Continue for 0.5m and turn right up Harbury Ln. M40 junct 14 S-bound. Follow A452 for Leamington. At 2nd rdbt take left into Harbury Ln **Parking:** 50

STRATFORD-UPON-AVON   MAP 10 SP25

◉◉ Billesley Manor Hotel

Modern British

Modern food in a fine historic setting

☎ 01789 279955 & 767103 Billesley, Alcester B49 6NF
e-mail: enquiries@billesleymanor.co.uk
web: www.billesleymanor.co.uk

Set in 11 acres of delightful grounds and parkland with a yew topiary garden and fountain, this impressive Elizabethan manor house is close to Stratford-upon-Avon and Shakespeare is believed to have written part of *As You Like It* here. The Stuart restaurant is a splendid oak-panelled room with a huge stone fireplace, chandeliers and silver pheasants, enjoying pleasant views across the gardens. A modern approach is taken to food and ingredients are carefully sourced. You might start with crab and spring onion risotto with lemon vinaigrette, before moving on to a main course of braised blade of beef, with roasted root vegetables, horseradish rösti and thyme. Caramelised banana bavarois might proving a fitting finale.

Chef: Christopher Short **Owners:** Paramount **Times:** 12.30-2/7-9.30 **Prices:** Fixed L £15, Fixed D £37.50, Starter £6-£12.50, Main £11-£22, Dessert £6-£12, Service added but optional 5% **Notes:** Dress Restrictions, No denims, trainers or T-shirts, Civ Wed 73 **Seats:** 42, Pr/dining room 40 **Children:** Menu, Portions **Rooms:** 72 (72 en suite) ★★★★ HL **Directions:** M40 junct 15, then take A46 S towards Stratford/Worcester. Follow the A46 E over three rdbts. Continue for 2m then take a right for Billesley **Parking:** 100

◉ Macdonald Alveston Manor

Modern British

Modern dining in Elizabethan manor

☎ 01789 205478 Clopton Bridge CV37 7HP
e-mail: events.alvestonmanor@macdonald-hotels.co.uk
web: www.macdonald-hotels.co.uk/alvestonmanor

A striking red-brick and half-timbered façade, well-tended grounds and a giant cedar - under which it's said that *A Midsummer Night's Dream* was first performed - all contribute to the charm of this well-established hotel. The main house retains much of its Elizabethan charm, with leaded light windows and splendid original panelling. In the traditional country-house style restaurant you can enjoy reliable modern British dishes on a daily-changing menu, perhaps wild mushroom soup followed by roast salmon and béarnaise sauce, or slow-roasted vine tomatoes with grilled English croûte, and apple clafoutis with honey and almond florentine to finish.

Times: 12-2.30/6-9.30, Closed L Mon-Sat **Rooms:** 113 (113 en suite) ★★★★ HL **Directions:** 6m from M40 junct 15, just on edge of town, across Clopton Bridge towards Banbury

◉◉ Mercure Shakespeare

British

Modern cooking behind a Tudor-timbered façade

☎ 0870 400 8182 01789 294997 Chapel St CV37 6ER

This 17th-century building is just what you would expect to see in Shakespeare's home town, with its Tudor-timbered façade. Inside it's just as authentic, with lots of original beams, and open fires lit in winter. The smart décor uses rich, deep fabrics, giving a traditional feel

throughout. The cooking, however, is up to the minute using the best of fresh ingredients. Think olive oil poached sea bass accompanied by a roast butternut squash risotto, crab and tarragon, or perhaps a breast of guinea fowl with braised endive, fondant potato and pink peppercorns. Save room for glazed lemon tart with vanilla ice cream, or a chocolate fondant with banana and Muscovado ice cream to finish.

Chef: Jon Wood **Times:** 12-2/6-9.30, Closed L Mon-Sat (ex by arrangement) **Prices:** Fixed L £15.95, Fixed D £24.95, Starter £6.50-£9.50, Main £15.50-£22.95, Dessert £6, Service optional **Wine:** 84 bottles over £20, 25 bottles under £20, 12 by the glass **Notes:** Fixed L 3 courses, Dress Restrictions, Smart casual, Civ Wed 100 **Seats:** 80, Pr/dining room 25 **Children:** Portions **Rooms:** 74 (74 en suite) ★★★★ HL **Directions:** Follow signs to town centre. Round one-way system, into Bridge St. At rdbt turn left. Hotel 200yds on left **Parking:** 35

◉ Stratford Manor

Traditional British

Assured cooking in a contemporary environment

☎ 01789 731173 Warwick Rd CV37 0PY
e-mail: stratfordmanor@marstonhotels.com
web: www.marstonshotels.com

This is a modern, purpose-built hotel located just 3 miles from Stratford-upon-Avon in attractive countryside. It offers a range of facilities including conference rooms, a leisure centre with a gym, pool, spa, sauna and tennis courts. The stylish dining room is decorated in calm colours; the atmosphere is relaxed and the service polished. The menus offer interesting, well-executed dishes, such as mussel and crab chowder, calves' liver with red onion confit and red wine jus, and vanilla pannacotta with stewed rhubarb. Light meals are served in the Terrace Bar.

Times: 12-2.30/6-9.30, Closed L Sat **Rooms:** 104 (104 en suite) ★★★★ HL

◉ Stratford Victoria

British, Mediterranean

Victorian-style modern hotel serving classic cuisine

☎ 01789 271000 Arden St CV37 6QQ
e-mail: stratfordvictoria@qhotels.com
web: www.qhotels.com

An old-fashioned red telephone box makes a curious statement in this otherwise modern hotel with a Victorian appearance, an easy walk from the town centre. Inside you'll find leather chesterfields and a relaxing décor; the Traditions restaurant comes with exposed beams and ornately carved furniture. The food remains consistently accomplished, with dish presentation and the quality of ingredients taken seriously. The crowd-pleasing range of British and European dishes might include baked pork fillet served with minted pea purée, black pudding, apple and herb mash, crispy pancetta and a red wine jus, and to finish, perhaps an apple and cinnamon tartlet with vanilla ice cream.

Chef: Mark Grigg **Owners:** QHotels **Times:** 12.30-2/6-9.45 **Prices:** Starter £6.95, Main £19.25, Dessert £5.95, Service included **Wine:** 31 bottles over £20, 20 bottles under £20, 9 by the glass **Notes:** Sun L carvery 4 courses £17.50 inc coffee, Civ Wed 160, Air con **Seats:** 90, Pr/dining room 90 **Children:** Menu, Portions **Rooms:** 102 (102 en suite) ★★★★ HL **Directions:** From town centre, follow A3400 to Birmingham. Turn left at lights towards Arden Street, hotel 150yds on right **Parking:** 102

STRATFORD-UPON-AVON Continued

🖥 Coconut Lagoon

☎ 0870 755 7746 23 Sheep St CV37 6EF
web: www.theaa.com/travel/index.jsp

Southern Indian cuisine from Goa, Kerala, Karnataka, and Andhra Pradesh.

🖥 Georgetown

☎ 01789 204 445 23 Sheep St CV37 6EF
web: www.theaa.com/travel/index.jsp

Named after the East India Company's trading port in Malaysia, the restaurant offers Tamil Indian Malaysian, Chinese Malaysian, and more purely Malay dishes.

Lambs of Sheep Street

☎ 01789 292554 12 Sheep Streeet CV37 6EF
Modern British fare handy for the theatre.

The Opposition

☎ 01789 269980 13 Sheep St CV37 6EF
Related to Lambs above and similar in style.

WARWICK

MAP 10 SP26

⊛⊛ The Lodge Restaurant at Ardencote Manor

Modern International
Refurbished lakeside restaurant

☎ 01926 843111 & 843939 Lye Green Rd CV35 8LT
e-mail: hotel@ardencote.com
web: www.ardencote.com

The Lodge Restaurant has been strikingly refurbished in contemporary style - its sleek, light, open-plan layout has a modern bistro look. Plentiful windows and patio doors open on to the waterside terrace offering terrific views over the lake, and, on less clement days, there's a bar at the restaurant's entrance and a huge stone fireplace at the far end of the dining room. The menu's modern approach fits the surroundings and includes a 'La Plancha' selection that offers simply prepared dishes with a choice of sauces and vegetables, while the more elaborate carte delivers the likes of a pencil fillet of lamb glazed with pear cider and served with a sweet potato fondant and elderflower and summer berry sauce.

Chef: Yavor Kostadinov **Owners:** TSB Developments Ltd **Times:** 12-3/6-11
Prices: Fixed L £10-£25, Starter £5.95-£6.75, Main £14.75-£19.75, Dessert £5.75-£6.50, Service included **Wine:** 50 bottles over £20, 40 bottles under £20, 8 by the glass **Notes:** Sun L 1-3 courses £9.95-£16.95, Vegetarian available, Civ Wed 180 **Children:** Menu, Portions **Rooms:** 75 (75 en suite)
★★★★ HL **Directions:** Off A4189. In Claverdon follow signs for Shrewley & brown tourist signs for Ardencote Manor. Approx 1.5m **Parking:** 200

🖥 Robbie's Restaurant

☎ 01926 400470 74 Smith St CV34 4HU
web: www.theaa.com/travel/index.jsp

More like a dinner party than a formal restaurant, Robbie's is friendly, with chatty staff, an upbeat atmosphere, and a monthly-changing modern British menu.

WISHAW   MAP 10 SP19

⊛ The De Vere Belfry

Modern British, French
Fine cooking at celebrated golf hotel

☎ 01675 470301   B76 9PR
e-mail: enquiries@thebelfry.com
web: www.thebelfry.com

A busy hotel complex designed to meet the needs of international conference delegates and top-level golfers, boasting no fewer than three championship courses in its 370-acre grounds. The luxuriously furnished restaurant overlooks the gardens and is a relaxed setting for delicious cuisine. Menus range from a short fixed-price option, through to a carte, a tasting menu and a good-value Sunday lunch menu, with dishes ranging from old favourites (glazed rack of lamb with Pommery mustard, carrot, red wine and rosemary jus) to more adventurous offerings like nitrogen-cooled Bloody Mary with langoustine carpaccio, or apple and wensleydale crumble with clotted cream.

Chef: Darren Rowe **Times:** 12.30-2/7.30-10, Closed L Mon-Sat **Prices:** Fixed D £34.95, Starter £8.50-£10.95, Main £16.95-£29.95, Dessert £8.50-£10.50, Service added but optional 12.5% **Notes:** Vegetarian available, Dress Restrictions, Smart casual, Civ Wed 300, Air con **Seats:** 80 **Children:** Min 14 yrs **Rooms:** 324 (324 en suite) ★★★★ HL **Directions:** At junct of A446 & A4091, 1m NW of M42 junct 9, adjacent to M6 toll junct T2 **Parking:** 915

WEST MIDLANDS

BALSALL COMMON   MAP 10 SP27

⊛ Isobels Restaurant

Modern British
Friendly, popular modern restaurant

☎ 01676 533004   Haigs Hotel, Kenilworth Rd CV7 7EL
e-mail: info@haigshotel.co.uk
web: www.haigshotel.co.uk

A smart, black-and-white half-timbered exterior hides the chic modern interior of this popular hotel and restaurant, within easy reach of the NEC and motorway. Privately-owned and family-run, the hotel prides itself on its levels of comfort and service. The modern British cuisine draws praise from regulars and visitors alike, offering some interesting combinations, and Sunday lunch is a big occasion with an extensive menu on offer. The seasonally-changing carte includes a good selection of vegetarian options. You might start with a tart of warm wild mushrooms, sun-blushed tomatoes and ricotta cheese, and move on to pan-seared gnocchi with baby spinach and walnuts. A global wine list produces an interesting selection of fine wines and champagnes.

Chef: Jenny Goff **Owners:** Bill & Diane Sumner **Times:** 12.30-2.30/7-9.30, Closed L Mon-Sat, D Sun **Prices:** Fixed L £13.95, Starter £3.50-£5.50, Main £8.75-£15.50, Dessert £4.50, Service optional **Wine:** 15 bottles over £20, 20 bottles under £20, 4 by the glass **Notes:** Vegetarian available **Seats:** 60, Pr/dining room 28 **Children:** Portions **Rooms:** 23 (23 en suite) ★★★ HL **Directions:** On A452, 6m SE of NEC/airport, on left before village centre **Parking:** 25

⊛⊛ *Nailcote Hall*

Modern
Delightful cooking in an attractive country house with great facilities

☎ 024 7646 6174   Nailcote Ln, Berkswell CV7 7DE
e-mail: info@nailcotehall.co.uk
web: www.nailcotehall.co.uk

Dating back as far as 1640, Nailcote Hall stands in 15 acres of grounds in a rural location, yet is just a few minutes from the Midlands motorway network. The Oak Room restaurant is spacious and comfortable, the tartan carpeting and dark oak beams perfectly in keeping with the style of the house. The food is both ambitious and accomplished, delivering seared king scallops with leek mash and a duo of Clonakilty puddings for example, or a main of roasted halibut with braised oxtail ravioli, Puy lentils and truffle dressing. Round your meal off in style with baked cookie dough cheesecake with muffin, blueberry sauce and blueberry sorbet. Extras such as home-made bread, a pre-dessert and petits fours all add to the dining experience.

Times: 12-2/7-9.30, Closed L Sat, D Sun **Rooms:** 40 (40 en suite) ★★★★ HL **Directions:** On B4101 towards Tile Hill/Coventry, 10 mins from NEC/Birmingham Airport

BARSTON   MAP 10 SP27

⊛ The Malt Shovel at Barston
Popular local foodie pub in a rural setting

☎ 01675 443223   Barston Ln B92 0JP
web: www.themaltshovelatbarston.com

Old country pub surrounded by fields, with stripped wooden floors, open fires, lime green paintwork and heavy fabrics. A separate dining area is slightly more formal. Portions are plentiful and the quality sound, with fish of all kinds featuring strongly. The bar menu is supplemented by blackboard specials from the restaurant. Take a starter of hot smoked mackerel with mascarpone risotto and rocket, followed by pan-fried monkfish with paprika-roasted butternut squash and ginger yogurt, and to finish, an irresistible stack of Kirsch blinis with plum and apricot chutney and caramelita ice cream. Vegetarians have interesting options too - try sweet potato and red onion korma with saffron and raisin rice and poppadom.

Chef: Max Murphy **Owners:** Caroline Furby & Chris Benbrook **Times:** 12-2.30/6.30-9.30, Closed 25 Dec, Closed D Sun **Prices:** Fixed L £21-£24, Fixed D £25-£28, Starter £2.95-£6.95, Main £9.95-£17.95, Dessert £5.50, Service optional, Group min 6 service 10% **Wine:** 12 bottles over £20, 14 bottles under £20, 6 by the glass **Notes:** Sun L £11.95, Vegetarian available, Air con **Seats:** 40 **Children:** Min 10 yrs, Portions **Directions:** M42 junct 5, take turn towards Knowle. 1st left on Jacobean Lane, right turn at T-junct (Hampton Lane). Sharp left into Barston Lane. Restaurant 0.5m **Parking:** 30

BIRMINGHAM

MAP 10 SP08

◉ Bank Restaurant & Bar

Modern European 🖥

Contemporary canal-side brasserie cuisine

☎ 0121 633 4466   4 Brindley Place B1 2JB
e-mail: birmres@bankrestaurants.com
web: www.bankrestaurants.com

Allied to the smart London restaurants of the same name, this chic canal-side eatery does a brisk trade with shoppers and suits alike. It's a light-and-airy affair conjured from glass and steel, with red leather seating, two lively cocktail bars for pre-dinner drinks and a busy terrace for alfresco summer dining. Crowd-pleasing modern European brasserie-style dishes predominate, plus a few old favourites, all using well-sourced, fresh ingredients. Take confit pork belly served with celeriac purée and carrot vinaigrette, or perhaps grilled sea bass with confit fennel and potato and a black olive dressing. There's a good-value fixed-price menu too, and it's also open for breakfast.

Chef: Stephen Woods **Owners:** Bank Restaurant Group plc **Times:** 12-2.45/5.30-10.30, Closed 26 Dec, 1-2 Jan, 1 May, BHs, Closed D 25 Dec **Prices:** Fixed L £12.50, Fixed D £15, Starter £4.20-£10.50, Main £12-£22, Dessert £4.75-£4.95, Service added but optional 12.5% **Wine:** 65 bottles over £20, 16 bottles under £20, 14 by the glass **Notes:** Vegetarian available, Air con **Seats:** 150, Pr/dining room 100 **Children:** Menu, Portions **Directions:** Located off Broad St (A456) **Parking:** 100 yds away (Sheepcoat St)

◉ Birmingham Marriott

Modern British

Elegant brasserie in traditional hotel

☎ 0121 452 1144   12 Hagley Rd, Five Ways B16 8SJ
e-mail: pascal.demarchi@marriotthotels.co.uk
web: www.marriott.co.uk/bhxbh

This large Edwardian hotel is located on the outskirts of the city centre. There's a real feel of fin-de-siècle elegance throughout. Comfortable, well-presented public areas include an informal restaurant, West 12, popular with the city's businessmen and leisure guests alike. Service is typically up-front and helpful for the UK's second city. The brasserie-style menu comprises traditional dishes with some modern influences. Start with crab and leek tart with poached egg before trying either the 35-day aged Scotch rib-eye or calves' liver served with bubble-and-squeak and Madeira sauce. Finish with banana and rosemary tarte Tatin.

Times: 12-2.30/6-10, Closed L Sat **Rooms:** 104 (104 en suite) ★★★★ HL **Directions:** City end of A456, at the Five Ways rdbt

◉ Chung Ying Garden

Traditional Chinese V

Cantonese restaurant with an amazing choice of dishes

☎ 0121 666 6622 & 622 1668   17 Thorp St B5 4AT
e-mail: chungyinggarden@aol.com
web: www.chungying.co.uk

Former barracks have been pressed into service to provide a large restaurant for over 380 people on two levels. There are function rooms, a dance floor, DJ facilities and in-house karaoke and disco, offering an authentic taste of Hong Kong in Birmingham. The vast menu of traditional Cantonese cuisine is said to be the largest in England with around 400 dishes including sweet and sours, sizzlers and live seafood. There's also a selection of banquets for four or six people and set dinners for two, three, four or five people.

Chef: Mr Siu Chung Wong **Owners:** Mr S C Wong **Times:** Noon/midnight, Closed 25 Dec **Prices:** Fixed L £14-£32, Fixed D £14-£32, Starter £2.40-£36, Main £7-£180, Dessert £1.50-£5, Service optional **Wine:** 9 bottles over £20, 21 bottles under £20, 4 by the glass **Notes:** Fixed D 2 courses, Additional dim sum dishes on Sun, Vegetarian menu, Smart casual preferred, Air con **Seats:** 380, Pr/dining room 200 **Directions:** City centre, just off Hurst St, near Hippodrome Theatre & shopping centre, just off A38 **Parking:** 50

◉ Hotel Du Vin

Mediterranean, French

Chic hotel with a winning bistro menu

☎ 0121 200 0600 25 Church St B3 2NR
e-mail: info@birmingham.hotelduvin.com
web: www.hotelduvin.com

Located in the Jewellery Quarter, Birmingham's outpost of the Hotel du Vin chain is as chic and trendy as its sister establishments. A former eye hospital, the building dates from the early Victorian era and retains many original features including a sweeping staircase and granite pillars. The hotel's well-stocked bar is popular with residents and locals alike, while its bistro upholds the classic Hotel du Vin philosophy of quality food cooked simply from the freshest ingredients and good attention to detail. Mains might include a perfectly chargrilled rib-eye steak with pommes frites and sauce béarnaise, or pan-fried sea bass with baby fennel and green asparagus in a chive velouté.

Chef: Nick Turner **Times:** 12-2/6-10 **Prices:** Fixed L £14.50, Starter £6.50, Main £15.50, Dessert £6.75, Service added but optional 10% **Wine:** 600 bottles over £20, 40 bottles under £20, 16 by the glass **Notes:** Sun L £22.50, Vegetarian available, Civ Wed 80 **Seats:** 85, Pr/dining room 120 **Children:** Menu, Portions **Rooms:** 66 (66 en suite) ★★★★ TH **Directions:** Telephone for directions **Parking:** 20

◉◉ Jessica's

British V

Discreet suburban dining meets bold, accomplished cooking

☎ 0121 455 0999 1 Montague Rd, Edgbaston B16 9HN
web: www.jessicasrestaurant.co.uk

Jessica's pretty courtyard entrance is just off the busy Hagley Road in a leafy suburb, and offers unexpected privacy. The conservatory-style restaurant with views over the garden has a minimalist edge, decked out with pale-wood floors, white walls hung with modern art, and rich purple chairs contrasting with the white-clothed tables. The kitchen takes a modern approach to food, which is prepared with a high level of technical skill. Top-quality ingredients and innovative combinations are features of the menu, with dishes such as slow-cooked lamb shoulder in lavender honey, or sea bass with braised celery and pig's trotter ravioli. Finish with a dessert of lemon and lime posset, cardamom and tamarilo with tamarilo sorbet, or perhaps double chocolate mousse with apple and mint, apple sorbet and chocolate crisps.

Chef: Glynn Purnell **Owners:** Mr K & Mrs D Stevenson, Glynn Purnell **Times:** 12.30-2.30/7-10.30, Closed 1 wk Xmas, 1 wk Etr, last 2 wks Jul, Sun, Closed L Sat & Mon **Prices:** Fixed L £24.50, Service added but optional 12.5% **Wine:** 50 bottles over £20, 6 bottles under £20, 8 by the glass **Notes:** Fixed L 4 courses, Fixed ALC £36.95, Vegetarian menu, Dress Restrictions, Smart casual, Air con **Seats:** 36 **Children:** No children **Parking:** On street

◉ Malmaison Birmingham

Traditional, Modern

Buzzing brasserie in the heart of Birmingham's Mailbox

☎ 0121 246 5000 1 Wharfside St, The Mailbox B1 1RD
e-mail: birmingham@malmaison.com
web: www.malmaison.com

Malmaison Birmingham is part of The Mailbox complex, a 1960s former Royal Mail sorting office, which also includes a host of designer stores and array of eating outlets. The contemporary hotel's public rooms include a stylish bar and brasserie, where dark brown tones, mood lighting, and small alcoves and corners set the scene. The appealing repertoire of quality, fresh ingredients is simply prepared and offered at affordable prices. Think pan-fried skate beurre noisette with Parmentier potatoes, or, from the chargrill, calves' liver and bacon with mashed potato and onion gravy. And to finish, perhaps a rich assiette of chocolate - dark chocolate tart, chocolate fondant and white chocolate ice cream.

Chef: Patrick Harness **Owners:** Malmaison Ltd **Times:** 12-2.30/6-10.30 **Prices:** Fixed L £13.50, Fixed D £19.50, Starter £4.95-£8, Main £10.50-£25, Dessert £5.95, Service added but optional 10% **Wine:** 250 bottles over £20, 20 bottles under £20, 26 by the glass **Notes:** Home grown & local menu Fixed 2-3 courses, Vegetarian available, Air con **Seats:** 155, Pr/dining room 40 **Children:** Portions **Rooms:** 189 (189 en suite) ★★★ HL **Directions:** M6 junct 6, follow the A38 towards Birmingham, hotel is located within The Mailbox **Parking:** Mailbox carpark

◉◉ Opus Restaurant

Modern British

Chic modern eatery with crustacea counter

☎ 0121 200 2323 54 Cornwall St B3 2DE
e-mail: restaurant@opusrestaurant.co.uk
web: www.opusrestaurant.co.uk

This spacious contemporary restaurant is close to the City Chambers in Birmingham city centre. Wood flooring, wine racks and a crustacea counter set the scene for an upbeat modern dining experience, while warm colours, a large window frontage and rear atrium flood the restaurant with light during the day. Service is friendly but professional, the atmosphere relaxed. Well-sourced, quality seasonal ingredients - including freshly caught wild fish delivered daily (shellfish is a speciality here) and commitment to free-range meats - drive the accomplished kitchen's modern approach. Start with the likes of Carlingford rock oysters, and maybe follow up with pan-fried scallops and belly pork with a spring onion mousseline and Puy lentil and leek sauce, or fillets of Cornish lamb served with brinjal potatoes and baby spinach.

Chef: Dean Cole, David Colcombe **Owners:** Ann Tonks, Irene Allan, Dean Cole, David Colcombe **Times:** 12-2.30/6-10, Closed between Xmas and New Year, Sun, Closed L Sat **Prices:** Fixed L £15.50, Fixed D £17.50, Starter £6.50-£12.50, Main £12.50-£19.50, Dessert £5-£6, Service added but optional 12.5% **Wine:** 65 bottles over £20, 12 bottles under £20, 28 by the glass **Notes:** Vegetarian available, Air con **Seats:** 85, Pr/dining room 64 **Children:** Menu, Portions **Directions:** Telephone for directions

BIRMINGHAM CONTINUED

◉◉◉ **Simpsons**

see below

◉ **Thai Edge Restaurant**

Thai V 💻

Authentic Thai cooking in a contemporary setting

☎ 0121 643 3993 Brindley Place B1 2HS
e-mail: manager777@btconnect.com
web: www.thaiedge.co.uk

This contemporary oriental restaurant is decorated with authentic Thai artefacts and the open-plan space is divided up with glass and wooden screens. Well-spaced, linen-dressed tables and smart, authentically-attired staff complete the picture. Authentic Thai dishes from the four main regions of Thailand are presented on the typically lengthy menu, each with its own unique style, and clear translations. There's no running order to the Thai meal so all the dishes are served together and are ideal for sharing. There's a series of set options for novices, pairs or groups, plus good choices for vegetarians, and well-informed staff are on hand to help. Why not try deep-fried lobster with garlic and chilli, or perhaps steamed sea bass fillet with spicy and sour sauce.

Thai Edge Restaurant

Chef: Mit Jeensanthia **Owners:** Harish Nathwani **Times:** 12-2.30/5.30-11, Closed 25-26 Dec, 1 Jan **Prices:** Fixed L £7.95, Fixed D £19.95-£39.95, Starter £4.50-£8.50, Main £7.50-£18.95, Dessert £4.50-£5.50, Service added but optional 10% **Wine:** 14 bottles over £20, 26 bottles under £20, 6 by the glass **Notes:** Sun buffet available £12.95, Vegetarian menu, Air con **Seats:** 100 **Directions:** Brindley Place is just off Broad St (approx 0.5m from B'ham New Street station) **Parking:** Brindley Place

---

◉◉◉

Simpsons

BIRMINGHAM   **MAP 10 SP08**

Modern V 🍷 NOTABLE WINE LIST

A serious restaurant with sophisticated cuisine

☎ 0121 454 3434 20 Highfield Rd B15 3DU
e-mail: info@simpsonsrestaurant.co.uk
web: www.simpsonsrestaurant.co.uk

Set in a Grade II listed Georgian building in Edgbaston, Simpsons is widely regarded as one of the best restaurants in the Birmingham area. It's the epitome of good taste - chic and subtle hues of cream and beige, artful floral arrangements in the bar and salon, and contemporary artwork adorning the walls. There are four individually-themed dining rooms - French, Venetian, Oriental and Colonial - adding a hint of the theatrical to the surroundings, with the sense of occasion heightened by discreetly attentive service from professional staff who demonstrate their skill admirably when advising on the serious wine list.

The modern menu focuses on quality seasonal ingredients from the best UK sources (Salcombe crab, Lyme Bay lemon sole, Aberdeenshire beef, Loch Fyne smoked salmon, etc) presented in dishes cooked with a high degree of culinary expertise by a talented team. Expect day-boat turbot with a sesame crust, Puy lentils, salad and grilled endives, lemon confit and sauce oriental, or perhaps a roast rack of Cornish lamb served with celeriac fondant, pink grapefruit, melon and rosemary, and to finish, maybe a rhubarb crumble soufflé with lemon ice cream.

Chef: Andreas Antona, Luke Tipping **Owners:** Andreas & Alison Antona **Times:** 12.30-2/7-10, Closed 24-26, 31 Dec, 1-2 Jan, BHs, Closed D Sun **Prices:** Fixed L £20, Fixed D £30, Starter £11.50-£13, Main £22-£27.50, Dessert £7.50, Service added but optional 12.5% **Wine:** 600 bottles over £20, 13 by the glass **Notes:** Fixed L 3 courses, Tasting menu 6 courses £65, Vegetarian menu, Dress Restrictions, Smart casual, Air con **Seats:** 70, Pr/dining room 18 **Children:** Menu, Portions **Directions:** 2m from city centre, opposite St Georges Church, Edgbaston **Parking:** 20

🖳 The Bucklemaker

☎ 0121 200 2515 30 Mary Ann St, St Paul's Square B3 1RL

web: www.theaa.com/travel/index.jsp

Tucked into a former Georgian silversmiths' workshop, this delightful restaurant is traditional, contemporary and welcoming all at once. The atmosphere is businessy at lunch, romantic in the evenings, with modern European menus and a friendly, buzzy bar area.

🖳 Henry's Cantonese Restaurant

☎ 0121 200 1136 27 St Paul's Square B3 1RB

web: www.theaa.com/travel/index.jsp

A topflight, slightly formal Cantonese restaurant. Bright and spacious with a relaxed atmosphere, Henry's is popular with a professional crowd. You'll find all your favourites, plenty of veggie dishes and five set menus.

Imran's Balti

☎ 0121 449 1370 264-266 Ladypool Rd, Sparkbrook B12 8JU

Longstanding balti famous for its family-sized naan.

Maharaja

☎ 0121 622 2641 23-25 Hurst St B5 4AS

Indian serving superior versions of familiar dishes.

🖳 Metro Bar and Grill

☎ 0121 200 1911 73 Cornwall St B3 2DF

web: www.theaa.com/travel/index.jsp

A sumptuous, modern meeting and eating place that attracts a loyal crowd of regulars. The bright, slightly rustic modern European menu seems to please just about everyone, and there are daily blackboard specials.

San Carlo

☎ 0121 633 0251 4 Temple St B2 5BN

Traditional Italian with pizzas, pasta and good fish.

DORRIDGE   MAP 10 SP17

◎◎ Forest Hotel

Modern European

Reliable cooking in a modern, boutique hotel

☎ 01564 772120 25 Station Approach B93 8JA
e-mail: info@forest-hotel.com
web: www.forest-hotel.com

The red-brick, boutique-style Forest Hotel cuts a sophisticated modern dash in this south-eastern suburb of Birmingham, with its designer décor and airy downstairs restaurant and bar. The crowd-pleasing, broadly European style of cooking suits the contemporary surroundings and a good choice is offered from the rapide lunch, prix-fixe dinner and carte menus. Well-conceived dishes are prepared from quality seasonal ingredients, and cooking is precise, simple and intelligent. A good example of a starter is beetroot, tomato and parmesan tart, or crab and dill risotto with spiced crab samosa, while mains might include grilled sea bass, thyme risotto and shellfish broth,

with egg custard tart and Earl Grey ice cream to finish. Competitive pricing and informal, professional service hit just the right note, too.

Chef: Dean Grubb **Owners:** Gary & Tracy Perkins **Times:** 12-2.30/6.30-10, Closed 25 Dec, Closed D Sun **Prices:** Fixed L £12, Fixed D £15, Starter £4-£7.50, Main £7.50-£17.50, Dessert £4.75-£5.50, Service added but optional 10% **Wine:** 12 bottles over £20, 30 bottles under £20, 9 by the glass **Notes:** Sun L 2 courses £14, 3 courses £17.50, Vegetarian available, Civ Wed 100, Air con **Seats:** 70, Pr/dining room 150 **Children:** Menu, Portions **Rooms:** 12 (12 en suite) ★★★★ RR **Directions:** From M42 junct 5, go through Knowle village, right to Dorridge village, turn left before bridge **Parking:** 40

HOCKLEY HEATH   MAP 10 SP17

◎◎ Nuthurst Grange Country House Hotel

British, French

Fine dining with all the trimmings in country-house style

☎ 01564 783972 Nuthurst Grange Ln B94 5NL
e-mail: info@nuthurst-grange.com
web: www.nuthurst-grange.com

An imposing country house with a tree-lined drive and lovely views over extensive landscaped gardens and woodland. In the sunny dining room guests are comfortably seated at large round tables set with crystal glassware and orchids. A range of highly imaginative classic and modern French and British cuisine is offered from a choice of fixed-price menus, with a separate Sunday roast menu. With well balanced flavours and artistic flair, typical dishes include Jerusalem artichoke soup with apple beignet crisps, followed by a trio of Gloucester Old Spot pork (confit belly, smoked fillet and chou farci) and vanilla crème brûlée with peach purée and ice cream. Well-presented selection of canapés and amuse-bouche.

Times: 12-2/7-9.30, Closed 25-26 Dec, Closed L Sat **Rooms:** 15 (15 en suite) ★★★ HL **Directions:** Off A3400, 0.5 mile S of Hockley Heath, turn at sign into Nuthurst Grange Lane

MERIDEN   MAP 10 SP28

◎ Manor Hotel

Modern British, French

Satisfying food cooked with skill in Georgian manor

☎ 01676 522735 Main Rd CV7 7NH
e-mail: reservations@manorhotelmeriden.co.uk
web: www.manorhotelmeriden.co.uk

This sympathetically extended Georgian manor house is located in the heart of this sleepy village within easy reach of the National Exhibition Centre and close to the medieval cross that supposedly marks the centre of England. There are two dining options - the informal Triumph Buttery for light lunches and snacks and the more formal Regency Restaurant for fine dining. The latter specialises in classically-inspired dishes with a light, modern touch and good presentation. Try roasted fillet of turbot with lobster ravioli and langoustine sauce, or a cannon of lamb served with shepherd's pie, fine ratatouille and a basil and lamb jus.

Chef: Peter Griffiths **Owners:** Mr R Richards **Times:** 12-2/7-9.45, Closed 27-30 Dec, Closed L Sat **Prices:** Fixed L £23-£24, Fixed D £27-£28, Starter £6.50-£11.50, Main £12.95-£19.95, Dessert £5.50-£5.95, Service included **Wine:** 11 bottles over £20, 28 bottles under £20, 6 by the glass **Notes:** Sun L £18.75, Civ Wed 120, Air con **Seats:** 150, Pr/dining room 220 **Children:** Menu, Portions **Rooms:** 110 (110 en suite) ★★★ HL **Directions:** M42 junct 6 take A45 towards Coventry then A452, signed Leamington. At rdbt join B4102, signed Meriden, hotel 0.5m on left **Parking:** 180

ENGLAND

SOLIHULL   MAP 10 SP17

◉ The Town House Restaurant & Bar

Modern European

Cosmopolitan city-centre bar and brasserie

☎ 0121 704 1567 & 713 9315 727 Warwick Rd B91 3DA
e-mail: reservations@thetown-house.com
web: www.thetown-house.com

A cosmopolitan brasserie housed in an elegant building, opposite the main shopping centre. Expect a contemporary, open-plan interior, beautifully designed and furnished with an abundance of leather, steel, stylish objets d'art, fresh flowers, and gleaming glasses on polished wooden tables. A relaxed and informal atmosphere prevails for light meals, serious dining, or just a glass of wine. Modern, classic bistro-style cooking takes in open sandwiches, set and Sunday lunch menus, a taster menu, and a carte offering the likes of crab and sweet potato fishcakes with mango salsa, followed by roast cod fillet with Boston clam chowder, and Bailey's crème brûlée with honeycomb ice cream.

Chef: Rob Wear **Owners:** John & Jayne O Malley/John & Heidi Billane
Times: 12-3/6-10, Closed 1 Jan **Prices:** Fixed L £12.50-£13.50, Fixed D £15.50-£16.50, Starter £5.25-£7, Main £12.50-£22, Dessert £5.25-£6, Service added but optional 8% **Wine:** 25 bottles over £20, 17 bottles under £20, 21 by the glass **Notes:** Fixed L/D Mon-Fri, Tasting menu available, Sun L/D £12.95, Vegetarian available, Dress Restrictions, No caps/hoods **Seats:** 95, Pr/dining room 60 **Children:** Menu, Portions **Directions:** M42 junct 5. Take A41 to town centre **Parking:** 45

SUTTON COLDFIELD   MAP 10 SP19

◉◉ New Hall

Modern European V NEW

Moated manor house oozing character and accomplished cuisine

☎ 0121 378 2442 Walmley Rd B76 1QX
e-mail: mmaguire@newhalluk.com
web: www.newhalluk.com

Standing in mature grounds, New Hall is reputed to be the oldest inhabited moated house in England, its 900-year history providing a magical glimpse of a bygone age, while sympathetic renovation delivers all the modern comforts yet retaining oodles of character. Think flagstone floors, open fires, exposed beams and mullioned windows for openers, while quality décor and furnishings highlight its intrinsic charm. There are two restaurants with The Bridge restaurant being the fine-dining option. Service is from a professional team, while

the kitchen's fixed-price menus focus around seasonality and quality produce, the cooking showing intelligent restraint and concentrating on flavour, balance and texture. Think a duo of pork (loin and belly) served with red cabbage and caramelised apples, or carpaccio of Balmoral venison, and perhaps a dark chocolate cone with lavender and milk chocolate mousse.

Chef: Wayne Thompson **Owners:** Bridgehouse Hotels **Times:** 12-2/7-9.30, Closed L Sat **Prices:** Fixed D £45, Service optional **Wine:** 37 bottles over £20, 22 bottles under £20, 12 by the glass **Notes:** Sun L £25, Vegetarian menu, Civ Wed 150 **Seats:** 30, Pr/dining room 50
Children: Portions **Rooms:** 60 (60 en suite) ★★★★ HL
Directions: On B4148, E of Sutton Coldfield, close to M6 & M42.
Parking: 60

WALSALL   MAP 10 SP09

◉◉ Fairlawns Hotel and Spa

Modern British

Elegant hotel with robust modern cooking

☎ 01922 455122 178 Little Aston Rd, Aldridge WS9 0NU
e-mail: reception@fairlawns.co.uk
web: www.fairlawns.co.uk

Set in 9 acres of landscaped gardens, this popular family-run hotel is located in an extended Victorian building, complete with fitness centre and spa. The restaurant's contemporary elegance, with cream décor, comfortable seating and white-clothed tables, sets the scene for some accomplished cooking. International influences are evident on the essentially British menu, which makes the most of fresh, seasonal ingredients from local producers where possible. Simply prepared yet imaginative and well presented dishes are available on the two- and three-course dinner menus, and on the wide-ranging brasserie-style lunch menu available Monday to Friday. For mains, take pot-roast blade of local beef, with bubble-and-squeak and pepper and Cognac sauce, and finish with chocolate and orange bread-and-butter pudding with whisky anglaise, or iced pistachio soufflé with toffee sauce.

ENGLAND

Chef: Neil Atkins **Owners:** John Pette **Times:** 12-2/7-10, Closed 25-26 Dec, 1 Jan, Good Fri, Etr Mon, May Day, BH Mon, Closed L Sat **Prices:** Fixed L £19.95, Fixed D £24.50-£32.50, Service optional **Wine:** 32 bottles over £20, 34 bottles under £20, 18 by the glass **Notes:** Sun menu £19.50 before 6.30pm, £22.50 after 6.30pm, Vegetarian available, Dress Restrictions, No jeans, trainers, sports clothing, Civ Wed 100, Air con **Seats:** 80, Pr/dining room 100 **Children:** Menu, Portions **Rooms:** 59 (59 en suite) ★★★ HL **Directions:** Outskirts of Aldridge, 400 yds from junction of A452 (Chester Rd) & A454 (Little Aston Road) **Parking:** 120

WIGHT, ISLE OF

FRESHWATER   MAP 05 SZ38

◉ Farringford

Modern V

Country-house hotel overlooking Tennyson Downs

☎ 01983 752500 Bedbury Ln PO40 9PE
e-mail: enquiries@farringford.co.uk
web: www.farringford.co.uk

Set in 33 acres of mature parkland, this former home of Alfred, Lord Tennyson remains a relaxed and sophisticated country-house retreat, with its cosy log fires in winter and marvellous views all-year round. The restaurant brings a modern touch to the period property, with its large picture windows and attentive, friendly young staff. Generous portions of the straightforward modern British cooking are served up using quality fresh ingredients; take baked fillet of New Forest barramundi served with smoke cherry tomatoes, haloumi cheese and pomme gauffrette, and to finish, perhaps sticky toffee pudding - this version accompanied by vanilla ice cream and mint anglaise.

Chef: Ross Hastings **Times:** 12-2/6.30-9 **Prices:** Fixed L £12, Fixed D £29-£30, Starter £4.50-£9.95, Main £13.75-£29, Dessert £6.50, Service optional **Wine:** 30 bottles over £20, 39 bottles under £20, 5 by the glass **Notes:** Vegetarian menu, Dress Restrictions, No sports clothes or denim, Civ Wed 150 **Seats:** 100, Pr/dining room 20 **Children:** Menu, Portions **Rooms:** 18 (18 en suite) ★★★ HL **Directions:** Follow signs for Yarmouth, over bridge for 1m, take left at Pixie Hill. Continue for 2m. At rdbt take left into Afton Rd. Turn left at the bay. Turn into Bedbury Ln. Farringford is 0.5m from bay **Parking:** 50

GODSHILL   MAP 05 SZ58

◉◉ The Essex

Modern British NEW ⬩

Thatched restaurant with modern seasonal cooking

☎ 01983 840232 High St PO38 3HH
e-mail: info@godshillparkfarm.uk.com
web: www.godshillparkfarm.uk.com

Set in the picturesque village, this Grade II listed cottage comes thatched and redecorated. There are leather sofas in the lounge area, while wooden flooring, upholstered chairs and white linen characterise the comfortable, light and airy dining area. Plain walls are hung with local prints and there's a patio area to the rear. Service is suitably relaxed and friendly. The kitchen takes a modern line with its seasonal-changing, fixed-price menus making the best of local organic produce. Lunch is bolstered by a light-bite medley, while dinner cranks things up a gear, with the likes of seared Aberdeen Angus fillet and braised shin served with summer greens, dauphinoise and Madeira jus, or

venison Wellington, with perhaps a chocolate fondant tart finish, accompanied by champagne sorbet and iced doughnuts.

The Essex

Chef: Steve Harris **Owners:** K A & M J Domaille **Times:** 12-4/6-11, Closed L Mon-Tue (winter), D Sun **Prices:** Fixed L £16, Fixed D £32, Service optional **Wine:** 20 bottles over £20, 46 bottles under £20, 5 by the glass **Seats:** 36 **Children:** Portions **Directions:** On A3020 6m S of Newport **Parking:** Car park 200mtrs

SEAVIEW   MAP 05 SZ69

◉ Priory Bay Hotel

Modern

Tranquil country-house dining with wonderful views

☎ 01983 613146 Priory Dr PO34 5BU
e-mail: enquiries@priorybay.co.uk
web: www.priorybay.co.uk

This peaceful hotel has much to offer, with its own stretch of beach, 6-hole golf course and an outdoor swimming pool. Once a priory in the 14th century that housed a community of monks, the house enjoys remarkable views of the Solent and Spithead. The sumptuous, Regency-styled, candlelit Island Room makes for a romantic dinner setting, with fantastic views of the gardens and the sea. Dishes allow good quality ingredients to speak for themselves with fresh flavours throughout - try chargrilled yellow fin tuna with papaya salsa to start, then move on to fillet of turbot with baby bok choy and lemon-crushed new potatoes.

Chef: Chris Turner **Owners:** Mr R Palmer & Mr J Palmer **Times:** 12.30-2.15/7-9.30 **Prices:** Food prices not confirmed for 2008. Please telephone for details **Wine:** 29 bottles over £20, 14 bottles under £20, 8 by the glass **Notes:** Vegetarian available, Dress Restrictions, Smart/smart casual recommended, Civ Wed 100 **Seats:** 70, Pr/dining room 50 **Children:** Menu, Portions **Rooms:** 31 (31 en suite) ★★★ HL **Directions:** On B3330 to Nettlestone, 0.5 miles from St Helens **Parking:** 50

SEAVIEW Continued

◎◎ Seaview Hotel & Restaurant

Modern British

Bright and lively hotel with a choice of restaurants

☎ 01983 612711 High St PO34 5EX
e-mail: reception@seaviewhotel.co.uk
web: www.seaviewhotel.co.uk

A recently refurbished and expanded hotel with a timeless quality tucked away from the seafront but offering fabulous glimpses of the Solent from selected vantage points. There are two dining options - the cosy Front restaurant is traditional and quaint, while the smart Sunshine restaurant and Regatta Room is brasserie-style in nautical blue and white. The seasonally-inspired menus, including a five-course gastronomic menu, list the modern choices. Kick off with pan-seared hand-dived scallops with snow pea and fennel salad and confit lemon oil, and move on to fillets of John Dory, braised chicory, bacon, peas and Jerusalem artichoke purée. Tempting desserts might feature dark chocolate and pistachio torte with crème fraîche and rosewater syrup. A children's menu is available, and smartly dressed staff provide excellent service.

Chef: Graham Walker **Owners:** Techaid Facilities Ltd **Times:** 12-2/7-9.30, Closed L weekdays during winter **Prices:** Starter £6.50-£9, Main £16.50-£24, Dessert £6.25, Service optional **Wine:** 22 bottles over £20, 14 bottles under £20, 4 by the glass **Notes:** Sun L/D 2 courses £13.95, 3 courses £16.95, Vegetarian available, Air con **Seats:** 80, Pr/dining room 100 **Children:** Min 5 yrs, Menu, Portions **Rooms:** 24 (24 en suite) ★★★ HL **Directions:** Take B3330 from Ryde to Seaview, left into Puckpool Hill & follow signs for hotel **Parking:** On street, car park nearby

---

VENTNOR   MAP 05 SZ57

◎◎ Hambrough Hotel

Modern European

Skilful cooking in stylishly renovated seaside hotel

☎ 01983 856333 Hambrough Rd PO38 1SQ
e-mail: info@thehambrough.com
web: www.thehambrough.com

Chic hotel and restaurant set on a hillside overlooking Ventnor with stunning views out to sea. The interior is modern and stylish, decorated in minimalist style in creams, fawns and browns. Both the bar and restaurant enjoy sea views, the latter being the venue for some skilful and imaginative cooking. The short fixed-price menu makes good use of local seasonal ingredients, with dishes allowing the main ingredients to shine through. The kitchen's passion for food is revealed in a beautifully presented starter of organic salmon, rolled in

herbs and served with pickled cauliflower, bacon crème caramel and smoked herring roe, and an equally impressive main course of roast beef fillet with creamed garlic, wild mushroom tortellini, truffled gnocchi and Madeira jus.

Chef: Craig Atchinson **Owners:** Jo Dos Santos **Times:** 12-2.30/7-10, Closed Tue, Closed D Sun **Prices:** Fixed L £14.50, Fixed D £38.50, Service optional, Group min 8 service 10% **Wine:** 80 bottles over £20, 20 bottles under £20, 6 by the glass **Notes:** Sun L 3 courses £14.95, Tasting menu £55, Air con **Seats:** 26, Pr/dining room 14 **Children:** Portions **Rooms:** 7 (7 en suite) **Directions:** Telephone for directions **Parking:** On street

◎ The Pond Café

Modern European

Accomplished restaurant in scenic village setting

☎ 01983 855666 Bonchurch Village Rd, Bonchurch PO38 1RG
e-mail: info@thepondcafe.com
web: www.thepondcafe.com

The pond in the title is just across the road from this Victorian property, and on fine days it can be admired from the patio tables. Inside, the pastel decorations and wooden flooring are pleasantly understated. There's an exciting element to the uncomplicated modern European cooking, thanks to the skills of the kitchen. The imaginative preparation and presentation of dishes like roast halibut with mussel and horseradish foam, chicken breast with spring onion risotto, and caramelised rice pudding with prune and Armagnac compôte are what brings people back.

Chef: Luke Borley **Owners:** Jo Dos Santos **Times:** 12-2.30/7-9.30, Closed Mon **Prices:** Starter £3.25-£3.95, Main £10.50-£13.50, Dessert £3.25-£3.95, Service optional **Wine:** 27 bottles over £20, 8 bottles under £20, 6 by the glass **Notes:** Sun L £10.95 **Seats:** 26 **Children:** Portions **Directions:** Telephone for directions **Parking:** On street

◎◎ The Royal Hotel

Modern British

Sophisticated cuisine in smart surroundings

☎ 01983 852186 Belgrave Rd PO38 1JJ
e-mail: enquiries@royalhoteliow.co.uk
web: www.royalhoteliow.co.uk

High ceilings, crystal chandeliers, heavily draped curtains, large oil paintings and candles add to the stately, old-fashioned ambience of this Victorian seaside hotel. It is quite formal, with a sophisticated atmosphere and smartly attired staff. Modern British and French influenced cuisine makes the best use of fine local produce like asparagus from the Arreton Valley, local Ventnor lobster and Godshill free-range chicken. You could try a starter of chicken liver and foie gras parfait, served with apricot and ginger chutney. Main courses might take in pancetta-wrapped monkfish with wild mushroom, chorizo and pea risotto or chargrilled beef fillet with Madeira sauce, with hot chocolate fondant among the puddings.

Chef: Alan Staley **Owners:** William Bailey **Times:** 12-1.45/6.45-9, Closed 2 wks Jan, Closed L Mon-Sat in Apr-Oct **Prices:** Fixed L £22-£25, Fixed D £35-£50, Service optional **Wine:** 46 bottles over £20, 18 bottles under £20, 6 by the glass **Notes:** Dress Restrictions, Smart casual, no shorts, Civ Wed 150 **Seats:** 100, Pr/dining room 40 **Children:** Min 5 yrs, Portions **Rooms:** 55 (55 en suite) ★★★★ HL **Directions:** On A3055 coastal road, into Ventnor. Follow the one way system, turn left at lights into Church St. At top of hill bear left into Belgrave Rd, hotel on right **Parking:** 50

YARMOUTH MAP 05 SZ38

◉◉ Brasserie at The George Hotel

Mediterranean NEW

Imaginative food meets relaxed setting and sea views

☎ 01983 760331 The George Hotel, Quay St PO41 0PE
e-mail: jeremy@thegeorge.co.uk
web: www.thegeorge.co.uk

At the time of going to press, this sunny brasserie, situated in the 17th-century George Hotel, was soon to be extended, as it is now the hotel's only restaurant. Located at the rear of the water's-edge property, a haven of rich character, window tables enjoy great views of the Solent. Recently arrived head chef, Jose Graziosi, hails from Abruzzo, and spent 5 years as senior sous chef at Rick Stein's Seafood Restaurant. Needless to say, this talented chef will be taking the food in an Italian direction. Expect an antipasto of salumi, burrata cheese, pan-fried foie gras with mostarda di Cremona, organic pork, Aberdeen Angus beef and, of course, risotto. All dishes utilise top-notch ingredients, often local, many organic and several especially sourced from Italy.

Chef: Jose Graziosi **Owners:** John Illsley, Jeremy Willcock
Times: 12.30/7-10 **Prices:** Starter £7.50-£12, Main £16.50-£35, Dessert £7-£8, Service optional **Wine:** 40 bottles over £20, 20 bottles under £20
Seats: 60, Pr/dining room 20 **Rooms:** 17 (17 en suite)★★★ HL
Directions: Situated between the castle and pier **Parking:** The Square

WILTSHIRE

BRADFORD-ON-AVON MAP 04 ST86

◉◉ The Tollgate Inn

Modern British

Traditional character inn offering notable cooking

☎ 01225 782326 Ham Green BA14 6PX
e-mail: alison@tollgateholt.co.uk
web: www.tollgateholt.co.uk

A roadside inn with two restaurant areas - downstairs, once a weavers' shed, is an intimate dining room with a wood-burning stove, furnished with pews and cushions. The first-floor restaurant is larger with an open fire, wooden beams and high-backed leather chairs, and was the adjoining Baptist church. The fine modern British cuisine with Mediterranean influences specialises in local produce and each item is carefully sourced - beef from Church Farm, Broughton Gifford, game from local shoots, and village-grown vegetables. All this makes for some excellent dishes, perhaps crab soufflé with bisque sauce to start, followed by roast venison with juniper and port sauce, and sticky toffee pudding to finish.

The Tollgate Inn

Chef: Alexander Venables **Owners:** Alexander Venables, Alison Ward-Baptiste **Times:** 11-2.30/5.30-11, Closed Dec 25-26, Mon, Closed D Sun
Prices: Fixed L £10.95-£13.95, Starter £4.50-£8, Main £13.50-£19.50, Dessert £4.50-£5.95, Service optional, Group min 6 service 10% **Wine:** 12 bottles over £20, 23 bottles under £20, 7 by the glass **Seats:** 60, Pr/dining room 38 **Children:** Min 12 yrs **Rooms:** 4 (4 en suite) ★★★★ INN
Directions: M4 junct 18, take A46 and follow signs for Bradford-on-Avon, take A363 then turn left onto B3105, in Holt turn left onto B3107 towards Melksham. The Tollgate Inn is 100 yds on right **Parking:** 40

◉ Widbrook Grange

Modern British

Imaginative British cooking in comfortable country house

☎ 01225 864750 Trowbridge Rd, Widbrook BA15 1UH
e-mail: stay@widbrookgrange.com
web: www.widbrookgrange.com

Nestling by the Kennet and Avon Canal near the delightful town of Bradford-on-Avon, this family-owned 18th-century Georgian country house is relaxed, friendly and classy. The cinnamon, sage and cream-coloured décor of the Medlar Tree restaurant is named after an ancient tree in the gardens and offers an intimate fine-dining experience. High quality ingredients are sourced by a kitchen that concentrates on modern dishes like mussels, oyster and crevettes on a bed of linguine with garlic, parsley and white wine sauce, or grilled fillet of hake with tomato, black olive, anchovy and parsley dressing.

Chef: Robert Harwood **Owners:** Peter & Jane Wragg **Times:** 7-11, Closed 21-30 Dec, Closed L Mon-Sat **Prices:** Starter £5-£7.50, Main £13-£18.50, Dessert £5.50, Service included **Wine:** 15 bottles over £20, 13 bottles under £20, 4 by the glass **Notes:** Dress Restrictions, Smart casual, Civ Wed 50 **Seats:** 45, Pr/dining room 10 **Children:** Menu, Portions **Rooms:** 20 (20 en suite) ★★★ CHH **Directions:** 1m S of Bradford-on-Avon on A363 **Parking:** 50

The Bybrook at the Manor

CASTLE COMBE MAP 04 ST87

Modern British 🖥

Innovative cooking in imposing surroundings

☎ 01249 782206   Manor House Hotel SN14 7HR
e-mail: cdumeige@manorhouse.co.uk
web: www.exclusivehotels.co.uk

Dating back to the 14th century, this charming manor house sits in peaceful grounds in the village of Castle Combe, complete with Italian gardens and lawns sweeping down to the Bybrook river. Curl up with a book by the fire or work up an appetite with a round of golf or croquet, and then take a seat in the restaurant, an atmospheric room hung with tapestries that boasts many original features including stained-glass windows and carved stonework.

If you can take your eyes off the pretty views, you'll find a menu as accomplished as the setting demands. Expect artful modern dishes from a kitchen that knows its stuff and consistently impresses with its imaginative approach, quality ingredients, and clever combinations. Local produce is used where possible, with vegetable and herbs often arriving courtesy of the manor's gardens.

A salad of hand-dived roast scallops is a typical starter, served with salt cod crème fraîche, cauliflower pannacotta and three preparations of lemon, followed by slow-roast belly of Gloucestershire Old Spot pork with prune purée, confit potatoes, red cabbage jam, liquorice jus and crackling, and desserts such as warm caramelised pear tart with caramel ice cream and pear foam.

Chef: David Campbell
Owners: Exclusive Hotels
Times: 12-2/7-10, Closed L Sat
Prices: Fixed L £16, Fixed D £49.50, Service optional
Wine: 80 bottles over £20, 10 bottles under £20, 175 by the glass
Notes: Tasting menu 6 courses £65-£95, Vegetarian available, Dress Restrictions, Smart casual, Civ Wed 90
Seats: 80, Pr/dining room 90
Children: Menu, Portions
Rooms: 48 (48 en suite)★★★★ CHH
Directions: M4 junct 17, follow signs for Castle Combe via Chippenham
Parking: 175

BRADFORD-ON-AVON CONTINUED

◎◎ Woolley Grange

Modern British, French

Child-friendly atmosphere and excellent dining

☎ 01225 864705 Woolley Green BA15 1TX
e-mail: info@woolleygrangehotel.co.uk
web: www.woolleygrangehotel.co.uk

This splendid Jacobean Cotswold manor house is set in attractive, peaceful gardens amid beautiful countryside. Children are made especially welcome - with a trained nanny on duty in the nursery and other child-friendly facilities. The restaurant itself is split into two rooms - the Orangery leading on to the garden, and the main dining room, with its fun pictures of life at Woolley. The accomplished food is modern with international influences using quality seasonal produce, including ingredients from the hotel's own garden. Think roast fillet of pork served with confit belly, a casserole of root vegetables and mustard and port mash, and perhaps a millefeuille of confit apple and vanilla bean ice cream to finish.

Chef: Paul Burfords **Owners:** Luxury Family Hotels & von Essen Hotels **Times:** 12-2/7-9.30 **Prices:** Fixed D £35.50, Starter £10, Main £20.50, Dessert £5, Service optional **Wine:** 72 bottles over £20, 10 bottles under £20, 8 by the glass **Notes:** Sun L 3 courses £21.50, Vegetarian available, Dress Restrictions, Smart casual, Civ Wed 50 **Seats:** 40, Pr/dining room 22 **Children:** Menu, Portions **Rooms:** 26 (26 en suite) ★★★ HL **Directions:** Telephone for directions **Parking:** 25

CASTLE COMBE   MAP 04 ST87

◎◎◎ The Bybrook at the Manor

see opposite

COLERNE   MAP 04 ST87

◎◎◎ Lucknam Park

see page 512

HIGHWORTH   MAP 05 SU29

◎◎ Jesmonds of Highworth

Modern European NEW

Stylish, contemporary restaurant with skilfully prepared cuisine to match

☎ 01793 762364 Jesmond House SN6 7HJ
e-mail: info@desmondsofhighworth.com
web: www.jesmondsofhighworth.com

The stylish and contemporary refurbishment of this Grade II listed restaurant with rooms, on the edge of the Cotswolds, is a successful blend of old and new. From the modern bar to lounge and restaurant, the upbeat theme is set, backed by professional but friendly service. The enthusiastic kitchen team has pedigree, their modern European approach driven by high-quality produce and delivering intelligently simply, skilfully prepared dishes with a fine combination of textures and flavours. There are various menu options, including lunch, lite bite and square meal offerings, while the dinner carte might deliver a rump of local beef with braised oxtail and white onion soubise, and to finish, perhaps an orange crème brûlée with poached rhubarb and ginger ice cream.

Times: 12-2.30/7-9.15, Closed Mon, Closed D Sun

LITTLE BEDWYN   MAP 05 SU26

◎◎◎ The Harrow Inn at Little Bedwyn

see page 513

LOWER CHICKSGROVE   MAP 04 ST92

◎ Compasses Inn

Traditional British

Carefully prepared, quality produce in delightful country inn

☎ 01722 714318 SP3 6NB
e-mail: thecompasses@aol.com
web: www.thecompassesinn.com

This 14th-century thatched inn comes brimful of character and atmosphere. Its original beams derive from decommissioned galleons, while stone walls, uneven flagstones and high settle booths add further charm, and, with only two windows, candlelight adds to the timeless quality, punctuated with helpings of relaxed and friendly service. The cooking's certainly not stuck in a time warp though, the modern approach making intelligent use of carefully sourced produce, including fish from Brixham. Menus come chalked up on blackboards, changing regularly to focus on seasonal and local availability; perhaps sea bass fillet with scallops and a crabmeat sauce, or slow-roast pork belly served with an apricot and apple compôte and cider sauce.

Chef: Ian Evans, Ian Chalmers **Owners:** Alan & Susie Stoneham **Times:** 12-3/6-11, Closed 25 & 26 Dec **Prices:** Starter £5-£7, Main £9-£18, Dessert £4.50-£6, Service optional **Wine:** 17 bottles over £20, 19 bottles under £20, 6 by the glass **Notes:** Vegetarian available **Seats:** 50, Pr/dining room 14 **Children:** Menu, Portions **Rooms:** 5 (5 en suite) ★★★★ INN **Directions:** On A30 W of Salisbury, take 3rd right after Fovant, after 1/2m turn left into Lagpond Lane, Inn 1m on left **Parking:** 35

Lucknam Park

COLERNE MAP 04 ST87

Modern British

Faultless country-house cuisine

☎ 01225 742777   SN14 8AZ
e-mail: reservations@lucknampark.co.uk
web: www.lucknampark.co.uk

Set in 500 acres of parkland and beautiful gardens, this magnificent Palladian mansion - now a notable country-house hotel - exudes luxury. A choice of lounge areas, from the luxurious splendour of the 17th-century drawing room with its chandeliers, ornate cornicing, oil paintings and deep sofas to the atmospheric library, deliver the anticipated comforts and style. The formal dining room, in the mansion's former ballroom, is an elegant bow-fronted affair with lovely views across the estate, gardens and that avenue of trees. Well-spaced tables, crisp napery and fine glassware fit the bill, as does the attentive, professional and knowledgeable service, while chef Hywel Jones's highly accomplished, clean-cut cooking more than matches expectations.

The approach is modern-focused, underpinned by a classical French theme, with great emphasis placed on sourcing high-quality seasonal ingredients. The fixed-price menus come dotted with luxury; think caramelised veal sweetbreads, lasagne of wild mushrooms, langoustines, Sauternes and rosemary foam to start, followed by loin of Brecon venison with creamed cabbage, oxtail and sloe gin sauce, or perhaps roast fillet of Cornish John Dory with braised free-range pork belly, white onion purée and baby leeks.

Chef: Hywel Jones
Owners: Lucknam Park Hotels Ltd
Times: 12.30-2.30/6.45-10, Closed L Mon-Sat
Prices: Fixed L £20, Fixed D £60, Service included
Notes: Sun L 3 courses £30, Dress Restrictions, Smart casual, no denim or trainers, Civ Wed 64
Seats: 80, Pr/dining room 30
Children: Min 5 yrs, Menu, Portions
Rooms: 41 (41 en suite)★★★★★ CHH
Directions: From M4 junct 17 take A350 to Chippenham, then A420 towards Bristol for 3m. At Ford turn towards Colerne. After 4m turn right into Doncombe Ln, then 100yds on right
Parking: 80

The Harrow Inn at Little Bedwyn

LITTLE BEDWYN   MAP 05 SU26

Modern British v ▲NOTABLE WINE LIST 🕮

Emphasis on stunning seafood and wine

☎ 01672 870871   SN8 3JP
e-mail: bookings@harrowinn.co.uk
web: www.harrowinn.co.uk

Secreted away down winding country lanes in the hamlet of
Little Bedwyn, what was once the village pub is now a
classy country restaurant of some note. The dining room -
split into two sections - is bright and contemporary, featuring
dark-leather high-backed chairs and neatly dressed tables laid
with Riedel glasses and colourful Villeroy crockery. Service,
led by Sue Jones, is friendly and relaxed, and husband Roger
mans the stove. There's also a small garden at the rear for
summer alfresco dining and aperitifs.
Roger's approach in the kitchen is equally modern, with much
emphasis placed on the freshness and sourcing of quality
ingredients. Fish is caught on day boats landed at Brixham,
while meat is from specialist farmers and butchers (perhaps
28-day hung Aberdeen Angus from Moray) and salads and
herbs are specifically grown in North Devon. Thus Roger's
cooking style is intelligently straightforward, allowing
ingredients to shine with clean-cut flavours. Expect the likes
of grilled diver-caught scallops with chorizo, pea purée and
pea shoots, a roast faggot and caramelised suckling pig with
apple sauce and perhaps a treacle tart to finish. A stunning
wine list of passion and high quality, plus an excellent range
of cheeses, provide exceptional accompaniment.

Chef: Roger Jones
Owners: Roger & Sue
Jones
Times: 12-3/7-11, Closed 3
wks Jan & Aug, Mon-Tue,
Closed D Sun
Prices: Fixed L £30, Fixed
D £40, Starter £12-£15,
Main £22-£25, Dessert
£7.50-£10, Service optional
Wine: 800 bottles over
£20, 25 bottles under £20,
14 by the glass
Notes: Fixed L 3 courses,
Fixed D 4 courses, Tasting
menu £60, Vegetarian
menu, Dress Restrictions,
Smart casual
Seats: 34
Children: Menu, Portions
Directions: Between
Marlborough &
Hungerford, well signed
Parking: On street

MALMESBURY   MAP 04 ST98

⊛ Best Western Mayfield House Hotel
Modern British NEW
Fresh, modern dishes in a country-house setting

☎ 01666 577409   Crudwell SN16 9EW
e-mail: reception@mayfieldhousehotel.co.uk
web: www.mayfieldhousehotel.co.uk

Situated in a small Cotswold village, this stone-built country-house hotel has a spacious walled garden. The chef takes a modern approach to cooking and presentation, turning out imaginative, fresh dishes. Starters might include the likes of seared wood pigeon salad with a sherry and prune dressing, while main courses typically feature dishes like rump of new season lamb, served sliced and pink, on a round of crushed and minted new potatoes, with seasonal vegetables. For dessert, try something truly indulgent, like a dark chocolate brownie with pistachio ice cream.

Chef: Paul Trewin **Owners:** Max Strelling, Chris Marston **Times:** 12-2/6.15-9, Closed L Mon-Sat **Prices:** Starter £3.75-£6.75, Main £10.95-£18, Dessert £4.50-£5, Service optional **Wine:** 10 bottles over £20, 24 bottles under £20, 5 by the glass **Notes:** Vegetarian available **Seats:** 50, Pr/dining room 40 **Children:** Menu, Portions **Rooms:** 26 (26 en suite) ★★★ HL **Directions:** 3m N of Malmesbury on A429, in the village of Crudwell. Hotel is on left **Parking:** 40

⊛⊛ Old Bell Hotel
Traditional French
Skilful cooking in elegant Edwardian surroundings

☎ 01666 822344   Abbey Row SN16 0BW
e-mail: info@oldbellhotel.com
web: www.oldbellhotel.com

Reputedly the oldest purpose-built hotel in England, The Old Bell has provided rooms and food since 1220. Visitors will note that facilities have improved greatly since then! Older rooms are furnished with antiques - new ones have a more contemporary feel. Service is friendly and efficient. The dining room is an elegant Edwardian addition offering imaginative dishes using local ingredients. To start try stilton, pear and endive salad with glazed walnuts and parmesan or marinated smoked salmon and crab with spring onion, ginger and lemon, followed by Scottish beef fillet, rösti potatoes, broad beans, morels and truffle jus. Comforting desserts include bread-and-butter pudding, warm chocolate fondant or an 'indulgence' of all five dessert offerings.

Chef: Tom Rains **Owners:** The Old Bell Hotel Ltd **Times:** 12.15-2/7-9.30 **Prices:** Starter £6.50-£8.95, Main £15.50-£21.50, Dessert £6.50-£6.75,

Service optional **Wine:** 109 bottles over £20, 8 bottles under £20, 8 by the glass **Notes:** Tasting menu 7 courses available, Vegetarian available, Dress Restrictions, Smart dress preferred, Civ Wed 80 **Seats:** 60, Pr/dining room 24 **Children:** Menu, Portions **Rooms:** 31 (31 en suite) ★★★ HL **Directions:** In town centre, next to Abbey. 5 m from M4 junct 17 **Parking:** 31

⊛⊛ The Rectory Hotel
British
Traditional country-house hotel with a close eye on contemporary style

☎ 01666 577194   Crudwell SN16 9EP
e-mail: info@therectoryhotel.com
web: www.therectoryhotel.com

The original Cotswold stone-built rectory dates from the 16th century but has additional Victorian wings, and 3 acres of walled gardens provide a delightful setting beside the village church. The hotel is elegant with stylish period furnishings and sympathetic décor. The restaurant overlooks the attractive gardens and features some impressive wood panelling. The dinner menu features British cuisine with some good straightforward dishes accurately cooked. Try the likes of Coln Valley smoked salmon served with champ potato cake, a poached egg and hollandaise sauce, followed by whole Bilbury trout with new potatoes and a lemon and caper dressing. Desserts are traditional and delicious - Eton Mess, or elderberry-scented summer berry trifle might be on offer, or perhaps try a refreshing Pimms jelly with poached peaches and vanilla cream. Children have their own menu.

Times: 12-2/7-9.30, Closed L 31 Dec **Rooms:** 12 (12 en suite) ★★★ **Directions:** Follow A429 to Cirencester. Rectory is in Crudwell village centre, next to church

⊛⊛⊛ Whatley Manor
see opposite

OAKSEY   MAP 04 ST99

⊛⊛ The Wheatsheaf Inn
Modern British
Friendly gastro-pub in tranquil village setting

☎ 01666 577348   Wheatsheaf Ln SN16 9TB

Dating back to the 14th century, this Cotswold stone pub in the pretty village of Oaksey has a big inglenook fireplace, a wooden-fronted bar and dark beams. The restaurant has a light, modern feel with sisal carpet, wooden tables and painted walls decorated with wine racks and jars of preserved vegetables. Modern British pub food is the order of the day, from a kitchen team with a strong commitment to local produce. Starters include salmon fishcake with a sweet-and-sour sauce, which may be followed by guinea fowl with fondant potato and bacon, or sea bass with crab and basil terrine, and a mussel and herb sauce.

Chef: Tony Robson-Burrell/Guy Opie **Owners:** Tony & Holly Robson-Burrell **Times:** 12-2/6.30-9.30, Closed Mon **Prices:** Starter £4.25-£6.50, Main £10.25-£17.95, Dessert £4.95-£5.50, Service optional **Wine:** 12 bottles over £20, 16 bottles under £20, 7 by the glass **Notes:** Sun L £13.95 3 courses **Seats:** 44, Pr/dining room 8 **Children:** Portions **Directions:** Off A429 towards Cirencester, near Kemble **Parking:** 15

Whatley Manor

MALMESBURY　　　　　　　　　MAP 04 ST98

Modern French 🍷 NOTABLE WINE LIST

French cuisine in new-style, luxury country-house hotel

☎ 01666 822888　Easton Grey SN16 0RB
e-mail: reservations@whatleymanor.com
web: www.whatleymanor.com

Nestling in 12 acres of gardens, meadows and woodland, this stunning Cotswold-stone country house has been lovingly renovated by its Swiss owners to provide the highest levels of luxury. Designed to soothe and restore, with luxurious furnishings and fabrics, beautiful gardens and a magnificent spa, complemented by professional yet understated service. There's a choice of restaurants, too: Le Mazot (named after and reflecting the old-fashioned Swiss mountain chalet) is the more informal brasserie (though suitably sophisticated in its own right with an appealing menu) and is open daily for lunch and dinner; while the elegant Dining Room is the intimate, dinner-only fine-dining option, resplendent in silk-clad walls, luxurious table settings and low-level lighting. Its cuisine is classic French with a contemporary theme, focusing on top-class produce, and, like everything else here, luxury. Light, complex, beautifully presented dishes are delivered via a fixed-price carte and tasting option. You might take a main course of pan-fried loin of Balmoral Estate venison with Epoisses and potato gratin and a chocolate gel and port reduction, while to finish, perhaps a caramel soufflé served with popcorn ice cream and mandarin smoothie. Ancillaries like canapés, amuse-bouche, pre-dessert, breads and petits fours all hold top form, while a notable wine list provides the perfect complement.

Chef: Martin Burge　**Owners:** Christian Landolt　**Times:** 7-10, Closed Mon-Tues, Closed L all week　**Prices:** Fixed D £65, Service added but optional 10%　**Wine:** 13 by the glass　**Notes:** Tasting menu £80, incl. wine £140, Vegetarian available　**Seats:** 40, Pr/dining room 30　**Children:** Min 12 yrs, Portions　**Rooms:** 23 (23 en suite)★★★★★ HL　**Directions:** Please telephone for directions　**Parking:** 120

PURTON　　　　　　　　　MAP 05 SU08

◎◎ **The Pear Tree at Purton**

Modern British 💻

Charming Cotswold stone hotel with superior food

☎ 01793 772100　Church End SN5 4ED
e-mail: stay@peartreepurton.co.uk
web: www.peartreepurton.co.uk

Surrounded by rolling Wiltshire farmland, this 15th-century former vicarage, once belonging to the unique twin towers church of St Mary's in Purton, looks out over 7.5 acres of well-tended gardens. The airy conservatory restaurant perfectly complements the serene setting, with fine linen and elegant tableware adding to the air of genteel refinement. The kitchen takes a suitably modern approach using quality ingredients - many locally sourced - cooked simply, marrying flavours with obvious expertise and flair. Take a starter of crispy sea bass with chilli and peanut salad, followed by steamed halibut with crispy bacon and an olive and caper salsa, or perhaps a rack of lamb partnered with a tomato and basil jus, and to finish, a prune and almond tart served with caramel ice cream.

Chef: Alan Postill　**Owners:** Francis and Anne Young　**Times:** 12-2/7-9.15, Closed 26-30 Dec, Closed L Sat　**Prices:** Fixed L £19.50, Fixed D £34.50, Service optional　**Wine:** 69 bottles over £20, 29 bottles under £20, 11 by the glass　**Notes:** Fixed L 3 courses, Fixed D 4 courses, Vegetarian available, Dress Restrictions, No shorts, Smart casual, Civ Wed 50　**Seats:** 50, Pr/dining room 50　**Children:** Portions　**Rooms:** 17 (17 en suite) ★★★ HL　**Directions:** From M4 junct 16, follow signs to Purton. Turn right at Spa shop, hotel 0.25m on right　**Parking:** 70

ROWDE　　　　　　　　　MAP 04 ST96

◎ **George & Dragon**

Modern British

Charming old pub with a relaxed gastro-pub atmosphere

☎ 01380 723053　High St SN10 2PN
e-mail: thegandd@tiscali.co.uk
web: www.thegeorgeanddragonrowde.co.uk

This charming old inn mixes original features with a relaxed gastro-pub atmosphere. With dark wooden beams throughout, a log fire strikes a homely note in the bar, while the restaurant is decked out with wooden furniture and simple table appointments. The carte is supplemented by blackboard specials, plus a separate fish menu featuring the likes of whole grilled lemon sole, or Scottish langoustines with mayonnaise. Expect mains such as rack of lamb with garlic mash, or warm duck breast salad with onion marmalade and sautéed potatoes, then finish with an old fashioned pudding: treacle tart with clotted cream for example, or chocolate bread-and-butter pudding.

Chef: Christopher Day　**Owners:** Mr & Mrs Hale & Mr C Day　**Times:** 12-3/6-11, Closed 1-8 Jan, Mon, Closed D Sun　**Prices:** Fixed L £13, Starter £5-£8, Main £9.50-£18.50, Dessert £5.50, Service optional　**Wine:** 34 bottles over £20, 16 bottles under £20, 10 by the glass　**Notes:** Sun L 3 courses £15.50　**Seats:** 35　**Children:** Portions　**Directions:** 1.5m out of Devizes towards Chippenham on A342　**Parking:** 12

SALISBURY
MAP 05 SU12

◉ Anokaa
Modern Indian
Contemporary Indian cuisine in colourful, stylish surroundings

☎ 01722 414142 60 Fisherton St SP2 7RB
e-mail: info@anokaa.com
web: www.anokaa.com

This modern split-level restaurant boasts an unfussy décor, with only subtle references to India visible. With waiters wearing traditional Moghul costumes, service is slick and confident - both factors very much in keeping with the forward-looking approach of the fusion Indian food. Dishes are all freshly prepared and each is distinctively spiced - baby squid tossed with fresh ground coconut, cumin and curry leaves, for example, or modu murg - corn-fed chicken breast cooked with honey and coconut in mild spices. The lunch menu is a real bargain - and ensures tables are full, so arrive early!

Chef: Vijindra Singh Rawat **Owners:** Mohammed Odud, Solman Farsi **Times:** 12-2/5.30-10.30, Closed 25-26 Dec **Prices:** Fixed L £7.25-£29, Fixed D £20-£40.50, Starter £3.95-£7.95, Main £8.90-£26, Dessert £3.55-£6.90, Service optional, Group min 12 service 10% **Wine:** 10 bottles over £20, 16 bottles under £20, 7 by the glass **Notes:** Vegetarian available, Dress Restrictions, Smart casual, Air con **Seats:** 80 **Children:** Min 5 yrs **Directions:** Adjoined to The Salisbury Playhouse & City Hall **Parking:** Main car park to rear of restaurant

◉ Best Western Red Lion Hotel
Modern European
Imaginative cooking in eclectic surroundings

☎ 01722 323334 Milford St SP1 2AN
e-mail: reception@the-redlion.co.uk
web: www.the-redlion.co.uk

Built to accommodate draughtsmen working on Salisbury Cathedral 750 years ago, the Red Lion is thought to be the oldest purpose-built hotel in Britain, and has been in the same family for 100 years. The old and the new mingle cheerfully in relaxed surroundings, and the ancient wattle-and-daub wall in the Vine restaurant makes a talking point amid the elegant settings. The menu, too, offers an interesting mixture of modern and traditional dishes, with English and continental influences, using fresh produce, local wherever possible.

Chef: Noel Malone **Owners:** Maidment Family **Times:** 12.30-2/7-9.30, Closed L Mon-Sat **Prices:** Fixed L £14.50-£15.50, Fixed D £24.95-£25.95,

Starter £4.95-£6.50, Main £13.50-£19.50, Dessert £5-£5.95, Service included **Wine:** 9 bottles over £20, 22 bottles under £20, 9 by the glass **Notes:** Civ Wed 60 **Seats:** 85, Pr/dining room 80 **Children:** Portions **Rooms:** 51 (51 en suite) ★★★ HL **Parking:** Pay & display car park

◉ 206 Brasserie
British NEW
Modern setting for straightforward, honest cooking

☎ 01722 417411 & 424111 Milford Hall Hotel, 206 Castle St SP1 3TE
e-mail: simonhughes@milfordhallhotel.com
web: www.milfordhallhotel.com

The smart brasserie-style restaurant adjoins the hotel and has the feel of a substantial conservatory. External decking provides space for outside seating in summer. The interior is light and airy with pastel rag-rolled walls and ceiling, and the tables are simply set. It's a great place to bring the family - not too formal - knowing you'll be well looked after and enjoy your meal. Simple, honest and skilfully cooked dishes include a starter of tempura scallops with sweet chilli jam, followed by whole sea bass with sea salt, new potatoes, vodka and dill beurre blanc, or pan-fried fillet steak on a rosemary croûte with Portobello mushrooms.

Chef: Chris Gilbert **Owners:** Simon Hughes **Times:** 12-2/6.30-10, Closed 26 Dec **Prices:** Starter £4.25-£6.75, Main £9.95-£16.50, Dessert £4.50-£6.50, Service optional **Wine:** 6 bottles over £20, 27 bottles under £20, 6 by the glass **Notes:** Sun L 3 courses £14.95, Vegetarian available, Civ Wed 50 **Seats:** 40, Pr/dining room 20 **Children:** Menu, Portions **Rooms:** 35 (35 en suite) ★★★ HL **Directions:** From A36 at rdbt on Salisbury ring road, right onto Churchill Way East. At St Marks rdbt left onto Churchill Way North to next rdbt, left in Castle St **Parking:** 50

SWINDON
MAP 05 SU18

▭ Pagoda Palace
☎ 01793 877888 Pepperhill Box, Meadway, Peatmoor SN5 5YZ
web: www.theaa.com/travel/index.jsp

An impressive traditional-style temple overlooking the tranquil Peatmoor Lagoon in West Swindon. The menu lists a feast of speciality Szechwan, Cantonese and Peking dishes. Excellent dim sum.

WARMINSTER
MAP 04 ST84

◉◉ Bishopstrow House Hotel
Modern British V
Enjoyable food in pleasant country-house environs

☎ 01985 212312 BA12 9HH
e-mail: info@bishopstrow.co.uk
web: www.bishopstrow.co.uk

Part of the von Essen group of hotels, this refurbished Georgian country house is set in 27 acres of landscaped grounds and houses one of the biggest collections of antique firearms in the country, as well as a host of period features complemented by a sensitive, modern approach to décor. The modern menu consists largely of tried-and-tested combinations delivered with consummate skill with the classical French influence never far from view. Take a starter of pan-fried fillet of rainbow trout with a risotto of peas and organic cress, followed by a main course of roast halibut served with crushed new potatoes, poached Scottish lobster and sugar snap peas, and for dessert champagne and strawberry terrine with clotted cream brûlée and pistachio caramel.

Chef: Luke Richards **Owners:** von Essen Hotels **Times:** 12-2.30/7-9.30 **Prices:** Fixed L £12-£26, Fixed D £24-£38, Starter £9, Main £20, Dessert £9, Service added but optional 15% **Wine:** 180 bottles over £20, 5 bottles under £20, 9 by the glass **Notes:** Tasting menu 7 courses £50, Sun L 3 courses £18.50, Vegetarian menu, Dress Restrictions, Smart casual, Civ Wed 70 **Seats:** 65, Pr/dining room 28 **Children:** Menu, Portions **Rooms:** 32 (32 en suite) ★★★★ HL **Directions:** From Warminster take B3414 (Salisbury). Hotel is signed **Parking:** 100

WHITLEY   MAP 04 ST86

◉◉ The Pear Tree Inn

Modern British

Attractive inn serving local produce

☎ 01225 709131 Top Ln SN12 8QX
e-mail: enquiries@thepeartreeinn.com
web: www.thepeartreeinn.com

The inn was once a farm and the décor reflects its history, using old agricultural implements and simple stripped wooden tables. The mellow stone building has been transformed with a rustic yet contemporary feel and is set in lovely grounds. The interior is divided into a bar, dining area and garden room. Modern British cuisine with European influences and fresh, locally-sourced seasonal produce are the draw here. Dishes are straightforward and the menu offers an appealing choice; think baked rump of lamb and braised rolled shoulder with caponata, buttery mash and a black olive dressing, or fillet of wild Cornish black bream served with pan-fried gnocchi, tomato and herb sauce, grilled courgettes and pesto, while puddings might include a dark chocolate brownie with clotted cream.

Chef: Kevin Chandler **Owners:** Martin & Debbie Still **Times:** 12-2.30/6.30-9.30, Closed 25-26 Dec, 1 Jan **Prices:** Fixed L £13.50-£15.50, Starter £4.95-£7.95, Main £11.50-£18.95, Dessert £5.50, Service optional **Wine:** 28 bottles over £20, 26 bottles under £20, 12 by the glass **Seats:** 60, Pr/dining room 40 **Children:** Menu, Portions **Rooms:** 8 (8 en suite) ✦✦✦✦✦ RR **Directions:** Telephone for directions **Parking:** 60

WORCESTERSHIRE

ABBERLEY   MAP 10 SO76

◉◉ The Elms Hotel & Restaurant

Modern, Traditional British

English country elegance and fining dining with excellent ingredients

☎ 01299 896666 Stockton Rd WR6 6AT
e-mail: info@theelmshotel.co.uk
web: www.theelmshotel.co.uk

Built in 1710 by Gilbert White (a pupil of Sir Christopher Wren), this stunning Queen Anne house overlooks beautifully manicured lawns to the countryside beyond. The lavish interiors are very much in keeping with the grandiose exteriors, with ornate plaster ceilings, carved fireplaces, antique furnishings and stained-glass windows evoking a sense of historical glamour. The kitchen shows a high level of technical skill and the accomplished modern British cooking aspires to greater heights through clear flavours and the imaginative use of first-class ingredients. You might expect a starter of seared scallops with sweet potato, pineapple and Asian spiced foam, followed perhaps by roast monkfish with pancetta, langoustine, lemongrass and ginger, with raspberry and Pol Roger champagne jelly accompanied by its own sorbet to finish.

Chef: Daren Bale **Owners:** von Essen Hotels **Times:** 12-2.30/7-9.30 **Prices:** Fixed L £13.50, Fixed D £35, Starter fr £9.50, Main fr £22.50, Dessert fr £9.50, Service optional **Wine:** 111 bottles over £20, 21 bottles under £20, 10 by the glass **Notes:** Sun L £24.95, Tasting menu £57.50, Dress Restrictions, Smart casual, no jeans, no T-shirts, Civ Wed 70 **Seats:** 50, Pr/dining room 50 **Children:** Menu, Portions **Rooms:** 21 (21 en suite) ★★★ HL **Directions:** Located on A443 near Abberley, 11m NW of Worcester **Parking:** 40

BROADWAY   MAP 10 SP03

◉◉ *Dormy House Hotel*

British, French

Enjoyable dining at this luxurious Cotswold retreat

☎ 01386 852711 Willersey Hill WR12 7LF
e-mail: reservations@dormyhouse.co.uk
web: www.dormyhouse.co.uk

This sympathetically converted 17th-century farmhouse overlooks the Cotswold town of Broadway. Luxurious rooms and a traditional approach to dining make a winning combination. Smart dress is

CONTINUED

ENGLAND

BROADWAY CONTINUED

required, but there's no stuffiness here. Those looking for a less formal meal can always opt for the gastro-pub menu in the Barn Owl bar. Staff throughout provide excellent, friendly service. High-quality, locally-sourced produce is used to create simple yet elegant traditional dishes with the occasional contemporary twist. Smoked salmon tartare with dill mayonnaise might precede a bouillabaisse of seafood and shellfish with chive risotto and solfrino of vegetables, or perhaps globe artichoke, goat's cheese and sun-blushed tomato with butternut squash caviar and red pepper emulsion. Finish with ever-popular sticky toffee pudding and vanilla ice cream.

Times: 12-2/7-9.30, Closed 24-27 Dec, Closed L Mon-Sat **Rooms:** 45 (45 en suite) ★★★ HL **Directions:** From A44 take turn signed Saintbury, after 0.5m turn left

◉◉ The Lygon Arms

Modern European 🖥

Accomplished cuisine with a sense of occasion

☎ 01386 852255 & 854400 High St WR12 7DU
e-mail: info@thelygonarms.co.uk
web: www.paramount-hotels/thelygonarms.co.uk

The recently renovated Elizabethan-era Great Hall - with its oak floor, barrel-vaulted ceiling, minstrels' gallery, huge stone fireplace, suits of armour and stags' heads - is the baronial-themed main dining room at this landmark, 16th-century former inn turned country-house hotel. Here a wealth of historic charm and character parades alongside more modern comforts, like the sophisticated fabrics and tailor-made furnishings in the Great Hall, which lend a sense of drama and occasion to the dining experience. The cooking takes a modern approach, driven by the best possible quality ingredients in skilful, well-executed dishes; take roast rack of Lighthorne lamb with confit neck fillet wrapped in a crisp potato coil and served with a light olive-flavoured jus and wild rice risotto.

Chef: Chris Lelliot **Owners:** Paramount Hotels **Times:** 12-2/7-9.30, Closed L Mon-Fri **Prices:** Fixed L £15, Fixed D £39.50, Starter £6.50-£15, Main £13.50-£19, Dessert £6.50-£8.50, Service optional **Wine:** 100+ bottles over £20, 4 bottles under £20, 14 by the glass **Notes:** Sun L £26.50, Dress Restrictions, Smart casual, no jeans, Civ Wed 80, Air con **Seats:** 80, Pr/dining room **Children:** Menu, Portions **Rooms:** 69 (69 en suite) ★★★★ HL **Directions:** A44 to Broadway. **Parking:** 150

◉◉ Russell's

British, Mediterranean

Indulgent cuisine in a stylish restaurant with rooms

☎ 01386 853555 20 High St WR12 7DT
e-mail: info@russellsofbroadway.com
web: www.russellsofbroadway.com

On the high street of a picturesque village, this chic restaurant with rooms blends period features with muted modern décor and contemporary art. A stone fireplace takes centre stage in the front room, but rather than having a real fire, it is used as a showcase for the hotel's fine wines. In summer you can eat outside on the terrace. The fixed-price menu and carte offer a good range of contemporary British dishes with international influences. Try a starter of grilled sea bass with fragrant aubergines, almonds and garlic sauce, for example. Main courses feature the likes of grilled cutlet of pork with parsnip mash, black pudding, sage gravy and a toffee apple.

Chef: Matthew Laughton **Owners:** Andrew Riley, Barry Hancox **Times:** 12-2.30/6-9.30, Closed D Sun **Prices:** Fixed L £14.95, Fixed D £22.95, Starter £7-£10.50, Main £15-£25, Dessert £5.60-£8.50, Service optional **Wine:** 38 bottles over £20, 12 bottles under £20, 12 by the glass **Notes:** Vegetarian available, Air con **Seats:** 55, Pr/dining room 14 **Children:** Portions **Rooms:** 4 (4 en suite) ★★★★★ RR **Directions:** A44 follow signs to Broadway, restaurant on High St opposite village green **Parking:** 16

BROMSGROVE   MAP 10 SO97

◉ Epic' Bar Brasserie

Modern International

Stylish, modern brasserie with high-quality cooking

☎ 01527 871929 68 Hanbury Rd, Stoke Prior B60 4DN
e-mail: epic.bromsgrove@virgin.net
web: www.epicbrasseries.co.uk

The stylish and retro-modern interior of this converted roadside inn delivers leather seating, stripped wooden floors, spotlights, polished wood tables and friendly service to this local hub of gastronomy. The extensive menu is fashionable, flexible and plays to the gallery (with a selection of dishes available as starter or main-course portions) and comes with an appealing nod to the Mediterranean and beyond. Take Thai-spiced salmon fishcakes served with chilli jam, or slow-roasted belly pork with caramelised apple and prunes, and lemon pannacotta with biscotti and limoncello syrup to finish. Cooking is direct, unfussy and flavour driven, presentation simple yet striking.

Chef: Jason Lynas **Owners:** Patrick McDonald **Times:** 12-3/6.30-10, Closed 26 Dec, 1 Jan, Closed D Sun **Prices:** Fixed L £9.95, Starter £5-£9, Main £9.95-£20, Dessert £5-£7.50, Service added but optional 10% **Wine:** 10 bottles over £20, 14 bottles under £20, 10 by the glass **Notes:** Fixed L/D Mon-Thu only, Vegetarian available **Seats:** 72, Pr/dining room 10 **Children:** Menu, Portions **Directions:** Telephone for directions **Parking:** 60

◉ Grafton Manor Restaurant

Modern Indian V

Modern cuisine dotted with Indian dishes in elegant period setting

☎ 01527 579007 Grafton Ln B61 7HA
e-mail: stephen@graftonmanorhotel.co.uk
web: www.graftonmanorhotel.co.uk

This impressive 16th-century manor house is set in manicured grounds and retains many original features. Moulded ceilings, open fires and a sumptuous period drawing room set the scene, together with the country-house style dining room finished with crisp white linen. The modern menu has a strong Indian influence (think Bombay prawns, or lamb with chickpeas), and there's a separate vegetarian menu (roast pepper with cottage cheese). A favourite dessert is Lord of Grafton's whisky steamed pudding with whisky cream. The hotel holds an annual Indian food festival.

Chef: Adam Harrison, Tim Waldon **Owners:** The Morris Family **Times:** 12.30-1.30/7-9.30, Closed BHs, Closed L Sat, D Sun **Prices:** Fixed L £18.50-£20.50, Fixed D £27.85, Service optional **Wine:** 46 bottles over £20, 24 bottles under £20, 3 by the glass **Notes:** Fixed L 3 courses, Vegetarian menu, Dress Restrictions, Smart casual, Civ Wed 120 **Seats:** 60, Pr/dining room 60 **Children:** Portions **Directions:** Off B4091, 1.5m SW of Bromsgrove **Parking:** 60

CHADDESLEY CORBETT   MAP 10 SO87

⑳⑳ Brockencote Hall

Modern French V

French provincial country-house dining

☎ 01562 777876   DY10 4PY
e-mail: info@brockencotehall.com
web: www.brockencotehall.com

This converted Victorian family residence now houses a comfortable hotel. Decorated in French country-house style, there are lots of pastel shades, chandeliers, fireplaces and a large refurbished conservatory and bar. With its formal settings and attractive views across the grounds, the elegant dining room is a popular venue. Ingredients are sourced locally and also direct from the chef's home country of France. The menu features classically-based dishes with a modern twist; take a fillet of line-caught Brixham turbot and langoustine with olive oil crushed potato, garden pea mousseline and winter truffles. A hot soufflé of the day, or bitter chocolate tart with Tahitian vanilla ice cream and amaretto crème anglaise, might feature on the dessert menu.

Chef: Didier Philipot   **Owners:** Mr & Mrs Petitjean   **Times:** 12-1.30/7-9.30, Closed L Sat   **Prices:** Fixed L £15, Fixed D £16.50, Starter £12.50-£14.50, Main £21.50-£22.50, Dessert £9.50, Service included   **Wine:** 160 bottles over £20, 26 bottles under £20, 13 by the glass   **Notes:** Dégustation menu 6 courses £55, Sun 3 courses L £24.50, Vegetarian menu, Dress Restrictions, Smart casual, no jeans, Civ Wed 70   **Seats:** 60, Pr/dining room 30   **Children:** Menu, Portions   **Rooms:** 17 (17 en suite)★★★ HL   **Directions:** On A448 just outside village, between Kidderminster & Bromsgrove   **Parking:** 45

EVESHAM   MAP 10 SP04

⑳ Best Western Northwick Hotel

British NEW

Traditional dining in welcoming hotel

☎ 01386 40322   Waterside WR11 1BT
e-mail: enquiries@northwickhotel.co.uk
web: www.northwickhotel.co.uk

Set close to the town centre, this modernised but classically designed hotel overlooks the River Avon and its adjacent park. Its aptly-named Courtyard restaurant has an airy garden feel, overlooking the courtyard and raised beds and pond. The straightforward carte delivers simple, well-presented, traditional dishes of flavour, based on home-made and local ingredients. Take grilled duck breast with crushed new Jersey potatoes and a cranberry and orange jus, or perhaps cod steak topped with green pesto and cooked in a chive cream sauce, and to finish, maybe a passionfruit cheesecake.

Times: Please telephone for details   **Prices:** Food prices not confirmed for 2008. Please telephone for details   **Rooms:** 29 (29 en suite) ★★★ HL

⑳ The Evesham Hotel

International V ♟ NOTABLE WINE LIST

Relaxed Georgian style, with plenty of choice

☎ 01386 765566   Coopers Ln, Off Waterside WR11 1DA
e-mail: reception@eveshamhotel.com
web: www.eveshamhotel.com

Built in 1540 as a fine Tudor farmhouse and modernised in 1810 in Georgian style, this is not your run-of-the-mill hotel. Owned and managed by the Jenkinson family since the mid-1970s, it delivers a humorously eccentric but always innovative experience. The aptly-named Cedar restaurant - an elegant Georgian room that looks out on to a 180-year-old Cedar of Lebanon - has a menu that is deliberately lengthy and wide-ranging. The cooking style is straightforward, delivering the likes of walnut lamb chops (dipped in egg and walnut breadcrumbs, pan-fried and served with a mint and lemon sauce), with perhaps a banoffee pie finish.

Chef: Sue James   **Owners:** John Jenkinson   **Times:** 12.30-2/7-9.30, Closed 25-26 Dec   **Prices:** Starter £3.50-£8.75, Main £12-£20, Dessert £3.60-£5.20, Service included   **Wine:** 100 bottles under £20, 5 by the glass   **Notes:** Buffet L available £9.00, Vegetarian menu   **Seats:** 55, Pr/dining room 12   **Children:** Menu, Portions   **Rooms:** 40 (40 en suite) ★★★ HL   **Directions:** Coopers Lane is off road along River Avon   **Parking:** 45

ENGLAND

EVESHAM CONTINUED

◉◉ *Riverside Hotel*

Traditional British

Fine dining with fabulous river views

☎ 01386 446200 The Parks, Offenham Rd WR11 8JP
e-mail: info@river-side-hotel.co.uk
web: www.river-side-hotel.co.uk

Beautifully located hotel overlooking the River Avon, set amid 3 acres of gardens in the ancient deer park of Evesham Abbey. Smart public areas include the lounge, where a live pianist plays, and the luxuriously appointed restaurant. A meal on the terrace watching the boats go by is a treat in fine weather. Fresh ingredients, organic where possible, form the basis of the menu, with good fresh fish (whole grilled sea bass on crushed potatoes with sweet chilli sauce) and chargrilled Hereford prime rib-eye steak. At lunch you can choose between the carte and a lighter option. Themed events are a regular occurrence, such as Italian, Greek, wine and champagne evenings.

Times: 12-2/7-9, Closed L Mon, D Sun **Rooms:** 10 (7 en suite) ★★ HL
Directions: From A46 Evesham follow signs for Offenham, then take a right onto B4510. Hotel 0.5m on left down private drive

KIDDERMINSTER   MAP 10 SO87

◉ **The Granary Hotel & Restaurant**

Modern European

Modern cuisine in a setting to match

☎ 01562 777535 Heath Ln, Shenstone DY10 4BS
e-mail: info@granary-hotel.co.uk
web: www.granary-hotel.co.uk

Modern hotel with an airy contemporary restaurant decorated in dark woods and muted colours, and furnished with Lloyd Loom chairs and well-spaced tables. A wallet-friendly carvery is served on weekday lunchtimes, but evenings bring a tempting menu of modern European dishes: suckling pig served with apricot and apples for example, or pan-fried calves' liver with creamed potatoes, onion gravy and crispy bacon. Those in the mood for simpler fare can tuck into a succulent steak and there's also a separate fish menu which features mains such as sea bass with braised fennel and shrimp chive butter or oven-baked monkfish wrapped in Parma ham.

Chef: Tom Court **Owners:** Richard Fletcher **Times:** 12-2.30/7-11, Closed 25 Dec, Closed L Mon/Sat, D Sun **Prices:** Fixed L £9.25, Fixed D £16-£17, Starter £4.95-£8.95, Main £10.95-£24.50, Dessert £4.50-£4.95, Service optional **Wine:** 10 bottles over £20, 31 bottles under £20, 8 by the glass
Notes: Vegetarian available, Civ Wed 200, Air con **Seats:** 60, Pr/dining room 40 **Children:** Portions **Rooms:** 18 (18 en suite) ★★★ HL
Directions: Situated on A450 between Worcester and Stourbridge. 2m outside Kidderminster **Parking:** 95

MALVERN   MAP 10 SO74

◉◉ **Cottage in the Wood Hotel and Restaurant**

British 🍷 NOTABLE WINE LIST

Country retreat with imaginative food and stunning views

☎ 01684 575859 Holywell Rd, Malvern Wells WR14 4LG
e-mail: proprietor@cottageinthewood.co.uk
web: www.cottageinthewood.co.uk

A relaxing, family-run hotel in a glorious setting, with arguably the 'best view in England', looking out over the Severn Plain from high on the steep wooded slopes of the Malvern Hills. The Cottage is a cluster of three white-painted buildings, with the classically decorated restaurant located in the heart of the elegant Georgian dower house. Views from window tables are stunning but the ambitious cooking does its best to distract, with a modern British menu that focuses on quality local seasonal produce. Take turbot with Bayonne ham, roast cherry tomatoes, Puy lentils and a tomato fondue, or perhaps pork loin served with rosemary-poached apples, boudin noir and pommery mash potatoes. The thoughtfully compiled wine list is packed with interest, enthusiasm and a refreshing lack of pretension.

Chef: Dominic Pattin **Owners:** The Pattin Family **Times:** 12.30-2/7-9.30 **Prices:** Starter £5-£12, Main £9-£22, Dessert £5-£10 **Wine:** 374 bottles over £20, 59 bottles under £20, 9 by the glass **Notes:** Sun L 3 courses £21.95 incl coffee, Air con **Seats:** 70, Pr/dining room 20 **Children:** Portions **Rooms:** 31 (31 en suite) ★★★ HL **Directions:** 3m S of Great Malvern off A449. From Great Malvern, take 3rd turning on right after Railway pub **Parking:** 40

⊛ Holdfast Cottage Hotel

Modern
Beautifully simple, quality dishes in a charming cottage setting

☎ 01684 310288 Marlbank Rd, Welland WR13 6NA
e-mail: enquiries@holdfast-cottage.co.uk
web: www.holdfast-cottage.co.uk

Set at the foot of the Malvern Hills, this lovely 17th-century wisteria-clad cottage was enlarged in Victorian times and boasts wonderful gardens and woodland. The cottage feel is carried through to the restaurant, where oak tables, fresh flowers and simple cutlery and glassware set the mood and service is relaxed and welcoming. Simple presentation and an emphasis on seasonality and quality are evident on the set four-course menu. Dishes like crab and basil risotto, and fillet of Herefordshire beef with bubble-and-squeak and peppercorn aïoli show the style, accompanied by some good vegetarian options.

Chef: Adam Cambridge **Owners:** Guy & Annie Dixon **Times:** 12-2.30/7-9 **Prices:** Fixed L £19.95, Fixed D £27.50, Service optional **Wine:** 2 bottles over £20, 27 bottles under £20, 2 by the glass **Notes:** Fixed D 4 courses, Sun L 2 courses £15.95, 3 courses £18.95, Civ Wed 30 **Seats:** 30, Pr/dining room 18 **Children:** Portions **Rooms:** 8 (8 en suite) ★★ HL **Directions:** On A4104 midway between Welland & Little Malvern **Parking:** 20

⊛⊛ Seasons Restaurant at Colwall Park Hotel

Modern British ✿
Stylish restaurant serving excellent local produce

☎ 01684 540000 Walwyn Rd, Colwall WR13 6QG
e-mail: hotel@colwall.com
web: www.colwall.com

An attractive hotel with a country-house look, Colwall Park is located at the heart of a small village with views of the Malvern Hills from the gardens. In contrast to the generally traditional décor in the public rooms, the restaurant is quite contemporary in shades of cream with light-oak panelling and bespoke artwork. The kitchen delivers accomplished, technically well-executed dishes, with good use made of seasonal produce and local producers are acknowledged. Typical options might include pan-seared fillet of halibut with crushed new potatoes, buttered spinach and a white wine froth, while a warm cinnamon apple tarte Tatin - served with vanilla ice cream - could catch the eye at dessert. There is also an impressive British cheeseboard.

Chef: James Garth **Owners:** Mr & Mrs I Nesbitt **Times:** 12-2/7-9, Closed L all week ex by arrangement **Prices:** Fixed L £16.95, Starter £6.25-£7.95, Main £17.25-£19.95, Dessert £6.50-£7.50, Service included **Wine:** 34 bottles over £20, 36 bottles under £20, 9 by the glass **Seats:** 40, Pr/dining room 100 **Children:** Menu, Portions **Rooms:** 22 (22 en suite) ★★★ HL **Directions:** On B4218, off A449 from Malvern to Ledbury **Parking:** 40

OMBERSLEY   MAP 10 SO86

⊛⊛ The Venture In Restaurant

British, French
Modern British dining in medieval draper's house

☎ 01905 620552 Main Rd WR9 0EW

Dating back to 1430, this restaurant has a wealth of beamed ceilings and inglenooks as well as a resident ghost. Fresh flowers and gentle colours make this an inviting and comfortable dining venue with attentive and thoughtful service. The excellent breads, ice creams and petits fours are made in-house. Dishes use best-quality ingredients, skilfully prepared and simply garnished. Precede the main course of roast best end of lamb, roast pumpkin, gnocchi and rosemary and garlic sauce with a starter of pan-fried squid served with roasted peppers and rocket salad, or maybe seared West Coast scallops with steamed asparagus and a shellfish foam. To finish, there's a glazed orange tart with chocolate sorbet, or perhaps pineapple Tatin served with vanilla ice cream.

Chef: Toby Fletcher **Owners:** Toby Fletcher **Times:** 12-2/7-9.30, Closed 25 Dec-1 Jan, 2 wks summer & 2 wks winter, Mon, Closed D Sun **Prices:** Fixed L £20.50, Fixed D £34, Service optional **Wine:** 40 bottles over £20, 20 bottles under £20, 6 by the glass **Notes:** Dress Restrictions, Smart casual, Air con **Seats:** 32, Pr/dining room 32 **Children:** Min 12 yrs D **Directions:** From Worcester N towards Kidderminster - A449 (approx 5m). Turn left at Ombersley turning - 0.75m on right **Parking:** 15

TENBURY WELLS   MAP 10 SO56

ⓦ Cadmore Lodge

Modern British

Enjoyable dining in rural retreat

☎ 01584 810044 Berrington Green, St Michaels
WR15 8TQ
e-mail: info@cadmorelodge.co.uk
web: www.cadmorelodge.co.uk

This friendly, family-run hotel - once a fishing lodge - has a country-style restaurant with great lake and valley views, warm colours and a log fire. The surrounding 70-acre estate gives this restaurant a peaceful and relaxing atmosphere, helped by friendly, welcoming staff. The daily-changing dinner menu takes a modern approach; think tea-smoked venison with pomegranate dressing to start, perhaps pan-fried duck breast served with spiced red cabbage and a sweet chilli jus to follow, while a tequila sunrise brûlée with sugar curl and vanilla cream might catch the eye at dessert.

Chef: Mark Griffiths, Russell Collins **Owners:** Mr & Mrs J Weston **Times:** 12-2/7-9.15, Closed 25 Dec, Closed L Mon **Prices:** Fixed L £10.50-£11.50, Fixed D £22.50-£27.50 **Wine:** 3 bottles over £20, 13 bottles under £20, 6 by the glass **Notes:** Vegetarian available, Civ Wed 100, Air con **Seats:** 50, Pr/dining room 50 **Children:** Menu, Portions **Rooms:** 15 (14 en suite) ★★ HL **Directions:** Off A4112 from Tenbury Wells to Leominster. 2m from Tenbury Wells, turn right opposite St Michael's Church **Parking:** 100

ⓦⓦ Whites @ the Clockhouse

Modern British NEW

Modern, high-street bistro with cooking to match

☎ 01584 811336 14 Market St WR15 8BQ
e-mail: whites@theclockhouse.net
web: www.whites@theclockhouse.net

A contemporary bistro, Whites sits on the town's pretty main street and delivers modern cooking with lashings of friendly service and warm, welcoming hospitality. In the corner of the ground-floor wine bar (serving a tapas menu), a spiral staircase leads up to the main light-and-airy, loft-style restaurant, with its wooden floors and polished-wood tables. Here high-quality fresh local produce, accomplished skills and stylish presentation combine in well-executed dishes of balanced combination and clean flavour. Take slow-cooked belly of pork served with black pudding and an apple, sage and cider sauce, or perhaps steamed fillet of halibut with a prawn and roasted pepper brochette, and to finish, maybe a ginger-scented pannacotta with rhubarb jelly.

Chef: Jonathon Waters **Owners:** Sarah MacDonald, Chris Whitehead **Times:** 10.30am/11pm, Closed 2wks mid Jan, last wk Aug, 1st wk Sep, Mon, Closed L Tue-Wed, D Sun **Prices:** Fixed L £12.95, Starter £4.95-£6.95, Main £12.50-£18.50, Dessert £5-£6, Service optional **Wine:** 15 bottles over £20, 20 bottles under £20, 6 by the glass **Seats:** 45 **Children:** Menu, Portions **Directions:** A456/A4112 into Tenbury Wells. Continue over the bridge and along the main street. Restaurant on right adjacent to The Royal Oak **Parking:** On street, car park on Teme St

UPTON UPON SEVERN   MAP 10 SO84

ⓦ White Lion Hotel

Modern British

Historic coaching inn with appealing food

☎ 01684 592551 21 High St WR8 0HJ
e-mail: info@whitelionhotel.biz
web: www.whitelionhotel.biz

Famed for playing home to author Henry Fielding during the writing of *Tom Jones*, this coaching inn dates back to 1510 and has a colourful history. Period details - exposed timbers, lathe and plaster walls - have been sensitively incorporated into the modern décor which maintains a traditional feel. Slick presentation and quality ingredients lift its extensive restaurant menu out of the ordinary. Start with seared monkfish with crispy pancetta and a mango, paw paw and chilli salsa, and then tuck into hearty mains such as pan-fried calves' liver with white pudding, smoked bacon and mushrooms, or mustard and herb-crusted lamb with honey-glazed vegetables and rosemary jus.

Chef: Jon Lear, Richard Thompson **Owners:** Mr & Mrs Lear **Times:** 12-2/7-9.15, Closed 31 Dec-1 Jan, Closed L few days between Xmas & New Year **Prices:** Starter £7.25, Main £15.25-£19.25, Dessert £5.95, Service optional **Wine:** 5 bottles over £20, 26 bottles under £20, 4 by the glass **Notes:** Sun L 2 courses £13.25, 3 courses £16, Vegetarian available **Seats:** 45 **Children:** Portions **Rooms:** 13 (13 en suite) ★★★ HL **Directions:** From A422 take A38 towards Tewkesbury. After 8m take B4104 for 1m, after bridge turn left to hotel **Parking:** 16

WORCESTER   MAP 10 SO85

ⓦ Brown's Restaurant

Modern International V

Skilful modern cooking in former corn mill

☎ 01905 26263 The Old Cornmill, South Quay
WR1 2JJ
e-mail: enquiries@brownsrestaurant.co.uk
web: www.brownsrestaurant.co.uk

In a stunning setting overlooking the Severn river, this former Victorian corn mill retains some of its original architectural features in its new incarnation as a restaurant. The chic, modern décor, complete with mezzanine balcony, falls in line with the cuisine's modern approach. Mediterranean and classical influences also catch the eye on the appealing repertoire, which makes good use of locally-sourced fresh ingredients. Think clean-cut dishes like a duo of lamb (roast loin and merguez sausage) with aubergine caviar and tomato and rosemary jus, or pan-fried escalope of veal with red onion marmalade, morel mushrooms and Madeira jus, while a trio of rhubarb (crème brûlée, soup and ice cream) might feature at dessert.

Chef: Lawson Shuttleworth **Owners:** Mr & Mrs R Everton **Times:** 12-2.30/6.30-10, Closed Mon **Prices:** Fixed L £17.50, Fixed D £30.95-£39.95, Service optional **Wine:** 93 bottles over £20, 30 bottles under £20, 7 by the glass **Notes:** Fixed D 5 courses, Tasting menu on request, Sun L £30.95, Vegetarian menu, Dress Restrictions, Smart casual preferred, Civ Wed 80 **Seats:** 110, Pr/dining room 20 **Children:** Portions **Directions:** From M5 junct 7 to city centre. At lights turn into Copenhagen St **Parking:** Large car park adjacent to the restaurant

◉◉ The Glasshouse

Modern British NEW

Bustling town-centre brasserie with cathedral views

☎ 01905 611120 55 Sidbury WR1 2HU
e-mail: eat@theglasshouse.co.uk
web: www.theglasshouse.co.uk

Shaun Hill's latest exciting venture occupies a renovated former antique shop in the centre of town. Immediately beyond the large plate-glass windows is a small bar leading through into the downstairs dining area with its striped banquette seating and light grey/blue leather chairs. The upstairs dining room, with views of the cathedral, is open to the ground floor and retains the great atmosphere. A Shaun Hill-designed menu is always going to be about good ingredients and simplicity of cooking and presentation. The choice is extensive - perfectly-timed calves' sweetbreads with potato and olive cake, or sautéed monkfish with mustard and cucumber sauce, are fine examples of what is on offer. Try the expertly made caramel and apple tart served with cinnamon ice cream for a grand finale.

Chef: Shaun Hill, Calum MacRimmon **Owners:** Brandon Weston, Shaun Hill **Times:** 12-2.30/5.30-10, Closed D Sun **Prices:** Starter £5-£11, Main £11-£19, Dessert £6-£12, Group min 8 service 10% **Wine:** 18 bottles over £20, 5 bottles under £20, 4 by the glass **Seats:** 100, Pr/dining room 16 **Children:** Portions **Directions:** M5 junct 7 towards Worcester. Continue straight over 2 rdbts, through 3 sets of lights. At 3rd set of lights turn left into car park, restaurant is opposite **Parking:** Pay & display 100yds

YORKSHIRE, EAST RIDING OF

BEVERLEY MAP 17 TA03

◉◉ The Manor House

Modern, Traditional

City style in country-house setting

☎ 01482 881645 Northlands, Walkington HU17 8RT
e-mail: info@walkingtonmanorhouse.co.uk
web: www.walkingtonmanorhouse.co.uk

Late Victorian country-house hotel standing in well-tended gardens, with two different style dining rooms making up its restaurant. The Blue Room boasts crystal chandeliers and silk wallpaper, while the larger, airier conservatory overlooks the south terrace and manicured lawns. Both have elegant table settings and comfortable seating, and deliver the same fine-dining experience. As well as two dining rooms, there are two fixed-price menus to match, both delivering modern-focused dishes showcasing quality ingredients, clear flavours and accomplished technical skill. Think pressed belly pork with a tarte Tatin of caramelised Bramleys and sage cream, or brioche and tomato-crusted cod loin with a nero and pancetta risotto, and to finish, perhaps a lemon sabayon pine nut tart with honey-roasted fig.

Chef: Neil Armstrong **Owners:** Ann Pickering **Times:** 12-2.30/6-9.15, Closed D Sun **Prices:** Fixed L £9.95, Fixed D £15-£36.50, Service optional **Wine:** 30 bottles over £20, 25 bottles under £20, 4 by the glass **Notes:** Civ Wed 70 **Seats:** 60, Pr/dining room 30 **Children:** Menu, Portions **Rooms:** 7 (7 en suite) ★★ HL **Directions:** From Hull towards York, at end of Beverley bypass left at rdbt towards Walkington, right at x-rds, on left **Parking:** 30

◉ The Pipe and Glass Inn

Modern British V NEW

Charming countryside inn serving hearty food

☎ 01430 810246 West End, South Dalton HU17 7PN
e-mail: email@pipeandglass.co.uk
web: www.pipeandglass.co.uk

This smart country inn effortlessly blends modern and traditional styles. In the cosy bar, there are church candles on the tables, whilst the small lounge area boasts dark burgundy leather sofas and a chalkboard menu above the fire. With a contemporary brown and cream colour scheme, the airy restaurant is divided into three areas with traditional pictures on the walls and fresh flowers on the chunky wood tables. The menus are seasonal including a separate vegetarian one. Expect rustic, hearty dishes like cold pressed terrine of local hare, ham hock and foie gras, and braised Harpham lamb with champ and a pot of mutton and kidney casserole.

Chef: James MacKenzie **Owners:** James MacKenzie, Kate Boroughs **Times:** 12-2/6.30-9.30, Closed 25 Dec, 2 wks Jan, Mon, Closed D Sun **Prices:** Starter £3.65-£8.95, Main £8.95-£18.95, Dessert £5.45-£7.95, Service optional **Wine:** 71 bottles over £20, 26 bottles under £20, 10 by the glass **Notes:** Traditional roasts available Sun, Vegetarian menu, Air con **Seats:** 70, Pr/dining room 26 **Children:** Menu, Portions **Parking:** 60

◉◉ Tickton Grange Hotel

Modern British

Elegant Georgian country-house retreat with exciting dining

☎ 01964 543666 Tickton HU17 9SH
e-mail: info@ticktongrange.co.uk
web: www.ticktongrange.co.uk

This charming Georgian country-house hotel dates from the 1820s and has 4 acres of grounds and attractive gardens. Its elegantly modern dining room has bay windows and hill views, and staff here are both efficient and friendly, while suppliers of the kitchen's local produce get a prominent listing on menus. These carefully selected, fresh seasonal ingredients are skilfully transformed into light modern British dishes notable for imaginative combinations, clear flavours and attractive presentation. Expect Kelleythorpe beef fillet with cottage pie, red onion marmalade and a Wold Top ale jus, and to finish, perhaps a white chocolate and mint marquise with bitter chocolate sorbet and cinnamon brûlée, plus there are wonderful Tickton truffles to enjoy over coffee. For a special occasion, there's the Taittinger champagne dinner.

Chef: David Nowell, John MacDonald **Owners:** Mr & Mrs Whymant **Times:** 12-2/5-9.30, Closed 26 Dec **Prices:** Fixed L £16.50, Fixed D £36.50, Starter £5.95-£6.95, Main £16.95-£21.95, Dessert £6.50-£8.50, Service optional **Wine:** 33 bottles over £20, 32 bottles under £20 **Notes:** Fixed D 4 courses, Sun L £16.95, Twilight menu 2 courses £15, Civ Wed 150 **Seats:** 45, Pr/dining room 20 **Children:** Menu, Portions **Rooms:** 17 (17 en suite) ★★★ HL **Directions:** From Beverley take A1035 towards Bridlington. After 3m hotel on left, just past Tickton **Parking:** 75

KINGSTON UPON HULL   MAP 17 TA02

◉ Boars Nest

Traditional British NEW

Accomplished cooking in a one-time butcher's shop

☎ 01482 445577 22 Princes Av HU5 3QA
e-mail: boarsnest@boarsnest.karoo.co.uk
web: www.theboarsnesthull.com

Once an old butcher's shop, complete with ceramic wall-and-floor tiles, the Boars Nest sits in a rejuvenated area of fashionable boutiques, artisan and ethnic food shops and popular eateries. The old front 'shop' is filled with smaller tables, while the former drawing room at the back acts as an intimate dining area and upstairs parades as a sumptuous aperitif and coffee lounge. The kitchen shows pedigree and skill via a lengthy flavour-driven British repertoire. Take Goosnargh corn-fed breast of duck, parsnip and goat's cheese glazed cottage pie and perhaps a hot chocolate pudding with clotted cream finish.

Chef: Simon Rogers, Andrew Young, Richard Bryan **Owners:** Simon Rogers, Dina Hanchett **Times:** 12-2/6.30-10, Closed 26 Dec **Prices:** Fixed L £9, Starter £4.95-£6.95, Main £10-£17.95, Dessert £5-£6.95, Service added but optional 10% **Wine:** 9 bottles over £20, 15 bottles under £20, 9 by the glass **Notes:** Vegetarian available, Dress Restrictions, Smart casual **Seats:** 34, Pr/dining room 16 **Directions:** 1m from Hull city centre

---

WILLERBY   MAP 17 TA03

◉◉ Best Western Willerby Manor Hotel

Modern European

Quality cooking in a slick, modern setting

☎ 01482 652616 Well Ln HU10 6ER
e-mail: willerbymanor@bestwestern.co.uk
web: www.willerbymanor.co.uk

This popular hotel boasts two dining options - the Everglades brasserie in a sunny conservatory, or the more formal Icon restaurant in a thoroughly contemporary dining room. The latter leans toward the Mediterranean in style: think herb-crusted salmon with warm potato and dill salad and Dijon mustard, or rack of lamb with provençale vegetables, roast shallots and walnuts and a thyme jus. Rather than the traditional separation into starters and mains, the menu gives the option of small or large portions for several of the dishes - a nice idea. It all takes place in an attractive manor house which once played home to a wealthy shipping merchant and has been renovated in sympathetic modern style.

Chef: David Roberts, Ben Olley **Owners:** Alexandra Townend **Times:** 12.30-2.30/7-9.30, Closed 1st wk Jan, last 2 wks Aug, BHs, Sun, Closed L Mon-Sat **Prices:** Fixed D £23.50, Starter £4.60-£5.75, Main £12.55-£15.20, Dessert £4.50-£4.70, Service optional **Wine:** 7 bottles over £20, 23 bottles under £20, 4 by the glass **Notes:** Vegetarian available, Civ Wed 300, Air con **Seats:** 40, Pr/dining room 40 **Children:** Portions **Rooms:** 51 (51 en suite) ★★★ HL **Directions:** M62/A63, follow signs for Humber Bridge, then signs for Beverley until Willerby Shopping Park. Hotel signed from rdbt next to MacDonald's **Parking:** 200

YORKSHIRE, NORTH

ALDWARK   MAP 19 SE46

◉◉ Aldwark Manor

British, European

19th-century manor house with a contemporary dining room

☎ 01347 838146 838251 YO61 1UF
e-mail: aldwarkmanor@qhotels.co.uk
web: www.qhotels.co.uk./hotels/aldwark-manor-york-yorkshire/

Within easy reach of York and Harrogate, this rambling country manor house dates from 1865 and is an interesting mix of old and new, set amid 100 acres of parkland on the River Ure. Located in the bright and airy modern extension, the restaurant's minimalist décor makes full use of the picture window overlooking the 18-hole golf course, and large modern artwork depicting wine bottles dominates the room. The cooking style is modern with good saucing, and there's a focus on local and British produce. The set three-course menu might include English asparagus with fresh hollandaise, followed by turbot with chive cream sauce and lemon-scented crushed Jersey Royals. The tangy lemon tart makes a refreshing dessert.

Times: 12-2.30/7-9.30 **Rooms:** 55 (55 en suite) ★★★★ HL **Directions:** From A1, A59 towards Green Hammerton, then B6265 towards Little Ouseburn, follow signs Aldwark Bridge/Manor. A19 through Linton on Ouse to Aldwark.

ARNCLIFFE   MAP 18 SD97

Amerdale House Hotel

British, European

Imaginative modern cuisine in a gorgeous Dales village

☎ 01756 770250 BD23 5QE
e-mail: amerdalehouse@littondale.com
web: www.amerdalehouse.co.uk

The setting here is a big wow-factor - this charming Victorian manor house is within an Area of Outstanding Natural Beauty and surrounded by immaculately maintained gardens. The house itself retains many original features, beautiful décor and period furniture, while the dining room has a more Regency style. The menu is very much influenced by seasonality and freshness with home-grown and local ingredients making appearances throughout. The chef's modern British approach leans toward the traditional with consistently well-cooked and thoughtful dishes - rack of new season spring lamb with black pudding or natural Whitby smoked haddock risotto might be on offer. At the time of going to press we understood there was a change of ownership taking place. Please visit www.theAA.com for further details.

Times: 7.30-8.30, Closed mid Nov-mid Mar, Closed L all week **Rooms:** 10 (10 en suite) **Directions:** On the outskirts of village.

ASENBY · MAP 19 SE37

◉◉ Crab and Lobster Restaurant

British, European

Character restaurant serving mainly seafood

☎ 01845 577286 Dishforth Rd YO7 3QL
e-mail: enquiries@crabandlobster.co.uk
web: www.crabandlobster.co.uk

Quirky and unconventional are just two words that come to mind when describing the décor at this thatched restaurant. From its low-ceilinged bar to dining room and pavilion conservatory, all is festooned in a riot of 'collectable anything' memorabilia. And, as the name suggests, seafood is the speciality of the lengthy, crowd-pleasing modern-themed repertoire that cleverly merges the traditional and more unusual. Take steamed Shetland mussels with apple, brandy, bacon and cream, followed by crab-crusted salmon on baby spinach with shellfish cream, with warm chocolate fondant with saffron ice cream to finish. Dishes are accomplished and well conceived, portions generous and the atmosphere's relaxed.

Chef: Steve Dean **Owners:** Vimac Leisure **Times:** 12-2.30/7-9.30
Prices: Fixed L £14.50, Fixed D £31.50, Starter £5-£11.50, Main £9.50-£22.50, Dessert £6.30-£9.50, Service optional **Wine:** 8 bottles over £20, 8 bottles under £20, 8 by the glass **Notes:** Vegetarian available, Civ Wed 24 **Seats:** 55, Pr/dining room 24 **Children:** Portions **Directions:** From A19/A168 take A167, drive through Topcliffe follow signs for A1. On left, 8m from Northallerton **Parking:** 80

AUSTWICK · MAP 18 SD76

◉ The Austwick Traddock

Modern British V

Organic cooking at a charming country-house hotel

☎ 015242 51224 Nr Settle LA2 8BY
e-mail: info@austwicktraddock.co.uk
web: www.austwicktraddock.co.uk

Once a gentleman's residence, this intimate Georgian country-house hotel is set in the midst of the Yorkshire Dales National Park. Relax by the fire with a book or board game in one of two comfortable lounges, or take a walk in the stunning countryside. Certified by the Soil Association, the cosy candlelit restaurant, the former library, prides itself on using only organic and wild ingredients. The menu offers modern British dishes, such as fillet of fennel-braised sea bass with crabmeat cream sauce, followed by lemon soufflé with Yorkshire curd sorbet, or an assiette of chocolate.

Chef: Tom Eunson **Owners:** Bruce & Jane Reynolds **Times:** 12.30-3/6.45-9.15 **Prices:** Starter £5-£9, Main £9-£25, Dessert £6-£14, Service optional **Wine:** 18 bottles over £20, 27 bottles under £20, 8 by the glass **Notes:** Sun L 2 courses £14, 3 courses £18, Vegetarian menu **Seats:** 36, Pr/dining room 16 **Children:** Portions **Rooms:** 10 (10 en suite) ★★ SHL **Directions:** From Skipton take A65 towards Kendal, 3m after Settle take right signed Austwick, cross hump back bridge, hotel 100yds on left **Parking:** 20

BILBROUGH · MAP 16 SE54

◉◉ The Three Hares Country Inn & Restaurant

Traditional British

Traditional inn with supremely satisfying food

☎ 01937 832128 Main St YO23 3PH
e-mail: info@thethreehares.co.uk
web: www.thethreehares.co.uk

This traditional stone-built inn is the only pub in the village, and so serves the dual purpose of cosy local combined with superior gastro-pub. There are three distinct areas to the Three Hares - a comfortable modern bar, the Red Room that has a definite racing theme, and the Old Village Forge with its attractive stone-flagged floor. The British menu keeps things relatively simple with successful updates or revisions of classic dishes cooked with undeniable skill. Try pan-fried sea bass fillets with baby vegetables, saffron potatoes and red wine jus, or maybe an open lasagne of wild mushrooms with white wine cream and herbs, followed by a selection of home-made ice creams.

Chef: Dan Simpson **Owners:** Charles Oliver **Times:** 12-2.30/7-9, Closed Mon (ex BHs), Closed D Sun **Prices:** Food prices not confirmed for 2008. Please telephone for details **Seats:** 60, Pr/dining room 16 **Children:** Portions **Directions:** From York take A64 towards Leeds and follow signs for Bilbrough on right **Parking:** 35

BOLTON ABBEY · MAP 19 SE05

◉◉◉◉ The Burlington Restaurant
see page 526

BOROUGHBRIDGE · MAP 19 SE36

◉◉ The Dining Room

Modern British, Mediterranean

Quality cooking in relaxed surroundings

☎ 01423 326426 20 St James Square YO51 9AR
e-mail: chris@thediningrooms.co.uk

CONTINUED ON PAGE 527

ENGLAND

The Burlington Restaurant

BOLTON ABBEY MAP 19 SE05

Modern French V NOTABLE WINE LIST

Beautiful country-house hotel fine dining

☎ 01756 718111 & 710441 The Devonshire Arms Country House Hotel & Spa BD23 6AJ
e-mail: res@devonshirehotels.co.uk
web: www.devonshirehotels.co.uk

Chef: Michael Wignall
Owners: Duke & Duchess of Devonshire
Times: 12.30-2.30/7-10, Closed Mon, Closed L Tue-Sat **Prices:** Fixed L £33, Fixed D £58-£75, Service added but optional 10%
Wine: 2,300 bottles over £20, 30 bottles under £20, 12 by the glass
Notes: Fixed L 3 courses, Fixed D 4 courses, Tasting menu £68, Vegetarian menu, Smart dress, Civ Wed 90 **Seats:** 70, Pr/dining room 90
Children: Menu
Rooms: 40 (40 en suite)★★★★ HL
Directions: On B6160 to Bolton Abbey, 250 yds N of junct with A59 rdbt junct
Parking: 100

Set on the Duke and Duchess of Devonshire's 30,000-acre Bolton Abbey Estate, this classic country-house hotel has stunning views of the delightful Wharfedale countryside. Originally a 17th-century coaching inn, it oozes the atmosphere of a private country mansion - think sumptuous lounges, antique furniture and large Devonshire family oil paintings. The fine-dining Burlington Restaurant continues the theme, with its refined, traditional edge, where large, highly-polished antique tables come appropriately set with the finest table appointments and service is professional but friendly. The dining room spreads over into the extended conservatory, with its wicker chairs and stone floor and views over the Italian courtyard garden. Executive Head Chef Michael Wignall brings an impressive track record to his highly accomplished kitchen, with time spent with Paul Heathcote, Marco Pierre White and John Burton Race and previously as head chef at Cliveden's Waldo's (see entry). His carefully crafted, complex but elegantly light dishes ooze modern French influence - underpinned by high-level technical skill - and come dressed to thrill, littered with top-notch, luxury ingredients and precise and intense flavours. His approach is via an appealing, fixed-price carte and ten-course tasting option (Menu Prestige). Expect the likes of slow-poached salt marsh lamb with Scottish langoustines, pork belly, pepper syrup and lovage oil, followed by praline parfait, mocha butter, caramelised filo, coffee brûlée and liquorice ice cream. A truly outstanding wine list is full of top-class producers.

BOROUGHBRIDGE CONTINUED

Behind the bow-fronted, shop-style frontage of this restaurant there's a traditional-style lounge and bar for aperitifs, while in contrast, the eponymous dining room is a more modern affair, decked out with beams, high-backed chairs, linen-dressed tables and quality crockery. A new terrace is perfect for alfresco dining. Chef-patron Chris Astley is passionate about his cooking, his intelligently compact menus (bolstered by specials) deliver fresh, clean-flavoured dishes utilising quality ingredients. Take wild mushroom risotto, confit of duck with belly of pork and glazed lemon tart. There is ongoing refurbishment taking place at this restaurant which will reinstate original features, but not affect opening times.

Chef: Christopher Astley **Owners:** Mr & Mrs C Astley **Times:** 12-2/7-9.30, Closed 25-27 Dec, 1 Jan, BHs, Mon, Closed L Tue-Sat, D Sun **Prices:** Fixed D £25, Starter £4.25-£5.50, Main £10.95-£13.50, Dessert £5.25, Service optional **Wine:** 48 bottles over £20, 37 bottles under £20, 7 by the glass **Notes:** Vegetarian available **Seats:** 32 **Children:** Min 3 yrs, Portions **Directions:** A1(M), Boroughbridge junct, sign to town. Opposite fountain in the town square **Parking:** On street/Private on request

BURNSALL   MAP 19 SE06

◎ Red Lion Hotel

Modern British

Picturesque old inn serving hearty favourites

☎ 01756 720204 By the Bridge BD23 6BU
e-mail: info@redlion.co.uk
web: www.redlion.co.uk

This delightful, 16th-century Dales village inn - beside a five-arch bridge over the River Wharfe - has avoided the trend to modernise, and retains real charm and character. So you'll see flagstone floors, hand-pump ales, roaring fires, low ceilings and exposed beams. Dine in the elegant restaurant, or more casually in the oak-panelled bar. The cooking is straightforward, bold and value-driven from a committed kitchen. Fresh local ingredients enhance traditional fare with its modern twist and eye-catching daily specials. Look out for Whitby crab risotto, steak and kidney pie braised in Theakstons ale or the pan-fried fillet of venison with wild mushrooms and baked kohlrabi.

Times: 12-2.30/6-9.30 **Rooms:** 15 (15 en suite) ★★ HL
Directions: 10m from Skipton on B6160

CRATHORNE   MAP 19 NZ40

◎◎ Crathorne Hall Hotel

British

Edwardian country house with impressive cuisine

☎ 01642 700398 TS15 0AR
e-mail: crathornehall@handpicked.co.uk
web: www.handpicked.co.uk

Savour the period elegance of Crathorne Hall, a magnificent Edwardian property set in 15 acres of grounds with views of the Leven Valley and the Cleveland Hills. Wood panelling, an impressive carved stone fireplace, ornate ceilings and imposing oil paintings are just some of the original features in the formal Leven restaurant. Impressive British cooking is characterised by interesting combinations, high-quality ingredients and an accomplished simplicity. Take a stroll

through the glorious grounds before an enjoyable dinner: perhaps chicken and lobster terrine with mango and coriander, followed by fillet of Grand Reserve beef with salted brisket and stuffed cabbage, and for dessert, a dark chocolate fondant won't fail to impress.

Chef: James Cooper **Owners:** Hand Picked Hotels **Times:** 12.30-2.30/7-10 **Prices:** Fixed L £15-£20, Fixed D £35-£45, Service optional **Wine:** 85 bottles over £20, 4 bottles under £20, 20 by the glass **Notes:** Fixed L 3 courses £19.50-£25, Civ Wed 120 **Seats:** 45, Pr/dining room 26 **Children:** Menu, Portions **Rooms:** 37 (37 en suite) ★★★★ HL **Directions:** Off A19, 2m E of Yarm. Access to A19 via A66 or A1, Thirsk **Parking:** 80

ESCRICK   MAP 16 SE64

◎ The Parsonage Country House Hotel

British, International V

Quality service and cooking in a delightful country house

☎ 01904 728111 York Rd YO19 6LF
e-mail: sales@parsonagehotel.co.uk
web: www.parsonagehotel.co.uk

This 19th-century former parsonage set in beautiful grounds has been lovingly restored and extended. Inside, there are comfortable lounges, a bar and the elegant fine-dining restaurant. Here diners are a mix of residents and visitors, all enjoying well-sourced produce from the 'Yorkshire Farmers' menu. Dishes are nicely presented, and might include a starter of boudin of Whitby crab with lemon-scented courgette ribbons and pink peppercorn sauce, followed by hot pot of baked cod fillet with fricassée of peas, bacon and thyme. Desserts might feature home-made mini doughnuts with Bramley apple compôte and nutmeg crème brûlée, or morello cherry clafoutis.

Chef: Neal Birtwell **Owners:** P Smith **Times:** 12-2/7-9, Closed L Sat **Prices:** Fixed L £12.50, Fixed D £24-£33.95, Starter £4.50-£6.50, Main £14.75-£18.95, Dessert £4.75-£8.50, Service included **Wine:** 20 bottles over £20, 26 bottles under £20, 10 by the glass **Notes:** Sun L £15.95, Sun D £17.95, Vegetarian menu, Dress Restrictions, No jeans, Civ Wed 100 **Seats:** 50, Pr/dining room 20 **Children:** Portions **Rooms:** 48 (48 en suite) ★★★ HL **Directions:** S from York on A19, Parsonage on right, 4m out of town in Escrick village **Parking:** 80

GREAT AYTON   MAP 19 NZ51

◎◎ The Cook's Room

Modern British NEW

Confident cuisine at popular, stylish and relaxed village restaurant

☎ 01642 724204 113a High St TS9 6BW
e-mail: thecooksroom@yahoo.co.uk

Overlooking the village green and appropriately looking down on the statue of Captain Cook, this popular village restaurant is accessed off the high street and up a flight of stairs. The décor is modern with splashes of colour coming from artwork, while pale wood, white fittings and paintwork (which change tone in different lights) cut a relaxed, stylish atmosphere. From the unclothed tables you might catch a glimpse of chef-patron Neal Bullock at the kitchen counter adding the finishing touches to his accomplished, classically-inspired,

CONTINUED

ENGLAND

GREAT AYTON CONTINUED

modern British with international influences cooking. Quality local seasonal produce is prepared with skill and enthusiasm; think pan-seared duck breast with roasted peach and cinnamon compôte served with a red onion tarte Tatin and foie gras sauce.

Chef: Neal Bullock **Owners:** Neal & Fiona Bullock **Times:** 12-3/6.30-10, Closed 1st wk Jan, Mon, Tue, Closed L Sat, Wed, D Sun **Prices:** Fixed D £27.95, Starter £3.95-£6.95, Main £8.95-£15.95, Dessert £4.95, Service optional **Wine:** 4 bottles over £20, 6 bottles under £20, 4 by the glass **Notes:** Sun L 2 courses £12.95, 3 courses £15.95 **Seats:** 46 **Children:** Portions **Directions:** Take A172 from Middlesbrough signed to Stokesley, take B1292 to Great Ayton. **Parking:** On street

GUISBOROUGH   MAP 19 NZ61

◉ Macdonald Gisborough Hall

Modern British

Well-prepared local produce at an elegant Victorian house

☎ 0870 400 8191 Whitby Ln TS1 6PT
e-mail: general.gisboroughhall@macdonald-hotels.co.uk
web: www.macdonald-hotels.co.uk

A Victorian country-house hotel situated on the edge of the North Yorkshire Moors, close to the historic market town of Guisborough, that has retained its charm and character. Tockett's dining room has a smart, traditional feel and its large windows overlook the stunning formal gardens. Service is friendly, and the menus - including carte, fixed-price and seasonal - feature classically-based cuisine with a modern slant. Go for salmon and sole presse with dill pesto, followed by breast of Harome organic chicken filled with wild mushroom and sorrel mousse, ragout of vegetables and a red wine sauce. Sticky toffee pudding with butterscotch sauce might prove a fitting finale.

Rooms: 71 (71 en suite) ★★★★ HL

◉ Pinchinthorpe Hall

Modern British

Cooking with a punch in a vibrant bistro setting

☎ 01287 630200 Pinchinthorpe TS14 8HG
e-mail: nybrewery@pinchinthorpe.wanadoo.co.uk
web: www.pinchinthorpehall.co.uk

This 17th-century country-house hotel is located in a spectacular woodland setting. The Brewhouse Bistro has its own organic micro brewery and offers unpretentious fare in a rustic setting, complete with flagstone floors, bare brick walls and unclothed timber tables. The Manor restaurant is a more formal affair, offering a weekly-changing menu using organic herbs and vegetables from the kitchen garden. The menu includes the likes of Dexter beef and pork rillettes wrapped in kale and smoked bacon, or honey-roast rack of venison served with a liver and boudin noir gâteau. Desserts might include Bailey's crème brûlée and Yorkshire shortcake biscuit.

Chef: Kevin Mulraney **Owners:** George Tinsley, John Warnock & Alison Foster **Times:** noon-9.30pm **Prices:** Fixed L £8.95-£15.95, Fixed D £15.95, Starter £3.95-£6.95, Main £9.95-£17.95, Dessert £4.50, Service optional **Wine:** 20 bottles over £20, 50 bottles under £20, 8 by the glass **Notes:** Fixed L 3 courses, Vegetarian available, Smart casual, Civ Wed 80 **Seats:** 45, Pr/dining room 40 **Children:** Portions **Rooms:** 6 (6 en suite) ★★★★ RR **Directions:** 10m S of Middlesbrough **Parking:** 150

HAROME   MAP 19 SE68

◉◉ The Star Inn

Traditional British ♦NOTABLE WINE LIST

Creative cuisine at a popular village inn

☎ 01439 770397 YO62 5JE
e-mail: starinn@bt.openworld.com
web: www.thestaratharome.co.uk

Run by a committed family team, this pretty thatched inn is a gastronomic haven that's always busy with an appreciative crowd of locals and foodies alike. It's a cosy haunt, full of candlelit nooks, ancient beams and open fires, and recent expansions have seen the opening of a shop, selling their dishes and local produce. If the restaurant is full you can eat in the small bar area, furnished with Robert Thompson 'Mouseman' furniture, while for private dining there's the Loft with its distinctive criss-crossed beams. The kitchen consistently delivers top-notch British dishes. Expect innovative creations with a strong emphasis on local ingredients: risotto of Sand Hutton asparagus and Yoadwath oak-smoked salmon perhaps, or steamed suet pudding of beef with a deep-fried Loch Fyne oyster.

Chef: Andrew Pern **Owners:** A & J Pern **Times:** 11.30-3/6.30-11, Closed 25 Dec, 2 wks early spring, BHs, Mon, Closed D Sun **Prices:** Food prices not confirmed for 2008. Please telephone for details **Wine:** 10 by the glass **Notes:** Civ Wed 50 **Seats:** 36, Pr/dining room 10 **Children:** Portions **Directions:** From Helmsley take A170 towards Kirkbymoorside, after 0.5m turn right towards Harome. After 1.5m Inn is 1st building on right

HARROGATE   MAP 19 SE35

◉◉ The Boar's Head Hotel

Modern British V

Charming British setting and food

☎ 01423 771888 Ripley Castle Estate HG3 3AY
e-mail: reservations@boarsheadripley.co.uk
web: www.boarsheadripley.co.uk

A former coaching inn with an aristocratic elegance, the Boar's Head is set in the private village of Ripley belonging to the Ripley Castle Estate. It's owned by the current castle occupiers, Sir Thomas and Lady Ingilby, who donated some of their paintings, including those of past Ingilby ancestors. The dining room walls fetchingly come in a vibrant deep red, while comfortable seating and well-trained staff all fit the bill. The kitchen's modern approach is fittingly inspired by British cuisine and uses fresh, quality ingredients with flair in well-presented dishes. Think a classic beef Wellington, or perhaps grilled fillet of pork served with cider and thyme-scented fondant potatoes. (The Bistro here offers less formal surroundings and a simpler menu.)

Chef: Marc Guilbert **Owners:** Sir Thomas Ingilby & Lady Ingilby **Times:** 12-2/7-9 **Prices:** Fixed L £16, Fixed D £30-£40, Service optional **Wine:** 50 bottles over £20, 20 bottles under £20 **Notes:** Vegetarian menu, Dress Restrictions, Smart casual, Civ Wed 150 **Seats:** 40, Pr/dining room 40 **Children:** Menu, Portions **Rooms:** 25 (25 en suite) ★★★ HL **Directions:** On A61 (Harrogate/Ripley road). In village centre **Parking:** 45

◉ Bower's Bistro

Modern International NEW

Charming, intimate bistro setting for accomplished cuisine

☎ 01423 565806 31 Cheltenham Crescent HG1 1DH
e-mail: info@bowersbistro.co.uk
web: www.bowersbistro.co.uk

Just a few minutes walk from the famous Bettys (tea shop) and just round the corner from the town's buzzy exhibition centre, Bower's shouldn't be overlooked. The bistro format sees the interior floored and furnished in wood with wicker-style seating and the bar being the room's focal point. French scenes and interesting art catch the eye and add a certain je ne sais quoi to the proceedings, while the kitchen's modern approach suits the concept, delivering quality produce with skill and interest; take chargrilled beef fillet with rösti potato, watercress purée and Madeira jus.

Chef: Martin Colley **Owners:** James Bolier **Times:** 12-2/6-10, Closed 25 Dec, 1 Jan, BHs, Sun-Mon **Prices:** Fixed D £16.75, Starter £3.95-£6.50, Main £11.95-£17.50, Dessert 90p-£12, Service optional, Group min 8 service 10% **Wine:** 6 bottles over £20, 14 bottles under £20, 6 by the glass **Seats:** 50 **Children:** Portions **Directions:** 11m from Leeds, 5mins walk from Harrogate train station **Parking:** NCP, on street

◉◉ Clocktower

Modern British

Elegant, modern hotel with excellent dining to match

☎ 01423 871350 Rudding Park, Follifoot HG3 1JH
e-mail: sales@ruddingpark.com
web: www.ruddingpark.com

You'll find the refurbished Clocktower restaurant in the converted stable block of Rudding Park House, an elegant and stylish modern hotel set in 200-year-old landscaped parkland. The striking, contemporary dining room has bare-wood tables with quality settings and glassware, modern artwork on the walls, and an adjacent lively bar area. A relaxed and happy air prevails and staff are friendly and professional. The seasonal menu uses oodles of fresh Yorkshire produce and offers modern British dishes with plenty of creativity. Think Nidderdale lamb shank with bubble-and-squeak mash and mulled wine braised red cabbage, or a bread-and-butter pudding finish, with Yorkshire clotted cream. The conservatory - with its 400-year-old olive tree - offers an informal area for Yorkshire tapas. There's a vast alfresco terrace, too.

Chef: Stephanie Moon **Owners:** Simon Mackaness **Times:** 12-3/7-9.30 **Prices:** Starter £5-£9.50, Main £13-£19.50, Dessert £6.50, Service included **Wine:** 50 bottles over £20, 20 bottles under £20, 14 by the glass **Notes:** Vegetarian available, Civ Wed 180, Air con **Seats:** 170, Pr/dining room 250 **Children:** Menu, Portions **Rooms:** 49 (49 en suite) ★★★★ HL **Directions:** A61 at rdbt with A658 follow signs 'Rudding Park' **Parking:** 250

◉ The Courtyard Restaurant

Modern British

Trendy venue in a former stable block

☎ 01423 530708 1 Montpellier Mews HG1 2TQ

This converted Victorian stable block in an attractive courtyard of trendy shops is complete with original Jacob's ladder leading to the hayloft upstairs. Nowadays the restaurant boasts contemporary pastel décor, beech furniture and candlelight in the evening. You can dine outside in the cobbled courtyard garden in summer. The menu offers contemporary British cuisine with classical influences and local, seasonal produce is sourced wherever possible. Expect dishes like Cornish crab, dill and sesame ballotine or garlic corn-fed chicken, thyme-roasted onions and chorizo cream. Early bird menus are also available.

Chef: Ryan Sadler **Owners:** Martin Wilks **Times:** 12-2/6-9.30, Closed 25-26 Dec, 1 Jan, Sun **Prices:** Starter £4.95-£9, Main £12.50-£20, Dessert £5.95, Service optional, Group min 10 service 10% **Notes:** Vegetarian available **Seats:** 28 **Children:** Portions **Directions:** City centre location, Montpellier Quarter next to Royal Baths **Parking:** On street

HARROGATE CONTINUED

◉ Harrogate Brasserie with Rooms

Modern British

A great place to eat and enjoy some jazz

☎ 01423 505041 28-30 Cheltenham Pde HG1 1DB
e-mail: info@brasserie.co.uk
web: www.brasserie.co.uk

This continental-style restaurant with rooms has live jazz nights on Wednesday, Friday and Sunday. The brasserie extends through three cosy, richly decorated dining areas, all adorned with artefacts - mainly on the jazz theme. The menu, supplemented by daily specials from the blackboard, offers modern British cooking. Think medallions of pork fillet served with creamy mash and a wholegrain mustard sauce, or perhaps salmon fillet with lemon and chive butter and saffron rice, while a treacle sponge with crème anglaise or apple and cinnamon crumble and ice cream might catch the eye at dessert.

Chef: Jeremy Foster **Owners:** Mr & Mrs R Finney **Times:** 6-9.45, Closed 26 Dec, 1 Jan, BHs, Closed L all week (ex residents) **Prices:** Fixed L £17.50, Fixed D £22.50, Service optional **Wine:** 11 bottles over £20, 22 bottles under £20, 9 by the glass **Notes:** Vegetarian available **Seats:** 72, Pr/dining room 26 **Children:** Portions **Rooms:** 17 (17 en suite) ★★★ RR **Directions:** In town centre, 500mtrs from railway station, behind theatre, 150mtrs from Conference Centre **Parking:** 12

◉ Hotel du Vin & Bistro

British, Mediterranean

Luxurious surroundings for fine food and wine

☎ 01423 856800 Prospect Place HG1 1LB
e-mail: info@hotelduvin.com
web: www.hotelduvin.com

Originally created from a row of eight Georgian-styled houses overlooking The Stray, which have operated as a hotel since the 1930s, Hotel du Vin Harrogate provides a luxurious experience. Both food and wine are very important here, the bistro menu changes daily and is available throughout the day. Classic dishes are featured, supporting the HdV philosophy of quality food cooked simply, with the freshest of local ingredients. Kick off with Serrano ham, figs and Manchego to start, followed by a simple classic such as veal saltimbocca or steak tartare, or more elaborate fare such as roast venison with pomme fondant and wild mushroom jus. Wine events held throughout the year.

Times: 12-1.45/6.30-9.45 **Rooms:** 43 (43 en suite) ★★★★ TH **Directions:** From A1 follow signs for Harrogate & town centre. Take 3rd exit on Prince of Wales rdbt (marked town centre). Hotel is 400yds on right

◉ Orchid Restaurant

Pacific Rim NEW

Authentic Pacific Rim cuisine in stylish setting

☎ 01423 560425 Studley Hotel, 28 Swan Rd HG1 2SE
e-mail: info@orchidrestaurant.co.uk
web: www.orchidrestaurant.co.uk

Close to the town centre, this friendly hotel is renowned for its ground-floor Orchid Restaurant, which provides a dynamic and authentic approach to Pacific Rim and Asian cuisine. The smart décor is contemporary with Asian influences - think elegant darkwood lacquered tables, authentic rattan bamboo steamers and Asian clay pots. The kitchen's repertoire sets the taste buds alight with a culinary trip through Asia, delivering well-balanced, accurately cooked dishes using high-quality ingredients - some coming direct from Thailand. Start with Szechuan kao yang (chargrilled lamb satay), followed by Thai ped ma kham (sliced roast duck breast with tamarind and honey sauce on a bed of pak choi). Sushi and sashimi are served on Tuesdays, and there's a good-value buffet lunch on Sundays.

Chef: Kenneth Poon **Owners:** Bokmun Chan **Prices:** Fixed L £8.50, Fixed D £19.95-£22.95, Starter £4-£8, Main £7-£22, Dessert £4-£5, Service added but optional 10% **Wine:** 13 bottles over £20, 15 bottles under £20, 8 by the glass **Notes:** Tue D sushi & sashimi, Sun brunch available, Vegetarian available, Air con **Seats:** 72, Pr/dining room 18 **Rooms:** 36 (36 en suite) ★★★ HL **Parking:** 18

◉ Quantro

Modern European

Stylish town-centre restaurant with skilful cooking

☎ 01423 503034 3 Royal Pde HG1 2SZ
e-mail: info@quantro.co.uk
web: www.quantro.co.uk

This popular, informal, glass-fronted town-centre venue is modern and sophisticated, with a lime and aubergine interior that comes fashionably decked out with banquettes, darkwood tables, ambient lighting, wooden floors and large wall mirrors. With relaxed, friendly service, the kitchen's sensibly-priced, modern European menus have a brasserie format and are delivered with panache and the use of good-quality ingredients. Expect seared calves' liver served with braised cabbage, smoked prunes and boulangère potatoes, or jasmine-smoked duck breast with oyster mushroom risotto, and perhaps a baked chocolate tart with sweet mango salsa to finish. (Cheaper light-lunch and early-evening menus offer exceptionally good value.)

Chef: Neil Ballinger **Owners:** T & K Burdekin **Times:** 12-2/6-10, Closed 25-26 Dec, 1 Jan, Sun **Prices:** Fixed L £10.95-£11.95, Fixed D £13.95-£14.95, Starter £4.90-£6.20, Main £11.40-£17, Dessert £3.50-£4.50, Service added but optional 10% **Wine:** 38 bottles under £20, 10 by the glass **Notes:** Vegetarian available, Smart casual preferred, Air con **Seats:** 40 **Children:** Min 8 yrs **Directions:** Telephone for directions **Parking:** On street

HELMSLEY MAP 19 SE68

◎◎ Feversham Arms Hotel

British, French NEW

Refined dining in smart and friendly hotel

☎ 01439 770766 1 High St YO62 5AG

e-mail: info@fevershamarmshotel.com

web: www.fevershamarmshotel.com

This old coaching inn, formerly owned by the Feversham family, is now a well-established hotel and the ideal base for exploring the North Yorkshire moors and the many stately homes in the area. With its high ceilings, the light-and-airy conservatory restaurant overlooks the landscaped terrace at the rear of the hotel. The menu changes every few days and quality ingredients appear in dishes like pan-fried scallops with Jerusalem artichoke purée and Parma ham, followed by corn-fed Goosnargh duck breast with endive and gooseberry tian and violet potatoes, or poached guinea fowl with roast garlic gnocchi, apple fondant and walnuts. Innovative desserts include chocolate and five-spice mousse with cinnamon ice cream and fig compôte. Service is relaxed and friendly.

Chef: Simon Kelly **Owners:** Simon Rhatigan **Times:** 12-2/7-9.30 **Prices:** Fixed D £32, Starter £8.25-£12.25, Main £17.50-£23.50, Dessert £8.50, Service optional **Wine:** 22 bottles under £20, 12 by the glass **Notes:** Sun L available, Dress Restrictions, Smart casual, No jeans, no T-shirts, Civ Wed 120 **Seats:** 50, Pr/dining room 25 **Children:** Menu, Portions **Rooms:** 19 (19 en suite) ★★★ HL **Directions:** From A1(M) take A168 to Thirsk then A170 for 14 miles to Helmsley **Parking:** 50

HOVINGHAM MAP 19 SE67

◎ Worsley Arms Hotel

British

A good traditional spa hotel restaurant

☎ 01653 628234 High St YO62 4LA

e-mail: worsleyarms@aol.com

web: www.worsleyarms.com

A 19th-century hotel overlooking the village green with a history dating back to the time when Sir William Worsley decided it would be a good idea to turn the village into a spa town - sadly an enterprise that failed. The restaurant, decorated in soothing reds and greens, has efficient and friendly service. Good, locally-sourced ingredients are used extensively; take slow-roast half shoulder of lamb served with black pudding mash and redcurrant jus, or perhaps a duo of fish with crushed potatoes, spinach and a cream sauce. Less formal dining is available in the Cricketers' Bar and Bistro at the rear.

Chef: Anthony Finn **Owners:** Mr & Mrs A Finn **Times:** 12-2/6.30-9, Closed L Mon-Sat **Prices:** Fixed L £16-£18, Fixed D £22.50-£30, Starter £6-£9, Main £15-£22, Dessert £5-£6.50, Service optional **Wine:** 8 by the glass **Notes:** Sun L 2 courses £16, 3 courses £18.50, Vegetarian available, Civ Wed 90 **Seats:** 70, Pr/dining room 40 **Children:** Portions **Rooms:** 20 (20 en suite) ★★★ HL **Directions:** 20 mins N of York on the B1257, between Malton and Helmsley **Parking:** 30

KIRKHAM MAP 19 SE76

◎ Stone Trough Inn

Modern British

Satisfying gastro-pub dining amid splendid scenery

☎ 01653 618713 Kirkham Abbey, Whitwell on the Hill YO60 7JS

e-mail: info@stonetroughinn.co.uk

web: www.stonetroughinn.co.uk

This red-roofed, yellow stone country inn occupies a wonderful elevated position close to Kirkham's romantic castle ruins. Log fires, flagstone floors, walls full of bric-à-brac or country-pursuit cartoons and comfortable seating fill its labyrinth of cosy rooms and restaurant, making this a popular dining destination. Service is thoughtful and friendly. The hard-working kitchen takes a modern approach producing dishes like pan-fried calves' liver on black pudding mash with crisp pancetta and sage and redcurrant jus, or roast rack of Flaxton lamb with crab apple sauce and mint, with a warm apricot and frangipane tart to finish. Home-made breads, brioches and petits fours bolster the accomplished act.

Chef: Adam Richardson **Owners:** Adam & Sarah Richardson **Times:** 12-2.15/6.45-9.30, Closed 25 Dec, 2-5 Jan, Mon, Closed L Tue-Sat, D Sun **Prices:** Starter £4.75-£8.50, Main £10.95-£19.95, Dessert £4.50-£4.95, Service optional, Group min 25 service 10% **Wine:** 20 bottles over £20, 45 bottles under £20, 14 by the glass **Notes:** Vegetarian available **Seats:** 55, Pr/dining room 14 **Children:** Menu, Portions **Directions:** 1.5m off the A64, between York & Malton **Parking:** 100

KNARESBOROUGH   MAP 19 SE35

◉◉ General Tarleton Inn

Modern British V ☺

Foodie destination in North Yorkshire countryside

☎ 01423 340284 Boroughbridge Rd, Ferrensby HG5 0PZ
e-mail: gti@generaltarleton.co.uk
web: www.generaltarleton.co.uk

Owned by the team behind the Angel Inn at Hetton (see entry), this is a destination for food-lovers trying exciting pub dining in the bar brasserie, or enjoying the more formal atmosphere of the dining room restaurant. The restaurant was originally a land-locked boatyard, but you would never guess from its smart, comfortable seating, exposed brickwork and beamed ceiling. Here you will find honest modern British cooking with the emphasis firmly on seasonal local and regional produce. A typical main course might be a roast rack, confit shoulder and mini shepherd's

pie of Yorkshire Dales lamb. For dessert you could try a warm Valrhona chocolate fondant with home-made vanilla ice cream.

Chef: John Topham, Robert Ramsden **Owners:** John & Claire Topham
Times: 12-1.45/6-9.15, Closed L Mon-Sat, D Sun **Prices:** Fixed L £22.95,
Fixed D £32.50, Service optional **Wine:** 70 bottles over £20, 29 bottles
under £20, 19 by the glass **Notes:** Fixed L 3 courses, Vegetarian menu,
Dress Restrictions, Smart casual **Seats:** 64, Pr/dining room 36
Children: Menu, Portions **Rooms:** 14 (14 en suite) ★★★★★ RR
Directions: A1(M) junct 48 at Boroughbridge, take A6055 to
Knaresborough. Continue into Ferrensby inn on right **Parking:** 40

MARTON   MAP 19 SE78

◉ The Appletree

Modern British

Quality food in cosy, country gastro-pub

☎ 01751 431457 YO62 6RD
e-mail: appletreeinn@supanet.com
web: www.appletreeinn.co.uk

Once a working farm, The Appletree evolved into a pub when the farmer's wife began serving beer to workers in the front room. Today, hundreds of candles and a roaring fire create a cosy ambience for diners, whose well-spaced tables are tucked away in private nooks and window alcoves throughout the ground floor. The daily-changing menu takes in some specials, offering simple and unfussy dishes with some unusual flavour combinations and good use of local seasonal produce. Start with brûléed English goat's cheese with tomato salsa perhaps, before moving on to braised thick flank of Marton beef with red onion marmalade and horseradish cream, or smoked haddock with lemon and pea risotto.

◉◉◉

Samuel's at Swinton Park

MASHAM   MAP 19 SE28

Modern British V ♦ NOTABLE WINE LIST

Elegant and atmospheric luxury castle hotel

☎ 01765 680900 HG4 4JH
e-mail: enquiries@swintonpark.com
web: www.swintonpark.com

Swinton Park has been a family home since the late 1800s although the earliest part of the castle dates from the late 1600s. Though extended during the Victorian and Edwardian eras, the original part of this castle hotel comes complete with turrets, gatehouse, sweeping drive and a 200-acre estate. Everything about Swinton Park oozes elegance; beautiful day rooms, huge windows, high ceilings, heavy drapes, antiques and portraits, and swish sofas. There's a real sense of grandeur, and Samuel's restaurant doesn't disappoint, with its ornate gold-leaf ceiling, comfortable seating, crisp white linen, impeccable service and sweeping views over lake and parkland.
The cooking draws heavily on fresh produce from the walled kitchen garden and estate, particularly game, herbs and vegetables. Clean, distinct flavours, fine combinations and balance, seasonality and luxury parade on the fixed-price menu repertoire, which at dinner includes a carte and tasting option. So expect a ravioli of Whitby crab with roasted salsify and shellfish dressing, followed by breast of Swinton

pheasant with game faggot, creamed garden kale and carrot purée, and perhaps pear tarte Tatin with almond ice cream to finish. There's an impressive cheese trolley, too.

Chef: Andrew Burton **Owners:** Mr and Mrs Cunliffe-Lister **Times:** 12.30-
2/7-9.30 **Prices:** Fixed L £17, Fixed D £39, Service optional **Wine:** 120
bottles over £20, 18 bottles under £20, 10 by the glass **Notes:** Fixed D 4
courses, Tasting menu 7 courses £48, Vegetarian menu, Civ Wed 100
Seats: 60, Pr/dining room 20 **Children:** Min 8 yrs D, Menu, Portions
Rooms: 30 (30 en suite)★★★★ HL **Directions:** A1 take B6267, from
Masham follow brown signs for Swinton Park **Parking:** 80

Chef: TJ Drew **Owners:** TJ & Melanie Drew **Times:** 12-2/6-9.30, Closed Xmas, 2 weeks Jan, Mon-Tue **Prices:** Starter £4-£7.50, Main £10-£19, Dessert £3-£7, Service optional **Wine:** 36 bottles over £20, 52 bottles under £20, 12 by the glass **Notes:** Booking essential, Mineral water complimentary **Seats:** 24, Pr/dining room 8 **Children:** Portions **Directions:** 2m from Kirkbymoorside on A170 towards Pickering, turn right to Marton **Parking:** 18

MASHAM   MAP 19 SE28
◉◉◉ Samuel's at Swinton Park
see opposite

◉◉ Vennell's
Modern British NEW
Small, traditional-styled local serving accomplished modern fare

☎ 01765 689000 7 Silver St HG4 4DX
e-mail: info@vennellsrestaurant.co.uk
web: www.vennellsrestaurant.co.uk

This eponymous, small, shopfront-style restaurant (formerly the Floodlite) overlooks the main street through the village. The décor in this Grade II listed property is traditional and comes in muted shades of beige, with the wallpaper, carpet and swag-and-tail curtains offering a homely feel, while plenty of artwork adorns the walls. There's a snug-style lounge downstairs to peruse the sensibly concise, appealing, classically-inspired menus and, while wife Laura runs front of house, chef-patron Jon (who worked for many years at Haley's Hotel in Leeds) is at the stove. Quality local ingredients and assured skill are evident throughout; think cured belly pork served with mustard mash, velouté, crackling, broad beans and apple, or steak and oxtail suet pudding with glazed vegetables.

Chef: Jon Vennell **Owners:** Jon & Laura Vennell **Times:** 12-2/7.15-9.15, Closed 26-29 Dec, 1-14 Jan, 1 wk Sep, BHs, Mon, Closed L Tue-Thu, D Sun **Prices:** Fixed L £16.95, Fixed D £24.90, Service optional **Wine:** 54 bottles over £20, 18 bottles under £20, 4 by the glass **Notes:** Sun L 3 courses £19.95 inc coffee **Seats:** 30 **Children:** Min 4 yrs, Portions **Directions:** 8m from A1 Masham exit **Parking:** On street and in Market Sq

MIDDLESBROUGH   MAP 19 NZ41
◉ Best Western Highfield Hotel
French, British
French brasserie-style restaurant

☎ 01642 817638 Marton Rd TS4 2PA
e-mail: info@thehighfieldhotel.co.uk
web: www.thehighfieldhotel.co.uk

The hotel's La Terrasse restaurant has an authentic brasserie feel, complete with Parisian prints and photographs on the walls, café-style chairs and linen cloths. The cuisine, like the décor, is classic French brasserie style with international influences, and there's a strong emphasis on seafood. You might start with Whitby crab served with Belgium endive and passionfruit salad, and move on to a lightly poached pavé of turbot, accompanied by sweet potato dauphinoise, vanilla-scented nage, broccoli purée and asparagus. A tasting of chocolate, or an interesting mulled wine risotto with cranberry compôte and cinnamon tuile might feature at dessert.

Chef: Stuart White **Owners:** Oakwell Leisure **Times:** 12-2.30/6-10 **Prices:** Fixed L £14.95, Starter £4.95-£7.95, Main £13.95-£16.95, Dessert £4.95-£5.95, Service included **Wine:** 50 bottles over £20, 20 bottles under £20, 12 by the glass **Notes:** Civ Wed 70 **Seats:** 80, Pr/dining room 25 **Children:** Menu, Portions **Rooms:** 23 (23 en suite) ★★★ HL **Directions:** Telephone for directions **Parking:** 100

PICKERING   MAP 19 SE78
◉ Fox & Hounds Country Inn
Modern British
Village pub with interesting menu

☎ 01751 431577 Main St, Sinnington YO62 6SQ
e-mail: foxhoundsinn@easynet.co.uk
web: www.thefoxandhoundsinn.co.uk

In a quiet village setting, this mellow-stone 18th-century coaching inn has an old mounting block outside and some of the original window frames bear old - often risqué! - inscriptions. The beamed bar has an intimate atmosphere and is popular with locals, while the restaurant is light and extends to the rear of the inn, with well-spaced tables, upholstered chairs and oak panelling. Traditional, flavoursome dishes might include the likes of roast fillet of salmon, with scallion-crushed potatoes and Yorkshire asparagus, followed by apricot clafoutis, stem ginger and honey ice cream.

Chef: Mark Caffrey **Owners:** Mr & Mrs A Stephens **Times:** 12-2/6.30-9, Closed 25-26 Dec **Prices:** Starter £4.75-£7.50, Main £10.25-£19.95, Dessert £4.95-£5.50 Service option **Seats:** 40 **Children:** Menu **Rooms:** 10 (10 en suite) ★★ HL **Directions:** In centre of Sinnington, 300 yds off A170 between Pickering & Helmsley **Parking:** 45

ENGLAND

Yorke Arms

RAMSGILL MAP 19 SE17

British ♦ NOTABLE WINE LIST

Character restaurant dedicated to quality

☎ 01423 755243   HG3 5RL
e-mail: enquiries@yorke-arms.co.uk
web: www.yorke-arms.co.uk

Dominating its tiny Dales hamlet, this creeper-clad restaurant with rooms overlooks the village green. A former pub, it oozes character and charm, boasting a comfy lounge and a cosy snug for winter evenings. A large antique mirror gives the dining room a touch of sophistication, while polished floorboards, rugs, a large oak dresser and wooden furniture provide plenty of traditional charm. As well as the main restaurant, there's a smaller affair for quieter nights, with a roaring fire when it's cold. Service is suitably professional and attentive from a young team.

Frances Atkins is a highly experienced chef who delivers an accomplished menu of modern dishes underpinned by classical techniques. There's great emphasis here on quality throughout, with tip-top wild and organic produce provided wherever possible from the abundant local larder. Expect clean flavours and a deceptively simple approach from a kitchen that lets its ingredients do the talking: a dish of Yorkshire grouse arrives with heather-scented jus, for example, served with wild moorland bilberries, while a blanquette and pastry of local mutton is served with pearl barley, apple and capers. A surprise six-course tasting menu is available. Book ahead.

Chef: Frances Atkins, Roger Olive
Owners: Mr & Mrs G Atkins
Times: 12-2/7-9, Closed D Sun (ex residents)
Prices: Fixed L £17.50-£26, Starter £6-£10, Main £18-£25, Dessert £6-£8.50, Service optional
Wine: 171 bottles over £20, 6 bottles under £20, 12 by the glass
Notes: Tasting menu 6 courses £50, Vegetarian available, Dress Restrictions, No jeans or trainers, jacket & tie preferred
Seats: 60, Pr/dining room 20
Children: Min 12 yrs
Rooms: 14 (14 en suite) ★★★★★ RR
Directions: From Pateley Bridge, turn right onto Low Wath road and continue for 5m, turn right into Ramsgill, Yorke Arms is beside village green
Parking: 20

PICKERING CONTINUED

⚜ The White Swan Inn

Traditional V ☺

Welcoming inn with pleasing food

☎ 01751 472288 Market Place YO18 7AA
e-mail: welcome@white-swan.co.uk
web: www.white-swan.co.uk

This charming 16th-century coaching inn has been in the Buchanan family for over 20 years and was taken over by the current generation in 1996. A place of great character with flagstone floors, log fires and a cosy, intimate dining room, it was once a refuge for salt smugglers. The classic gastro-pub style cooking features locally-sourced ingredients, including meat produce from The Ginger Pig in Levisham. Dishes include Sand Hutton asparagus with a poached egg and Maltaise sauce, and marinated leg of Levisham spring lamb with potato rösti.

Chef: Darren Clemmit **Owners:** The Buchanan Family **Times:** 12-2/6.45-9 **Prices:** Fixed L £10, Starter £4.25-£10.25, Main £10.95-£16.95, Dessert £5.25-£5.50, Service optional **Wine:** 128 bottles over £20, 41 bottles under £20, 13 by the glass **Notes:** Fixed L Mon-Fri, Vegetarian menu, Civ Wed 50 **Seats:** 50, Pr/dining room 18 **Children:** Menu, Portions **Rooms:** 21 (21 en suite) ★★★ HL **Directions:** A1/A19 towards Thirsk, then A170 to Pickering. Between the church and steam railway station **Parking:** 35

RAMSGILL   MAP 19 SE17

⚜⚜⚜ Yorke Arms

see opposite

RICHMOND   MAP 19 NZ10

⚜ Frenchgate Hotel

Modern British

Restored gentleman's residence with a modern menu

☎ 01748 822087 59-61 Frenchgate DL10 7AE
e-mail: info@thefrenchgate.co.uk
web: www.thefrenchgate.co.uk

The hotel is a three-storey Georgian townhouse set in a quiet cobbled street. The building has been beautifully restored, and there are period features, antique furniture throughout, and works of art. The restaurant is a mix of traditional and contemporary, with oak tables, chairs and restored floorboards, with sophisticated lighting and fine table appointments. Modern British cooking with a continental twist includes carpaccio of venison with a fig chutney and Swaledale Blue dressing, and pan-fried breast of guinea fowl with seared foie gras, creamed cabbage, and ham hock velouté.

Frenchgate Hotel

Chef: Matt Allen **Owners:** David & Luiza Todd **Times:** 12-2.30/7-10, Closed Mon **Prices:** Fixed D £29, Service optional **Wine:** 58 bottles over £20, 36 bottles under £20, 9 by the glass **Seats:** 24, Pr/dining room 16 **Children:** Min 6 yrs D, Portions **Rooms:** 8 (8 en suite) ★★ HL **Directions:** Please telephone for details **Parking:** 12

SCARBOROUGH   MAP 17 TA08

⚜ Beiderbecke's Hotel

Modern International

Buzzing atmosphere with jazz music while you eat

☎ 01723 365766 1-3 The Crescent YO11 2PW
e-mail: info@beiderbeckes.com
web: www.beiderbeckes.com

Marmalade's restaurant in this hotel, named after a famous American jazz cornetist, offers international cuisine with a modern twist. It hosts live music acts at weekends, including the resident jazz band. This is reflected in the décor with red walls setting off jazz pictures and a stage for the musicians. Diners can enjoy the lively atmosphere while they choose from an extensive menu and range of daily specials. Typical dishes include Whitby fish soup or goat's cheese wontons to start, followed by breast of duck with shallot and spinach tartlet.

Chef: Nick Poole **Owners:** Vladimir Kishenin **Times:** 6-9.30, Closed L Mon-Sat **Prices:** Fixed D £19.50, Starter £4.95-£7.50, Main £11.95-£17.50, Dessert £5.50-£7.50, Service included **Wine:** 12 bottles over £20, 20 bottles under £20, 6 by the glass **Notes:** Sun L 3 courses £12.50, Vegetarian available, Dress Restrictions, Smart casual, Air con **Seats:** 100, Pr/dining room 20 **Children:** Menu, Portions **Rooms:** 27 (27 en suite) ★★★ HL **Directions:** 200mtrs from rail station **Parking:** 15

ENGLAND

ENGLAND

SCARBOROUGH CONTINUED

◉ Pepper's Restaurant

Modern, Traditional British NEW

Carefully sourced produce served in a welcoming atmosphere

☎ 01723 500642 11 York Place YO11 2NP
e-mail: peppers.restaurant@virgin.net
web: www.peppersrestaurant.co.uk

An imposing Georgian townhouse with split-level dining and a cellar bar area. The friendly team show you to generous wooden tables where you can enjoy the artwork on display while perusing the menu. Traditional British and European dishes are reinterpreted using classical techniques and taking advantage of the best seasonal produce from the local area. Freshly baked bread speaks volumes for the attention to detail, a simple white roll transformed with mushroom and thyme. Starters might include a special of marinated line-caught mackerel, while seared Scarborough landed sea trout with crushed peas in vinaigrette, crab fritter and chilled hollandaise may be on offer as a seafood main course.

Chef: Jonothon Smith **Owners:** Jonothon & Katherine Smith **Times:** 12-2/6-10, Closed 5 days over Xmas, Sun-Mon, Closed L Tue-Wed **Prices:** Fixed D £20, Starter £5.50-£8, Main £13-£19, Dessert £6, Service optional **Wine:** 10 bottles over £20, 13 bottles under £20, 6 by the glass **Seats:** 45 **Children:** Menu, Portions **Parking:** On street

---

SUTTON-ON-THE-FOREST   MAP 19 SE56

◉ The Blackwell Ox Inn

Modern European

Gastro-pub cooking in refurbished village inn

☎ 01347 810328 & 690758 Huby Rd YO61 1DT
e-mail: enquiries@blackwelloxinns.com
web: www.blackwelloxinn.co.uk

Dating back to the 1820s, the inn is named after a famous Shorthorn Teeswater ox weighing in at 2,278lb. Today the inn has been modernised and refurbished to provide a bar, lounge bar and smart restaurant. Based on prime local produce and regional cookery from France with a Spanish influence, the menu offers big rustic flavours, rich stews, light shellfish dishes and a great range of charcuterie and cheeses. Think home-farmed venison casserole served with herby suet dumplings, perhaps monkfish and oxtail bourguignon, or roast fillet of cod with olive oil mash, gremolata and provençal tomatoes.

Chef: Steven Holding **Owners:** Blackwell Ox Inns (York) Ltd
Times: 11.30-2/6-9.30 **Prices:** Fixed L £8.50, Fixed D £13.50, Starter £3.95-

£7.50, Main £9.95-£18.50, Dessert £3.50-£7.50, Service optional **Wine:** 24 bottles over £20, 31 bottles under £20, 9 by the glass **Seats:** 36, Pr/dining room 16 **Children:** Portions **Rooms:** 5 (5 en suite) ★★★★ INN **Directions:** A1237 take B1363 to Sutton-on-the-Forest, turn left at T-junct, Inn 50m on right **Parking:** 19

see advert opposite

◉ Rose & Crown

Modern British

Relaxed, country-dining pub

☎ 01347 811333 Main St YO61 1DP
e-mail: ben@rosecrown.co.uk
web: www.rosecrown.co.uk

This dining pub in a village setting midway between York and Helmsley has a simple beamed interior with wooden floors and tables and open fires. The warm and cosy décor of the dining room has contemporary features and has been extended into a conservatory. There are African-inspired thatched gazebos on the terrace where you can enjoy alfresco dining. Dishes are attractively presented and there is an emphasis on fresh fish and seafood. Expect the likes of monkfish wrapped in Parma ham with buttered asparagus and mixed herb pesto, or haunch of venison with braised red cabbage and red wine jus.

Chef: Adam Jackson, Danny Jackson **Owners:** Ben & Lucy Williams **Times:** 12-2/6-9.30, Closed 1st 2wks Jan, Mon, Closed D Sun **Prices:** Fixed L £12.50-£20, Fixed D £15-£30, Starter £4.25-£7.95, Main £9.50-£26, Dessert £4.95-£6.50, Service optional **Wine:** 50 bottles over £20, 20 bottles under £20, 12 by the glass **Notes:** Sun L 1-3 courses, £10.95-£18.95 **Seats:** 80 **Children:** Portions **Directions:** 8m N of York towards Helmsley on B1363 **Parking:** 12

TADCASTER   MAP 16 SE44

◉◉ Restaurant Anise

Modern European

Modern brasserie in a converted castle hotel

☎ 01937 535317 Hazlewood Castle, Paradise Ln, Hazlewood LS24 9NJ
e-mail: info@hazlewood-castle.co.uk
web: www.hazlewood-castle.co.uk

This hotel has been imaginatively converted from a 950-year-old castle and stands in 77 acres of parkland. Yet Restaurant Anise (located in the basement) is not quite what you'd expect from a castle dining room - an informal, funky, stylish, modern, eye-catching, bold-coloured French-themed brasserie incorporating a bar. Unclothed black tables, leather chairs, exposed stonework, original beams, wooden flooring and an elegant terrace overlooking the delightful gardens complete an upbeat picture. The cuisine is Mediterranean-styled with French classics (from a French chef) finding their place on the accomplished repertoire that displays an emphasis on freshness and flavour. Take pan-fried rump of lamb served with rustic ratatouille, rosemary polenta and its own jus, or fillet steak with forestière garnish, baby onions, cocotte potatoes and a Madeira sauce.

Chef: Valerie Hamelin **Owners:** Hazlewood Castle Ltd **Times:** 12-2/6-9, Closed 25 Dec **Prices:** Starter £5-£8, Main £14-£18, Dessert £5-£8 **Notes:** Sun L 3 courses £24.95, Civ Wed 120 **Seats:** 50 **Children:** Menu, Portions **Rooms:** 21 (21 en suite) ★★★ HL **Directions:** Signed from A64, W of Tadcaster, 0.5m from A1/M1 **Parking:** 120

WEST WITTON   MAP 19 SE08

◉ The Wensleydale Heifer

Traditional, International V

Great seafood restaurant in the Dales

☎ 01969 622322 DL8 4LS
e-mail: info@wensleydaleheifer.co.uk
web: www.wensleydaleheifer.co.uk

Behind the coach house inn frontage there is a smart, modern seafood restaurant offering two different dining experiences. The fish bar is less formal, with its seagrass flooring, wooden tables and rattan chairs, while the restaurant has a contemporary tone with chocolate leather chairs, linen cloths and Doug Hyde pictures. The kitchen shows its pedigree via a repertoire awash with the fruits of the sea. Well-sourced, high-quality fresh fish and seafood are handled with simplicity and come full of flavour. Take blue swimmer, crab-crusted wild Pacific halibut fillet with crushed new potatoes, buttered spinach and asparagus cream, or Thai shellfish curry. (Meat dishes also available.)

Chef: David Moss **Owners:** David & Lewis Moss **Times:** 12-2.30/6-9.30 **Prices:** Fixed L £13.50, Starter £6-£10.50, Main £11.50-£19.50, Dessert £5.50, Service added but optional 10% **Wine:** 24 bottles over £20, 29 bottles under £20, 11 by the glass **Notes:** Sun L 2 courses £14.95, 3 courses £17.95, Vegetarian menu **Seats:** 70 **Children:** Menu, Portions **Rooms:** 9 (9 en suite) ★★ HL **Directions:** On A684 (3m W of Leyburn) **Parking:** 30
see advert on this page

WHITBY   **MAP 19 NZ81**

◉ Dunsley Hall

Modern, Traditional V

Modern culinary delights in a fine country house

☎ 01947 893437 Dunsley YO21 3TL
e-mail: reception@dunsleyhall.com
web: www.dunsleyhall.com

This delightful mellow-stone Victorian country-house hotel is set amid 4 acres of landscaped gardens on the Whitby coastline. The traditional-style dining room comes complete with original wooden panelling and fireplaces; there's also a separate bar, and the atmosphere is relaxed and friendly. An amuse-bouche and an intermediate course inject an unhurried feel, and the modern menus with French influences are well worth lingering over. An enthusiastic team makes the most of the fine produce harvested locally from the land and sea. A sample menu offers starters like crab and prawn platter with capers, lemon and petit salad, or seared diver pickled scallops with pea and lemongrass cream, truffled asparagus and pea shoots, while mains include grilled Whitby crab with fresh tomato fondue, wilted spinach and crayfish tails.

Chef: Wayne Newsome **Owners:** Mr & Mrs W Ward **Times:** 12-2/7.30-9.30 **Prices:** Fixed L £12.95-£18.95, Fixed D £29-£35, Starter £4-£7, Main £15-£21, Dessert £6-£9, Service optional **Wine:** 10 bottles over £20, 10 bottles under £20, 10 by the glass **Notes:** Vegetarian menu, Dress Restrictions, Smart casual, no jeans or shorts, Civ Wed 100 **Seats:** 85, Pr/dining room 30 **Children:** Min 5 yrs, Menu, Portions **Rooms:** 18 (18 en suite) ★★★ CHH **Directions:** 3.5m from Whitby off A171 Teeside road **Parking:** 30

◉ Estbek House

Modern British

Restaurant with rooms by the sea

☎ 01947 893424 East Row, Sandsend YO21 3SU
e-mail: info@estbekhouse.co.uk
web: www.estbekhouse.co.uk

This popular restaurant with rooms occupies an impressive listed building on the seafront of a small coastal village not far from Whitby. Dine alfresco in a pretty cobbled courtyard in summer or upstairs in the contemporary restaurant - a chic and romantic room decked out with mirrors, sparkling glassware and high-backed leather chairs. Local fish is the mainstay of the menu, but there's plenty of other fare to tempt including a wild mushroom basket starter and mains such as loin of lamb with a raspberry and rosemary sauce. Start with sweet-cured Orkney herring fillets in Madeira, and then tuck into cod Mornay, or lobster and crab ravioli with king scallop, with hot Kirsch cherries and vanilla pod ice cream to finish.

Chef: Tim Lawrence, James Nelson **Owners:** D Cross, T Lawrence **Times:** 6-9 **Prices:** Starter £5.95-£8.75, Main £13.95-£28.95, Dessert £5.50, Service optional **Wine:** 55 bottles over £20, 20 bottles under £20, 10 by the glass **Notes:** Tasting menu available, Vegetarian available **Seats:** 36, Pr/dining room 16 **Children:** Min 14 yrs **Rooms:** 4 (3 en suite) ★★★★ RR **Directions:** From Whitby follow A174 towards Sandsend, Estbek just before bridge **Parking:** 6
see advert on this page

⊛ The White Horse & Griffin

Modern, Traditional European

Bistro fare in historic coaching inn

☎ 01947 825026 & 604857   Church St YO22 4BH
e-mail: info@whitehorseandgriffin.co.uk
web: www.whitehorseandgriffin.co.uk

Dating from the 17th century, this former coaching inn retains many original features. There are three dining areas, each with a different mood, and the kitchen delivers crowd-pleasing bistro cooking using locally-sourced meat and fish direct from the boats. Good quality breads are freshly made daily, alongside dishes such as seafood medley on a stick with rocket and wasabi mayo, or pot-roast pheasant with cider, creamed cabbage and good old-fashioned mashed potato. A fun dessert for two or more diners is Swiss chocolate fondue with exotic fruits.

Chef: S Perkins, K Healy, C Eddon, A Pearson   **Owners:** June & Stewart Perkins   **Times:** 12-3/5-9, Closed D 25 Dec   **Prices:** Starter £5.95-£9.95, Main £7.95-£30, Dessert £6.95-£10   **Wine:** 13 bottles over £20, 23 bottles under £20, 12 by the glass   **Notes:** Vegetarian available   **Seats:** 75, Pr/dining room 36   **Children:** Menu, Portions   **Rooms:** 10 (10 en suite) ★★★ RR   **Parking:** 3

Magpie Café

☎ 01947 602058   14 Pier Rd YO21 3PU

Overlooking Whitby harbour, this is an ideal location to enjoy local fish, seafood and Magpie Café specialities.

YARM   **MAP 19 NZ41**

⊛⊛⊛ Judges Country House Hotel

see below

YORK   **MAP 16 SE65**

⊛ Best Western York Pavilion Hotel

Modern European 🖥

Relaxed, brasserie-style dining in Georgian surroundings

☎ 01904 622099   45 Main St, Fulford YO10 4PJ
e-mail: reservations@yorkpavilionhotel.com
web: www.yorkpavilionhotel.com

The Pavilion is an elegant Grade II Georgian property just over a mile from the city walls. The hotel's Langton Brasserie is just what its name suggests, with floorboards, polished-wood tables and lots of prints and pictures in true brasserie style. It's light and airy, too, thanks to high ceilings and large garden windows. The imaginative, sensibly compact menu includes dishes such as lemon and dill home-cured salmon with lamb's leaf and baby spinach salad, beetroot crisps and caper dressing, or garlic-infused rump of lamb with roast Charentais carrots, mint pesto and red wine jus.

Chef: Stuart Mills   **Owners:** Irene & Andrew Cossins   **Times:** 12-1.45/6.30-9.30   **Prices:** Fixed L £14.95, Fixed D £25-£35, Starter £3.95-£5.25, Main £11.95-£16.95, Dessert £3.95-£4.95, Service optional   **Wine:** 25 bottles over £20, 20 bottles under £20, 11 by the glass   **Notes:** Sun L 3 courses £16.95, Civ Wed 90   **Seats:** 60, Pr/dining room 150   **Children:** Menu, Portions   **Rooms:** 57 (57 en suite) ★★★ HL   **Directions:** S from York city centre on A19 (Selby), hotel 2m on left. On A1 from N or S take A64 to York, then take Selby/York City Centre A19 junct   **Parking:** 50

⊛⊛⊛

Judges Country House Hotel

YARM   **MAP 19 NZ41**

Modern French NOTABLE WINE LIST

Delightful conservatory restaurant offering bold, accomplished cooking

☎ 01642 789000   Kirklevington TS15 9LW
e-mail: enquiries@judgeshotel.co.uk
web: www.judgeshotel.co.uk

This gracious Victorian mansion with its 42 acres of landscaped grounds offers diners a haven of peace and tranquility. Once the sumptuous lodging for circuit court judges - hence its name - it still proves an ideal country retreat for calm deliberation. The lounge has plump-cushioned armchairs and roaring winter fires, while the elegant, airy conservatory restaurant offers views over the lovely gardens. Classical décor, a friendly atmosphere and attentive, professional staff enhance the experience.

The accomplished kitchen's modern approach comes underpinned by a classical French theme, delivered by crisply-scripted fixed-price menus that bring fresh, local seasonal produce to the plate with clean flavours, assured balance, fine presentation and innovation. Take hand-dived scallops with cauliflower textures, boudin noir and jus 'coq au vin' to start, and perhaps cumin-spiced turbot with lamb shank and Moroccan flavours or Mount Grace Farm pork served with pommes

mousseline, turnips, passionfruit, sage and a beurre blanc to follow. Finish with lemongrass and cardamom soup with plum compôte and chilli sorbet, or apple and raisin soufflé accompanied by a champagne sorbet.

Chef: John Schwarz   **Owners:** Mr M Downs   **Times:** 12-2/7-9.30   **Prices:** Fixed L £14.50, Fixed D £44-£52.50, Service optional   **Wine:** 117 bottles over £20, 45 bottles under £20, 12 by the glass   **Notes:** Vegetarian available, Dress Restrictions, Jacket & tie preferred, No jeans, Smart dress, Civ Wed 200   **Seats:** 60, Pr/dining room 50   **Children:** Menu, Portions   **Rooms:** 21 (21 en suite) ★★★ HL   **Directions:** 1.5m from junct W A19, take A67 towards Kirklevington, hotel 1.5m on left   **Parking:** 110

ENGLAND

YORK CONTINUED

◉ Blue Bicycle

Modern European 🖥

Popular bistro-style city-centre restaurant

☎ 01904 673990 34 Fossgate YO1 9TA
e-mail: info@thebluebicycle.com
web: www.thebluebicycle.com

One of York's best-loved restaurants, this buzzy city-centre eatery has an intimate atmosphere. You'll easily spot the namesake blue bicycle propped up outside the bright shop-front style window and entrance to the two-floored restaurant. The kitchen brings creative touches to popular dishes, delivering a wide-ranging modern European menu with an emphasis on local ingredients, including fish and game in season. Think chargrilled chicken breast with parsnip purée, buttered baby vegetables and saffron dressing, or perhaps grilled fillets of sea bass with crayfish and thyme risotto with cucumber spaghetti and red pepper coulis.

Blue Bicycle

Chef: Simon Hirst **Owners:** Lawrence Anthony Stephenson **Times:** 12-2.30/6-9.30, Closed 24-26 Dec, 1-2 Jan, Closed L 31 Dec **Prices:** Starter £6-£9.75, Main £14.50-£19.75, Dessert £6.50-£9, Service added but optional 10% **Wine:** 38 bottles over £20, 36 bottles under £20, 19 by the glass **Notes:** Vegetarian available **Seats:** 83, Pr/dining room **Directions:** Located in centre of York, just off Parliament St **Parking:** On street & NCP

see advert below

◎◎ D.C.H

Modern 🖥

Fine dining with great views of York Minster

☎ 01904 625082 Best Western Dean Court Hotel, Duncombe Place YO1 7EF
e-mail: sales@deancourt-york.co.uk
web: www.deancourt-york.co.uk

Originally built to house the clergy, this smart hotel enjoys an enviable location overlooking York Minster. It's been sensitively refurbished in an elegant, contemporary style and offers two dining options - the popular D.C.H. restaurant for fine dining and the café-bistro, The Court. The former offers a fairly extensive menu with a wonderful array of modern British favourites cooked expertly - fish and chips in the form of seared scallops on minted pea purée served with home-made miniature chips to start, for example, followed by game pie of local game cooked in Black Sheep Ale. Finish with a classic crème caramel or creamy rice pudding with nutmeg and fruit compôte.

Chef: Andrew Bingham **Owners:** Mr B A Cleminson **Times:** 12.30-2/7-9.30, Closed L 31 Dec, D 25 Dec **Prices:** Fixed L £13, Starter £5.25-£8.25, Main £14.50-£21, Dessert £5.75 **Wine:** 94 bottles over £20, 32 bottles under £20, 18 by the glass **Notes:** Sun L 3 courses £18.75, Vegetarian available, Civ Wed 54, Air con **Seats:** 60, Pr/dining room 40
Children: Menu, Portions **Rooms:** 37 (37 en suite) ★★★ HL
Directions: City centre, directly opposite York Minster **Parking:** Car park nearby

◎◎ Ivy Brasserie

Modern British, European

Ambitious modern-brasserie cooking in a Regency townhouse

☎ 01904 644744 The Grange Hotel, 1 Clifton YO30 6AA
e-mail: info@grangehotel.co.uk
web: www.grangehotel.co.uk

Located within walking distance of the city centre, this smart, bustling Regency townhouse hotel has revamped its previous three dining options into one, namely the Ivy Brasserie. Refurbished, though still retaining its striking wall murals reflecting the city's racing history, it comes decked out with wooden floors and tables, leather banquettes and matching leather chairs. The other half of the brasserie has red wallpaper and elegant drapes adapted from the once fine-dining restaurant. The kitchen makes good on its promise of modern, brasserie-style cooking, the crisply-scripted menus delivering flair and creativity; take rib-eye with slow-roasted tomato and parsley snail butter, perhaps hare Wellington with quinoa, or a fillet of zander with freshwater crayfish and saffron potatoes. The same menu is also served in the more informal Cellar Bar.

Chef: James Brown **Owners:** Jeremy & Vivien Cassel **Times:** 12-2/6-10, Closed L Mon-Sat, D Sun **Prices:** Fixed L £12.50, Fixed D £25, Starter £4.50-£9.50, Main £13.50-£19, Dessert £4.50-£7.50, Service optional
Wine: 19 bottles over £20, 24 bottles under £20, 14 by the glass
Notes: Civ Wed 60 **Seats:** 60, Pr/dining room 60 **Children:** Portions
Rooms: 30 (30 en suite)★★★ HL **Directions:** A19 York/Thirsk road, approx 400 yds from city centre **Parking:** 30

ENGLAND

YORK CONTINUED

◉◉ Melton's

British

Carefully prepared modern dishes in a family-run, relaxed setting

☎ 01904 634341 7 Scarcroft Rd YO23 1ND
e-mail: greatfood@meltonsrestaurant.co.uk
web: www.meltonsrestaurant.co.uk

The Victorian terraced frontage conceals a bright and modern dining room with a bustling ambience. Long and narrow, its walls are covered with mirrors and a couple of large murals depicting the chef and his customers going about their business to a backdrop of city scenes. Unclothed tables, polished-wood floors, banquette seating or chairs and friendly service contribute to the relaxing atmosphere. The kitchen's modern, intelligently simple approach delivers carefully prepared dishes where flavour is everything; think pan-fried fillet of grey mullet slashed with fresh herbs and served with fresh lovage pasta, and perhaps a hot summer berry soufflé finale.

Chef: Michael Hjort, Annie Prescott **Owners:** Michael & Lucy Hjort
Times: 12-2/5.30-10, Closed 3 wks Xmas, 1wk Aug, Sun, Closed L Mon
Prices: Fixed L £17.50, Starter £6.40-£7.90, Main £12.50-£21.50, Dessert £5.60-£6.90, Service optional **Wine:** 69 bottles over £20, 28 bottles under £20, 6 by the glass **Seats:** 30, Pr/dining room 16 **Children:** Portions **Directions:** South from centre across Skeldergate Bridge, restaurant opposite Bishopthorpe Road car park **Parking:** Car park opposite

◉◉ Middlethorpe Hall & Spa

Modern British V ⬥ NOTABLE WINE LIST 🖥

Luxurious dining in an historic setting

☎ 01904 641241 Bishopthorpe Rd, Middlethorpe YO23 2GB
e-mail: info@middlethorpe.com
web: www.middlethorpe.com

Built for a prosperous master cutler keen to play the gentleman, Middlethorpe is a magnificent example of a William and Mary country house. It sits in red-brick splendour adjacent to York racecourse amid 20 acres of carefully tended estate that includes a kitchen garden and luxury spa. Quality glassware sparkles in candlelight and long windows overlook the grounds in the elegant oak-panelled restaurant. Expect accomplished cooking rooted in classical and regional cuisine that's studded with a liberal sprinkling of luxury ingredients; think roast lamb cutlet served with shepherd's pie, braised lentils and a caramelised garlic jus, or perhaps pan-fried zander with confit chicken, celeriac fondant, salsify, baby spinach and a thyme jus.

Chef: Nicholas Evans **Owners:** Historic House Hotels Ltd **Times:** 12.30-2.15/7-9.45 **Prices:** Fixed L £17, Fixed D £41.50, Service included
Wine: 221 bottles over £20, 17 bottles under £20, 9 by the glass
Notes: Tasting menu 6 courses £55, Sun L 3 courses £26, Vegetarian menu, Dress Restrictions, Smart, no trainers, tracksuits or shorts, Civ Wed 56
Seats: 60, Pr/dining room 56 **Children:** Min 6 yrs **Rooms:** 29 (29 en suite)★★★★ HL **Directions:** 1.5m S of York, beside York racecourse
Parking: 70

⊛ *One 19 The Mount*

British

Quality cooking in a popular hotel

☎ 01904 619444 Mount Royale, The Mount YO24 1GU
web: www.mountroyale.co.uk

Its position in a hotel close to the town centre makes this an ideal dining venue for tourists, locals and business people alike. Delightful gardens overlooked by a bright, modern restaurant and separate bar have their own appeal, while beauty treatments, swimming pool, sauna and hot tub are attractions for residents. The menu offers a good balance with daily specials and vegetarian choices, and the modern cooking is based on sound ingredients and good technical skills. Expect the likes of sautéed king scallops or Thai fishcakes to start, with mains such as sea bass provençale or succulent rack of lamb.

Times: 12-2.30/6-9.30, Closed 1-6 Jan, Sun **Rooms:** 24 (24 en suite)
★★★ HL **Directions:** W on B1036, towards racecourse

▭ **The Lime House**

☎ 01904 632734 55 Goodramgate YO1 7LS
web: www.theaa.com/travel/index.jsp

Excellent food and wine, a relaxed and friendly atmosphere and a regularly-changing menu with an international flavour. Good vegetarian choices too.

YORKSHIRE, SOUTH

CHAPELTOWN   MAP 16 SK39

⊛ **Greenhead House**

European

Exciting food of consistent quality in country-style restaurant

☎ 0114 246 9004 84 Burncross Rd S35 1SF
web: www.thebigmenu.co.uk

A small, 17th-century country house on the outskirts of Sheffield set in a large walled garden. Retaining many of its original features, inside you'll find country-style furnishings, a comfortable lounge, oak beams and an open fire. European cooking is carefully prepared by a skilled kitchen team using the best of local produce. Fancy presentation is eschewed; this is good, tasty food served hot as soon as it's ready. The set monthly-changing menu might offer mackerel rillettes served with a salad of pickled porcini, green beans and a tomato and caper confit, followed by roast saddle of hare wrapped in Parma ham.

Chef: Neil Allen **Owners:** Mr & Mrs N Allen **Times:** 12-1/7-9, Closed Xmas-New Year, 2wks Etr, 2wks end Aug, Sun-Tue, Closed L Wed, Thu & Sat

Prices: Fixed L £12-£17, Fixed D £39.50-£44, Service included **Wine:** 30 bottles over £20, 15 bottles under £20, 7 by the glass **Notes:** Fixed D 4 courses **Seats:** 32 **Children:** Min 7 yrs, Portions **Directions:** 1m from M1 junct 35 **Parking:** 10

ROSSINGTON   MAP 16 SK69

⊛ **Best Western Mount Pleasant Hotel**

British

Country-house hotel with a tempting menu

☎ 01302 868696 & 868219 Great North Rd, Rossington DN11 0HW
e-mail: reception@mountpleasant.co.uk
web: www.mountpleasant.co.uk

Comfortable country-house hotel set in 100 acres of wooded parkland and well-tended gardens. Its elegant restaurant is decorated with tapestries and delivers a traditional menu of well-cooked, flavoursome dishes. Kick things off with smoked chicken and apricot terrine, before moving on to mains such as roasted pork fillet with Puy lentils, black pudding and a spicy apple compôte, or coconut-battered sea bass with sweet potato chips and sweet chilli jam. If simpler fare is the order of the day, steaks and chops are available from the grill with a variety of sauces. Round things off with red berry pannacotta, before relaxing with a drink in one of the hotel's many characterful lounges.

Chef: Dave Booker **Owners:** Richard McIlroy **Times:** 12-2/6.45-9.30, Closed 25 Dec **Prices:** Fixed L £16.50, Fixed D £25.50-£35, Starter £4.95-£7.95, Main £14.50-£24.95, Dessert £6.25, Service optional **Wine:** 38 bottles over £20, 15 bottles under £20, 7 by the glass **Notes:** Sun D £18.95, Dress Restrictions, Smart casual preferred, Civ Wed 150, Air con **Seats:** 72, Pr/dining room 200 **Children:** Menu, Portions **Rooms:** 57 (57 en suite)
★★★★ HL **Directions:** Located S of Doncaster, adjacent to Robin Hood Airport, on A638 between Bawtry and Doncaster **Parking:** 140

SHEFFIELD   MAP 16 SK38

⊛⊛ **Artisan**

British, European

Classic, chic Parisian-style bistro

☎ 0114 266 6096 32-34 Sandygate Rd, Crosspool S10 5RY
e-mail: info@artisan.com
web: www.artisanofsheffield.com

Occupying the ground floor of Richard Smith's one-time Thyme restaurant (now refurbished and split into two venues with the seafood restaurant Catch - see entry - upstairs), Artisan's décor comes bathed in the Parisian bistro-chic. Think darkwood floors, dark brown leather chairs and foodie memorabilia adorning walls, while there's a bar at the front and a semi open-plan kitchen at the rear. The service suits the surroundings, is fittingly friendly, attentive but relaxed like the atmosphere. The kitchen delivers rustic, accomplished dishes where the freshness of local produce is showcased at its best. Expect the likes of a classic blanquette of veal with courgette fritters and summer truffle mash, or perhaps duck shepherd's pie with spicy cabbage.

Chef: Simon Wild **Owners:** Richard & Victoria Smith, Simon Wild **Times:** 12-2.30/6-10, Closed 25, 26 Dec **Prices:** Fixed L £12-£15, Fixed D £15-£24, Starter £5-£12, Main £12-£24, Dessert £5-£8, Service optional **Wine:** 60 bottles over £20, 60 bottles under £20, 12 by the glass **Notes:** Sun L 3 courses £15 , children under 12yrs eat free, Vegetarian available, Air con **Seats:** 60 **Children:** Portions **Directions:** Just off A57, in Crosspool shopping centre **Parking:** On street

ENGLAND

SHEFFIELD *Continued*

◉◉ Catch Seafood Café

Modern, Traditional

Modern, vibrant seafood café

☎ 0114 266 6096 34 Sandygate Rd, Crosspool S10 5RY
web: www.catchofsheffield.com

Tucked above a Parisian bistro in a parade of shops on Sandygate, this aptly-named eatery is styled as a modern seafood café and has a buzzy, laidback feel. A fish market provides the inspiration for the interior design, with metal-topped tables, white-tiled walls and daily-changing blackboard menus suspended from metal racks by meat hooks. Its kitchen is dedicated to delivering fresh, high-quality seafood and has its own in-house fishmonger who buys-in daily. Whether you come for a quick snack or a leisurely meal, you'll find bold and accomplished cooking distinguished by influences from around the globe: seared tuna sashimi with red chilli salad and oriental dressing, for example, or spaghetti with langoustines, rocket and crème fraîche.

Chef: Simon Wild **Owners:** Richard & Victoria Smith, Simon Wild
Times: 12-3/6-10, Closed 25-26 Dec, Sun **Prices:** Fixed L £12-£15, Fixed D £15, Starter £4-£15, Main £10-£30, Dessert £4-£5, Service optional
Wine: 20 bottles over £20, 20 bottles under £20, 10 by the glass
Notes: Fixed D 2 courses, Air con **Seats:** 30, Pr/dining room 30
Children: Portions **Directions:** Just off A57, in Crosspool shopping centre
Parking: On street

◉ Nonna's Ristorante

Modern Italian NEW

Friendly, relaxed trattoria with a passion for Italian cooking

☎ 0114 268 6166 535-41 Ecclesall Rd S11 8PR
e-mail: info@nonnas.co.uk
web: www.nonnas.co.uk

If you enjoy the food and wine at this popular trattoria, you can take many of the high-quality ingredients home with you, courtesy of a deli at the back of the property. In the front, there's a bar with window seats for a quick espresso or leisurely latte, but it's the bustling restaurant that's the main draw as local foodies are well aware. Many of the ingredients come direct from Italy, arriving at the table in classic dishes such as melanzana parmigiana, pasta puttanesca, and tiramisù. And there's less familiar fare too, including regional specialities from a different area every week. Authentic cooking from a kitchen with heart.

Chef: Jamie Taylor **Owners:** Gian Bohian, Maurizio Mori **Times:** 12-3.30/6-9.45, Closed 25 Dec, 1 Jan **Prices:** Fixed D £30, Starter £4.75-£8.95, Main £8.95-£19.95, Dessert £5.75-£5.95, Service optional **Wine:** 90 bottles

over £20, 23 bottles under £20, 18 by the glass **Notes:** Fixed D 4 courses, Vegetarian available, Air con **Seats:** 75, Pr/dining room 32
Children: Menu, Portions **Directions:** Large red building situated on Eccleshall Rd **Parking:** On street

◉◉ Rafters Restaurant

Modern European

Popular neighbourhood restaurant in a leafy area

☎ 0114 230 4819 220 Oakbrook Rd, Nethergreen S11 7ED
web: www.raftersrestaurant.co.uk

This popular restaurant is located above a parade of shops in a well-known and quieter suburb of the city. Original rafters echo the restaurant's name, while oak beams and exposed brickwork feature too, along with contemporary soft furnishings and overhanging lighting to create a bright and cosy vibe. The fixed-price menus make good reading and take a fashionably modern approach dotted with influences from around the world. Take sautéed medallions of monkfish served on aromatic Indian rice with a smoked roasted pepper sauce and prawn tempura, while frosted berries with a hot white chocolate sauce and blood orange and star anise jelly might catch the eye at dessert.

Chef: Marcus Lane, Michael Sabin **Owners:** Marcus Lane, Michael Sabin
Times: 7-10, Closed 25-26 Dec, 1wk Jan, 2 wks Aug, Sun, Tue, Closed L all week **Prices:** Fixed D £32.50, Service optional, Group min 8 service 10%
Wine: 20 bottles over £20, 25 bottles under £20, 7 by the glass
Notes: Dress Restrictions, Smart casual, No jeans, Air con **Seats:** 38
Children: Min 5 yrs, Portions **Directions:** 5 mins from Eccleshall Rd, Hunters Bar rdbt **Parking:** 15

◉ Staindrop Lodge Hotel

British, European

Art deco-style brasserie in a smart hotel

☎ 0114 284 3111 Ln End, Chapeltown S35 3UH
e-mail: info@staindroplodge.co.uk
web: www.staindroplodge.co.uk

Bar, brasserie and hotel occupying an extended and refurbished 200-year-old building on the north side of the city, handy for the M1. The split-level restaurant is in art deco style with lots of glass and a solid floor. The menu reflects influences from around the world, with dishes such as duck wontons with a spaghetti of cucumber, sliced spring onions and hoi sin sauce, and cannon of English lamb with potato and mint soufflé and sautéed pak choi. A similar menu is also available in the bar.

Times: 12/9.30 **Rooms:** 32 (32 en suite) ★★★ HL **Directions:** Take A629 towards Huddersfield, go straight at first rdbt, at mini rdbt take right fork. Restaurant is 0.5 miles on the right

YORKSHIRE, WEST

CLIFTON   MAP 16 SE12

◉ Black Horse Inn Restaurant with Rooms

British, Mediterranean

Welcoming Yorkshire coastal inn with enjoyable dining

☎ 01484 713862   HD6 4HJ
e-mail: mail@blackhorseclifton.co.uk
web: www.blackhorseclifton.co.uk

A traditional village inn with a cheerful pub atmosphere and good coastal views. The white linen tablecloths and brown leather chairs, mixing easily with the oak beams and open fires, might seem out of place in this former Luddite meeting house. Gone are Shirley Bassey, Roy Orbison, Showaddywaddy and other celebrity guests of the 1960s and 1970s. Today's guests come here for traditional dishes with the occasional Mediterranean flourish, such as beer-battered Whitby haddock with chunky chips and minted pea purée, or Japanese-style lemon and star anise lobster spring roll.

Chef: Darren Marshall **Owners:** Andrew & Jane Russell **Times:** 12-3/5.30-9.30, Closed D 25-26 Dec **Prices:** Fixed D £16.95, Starter £4.50-£8.50, Main £12.75-£18, Dessert £5.50-£7, Service optional **Wine:** 18 by the glass **Notes:** Dress Restrictions, Smart casual, Civ Wed 60 **Seats:** 80, Pr/dining room 60 **Children:** Menu, Portions **Directions:** M62 junct 25, Brighouse and follow signs **Parking:** 60

DEWSBURY   MAP 16 SE22

◉ Healds Hall Hotel

Modern British

Charming 18th-century family-run hotel with bistro and restaurant

☎ 01924 409112   Leeds Rd, Liversedge WF15 6JA
e-mail: enquire@healdshall.co.uk
web: www.healdshall.co.uk

This attractive, stone-built 18th-century country house set in peaceful gardens was formerly a mill owner's grand house and has links to the Brontë family. There's a lively, modern bistro and cosy bar, but it's the classic, fine-dining Harringtons restaurant that's at its heart. The cooking has a strong emphasis on using quality local produce. Take a starter of pan-fried king scallops with pancetta, Jerusalem artichokes, peas and herb dressing, followed by grilled fillet of sea bass with a stew of Scottish mussels, tomatoes, olives and basil. Daily blackboard specials, a good range of Yorkshire cheeses and polite, friendly service bolster the act.

Chef: Phillip McVeagh, David Winter **Owners:** Mr N B & Mrs T Harrington **Times:** 12-2/6-10, Closed 1 Jan, BHs, Closed L Sat, D Sun (ex residents) **Prices:** Fixed L £7.50, Starter £3.95-£6.50, Main £12-£18.95, Dessert £4.25-£4.75, Service optional **Wine:** 21 bottles over £20, 31 bottles under £20, 8 by the glass **Notes:** Sun L £16.50, Vegetarian available, Civ Wed 100, Air con **Seats:** 46, Pr/dining room 30 **Children:** Portions **Rooms:** 24 (24 en suite) ★★★ HL **Directions:** M1 junct 40, A638, From Dewsbury take the A652 (signed Bradford). Turn left at A62 and then 50 yds on right **Parking:** 90

HALIFAX   MAP 19 SE02

◉◉ Holdsworth House Hotel

Modern British

Magnificent Jacobean manor-house dining

☎ 01422 240024   Holdsworth HX2 9TG
e-mail: info@holdsworthhouse.co.uk
web: www.holdsworthhouse.co.uk

Of particular interest at this 17th-century manor house is the stone cross of St John above the centre gable of the house. It's a delightful property, set in well-tended gardens, with exposed beams, crooked floors, real fires and oil paintings. The restaurant comprises three interconnecting, aptly-named rooms - the oak-panelled Panel Room, the Mullion Room with its leaded windows, and the informal Stone Room. The kitchen offers a traditional style of cooking, catering for both business guests and those celebrating a special occasion. Try Holdsworth House oak-smoked chicken, or maybe Holme farmed venison with Savoy cabbage and streaky bacon. A grand selection of delicious desserts rounds things off in style.

Chef: Jamie Cann **Owners:** Gail Moss, Kim Wynn **Times:** 12-2/7-9.30, Closed Xmas (open 25-26 Dec L only), Sun, Closed L Sat **Prices:** Fixed L £13.95, Starter £4.95-£7.45, Main £11.50-£19.25, Dessert £6-£11.25, Service optional, Group min 10 service 10% **Wine:** 40 bottles over £20, 32 bottles under £20, 13 by the glass **Notes:** Early supper 5.30-6.30 2 courses £13.95, 3 courses £16.95, Vegetarian available, Dress Restrictions, Smart casual, No shorts, Civ Wed 120 **Seats:** 45, Pr/dining room 120 **Children:** Portions **Rooms:** 40 (40 en suite) ★★★ HL **Directions:** From Halifax take A629 (Keighley), 2m turn right at garage to Holmfield, hotel 1.5m on right **Parking:** 60

◉ The Old Bore at Rishworth

Modern European V

Traditional coaching inn with a growing reputation for fine food

☎ 01422 822291   Oldham Rd, Rishworth HX6 4QU
e-mail: chefhessel@aol.com
web: www.oldbore.co.uk

This recently converted 200-year-old coaching inn has a roadside location in pretty countryside. The traditional décor comes replete with flagstone floors, stuffed animals and antler chandeliers, while in the restaurant area there's a more formal tone, with oak floors, exposed wooden beams, antique or high-backed leather chairs, candlelight and white linen - all in the style of a shooting lodge. The well-conceived menu delivers a modern cooking style with a nod to seafood, fish and game, while quality ingredients are sourced from a strong network of local suppliers. Rabbit saddle served with acorn-fed ham, spring greens, pearl barley and morel risotto is a fine example of the fare.

Chef: Scott Hessel **Owners:** Scott Hessel **Times:** 12-2.15/6-9.30, Closed 2 wks in Jan, Mon-Tue **Prices:** Fixed L £11.95, Fixed D £11.95, Starter £6.45-£9.95, Main £12.95-£21.95, Dessert £5.95-£6.95, Service optional **Notes:** Fixed D 2 courses, Sun L 2 courses £14.95. 3 courses £17.95, Vegetarian menu **Seats:** 80, Pr/dining room 20 **Children:** Portions **Directions:** M62 junct 22 take A672 towards Halifax, 3m on left after reservoir **Parking:** 20

HALIFAX CONTINUED

🏵 Shibden Mill Inn

Modern British

Secluded inn with a menu to draw the crowds

☎ 01422 365840 Shibden Mill Fold, Shibden HX3 7UL
e-mail: enquiries@shibdenmillinn.com
web: www.shibdenmillinn.com

A world away from the hustle and bustle of Halifax, this popular 17th-century inn enjoys an appealing and peaceful setting in the Shibden Valley beside Red Beck. You can dine in both the beamed lounge-style bars, warmed by log fires, and the candlelit loft conversion beneath a raftered ceiling and chandeliers, or even outside on the riverside terrace in summer. Expect an appealing, crowd-pleasing menu with imaginative modern twists to classic combinations using quality produce; take sea bream served with celeriac purée, a red wine sauce and crispy Parma ham. Quality bar meals complete the culinary picture.

Chef: Steve Evans **Owners:** Mr S D Heaton **Times:** 12-2/6-9.30, Closed 25 Dec (Eve), Closed D 26 Dec, 31 Dec **Prices:** Fixed L £9.95, Fixed D £9.95, Starter £3.75-£5.95, Main £11.50-£17.95, Dessert £5.25-£5.95, Service optional **Wine:** 16 bottles over £20, 38 bottles under £20, 12 by the glass **Notes:** Fixed D 2 courses, Sun L £9.95, Vegetarian available **Seats:** 50, Pr/dining room 10 **Children:** Menu, Portions **Rooms:** 11 (11 en suite) ★★★★ INN **Directions:** Telephone for directions **Parking:** 100

HAWORTH   MAP 19 SE03

🏵 Weavers Restaurant with Rooms

Modern, Traditional British 🍃

Friendly family-run place with a Northern flavour

☎ 01535 643822 15 West Ln BD22 8DU
e-mail: weaversinhaworth@aol.com
web: www.weaversmallhotel.co.uk

As its name suggests, this informal family-run bar and restaurant is converted from 18th-century weavers' cottages. An eclectic collection of mismatched furniture sets the scene and the atmosphere is very relaxed. Northern regional food is on offer, including new ideas cooked with flair and creativity, traditional dishes, and old favourites that are popular with the regulars. Using ingredients sourced from excellent local suppliers, typical options are McKenzie's ale-cured Dales beef carpaccio with celeriac and horseradish coleslaw, followed by griddled Dales-bred beef fillet with red wine reduction and caramelised onion potato cake, and baked lemon cheesecake with lemon curd sauce for dessert. Service is provided by young, friendly staff.

Chef: Colin, Tim & Jane Rushworth **Owners:** Colin & Jane Rushworth **Times:** 11.30-2.30/6.30-9.30, Closed 10 days Xmas/New Year, Mon, Closed L Tue & Sat, D Sun **Prices:** Fixed L £12.95, Fixed D £15.95, Starter £4.50-£6.50, Main £10.50-£17.50, Dessert £4.50-£5.50, Service optional, Group min 6 service 10% **Wine:** 8 bottles over £20, 56 bottles under £20, 8 by the glass **Notes:** Dress Restrictions, Clean & tidy, Air con **Seats:** 65, Pr/dining room 14 **Children:** Portions **Rooms:** 3 (3 en suite) ★★★ RR **Directions:** From A629 take B6142 towards Haworth, follow signs for Brontë Parsonage Museum, use museum car park **Parking:** Brontë Museum car park (free 6pm-8am)

HUDDERSFIELD   MAP 16 SE11

🏵🏵 The Weavers Shed Restaurant with Rooms

Modern British 🍷 NOTABLE WINE LIST

Enjoyable regional dining with home-grown ingredients

☎ 01484 654284 86-88 Knowl Rd, Golcar HD7 4AN
e-mail: info@weaversshed.co.uk
web: www.weaversshed.co.uk

This converted 18th-century wool mill has undergone refurbishment. Contemporary in style, there are still plenty of original features, including stone and bare wood. The comfortable lounge leads on to an atmospheric, barn-style dining room with banquettes and chairs and clothed tables. There's a wonderful kitchen garden to drive the kitchen, which provides fowl, fruit, vegetables and over 70 varieties of wild edibles. Dishes are cooked in the modern British style and based almost without exception on home-grown and local produce. Expect chargrilled calves' liver served with cavolo nero cabbage, a cassoulet of haricot beans with parsley and pearl onions and roast veal jus, and to close, perhaps a bitter chocolate biscuit sandwich with malt ice cream and cocoa syrup.

Chef: S Jackson, I McGunnigle, C Sill **Owners:** Stephen & Tracy Jackson **Times:** 12-2/7-9, Closed 25 Dec-7 Jan, Sun, Mon, Closed L Sat **Prices:** Fixed L £13.95, Starter £7.95-£12.95, Main £16.95-£25.95, Dessert £8.50-£9.95, Service optional **Wine:** 56 bottles over £20, 22 bottles under £20, 6 by the glass **Seats:** 26, Pr/dining room 16 **Rooms:** 5 (5 en suite) ★★★★ RR **Directions:** 3m W of Huddersfield off A62. (Please telephone for further directions) **Parking:** 30

ILKLEY   MAP 19 SE14

🏵🏵 Best Western Rombalds Hotel & Restaurant

Modern International

Modern cuisine in a relaxing atmosphere

☎ 01943 603201 11 West View, Wells Rd LS29 9JG
e-mail: reception@rombalds.demon.co.uk
web: www.rombalds.co.uk

Modern European cooking with just a nod to Pacific Rim cuisine is the order of the day at this elegant Georgian townhouse on the edge of Ilkley Moor. Its attractive restaurant has a relaxed atmosphere and a commitment to local produce, delivering starters such as a terrine of mixed Yorkshire game with balsamic roast figs and a port reduction, followed by roast Yorkshire partridge with ravioli of partridge leg, girolles, beetroot and apple boulangère. Expect complex and ambitious dishes from a kitchen that likes to impress: pan-fried chicken stuffed with Whitby crab, feta couscous and bois boudrin sauce for example, or a lemon sole and salmon tower, with crushed tarragon new potatoes, and cucumber and chive cream.

Best Western Rombalds Hotel & Restaurant

Chef: Andrew Davey **Owners:** Colin & Jo Clarkson **Times:** 12-2/6.30-9, Closed 28 Dec-2 Jan **Prices:** Fixed L £12.95, Fixed D £14.95-£16.95, Starter £4.95-£6.75, Main £12.65-£18.95, Dessert £5.25, Service optional **Wine:** 50 bottles over £20, 62 bottles under £20, 6 by the glass **Notes:** Smart casual, Civ Wed 70 **Seats:** 34, Pr/dining room 50 **Children:** Menu, Portions **Rooms:** 15 (15 en suite) ★★★ HL **Directions:** From Leeds take A65 to Ilkley. At 3rd main lights turn left & follow signs for Ilkley Moor. At junct take right onto Wells Rd, by bank. Hotel 600yds on left **Parking:** 22

@@@ **Box Tree**

see below

KEIGHLEY
◉ The Harlequin Restaurant
Modern British
Cosmopolitan cooking served in style

MAP 19 SE04

☎ 01535 633277 139 Keighley Rd, Cowling BD22 0AH
e-mail: enquiry@theharlequin.org.uk
web: www.theharlequin.org.uk

A stylish modern eatery in a converted traditional Yorkshire stone Victorian property, decked out with comfortable banquette seating and spacious, well-dressed tables. Simplicity is the watchword here; flavours are straightforward and enjoyable and draw diners from near and far. Start with crab and avocado tian with rocket salad and lemon mayonnaise, or poached pear with raspberry and goat's cheese salad, and then move on to mains such as slow-roast duckling served on a

CONTINUED

Box Tree

ILKLEY
Modern British, French 🍷 NOTABLE WINE LIST
Culinary legend that still delivers

MAP 19 SE14

☎ 01943 608484 35-37 Church St LS29 9DR
e-mail: info@theboxtree.co.uk
web: www.theboxtree.co.uk

Not far from the centre of Ilkley, this renowned restaurant occupies a 300-year-old farmhouse cottage and is decorated in homely, traditional style with art and antiques. Low ceilings, exposed beams and a huge stone fireplace give away its age and make for an intimate setting, while plush high-backed seats ensure dinner is a comfortable affair.

Now in the highly experienced hands of chef Simon Gueller, the kitchen delivers a range of bold and flavourful dishes cleverly constructed from the freshest of seasonal produce. A value prix-fixe lunch and dinner is bolstered by an appealing carte that comes dotted with luxury, and might see you dithering between veal sirloin steak with asparagus, Jabugo ham, pomme purée and thyme jus, and Gressingham duck breast with ceps, celeriac mash, onion fricassée, and Alsace bacon. Desserts are sure to tempt and might include a tangy lemon tartlet with passionfruit sorbet, or pineapple tarte Tatin, accompanied by an intriguing spoonful of black pepper ice cream and

a pineapple cigarette. Wash it all down with a tipple from the extensive wine list and you're all set for an evening worthy of the Box Tree's legendary reputation.

Chef: Mr S Gueller **Owners:** Mrs R Gueller **Times:** 12-2/7-9.30, Closed 27-31 Dec & 1-5 Jan, Mon, Closed L Tue-Thur, D Sun **Prices:** Fixed L £18, Fixed D £28, Starter £9-£17, Main £22-£30, Dessert £8.50, Group min 8 service 10% **Wine:** 256 bottles over £20, 8 bottles under £20, 7 by the glass **Notes:** Sun L £25, Dress Restrictions, Smart casual, Air con **Seats:** 50, Pr/dining room 16 **Children:** Min 10 yrs **Directions:** On A65 from Leeds through Ilkley, main lights approx. 200 yds on left **Parking:** NCP

KEIGHLEY CONTINUED

bed of apricot and Madeira sauce, or pork wrapped in Parma ham with grain mustard mash and a juniper berry jus. Desserts are a particular highlight, so leave some room to enjoy the likes of sticky toffee brûlée with fresh strawberries.

Chef: Mr R Gilbert **Owners:** Mr T Zebedee & Ms F McGowan **Times:** 12-3/5.30-11, Closed 4 days at Xmas, BHs, Mon-Tue **Prices:** Fixed L £12.50, Starter £5.50-£6.95, Main £11.50-£17.95, Dessert £4.95-£5.50 **Wine:** 42 bottles over £20, 39 bottles under £20, 11 by the glass **Notes:** Sun L 2-3 courses £12.50-£15.95 **Seats:** 42 **Children:** Min 6 yrs D, Portions **Directions:** On A6068 in Cowling village, between Crosshills and Colne. 6m from M65 **Parking:** 10

LEEDS   MAP 19 SE23

◉◉◉ Anthony's Restaurant

see below

◉◉ Brasserie Forty 4

British, European

Buzzing brasserie overlooking the canal

☎ 0113 234 3232 44 The Calls LS2 7EW
e-mail: info@brasserie44.com
web: www.brasserie44.com

Converted from an old grain store, this bustling eatery is situated on the waterfront with a balcony overlooking the canal. The stylish décor comes based around a modern colour scheme of cream and

terracotta, creating a warm, welcoming, airy feel that - coupled with a fashionable, cosmopolitan menu and informal, friendly service - plays to the gallery and offers appeal for all. Accomplished brasserie standards sit alongside more modish combinations to deliver an appealing nod to the Mediterranean; take classics like chicken liver parfait with brioche and apple chutney or vanilla crème brûlée, to the likes of pan-fried red snapper with Sicilian aubergine stew and salt and pepper squid, or spicy lamb parcel with cucumber spaghetti and mango pickle. An interesting wine list complements the upbeat package.

Chef: Antone Quentin **Owners:** Steve Ridealgh **Times:** 12-2/6-10, Closed BHs, Sun **Prices:** Fixed L £13.50, Fixed D £19.95, Starter £4.50-£6.50, Main £11.50-£19.50, Dessert £5, Service added but optional 10% **Wine:** 127 bottles over £20, 36 bottles under £20, 12 by the glass **Notes:** Fixed earlybird D incl 1/2 bottle wine, Air con **Seats:** 130, Pr/dining room 50 **Children:** Portions **Directions:** From Crown Point Bridge, left past Church, left into High Court Lane. On river **Parking:** On street, NCP

◉◉ Brontë Restaurant

Modern European

Grand dining room offering classic cuisine

☎ 0113 282 1000 De Vere Oulton Hall, Rothwell Ln, Oulton LS26 8HN
e-mail: oulton.hall@devere-hotels.com
web: www.devereonline.co.uk

Set amid delightful parkland, complete with its own 27-hole golf course, this Grade II listed mansion dates back over 150 years and has been lovingly restored to combine traditional features and modern

---

◉◉◉

Anthony's Restaurant

LEEDS   MAP 19 SE23

Modern European

One of the city's most exciting restaurants

☎ 0113 245 5922 19 Boar Ln LS1 6EA
e-mail: reservations@anthonysrestaurant.co.uk
web: www.anthonysrestaurant.co.uk

Chef Anthony Flinn's bold, modern cuisine sits well with the chic surroundings and both are designed to wow and excite diners at this ambitious and highly praised city restaurant. Stairs lead down from the swish ground-floor bar, with its floor-to-ceiling windows and large, deep leather sofas, to the curved basement dining room. Decorated in clean, modern minimalist lines, its simple colours of cream and chocolate contrast well with modern art and high-quality cutlery and glassware that grace well-spaced tables.

Anthony has an impressive pedigree, having trained with John Campbell (of The Vineyard at Stockcross, see entry) and worked at the internationally acclaimed El Bulli restaurant in Spain. The approach is via a compact, crisply-scripted carte, with the kitchen's superbly-presented, light style bursting with flavours and surprise. Think saddle of rabbit with celeriac remoulade and malt foam, or roast red mullet with coconut jelly and langoustines, while an apricot mousse with pink pepper cider toffee might head-up dessert offerings. Much effort goes

into the amazing tasters and inter-courses that pepper the repertoire, with pre-starters, amuse-bouche, pre-desserts, petits fours and breads all hitting top form. There's also a good-value fixed-price lunch option and a tasting menu (for the whole table) to complete the exciting package of this rising star.

Chef: Anthony Flinn **Owners:** Anthony Flinn **Times:** 12-2.30/7-9.30, Closed BH incl Tue, wk in Sep, 25 & 26 Dec, Sun, Mon, Closed L Tue-Thu **Prices:** Fixed L £19.95, Starter £7.50-£12.25, Main £21-£24.50, Dessert £6.45-£7.50, Service optional **Wine:** 100 bottles over £20, 5 bottles under £20, 4 by the glass **Notes:** Tasting menu £60, Air con **Seats:** 40 **Children:** Portions **Directions:** 500 yds from Leeds Central Station towards The Corn Exchange **Parking:** NCP 20 yds

comforts. The impressive scale of the hotel is apparent in the grand Brontë restaurant, with its velvet-clad walls and décor in shades of cream, dark red and claret. An impressive central feature light also creates a starlight effect, and mahogany pillars and panels add to the ambience. English and European cooking is on offer here on an extensive menu littered with fine ingredients. Signature dishes and matching wines are recommended at each course. Take a main course of roast guinea fowl served with a fricassée of thigh meat, baby leeks and tarragon, and follow with Valrhona griottine chocolate fondant with a Kirsch syrup and white chocolate sorbet. Main courses might include grilled steaks from the late Queen Mother's estate in the Castle of Mey.

Chef: Steve Collinson **Owners:** De Vere Hotels **Times:** 12.30-2/7-10 **Prices:** Fixed L £13.50, Fixed D £30, Starter £7.50-£12, Main £14-£28, Dessert £6-£9 **Wine:** 80 bottles over £20, 10 bottles under £20, 13 by the glass **Notes:** Tasting menu available 5 courses, Vegetarian available, Restrictions, Smart casual, no T-shirts or shorts, Civ Wed 100, Air con **Seats:** 180 **Children:** Menu, Portions **Rooms:** 152 (152 en suite) ★★★★★ HL **Directions:** M62 junct 30 signed Rothwell, or M1 junct 44 signed Pontefract **Parking:** 200

◎◎ Haley's Hotel & Restaurant

Modern European

Convivial restaurant in a conservation area

☎ 0113 278 4446 Shire Oak Rd, Headingley LS6 2DE
e-mail: info@haleys.co.uk
web: www.haleys.co.uk

A former manor house, this handsome Grade II listed building is located in leafy Headingley a couple of miles from the city centre. The restaurant exudes conviviality while maintaining privacy at the table. Service is technically efficient, delivered with large helpings of northern hospitality, and the setting is traditional with starched white linen, silver cutlery and floral arrangements. The kitchen takes a modern approach to British cooking with French influences, producing dishes along the lines of pan-fried langoustine, baby artichoke, hot barigoul and saffron jelly with eucalyptus foam, or pan-fried frogs' legs persillade style, with celery tart, tomato chutney, wild garlic emulsion, lemon crisps and meat jus.

Chef: Frederic Aumeinier **Owners:** Kiran Aujla **Times:** 12-2.30/7.15-9.30, Closed 26-30 Dec **Prices:** Fixed L £18, Fixed D £23, Starter £7-£9, Main £15-£21, Dessert £6-£7, Service optional **Wine:** 63 bottles over £20, 9 bottles under £20 **Notes:** Civ Wed 100, Air con **Seats:** 60, Pr/dining room 24 **Children:** Portions **Rooms:** 28 (28 en suite) ★★★ HL **Directions:** 2m N of city centre off A660, between HSBC & Starbucks

◎ Malmaison Hotel

Traditional French 🍷 NOTABLE WINE LIST

Funky French brasserie food in stylish hotel

☎ 0113 398 1000 & 398 1001 1 Swinegate LS1 4AG
e-mail: leeds@malmaison.com
web: www.malmaison.com

The Leeds offshoot of the chic modern hotel chain is located in an old converted tram company station on Sovereign Quay. It's stylish, intimate and design-led, a fashionable venue with a smart, contemporary interior that features funky bedrooms as well as a true

brasserie-style dining room, with panelling, stone floors and a relaxed atmosphere. Diners can choose between a substantial snack and a three-course meal on the crowd-pleasing, seasonally-changing menu. Uncomplicated but innovative cooking might offer a classic threesome like eggs Benedict, steak and frites and a crème brûlée finish.

Chef: John Malia **Owners:** Malmaison **Times:** 12-2.30/6-11 **Prices:** Fixed L £13.50, Fixed D £15.50, Starter £4.95-£8, Main £10.95-£25, Dessert £5.95, Service added but optional 10% **Wine:** 90% bottles over £20, 10% bottles under £20, 25 by the glass **Notes:** Vegetarian available, Air con **Seats:** 95, Pr/dining room 12 **Children:** Portions **Rooms:** 100 (100 en suite) ★★★ HL **Directions:** City centre. 5 mins walk from Leeds railway station. On junct 16 of Loop road, Sovereign St & Swinegate **Parking:** Criterion Place car park

◎◎ Simply Heathcotes Leeds

Modern French 🖵

Converted warehouse with a friendly bistro feel

☎ 0113 244 6611 Canal Wharf, Water Ln LS11 5PS
e-mail: leeds@heathcotes.co.uk
web: www.heathcotes.co.uk

This trendy brasserie is located in a former warehouse overlooking the Leeds-Liverpool canal - indeed, in its heyday, canal boats used to travel through the warehouse to unload. Nowadays the old stone walls and exposed beams are complemented by low-key modern décor with an upstairs bar lounge for reclining and imbibing. The food is contemporary in style with a bistro feel and plenty of comfort dishes. Using the best of local produce, the emphasis is still firmly on big, satisfying flavours as demonstrated in a starter of black pudding and ham hock salad with boiled egg and chive hollandaise and main courses such as pan-fried calves' liver, creamed potatoes, smoked ham and caramelised onion sauce.

Chef: Luke Culkin **Owners:** Paul Heathcote **Times:** 12-2.30/6-10, Closed 25-26 Dec, 1-2 Jan, BH Mons **Prices:** Fixed L £15, Fixed D £25-£35, Starter £3.95-£9, Main £12.50-£24, Dessert £4.95-£6, Service optional, Group min 8 service 10% **Wine:** 70 bottles over £20, 20 bottles under £20, 14 by the glass **Notes:** Vegetarian available, Air con **Seats:** 120 **Children:** Menu, Portions **Directions:** 0.5m from M621 junct 3; follow signs to city centre, left into Water Lane, right onto Canal Wharf. On Canal Basin **Parking:** 20

ENGLAND

LEEDS CONTINUED

ⓜ Thorpe Park Hotel & Spa

Modern British

Chic modern dining showcasing local produce

☎ 0113 264 1000 Century Way, Thorpe Park LS15 8ZB

e-mail: thorpepark@shirehotels.com

web: www.shirehotels.com

A modern hotel with state-of-the-art spa and contemporary comforts. The range of dining options includes a spacious open-plan restaurant furnished with lightwood and leather. There is an open fire lit in winter and a large alfresco terrace for summer dining. Cuisine reflects the Yorkshire area with maximum use of seasonal ingredients from local suppliers. Try a starter of 'Bleikers of Yorkshire' hot smoked salmon, braised and glazed Nidderdale lamb shank with roasted beets, followed by warm chocolate tart with espresso ice cream.

Times: 12-2/6.45-9.30, Closed L Sat & Sun **Rooms:** 123 (123 en suite) ★★★★ HL **Directions:** Telephone for directions

Bibis

☎ 0113 243 0905 Minerva House, 16 Greek St LS1 5RU

Bustling contemporary Italian.

💻 Georgetown

☎ 01926 863645 Dysons Clock Building, 24-26 Briggate LS1 6EP

web: www.theaa.com/travel/index.jsp

Restored Victorian emporium offering authentic Malaysian menu. The Singapore Slings are a must.

MARSDEN   MAP 16 SE01

ⓜⓜ Hey Green Country House Hotel

Modern British

Modern brasserie in elegant surroundings

☎ 01484 848000 Waters Rd HD7 6NG

e-mail: info@heygreen.com

web: www.heygreen.com

Situated in a cosy country-house hotel set in landscaped gardens close to Huddersfield Canal, Crowther's Brasserie is located in the oldest part of the building, with a superb flagstone floor and open fire burning throughout winter. An archway leads into smaller dining areas creating a sense of intimacy. Expect a tempting selection of modern British dishes with a comforting feel - wild boar and Yorkshire beer sausages with onion gravy and mash perhaps - from a creative kitchen that delivers exquisite combinations of the freshest ingredients. You might start with black pudding with poached egg and a mustard sauce, followed by chargrilled tuna with olive mash, and Granny Smith crème brûlée with cinnamon shortbread. Booking is essential.

Chef: Nigel Skinkis **Owners:** S Hunter, M Dolman **Times:** 12-2.30/6.30-9.30, Closed 1-4 Jan, Closed L Mon-Sat **Prices:** Fixed L £13.95-£15, Fixed D £20, Starter £4.25-£6.95, Main £7.95-£16.95, Dessert £4.50-£5.75, Service optional **Wine:** 16 bottles over £20, 20 bottles under £20, 12 by the glass **Notes:** Dress Restrictions, Smart casual, no jeans or T-shirts, Civ Wed 120 **Seats:** 44, Pr/dining room 20 **Children:** Menu, Portions **Rooms:** 12 (12 en suite) ★★ HL **Directions:** M62 junct 22, equal distance from Oldham and Huddersfield on A62 **Parking:** 70

ⓜ Olive Branch

Modern French

A very old pub serving restaurant food

☎ 01484 844487 Manchester Rd HD7 6LU

e-mail: mail@olivebranch.uk.com

web: www.olivebranch.uk.com

A relaxed pub-style establishment with restaurant quality food and service has been developed at this old coaching inn. The surrounding countryside has many historic attractions and pleasant walking. The modern French menu features classic sauces, fish on the bone, and luxury items such as lobster. Seasonal and local produce is cooked with flair and enthusiasm, and recommended dishes include parfait of foie gras and chicken liver with grenadine stewed onions and toasted babky bread, or rack of venison with chocolate and red wine sauce, followed by a classic crème brûlée.

Chef: Paul Kewley **Owners:** Paul Kewley & John Lister **Times:** 12-2/6.30-9.30, Closed 1st 2 wks Jan, Closed L Mon, Tue, Sat **Prices:** Fixed L £11.95, Fixed D £18.95, Starter £4.95-£9.50, Main £12.95-£21.95, Dessert £6.50, Service optional **Wine:** 100 bottles over £20, 30 bottles under £20, 16 by the glass **Seats:** 65, Pr/dining room 40 **Children:** Portions **Rooms:** 3 (3 en suite) ★★★★ RR **Directions:** Located on A62 between Slaithwaite and Marsden **Parking:** 20

OTLEY   MAP 19 SE24

ⓜ Chevin Country Park Hotel

Modern European

Scandinavia comes to Yorkshire

☎ 01943 467818 Yorkgate LS21 3NU

e-mail: reception@chevinhotel.com

web: www.chevinhotel.com

Conveniently located for both major road links and the airport, this log-built, Finnish-style hotel sits in attractive woodland by a lake. Its pine-clad modern restaurant makes an impact with black high chairs and white-clothed tables, and offers an extensive range of dishes with a set price for two or three courses. Kick things off with seared breast of pigeon with chargrilled endive and caramelised apple, before tucking into grilled rib-eye steak with a blue cheese glaze and rioja jus or roast rump of lamb with parsnip purée mash. Desserts are a highlight: save room for the likes of gingerbread sponge with caramel sauce and vanilla ice cream.

Times: 12-2/6.30-9.15, Closed L Mon, Sat **Rooms:** 49 (49 en suite) ★★★ HL **Directions:** Take A658 towards Harrogate. Left at 1st turning towards Carlton, turn 2nd left towards Yorkgate

PONTEFRACT — MAP 16 SE42

◉ Wentbridge House Hotel

Modern British V ⬛ NOTABLE WINE LIST

Classically-influenced cuisine in a country-house setting

☎ 01977 620444 Wentbridge WF8 3JJ
e-mail: info@wentbridgehouse.co.uk
web: www.wentbridgehouse.co.uk

A well-established hotel in 20 acres of landscaped gardens, with a choice of dining styles. The traditionally-styled Fleur de Lys restaurant offers polished service and a varied menu of interesting dishes, while the brasserie delivers a more relaxed alternative. Country-house dining is the order of the day with a combination of modern British and French classics. Produce is well sourced and the cooking shows attention to flavours in dishes like pan-roasted monkfish served with an oxtail and tarragon risotto. There's a little 'table theatre' on offer too, with some dishes prepared in the restaurant; think steak Diane, or flambéed black cherries with toasted almonds and cherry ice cream.

Chef: Steve Turner **Owners:** Mr G Page **Times:** 7.15-9.30, Closed 25 Dec eve, Closed L Mon-Sat, D Sun **Prices:** Fixed D £30, Starter £5-£15, Main £18-£30, Dessert £7-£9, Service optional **Wine:** 100 bottles over £20, 30 bottles under £20, 10 by the glass **Notes:** Vegetarian menu, Civ Wed 130 **Seats:** 60, Pr/dining room 24 **Children:** Portions **Rooms:** 18 (18 en suite) ★★★ HL **Directions:** 0.5m off A1, 4m S of M62/A1 junct **Parking:** 100

SHIPLEY — MAP 19 SE13

◉ Marriott Hollins Hall Hotel & Country Club

Traditional British

Traditional dining venue with formal service

☎ 01274 530053 Hollins Hill BD17 7QW
e-mail: mhrs.lbags.frontdesk@marriotthotels.com
web: www.marriott.com

Built in 1858, Hollins Hall was constructed by the first Baron of Park Gate in the Elizabethan style and is set in 200 acres of grounds. Set in the original drawing room, the cosy restaurant has wonderful views over the garden; the atmosphere is warm and relaxed, helped along by friendly and attentive staff. The menu delivers a balance of traditional and contemporary culinary styles with international influences. Expect the likes of lobster and crab galette, monkfish and rosemary skewers with saffron risotto or grilled halibut with poached seafood wontons.

Chef: Guy Gage **Owners:** Marriott International **Times:** 12-2/6.30-9.30, Closed L Sat, D BHs **Prices:** Fixed L £13.95, Fixed D £27.50, Starter £6.25-£7.85, Main £15.75-£18.95, Dessert £5.50, Service optional **Wine:** 33

bottles over £20, 31 bottles under £20, 15 by the glass **Notes:** Dress Restrictions, Smart casual, Civ Wed 120, Air con **Seats:** 120, Pr/dining room 30 **Children:** Menu, Portions **Rooms:** 122 (122 en suite) ★★★★ HL **Directions:** From A650 follow signs to Salt Mill. At lights in Shipley take A6038. Hotel 3m on left **Parking:** 250

WAKEFIELD — MAP 16 SE32

◉ *Best Western Waterton Park Hotel*

Modern European

Simple cooking in idyllic setting

☎ 01924 257911 Walton Hall, The Balk, Walton WF2 6PW
e-mail: watertonpark@bestwestern.co.uk
web: www.watertonparkhotel.co.uk

Set on an island surrounded by a 26-acre lake, this former private mansion was the home of an eccentric traveller and naturalist who created the world's first wildfowl reserve here. It's now a comfortable hotel and proves a popular choice for wedding functions. Guests can dine in the Bridgewalk restaurant where they might choose a starter of deep-fried avocado with sesame seeds and cranberry dressing, followed by poached fillet of salmon with lemon-crushed potatoes and Chardonnay cream or grilled leg of lamb steak with butter mash and sweet shallot jus.

Times: 12-2/7-9.30 **Rooms:** 68 (68 en suite) ★★★ HL **Directions:** From Wakefield follow A61 to Walton and follow brown signs. M1 junct 39, A638 (Crofton)

◉ Brasserie Ninety Nine

Modern British, European

Bright, fresh brasserie in a business park

☎ 01924 377699 Trinity Business Park WF2 8EF
e-mail: brasserie99@lawsonleisure.com

Stainless steel and glass are the chosen materials for the interior of this ultra-modern restaurant, unexpectedly located beyond the security gates of a high-tech business park. Within the silver and red colour scheme, the kitchen offers a comprehensive choice of modern European dishes made from the best available produce. Well-informed waiting staff serve up the likes of skewered pan-seared 'Black Pearl' scallops and slow-braised Nidderdale lamb shank. There's a more limited choice at lunchtime, but the atmosphere is always relaxed and friendly.

Chef: Matthew Richardson **Owners:** Steve Lawson **Times:** 12-2.30/5.30-10, Closed 25 Dec, 1 Jan, BHs, Sun, Closed L Sat, D Mon, Tue **Prices:** Starter £3.25-£6.50, Main £8.75-£18.75, Dessert £4.50, Service optional **Wine:** 6 bottles over £20, 20 bottles under £20, 6 by the glass **Notes:** Vegetarian available, Dress Restrictions, Smart casual, Air con **Seats:** 120, Pr/dining room 40 **Children:** Menu, Portions **Directions:** Please telephone for directions **Parking:** 40

ENGLAND

WETHERBY   MAP 16 SE44

⚜⚜ Wood Hall Hotel

Modern European V ⚑ NOTABLE WINE LIST

Classic country house with modern food and décor

☎ 01937 587271   Trip Ln, Linton LS22 4JA

web: www.handpicked.co.uk

Wood Hall has been a family home, a boys' school and even the first pastoral and ecumenical centre for Britain. In many respects it is a classic country house, a striking Georgian hall in 100 acres of parkland, but there is no mistaking the contemporary stamp of the décor, all calm, light and soothing. The modern theme extends to the cooking, with good use of local, seasonal products. Expect dishes such as wasabi-spiced tuna with soused vegetables, bouillabaisse with saffron potatoes, poached corn-fed chicken with truffle pearl barley broth, and banana mousse with mango sorbet, or prune and Armagnac soufflé to finish. Special gourmet events are a regular feature.

Chef: Darren Curson **Owners:** Hand Picked Hotels **Times:** 12-2.30/6.30-9.30, Closed L Mon-Sat **Prices:** Fixed L £16.50-£21, Fixed D £32.50-£35, Starter £8.50-£13.50, Main £18-£23.50, Dessert £7.50-£8.50, Service optional **Wine:** 78 bottles over £20, 4 bottles under £20, 21 by the glass **Notes:** Vegetarian menu, Dress Restrictions, Smart casual, no jeans or trainers, Civ Wed 100 **Seats:** 32, Pr/dining room 100 **Children:** Menu, Portions **Rooms:** 44 (44 en suite)★★★★ CHH **Directions:** From Wetherby take A661(Harrogate road) N for 0.5m. Left to Sicklinghall/Linton. Cross bridge, left to Linton/Woodhall, right opp Windmill Inn, 1.25m to hotel, (follow brown signs) **Parking:** 100

CHANNEL ISLANDS
GUERNSEY

CASTEL   MAP 24

⚜ La Grande Mare Hotel Golf & Country Club

Modern NEW

Resort hotel restaurant serving accomplished cuisine

☎ 01481 256576   The Coast Rd, Vazon Bay GY5 7LL

e-mail: simon@lagrandemare.com

web: www.lgm.guernsey.net

Set in 110 acres of private grounds, La Grande Mare is a family-owned and run resort hotel set next to a sandy bay and incorporating a golf course and health suite. With its granite fireplaces, the restaurant has several arches and oak floors, with friendly but professional service. New head chef Chris Sloan has pedigree, his modern approach driven by fresh seasonal produce and a passion for locally-caught fish. Intelligently simple dishes deliver clean flavours and eye-catching presentation; take pan-seared sea bass served with saffron risotto and red wine fumé, perhaps seared local scallops with Lyonnaise potatoes and a tomato and pesto dressing, or roast rack of lamb served with wilted spinach, pomme purée and tarragon jus.

Chef: Christopher Sloan **Owners:** The Vermeulen Family **Times:** 12-2/7-9.30 **Prices:** Fixed L £10-£25, Fixed D £20-£35, Starter £5.95-£8.95, Main £14.95-£18.95, Dessert £4.95-£8.50, Service optional **Wine:** 36 bottles over £20, 43 bottles under £20, 14 by the glass **Notes:** Sun L £16.95 **Seats:** 70, Pr/dining room 30 **Rooms:** 24 (24 en suite) ★★★★ HL **Directions:** From airport turn right. 5 mins to reach Coast Rd. Turn right again. Hotel another 5 min drive **Parking:** 200

COBO   MAP 24

⚜ Cobo Bay Restaurant

Modern International

Great views of the bay from this popular restaurant

☎ 01481 257102   GY5 7HB

e-mail: reservations@cobobayhotel.com

web: www.cobobayhotel.com

A traditional seaside holiday destination overlooking a picture-postcard bay, the hotel is comfortable and modern, but somehow recalls the golden age of British holiday-making. The food is undoubtedly a highlight for guests who enjoy contemporary cuisine prepared from fresh local ingredients. There's an emphasis on seafood, yet carnivores needn't feel left out, with dishes of pan-seared diver-caught scallops on sautéed baby spinach leaves, followed by medallions of beef fillet layered with creamed forest mushrooms and accompanied by a Guinness and grain mustard sauce, or grilled fillet of halibut on a bed of sautéed leaf spinach served with a dry vermouth cream.

Chef: John Chapman **Owners:** Mr D Nussbaumer **Times:** 12-2/7-9, Closed Jan & Feb, Closed L Mon-Sat **Prices:** Fixed L £16.50, Fixed D £22.50 **Wine:** 21 bottles over £20, 24 bottles under £20, 6 by the glass **Notes:** Sun L £16.50, Dress Restrictions, Smart casual, Air con **Seats:** 110 **Children:** Menu, Portions **Rooms:** 36 (36 en suite) ★★★ HL **Directions:** From St Peter Port follow signs for Castel/Cobo/West Coast. At coast road turn right, hotel 100m on right **Parking:** 50

PERELLE   MAP 24

⚜⚜ Atlantique Hotel

Modern European

Modern hotel restaurant with seriously good views

☎ 01481 264056   Perelle Bay GY7 9NA

e-mail: enquiries@perellebay.com

web: www.perellebay.com

You can watch the sun go down over the bay from this modern hotel dining room, and move into the comfortable lounge for a post-dinner coffee. Many diners choose to start the evening in the cocktail bar, where the appealing carte can be perused over a drink. The secret of the much-sung modern-British-meets-European cooking lies in the simple handling of quality produce - with local seafood delivered daily - by a skilled and adaptable team. Expect medallions of beef fillet served with sherry-glazed shallots, oxtail ravioli and a béarnaise sauce, or perhaps West Coast sea bass with pan-fried scallops, sweet potato rösti, sautéed spinach and a champagne and chive butter sauce, and to finish, a dark chocolate tart with milk sorbet and rosewater jelly.

Atlantique Hotel

Chef: Lee Woodend **Owners:** Nerne Trust/L'Atlantique 2003 Ltd
Times: 12-2/6.30-9.30, Closed 31 Oct-end Mar, Closed L Mon-Sat
Prices: Food prices not confirmed for 2008. Please telephone for details
Notes: Smart casual, Air con **Seats:** 80, Pr/dining room 40
Children: Portions **Rooms:** 23 (21 en suite) ★★★ HL **Directions:** Off
west coast road overlooking Perelle Bay **Parking:** 30

ST MARTIN   MAP 24

◉◉ The Auberge

Modern European NEW

Exciting modern cooking with stunning ocean views

☎ 01481 238485 Jerbourg Rd GY4 6BH
e-mail: auberge@cihospitality.com
web: www.theauberge.gg

The elevated setting of The Auberge and stunning views over the bay
to the neighbouring islands, proves every bit as memorable as the
cuisine. Its rather unassuming exterior belies the sleek, contemporary,
minimalist styling inside. A long bar dominates the entrance, which
leads into the conservatory-style dining area with its floor-to-ceiling
windows and decked terrace for alfresco eating. Tables are unclothed
and service is relaxed and efficient, while the exciting cooking matches
the contemporary styling and buzz of the place. It's innovative and
modern with the emphasis on using fresh, locally-sourced produce.
Think pan-fried sea bass on champ mash with a tomato and garlic
fondue, chargrilled artichoke hearts and tapenade sauce, or perhaps
Eton Mess to finish.

Chef: Daniel Green **Owners:** CI Hospitality **Times:** 12-2/7-9.30, Closed
25 Dec, 1 Jan **Prices:** Fixed L £14.95, Fixed D £24.50, Starter £5.50-£7.50,
Main £13.15-£16.95, Dessert £5.75-£5.95, Service optional **Wine:** 16 bottles
over £20, 19 bottles under £20, 6 by the glass **Notes:** Vegetarian available
Seats: 70 **Children:** Menu, Portions **Directions:** End of Jerbourg Rd at
Jerbourg Point **Parking:** 25

◉ La Barbarie Hotel

British, French

Quietly located hotel with a strong local reputation

☎ 01481 235217 Saints Rd, Saints Bay GY4 6ES
e-mail: reservations@labarbariehotel.com
web: www.labarbariehotel.com

An old stone priory houses this delightful small hotel, quietly located
in St Martin. Named after 17th-century pirates from the Barbary Coast
who kidnapped a previous owner, it promises a peaceful stay in its
cosy accommodation and brightly decorated restaurant. The fresh fish
and steak board attract a strong local following, with a short carte
adding to the variety. The kitchen takes a pride in its output, evidenced
by starters like tian of crab, avocado, couscous with sweet chilli
dressing, followed by pork loin steak, caramelised apple and Calvados
sauce.

Times: 12-1.45/6-9.30, Closed 29 Oct-9 Mar **Rooms:** 22 (22 en suite)
★★★ HL **Directions:** At traffic lights in St Martin take road to Saints Bay
- hotel on right at end of Saints Rd

◉ Hotel Jerbourg

Modern British

Cliff-top hotel restaurant specialising in seafood

☎ 01481 238826 Jerbourg Point GY4 6BJ
e-mail: stay@hoteljerbourg.com
web: www.hoteljerbourg.com

The Jerbourg is a cliff-top hotel set in pretty landscaped grounds with
a conservatory-style restaurant called Les Trois Isles - appropriately so
with its fabulous sea views towards Herm, Sark and Jersey. Not
surprisingly, the kitchen specialises in seafood (though there's plenty
of choice for meat-eaters, too), with dishes like grilled fillet of brill with
crushed new potatoes and béarnaise sauce, lobster thermidor, or
moules marinière, followed by glazed citrus crème brûlée with
shortbread fingers for dessert. Dining tables are neatly clothed, service
is relaxed but professional, and there's an elegant lounge for
pre-dinner drinks.

Chef: Kristian Gregg **Owners:** Ess Ltd **Times:** 12-2.30/6.30-9.30, Closed
Nov-Mar **Prices:** Fixed L £12.75-£15, Fixed D £19.50, Starter £6-£10, Main
£10-£18, Dessert £5-£7, Service optional **Wine:** 10 bottles over £20,
10 bottles under £20, 6 by the glass **Notes:** Fixed L 3 courses, Air con
Seats: 80, Pr/dining room 20 **Children:** Menu, Portions **Rooms:** 32 (32
en suite) ★★★ HL **Directions:** From St Peter Port follow signs for St
Martin, at lights by Manor stores turn left. Hotel at end of road on right
Parking: 30

ST PETER PORT   MAP 24

◉ The Absolute End

Mediterranean, International

Cottage restaurant serving fresh fish straight from the boat

☎ 01481 723822 Longstore GY1 2BG
e-mail: theabsoluteend@cwgsy.net

Housed in a converted fisherman's cottage, opposite the sea on the road out of town, the restaurant's main dining room has half-panelled walls on rough plaster dotted with small paintings, and upstairs there's a private dining room with a covered terrace. Candles and tablecloths formalise the atmosphere in the evening. The chef concentrates on fresh fish along with specials from his native Italy, and the results go down well with a loyal clientele. For starters, why not try the home-smoked seafood platter, including brill, scallops, salmon, mackerel and trout, while an impressive main course is the grilled local sea bass, perfectly timed, with a well-judged hollandaise sauce.

Chef: Antonio Folmi **Owners:** Antonio Folmi **Times:** 12-2/7-10, Closed Jan, Sun **Prices:** Fixed L £15, Fixed D £20, Starter £5.50-£12, Main £12.50-£24, Dessert £4.50 **Wine:** 17 bottles over £20, 35 bottles under £20, 3 by the glass **Notes:** Fixed L 3 courses, Fixed D 4 courses, Vegetarian available, Civ Wed 50, Air con **Seats:** 55, Pr/dining room 22 **Children:** Portions **Directions:** Less than 1m from town centre, going N on seafront road to St Sampson **Parking:** On street

◉◉ Christophe

Modern French NEW

Quality food, relaxed, friendly service and spectacular sea views

☎ 01481 230725 Fort Rd GB GY1 1ZP
web: www.christophe-restaurant.co.uk

Set just off the main road between the airport and St Peter Port, this hotel restaurant boasts a terraced area with stunning views out to Fermain Bay. The same outlook can be seen from the dining room itself with its full-size glass sliding doors. With square wood panelling around the walls, round wooden pillars, cappuccino-coloured leather chairs, white-linen clothed tables and quality table appointments, there is a contemporary air to the décor. The kitchen delivers modern French cooking, displaying some accomplished technical skills and eye-catching presentation. Flavours are clean, with quality ingredients allowed to speak up and be counted. Start with asparagus and morels with almond milk sauce or avocado with smoked salmon mousse, and follow with poached lobster in wild garlic butter or fish from the day's market. Desserts are a strong point, as displayed in warm fruit minestrone with balsamic jelly and strawberry and basil sorbet, or pineapple tarte Tatin with star anise pannacotta. A menu gourmand is available.

Chef: Christophe Vincent **Owners:** Christophe Vincent **Times:** 12-2/7-10, Closed 2 wks Nov, 2 wks Feb, BHs, Mon, Closed D Sun **Prices:** Fixed L £14.95, Starter £7-£12.50, Main £14-£25, Dessert £6.50-£8.50, Service optional **Wine:** 130 bottles over £20, 30 bottles under £20, 11 by the glass **Notes:** Gourmand menu 7 courses (incl wine) £50, Vegetarian available, Air con **Seats:** 60, Pr/dining room 14 **Children:** Portions **Parking:** 40

◉ Da Nello

Italian, Mediterranean

Popular Italian just off the High Street

☎ 01481 721552 46 Le Pollet GY1 1WF
e-mail: danello@cwgsy.net
web: www.where2eatguernsey.com

The narrow frontage of this old granite house opens out into a series of dining areas, leading to the pièce de résistance, a covered Mediterranean-style piazza decked out in marble and terracotta. Much extended and smartly renovated, the 500-year-old building is located on the site of an ancient Roman encampment, with pottery finds to prove it. The lengthy menu covers all the Italian favourites and has a separate fish section. Of particular note are carpaccio of beef with parmesan and rucola salad, or linguini with lobster for starters, followed by the likes of bass Livornese with basil, capers and tomato, or medallions of beef with Barolo sauce. Finish with prosecco and raspberry jelly.

Chef: Tim Vidamour **Owners:** Nello Ciotti **Times:** 12-2/6.30-10, Closed 25 Dec-23 Jan **Prices:** Fixed L £12.50-£14, Fixed D £22.95, Starter £4.25-£8.95, Main £9.50-£25, Dessert £4.75-£5.50, Service optional **Wine:** 19 bottles over £20, 31 bottles under £20, 4 by the glass **Notes:** Fixed L 3 courses, Menus change regularly, Vegetarian available, Air con **Seats:** 90, Pr/dining room 20 **Children:** Portions **Directions:** In town centre, 100 yds from North beach car park **Parking:** 900

⊛⊛ La Frégate

British, French
Relaxed, elegant dining with sea views and seafood

☎ 01481 724624 Les Cotils GY1 1UT
e-mail: enquiries@lafregatehotel.com
web: www.lafregatehotel.com

Enjoying stunning views over the island's capital and across to Sark, Herm and Jersey, this unique hotel combines modernity with the charm of an 18th-century manor house. The dining room continues the contemporary styling, with white-clothed tables and cream paintwork, curtains and leather chairs, set against a darkwood floor. Its wall of windows opens the room up to those views, and there's a terrace for alfresco dining. The kitchen makes fine use of fresh local ingredients, especially seafood - peppered monkfish and seared scallops with wilted spinach and a tomato and tarragon hollandaise, or perhaps fillet of brill set on a shellfish risotto with lobster cream and herb oil. Meat-eaters are also well catered for.

Chef: Neil Maginnis **Owners:** GSH Ltd **Times:** 12-2.30/6.30-9.45
Prices: Fixed L £12.95, Fixed D £27.50, Starter £4.50-£12.50, Main £9.50-£22, Dessert £4-£8, Service optional **Wine:** 40 bottles over £20, 70 bottles under £20, 10 by the glass **Seats:** 70, Pr/dining room 30
Children: Portions **Rooms:** 22 (22 en suite) ★★★ HL
Directions: Town centre, above St Julian's Ave **Parking:** 25

⊛⊛ Governor's

Traditional French
Formal dining with fine views over St Peter Port harbour

☎ 01481 738623 Old Government House Hotel, St Ann's Place GY1 2NU
e-mail: governors@theoghhotel.com
web: www.theoghhotel.com

Once the residence of the Governor of Guernsey, the property dates back to 1748 and has been a hotel since 1857. The location is superb, overlooking the harbour and town. The restaurant is an intimate, beautifully decorated room full of memorabilia and photographs of former island governors. Shaped seating, rich fabrics and patterned wallpaper recollect the glorious décor of the early 19th century. Traditional cooking is influenced by the French chef, who offers a seven-course dégustation surprise menu in addition to the carte. Local produce features strongly in dishes like trilogy of crab (tian, cake and bisque), or roasted sea bass with scallop scale, basil-crushed potato and olive tapenade, with a chocolate and caramel mousse millefeuille to finish.

Chef: Jerome Babbancon **Owners:** Kenneth W McVey **Times:** 12-2/7.30-10, Closed L Sat, Sun, D Mon **Prices:** Fixed L £12.50-£15.50, Fixed D £25, Starter £7.50-£9.50, Main £15-£18.50, Dessert £6-£8.50, Service optional **Wine:** 35 bottles over £20, 8 by the glass **Notes:** Tasting menu 7 courses £35, Vegetarian available, Air con **Seats:** 18, Pr/dining room 32
Children: Min 12 yrs **Rooms:** 60 (60 en suite) ★★★★ HL
Directions: Located off St Julian's Av, N of town centre **Parking:** 20

⊛ Mora Restaurant & Grill

British, French NEW
Contemporary eatery in remodelled former wine merchants overlooking the harbour

☎ 01481 715053 The Quay GY1 2LE
e-mail: eat@mora.gg

Set on the historic seafront beside Victoria Marina, Mora is the new sister venture to the town's Da Nello restaurant (see entry), and fills two storeys of a former vaulted wine cellar. Now totally refurbished, it boasts contemporary furnishings, with black and white portraits and scenes of local fishermen adorning the walls, and an open-plan kitchen on the first floor. But it's really two restaurants; the ground-floor Little Mora is the place to grab a lighter one-course lunch or dinner, while upstairs offers the full dining experience. Here classic cooking comes with contemporary influence driven on by fresh local ingredients and clean flavours; think fleur de sel crusted sea bass with asparagus, spring onion étuvée, saffron potatoes and sauce vièrge.

Chef: Réne Bisson **Owners:** Nello Ciotti **Times:** 12-2/6.30-10, Closed Sun **Prices:** Starter £5.50-£8.75, Main £13.50-£25, Dessert £5.50-£6, Service optional **Wine:** 24 bottles over £20, 35 bottles under £20, 6 by the glass **Notes:** Vegetarian available **Seats:** 90 **Children:** Portions **Directions:** Facing Victoria Marina **Parking:** On pier

⊛ Le Nautique Restaurant

Modern French V
Nautical-themed restaurant with sea views

☎ 01481 721714 Quay Steps GY1 2LE
web: lenautiquerestaurant.co.uk

Converted from a warehouse, this harbour-side establishment overlooks the marina, Castle Cornet and the islands beyond. The building has plenty of character with traditional décor in the downstairs dining room and a more chic, cosmopolitan look for the upper level. The menu offers French cooking with international influences, using fresh local produce where possible. Good clean flavours come through in dishes of Thai crab cakes with mango and banana salsa served with oriental salad, or perhaps a terrine of scallops, prawns and smoked salmon, with a herb yogurt dressing. Continue with seared fillet of sea bass, moist and succulent, accompanied by a good beurre blanc sauce.

Chef: G Botzenhardt & J Flemming **Owners:** Gunter Botzenhardt
Times: 12-2/6.30-10, Closed Sun, Closed L Sat **Prices:** Fixed L £12.50, Fixed D £18.50-£34.50, Starter £4.50-£8.50, Main £9.50-£17.50, Dessert £4.50-£14, Service optional **Wine:** 51 bottles over £20, 25 bottles under £20, 16 by the glass **Notes:** Vegetarian menu, Dress Restrictions, Smart casual, Air con **Seats:** 56, Pr/dining room 30 **Children:** Portions **Directions:** Seafront opposite harbour and Victoria Marina **Parking:** On street

ENGLAND

ST PIERRE PARK HOTEL

Tel: 01481 728282
E-mail: info@stpierreparkhotel.co.uk
Web: www.stpierreparkhotel.co.uk

The only true resort hotel in the Channel Islands, St Pierre Park is set in 45 acres of landscaped gardens and has a friendly and relaxed atmosphere throughout. The interior has seen some major refurbishment in both the bedrooms and public areas and a choice of restaurants is available. The fine dining option is the Victor Hugo restaurant; light and airy with well spaced tables. Fresh fish is a speciality of the regularly changing menus: à la carte and menu gourmand. A good sample menu is very fresh locally caught sea bass, accompanied by a creamy risotto, and black cherry flambé with pistachio parfait and nougatine tuile for dessert.

The chef is now *Jan Wilhelm.*

Opening times are dinner only Monday-Saturday 7.00pm-9.30pm, open Sunday evenings for dinner during the summer months.

ST PETER PORT CONTINUED

◉ Saltwater

Traditional, Seafood
Contemporary restaurant with great harbour views

☎ 01481 720823 Albert Pier GY1 1AD
e-mail: info@saltwater.gg
web: www.saltwater.gg

This popular local restaurant overlooks the outer harbour. Stylish décor with wooden floors, whitewashed panelled walls, a bright conservatory and an understated nautical theme achieve an unpretentious chic. The extensive carte, fixed-price menu and daily specials offer plenty of choice. As you might expect, the menu favours seafood dishes, many of the simple, classic variety like moules marinière or crab thermidor, or perhaps Thai-style fishcakes served with a citrus mayonnaise and chilli jam. For mains, tuck into an impressively fresh, moist sea bass with hollandaise sauce, while for dessert vanilla crème brûlée hits all the right notes for texture and creaminess.

Chef: Anthony Jeanes **Owners:** Jenny Meeks, Joanna Baker **Times:** 12-2/6-10, Closed 23 Dec-5 Jan, Closed L Sat (Nov-Mar), D Sun (Nov-Mar) **Prices:** Fixed L £10, Fixed D £10, Starter £3.95-£7.95, Main £8.50-£21.95, Dessert £3.25-£5.95, Service optional **Wine:** 30 bottles over £20, 10 bottles under £20, 4 by the glass **Notes:** Fixed D 2 courses, Sun L 3 courses £15, Vegetarian available, Air con **Seats:** 70 **Children:** Menu, Portions

◉◉ Victor Hugo Restaurant

Traditional European
Sophisticated hotel restaurant serving quality local produce

☎ 01481 728282 St Pierre Park Hotel, Rohais GY1 1FD
e-mail: info@stpierreparkhotel.com
web: www.stpierreparkhotel.com

Peacefully located on the outskirts of St Peter Port, this luxurious, yet friendly and relaxed, resort hotel is set amidst 45 acres of mature parkland. The interior has seen some major refurbishment in both the bedrooms and public areas and a choice of three dining experiences is available. The elegant Victor Hugo Restaurant is the fine-dining option; light and airy with well-spaced tables. Fresh fish and seafood are a speciality of the regularly-changing menus which feature set price, carte and menu gourmand. A good choice is baked monkfish with new potatoes, grilled artichokes, sun-blushed tomatoes and chorizo sausage, or perhaps fillet of beef with a glazed fondant potato and buttered asparagus. For dessert, why not try praline parfait served with soft fruit and red coulis.

Chef: Jan Wilhelm **Owners:** C I Traders **Times:** 6.30-9 **Prices:** Fixed D £23.50, Starter £5.50-£7, Main £11.50-£19, Dessert £6.50-£8, Service optional **Wine:** 22 bottles over £20, 42 bottles under £20, 6 by the glass **Notes:** Dress Restrictions, Smart casual, no trainers/jeans/sandals, Air con **Seats:** 50, Pr/dining room **Children:** Menu, Portions **Rooms:** 131 (131 en suite) ★★★★ HL **Directions:** Located 1.5m from St Peter Port on road to Cobo Bay **Parking:** 150
see advert above

see advert above

HERM

HERM   MAP 24

◉ White House Hotel

Modern, Mediterranean NEW
Island hotel with sea views and accomplished cooking

☎ 01481 722159   GY1 3HR
e-mail: hotel@herm-island.com
web: www.herm-island.com

Enjoying a unique island setting, this attractive hotel is set in well-tended gardens and offers lovely sea views. You can relax in one of several lounges, enjoy a drink in one of two bars and choose from two dining options. The main dining room is where the real culinary action takes place, a light-and-airy affair with those views enjoyed from most tables, while the conservatory section looks out over the garden too. Service is relaxed but attentive from smartly uniformed staff. The kitchen deals in a daily fixed-price, four-course dinner, perhaps featuring roast fillet of pork with mustard and brandy cream, or grilled butterfly smoked salmon steak and asparagus.

Chef: Neil Southgate **Owners:** Wood of Herm Island **Times:** 12.30-1.30/7-9, Closed Oct-Apr **Prices:** Fixed D £24, Starter £4.75-£7, Main £9.95-£16, Dessert £4.45-£5.95, Service optional **Wine:** 74 bottles over £20, 101 bottles under £20, 7 by the glass **Notes:** Fixed D 4 courses, Vegetarian available, Dress Restrictions, Jacket & tie at D **Seats:** 100 **Children:** Portions **Rooms:** 40 (40 en suite) ★★★ HL **Directions:** By regular 20 min boat trip from St Peter Port, Guernsey

JERSEY

GOREY   MAP 24

◉ Jersey Pottery, The Garden Restaurant
Mediterranean, International
Convivial conservatory restaurant
☎ 01534 850850 Gorey Village JE3 9EP
e-mail: enquiries@jerseypottery.com
web: www.jerseypottery.com

The much classier of two eateries at this Jersey institution, the Garden Restaurant - a vine-decked conservatory - has a convivial café ambience and is always busy with a mix of lunching ladies, family gatherings and chattering couples. Take a tour around the pottery, snap up a bargain in the shop, and then peruse the lengthy menu awash with local produce, especially fish and seafood plateau fruits de mer. Maybe a platter of Jersey lobster, gambas, oysters, langoustine and Chancre crab claws, otherwise try the likes of clay-baked bass with beurre blanc, spinach, green beans and Jersey Royals.

Chef: Tony Dorris **Owners:** The Jones Family **Times:** 12-2.30, Closed Xmas, Jan, mid Feb, Mon, Closed D (private functions only) **Prices:** Fixed L £12.50, Starter £6.50-£16.95, Main £8.95-£32.50, Dessert £3.95-£5.50, Service included **Wine:** 31 bottles over £20, 39 bottles under £20, 12 by the glass **Notes:** Vegetarian available, Dress Restrictions, Smart casual, Civ Wed 180 **Seats:** 180, Pr/dining room 180 **Children:** Menu, Portions **Directions:** On main road to Gorey Castle. Turn left before Gorey village. Follow signs **Parking:** 300

◉◉ Suma's
Modern Mediterranean
Sea views, skilful cuisine and excellent service
☎ 01534 853291 Gorey Hill JE3 6ET
e-mail: info@sumarestaurant.com
web: www.sumarestaurant.com

A superb location delivering outstanding views from inside and from the terrace - over Mont Orgueil Castle and Gorey's attractive fishing harbour - proves an irresistible drawcard at this baby sibling of Longueville Manor (see entry). Its simple, modern décor with appropriate blue theme is as bright and refreshing as the food-and wine-themed paintings and collages adorning the walls, while the mood is suitably relaxed and friendly. The kitchen's contemporary approach, with a dash of Mediterranean flair, suits the surroundings. Expect high-quality local produce and light, intelligently simple, clear-

flavoured and well-presented dishes; take local sea bass with aubergine caviar, truffled pomme purée, samphire and a bouillabaisse sauce, or perhaps bitter lemon tart with a Jersey crème fraîche sorbet and raspberry coulis to close.

Suma's

Chef: Daniel Ward **Owners:** Mrs Butts & Mr M Lewis **Times:** 12-2.30/6.15-9.30, Closed mid Dec-mid Jan (approx) **Prices:** Fixed L £15, Fixed D £17.50-£30, Starter £4.50-£11.50, Main £13.75-£25, Dessert £6.50-£10, Service included **Wine:** 49 bottles over £20, 22 bottles under £20, 13 by the glass **Notes:** Sun L £22, Dress Restrictions, Smart casual, Air con **Seats:** 40 **Children:** Menu, Portions **Directions:** Take A3 E, continue for 5m from St Helier to Gorey. Before castle take sharp left. Restaurant 100yds up hill on left. (Look for blue & white blind) **Parking:** On street

◉ The Village Bistro
Modern British, Mediterranean V
Friendly, relaxed restaurant in village surroundings
☎ 01534 853429 Gorey Village JE3 9EP
e-mail: thevillagebistro@yahoo.co.uk

This popular bistro in a converted church - located in the centre of the pretty seaside village - is a relaxed, family-run affair, with husband Sean front of house while wife Sarah cooks. It's simply furnished and decorated, with the bonus of alfresco dining in the front garden (under parasol or heater) and friendly French service. The cuisine has a careful, rustic style with the emphasis on quality produce and value for money. Fish has its say, perhaps roasted monkfish wrapped in Parma ham with marinated sun-blush tomatoes, sautéed potatoes and sugar snap peas.

Chef: Sarah Copp **Owners:** Sean & Sarah Copp **Times:** 12-2.30/7-10.30, Closed Mon, Closed D Sun **Prices:** Fixed L £14.50, Fixed D £17.50, Starter £4.95-£8.50, Main £12.50-£19.50, Dessert £5.25, Service optional, Group min 8 service 10% **Wine:** 14 bottles over £20, 20 bottles under £20, 4 by the glass **Notes:** Fixed L 3 courses, Fixed D 4 courses, Sun L £17.50, Vegetarian menu, Dress Restrictions, Smart casual **Seats:** 40 **Children:** Portions **Directions:** Take A3 E from St Helier to Gorey. Restaurant in village centre **Parking:** On street and public car park

ROZEL   MAP 24

⊚⊚ Château La Chaire

Traditional British, French
Luxurious surroundings for a gastronomic delight

☎ 01534 863354 Rozel Bay JE3 6AJ
e-mail: res@chateau-la-chaire.co.uk
web: www.chateau-la-chaire.co.uk

Originally a traditional Victorian mansion house, the château lends itself to its current incarnation as a hotel. The architecture and original features, such as oak panelling and ornate plasterwork, are truly impressive. The creative menu - served in two dining areas, one a light-and-airy conservatory - combines French romance and culinary techniques with traditional English dishes and ingredients. Take pan-fried fillet of sea bass served with a saffron and broad bean risotto, or perhaps roast fillet of beef teamed with rösti potato and a woodland mushroom sauce. You get the impression that time stands still here, so relax and enjoy a wonderful meal in these opulent surroundings.

Chef: Simon Walker **Owners:** The Hiscox Family **Times:** 12-3/7-10 **Prices:** Fixed L £12.50, Fixed D £32.50-£35.50, Starter £7.95-£10.95, Main £16.95-£25, Dessert £6.95-£9, Service added but optional 10% **Wine:** 51 bottles over £20, 18 bottles under £20, 12 by the glass **Notes:** Fixed D 4 courses, Dress Restrictions, No jeans, Jackets required evening, Civ Wed 60 **Seats:** 60, Pr/dining room 28 **Children:** Portions **Rooms:** 14 (14 en suite)★★★ HL **Directions:** From St Helier NE towards Five Oaks, Maufant, then St Martin's Church & Rozel; 1st left in village, hotel 100mtrs **Parking:** 30

ST AUBIN   MAP 24

⊚ The Boat House Restaurant & Bar

Modern European NEW
Modern, stylish seafront venue specialising in seafood

☎ 01534 744226 1 North Quay, Jersey JE3 8BS
e-mail: enquiries@jerseyboathouse.com
web: www.jerseyboathouse.com

Set on the harbour edge with stunning views, this brand new, striking, sleek modern venue is set over two floors and is situated on the site of a one-time boat repair yard. There's a bar with casual dining and an alfresco terrace on the ground floor, but it's the first floor where the real dining action takes place. Glass and wood is the theme here; think wooden floors, plate-glass windows and polished-wood tables, while a glass-enclosed kitchen and racks of wine catch the eye too. The modern European menu specialises in the fruits of the sea, its straightforward, modern approach focusing on the island's abundant local larder; perhaps grilled fillet of line-caught sea bass with sauce vièrge, spring onion mash and sugar snaps.

Chef: Adrian Goldsborough, John Benson-Smith **Owners:** Mill Holdings (St Brelade) Ltd **Times:** 12-2/7-9.30, Closed 25 Dec & 31 Dec to first week in Feb, Closed L Sat, D Sun **Prices:** Fixed L £16.95, Starter £7.50-£9.50, Main £14.50-£25, Dessert £5.50-£7, Service optional, Group min 8 service 10% **Notes:** Fixed L 3 courses **Seats:** 96 **Children:** Menu, Portions **Parking:** On street, public car park

---

⊚⊚ Somerville Hotel

Modern French
Stunning views over the bay, and serious modern cooking

☎ 01534 741226 Mont du Boulevard JE3 8AD
e-mail: somerville@dolanhotels.com
web: www.dolanhotels.com

Settings just don't come much better than this: on the hillside overlooking St Aubin's harbour, with glorious views over the gardens all the way to St Helier enjoyed from both the recently refurbished lounge and the smart, classic country-house atmosphere of the Tides restaurant. Service is formal and reserved, and the smart table settings are in keeping with this serious approach to dining. The extensive choice on the modern menu make fine use of the abundant local larder, including the fruits of the sea, in complex, accomplished dishes; take roast fillet of Jersey bass with a sauté of ceps, asparagus, Jersey Royals, broad beans, leeks and brown butter with prawns and caper berries.

Chef: Wayne Pegler **Owners:** Mr W Dolan **Times:** 12.30-2/7-9 **Prices:** Fixed L £13.50, Fixed D £27.50, Starter £5.95-£8.95, Main £15.95-£20, Dessert £6.95-£8.50, Service optional **Wine:** 24 bottles over £20, 28 bottles under £20, 8 by the glass **Notes:** Fixed L 3 courses, Fixed D 4 courses, Sun L £18.50, Vegetarian available, Dress Restrictions, Smart casual at D, Civ Wed 40, Air con **Seats:** 120 **Children:** Portions **Rooms:** 56 (56 en suite) ★★★ HL **Directions:** From village follow harbour, then take Mont du Boulevard **Parking:** 30

ST BRELADE   MAP 24

⊚ Hotel La Place

Modern British
Classic cooking in a beamed dining room

☎ 01534 744261 Route Du Coin, La Haule JE3 8BT
e-mail: hotlaplace@aol.com
web: www.hotellaplacejersey.com

This 16th-century farmhouse has been transformed into a comfortable hotel, and makes a good base for exploring the island. Take an aperitif in the cocktail bar overlooking the pool if the weather's clement, or by the log fire in the lounge in winter, and then head through to the Retreat restaurant, a traditional, beamed affair which overlooks a pretty private courtyard. The menu suits the setting and makes good use of local produce - tuck into flash-fried Jersey scallops, chilli mange-tout and chorizo, and apricot-and thyme-stuffed chicken breast with truffle risotto and Madeira jus.

Hotel La Place

Times: 12-2/7-9 **Rooms:** 42 (42 en suite) ★★★★ HL
Directions: Telephone for directions

◎◎ L'Horizon Hotel and Spa

British, French V

Modern, intimate dining room overlooking the bay

☎ 01534 743101 Route de la Baie JE3 8EF
e-mail: lhorizon@handpicked.co.uk
web: www.handpicked.co.uk

Plenty of glass and mirrors create an impression of light and space at this stylish hotel restaurant, while clever use of partitions and alcoves helps to impart an air of intimacy. A sliding glass door opens to reveal the wonderful views of St Brelade's Bay, while crisp white linen and small flower arrangements add a touch of formality. A classical base underpins the cooking, though the interpretation of most dishes is modern and light, especially when it comes to seafood. Quality produce, local where possible, is evident in the likes of seared fillet of brill with a beetroot risotto, mint dressing and carbonara bubble, or perhaps roasted wild pheasant breast served with prune purée, creamed cabbage and bread custard. Alfresco fine dining in summer proves a further drawcard.

Chef: Kevin Clark **Owners:** Hand Picked Hotels **Times:** 7-9.45, Closed Xmas, Sun-Mon, Closed L all wk **Prices:** Fixed D £41.50, Service included **Wine:** 75 bottles over £20, 14 bottles under £20, 8 by the glass **Notes:** Tasting menu available, Vegetarian menu, Civ Wed 200, Air con **Seats:** 46, Pr/dining room 250 **Children:** Min 12 yrs, Menu, Portions **Rooms:** 106 (106 en suite) ★★★★ HL **Directions:** 2m from Jersey Airport, 5m from St Helier **Parking:** 150

◎◎◎ Ocean Restaurant at the Atlantic Hotel

see page 560

ST CLEMENT
MAP 24

◎ Green Island Restaurant

Mediterranean

Contemporary beachside café with alfresco tables

☎ 01534 857787 Green Island JE2 6LS
e-mail: greenislandrestaurant@jerseymail.co.uk
web: www.greenislandrestaurant.com

A jazzed-up beach café/restaurant that's very popular locally, especially in the summer, and the takeaway window serving quality food does a roaring trade. The views out over Green Island are well worth

savouring, as is the stylish modern Mediterranean cooking with much emphasis on fresh fish dishes. Expect sardines, crab, and lobster to be on the menu. Fresh squid with soy sauce and sesame seeds with an oriental salad might be followed by an accurately cooked breast of chicken stuffed with emmental cheese and wrapped in Parma ham. Staff in white T-shirts and jeans are relaxed and helpful.

Times: 12-3/7-10, Closed 21 Dec-Mar, Mon, Closed D Sun
Directions: Telephone for directions

ST HELIER
MAP 24

◎◎◎◎ Bohemia

see page 561

◎◎ The Grand Jersey

Modern European NEW

Refurbished landmark hotel offering modern ambience and food to match

☎ 01534 722301 The Esplanade JE4 8WD
e-mail: kmcalpine@hilwoodresorts.com
web: www.grandjersey.com

A local landmark, the newly refurbished Grand hotel is set on The Esplanade with the bustling streets of St Helier to the rear and views across the bay at the front. The main restaurant is a stylish, chic and contemporary affair, with linen tablecloths and sophisticated, knowledgeable service, plus great views of the bay and Elizabeth Castle. (There's also an adjoining modern brasserie and Champagne Bar.) The kitchen's modern European cooking uses the finest available ingredients, offering a sophisticated yet intelligently simple approach that allows subtle flavours to shine. Think Jersey plaice fillets served with retro chips, new season peas and a mint foam, and to finish, perhaps a warm chocolate fondant with white chocolate air.

Times: Please telephone for details **Rooms:** 122 (122 en suite) ★★★★ HL **Directions:** On outskirts of town overlooking Victoria Park

◎◎ La Petite Pomme

Modern European

Convivial dining with good views

☎ 01534 880110 Pomme d'Or Hotel, Liberation Square JE1 3UF
e-mail: enquiries@pommedorhotel.com
web: www.pommedorhotel.com

La Petite Pomme restaurant, the hotel's fine-dining option, occupies the first floor of an historic hotel and overlooks Liberation Square and St Helier harbour. The décor is rich and so are the clientele who expect the best of food and service. Well-spaced tables with expensive linen and settings make this a popular venue with local businessmen. Dishes are modern, imaginative and skilfully prepared. Try salmon and king prawns with saffron sauce to start and follow with a main course of crispy-skinned sea bass with spinach, sweet potato, roasted spring vegetables and fennel sauce. Desserts include a light chocolate and passionfruit bavarois.

Chef: James Waters **Owners:** Seymour Hotels **Times:** 7-10, Closed 26-30 Dec, Sun, Closed L all week **Prices:** Fixed D £15-£18.95, Starter £4.95-£7.95, Main £8.95-£24.50, Dessert £5.50-£5.95, Service optional **Wine:** 17 bottles over £20, 41 bottles under £20, 10 by the glass **Notes:** Dress Restrictions, Smart casual, Air con **Seats:** 50, Pr/dining room 50 **Children:** Menu, Portions **Rooms:** 143 (143 en suite) ★★★★ HL **Directions:** 5m from Airport, 0.5m from ferry terminal **Parking:** 100 yds from hotel

Ocean Restaurant at the Atlantic Hotel

ST BRELADE MAP 24

Modern British

Sophisticated dining with Atlantic views

☎ 01534 744101   Le Mont de la Pulente JE3 8HE
e-mail: info@theatlantichotel.com
web: www.theatlantichotel.com

Chef: Mark Jordan
Times: 12.30-2.30/7-10, Closed 5 Jan-8 Feb
Rooms: 50 (50 en suite)★★★★ HL
Directions: From St Brelade take the road to Petit Port, turn into Rue de Sergente and right again, signed to hotel

Adjoining the manicured fairways of the La Moye championship golf course, this elegant, luxury, privately-owned hotel enjoys a peaceful setting amid sub-tropical gardens and with breathtaking views over St Ouen's Bay. The air of understated luxury continues in the sophisticated Ocean Restaurant, its modern design offering a nod to its coastal setting, while service achieves that perfect balance between professionalism and friendliness.

The kitchen's modern approach - from a chef of pedigree - combines intelligent simplicity alongside tip-top produce from the abundant local Jersey larder, including the fruits of the sea. The cooking's accurate, consistent, innovative and full of flavour. Think a tranche of turbot with braised oxtail, baby gem lettuce, caramelised parsnips and girolle mushrooms, or perhaps cutlets of new season lamb served with a stilton soufflé, tarragon rösti and lamb juices, and to finish, perhaps a crisp, thin mango tart with Bailey's reduction and coconut ice cream, while peripherals like amuse-bouche, breads and petits fours all hold form through to the end.

Bohemia

ST HELIER MAP 24

Modern French

Confident classical cooking in contemporary Jersey restaurant

☎ 01534 880588 The Club Hotel & Spa, Green St JE2 4UH
e-mail: bohemia@huggler.com
web: www.bohemiajersey.com

A swish, contemporary townhouse close to the centre of town, The Club Hotel & Spa plays host to the island's most trendy, and highly rated restaurant, Bohemia, with its chef Shaun Rankin delivering some seriously accomplished cuisine. A long, trendy bar runs the length of its plate-glass windows and attracts an equally trendy crowd, and behind it sits the restaurant. Decorated in shades of earthy brown, there's lots of wood, leather, Lalique glass, fresh flowers and elegant table appointments. Service is appropriately polished and attentive, yet unstuffy, from a friendly international team (with a super restaurant manager and sommelier). A buzzing venue with a vibrant see-and-be-seen vibe.

Shaun Rankin's kitchen takes a modern approach underpinned by a classical French theme; this is refined, top-notch, creative cooking at its best. Expect great use of seasonal and local produce from sea and land, bags of luxury (crab, lobster, oysters, Périgord truffles, caviar), great technical skills, lovely clean, clear flavours with fine textural combinations, and a sense of adventure. Think grilled local sea bass with scallop carpaccio, samphire, lime and sauce vièrge, or perhaps roast loin of Yorkshire venison teamed with chocolate tortellini, medjool dates and ginger-scented quinoa, and to finish, maybe a macerated raspberry and balsamic soufflé served with white chocolate fudge cannelloni. The repertoire is a fixed-price affair and includes a tasting option, while the fresh Jersey seafood proves a drawcard and peripherals - like tasters and inter-courses and fabulous petits fours - complete the experience. The hotel's Club Café upstairs serves less elaborate food, there are luxury rooms and a wonderful spa, too.

Chef: Shaun Rankin
Owners: Laurence Huggler
Times: 12-2.30/6.30-10, Closed Sun, Closed L Sat
Prices: Fixed L £16.50, Fixed D £49, Starter £17, Main £27-£33, Dessert £8.50, Service added but optional 10%
Wine: 110 bottles over £20, 12 bottles under £20, 21 by the glass
Notes: Tasting menu available, Vegetarian available, Dress Restrictions, Smart casual, Air con
Seats: 40, Pr/dining room 6
Children: Portions
Rooms: 46 (46 en suite)★★★★
Directions: Located on Green St in centre of St Helier
Parking: 20

Longueville Manor

ST SAVIOUR MAP 24

Modern British

Historic manor with sophisticated cuisine

☎ 01534 725501   JE2 7WF
e-mail: info@longuevillemanor.com
web: www.longuevillemanor.com

Dating from the 13th century, this grand Norman manor house is an imposing dinner venue and a hotel of international renown. Clad in wisteria, it stands in 15 acres of woodland that invite exploration - take a stroll before dinner and you may stumble across a game of croquet on the lawn, a spectacular rose garden, or a lake with a flock of majestic black swans. Inside, everything is decorated in understated country-house style, and guests are treated to very high standards of comfort and care.

The two dining rooms cater for different moods, from the Jacobean dark-panelled Oak Room to the more relaxed and modern Garden Room, rich in fabrics and antiques. Whichever you choose, you're in for a treat; the cuisine at Longueville is confident and accomplished, and makes intelligent use of top-notch ingredients from the walled kitchen garden and local area (Taste of Jersey menu available). Combinations are deft and flavours balanced; the result is an assured menu of classical dishes. You might start with sesame-coated seared tuna, served with rocket salad, horseradish cream and caviar sauce, followed by best end of lamb with slow-roast plum tomatoes, French beans and sauté sweetbreads, and then finish with vanilla crème brûlée, Granny Smith sorbet and apple soup.

Chef: Andrew Baird
Owners: Malcolm Lewis
Times: 12.30-2/7-10
Prices: Fixed D £52.50-£64, Service included
Wine: 300+ bottles over £20, 20 bottles under £20, 23 by the glass
Notes: Vegetarian available, Dress Restrictions, Smart casual, jacket minimum, Civ Wed 40
Seats: 65, Pr/dining room 22
Children: Menu, Portions
Rooms: 30 (30 en suite)★★★★ HL
Directions: From St Helier take A3 to Gorey, hotel 0.75m on left
Parking: 45

ST SAVIOUR   MAP 24

⦾⦾⦾ Longueville Manor

see opposite

TRINITY   MAP 24

⦾⦾ Water's Edge Hotel

Modern British

Stunning coastal setting for enjoyable cuisine

☎ 01534 862777   Bouley Bay JE3 5AS
e-mail: mail@watersedgehotel.co.je
web: www.watersedgehotel.co.je

There are breathtaking views over Bouley Bay from this art-deco style hotel, which certainly lives up to its name. You can even see as far as the French coastline on a good day. The split-level restaurant provides a wonderful setting in which to enjoy the carefully prepared dishes, but do try to get a window seat to make the most of the view. Choose from the carte or fixed-price market menu, both featuring local seafood, including live local lobster and Royal Grouville Bay oysters. For a touch of drama, try prime Angus sirloin fillet or crêpe Suzette from the flambé trolley. Formal service and crisp table linen complete the experience.

Chef: Gael Maratier **Owners:** Water's Edge Hotel Ltd **Times:** 12.30-2/7-9.15, Closed Nov-Mar, Closed L Mon-Sat **Prices:** Fixed L £16-£23, Fixed D £23-£25, Starter £5-£12, Main £16.50-£35, Dessert £6-£10, Service included **Wine:** 40 bottles over £20, 50 bottles under £20, 14 by the glass **Notes:** Fixed L 3 courses, Vegetarian available, Dress Restrictions, Smart casual, no trainers, jeans or T-shirts, Civ Wed 100 **Seats:** 100, Pr/dining room 40 **Children:** Min 7 yrs, Menu, Portions **Rooms:** 50 (50 en suite) ★★★ HL **Directions:** 10-15 mins from St Helier, A9 N to the A8 to the B31, follow signs to Bouley Bay **Parking:** 20

SARK

SARK   MAP 24

⦾ Hotel Petit Champ

Modern British

Relaxed, country-house dining with amazing sea views

☎ 01481 832046   GY9 0SF
e-mail: info@hotelpetitchamp.co.uk
web: www.hotelpetitchamp.co.uk

This secluded hotel on Sark's west coast has a fascinating history, having served as a private home, boatyard and German observation post during the Occupation. These days, the only things guests come to watch are the magnificent sea views, which are particularly stunning at sunset. The restaurant delivers a menu of modern British dishes with an international twist: lemon- and truffle-roasted breast of chicken served with morel jus, for example, or treacle-marinated fillet of lamb with a casserole of creamy summer vegetables. Fresh crab and lobster from the harbour are a speciality, the latter offered with an array of sauces, including chilli, coriander and coconut cream, and garlic butter.

Chef: Tony Atkins **Owners:** Chris & Caroline Robins **Times:** 12.15-1.45/8, Closed Oct-Etr **Prices:** Fixed D £20.75, Starter £3.75-£7.50, Main £10.75-£19.25, Dessert £3.40-£4.50, Service optional **Wine:** 11 bottles over £20, 66 bottles under £20, 4 by the glass **Notes:** Sun L 4 courses £12.50, Fixed D 5 courses, Vegetarian available, Dress Restrictions, Smart casual **Seats:** 50 **Children:** Min 7 yrs D, Menu, Portions **Rooms:** 10 (10 en suite)★★ HL **Directions:** 20 min walk from village, signed from Methodist Chapel

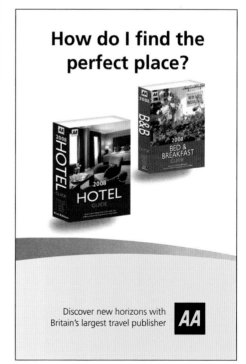

ENGLAND

SARK *Continued*

◎◎ La Sablonnerie
Modern International
Creative cuisine in a rustic setting

☎ 01481 832061 GY9 0SD
web: www.lasablonnerie.com

This cosy gem on the idyllic island of Sark has garnered a mantelpiece of awards over the years, thanks to a picture-perfect setting, attention to detail, and accomplished cuisine. Sark is car-free, so access comes courtesy of the hotel's horse and carriage which will deliver you to the door of a whitewashed cottage half-hidden in summer by a mass of flowers. The restaurant retains the original style and charm of the 400-year-old farmhouse, and delivers a menu of modern international dishes with a strong French influence: cannon of lamb in pancetta, for example, served with Bretonne potatoes, roasted root vegetables and a mint and tarragon jus, or seared tuna with a black-pepper crust and little gem fondue. Fresh fish and lobster are a speciality.

Chef: Martin Cross **Owners:** Elizabeth Perrée **Times:** 12-2.30/7-9.30, Closed mid Oct-Etr **Prices:** Fixed L £16.80-£22.30, Fixed D £23.60-£30.10, Starter £5.80-£7.80, Main £11-£14.50, Dessert £5.80-£6.80, Service added 10% **Wine:** 9 bottles over £20, 41 bottles under £20, 6 by the glass **Notes:** Vegetarian available **Seats:** 39 **Children:** Menu, Portions **Directions:** On southern part of island. Horse & carriage is transport to hotel

ISLE OF MAN

DOUGLAS   MAP 24 SC37

◎ Sefton Hotel
Modern European
Fine dining beside the sea

☎ 01624 645500 Harris Promenade IM1 2RW
e-mail: info@seftonhotel.co.im
web: www.seftonhotel.co.im

A Victorian seafront hotel with a contemporary, comfortable fine-dining restaurant, decorated with bright artwork and enjoying fine views out to sea. Modern cooking is the order of the day with fine ingredients in a mix of European-style and classic French dishes. Typically, start with caramelised pear and dolcelatte tart with roasted vine tomatoes and balsamic syrup, or pan-seared scallops coated with polenta, before moving on to pan-roasted fillet of Manx beef with celeriac and potato mash, onion marmalade tart, red wine and vegetable broth, or perhaps simply grilled Dover sole. Finish with hot chocolate pudding served with warm anglaise and vanilla pod ice cream.

Chef: Chris Swinden **Owners:** Sefton Hotel Plc **Times:** 12-2/6-10, Closed L Sun **Prices:** Fixed L £9.95-£20.95, Starter £5.25-£8.95, Main £14.50-£22.50, Dessert £5-£6.95, Service optional **Notes:** Vegetarian available, Dress Restrictions, Smart casual **Seats:** 25, Pr/dining room 40 **Children:** Portions **Rooms:** 96 (96 en suite) ★★★★ HL **Directions:** 1m along Promenade from the sea terminal **Parking:** 20

The valley of Dovedale, Peak District national Park

Scotland

CITY OF ABERDEEN

SCOTLAND

ABERDEEN   MAP 23 NJ90

◉ Atlantis at the Mariner Hotel

Modern British, Seafood V

Established hotel with excellent local seafood and meats

☎ 01224 588901 349 Great Western Rd AB10 6NW
e-mail: info@themarinerhotel.co.uk
web: www.themarinerhotel.co.uk

A family-run hotel to the west of the city centre. Dine in the Atlantis restaurant, a split-level affair with a conservatory area, subtle nautical theme, rich coloured furnishings and a wide-ranging menu. The emphasis is on fresh local seafood, including a cold seafood platter and selection of lobster dishes, and, inevitably for Aberdeen, there are steaks too. Portions are hearty and a light touch lets the quality of regional produce speak for itself. Take halibut thermidor served with duchess potatoes, or monkfish and Parma ham brochette with a barbecue sauce, and, for carnivores, perhaps roast fillet of lamb with a herb mash and redcurrant gravy. To close, sticky toffee pudding might catch the eye.

Chef: George Bennett **Owners:** The Edwards Family **Times:** 12-2/6-9.30, Closed 26 Dec, 1-2 Jan, Closed L Sat **Prices:** Fixed L £15, Fixed D £18, Starter £3.25-£8, Main £11-£32.50, Dessert £4.50, Service optional **Wine:** 28 bottles over £20, 17 bottles under £20, 3 by the glass **Notes:** Sun L 3 courses £14.50, Vegetarian menu **Seats:** 50 **Children:** Portions **Rooms:** 25 (25 en suite) ★★★ HL **Directions:** From S, 400yds right off A90 at Great Western Rd lights **Parking:** 50

◉◉ Copthorne Hotel Aberdeen

British 🛏

Traditional hotel restaurant serving simple British cuisine

☎ 01224 630404 122 Huntly St AB10 1SU
e-mail: reservations.aberdeen@mill-cop.com
web: www.copthorne.com

This granite building is a former grain warehouse found in the city's West End shopping district. A traditional hotel restaurant here, Poachers, serves high-quality, simply-prepared dishes, using the best local and Scottish ingredients. Service is relaxed and friendly so take your time to peruse the menu. You'll find the carte supplemented by options from the chargrill and side orders like sliced olive and herb potatoes. Typical starters include bradan rost mango and avocado salsa, or traditional Cullen skink. Main courses might include

pan-seared fillet of monkfish wrapped in Parma ham on a creamy Loch Fyne mussel chowder. Cheese and Scottish oatcakes make an alternative to desserts like iced tiramisù parfait.

Times: 7-9, Closed 25-26 Dec, Closed L all week **Rooms:** 89 (89 en suite) ★★★★ HL **Directions:** City centre. 200yds off Union St, at top of Huntly St

◉ Maryculter House Hotel

Traditional Scottish

Cosy dining in historic mansion house

☎ 01224 732124 AB12 5GB
e-mail: info@maryculterhousehotel.com
web: www.maryculterhousehotel.com

Once a seat of the Knights Templar, Maryculter House dates from 1225 and is set in 5 acres of woodland on the banks of the River Dee. These days it's a busy country-house hotel where guests can feast by candlelight in the stone-walled Priory restaurant. The Scottish menu lists prime local produce, including beef and salmon. Typical dishes are haggis, neeps and tatties wrapped in filo pastry and served with whisky cream, followed by collops of Highland venison with potatoes Lyonnaise, Savoy cabbage and red wine jus, with a dessert of iced parfait flavoured with Grand Marnier.

Chef: Sebastian Schroeder **Owners:** James Gilbert **Times:** 7-9.30, Closed Sun, Closed L all week **Prices:** Starter £3.25-£5.95, Main £14.95-£18.95, Dessert £4.95-£5.45, Service optional **Wine:** 20 bottles over £20, 16 bottles under £20, 1 by the glass **Notes:** Vegetarian available, Dress Restrictions, Smart casual, no jeans or T-shirts, Civ Wed 150 **Seats:** 40, Pr/dining room 180 **Children:** Min 4 yrs, Portions **Rooms:** 40 (40 en suite) ★★★ HL **Directions:** Off A90 to S of Aberdeen and onto B9077. Hotel is located 8m on right, 0.5m beyond Lower Deeside Caravan Park **Parking:** 150

◉ Norwood Hall

British, European

Fine dining on a grand scale

☎ 01224 868951 Garthdee Rd, Cults AB15 9FX
e-mail: info@norwood-hall.co.uk
web: www.norwood-hall.co.uk

An imposing Victorian mansion in 7 acres of grounds, with roaring winter fires, sweeping staircases and an oak-panelled dining room, aptly named the Tapestry restaurant after the ornate tapestry work on the walls. Well-spaced candlelit tables grace this richly furnished room, displaying fine crockery and glassware befitting the magnificent scale of the house. A selection of traditional and more adventurous dishes is the kitchen's style, driven by quality local seasonal produce, with an emphasis on game and seafood. The slick cooking majors on flavour and simplicity; perhaps medallions of beef served with a wild mushroom sauce and haggis, followed by chocolate brownie and vanilla ice cream finish.

Times: 12-2.30/7-9.45 **Rooms:** 37 (37 en suite) ★★★★ HL **Directions:** From S, off A90 at 1st rdbt cross bridge and turn left at rdbt into Garthdee Road, continue 1.5m

◎◎ The Silver Darling

French, Seafood
Romantic seafood restaurant with stunning harbour views

☎ 01224 576229 Pocra Quay, North Pier AB11 5DQ

The location of The Silver Darling is almost as good a talking point as the food. It stands at the entrance to Aberdeen harbour and was originally the customs house. From the large windows of the first-floor conservatory restaurant you can see passing ships and even dolphins. Given the name (a reference to herring), it's not surprising that fresh locally-landed seafood is the speciality here. The sophisticated evening menu is strongly French influenced and is typified by steamed wild sea bass served with seaweed linguini, carrot and fennel purée and bouillabaisse jus. Lunch is a simpler affair but there's no compromising the quality of ingredients, flavours and cooking skills.

Chef: Didier Dejean **Owners:** Didier Dejean & Karen Murray **Times:** 12-1.45/6.30-9.30, Closed Xmas-New Year, Sun, Closed L Sat **Prices:** Starter £8.50-£11.50, Main £18.50-£20.50, Dessert £7.50-£8.50, Service optional, Group min 10 service 10% **Wine:** 36 bottles over £20, 6 bottles under £20, 7 by the glass **Seats:** 50 **Children:** Portions **Directions:** Situated at Aberdeen Harbour entrance **Parking:** On quayside

🖳 Howies Restaurant - Chapel Street

☎ 01224 639500 50 Chapel St AB10 1SN
web: www.theaa.com/travel/index.jsp

The Aberdeen member of the successful Edinburgh-based group of modern Scottish restaurants. Monthly-changing menus of fantastic seasonal and local food made on the premises every day.

BALLATER   MAP 23 NO39

◎◎◎ Darroch Learg Hotel
see below

◎◎ The Green Inn

Modern British V NEW
Intimate, family-run conservatory-style restaurant

☎ 013397 55701 9 Victoria Rd AB35 5QQ
e-mail: info@green-inn.com
web: www.green-inn.com

Trevor O'Halloran is a larger than life character at front of house, while son Chris is in charge of the kitchen - ably assisted by mum Evelyn - to make this a real family affair. A comfortable lounge leads to the splendid conservatory that looks out on to the small, secluded garden and, with only seven well-spaced tables, the atmosphere is comfortable and relaxed at this dinner-only affair. Chris's cooking has a contemporary approach underpinned by a classical theme, reflecting a learning stint at Le Manoir aux Quat' Saisons (see entry), with impressive technical skills and artistic presentation to the fore in dishes utilising fresh, local produce. Take pan-roasted Atlantic halibut fillet with truffle-scented potato, broad bean purée and carrot broth, or raspberry soufflé with mascarpone sorbet to finish.

Chef: Chris & Evelyn O'Halloran **Owners:** Trevor & Evelyn O'Halloran **Times:** 7-9, Closed 2 wks Nov, 2 wks Jan, Sun, Mon **Prices:** Fixed D £36, Service optional **Wine:** 46 bottles over £20, 12 bottles under £20, 7 by the glass **Notes:** Vegetarian menu, Dress Restrictions, Smart casual **Seats:** 30, Pr/dining room 24 **Rooms:** 3 (3 en suite) ✫✫✫✫ RR **Parking:** On street

SCOTLAND

Darroch Learg Hotel

BALLATER   MAP 23 NO39

Modern Scottish V
Flawless cooking in stunning setting

☎ 013397 55443 Braemar Rd AB35 5UX
e-mail: info@darrochlearg.co.uk
web: www.darrochlearg.co.uk

Set high above the road in extensive wooded grounds, this long-established hotel offers superb views of Royal Deeside. Inside this renowned 19th-century country-house hotel, there are two comfortable, welcoming lounges, one with a crackling log fire, while the smart restaurant extends into a conservatory to make the best of those views. Decorated in bright modern style, with splashes of colour from contemporary prints, its well-appointed tables come dressed in white linen. The mood is relaxed and service knowledgeable and friendly, with the Franks themselves (the owners) involved with great effect.

The kitchen's modern approach is delivered via an appealing carte and seven-course tasting option that place great emphasis on high-quality produce from the abundant local Scottish larder, including venison, beef, salmon and scallops. The accurate, intelligently simple approach and light touch allow the quality ingredients to speak for themselves with clean, clear flavours and limited fuss. Take pan-fried

West Coast scallops with cauliflower, smoked salmon and capers, followed by vanilla parfait with hazelnut sponge and Agen prunes. And do take time to explore the wine list, as there's some great-value drinking to be enjoyed.

Chef: David Mutter **Owners:** The Franks Family **Times:** 12.30-2/7-9, Closed Xmas, last 3wks Jan, Closed L Mon-Sat **Prices:** Fixed L £24, Fixed D £41-£47, Service included **Wine:** 186 bottles over £20, 4 by the glass **Notes:** Fixed L 3 courses, Tasting menu £47, Vegetarian menu, Dress Restrictions, Smart casual **Seats:** 48 **Children:** Menu, Portions **Rooms:** 17 (17 en suite)★★★ SHL **Directions:** On A93 at the W end of village **Parking:** 15

BALLATER CONTINUED

⊛ Loch Kinord Hotel

Modern British NEW

Stylish, elegant dining in woodland setting

☎ 013398 85229 Ballater Rd, Dinnet AB34 5JY
e-mail: stay@kinord.com
web: www.kinord.com

This attractive, granite-faced roadside hotel stands in a woodland setting with pretty gardens and comes brimful of character and friendly atmosphere. Inside is cosy and informal with a choice of comfortable lounges and bars and a formally laid, elegant dining room with attentive service. The kitchen's style is intelligently uncomplicated, delivering neatly presented dishes and honest flavours that make good use of the abundant local larder. Take a breast of Gressingham duck with caramelised red cabbage and cranberry and port gravy, and perhaps a rich mocha chocolate mousse to finish.

Chef: Fraser Bell **Owners:** Andrew & Jenny Cox **Times:** 6.30-9, Closed L all week **Prices:** Starter £5-£8, Main £12-£17, Dessert £6, Service optional **Wine:** 15 bottles over £20, 15 bottles under £20, 4 by the glass **Notes:** Vegetarian available, Civ Wed 40 **Seats:** 30 **Children:** Menu, Portions **Rooms:** 20 (20 en suite) ★★★ HL **Directions:** From Aberdeen city take A93 Wt towards Braemar, hotel on A93 between Aboyne & Ballater **Parking:** 20

Glen Lui

☎ 013397 55402 Invercauld Rd AB35 5RP
Delightful country house set in lovely grounds.

BANCHORY   MAP 23 NO69

⊛⊛ Raemoir House Hotel

Scottish, French NOTABLE WINE LIST

Romantic and historic setting for accomplished cuisine

☎ 01330 824884 Raemoir AB31 4ED
e-mail: relax@raemoir.com
web: www.raemoir.com

A romantic setting in 3,500 acres of parkland and forest. The original 'Ha' Hoose' is of great historical importance and has been restored to become an annexe to the main house, a hotel since 1943. The sense of history is everywhere, but nowhere more so than in the amazing Oval Dining Room, now used as the restaurant. Here the unique tapestry-lined walls, curved doors and blazing log fire give out tremendous warmth and character. Cuisine is Scottish with French

influences and uses prime local produce. For example, take grilled sea bass served with a herb risotto, confit aubergine and shellfish cream, or perhaps breast of Raemoir pheasant teamed with a sweet potato pancake and game broth.

Chef: Grant Walker **Owners:** Mr & Mrs D Webster **Times:** 12-2/6.30-9, Closed 26-30 Dec **Prices:** Fixed L £18-£25, Fixed D £35-£42, Service optional **Wine:** 65 bottles over £20, 13 bottles under £20, 10 by the glass **Notes:** Vegetarian available, Dress Restrictions, Smart casual, no jeans/T-shirts, Civ Wed 60 **Seats:** 45, Pr/dining room 60 **Children:** Portions **Rooms:** 20 (20 en suite) ★★★ CHH **Directions:** A93 to Banchory then A980, hotel at x-rds after 2.5 m **Parking:** 50

Milton Restaurant

☎ 01330 844566 On A493 Royal Deeside Rd, E of Banchory AB31 5YR
Modish roadside restaurant with craft shop.

OLDMELDRUM   MAP 23 NJ82

⊛ Meldrum House Hotel Golf & Country Estate

Traditional British V

Elegant dining in a splendid country mansion

☎ 01651 872294 AB51 0AE
e-mail: enquiries@meldrumhouse.co.uk
web: www.meldrumhouse.com

A baronial country mansion set in 350 acres of woodland and parkland with a golf course as the centrepiece. The hotel has been tastefully restored to highlight its original character. The traditional Scottish cooking - with international twists - has a flare for presentation in well-constructed dishes using quality Scottish produce. Expect roasted monkfish with garlic, red pepper chutney and saffron rice, or perhaps collops of beef fillet with a pickled walnut sauce. Desserts like rhubarb crumble and custard, or lemon tart with boozy fruits provide the finish.

Chef: Gary Christie **Owners:** Sylvia Simpson **Times:** 12-2.30/6.30-9.30 **Prices:** Fixed L £18.50, Fixed D £32.50, Service optional **Notes:** Fixed L 3 courses, Fixed D 4 courses, Vegetarian menu, Dress Restrictions, Smart casual, Civ Wed 80 **Seats:** 40, Pr/dining room 16 **Children:** Menu, Portions **Rooms:** 9 (9 en suite) ★★★ CHH **Directions:** 11m N of Aberdeen, from Aberdeen to Dyce, follow A947 towards Banff, through Newmachen along outskirts of Oldmeldrum, main entrance is large white archway **Parking:** 60

STONEHAVEN   MAP 23 NO88

⊛ Tolbooth Restaurant

Modern, Mediterranean

Quay-side restaurant serving fish straight from the sea

☎ 01569 762287 Old Pier Rd AB39 2JU
web: www.tolbooth-restaurant.co.uk

Accessed via a steep outside staircase, this former prison and excise house on the harbour wall - now a popular restaurant - evokes a sense of the Mediterranean with its rustic whitewashed stone walls, wooden floors and modern table settings. Wonderfully fresh seafood includes the likes of spiced local crab parcels with garlic and chilli, and home-cured Scottish salmon gravad lax baked in the oven. Meat dishes are also available, and there's an especially good-value lunchtime menu. Tempting desserts include milk chocolate and peppermint crème brûlée and home-made tiramisù with Amaretto.

Chef: Robert Cleaver & Craig Sumers **Owners:** Robert Cleaver **Times:** 12-2/6-9.30, Closed 3 wks after Xmas, Sun & Mon **Prices:** Fixed L £12, Starter £3.15-£6.95, Main £10.95-£18.95, Dessert £5.95-£6.50, Service optional **Wine:** 22 bottles over £20, 13 bottles under £20, 3 by the glass **Seats:** 46 **Children:** Portions **Directions:** 15m S of Aberdeen on A90, located in Stonehaven harbour **Parking:** Public car park, 100 spaces

ANGUS

BRIDGEND OF LINTRATHEN   MAP 23 NO25

◉◉ Lochside Lodge & Roundhouse Restaurant

Modern British
Imaginative dishes in unique farm steading

☎ 01575 560340   DD8 5JJ
e-mail: enquiries@lochsidelodge.com
web: www.lochsidelodge.com

A 150-year-old converted farm steading, Lochside Lodge is set amid arguably the most picturesque of the Angus glens. There's a choice of two dining options: the Steading, which provides a more informal atmosphere, and the more formal, spacious Roundhouse Restaurant. The menu is modern Scottish with an emphasis on locally-sourced produce wherever possible. Start with an interesting dish like timbale of East Coast crab and mango salad, with gazpacho drizzle, or maybe a tranche of Shetland smoked salmon with an orange and vanilla

dressing. Follow with seared centre cut of Angus rib-eye beef glazed with organic Mull brie, set on creamed leeks in a red wine jus, and round things off with a pink champagne-poached pear with home-made honeycomb ice cream.

Chef: Graham Riley **Owners:** Graham & Gail Riley **Times:** 12-1.30/6.30-8.30, Closed 1-25 Jan, 23-27 Dec, 2nd wk Oct, Mon, Closed D Sun **Prices:** Fixed L £13-F15, Fixed D £35, Service optional, Group min 20 service 10% **Wine:** 20 bottles over £20, 16 bottles under £20, 6 by the glass **Notes:** Dress Restrictions, Smart casual, no jeans **Seats:** 35, Pr/dining room 48 **Children:** Portions **Rooms:** 6 (6 en suite) ★★★★ RR **Directions:** From Kirriemuir, take B591 towards Glenisla for 7m, turn left towards Lintrathen and follow to village, restaurant on left **Parking:** 40

GLAMIS   MAP 21 NO34

◉◉◉ Castleton House Hotel
see below

INVERKEILOR   MAP 23 NO64

◉◉ Gordon's

Modern British V
Scottish cooking from a friendly family team

☎ 01241 830364   Main St DD11 5RN
e-mail: gordonsrest@aol.com
web: www.gordonsrestaurant.co.uk

The name of this family-run establishment only tells part of the story, as the eponymous Gordon is joined in the kitchen by son Garry whose cooking is now cutting edge with that all-important wow-factor.

CONTINUED

◉◉◉

Castleton House Hotel

GLAMIS   MAP 21 NO34

Traditional British V ✋
Victorian country house with culinary flair

☎ 01307 840340   Castleton of Eassie DD8 1SJ
e-mail: hotel@castletonglamis.co.uk
web: www.castletonglamis.co.uk

The tall trees that surround this charming 100-year-old house create such a sense of exclusivity and tranquillity that once here it's difficult to imagine ever being able to leave. There is a croquet lawn and animals - ducks, chickens and pigs - roaming around these beautiful grounds complete with moat. A conservatory dining room with beautiful vases of seasonal flowers overlooks the gardens. With vegetables and herbs coming from the gardens too, the accomplished British cooking with French influences relies heavily on the quality - and provenance - of the ingredients, which if not home grown or home reared are sourced from the surrounding region. The result is simple, clear cooking with the flavours of the superb ingredients shining through at each course. The flawlessly-timed dishes might include a starter of tian of Skye salmon with lobster, caviar and hazelnut apple purée, followed by a main of roast loin of Glen Prosen venison with roast celeriac and muscovite sauce, and a dessert of warm plum tarte Tatin with caramel sauce and clotted cream ice cream.

Chef: Andrew Wilkie **Owners:** David & Verity Webster **Times:** 12-2/6.30-9, Closed New Year **Prices:** Fixed L £21.50, Fixed D £35, Starter £3.95-£6.95, Main £5.95-£15.95, Dessert £4.50, Service optional **Wine:** 32 bottles over £20, 21 bottles under £20, 7 by the glass **Notes:** Vegetarian menu, Smart casual, Civ Wed 50 **Seats:** 50, Pr/dining room 35 **Children:** Menu, Portions **Rooms:** 6 (6 en suite)★★★ CHH **Directions:** On A94 midway between Forfar & Coupar Angus, 3m W of Glamis **Parking:** 50

INVERKEILOR Continued

The imaginative, modern cooking is underpinned by a classical theme and makes good use of seasonal produce from the abundant Scottish larder on its appealing, sensibly compact menus. Loin of venison with red cabbage and pear compôte, roast salsify and jus, or a raspberry and Drambuie iced parfait with raspberry soup might be just the thing. It's a cosy affair with bags of character - beamed ceiling, huge open fire and rugs on wooden floors.

Chef: Gordon Watson & Garry Watson **Owners:** Gordon & Maria Watson **Times:** 12-1.45/7-9, Closed 1st 2 wks Jan, Mon, Closed L Tues, D Sun **Prices:** Fixed L £26, Fixed D £39, Service optional **Wine:** 19 bottles over £20, 25 bottles under £20, 3 by the glass **Notes:** Fixed L 3 courses, Fixed D 4 courses (both inc coffee), Vegetarian menu, Dress Restrictions, Smart casual **Seats:** 24, Pr/dining room 8 **Children:** Min 12 yrs **Rooms:** 3 (2 en suite) ★★★★ RR **Directions:** On A92, turn off at signs for village of Inverkeilor, between Arbroath and Montrose **Parking:** 6

ARGYLL & BUTE

ARDUAINE   MAP 20 NM71

◉◉ Loch Melfort Hotel

Modern British V

Wonderful views and a menu specialising in fresh seafood

☎ 01852 200233   PA34 4XG
e-mail: reception@lochmelfort.co.uk
web: www.lochmelfort.co.uk

In a spectacular location on the West Coast, this popular, family-run hotel enjoys outstanding views across Asknish Bay towards the islands of Jura, Scarba and Shuna. The setting is the perfect complement to the wonderful seafood on offer in the attractive dining room. An alternative dining choice, popular with visiting yachtsmen, the Skerry Bistro offers blackboard specials. Skilful cooking makes excellent use of local produce, particularly fresh fish and shellfish. Think grilled fillet of sea bream with chargrilled asparagus, Parisienne potatoes and a chive beurre blanc, or maybe pan-fried John Dory fillets with saffron-braised fennel and white wine, while meat-eaters might opt for pan-fried medallions of beef with Lyonnaise potatoes and green peppercorn sauce. Tantalising desserts include the likes of baked chocolate pudding with chocolate fudge sauce and vanilla ice cream, or summer fruit brûlée. The well-chosen wine list is also worth a look.

Chef: Colin Macdonald **Owners:** Kyle & Nigel Schofield **Times:** 7-9, Closed 2 Jan-15 Feb, Closed L all week **Prices:** Food prices not confirmed for 2008. Please telephone for details **Wine:** 25 bottles over £20, 40 bottles under £20, 4 by the glass **Notes:** Vegetarian menu, Dress

Restrictions, Smart casual, no jeans **Seats:** 75 **Children:** Menu, Portions **Rooms:** 25 (25 en suite) ★★★ HL **Directions:** From Oban, 20m S on A816; from Lochgilphead, 19m N on A816 **Parking:** 65

CARRADALE   MAP 20 NR83

◉ Dunvalanree

Scottish NEW

Local seafood in stunning location

☎ 01583 431226 Port Righ Bay PA28 6SE
e-mail: stay@dunvalanree.com
web: www.dunvalanree.com

An ideal base to explore the Mull of Kintyre, Dunvalanree enjoys stunning views across the Kilbrannan Sound to the hills of Arran. This is a genuine family-run operation with mum in the kitchen and father and daughter welcoming guests in the traditional restaurant. With skill and imagination, simple Scottish cuisine is conjured from the very best that the local larder has to offer and traditional dishes stand shoulder to shoulder with more innovative fare. The daily-changing menu might include crab cakes with dill mayonnaise followed by Kintyre venison fillet steak with roasted satsuma and rowan and port gravy, or scallop and monkfish skewers.

Times: 7, Closed L all week **Rooms:** 5 (5 en suite) ★★★★

CLACHAN   MAP 20 NR75

◉ Balinakill Country House Hotel

Scottish, French

Victorian setting for contemporary cuisine

☎ 01880 740206   PA29 6XL
e-mail: info@balinakill.com
web: www.balinakill.com

Set in grounds on the Kintyre peninsula and built by William Mackinnon, founder of the British India Line, this magnificent house was used as a school during World War II, came close to demolition in the 1970s, became a family home and was then rescued in its current incarnation as a hotel. There is little evidence of this varied past in the beautiful Victorian plasterwork and panelling, antiques and period pieces. The cooking is classical Scottish and French style, making use of free-range, organic and local produce. Try grilled Tarbert sole with paprika butter and creamed saffron potatoes.

Times: 7-9, Closed L all week **Rooms:** 10 (10 en suite) ★★ CHH
Directions: 10m S of Tarbert Loch Fyne. The entrance is located on the left off A83 travelling S towards Campbeltown

CLACHAN-SEIL

MAP 20 NM71

◉◉ Willowburn Hotel

British, French ⬥ NOTABLE WINE LIST 🍷

Friendly country-cottage hotel offering local produce and fine dining

☎ 01852 300276   PA34 4TJ

e-mail: willowburn.hotel@virgin.net
web: www.willowburn.co.uk

Enjoying a glorious setting with grounds running down to the water's edge of Clachan Sound, this friendly hotel has a warm, homely feel and you can watch the wildlife from the dining room window. Service is friendly and unobtrusive, and there's a dinner party atmosphere with all guests congregating at 7pm for aperitifs and canapés. The cooking style brings together French, Scottish and British cuisine, producing good clean flavours. Try a starter like Loch Etive mussels in tomato, herbs and wine, followed by a main course of delicious local crab dressed and topped with a herb and cheese crust. Finish with an interesting dessert like chocolate samosas with champagne ice cream. An excellent wine list completes the upbeat package.

Chef: Chris Wolfe   **Owners:** Jan & Chris Wolfe   **Times:** 7-8.30, Closed Dec-Feb   **Prices:** Fixed D £38-£40, Service optional   **Wine:** 74 bottles over £20, 64 bottles under £20, 4 by the glass   **Notes:** Fixed D 4 courses, Gourmet & wine wknds available   **Seats:** 20   **Children:** Min 8 yrs   **Rooms:** 7 (7 en suite) ★★   SHL   **Directions:** 11m S of Oban via A816 and B844 (Easdale) over Atlantic Bridge, restaurant 0.5m after bridge on left   **Parking:** 20

COVE

MAP 20 NS28

◉ Knockderry House Hotel

Modern Scottish, International NEW

Loch-side setting with cooking showcasing quality local ingredients

☎ 01436 842283   Shore Rd G84 0NX

e-mail: info@knockderryhouse.co.uk
web: www.knockderryhouse.co.uk

Overlooking Loch Long, Knockderry's restaurant is certainly in keeping with its Victorian country-house style; think wood-panelled walls, stained-glass windows and picture-postcard views of the Clyde sea lochs and beyond. The accomplished kitchen delivers two menus, a lighter, informal lounge bar menu, and the full-on evening dinner carte. Time and care are taken in sourcing quality local ingredients, with dishes showcasing good attention to detail, balance, flavour and consistency; take a chargrilled fillet of Rahane beef with fondant potato, wild mushrooms and roast garlic, or perhaps pan-fried Scottish salmon with basil risotto, buttered spinach and asparagus.

Chef: Beth MacLeod, Paul Deakin   **Owners:** Beth & Murdo MacLeod   **Times:** 12.30-2.30/5.30-9, Closed 25 Dec   **Prices:** Fixed L £12.95, Starter £3.95-£9.95, Main £9.95-£22, Dessert £4.95-£8.50, Service optional, Group min 8 service 10%   **Notes:** Sun L 2 courses £12.95, 3 courses £14.95, Dress Restrictions, Smart casual   **Children:** Menu, Portions   **Rooms:** 9 (9 en suite) ★★★   SHL   **Directions:** From A814 follow signs to Coulport, then take sharp left at rdbt and continue for 2m along Shore Rd

SCOTLAND

◉◉◉
Isle of Eriska

ERISKA

MAP 20 NM94

British ⬥ NOTABLE WINE LIST 🍷

Flawless blend of service, style and good food in luxurious surroundings

☎ 01631 720371   PA37 1SD

e-mail: office@eriska-hotel.co.uk
web: www.eriska-hotel.co.uk

It's hard to beat the Isle of Eriska as a destination. First, it's a private island with stunning sea views and amazing sunsets. Linked to the mainland by a causeway, it has a remote and secluded feel that belies its proximity to Glasgow and Edinburgh. Secondly, there's the house - a Scottish baronial pile decorated in an opulent yet tasteful style with rich colours, heavy curtains and plenty of dark, polished wood. Not to mention the thoroughly modern addition of a luxurious spa.
The restaurant continues the fine balance of old-school formality and current dining sensibilities with highly professional staff offering knowledgeable and friendly service, particularly the sommelier. The menu is modern, utilising some of the finest Scottish produce. Seared dried Mull scallops with lobster charlotte, tomato and vanilla dressing and fine bean salad, followed by crisp duck breast, rillette pithivier, sweet red onions and thyme leaf jus are good examples of what's on offer on the daily-changing menu, with a hot chocolate madeleine,

home-grown rhubarb compôte and gingerbread ice cream to finish. An impressive wine list pays due reverence to the memorable cuisine. Don't miss the badgers that come to feed at the terrace door in the evening.

Chef: Robert MacPherson   **Owners:** Mr Buchanan-Smith   **Times:** 12.30-1.30/8-9, Closed Jan   **Prices:** Fixed D £39.50, Service optional   **Wine:** 10 by the glass   **Notes:** Fixed D 4 courses, Dress Restrictions, Jacket & tie, Civ Wed 110, Air con   **Seats:** 40, Pr/dining room 20   **Children:** Menu, Portions   **Rooms:** 17 (17 en suite) ★★★★★   CHH   **Directions:** A82 from Glasgow to Tyndrum. A85 towards Oban; at Connel bridge take A828 to Benderloch village for 4m   **Parking:** 50

SCOTLAND

ERISKA   MAP 20 NM94

◉◉◉ Isle of Eriska

see page 573

KILCHRENAN   MAP 20 NN02

◉◉ The Ardanaiseig Hotel

French, British

An idyllic lochside location, with a rugged romantic feel and awesome food

☎ 01866 833333   by Loch Awe PA35 1HE
e-mail: info@ardanaiseig.com
web: www.ardanaiseig.com

The reward for a beautiful, long and winding drive down a single-track road is this early Victorian mansion, gloriously located on the shores of Loch Awe, amid truly breathtaking scenery. Interiors are very much in keeping with the period, with gorgeous antiques and fine art, all very understated and uncluttered. The kitchen produces innovative food, skilfully and faultlessly cooked with good use made of local produce. Dinner is a complete experience with little surprise extras really rounding off the meal - your five courses might include monkfish with champagne sauce, duck breast with Puy lentils, artichoke purée and truffle jus, followed by a perfect rhubarb soufflé with ginger anglaise, and delicious home-made petits fours. Exquisite.

Times: 12-2/7-9, Closed 2 Jan- 10 Feb   **Rooms:** 16 (16 en suite) ★★★ CHH   **Directions:** Take A85 to Oban. At Taynuilt turn left onto B845 towards Kilchrenan. In Kilchrenan turn left by pub. Hotel in 3m

◉◉ Taychreggan Hotel

British

Imaginative dining in Highland country house

☎ 01866 833211 833366   PA35 1HQ
e-mail: info@taychreggan.co.uk
web: www.taychregganhotel.co.uk

Good technique and high-quality ingredients distinguish the cooking at this comfortable country-house hotel, which has an enviable location on the shores of Loch Awe. A former old cattle drovers' inn, it's surrounded by stunning Highland scenery, and offers picture-perfect views from the arched windows of its elegant dining room. Service is courteous and winningly old fashioned, but the food is a more contemporary affair with dishes making extensive use of Scottish and locally sourced ingredients. Start with home-smoked salmon with a toasted pine nut and parsley risotto, parsnip crisps and red pepper

syrup, before tucking into baked fillets of sea bass with saffron potatoes and a black olive and herb butter sauce.

Times: 7.30-8.45   **Rooms:** 20 (20 en suite) ★★★ CHH   **Directions:** W from Glasgow on A82 to Crainlarich. W on A85 to Taynuilt. On B845 to Kilchrenan & Taychreggan

LOCHGILPHEAD   MAP 20 NR88

◉ Cairnbaan

British, European

Canal-side dining

☎ 01546 603668   Crinan Canal, Cairnbaan PA31 8SJ
e-mail: info@cairnbaan.com
web: www.cairnbaan.com

Delightfully located small hotel on the Crinan Canal, with wide picture windows making the most of the views. While alfresco dining is popular in the warmer months, winter is made cosy by the tartan décor in the restaurant, and a wealth of creature comforts. Fresh seafood is a powerful draw throughout the seasons, though it's not an exclusively fish-based menu. Smoked mackerel salad or haggis, neeps and tatties might kick things off, followed by deep-fried Tarbert haddock with chips or steak and ale pie. Maybe try the traditional Scottish pudding of Cranachan accompanied by hazelnut shortbread.

Times: 12-2.30/6-9.30   **Rooms:** 12 (12 en suite) ★★★ HL
Directions: Cairnbaan is 2m N of Lochgilphead on A83. Hotel first on left

LUSS   MAP 20 NS39

◉◉ Colquhoun's

Modern British

Stunning loch views and imaginative cuisine

☎ 01436 860201   The Lodge on Loch Lomond, Hotel & Restaurant G83 8PA
e-mail: res@loch-lomondhotel.co.uk
web: www.loch-lomond.co.uk

Set amidst some of Scotland's most idyllic and unspoilt areas, Colquhoun's is The Lodge on Loch Lomond's fine-dining venue, enjoying breathtaking, undisturbed views over the Loch. The newly refurbished restaurant has a Scandinavian-style décor of pinewood walls and pillars blended with traditional Scottish décor, and an open-plan split-level bar. Service is relaxed and friendly, and in summer guests can dine alfresco on the balconied terrace. The cuisine is modern British with strong Scottish influences, using fresh local produce. For starters, perhaps take braised ox cheek with lightly smoked spring onion and butter risotto, followed by a main course of grilled sea bream with French beans and artichokes. Finish off with a delicious warm honey and ginger pudding and lemon ice cream.

Colquhoun's

Chef: Donn Eadie **Owners:** Niall Colquhoun **Times:** 12-5/6-9.45 **Prices:** Fixed L £14.95-£16.95, Fixed D £32.95-£38.90, Starter £8-£9.95, Main £16.95-£22.90, Dessert £8-£9.95, Service optional **Wine:** 19 bottles over £20, 16 bottles under £20, 7 by the glass **Notes:** Civ Wed 100 **Seats:** 100, Pr/dining room 40 **Children:** Menu, Portions **Rooms:** 47 (47 en suite) ★★★ HL **Directions:** N of Glasgow on A82 **Parking:** 70

OBAN   MAP 20 NM82

◉ *Bachler's Conservatory*

French, International

Sophisticated dining overlooking Oban Bay

☎ 01631 571115 13 Dalriach Rd PA34 5EQ
e-mail: info@kimberley-hotel.com
web: www.kimberley-hotel.com

The stunning Bachler's Conservatory restaurant overlooks the garden, the harbour and the waters of Oban Bay, with a sophisticated décor of green tablecloths, red striped seating and plenty of fresh flowers. The building was a maternity hospital until 1995, and the hotel name is linked to the South African Kimberley Diamond Mine. The cooking has a distinctly modern French flair but the ingredients are decidedly top-of-the-range Scottish. Seafood straight from the sea is a strength (monkfish roasted in herbal butter with leaf spinach), but local game (roasted venison) and meat (Aberdeen Angus beef and Scottish lamb) are well represented too.

Times: 6-10, Closed Nov-Etr, Closed L all week **Rooms:** 14 (14 en suite) ★★ **Directions:** Telephone for directions

◉ *Eeusk*

Seafood

Impeccably fresh seafood and unrestricted sea views

☎ 01631 565666 North Pier PA34 5QD
e-mail: eeusk.fishcafe@virgin.net

In a fantastic location, right on one of Oban's piers, Eeusk is a modern building with large glass windows and unrestricted views of the bay and islands. The pier is busy with fishermen and visitors, so it's an interesting place to eat with plenty to see. Simple cooking makes the best of fine fresh produce, with a natural emphasis on local seafood. Recommendations include oven-baked wild halibut with creamed leeks, creamy smoked haddock chowder, or a seafood platter comprising oysters, langoustine, mussels, a scallop and fresh smoked salmon.

Chef: Wayne Keenan **Owners:** The Macleod Family **Times:** 12-2.30/ 6-9.30, Closed 25-26 Dec, 1 Jan, 2 wks mid Jan **Prices:** Starter £3.95-£9.95, Main £10.95-£19.95, Dessert £4.25-£6.95, Service optional, Group min 10 service 8% **Notes:** Vegetarian available **Seats:** 100, Pr/dining room 24 **Children:** Min 10 yrs D, Portions **Directions:** Close to ferry terminal **Parking:** Public car park at rear

◉ **Manor House Hotel**

Traditional European

Quality produce and classical elegance by the sea

☎ 01631 562087 Gallanach Rd PA34 4LS
e-mail: info@manorhouseoban.com
web: www.manorhouseoban.com

The dower house of the Duke of Argyll, dating from around 1780, stands overlooking the harbour. It admirably preserves the elegance of its bygone days, and the small dining room has great country-house appeal with deep green walls and heavy curtains. The kitchen makes fine use of local produce on a daily five-course dinner menu. Typical dishes are Loch Etive mussels in light Thai curry with coriander and coconut milk, and cutlet of West Coast lamb in a herb crust, with thyme jus, bacon and bean parcels and cauliflower roses.

Chef: Patrick Freytag, Shaun Squire **Owners:** Mr P L Crane **Times:** 12-3/9-12, Closed 25-26 Dec **Prices:** Fixed D £32.50, Starter £7, Main £14-£18, Dessert £7, Service optional **Wine:** 30 bottles over £20, 26 bottles under £20, 8 by the glass **Notes:** Fixed D 5 courses, Vegetarian available, Dress Restrictions, Smart casual **Seats:** 30 **Children:** Min 12 yrs, Portions **Rooms:** 11 (11 en suite) ★★★ HL **Directions:** 300 mtrs W of Oban ferry terminal **Parking:** 20

SCOTLAND

PORT APPIN   MAP 20 NM94

◉◉◉ Airds Hotel and Restaurant

see below

STRACHUR   MAP 20 NN00

◉ Creggans Inn

Modern British

Local produce showcased in spectacular lochside setting

☎ 01369 860279   PA27 8BX

e-mail: info@creggans-inn.co.uk

web: www.creggans-inn.co.uk

Set on the doorstep of some of the most remote and unspoilt countryside in Scotland, this delightful hotel boasts a picture-perfect location on the shores of Loch Fyne. Stunning views, open fires and a restaurant that showcases local produce make it a destination venue for tourists and business travellers alike. The dining room boasts stripped floors, terracotta walls and fabulous views. Scottish dishes predominate on a menu that offers hand-dived scallops as a starter, with mussels and a saffron cream sauce, followed perhaps by chicken served with baby haggis, mustard mash and a beetroot jus, and dark chocolate marquise with a blueberry coulis.

Chef: Calum Williamson   **Owners:** The Robertson Family   **Times:** 7-9, Closed 25-26 Dec, Closed L all week   **Prices:** Fixed D £32, Service optional **Wine:** 32 bottles over £20, 33 bottles under £20, 6 by the glass **Notes:** Fixed D 4 courses, Dress Restrictions, Smart casual   **Seats:** 35 **Children:** Min 8 yrs, Menu, Portions   **Rooms:** 14 (14 en suite) ★★★ HL **Directions:** From Glasgow A82, along Loch Lomond, then W on A83, onto

A815 to Strachur. Or by ferry from Gourock to Dunoon onto A815 **Parking:** 25

TIGHNABRUAICH   MAP 20 NR97

◉◉ An Lochan

Modern Scottish V ☺

Fresh seafood and game beside the loch

☎ 01700 811239   Shore Rd PA21 2BE

e-mail: info@anlochan.co.uk

web: www.anlochan.co.uk

Just yards from the loch shore, this family-run hotel offers jaw-dropping views over the waters of the Kyles of Bute from a choice of dining areas. The fine-dining Crustacean restaurant has an intimate, candlelit buzz, while there's a more relaxed brasserie-bar option, too. The modern Scottish approach has seafood at its heart and native produce its soul - with suppliers named. Seafood straight from the nets, game, or beef from the Duke of Buccleuch Estate are treated with integrity, the intelligently simple, accurate approach letting the quality, fresh produce do the talking. Start with salmon ballotine and follow on with sea bass with langoustines, saffron linguini and pea and parsley velouté. A Land and Sea tasting menu is available.

Chef: R McKie, L McKie   **Owners:** McKie Family   **Times:** 12-2.30/6-9 **Prices:** Fixed D £37.50, Starter £5-£9, Main £14-£21, Dessert £4-£9, Service optional   **Wine:** 50 bottles over £20, 14 bottles under £20, 6 by the glass **Notes:** Fixed D 4 courses, Vegetarian menu   **Seats:** 35, Pr/dining room 20 **Children:** Portions   **Rooms:** 11 (11 en suite) ★★★ SHL   **Directions:** From Strachur, on A886, turn right onto A8003 to Tighnabruaich. Hotel on right at bottom of hill. Dunoon ferry terminal take left onto B8000   **Parking:** 20

◉◉◉

Airds Hotel and Restaurant

PORT APPIN   MAP 20 NM94

Modern British V 🍷NOTABLE WINE LIST

Lochside gastronomic treat

☎ 01631 730236   PA38 4DF

e-mail: airds@airds-hotel.com

web: www.airds-hotel.com

Originally an 18th-century ferry inn, this small, luxury hotel sits at the edge of the waters of the Sound of Lismore with stunning views of Loch Linnhe. Inside, country-house comfort meets modern chic in a relaxed, intimate atmosphere. The sumptuous lounges are replete with cosy couches, log fires and interesting artwork, while the restaurant continues the theme with designer fabrics, candlelit tables and large windows to take advantage of the views. Service is highly professional, but retains a personal and welcoming touch, while the cooking takes a modern approach imbued with a Scottish twist. Tip-top ingredients are treated with due respect, the kitchen's intelligently simple, clean-cut style and uncomplicated combinations allowing the flavours of key ingredients to shine on the daily-changing, fixed-price menus. Try an assiette of cured local fish with a horseradish chantilly and sweet dill dressing as a starter, followed perhaps by roast loin of Scottish lamb and Stornoway black pudding with root vegetable Anna and Madeira sauce, or braised fillet of brill and scallops with wilted spinach and a vermouth velouté.

Chef: J Paul Burns   **Owners:** Mr & Mrs S McKivragan   **Times:** 12-1.45/7.30-9, Closed 12-30 Jan   **Prices:** Fixed D £49.50, Starter £3.50-£7.50, Main £13.50-£17.50, Dessert £7.50, Service optional   **Wine:** 140 bottles over £20, 5 bottles under £20, 6 by the glass   **Notes:** Fixed D 4 courses, Gourmet menu 7 courses £70, Vegetarian menu, Dress Restrictions, Smart casual at D, no jeans/trainers/T-shirts, Civ Wed 40   **Seats:** 36   **Children:** Min 8 yrs, Menu, Portions   **Rooms:** 11 (11 en suite)★★★★ HL   **Directions:** A828 Oban to Fort William road follow signs for Port Appin. Continue for 2.5m, Airds Hotel on left   **Parking:** 20

AYRSHIRE, EAST

SORN MAP 20 NS52

◉◉ The Sorn Inn

Modern British
Refurbished coaching inn offering modern cuisine

☎ 01290 551305 35 Main St KA5 6HU
e-mail: craig@sorninn.com
web: www.sorninn.com

A late 18th-century coaching inn on the outside, but bang up-to-date on the inside, with modern styling and a warm, rustic colour scheme throughout. There are two dining options, the more informal Chop House for bistro-style food in a cosy pub area and the fine-dining restaurant with its comfy leather seats and interesting artwork. Here you will find modern British cooking with the emphasis on fresh produce from the abundant local larder, including game, meat and fish. Expect pan-fried halibut served with saffron pasta, a black olive tapenade sauce and red pepper compôte, or perhaps a pavé of Scottish beef with confit new potatoes, creamed Savoy cabbage, wild mushrooms and a smoked garlic jus.

Chef: Craig Grant **Owners:** The Grant Partnership **Times:** 12-2.30/6.30-9.30, Closed 2 wks Jan, Mon, Closed D Sun **Prices:** Fixed L £12.95, Fixed D £21-£25, Service optional **Wine:** 34 bottles over £20, 28 bottles under £20, 13 by the glass **Notes:** Tasting menu available **Seats:** 42
Children: Menu, Portions **Rooms:** 4 (4 en suite) ★★★★ RR
Directions: From A77, take the A76 to Mauchline join B743, 4m to Sorn
Parking: 9

AYRSHIRE, NORTH

DALRY MAP 20 NS24

◉◉ Braidwoods

Modern Scottish
Creative flair in a beautiful setting

☎ 01294 833544 Drumastle Mill Cottage KA24 4LN
e-mail: keithbraidwood@btconnect.com
web: www.braidwoods.co.uk

This charming group of old millers' cottages, transformed into a modern-looking restaurant with two dining rooms, offers rustic dining in a relaxed yet formal environment. A popular venue for 'ladies who lunch', but equally a romantic setting for dinner. Skilled cooking by the chef-patron brings modern Scottish dishes of high quality and good value to the menu. Try a starter of smoked chicken, prawn and avocado salad with garlic and anchovy dressing. Main courses might include the likes of whole roasted boneless quail stuffed with black pudding or baked fillet of West Coast turbot on smoked salmon risotto. To finish, try vanilla pannacotta with passionfruit, pineapple and mango soup.

Times: 12-1.45/7-9, Closed 25-26 Dec, 1st 3 wks Jan, 1st 2 wks Sep, Mon, Closed L Tue (Sun Etr-Sep), D Sun **Directions:** 1 mile from Dalry on the Saltcoats road

AYRSHIRE, SOUTH

AYR MAP 20 NS32

◉◉ Enterkine Country House

Traditional NEW
Classic Scottish cuisine offering the best from the local and national larder

☎ 01292 520580 Annbank KA6 5AL
e-mail: mail@enterkine.com
web: www.enterkine.com

Positioned within its own 350-acre estate with views over woodland, meadows and the Ayr Valley, the restaurant itself is a large, open-plan room with low ceilings, a blazing fire in winter and Shaker-style panelling. The style of cooking is traditional country house with Scottish produce featuring heavily, cooked and presented in a modern fashion. For starters, why not try Scottish lobster and goat's cheese soufflé served with baby spinach, red pepper compôte and Meaux mustard, followed by a succulent fillet of organic Buccleuch beef for mains, served with parsnip purée, braised oxtail, spinach and a Madeira sauce. Wickedly tempting desserts include the likes of warm Valrhona chocolate fondant with stem ginger ice cream, or go for the savoury option and sample the selection of Scottish and French cheeses.

Chef: Paul Moffat **Owners:** Mr Browne **Times:** 12-2/7-9 **Prices:** Fixed L £16.50-£18.50, Fixed D £29.95-£45, Service optional **Wine:** 36 bottles over £20, 14 bottles under £20, 4 by the glass **Notes:** Fixed D 4 courses, Vegetarian available, Dress Restrictions, Jacket, Civ Wed 70 **Seats:** 40, Pr/dining room 12 **Children:** Menu, Portions **Rooms:** 6 (6 en suite) ★★★ CHH **Directions:** 5m E of Ayr on B743 **Parking:** 20

◉◉ Fairfield House Hotel

Traditional British
Modern, relaxed dining and great views

☎ 01292 267461 12 Fairfield Rd KA7 2AS
e-mail: reservations@fairfieldhotel.co.uk
web: www.fairfieldhotel.co.uk

Once home to a Glasgow tea merchant, this luxury seafront hotel has spectacular views across the Firth of Clyde to the Isle of Arran. Martins Bar and Grill has leather seating, Grecian-style pillars, feature plants and original artwork across the bar and restaurant areas, plus an outside deck making the most of the views. The cuisine style is simple using local produce to create Scottish dishes with a twist. Try scallops with a cauliflower cream and whisky caramel, followed by fillet of sea

SCOTLAND

CONTINUED

AYR CONTINUED

bass with sweet potato, mussels and lemon broth. Finish, perhaps, with chocolate pudding soufflé. There is a wide selection of fine wines, plus a good collection of single malts.

Chef: Charles Hilton **Owners:** G Martin **Times:** 11-9.30 **Prices:** Fixed L £12-£15, Fixed D £25, Starter £3.95-£9.95, Main £9.95-£22.95, Dessert £4.95-£7.95, Service optional **Wine:** 34 bottles over £20, 16 bottles under £20, 6 by the glass **Notes:** Vegetarian available, Civ Wed 150, Air con **Seats:** 80, Pr/dining room 12 **Children:** Menu, Portions **Rooms:** 44 (44 en suite) ★★★★ HL **Directions:** From A77 to Ayr South. Follow signs for town centre. Left into Miller Rd. At lights turn left, then right into Fairfield Rd **Parking:** 50

see advert opposite

Fouters

Rosettes not confirmed at time of going to press

French, Scottish

Intimate basement restaurant and ambitious cooking

☎ 01292 261391 2A Academy St KA7 1HS
e-mail: chef@fouters.co.uk
web: www.fouters.co.uk

It's easy to miss, along a cobbled lane, down a flight of steps to a series of intimate cellar rooms that once operated as a bank vault in the 18th century. The vaulted ceiling, flagstone floors, linen-clothed tables and colourful local seascapes give this family-run place an appealing atmosphere, and the service is relaxed and friendly. Fish landed at the local quay and meat and game from the surrounding hills are skilfully handled and the cooking honest and unpretentious, allowing the fresh flavours to shine through. As we went to press a change of chef and ownership had taken place.

Chef: George Ramage **Owners:** Tom Harwood, George Ramage **Times:** 12-2/6-9, Closed 2 wks Feb, 2 wks Nov, 1 Jan, Sun-Mon **Prices:** Fixed L £9.95, Starter £3.75-£7.95, Main £13.50-£21.95, Dessert £5.50-£5.65, Service optional **Wine:** 22 bottles over £20, 10 bottles under £20, 3 by the glass **Notes:** Tasting menu available Tue-Thu, Vegetarian available, Air con **Seats:** 36, Pr/dining room 22 **Children:** Min 5-10 yrs, Portions **Directions:** Town centre, opposite Town Hall, down Cobblestone Lane **Parking:** On street

◉ The Western House Hotel

Traditional British NEW

Race-goers' haven with winning formula and accomplished cuisine

☎ 0870 055 5510 2 Craigie Rd KA8 0HA
e-mail: msimpson@ayr-racecourse.co.uk
web: www.ayr-racecourse.co.uk

Set in attractive gardens, this impressive hotel proves a winner with horserace lovers, as it comes perched on the edge of Ayr racecourse. Light and airy, yet with an intimate note, its half oak-panelled restaurant is appropriately decked out with plenty of equestrian pictures, while dining to the backdrop of race-meeting action only adds to the atmosphere, with views over the parade ring and part of the course. The cooking is a sure bet too, the modern approach takes an intelligently straightforward approach; think Burns House smoked salmon with caviar starter, then halibut with garlic herb mash and mushrooms.

Chef: Charles Price **Owners:** Alan MacDonald, Richard Johnstone **Times:** 12.30-2/7-9.30 **Prices:** Fixed L £14-£16, Fixed D £21-£26, Starter £5-£6, Main £14-£21, Dessert £4-£5, Service optional **Wine:** 12 bottles over £20, 21 bottles under £20, 4 by the glass **Notes:** Vegetarian available, Dress Restrictions, Smart casual, Air con **Seats:** 40, Pr/dining room 60 **Children:** Portions **Rooms:** 49 (49 en suite) ★★★★ HL **Parking:** 200

BALLANTRAE MAP 20 NX08

◉◉◉ Glenapp Castle

see opposite

TROON MAP 20 NS33

◉◉◉ Lochgreen House

see page 580

◉◉ MaccCallums of Troon

Modern International

Seafood restaurant in a working harbour

☎ 01292 319339 The Harbour KA10 6DH

One-time pump house turned spacious modern restaurant with a stunning harbourside location, where you can see the fishing fleet come and go. The tasteful interior resembles a spacious boathouse, with high-raftered ceilings and walls brimful of memorabilia of the America's Cup. Wooden floors and darkwood tables and chairs add to the relaxed atmosphere, while service is friendly from smart, apron-clad staff. Expect a menu awash with fish from a kitchen confident enough to take a simple approach and let the freshness of its produce shine through. Chargrilled tuna is a typical main, served with mango and chilli lime salsa, or perhaps seared scallops with celeriac purée and truffle dressing.

Chef: Ewan McAllister, Adele Wylie **Owners:** John & James MacCallums **Times:** 12-2.30/6.30-9.30, Closed Xmas, New Year, Mon, Closed D Sun **Prices:** Starter £3.95-£8.95, Main £8.50-£26.50, Dessert £4.85-£5.85, Service optional, Group min 12 service 10% **Wine:** 9 bottles over £20, 17 bottles under £20, 4 by the glass **Seats:** 43 **Children:** Portions **Directions:** Please telephone for directions **Parking:** 12

TURNBERRY   MAP 20 NS20

◉ *Malin Court*

Scottish

Modern cooking with views of the Firth of Clyde

☎ 01655 331457   KA26 9PB
e-mail: info@malincourt.co.uk
web: www.malincourt.co.uk

Malin Court is situated beside the famous Turnberry golf course with views of the Kintyre courses. The hotel's restaurant, Cotters, has lounge areas, a real fire in the cooler months and wonderful views along the coast. A good-value lunch and supper menu is offered and a set six-course dinner including canapés and coffee. Modern British dishes are presented alongside traditional Scottish fare, all using quality local ingredients. Typical of these are mussels cooked in a saffron and coriander cream, and beef fillet with mustard dauphinoise, roasted tomatoes and onion confit.

Times: 12.30-2/7-9   **Rooms:** 18 (18 en suite) ★★★   HL   **Directions:** On A719 one mile from A77 on N side of village

◉◉◉

Glenapp Castle

BALLANTRAE   MAP 20 NX08

Modern British V

Elegant castle hideaway offering accomplished, innovative cuisine

☎ 01465 831212   KA26 0NZ
e-mail: info@glenappcastle.com
web: www.glenappcastle.com

Beautifully restored in recent years by Fay and Graham Cowan, this private castle dates back to 1870 and nowadays offers the perfect luxury retreat. The 30 acres of gardens and woodland are well worth exploring, and guests at the castle can enjoy the terraced formal gardens, azalea pond and walled garden with impressive 150ft Victorian glasshouses.
The dining room takes diners back to an age of elegance with its beautiful proportions, stately window dressings and immaculately clothed tables. The chef excels himself to produce an original and imaginative set six-course dinner menu each day, demonstrating a superb blend of traditional and modern cuisine. Skilful cooking brings out the best in high quality ingredients with seasonal garnishes and plenty of traditional Scottish produce. Where else could you find a menu interspersed with combinations like a ballotine of organic Loch Duart salmon with potato mousse and horseradish dressing, or a nage of locally caught halibut with Jerusalem artichokes and cucumber. Sublime desserts include the likes of tiramisù with white coffee ice cream. A simple lunch menu, on the other hand, offers a variety of dishes with some offered as a starter or main course portion.

Chef: Matt Weedon   **Owners:** Graham & Fay Cowan   **Times:** 12.30-2/7-9.30, Closed 2 Jan-1 Apr, Xmas   **Prices:** Fixed D £55, Service optional   **Wine:** 200 bottles over £20, 8 by the glass   **Notes:** Fixed D 6 courses, Vegetarian menu, Civ Wed 40   **Seats:** 34, Pr/dining room 20   **Children:** Min 5 yrs, Menu, Portions   **Rooms:** 17 (17 en suite) ★★★★★ HL   **Directions:** Drive through Ballantrae, over bridge, 1st right - 1m to gates and lodge house   **Parking:** 20

Lochgreen House

TROON   **MAP 20 NS33**

Modern British

Winning country-house hotel and highly rated restaurant

☎ 01292 313343   Monktonhill Rd, Southwood KA10 7EN
e-mail: lochgreen@costleyhotels.co.uk
web: www.lochgreenhouse.co.uk

Sympathetically restored and extended, this imposing country-house hotel stands in 16 acres of beautifully tended grounds with views across golf links to the sea and Ailsa Craig. It has a solid reputation for good Scottish food and you can expect a welcoming atmosphere. The light-and-airy, formal Tapestry restaurant comes with a high vaulted ceiling, stunning chandeliers, namesake wall-hung tapestries and furniture to match, and overlooks the fountain garden. Andrew Costley's cooking is in the classic vein but with a modern approach, his accomplished kitchen's precise handling and finesse with the freshest seasonal produce from the abundant Scottish larder responsible for consistent results. Rich, clear flavours and artistic presentation abound in dishes like seared king scallops with a carrot, sultana and ginger salad and sauce d'épice, or a duo of roast breast of duckling and ravioli of confit leg, served with Puy lentils and a fried apple and prune jus. To finish, perhaps warm milk chocolate tart with pistachio ice cream and golden syrup. A stroll in the carefully tended gardens pre- or post-meal is a Lochgreen requisite.

Chef: Andrew Costley **Times:** 12-2.30/7-9.30 **Rooms:** 38 (38 en suite)★★★★ CHH **Directions:** From A77 follow signs for Prestwick Airport, take B749 to Troon, Lochgreen is situated on left 1m from junct

---

TURNBERRY CONTINUED

◉◉ The Westin Turnberry Resort Hotel

Traditional

Fine dining with coastal views across famous golf courses

☎ 01655 331000   KA26 9LT
e-mail: turnberry@westin.com
web: www.westin.com/turnberry

This imposing hotel is a celebrated resort destination and comes with all mod cons, including a golf academy, spa, and a range of eateries to suit every mood. Book ahead for a window table in the elegant Turnberry restaurant, which offers dramatic sunset views of the Isle of Arran and misty Mull of Kintyre, and make your choice from a traditional selection of classic dishes, or a six-course Cuisine Creative menu that features more innovative contemporary cuisine. The cooking is faultless and based around the finest local ingredients: seared scallops, for example, served with foie gras, rhubarb compôte and a chicory, lemon and chive salad, or pan-roast venison with creamed cauliflower, beetroot compôte and artichoke gnocchi.

Times: 7-10, Closed Xmas, Closed L Mon-Sun **Rooms:** 219 (219 en suite)★★★★★ HL **Directions:** Just off A77 S towards Stranraer, through Maybole. 2m after Kirkoswald turn right & follow signs for Turnberry. Hotel 0.5m on right

DUMFRIES & GALLOWAY

AUCHENCAIRN   **MAP 21 NX75**

◉◉ Balcary Bay Hotel

Modern French V   NOTABLE WINE LIST

Great food in a romantic setting

☎ 01556 640217 & 640311   DG7 1QZ
e-mail: reservations@balcary-bay-hotel.co.uk
web: www.balcary-bay-hotel.co.uk

Set beside the beautiful bay from which it takes its name, Balcary has a genteel air that belies its shady 17th-century origins as the headquarters of a local smuggling racket. Its elegant dining room teams stunning sea views with top-notch cooking, delivering a menu of modern French cuisine that consistently impresses. Simple dishes such as home-cured salmon with French beans and rösti potatoes provide a culinary safety net, but there's more complex fare to enjoy too from a kitchen with no shortage of imagination. So, caramelised halibut arrives with braised ox shin, leeks and a red wine butter sauce, while black coffee jelly is a star dessert, served with doughnuts, fudge ice cream and caramel walnuts. A good vegetarian selection is also available.

Balcary Bay Hotel

Chef: Martin Avey **Owners:** Graeme A Lamb & Family **Times:** 12-2/7-8.30, Closed early Dec-early Feb, Closed L prior booking only Mon-Sat **Prices:** Fixed D £31.75, Starter £5.25-£7.95, Main £15.25-£18.50, Dessert £6.25, Service optional **Wine:** 60 bottles over £20, 25 bottles under £20, 3 by the glass **Notes:** Fixed L 3 courses, Fixed D 4 courses, Sun L £16.50, Vegetarian menu **Seats:** 55 **Children:** Menu, Portions **Rooms:** 20 (20 en suite) ★★★ HL **Directions:** Situated on the A711 between Dalbeattie & Kirkcudbright. On reaching Auhencairn follow signs to Balcary along the shore rd for 2m **Parking:** 45

CASTLE DOUGLAS MAP 21 NX76

Carlo's

☎ 01556 503977 211 King St DG7 1DT

Family-run Italian offering familiar dishes from pizza to shellfish stew.

Designs

☎ 01556 504552 179 King St DG7 1DZ

A popular lunch spot below the shop of the same name. Food has an organic slant.

DUMFRIES MAP 21 NX97

◎◎ *The Linen Room*

Modern French 🍷 NOTABLE WINE LIST

Refreshingly unpretentious restaurant with imaginative food

☎ 01387 255689 53 St. Michael St DG1 2QB

e-mail: enquiries@linenroom.com

web: www.linenroom.com

Just a short stroll from the centre of town, The Linen Room's décor is striking in its simplicity - black walls and carpet setting off fresh white table linen, white cushioned captain's-style chairs and black-and-white framed prints dotting the walls. Fine dining certainly, but refreshingly unpretentious with friendly, relaxed and informed service. The innovative cuisine makes good use of local seasonal produce in well-presented modern French dishes that reveal strong flavours and a light touch. Take a starter of hand-dived scallops with white onion, rocket hot shot, crunchy mushrooms and cep vinaigrette, followed by seared sea bass with salt cod brandade, mussels and tarragon, and to finish off, 'obsession in chocolate MkII'. Two tasting menus and a comprehensive wine list complete an assured package.

Times: 12.30-2.30/7-10, Closed 25 & 26 Dec, 1 & 2 Jan, 2 wks in Jan & Oct, Mon

---

◎ *Reivers Restaurant*

British, International

Interesting dishes based on local Borders produce

☎ 01387 254111 Cairndale Hotel & Leisure Club, English St DG1 2DF

e-mail: sales@cairndalehotel.co.uk

web: www.cairndalehotel.co.uk

Reivers Restaurant is named after the Border Reivers, telling the story of ongoing feuds between Scottish clans and English families either side of the border between the 13th and 17th centuries. The menu is firmly based around local produce, with some interesting combinations of ingredients. For a starter try a salad of marinated strips of Solway salmon, or maybe Isle of Skye scallops with a cauliflower pannacotta, while main courses might feature suprême of chicken stuffed with sundried tomato mousseline in a chive and vermouth sauce. Desserts like honeycomb brûlée, or lemon and vanilla pannacotta might prove too tempting to resist.

Times: 7-9.30, Closed Sun & Mon, Closed L Tue-Sat **Rooms:** 91 (91 en suite) ★★★ HL **Directions:** Telephone for directions

---

ESKDALEMUIR MAP 21 NY29

◎ Hart Manor

British

Wholesome country cooking in an idyllic setting

☎ 013873 73217 DG13 0QQ

e-mail: visit@hartmanor.co.uk

web: www.hartmanor.co.uk

An ideal base for hill walking, photography or a spot of golf, this immaculate former shooting lodge lies on a wooded hillside near a peaceful rural hamlet. Owners John and Kathleen Leadbeater ensure a warm welcome and hearty British country cooking; dishes are made to order using fresh, local ingredients - breakfasts are to die for. Starters include roasted red pepper and tomato soup, while typical mains include a melt-in-the-mouth roasted leg of lamb served with apricot and thyme stuffing and a hint of Glayva, or a comforting butter-baked haddock fillet with cream and parsley sauce. Don't miss the wonderful sherry-laden trifle.

Chef: Kathleen Leadbeater **Owners:** John & Kathleen Leadbeater **Times:** 7-7.30, Closed Xmas & New Year **Prices:** Fixed D £30 **Notes:** Fixed D 4 courses **Seats:** 12, Pr/dining room 10 **Children:** Min 10 yrs **Rooms:** 5 (5 en suite) ★★★★★ GA **Directions:** From M74 junct 17 follow signs for Eskdalemuir. Approx 14m. Through Eskdalemuir village, hotel approx 1m left on road to Langholm **Parking:** 10

SCOTLAND

GATEHOUSE OF FLEET   MAP 20 NX55

◉ Cally Palace Hotel

Traditional

Quality British cuisine in a grand setting

☎ 01557 814341   DG7 2DL
e-mail: info@callypalace.co.uk
web: www.callypalace.co.uk

Dating back to 1763 and set in 150 acres of woodland, this country manor is an imposing dinner destination. The opulent décor befits its stately past. The menu is concise, but changes daily and puts a winning emphasis on quality local ingredients, particularly fish. Expect British cooking; a starter of avocado, blue swimmer crab and crayfish salad, followed by pan-fried Scottish salmon served on fennel risotto, with spinach and barigoule sauce perhaps. Those with a sweet tooth should leave room for desserts such as strawberry and mascarpone cheesecake on a honeycomb base, or warm chocolate brownies with pistachio ice cream and chocolate sauce.

Times: 12-1/6.45-9, Closed 3 Jan-early Feb   **Rooms:** 55 (55 en suite) ★★★★ HL   **Directions:** From A74(M) take A75, at Gatehouse take B727. Hotel on left

KIRKBEAN   MAP 21 NX95

◉ Cavens

British, French

Hearty cooking at a country-house hideaway

☎ 01387 880234   DG2 8AA
e-mail: enquiries@cavens.com
web: www.cavens.com

Built in 1752 by a Glasgow tobacco baron with strong links to Robert Burns, this cosy country-house hotel is set in landscaped gardens not far from Dumfries and has just eight bedrooms. The dining room is an intimate affair with a limited number of well-spaced tables, making reservations essential. Expect a concise set menu of dinner-party fare, with a choice of two dishes offered at each course plus alternatives on request, and a number of ingredients courtesy of local artisan producers. Starters might include pan-fried scallops with lime and vermouth, followed by sea bass roasted with white wine and fennel, with pannacotta for dessert, or cheeses from the Loch Arthur Estate.

Chef: A Fordyce **Owners:** A Fordyce **Times:** 7-8.30, Closed Dec-1 Mar, Closed L all week **Prices:** Food prices not confirmed for 2008. Please telephone for details **Notes:** Dress Restrictions, Smart casual, Civ Wed 100 **Seats:** 14, Pr/dining room 20 **Children:** Min 12 yrs **Rooms:** 6 (6 en suite) ★★ CHH **Directions:** From Kirkbean, follow signs for Cavens **Parking:** 20

LOCKERBIE   MAP 21 NY18

◉ Dryfesdale Country House Hotel

Modern British

Country-house hotel serving modern cuisine

☎ 01576 202427   DG11 2SF
e-mail: reception@dryfesdalehotel.co.uk
web: www.dryfesdalehotel.co.uk

Set in manicured gardens, this 18th-century former manse even has a helicopter landing site for those who want to arrive in style. The airy Kirkhill restaurant, which extends into an attractive terrace, boasts a grand piano in one corner and tables are covered in crisp linen. In the formal dining room, a wide choice of cuisine is available. Good-value dinners may include chicken liver and black pudding pâté, home-made gnocchi with peas and mint dressed with a truffle sabayon and pear tart served with sultana anglaise and a mixed berry compôte.

Times: 12-2.30/6-9 **Rooms:** 16 (16 en suite) ★★★ HL **Directions:** M74 junct 17 (0.5m) to Lockerbie

MOFFAT   MAP 21 NT00

◉◉ Well View

Modern European V NEW

Intimate dining, lovely views and personal service

☎ 01683 220184   Ballplay Rd DG10 9JU
e-mail: johnwellview@aol.com
web: www.wellview.co.uk

As the name suggests, this nicely-appointed house - set in lovely gardens in a wonderful location on the Scottish Borders - offers those predicted outstanding views. Tastefully and traditionally decorated and furnished, it comes with many personal pieces. Service and attention to detail are key features, with the accomplished, traditionally-based fare personally cooked by the proprietors. The kitchen makes fine use of the abundant Scottish larder, with quality local produce a feature of the intimate restaurant's repertoire. Dining is dinner-party style with everyone seated around one large table. Take a starter of melon and home-cured gravad lax served with honey and mustard vinaigrette, and to follow, perhaps roast breast of partridge with coarse duck pâté wrapped in Parma ham and finished with a port wine and bramble jus. (Three well-presented bedrooms complete the package.)

Chef: Janet & Lina Schuckardt **Owners:** Janet & John Schuckardt **Times:** 12.30/7.30, Closed L Mon-Sat **Prices:** Fixed L £22, Fixed D £35, Service included **Notes:** Fixed L 3 courses, Fixed D 4 courses, Vegetarian menu, Dress Restrictions, Smart dress **Seats:** 10, Pr/dining room 10 **Children:** Min 6 yrs **Rooms:** 3 (3 en suite) ★★★★★ GA **Directions:** M74 junct 15, enter Moffat. Continue out of Moffat on A708 for 0.5m, turn left into Ballplay Rd, restaurant is 300 yds on right **Parking:** 4

NEWTON STEWART
MAP 20 NX46

◉◉ Kirroughtree House

Modern European V

Formal dining in Scottish mansion

☎ 01671 402141 Minnigaff DG8 6AN
e-mail: info@kirroughtreehouse.co.uk
web: www.kirroughtreehouse.co.uk

An imposing 18th-century mansion house in 8 acres of grounds where antiques and architectural features abound, including a 'modesty staircase' designed to hide a lady's ankles as she climbs the steps. Opulent, formal decoration extends to the dining rooms where good-quality china, linen and glassware combine with professional and friendly service. The chef seeks out local specialist suppliers to bring the best of Galloway's larder to his kitchen, such as Kirroughtree venison, Wigtown Bay wildfowl and Cairnsmore cheese. Otherwise, expect a breast of Gressingham duck served with fondant potato, turnips, spinach and a Cassis sauce, and to finish, perhaps a chocolate marquise with caramel sauce and vanilla ice cream.

Chef: Rolf Mueller **Owners:** Mr D McMillan **Times:** 12-1.30/7-9, Closed 2 Jan-mid Feb **Prices:** Fixed D £32.50, Starter £2.50-£5.50, Main £10.75-£15.25, Dessert £3.75-£4.50, Service optional **Wine:** 73 bottles over £20, 21 bottles under £20 **Notes:** Sun L 3 courses £16, Vegetarian menu, Dress Restrictions, Jacket must be worn after 6.30pm **Seats:** 45 **Children:** Min 10 yrs **Rooms:** 17 (17 en suite)★★★ HL **Directions:** From A75 turn onto A712 (New Galloway), hotel entrance 300 yds on left **Parking:** 50

PORTPATRICK
MAP 20 NW95

◉ Fernhill Hotel

British V

Conservatory restaurant with stunning views

☎ 01776 810220 Heugh Rd DG9 8TD
e-mail: info@fernhillhotel.co.uk
web: www.fernhillhotel.co.uk

Set high above the village of Portpatrick in secluded gardens, this smart hotel overlooks the harbour and the Irish Sea. An airy conservatory houses the restaurant, and with views across to the Irish coast on clear days, it's worth booking ahead for a window table. The concise menu changes daily and offers the likes of pan-fried lamb's liver with onion jam and pancetta followed by roast loin of Scottish venison with redcurrant jus. The selection of Scottish cheeses is particularly fine - or turn your attention to the sweet treats promised by the dessert menu.

Fernhill Hotel

Chef: Andrew Rankin **Owners:** McMillan Hotels **Times:** 12-1.45/6.30-9, Closed mid Jan-mid Feb **Prices:** Fixed L £13.50, Fixed D £32.50, Service included **Wine:** 17 bottles over £20, 38 bottles under £20, 3 by the glass **Notes:** Vegetarian menu, Dress Restrictions, No jeans or shorts, Civ Wed 40, Air con **Seats:** 70, Pr/dining room 24 **Children:** Menu, Portions **Rooms:** 36 (36 en suite) ★★★ HL **Directions:** A77 from Stranraer, right before war memorial. Hotel 1st left **Parking:** 45

◉◉◉ Knockinaam Lodge
see page 584

STRANRAER
MAP 20 NX06

◉ Corsewall Lighthouse Hotel

Modern Scottish V

Stunning lighthouse restaurant

☎ 01776 853220 Corsewall Point, Kirkcolm DG9 0QG
e-mail: info@lighthousehotel.co.uk
web: www.lighthousehotel.co.uk

This unique hotel is converted from buildings adjoining a listed 19th-century lighthouse. It offers dramatic views from its perch on the rocky coastline at the end of a single-track road. The daily-changing menu, served in the intimate restaurant, features local beef, lamb and seafood. Typical of the dishes offered are terrine of mixed coarse game from the Craufurdland Estate, enhanced with whisky, herbs and cream and served with oatcakes and chutney, followed by a main course of baked fillet of prime Shetland salmon finished in Pernod with tarragon-scented cream topped with Avruga caviar, or alternatively roast loin of Galloway lamb with a couscous timbale.

Chef: A Downie, D. McCubbin **Owners:** Gordon, Kay, & Pamela Ward **Times:** 12-2/7-9 **Prices:** Fixed L £10.60-£24.25, Starter £2.85-£5.75, Main £15.95-£19.50, Dessert £5.25, Service optional **Wine:** 4 by the glass **Notes:** Vegetarian menu, Dress Restrictions, Preferably no jeans, Civ Wed 28 **Seats:** 28 **Children:** Portions **Rooms:** 10 (10 en suite) ★★★ HL **Directions:** Take A718 from Stranraer to Kirkcolm, then follow B718 signposted Lighthouse **Parking:** 30

Knockinaam Lodge

PORTPATRICK   **MAP 20 NW95**

Modern Scottish V ▧ NOTABLE WINE LIST

Idyllic location with cooking of real grace and refinement

☎ 01776 810471   DG9 9AD

e-mail: reservations@knockinaamlodge.com

web: www.knockinaamlodge.com

Chef: Antony Pierce **Owners:** David & Sian Ibbotson **Times:** 12.30-2/7-9 **Prices:** Fixed L £37.50, Fixed D £50, Service optional **Wine:** 335 bottles over £20, 18 bottles under £20, 10 by the glass **Notes:** Fixed L 4 courses, Fixed D 5 courses, Vegetarian menu, Dress Restrictions, No jeans, Civ Wed 40 **Seats:** 32, Pr/dining room 18 **Children:** Min 12 yrs, Menu **Rooms:** 9 (9 en suite)★★★ HL **Directions:** From A75, follow signs to Portpatrick, follow tourist signs to Knockinaam Lodge **Parking:** 20

Set in glorious isolation in an idyllic cove with its own pebble beach, and sheltered by majestic cliffs and serene woodlands, this exquisite country-house hotel - a former Victorian lodge - has a simply stunning location. Conjuring up all the magic of a bygone era, the charming dining room overlooks the bay and is the perfect setting for modern Scottish cooking from a classically trained chef.

The precise cooking style tends to focus on one key element enhanced by complementary flavours, and presentation is kept succinct and unfussy. Many of the vegetables, herbs and flowers that adorn the dining room are home grown and are joined by locally-reared lamb, beef and game and seafood landed nearby. The six-course set menu gives a true overview of the cooking here: ravioli of veal sweetbreads with confit lemon, artichokes and thyme, and Luce Bay crab salad with citrus fruits and a beetroot vinaigrette, followed by jellied strawberry and champagne terrine with rosewater ice cream to finish.

De Vere Deluxe Cameron House

BALLOCH   **MAP 20 NS38**

Modern French

Fine dining on the shores of Loch Lomond

☎ 01389 755565   G83 8QZ

e-mail: reservations@cameronhouse.co.uk

web: www.devere.co.uk

scallops from the Sound of Mull or delicious Loch Fyne oysters, followed by a magnificent saddle of Scottish venison.

Owners: De Vere Hotels **Times:** 12-2.30/7-9.30, Closed Mon, Tue, Closed L Wed-Sat **Rooms:** 96 (96 en suite) ★★★★★ HL **Directions:** M8 junct 30, over toll bridge and follow signs for Loch Lomond (A82). Hotel is on right **Parking:** 250

Idyllically set on the shores of Loch Lomond, this elegant mansion boasts wonderful views and an array of facilities, including a spa and numerous restaurants. Built in the Scottish baronial style, it dates back to the 17th century and has played host to countless dignitaries, with Winston Churchill and Queen Victoria listed among former guests. Dinner in the elegant Lomonds restaurant offers a chance to sample the high-life; it's a traditional affair, decorated with chandeliers, rich fabrics and oil paintings, with well-spaced tables and pristine appointments. Despite the formality of the efficient service - the obligatory jacket and tie at dinner for gentlemen and staff clad in white gloves and starched aprons - there's a friendly, relaxed feel. The accomplished kitchen's modern approach, underpinned by a classical theme, works well with the surroundings, and makes fine use of the abundant, fresh local produce. Highly creative technical skills, precision and deft execution deliver a fixed-price repertoire that includes a six-course gourmet surprise menu. Expect diver-caught

SCOTLAND

STRANRAER Continued

🏵 North West Castle Hotel

British V

Family-run hotel with a traditional menu

☎ 01776 704413   DG9 8EH
e-mail: info@northwestcastle.co.uk
web: www.mcmillanhotels.com

This imposing manor house has two unexpected claims to fame, both of a chilly nature. Built in 1820 for the celebrated arctic explorer Sir John Ross, it was also the first hotel in the world to have its very own indoor curling rink. Its spacious dining room is decorated in traditional style with well-spaced tables and sparkling chandeliers, and is adjoined by a comfy lounge where you'll find a blazing fire in winter. The menu is in keeping with the setting and features mains such as fillet of Isle of Bute rainbow trout, with parsley-mashed potatoes and buttered spinach, followed by Scotch whisky and fruit tart with honey and whisky cream and vanilla ice cream.

Chef: Bruce McLean **Owners:** H C McMillan **Times:** 12-2/6.30-9 **Prices:** Fixed D £23.50, Starter £2.50-£4.95, Main £8-£15.85, Dessert £3, Service included **Wine:** 29 bottles over £20, 55 bottles under £20, 3 by the glass **Notes:** Vegetarian menu, Dress Restrictions, Smart casual, No jeans, Civ Wed 130 **Seats:** 130, Pr/dining room 180 **Children:** Menu, Portions **Rooms:** 72 (72 en suite) ★★★★ HL **Directions:** From Glasgow N take A77 to Stranraer. From S follow M6 to Gretna then A75 to Stranraer. Hotel in town centre opp ferry terminal **Parking:** 50

DUNBARTONSHIRE, WEST

BALLOCH   MAP 20 NS38

🏵🏵🏵 *De Vere Deluxe Cameron House*

see opposite

CLYDEBANK   MAP 20 NS47

🏵🏵 Arcoona at the Beardmore

Modern

Stylish modern dining on the banks of the Clyde

☎ 0141 951 6000   Beardmore Hotel, Beardmore St G81 4SA
e-mail: info@beardmore.scot.nhs.uk
web: www.thebeardmore.com

This impressive modern hotel on the banks of the Clyde offers fine dining in the newly refurbished Arcoona restaurant. The restaurant's name comes from a passenger ship built by William Beardmore & Co,

shipbuilders on the site in 1924. Décor is chic and stylish, while service is friendly and efficient. The menus focus on modern British and French-style cooking with classical elements - perhaps chicken liver parfait with gooseberry chutney, or roast rump of lamb with herb mash and pea cream sauce. Choose carefully as there are lots of extras like home-made vegetable crisps and warm nuts as well as a selection of great home-baked breads.

Arcoona at the Beardmore

Chef: Iain Ramsay **Owners:** Scottish Executive **Times:** 7-10, Closed Festive period, Sun, Mon, Closed L all week **Prices:** Starter £4.95-£8.95, Main £9.95-£22.75, Dessert £4.95-£8.95, Service optional **Wine:** 39 bottles over £20, 30 bottles under £20, 12 by the glass **Notes:** Civ Wed 174, Air con **Seats:** 60, Pr/dining room 16 **Children:** Min 12 yrs, Menu, Portions **Rooms:** 166 (166 en suite) ★★★★ HL **Directions:** M8 junct 19, follow signs for Clydeside Expressway to Glasgow road, then Dumbarton road (A814), then signs for Clydebank Business Park. Hotel on left **Parking:** 400

CITY OF DUNDEE

DUNDEE   MAP 21 NO43

🏵🏵 Alchemy Restaurant

Modern International

Creative cooking on the quayside

☎ 01382 202404   Apex City Quay Hotel & Spa,
1 West Victoria Dock Rd DD1 3JP
e-mail: reservations@alchemyrestaurant.co.uk
web: www.alchemyrestaurant.co.uk

The Apex City Quay is a stylish modern hotel at the heart of Dundee's regenerated quayside. Open-plan public areas offer panoramic views, while first-rate facilities include a decadent spa and range of restaurants. Alchemy is the hotel's fine-dining option with a modern menu based around quality Scottish produce. Dishes with an almost lyrical quality include lime-cured Scottish salmon with

CONTINUED

SCOTLAND

DUNDEE CONTINUED

buckwheat blinis to start, or an unusual roast four-carrot terrine with goat's cheese fondue, followed by a main course of Cairngorm venison loin with fig tartlet and beetroot emulsion. Finish with heather honey and lavender crème brûlée, or your choice of cheese with grape chutney, warm walnut loaf and oatcakes. Set Garden, Highland and Ocean tasting menus are also available.

Chef: Bruce Price **Owners:** Apex Hotels **Times:** 7-9.30, Closed 25 Dec-10 Jan, Sun-Mon, Closed L all week **Prices:** Fixed D £26, Service optional **Wine:** 1 bottle over £20, 1 bottle under £20, 4 by the glass **Notes:** 3 tasting menus available 4 courses £20-£28, Dress Restrictions, Smart casual, no jeans or T-shirts, Civ Wed 200 **Seats:** 30, Pr/dining room 12 **Children:** Min 14 yrs **Rooms:** 153 (153 en suite) ★★★★ HL **Directions:** A90 from Perth. A85 along riverside for 2m. With Discovery Quay on right, at rdbt follow signs for Aberdeen. At next rdbt turn right into city quay **Parking:** 150

CITY OF EDINBURGH

EDINBURGH   MAP 21 NT27

◉ Agua

Modern British NEW

Stylish, modern hotel bistro with food to match

☎ 0131 243 3456 Apex City Hotel, 61 Grassmarket EH1 2JF
e-mail: reservations@apexhotels.co.uk
web: www.apexhotels.co.uk

The stylish bistro here at the Apex City Hotel combines a popular bar with a lounge and dining room. Contemporary styling draws a hip crowd, and this theme is essentially carried through on the eye-catching menu that plays to the gallery with something for everyone; dishes allow for some mixing and matching and prices are competitively priced. Quality ingredients and light, clear flavours deliver in the likes of sea bream with fragrant rice and sweet-and-sour salsa, and a classic crème brûlée to finish. Friendly staff, keen to please, round off a consistent, modern-focused act.

Chef: John Paul Persighetti **Times:** 12-2/4-10, Closed 20-28 Dec **Prices:** Fixed D £10-£17, Starter £3.95-£6.95, Main £9.95-£17.95, Dessert £5.95, Service optional, Group min 8 service 10% **Wine:** 8 bottles over £20, 23 bottles under £20, 6 by the glass **Seats:** 60 **Children:** Menu **Rooms:** 119 (119 en suite) ★★★★ HL **Directions:** Continue towards W end of Princes St, at main junct turn into Lothian Rd, then turn left onto Kings Stables Rd which leads into Grassmarket **Parking:** 10

◉◉ Apex International Hotel

Modern Scottish NEW

Fabulous views and minimalist décor meet refined cooking

☎ 0131 300 3456 31/35 Grassmarket EH1 2HS
e-mail: reservations@apexhotels.co.uk
web: www.apexhotels.co.uk/eat

Located on the fifth floor of this boutique-styled hotel, the aptly-named Heights restaurant has panoramic views of Edinburgh Castle and across the city skyline. There are acres of glass and chrome, wood and marble, soft modern lighting and minimalist styling, while service

is sharp but friendly. The kitchen's concise carte has a modern approach that matches the surroundings and majors on quality ingredients from the Scottish larder, with plentiful seafood and game. Expect accomplished, refined and clear-flavoured dishes, like grilled carpaccio of lobster and Shetland scallop, seared John Dory with braised Black Angus ox cheek and celeriac mash, and a caramelised rice pudding finish, served with blueberry compôte.

Chef: John Paul Persighetti **Times:** 7-9.45, Closed Sun, Closed L all week **Prices:** Fixed D £22.50, Starter £6.50-£7.95, Main £15-£22.50, Dessert £5.95, Service optional **Wine:** 17 bottles over £20, 13 bottles under £20, 7 by the glass **Seats:** 85 **Rooms:** 171 (171 en suite) ★★★★ HL **Directions:** From Princes St turn into Lothian Rd and then King Stables Rd. Follow this road winding round the foot of the castle, then into Grassmarket **Parking:** 65

◉ The Atholl at The Howard Hotel

Modern British 🖥

Stylish townhouse with intimate dining room

☎ 0131 557 3500 34 Great King St EH3 6QH
e-mail: reception@thehoward.com
web: www.thehoward.com

Situated in a converted Georgian terraced townhouse near the city centre, there is an exclusive, clubby feel to this small, elegant restaurant. Before taking your place for dinner, why not peruse the menu over cocktails in the comfortable drawing room, and enjoy views over the wide cobbled streets. The kitchen delivers modern takes on classic dishes, taking in some traditional Scottish fare. Starters might include a terrine of duck foie gras with toasted pain de mie and peach chutney, followed perhaps by roast rump of Perthshire lamb with confit Mediterranean vegetables and a ravioli of its shoulder.

Chef: Steven Falconer **Owners:** Peter Taylor **Times:** 12-2/7-9, Closed 25 Dec **Prices:** Starter £6-£10.50, Main £15-£26, Dessert £6-£9, Service optional **Wine:** 40 bottles over £20, 6 bottles under £20, 10 by the glass **Notes:** Civ Wed 35 **Seats:** 18, Pr/dining room 40 **Children:** Portions **Rooms:** 18 (18 en suite) ★★★★ TH **Directions:** Telephone for directions **Parking:** 10

◉◉ Atrium

Modern Scottish 🏅 NOTABLE WINE LIST 🖥

Modish contemporary dining in the city centre

☎ 0131 228 8882 10 Cambridge St EH1 2ED
e-mail: eat@atriumrestaurant.co.uk
web: www.atriumrestaurant.co.uk

An atmospheric haunt in the heart of the city, this renowned Edinburgh restaurant is a chic, upmarket dining destination. Canvas and copper make for a warm and quirky décor, while candlelight flickers in the surfaces of darkwood tables. Ingredients are locally sourced where possible and deftly handled by a kitchen confident in its skills. Take a rump of Borders lamb served with tomato, roast pepper and black olive couscous, or a fillet of organic salmon teamed with poached oysters, wilted spinach and a saffron velouté, and to finish, perhaps a chocolate frangipane tart with vanilla ice cream and griottines. The modern menu changes daily and is complemented by an extensive and award-winning wine list.

Chef: N Forbes **Owners:** Andrew & Lisa Radford **Times:** 12-2/6-10, Closed 25-26 Dec, 1-2 Jan, Sun (apart from Aug), Closed L Sat (apart from Aug & international rugby matches) **Prices:** Fixed L £15.50, Fixed D £25, Starter £7.50-£12.50, Main £19.50-£23.50, Dessert £7, Service optional, Group min 5 service 10% **Wine:** 250+ bottles over £20, 10 bottles under £20, 250 by the glass **Notes:** Vegetarian available, Civ Wed 100, Air con **Seats:** 80, Pr/dining room 20 **Children:** Portions **Directions:** From Princes St, turn into Lothian Rd, 2nd left & 1st right, by the Traverse Theatre, Blu Bar Café and Usher Hall **Parking:** Castle Terrace Car Park and on Cambridge St

⊛ Bisque Bar & Brasserie

Modern British

Smart, contemporary hotel restaurant

☎ 0131 622 8163 Best Western Bruntsfield Hotel, 69 Bruntsfield Place EH10 4HH
e-mail: reservations@bisquebar.co.uk
web: www.bisquebar.co.uk

The new trendy, contemporary, cosmopolitan Bisque bar and brasserie at this stylish townhouse hotel enjoys a bustling, relaxed and friendly atmosphere. The cooking follows the theme, the kitchen's modern approach using locally-sourced Scottish produce on a diverse, crowd-pleasing all-day repertoire, delivering everything from breakfast croissants, to tapas and more hearty fare. For mains, expect the likes of breast of chicken stuffed with haggis and served with swede and carrot mash and a whisky cream sauce, or meat-eaters might opt for a classic grilled Aberdeen Angus beef fillet with roast tomato and thin-cut chips.

Chef: Martyn Dixon **Owners:** Mrs C A Gwyn **Times:** 5.30-9.30, Closed 25 Dec **Prices:** Starter £3.95-£6.95, Main £6.95-£16.95, Dessert £4.95-£6.95, Service optional **Wine:** 26 bottles over £20, 19 bottles under £20, 10 by the glass **Notes:** Vegetarian available, Dress Restrictions, No football colours, Civ Wed 75 **Seats:** 130, Pr/dining room 120 **Children:** Menu, Portions **Rooms:** 71 (71 en suite) ★★★ HL **Directions:** From S enter Edinburgh on A702. Continue for 3m. Hotel overlooks Bruntsfield Links Park. 1m S of the W end of Princes St

⊛ Le Café St Honore

Scottish, French

Rustic French food in genuine bistro

☎ 0131 226 2211 34 NW Thistle St Lane EH2 1EA
web: www.cafesthonore.com

Set in a quiet cobbled side street five minutes from Princes Street, this intimate eatery is the genuine article when it comes to authentic back-street Parisian-style bistros. Black and white tiled floors, smoked-glass mirrors and wine racks on the walls add to the charming Bohemian atmosphere of the place. As for the food, this isn't a place for faddish cooking, just simple rustic classics created from excellent Scottish ingredients; think a rack of lamb served with Stornoway black pudding, chickpeas, spinach and garlic confit, or steamed sea bass with prawns, mussels, fennel and saffron, and to close, perhaps hot plum crumble with cinnamon ice cream.

Chef: Chris Colverson, Bob Cairns **Owners:** Chris & Gill Colverson **Times:** 12-2.15/7-10, Closed 24-26 Dec, 3 days at New Year **Prices:** Fixed D £21, Starter £3.95-£10.40, Main £9.50-£22.50, Dessert £5.50, Service optional, Group min 8 service 10% **Wine:** 45 bottles over £20, 19 bottles under £20, 9 by the glass **Notes:** Vegetarian available **Seats:** 56, Pr/dining room 18 **Children:** Portions **Directions:** City centre, between Hanover & Frederick St **Parking:** On street - Thistle St

⊛⊛ Channings Bar and Restaurant

Modern British 🖥

Honest, well-prepared food in a bright basement restaurant

☎ 0131 315 2225 15 South Learmonth Gardens EH4 1EZ
e-mail: restaurant@channings.co.uk
web: www.channings.co.uk

Channings is the former home of the polar explorer Sir Ernest Shackleton, a traditional townhouse property offering a peaceful retreat just minutes from the city centre. The hotel's modern basement restaurant is next to the bar facing the terraced gardens. The kitchen takes a refreshingly simple approach to the cooking of quality local produce, with uncluttered presentation and an emphasis on flavour. The style is modern brasserie with a nod to the Mediterranean; take pan-fried sea bream served with olive oil mash and salsa verde, or perhaps leek, chervil and tarragon risotto with a parmesan tuile, while desserts might be headed-up by a plum bread-and-butter pudding served with vanilla custard, or perhaps a dark chocolate pot might catch the eye.

Chef: Hubert Lamort **Owners:** Mr P Taylor **Times:** 12-2.30/6-10 **Prices:** Fixed L £12, Starter £4.50-£7.50, Main £11-£23, Dessert £4-£6.50,

CONTINUED

EDINBURGH CONTINUED

Service optional, Group min 10 service 10% **Wine:** 26 bottles over £20, 16 bottles under £20, 6 by the glass **Notes:** Sun L available **Seats:** 40, Pr/dining room 30 **Children:** Portions **Rooms:** 41 (41 en suite)★★★★ TH **Directions:** From Princes St follow signs to Forth Bridge (A90), cross Dean Bridge and take 4th right into South Learmonth Ave. Follow road to bottom of hill **Parking:** on street

⑧⑧ Dalhousie Castle and Aqueous Spa

Modern European

Creative cuisine in a truly unique setting

☎ 01875 820153 Bonnyrigg EH19 3JB
e-mail: info@dalhousiecastle.co.uk
web: www.dalhousiecastle.co.uk

This stunning castle is a popular choice for weddings, and the atmospheric Dungeon restaurant - in the part that dates back to the 13th century - certainly makes a unique setting for dinner whatever the occasion. Think high-arched stone-vaulted ceilings, suits of armour, antique swords and tapestries, and bountiful candlelight all adding to the atmosphere. But, before descending the ancient steps to the restaurant, you can enjoy a complimentary glass of champagne in the wood-panelled library, which hides a secret bar. The menu showcases modern French dishes and some creative combinations; take a loin of venison with a raspberry garnish, dauphinoise potato and wilted spinach, or perhaps a roast loin of monkfish served with a mussel beurre blanc, Puy lentils and parsley purée. The wine list is well chosen.

Chef: Francois Graud **Owners:** von Essen Hotels **Times:** 7-10, Closed L all week **Prices:** Fixed D £38, Service optional **Notes:** Smart casual, Civ Wed 100 **Seats:** 45, Pr/dining room 100 **Children:** Portions **Rooms:** 36 (36 en suite) ★★★ HL **Directions:** From A720 (Edinburgh bypass) take A7 south, turn right onto B704. Castle 0.5m on right **Parking:** 150

⑧ Duck's at Le Marché Noir

Modern Scottish, French NOTABLE WINE LIST

Modern cooking in inviting restaurant

☎ 0131 558 1608 14 Eyre Place EH3 5EP
e-mail: enquiries@ducks.co.uk
web: www.ducks.co.uk

A charming Edinburgh eatery that can be both intimate or vibrant, with its friendly but formal table service blending well with white linen and evening candlelight. Ducks feature everywhere, from décor to a frequent option on the menu, thanks to namesake owner Malcolm Duck. The good-value repertoire shows a hint of French-brasserie style with a modern Scottish flavour. Take West Coast scallops with quince, salsa verde and Avruga caviar, or confit duck leg with braised chicory, onion soubise and rosemary sauce.

Chef: Stuart Lynch **Owners:** Mr M K Duck **Times:** 12-2.30/7-10.30, Closed 25-26 Dec, Closed L Sat-Mon **Prices:** Fixed L £16, Fixed D £19.50, Starter £5-£7.50, Main £12.50-£24.50, Dessert £4-£6.40, Service optional, Group min 8 service 10% **Wine:** 150 bottles over £20, 28 bottles under £20, 7 by the glass **Seats:** 60, Pr/dining room 51 **Directions:** Princes St, Hanover St, Dundas St, right at lights **Parking:** On street

⑧⑧ La Garrigue

Traditional French 💻

Authentic French regional cuisine with fine views

☎ 0131 557 3032 31 Jeffrey St EH1 1DH
e-mail: lagarrigue@btconnect.com
web: www.lagarrigue.co.uk

With outstanding hill views, a little piece of Languedoc can be found here, recreating a traditional French neighbourhood restaurant, but also featuring Tim Stead furniture and Andrew Walker original South of France paintings. The wooden floor, chunky wooden tables and chairs and cool blue walls give a sophisticated Mediterranean feel, while the atmosphere is relaxed and friendly and the restaurant deservedly popular. The authentic regional cooking style offers simple, rustic dishes using fresh local produce as well as specialist ingredients sourced by the chef. Signature offerings include the likes of bouillabaisse, cassoulet and pot-au-feu, otherwise try a saddle of rabbit served with sautéed apple, black pudding and potatoes.

Chef: Jean Michel Gauffre **Owners:** J M Gauffre **Times:** 12-3/6.30-10.30, Closed 25-26 Dec, 1-2 Jan, Sun **Prices:** Fixed L £12.50, Fixed D £26.50, Service added but optional 10% **Wine:** 24 bottles over £20, 10 bottles under £20, 11 by the glass **Seats:** 48, Pr/dining room 11 **Children:** Portions **Directions:** Halfway down Royal Mile towards Holyrood Palace, turn left at lights into Jeffrey St **Parking:** On street, NCP

SCOTLAND

⊛ Hadrians

Modern International 🍷 NOTABLE WINE LIST

Buzzy, stylish brasserie with a cosmopolitan menu

☎ 0131 557 5000 & 556 2414 The Balmoral Hotel,
1 Princes St EH2 2EQ
e-mail: hadrians@roccofortehotels.com
web: www.roccofortehotels.com

Located on the ground floor of The Balmoral Hotel, this slick urban
brasserie has a distinct art deco influence, with walnut floors and walls
painted in lime and African violet - a combination inspired by the
natural landscapes of Edinburgh. A palette of Scottish produce is used
to create dishes with European scope. Take seared scallops served
with creamy mash and sauce vierge, or Scottish lamb cutlets with
roasted tomatoes and a feta and mint salad. From the grill, perhaps
Dover Sole or rib-eye with a choice of sauces - from peppercorn to
tartare by way of béarnaise or hollandaise.

Chef: Jeff Bland **Owners:** Rocco Forte Hotels **Times:** 12-2.30/6.30-10.30
Prices: Fixed L £25-£30, Fixed D £27.50-£40, Starter £6.50-£11, Main £9.25-
£27.50, Dessert £6.50-£7.95, Service optional, Group min 8 service 10%
Wine: 42 bottles over £20, 5 bottles under £20, 8 by the glass **Notes:** Sun
L £14.95, Vegetarian available, Dress Restrictions, Smart casual, Civ Wed 60,
Air con **Seats:** 100, Pr/dining room 30 **Children:** Menu, Portions
Directions: Hotel at beginning of Princes Street, next to Waverley station
Parking: 40

⊛⊛ Haldanes

Modern 🖥

*Intimate basement restaurant in an Edinburgh
townhouse*

☎ 0131 556 8407 13B Dundas St EH3 6QG
e-mail: dinehaldanes@aol.com
web: www.haldanesrestaurant.com

This quirky, popular basement restaurant provides an elegant and
intimate setting, with Vettriano prints, smart white-clothed tables,
subdued lighting and exposed natural stone all adding to the
contemporary vibe. Three small interconnected eating areas make for
cosy dining, while upstairs there's a lounge bar for pre-dinner drinks,
and during the day it's used mainly for casual meals, serving coffees,
pastries and good-value lunches in the French café-bar style. The
finest seasonal Scottish produce features on a monthly-changing
menu of modern dishes, simply prepared. For starters, take a warm
salad of West Coast scallops with sautéed charlotte new potatoes and
Parma ham, and follow with a grilled fillet of halibut with a panaché of
sweet potatoes and purple sprouting broccoli, served with cherry
tomato confit and red pepper dressing.

Chef: George Kelso **Owners:** Mr and Mrs G Kelso **Times:** 12-2.15/5.30-
10.15, Closed Mon, Closed L Sat-Sun **Prices:** Starter £7.25-£15, Main
£17.95-£27.50, Dessert £6.95-£10, Service optional, Group min 10 service
10% **Wine:** 67 bottles over £20, 16 bottles under £20, 9 by the glass
Notes: Dress Restrictions, Smart casual preferred **Seats:** 60, Pr/dining
room 32 **Children:** Portions **Directions:** Telephone for directions
Parking: On street

⊛ Iggs

Spanish 🍷 NOTABLE WINE LIST

*Convivial and welcoming taste of Spain near the Royal
Mile*

☎ 0131 557 8184 15 Jeffrey St EH1 1DR
e-mail: iggsbarioja@iggsbarioja.force9.co.uk
web: www.iggs.co.uk

Just a stone's throw from the Royal Mile, this modern glass-fronted
restaurant is the more formal dining option to the next-door tapas bar
(Barioja) under the same ownership. Bringing a touch of the
Mediterranean to the city, the restaurant's décor in warm shades of
terracotta is complemented by large cast-iron candlesticks and antique
dressers, with oils and mirrors adorning the walls. The cooking also
speaks with a Spanish accent, creating simple, well-constructed
modern dishes that deliver quality ingredients and good flavours.
Think Almejas y Mejillones, or clams and mussels if you prefer,
steamed with tomatoes and white wine. The wine list is equally
patriotic.

Chef: Leon Quate **Owners:** Mr I Campos **Times:** 12-2.30/6-10.30, Closed
Sun **Prices:** Fixed L £13-£16, Fixed D £23.50, Starter £4.50-£9.50, Main
£14.50-£25, Dessert £6.50-£8, Service optional **Wine:** 10 by the glass
Notes: Vegetarian available **Seats:** 80, Pr/dining room 40
Children: Portions **Directions:** At the heart of Edinburgh's Old Town
0.5m from castle, just off the Royal Mile **Parking:** On street, NCP

SCOTLAND

EDINBURGH *Continued*

◉ The Indian Cavalry Club

Indian V **NEW**

Settle in for the night and enjoy a traditional Indian feast

☎ 0131 228 3282 & 228 2974 3 Atholl Place EH3 8HP
web: www.indiancavalryclub.co.uk

Although this is a private club, the 'Officer's Mess' restaurant is open to everyone. High ceilings and tall windows swathed and draped with curtains and a black and white tiled floor make quite an impression. That's until you see the menu (around 16 pages) - you might get through a drink and a few poppadoms just deciding what to order. Luckily the extensive selection is helpfully annotated with suggested side orders and drinks for each dish. Offering a modern taste of India, the dishes are lighter and rely on the finest of ingredients. There are various banquet options and also a truly wide-ranging carte offering authentic tandoori, biryani, vegetarian, chicken, lamb and seafood dishes.

Chef: Muktar Miah, Firoz Hossain **Owners:** Shahid Choudhury
Times: 12-2/5.30-11 **Prices:** Fixed D £16.95-£23.50, Starter £3.85-£7.85, Main £8.85-£9.95, Dessert £3.85-£5.85, Service added but optional 10%
Wine: 15 bottles over £20, 16 bottles under £20, 2 by the glass
Notes: Fixed D 4 courses, Vegetarian menu **Seats:** 120, Pr/dining room 30
Directions: 3 mins walk from Haymarket Railway Stn on west end of Princess St **Parking:** On street

◉◉◉ The Kitchin

see below

◉ Macdonald Holyrood Hotel

Modern British

Relaxed dining in the shadow of Holyrood Palace

☎ 0131 550 4500 Holyrood Rd EH8 6AU
e-mail: holyrood@macdonald-hotels.co.uk
web: www.macdonaldhotels.co.uk

Just a short stroll from the new Scottish Parliament Building, this impressive hotel is located in the heart of Edinburgh's Old Town. The split-level Opus 504 restaurant showcases a wide range of prime Scottish produce on its 'wild fish & chophouse' menu, and keen staff impart detailed knowledge of this. Traditional dishes with a modern twist vie for diners' attention; take grilled fillet of wild sea bass scented with lemon thyme and served with Mediterranean vegetables, or traditionally aged, hand-cut Scottish beef fillet, and perhaps a sticky toffee pudding to finish, served with butterscotch sauce.

Chef: John Forestier **Owners:** Macdonald Hotels **Times:** 12-2/6.30-10, Closed L all week (ex group bookings), D 25 Dec **Prices:** Starter £6.95-£9.50, Main £13-£26, Dessert £5.50-£7.95, Service optional **Wine:** 43 bottles over £20, 3 bottles under £20, 9 by the glass **Notes:** Vegetarian available, Dress Restrictions, Smart casual, Civ Wed 120, Air con
Seats: 95, Pr/dining room 20 **Children:** Menu, Portions **Rooms:** 156 (156 en suite) ★★★★ HL **Directions:** City centre near the Royal Mile
Parking: 20

◉◉◉

The Kitchin

EDINBURGH   **MAP 21 NT27**

Scottish, French NEW

Slick, modern décor and cooking on the waterfront

☎ 0131 555 1755 78 Commercial Quay, Leith EH6 6LX
e-mail: info@thekitchin.com
web: www.thekitchin.com

The Kitchin - thankfully not some glib play on words - is home to chef-patron, Tom Kitchin, whose impressive CV includes stints in the lofty kitchens of the likes of Pierre Koffmann in London and Alain Ducasse and Guy Savoy in France. Set on Leith's rejuvenated waterfront, The Kitchin has a fine outlook on to the smart maritime piazza. It's a delightful modern dining venue, with funky, striking colours and fabrics and high-quality furniture, together with a feature glass-walled theatre kitchen allowing views of the brigade at work. Simple table appointments, soft lighting, highly comfortable leather seating and refreshingly informal but attentive and knowledgeable service complete the upbeat package.

Meanwhile, the slick, modern cooking showcases a successful marriage of fresh, seasonal quality Scottish produce and classical French technique. From 'nature to plate' is Tom's strapline and cooking philosophy here. It's ambitious with impressive presentation to create a focal point on every plate; red mullet upside down with roasted squid, cumin-flavoured aubergine, caviar and spiced sauce, and to finish, perhaps an iced Perthshire honey parfait with kumquats and cardamom brandy snaps.

Chef: Tom Kitchin **Owners:** T & M Kitchin **Times:** 12.30-2.30/7.30-10
Prices: Food prices not confirmed for 2008. Please telephone for details
Notes: Vegetarian available **Directions:** Please telephone for details

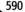

◉ Malmaison Hotel & Brasserie

Scottish, French 🖥

Slick style, simple food and friendly service

☎ 0131 468 5000 One Tower Place, Leith EH6 7DB
e-mail: edinburgh@malmaison.com
web: www.malmaison.com

Built in 1883 as a seaman's mission on the water of Leith, this hotel has a castle-like appearance. Inside you'll find slick French style throughout with wooden floors, leather chairs and banquettes. The ground-floor brasserie looks out across a cobbled concourse to the quayside. Classic, simple dishes are cooked using fresh local ingredients (many suppliers listed on the Home-grown and Local menu), try leek and gruyère tart with hollandaise, pork fillet medallions with Agen prunes and grain mustard sauce, or grilled halibut with warm squid and caper salad. Service is relaxed and friendly - why not go for a laid-back Sunday brunch.

Chef: Lindsay Wood **Owners:** Malmaison Hotels Ltd **Times:** 12-2/6-10.30, Closed D 25 Dec **Prices:** Fixed L £13.50, Starter £4.95-£7.50, Main £12.50-£25, Dessert £5.95, Service added but optional 10%, Group min 8 service 10% **Wine:** 146 bottles over £20, 14 bottles under £20, 12 by the glass **Notes:** Sun brunch menu, Vegetarian available, Air con **Seats:** 62, Pr/dining room 60 **Children:** Portions **Rooms:** 100 (100 en suite) ★★★ HL **Directions:** From the city centre follow Leith Docklands, through 3 sets of lights and left into Tower St **Parking:** 48

◉◉ *Marriott Dalmahoy Hotel & Country Club*

Modern European

Intimate fine dining in Georgian splendour

☎ 0131 333 1845 Kirknewton EH27 8EB
e-mail: fandb.dalmahoy@marriotthotels.co.uk
web: www.marriott.co.uk/edigs

Many of the original features have been retained in the fine Adam-designed mansion, which is bounded by two championship golf courses, expansive grounds, and the rolling Pentland Hills. In addition, there is an impressive health and beauty spa and a choice of formal and informal drinking and dining options. The smart, classically furnished Pentland restaurant, overlooking the 18th hole, is where the serious eating takes place. Cooking successfully combines a strong Scottish theme, with the use of quality seafood and game, classic dishes as seen in the retro roast trolley, or perhaps simply grilled Dover sole, and more contemporary dishes, such as lamb with black pudding mash and pulse casserole.

Times: 12.30-2/7-10, Closed L Sat & Sun **Rooms:** 215 (215 en suite) ★★★★ HL **Directions:** On A71 city bypass. Take Calder exit & follow signs for A71. 7m and hotel clearly signed on left.

◉◉◉ Norton House Hotel

see below

◉◉◉

Norton House Hotel

EDINBURGH   **MAP 21 NT27**

Modern British

Small, sophisticated restaurant in elegant hotel

☎ 0131 333 1275 Ingliston EH28 8LX
e-mail: nortonhouse@handpicked.co.uk
web: www.handpicked.co.uk

Situated outside the city and convenient for the airport, this extended Victorian mansion is set in 55 acres of parkland. Original features blend with a relaxed, contemporary edge. Visitors to the fine-dining Ushers restaurant can make use of the refurbished drawing room, while hotel brasserie users can relax in the conservatory bar lounge. Ushers is an intimate 22-seat affair, smartly decked out with pale walls, subdued lighting and maroon tablecloths with white runners.
The kitchen's modern approach is underpinned by a classical theme, delivered via an appealing, sensibly compact carte. Skilled, precise cooking allows fine-quality Scottish ingredients to shine with deceptive simplicity and clean, clear, balanced flavours. Expect twice-baked Scottish crab soufflé served with langoustines and a soy and lime dressing to start, followed by a main course of pan-fried fillet of wild sea bass with langoustine tortellini, olive gnocchi, shiitake mushrooms, purple sprouting broccoli, chorizo purée and a tomato caper dressing, while a warm pear tarte Tatin served with red apple skin sorbet and a raisin anglaise might catch the eye at dessert. A good cheese selection, first-class breads and interesting canapés hold up standards, and make a walk around the grounds almost mandatory.

Chef: Graeme Shaw & Glen Bilins **Owners:** Hand Picked Hotels **Times:** 7-9.30, Closed 26 Dec, 1 Jan, Sun-Mon, Closed L all week **Prices:** Starter £7.50-£11.95, Main £18.50-£23.95, Dessert £7.50, Service optional **Wine:** 168 bottles over £20, 12 by the glass **Notes:** Civ Wed 140, Air con **Seats:** 22, Pr/dining room 40 **Children:** Portions **Rooms:** 47 (47 en suite) ★★★★ HL **Directions:** M8 junct 2, off A8, 0.5m past Edinburgh Airport **Parking:** 100

SCOTLAND

SCOTLAND

EDINBURGH CONTINUED

⊚⊚⊚ *Number One, The Balmoral Hotel*
see below

⊚⊚ Off the Wall Restaurant
British, French 🖥
Stylish dining along the Royal Mile

☎ 0131 558 1497 105 High St, Royal Mile EH1 1SG
e-mail: otwedinburgh@aol.com
web: www.off-the-wall.co.uk

Arched leaded-glass windows look out across the Royal Mile from this sophisticated restaurant housed in one of the oldest buildings on the famous thoroughfare. A tasteful, simple décor with plum and white walls creates a soothing ambience that contrasts with the hustle and bustle of the street below. Cooking is consistent and skilful, classically based but with a modern approach, using quality local and seasonal produce. Dishes come intelligently simply presented allowing key flavours to shine; take a saddle of Scottish lamb served with baby spinach and ragout of carrots, dauphinoise potato and a port sauce, and perhaps a chocolate torte with chocolate sauce and mint ice cream to finish. Service is fittingly refined and friendly.

Chef: David Anderson **Owners:** David Anderson/Aileen Wilson
Times: 12-2/6.30-10, Closed 25-26 Dec, 1-2 Jan, Sun **Prices:** Fixed L £16.50, Starter £10.50-£12.95, Main £19.95-£21.95, Dessert £6.95, Service optional **Wine:** 35 bottles over £20, 8 bottles under £20, 5 by the glass
Notes: Tasting menu pre-booked 2+ persons, Fixed 3 course L £19.50

Seats: 44, Pr/dining room 20 **Children:** Portions **Directions:** On Royal Mile near John Knox House - entrance via stairway next to Baillie Fyfes Close (first floor) **Parking:** NCP

The Plumed Horse
Modern NEW
Location change for a well established favourite

☎ 0131 554 5556 50-54 Henderson St, Leith EH6 6DE
e-mail: plumedhorse@aol.com
web: www.plumedhorse.co.uk

Relocated from Castle Douglas to Leith, The Plumed Horse is the brainchild of dynamic chef/proprietor Tony Borthwick. The imaginative menu has lost nothing in its relocation, still boasting impressively modern cuisine with a good classical twist and perfectly executed presentation. As we went to press, this restaurant was due to be inspected. Please visit www.theAA.com for up-to-date information.

Chef: Tony Borthwick **Times:** 12-1.30/7-9, Closed Sun-Mon
Directions: Fom city centre N on Leith Walk, left into Great Junction St and 1st right into Henderson St. Restaurant 200mtrs on right

---

⊚⊚⊚

Number One, The Balmoral Hotel

EDINBURGH MAP 21 NT27
Modern Scottish, French
Fine dining in luxury hotel

☎ 0131 557 6727 1 Princes St EH2 2EQ
e-mail: numberone@thebalmoralhotel.com
web: www.roccofortehotels.com

Opulence, comfort, courtesy and elegance are the bywords at this luxurious hotel that dominates the east end of Princes Street, with fine views over the city and castle. The grand Edwardian building includes a Roman-style health spa, a choice of two bars (one stocking 30 different champagnes) and two very different dining options. Whereas Hadrians is a bustling, informal brasserie, the chic basement restaurant Number One is the place for a romantic meal and some seriously creative cuisine. Styled by Olga Polizzi, rich red walls hold numerous colourful prints and large, well-spaced tables, and gold velvet chairs enhance the exclusive feel.

Well-drilled staff ensure refined service which is matched by classical French cooking with modern influences. A large amount of Scottish produce is used in innovative combinations of flavours and textures. A starter of peanut-encrusted scallops, served with curried oxtail and parsnip purée, may kick off a memorable meal that continues with a deliciously tender fillet of beef with truffle mash. Desserts like a

chocolate and orange tart with five differing styles of orange are precise and well executed. Wonderful canapés, amuse-bouche, pre-dessert and petits fours all add to the dining experience.

Chef: Jeff Bland **Owners:** Rocco Forte Hotels **Times:** 12-2/7-10, Closed 1st 2 wks Jan, Closed L Mon-Tue, Sat-Sun **Rooms:** 188 (188 en suite)
★★★★★ HL **Directions:** Hotel at E end of Princes St, next to Waverley station

AA Hotel of the Year for Scotland

◎◎ *The Restaurant at the Bonham*

Modern Scottish 🖥

Enjoyable dining in stylish urban setting

☎ 0131 274 7444 35 Drumsheugh Gardens EH3 7RN
e-mail: restaurant@thebonham.com
web: www.thebonham.com

Set in the heart of trendy New Town, this converted Victorian townhouse is now home to a spacious and stylish dining room. Wooden floors and panelling sit comfortably with modern furniture, minimalist décor and modern artworks. Attractive wooden tables are set with fine glassware, cutlery, linen napkins and candles, and staff provide attentive service. The French chef uses his classical training to transform local and seasonal ingredients into dishes with flair and individualism. The short menu avoids the agony of indecision. Simpler starters like roast loin of rabbit salad with lemon gnocchi precede main courses of oven-roasted poussin with its own confit legs, swede and potato cake and wilted Savoy cabbage, rounded off with praline crème brûlée with lemon macaroon.

Times: 12-2.30/6.30-10 **Rooms:** 48 (48 en suite) ★★★★ TH
Directions: Located to the W end of Princes St

◎◎◎◎ **Restaurant Martin Wishart**
see page 594

◎◎ **Rhubarb - the Restaurant at Prestonfield**

Traditional British 🖥

Opulent setting for impressive food

☎ 0131 225 1333 Prestonfield, Priestfield Rd EH16 5UT
e-mail: reservations@prestonfield.com
web: www.rhubarb-restaurant.com

Richly decadent, stylish and very glamorous, Prestonfield's interior is the epitome of opulence. Situated within a remarkable Regency house set in its own 20-acre parkland, Rhubarb is the luxurious and comfortable restaurant within the hotel and comprises two separate dining rooms, both with fine views and crisp linen on the tables. Four separate rooms available for pre- and post-dinner drinks are as atmospheric and indulgent as the rest of the hotel. The very best Scottish produce is handled with flair and panache, in creative dishes like West Coast crab with scallop céviche, or pan-fried fillet of sea bass with artichoke ravioli and a barigoule dressing. Warm dark chocolate fondant with basil anglaise and Greek yogurt ice cream might feature at dessert, or choose from a selection of British and continental artisan cheeses.

Chef: John MacMahon **Owners:** James Thomson OBE **Times:** 12-2/6-11
Prices: Fixed L £16.95, Starter £8.50-£13.95, Main £19.50-£30, Dessert £6.95-£9.95, Service optional, Group min 8 service 10% **Wine:** 400 bottles over £20, 20 bottles under £20, 12 by the glass **Notes:** Theatre D 2 courses £16.95, Vegetarian available, Civ Wed 500 **Seats:** 90, Pr/dining room 500 **Children:** Min 12 yrs, Portions **Rooms:** 24 (24 en suite)★★★★★ TH **Directions:** Leave city centre on Nicholson St, join Dalkeith Rd. At lights turn left into Priestfield Rd. Prestonfield is on the left **Parking:** 200

◎◎ *Santini*

Italian

Chic venue for modern Italian food

☎ 0131 221 7788 8 Conference Square EH3 8AN

Santini is a fresh, modern and elegant Italian restaurant and bistro that provides an informal dining venue for the Sheraton Grand's impressive One Spa. The two operations share a spacious entrance dominated by a large cocktail bar; the bistro has diners sitting high on padded stools, while more traditional seating fills the restaurant - a bright, contemporary space, decked out in glass, chrome and low-key neutral shades, and presided over by attentive staff. Dishes are well executed using Scottish ingredients and full of Italian flavours. Menus follow a traditional format (antipasti, primi, pesce and carne), typically including smoked swordfish starter, served with pear, pink peppercorns and Grappa Williams, while mains might include mushroom risotto and spaghetti vongole, as well as more modern options such as sea bass with rosemary and balsamic vinegar sauce.

Times: 12-2.30/6.30-10.30, Closed 1 Jan, Sun, Closed L Sat

SCOTLAND

SCOTLAND

Restaurant Martin Wishart

EDINBURGH MAP 21 NT27

Modern French V 🍷 NOTABLE WINE LIST 🖥️

Imaginative, memorable French cooking in intimate, fashionable waterfront venue

☎ 0131 553 3557 54 The Shore, Leith EH6 6RA
e-mail: info@martin-wishart.co.uk
web: www.martin-wishart.co.uk

Chef: Martin Wishart
Owners: Martin Wishart
Times: 12-2/6.30-10, Closed 25 Dec, 1 wk Jan, Sun-Mon
Prices: Fixed L £22.50, Fixed D £50, Service optional, Group min 6 service 10%
Wine: 200+ bottles over £20, 2 bottles under £20, 16 by the glass
Notes: Fixed L 3 courses, Tasting menu 7 courses £60, Vegetarian menu, Dress Restrictions, Smart casual
Seats: 50
Children: Portions
Directions: Telephone for directions/map on website
Parking: On street

This unassuming shopfront-style restaurant on the fashionable, rejuvenated Leith dockland waterfront could easily be overlooked, yet the informed know it's home to one of Scotland's top chefs and a colossus on the culinary map. As one enters the glass-enclosed foyer is brimming with the smell of lilies and you realise you've arrived somewhere special. Soft muted shades of beige and browns, suede and leather, clever lighting and eye-catching contemporary artworks grace the intimate, modern, minimalist-styled room that oozes style and refinement. Crisp white linen, impeccable table appointments, comfortable seating and polished, professional service add class and sophistication. Chef-patron Martin Wishart is a true flavour-smith, his kitchen's elaborate modern French style aptly befits the surroundings, while making fine use of impeccably sourced seasonal produce (local where possible) to deliver sublime, fresh, intense, dynamic flavours. Flawless execution, invention and flair find their place in complex, refined dishes that also pay due homage to texture, balance and combination. The approach is via an eye-catching fixed-price repertoire that comes dotted with luxury and includes a superb value lunch, plus tasting menu (including a separate vegetarian version and the option of selected wines) and an enticing carte (plus its vegetarian alternative). Think baked turbot served with scallops, ceps and hazelnut, or perhaps poached Anjou pigeon paired with peas, girolles, figs and a redcurrant jus, and to finish, a cracking coconut pannacotta with fromage frais sorbet and mango and pineapple ravioli. Peripherals like canapés, breads, amuse-bouche and petits fours all hold top form, while an impressive wine list pays due reverence to the memorable cuisine.

◎◎ The Scotsman

Modern Scottish

Stylish setting for relaxed, modern fine dining

☎ 0131 556 5565 20 North Bridge EH1 1YT
e-mail: reservations@thescotsmanhotelgroup.co.uk
web: www.thescotsmanhotel.co.uk

This magnificent Victorian building was formerly the headquarters of *The Scotsman* newspaper - hence the name. Combining the best of the original features with cutting-edge design, the restaurant entices guests in with a grand marble staircase and then to the stylish and intimate, fine-dining Vermilion restaurant in what was once the newspaper's features room (one imagines a similar buzz close to deadline as current diners create on a busy lunch or dinner). The kitchen here is both technically accomplished and creative, making good use of quality Scottish produce on its sensibly compact, fixed-price menus. Typical dishes could be fillet of beef with oxtail bread pudding, dressed crab with breaded langoustines and tomato and herb salad, with vanilla custard tart and poached rhubarb to finish.

Chef: Geoff Balharrie, Ian Henderson **Owners:** The Scotsman Hotel Group **Times:** 7-10, Closed Mon & Tue, Closed L all week **Prices:** Fixed D £35-£55, Starter £7-£14, Main £16-£30, Dessert £7, Service optional **Wine:** 109 bottles over £20, 5 bottles under £20, 6 by the glass **Notes:** Tasting menu available Fri-Sat, Civ Wed 80 **Seats:** 32, Pr/dining room 80 **Children:** Min 12 yrs, Portions **Rooms:** 69 (69 en suite) ★★★★★ HL **Directions:** Town centre, next to railway station **Parking:** Station car park

◎◎ The Sheraton Grand Hotel & Spa

Modern International V

Classic Scottish dishes in luxurious surroundings

☎ 0131 221 6422 1 Festival Square EH3 9SR
e-mail: grandedinburgh.sheraton@sheraton.com
web: www.sheraton.com/grandedinburgh

Prices and service are pitched at the same high level at the Sheraton's flagship fine-dining Grill Room, while the décor leaves no doubt as to where you're dining. Tartan walls, oak panelling, Scottish prints and paintings on grand Scottish themes never undermine the intimacy of the crisply-dressed tables with formal settings and fresh flowers. Fresh local produce is the basis of complex, well-presented modern and classical dishes. Think saffron-scented monkfish with a lobster and vanilla risotto and watercress foam, and, from The Grill, perhaps a rib of beef or swordfish (served with a choice of sauces). To finish, maybe a Macadamia nut tart with crispy banana fritter and toasted coconut ice cream.

Chef: Malcom Webster **Owners:** Hotel Corporation of Edinburgh **Times:** 12-2/7-10, Closed Jan, Sun & Mon, Closed L Sat **Prices:** Fixed L £16.95, Starter £6.50-£14.50, Main £17.50-£42.50, Dessert £7.50, Service optional **Notes:** Vegetarian menu, Dress Restrictions, Smart casual, Civ Wed 250, Air con **Seats:** 40 **Children:** Min 14 yrs **Rooms:** 260 (260 en suite) ★★★★★ HL **Directions:** Off Lothian Road. Entrance to hotel behind Standard Life building **Parking:** 121

◎ Stac Polly

Modern Scottish

Modern Scottish cuisine in relaxed atmosphere

☎ 0131 229 5405 & 558 3083 8-10 Grindlay St EH3 9AS
e-mail: bookings@stacpolly.com
web: www.stacpolly.co.uk

This Edinburgh chain has proved so successful with tourists and locals alike, it's just opened a third branch to go with its two existing eateries on Dublin Street (see below) and Grindlay Street. The latter outpost is within strolling distance of the Princes Street shops, and hides a convivial warren of richly furnished and softly lit rooms behind an unassuming façade. Modern Scottish cooking dominates the menu, conjured from local seasonal produce where possible and distinguished by accomplished technique and honest flavours. A twice-baked smoked cheddar cheese soufflé is complemented by gooseberry chutney, while oven-baked monkfish arrives wrapped in Parma ham and filled with aubergine confit.

Chef: Steven Harvey, Stanislas Andre **Owners:** Roger Coulthard **Times:** 12-2/6-10, Closed Xmas, New Year, Sun, Closed L Sat **Prices:** Fixed L £15.95, Starter £6.95-£8.45, Main £17.95-£21.95, Dessert £6.55, Service added but optional 10% **Notes:** Vegetarian available **Seats:** 98, Pr/dining room 50 **Children:** Portions **Directions:** In town centre. Situated beneath the castle, near Lyceum Theatre **Parking:** NCP - Castle Terrace

◎ Stac Polly

Modern Scottish

Modern Scottish cuisine in atmospheric surroundings

☎ 0131 556 2231 29-33 Dublin St EH3 6NL
e-mail: enquiry@stacpolly.com
web: www.stacpolly.co.uk

Taking its name from a Scottish mountain, there are two restaurants of this name in the city centre (see above). Set in a 200-year-old building at basement level, this restaurant features a labyrinth of rough stone-walled cellars, combining traditional and modern décor. The same menu is served at both restaurants, and features modern Scottish dishes with a traditional twist and some French influences. Take baked filo parcels of finest haggis served on a sweet plum and red wine sauce, followed by a mouthwatering main course of roast breast of mallard with confit leg, honey-roast vegetables and delicious game sauce.

Chef: Andre Stanislas **Owners:** Roger Coulthard **Times:** 12-2/6-10, Closed 25-26 Dec, 1 Jan, Sun, Closed L Sat **Prices:** Fixed L £16.95, Starter £7.95-£8.35, Main £18.95-£21.95, Dessert £6.55-£8.55, Service added but optional 10% **Notes:** Vegetarian available **Seats:** 100, Pr/dining room 54 **Children:** Portions **Directions:** On corner of Albany St and Dublin St **Parking:** On street - after 6.30 pm

SCOTLAND

SCOTLAND

EDINBURGH CONTINUED

⊛ Tower Restaurant & Terrace

Modern British

Cultural and culinary delights combined in a striking modern venue

☎ 0131 225 3003 Museum of Scotland, Chambers St EH1 1JF
e-mail: reservations@tower-restaurant.com
web: www.tower-restaurant.com

Situated on the top floor of the Museum of Scotland, this elegant, contemporary restaurant enjoys impressive views over the castle and cathedral, with an outside terrace for summer dining. The colourful décor is chic and luxurious, with striking aluminium furniture and banquettes creating a clubby feel. The equally modern menu offers the likes of seared pigeon with beetroot jam and wilted chard, and gilt head bream with shiitake mushrooms and stir-fry bok choy. Superb quality beef comes prepared in a variety of ways. A couple of light menus at lunchtime and early evening offer terrific value.

Chef: Gavin Elder **Owners:** James Thomson OBE **Times:** 12/12-11, Closed 25-26 Dec **Prices:** Fixed L £12.95, Starter £6.50-£14.50, Main £15-£29, Dessert £4-£7, Service optional, Group min 8 service 10% **Wine:** 150 bottles over £20, 30 bottles under £20, 14 by the glass **Notes:** Theatre supper £12.95, Vegetarian available, Air con **Seats:** 96, Pr/dining room 90 **Directions:** Above the Museum of Scotland building at corner of George IV Bridge & Chambers St, on level 5 **Parking:** On street

⊛⊛ The Vintners Rooms

French, Mediterranean V

Candlelit restaurant with vintage charm

☎ 0131 554 6767 The Vaults, 87 Giles St, Leith EH6 6BZ
e-mail: enquiries@thevintnersrooms.com
web: www.thevintnersrooms.com

Lit by flickering candles, this romantic restaurant has character a-plenty. A former warehouse dating from the 15th century, it's exquisitely adorned with hand-worked stucco, and sits above cellars that have stored imported barrels of fine tipples from France since the 11th century. There's a touch of the 'auld alliance' about the food too, with modern French dishes conjured from quality Scottish produce; think Aberdeen Angus fillet with a Périgord truffle sauce, or steamed wild halibut served with a mussel broth. This is rustic cuisine, presented with great artistry, and fittingly complemented by an extensive wine list.

Chef: P Ginistière **Owners:** Patrice Ginistière **Times:** 12-2/7-10, Closed 1-16 Jan, Sun-Mon **Prices:** Fixed L £16, Starter £6.50-£11.50, Main £17-£25, Dessert £5.50, Service added but optional 10%, Group min 5 service 10% **Wine:** 160 bottles over £20, 12 bottles under £20, 4 by the glass **Notes:** Vegetarian menu **Seats:** 64, Pr/dining room 34 **Children:** Portions **Directions:** At the end of Leith Walk; left into Great Junction St, right into Henderson St. Restaurant in old warehouse on right **Parking:** 4

⊛ The Witchery by the Castle

Traditional Scottish

Destination dining in historic location

☎ 0131 225 5613 Castlehill, Royal Mile EH1 2NF
e-mail: mail@thewitchery.com
web: www.thewitchery.com

Dating back to 1595, The Witchery takes its name from the hundreds of people burnt at the stake as witches on Castlehill in the 16th and 17th centuries. Now a renowned romantic hotel, the unique combination of décor reflects the building's fascinating past. Choose between the rich baroque surroundings of the oak-panelled Witchery, or the elegant charms of the Secret Garden, reached via a stone staircase from the courtyard above. The very best of Scottish produce, including Angus beef, lamb, game and seafood, features on a classic menu with a relaxed and unfussy style, accompanied by a world-class wine list. Scottish lobster and rock oysters sit alongside Witchery classics like hot smoked salmon with leeks and hollandaise, while main courses might include the likes of Angus beef fillet with smoked garlic broth, or a jambonette of Borders guinea fowl served with a blanquette of baby vegetables, caramelised apple and smoked garlic. The sense of quality, luxury and theatre cannot help but impress.

The Witchery by the Castle

Chef: Douglas Roberts **Owners:** James Thomson OBE **Times:** 12-4/5-11.30, Closed 25-26 Dec **Prices:** Fixed L £12.95, Starter £6.50-£12.95, Main £15-£29, Dessert £7-£9, Service optional, Group min 8 service 10% **Wine:** 700+ bottles over £20, 20 bottles under £20, 14 by the glass **Notes:** Theatre supper £12.95, Vegetarian available, Air con **Seats:** 120, Pr/dining room 70 **Children:** Min 12 yrs **Rooms:** 7 (7 en suite) ★★★★★ RR **Directions:** At the gates of Edinburgh Castle, at the top of the Royal Mile

🖥 Bellini - Edinburgh
☎ 0131 476 2602 8b Abercromby Place EH3 6LB
web: www.theaa.com/travel/index.jsp

Regional Italian cuisine in a Georgian dining room in the heart of New Town, with a relaxed and friendly atmosphere.

🖥 Daniel's Restaurant
☎ 0131 553 5933 88 Commercial St EH6 6LX
web: www.theaa.com/travel/index.jsp

A bright, light warehouse conversion on the lovely Leith waterfront, offering consistently high-quality French and Scottish food and a friendly atmosphere.

David Bann
☎ 0131 556 5888 56/58 St Mary St EH1 1SX
Smart vegetarian restaurant and bar, off the Royal Mile.

🖥 First Coast
☎ 0131 313 4404 97-101 Dalry Rd EH11 2AB
web: www.theaa.com/travel/index.jsp
An intimate, relaxed shop-front restaurant with a frequently-changing modern Scottish menu, offering meat and fowl as well as fish. Short, thoughtful wine list, good vegetarian choices and warm service.

🖥 Fishers Bistro
☎ 0131 554 5666 1 The Shore, Leith EH6 6QW
web: www.theaa.com/travel/index.jsp
A long-time favourite in Leith, with views over the water. From superb raw Loch Fyne oysters, to seared tuna steak with chilli and lime couscous salad, the fish, as you would expect, is excellent.

🖥 Fishers in the City
☎ 0131 225 5109 58 Thistle St EH2 1EN
web: www.theaa.com/travel/index.jsp
A smart, stylish, modern bistro in New Town with all the virtues of the original Fishers Bistro in Leith: superb ingredients, memorable cooking, swift, caring service, and a great atmosphere.

🖥 The Gallery Restaurant & Bar
☎ 0131 624 6579 National Gallery, The Mount EH2 2EL
web: www.theaa.com/travel/index.jsp
A fantastic location and great views in the stunning new Weston link joining the National Gallery and the Royal Scottish Academy. Décor is smart and up to the minute, and so is the modern Scottish menu.

Henderson's Salad Table
☎ 0131 225 2131 94 Hanover St EH2 1DR
Pioneering vegetarian/health food restaurant with deli and farm shop.

🖥 Howies Restaurant - Alva Street
☎ 0131 225 5553 1a Alva St EH2 4PH
web: www.theaa.com/travel/index.jsp
Monthly-changing menus offer modern Scottish dishes, superb local ingredients and seasonal fare. As much as possible - desserts and warm crusty bread included - is made on the premises.

🖥 Howies Restaurant - Victoria Street
☎ 0131 225 1721 10-14 Victoria St EH1 2HG
web: www.theaa.com/travel/index.jsp
Part of a thriving chain of acclaimed modern Scottish restaurants, this branch is characteristically modern and atmospheric; popular for quick lunches by day, and leisurely candlelit dinners by night.

SCOTLAND

EDINBURGH CONTINUED

🖳 Howies Restaurant - Waterloo Place

☎ 0131 556 5766 29 Waterloo Place EH1 3BQ
web: www.theaa.com/travel/index.jsp

This particular Howies occupies a 200-year-old Georgian building and reliably serves up the classic Howies' mix of a laidback atmosphere and quality, good-value modern Scottish cooking served by friendly staff in bright, light surroundings.

🖳 No.3 Restaurant

☎ 0131 477 4747 3 Royal Ter EH7 5AB
web: www.theaa.com/travel/index.jsp

A narrow, airy dining room serving great Scottish produce.

🖳 The Olive Branch Bistro

☎ 0131 557 8589 91 Broughton St EH1 3RX
web: www.theaa.com/travel/index.jsp

Lunch, dinner, weekend brunches all from a Mediterranean menu. Informal, relaxed, friendly and romantic.

🖳 Petit Paris

☎ 0131 226 1890 17 Queensferry St EH2 4QP
web: www.theaa.com/travel/index.jsp

A cosy, traditional French bistro with a whitewashed dining room and checked tablecloths.

🖳 The Stockbridge Restaurant

☎ 0131 226 6766 54 St Stephens St EH3 5AL
web: www.theaa.com/travel/index.jsp

Romantic basement is an intimate showcase for exciting modern European cooking.

VinCaffe

☎ 0131 557 0088 11 Multrees Walk EH1 3DQ

A popular Italian restaurant offering good range of menu choices.

FALKIRK

BANKNOCK   MAP 21 NS77
◎◎ Glenskirlie House and Castle
Modern British
Elegant hotel with an imaginative kitchen

☎ 01324 840201 Kilsyth Rd FK4 1UF
e-mail: macaloneys@glenskirliehouse.com
web: www.glenskirliehouse.com

Luxurious fabrics and striking wall coverings give the dining room of this refined country house an elegant feel, while well-spaced tables and unobtrusive staff make it an ideal destination for both romantic and business assignations. And the food's good too: a blend of classic and contemporary cuisine, conjured from the finest Scottish ingredients. Starters might include scallops with pea and mint gnocchi and cauliflower purée, or lobster thermidor baked in a soft pastry pie with baby capers, beetroot, daikon and shiso cress salad. Main dishes range from complex concoctions such as suprême of organic chicken stuffed with truffle butter, served with potato galette, turnip confit, kohlrabi, baby onion and fresh tarragon sauce, to simpler fare like fillet steak with sautéed mushrooms and onion rings.

Chef: Daryl Jordan **Owners:** John Macaloney, Colin Macaloney
Times: 12-2/6-9.30, Closed 26-27 Dec, 1-3 Jan, Closed D Mon
Prices: Fixed L £17.50-£19.50, Starter £7.50-£12.50, Main £19-£25, Dessert £8.50, Service optional **Wine:** 40 bottles over £20, 20 bottles under £20, 8 by the glass **Notes:** Civ Wed 94, Air con **Seats:** 54, Pr/dining room 150
Children: Menu, Portions **Directions:** From Glasgow take A80 towards Stirling. Continue past Cumbernauld, at junct 4 take A803 signed Kilsyth/Bonnybridge. At T-junct turn right. Hotel 1m on right **Parking:** 100

GRANGEMOUTH   MAP 21 NS98
◎◎ The Grange Manor
Modern
Family-run manor-house hotel with innovative cuisine

☎ 01324 474836 Glensburgh FK3 8XJ
e-mail: info@grangemanor.co.uk
web: www.grangemanor.co.uk

This stylish, country-house hotel is set in lovely gardens on the outskirts of Grangemouth. There's a choice of two dining venues: Wallace's bistro bar, serving popular international dishes, and Le Chardon, an elegant restaurant for more formal dining. The latter offers some adventurous cooking, beautifully presented, using the finest local ingredients. Sweet seared scallops are served with lavender and pumpkin purée and black pudding, dressed with infused raspberry and champagne balsamic. Garlic-crusted suprême of chicken is another elaborate and well-flavoured dish, stuffed with a leek and tarragon farcie on Chinese greens with a chive velouté.

The Grange Manor

Chef: Paul Cook **Owners:** Monument Leisure Ltd **Times:** 12-2/7-9.30, Closed 26 Dec, 1-2 Jan, Sun, Closed L Sat **Prices:** Fixed L £10.95-£15.95, Starter £3.95-£9.95, Main £9.95-£24.95, Dessert £3.95-£6.95, Service optional **Wine:** 30 bottles over £20, 25 bottles under £20, 9 by the glass **Notes:** Dress Restrictions, Smart casual, Civ Wed 160, Air con **Seats:** 65, Pr/dining room 40 **Children:** Menu, Portions **Rooms:** 36 (36 en suite)
★★★★ HL **Directions:** M9 (eastward) junct 6 200 mtrs on right, M9 (westward) junct 5, then A905 for 2m **Parking:** 150

FIFE

ANSTRUTHER   MAP 21 NO50
◎◎◎ Cellar Restaurant
see page 600

SCOTLAND

SCOTLAND

Cellar Restaurant

ANSTRUTHER MAP 21 NO50

Seafood, European

Superb seafood served in atmospheric restaurant

☎ 01333 310378 24 East Green KY10 3AA

Peter Jukes' well-known seafood restaurant is a 400-year-old former cooperage, where barrels were made for the herring industry, and retains an old, rustic feel with roaring log fires, beams, stone floors and walls, and an eclectic décor featuring local art and pottery. You'll find it tucked away in a cobbled courtyard close to the harbour.

The real draw is of course the food and the restaurant has an established reputation, so it's worth booking in advance. The philosophy is simple and extremely successful, the very best fresh fish and other produce, cooked with care to allow the flavours to shine through. A daily-changing array of dishes uses consistently excellent produce - signature classics such as crayfish bisque gratin, River Forth langoustines, roasted whole with either lemon or garlic butter, or fillet of wild Channel Isle sea bass served with crushed potatoes flavoured with chopped black olives, garlic, mint and oregano and Niçoise dressing. There are a few alternatives to seafood, as well as some delicious desserts. Front of house, Susan Dukes offers a warm welcome and can help you match suitable wines with the various dishes from a well-chosen list.

Chef: Peter Jukes
Owners: Peter Jukes
Times: 12.30-1.30/7-9.30, Closed Xmas, Sun, Mon, Closed L Tue
Prices: Food prices not confirmed for 2008. Please telephone for details
Seats: 40
Directions: Located behind Scottish Fisheries Museum
Parking: Outside

CUPAR   MAP 21 NO31

◉◉ Ostlers Close Restaurant

Modern British

Modern, elegant restaurant making good use of excellent local ingredients

☎ 01334 655574   Bonnygate KY15 4BU
web: www.ostlersclose.co.uk

Tucked away down the eponymous close, this long-established, family-run restaurant attracts a loyal coterie of local food enthusiasts - as well as those drawn from further afield - with its well-deserved reputation for charming service and assured cooking. The owners have a passion for fresh, local ingredients (many of which are grown in their garden) and in particular for wild mushrooms which they pick themselves from local woodland, plus there's always locally-landed sea-fresh fish on the menu. Take a fillet of Pittenweem halibut, for instance, served with St Andrews Bay lobster, or a saddle of roe venison teamed with wild mushrooms and a celeriac rösti, while an apple tarte Tatin with apple ripple ice cream might head-up desserts.

Chef: James Graham   **Owners:** James & Amanda Graham   **Times:** 12.15-1.30/7-9.30, Closed 25-26 Dec, 1-2 Jan, 2 wks Oct, 2 wks Etr, Sun-Mon, Closed L Tue-Fri   **Prices:** Starter £5-£10.50, Main £11-£20, Dessert £5.75-£6.75, Service optional   **Wine:** 60 bottles over £20, 31 bottles under £20, 6 by the glass   **Seats:** 26   **Children:** Min 6 yrs D, Portions   **Directions:** In small lane off main street, A91   **Parking:** On street, public car park

DUNFERMLINE   MAP 21 NT08

◉ Cardoon

Modern, Traditional

Contemporary cooking in relaxed conservatory restaurant

☎ 01383 736258   Best Western Keavil House, Crossford KY12 8QW
e-mail: sales@keavilhouse.co.uk
web: www.keavilhouse.co.uk/ConservatoryRestaurant.asp

A 16th-century former manor house plays host to the Keavil House Hotel and its stylish, conservatory restaurant, Cardoon, which overlooks the gardens and has a terrace for fair-weather aperitifs. Rich colours and a bright, airy, relaxed atmosphere create the mood, while the kitchen's crowd-pleasing, modern, brasserie-style repertoire suits the surroundings, the conventional three-course format enhanced by a range of light dish options and grills. Expect pan-fried sea bass with baby pak choi and fennel and orange salad, and perhaps a cherry and frangipane tart teamed with pecan nut and butterscotch ice cream to finish.

Chef: Phil Yates   **Owners:** Queensferry Hotels Ltd   **Times:** 12-2/6.30-9.30   **Prices:** Fixed D £12.50, Starter £5.95-£6, Main £12.25-£19.95, Dessert £4, Service optional   **Wine:** 11 bottles over £20, 23 bottles under £20, 6 by the glass   **Notes:** Vegetarian available, Dress Restrictions, No football colours, Civ Wed 200   **Seats:** 65, Pr/dining room 22   **Children:** Menu, Portions   **Rooms:** 47 (47 en suite) ★★★ HL   **Directions:** M90 junct 3, 7m from Forth Road Bridge, take A985, turning right after bridge. From Dunfermline, 2m W on A994   **Parking:** 175

ELIE   MAP 21 NO40

◉◉ Sangsters

Modern British

Enjoy great Scottish dishes in relaxed surroundings

☎ 01333 331001   51 High St KY9 1BZ
e-mail: bruce@sangsters.co.uk
web: www.sangsters.co.uk

A seaside village restaurant, Sangsters has a relaxed and peaceful atmosphere with a comfortable lounge for pre-dinner drinks and after-dinner coffees. The dining room has bright, clean and simple lines, the walls hung with local prints and watercolours. Cooking is precise, showing attention to detail and considerable skill in a menu of modern British cooking prepared from quality raw ingredients. Impressive dishes include Ross-shire diver scallops with ginger, lime and peppercorn butter, served with Thai coconut sauce, followed by oven-baked fillet of North Sea halibut, the sea-fresh fish complemented by an Arbroath smokie and chive crust with a vegetable risotto and vermouth sauce. Cinnamon pannacotta with apple vanilla and lemon compôte and an apple and cider sorbet might catch the eye at dessert, or chocolate-lovers might succumb to the chocolate cheesecake with cherry compôte home-made ice cream.

Chef: Bruce R Sangster   **Owners:** Bruce & Jacqueline Sangster   **Times:** 12.30-1.30/7-9.30, Closed 25-26 Dec, early Jan, mid Feb/Oct, mid Nov, Mon, Closed L Tue & Sat, D Sun   **Prices:** Fixed L £18.75, Fixed D £32.50, Service optional   **Wine:** 44 bottles over £20, 13 bottles under £20, 7 by the glass   **Notes:** Sun L 3 courses £25, Dress Restrictions, Smart casual   **Seats:** 28   **Children:** Min 12 yrs   **Directions:** From St Andrews on the A917, take the B9131 to Anstruther, turn right at rdbt and follow A917 to Elie. 11m from St Andrews   **Parking:** On street

KIRKCALDY MAP 21 NT29

◉ Dunnikier House Hotel

Traditional V

Local flavours in Adam-style dining room

☎ 01592 268393 Dunnikier Park KY1 3LP
e-mail: recp@dunnikier-house-hotel.co.uk
web: www.dunnikier-house-hotel.co.uk

The Oswald Room is an elegant Adam-style dining room in this converted 18th-century manse house. Elegant panelling, efficient service, good-quality settings and smart high-backed chairs create a formal backdrop to the contemporary menus. Scottish dishes use lots of local, seasonal produce such as starters of mushroom provençale in a pastry case and main courses of either peppered venison with grilled vegetables or salmon steak with a sesame seed crust, and roasted cherry tomatoes with leek and white wine sauce. Finish with lemon and blackcurrant crème brûlée.

Chef: Simon Bain **Owners:** Brian & Jane Maloney **Times:** 12-2/6-9 **Prices:** Fixed L £15, Fixed D £24, Starter £3.95-£5.50, Main £12.25-£18.50, Dessert £2.50-£5.95, Service optional **Wine:** 4 bottles over £20, 4 bottles under £20, 2 by the glass **Notes:** Fixed L 3 courses £24, Fixed D 3 & 4 courses £24, Vegetarian menu, Civ Wed 150 **Seats:** 22, Pr/dining room 15 **Children:** Menu, Portions **Rooms:** 15 (15 en suite) ★★★ HL **Directions:** Turn off A92 at Kirkcaldy West, take 3rd exit at rdbt signed hospital/crematorium, then 1st left past school **Parking:** 100

MARKINCH MAP 21 NO20

◉◉ Balbirnie House

Classic 🍷 NOTABLE WINE LIST

Top-notch cooking in a sophisticated setting

☎ 01592 610066 Balbirnie Park KY7 6NE
e-mail: info@balbirnie.co.uk
web: www.balbirnie.co.uk

Despite being one of Scotland's most important Grade A listed buildings, this hotel describes itself as 'swanky but not snooty!'. It boasts a choice of restaurants to suit your mood, serving delicious dishes in both its orangery restaurant and more informal bistro. Expect accomplished cooking rooted in classical cuisine: duck with orange sauce, dauphinoise potatoes and French beans perhaps, or grilled halibut with chive mash, spinach, Mull cheddar and parsley cream sauce. Between the starter and main you can enjoy a light intermediate course such as shellfish bisque with saffron aïoli, or Granny Smith sorbet with Calvados, while desserts might include raspberry and Drambuie parfait.

Chef: Ian MacDonald **Owners:** The Russell family **Times:** 12-1.30/7-9 **Prices:** Fixed L £13.50, Fixed D £36, Starter £3.95-£7.95, Main £8.50-£17.50, Dessert £4.50, Service optional **Wine:** 100 bottles over £20, 43 bottles under £20, 10 by the glass **Notes:** Fixed D 4 courses, Civ Wed 200, Air con **Seats:** 65, Pr/dining room 216 **Children:** Menu, Portions **Rooms:** 30 (30 en suite)★★★★ HL **Directions:** M90 junct 13, follow signs for Glenrothes and Tay Bridge, right onto B9130 to Markinch and Balbirnie Park **Parking:** 100

PEAT INN MAP 21 NO40

◉◉ The Peat Inn

Modern British

The original restaurant with rooms

☎ 01334 840206   KY15 5LH
e-mail: stay@thepeatinn.co.uk
web: www.thepeatinn.co.uk

You only have to step inside this 300-year-old whitewashed coaching inn to discover a gastro-pub that pays serious homage to fine dining. Modest on the outside, inside sumptuous fabrics, gleaming crystal glasses and polished silver cutlery combine with high-backed chairs, tapestries and beams in a smartly decorated dining room. Recently refurbished, there are three separate dining areas, each with its own character in the style of a French auberge. The highly accomplished cooking shows great attention to detail with a focus on flavour, presentation and sourcing of quality produce, while intelligently simple, appealing, balanced combinations are delivered in fine style on the menu of the day, tasting option and carte. Take wild halibut served with wilted greens and a braised oxtail and horseradish velouté, and to close, perhaps a pavé of Amedei chocolates with praline ice cream.

Chef: Geoffery Smeddle **Owners:** Geoffery & Katherine Smeddle **Times:** 12.30-2/7-9.30, Closed 25-26 Dec, 1-4 Jan, Sun-Mon **Prices:** Fixed L £22, Fixed D £32, Starter £8-£13, Main £16-£20, Dessert £8, Service optional **Wine:** 250 bottles over £20, 10 bottles under £20, 9 by the glass **Notes:** Fixed L 3 courses, Tasting menu 6 courses £48, incl coffee **Seats:** 40, Pr/dining room 14 **Rooms:** 8 (8 en suite) ★★★★ RR **Directions:** At junction of B940/B941, 6m SW of St Andrews **Parking:** 24

ST ANDREWS MAP 21 NO51

◉◉ Fairmont St Andrews

Mediterranean V NEW

Mediterranean cooking in luxuriously appointed hotel restaurant

☎ 01334 837000   KY16 8PN
e-mail: standrews.scotland@fairmont.com
web: www.fairmont.com

Overlooking the bay and flanked by its two golf courses, a central atrium is the focal point of this resort hotel. Esperante is the well-presented restaurant overlooking the atrium with an opulent Mediterranean atmosphere, deep ruby and red décor and luxurious upholstery. Staff are professional and friendly. The generous menu is heavily influenced by French and Italian classics with contemporary British touches. Dishes are prepared with skill and care, and good use is made of top-quality ingredients. Take lobster ravioli with braised lettuce and crushed peas in basil butter sauce, followed perhaps by sautéed monkfish tail with braised oxtail, salsify and ceps, or sea bass with coriander couscous, tortellini of langoustines and a vine tomato cappuccino, and to finish, a classic warm chocolate fondant or tiramisù.

Fairmont St Andrews

Times: 7.30-9.30, Closed Mon-Tues, Closed L all wk **Prices:** Fixed D £43.50, Service optional **Wine:** 67 bottles over £20, 3 bottles under £20, 6 by the glass **Notes:** Dégustation menu available with selected wines, Vegetarian menu, Dress Restrictions, No denim, Civ Wed 600, Air con **Seats:** 60, Pr/dining room 80 **Children:** Min 14 yrs **Rooms:** 217 (217 en suite) ★★★★★ HL **Directions:** 1.5m outside St Andrews on A917 towards Crail **Parking:** 250

⊛⊛ Inn at Lathones

British, French 🍷 NOTABLE WINE LIST 💻

Exquisite local produce, imaginative menus and an ancient inn

☎ 01334 840494 Largoward KY9 1JE
e-mail: lathones@theinn.co.uk
web: www.theinn.co.uk

Don't let the resident ghosts put you off - it's just part of the charm of St Andrews' oldest coaching inn. Over 400 years old, the premises have been extended over the years to provide accommodation and meeting rooms; décor mixes modern style with traditional country-house flair, with a relaxed and friendly atmosphere pervading throughout. Modern British cooking with French influences and refined techniques makes the best of the larder that the area has to offer. Starters might include pan-fried foie gras with a sweet grape sauce, followed by grilled lamb cutlets with celeriac purée, crispy leek and a light jus. The Market menu, à la carte and intriguing Trilogy menu provide the best ways of sampling the kitchen's skill and creativity.

Inn at Lathones

Chef: Marc Guibert **Owners:** Mr N White **Times:** 12-2.30/6-9.30, Closed 25-26 Dec, 4-18 Jan **Prices:** Fixed L £14.50, Starter £3.95-£8, Main £18-£26, Dessert £7-£8.50, Service optional **Wine:** 89 bottles over £20, 17 bottles under £20, 9 by the glass **Notes:** Dress Restrictions, Smart casual, Civ Wed 40 **Seats:** 34, Pr/dining room 30 **Children:** Menu, Portions **Rooms:** 13 (13 en suite) ★★★★ INN **Directions:** 5m SW of St Andrews on A915. In 0.5m before Largoward on left, just after hidden dip **Parking:** 34

⊛⊛ Macdonald Rusacks Hotel

Traditional British

Accomplished cooking in legendary golfing setting

☎ 0870 400 8128 Pilmour Links KY16 9JQ
e-mail: general.rusacks@macdonald-hotels.co.uk
web: www.macdonald-hotels.co.uk

Just a short chip from the 18th hole, this St Andrews' veteran offers unrivalled views of the famous golf course. The food's not bad either; take your eyes off the green and you'll find a tempting range of sophisticated, contemporary, weekly-changing dishes, including the likes of grilled rainbow trout with Arbroath smokie fishcake, served with sautéed red pepper and leek fondue, or pot-au-feu guinea fowl with dhal and winter root vegetables; vegetarians might like butternut squash and red pepper lasagne with goat's cheese gratin. For those with a sweet tooth, the Bailey's and espresso brûlée with white chocolate cookies is sure to appeal.

Times: 12-2.30/6.30-9 **Rooms:** 68 (68 en suite) ★★★★ HL **Directions:** From M90 junct 8 take A91 to St Andrews. Hotel on left on entering the town

⊛⊛⊛ The Road Hole Grill

see page 604

◉◉◉

The Road Hole Grill

ST ANDREWS   MAP 21 NO51

British 🍷 NOTABLE WINE LIST

Sumptuous dining in golfing heaven

☎ 01334 474371 Old Course Hotel, Golf Resort & Spa
KY16 9SP

e-mail: reservations@oldcoursehotel.co.uk
web: www.oldcoursehotel.co.uk

Situated on the fourth floor of the Old Course Hotel, one of the most famous golfing hotels in the world, this elegant, traditional grill room commands stunning views over the course and St Andrews Bay. Luxury and comfort are bywords in the grand hotel, no more so than in this traditional fine-dining venue, with its elegant oak panelling, crisp linen-clothed tables and open-to-view theatre kitchen. Friendly staff deliver exacting service and advice as befits the five-star setting. Well-balanced menus make full use of quality seasonal, local Scottish produce, with a welcome focus on luxury ingredients from the land and sea, with the likes of foie gras, langoustines, scallops, oysters and Glen Lochry venison perhaps making an appearance on the impressive carte. Beautifully presented, traditional classics are given a modern twist; take a fillet of Speyside beef with braised oxtail, root vegetables and a red wine and horseradish fumet, or perhaps pan-roast, line-caught sea bass with fennel gnocchi, a fricassée of leek and crab and saffron and vanilla sauce, while a warm Dundee marmalade cake - served with clotted cream ice cream and Dalwhinnie sabayon - might catch the eye at dessert.

Chef: Drew Heron **Owners:** Kohler Company **Times:** 7-10, Closed 23-26 Dec (residents only), Closed L all week **Prices:** Fixed D £43-£45, Starter £12-£16, Main £19-£28, Dessert £8.50-£13 **Wine:** 220 bottles over £20, 8 by the glass **Notes:** Vegetarian available, Dress Restrictions, Smart dress, no jeans, jacket & tie, Civ Wed 200 **Seats:** 60, Pr/dining room 20 **Children:** Menu, Portions **Rooms:** 144 (144 en suite)★★★★★ HL **Directions:** M90 junct 8, close to A91. 5 mins from St Andrews **Parking:** 100

ST ANDREWS Continued

◎◎ Rufflets Country House & Garden Restaurant

Modern British 🍷 NOTABLE WINE LIST

Stylish country-house dining in a friendly atmosphere

☎ 01334 472594 Strathkinness Low Rd KY16 9TX
e-mail: reservations@rufflets.co.uk
web: www.rufflets.co.uk

This stylish Edwardian country house with delightful formal gardens and woodland makes a wonderful retreat. The restaurant features simple and stylish traditional décor with lots of colourful artwork. Service is particularly friendly and attentive making the diner feel really at ease. The chef cooks modern cuisine with influences from the Mediterranean, using the freshest local produce available. Typical dishes include a starter of Inverawe smoked salmon with pickled cucumber, crispy capers and lemon vinaigrette. Likewise, a main course might be roast suprême of guinea fowl stuffed with chestnut on honey-glazed carrots, with fondant potatoes and Calvados café au lait. Scottish cheeses like Dunsyre Blue and Gruth Dhu Stone might appear on the cheeseboard.

Chef: Mark Nixon **Owners:** Ann Murray-Smith **Times:** 12.30-2/7-9, Closed L Mon-Sat **Prices:** Fixed L £10-£16.50, Fixed D £38.50-£50, Service optional, Group min 20 service 10% **Wine:** 88 bottles over £20, 18 bottles under £20, 9 by the glass **Notes:** Dress Restrictions, No shorts, Civ Wed 45 **Seats:** 80, Pr/dining room 80 **Children:** Menu, Portions **Rooms:** 24 (24 en suite)★★★★ HL **Directions:** 1.5m W of St Andrews on B939 **Parking:** 50

◎ Russell Hotel

Scottish, International

Imaginative cooking in an intimate setting

☎ 01334 473447 26 The Scores KY16 9AS
e-mail: russellhotel@talk21.com
web: www.russellhotelstandrews.co.uk

This comfortable and intimate hotel restaurant prides itself on the sort of convivial atmosphere and closely-arranged tables usually only found in Paris bistros. The international cooking draws on French and British influences and high-quality local ingredients appear in bradan rost kiln-smoked salmon from Loch Fyne, roast loin of Highland venison, or roast cannon of Perthshire lamb and lamb's kidneys with sweet potato purée and light Madeira jus. Desserts could include rhubarb and custard cheesecake or pannacotta with a tuile basket and fruit coulis.

Russell Hotel

Chef: Michael Smith **Owners:** Gordon De Vries **Times:** 12-2/6.30-9.30, Closed Xmas **Prices:** Fixed L £9.95-£17, Fixed D £29.50, Service optional **Wine:** 17 bottles over £20, 23 bottles under £20, 12 by the glass **Notes:** Vegetarian available, Civ Wed 40, Air con **Seats:** 40, Pr/dining room 10 **Children:** Menu, Portions **Rooms:** 10 (10 en suite) ★★ HL **Directions:** A91 to St Andrews. At 2nd rdbt take 1st exit onto Golf Place. After 200 yds turn right into The Scores, hotel is 200 yds on right **Parking:** 80

◉◉ St Andrews Golf Hotel

Scottish
Modern Scottish fine-dining restaurant

☎ 01334 472611 40 The Scores KY16 9AS
e-mail: reception@standrews-golf.co.uk
web: www.standrews-golf.co.uk

A friendly, family-run hotel with amazing views of the famous golf course and the coastline. Dunes Restaurant is a formal dining room where professional staff are on hand, serving at smartly-set tables. Skilful cooking produces pleasingly simple dishes based on fine Scottish produce. A hard day on the golf course will be well rewarded here with hearty portions. Try warm St Andrews Bay crab cake with rocket and basil salad, followed by seared scallop of venison, spinach and dauphinoise potatoes and shallot jus. As we went to press we understand that the hotel was completing a refurbishment.

Chef: Craig Hart **Owners:** Justin Hughes **Times:** 12.30-2/7-9.30, Closed 26-28 Dec **Prices:** Food prices not confirmed for 2008. Please telephone for details **Notes:** Dress Restrictions, No jeans, shorts, trainers, baseball caps, Civ Wed 180, Air con **Seats:** 60, Pr/dining room 20 **Children:** Menu, Portions **Rooms:** 22 (22 en suite) ★★★ HL **Directions:** Enter town on A91, cross both mini rdbts, turn left at Golf Place and 1st right into The Scores. Hotel 200 yds on right **Parking:** 6

◉ Sands Restaurant

International, Mediterranean NOTABLE WINE LIST
Elegant, stylish restaurant within golf-resort hotel complex

☎ 01334 474371 & 468228 The Old Course Hotel, Golf Resort & Spa KY16 9SP
e-mail: reservations@oldcoursehotel.co.uk
web: www.oldcoursehotel.co.uk

The hotel borders the 17th fairway of the legendary Old Course, and the Sands Restaurant is its second dining option. It has a stylish, sophisticated décor with lots of dark wood and black leather - shades

of a luxury ocean-going liner of yesteryear - and an upbeat atmosphere. The cooking is unpretentious with a good smattering of Mediterranean-influenced brasserie-style dishes. Perhaps pan-seared North Atlantic halibut with roasted vine cherry tomatoes, baby leeks and a white wine nage, or grilled Speyside sirloin steak with horseradish mash and a fricassée of vegetables. Attentive, professional table service.

Chef: Mark Lindsey **Owners:** Kohler Company **Times:** 12-6/6-10, Closed 23-26 Dec (residents only) **Prices:** Starter £5.75-£10.50, Main £13.50-£19.50, Dessert £5.50, Service included **Wine:** 22 bottles over £20, 8 by the glass **Notes:** Vegetarian available, Smart casual, Civ Wed 200 **Seats:** 80, Pr/dining room 40 **Children:** Menu, Portions **Rooms:** 144 (144 en suite) ★★★★★ HL **Directions:** M90 junct 8. Situated close to A91 and 5 mins walk from St Andrews **Parking:** 100

◉◉◉ The Seafood Restaurant
see page 606

ST MONANS   MAP 21 NO50

◉◉ The Seafood Restaurant

Modern Scottish ❦
The freshest seafood by the harbour

☎ 01333 730327 16 West End KY10 2BX
e-mail: info@theseafoodrestaurant.com
web: www.theseafoodrestaurant.com

The restaurant occupies an old fisherman's cottage and features an 800-year-old freshwater well with mythical healing powers. There's an open fire in the Victorian bar, a terrace for sitting outside, and picture windows in the modern restaurant extension overlooking the harbour and the Firth of Forth across the Isle of May. The cooking deals in the freshest fish simply cooked, a light touch allowing the main ingredient to dominate on the plate. Think pan-seared scallops served with a pancetta and herb risotto, or grilled fillet of halibut with anchovy-crushed potatoes, spinach and a grain mustard sauce, and to finish, perhaps a baked lime cheesecake with blueberries and flaked almonds. There's usually one dish on the fixed-price repertoire for meat-eaters too.

Chef: Andy Simpson **Owners:** Craig Millar, Tim Butler **Times:** 12-2.30/6-9.30, Closed 25-26 Dec, 1-2 Jan, Mon, Tues **Prices:** Fixed L £20, Fixed D £30-£35, Service included **Wine:** 40 bottles over £20, 18 bottles under £20, 6 by the glass **Seats:** 44 **Children:** Portions **Directions:** Take A959 from St Andrews to Anstruther, then head W on A917 through Pittenweem. In St Monans to harbour then right **Parking:** 10

The Seafood Restaurant

ST ANDREWS MAP 21 NO51

Modern Seafood 🍷 NOTABLE WINE LIST 🕯

Accomplished cooking in a stunning glass building by the bay

☎ 01334 479475 The Scores KY16 9AS
e-mail: info@theseafoodrestaurant.com
web: www.theseafoodrestaurant.com

Once an open-air theatre, this restaurant is a stunning modern, glass-walled building, virtually suspended over the bay to give uninterrupted views of the sea and coastline. Uncompromisingly contemporary and upmarket in style, the bright, clean-lined interior combines traditional high-quality table settings with a funky style of seating and napery. The open-plan kitchen not only provides a striking feature but also allows tantalising aromas to drift into the restaurant and heighten expectancy.

As the names suggests, seafood dominates the menu, a fixed-price affair with a good-value alternative set meal in winter. The clean, crisp cooking style is flavour-driven, allowing the wonderfully fresh produce to shine. Think smoked haddock rarebit with creamed leeks and pancetta, or grilled fillet of John Dory served with braised oxtail, wilted green vegetables, truffle and pea foam. This is sister to The Seafood Restaurant at St Monans, down the coast, where Tim Butler and Craig Millar first joined forces (see entry) and is a recent AA Wine Award winner for Scotland.

Chef: Craig Millar, Neil Clarke, Scott Miller
Owners: Craig Millar, Tim Butler
Times: 12-2.30/6.30-10, Closed 25-26 Dec, Jan 1
Prices: Fixed L £21, Fixed D £35-£45, Group min 8 service 10%
Wine: 180 bottles over £20, 5 bottles under £20, 8 by the glass
Notes: Oct-Mar fixed L menu 3 courses £12.95 Mon-Fri, Air con
Seats: 60
Children: Min 12 yrs, Portions
Directions: Please telephone for directions
Parking: 50mtr away

CITY OF GLASGOW

GLASGOW   **MAP 20 NS56**

⊛ An Lochan

Modern V 🖥 ✆ NEW

Simple café style in a trendy residential area, serving Scottish produce

☎ 0141 338 6606 340 Crow Rd G11 7HT
web: www.anlochan.co.uk

Formerly a bank, this bustling shop-front style establishment has tables on the pavement, but inside you'll find cheery bistro-style décor with blue gingham tablecloths, blue walls and a seafood theme. Named after one of its restaurants that is situated by a loch, the restaurant serves modern Scottish food ranging from light snacks, a blackboard tapas menu and pre-theatre dinners to an evening carte. Majoring on seafood, a sample evening menu might include smoked haddock chowder with a poached oyster for starters, then continue with steamed West Coast mussels, clams and scallops, or a platter of seafood. Simple cooking that makes the most of fresh, local produce. Service is relaxed and friendly.

Chef: Claire Mckie **Owners:** The McKie Family **Times:** 12-3/6-11.30, Closed 25 & 26 Dec, 1-4 Jan, Mon, Closed D Sun **Prices:** Fixed L £8.95-£11.95, Fixed D £15.95, Starter £4.95-£8.95, Main £15.95-£26.95, Dessert £4.50-£4.95, Service optional **Wine:** 9 bottles over £20, 10 bottles under £20, 3 by the glass **Notes:** Fixed D 5 courses £32.50 available Fri-Sat, Vegetarian menu, Air con **Seats:** 40 **Children:** Portions
Directions: Telephone for directions

⊛ Brian Maule at Chardon d'Or

British, French V 🏆 NOTABLE WINE LIST 🖥

Confident cooking in a slick city-centre venue

☎ 0141 248 3801 176 West Regent St G2 4RL
e-mail: info@brianmaule.com
web: www.brianmaule.com

A blend of modern and traditional works well in this converted city-centre Georgian townhouse. Suede and leather banquette seating, cream walls and vibrant pictures contrast with high ceilings and other original features. Attentive, friendly service adds to the relaxed ambience, where classic French and British cuisine - with a modern twist - dominates a menu created from high-quality ingredients. Try roast fillet of lamb served with spiced pastille and aubergine caviar, or baked halibut with a tomato fondue, herb crust and white wine cream sauce, while a tarte Tatin of apple with vanilla ice cream might provide the finish.

Chef: Brian Maule **Owners:** Brian Maule at Chardon d'Or **Times:** 12-2/6-10, Closed 2 wks Jan, BHs, Sun, Closed L Sat **Prices:** Fixed L £15.50, Starter £6.75-£9.95, Main £19.85-£24, Dessert £6.95-£7.50, Service optional
Wine: 280 bottles over £20, 6 by the glass **Notes:** Tasting menu 6 courses £48.50, Vegetarian menu, Air con **Seats:** 90, Pr/dining room 60
Children: Portions **Directions:** 10-minute walk from Glasgow central station **Parking:** Metered parking on street

⊛⊛ The Buttery

Modern British

Vibrant flavours in Glaswegian grandee

☎ 0141 221 8188 652 Argyle St G3 8UF
e-mail: the_buttery@hotmail.co.uk
web: www.eatbuttery.com

This revitalised Glasgow institution - a timbered 19th-century former wine merchant's premises and tavern set in a city tenement - has a surprisingly unassuming exterior. But inside is quite a different matter, its rich and luxurious décor combine original Victorian fittings with fashionable modern touches. Think oak-panelled walls, high ornate ceilings, stained-glass windows, deeply comfortable seating, crisp white linen and a stunning marble-topped bar. The kitchen's modern approach deals in quality ingredients from the abundant Scottish larder, its balanced, appropriately refined dishes showcasing clean, clear flavours. Think grilled fillet of West Coast turbot rolled in salsa Romesco on confit leeks with a smoked haddock and saffron cream sauce, and a brandy crème brûlée finish, served with fudge ice cream and vanilla sauce.

Chef: Christopher Watson **Owners:** Ian Fleming **Times:** 12-2/5.30-10, Closed 1-7 Jan, Sun, Mon, Closed L Sat **Prices:** Fixed L £16, Fixed D £50, Starter £8.50-£18, Main £16.50-£36, Dessert £6.50-£18, Service optional
Notes: Fixed D 4 courses, Air con **Seats:** 60, Pr/dining room 40
Children: Portions **Directions:** From St Vincent St (city centre) first left onto Elderslie St, at rdbt, left onto Argyle St. Restaurant 600 yds on left
Parking: 36

⊛⊛ Gamba

Scottish, Seafood 🖥

One of Glasgow's most established fish restaurants

☎ 0141 572 0899 225a West George St G2 2ND
e-mail: info@gamba.co.uk
web: www.gamba.co.uk

Located right in the city centre, this perennial seafood favourite ('gamba' being Spanish for prawn) continues to provide attentive service and consistent food in a comfortable, stylish basement setting. Unsurprisingly, there's a striking Mediterranean theme to the décor - warm colours, terracotta floor tiles, stylish fish artwork and polished-wood tables, plus a cosy cocktail area. The Mediterranean theme extends to the food - though with some subtle Asian influence too - on the well-balanced menu. But it's the classics, such as the Gamba fish soup - for which they are deservedly renowned - that win the day. Otherwise, you might try roast fillet of cod served with a smoked haddock, shrimp and pea curry, or perhaps seared scallops with sticky rice and black bean dipping sauce.

CONTINUED

SCOTLAND

SCOTLAND

GLASGOW CONTINUED

Chef: Derek Marshall, Wayne Shannon **Owners:** Mr A C Tomkins & Mr D Marshall **Times:** 12-2.30/5-10.30, Closed 25-26 Dec, 1-2 Jan, BHs, Sun **Prices:** Food prices not confirmed for 2008. Please telephone for details **Seats:** 66 **Children:** Min 14 yrs **Directions:** Telephone for directions

◉◉ Hotel du Vin Bistro at One Devonshire Gardens

British, European NEW

Elegant bistro with modern food and notable wines in stylish townhouse hotel

☎ 0141 339 2001 1 Devonshire Gardens G12 0UX
e-mail: events@onedevonshiregardens.com
web: www.onedevonshiregardens.com

Set in a series of Victorian townhouses on a tree-lined terrace in Glasgow's West End, the Hotel du Vin group have remodelled this contemporary boutique hotel in their usual fine style. The refurbished interior is sympathetic to the original architecture while adding all the modern comforts. The bar-lounge has deep sofas and comfortable chairs, while the popular, atmospheric, oak-panelled bistro follows the theme. The kitchen's repertoire of modern and classic dishes supports the group's philosophy; quality food cooked simply with the freshest local ingredients and attractive presented. And, as the hotel name suggests, wine is a hallmark theme, with a list to delight backed by knowledgeable, friendly and relaxed service. So expect dishes like cannelloni of blade of beef wrapped in turnip with roasted garlic and Morteau sauce or butter-roasted, line-caught halibut. There is also a cosy and inviting whisky snug.

Chef: Paul Tamburrini **Times:** 6.30-9.30, Closed 25-26 Dec, Closed L Private lunches only **Prices:** Food prices not confirmed for 2008. Please telephone for details **Wine:** 70 bottles over £20, 7 by the glass **Notes:** Civ Wed 48 **Children:** Portions **Rooms:** 35 (35 en suite) ★★★★ TH **Directions:** M8 junct 17, follow signs for A82 after 1.5 miles turn left into Hyndland Rd **Parking:** Parking available, residential area

◉ Ho Wong Restaurant

Chinese

Stylish design with welcoming Chinese hospitality and an emphasis on seafood

☎ 0141 221 3550 & 221 4669 82 York St G2 8LE
e-mail: ho.wong@amserve.com
web: www.ho-wong.com

There's quite a buzz to this popular, upmarket, street-level restaurant close to the city centre. Friendly, skilled and attentive staff, stylish modern décor and impressive surroundings all contribute to the relaxed atmosphere. Fish dishes are a real highlight on the sophisticated, traditional Cantonese-style menu. Push the boat out with fresh lobster (perhaps baked in ginger and spring onion), or maybe try monkfish with black bean sauce, or fillet of beef gumbo. Quality fish is sourced from MacCallums of Troon, while a series of set-menu options are available for two or more diners.

Chef: S Wong **Owners:** David Wong **Times:** 12-2.15/6-11.30, Closed L Sun **Prices:** Fixed L £9.50, Fixed D £18-£23, Starter £4-£7, Main £10-£18, Dessert £2.80-£3.90, Service optional, Group min 8 service 10% **Wine:** 42 bottles over £20, 30 bottles under £20, 4 by the glass **Notes:** Vegetarian available, Air con **Seats:** 90, Pr/dining room 35 **Directions:** Off Argyle St. 2 mins from Glasgow Central station **Parking:** 8

◉ Killermont Polo Club

Traditional Indian

Accomplished Indian dining in a polo-inspired setting

☎ 0141 946 5412 2002 Maryhill Rd, Maryhill Park G20 0AB
web: www.killermontpoloclub.com

Dum pukht is the speciality of this stylish eatery - an unusual cuisine thought to have originated with the arrival of the moghul emperors in India. It's said they blended the best of Indian spices with those they'd brought with them from the legendary city of Samarkand in Uzbekhistan to create a flavourful new style of cooking. Nearby Glasgow might seem an odd place for their culinary legacy to take root, but the Killermont does its best to transport you to a different time and place, delivering a great-value menu (particularly at lunchtime) in a setting fit for a maharaja. Start with sakhat kabar (minced lamb with cheese coasted in batter and fried), followed perhaps by chicken dhansak or Kashmiri korma.

Chef: Belbir Farwaha **Owners:** P Thapar **Times:** 12-2.30/5-11.30 **Prices:** Starter £2.95-£6.95, Main £6.50-£14.95, Dessert £2.50-£3.50 **Notes:** Vegetarian available, Dress Restrictions, Smart casual **Seats:** 80, Pr/dining room 30 **Children:** Menu, Portions **Directions:** Telephone for directions or visit website **Parking:** 40

◉◉ Langs Hotel

Modern Scottish

Glitzy and unforgettable modern restaurant with contemporary Scottish cuisine

☎ 0141 333 1500 2 Port Dundas Place G2 3LD
e-mail: neil.raw@langshotels.co.uk
web: www.langshotels.co.uk

A sharply-styled, modern city-centre hotel whose Aurora restaurant makes a bold and colourful statement set in its own secluded environment. The mood lighting is cool and trendy, enhanced by candles on the spacious tables for a touch of intimacy. Staff are casually uniformed and knowledgeable. The cooking is modern Scottish using the finest local ingredients whenever possible. Careful preparation and eye-catching presentations prepare you for the sumptuous flavours that come from a seriously focused kitchen. Alternative eating is in Oshi offering a Euro-fusion style of menu.

Times: 5-10, Closed Sun, Mon, Closed L all wk **Rooms:** 100 (100 en suite) ★★★★ HL **Directions:** Telephone for directions

◉ The Living Room

Modern International 🖥

Laid-back bar that aims to please

☎ 0870 220 3028 150 St Vincent St G2 5NE
e-mail: glasgow@thelivingroom.co.uk
web: www.thelivingroom.co.uk

More Manhattan than Glasgow, this achingly chic bar offers secluded booths and alcoves, decent music and a menu to suit all comers. Its lengthy selection runs from comfort food to fine cuisine, so whether you're in the mood for fish and chips or organic salmon with piperade, wild rocket and paprika, you'll find something to suit. There's a good mix of local and international dishes including mains such as 21-day aged British fillet steak with mash, and Thai red chicken curry. It's great value too, particularly at lunchtime, and there's an extensive range of cocktails and wines by the glass. Sit back and relax.

Chef: Alan Watts **Owners:** Living Ventures **Times:** 11-3/5-11, Closed 25-26 Dec, 1-2 Jan **Prices:** Starter £3.25-£7.75, Main £8.95-£18.95, Dessert £4.50-£4.95, Service optional, Group min 6 service 10% **Wine:** 24 bottles over £20, 14 bottles under £20, 12 by the glass **Notes:** Vegetarian available, Dress Restrictions, Smart casual, no sportswear, Air con **Seats:** 140, Pr/dining room 11 **Children:** Menu, Portions **Directions:** City Centre location between Hope St & Wellington St **Parking:** On street

◉◉ Lux

Modern Scottish V

Stylish, formal fine dining in a converted railway station

☎ 0141 576 7576 1051 Great Western Rd G12 0XP
e-mail: luxstazione@bt.connect.com
web: www.luxstazione.co.uk

Once Kelvinside railway station, this JJ Burnet listed Victorian building has been converted into two stylish restaurants. Situated on the upper floor, Lux's dining room has a modern, minimalist style, with wood floors, comfortable leather chairs, subtle lighting and a muted colour scheme creating a relaxed ambience. The food is resolutely modern with a variety of influences shining through. Dishes bring together unusual combinations of ingredients cooked with obvious technical skill, as in flash-fried king prawns on Swedish potato salad with roast cherry tomatoes and lemon thyme, or fillet of Orkney salmon wrapped in smoked salmon on spinach and lemon cream. For dessert, try coconut and Malibu parfait with vanilla and pineapple compôte, or perhaps poached pear on dark chocolate ice cream with Drambuie caramel. Great service is the icing on the cake.

Chef: Stephen Johnson **Owners:** Stephen Johnson **Times:** 6-until late, Closed 25-26 Dec, 1-2 Jan, Sun ex by arrangement, Closed L all week ex by arrangement **Prices:** Fixed D £33.50, Service optional, Group min 6 service 10% **Wine:** 60 bottles over £20, 6 bottles under £20, 4 by the glass **Notes:** Vegetarian menu, Smart casual, Air con **Seats:** 64, Pr/dining room 14 **Children:** Min 12 yrs **Directions:** At traffic lights signed Gartnavel Hospital, on Great Western Rd. 0.25m E of Anniesland Cross **Parking:** 16

◉ Malmaison

French, British 🍷NOTABLE WINE LIST 💻

French brasserie in a stylish church conversion

☎ 0141 572 1001 278 West George St G2 4LL
e-mail: glasgow@malmaison.com
web: www.malmaison.com

This smart, contemporary hotel is built around a 19th-century former Greek Orthodox church in the historic Charing Cross area of the city. The restaurant, located in the crypt, is packed with atmosphere and comes decked out in modern styling - leather banquettes and chairs, wooden flooring and subtle lighting. The French brasserie-style food is simple but accomplished and uses quality local ingredients; expect steak frites (naturally reared, grass-fed dry-aged rump with home-made chips), veal milanese with tagliatelle and tomato fondue, and perhaps a chocolate fondant with pistachio ice cream to finish.

Chef: Donald McInnes **Owners:** Malmaison Hotels Ltd **Times:** 12-2.30/5.30-10.30 **Prices:** Fixed L £13.50, Fixed D £15.50-£39.95, Starter £4.95-£8.95, Main £10.95-£25, Dessert £5.95, Service added but optional 10%, Group min 10 service 10% **Wine:** 160 bottles over £20, 20 bottles under £20, 20 by the glass **Notes:** Sun Brunch available, Vegetarian available **Seats:** 85, Pr/dining room 22 **Children:** Menu, Portions **Rooms:** 72 (72 en suite) ★★★ HL **Directions:** From George Square take St.Vincent St to Pitt St. Hotel on corner with West George St **Parking:** Q Park Waterloo St

◉ Manna Restaurant

Modern 💻

New style at city-centre bistro

☎ 0141 332 6678 104 Bath St G2 2EN
e-mail: info@mannarestaurant.co.uk
web: www.mannarestaurant.co.uk

Formerly known as Papingo, this restaurant presents a new image and a welcome to a new head chef. The décor has clean lines with cream walls, leather banquette seating and clothed tables. Much attention is focussed on sourcing Scottish produce as the Buccleuch Estate steaks bear witness - Chateaubriand for two, fillet, sirloin and rib-eye are all offered on the menu. Other dishes might be a starter of well-balanced spiced carrot, coriander and coconut soup, followed by perfectly cooked cod on a bed of king prawns, chickpea and wilted spinach curry. Tempting desserts could include warm chocolate sponge with orange ice cream and bitter chocolate sauce.

Chef: John Gillespie **Owners:** Alan Tomkins **Times:** 12-2.30/5-10.30, Closed 25-26 Dec, 1-2 Jan, Closed L Sun **Prices:** Fixed L £9.95, Starter £4-£9, Main £10-£24, Dessert £4-£6, Group min 6 service 10% **Notes:** Pre-theatre D £11.95, Air con **Seats:** 80 **Children:** Min 14 yrs, Portions **Directions:** City centre. At junct of Bath St & Hope St

GLASGOW Continued

◉◉ Michael Caines Restaurant

Modern European V 💻

Concept hotel with stylish décor and accomplished cuisine

☎ 0141 572 6011 & 572 6006 Abode Hotel Glasgow,
129 Bath St G2 2SZ
e-mail: restaurantmanagerglasgow@michaelcaines.com
web: www.michaelcaines.com

Housed in former Department of Education offices, this stylish hotel, with original Edwardian features, boasts a café-bar with low-level lighting, leather seating, table service and a cocktail menu for pre-dinner drinks. The accomplished cooking in the Michael Caines Restaurant has a growing reputation. Here you'll find darkwood flooring, comfortable chairs and banquettes, stylish table appointments, and an eye-catching glass-screened wine cave. A starter of raviolo of pheasant and foie gras with Stornoway black pudding and red wine sauce, followed by saddle of wild red deer with caramelised swede, kohlrabi, braised salsify and mixed berries sets the style. The hot chocolate Earl Grey fondant makes a fabulous finale.

Chef: Martin Donnelly **Owners:** Abode Hotels **Times:** 12-2.30/7-10, Closed 1-2 Jan, Sun **Prices:** Fixed L £12.50, Fixed D £25, Starter £9.50-£13.50, Main £15.95-£23.95, Dessert £7, Service optional **Wine:** 100 bottles over £20, 8 bottles under £20, 8 by the glass **Notes:** Tasting menu £55, Vegetarian menu, Air con **Seats:** 40, Pr/dining room 40
Children: Min 5 yrs, Portions **Rooms:** 60 (60 en suite) ★★★★ HL

◉ Millennium Hotel Glasgow

Modern 💻

Superb-quality ingredients in modern, stylish brasserie

☎ 0141 332 6711 George St G2 1DS
e-mail: reservations.glasgow@mill-cop.com
web: www.millenniumhotels.com

Smack in the heart of the city in pride of place overlooking George Square, the Millennium's contemporary, minimalist-designed interior comes complete with a stylish, relaxed, eye-catching dining room. Think shades of beige and brown, stripped wooden floor, leafy palms, smartly-appointed tables and friendly, unstuffy service. The modern focus extends to the brasserie-style cuisine, where the emphasis is on quality produce from the abundant Scottish larder. Expect a platter of Loch Fyne mussels, langoustine, scallops, bradan rost, salmon and oysters with a chive beurre blanc, and perhaps a trio of chocolate to finish.

Times: 12-2.15/6-10.15, Closed 25-26 Dec, Closed L Sun **Rooms:** 117 (117 en suite) ★★★★ HL **Directions:** M8 junct 15, follow directions to George Sq, brasserie is in Millennium Hotel

◉◉ Rococo

Modern European 💻

Intimate, stylish place to be seen and enjoy impressive cuisine

☎ 0141 221 5004 202 West George St G2 2NR
e-mail: info@rococoglasgow.co.uk
web: www.rococoglasgow.co.uk

This well-established basement restaurant - complete with fibre optic-lit ceiling, marble-tiled floors, blown glass art and trendy oversized leather seats - is one of the most stylish eateries in the city centre. The cooking style is modern British with French and Italian influences, and there is a firm emphasis on fine quality seasonal, local produce. Pan-roasted Oban scallops with pak choi and shiitake mushrooms might feature on the dinner menu, or perhaps roast fillet of Scottish beef with rosemary and parmesan polenta cake. Round things off with a dessert of millefeuille of winter berries, or a delice of Scottish raspberries and champagne. The more simple lunch menu is excellent value for money.

Chef: Mark Tamburrini **Owners:** Alan & Audrey Brown **Times:** 12-3/5-10, Closed 26 Dec, 1 Jan **Prices:** Fixed L £15, Fixed D £39.50-£44.50, Starter £4.25-£8.50, Main £11.50-£18.75, Dessert £4.75-£5.25, Service added but optional 10%, Group min 6 service 10% **Wine:** 100 bottles over £20, 12 by the glass **Notes:** Tasting menu 6 courses £65 **Seats:** 60, Pr/dining room 30
Children: Menu **Directions:** City centre **Parking:** On street parking or NCP
see advert opposite

◉ Saint Jude's

Modern British

Popular restaurant and bar complex

☎ 0141 352 8800 190 Bath St G2 4HG
e-mail: reservations@saintjudes.com
web: www.saintjudes.com

This modern first-floor restaurant and basement bar complex is hidden away in a creeper-clad Victorian townhouse. Its minimalist décor and modern art strike a contemporary note that's also reflected in the food's brasserie style and presentation, with a short, speedy midday menu giving way to a more expansive dinner carte. Starters and desserts really stand out. Kick off with classic moules marinière, followed by roast salmon on French beans, served with sautéed potatoes and provençale sauce, or confit of duck scented with anise on herb mash, in a Burgundy jus. Continue the French theme with crêpes Suzette for dessert.

Times: 12-2.30/5-10.30, Closed 25 Dec, 1-2 Jan, Closed L Sat-Sun **Directions:** City centre

SCOTLAND

⊛ Shish Mahal

British, Indian V

Consistently hitting the mark with fine Indian cuisine

☎ 0141 339 8256 & 334 7899 60-68 Park Rd G4 9JF
e-mail: reservations@shishmahal.co.uk
web: www.shishmahal.co.uk

The Shish Mahal remains unaltered and continues to go from strength to strength after more than 30 years. In three sections, including a mezzanine level, the décor has a Moorish theme, and this consistently good Indian restaurant fills quickly with local residents, business people and students. Service is attentive from uniformed staff. The modern Punjabi cooking style shows great depth of flavour with all the extras meeting the same high standards. Lunch is especially good value. Dinner offers a huge selection of chicken, fish, lamb and vegetarian dishes - try delicious fish pakora with spiced tomato sauce to begin.

Chef: Mr I Humayun **Owners:** Ali A Aslam, Nasim Ahmed **Times:** 12-2/5-11, Closed 25 Dec, Closed L Sun **Prices:** Fixed L £5.50-£6.75, Fixed D £12.95-£16.95, Starter £2.50-£7.95, Main £6.50-£15.95, Dessert £1.90-£3.95, Service optional, Group min 5 service 10% **Wine:** 3 bottles over £20, 13 bottles under £20, 1 by the glass **Notes:** Fixed L 3 courses, Vegetarian menu, Air con **Seats:** 95, Pr/dining room 14 **Children:** Portions **Directions:** From M8/A8 take exit towards Dumbarton, drive along Great Western Rd and turn 1st left into Park Rd **Parking:** Side street, Underground station car park

⊛⊛ Stravaigin

Modern International 🖥

Lively, relaxed basement restaurant with eclectic cooking

☎ 0141 334 2665 30 Gibson St G12 8NX
e-mail: bookings@stravaigin.com
web: www.stravaigin.com

A modern exterior with chrome and blue lighting creates a positive first impression at this popular, refurbished restaurant. The style is distinctly contemporary, with a lacquered tiled floor, stone and leather-covered walls - decorated with modern art and quirky antiques - and lightwood tables throughout. Whether eating in the informal vibe of the bar or the main basement dining area, the wide range of eclectic dishes proves a crowd-pleaser. Imaginative, unusual, fun and exciting fusion food is the thing, something you won't find elsewhere in the city; take Smitton's lamb shoulder with pan-fried Rosevale potatoes, yellow beans, kalamata olives and smoked aubergine purée, or perhaps Szechuan-peppered pineapple carpaccio with coconut sorbet to finish. Interesting vegetarian dishes available.

Stravaigin

Chef: Daniel Blencowe **Owners:** Colin Clydesdale **Times:** 12/11, Closed 25-26 Dec, 1 Jan, Closed L Tue-Thu **Prices:** Starter £3.45-£6.45, Main £12.65-£22.50, Dessert £4.95-£5.95, Service optional **Wine:** 24 bottles over £20, 26 bottles under £20, 11 by the glass **Notes:** Sun brunch available, Vegetarian available, Air con **Seats:** 76 **Children:** Menu, Portions **Directions:** Next to Glasgow University. 200 yds from Kelvinbridge underground **Parking:** On street, car park 100yds

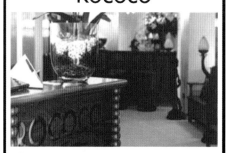

GLASGOW CONTINUED

◎ Two Fat Ladies

Modern seafood

Cosy seafood restaurant offering good-value dishes in the city centre

☎ 0141 847 0088 118a Blytheswood St G2 4EG

The name of this small street-level restaurant comes from its founding premises at 88 Dumbarton Road (two fat ladies - 88). It has a polished parquet floor and the yellow walls are hung with colourful paintings of coastal scenes. The variety and freshness of the food dictate the style of cooking. Seafood is the speciality, presented in uncomplicated dishes with a degree of innovation. Expect the likes of pan-fried fillet of sea bass with turnip and thyme mash and red wine glaze, halibut fillet on Savoy cabbage with a mussel and chervil cream or king prawns cooked in chilli butter.

Times: 12-3/5.30-10.30
Directions: Telephone for directions

◎◎ Ubiquitous Chip

Traditional Scottish 🍷 NOTABLE WINE LIST

Impressive Scottish cuisine in a unique setting

☎ 0141 334 5007 12 Ashton Ln G12 8SJ
e-mail: mail@ubiquitouschip.co.uk
web: www.ubiquitouschip.co.uk

A Glasgow institution for over 30 years, this unusual restaurant is set in a spectacular glass-covered courtyard in a cobbled mews with a fabulous array of lush green plants. A mezzanine level overlooks the tables and foliage below, and there's also a more formal dining room. There are three bars, too, each with its own atmosphere. The cooking is a mixture of traditional and original Scottish recipes using local ingredients. Menus are constantly evolving with the seasons, but three favourite dishes are tartare of finnan haddie with avocado and poached grapes, organic Orkney salmon marinated in honey and tamari with mashed potatoes and spinach sauce, and whisky and green ginger parfait with poached rhubarb.

Chef: Ronnie Clydesdale **Owners:** Ronnie Clydesdale **Times:** 12-2.30/5.30-11, Closed 25 Dec, 1 Jan **Prices:** Fixed L £22.85, Fixed D £39.85, Service optional **Wine:** 301 bottles over £20, 25 bottles under £20, 35 by the glass **Notes:** Sun L £18.65 3 courses inc. wine, Civ Wed 60, Air con **Seats:** 200, Pr/dining room 45 **Children:** Menu, Portions **Directions:** In the West End of Glasgow, off Byres Rd. Beside Hillhead subway station **Parking:** Lilybank gardens (50m)

◎◎ Urban Bar and Brasserie

Modern French NEW

Contemporary bar-brasserie with food to match

☎ 0141 248 5636 23/25 St Vincent Place G1 2DT
e-mail: info@urbanbrasserie.co.uk
web: www.urbanbrasserie.co.uk

Occupying the premises of a former financial institution in the City's commercial heart, the Urban Bar and Brasserie has bags of style and modern good looks. A grand façade and imposing entrance sets the scene and leads into the large bar, off which is an intimate lounge and spacious dining area. Here white walls are hung with colourful modern artwork, and there's brown banquette seating, smart wood flooring, a glass skylight and tables dressed in their best whites. The kitchen's accomplished approach is in harmony with the surroundings, delivering the likes of roasted monkfish with mussel stew, onion, lemon and thyme, or peppered rib-eye beef with fries. Flavours are clean, the produce well sourced and the wine list well chosen.

Chef: Derek Marshall **Owners:** Alan Tomkini, Derek Marshall **Times:** 12-10/12-10, Closed 25 & 26 Dec, 1 & 2 Jan **Prices:** Fixed L £13.95, Starter £5-£10, Main £10-£24, Dessert £6-£7, Group min 6 service 10% **Wine:** 60 bottles over £20, 20 bottles under £20, 10 by the glass **Notes:** Pre-theatre menu 5-6pm £12.95, Air con **Seats:** 110, Pr/dining room 18 **Children:** Min 14 yrs, Portions

🖳 The Big Blue

☎ 0141 357 1038 445 Great Western Rd G12 8HH
web: www.theaa.com/travel/index.jsp

The entrance is on one of the West End's busier streets, but this bar is three flights down, in an old archway which opens out on to the Kelvin walkway and overlooks the river. The menu is predominantly Italian with a few seafood dishes thrown in.

Bouzy Rouge

☎ 0141 221 8804 11 West Regent St G2 2RU
Relaxed bistro with a great buzz.

Café Gandolfi

☎ 0141 552 6813 65 Albion St G1 1NY
Hugely popular cross between a traditional Glasgow tea room and a continental-style restaurant.

Mother India

☎ 0141 221 1663 28 Westminster Ter, Sauchiehall St G3 7RU
Popular, cosy Indian.

🖳 Red Onion

☎ 0141 221 6000 257 West Campbell St G2 4TT
web: www.theaa.com/travel/index.jsp

A charming restaurant in the heart of the City, with an eclectic menu and open from breakfast throughout the day.

SCOTLAND

HIGHLAND

ACHILTIBUIE   MAP 22 NC00

◉◉ The Summer Isles Hotel

Modern British

Food from land and sea in stunning location

☎ 01854 622282   IV26 2YG
e-mail: info@summerisleshotel.co.uk
web: www.summerisleshotel.co.uk

This one-time fishing inn has retained a friendly and informal feel despite its transformation into a chic and comfortable hotel. Run by the same family since the late 1960s, it's a perfect base for exploring the stunning scenery of Achiltibuie, particularly during the summer when the long northern days stretch until 10.30pm. A single five-course menu is served every night, but with cooking this good you're in safe hands; flavours are clean, combinations refreshingly straightforward, and almost all the ingredients are home produced or locally caught. Warm scallop mousse with herb and tomato loaf, followed by grilled fillet of Lochinver halibut with local mussels steamed in saffron and white wine are fine examples of the fare.

Chef: Chris Firth-Bernard **Owners:** Mark & Gerry Irvine **Times:** 12.30-2/8, Closed mid Oct-Etr **Prices:** Fixed D £51, Service included **Wine:** 4 by the glass **Notes:** Fixed D 5 courses **Seats:** 28 **Children:** Min 8 yrs, Portions **Directions:** 10 m N of Ullapool. Turn left off A835 onto single track road. 15m to Achiltibuie. Hotel 100 yds after post office on left **Parking:** 15

BOAT OF GARTEN

◉◉ Boat Hotel - The Capercaille

Modern

Scottish cuisine with a modern twist

☎ 01479 831258   Deshar Rd PH24 3BH
e-mail: holidays@boathotel.co.uk
web: www.boathotel.co.uk

Situated in breathtaking scenery in the Spey Valley, next to the Speyside Steam Railway, this Victorian station hotel has been tastefully modernised while retaining many period features. The intimate, stylish restaurant is lit by a fire and wall sconces, emphasising the dark blue walls and striking avant-garde artwork, and there's a refurbished bar and comfortable lounge in which to enjoy canapés or after-dinner drinks. Scottish cuisine is prepared with a contemporary twist, making the most of local produce. Interesting combinations might include a starter of pan-fried jumbo Moray Coast scallops on a leek and butter bean ragout with saffron, or toasted Crowdie cheese with plums and red onion marmalade on a sage and hazelnut brioche croûton.

Owners: Mr J Erasmus & Mr R Drummond **Times:** 7-9.30, Closed last 2 wks in Jan, Closed L all week **Prices:** Fixed D £35.50, Service optional **Wine:** 40 bottles over £20, 6 bottles under £20, 4 by the glass **Notes:** Vegetarian available, Dress Restrictions, No jeans **Seats:** 40, Pr/dining room 40 **Children:** Min 8 yrs **Rooms:** 22 (22 en suite) **Directions:** Turn off A9 N of Aviemore onto A95. Follow signs to Boat of Garten **Parking:** 36

BRORA   MAP 23 NC90

◉ Royal Marine Hotel

Modern British

Traditional Highland hotel with reliable cooking

☎ 01408 621252   Golf Rd KW9 6QS
e-mail: info@highlandescape.com
web: www.highlandescapehotels.com

This Edwardian country house has been sensitively restored and is a popular choice with the many tourists lured by the area's reputation for good shooting, fishing, golf and whisky. Three dining options are on offer: a bustling bistro, a café-bar overlooking the pool, and the formal Lorimer Dining Room, which delivers a modern British menu of solid, dependable fare with a sprinkling of traditional Scottish favourites. You might start with Cullen skink or hot-smoked roast and whisky-cured salmon, and then tuck into collops of best Scottish beef, pan-fried and served on a crispy haggis cake with a creamy malt whisky sauce.

Chef: Fiona Beattie **Owners:** Duncraggie Ltd **Times:** 12-2/6.30-8.45, Closed L (pre booking only) **Prices:** Fixed D £25-£30, Starter £4-£9, Main £13-£19, Dessert £4-£5 **Wine:** 35 bottles over £20, 35 bottles under £20, 10 by the glass **Notes:** Vegetarian available, Civ Wed 60 **Seats:** 50, Pr/dining room 12 **Children:** Menu, Portions **Rooms:** 22 (22 en suite) ★★★ HL **Directions:** Turn off A9 in village toward beach and golf course **Parking:** 40

CONTIN   MAP 23 NH45

◉ Achilty Hotel

Traditional, Mediterranean NEW

Traditional Scottish fare in a family-run hotel

☎ 01997 421355   IV14 9EG
e-mail: info@achiltyhotel.co.uk
web: www.achiltyhotel.co.uk

Originally a drovers' inn dating back to the 1700s, this family-run restaurant and hotel offers a traditional Scottish menu in a spacious open-plan restaurant located in a former still, which lends the restaurant a traditional appearance with high ceilings and stone walls. Tables are well appointed and the service is attentive and friendly, while the food has a strong Scottish influence. Take a starter of traditional Cullen skink made with smoked haddock, leeks, potatoes, cream and parsley, while for mains you might try seared fillet of Scottish salmon, topped with a tomato, red onion and pepper chutney with mozzarella cheese, served with leek and potato mash.

SCOTLAND

CONTIN CONTINUED

Chef: Christopher Slater **Owners:** Christopher & Ethel Slater **Times:** 12-2/5-8.30, Closed L Mon-Tue **Prices:** Fixed L £9.95, Fixed D £11.95, Starter £2.90-£8.95, Main £10.55-£19.95, Dessert £4.25-£7.35, Service optional **Wine:** 9 bottles over £20, 26 bottles under £20, 7 by the glass **Notes:** Fixed D 2 courses Mon-Sat 5-7pm, Sun L 3 courses £9.95 **Seats:** 32, Pr/dining room 30 **Children:** Portions **Rooms:** 11 (11 en suite) ★★★ SHL **Directions:** A9 N of Inverness onto A835 to Contin, hotel is 0.5m W of village **Parking:** 50

◉ Coul House Hotel

Modern British V NEW

Relaxed country-house setting for fine food and wines

☎ 01997 421487 IV14 9ES
e-mail: stay@coulhousehotel.com
web: coulhousehotel.com

This fine country house is set in 8 acres of grounds with beautiful mountain views. The hotel boasts lots of period features and an open fire in the entrance hall. Two comfortable reception rooms, each with open fires, provide a bar area and room to relax. The menu in the unique octagonal dining room offers a mix of modern British and classical French dishes, complemented by an extensive wine list. Choose from starters such as seared home-cured salted and smoked treacle pork belly and mains such as roasted miniature leg of lamb with savoury mash, roasted parsnips, caramelised onion jus and broccoli.

Chef: G Kenley **Owners:** Stuart MacPherson **Times:** 12-2.30/6.30-9 **Prices:** Starter £4-£10.50, Main £10.50-£21, Dessert £4.95-£7.50, Service optional **Wine:** 38 bottles over £20, 17 bottles under £20, 8 by the glass **Notes:** Vegetarian menu, Civ Wed 120 **Seats:** 76, Pr/dining room 40 **Children:** Menu, Portions **Rooms:** 20 (20 en suite) ★★★ CHH **Directions:** A835 signed Ullapool, 12m Contin. Hotel drive 100yds right after petrol station **Parking:** 60

DORNOCH   MAP 23 NH78

◉ Dornoch Castle Hotel

Modern Scottish

Refreshing brasserie food in the castle conservatory

☎ 01862 810216 Castle St IV25 3SD
e-mail: enquiries@dornochcastlehotel.com
web: www.dornochcastlehotel.com

A conservatory restaurant, attached to the fine old castle and overlooking the garden, successfully marries traditional and modern styles. The modern Scottish menu offers a straightforward brasserie-style choice using quality ingredients, locally sourced wherever possible. Dinner may take in trout pâté with citrus coulis and toasted lemon bread to start, with roast lamb shank cooked in red wine and served with red onion marmalade mash, or Loch Duart salmon with basil risotto and tarragon butter for main course. For dessert, try the banoffee cream parfait. Service is informal, but attentive.

Chef: Grant MacNicol **Owners:** Colin Thompson **Times:** 12-3/6-9.30 **Prices:** Fixed L £8.95, Fixed D £20-£30, Starter £4.25-£7.95, Main £9.95-£22, Dessert £4.25-£5.95, Service optional **Wine:** 25 bottles over £20, 22 bottles under £20, 6 by the glass **Seats:** 75, Pr/dining room 25 **Children:** Menu, Portions **Rooms:** 21 (21 en suite) ★★★ HL **Directions:** 2m from A9 in the centre of Dornoch **Parking:** 12

◉◉ 2 Quail Restaurant & Rooms

International

Classic cooking in tiny Highland restaurant

☎ 01862 811811 Inistore House, Castle St IV25 3SN
e-mail: theaa@2quail.com
web: www.2quail.com

You'll need to make a reservation ahead at this small, book-lined restaurant. Located in a Victorian Highland townhouse, it has a homely feel and as it's run by a husband-and-wife team, you can be sure of personal attention. Everything is made in-house using locally-sourced produce where possible. The four-course dinner menu offers a choice between dessert and cheese, with the other dishes being fixed. You might start with fricassée of quail and foie gras with grilled fig and sage gravy, then suprême of halibut with chicory and tarragon butter sauce, followed by roast Ross-shire lamb with roasted vegetables and dauphinoise potatoes. Good quality wines are served by the glass or bottle.

Chef: Michael Carr **Owners:** Michael and Kerensa Carr **Times:** 7.30-9.30, Closed Xmas, 2 wks Feb-Mar, Sun-Mon **Prices:** Fixed D £37.50, Service optional **Wine:** 47 bottles over £20, 10 bottles under £20, 8 by the glass **Notes:** Fixed D 4 courses, Dress Restrictions, Smart casual **Seats:** 14 **Children:** Min 10 yrs **Rooms:** 3 (3 en suite) ★★★★★ RR **Directions:** 200 yds past war memorial on left side of main street, just before Cathedral **Parking:** On street

---

FORT WILLIAM   MAP 22 NN17

◉◉◉ Inverlochy Castle Hotel

see opposite

◉ Moorings Hotel

Modern

Contemporary cuisine in the heart of the Highlands

☎ 01397 772797 Banavie PH33 7LY
e-mail: reservations@moorings-fortwilliam.co.uk
web: www.moorings-fortwilliam.co.uk

Popular business and tourist hotel located beside Neptune's Ladder, a series of locks on the Caledonian Canal, and boasting magnificent views of Ben Nevis. A four-course dinner is offered in the spacious Jacobean-styled restaurant. The finest local produce, including West Coast seafood and Highland game, is used to good effect in contemporary British and European dishes. A typical meal might kick off with a tian of crab and avocado, or maybe scallops with sage, followed by sesame-crusted sea bass in an aromatic broth, or wild mushroom lasagne. Puddings include a delicious whisky fruit tart accompanied by whisky ice cream.

◎◎◎

Inverlochy Castle Hotel

FORT WILLIAM   MAP 22 NN17

Modern British 🏆 NOTABLE WINE LIST

Luxurious Highland castle setting for fine dining

☎ 01397 702177   Torlundy PH33 6SN
e-mail: info@inverlochy.co.uk
web: www.inverlochycastlehotel.com

This majestic castle, nestling in the foothills of Ben Nevis and set in over 500 acres of gardens, is a truly impressive setting for fine dining. Now a luxury hotel, it's lavishly appointed in classic country-house style: aperitifs are taken in the sumptuous lounge, whilst the restaurant is furnished with elaborate period furniture and offers stunning mountain views. Genuine comfort and luxury abound, while service is highly professional but with a relaxed and friendly note. The kitchen's accomplished modern approach - underpinned by a classical theme - suits the surroundings and makes fine use of the abundant Highland larder, as well as produce from the estate's walled garden, on its repertoire of daily-changing, five-course dinner and tasting menus. Expect high-level technical skill and clear flavours in dishes like caramelised Skye scallops with onion compôte and Puy lentils, or a tian of Isle of Barra crab with its own consommé and mustard seed bread, followed perhaps by grilled tranche of turbot with truffled Jerusalem artichoke and caviar velouté, or truffle-crusted shoulder of

beef with buttered spinach and wild mushrooms. Finish with a delicious pineapple tarte Tatin, served with pistachio ice cream and caramel sauce. There's a notable wine list with an extensive range of half bottles to enjoy, but remember your jacket and tie gentlemen, it's the required dress code here.

Chef: Matthew Gray **Owners:** Inverlochy Ltd **Times:** 12.30-1.15/6.30-10 **Prices:** Fixed L £28.50, Fixed D £65, Service optional **Wine:** 283 bottles over £20, 8 by the glass **Notes:** Fixed D 4 courses, Dress Restrictions, Jacket & tie for D, Civ Wed 80 **Seats:** 40, Pr/dining room 20 **Children:** Menu, Portions **Rooms:** 17 (17 en suite)★★★★★ CHH **Directions:** 3m N of Fort William on A82, just past Golf Club **Parking:** 20

Chef: Paul Smith **Owners:** Mr S Leitch **Times:** 7-9.30, Closed 24-26 Dec, Closed L all week **Prices:** Fixed D £26, Starter £4-£10, Main £9-£19, Dessert £4-£7, Service optional **Wine:** 17 bottles over £20, 28 bottles under £20 **Notes:** Dress Restrictions, Smart casual **Seats:** 60, Pr/dining room 120 **Children:** Portions **Rooms:** 27 (27 en suite) ★★★ HL **Directions:** From A82 take A830 W for 1 mile. 1st right over Caledonian Canal on B8004 **Parking:** 50

GLENFINNAN   MAP 22 NM88

◎◎ **The Prince's House**

Modern British

Accomplished Scottish cuisine and a warm welcome

☎ 01397 722246   PH37 4LT
e-mail: princeshouse@glenfinnan.co.uk
web: www.glenfinnan.co.uk

Dating back to the 17th century, this traditional country house was allegedly used by Bonnie Prince Charlie at the start of the Jacobite uprising. Family-run and blessed with a marvelous romantic setting surrounded by mountains and woodland, the hotel is very strong on hospitality and is simply furnished with natural floor coverings and hardwood panelling on the walls. Simple dishes are well executed with superb quality ingredients - local sourcing and seasonality playing a key role on the modern menu. Think poached fillets of turbot served with braised fennel and a West Coast shellfish broth, with perhaps a strawberry and Drambuie Eton Mess to finish. A winter log fire burns in the hearth, while the adjoining conservatory offers a tranquil spot for coffee.

Chef: Kieron Kelly **Owners:** Kieron & Ina Kelly **Times:** 7-9, Closed Xmas, Jan-Feb, Low season - booking only, Closed L all wk **Prices:** Fixed D £30-£35, Service included **Wine:** 30 bottles over £20, 10 bottles under £20, 6 by the glass **Seats:** 30 **Children:** Portions **Rooms:** 9 (9 en suite) ★★ SHL **Directions:** From Fort William N on A82 for 2 m. Turn left onto A830 Mallaig Rd for 15 m to hotel **Parking:** 18

GRANTOWN-ON-SPEY   MAP 23 NJ02

◎◎ **Craggan Mill**

Modern Scottish, International NEW 🍂

A 17th-century mill restaurant serving carefully-prepared modern fare

☎ 01479 872288   PH26 3NT
e-mail: info@cragganmill.co.uk
web: www.cragganmill.co.uk

Just south of town, with outstanding views of the Cairngorm Mountains and Cromdale Hills, this restored former 17th-century mill comes brimful of rustic character including a working wheel, and now plays host to a restaurant and art gallery. Natural wood predominates; think lounge tables from cross cuts of large mature trees, pitched-raftered ceiling and natural-wood dining tables with place mats made from ends of French wine boxes. The kitchen makes excellent use of the abundant Scottish larder, its modern approach encompassing some international influences as well as an impressive choice of vegetarian options in clear-flavoured, well-executed dishes. Expect Straithaird salmon en croûte with Drambuie and orange sauce, or rack of Highland venison with bramble, red wine, chocolate and chilli sauce.

CONTINUED

GRANTOWN-ON-SPEY CONTINUED

Craggan Mill

Chef: Graham Harvey & Sheila McConachie **Owners:** Graham Harvey & Sheila McConachie **Times:** 12-2.30/6-11, Closed Tues **Prices:** Starter £3.25-£7.95, Main £9.95-£22.95, Dessert £3.95-£6.95, Service optional **Wine:** 16 bottles over £20, 25 bottles under £20, 8 by the glass **Notes:** Sun L 3 courses £18.85, Vegetarian available **Seats:** 50, Pr/dining room 20 **Children:** Menu, Portions **Directions:** 1m S of Grantown-on-Spey **Parking:** 18

⊛ Culdearn House

Traditional Scottish V ⚑ NOTABLE WINE LIST

Quality local ingredients cooked with flair in homely small hotel

☎ 01479 872106 Woodlands Ter PH26 3JU
e-mail: enquiries@culdearn.com
web: www.culdearn.com

This large Victorian villa set in a quiet residential street has beautifully proportioned rooms with ornate ceilings, marble fireplaces and many other period features. The small dining room at the front of the house is colourful and comfortable, offering lovely views of the garden from white-clothed tables. Good-quality local ingredients are simply cooked with care and skill, especially beautifully fresh fish and fully traceable beef. Think a fillet of sea bass with a Pernod and fennel cream, or prime fillet of Highland beef served with mushrooms and a Drambuie sauce. Service is efficient but unobtrusive making this a relaxing place to dine. The wine list includes interesting information.

Chef: Sonia Marshall **Owners:** Mr & Mrs Marshall **Times:** 7, Closed Feb, Closed L all week **Prices:** Fixed D £32, Service optional **Wine:** 28 bottles over £20, 9 bottles under £20, 4 by the glass **Notes:** Fixed D 4 courses, Vegetarian menu, Dress Restrictions, Smart casual, no jeans, sportswear/T-shirts **Seats:** 14 **Children:** Min 10 yrs **Rooms:** 7 (7 en suite) ★★ SHL **Directions:** Enter Grantown from SW on A95, left at 30mph sign **Parking:** 11

⊛⊛ The Glass House Restaurant

Modern British V

Ambitious cooking in a conservatory setting

☎ 01479 872980 Grant Rd PH26 3LD
web: www.theglasshouse-grantown.co.uk

Tucked away down a quiet residential street, this conservatory restaurant has attracted some rave local reviews. Its clean lines, leafy plants and large windows create a light, contemporary setting for an accomplished menu of modern British dishes. The range is limited - only three or four choices per course - but you're in safe hands; the

food here is full of flavour and makes good use of seasonal local produce. Better still, it's great value for money even in the evening, when the cooking gets more adventurous. Kick off with seared scallops with pak choi and sorrel cream perhaps, followed by confit duck leg with roast butternut squash, and bread-and-butter pudding with ginger ice cream.

Chef: Stephen Robertson **Owners:** Stephen and Karen Robertson **Times:** 12-1.45/7-9, Closed 2 wks Nov, 1 wk Jan, 25-26 Dec, 1-2 Jan, Mon, Closed L Tue, D Sun **Prices:** Fixed L £9.95, Starter £3.95-£4.95, Main £15.95-£18.95, Dessert £4.95-£5.50, Service optional **Wine:** 10 bottles over £20, 12 bottles under £20, 2 by the glass **Notes:** Oct-Mar 2 courses £9.95, 3 courses £13.50, Vegetarian menu **Seats:** 30 **Children:** Portions **Directions:** Turn off High St between the bank and Co-op into Caravan Park Rd. First left onto Grant Rd. **Parking:** 10

INVERGARRY MAP 22 NH30

⊛ Glengarry Castle

British, International

Scottish country-house style in a dramatic setting

☎ 01809 501254 PH35 4HW
e-mail: castle@glengarry.net
web: www.glengarry.net

There are great views to be had from this charming Victorian property, set on the shores of Loch Oich in 50 acres of grounds. A panelled reception hall, marble fireplaces and an elegant dining room are features of this comfortable and welcoming hotel. The innovative menu showcases the best of Scottish produce in dishes like smoked Orkney salmon cheesecake on a savoury biscuit base with tomato and dill dressing, and pan-seared breast of duckling enhanced by a honey and forest mushroom sauce. Finish with bread-and-butter pudding served with Drambuie custard.

Chef: John McDonald **Owners:** Mr & Mrs MacCallum **Times:** 7-8.30, Closed mid Nov to mid Mar, Closed L Mon-Sun **Prices:** Fixed D £29, Service included **Wine:** 29 bottles over £20, 25 bottles under £20, 9 by the glass **Notes:** Fixed D 4 courses **Seats:** 40 **Children:** Menu, Portions **Rooms:** 26 (26 en suite) ★★★ CHH **Directions:** 1m S of Invergarry on A82 **Parking:** 30

INVERGORDON MAP 23 NH76

⊛ Kincraig House Hotel

Modern French NEW

Fine dining in a lovingly restored period house

☎ 01349 852587 IV18 0LF
e-mail: info@kincraig-house-hotel.co.uk
web: www.kincraig-house-hotel.co.uk

A charming country house set in landscaped grounds with sea views, the hotel has been totally refurbished in recent years. The restaurant, looking over the grounds to the Cromarty Firth, boasts a large original fireplace, while crisp white linen, sparkling glassware and fresh flowers all add to the ambience. Skilfully prepared dishes make use of the finest Scottish produce. Original presentation particularly appeals in a main course of grilled halibut with braised fennel, crispy polenta parcels and sauce vierge, followed by an equally impressive tarte Tatin with excellent vanilla ice cream. The sympathetically restored lounge has open fires and comfortable seating, as does the bar, where informal meals are served.

Chef: Mikael Helies **Owners:** Kevin Wickman **Times:** 12.30-2/6.45-9
Prices: Fixed L £14.50, Fixed D £32.50, Service optional **Wine:** 29 bottles
over £20, 23 bottles under £20, 4 by the glass **Notes:** Dress Restrictions,
Smart casual, Civ Wed 50 **Seats:** 30, Pr/dining room 40 **Children:** Menu,
Portions **Directions:** Situated off A9, past Alness towards Tain. Hotel is
0.25m on left past church **Parking:** 40

INVERNESS
MAP 23 NH64

Bunchrew House Hotel

Modern

Confident cooking in imposing Highland manor

☎ 01463 234917 Bunchrew IV3 8TA
e-mail: welcome@bunchrew-inverness.co.uk
web: www.bunchrew-inverness.co.uk

A fine-looking 17th-century Scottish baronial mansion set alongside
the Beauly Firth in 20 acres of woodland and pretty gardens. The
stately, well-proportioned restaurant makes the most of the view
towards Ben Wyvis and the Black Isle across the water - book ahead
for a window table as the summer sunsets are stunning. There's
nothing whimsical about the food or the dedication to combining
quality Scottish ingredients with accomplished technique.
Contemporary dishes on daily dinner menus may include roast loin of
lamb encased in a smoked guinea fowl mousse with confit garlic,
sweet potato purée, asparagus and a camomile sauce, and to finish,
perhaps a pineapple tart Tatin served with ginger butterscotch ice
cream and coconut sabayon.

Times: 12-1.45/7-8.45, Closed 22-28 Dec **Rooms:** 16 (16 en suite)
★★★★ CHH **Directions:** 3m W of Inverness on A862 towards Beauly

Culloden House Hotel

Traditional British

Serious Scottish cuisine in historic setting

☎ 01463 790461 Culloden IV2 7BZ
e-mail: info@cullodenhouse.co.uk
web: www.cullodenhouse.co.uk

'Bonnie' Prince Charlie lodged at this grand Palladian mansion before
the battle of Culloden Moor in 1746. High ceilings and intricate
cornices are particular features of the public rooms, including the
elegant Adam dining room. Scottish produce is served in a five-course
extravaganza, commencing with canapés and finishing with hand-
made petits fours. Perfectly cooked risotto of smoked haddock is
served with a lemon dressing, to cut through the strong fish flavour,
and another well balanced dish is grilled fillet of halibut set on
courgette provençale with tomato jus. For dessert, an interesting
combination of flavours comes together in an attractively presented
lemon crème brûlée with cardamom and pistachio ice cream.

Chef: Michael Simpson **Owners:** Culloden House Ltd **Times:** 12.30-2/7-
9, Closed 2 wks Jan/Feb **Prices:** Food prices not confirmed for 2008.
Please telephone for details **Wine:** 7 by the glass **Notes:** Vegetarian
available, Dress Restrictions, Smart casual, Civ Wed 65 **Seats:** 50, Pr/dining
room 17 **Children:** Min 10 yrs, Portions **Rooms:** 28 (28 en suite)
★★★★ HL **Directions:** From A96, take left turn at junction of Balloch,
Culloden, Smithton. Continue for 2m, hotel is on right **Parking:** 50

The Drumossie Hotel

Modern British

Country-house hotel producing high-quality food

☎ 01463 236451 Old Perth Rd IV2 5BE
e-mail: stay@drumossiehotel.co.uk
web: www.drumossiehotel.co.uk

An art deco building on a hillside south of Inverness houses this
comfortable hotel. It has been refurbished to country-house standard,
and features an elegant restaurant with well-dressed tables where the
crisp white linen and polished silverware lend a touch of formality.
The food is several notches above the ordinary, and has been very
well received locally. Notable among the daily-changing set dishes are
an Isle of Skye fish pie featuring salmon, halibut and sole, and a
seared tournedos of Castle Mey tenderloin of beef and braised ribs
with caramelised red onion and Burgundy infusion. Dessert may come
in the form of pear tarte Tatin with liquorice ice cream and star anise
anglaise.

Times: 12.30-2/7-9.30 **Rooms:** 44 (44 en suite) ★★★★ HL
Directions: Telephone for directions

Glenmoriston Town House Hotel
see page 618

Reserve

Modern European

*Lively cosmopolitan atmosphere meets classic dishes
with contemporary twist*

☎ 01463 717274 Rocpool Reserve, 1 Ness Walk IV3 5NE
web: www.rocpool.com

A busy city-centre brasserie with sleek contemporary interior, riverside
views and an energetic atmosphere, Rocpool Reserve brings a touch
of modern style and glamour to town. Lots of wood and glass - with
windows the entire length of the long, slim room - come decked out
with wood tables, crisp white linen and leather banquettes, backed by
attentive but unobtrusive service. The food is equally fashionable,
modern European, delivering quality ingredients cooked with flair.
Dishes come attractively presented but sensibly not over embellished
as in a risotto of Kyle langoustine, hand-picked crab and roasted vine
tomatoes as a starter, with slow-roasted organic lamb, spiced liver and
braised shoulder with sweet potato, aubergine and cumin for a main
course.

Times: 12-2.30/5.45-10, Closed 25 Dec, 1 Jan, Sun **Directions:** Telephone
for details

SCOTLAND

Glenmoriston Town House Hotel

INVERNESS   MAP 23 NH64

Modern French V

Refined French dining in elegant townhouse hotel

☎ 01463 223777 20 Ness Bank IV2 4SF
e-mail: reception@glenmoristontownhouse.com
web: www.glenmoristontownhouse.com

Bold contemporary designs blend seamlessly with the classical architecture of this stylish townhouse hotel on the banks of the River Ness. Stylishly-dressed tables, quality glassware, lots of wood and leather, mood lighting and fresh flowers contribute to the chic modern elegance of the sophisticated restaurant Abstract, which has been refurbished and now includes Scotland's first chef's table in its kitchen. Service is friendly and attentive, while the fine-dining experience offers a refined modern-French flavour.

High-quality Scottish ingredients - with a strong emphasis on seasonality - are prepared and presented with flair, skill and attention to detail, with interesting combinations that don't overpower the principal ingredient. There's an eight-course tasting menu too, bolstering an appealing carte, while excellent ancillaries - including amuse-bouche, pre-dessert and petits fours - all hold form. Expect lightly-smoked roe deer fillet with foie gras croûton, poached quail's egg and parsnip purée to start, perhaps followed by roasted North Sea halibut served with a fine bean and streaky bacon fricassée, oatmeal cake and hazelnut meat jus, while a magnum of hot passionfruit soufflé with coconut sauce and an exotic fruit coulis might catch the eye at dessert. The hotel's bistro-style restaurant Contrast offers a stylish but less formal alternative.

Chef: Loic Lefebvre, Geoffery Malmedy **Owners:** Larsen & Ross South
Times: 7-10, Closed 26-28 Dec, Sun, Closed L all week **Prices:** Starter £4-£14, Main £14-£22, Dessert £6-£8, Service optional, Group min 6 service 12.5% **Wine:** 90% bottles over £20, 10% bottles under £20, 11 by the glass **Notes:** Vegetarian menu, Dress Restrictions, Smart casual **Seats:** 50, Pr/dining room 15 **Children:** Menu, Portions **Rooms:** 30 (30 en suite)
★★★ HL **Directions:** 2 mins from city centre, on river opposite theatre
Parking: 50

INVERNESS *Continued*

◉ Riverhouse

British

Relaxed riverside dining

☎ 01463 222033 1 Greig St IV3 5PT
e-mail: riverhouse@netbreeze.co.uk

This small bistro-style restaurant is situated on the banks of the River Ness, close to the city centre and near the main shopping district. The wood-panelled interior has an intimate atmosphere and you can even watch the chefs cooking in the open kitchen. Classic dishes are simply prepared using quality produce: Loch Fyne oysters washed down with a glass of Black Isle ale, followed by chargrilled fillet of local beef topped with coarse farmhouse pâté and finished with Madeira jus, with a seasonal berry bruschetta topped with mascarpone cream to finish. The lunch and early supper menu offers particularly good value.

Times: 12-2.15/5.30-10, Closed Mon, Closed L Sun **Directions:** On corner of Huntly Street and Greig Street

Café 1

☎ 01463 226200 75 Castle St IV2 3EA

Modern-style city-centre restaurant with a good range of contemporary dishes.

Harry Ramsden's

☎ 01463 713345 Inshes Retail Park IV2 3TW

Famous fish & chip shop.

KINGUSSIE   MAP 23 NH70

◉◉◉ The Cross at Kingussie

see opposite

KYLE OF LOCHALSH   MAP 22 NG72

◉ The Seafood Restaurant

Seafood NEW

Wonderful setting for fine food and great views

☎ 01599 534813 Railway Station Buildings, Station Rd IV40 8AE
e-mail: seafoodrestaurant@btinternet.com

This restaurant is found in one of the railway buildings on the pier, looking over one platform towards the Skye bridge, and across the other towards Loch Duich. Parking is on the pier at the end of the buffers. The simply furnished restaurant seats 35 at pinewood tables and there is a dispense bar with counter. Naturally the menu relies heavily on fresh seafood and the portions are generous. Try the seafood chowder to start, served piping hot. Main courses might include Isle of Skye smoked haddock with clapshot and a white wine and parsley sauce.

Chef: Clare Mansfield, Jann MacRae **Owners:** Jann MacRae **Times:** 11-3/5-9.30, Closed end Oct-begin Mar, Closed L Sun **Prices:** Food prices not confirmed for 2008. Please telephone for details **Wine:** 2 bottles over £20, 15 bottles under £20, 2 by the glass **Notes:** Vegetarian available **Seats:** 35 **Children:** Portions **Directions:** Off A87 **Parking:** 5

The Cross at Kingussie

KINGUSSIE MAP 23 NH70

Modern Scottish 🍷 NOTABLE WINE LIST 🐦

Top-notch restaurant with rooms in a pretty setting

☎ 01540 661166 Tweed Mill Brae, Ardbroilach Rd PH21 1LB
e-mail: relax@thecross.co.uk
web: www.thecross.co.uk

Once a water-powered tweed mill, this inviting restaurant with rooms sits beside the tumbling River Gynack amid wildflower gardens and woodland. David Young and his wife Katie offer a warm welcome, cosy lounges and comfortable accommodation, but the heart of the operation is undoubtedly the restaurant, with its whitewashed walls, wooden beams and open fire. Major refurbishment and redecoration has installed new flooring, natural-wood tables with slate tablemats and Riedel glassware, and there's also a sunny terrace for alfresco dining.
The cooking is refreshingly unfussy and deceptively straightforward, with great attention paid to seasonality and careful sourcing of prime ingredients from the abundant Scottish larder. Expect balanced, clear-flavoured dishes and some sublime combinations from the fixed-price, daily-changing menus. Corn-fed organic chicken is a typical main course, served with vine tomato risotto, caramelised onion and wilted rocket, or you might plump for Scrabster cod, with vanilla, braised little gems and potato purée. Heading-up desserts, perhaps a lemon tart served with raspberry sorbet, or chocolate truffle cake with Pedro Ximenez and raisin ice cream.

Chef: Becca Henderson, David Young
Owners: David and Katie Young
Times: 7-8.30, Closed Xmas & Jan (excl New Year), Sun-Mon, Closed L all week
Prices: Fixed D £41-£45, Service included, Group min 6 service 10%
Wine: 200 bottles over £20, 20 bottles under £20, 4 by the glass
Notes: Fixed D 4 courses
Seats: 20
Children: Min 10 yrs
Rooms: 8 (8 en suite)
★★★★★ RR
Directions: From lights in centre of Kingussie, uphill along Ardbroilach Rd for 300 mtrs
Parking: 12

SCOTLAND

SCOTLAND

The Boath House

NAIRN MAP 23 NH85

Traditional V 🖐

Stunning food and effortless service in small country-house hotel

☎ 01667 454896 Auldearn IV12 5TE
e-mail: wendy@boath-house.com
web: www.boath-house.com

This lovingly restored, classic Georgian mansion - one of Scotland's finest small hotels - sits in 20 acres of peaceful lawns, mature woodlands and streams. Its walled garden provides produce for chef Charles Lockley's inspired cooking, while ebullient, hands-on owners the Mathesons greet guests and diners like old friends. The lake here is stocked with brown and rainbow trout (in the early evening, when the flies are about, they can be seen jumping), while in the grounds, badgers and roe deer can be spotted. Inside, open fires flicker, while lounges and dining room abound with colourful ceramics and vibrant paintings - Boath acting as a permanent exhibition for contemporary Highland art. The elegant, candlelit dining room comes with well-spaced tables, high-quality appointments and comfortable high-backed chairs, with views over garden and lake. Service suits the winning formula here, being attentive, skilled and efficient but suitably relaxed and friendly.

Charles Lockley's modern approach is classically based with a strong Scottish influence, using high-quality produce from the abundant Highland larder. Think braised blade of Aberdeenshire Angus delivered with baby leeks and parsnip purée, or perhaps a fillet of halibut with cep gnocchi, langoustines and kohlrabi, while a chocolate and Agen prune clafoutis with nutmeg ice cream might feature at dessert. The approach at dinner is a fixed-price, five-course set affair, but with a choice offered at mains and dessert. The emphasis here is on allowing the superb-quality produce to shine. High technical skills, imagination, balance, a light touch and clean, clear flavours parade in style. Make a night of it and stay in one of six beautiful bedrooms, enjoy a spa treatment, or just stroll in the lovely grounds.

Chef: Charles Lockley
Owners: Mr & Mrs D Matheson
Times: 12.30-1.45/7-8.30, Closed Xmas, Closed L Mon-Wed
Prices: Fixed L £19.50, Fixed D £48, Service optional
Wine: 146 bottles over £20, 11 bottles under £20, 7 by the glass
Notes: Fixed D 5 courses, Vegetarian menu, Dress Restrictions, Smart casual, no shorts/T-shirts/jeans, Civ Wed 30
Seats: 28, Pr/dining room 8
Children: Portions
Rooms: 6 (6 en suite)★★★ HL
Directions: 2 miles E of Nairn on A96 (Inverness to Aberdeen road)
Parking: 20

LOCHINVER — MAP 22 NC02

◉ Inver Lodge

Modern Scottish

Relaxed fine dining in wonderful location

☎ 01571 844496 IV27 4LU
e-mail: stay@inverlodge.com
web: www.inverlodge.com

Diners at this delightful, modern hotel are treated to spectacular views over the small harbour and the ocean beyond. On a clear day, the Western Isles can be seen through the restaurant's large picture windows. The kitchen makes sound use of the abundant local larder - fish is landed at the quayside below, while Aberdeen Angus beef might also feature on the fixed-price, daily-changing dinner menu. Descriptions are not short on adjectives and the cooking's equally ambitious; take flash-roasted rump of lamb sliced over a rosemary jus and served with herb-roast potatoes, garlic-buttered broccoli and fresh apricots in a mint syrup.

Chef: Peter Cullen **Owners:** Anne & Edmund Vestey **Times:** 7-9, Closed Nov-Mar, Closed L Mon-Sun **Prices:** Food prices not confirmed for 2008. Please telephone for details **Wine:** 23 bottles over £20, 41 bottles under £20, 5 by the glass **Notes:** Dress Restrictions, No jeans, shorts, tracksuit trousers, Civ Wed 60 **Seats:** 50 **Children:** Min 10 yrs, Portions **Rooms:** 20 (20 en suite)★★★★ HL **Directions:** A835 to Lochinver, left at village hall, private road for 0.5m **Parking:** 30

MUIR OF ORD — MAP 23 NH55

◉ Ord House Hotel

Traditional French

Home comforts and fresh local produce in listed country house

☎ 01463 870492 IV6 7UH
e-mail: admin@ord-house.co.uk
web: www.ord-house.co.uk

Built in 1637 as the laird's house and set in 60 acres of grounds, the property is now a comfortable country-house hotel. Husband-and-wife team John and Eliza Allen offer a warm welcome and encourage guests and diners to enjoy the grounds, which provide some of the fruit, vegetables and herbs used in the cooking. Sporting pursuits are recommended locally and you'll find game, fish and local beef and lamb on the menu. Straightforward British and French cooking styles are used in dishes like chargrilled salmon fillet served with wild mushrooms, or perhaps hot whisky cream with fresh berries to finish.

Chef: Eliza Allen **Owners:** Eliza & John Allen **Times:** 12-2/7-9, Closed Nov-end Feb **Prices:** Fixed L £14, Fixed D £26, Starter £5.50-£9.50, Main £12-£19, Dessert £2.50-£6, Service included **Wine:** 14 bottles over £20, 18 bottles under £20, 4 by the glass **Notes:** Fixed D 4 courses **Seats:** 26 **Children:** Portions **Rooms:** 12 (12 en suite) ★★ HL **Directions:** A832 to Muir of Ord. Over x-rd and rail bridge, 1st left signed Ullapool & Ord Distillery. Hotel 0.5m on left **Parking:** 24

NAIRN — MAP 23 NH85

◉◉◉◉ The Boath House

see opposite

NETHY BRIDGE — MAP 23 NJ02

◉◉ The Restaurant at The Mountview Hotel

Modern British

Confident Highland cooking amidst amazing scenery

☎ 01479 821248 Grantown Rd PH25 3EB
e-mail: mviewhotel@aol.com
web: www.mountviewhotelnethybridge.co.uk

This Edwardian country-house hotel offers wonderful views of the Cairngorms from its elevated position on the edge of the village. Built in 1896, the building has been sensitively extended with a modern dining room with large picture windows allowing guests to drink in the breathtaking scenery. The cooking is characterised by flashes of contemporary flair underpinned by traditional influences and wonderful seasonal ingredients from a region renowned for its produce, including the hotel's own organic kitchen garden. Expect assured, imaginative cooking on a menu that might include starters such as baked peat-smoked haddock on a bed of crushed peas, followed by roast fillet of venison on potato and celeriac gratin and a sticky pear and chocolate pudding to finish things off.

Chef: Lee Beale **Owners:** Kevin & Caryl Shaw **Times:** 12-2/6-11, Closed 25-26 Dec, Mon-Tue, Closed L Mon-Sat **Prices:** Starter £4.50-£5.95, Main £13.50-£17.95, Dessert £5.25-£5.75, Service optional **Wine:** 4 by the glass **Seats:** 24 **Children:** Menu, Portions **Rooms:** 12 (11 en suite) ★★ HL **Directions:** From Aviemore follow signs for Nethy Bridge, through Boat-of-Garten. In Nethy Bridge over humpback bridge & follow hotel signs **Parking:** 20

ONICH — MAP 22 NN06

◉ Lodge on the Loch Hotel

British, European

Stunning lochside setting for ambitious cuisine

☎ 01855 821237 PH33 6RY
e-mail: info@lodgeontheloch.com
web: www.lodgeontheloch.com

Enjoying fine views over Loche Linnhe, this aptly-named hotel in a Victorian property combines striking design with country-house comforts, and offers first-class Highland hospitality. Friendly but professional service is complemented by white-clothed tables and formal settings, while stunning views can be enjoyed from the restaurant - book a window seat if you can. Modern Scottish cooking is the style with European influences and Asian seafood, classically rooted, complex and ambitious with clever presentation, while a few dishes for two (perhaps a starter tasting plate or dessert assiette) are featured on the generous menu. Sample dishes start with a white pudding of scallops on potato salad, with garden leaves and home-made curry ketchup, and follow on with best end of Speyside beef with ginger, onions and roasted peppers, served with mashed tatties and Szechuan pepper.

Chef: Vaclav Stanek **Owners:** Daniel Goh **Times:** 6.30-9, Closed Mon-Fri Nov-Etr, (Open 23 Dec-5 Jan), Closed L all week **Prices:** Fixed D £19-£34, Starter £5-£8, Main £10-£20, Dessert £4-£6.50, Service optional **Wine:** 21 bottles over £20, 13 bottles under £20, 6 by the glass **Notes:** Dress Restrictions, Smart casual, Civ Wed 72 **Seats:** 60 **Children:** Min 14 yrs **Rooms:** 15 (15 en suite) ★★★ HL **Directions:** Off A82 between Glasgow and Inverness **Parking:** 17

SCOTLAND

ONICH CONTINUED

◉ Onich Hotel

Traditional

Formal dining with wonderful sea views

☎ 01855 821214   PH33 6RY
e-mail: enquiries@onich-fortwilliam.co.uk
web: www.onich-fortwilliam.co.uk

Friendly hotel set in pretty gardens on the shores of Loch Linnhe. A choice of inviting public rooms includes a cocktail bar and a sun lounge with panoramic views of the lake, which can also be enjoyed from the attractive restaurant. Using local produce such as seafood from the West Coast and Highland game, there's plenty on the menu to tempt - steak and ale pie for example, or bangers and mash with onion gravy - as well as more complex dishes, such as bacon-wrapped chicken stuffed with haggis and served with whisky sauce and mash. Lighter snacks are available in the bar, and in summer you can dine alfresco in the hotel's landscaped grounds.

Chef: Alan Pearson **Owners:** Mr S Leitch **Times:** 7-9, Closed Xmas, Closed L all week **Prices:** Food prices not confirmed for 2008. Please telephone for details **Notes:** Dress Restrictions, Smart casual **Seats:** 50, Pr/dining room 24 **Children:** Menu, Portions **Rooms:** 26 (26 en suite) ★★★ HL **Directions:** Beside A82. Located in village of Onich, 9m S of Fort William **Parking:** 50

POOLEWE   MAP 22 NG88

◉◉ Pool House Hotel

British, French

Stunning location for fine Scottish cuisine

☎ 01445 781272   IV22 2LD
e-mail: enquiries@poolhousehotel.com
web: www.poolhousehotel.com

Set on the shores of Loch Ewe, this country-house hotel has an unassuming façade that hides a stunning interior. A recent refurbishment has only added to the wow factor, so it's worth visiting now before word gets round and everyone wants to dine here. Panoramic views of Loch Ewe form the backdrop for imaginative cuisine in the stylish North By North West dining room, and when you're done dithering over the menu, you can try spotting otters and seals. A concise menu provides a limited choice, but you're in safe hands: expect honest and accurate cooking based on the finest local ingredients. Whet your appetite with cream of lentil soup perhaps, before moving on to roast lamb with bubble-and-squeak potato, glazed parsnips and red wine gravy.

Times: 6.30-8.30, Closed Jan **Rooms:** 7 (7 en suite) ★★★ SHL
Directions: 6M N of Gairloch on A832. Hotel by bridge on River Ewe

---

ROY BRIDGE   MAP 22 NN28

◉ Best Western Glenspean Lodge Hotel

Modern British

Crowd-pleasing cuisine at this former hunting lodge

☎ 01397 712223   PH31 4AF
e-mail: reservations@glenspeanlodge.com
web: www.glenspeanlodge.com

Built as a hunting lodge in the 1880s and nestled in 5 acres of gardens and woodland, this peaceful country-house hotel offers dramatic panoramas of the Spean Valley and the Nevis range from its spacious dining room. The food looks good too - expect accomplished modern Scottish cooking from a kitchen that aims to please: seared Islay scallops with a lobster and crab cake, served with tomato and cucumber salsa perhaps or roast breast of pheasant with game sausage, haggis and wine sauce. A less formal menu is served in the Mackintosh Lounge.

Times: 5-9, Closed Jan **Rooms:** 17 (17 en suite) ★★★ HL
Directions: A86, 2m past Roy Bridge

SHIELDAIG   MAP 22 NG85

◉◉ Tigh an Eilean Hotel Restaurant

Modern Scottish V

Accomplished cooking in a welcoming hotel

☎ 01520 755251   IV54 8XN
e-mail: tighaneilean@keme.co.uk

However long your journey to reach Sheildaig, an 18th-century fishing village perched on the shore of Loch Torridon, you'll know it was worth it when you arrive at this delightful white-painted hotel. The restaurant is airy and light, with an atmosphere of relaxed chic, and fabulous views across the loch to the open sea beyond. The hotel centres around the original substantial house, built around 1800 when the village was constructed using a government grant. Modern Scottish cuisine with French influences offers straightforward, accurately prepared dishes where nothing is more important than flavour. Daily-changing menus rely on local produce, demonstrating a passion for fine ingredients and a commitment to quality. Expect a main course of walnut-encrusted escalope of organic salmon with an orange sauce, followed perhaps by griottine cherry and almond clafoutis.

Chef: Christopher Field **Owners:** Christopher & Cathryn Field **Times:** 7-8.30, Closed end Oct-mid Mar (except private booking), Closed L all week **Prices:** Fixed D £42.50, Service optional **Wine:** 45 bottles over £20, 20 bottles under £20, 8 by the glass **Notes:** Vegetarian menu, Smart casual, Civ Wed 40 **Seats:** 28, Pr/dining room 28 **Children:** Menu, Portions **Rooms:** 11 (11 en suite) ★ SHL **Directions:** From A896 follow signs for Shieldaig. Hotel in village centre on water's edge

SOUTH BALLACHULISH   MAP 22 NN05

◎◎ *Ballachulish House*

Modern Scottish
Magnificent dining in Highland house-party setting

☎ 01855 811266   PH49 4JX
e-mail: mclaughlins@btconnect.com
web: www.ballachulishhouse.com

A sympathetically restored and imposing 17th-century laird's loch-side residence with superb mountain views, this archetypal country-house hotel has a classic dining room furnished with antiques and crisply clothed tables. The three-hour dining experience has a house-party atmosphere. Canapés enjoyed by the drawing room fire are often accompanied by a piper. The five-course menu comprises dishes based on the very best Scottish fare. Tried and trusted combinations allow the skilful kitchen to concentrate on keeping flavours fresh and vibrant with attention to detail with flavours and textures. A main course of poached fillet of John Dory, for example, is served with perfectly cooked langoustine and garlic beignets and sauce hollandaise.

Times: 12-2.15/7-8   **Rooms:** 8 (8 en suite) ★★★★★ GA
Directions: Take A82 to Ballachulish rdbt, then A828 (Oban) for approx 0.25m. Hotel on L & signed

---

SPEAN BRIDGE   MAP 22 NN28

◎ Old Pines Hotel

Modern British V
Scandinavian-style setting for Scottish cuisine

☎ 01397 712324   PH34 4EG
e-mail: enquiries@oldpines.co.uk
web: www.oldpines.co.uk

This Scandinavian-style pine chalet hotel enjoys wonderful views of the Ben Nevis range and has a backdrop of ancient pine trees creating a dramatic setting. The restaurant prides itself on offering modern Scottish cuisine using locally-sourced ingredients, organic wherever possible. Dinner is a fixed-price, four-course affair starting with home-made canapés and finishing with organic chocolate truffles. In between, you might sample a fillet of West Coast cod, seared langoustine and scallop and shellfish brandy bisque, and perhaps a warm chocolate and raspberry brownie dessert, served with a white chocolate sauce and raspberry ice cream. Service is relaxed, friendly and semi-formal. Excellent vegetarian menu available.

Chef: Imogen Dalley   **Owners:** Imogen & Ken Dalley   **Times:** 12-3/6.30-9
Prices: Fixed D £34.50, Service optional   **Wine:** 15 bottles over £20, 50 bottles under £20, 12 by the glass   **Notes:** Vegetarian menu, Dress Restrictions, Smart casual, no jeans to D, Civ Wed 30   **Seats:** 30
Children: Menu, Portions   **Rooms:** 8 (8 en suite) ★★★
Directions: 10m N of Fort William, 400yds from A82 at Commando Memorial   **Parking:** 10

◎◎ Russell's at Smiddy House

Modern Scottish
Top-notch cooking in a convivial setting

☎ 01397 712335   Roy Bridge Rd PH34 4EU
e-mail: enquiry@smiddyhouse.co.uk
web: www.smiddyhouse.co.uk

Prominently located on the ground floor of this large house in the centre of town, formerly the village blacksmith, the candlelit Russell's restaurant occupies two front rooms and seats its diners at tables decked with sparkling glasses, quality china and fresh flowers. It's an intimate venue with modern-classic design, and the knack for turning the best of local seasonal produce into high-quality, well-presented and well-balanced cuisine. The concise, fixed-price menu stays true to its roots, featuring dishes such as a rack of Highland lamb served with sweet potato and parsnip mash and a red wine jus, or peppered Highland venison with oatmeal stuffing and a confit of beetroot, while to finish, perhaps a warm pear and gingerbread pudding with warm toffee sauce.

Chef: Glen Russell   **Owners:** Glen Russell/Robert Bryson   **Times:** 6-9, Closed 2 wks Jan, 2 wks Nov, 2 days a week (Nov-Apr), Closed L all week
Prices: Fixed D £27.95-£34.45, Service optional   **Wine:** 14 bottles over £20, 16 bottles under £20, 3 by the glass   **Notes:** Dress Restrictions, Smart casual   **Seats:** 38   **Children:** Menu, Portions   **Rooms:** 4 (4 en suite)
★★★★ GH   **Directions:** Located in Spean Bridge, 9m N of Fort William, on A82 towards Inverness   **Parking:** 15

STEIN   MAP 22 NG25

◎ Loch Bay Seafood Restaurant

British, Seafood
Excellent local seafood in a simple setting

☎ 01470 592235   IV55 8GA
e-mail: david@lochbay-seafood-restaurant.co.uk
web: www.lochbay-seafood-restaurant.co.uk

A terrace of 18th-century fishermen's cottages is the setting for this intimate seafood restaurant, located close to the loch shore near Waternish Point. The wonderfully welcoming atmosphere is another part of its allure, and the need to book for both lunch and dinner really says it all. The blackboard advertises the freshest of seafood from the catch landed at nearby Dunvegan, and supplements an extensive carte. Everything is simply cooked with almost nothing added to mask the natural flavours. Sautéed scallops with lime and coriander are a good place to start, followed perhaps by whole Dover sole, or Wild Esk salmon, and Drambuie pannacotta with exotic fruit syrup to finish.

Chef: David Wilkinson   **Owners:** David & Alison Wilkinson   **Times:** 12-2/6-9, Closed Nov-Easter (excl. 1wk over Hogmanay), Sun-Mon, Etr-mid May, mid Sep-Nov, Closed L Mon   **Prices:** Starter £3.25-£9, Main £10-£18, Dessert £3.80-£5, Service optional   **Wine:** 11 bottles over £20, 21 bottles under £20, 4 by the glass   **Notes:** Extensive blackboard choices
Seats: 26   **Children:** Portions   **Directions:** 4m off A850 by the B886 **Parking:** 6

SCOTLAND

STRONTIAN   MAP 22 NM86

◉◉ Kilcamb Lodge Hotel

Modern European V

Tranquil lochside setting for accomplished cuisine

☎ 01967 402257   PH36 4HY

e-mail: enquiries@kilcamblodge.co.uk

web: www.kilcamblodge.co.uk

Used as a barracks during the Highland Clearances, Kilcamb Lodge is now a delightful haven for guests seeking a peaceful retreat in a lovely lochside setting. Accomplished country-house cooking sees careful sourcing of fine fresh ingredients from local suppliers. Typically, you'll find well-executed starters like Inverawe smoked salmon and dill bavarois with smoked salmon remoulade and cucumber relish, and well-flavoured main courses like fillet of Mallaig halibut with Loch Fyne oyster beignet, sautéed spinach, a panaché of vegetables and shellfish velouté sauce. Desserts might feature lemon curd brûlée with vanilla pod ice cream served in an almond tuile. Round off an enjoyable meal with freshly ground cafetière coffee and home-made petits fours.

Chef: Gordon Smillie   **Owners:** Sally & David Fox   **Times:** 12-2.30/7.30-9.30, Closed 3 Jan-15 Feb, Mon-Tue (Nov & Feb), Closed L Mon **Prices:** Fixed L £14.95-£18.95, Fixed D £45, Starter £4.95-£7.95, Main £8.95-£16.95, Dessert £5.75, Service optional, Group min 5 service 10% **Wine:** 40 bottles over £20, 40 bottles under £20, 8 by the glass **Notes:** Fixed L 3 courses, Fixed D 4 courses, Vegetarian menu, Dress Restrictions, Smart casual, Civ Wed 60 **Seats:** 26 **Children:** Min 12 yrs **Rooms:** 12 (12 en suite)★★★ CHH **Directions:** Take the Corran ferry off A82. Follow A861 to Strontian. First left over bridge after village. **Parking:** 28

TAIN   MAP 23 NH78

◉◉ Glenmorangie Highland Home at Cadboll

French, European ▪NOTABLE WINE LIST

Home-from-home dining from Scotland's larder

☎ 01862 871671   Cadboll, Fearn IV20 1XP

e-mail: relax@glenmorangieplc.co.uk

web: www.theglenmorangiehouse.com

More than a country house, this Highland home - owned by the Glenmorangie whisky company - is formed from a 17th-century farmhouse and an 18th-century castle, with its own beach, grounds and walled orchards and gardens providing produce for the house. Guests and diners sit down together house-party style around one long table, after being introduced in the drawing room over whiskies, and it's the ideal place to take your own group of friends or family.

Impressive cuisine capitalises on the availability of wonderful local produce like fresh seafood and venison from neighbouring shooting estates. Dinner is a six-course affair (with just one choice at an interim course), but expect the likes of a mains roast fillet of beef and braised shin served with fondant potatoes and a port wine jus.

Chef: David Graham   **Owners:** Glenmorangie Ltd   **Times:** 8, Closed 23-26 Dec, 4-27 Jan, Closed L by prior arrangement **Prices:** Fixed D £45, Service optional **Notes:** Fixed D 5 courses, Dress Restrictions, Smart casual, no jeans or T-shirts, Civ Wed 60 **Seats:** 30, Pr/dining room 30 **Children:** Min 16 yrs, Portions **Rooms:** 9 (9 en suite)★★ CHH **Directions:** N on A9, at Nigg Rdbt turn right onto B9175 (before Tain) & follow signs for hotel **Parking:** 60

TONGUE   MAP 23 NC55

◉ Ben Loyal Hotel

Modern Scottish

Food with flair in a magnificent setting

☎ 01847 611216   Main St IV27 4XE

e-mail: benloyalhotel@btinternet.com

web: www.benloyal.co.uk

Arriving here after a stunning highland and coastal drive, guests eating in the restaurant can take in the magnificent views of the Kyle of Tongue. With informal, friendly service, an extensive range of modern dishes is offered, featuring expertly cooked local ingredients - try Ben Loyal potted venison or Kyle of Tongue oysters, followed by beef bourguignon with herb dumplings, or haddock on champ with cheddar cheese cream. Then round off with orange and whisky-scented bread-and-butter pudding. The bar offers a bistro menu and is a popular choice for locals and tourists.

Owners: Mr & Mrs P Lewis   **Times:** 12-2.30/6-8.30, Closed 30 Nov - 1 Mar, Closed L all week **Prices:** Starter £4.50-£6, Main £10-£15, Dessert £5, Service optional **Wine:** All bottles under £20, 4 by the glass **Notes:** Vegetarian available **Seats:** 50 **Children:** Menu, Portions **Rooms:** 11 (11 en suite) ★★ HL **Directions:** Hotel in centre of village at junction of A836 & A838 **Parking:** 20

◉ Borgie Lodge Hotel

Modern British

Cosy hotel offering accomplished cooking

☎ 01641 521332   Skerray KW14 7TH

e-mail: info@borgielodgehotel.co.uk

web: www.borgielodgehotel.co.uk

This Victorian sporting lodge lies in a glen close to the river of the same name, and continues to provide a welcome retreat for today's sportsmen, particularly anglers. There's a relaxed and friendly atmosphere in the cosy lounge and bar, where you can settle down by the fire and listen to tales about 'the one that got away'! A skilful kitchen makes good use of local produce in modern British and Scottish dishes. The concise menu changes daily depending on what's in season, but might include crab claws with pink grapefruit and herb dressing, followed by fillet of local beef with onion marmalade and port sauce, and bitter chocolate fondant pudding.

Chef: Daniel Stickland   **Owners:** RJ, DA & BF Stickland   **Times:** 12-2/7-8.30, Closed 25 Dec **Prices:** Fixed D £32, Service optional **Wine:** 9 bottles over £20, 16 bottles under £20, 4 by the glass **Notes:** Fixed D 4 courses, Dress Restrictions, Smart casual, no jeans **Seats:** 16 **Children:** Min 12 yrs **Rooms:** 8 (7 en suite) ★★ HL **Directions:** 0.5m off A836 6m from Tongue **Parking:** 15

TORRIDON   MAP 22 NG95

⊚⊚ The Torridon Restaurant

Modern British V ⦾ NOTABLE WINE LIST ✑

Country house with stunning views and accomplished cooking

☎ 01445 791242   Loch Torridon Country House Hotel IV22 2EY
e-mail: info@thetorridon.com
web: www.thetorridon.com

Expect to be wowed by the magnificent lochside setting and awe-inspiring mountain scenery at this beautifully restored Victorian country-house hotel. Once a shooting lodge, it makes a perfect setting for a romantic break or to escape the pressures of life. Original Scottish pine panelling and ornate ceilings cut a formal yet relaxed tone in the restaurant, with its friendly and attentive kilted staff, while the conservatory area takes in the scenery. There's a clubby bar boasting 300 malt whiskies and a serious wine list, too. The modern approach to cooking delivers a progressive take on a classical French theme, with intricate, appealing, accomplished dishes employing top-notch local ingredients, including produce from the hotel's potager and beef from their own herd. A roast saddle of wild venison with pear tart Tatin, langoustine and liquorice, or roast brill with a poppy seed and sesame crunch, grapefruit jam, courgette and mung beans are fine examples of the fare.

Chef: Kevin Broome   **Owners:** Daniel & Rohaise Rose-Bristow   **Times:** 12-2/7-9, Closed 2 Jan for 3 wks, Closed L Bar only   **Prices:** Fixed D £40-£65, Service optional   **Wine:** 156 bottles over £20, 27 bottles under £20, 8 by the glass   **Notes:** Fixed D 4 courses, Tasting menu available, Vegetarian menu, Dress Restrictions, No jeans or trainers, Civ Wed 42   **Seats:** 38, Pr/dining room 16   **Children:** Min 10 yrs, Menu, Portions   **Rooms:** 19 (19 en suite)★★★ CHH   **Directions:** From Inverness take A9 N, follow signs to Ullapool (A835). At Garve take A832 to Kinlochewe; take A896 to Torridon. Do not turn off to Torridon Village. Hotel on right after Annat village   **Parking:** 20

LANARKSHIRE, SOUTH

BIGGAR   MAP 21 NT03

⊚⊚ Chancellors at Shieldhill Castle

Modern, International ⦾ NOTABLE WINE LIST

Fine food and wine in historic fortified country mansion

☎ 01899 220035   Quothquan ML12 6NA
e-mail: enquiries@shieldhill.co.uk
web: www.shieldhill.co.uk

Set in rolling countryside and 7 acres of lawns and woodland, Shieldhill is a fortified mansion that can trace its history from 1199. This imposing building provides a fusion of historic architecture with modern cooking and friendly service. Atmospheric public areas include the oak-panelled lounge and Chancellor's restaurant, a classic high-ceilinged room resplendent in its baronial furnishings. A technically accomplished kitchen delivers simple, full-flavoured, imaginative dishes that utilise fresh local seasonal produce - including the estate game - combined with an award-wining wine list designed by the proprietors. The flexible carte teams the two, providing a choice of wines to accompany every dish - all of which are available as starters or mains. Take aromatic turbot served with a sun-blushed tomato and shallot risotto and lime and herb dressing, or Sheildhill Castle sporting venison with confit of carrot, oxtail pudding, broad beans and a wood sorrel dressing.

Chef: Christina Lamb   **Owners:** Mr & Mrs R Lamb   **Times:** 12-1.45/7-8.45   **Prices:** Fixed L £15.95, Fixed D £19.95, Starter £6.95-£13.95, Main £12.95-£29.95, Dessert £7.95-£9.45, Service optional, Group min 10 service 5%   **Wine:** 20 bottles under £20, 30 by the glass   **Notes:** Vegetarian available, Civ Wed 150   **Seats:** 52, Pr/dining room 30   **Children:** Portions   **Rooms:** 16 (16 en suite) ★★★ CHH   **Directions:** From Biggar take B7016 to Carnwath. After approx 2.5m turn left onto Shieldhill Road. Castle is 1m on right   **Parking:** 60

⊚ Fifty Five

Modern Scottish

Contemporary Scottish dining

☎ 01899 221555   55 High St ML12 6DA
e-mail: info@fiftyfive.uk.com
web: www.fiftyfive.uk.com

This High Street restaurant offers contemporary rustic décor, where vibrant pictures and prints and cream and chocolate brown furnishings contrast with bare stonework. The modern Scottish cuisine suits the surroundings; the 55 Menu offers a fixed-price tasting selection for two, while the carte has an appealing range of dishes at each turn, and there are early evening and kids' menus, too. Expect roast rump of lamb served with stewed tomatoes, peppers and chorizo, or perhaps grilled Dover sole with new potatoes, creamed spinach and buttered asparagus, while a passionfruit crème brûlée might provide the finish.

Chef: Jimmy Guldberg   **Owners:** Warren, Lee & Wayne Godfrey   **Times:** 12-2.30/5.30-9.30, Closed 2-12 Jan, Mon, Closed L Tues-Fri   **Prices:** Fixed L £17.50, Fixed D £55, Starter £5.50-£10.50, Main £14-£21, Dessert £4.50-£5.50, Service optional   **Wine:** 60 bottles over £20, 19 bottles under £20, 7 by the glass   **Notes:** Early D 2 courses £16, 3 courses £19   **Seats:** 34   **Children:** Menu, Portions   **Directions:** In centre along A702   **Parking:** 3

EAST KILBRIDE   MAP 20 NS65

◉ Macdonald Crutherland House

Scottish, International

Honest, clear flavours in country-house hotel

☎ 01355 577000 Strathaven Rd G75 0QZ
e-mail: general.crutherland@macdonald-hotels.co.uk
web: www.macdonald-hotels.co.uk

Set in peaceful countryside just 20 minutes from the centre of Glasgow, this upmarket hotel is deservedly popular with the conference market. Its richly furnished dining room is a haven of elegant good taste and offers an extensive range of dishes. Those on the carte showcase the kitchen's flair, while a fixed-price selection offers simpler choices at keener prices. Expect honest, flavourful cooking - chargrilled rib-eye steak, tomato confit, hand-cut chips and garlic butter, or wild sea bass with saffron risotto. Banana parfait with spiced compôte to finish, maybe.

Chef: Joe Queen **Owners:** Macdonald Hotels **Times:** 12-2.30/6-9.30
Prices: Fixed L £9.95-£14, Fixed D £25-£29.50, Starter £5.95-£7.50, Main £14.25-£22.95, Dessert £6.25-£7.50, Service optional **Wine:** 62 bottles over £20, 14 bottles under £20, 14 by the glass **Notes:** Gourmet dinners available, Civ Wed 250, Air con **Seats:** 80, Pr/dining room 200
Children: Menu, Portions **Rooms:** 75 (75 en suite) ★★★★ HL
Directions: From East Kilbride take A726 towards Strathaven. 1.5m, & beyond Torrance rdbt, hotel on left **Parking:** 60

STRATHAVEN   MAP 20 NS74

◉ Rissons at Springvale ·

Modern Scottish

Relaxed restaurant with modern Scottish cuisine

☎ 01357 520234 & 521131 18 Lethame Rd ML10 6AD
e-mail: rissons@msn.com
web: www.rissonsrestaurant.co.uk

Located just outside the town, this light-and-airy, modern-styled restaurant comes with an intimate conservatory overlooking the local park. The atmosphere is relaxed and friendly, and the service informed, while the kitchen's modern-bistro output matches the mood, delivering simple, unfussy, well-presented dishes that concentrate on clean flavours and the use of quality produce. Typically, twice-baked peat-smoked haddock soufflé with Ayrshire bacon, or perhaps a haunch of venison with sweet red cabbage, crispy bacon and a port wine sauce, while baked citrus cake with fresh lemon curd could catch the eye at dessert.

Chef: Scott Baxter, Leonard Allen **Owners:** Scott Baxter, Anne Baxter
Times: 5.30-9.30, Closed New Year, 1 wk Jan, 1st wk July, Mon-Tue, Closed L Wed-Sat **Prices:** Starter £4-£8, Main £8-£17, Dessert £4-£5.50, Service optional **Wine:** 13 bottles over £20, 23 bottles under £20, 6 by the glass **Notes:** Early evening D 2 courses £12.95, 3 courses £14.95, Vegetarian available **Seats:** 40 **Children:** Menu, Portions **Rooms:** 11 (11 en suite)
★★★ RR **Directions:** From M74 junct 8 follow A71, through Stonehouse and onto Strathaven **Parking:** 10

DIRLETON   MAP 21 NT58

◉ The Open Arms Hotel

Modern Scottish

Charming country hotel with relaxing atmosphere and enjoyable dining

☎ 01620 850241 EH39 5EG
e-mail: openarmshotel@clara.co.uk
web: www.openarmshotel.com

This well-established hotel lies across the green from Dirleton Castle. The inviting interior includes the popular Deveau's brasserie and the more formal Library restaurant. The latter has soft lighting, clothed tables and formal settings. Staff are helpful and friendly, serving carefully-prepared modern and traditional dishes like starters of pan-fried breast of pigeon with creamed leek fondue and redcurrant jus, and main courses like rack of lamb with honey and ginger, or baked fillet of monkfish wrapped in pancetta with chervil and champagne cream sauce. Finish with Bailey's crème brûlée with cranachan ice cream, or try the good selection of Scottish farmhouse cheeses.

Times: 12-2/7-9, Closed D Sun **Rooms:** 10 (10 en suite) ★★★ SHL
Directions: From A1 (S) take A198 to North Berwick, then follow signs for Dirleton - 2 miles W. From Edinburgh take A6137 leading to A198

GULLANE   MAP 21 NT48

◉◉◉ Greywalls Hotel

see opposite

◉◉ La Potinière

Modern British

Ambitious cooking in cottage-style restaurant

☎ 01620 843214 Main St EH31 2AA
web: www.la-potiniere.co.uk

A delightful cottage-style restaurant of fairytale proportions, La Potinière is a two-partner operation, both sharing the kitchen, while Keith also acts as host and wine waiter. Accordingly, the meal is a leisurely four-course affair at dinner, plus an amuse-bouche and pre-dessert, and three courses at lunch. Smart, crisp linen and quality tableware reinforce the kitchen's serious intent, while the cooking lends a contemporary touch with artistic presentation and makes fine use of local seasonal produce. There are just two choices at each course, perhaps featuring cream of Jerusalem artichoke soup followed by warm guinea fowl timbale with wild mushrooms, or roast loin of Scottish venison with a truffle dauphinoise and beetroot fondant. Round things off in style with champagne rhubarb or white chocolate and Bailey's mousse.

Chef: Mary Runciman & Keith Marley **Owners:** Mary Runciman
Times: 12.30-1.30/7-8.30, Closed Xmas, BHs, Mon-Tue, Closed D Sun (Oct-Apr) **Prices:** Fixed L £17.50, Fixed D £38, Service optional **Wine:** 28 bottles over £20, 8 bottles under £20, 4 by the glass **Notes:** Fixed D 4 courses, Vegetarian available, Dress Restrictions, Smart casual **Seats:** 30
Children: Portions **Directions:** 20m SE of Edinburgh. 3m from North Berwick on A198 **Parking:** 10

SCOTLAND

⊚⊚⊚
Greywalls Hotel

GULLANE   MAP 21 NT48
Modern British
Fine cooking in a quintessential country house

☎ 01620 842144   Muirfield EH31 2EG
e-mail: hotel@greywalls.co.uk
web: www.greywalls.co.uk

Greywall's enviable location overlooking the famous Muirfield golf course has long made it a destination hotel for sporting types, and these days it also lures foodies from far and wide with its imaginative Scottish cuisine. A dignified Lutyens country house with pretty gardens created by Gertrude Jekyll, it offers elegant Edwardian comfort in the form of sumptuous sitting rooms whose deep sofas beckon for pre- and post-dinner drinks. The restaurant is comprised of two peaceful rooms with well-spaced, well-appointed tables and comfortable chairs, and more views over the golf course. Traditional formalities mean jackets and ties for gentlemen and formal, though friendly, service. The kitchen's modern Scottish approach is underpinned by classical French techniques and combinations, the cooking focusing on high-quality produce from the abundant Scottish larder. You might start with honey and lime roast quail with pea purée, bacon and lettuce, or a salad of rare roast beef with gherkins, olives and pesto, followed by roast organic salmon with a lentil cassoulet, foie gras and Sévruga caviar, or saffron and gold leaf risotto with langoustines, fine beans and cress.

Chef: David Williams **Owners:** Mr & Mrs G Weaver **Times:** 12-2/7-9.30, Closed Jan-Feb, Closed L Mon-Thu, D Sun **Prices:** Fixed L £20, Fixed D £45, Service optional **Wine:** 200 bottles over £20, 10 bottles under £20, 12 by the glass **Notes:** Fixed D 4 courses, Dress Restrictions, Jacket requested, Civ Wed 40 **Seats:** 40, Pr/dining room 20 **Children:** Portions **Rooms:** 23 (23 en suite)★★★ HL **Directions:** From Edinburgh take A1 to North Berwick slip road, then follow A198 along coast to far end of Gullane - Greywalls in last road on left **Parking:** 40

SCOTLAND

HADDINGTON   MAP 21 NT57
⊚⊚ **Bonars Restaurant**
Contemporary
Clean, contemporary cuisine in former watermill

☎ 01620 822100   Poldrate Mill, Tyne House EH41 4AD
e-mail: info@bonars.co.uk
web: www.bonars.co.uk

An old watermill on the banks of the Tyne provides the idyllic setting for this popular restaurant, which offers a great-value menu, as well as cookery courses and theme nights. The Mediterranean-style room has stone walls, spotlights and terracotta tiles. Dishes are straightforward and full of flavour, and arrive at the table in stunning arrangements; start with a delectable chicken liver parfait, perhaps, and then move on to red wine venison with beignets of haggis, or a mouthwatering dessert such as twice-baked chocolate torte with bitter chocolate and raspberry ice cream. An attached brasserie provides lighter options if you're in the mood for more informal fare.

Times: 12-2.30/6-9, Closed Mon, Tues

Waterside Bistro
☎ 01620 825674   1-5 Waterside EH41 4AT

Relatively formal eatery located in a picturesque setting and known for generous portions.

NORTH BERWICK   MAP 21 NT58
⊚ **Macdonald Marine Hotel**
British NEW
Fantastic location for an impressive hotel with fine-dining restaurant

☎ 0870 400 8129   Cromwell Rd EH39 4LZ
e-mail: sales.marine@macdonald-hotels.co.uk
web: www.macdonaldhotels.co.uk/marine

A full refurbishment has transformed this stylish hotel, now offering extensive leisure and conference facilities in addition to the championship golf course in front of it and views across the sea to the Firth of Forth. The restaurant has an equally impressive setting, the formal décor with oak panelling, deep plum coloured walls and portraits has a regal feel. Diners enjoy canapés and pre-starters in addition to choices from the classically-based menu. Lamb rillette, tomato confit and truffles is a typical starter. Main courses might feature suprême of guinea fowl or perhaps wild salmon.

Times: 12.30-2.30/6.30-9.30 **Rooms:** 83 (83 en suite) ★★★★ HL

LOTHIAN, WEST

LINLITHGOW   MAP 21 NS97

◉◉ Champany Inn

Traditional British

Unrivalled steak restaurant in a country lodge

☎ 01506 834532 & 834388   EH49 7LU
e-mail: reception@champany.com
web: www.champany.com

Several cottages and an ancient watermill comprise this unusual hotel. The restaurant itself is an octagonal affair with exposed stone walls and timbered ceiling, while tapestries, gleaming copper and elegant portraits abound alongside an open kitchen. The small lounge boasts leather seating and antiques, while the extensive wine choice is stored on a mezzanine floor. A temple to prime beef and the Rolls Royce of steakhouses, Champany specialises in cuts from cattle sourced and prepared by the restaurant's own butchery and hung for three weeks. West Coast seafood also finds its place, but it's the full-flavoured, tender beef that takes pride of place, such as Aberdeen Angus sirloin, fillet or rib-eye. The farmer's cottage has now been converted into a shop selling Champany produce, while the Chop and Ale House serves a bistro-style menu.

Chef: C Davidson, D Gibson, C Hart **Owners:** Mr & Mrs C Davidson **Times:** 12.30-2/7-10, Closed 25-26 Dec, 1-2 Jan, Sun, Closed L Sat **Prices:** Fixed L £19.50, Starter £9-£15, Main £20-£42, Dessert £7.50, Service added 10% **Wine:** 650 bottles over £20, 8 bottles under £20, 8 by the glass **Notes:** Dress Restrictions, No jeans **Seats:** 50, Pr/dining room 30 **Children:** Min 8 yrs **Directions:** 2m NE of Linlithgow. From M9 (N) junct 3, at top of slip road turn right. Champany is 500yds on right **Parking:** 50

◉◉ Livingston's Restaurant

Modern Scottish

Superb Scottish cooking in a delightful rural restaurant

☎ 01506 846565   52 High St EH49 7AE
e-mail: contact@livingstons-restaurant.co.uk
web: www.livingstons-restaurant.co.uk

Tucked away at the end of a semi-hidden 'ginnel' or lane, Livingston's provides an authentic Scottish experience. Ruby red fabrics, tartan carpets and soft candlelight conspire to create a relaxed and intoxicatingly Caledonian atmosphere that enhances the offerings on a menu which trumpets local ingredients such as Inverurie lamb and Highland venison. Among the highlights are dishes such as warm Stornoway black pudding tart with crispy pancetta and herb salad, roast halibut on wilted spinach with rosemary and red wine jus or try saddle of wild Highland venison with red cabbage and bitter chocolate sauce. Make room for the assiette of Livingston's puddings. The well-chosen wine list has interesting tasting notes.

Chef: Julian Wright **Owners:** Ronald & Christine Livingston **Times:** 12-2.30/6-9.30, Closed 1 wk Jun, 1 wk Oct, 2wks Jan, Sun (except Mothering Sun)-Mon **Prices:** Fixed L £17.95, Fixed D £33.95, Service optional, Group min 8 service 10% **Wine:** 37 bottles over £20, 24 bottles under £20, 6 by the glass **Notes:** Vegetarian available, Dress Restrictions, Smart casual **Seats:** 40 **Children:** Min 8 yrs, Portions **Directions:** Opposite post office **Parking:** NCP Linlithgow Cross, on street

Chop & Ale House

☎ 01506 834532   EH49 7LU
web: www.champany.com

A popular place to eat where traditional cooking blends with modern.

Marynka

☎ 01506 840123   57 High St EH49 7ED

Glass-fronted restaurant with modern Scottish cooking.

UPHALL   MAP 21 NT07

◉ Macdonald Houstoun House

Traditional British

Fine dining in beautiful surroundings

☎ 0870 194 2107   EH52 6JS
e-mail: houstoun@macdonald-hotels.co.uk
web: www.macdonaldhotels.co.uk/houstoun.house

Set in beautifully-landscaped grounds and gardens, this 17th-century tower house boasts a modern leisure club and spa, and comes with a choice of dining options, including a vaulted cocktail bar with an impressive selection of whiskies, and an elegant period-style dining room with formally-set tables. The fixed-price menu provides good value with traditional choices, while the carte is a little more adventurous. Dishes remain flavour-driven through good, honest and uncomplicated cooking using the finest Scottish ingredients. Expect mains like pan-fried fillet of Scottish beef with fondant potato, roast shallots and pancetta, followed by wild strawberry and pistachio parfait with forest fruit syrup to finish.

Chef: John Paul McLachlan **Owners:** Macdonald Hotels **Times:** 12-2/7-9.30, Closed L Sat **Prices:** Fixed L £18.50-£23.50, Fixed D £29.50-£32.50, Service optional **Wine:** 74 bottles over £20, 16 bottles under £20, 13 by the glass **Notes:** Dress Restrictions, Smart casual, no jeans or trainers, Civ Wed 200 **Seats:** 65, Pr/dining room 30 **Children:** Menu, Portions **Rooms:** 71 (71 en suite) ★★★★ HL **Directions:** M8 junct 3 follow signs for Broxburn. Continue straight over rdbt the turn right at mini rdbt towards Uphall, Hotel 1m on right **Parking:** 200

MORAY

ARCHIESTOWN   MAP 23 NJ24

◉ Archiestown Hotel

Modern British

Well-prepared local produce at a small, friendly hotel

☎ 01340 810218   AB38 7QL
e-mail: jah@archiestownhotel.co.uk
web: www.archiestownhotel.co.uk

This small Victorian country house is located in the village square, in the heart of the whisky and salmon fishing country of Speyside, and comes with a delightful walled garden. Popular with locals and visitors alike, the cosy bistro-style restaurant offers a seasonally-changing menu full of interesting dishes. Twice-baked crab soufflé with Mull of Kintyre cheddar makes an impressive starter, followed by an equally enjoyable main course of pan-charred fillet steak with a mushroom and stilton glaze, served with shallots and rowan jelly jus. Puddings are satisfyingly traditional - you might try iced cranachan with raspberry compôte and home-made pecan meringue.

Chef: Robert Aspden, Ian Fleming **Owners:** Alan & Jane Hunter
Times: 12-2/7-9, Closed Xmas, 3 Jan-10 Feb **Prices:** Fixed L £9-£18.50, Fixed D £26.50-£37, Starter £4.50-£8.50, Main £16.50-£23, Dessert £5.50-£6, Service optional, Group min 10 service 10% **Wine:** 24 bottles over £20, 11 bottles under £20, 6 by the glass **Notes:** Vegetarian available, Smart casual, Civ Wed 20 **Seats:** 35, Pr/dining room 16 **Children:** Portions **Rooms:** 11 (11 en suite) ★★ SHL **Directions:** Turn off A95 onto B9102 at Craigellachie **Parking:** 30

CRAIGELLACHIE   MAP 23 NJ24

◉◉ *Craigellachie Hotel*

Traditional Scottish

Formal dining with Scottish flavour and atmosphere

☎ 01340 881204   AB38 9SR
e-mail: info@craigellachie.com
web: www.craigellachie.com

Impressive Victorian hotel in the heart of Speyside's whisky distilling area - no surprises then that the bar features more than 600 malts. Log fires, hunting and fishing paraphernalia, and traditional Scottish décor make for a relaxing experience. The Ben Aigan Restaurant encompasses several rooms, each with its own decorative style, backed by efficient, friendly service. A Scottish approach to cooking, with both French and international influences, delivers excellent flavours via dishes graced by fresh, high-quality produce from the abundant Scottish larder - prime Aberdeen Angus beef, Cabrach lamb, Moray Firth seafood and shellfish, river salmon and game. Braised shank of Cabrach lamb slowly cooked in red wine and sage reduction or fillet of Aberdeen Angus beef on smoked bacon champ, roasted vegetables and whisky jus are fine examples of the fare.

Times: 12-2/6-10 **Rooms:** 26 (26 en suite) ★★★ HL **Directions:** 12m S of Elgin, in the village centre

CULLEN   MAP 23 NJ56

◉ Cullen Bay Hotel

Traditional Scottish NEW

Restaurant with views and traditional local Scottish fare

☎ 01542 840432   AB56 4XA
e-mail: stay@cullenbayhotel.com
web: www.cullenbayhotel.com

True to its name, this small family-run hotel sits on a hillside west of the town and offers lovely views over the bay, taking in beach, golf course and Moray Firth. Its spacious, relaxed, traditionally-styled restaurant makes the best of the panoramas. The kitchen's simply prepared and presented traditional food with modern twists focuses on quality Scottish produce, especially seafood from the local port. Cullen skink is an essential start, and to follow, perhaps oven-baked fillet of sea bass topped with a herb crust and served with a rich pesto. Desserts from the sweet trolley, or perhaps a speciality Cranachan rice pudding.

Chef: Gail Meikle **Owners:** Mr & Mrs Tucker & Sons **Times:** 12-2/6.30-9, Closed From 2 Jan for 10 days **Prices:** Starter £3.50-£5.25, Main £9.50-£22.50, Dessert £4.25-£4.75, Service optional **Wine:** 5 bottles over £20, 48 bottles under £20, 8 by the glass **Notes:** ALC D prices, Vegetarian available, Civ Wed 150 **Seats:** 46, Pr/dining room 40 **Children:** Menu, Portions **Rooms:** 14 (14 en suite) ★★★ SHL **Directions:** On A98, 0.25 m W of Cullen **Parking:** 100

SCOTLAND

Andrew Fairlie @ Gleneagles

AUCHTERARDER MAP 21 NN91

Modern French

Dramatic setting, inspired food

☎ 01764 694267   PH3 1NF
e-mail: andrew.fairlie@gleneagles.com
web: www.gleneagles.com

Chef: Andrew Fairlie
Owners: Andrew Fairlie
Times: 6.30-10, Closed 24-25 Dec, 3 wks Jan, Sun, Closed L all week, D Sun
Prices: Fixed D £65, Service optional
Wine: 250 bottles over £20, 12 by the glass
Notes: Tasting Menu 6 courses £85, Dress Restrictions, Smart casual, Air con
Seats: 54
Children: Min 12 yrs
Directions: Take Gleneagles exit from A9, continue for 1m
Parking: 300

This is fine dining through and through! Set between this luxurious, world-famous golfing hotel's main bar and the Strathearn restaurant, Andrew Fairlie's is an independent business and dinner-only affair that attracts a well-heeled, five-star international clientele. A small bar leads through to the intimate, elegant, high-ceilinged dining room that provides the ultimate in discerning interior design. Boldly decorated with black walls hung with bespoke artworks by Archie Forrest, floor-to-ceiling raw silk drapes and opulent fabrics deliver that expected wow-factor. Well-spaced, elegantly-appointed tables - with dramatic, strategically placed down-lighters that angle pools of illumination onto the crisp tableware - and comfortable seating are set to a subtle jazz backing track that lends a smooth vibe to proceedings. The service is pin-sharp and highly professional - the anticipation of the diner's needs is supreme. The menu and serious wine lists are lavish and user-friendly affairs, their presentation further echoing the décor and sense of occasion. One of Scotland's leading chefs, Andrew Fairlie's modern approach comes underpinned by a classical French theme (classics given a modern makeover) and celebrates the union of dazzling technique and top-notch ingredients. The style is complex and bold, the emphasis on flavour with dishes delivered dressed to thrill. Menus are crisply scripted and come brimful of luxury items, the menu du marché and carte are bolstered by a dégustation option (all fixed-price affairs) that seduce with an agony of choice. Think roast hand-dived scallops with caramelised cauliflower risotto, perhaps followed by an assiette de porc Gascony with jus rôti, or pan-roast fillet of John Dory served with beetroot bordelaise to follow, and to finish, a hot Valrhona chocolate biscuit with mango sorbet.

PERTH & KINROSS

AUCHTERARDER — MAP 21 NN91

◉◉◉◉ Andrew Fairlie @ Gleneagles
see opposite

◉ Cairn Lodge
British, International
Stylish dining in comfortable country house

☎ 01764 662634 Orchil Rd PH3 1LX
e-mail: email@cairnlodge.co.uk
web: www.cairnlodge.co.uk

This twin-turreted country house on the edge of town makes a delightful boutique hotel, with its wooded grounds close to Gleneagles and dozens of other golf courses. The Cairn Bar offers meals throughout the day, but the Capercaillie restaurant is the main dining focus here. Comfortable seating, helpful staff, bold décor and silver service set the tone. The kitchen's modern approach make good use of the abundant Scottish larder; take Scottish beef Wellington with honey-roasted vegetables and redcurrant juices, or perhaps grilled fillet of sea bass served with fragrant rice and lobster essence. Leave room for dark and white chocolate Genoese mousse topped with a fresh berry glaze.

Chef: Ben Mailer **Owners:** Ridi Stackis Christie **Times:** 12-2/6-10, Closed Mon-Thu (winter) **Prices:** Fixed L £12-£14, Starter £3-£5, Main £12-£20, Dessert £4-£5, Service optional **Wine:** 48 bottles over £20, 26 bottles under £20, 16 by the glass **Notes:** Vegetarian available, Civ Wed 50 **Seats:** 45, Pr/dining room 20 **Children:** Menu, Portions **Rooms:** 10 (10 en suite) ★★ **Directions:** From A9 take A824 (Auchterarder). Hotel at S end of town; on road to Gleneagles **Parking:** 50

◉◉ The Strathearn
Classic
Classic dining where service is as memorable as the food

☎ 01764 694270 The Gleneagles Hotel PH3 1NF
e-mail: resort.sales@gleneagles.com
web: www.gleneagles.com

There is only one Gleneagles, but there are several options when it comes to dining. The Strathearn remains a bastion of classical elegance and traditional values - it surely must be one of the last grand dining rooms in Britain. The space is massive, with high ceilings and pillars in the grand ballroom style. Formal service is provided by a full brigade in the good old-fashioned way, but is absolutely delightful and in no way stuffy. The seasonal menu offers a blend of classical dishes and modern presentation. Take seared West Coast scallops with caramelised leeks, cauliflower and truffle velouté, followed by smoked cannon of Caithness lamb with tapenade jus, with a superb light-textured chocolate orange tart to finish.

Times: 12.30-2.30/7-10, Closed L Mon-Sat **Rooms:** 266 (266 en suite)★★★★★ HL **Directions:** Just off A9, well signed. Between Stirling and Perth

COMRIE — MAP 21 NN72

◉ Royal Hotel
Traditional British
Traditional food in an elegant environment

☎ 01764 679200 Melville Square PH6 2DN
e-mail: reception@royalhotel.co.uk
web: www.royalhotel.co.uk

Behind the façade of this 18th-century coaching inn, on Comrie's central square, lies an elegant interior of polished-wood floors, stylish soft furnishings, log fires and antique pieces. There's a choice of dining venues, including the lounge bar, a colonial-look conservatory brasserie, the open-hearthed library and the beautifully appointed formal dining room. In fine weather you can eat outside in the walled garden. Scottish fare is skilfully prepared from local produce, with prime Scottish beef, venison, salmon, game and seafood figuring strongly.

Chef: David Milsom **Owners:** The Milsom Family **Times:** 12-2/6.30-9, Closed Xmas **Prices:** Fixed L £14.50-£21, Fixed D £19-£26.50, Starter £3.75-£7.95, Main £9.75-£17.50, Dessert £4.95, Service optional **Wine:** 46 bottles over £20, 47 bottles under £20, 7 by the glass **Notes:** Sun L roast £10.95, Vegetarian available **Seats:** 60 **Children:** Portions **Rooms:** 11 (11 en suite) ★★★ HL **Directions:** In main square, 7m from Crieff, on A85 **Parking:** 25

COUPAR ANGUS — MAP 21 NO23

◉ Enverdale House
Traditional British NEW
Traditional country-house style dining offering local fare

☎ 01828 627606 6 Pleasure Rd PH13 9JB
web: www.enverdale.co.uk

Situated in a small rural town, this popular hotel occupies a large period property with lovely high ceilings, a comfortable bar area and spacious reception rooms. The traditional, country-house style

CONTINUED

COUPAR ANGUS CONTINUED

restaurant is staffed by an enthusiastic and friendly young team, serving up classical-style dishes with the emphasis firmly on local produce and popular combinations. A typical main course might consist of succulent loin of local lamb with light, fragrant minted peas and crushed potatoes, lightly glazed carrots and rosemary jus.

Times: 12-2/5-9 **Prices:** Fixed L £12.95, Fixed D £16.95, Starter £4.25-£5.95, Main £11.50-£15.75, Dessert £4.95, Service optional **Seats:** 48 **Children:** Menu **Rooms:** 5 (5 en suite) ★★★ GH **Directions:** Just off A94

CRIEFF   MAP 21 NN82

◎◎ **The Bank Restaurant**

British, French

Original features and classic cuisine

☎ 01764 656575 32 High St PH7 3BS

e-mail: mail@thebankrestaurant.co.uk

web: www.thebankrestaurant.co.uk

As the name suggests, this restaurant had a former existence as a banking hall. An ornate, red sandstone listed building - set in a prominent position on the main street - was the work of Washington Brown, who also designed the Caledonian Hotel in Edinburgh. Today, the original wood panelling and cornices can still be seen in the charming, genteel atmosphere of the dining room, with its wooden floors, lofty ceiling and print-adorned walls. Run by a husband-and-wife team, the kitchen takes a fittingly serious approach to cooking. Its accomplished classical French-influenced cuisine delivers the likes of a

fillet of East Coast halibut with saffron mash, mixed greens and a lobster and brandy sauce, followed by warm Valrhona chocolate cake with orange curd ice cream.

The Bank Restaurant

Chef: Bill McGuigan **Owners:** Mr B & Mrs L McGuigan **Times:** 12-1.30/7-9.30, Closed 25-26 Dec, 2 wks mid Jan, 1 wk Jul, Mon/Sun, booking essential for L and D **Prices:** Starter £3.50-£7, Main £10.25-£17, Dessert £3.95-£5.25, Service included **Wine:** 24 bottles over £20, 26 bottles under £20, 4 by the glass **Seats:** 22 **Children:** Portions **Directions:** Telephone for directions **Parking:** Parking available 150 yds

---

DUNKELD   MAP 21 NO04

◎◎◎ **Kinnaird**

see below

◎◎◎

Kinnaird

DUNKELD   MAP 21 NO04

Modern European 🍷 NOTABLE WINE LIST

Exquisite country house in remote setting serving innovative food

☎ 01796 482440 Kinnaird Estate PH8 0LB

e-mail: enquiry@kinnairdestate.com

web: www.kinnairdestate.com

An imposing Edwardian baronial mansion on a grand scale, Kinnaird is set in breathtaking countryside in a magnificent 7,000-acre estate overlooking the River Tay valley. A haven of relaxed and civilised charm, it oozes all the lavish trappings of a fine country-house hotel, complete with rare antiques, an impressive collection of art and inviting sitting rooms with deep-cushioned sofas and open fires. The dining room is quite stunning, with original Italianate frescoed walls, marble fireplace, ornate chandelier and breathtaking views through its picture windows. Despite the grandeur, the formality of the service and the obligatory jacket and tie at dinner, the mood is surprisingly unstuffy, tranquil and relaxed.

The food is creative and imaginative to match the surroundings. Classically-based cooking with modern twists delivers on a compact, inspirational menu using the very best of locally-sourced produce from the abundant Scottish larder. There's good emphasis on texture

variation and fresh, vibrant, clean flavours. Precision, high skill and accuracy abound in comfortable adventure; take halibut roasted over aromats, scallop, saffron potatoes, asparagus, fennel confit and a beurre blanc, and to finish, perhaps a sticky toffee pudding soufflé with warm caramel sauce. An excellent wine list completes the upbeat package.

Chef: Trevor Brooks **Owners:** Mrs C Ward **Times:** 12-1.45/7-9.30, Closed L Mon-Tue (light L only) **Prices:** Fixed L £18-£21, Fixed D £55, Service optional **Wine:** 250 bottles over £20, 1 bottle under £20, 6 by the glass **Notes:** Dress Restrictions, Jackets for gentlemen at D, Civ Wed 45 **Seats:** 35, Pr/dining room 20 **Children:** Min 8 yrs **Rooms:** 9 (9 en suite)★★★★ HL **Directions:** From A9 N take B898 for 4.5m. Hotel on right **Parking:** 15

GLENDEVON　　　　　MAP 21 NN90
◉ An Lochan Tormaukin
Modern Scottish NEW

High-quality local produce served in relaxed, rustic surroundings

☎ 01259 781252　FK14 7JY
e-mail: enquiries@tormaukin.co.uk
web: www.anlochan.co.uk

A delightful country inn dating back to the 17th century, set amongst rolling hills in a secluded location close to Gleneagles. Open wood-burning fires, bare stone walls and wooden tables are enlivened by vibrant artwork. Both table settings and service are suitably relaxed and informal, while the honest modern Scottish fare is driven by high-quality, well-sourced local seasonal produce. Both carte and fixed-price menus offer generous portions and bags of attention to detail; take a rump of Glenearn lamb served with Stornoway black-pudding mash and redcurrant jus, and perhaps an apple and Calvados steamed pudding to finish.

Chef: Gary Noble　**Times:** Please telephone for details

KENMORE　　　　　MAP 21 NN74
◉ Kenmore Hotel
Traditional British NEW

Tay views and quality Scottish fare

☎ 01887 830205　The Square PH15 2NU
e-mail: reception@kenmorehotel.co.uk
web: www.kenmorehotel.co.uk

Built in 1572, the Kenmore is Scotland's oldest inn. The historic building has a cosy bar with a log fire, while the modern restaurant is surrounded by glass and enjoys panoramic views over the River Tay and the surrounding forests. Seasonality plays a big part in the menu composition, and dishes prepared from fresh local ingredients are simply and cleanly presented, as in oven-roasted Scottish salmon filled with Islay whisky-flavoured haggis soufflé and leek sauce, or roast breast of duckling with a nice crisp skin, coated with lemongrass and honey sauce and accompanied by stir-fried pak choi. For dessert, baked rice pudding, with scented vanilla, pineapple compôte and coconut ice cream.

Chef: Peter Backhouse　**Owners:** Kenmore Estates Ltd　**Times:** 12-17/17-9.30　**Prices:** Fixed L £12-£18, Fixed D £18-£31, Starter £4.60-£5.95, Main £10.25-£18.95, Dessert £4.50-£4.95, Service optional　**Wine:** 14 bottles over £20, 35 bottles under £20, 11 by the glass　**Notes:** Sun L £9.95, Taste of Scotland menu £29.50, Vegetarian available, Civ Wed 80, Air con　**Seats:** 100, Pr/dining room 80　**Children:** Menu, Portions　**Directions:** A9 N, A827 Ballinluig, A827 into Kenmore, hotel is at centre of village　**Parking:** 40

KILLIECRANKIE　　　　　MAP 23 NN96
◉◉ Killiecrankie House Hotel
Modern Scottish V ◉ NOTABLE WINE LIST ▭
AA Wine Award Winner for Scotland

☎ 01796 473220　PH16 5LG
e-mail: enquiries@killiecrankiehotel.co.uk
web: www.killiecrankiehotel.co.uk

A relaxing small country hotel, built as a dower house in 1840, and set in mature landscaped gardens overlooking the River Garry and the Pass of Killiecrankie. Enthusiastically run, the hotel maintains consistently high standards and a sound reputation for accomplished modern Scottish cooking. The compact fixed-price dinner menu changes daily and is driven by fresh local produce, including game and fish as well as herbs and vegetables from the kitchen garden. Suggested wine matches (from a spectacular list) accompany mains like grilled fillet of salmon and halibut with seared king scallops, roasted Mediterranean vegetables, roasted potatoes and pesto, while desserts might feature a banana and toffee tartlet baked with amaretti.

Chef: Mark Easton　**Owners:** Mr & Mrs Waters　**Times:** 7-11, Closed Jan-Feb, Closed L all week　**Prices:** Fixed D £28, Starter £6, Main £16, Dessert £6, Service optional, Group min 6 service 10%　**Wine:** 163 bottles over £20, 44 bottles under £20, 8 by the glass　**Notes:** Vegetarian menu, Dress Restrictions, No shorts　**Seats:** 30, Pr/dining room 12　**Children:** Min 9 yrs, Menu, Portions　**Directions:** From A9 take B8079 N of Killiecrankie, hotel is 3m on right, just past village signpost　**Parking:** 20　(See page 634.)

KINCLAVEN　　　　　MAP 21 NO13
◉◉ Ballathie House Hotel
Modern Scottish V ◉ NOTABLE WINE LIST
Romantic Tayside hotel dining

☎ 01250 883268　PH1 4QN
e-mail: email@ballathiehousehotel.com
web: www.ballathiehousehotel.com

This Victorian shooting lodge remained a private house until 1970. Service is friendly and attentive, and the traditionally decorated dining room has excellent views across the estate over the tree-lined lawns and down to the River Tay. Ingredients for the creative menus are either home grown on the estate or Scottish. To start, try excellent sautéed langoustines with mussels and tagliatelle in lemongrass and coriander sauce. Main courses include roast rack of Uist lamb on a cassoulet of pulses with potato dauphinoise and rosemary jus, followed by apple sultana parfait with warm apple crumble and petit toffee apple. An excellent wine list completes the experience.

CONTINUED

SCOTLAND

Scotland

Wine Award Winner

Killiecrankie House Hotel

Page 633

KINCLAVEN CONTINUED

Chef: Jonny Greer **Owners:** Ballathie House Hotel Ltd **Times:** 12.30-2/7-9 **Prices:** Fixed L £19.50, Fixed D £42, Service optional **Wine:** 236 bottles over £20, 14 bottles under £20, 6 by the glass **Notes:** Vegetarian menu, Dress Restrictions, Jacket & tie preferred, no jeans/T-shirts, Civ Wed 75 **Seats:** 70, Pr/dining room 32 **Children:** Min 12 yrs, Portions **Rooms:** 41 (41 en suite) ★★★★ CHH **Directions:** From A9 take Luncarty/Stanley exit, follow the B9099 through Stanley, follow signs for Ballathie after 0.5m **Parking:** 100

KINLOCH RANNOCH   MAP 23 NN65

❀ Dunalastair Hotel

Modern British

Accomplished cuisine in traditional Highland hotel with a Scottish baronial feel

☎ 01882 632323   PH16 5PW
e-mail: info@dunalastair.co.uk
web: www.dunalastair.co.uk

This traditional Highland hotel was built as a retreat for soldiers. The magnificent wood-panelled Schiehallion restaurant, complete with roaring log fire and lighting made from red deer antlers, has a real baronial feel. The kitchen adds a modern touch to traditional dishes making use of excellent Scottish ingredients. The cooking and presentation are beautiful in their simplicity with a great balance of flavours and no superfluous elements. Try roast celeriac soup followed by Scottish lamb rump set on red cabbage with port jus or wild mushroom and parmesan risotto.

Chef: Kevin Easingwood **Owners:** R Gilmour **Times:** 12-2.30/6.30-9 **Prices:** Fixed L £12-£15, Fixed D £29.50-£36, Starter £4.95-£7.95, Main £12.95-£19.95, Dessert £3.95-£5 **Wine:** 55 bottles over £20, 25 bottles under £20, 6 by the glass **Notes:** Civ Wed 70 **Seats:** 70, Pr/dining room 20 **Children:** Portions **Rooms:** 28 (28 en suite) ★★★ HL **Directions:** From Pitlochry N, take B8019 to Tummel Bridge then B846 to Kinloch Rannoch **Parking:** 50

KINROSS   MAP 21 NO10

❀ The Green Hotel

Modern International NEW

Contemporary restaurant with classic-based, modern cuisine

☎ 01577 863467   2 The Muirs KY13 8AS
e-mail: reservations@green-hotel.com
web: www.green-hotel.com

Aptly named, this hotel comes with its own golf course and sits at the heart of the small town in extensive grounds and gardens. Basil's is its bright and spacious contemporary restaurant, with colourful artwork and floral displays adding interest. There's a small cocktail bar for aperitifs with views over a landscaped courtyard, too. Service is friendly, while the accomplished kitchen's modern approach - underpinned by a French classical theme - delivers on a seasonal menu backed by daily specials. Take tournedos of Angus fillet served with horseradish rösti and a gratin of wild mushrooms, or perhaps a warm chocolate fondant finish, served with white chocolate and thyme ice cream.

Rooms: 46 (46 en suite) ★★★★ HL
see advert above

SCOTLAND

SCOTLAND

⚘⚘ Acanthus Restaurant

Modern Scottish

Enjoyable seasonal cooking in Victorian dining room

☎ 01738 622451 Parklands Hotel, St Leonards Bank PH2 8EB
e-mail: info@acanthusrestaurant.com
web: www.acanthusrestaurant.com

This one-time home of the Lord Provost stands conveniently close to the centre of town yet has great views across the South Inch. The stylish Victorian Acanthus Restaurant is the fine dining option of the Parklands Hotel. Formal service keeps diners supplied with imaginative and well-prepared dishes based on quality local and seasonal ingredients. There's good use of game such as the medallions of Strathspey venison and Angus beef with port and juniper jus, or the potted confit of duck starter, served with chilli oranges. Pot-roasted chicken is served with mushroom ravioli, lemon thyme polenta and tarragon jus. Good rich flavours are finished off with stylish desserts like apple tarte Tatin.

Chef: Graeme Pallister **Owners:** Scott and Penny Edwards **Times:** 7-9, Closed 26th Dec, 1st & 2nd Jan, Sun-Tue, Closed L Wed-Sat **Prices:** Fixed D £27.95-£33.50, Service optional, Group min 8 service 8% **Wine:** 30 bottles over £20, 53 bottles under £20, 6 by the glass **Notes:** Dress Restrictions, Smart casual, no shorts or jeans, Civ Wed 30 **Seats:** 36, Pr/dining room 22 **Children:** Menu, Portions **Rooms:** 14 (14 en suite) ★★★ HL **Directions:** Adjacent to Perth station, overlooking South Inch Park **Parking:** 25

⚘⚘ Best Western Huntingtower Hotel

Traditional British

Impressive cuisine in wonderful setting

☎ 01738 583771 Crieff Rd PH1 3JT
e-mail: reservations@huntingtowerhotel.co.uk
web: www.huntingtowerhotel.co.uk

Originally built as a mill owner's house in 1892, this is now a country-house hotel, set in six acres of magnificent landscaped gardens. Traditional décor and period features are in keeping with the style of the hotel, where the conservatory is used for lunch and the traditional oak-panelled dining room for dinner. Scottish cuisine with a French twist sees dishes like Arbroath smokie and cheese soufflé or ham hock, spinach and mushroom terrine to start. Main courses might feature loin of pork with onion marmalade, black pudding fritters, mustard mash, caramelised apple and green peppercorn sauce or fillet of beef with seared foie gras. Try classic vanilla pannacotta for dessert.

Chef: Bill McNicoll **Times:** 12-2/6-9.30 **Prices:** Fixed L £12.95, Fixed D £27.50, Starter £4.50-£7.95, Main £9.95-£16.95, Dessert £4.95-£5.95, Service optional **Wine:** 23 bottles over £20, 26 bottles under £20, 4 by the glass **Notes:** Vegetarian available, Civ Wed 135 **Seats:** 34, Pr/dining room 24 **Children:** Menu, Portions **Rooms:** 34 (34 en suite) ★★★ HL **Directions:** 10 minutes from Perth on A85 towards Crieff **Parking:** 200

⚘⚘ Deans@Let's Eat

Scottish

Modern bistro serving simple, quality food

☎ 01738 643377 77/79 Kinnoull St PH1 5EZ
e-mail: deans@letseatperth.co.uk
web: www.deans@letseatperth.co.uk

Housed in a former 19th-century theatre, this lively bistro is run by a husband-and-wife team and has recently been fully refurbished throughout. A cosy and informal venue, large sofas beckon guests for pre- or post-dinner drinks, and the warm, rich décor creates a cosy atmosphere. Vibrant, contemporary Scottish cooking makes the most of the best seasonal ingredients, sourced locally where possible, and everything from bread to chocolates is home made. Start with seared scallops on aubergine caviar and a lemongrass and tomato reduction, followed perhaps by fillet of sea bass and langoustine, with fennel and vine tomatoes, fried potatoes and apple balsamic dressing. A great favourite with the locals, so be sure to book ahead.

Chef: Willie Deans, Simon Lannan **Owners:** Mr & Mrs W Deans **Times:** 12-2/6.30-9.45, Closed 1 wk Jan, 1 wk summer, Sun-Mon **Prices:** Fixed L £11.95, Starter £3.95-£7.95, Main £10.95-£18.95, Dessert £5-£6.25, Service optional **Wine:** 33 bottles over £20, 22 bottles under £20, 7 by the glass **Notes:** Vegetarian available, Dress Restrictions, Smart casual **Seats:** 65 **Children:** Portions **Directions:** On corner of Kinnoull Street & Atholl Street, close to North Inch **Parking:** Multi-storey car park (300 yds)

⚘⚘ Murrayshall Country House Hotel

Traditional

Scottish dining in country-house golfing destination

☎ 01738 551171 New Scone PH2 7PH
e-mail: info@murrayshall.co.uk
web: www.murrayshall.co.uk

Set on a hillside in 350 acres of grounds, this impressive country house boasts lovely views of the Grampian Hills. Work up an appetite on one of the hotel's two golf courses and then pay a visit to the Old Masters restaurant, an elegant dining room with well-spaced tables and a traditional décor. Its friendly and attentive staff foster a relaxed ambience and deliver an accomplished menu of Scottish cuisine distinguished by plenty of high-quality ingredients. Expect conventional combinations from a kitchen that keeps things simple: honey and lime-basted breast of duck with rösti potato perhaps, or herb-crusted halibut with buttered asparagus and saffron cream.

Chef: Clive Lamb **Owners:** Old Scone Ltd **Times:** 12-2.30/7-9.45, Closed 26 Dec, Closed L Sat **Prices:** Fixed L £11.50, Fixed D £26-£28.25, Service optional **Wine:** 8 by the glass **Notes:** Vegetarian available, Civ Wed 100, Air con **Seats:** 55, Pr/dining room 40 **Children:** Menu, Portions **Rooms:** 41 (41 en suite) ★★★ HL **Directions:** From Perth A94 (Coupar Angus) turn right signed Murrayshall before New Scone **Parking:** 90

◎◎ 63 Tay Street

Modern Scottish

Chic city dining in Tayside

☎ 01738 441451   63 Tay St PH2 8NN
e-mail: info@63taystreet.com
web: www.63taystreet.co.uk

This stylish, modern restaurant is housed in a fine old building in the centre of Perth, overlooking the River Tay. Accessed via a flight of steps next door to Perth's council offices, it's a popular choice for both dinner and the great-value lunch, with friendly and attentive waiting staff. Modern Scottish cooking provides a showcase for local produce, as in a starter of hand-dived Shetland scallops, sesame pork and marinated skate wing, or a traditional-sounding main course of braised lamb neck, served with caramelised neeps and burnt butter spinach. At the time of going to press we understand that a change of ownership and chef had taken place.

Chef: Graeme Pallister **Owners:** Scott & Penny Edwards, Graeme Pallister **Times:** 12-2/6.30-9, Closed Xmas, New Year, 1st wk Jul, Sun, Mon **Prices:** Fixed L £14.95, Fixed D £27.95, Service optional, Group min 6 service 10% **Wine:** 59 bottles over £20, 25 bottles under £20, 8 by the glass **Seats:** 35 **Children:** Portions **Directions:** In town centre, on river

---

PITLOCHRY   MAP 23 NN95

◎ Donavourd House

International

Wonderful views and sound cooking in lovely country house

☎ 01796 472100   PH16 5JS
e-mail: reservations@donavourdhousehotel.co.uk
web: www.donavourdhousehotel.co.uk

Once home to the local laird, this attractive country house sits in its own gardens in a quiet, elevated location overlooking Strathtummel. Decorated in a period style, the dining room has crisp linen and fine glassware, which complements the traditional, classic cooking here. A short menu boasts simple dishes with an emphasis on local produce. A starter of lightly dressed salad greens topped with crumbled stilton, toasted walnuts and sliced pears may be followed by pan-seared breast of duck served with roasted aubergine, chickpea and rice medley and pomegranate molasses sauce.

Times: 6.30-8.30, Closed Jan, Feb, Closed L all week **Rooms:** 9 (9 en suite) **Directions:** Southbound on main rd from Pitlochry, before entrance to A9 follow signs to hotel. Take Pitlochry exit off A6 northbound, turn right under railway bridge and follow signs

◎ Green Park Hotel

Modern, Traditional British

Fine cuisine in a lochside country-house hotel

☎ 01796 473248   Clunie Bridge Rd PH16 5JY
e-mail: bookings@thegreenpark.co.uk
web: www.thegreenpark.co.uk

This family-run country-house hotel enjoys an enviable location on the shore of Loch Faskally. The traditional dining room - in soothing colours of beige and purple - looks out over gardens towards the loch, providing a relaxing setting for some fine traditional-inspired cuisine. The menu makes the most of local and specialist produce - so seafood and game feature strongly - alongside seasonal herbs and salads from the kitchen garden. Think a salad of hot roast guinea fowl suprême served with coleslaw, plum tomatoes and olive oil dressing, or perhaps a roast rib of beef with horseradish mash and onion and sherry gravy.

Chef: Chris Tamblin **Owners:** Green Park Ltd **Times:** 12-2/6.30-8.30, Closed L all week (ex residents) **Prices:** Fixed D £21, Main £25, Service optional **Wine:** 10 bottles over £20, 65 bottles under £20, 8 by the glass **Notes:** Fixed ALC 4 courses inc cheese, Dress Restrictions, Reasonably smart dress **Seats:** 100 **Children:** Menu, Portions **Rooms:** 51 (51 en suite) ★★★ CHH **Directions:** Off A9 at Pitlochry, follow signs along Atholl road to Inverness **Parking:** 52

◎ Pine Trees Hotel

Modern

Honest food in elegant hotel

☎ 01796 472121   Strathview Ter PH16 5QR
e-mail: info@pinetreeshotel.co.uk
web: www.pinetreeshotel.co.uk

Set within spacious grounds on the edge of the Victorian spa town of Pitlochry, this elegant hotel has a formal dining room overlooking the attractive gardens. The Scottish-influenced food is cooked with expertise and presented with flair, with friendly front-of-house staff clearly taking a pride in their work. The cooking here is confident and simple dishes generate bold flavour. Think beef carpaccio or smoked salmon for starters followed by roast saddle of Perthshire venison with red cabbage, and warm sticky toffee pudding for dessert.

Times: 12/6.30, Closed L Mon-Sat **Rooms:** 20 (20 en suite) ★★★ CHH **Directions:** N through Pitlochry to far end of town, turn R into Larchwood Road. Hotel on L just below golf course

---

ST FILLANS   MAP 20 NN62

◎ Achray House Hotel

Modern, Traditional NEW

Family-run hotel, loch views and traditional cooking

☎ 01764 685231   PH6 2NF
e-mail: info@achray-house.co.uk
web: www.achray-house.co.uk

Achray House is a family-run affair and comes picturesquely set in pretty gardens at the eastern end of Loch Earn. Pleasantly uncommercial, there's a choice of two dining rooms as well as a conservatory-style bar that offers the best of the views. Service is fittingly friendly and relaxed, while the food is an essential part of any

Continued

SCOTLAND

ST FILLANS CONTINUED

visit, with the accomplished kitchen making intelligent use of the abundant local Scottish larder. With daily-changing menus, think slow-cooked Strathearn lamb shank with mushrooms and rosemary, or perhaps roasted monkfish with pancetta, garlic and tomato. Good vegetarian choices available.

Chef: Andrew J Scott **Owners:** Andrew J Scott **Times:** 12-2.30/6-8.30, Closed 3-31 Jan **Prices:** Fixed L £14.95-£16.95, Fixed D £24.95-£29.95, Starter £4.45-£6.50, Main £9.95-£18.95, Dessert £3.95-£5.95, Service optional **Wine:** 11 bottles over £20, 2 bottles under £20, 9 by the glass **Notes:** Vegetarian available **Seats:** 70, Pr/dining room 30 **Children:** Menu, Portions **Rooms:** 10 (10 en suite) ★★★ SHL **Parking:** 20

◉◉ The Four Seasons Hotel

Modern European

Breathtaking scenery and bold cuisine

☎ 01764 685333 Loch Earn PH6 2NF
e-mail: info@thefourseasonshotel.co.uk
web: www.thefourseasonshotel.co.uk

Tucked away beneath steeply forested hills on the edge of Loch Earn, this hotel has a range of comfortable lounges, log fires and stunning views where you really can appreciate the seasons throughout the year. Originally built in the early 1800s for the manager of the limekilns, it was also a schoolmaster's house before becoming a hotel. The lochside Meall Reamhar fine-dining restaurant serves up modern Scottish and European dishes based on great Scottish produce. Bold flavours and imaginative combinations might produce a signature starter of hand-dived Scrabster sea scallops with an orange and tarragon butter sauce. Soup or sorbet precede main courses such as fillets of Ayrshire pork served with garlic and crème fraîche, sweet potato and a Dijon mustard sauce.

Times: 12-2.30/6-9.30, Closed Jan-Feb **Rooms:** 18 (18 en suite) ★★★ HL **Directions:** From Perth take A85 W, through Crieff & Comrie. Hotel at west end of village

SPITTAL OF GLENSHEE   MAP 23 NO17

◉◉ Dalmunzie House Hotel

Traditional, British

Cooking worthy of the laird in a highland mansion

☎ 01250 885224 PH10 7QG
e-mail: reservations@dalmunzie.com
web: www.dalmunzie.com

A former Highland laird's mansion, complete with turrets, set on an estate of 6,500 acres. Within easy reach of the ski slopes at Glenshee, this could be the perfect destination after a hard day on the piste. The house is furnished with antiques, and logs burn in the original fireplaces. The spacious dining room has well-appointed tables and a classic blue and cream colour scheme where you can soak up the fine-dining experience, or have a more relaxed bite in the bar. Top-quality, seasonal ingredients are sourced for dishes with a British approach, underpinned by classic French influences. Take chargrilled venison loin served with baby spinach, cauliflower purée and an elderflower wine jus, or perhaps a sticky toffee pudding with butterscotch sauce and malt whisky ice cream to finish.

Chef: Michelle Metten **Owners:** Scott & Brianna Poole **Times:** 12-2.30/7-9, Closed 1-28 Dec **Prices:** Fixed D £36, Service included **Wine:** 45 bottles over £20, 17 bottles under £20, 4 by the glass **Notes:** Fixed D 4 courses, Dress Restrictions, Smart casual, jacket & tie preferred, Civ Wed 70 **Seats:** 40, Pr/dining room 18 **Children:** Portions **Rooms:** 17 (17 en suite) ★★★ CHH **Directions:** N of Blairgowrie on A93 at the Spittal of Glenshee **Parking:** 40

RENFREWSHIRE

HOWWOOD   MAP 20 NS36

◉ Country Club Restaurant

Modern British

Stylish modern cooking in old-world surroundings

☎ 01505 705225 Bowfield Hotel & Country Club PA9 1DZ
e-mail: enquiries@bowfield.co.uk
web: www.bowfieldcountryclub.co.uk

Occupying a converted 17th-century bleaching mill, this hotel oozes character, with beamed ceilings, brick and white-painted walls and open fires. The atmosphere is friendly and the staff are keen to please. Simple, clear presentation belies the complexity of the cooking, but all the skill and effort is evident in the flavours. Seasonal produce is respectfully prepared and there are lots of Scottish elements to the dishes, with an emphasis on local fish, game and shellfish. West Coast scallops are served as a starter with Orkney black pudding and pancetta salad, followed by loin of Perthshire lamb with skirlie, celeriac and butternut squash gratin, spinach and red wine jus.

Chef: Ronnie McAdam **Owners:** Bowfield Hotel & Country Club Ltd **Times:** 12-2.30/6.30-9 **Prices:** Fixed L £9.50, Fixed D £25, Service optional **Wine:** 39 bottles over £20, 24 bottles under £20, 11 by the glass **Notes:** Dress Restrictions, Smart casual, Civ Wed 120 **Seats:** 40, Pr/dining room 20 **Children:** Menu, Portions **Rooms:** 23 (23 en suite) ★★★ HL **Directions:** From M8. Take A737 (Irvine Rd), exit at Howwood, take 2nd right up country lane, turn right at top of hill **Parking:** 100

RENFREWSHIRE, EAST

UPLAWMOOR   MAP 10 NS45

◉◉ Uplawmoor Hotel

Modern Scottish

Friendly inn serving traditional and modern Scottish cuisine

☎ 01505 850565 Neilston Rd G78 4AF
e-mail: info@uplawmoor.co.uk
web: www.uplawmoor.co.uk

An 18th-century coaching inn and one-time haunt of smugglers, the hotel was extended in 1958 by architect James Gray, who added the Charles Rennie Mackintosh-inspired exterior. The beamed interior is cosy and atmospheric with subtle lighting and rich furnishings. Menus (a regular carte and monthly-changing fixed-price) offer both traditional and modern Scottish fare with an emphasis on red meat and game. Excellent meat is supplied by five local farms and herbs are home grown. Recommendations include seared king scallops with crispy bacon, Stornoway black pudding and balsamic dressing, or flamed fillet steak with haggis croûton, and onion and garlic jus. Finish with a delicious, traditional dessert like sticky toffee pudding, or hot chocolate fudge cake and Italian ice cream. A menu of traditional bar food is also available.

Chef: Paul Brady **Owners:** Stuart & Emma Peacock **Times:** 12-3/6-9.30, Closed 26 Dec, 1 Jan, Closed L Mon-Sat **Prices:** Fixed L £13, Fixed D £16-£23, Starter £4-£8.50, Main £12.50-£21, Dessert £5.25, Service optional **Wine:** 5 bottles over £20, 18 bottles under £20, 9 by the glass **Notes:** Vegetarian available, Dress Restrictions, Smart casual **Seats:** 30 **Children:** Min 12 yrs, Menu, Portions **Rooms:** 14 (14 en suite) ★★ HL **Directions:** From Glasgow follow M8 & M77 to junct 2, follow signs for Barrhead & Irvine A736. 5m past Barrhead take village road left signposted to Uplawmoor **Parking:** 38

SCOTTISH BORDERS

EDDLESTON   MAP 21 NT24

⊚⊚⊚ **The Horseshoe Inn**

see below

KELSO   MAP 21 NT73

⊚⊚ **The Roxburghe Hotel & Golf Course**

Modern, Traditional

Traditional sporting destination with fine Scottish dining and impressive wine list

☎ 01573 450331 TD5 8JZ

e-mail: hotel@roxburghe.net

web: www.roxburghe.net

Owned by the Duke of Roxburghe, this imposing Jacobean mansion has 500 acres of mature wood and parkland incorporating a championship golf course. The interior is luxuriously furnished, replete with log fires, high ceilings and rich fabrics and furnishings. The dining room has quality table appointments and settings with discreet and efficient service. The skilful kitchen uses many ingredients from the estate and provides diners with traditional Scottish starters of warm crayfish tails with shallot butter sauce and puff-pastry case. Main courses might include seared West Coast scallops, bubble-and-squeak cake, spiced tomatoes and roasted tiger prawns. For dessert, there's rhubarb mousse with rhubarb and yogurt sorbet and poached apricots.

Chef: Keith Short **Owners:** Duke of Roxburghe **Times:** 12.30-2/7.30-9.45 **Prices:** Fixed L £16-£20, Fixed D £37-£40, Service optional **Wine:** 120 bottles over £20, 12 bottles under £20, 6 by the glass **Notes:** Vegetarian available, Dress Restrictions, No jeans or trainers, Civ Wed 50 **Seats:** 35, Pr/dining room 40 **Children:** Menu, Portions **Rooms:** 22 (22 en suite) ★★★ HL **Directions:** From A68, 1m N of Jedburgh, take A698 for 5m to Heiton **Parking:** 150

The Horseshoe Inn

EDDLESTON   MAP 21 NT24

French NEW

AA Restaurant of the Year for Scotland

☎ 01721 730225 EH45 8QP

e-mail: reservations@horseshoeinn.co.uk

web: www.horseshoeinn.co.uk

A converted village blacksmiths houses the operation's luxurious fine-dining Bardoulet's restaurant, a bistro/bar and lounge areas. The décor's striking, a combination of traditional with a modern twist; vibrant colours juxtapose soft-toned fabrics, with fabulous table appointments, gilt-edged mirrors and character stone floors all adding to the ambience. Staff are refreshingly helpful, knowledgeable, relaxed but attentive, while the highly accomplished kitchen under Patrick Bardoulet draws on his native homeland to deliver a modern French approach with a nod to traditional Scottish fare.

Quality, local fresh seasonal ingredients are combined with flair and vision, while technical skills and execution are top drawer. Think a loin of roe deer served with onion roasted in liquorice, celeriac purée, potato croquette and game jus, or meunière of Dover sole with parsnip purée, razor clams, samphire and a noisette butter sauce, while to finish, perhaps choose between an assiette of honey desserts (soufflé, millefeuille and ice cream) and an iced praline parfait served

with lemon shortbread, crushed meringue and champagne custard.

Chef: Patrick Bardoulet **Owners:** Border Steelwork Structures Ltd **Times:** 12-2.30/7-9, Closed 25 Dec, 3-11 Jan, 18-31 Oct, Mon, Closed D Sun **Prices:** Fixed L £20, Starter £5.50-£9.50, Main £13.50-£23.50, Dessert £6.50-£8.50, Service optional **Wine:** 55 bottles over £20, 32 bottles under £20 **Notes:** Fixed L 3 courses, Sun L 2 courses £14.95, 3 courses £18.50, Dress Restrictions, Smart casual, Jackets for men preferred **Seats:** 40 **Rooms:** 8 (8 en suite) ★★★★ RR **Directions:** On A703, 5m N of Peebles **Parking:** 20

MELROSE   MAP 21 NT53

◉◉ Burt's Hotel

Modern British

Contemporary cooking in a sophisticated setting

☎ 01896 822285 The Square TD6 9PL

e-mail: burtshotel@aol.com

web: www.burtshotel.co.uk

Set in Melrose's picturesque 18th-century market square, with a distinctive white-painted façade, Burt's has been in the same family for 35 years and its hospitality is a byword locally. Originally home to a local dignitary, today it still retains much of its period charm, and the elegant restaurant has a smart, clubby feel, with dark green striped wallpaper, sporting prints, and high-backed chairs. Here the modern British menu takes in the likes of salmon and crayfish ravioli, with étuvée of leek and céviche of scallop, or perhaps a tranche of halibut, saffron mash, langoustine tortellini and bouillabaisse sauce. There's a great choice of grills boasting matured Scottish lamb and beef, and an excellent cheeseboard including a number of local and speciality products. Lunch and supper are also served in the relaxing Bistro Bar.

Chef: David McCallum **Owners:** The Henderson Family **Times:** 12-2/7-9, Closed 26 Dec, 3-5 Jan **Prices:** Fixed L £16-£22, Fixed D £32.75, Starter £6.50-£12, Main £16.50-£28, Dessert £7.50-£9.50, Service optional **Wine:** 40 bottles over £20, 20 bottles under £20, 6 by the glass **Notes:** Sun L available, Dress Restrictions, Jacket & tie preferred **Seats:** 50, Pr/dining room 25 **Children:** Min 10 yrs, Portions **Rooms:** 20 (20 en suite) ★★★ HL **Directions:** Town centre in Market Sq **Parking:** 40

PEEBLES   MAP 21 NT24

◉◉ Castle Venlaw Hotel

Traditional British

Classical dining in a romantic environment

☎ 01721 720384 Edinburgh Rd EH45 8QG

e-mail: stay@venlaw.co.uk

web: www.venlaw.co.uk

Built in 1742 on the site of Old Smithfield Castle, this family-owned castle-style hotel is located in the scenic Borders, overlooking the historic town of Peebles. The elegant restaurant boasts tall windows, an ornamental fireplace and corniced ceiling, and the hotel comes complete with a cosy library bar where you can enjoy a snack or dishes from the restaurant menu at lunchtime. The kitchen's technical skills are evident in well-balanced, full-flavoured dishes offered on traditional British and Scottish fixed-price menus, with the occasional nod to the Mediterranean. House specialities include starters like hot

oak-smoked Scottish salmon rosette served with horseradish beurre blanc, with chargrilled fillet of Scottish beef accompanied by thyme fondant potatoes, wild mushrooms and port-glazed onions to follow. Service is friendly and obliging, while the wine list is thoughtfully prepared and has good tasting notes.

Chef: David Harrison **Owners:** Mr & Mrs J Sloggie **Times:** 12-2.30/7-9 **Prices:** Fixed D £30-£40, Service optional **Wine:** 6 by the glass **Notes:** Vegetarian available, Dress Restrictions, Smart casual, Civ Wed 35 **Seats:** 35, Pr/dining room 30 **Children:** Min 5 yrs, Menu, Portions **Rooms:** 12 (12 en suite) ★★★ CHH **Directions:** From Peebles at east end of High Street, turn left at rdbt signed A703 to Edinburgh. After 0.75m hotel is signed on right **Parking:** 25

◉◉ Cringletie House

Modern French

Enjoyable Scottish dining in baronial surroundings

☎ 01721 725750 Edinburgh Rd EH45 8PL

e-mail: enquiries@cringletie.com

web: www.cringletie.com

Set in 28 acres of gardens and woodlands, this traditional Scottish turreted baronial mansion retains all the warmth of a family home. The stately dining room enjoys views over the countryside, and oak floors, staircases and painted ornamental ceilings, combined with contemporary styling in fabrics and furniture, create an atmosphere of timeless elegance. There's a strong emphasis on local Scottish produce, with much of the fruit and vegetables coming from the kitchen garden. Imaginative dishes might include a starter like roasted scallops in the shell, with brunoise of celeriac and black truffle, followed by fillet of turbot with oyster tartare, spaghetti of vegetable and oyster and champagne sauce. Clementine and rose soup with blood orange jelly and Glenkinchie sorbet might prove an interesting dessert.

Chef: Jimmy Desrivieres **Owners:** Jacob & Johanna van Houdt **Times:** 12-2/7-9 **Prices:** Fixed L £17.50, Fixed D £42.50, Starter £15, Main £23, Dessert £7.50, Service optional **Wine:** 68 bottles over £20, 10 bottles under £20, 5 by the glass **Notes:** Dégustation menu fr £60, Sun L fr £25, Dress Restrictions, Smart/casual, no jeans, no trainers, Civ Wed 45 **Seats:** 60, Pr/dining room 12 **Children:** Portions **Rooms:** 13 (13 en suite)★★★★ CHH **Directions:** 2.5m N of Peebles on A703 **Parking:** 30

SCOTLAND

Macdonald Cardrona Hotel Golf & Country Club

Scottish NEW

Accomplished cooking with stunning views

☎ 0870 1942114 Cardrona Mains EH45 6LZ
e-mail: general.cardrona@macdonald-hotels.co.uk
web: www.macdonald-hotels.co.uk

Diners can enjoy glorious views from the second-floor Renwicks restaurant of this smart hotel. You can keep an eye on the fairways and greens, or cast your eyes further to the surrounding hills. The set-price seasonal menu offers excellent Scottish produce like fresh seafood and well-hung game. The cooking style is crisp and precise so simple concepts are delivered with a high degree of accuracy. Try a main course like chargrilled fillet of beef with flat cap mushroom, pomme frite, tomato confit and béarnaise sauce. Service is delightful from a strong, professional team.

Times: Please telephone for details **Rooms:** 99 (99 en suite) ★★★★ HL

ST BOSWELLS   MAP 21 NT53

The Tweed Restaurant

Traditional Scottish

Scottish cuisine in the breathtaking Borders countryside

☎ 01835 822261 Dryburgh Abbey Hotel TD6 0RQ
e-mail: enquiries@dryburgh.co.uk
web: www.dryburgh.co.uk

This red-stone baronial mansion sits on the banks of the Tweed beside Dryburgh Abbey, the last resting place of Sir Walter Scott. It's an imposing property with a well-earned reputation for hospitality and fine food. Enjoy a pre-dinner drink in the lounge, and then move through to the spacious Tweed Restaurant, with its high ceilings, ornate chandeliers and first-floor river views. Traditional Scottish dishes using the best local produce is the cooking style; take a roast loin of pork from the Borders region, served with a compôte of apples, grain mustard mash and sage-flavoured juices.

Chef: Scott Hume **Owners:** The Grose Family **Times:** 12-2/7-9.15, Closed L Mon-Sat **Prices:** Fixed L £15.95, Fixed D £32.50, Starter £5.50-£6.50, Main £16-£19, Dessert £5-£6.50, Service included **Wine:** 52 bottles over £20, 28 bottles under £20, 11 by the glass **Notes:** Fixed D 4 courses, Vegetarian available, Dress Restrictions, No jeans or sportswear, Civ Wed 110 **Seats:** 78, Pr/dining room 40 **Children:** Menu, Portions **Rooms:** 38 (38 en suite) ★★★ HL **Directions:** 4m from the A68 **Parking:** 50

SWINTON   MAP 21 NT84

The Wheatsheaf at Swinton

Modern British

Tempting cooking at a classic village inn

☎ 01890 860257 Main St TD11 3JJ
e-mail: reception@wheatsheaf-swinton.co.uk
web: www.wheatsheaf-swinton.co.uk

Most people know this traditional country inn as a destination food venue, but The Wheatsheaf is still very much at the heart of village life. A pine-clad conservatory dining room and traditional bar lounge

are among the cosy eating areas, warmed by log fires in winter. The menu is broad and appeals to all appetites. Dishes reflect the seasons and are rotated and replaced regularly, and an additional selection is provided by the daily specials board. Fresh local ingredients are sourced within the region and the keen eye for provenance is evident in dishes like roast rack of border lamb with a basil and mustard crust on rosemary-scented juices, Fyemouth langoustines, or Teviotdale smoked salmon with a gruyère and herb crust served on savoury spinach and roast vine tomatoes.

Chef: John Kier **Owners:** Mr & Mrs Chris Winson **Times:** 12-2/6-9, Closed 25-27 Dec, Closed D Sun (Dec, Jan) **Prices:** Starter £4.50-£6.50, Main £11.50-£21, Dessert £5.50-£6.50, Service optional, Group min 12 service 10% **Wine:** 82 bottles over £20, 49 bottles under £20, 10 by the glass **Notes:** Vegetarian available, Civ Wed 50 **Seats:** 45, Pr/dining room 29 **Children:** Menu, Portions **Rooms:** 10 (10 en suite) ★★★★ RR **Directions:** From Edinburgh turn off A697 onto B6461. From East Lothian turn off A1 onto B6461 **Parking:** 6

STIRLING

CALLANDER   MAP 20 NN60

Roman Camp Country House Hotel

see page 642

STRATHYRE   MAP 20 NN51

Creagan House

French, Scottish V ⬛ NOTABLE WINE LIST

Impressive food from a local institution

☎ 01877 384638 FK18 8ND
e-mail: eatandstay@creaganhouse.co.uk
web: www.creaganhouse.co.uk

Once a working farm, this 17th-century house has been sympathetically restored, with a large, baronial-style dining hall - complete with grand fireplace and polished refectory tables - that manages to balance grandiosity with a romantic intimacy. Service is very friendly, with the owners making every diner feel special. The food is classical French with strong Scottish overtones. Fine produce is important to the kitchen - all their meat is sourced from farms within Perthshire and herbs are grown in the gardens. Expect a roast loin of local Blackface lamb with shoulder, kidney and caper cake served in a Madeira and nutmeg gravy, or perhaps baked halibut with Jerusalem artichoke purée and a dry vermouth and prawn sauce. The great selection of whiskies and excellent wine list should not be overlooked.

Chef: Gordon Gunn **Owners:** Gordon & Cherry Gunn **Times:** 7.30-8.30, Closed 2-21 Nov, Xmas, 20 Jan-7 Mar, Wed, Closed L (ex parties), D Thu **Prices:** Fixed D £28-£31, Service optional **Wine:** 40 bottles over £20, 35 bottles under £20, 8 by the glass **Notes:** Vegetarian menu, Dress Restrictions, Smart casual, Civ Wed 35 **Seats:** 15, Pr/dining room 6 **Children:** Min 10 yrs, Portions **Rooms:** 5 (5 en suite) ★★★★★ RR **Directions:** 0.25m N of village, off A84 **Parking:** 25

SCOTLAND

Roman Camp Country House Hotel

CALLANDER MAP 20 NN60

Modern French V

Innovative cooking in splendid riverside setting

☎ 01877 330003   FK17 8BG
e-mail: mail@romancamphotel.co.uk
web: www.romancamphotel.co.uk

Set in 20 acres of tranquil woodland gardens and grounds leading down to the River Teith, this charming, long-established hotel has a rich history. Built as a hunting lodge in 1625 for the Dukes of Perth, the Roman Camp Country House Hotel was developed in 1939. Real fires warm the atmospheric public rooms in expected country-house fashion, while decorative tapestries grace the walls of the oval dining room. Softly decorated in a modern, classical style, well-spaced tables come lit by candlelight and decorated with fresh flowers, while the service is suitably professional yet friendly. The talented kitchen's modern approach is underpinned by a classical theme, the repertoire dominated by high-quality Scottish produce from the abundant local larder that's treated with due reverence. Expect creative, exciting and innovative dishes with clear flavours, like John Dory and scallops with a risotto of coriander and spring onions, and to follow perhaps Black Gold beef fillet with tongue and cheek, horseradish pomme purée and bone marrow sauce. Finish off with a dessert of warm chocolate crumpet with Agen prunes and Jack Daniel's milk. An extensive wine list and peripherals like canapés, pre-desserts and petits fours hold form through to the end.

Chef: Ian McNaught
Owners: Eric Brown
Times: 12.30-1.45/7-8.30
Prices: Fixed L £25-£28, Fixed D £44-£49, Starter £9.95-£17, Main £26-£30, Dessert £8.50-£11.50, Service optional
Wine: 180 bottles over £20, 20 bottles under £20, 16 by the glass
Notes: Fixed L 3 courses, Fixed D 4 courses, Vegetarian menu, Civ Wed 100
Seats: 120, Pr/dining room 36
Children: Portions
Rooms: 14 (14 en suite) ★★★ HL
Directions: N on A84 through Callander Main St turn right at East End into drive
Parking: 80

SCOTTISH ISLANDS ARRAN, ISLE OF

BRODICK   MAP 20 NS03

◎◎ Auchrannie Country House Hotel

Modern, Traditional

Fine dining on Arran Isle

☎ 01770 302234   KA27 8BZ
e-mail: info@auchrannie.co.uk
web: www.auchrannie.co.uk

The Isle of Arran is the romantic setting for this imposing country-house hotel, part of a luxury resort complex. The Garden restaurant is tastefully housed in the conservatory, where beautiful table settings and subtle lighting create an appealing atmosphere for the fine Scottish dining. Traditional recipes - using the best of local produce - are given a modern makeover on the short monthly-changing menu, with a couple of daily specials at each course thrown in for added interest. Take a starter of spiced warm potato and Arran cheese terrine, followed by breast of Gressingham duck with ginger, blackcurrants and parsnip and mustard purée, or perhaps grilled fillet of halibut served with fennel and white onion confit and black olive tapenade.

Chef: Gregg Russell   **Owners:** Mr I Johnston   **Times:** 6.30-9.30, Closed L all week   **Prices:** Fixed D £27.95, Service optional   **Wine:** 25 bottles over £20, 20 bottles under £20, 6 by the glass   **Notes:** Smart casual, Civ Wed 100   **Seats:** 52, Pr/dining room 22   **Children:** Menu, Portions   **Rooms:** 28 (28 en suite) ★★★★ HL   **Directions:** From Brodick Pier turn right onto main road. Continue for 0.5m, turn left at signs for Auchrannie
Parking: 25

◎◎ Kilmichael Country House Hotel

Modern British

Exciting local dining in country-house surroundings

☎ 01770 302219   Glen Cloy KA27 8BY
e-mail: enquiries@kilmichael.com
web: www.kilmichael.com

The oldest house on the island, the hotel has period features throughout and is furnished with a mixture of antiques and artefacts collected during the owners' extensive travels. Drinks are served in two elegant drawing rooms, both with open fires and one with a grand piano. There are also 4 acres of fascinating gardens. The restaurant is elegant and semi-formal but with an emphasis on guests' comfort and relaxation. Everything is made in-house using fresh produce from the hotel's own gardens or from the island. Recommended dishes are rack of lamb with rosemary and redcurrants, or turban of sea bass and tiger prawns with lemongrass and ginger butter.

Chef: Antony Butterworth   **Owners:** G Botterill & A Butterworth   **Times:** 7-8.30, Closed Nov-Mar, Tue   **Prices:** Fixed D £38.50, Service optional   **Wine:** 32 bottles over £20, 23 bottles under £20, 3 by the glass   **Notes:** Fixed D 4 courses, Dress Restrictions, Smart casual, no T-shirts or bare feet   **Seats:** 18   **Children:** Min 12 yrs   **Rooms:** 7 (7 en suite)★★★ HL   **Directions:** Turn right on leaving ferry terminal, through Brodick & left at golf club. Follow brown sign. Continue past church & onto private drive
Parking: 12

HARRIS, ISLE OF

SCARISTA   MAP 22 NG09

◎◎ Scarista House

Modern Scottish V

Country house with great views and island produce

☎ 01859 550238   HS3 3HX
e-mail: timandpatricia@scaristahouse.com
web: www.scaristahouse.com

A former manse, Scarista House is now a haven for food lovers who seek to explore the magnificent island of Harris. The house enjoys breathtaking views of the Atlantic and is just a short stroll from miles of sandy beaches. The dining room is elegantly presented with silver cutlery and candlesticks, oak dining tables and original art on the walls. Drinks are served in two sitting rooms, both with open fires. Immediately available island seafood, lamb, beef and game are cooked with natural skill to produce dishes of Cullen skink with smoked halibut, followed by roasted fillet of Aberdeen Angus beef with Burgundy reduction and celeriac mash, and brown bread ice cream with glazed fresh figs and port syrup.

Chef: Tim Martin   **Owners:** Tim & Patricia Martin   **Times:** 7.30-8, Closed 25 Dec, Jan-Feb   **Prices:** Fixed D £39.50, Service optional   **Wine:** 25 bottles over £20, 25 bottles under £20, 2 by the glass   **Notes:** Vegetarian menu, Civ Wed 40   **Seats:** 20, Pr/dining room 14   **Children:** Min 7 yrs, Menu, Portions   **Rooms:** 5 (5 en suite) ★★★★ RR   **Directions:** On A859 15m S of Tarbert   **Parking:** 10

SCOTLAND

ISLAY, ISLE OF

BOWMORE
MAP 20 NR35

◎◎ The Harbour Inn

Scottish, International
Must-visit dining experience on this magnificent island with wonderful views

☎ 01496 810330   The Square PA43 7JR
e-mail: info@harbour-inn.com
web: www.harbour-inn.com

The humble exterior of this whitewashed inn in a pretty fishing village - with views over the harbour to the loch beyond - belies an interior which houses a sizeable modern restaurant decorated with sympathetic sophistication. The menu relies heavily on premium local produce with many of the dishes focusing around one or two key ingredients, and thus wholly dependent on this picturesque island's abundant larder, including world-class seafood and fish and fantastic cheeses. The wide variety on the menu provides an agony of choice; take medallions of monkfish served with a spinach mousseline, fresh samphire and an elderflower dressing, or perhaps prime Islay fillet steak with Lochaber haggis, mushroom duxelle and single malt sauce. (Lunch is a lighter affair.)

Chef: Paul Lumby **Owners:** Carol Scott, Neil Scott **Times:** 12-2.30/6-9.30
Prices: Starter £3.95-£12.50, Main £16.50-£25, Dessert £4.25-£6.50, Service optional **Wine:** 27 bottles over £20, 25 bottles under £20, 8 by the glass
Notes: Vegetarian available, Dress Restrictions, Smart casual **Seats:** 44
Children: Min 10 yrs, Portions **Rooms:** 7 (7 en suite) ★★★★★ RR
Directions: Bowmore is situated approx 8m from both ports of Port Ellen & Port Askaig

MULL, ISLE OF

TOBERMORY
MAP 22 NM55

◎◎ Highland Cottage

Modern Scottish, International
A traditional Mull hotel with enticing local menu

☎ 01688 302030   Breadalbane St PA75 6PD
e-mail: davidandjo@highlandcottage.co.uk
web: www.highlandcottage.co.uk

Small, family-run hotel in the conservation area of Tobermory and close to the working fishermen's pier. This restaurant has a loyal local following and, with its country-style décor and large oak fireplace, is

perfect for special-occasion dining. The resident hosts make every effort on behalf of their guests and there's a welcoming atmosphere. In the winter months they travel and research new dishes and ideas. A commitment to local produce is evident on the Scottish menu with international influences. Start with either Croig crab cakes or Inverlussa smoked mussels with mango mayonnaise. Main courses include roast monkfish with sauté leeks, tomato and crayfish sauce or pan-fried peppered Aberdeen Angus fillet with seasonal vegetables and peppercorn sauce.

Highland Cottage

Chef: Josephine Currie **Owners:** David & Josephine Currie **Times:** 7-9, Closed Nov-Feb, Closed L all week **Prices:** Fixed D £40, Service included
Wine: 33 bottles over £20, 21 bottles under £20, 11 by the glass
Notes: Fixed D 4 courses, Vegetarian available, Dress Restrictions, Smart casual **Seats:** 24 **Children:** Min 10 yrs, Portions **Rooms:** 6 (6 en suite)★★★ SHL **Directions:** Opposite fire station. Main St up Back Brae, turn at top by White House. Follow road to right, left at next junct
Parking: On street

◎ Tobermory Hotel

Modern Scottish
Delightful seafront retreat on the Isle of Mull

☎ 01688 302091   53 Main St PA75 6NT
e-mail: tobhotel@tinyworld.co.uk
web: www.thetobermoryhotel.com

With its pretty pink frontage, this friendly, small hotel sits on the seafront amid the famous picture-postcard, brightly-coloured cottages overlooking Tobermory Bay. The attractive and aptly-named Water's Edge restaurant is laid out with solid-wood furniture, while specially commissioned wall lights on a fish theme prove a talking point. The kitchen follows an intelligent and refreshingly simple modern line, allowing the quality local produce to shine. Tobermory smoked trout with scrambled eggs, Isle of Mull cheddar and spring onion muffin, or a platter of local seafood are typical examples of the fare.

Chef: Helen Swinbanks **Owners:** Mr & Mrs I Stevens **Times:** 6-9, Closed Xmas, Closed L all week **Prices:** Fixed D £21.50-£29.50, Service optional
Wine: 11 bottles over £20, 31 bottles under £20, 4 by the glass **Seats:** 30
Children: Menu, Portions **Rooms:** 16 (15 en suite) ★★ HL
Directions: Telephone for directions **Parking:** On street

The Anchorage

☎ 01688 302313   Main St PA75 6NU

Great local shellfish, plus game and vegetarian options.

ORKNEY ISLANDS

ST MARGARET'S HOPE   MAP 24 ND49

◉◉ Creel Restaurant

Modern, Seafood

Family-run seafront restaurant

☎ 01856 831311 Front Rd KW17 2SL

e-mail: alan@thecreel.freeserve.co.uk

web: www.thecreel.co.uk

The Creel is a charming island restaurant with rooms, specialising in local produce. The dining room is informal in style and looks out over the seafront in the pretty village of St Margaret's Hope. A large collection of local artwork is displayed on the walls, and the atmosphere is warm and friendly. Fresh and simple is the philosophy behind the cooking and the menu is constantly changing according to the supply of seafood, Orkney meat and vegetables. Seafood figures strongly, and favourites are brandade of salt ling with basil mayonnaise and avocado salsa, or pan-fried sea trout fillets with langoustine bisque. For a fitting finish, try a trio of rhubarb.

Chef: Alan Craigie **Owners:** Alan & Joyce Craigie **Times:** 7-9, Closed Jan-Mar, Nov, Mon & Tues (Apr, May, Sep, Oct), Closed L all week **Prices:** Starter £7-£8.50, Main £18.50-£19.50, Dessert £6.50, Service optional **Wine:** 10 bottles over £20, 18 bottles under £20, 4 by the glass **Seats:** 34, Pr/dining room 14 **Children:** Portions **Directions:** 13m S of Kirkwall on A961, on seafront in village **Parking:** 12

SKYE, ISLE OF

COLBOST   MAP 22 NG24

◉◉◉ The Three Chimneys

see page 646

ISLEORNSAY   MAP 22 NG71

◉◉ Hotel Eilean Iarmain

Traditional Scottish

Impressive cuisine on Skye

☎ 01471 833332 IV43 8QR

e-mail: hotel@eileaniarmain.co.uk

web: www.eileaniarmain.co.uk

The hotel is built around a 19th-century inn, set above the beach by the pier, overlooking the bay and sea lochs beyond. Enjoy pre-dinner drinks in front of a roaring fire in the cosy lounge before moving into the elegant panelled restaurant with its view of Ornsay Lighthouse. Scottish fare prepared from high-quality local ingredients is offered from a daily menu, including venison from their own estate. Specialities include hand-dived scallops in a dill and vermouth cream with baby spinach leaves and grated parmesan, or West Highland pink roasted lamb in a garlic and rosemary jus with a vegetable bouquet and carrot and parsnip purée.

Chef: Steffen Bux **Owners:** Sir Ian Andrew Noble **Times:** 12-2.30/6.30-8.45, Closed L all week (ex bookings), D (open until 10 summer) **Prices:** Fixed L £12-£17.50, Fixed D £31-£35, Starter £2.50-£5.95, Main £6-

£15, Dessert £3.95-£4.75, Service optional **Wine:** 60 bottles over £20, 10 bottles under £20, 6 by the glass **Notes:** Fixed L 3 courses, D 4 courses, Dress Restrictions, Smart casual, Civ Wed 80 **Seats:** 40, Pr/dining room 22 **Children:** Min 8 yrs, Menu **Rooms:** 16 (16 en suite) ★★ SHL **Directions:** Overlooking harbour - cross bridge at Kyle of Lochalsh then take A850 and A851, then to harbour front

◉ Iona Restaurant

Modern Scottish

Stylish haven of peace serving Skye's wonderful produce

☎ 01471 820200 & 833231 Toravaig House Hotel, Knock Bay IV44 8RE

e-mail: info@skyehotel.co.uk

web: www.skyehotel.co.uk

A haven of tranquillity, this refurbished, stylish hotel enjoys panoramic views as far as the Knoydart Hills. The elegant Iona Restaurant comes with white-clothed tables, high-backed modern leather chairs and relaxed but efficient service. The emphasis is on the freshest ingredients from the abundant Highland larder. Enjoy Skye's wonderful fish, game or lamb in dishes such as a loin fillet of monkfish wrapped in Argyle ham with a ragout of leeks, broad beans and mussels and a lemon butter sauce. The style is straightforward, with clear flavours that intelligently allow the quality produce to take centre stage.

Chef: Peter Woods **Owners:** Anne Gracie & Ken Gunn **Times:** 12-2/6.30-8.30 **Prices:** Fixed D £32.50, Service optional **Wine:** 22 bottles over £20, 15 bottles under £20, 5 by the glass **Notes:** Fixed D 4 courses, Trilogy tasting menu 3 courses £42.50 **Seats:** 28 **Children:** No children **Rooms:** 9 (9 en suite) ★★★ SHL **Directions:** Travel to Isle of Skye by bridge, continue towards Broadford for 4m, turn left for Armadale & Sleat. Torvaig is on main A851, 11m beyond this junct **Parking:** 12

see advert on page 647

SCOTLAND

The Three Chimneys

COLBOST MAP 22 NG24

Modern Scottish 🌿

Foodie hideaway on Skye serving the freshest seafood

☎ 01470 511258   IV55 8ZT
e-mail: eatandstay@threechimneys.co.uk
web: www.threechimneys.co.uk

Housed within the stone walls of an original crofter's cottage, close to the shores of Loch Dunvegan, The Three Chimneys is worth the long journey. This magical little restaurant is set in glorious wilderness, nestled between the hills and the sea. The whitewashed building's interconnecting rooms pick up on the natural theme to create a feeling of chic simplicity. Take the candlelit restaurant's bare stone walls, low ceilings and polished-wood tables, with their slate tablemats and high-backed chairs. It's intimate and cosy, while service is suitably relaxed and friendly, but professional and well informed.

As you'd expect, the menus change daily to make the best of the abundant local larder, with seafood a highlight. Superb quality produce is simply cooked to let the freshness and quality shine through. The finely-tuned style marries traditional Scottish ideas with a more modern approach, delivering skilful combinations and clean, crisp flavours - as in a Broadford smoked haddock and Borreraig Farm duck egg omelette with radish leaves and smoked herring roe or grilled loin of Glen Hinnisdal lamb with kidneys and slow-roast shoulder, rosemary polenta, neeps and lamb gravy. For dessert, expect the likes of warm rhubarb and almond tart with rhubarb and blood orange sorbet. Add an impressive wine list and fantastic views that money can't buy, and a walk along the loch to see the seals is a must.

Chef: Michael Smith
Owners: Eddie & Shirley Spear
Times: 12.30-2/6.30-9.30, Closed 6-25 Jan, Closed L end Oct-Easter
Prices: Fixed L £22, Fixed D £50-£60, Service optional, Group min 8 service 10%
Wine: 9 by the glass
Notes: Tasting menu 7 courses, Dress Restrictions, Smart casual preferred **Seats:** 32
Children: Min 8 yrs D, Portions
Rooms: 6 (6 en suite)
★★★★★ RR
Directions: 5m W of Dunvegan take B884 signed Glendale. On left beside loch

SCOTLAND

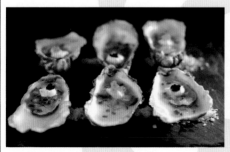

Scottish Island Hotel of the Year 2007

Tourism Excellence 2006

Excellent Service 2006

Toravaig House Hotel, an Award winning small hotel situated on the Isle of Skye
Personally run by *Capt. Ken Gunn and Anne Gracie*,
Toravaig House has gained a splendid reputation for it's food, hospitality and service. All dishes are freshly prepared to order using only the freshest of local produce. Daily Yachting excursions are offered exclusive to residents taking them to inlets on the mainland inaccessible by car.

Toravaig House Hotel, Knock Bay, Sleat, ISLE of SKYE, IV44 8RE
Tel. 0845 055 1117   Fax. 01471 833 231
Email: info@skyehotel.co.uk   Web: www.skyehotel.co.uk <http://www.skyehotel.co.uk>

SCOTLAND

PORTREE

MAP 22 NG44

◎◎ Bosville Hotel

Modern British

Masterful cooking using truly local produce

☎ 01478 612846 Bosville Ter IV51 9DG
e-mail: bosville@macleodhotels.co.uk
web: www.macleodhotels.co.uk/bosville

A popular hotel with fine views over Portree Harbour, the Bosville offers stylish public areas including a smart bar, bistro and the Chandlery restaurant. The restaurant draws on an abundance of fresh local produce, especially seafood and game. Great produce, skilful cooking techniques and inspirational combinations are evident in dishes such as hand-dived scallops from Loch Sligachan on a carrot purée with roast beetroot, garnished with lardons of Stornoway black pudding accompanied by an apple and lemon emulsion, or pan-seared estate venison loin served on a confit of tomatoes, beans and Orbost garlic chives, Glendale wilted greens, a little rabbit bridie and Waternish shiitake mushroom fricassée.

Chef: John Kelly **Owners:** Donald W Macleod **Times:** 6.30-9.30, Closed L all week **Prices:** Fixed D £40, Service optional **Wine:** 12 bottles over £20, 30 bottles under £20 **Notes:** Fixed D 4 courses, Vegetarian available **Seats:** 30 **Children:** Portions **Rooms:** 19 (19 en suite) ★★★ HL **Directions:** 200mtrs from bus station, overlooking Portree Harbour **Parking:** 10

◎◎ Cuillin Hills Hotel

Modern French

Highland hotel with stunning views and fine local produce

☎ 01478 612003   IV51 9QU
e-mail: info@cuillinhills-hotel-skye.co.uk
web: www.cuillinhills-hotel-skye.co.uk

Set in 15 acres of mature grounds, this former Victorian hunting lodge is located in a small fishing village, and enjoys superb views of Portree Bay and the Cuillin Hills beyond from its split-level restaurant. In summer you can enjoy drinks on the lawn, and service is friendly and professional. The imaginative cuisine combines modern European and classical French dishes, and takes full advantage of fresh, local produce, including local seafood, Highland game and home-made breads. Traditional Scottish dishes such as Cullen skink are set

CONTINUED

PORTREE CONTINUED

alongside the likes of tenderloin of Highland venison and wood pigeon, served with grilled white pudding and red onion compôte, finished off with a dessert of dark chocolate parfait with caramelised bananas. There's an extensive wine list.

Chef: Robert Macaskill **Owners:** Wickman Hotels Ltd **Times:** 12-2/6.30-9, Closed 6-26 Jan, Closed L Mon-Sat **Prices:** Fixed D £32.50-£35, Service optional **Wine:** 30 bottles over £20, 12 bottles under £20, 6 by the glass **Notes:** Civ Wed 70 **Seats:** 48, Pr/dining room 20 **Children:** Menu, Portions **Rooms:** 27 (27 en suite) ★★★ HL **Directions:** 0.25 miles N of Portree on A855 **Parking:** 56

◉ Rosedale Hotel

Traditional Scottish

Local produce by the seafront

☎ 01478 613131 Beaumont Crescent IV51 9DB
e-mail: rosedalehotelsky@aol.com
web: www.rosedalehotelskye.co.uk

This charming, family-run harbourside hotel has good views of the water from the attractive first-floor restaurant. It was once a set of fishermen's cottages, and the décor has preserved the intimate atmosphere - a labyrinth of stairs and corridors connects the lounges, bar and dining room. Local produce is handled with flair on an imaginative Scottish menu priced by the number of courses, with seafood a speciality. Expect locally-caught fillet of Skye cod with a chilli and parmesan crust and lemon and chive beurre blanc, or a cannon of Highland lamb with haggis mash and a red wine and mint jus.

Chef: Kirk Moir **Owners:** Mr & Mrs P Rouse **Times:** 7-9, Closed 1 Nov-1 Mar, Closed L all week **Prices:** Fixed D £26-£30, Service optional **Wine:** 10 bottles over £20, 20 bottles under £20, 7 by the glass **Seats:** 30 **Children:** Menu, Portions **Rooms:** 18 (18 en suite) ★★ HL **Directions:** On harbour front **Parking:** On street

STRUAN   MAP 22 NG33

◉◉ Ullinish Country Lodge

Modern French V

Tranquillity, candlelit dinners and imaginative cuisine

☎ 01470 572214 IV56 8FD
e-mail: ullinish@theisleofskye.co.uk
web: www.theisleofskye.co.uk

Set at the end of a track with lochs on three sides and breathtaking views of the Black Cuillins and MacLeods Tables, Ullinish Lodge is quite the haven of peace and boasts Samuel Johnson as a former guest. The interior unsurprisingly has a country-house feel, with a peaceful lounge and efficient, pleasant service. Tables in the wood-panelled dining room feature pristine white linen against a backdrop of tartan carpet and curtains, the intimate atmosphere heightened by candlelight. The chef's modern ideas make use of fresh local produce from the ever-abundant Highland larder; perhaps loin of Orbost Estate venison, risotto of ebly wheat, beetroot sorbet, jellied balsamic and peanut butter foam, while to finish, a soufflé of rum and raisin with crème brûlée ice cream and sea blackthorn jelly.

Chef: Bruce Morrison, Craig Halliday **Owners:** Brian & Pam Howard **Times:** 12-2.30/7-8.30, Closed Jan **Prices:** Fixed L £12.95, Fixed D £39.50, Service optional **Wine:** 24 bottles over £20, 14 bottles under £20 **Notes:** Fixed D 6 courses, Vegetarian menu, Dress Restrictions, Smart casual, no T-shirts **Seats:** 22 **Children:** Min 16 yrs **Rooms:** 6 (6 en suite) ★★★★★ **Directions:** 9m S of Dunvegan on A863 **Parking:** 10

Loch an Eilean

Wales

WALES

ANGLESEY, ISLE OF

BEAUMARIS   MAP 14 SH67

◉ Bishopsgate House Hotel

Traditional Welsh

Fine Welsh cooking in a historic setting

☎ 01248 810302 54 Castle St LL58 8BB
e-mail: hazel@bishopsgatehotel.co.uk
web: www.bishopsgatehotel.co.uk

An 18th-century Georgian townhouse, believed to have been built as a dower house for a wealthy local family, and now transformed into a small hotel. The popular restaurant offers fresh local produce including fish, salt marsh lamb and beef from the Lleyn Peninsula. Traditional Welsh cooking is epitomised in dishes like grilled local goat's cheese with organic tomato chutney, followed by Welsh Black rib-eye steak with onion purée and red wine sauce, or rack of lamb with honey and rosemary jus. Leave some room for a delicious dessert like lemon bavarois.

Chef: H Johnson Ollier & I Sankey **Owners:** Hazel Johnson Ollier
Times: 12.30-2.30/7-9.30, Closed L Mon-Sat **Prices:** Fixed L £12.95, Fixed D £17.50, Starter £4.50-£5.95, Main £9.50-£17.25, Dessert £4.75, Service optional **Wine:** 14 bottles over £20, 20 bottles under £20, 3 by the glass
Notes: Sun L 2 courses £10.95, 3 courses £12.95, Dress Restrictions, Smart dress **Seats:** 40 **Children:** Portions **Rooms:** 9 (9 en suite) ★★ HL
Directions: From Britannia Bridge follow A545 into Beaumaris town centre. Hotel is 2nd on left in the main street **Parking:** 10

◉◉ Ye Olde Bulls Head Inn

Modern British

Historic place with punchy food

☎ 01248 810329 Castle St LL58 8AP
e-mail: info@bullsheadinn.co.uk
web: www.bullsheadinn.co.uk

Ye Olde Bulls Head Inn

Charles Dickens and Samuel Johnson were both regular visitors to this historic coaching inn. Originally built in the late 1400s, there are still exposed beams and antique weaponry linking it to its heritage, although the rest of the décor is smart and contemporary, particularly the Loft restaurant, the more formal of the two dining options. The food is confident, progressive and demonstrates creativity - ravioli of girolle mushrooms, aged parmesan, white truffle and wild mushroom ragout to start, then a main of line-caught sea bass with purple broccoli, crab risotto, champagne and sorrel cream and oyster tempura. To finish, Valrhona dark chocolate tart with roasted pistachio ice cream and chocolate sauce.

Chef: Keith Rothwell, Craig Yardley **Owners:** D Robertson, K Rothwell
Times: 7-9.30, Closed 25-26 Dec, 1 Jan, Sun, Closed L Mon-Sat
Prices: Fixed D £37-£38.50, Service optional **Wine:** 87 bottles over £20, 25 bottles under £20, 6 by the glass **Seats:** 45 **Children:** Min 7 yrs
Rooms: 13 (13 en suite) ★★ HL **Directions:** Town centre, main street
Parking: 10

CARDIFF

CARDIFF   MAP 09 ST17

◉ Ana Bela Bistro

Modern European NEW

Bijou bistro delivering a nod to the Mediterranean

☎ 029 2023 9393 5 Pontcanna St, Pontcanna CF11 9HQ
e-mail: eat@delightfulbistro.co.uk
web: www.delightfulbistro.co.uk

Set on the outskirts of the city, this bijou bistro comes with a couple of tables outside for fair-weather alfresco dining. Inside is decorated and furnished in a modern style, with a hint of the Mediterranean. No surprise perhaps, as chef Ana Bela hails from Portugal, and her modern approach echoes the European theme, too. Flavours are clean and the cooking's not over-worked, intelligently allowing the quality fresh organic produce to shine. Take a sirloin of pork with creamy Calvados sauce, served with braised red cabbage, sautéed green apples and caramelised roast parsnips, and to finish, perhaps a brioche-and-butter pudding laced with Bailey's.

Chef: Ana Bela Teixeira **Owners:** Inness Mitchell & A B Teixeira
Times: 12-3/7-11.30, Closed 2 wks Aug, Xmas, New Year, Sun-Mon
Prices: Fixed L £15.25, Starter £4.75-£6.95, Main £14.25-£24.95, Dessert £5.75, Group min 6 service 10% **Wine:** 12 bottles over £20, 19 bottles under £20, 5 by the glass **Seats:** 34 **Children:** Portions
Directions: With castle on right (across the river) turn right into Cathedral Rd. Pontcanna St is 1m on left after 2nd pedestrian crossing **Parking:** On street

◎ Best Western New House Country Hotel

British, International
Enjoyable seasonal dining with excellent views

☎ 029 2052 0280 Thornhill CF14 9UA
e-mail: enquiries@newhousehotel.com
web: www.newhousehotel.com

From its elevated position, this country-house hotel has wonderful views of nearby Cardiff and, on clear days, the sea beyond. Good public rooms include a reassuringly traditional, elegantly decorated restaurant that has a patio area for alfresco dining. Specialising in dishes based on local, seasonal produce, there is minimal intervention by the kitchen, resulting in simply prepared, effective dishes. Expect starters such as fresh pea and broad bean fricassée with gnocchi and ricotta cheese. Main courses might include cannon of Welsh lamb on aubergine and Madeira risotto, finishing with chocolate pudding served with white chocolate sauce and cherries in Kirsch.

Times: 12-2/6-9.45, Closed 26 Dec, 1 Jan **Rooms:** 36 (36 en suite) ★★★ HL **Directions:** Take A469 to N of city. Entrance on left shortly after crossing M4 flyover

◎◎ da Venditto

Italian
Traditional Italian style in modern surroundings in the heart of Cardiff

☎ 029 2023 0781 7-8 Park Place CF10 3DP

There may be just a sign and menu case on street-level at this eponymous restaurant, but don't overlook it, as it's something of a hidden gem of an Italian. Inside, the basement premises offer clean contemporary lines, with stainless steel, marble and cherrywood cutting a chic but casual edge. The classic Italian cooking suits the surroundings, its approach placing emphasis on quality ingredients and clear-flavoured, sophisticated dishes. The fixed-price lunch and traditional but flexible-format carte allows some pasta and risotto options to be taken as starter, intermediate or main course. The crab risotto is especially recommended. Other dishes might include succulent lobster on linguine with garlic and tomato sauce.

Times: 12-2.30/5.30-10.45, Closed Xmas, New Yr, BHs, Sun **Directions:** In the city centre, opposite the new theatre

◎◎ Elements

Modern V NEW
Deft cooking at a popular restaurant and champagne bar on Cardiff Bay

☎ 029 2047 0780 Harbour Dr (off Pierhead St), Cardiff Bay CF10 4DQ
web: www.elementscardiffbay.com

It's a wise chef who knows not to overwork the ingredients and it's that restraint which distinguishes the cooking at this glass-fronted restaurant and champagne bar on the edge of Cardiff Bay. With contemporary art on the walls and long, hanging lighting, tables are well spaced and glass topped with the restaurant's insignia. Fresh local produce arrives at the table in well-judged and flavourful combinations. Brunch is served from 8am till 2pm (American pancakes, boiled eggs and Marmite soldiers, Welsh rarebit and proscuitto), with a combined grazing menu and à la carte, and nine-course tasting extravaganza available in the evening. Roast sea bass with beetroot, pine nut and dill crème fraîche, or rib-eye steak accompanied by braised oxtail and horseradish beignet, are fine examples of the fare.

Times: 8/mdnt, Closed Sun, Closed L Sat, D Mon-Tue **Notes:** Vegetarian menu

◎◎ Le Gallois-Y-Cymro

French, European
Popular culinary venue in Cardiff's Canton district

☎ 029 2034 1264 6-10 Romilly Crescent CF11 9NR
e-mail: info@legallois-ycymro.com
web: www.legallois-ycymro.com

This Franco-Welsh family-run restaurant has built up a loyal following over the years by offering carefully cooked modern European dishes. The décor is minimalist, with the glass shopfront and large mirrors bringing lots of light into the split-level dining area. The French and Welsh staff are welcoming and knowledgeable, serving dishes based on innovative combinations, with quality ingredients being the guiding factor. Take a starter of crab and sweetcorn soup with crab cake and spring roll, or maybe caramelised Scottish scallops with garlic crostini and Bloody Mary ketchup. Follow with pan-fried sea bream served with parsnip and caramelised garlic purée, Savoy cabbage and fondant kohlrabi, and for dessert, raspberry and goat's cheese soufflé and goat's milk ripple ice cream.

Chef: Padrig Jones **Owners:** The Jones & Dupuy Family **Times:** 12-2.30/6.30-10.30, Closed Xmas, 1 wk Aug, New Year, Sun **Prices:** Fixed L £14.95, Starter £6-£18, Main £10.95-£27, Dessert £5-£7, Service optional, Group min 6 service 10% **Wine:** 45 bottles over £20, 21 bottles under £20, 6 by the glass **Notes:** Smart casual, Air con **Seats:** 60 **Children:** Portions **Directions:** From town centre, follow Cowbridge Rd East. Turn right to Wyndham Crescent, then to Romilly Crescent. Restaurant on right **Parking:** 7

◉◉ Gilby's Restaurant

Modern European

Enjoyable dining in this Cardiff institution

☎ 029 2067 0800 Old Port Rd, Culverhouse Cross
CF5 6DN
e-mail: info@gilbysrestaurant.co.uk
web: www.gilbysrestaurant.co.uk

This converted tithe barn on the outskirts of Cardiff is a local dining destination. Fresh fish are displayed inside cold cabinets, and in the background the busy kitchens can be glimpsed, while friendly staff dart between the darkwood tables and balustrades that divide up the dining room. The best of local fish and Welsh produce are emphasised on the modern European menu. Take grilled fillets of gilt head bream served with roasted fennel, baby tomatoes, caramelised red onion Lyonnaise and a cucumber and dill velouté, and to finish, perhaps an apple tarte Tatin with vanilla ice cream. Excellent home-baked breads and good-value lunch and early-evening menus complete a popular package.

Chef: Anthony Armelin, Zin Michael Thant **Owners:** Mr A Armelin
Times: 12-2.30/5.45-10, Closed 1 wk Jan, 1 wk Whitsun, 2 wks Sep, BHs, Mon, Closed D Sun **Prices:** Fixed L £13.95, Fixed D £18.95, Starter £5-£12.95, Main £12.95-£19.95, Dessert £5.50, Service optional **Wine:** 22 bottles over £20, 18 bottles under £20, 12 by the glass **Notes:** Sun L 3 courses £19.95 **Seats:** 100 **Children:** Min 8 yrs, Portions
Directions: From M4 junct 33 follow signs for Airport/Cardiff West. Take A4050 Barry/Airport road and right at 1st rdbt **Parking:** 50

◉ The Laguna Kitchen & Bar

Modern British

Enjoyable dining in contemporary surroundings

☎ 029 2011 1103 Park Plaza Cardiff, Greyfriars Rd
CF10 3AL
e-mail: ppcres@parkplazahotels.co.uk
web: www.parkplazacardiff.com

Laguna is far from your typical hotel restaurant, a large contemporary space in a new-build hotel, with wooden floors, low lighting, unclothed tables, an open-plan kitchen at one end and huge windows affording river views. The extensive menu lists simple snacks alongside skilfully-prepared dishes, but quality ingredients bring out vibrant flavours throughout. Choose small or large plates of dishes like brown shrimp and sweet chilli risotto, or pappardelle, Parma ham and wild mushrooms, and mains like slow-roasted Welsh lamb shank with bubble-and-squeak, or fish with hand-cut chips and mushy peas.

Chef: Mark Freeman **Owners:** Martin Morris **Times:** 12-2.30/5.30-10.30
Prices: Fixed L £12.50, Starter £3-£6, Main £8-£19.50, Dessert £4.50, Service added but optional 10% **Wine:** 44 bottles over £20, 36 bottles under £20, 9 by the glass **Notes:** Sun L 2 courses £11.50, 3 courses £14.50, Vegetarian available, Civ Wed 140, Air con **Seats:** 110
Children: Menu, Portions **Rooms:** 129 (129 en suite) ★★★★ HL
Directions: City centre, next to New Theatre **Parking:** NCP

◉ Manor Parc Country Hotel & Restaurant

Traditional European

Welcoming hotel with an approachable menu

☎ 029 2069 3723 Thornhill Rd, Thornhill CF14 9UA
e-mail: enquiry@manorparc.com
web: www.manorparc.com

Traditional hospitality and service are the hallmarks of this delightful hotel, set in open countryside on the outskirts of Cardiff. A rather grand affair, it boasts a light orangery-style restaurant which is decorated in sumptuous style and overlooks the well-tended grounds. Smoked duck salad is a typical starter, served with a walnut, apple and leaf salad, while mains range from old favourites like sausage and mash, to classier fare such as pheasant with red cabbage and cranberry, or honey-roast duck with sweet-and-sour orange sauce. Finish your meal with one of the daily choice of delicious home-made desserts from the trolley.

Chef: Mr D Holland, Alun Thomas **Owners:** Mr S Salimeni & Mrs E A Salimeni **Times:** 12-2/6-9, Closed 26 Dec-2 Jan, Closed D Sun
Prices: Fixed L £19, Fixed D £19-£27, Service optional, Group min 6 service 10% **Notes:** Vegetarian available, Civ Wed 100 **Seats:** 70, Pr/dining room 100 **Children:** Portions **Rooms:** 21 (21 en suite) ★★★ HL
Directions: Off A469 Cardiff-Caerphilly road **Parking:** 85

WALES

◉◉ Mercure Holland House

Modern European

European cooking to match a stylish modern hotel restaurant

☎ 0870 122 0020 24-26 Newport Rd CF24 0DD

There's an exciting buzz at this modern tower-block city-centre hotel, not least in the First Floor restaurant where there are views over city life through floor-to-ceiling windows. Contemporary styling - with bags of natural light by day and coloured lighting by night casting a glow on high-quality furnishings (bistro-style seating and unclothed tables), décor and the open theatre kitchen. The menu provides plenty of Welsh produce, given contemporary appeal with European inspiration; take a loin of Welsh lamb with anchovy crust and braised shoulder, served with a white bean purée, confit of baby leeks, butternut squash, baby fondant potatoes and a rosemary-garlic jus, and to finish, perhaps a pear and thyme tart partnered by chocolate and cardamom ice cream.

Times: 12-2/6-10 **Rooms:** 165 (165 en suite) ★★★★ HL
Directions: Please telephone for directions

◉ Raglans Restaurant

Modern European

Modern hotel with agreeable fine-dining restaurant

☎ 029 2059 9100 Copthorne Hotel Cardiff,
Copthorne Way, Culverhouse Cross CF5 6DH
e-mail: sales.cardiff@mill-cop.com
web: www.copthornehotels.com

Located just 4 miles from the city centre in an out-of-town shopping centre, and within easy reach of the airport and motorway, this modern purpose-built hotel enjoys a pleasant setting with views over the adjacent lake and well-tended grounds from the Raglans Restaurant. Wood panelling, stained glass and comfortable seating create a traditional feel, while service is attentive and friendly. The unfussy modern European cuisine includes some refined touches, and may include the likes of a ballotine of chicken and basil mousse with mild garlic and onion ice cream, followed by a medallion of Welsh Black beef with turmeric and shallot butter crust. Finish perhaps with a dessert of lemon thyme-infused pannacotta.

Chef: Daniel James **Owners:** Millennium & Copthorne Hotels
Times: 12.30-2/6.30-9.45, Closed 25 Dec, Closed L Sat **Prices:** Fixed L £15-£25, Fixed D £33.50-£35, Starter £6.50-£10.50, Main £14-£28, Dessert £6-£9, Service optional **Wine:** 26 bottles over £20, 25 bottles under £20, 13 by the glass **Notes:** Fixed L 3 courses, Dress Restrictions, Smart casual, Civ Wed 120, Air con **Seats:** 100, Pr/dining room 180 **Children:** Menu, Portions **Rooms:** 135 (135 en suite) ★★★★ HL **Directions:** M4 junct 33 take A4232 (Culverhouse Cross), 4th exit at rdbt (A48), 1st left **Parking:** 225

◉◉ The St David's Hotel & Spa

Modern International

Modern brasserie dining in impressive Cardiff Bay setting

☎ 029 2045 4045 Havannah St, Cardiff Bay CF10 5SD
web: www.thestdavidshotel.com

Situated on the waterfront with dramatic views overlooking Cardiff Bay, Tides Bar & Grill incorporates an impressive floor-to-ceiling glass-backed atrium that creates a thoroughly dynamic and contemporary ambience. Alfresco dining on the terrace is available during warmer months. The brasserie-style menu translates fresh, seasonal produce into modern dishes with strong Welsh influences. Take for example Portobello mushroom risotto with Welsh Blue goat's cheese, followed by Welsh Black beef medallion with tiger prawn tails, new potatoes and pak choi, or peppered fillet of monkfish with mange-tout mash and red wine butter. Finish with lemon pie and Malibu sherbet, or chocolate-lovers might opt for bitter sweet chocolate and passionfruit tart with raspberry coulis. As we went to press we understand a change of ownership had taken place.

Chef: Georg Fuchs **Owners:** Principal Hotels **Times:** 12.30-2.15/6.30-10.30 **Prices:** Fixed L £18.50-£22.50, Fixed D £35, Starter £7.50-£14.50, Main £16.75-£28, Dessert £7-£8.50, Service added but optional 10% **Wine:** 100+ bottles over £20, 12 bottles under £20, 20 by the glass **Notes:** Vegetarian available, Dress Restrictions, Smart casual, Civ Wed 160, Air con **Seats:** 98, Pr/dining room 40 **Children:** Menu, Portions **Rooms:** 132 (132 en suite) ★★★★★ HL **Directions:** From M4 junct 33 take A432, 9m to Cardiff Bay. At rdbt over Queens Tunnel take 1st left, then immediate right **Parking:** 60

WALES

CARDIFF CONTINUED

◉ Woods Brasserie

Modern European

Contemporary-style brasserie in Cardiff Bay

☎ 029 2049 2400 Pilotage Building, Stuart St,
Cardiff Bay CF10 5BW
web: www.woods-brasserie.com

This contemporary brasserie is a former customs and excise office on the edge of the regenerated Cardiff Bay area. Enormous glass windows enhance the restaurant's sense of light and space, and outdoor seating on the patio is great for alfresco dining. There's a strong French influence to the modern European cooking, the variety of which appeals to shoppers, businessmen and tourists alike. Among the favourite dishes are pan-seared squid carbonara, chargrilled rib-eye steak with Lyonnaise potatoes and red wine jus, and apple and custard tart with cinnamon ice cream.

Chef: Sean Murphy **Owners:** Choice Produce **Times:** 12-2/5.30-10, Closed 25-26 Dec & 1 Jan, Closed D Sun (Sep-May) **Prices:** Fixed L £13.50, Fixed D £35, Starter £4.45-£9.25, Main £9.95-£19.95, Dessert £5.50, Service optional, Group min 6 service 10% **Wine:** 35 bottles over £20, 25 bottles under £20, 20 by the glass **Seats:** 90, Pr/dining room 40 **Children:** Menu, Portions **Directions:** In heart of Cardiff Bay. M4 junct 33, then towards Cardiff Bay, big stone building on the right **Parking:** Multi-storey car park opposite

La Brasserie

☎ 029 2023 4134 60 Saint Mary St CF1 1FE
Bustling venue offering quality meats and seafood.

Juboraj

☎ 029 2062 8894 11 Heol-y-Deri, Rhiwbina CF14 6HA
Interesting and varied Bangladeshi cooking.

Le Monde Fish Bar & Grill

☎ 029 2038 7376 60-62 Saint Mary St CF10 1FE
Seafood restaurant, where food is cooked in a bustling open kitchen.

CARMARTHENSHIRE

CARMARTHEN   MAP 08 SN42

◉ Falcon Hotel

Modern, Traditional British, Mediterranean

Local food in a family-run hotel restaurant

☎ 01267 234959 & 237152 Lammas St SA31 3AP
e-mail: reception@falconcarmarthen.co.uk
web: www.falconcarmarthen.co.uk

Owned by the Exton family for over 45 years, the Falcon is a small friendly hotel in the centre of Carmarthen. The restaurant is light, airy and spacious and has an adjacent bar and lounge. The cooking style is straightforward and the menu offers a selection of dishes making good use of local produce. Chef's meat terrine and mango chutney with balsamic dressing is a house speciality to start, followed by braised venison, Towey Valley lamb, or Welsh beef rump in Felinfoel beer with lardons of bacon and shallots.

Chef: David Frolik **Owners:** J R Exton **Times:** 12-2.15/6.30-9, Closed 26-27 Dec, Closed D Sun, 25 Dec **Prices:** Fixed L £9.95, Fixed D £19.95, Starter £3.95-£6.50, Main £11.95-£19.95, Dessert £4.50 **Wine:** 8 bottles over £20, 26 bottles under £20, 6 by the glass **Notes:** Sun L 3 courses £15.95, Air con **Seats:** 100,,Pr/dining room 25 **Children:** Portions **Rooms:** 16 (16 en suite) ★★ HL **Directions:** Located in the centre of Carmarthen, 200 yds from bus station **Parking:** 40

LAUGHARNE   MAP 08 SN31

◉◉ The Cors Restaurant

Modern

Great food in a quirky former vicarage

☎ 01994 427219 Newbridge Rd SA33 4SH
e-mail: nickpriestland@hotmail.com
web: www.the-cors.co.uk

Set down a lane, the unremarkable exterior of this former vicarage in the village made famous by Dylan Thomas doesn't prepare first-time visitors for what's inside. With no draught beer, no optics, no credit cards, no printed menus and walls painted with bold colours, this quirky place has a Bohemian air about it. It all makes sense as soon as the food emerges from the kitchen which makes fine use of produce from the region: roasted butternut squash appears with Carmarthen ham, parmesan and balsamic, while tournedos of Pembrokeshire Black beef fillet is served with green peppercorns and a red wine jus.

Times: 7-9.30, Closed Sun-Wed, 25 Dec **Directions:** From Carmarthen follow A40, turn left at St Clears & 4m to Laugharne

see advert opposite

LLANDEILO   MAP 08 SN62

◉◉ The Angel Salem

British

Hearty food in a delightful rural location

☎ 01558 823394 Salem SA19 7LY

It's well worth a trip into the Carmarthenshire countryside to find this welcoming inn, with its big comfy sofas and an interesting mixture of modern and antique furniture. People come for the pleasant surroundings and friendly service, but above all for the carefully prepared food made from quality produce. Contemporary dishes with classical influences are offered from lunchtime blackboard specials and a regularly-changing carte. Recommendations are the soufflé of Welsh goat's cheese and walnut to start, a main course of cumin-braised shoulder of Welsh lamb with onion and raisin jus and minted yogurt, and dessert of white chocolate and raspberry trifle. Everything is home made including the excellent breads.

Chef: Rod Peterson **Owners:** Rod Peterson & Liz Smith **Times:** 12-3/7-9, Closed 2 wks in Jan, Sun-Mon (ex BHs), Closed L Tues **Prices:** Starter £4.25-£7.50, Main £15-£19, Dessert £5.50-£7.95, Service optional **Wine:** 18 bottles over £20, 21 bottles under £20, 5 by the glass **Seats:** 70 **Children:** Portions **Directions:** Please telephone for directions **Parking:** 25

LLANELLI   MAP 08 SN50

◉ Fairyhill Bar & Brasserie

Modern ⚑NOTABLE WINE LIST

Modern brasserie with views over the Estuary

☎ 01554 744994 Machynys Golf Club, Nicklaus Av SA15 2DG

e-mail: machynys@fairyhill.net

web: www.fairyhill.net

This stylish bar brasserie is located on the Machynys Peninsula in the impressive clubhouse of the Jack Nicklaus-designed golf course. Views over the course and bay are excellent, and staff make guests feel even more relaxed, with efficient, informal service. Everything on the menu is fairly easy on the pocket, with local produce and specialities brought to the fore in dishes like roast vegetable and Welsh cheese salad, or cockles, laverbread and Welsh bacon, followed perhaps by baked hake with spaghetti and leek in garlic cream sauce. Finish with warm apple and almond pie with vanilla custard. Good hearty fare, guaranteed to please.

Chef: Nick Jones **Owners:** Paul Davies, Andrew Hetherington **Times:** 12-3/6-10, Closed 25 Dec **Prices:** Fixed L £10.95, Starter £3.25-£5.55, Main £9.95-£16.95, Dessert £3.55-£5.55, Service included **Wine:** 12 bottles over £20, 18 bottles under £20, 4 by the glass **Seats:** 70, Pr/dining room 125 **Children:** Min 5 yrs **Directions:** M4 junct 48 onto A4138 towards Llanelli. Follow signs to Machynys Golf Club **Parking:** 100

The Cors Restaurant
Newbridge Road   Laugharne
Carmarthenshire
SA33 4SH
Tel: 01994 427219

"Very special, very romantic and quirky, The Cors is famous among locals for its candlelit intimacy, its beautiful setting and the inspired cooking of its chef-proprietor, Nick Priestland, which is pleasingly free from fuss and frills'.

The Times Feb 11th 2006.

NANTGAREDIG   MAP 08 SN42

◉◉ Y Polyn

British, French NEW

A simple, unpretentious regional restaurant of distinction

☎ 01267 290000 SA32 7LH

e-mail: ypolyn@hotmail.com

web: www.ypolyn.co.uk

This modest, white-painted former inn sits in peaceful countryside a few miles outside Carmarthen. Today though, Y Polyn is a cosy bar and restaurant with a serious approach to food, and a setting which oozes rustic, unpretentious charm. Think shabby chic, with solid farmhouse-style tables and a miscellany of comfy chairs set on quarry-tiled floors and sisal-style carpet runners, and dark terracotta painted walls hung with paintings or menus from renowned restaurants. Service is very personable, suitably relaxed but efficient. The kitchen delivers modern, British-themed bistro-style fare using the best local produce from the abundant Welsh larder. Dishes and flavours are clean cut and not overworked, with the main ingredient allowed to shine; think Pembrokeshire organic Welsh Black fillet steak with béarnaise sauce, or skate with black butter, and do save room for the excellent home-made breads.

Chef: Susan Manson, Maryann Wright **Owners:** Mark & Susan Manson, Simon & Maryann Wright **Times:** 12-2/7-9, Closed Mon, Closed L Sat, D Sun **Prices:** Fixed D £27.50-£31.50, Starter £4-£7.50, Main £8.50-£14.50, Dessert £5.50, Service optional **Wine:** 20 bottles over £20, 31 bottles under £20, 7 by the glass **Notes:** Alc L only **Seats:** 40 **Children:** Portions **Directions:** Follow brown tourist signs to National Botanic Gardens, Y Polyn is signed **Parking:** 25

WALES

CEREDIGION

ABERAERON — MAP 08 SN46

⊕ Harbourmaster Hotel

Modern Welsh ☺

Enjoyable Welsh cuisine in an historic harbourside hotel

☎ 01545 570755 Pen Cei SA46 0BA
e-mail: info@harbour-master.com
web: www.harbour-master.com

A Grade II listed harbourmaster's house, sympathetically updated and with a dramatic quayside location. Eat at the bar tables or in the bright, airy brasserie with its ships' chandlery wall décor and magnificent spiral staircase. Relaxed, bilingual service delivers modern Welsh dishes based on local produce to eager diners. Start with ham hock terrine with beetroot relish before trying a main course of roast rack of Ystwyth Valley lamb with sweet potato and chilli lentils or roast cod with parsley mash, cockle, leek and white wine sauce. Try some excellent Welsh cheeses to finish.

Chef: Stephen Evans **Owners:** Glyn & Menna Hevlyn **Times:** 12-2/6.30-9, Closed 24 Dec-9 Jan, Closed L Mon, D Sun **Prices:** Starter £5.50-£8.50, Main £13.50-£19.50, Dessert £5-£5.50, Service optional, Group min 6 service 10% **Wine:** 25 bottles over £20, 25 bottles under £20, 10 by the glass **Seats:** 40 **Children:** Portions **Rooms:** 9 (9 en suite) ★★★★★ INN **Directions:** A487 coastal road, follow signs for town-centre tourist information centre **Parking:** 3

⊕⊕ Ty Mawr Mansion

Modern British NEW

Peaceful, relaxed country-house dining showcasing quality local produce

☎ 01570 470033 Cilcennin SA48 8DB
e-mail: info@tymawrmansion.co.uk
web: www.tymawrmansion.co.uk

Set in 12 acres of countryside grounds, this recently refurbished, Grade II listed mansion offers a true country-house experience where peace and tranquility are key. There's a choice of three lounges for aperitifs, each with its own theme, while the restaurant comes smartly decked out in polished-oak flooring and bold blue colours that coordinate with furnishings, pictures and prints. Service is relaxed and friendly, while the kitchen deals in fresh, locally-sourced, seasonal produce, including herbs from the mansion's garden. The cooking style has a classical theme but with a contemporary Welsh twist; take a fillet of Welsh beef served with horseradish pomme purée, creamed leeks, oxtail ravioli and foie gras espuma, or loin of venison with caramelised cauliflower, braised red cabbage and chestnut and rowanberry jus.

Ty Mawr Mansion

Chef: Paul Owens **Owners:** Martin & Catherine McAlpine **Times:** 7-9, Closed 26 Dec-7 Jan, Sun-Mon, Closed L all week **Prices:** Fixed D £32-£42 **Wine:** 23 bottles over £20, 13 bottles under £20, 6 by the glass **Notes:** Dress Restrictions, Smart casual **Children:** Min 12 yrs **Rooms:** 9 (9 en suite) ★★★★★ RR **Directions:** 4m from Aberaeron on A482 to Lampeter road **Parking:** 20

AA Guest Accommodation of the Year for Wales

ABERYSTWYTH — MAP 08 SN58

Conrah Hotel

Rosettes not confirmed at time of going to press

British, International

Innovative food at a lovely country hotel

☎ 01970 617941 Ffosrhydygaled, Chancery SY23 4DF
e-mail: enquiries@conrah.co.uk
web: www.conrah.co.uk

Now under new ownership, this hotel is undergoing a total refurbishment, but guests can still enjoy a country-house hotel atmosphere and, of course, wonderful views of the Ystwyth Valley. The uncomplicated, modern British dishes rely extensively on Welsh produce including much grown in the hotel's own garden. Try a starter of pan-fried red snapper with creamed leeks and saffron sauce, followed by duck 'two ways' - duck breast and confit of leg - served with roast baby beetroot and Dijon sauce. As we went to press a change of ownership had taken place.

Times: 12-2/7-9, Closed 1 wk Xmas, Closed D Sun (low season) **Rooms:** 17 (17 en suite) ★★★ CHH **Directions:** On A487, 3m S of Aberystwyth

⊕ Harry's

Modern

Classic bistro with French-inspired dishes

☎ 01970 612647 40-46 North Pde SY23 2NF
e-mail: mail@harrysaberystwyth.com
web: www.harrysaberystwyth.com

Close to the shopping area and the seafront, Harry's is a friendly restaurant with rooms. Recently changed into a more informal French bistro, the rustic interior comprises two dining areas each decked out with chunky wooden furniture, stripped floors and brightly painted walls. French-inspired menus make good use of local and seasonal produce that bring depth and flavour to the dishes. Typical starters might include pan-seared squid with tomato fondue and herb crust, followed by pan-fried Welsh Black beef medallion, celeriac purée, cocotte potatoes and Madeira jus, or perhaps a selection of tempura-battered seafood with home-made tartare sauce and rocket salad.

Chef: Chris Williams **Owners:** Harry Hughes **Times:** 12-2/6-9.30, Closed 25-26 Dec **Prices:** Starter £3.60-£6.50, Main £7.50-£14.50, Dessert £5, Service included **Wine:** 2 bottles over £20, 21 bottles under £20, 4 by the glass **Notes:** Vegetarian available **Seats:** 120, Pr/dining room 40 **Children:** Portions **Rooms:** 22 (22 en suite) ★★ HL **Directions:** Town centre **Parking:** 14

⊛ Le Vignoble

Modern British, French NEW

Stylish, welcoming restaurant with a flavour of France

☎ 01970 630800 31 Eastgate St SY23 2AR
e-mail: info@orangery.uk.com
web: www.orangery.uk.com

The Vignoble restaurant is round the corner from its sister establishment, the Orangery Bistro and wine bar. British cuisine with a French flavour is served in contemporary surroundings enhanced by beautiful photographs of the French countryside. The open-plan kitchen means diners can see the chef at work. A two- or three-course fixed lunch menu gives way to a longer carte in the evenings. Here you might find a main course like half a local lobster, served with saffron aïoli, chips and mixed leaves, or fillet steak with stilton mousse. For dessert, try dark chocolate marquise with vanilla cream and raspberry sorbet.

Chef: Cheuk Kong **Owners:** Robert Hadaway **Times:** 12-2/6-10, Closed 25 Dec, 1 Jan, Sun, Mon, Closed L Tue **Prices:** Fixed L £12.50, Starter £4-£8, Main £10.50-£21, Dessert £2.50-£6, Service optional, Group min 8 service 10% **Wine:** 21 bottles over £20, 37 bottles under £20, 5 by the glass **Seats:** 35 **Children:** Portions **Directions:** Located on Eastgate St which runs parallel to The Promenade

EGLWYSFACH   MAP 14 SN69

⊛⊛⊛ Ynyshir Hall

see below

LAMPETER   MAP 08 SN54

⊛⊛ Best Western Falcondale Mansion

Modern British

Mansion house offering fine dining with local produce

☎ 01570 422910 SA48 7RX
e-mail: info@falcondalehotel.com
web: www.falcondalehotel.com

This charming Victorian mansion - built in the Italianate style - is set in 14 acres of gardens and parkland containing many rare varieties of exotic and native trees and shrubs. It was originally the country residence of the Harford family, founders of the NatWest bank. Now transformed into a country hotel, you'll find Peterwells brasserie offering informal dining, while the candlelit Valley restaurant is the main act with its daily-changing menu using fine local produce. Expect fillet of sea bass with prawn and Welsh cheese risotto and saffron

CONTINUED

WALES

Ynyshir Hall

EGLWYSFACH   MAP 14 SN69

Modern British V ⊛

Adventurous and stunning country-house cuisine

☎ 01654 781209 SY20 8TA
e-mail: ynyshir@relaischateaux.com
web: www.ynyshir-hall.co.uk

This charming, white-painted Tudor manor-house hideaway, set in 14 acres of glorious gardens amid the splendour of the Dovey estuary and once owned by Queen Victoria as a shooting lodge, offers one of Wales' great gastronomic and country-house experiences. The original 1,000-acre estate that surrounds the hotel is now an RSPB reserve, while Ynyshir's gardens are ablaze with azaleas and rhododendrons in spring, and the drive is flanked by sequoia and Wellingtonia trees. An intimate retreat of high quality, though there's a modern twist on the country-house theme here, with a bold and vibrant colour scheme and walls adorned with bright canvasses.

The restaurant is the epitome of a country-house dining room, small and decked out with crisp white linen and comfortable high-backed chairs, while offering views over the garden. Head chef Shane Hughes' cooking oozes pedigree, his modern approach underpinned by classical technique and driven by high-quality Welsh produce, including herbs and vegetables from Ynyshir's walled garden. His

innovative, creative, sharp cooking might deliver beef fillet and mushroom ravioli with celery, parsnip and black pepper, or perhaps monkfish and squid teamed with fennel risotto, cherry tomatoes and kohlrabi.

Chef: Shane Hughes **Owners:** Rob & Joan Reen **Times:** 12.30-1.30/7-8.45, Closed Jan **Prices:** Fixed L £21, Fixed D £65, Service optional **Wine:** 250 bottles over £20, 5 bottles under £20, 14 by the glass **Notes:** Fixed D 4 courses, Tasting menu £65-£75, Vegetarian menu, Dress Restrictions, No jeans, beachwear or shorts, Civ Wed 40 **Seats:** 30, Pr/dining room 16 **Children:** Min 9 yrs **Rooms:** 9 (9 en suite) ★★★ CHH **Directions:** On A487, 6m S of Machynlleth **Parking:** 15

LAMPETER CONTINUED

sauce, or perhaps a tartlet of roasted Mediterranean vegetables, asparagus spears, poached egg and béarnaise sauce. To finish, an indulgent melting chocolate pudding with white chocolate sauce might catch the eye.

Chef: Michael Green, Stephane Biteau **Owners:** Chris & Lisa Hutton **Times:** 12-2/7-9, Closed L 1 Jan **Prices:** Fixed D £32, Service optional, Group min 10 service 10% **Wine:** 15 bottles over £20, 35 bottles under £20, 12 by the glass **Notes:** Fixed D 4 courses, Sun L £16.95, Dress Restrictions, Smart casual, Civ Wed 60 **Seats:** 40, Pr/dining room 28 **Children:** Portions **Rooms:** 20 (20 en suite) ★★★ CHH **Directions:** 1m from Lampeter take A482 to Cardigan, turn right at petrol station, follow for 0.75m **Parking:** 60

CONWY

ABERGELE
MAP 14 SH97

◉ The Kinmel Arms

Modern Welsh NEW
Popular gastro-pub serving regional produce

☎ 01745 832207 The Village, St George LL22 9BP
e-mail: info@thekinmelarms.co.uk
web: www.thekinmelarms.co.uk

Set in the beautiful Elwy valley, light open-plan spaces have been created by the conversion of this 17th-century inn. Featuring oak floors, a conservatory with marble tables and a central slate-topped bar with a stained-glass header, mountain photography and paintings by the owner adorn the walls, reflecting an interest in climbing and travel. The food is well balanced and presented, based on local ingredients, and offered alongside a good wine selection and real ales. With daily fish specials, recommendations include Conwy crab and salmon cake with crunchy Asiatic salad and mango salsa, or rump of spring organic Welsh lamb with a timbale of chargrilled Mediterranean vegetables.

Chef: Arwel Jones **Owners:** Tim & Lynn Watson **Times:** 12-2/6.30-9.30, Closed 25 Dec, 1-2 Jan, Mon, Closed D Sun **Prices:** Fixed L £16.95, Fixed D £19.95, Starter £3.95-£8.45, Main £10.95-£19.95, Dessert £5.45-£6.45, Service optional **Wine:** 26 bottles over £20, 26 bottles under £20, 16 by the glass **Notes:** Tasting menu £35-£75, Sun L 1-3 courses £11.95-£17.95, Vegetarian available **Seats:** 70 **Children:** Menu, Portions **Parking:** 60

BETWS-Y-COED
MAP 14 SH75

◉ Craig-y-Dderwen Riverside Hotel & Restaurant

Traditional, International NEW
Fine local produce in a country-house dining room

☎ 01690 710293 LL24 0AS
e-mail: info@snowdoniahotel.com
web: www.snowdoniahotel.com

A country-house hotel set in 16 acres of peaceful gardens and grounds beside the Conwy River, which you can see from the formal dining room. Here a two- or three-course menu features local seasonal produce in skilfully prepared dishes. Interesting combinations feature in a starter like Thai crab cake with a chilli, banana and mango chutney. Traditional main courses are given a local touch in dishes like fillet of Welsh beef, pan-fried in truffle oil, and served on a bed of wild

mushrooms, glazed with Snowdon cheese. The wine list is extensive and has useful tasting notes.

Chef: Paul Goosey **Owners:** Martin Carpenter **Times:** 12-2.30/5.30-9.30, Closed 25 Dec, 2 Jan-1 Feb, Closed L Mon-Fri **Prices:** Starter £4.25-£7.50, Main £12.25-£17.75, Dessert £4.95-£6.50, Service optional **Wine:** 52 bottles over £20, 40 bottles under £20, 2 by the glass **Notes:** Dress Restrictions, Smart casual, Civ Wed 50 **Seats:** 82, Pr/dining room 40 **Children:** Menu, Portions **Rooms:** 16 (16 en suite) ★★★ CHH **Directions:** On A5 near Waterloo Bridge **Parking:** 50

◉ Llugwy Restaurant

Modern British, Welsh
Upmarket Welsh cooking in a popular Snowdonian hotel

☎ 01690 710219 The Royal Oak Hotel, Holyhead Rd LL24 0AY
e-mail: royaloakmail@btopenworld.com
web: www.royaloakhotel.net

This former coaching inn situated in the pretty village of Betws-y-Coed was once home to a 19th-century artists' colony, whose members included JMW Turner. These days The Royal Oak caters to a wider clientele as hotel guests breakfast alongside mountain trekkers in the modern bistro. Through the comfortable bar with its antique furniture, there's a Victorian dining room with ornate plaster ceiling and linen-clothed tables. Helpful staff serve carefully prepared starters of home-cured gravad lax with coarse grain mustard and crème fraîche dressing, followed by noisettes of Welsh venison on wilted spinach with damson and red wine jus.

Chef: Dylan Edwards **Owners:** The Royal Oak Hotel **Times:** 12-3/6.30-9, Closed 25, 26 Dec, Mon-Tue, Closed L Wed-Sat, D Sun **Prices:** Fixed L £9.95-£12.25, Fixed D £17.50-£24.50, Starter £4.95-£7.85, Main £12.95-£18.95, Dessert £4.95, Service optional **Wine:** 16 bottles over £20, 39 bottles under £20, 11 by the glass **Notes:** Vegetarian available, Dress Restrictions, Smart casual, Civ Wed 85 **Seats:** 60, Pr/dining room 20 **Children:** Menu, Portions **Rooms:** 27 (27 en suite) ★★★ HL **Directions:** Situated on A5 trunk road **Parking:** 100

WALES

Tan-y-Foel Country House

BETWS-Y-COED MAP 14 SH75

Modern British
Gourmet sanctuary in Snowdonia

☎ 01690 710507 Capel Garmon LL26 0RE
e-mail: enquiries@tyfhotel.co.uk
web: www.tyfhotel.co.uk

Perched in the hills above the pretty village of Betws-y-Coed, this family-run hotel offers stunning views of the Conwy valley. Its unassuming 17th-century façade conceals a chic and sophisticated interior which blends country-house comfort with minimalist modern design in a series of intimate and individual rooms, including a cosy restaurant which seats only a dozen diners at a time.
Daughter Kelly and husband Peter serve, while mum Janet (Pitman) conjures up some of the finest cuisine in Wales, allowing quality local organic produce to speak for itself in mains such as a fillet of Welsh Black beef, perhaps served with pomme rösti, sautéed shiitake and oyster mushrooms, butter beans and a rich oxtail jus. The compact fixed-price menu changes daily and features a choice of two dishes at each course, with wine recommendations accompanying mains. Start with seared scallops with a liquorice sauce and crisp-fried greens, maybe take the wild turbot main course, teamed with fennel purée, sautéed potatoes, celeriac fritter and a red wine cream sauce, and to

finish, perhaps pannacotta with roasted plum and almond purée and Anglesey biscuit will catch the eye.

Chef: Janet Pitman **Owners:** Mr & Mrs P Pitman **Times:** 7.30-8.15, Closed Dec/Jan, Mon, Closed L all week **Prices:** Fixed D £39-£42, Service optional **Wine:** 81 bottles over £20, 2 bottles under £20, 7 by the glass **Notes:** Dress Restrictions, No jeans, trainers, tracksuits, walking boots **Seats:** 12 **Children:** Min 12 yrs **Rooms:** 6 (6 en suite) ★★★★★ GH **Directions:** A5 onto A470; 2m N towards Llanrwst, then turning for Capel Garmon. Country House on left 1m before village **Parking:** 14

WALES

Tan-y-Foel Country House
see above

CONWY MAP 14 SH77

Castle Hotel Conwy

Modern British
An ideal venue for special occasions

☎ 01492 582800 High St LL32 8DB
e-mail: mail@castlewales.co.uk
web: www.castlewales.co.uk

This family-run coaching inn - set in the Unesco World Heritage town with its imposing 13th-century castle - is itself one of Conwy's most distinguished buildings. A popular modern bar offers light meals, but Shakespeare's is the main event, a fine-dining restaurant that takes its

name from a set of theatrical scenes painted for the hotel by the distinguished Victorian artist John Dawson-Watson in exchange for his supper. The lengthy carte of modern British dishes features the likes of chargrilled fillet of Welsh beef with steamed oxtail pudding, creamed vanilla shallots, parsley and horseradish mash, and a rich shallot sauce, with perhaps bread-and-butter pudding to finish, served with crème Chantilly and a sticky apricot compôte.

Castle Hotel Conwy

Chef: Graham Tinsley **Owners:** Lavin Family & Graham Tinsley **Times:** 12.30-2/7-9.30, Closed L Sat **Prices:** Fixed L £12.95-£15.45, Starter £6-£9, Main £17-£20, Dessert £6-£8, Service added but optional 10% **Wine:** 25 bottles over £20, 24 bottles under £20, 12 by the glass **Notes:** Vegetarian available, Dress Restrictions, Smart casual, no collarless T-shirts **Seats:** 50 **Children:** Menu, Portions **Rooms:** 28 (28 en suite) ★★★ HL **Directions:** From A55 junct 18 towards town centre. Follow signs for town centre and continue on one-way system. Hotel halfway up High St **Parking:** 36

CONWY CONTINUED

⑯ The Groes Inn

Traditional

Honest, wholesome food in an intimate inn

☎ 01492 650545 Tyn-y-Groes LL32 8TN
web: www.groesinn.com

Dating back to the 15th century, this ancient inn oozes charm and character. Reputedly the first inn to be granted a licence in Wales, its cosy warren of nooks and crannies preserves an authentic sense of history. A warm welcome is part of the appeal, enhanced by a beautiful restaurant with a conservatory extending into the garden with stunning mountain views. Fresh ingredients, creatively handled, make for an irresistible choice. Look out for Welsh lamb and beef, pheasant and game from nearby estates, as well as Conwy crab and plaice, wild salmon, oysters and mussels from nearby waters. For mains, expect the likes of sweet organic Bryn Dowsi lamb knuckle, slowly baked with capers and garlic in a redcurrant jus, followed by a hearty-warming apple crumble.

Chef: Ray Jones **Owners:** Dawn & Justin Humphreys **Times:** 12-2.15/6.30-9, Closed 25 Dec **Prices:** Fixed D £28, Starter £4.50-£7.50, Main £8.25-£17.45, Dessert £4.95-£5.50, Service optional, Group min 8 service 10% **Wine:** 10 by the glass **Notes:** Fixed D 4 courses, Vegetarian available, Dress Restrictions, Smart casual **Seats:** 54, Pr/dining room 20 **Children:** Min 12 yrs **Rooms:** 14 (14 en suite) ★★★ HL **Directions:** On B5106, 3m from Conwy **Parking:** 100

The Mulberry

☎ 01492 583350 Morfa Dr, Conwy Marina LL32 8EP

Pub with scenic views overlooking the Conwy estuary. Food includes fresh fish and local mussels.

DEGANWY   MAP 14 SH77

⑯ Quay Hotel & Spa

Modern International NEW

Panoramic views, contemporary surroundings and innovative dishes

☎ 01492 564100 Deganwy Quay LL31 9DJ
e-mail: toni.riley@quayhotel.com
web: www.quayhotel.com

As its name might suggest, this modern waterside hotel offers fabulous views over the estuary and Conwy Castle. Clean-cut styling epitomises the cool, sophisticated design, with the Quay's first-floor restaurant - aptly called The Vue - continuing the contemporary approach, its two dining areas separated by cleverly lit glass partitions that bring the

nautical theme indoors. It's an informal, brasserie-style experience, backed by relaxed and friendly service. The cooking is suitably modern too, focusing on quality local produce; take a rump of lamb with creamed cabbage and potatoes dauphinoise.

Times: 12-3/6-10 (last orders 9.45) **Rooms:** 74 (74 en suite) ★★★★ HL
AA Hotel of the Year for Wales

LLANDUDNO   MAP 14 SH78

⑯⑯⑯ Bodysgallen Hall and Spa

see opposite

⑯ Empire Hotel

Modern British

Family-run hotel restaurant offering traditional cuisine

☎ 01492 860555 Church Walks LL30 2HE
e-mail: reservations@empirehotel.co.uk
web: www.empirehotel.co.uk

Built in 1854 as the town's first block of shops, the building was reconstructed in 1904 as the Empire Hotel. It has been owned by the same family for 60 years. The elegant restaurant was formerly a wine and spirits merchants and now showcases traditional cooking using modern techniques and extensive sourcing of local produce. Typical dishes include chicken liver and orange pâté with Cumberland sauce, which might be followed by a pepper-crusted rib-eye steak with red wine sauce or slow-braised shoulder of Welsh lamb with wholegrain mustard mash.

Chef: Michael Waddy, Larry Mutisyo **Owners:** Len & Elizabeth Maddocks **Times:** 12.30-2/6.45-9.30, Closed 16-28 Dec, Closed L Mon-Sat **Prices:** Fixed D £19.75-£25, Service optional **Wine:** 39 bottles over £20, 47 bottles under £20, 7 by the glass **Notes:** Sun L £13.50-£15.50, Fixed D 4 courses, Dress Restrictions, Smart casual, Air con **Seats:** 110, Pr/dining room 18 **Children:** Portions **Rooms:** 54 (54 en suite) ★★★ HL **Directions:** From Chester take A55 junct 19, then follow signs towards Llandudno. Follow signs to town centre, head through town centre to Millennium rdbt, take 2nd exit, hotel at end facing main street **Parking:** 44

WALES

Bodysgallen Hall and Spa

LLANDUDNO MAP 14 SH78

Modern 🍷 NOTABLE WINE LIST

Sumptuous dining in classic country-house setting

☎ 01492 584466   LL30 1RS
e-mail: info@bodysgallen.com
web: www.bodysgallen.com

Standing in over 200 acres of its own parkland to the south of Llandudno with spectacular views of Snowdonia, Bodysgallen Hall started life as a look-out tower for nearby Conwy Castle. This traditional country-house hotel grew to its current proportions in the 17th century and today still enjoys a wonderful position in extensive grounds with views of the surrounding countryside. There is a comfortable and welcoming foyer lounge doubling as a bar with two formal yet intimate dining rooms. The well-established service makes this a wonderful dining venue with staff operating like a well-oiled machine.

The best of North Welsh produce is competently showcased on the fixed-price menus of modern British dishes. A starter of seared sea scallops with golden raisin purée and cauliflower cream displays considerable technical skill and an ability to handle delicate flavours, while a main course of pan-fried sea bass with garlic and lemon purée, wild rocket, caper and tomato dressing shows accurate cooking. Round things off in style with an exemplary dessert like apple and Calvados charlotte with clove ice cream. Special mention has to be made of the canapés, home-made breads and exceptional wine list.

Chef: John Williams
Owners: Historic House Hotels Ltd
Times: 12.30-1.45/7-9.30
Prices: Fixed L £18-£24, Fixed D £40-£47, Service included
Wine: 100 bottles over £20, 30 bottles under £20, 8 by the glass
Notes: Vegetarian available, Dress Restrictions, Smart casual, no trainers/T-shirts/tracksuits, Civ Wed 55, Air con
Seats: 60, Pr/dining room 40
Children: Min 6 yrs, Portions
Rooms: 33 (33 en suite)★★★★ HL
Directions: From A55 junct 19 follow A470 towards Llandudno. Hotel 2m on right
Parking: 40

WALES

LLANDUDNO CONTINUED

◉ Imperial Hotel

Modern British

Trustworthy cooking with a Welsh bias

☎ 01492 877466 The Promenade LL30 1AP

e-mail: reception@theimperial.co.uk

web: www.theimperial.co.uk

There's something quintessentially Victorian about this imposing hotel - perhaps it's the seaside location, set back on the promenade in Llandudno, or perhaps it's the grandiose façade. Interiors are decorated in a more unassuming contemporary style. The menu at the elegant Chantrey's restaurant changes monthly and takes full advantage of local produce; expect reliable cooking and a range to suit most tastes. A starter of pan-seared scallops is flavoured with lemon, lime and coriander, while a main course dish of Welsh valley lamb arrives with minted sweet potato boulangère, parsnip purée, winter greens and redcurrant jus. Those in the mood for simpler fare might enjoy a steak from the grill.

Chef: Arwel Jones, Wayne Roberts, Joanne Williams **Owners:** Greenclose Ltd **Times:** 12.30-3/6.30-9.30 **Prices:** Fixed D £25, Service included **Notes:** Dress Restrictions, Smart casual, Civ Wed 120 **Seats:** 150, Pr/dining room 30 **Children:** Menu, Portions **Rooms:** 100 (100 en suite) ★★★ HL **Directions:** On the Promenade **Parking:** 20

◉ Osborne House

Modern British

Small luxury hotel with bistro-style food

☎ 01492 860330 17 North Pde LL30 2LP

e-mail: sales@osbornehouse.com

web: www.osbornehouse.co.uk

A luxurious Victorian townhouse overlooking the seafront at Llandudno, smartly decorated with rich fabrics, dark woods and Roman-style pillars that add a Palladian glamour to the elegant dining room. Helpful, formal service, which despite the grand surroundings manages to feel both personal and pleasantly relaxed, comes from uniformed staff. The bistro-style menu consists largely of modern standards, using local ingredients wherever possible. Typically, order roasted shallot and goat's cheese tart to start, follow with Conwy Valley lamb shank with mint gravy, or grilled plaice with lemon butter, and finish with warm dark chocolate pudding.

Chef: Michael Waddy & Rob Parry **Owners:** Len & Elizabeth Maddocks **Times:** 12-4/5-10, Closed 16-28 Dec **Prices:** Fixed D £17.95-£21.50, Starter £4-£9, Main £9-£15.50, Dessert £3.50-£5, Service optional, Group min 12 service 10% **Wine:** 17 bottles over £20, 24 bottles under £20, 6 by the glass **Seats:** 70, Pr/dining room 18 **Children:** Portions **Rooms:** 6 (6 en suite)★★★★ TH **Directions:** A55 at junct 19, follow signs for Llandudno then Promenade, at War Memorial turn right, Osborne House on left opposite entrance to pier **Parking:** On street

◉ St George's Hotel

Modern, Traditional NEW

Refined dining in luxurious surroundings

☎ 01492 877544 The Promenade LL30 2LG

e-mail: events.stgeorges@macdonald-hotels.co.uk

web: www.stgeorges.co.uk

This recently refurbished seafront hotel offers two eating options, the elegant and contemporary-style Terrace restaurant, with sea views, and the magnificent Wedgwood room, with ornate Jasper-style Wedgwood décor. The same menu is served in both rooms under the watchful eye of head chef Robin Lawton. Creative dishes are offered, making good use of local and national produce. Starters might feature smoked salmon, crab and laverbread terrine, while mains could include suprême of chicken with herb polenta and cream jus reduction. Desserts like pear crumble tart with vanilla custard complete the meal.

Chef: Robin Lawton **Owners:** Anderbury Ltd **Times:** 6.30-9 **Prices:** Fixed L £13.95, Fixed D £23.95, Starter £5-£8, Main £14-£23, Dessert £5-£8, Service optional **Wine:** 18 bottles over £20, 32 bottles under £20, 10 by the glass **Notes:** Dress Restrictions, Smart casual, Civ Wed 150, Air con **Seats:** 110, Pr/dining room 12 **Children:** Menu, Portions **Rooms:** 75 (75 en suite) ★★★★ HL **Directions:** A55 exit at Glan Conwy for Llandudno. A470 follow signs for seafront, look out for distinctive tower to locate hotel **Parking:** 36

◉◉ St Tudno Hotel and Restaurant

Modern British
Accomplished cuisine in elegant surroundings

☎ 01492 874411 The Promenade LL30 2LP
e-mail: sttudnohotel@btinternet.com
web: www.st-tudno.co.uk

Perched on the seafront opposite the Victorian pier, this elegant establishment caters to a genteel clientele, offering classical cuisine and a magnificent afternoon tea. Ornate columns and arches provide glimpses of Lake Como - in mural form, prettily complemented by imposing Italian chandeliers and a working fountain. Quality ingredients are brought together in intriguing combinations to form an appealing modern seasonal carte, plus a list of daily specials. Expect line-caught sea bass to be served with Asian greens, lemongrass and a coconut velouté, or perhaps a rump of Welsh lamb teamed with tomato couscous, fried courgettes and a minted butter sauce, while an orange yogurt pannacotta with orange sherbet and candied kumquat might catch the eye at dessert.

Chef: Stephen Duffy **Owners:** Mr Bland **Times:** 12.30-1.45/7-9.30
Prices: Fixed L £15, Fixed D £38.50, Service optional **Wine:** 194 bottles over £20, 32 bottles under £20, 13 by the glass **Notes:** Vegetarian available, Dress Restrictions, Smart casual, no shorts or tracksuits, Air con **Seats:** 60 **Children:** Min 6 yrs D, Menu, Portions **Rooms:** 18 (18 en suite)★★ HL **Directions:** Town centre, on Promenade opposite the pier entrance (near the Great Orme) **Parking:** 9

DENBIGHSHIRE

LLANDRILLO   MAP 15 SJ03

◉◉ Tyddyn Llan

Modern British V 🍷 NOTABLE WINE LIST
Relaxed and stylish North Wales dining destination

☎ 01490 440264 LL21 0ST
e-mail: tyddynllan@compuserve.com
web: www.tyddynllan.co.uk

This stylish restaurant with rooms is situated in a quiet corner of North Wales in an elegant Georgian house that was once a shooting lodge for the Duke of Westminster. Comfortable, thoughtfully furnished bedrooms and lounges provide every excuse to stay over. The dining room has particularly attractive views over the surrounding gardens (perfect for a post-meal stroll or summer alfresco dining on the terrace), while service is informal and efficient. The emphasis is on quality local produce with the chef-proprietor offering a daily-changing repertoire to reflect availability, with a tasting option bolstering the choice. Expect the likes of a loin of local lamb with tapenade and braised peppers, or a fillet of aged Welsh Black beef au poivre, while an impressive wine list rounds things off in fine style.

Chef: Bryan Webb **Owners:** Bryan & Susan Webb **Times:** 12.30-2.30/7-9.30, Closed 3 wks Jan/Feb, Closed L Mon-Thu **Prices:** Fixed L £21.50, Fixed D £45 **Wine:** 184 bottles over £20, 24 bottles under £20, 16 by the glass **Notes:** Tasting menu £60, Sun L £23.50, Vegetarian menu, Civ Wed 40 **Seats:** 40, Pr/dining room 40 **Children:** Portions **Rooms:** 13 (13 en suite) ★★★★ RR **Directions:** Take B4401 from Corwen to Llandrillo. Restaurant on right leaving village **Parking:** 20

LLANGOLLEN   MAP 15 SJ24

The Wild Pheasant Hotel & Restaurant
Rosettes not confirmed at time of going to press
Modern British
Country house with a striking modern wing and beautiful setting

☎ 01978 860629 Berwyn Rd LL20 8AD
e-mail: wild.pheasant@talk21.com
web: www.wildpheasanthotel.co.uk

The Wild Pheasant is a much extended 19th-century country house with views of Castell Dinas Bran, the Berwyn Mountains and the Vale of Llangollen. It is smartly presented throughout with wide-ranging facilities. Food is served in the informal Chef's Bistro & Bar or the Cinnamon restaurant. As we went to press we were told of a change of ownership at this establishment. Please visit www.theAA.com for further details.

Times: 12.30-2.30/6.30-9.30, Closed L Mon-Sat **Rooms:** 46 (46 en suite)
Directions: 1.5m outside Llangollen on the A5 towards Holyhead

WALES

RHYL — MAP 14 SJ08

◉◉ Barratt's at Ty'n Rhyl

British, French

Historic house serving imaginative food

☎ 01745 344138 & 0773 095 4994 Ty'n Rhyl,
167 Vale Rd LL18 2PH
e-mail: EBarratt@aol.com

A family-run establishment, this stone-built 16th-century property is set well back from the road surrounded by mature gardens. Bard Angharad Llwyd once lived here and the house - the oldest in Rhyl - is full of charm with oak panelling, comfortable sofas and a separate bar. The soft lemon-coloured restaurant is country house in style with original wooden floors, well-spaced tables and crisp linen. The daily-changing menu utilises local ingredients and reflects the seasons with well-balanced dishes and classic sauces. Good examples are crab and dill cakes with spinach for starters, followed by the likes of pigeon breast with a blackcurrant and fennel sauce, or fillet of Welsh Black beef with caramelised onion and truffle-flavoured jus. For dessert, why not try creamed rhubarb tart with red wine ice cream, or perhaps passionfruit crème brûlée.

Chef: David Barratt **Owners:** David Barratt **Times:** 12-2.30/7.30-9, Closed 26 Dec, 1 wk for holiday **Prices:** Fixed L £10, Fixed D £25, Service optional **Notes:** Dress Restrictions, Smart casual **Seats:** 24, Pr/dining room 16 **Children:** Portions **Rooms:** 3 (3 en suite) ★★★★ RR **Directions:** From A55 take Rhyl exit onto A525. Continue past Rhuddlan Castle, supermarket, petrol station, 0.25 on right **Parking:** 20

RUTHIN — MAP 15 SJ15

◉ Ruthin Castle

Modern British

Upmarket modern cooking in historic surroundings

☎ 01824 702664 Castle St LL15 2NU
e-mail: reservations@ruthincastle.co.uk
web: www.ruthincastle.co.uk

The main part of this impressive castle was built in the early 19th century, though it dates from the 13th century, and makes the perfect setting for a luxury hotel, complete with a ghostly grey lady strolling the battlements. Elegant public rooms include a bar, medieval banqueting hall and a wood-panelled restaurant with five chandeliers. A sophisticated British menu makes the most of local ingredients, as in seared hand-dived Anglesey scallops with lobster soufflé, confit of Llywcrychddod organic duck leg en croûte, and wild raspberry soufflé with kir royale sorbet.

Ruthin Castle

Chef: James Peter Cooke **Owners:** Mr & Mrs Saint Claire **Times:** 12.30-2/7-9.30, Closed L Sat **Prices:** Fixed L £10.50-£14.50, Fixed D £28.75-£31.50, Starter £6-£9.25, Main £17.50-£22.50, Dessert £5.25-£7.50, Service optional **Wine:** 60 bottles over £20, 30 bottles under £20, 12 by the glass **Notes:** Gourmet menu available 5 courses, Sun L £14.50, Vegetarian available, Dress Restrictions, Smart casual, Civ Wed 120 **Seats:** 60, Pr/dining room 26 **Children:** Portions **Rooms:** 22 (22 en suite) ★★★ HL **Directions:** Telephone for directions **Parking:** 120

◉◉ Woodlands Hall Hotel

Modern European

Fresh ingredients and full flavoured cuisine in oak-panelled splendour

☎ 01824 705107 Llanfwrog LL15 2AN
e-mail: info@woodlandshallhotel.co.uk
web: www.woodlandshallhotel.co.uk

Standing in 30 acres of parkland, this attractive timber-framed house has lovely views over the Vale of Clwyd. The interior is adorned with intricately carved woodwork, and offers two dining options; the formal, oak-panelled surroundings of Bremner's restaurant is the serious choice, while there's a relaxed conservatory alternative with a lighter menu. The modern approach from a skilled kitchen uses fresh, quality produce to deliver dishes with full flavours on Bremner's sensibly compact, appealing carte. Expect a duo of Welsh lamb (noisette and pavé) with a redcurrant and rosemary jus, or perhaps a fillet of skate wing served with pak choi and soy sauce.

Chef: Gordon Hogsflesh **Owners:** Gordon Hogsflesh & Tracy Woolliscroft **Times:** 12-2/6.45-9.15, Closed 2 wks end Feb, Sun, Mon (except residents) **Prices:** Starter £4-£7.50, Main £12.95-£19, Dessert £4.85-£6.25, Service optional **Wine:** 10 bottles over £20, 16 bottles under £20, 13 by the glass **Notes:** Dress Restrictions, Smart casual, no T-shirts **Seats:** 20, Pr/dining room 20 **Children:** Min 14 yrs **Rooms:** 6 (6 en suite) ★★ HL **Directions:** From Ruthin take B5105, turn right at Cross Keys Inn signed Bontuchel. The hall is signed 0.75m on left **Parking:** 20

◉◉ The Wynnstay Arms

Traditional, International

Popular town-centre brasserie

☎ 01824 703147 Well St LL15 1AN
e-mail: reservations@wynnstayarms.wanadoo.co.uk
web: www.wynnstayarms.com

This 16th-century former coaching inn was once a secret Jacobite meeting place. Today extensive renovation has transformed it into a

WALES

smart hotel with good-quality accommodation, an attractive café-bar and the smart Fusions brasserie. Here service is friendly and informal, but always professional. The uncomplicated cooking style focuses on fresh produce, locally-sourced where possible, to deliver starters such as tian of crab, avocado, prawns and lemon, with dill sauce, and mains of tender roast rack of Welsh lamb with a herb crust and red wine sauce. Among the tempting desserts you might find lemon and raspberry pannacotta or an exotic fruit knickerbocker glory. A selection of lighter bites is served at lunchtime, including fresh sandwiches on bloomer bread and hot paninis.

Chef: Jason Jones **Owners:** Jason & Eirian Jones, Kelvin & Faye Clayton **Times:** 12-2/6-9.30 **Prices:** Fixed L £13.50-£14.50, Fixed D £16.50-£23.50, Starter £4.25-£6.50, Main £13.50-£19.95, Dessert £4.50-£5.50, Service optional **Wine:** 6 bottles over £20, 31 bottles under £20, 6 by the glass **Notes:** Fixed L 3 courses, Vegetarian available **Seats:** 40 **Children:** Menu **Rooms:** 6 (6 en suite) ★★★★ RR **Directions:** Telephone for directions **Parking:** 12

ST ASAPH   MAP 15 SJ07

◉ Oriel House Hotel

Modern British NEW

Formal dining in fabulous surroundings

☎ 01745 582716 Upper Denbigh Rd LL17 0LW
e-mail: reservations@orielhousehotel.com
web: www.orielhousehotel.com

Dating back to 1780, the building was originally a country home, but became a hotel in the early 1970s. Since changing hands in 1998, the hotel has been refurbished and given a new lease of life. The stylish formal restaurant adjoins a sunny terrace where you can dine alfresco. Imaginative food is served here, relying on fresh local produce in dishes like rack of Welsh lamb with seasonal vegetables, or pot-roast pheasant with shallots, caramelised apples, château potatoes and baby turnips. Desserts might feature a traditional-style strawberry cheesecake.

Times: 12-6/6-9.30 **Rooms:** 39 (39 en suite) ★★★ HL

FLINTSHIRE

EWLOE   MAP 15 SJ36

◉ De Vere St David's Park

Modern European

Leisure hotel offering imaginative cooking

☎ 01244 520800 St David's Park CH5 3YB
e-mail: reservations.stdavids@devere-hotels.com
web: www.devere.co.uk

Superb leisure facilities include an 18-hole championship golf course and a spa at this purpose-built resort hotel, located within easy reach of Chester and Liverpool, on the edge of beautiful countryside. There's a new conservatory overlooking the garden courtyard and ornamental fish pond, and the Borders restaurant is contemporary in style, modern and chic. The kitchen likes to take classic dishes in new directions, and recommendations include pressed ham hock terrine with pease pudding and home-made piccalilli, followed by a main course of smoked haddock topped with Welsh rarebit and served with black pudding mash.

De Vere St David's Park

Chef: Rhys Faulkner-Walford **Owners:** De Vere Hotels **Times:** 12.30-2/7-10, Closed L Sat **Prices:** Fixed L £12.95, Fixed D £22-£25, Starter £5.50-£9.50, Main £13.95-£29.95, Dessert £6.50, Service optional **Wine:** 12 bottles over £20, 19 bottles under £20, 17 by the glass **Notes:** Dress Restrictions, No T-shirts or trainers, Civ Wed 220, Air con **Seats:** 184, Pr/dining room 45 **Children:** Menu, Portions **Rooms:** 147 (147 en suite) ★★★★ HL **Directions:** 1m from Hawarden station. Hotel just off junct for B5127 **Parking:** 220

GWYNEDD

ABERDYFI   MAP 14 SN69

◉ Penhelig Arms Hotel Restaurant

Modern British ⚱ NOTABLE WINE LIST

Fresh fish and local produce at the water's edge

☎ 01654 767215 LL35 0LT
e-mail: info@penheligarms.com
web: www.penheligarms.com

A delightful old inn right at the water's edge in the picturesque resort of Aberdyfi, with lovely views over the tidal Dydi estuary. The wood-panelled bar is a favourite haunt of locals and tourists alike who come for the real ales and great wines by the glass, while those arriving to dine in the more contemporary restaurant are drawn by the reputation of the fresh fish as well as quality local meats. Take pan-fried halibut served with a saffron and pea mash and prawn velouté, or perhaps chargrilled lamb's liver and bacon with leek and black pudding mash and gravy.

Chef: J Griffith, B Shaw **Owners:** Mr & Mrs R Hughes **Times:** 12-2.30/6-9.30, Closed 25-26 Dec **Prices:** Fixed L £14.50, Fixed D £29, Service optional **Wine:** 160 bottles over £20, 125 bottles under £20, 28 by the glass **Notes:** Sun L 3 courses £18, Air con **Seats:** 36, Pr/dining room 22 **Children:** Portions **Rooms:** 15 (15 en suite) ★★ SHL **Directions:** From Machynlleth take A439 coastal route (9m) **Parking:** 12

WALES

ABERSOCH
MAP 14 SH32

◉ Neigwl Hotel

British, European
Well-established hotel with a sound reputation

☎ 01758 712363 Lon Sarn Bach LL53 7DY
e-mail: relax@neigwl.com
web: www.neigwl.com

This delightful hotel offers magnificent views over Abersoch Bay from both its restaurant and comfortable lounge. It's privately owned and run, and is located just a short stroll from the town, harbour and beach. Tried-and-tested favourites are the mainstay of its British menu with European influences; starters might include grilled goat's cheese with mixed leaf salad and capers, while mains range from rack of Welsh lamb with basil, tomato and oregano to fillet of fresh cod provençale. Book ahead for a window table.

Times: 7-9, Closed Jan, Closed L all week **Rooms:** 9 (9 en suite) ★★ HL
Directions: A499 from Pwllheli to Abersoch. On entering village turn right at bank. Hotel is 400yds on left

◉◉ Porth Tocyn Hotel

Modern, Traditional
Ambitious cooking in country hotel with stunning views

☎ 01758 713303 Bwlch Tocyn LL53 7BU
e-mail: bookings@porthtocyn.fsnet.co.uk
web: www.porth-tocyn-hotel.co.uk

Originally converted from a row of lead miners' cottages, this welcoming hotel has been run by the same family for over 50 years. Marine watercolours adorn the walls of the dining room, with large picture windows providing impressive views over Cardigan Bay and across to Snowdonia. A daily-changing menu is short, contemporary and dictated by local, seasonal produce. Bold flavours can be enjoyed in simple dishes like pan-fried quail with soft parmesan polenta, wilted greens and balsamic reduction, or pan-fried Welsh lamb fillet with woodland mushrooms, green fig compôte, minted crushed potatoes and red wine jus, with orange and almond sponge pudding to finish. Service is relaxed and friendly from hands-on owners.

Chef: L Fletcher-Brewer, J Bell **Owners:** The Fletcher-Brewer Family
Times: 12.15-2/7.30-9, Closed mid Nov, 2 wks before Etr, Closed L Mon-Sat
Prices: Fixed L £22.25, Fixed D £32.50, Service included **Wine:** 48 bottles over £20, 32 bottles under £20, 4 by the glass **Notes:** Fixed D 2 courses, Vegetarian available **Seats:** 50 **Children:** Min 7 yrs D, Portions
Rooms: 17 (17 en suite) ★★★ CHH **Directions:** 2m S of Abersoch, through Sarn Bach & Bwlch Tocyn. Follow brown road signs

BALA
MAP 14 SH93

◉ Palé Hall Country House

Modern British, French V
Formal dining in delightful mansion

☎ 01678 530285 Palé Estate, Llandderfel LL23 7PS
e-mail: enquiries@palehall.co.uk
web: www.palehall.co.uk

Set in extensive grounds, this enchanting 19th-century mansion, which was once visited by Queen Victoria, is steeped in history and brimming with character. The magnificent entrance hall with its high ceilings and galleried oak staircase is immediately impressive, as are the elegant lounges and oak-panelled restaurant. Service is formal and the cooking style is modern, with a good use of local meat and game in season. Dinner may include ham hock and foie gras terrine with red onion marmalade, followed by a duo of sea bass and John Dory on a confit of vine tomato and basil, with an apple and almond gratin with sultanas and Calvados ice cream to finish.

Chef: Gilles Mignon **Owners:** Mr Saul Nahed **Times:** 12-1.30/7-8.30
Prices: Fixed L £21, Fixed D £33 **Wine:** 15 bottles under £20
Notes: Fixed L 3 courses, Fixed D 2 courses, Vegetarian menu, Dress Restrictions, Smart dress preferred, Civ Wed 40 **Seats:** 28, Pr/dining room 24 **Rooms:** 17 (17 en suite) ★★★ CHH **Directions:** Just off B4401, 4m from Llandrillo **Parking:** 40

WALES

BARMOUTH
MAP 14 SH61

◉ Bae Abermaw

Modern British
Modern cuisine and wonderful sea views

☎ 01341 280550 Panorama Rd LL42 1DQ
e-mail: enquiries@baeabermaw.com
web: www.baeabermaw.com

The Bay View restaurant here is aptly named, enjoying stunning views across Cardigan Bay, with French doors that open on to the garden. From the outside, the dark-stone Victorian building gives no hint of its wonderfully bright, contemporary interior. Wooden floors, fresh white walls, exposed brickwork, marble and slate fireplaces and modern art prints set the upbeat scene. The fittingly modern British cuisine comes with French influences and makes fine use of local produce, including herbs from the garden. Think pan-fried tenderloin of Gwynedd pork served with creamed mushrooms, apple and lemon jus and garlic-scented potatoes.

Chef: Aaron Brading, David Banks **Owners:** Richard & Connie Drinkwater **Times:** 7-9, Closed 2 wks Jan, Mon, Closed L all week (ex parties of 10+ pre booked) **Prices:** Starter £5.50-£7.70, Main £15-£20, Dessert £5.75-£8, Service optional **Wine:** 28 bottles over £20, 18 bottles under £20, 6 by the glass **Notes:** Vegetarian available, Dress Restrictions, Smart casual, Civ Wed 100 **Seats:** 28, Pr/dining room 80 **Children:** Menu, Portions **Rooms:** 14 (14 en suite) ★★★ HL **Directions:** From Barmouth centre towards Dolgellau on A496, 0.5m past garage turn left into Panorama Rd, restaurant 100yds **Parking:** 40

CAERNARFON
MAP 14 SH46

◉◉ Seiont Manor Hotel

Traditional British V
Culinary hideaway near Snowdonia

☎ 01286 673366 Llanrug LL55 2AQ
e-mail: seiontmanor@handpicked.co.uk
web: www.handpicked.co.uk

Imaginatively developed from the old farmstead of a Georgian manor house, this friendly hotel extends a warm welcome that makes you feel instantly at home. Contemporary fabrics and pastel colours are teamed with original features such as stone slabs and exposed brickwork in the public areas, while the beamed dining room is traditionally appointed with crisp linen cloths, fresh flowers and sparkling glassware. Simple cooking and effective presentation allow local produce to really shine: start with home-made haddock and leek fishcakes, with a tarragon and lemon mayonnaise, before moving on

to succulent duck, pan seared and served on a bed of garlic rösti, with spaghetti vegetables and sautéed wild mushrooms. After dinner, relax in the cosy bar or library.

Chef: Martin Williams **Owners:** Hand Picked Hotels **Times:** 12-2/7-9.30 **Prices:** Fixed L £13.50, Fixed D £29.50, Service optional **Wine:** 89 bottles over £20, 7 bottles under £20, 11 by the glass **Notes:** Vegetarian menu, Dress Restrictions, Smart casual, Civ Wed 100 **Seats:** 55, Pr/dining room 20 **Children:** Menu, Portions **Rooms:** 28 (28 en suite)★★★ CHH **Directions:** From Bangor follow signs for Caernarfon. Leave Caernarfon on A4086. Hotel 3m on left **Parking:** 40

CRICCIETH
MAP 14 SH53

◉ Bron Eifion Country House Hotel

British
Stylish dining in conservatory restaurant

☎ 01766 522385 LL52 0SA
e-mail: broneifion@bestwestern.co.uk
web: www.broneifion.co.uk

An imposing Grade II listed country house set in peaceful grounds that run down to the sea. Enjoy a pre-dinner drink in the Great Hall, a stately room with minstrels' gallery and lofty timbered roof. Dine in the elegant, candlelit conservatory restaurant in comfortable surroundings enhanced by soft music. British and international cuisine features dishes like cream of parsnip and honey soup followed by fillet of lemon sole baked in a prawn and scallop sauce or Welsh lamb shank braised in Madeira-scented jus. Traditional sticky toffee pudding or vanilla-poached pear might catch the eye at dessert.

Times: 12-2.30/7-9.30 **Rooms:** 19 (19 en suite) ★★★ CHH **Directions:** A497 Between Porthmadog and Pwllheli

DOLGELLAU
MAP 14 SH71

◉ Dolserau Hall Hotel

Traditional
A peaceful setting for enjoyable hotel cuisine

☎ 01341 422522 LL40 2AG
e-mail: welcome@dolserau.co.uk
web: www.dolserau.co.uk

Built in 1863, this impressive country house in a wooded setting has enjoyed a number of uses, from Quaker meeting place to retirement flats, before its current incarnation as a charming hotel. Food is a major focus for the owners and the daily-changing dinner menu in the Winter Garden restaurant features Welsh lamb and Black beef, game, fish and locally-produced vegetables and fruit. Typical dishes might range from a starter of Welsh farmhouse vegetable soup to a main course of rump of Welsh lamb braised in ale with onions and mushrooms, rounded off with Dolserau bread-and-butter pudding.

Times: 7-9, Closed Nov-Feb, Closed L all week **Rooms:** 20 (20 en suite) ★★★ HL **Directions:** 1.5m from Dolgellau on unclass road between A470/A494 to Bala

DOLGELLAU CONTINUED
◎◎ Penmaenuchaf Hall Hotel
Modern British 🏆NOTABLE WINE LIST

Enjoyable dining in Victorian mansion

☎ 01341 422129 Penmaenpool LL40 1YB
e-mail: eat@penhall.co.uk
web: www.penhall.co.uk

Nestling in the foothills of Cader Idris, and set in 21 acres of terraced gardens and woodland, this impressive Victorian manor house has splendid views over the Mawddach Estuary. Take a pre-meal stroll in the grounds before taking your seat in the recently opened contemporary Garden Room restaurant with its Gothic windows and high ceiling. Here the tables are draped in heavy cream linen, with silver, crystal and fresh flower displays setting the scene, backed up by relaxed and pleasant service from smartly attired staff. Fresh local produce, including herbs from the garden, are delivered with a modern approach, the cooking assured and flavour driven. Take slow-roasted rump of Bala lamb served with Puy lentils, root vegetables and a rosemary jus, and a Penmaenuchaf apple tart with cinnamon ice cream to close.

Chef: J Pilkington, T Reeve **Owners:** Mark Watson, Lorraine Fielding **Times:** 12-2/7-9.30 **Prices:** Fixed L £15.95, Fixed D £35, Starter £7.50-£8.50, Main £19.95-£24.50, Dessert £7-£8.50, Service optional **Wine:** 65 bottles over £20, 37 bottles under £20, 5 by the glass **Notes:** Fixed D 4 courses, Dress Restrictions, Smart casual, no jeans or T-shirts, Civ Wed 50 **Seats:** 36, Pr/dining room 16 **Children:** Min 6 yrs, Portions **Rooms:** 14 (14 en suite) ★★★ HL **Directions:** From A470 take A493 (Tywyn/Fairbourne), entrance 1.5m on left by sign for Penmaenpool **Parking:** 36

HARLECH MAP 14 SH63
◎◎ Maes y Neuadd Country House Hotel
Modern, Traditional 🏆NOTABLE WINE LIST

Family-run hotel with fine food

☎ 01766 780200 LL47 6YA
e-mail: maes@neuadd.com
web: www.neuadd.com

With origins in the 14th century, this pretty and enticing manor house has been added to over the centuries and yet all parts of the building sit together in harmony. Comfortable and tranquil, the house is furnished with antiques throughout, while service is formal but with a friendly, family feel. The elegant Georgian panelled dining room is decorated in deep blue and gold, while the menu showcases top-quality Welsh produce, with many of the vegetables and herbs coming from the hotel's extensive gardens. The four-course dinner menu might feature a fillet of Welsh beef with braised potato, mushroom ragout and pickled walnut jus, and perhaps a bara brith pudding with cinnamon ice cream and compôte of fruits to close. Look out for the notable wine list and fine Welsh cheeses.

Chef: Peter Jackson, John Owen Jones **Owners:** Mr & Mrs Jackson & Mr & Mrs Payne **Times:** 12-1.45/7-8.45 **Prices:** Fixed D £33, Service optional, Group min 15 service 10% **Wine:** 100 bottles over £20, 46 bottles under £20, 10 by the glass **Notes:** Sun L 3 courses £16.50, Smart casual, no jeans for D or Sun L, Civ Wed 65 **Seats:** 50, Pr/dining room 12 **Children:** Menu, Portions **Rooms:** 15 (15 en suite) ★★★ HL **Directions:** 3m NE of Harlech, signed off B4573 **Parking:** 60

LLANBERIS MAP 14 SH56
◎ Y Bistro
Modern British

Well-established restaurant serving hearty modern dishes

☎ 01286 871278 Glandwr, 43-45 Stryd Fawr (High Street) LL55 4EU
e-mail: ybistro@fsbdial.co.uk
web: www.ybistro.co.uk

This high-street restaurant with attractive frontage has been under the same ownership for 25 years, and it continues to promote fresh Welsh produce in a relaxing atmosphere. The cosy dining room, with high-backed leather chairs, has Tiffany-style lighting and local art and prints. Modern British cooking is influenced by the owner's travels. Dishes are described in Welsh with translations, and portions are hearty. Smoked and fresh salmon and crayfish potato cake with sweet dill pickled cucumber or rib-eye of Welsh beef with garlic, mushroom and port wine sauce are fine examples of the fare.

Chef: Nerys Roberts **Owners:** Danny & Nerys Roberts **Times:** 7.30-10.15, Closed 2 wks Jan, Sun (Mon in winter), Closed L except for functions, D Sun (Mon in winter) **Prices:** Starter £6-£10, Main £14-£19.50, Dessert £6, Service optional **Wine:** 10 bottles over £20, 43 bottles under £20, 5 by the glass **Notes:** Dress Restrictions, Smart casual **Seats:** 40 **Children:** Portions **Directions:** In the centre of the village at the foot of Mount Snowdon by Lake Padam **Parking:** On street

PORTMEIRION MAP 14 SH53
◎ Castell Deudraeth
Modern Welsh

Stylish hotel dining in awe-inspiring North Wales fantasy village

☎ 01766 772400 LL48 6EN
e-mail: castell@portmeirion-village.com
web: www.portmeirion-village.com

This castellated mansion, set in the heart of Clough Williams-Ellis' Italianate village, has a smart, light brasserie-themed dining room affording serene views of the garden and distant sea. Wooden tables, upholstered chairs and simple settings lend an air of informality to meals here. Using the best of local produce, especially seafood, why not start with grilled lobster with mayonnaise and follow with roast cod wrapped in Carmarthen ham on chargrilled vegetables, or braised Welsh lamb Henry with lentils and minted dumplings. To finish, there's rhubarb crumble or baked Alaska.

Chef: Peter Hedd Williams **Owners:** Portmeirion Ltd **Times:** 12-2/6-9.30
Prices: Fixed L £12.50-£14.50, Fixed D £21.50, Service optional
Notes: Vegetarian available, Civ Wed 40, Air con **Seats:** 80, Pr/dining
room 40 **Children:** Menu, Portions **Rooms:** 11 (11 en suite) ★★★★
HL **Directions:** Off A487 at Minffordd. Between Porthmadog &
Penryndeudraeth **Parking:** 40

◉ Hotel Portmeirion

Modern Welsh

Delightful Italianate setting for accomplished local dining

☎ 01766 770000 & 772440   LL48 6ET
e-mail: hotel@portmeirion-village.com
web: www.portmeirion-village.com

Built on a river estuary, this main hotel in Clough Williams-Ellis'
Italianate village was opened in 1926. Its fame was secured when the
cult series, *The Prisoner*, was filmed here in the 1960s. The bright
curvilinear dining room comes with new Terence Conran design and
has an art deco feel and the atmosphere of a grand cruise liner, with
columns, large windows, clothed tables and views across the estuary.
Bilingual staff serve modern Welsh dishes with the emphasis on
quality local produce. Expect a marinated loin of Pen Lyn lamb with
kohlrabi fondant, spinach purée and spicy black pudding fritters,
followed by ice nougatine parfait with a tuile biscuit.

Chef: David Doughty **Owners:** Portmeirion Ltd **Times:** 12-2/6.30-9,
Closed 8-19 Jan **Prices:** Fixed L £16.50-£19.50, Fixed D £27.50-£39.50,
Starter £4.50-£11.50, Main £11.50-£21.50, Dessert £4.50-£8.50, Service
optional **Wine:** 60 bottles over £20, 40 bottles under £20, 8 by the glass
Notes: Fixed L 3 courses, Dress Restrictions, Smart dress, no trainers,
T-shirts, Civ Wed 100 **Seats:** 100, Pr/dining room 30 **Children:** Menu,
Portions **Rooms:** 42 (42 en suite) ★★★★ HL **Directions:** Off A487 at
Minffordd **Parking:** 100

PWLLHELI   MAP 14 SH33

◉◉ Plas Bodegroes

Modern British

Destination restaurant with rooms on the Llyn Peninsula

☎ 01758 612363   Nefyn Rd LL53 5TH
e-mail: gunna@bodegroes.co.uk
web: www.bodegroes.co.uk

Once a Georgian residence, this sympathetically converted restaurant
with rooms occupies a secluded corner of the beautiful Llyn Peninsula.
There's a covered terrace, a walled garden and a ha-ha. The elegant,
contemporary dining room doubles as a showcase for paintings by
famous local artists. Service is personable and efficient. Modern British
dishes are cooked with care and flavours are deftly balanced using the
best of North Welsh produce. Start perhaps with seared Cardigan Bay
scallops with caramelised chicory and vanilla sauce before griddled
sirloin of Welsh Black beef with glazed shallots and a steak-and-kidney
pudding. Finish with a cinnamon biscuit of rhubarb and apple with
elderflower custard.

Chef: Chris Chown **Owners:** Mrs G Chown & Chris Chown **Times:** 12-
2.30/7-9, Closed Dec-Feb, Mon, Closed L Tue-Sat, D Sun **Prices:** Fixed D
£40, Service optional **Wine:** 261 bottles over £20, 72 bottles under £20,
4 by the glass **Notes:** Fixed D 4 courses, Sun L 3 courses £18.50
Seats: 40, Pr/dining room 16 **Directions:** On A497, 1m W of Pwllheli
Parking: 30

MONMOUTHSHIRE

ABERGAVENNY   MAP 09 SO21

◉ Angel Hotel

European

Friendly modern restaurant to suit all tastes

☎ 01873 857121   15 Cross St NP7 5EN
e-mail: mail@angelhotelabergavenny.com
web: www.angelhotelabergavenny.com

A long-established and popular venue with locals and visitors alike, the
Angel combines Georgian elegance with contemporary style. Dining
options include a candlelit restaurant, comfortable bar and pretty
courtyard, and a pianist plays for diners on Friday and Saturday nights.
There's no sacrifice of quality to quantity in the extensive menu, which
includes sections for fish and shellfish, grills, salads, and pasta and
rice, with dishes like moules marinière, flash-fried calves' liver with
pancetta and red wine gravy, or mushroom risotto. Afternoon tea here
is a great treat.

Chef: Mark Turton, Marc Corfield **Owners:** Caradog Hotels Ltd
Times: 12-2.30/7-10, Closed 25 Dec, Closed D 24 & 26 Dec **Prices:** Starter
£4.80-£8.40, Main £9.60-£18, Dessert £4.80-£5.20, Service optional
Wine: 50 bottles over £20, 48 bottles under £20, 6 by the glass
Notes: Sun L 3 courses £16.80, Vegetarian available, Civ Wed 200
Seats: 80, Pr/dining room 120 **Children:** Portions **Rooms:** 29 (29 en
suite) ★★★ HL **Directions:** From A4042/A465/A40 rdbt S of
Abergavenny, follow signs for town centre. Continue past railway and bus
station on left **Parking:** 40

◉◉ The Foxhunter

Modern ⬧NOTABLE WINE LIST

*A delightful combination of service, surroundings and
excellent food*

☎ 01873 881101   Nantyderry NP7 9DN
e-mail: info@thefoxhunter.com
web: www.thefoxhunter.com

This charming restaurant is set in an old stationmaster's house that
has been sensitively restored and decorated in contemporary style.
The owners have recently added a separate cottage for overnight
stays. The Foxhunter has an excellent reputation both locally and
nationally with a combination of impressive and imaginative food and
engaging service. The menu is difficult to choose from as all the
dishes sound equally appealing - you could start with white onion and
thyme soup with a poached egg, then move on to confit duck leg with
balsamic braised radicchio and pancetta. Save room for the likes of
cherry and almond sponge pudding with clotted cream. Classy,
forward-thinking food and superb wine list.

Chef: Matt Tebbutt **Owners:** Lisa & Matt Tebbutt **Times:** 12-2.30/7-9.30,
Closed Xmas, 1 Jan, 2 wks Feb, Sun-Mon (exceptions apply) **Prices:** Fixed
L £17.95, Starter £5.95-£10.95, Main £11.95-£18.95, Dessert £5.95-£6.95,
Service optional, Group min 8 service 10% **Wine:** 50 bottles over £20,
26 bottles under £20, 8 by the glass **Seats:** 50, Pr/dining room 30
Children: Portions **Directions:** Just off A4042 between Usk &
Abergavenny **Parking:** 25

WALES

WALES

ABERGAVENNY CONTINUED

⊛⊛ The Hardwick

Modern British NEW

Modern gastro-pub style dining from a renowned chef

☎ 01873 854220 Old Raglan Rd NP7 9AA

Located just outside town, this one-time roadside inn has been totally refurbished, though admirably retains its former character alongside the modern ambience and style of a restaurant-cum-gastro-pub. It has been creating waves on the local dining scene and that's hardly a surprise - with renowned chef Stephen Terry at the helm, there's deservedly a real buzz about the place. Bare wooden tables come well spaced, some offering views over the surrounding countryside, while service is friendly and welcoming, and the atmosphere relaxed. Stephen's accomplished, simply-prepared, bold and appealing cooking offers something for everyone and utilises quality local ingredients; think home-made Gloucestershire Old Spot pork sausages with fresh Italian borlotti beans, braised fennel, polenta, rocket, gravy dressing and parmesan, and perhaps a panettone crème brûlée finish.

Chef: Stephen Terry **Times:** 12-3/6.30-10, Closed Mon (exc BHs), Closed D Sun

⊛⊛ Llansantffraed Court Hotel

Modern British 🍷 NOTABLE WINE LIST

Stylish country-house hotel with winning menus

☎ 01873 840678 Llanvihangel Gobion, Llytha NP7 9BA
e-mail: reception@llch.co.uk
web: www.llch.co.uk

A Grade II listed former manor house set in 20 acres of landscaped gardens, this country-house hotel has lovely views, sumptuous lounges and roaring fires. There's a comfortable bar and a beamed dining room with country-style furniture and pretty floral prints. Attentive but friendly service, crisp linen and candles make this a romantic affair, and there's a south-facing terrace for summer alfresco dining. The menu comprises stylish classical dishes with unfussy modern presentation based on quality local and home-grown produce. Think Welsh Black beef fillet served with rich oxtail ravioli, or Old Spot pork in apple juice with a gratin mustard and chive sauce, and then banana tarte Tatin with rum-and-raisin ice cream.

Chef: Simon King **Owners:** Mike Morgan **Times:** 12-2/7-8.45
Prices: Fixed L £14.50-£19.50, Fixed D £29.50-£42.50, Starter £4.50-£9.50, Main £13.50-£21, Dessert £5-£9, Service optional **Wine:** 57 bottles over £20, 25 bottles under £20, 22 by the glass **Notes:** Tasting menu 8 courses £42.50, Sun L 4 courses £22.50, Vegetarian available, Civ Wed 150 **Seats:** 50, Pr/dining room 30 **Children:** Menu, Portions **Rooms:** 21 (21

en suite) ★★★ CHH **Directions:** From junction of A40 & A465 at Abergavenny, take B4598 signed to Usk. Hotel 4.5m on left (with white gates). 0.5m along drive **Parking:** 250

⊛ Llanwenarth Hotel & Riverside Restaurant

British, European

Stylish riverside dining

☎ 01873 810550 Brecon Rd NP8 1EP
e-mail: info@llanwenarthhotel.com
web: www.llanwenarthhotel.com

Situated in the Brecon Beacons National Park, with spectacular views of the Usk Valley, this 16th-century former coaching inn is midway between the market towns of Abergavenny and Crickhowell. The majority of the bedrooms overlook the River Usk, as does the large, popular restaurant with its floor-to-ceiling windows, well-spaced tables and terrace. Local, seasonal produce is carefully prepared and there are some well thought out combinations of ingredients and flavours on the lengthy modern British menu with European influences. Take best end of Welsh lamb teamed with oaty black pudding and a lamb and mint jus, and perhaps a star anise-infused pannacotta to finish, served with fresh poached fruits.

Chef: Rob Scrimgeour **Owners:** Richard Wallace & Jon West **Times:** 12-2/5.30-9.30, Closed 26 Dec, 1 Jan **Prices:** Fixed L £11.45, Fixed D £14.25, Starter £1.95-£5.95, Main £9.25-£14.95, Dessert £4.25, Service optional **Wine:** 10 bottles over £20, 25 bottles under £20, 4 by the glass **Notes:** Sun L 2 courses £12.25, 3 courses £14.25, Air con **Seats:** 60 **Rooms:** 17 (17 en suite) ★★ HL **Directions:** A40 from Abergavenny towards Brecon, hotel 3m past hospital on left **Parking:** 30

LLANTRISANT MAP 09 ST39

⊛ Brookes Restaurant & Private Dining Room

Modern International

Welcoming restaurant offering globally-influenced dining

☎ 01443 239600 79-81 Talbot Rd, Talbot Green CF72 8AE
e-mail: staffbrookes@btconnect.com
web: www.brookes-restaurant.co.uk

With its bright blue frontage, it's hard to miss this buzzy eatery. The chic dining room is equally bold and contemporary, with glass block surfaces and striking whitewashed walls adorned with modern art. The extensive menu offers a selection of innovative dishes, fusing traditional and modern styles with a mix of Italian, British, French and even Thai cuisine. Try wok-fried beef with noodles, followed by seared fillet of sea bass on roast fennel, baby plum tomatoes, spinach, sweet potato with tempura of king scallop and herb beurre blanc. For dessert, take orange and vanilla cheesecake with honeycomb praline, mango sauce and white chocolate ice cream. The upstairs café-bar is popular with shoppers.

Chef: Craig Brookes **Owners:** Craig & Kevin Brookes **Times:** 12-2.30/7-10.30, Closed 24 Dec, 1 Jan & BHs, Mon, Closed L Sat, D Sun **Prices:** Fixed L £12.95-£16.90, Starter £4.95-£8.95, Main £15.95-£19.95, Dessert £5.50, Service optional **Wine:** 25 bottles over £20, 20 bottles under £20, 2 by the glass **Notes:** Vegetarian available, Air con **Seats:** 91, Pr/dining room 26 **Children:** Portions **Directions:** M4 junct 34, follow signs for Llantrisant, turn left at 2nd lights **Parking:** On street

ROCKFIELD   MAP 09 SO41

◉◉ The Stonemill & Steppes Farm Cottages

British, French NEW ⊘

A unique dining experience with modern, flavour-driven cooking

☎ 01600 716273   NP25 5SW
e-mail: enquiries@thestonemill.co.uk
web: www.thestonemill.co.uk

This beautiful 16th-century barn, just a couple of miles outside Monmouth, has been tastefully converted with a modern twist. Think oak beams, vaulted ceilings and an old cider press, blending effortlessly with trendy furnishings. Tables are bare wood, the atmosphere's relaxed and service is first class. The kitchen's modern approach makes fine use of fresh local produce, with accomplished, well-presented wholesome dishes of clean, crisp flavours. Take a cannon of Welsh lamb with a citrus crust, fricassée of braised shoulder and kidney, lamb jus and dauphinoise potatoes, while a liquorice parfait with poached comice pear and lime syrup might catch the eye at dessert. Accommodation is available in farmhouse cottages in the grounds.

Chef: Mr Michael Fowler **Owners:** Mrs M L Decloedt **Times:** 12-2/6-9, Closed 25-26 Dec, 2 wks Jan, Mon, Closed D Sun **Prices:** Fixed L £11.95, Fixed D £17.95, Starter £5.95-£8.95, Main £13.95-£18.95, Dessert £5.95-£6.95, Service optional **Wine:** 15 bottles over £20, 28 bottles under £20, 8 by the glass **Notes:** Sun L 2 courses £15.50, 3 courses £17.50, Vegetarian available, Civ Wed 60 **Seats:** 56, Pr/dining room 12 **Children:** Portions **Rooms:** 6 (6 en suite) ★★★★ GA **Directions:** B4233, 2.5m from Monmouth town **Parking:** 40

SKENFRITH   MAP 09 SO42

◉◉ The Bell at Skenfrith

British ⦿ NOTABLE WINE LIST ⊘

AA Wine Award Winner for Wales

☎ 01600 750235   NP7 8UH
e-mail: enquiries@skenfrith.co.uk
web: www.skenfrith.co.uk

Standing beside the River Monnow in a lovely village setting, this stylishly refurbished former coaching inn still retains much charm and character. Beams, flagstone floor and big fires blend with plain walls and simple wooden tables that contribute to the understated elegance, backed by relaxed, friendly and efficient service. The menu follows a modern British approach, with keen attention to seasonality and the use of quality local produce - with the herbs used in the kitchen's well-presented dishes grown in The Bell's own garden. Think a fillet of Brecon beef with fondant potato, creamed leeks and spinach, green beans and a pancetta, mushroom and shallot tortellini served in a red wine jus. The award-winning wine list shows great enthusiasm with well-written notes (see page 674).

Chef: David Hill **Owners:** Mr & Mrs W Hutchings **Times:** 12-2.30/7-9.30, Closed Last wk Jan 1st wk Feb, Mon (Nov-Mar) **Prices:** Starter £4.50-£7.95, Main £14.25-£18.50, Dessert £5.75, Service optional **Wine:** 142 bottles over £20, 39 bottles under £20, 13 by the glass **Seats:** 55, Pr/dining room 40 **Children:** Min 8 yrs **Rooms:** 8 (8 en suite) ★★★★★ RR **Directions:** N of Monmouth on A466 for 4m. Left on B4521 towards Abergavenny, 3m on left **Parking:** 35

USK   MAP 09 SO30

◉ The Newbridge Inn

Modern British, International

Friendly gastro-pub on the banks of the Usk

☎ 01633 451000   Tredunnock NP15 1LY
e-mail: eatandsleep@thenewbridge.co.uk
web: www.thenewbridge.co.uk

Idyllically set on the meandering banks of the River Usk, this 200-year-old inn has been sympathetically transformed into a spacious restaurant on two levels. There's a touch of the Mediterranean about the place that sets a friendly rustic tone, while smart table settings and efficient service indicate you're in capable hands. Dishes are modern British in style with the occasional nod to more exotic climes. Local meats feature heavily, while a specials board offers fish options direct from the Cornish quayside. Tuck into Old Spot pork loin with braised Savoy cabbage and mustard mash, or steak and ale pie.

WALES

CONTINUED

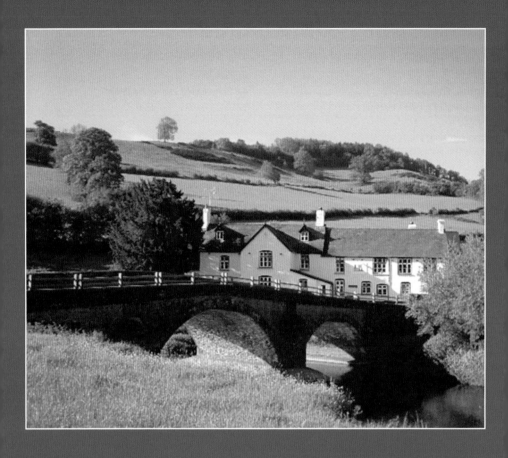

Wales

Wine Award Winner

The Bell at Skenfrith

Page 673

USK CONTINUED

Chef: Iain Sampson **Owners:** Glen Rick Court Ltd **Times:** 12-2.30/6.30-9.30, Closed 26 Dec, 1st wk Jan **Prices:** Fixed L £10, Starter £4.50-£9, Main £12.50-£20, Dessert £4.50-£5.75, Service optional **Wine:** 8 by the glass **Notes:** Vegetarian available, Dress Restrictions, Smart casual, Civ Wed 60, Air con **Seats:** 80, Pr/dining room 16 **Children:** Portions **Rooms:** 6 (6 en suite) ★★★★ RR **Directions:** A449 towards Usk. Continue through Usk and take B route to Llangibby for approx 5m. From Llangibby continue for approx. 0.5m until sign for Tredunnock. Turn left through Tredunnock to the back of the river **Parking:** 60

Raglan Arms
Modern
Unpretentious restaurant offering substantial portions

☎ 01291 690800 Llandenny NP15 1DL

e-mail: raglanarms@aol.com

This friendly, two-storey flint-built inn, located in a beautiful village setting in scenic Monmouthshire, is a cosy, stone-floored pub with restaurant seating around the bar and in a conservatory extension. The solid, unpretentious home cooking keeps an eye on seasonality and uses local, organic produce wherever possible. Come hungry, as portions are substantial - especially bolstering winter dishes like oxtail crepinette with celeriac purée and cinnamon jus, which could be followed by local rib-eye of Longhorn beef with grilled field mushroom, fries and rosemary jus.

Chef: Giles Cunliffe, Sebastian Talle **Owners:** Giles Cunliffe, Sebastian Talle, Charlott Fagergard **Times:** 12-2.30/7-9.30, Closed 25-26 Dec, Mon except BHs, Closed D Sun **Prices:** Starter £4.75-£7, Main £10-£20, Dessert £4.50-£6, Service optional **Wine:** 26 bottles over £20, 35 bottles under £20, 13 by the glass **Notes:** Sun L 2 courses £15.50, 3 courses £20 **Seats:** 50 **Children:** Portions **Directions:** M4 junct 26. Llandenny is situated halfway between the market towns of Usk and Raglan **Parking:** 30

WHITEBROOK   MAP 04 SO50

Crown at Whitebrook
Modern French ⚑ NOTABLE WINE LIST
Superb technical skills and exhilarating recipes in stylishly renovated inn

☎ 01600 860254 NP25 4TX

e-mail: info@crownatwhitebrook.co.uk

web: www.crownatwhitebrook.co.uk

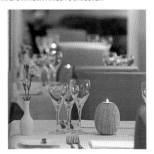

An old drover's inn set well off the beaten track at the heart of the Wye Valley, but well worth the effort to find. Many of the original 17th-century features remain, like old beams (though now washed white with lime ash), while the elegantly dressed tables, minimalist décor and original artwork are firmly 21st century. The menu offers a bold interpretation of modern British ideas - underpinned by a classical French theme and the intelligent use of fresh local produce - to produce some exciting results. Think pan-seared John Dory with oxtail, braised little gem and lemon oil, or perhaps roast loin of venison served with venison tortellini and vanilla jus, and to finish, a hot chocolate and peanut brownie with peanut-butter ice cream.

Chef: James Sommerin **Owners:** Well Oiled Ltd **Times:** 12-2/7-9.30, Closed 2 wks Xmas, New Year, Mon-Tue, Closed D Sun **Prices:** Fixed L £22.50-£27, Fixed D £39.95-£47.95, Service optional, Group min 6 service 12.5% **Wine:** 190 bottles over £20, 17 bottles under £20, 11 by the glass **Notes:** Tasting menu 8 courses £65, Sun L £25, Vegetarian available, Dress Restrictions, Smart casual, no T-shirts, shorts or sandles **Seats:** 36, Pr/dining room 12 **Children:** Min 12 yrs **Rooms:** 8 (8 en suite) ★★★★★ RR **Directions:** From Monmouth take B4293 towards Trellech, continue for 2.7m. Take left towards Whitebrook, continue for 2m **Parking:** 20

NEWPORT

NEWPORT   MAP 09 ST38

The Chandlery
Modern, Traditional
Skilful cooking in historic maritime surroundings

☎ 01633 256622 77-78 Lower Dock St NP20 1EH

e-mail: food@thechandleryrestaurant.com

web: www.thechandleryrestaurant.com

This Grade II listed Georgian ships' chandlery building in Newport's commercial centre has now been sympathetically converted into a restaurant. Original features mix well with the smart décor. There's a comfortable bar area and well-spaced tables in the light-and-airy dining rooms. Service is attentive and friendly. Modern dishes are all carefully prepared and presented in a modern unfussy way using top-quality local and Welsh produce. Try a starter of rabbit, leek and smoked bacon terrine with prune chutney, followed by a lightly poached selection of fish and shellfish. To finish there's hot chocolate fondant with Merlyn liqueur ice cream or Bakewell tart with griottine cherry ice cream.

Chef: Simon Newcombe, Carl Hammet **Owners:** Simon Newcombe, Jane Newcombe **Times:** 12-2/7-10, Closed 1 wk Xmas, Sun-Mon, Closed L Sat **Prices:** Fixed L £9.95, Starter £3.95-£7.95, Main £9.50-£16.95, Dessert £4.95-£5.95, Service optional, Group min 6 service 10% **Wine:** 19 bottles over £20, 21 bottles under £20, 6 by the glass **Notes:** Tasting menu available, Vegetarian available, Air con **Seats:** 80, Pr/dining room 60 **Children:** Portions **Directions:** Situated on A48, 0.5m from the Royal Gwent Hospital at the foot of George St Bridge **Parking:** 20

WALES

NEWPORT CONTINUED

⊛ Junction 28

Modern European NEW

Busy, popular, informal dining just a diversion from the M4

☎ 01633 891891 Station Approach, Bassaleg NP10 8LD
e-mail: enquiries@junction28.com
web: www.junction28.com

Taking its name from the nearby M4 motorway junction, this large, highly popular, informal restaurant (formerly a railway station) draws the crowds with its extensive repertoire while managing to maintain a professional and welcoming approach to service and hospitality. The brasserie-style dishes play to the gallery with something for everyone, delivered via value fixed-price lunch and evening 'Flying all Night' menus that come bolstered by an equally generous carte. Expect the likes of fillet of sea bass with seafood lasagne, beurre blanc of mussels and tarragon, and a more traditional range of grills and homely puddings like treacle suet pudding or apple crumble.

Chef: Jon West **Owners:** Jon West/Richard Wallace **Times:** 12-2/5.30-9.45, Closed last wk July, 1st wk Aug, Closed D Sun **Prices:** Fixed L £11.95, Fixed D £16.25-£19.95, Starter £4.95-£7.95, Main £10.95-£16.50, Dessert £2.95-£4.95, Service optional **Wine:** 23 bottles over £20, 38 bottles under £20, 6 by the glass **Notes:** Vegetarian available, Dress Restrictions, Smart casual, Air con **Seats:** 165, Pr/dining room 12 **Children:** Portions **Directions:** M4 junct 28, follow signs Risca-Brymawr, then left in 0.5m signed Caerphilly. Right at mini rdbt, then 1st left beyond St Basil's church **Parking:** 50

⊛⊛ Owens at the Celtic Manor Resort

Modern European V

Fine dining at a luxury resort hotel

☎ 01633 410262 & 413000 Coldra Woods NP18 1HQ
e-mail: reservations@celtic-manor.com
web: www.celtic-manor.com

Owens is the Resort's fine-dining flagship, an intimate venue serving award-winning food using the finest Welsh organic produce. Owens Lounge Bar provides a private area for Owens' diners to meet for a drink before dinner, with luxurious black leather chairs set against cool granite and limed oak tables, linking perfectly with the restaurant décor. A wide choice is offered on the carte, tasting menu and separate vegetarian carte. The contemporary cooking has an international feel and fuses modern and classic styles, as seen in

organic salmon mi-cuit with spiced lentils, apple compôte and fig chutney, followed by pan-fried dorade with sautéed scallops, crushed potatoes, fennel purée and light vanilla foam, or braised turbot with horseradish purée, roast salsify and oxtail persillade.

Chef: Lee Milne **Owners:** Sir Terence Matthews **Times:** 7-10.30, Closed 1-12 Jan, Sun, Closed L all week **Prices:** Fixed D £47.50, Service optional **Wine:** 200 bottles over £20, 4 bottles under £20, 9 by the glass **Notes:** Tasting menu 8 courses £65, with wine add £35, Vegetarian menu, Dress Restrictions, Smart casual, no jeans or trainers, Civ Wed 100, Air con **Seats:** 45, Pr/dining room 26 **Children:** No children **Rooms:** 400 (400 en suite) ★★★★★ HL **Directions:** From M4 junct 24 take B4237 towards Newport, turn right after 300yds **Parking:** 1,000

ST BRIDES WENTLOOGE   MAP 09 ST28

⊛ The Inn at the Elm Tree

Modern British ☺

Modern-style inn serving fresh local produce in peaceful location

☎ 01633 680225 St Brides Wentlooge NP10 8SQ
e-mail: inn@the-elm-tree.co.uk
web: www.the-elm-tree.co.uk

Situated in the tranquil setting of Wentlooge Flats, this stylish barn conversion is quite an unexpected find. Its modern restaurant has a cool minimalist note with relaxed, attentive service, and the lovely tropical courtyard is the perfect place to be on warm summer evenings. The kitchen's modern approach follows the contemporary theme and makes good use of fresh local produce, including the fruits of the sea. Expect the likes of smoked salmon and cream cheese roulade to start, followed by pan-fried tuna steak served with mixed caponata, and maybe tempura banana with butterscotch, or bread-and-butter pudding with crème anglaise to round things off.

Chef: David Goddard **Owners:** Shaun Ellis **Times:** 12-2.30/6-9.30 **Prices:** Fixed L £7.50, Fixed D £15, Starter £4.60-£8.95, Main £12.50-£18.95, Dessert £4.95-£6.50, Service optional **Wine:** 16 bottles over £20, 27 bottles under £20, 11 by the glass **Notes:** Civ Wed 60 **Seats:** 45, Pr/dining room 20 **Children:** Min 12 yrs **Rooms:** 10 (10 en suite) ★★★★★ INN **Directions:** From M4 junct 28 take A48 towards Castleton. At 1st rdbt turn left, continue 1.5m, right onto Morgan Way. Turn right at T-junct onto B4239. Inn 2.5m **Parking:** 30

PEMBROKESHIRE

HAVERFORDWEST
MAP 08 SM91

◉ Wolfscastle Country Hotel

Traditional, International ◔

Freshly cooked local food in comfortable surroundings

☎ 01437 741225 & 741688 Wolf's Castle SA62 5LZ
e-mail: info@wolfscastle.com
web: www.wolfscastle.com

Dating from the mid-19th century, this large stone-built property commands a prominent position in the village. The hotel has a good reputation for its food and the same menu is offered in the bar and restaurant. The menu divides into a choice of traditional dishes like Thai red chicken curry, local pork sausages, or deep-fried breaded fillet of plaice, and a more International selection of starters and mains like pan-fried king prawns, collops of monkfish flamed in Grand Marnier with mango and cream on a bed of wilted spinach, or leek and mushroom croustade with a Mediterranean tomato compôte and parsnip crisp.

Chef: Steve Brown **Owners:** Mr A Stirling **Times:** 12-2/7-9, Closed 24-26 Dec **Prices:** Starter £3.80-£7.95, Main £7.75-£19.95, Dessert £4.95, Service optional **Wine:** 20 bottles over £20, 44 bottles under £20, 9 by the glass **Notes:** Vegetarian available, Civ Wed 60 **Seats:** 55, Pr/dining room 32 **Children:** Menu, Portions **Rooms:** 21 (21 en suite) ★★ CHH **Directions:** From Haverfordwest take A40 towards Fishguard. Hotel in centre of Wolf's Castle **Parking:** 75

PORTHGAIN
MAP 08 SM83

◉ The Shed

Traditional British, Mediterranean

Local seafood dining in sea-going surroundings

☎ 01348 831518 SA62 5BN
e-mail: caroline@theshedporthgain.co.uk
web: www.theshedporthgain.co.uk

This former carpenter's workshop and fisherman's lock-up is now an atmospheric quayside restaurant in this picturesque port village. Decorated in the flotsam and jetsam style, it's a great setting to enjoy local seafood, much of it caught by the owners. Expect starters like Penclawdd cockle chowder, followed by main courses of pan-fried fillet of John Dory with sauce vièrge or a bowl of delicious bouillabaisse. Finish with hot apple tarte Tatin with ground cloves.

Chef: Caroline Jones **Owners:** Rob & Caroline Jones **Times:** 11-4.30/6-11.30, Closed Nov-Apr open only weekends, subject to bookings **Prices:** Starter £5.95-£7.95, Main £18.95-£22.95, Dessert £5.95-£6.95 **Wine:** 26 bottles under £20, 6 by the glass **Notes:** Children's menu available L only **Seats:** 36 **Children:** Menu, Portions **Directions:** 7m from St David's. Off A40 **Parking:** On village street

ST DAVID'S
MAP 08 SM72

◉ Morgan's

Modern British ◔

Family-run restaurant serving fresh local fare

☎ 01437 720508 20 Nun St SA62 6NT
e-mail: eat@morgans-restaurant.co.uk
web: www.morgans-restaurant.co.uk

A schoolhouse, dentist and laundrette in its time, this 19th-century building now serves the inhabitants of Britain's smallest city as a chic little eatery. Husband-and-wife team Tara and David run the show, offering a modern British menu that makes the most of fresh local ingredients. Twice-baked Caerfai cheese soufflé gets things started, followed by Gressingham duck with a Seville orange and Grand Marnier sauce, or Welsh beef with Madeira jus, parsley cream and truffled potato boulangère. Save room for the likes of banana and butterscotch crumble with honey ice cream and raspberry sauce, or lemon tart with lemon curd milkshake.

Chef: Tara Pitman **Owners:** David & Tara Pitman **Times:** 12-2.30/6.30-11.30, Closed Jan, Tue, Closed L all week (May-Aug), Mon-Thu (Sep-Apr), D Tue (Apr-Aug), Tue-Wed (Sep-Mar) **Prices:** Starter £4.75-£8.75, Main £12.50-£20, Dessert £4.50-£6.50, Service optional **Wine:** 5 bottles over £20, 22 bottles under £20, 4 by the glass **Notes:** Vegetarian available, Dress Restrictions, Smart casual **Seats:** 36, Pr/dining room 12 **Children:** Portions **Directions:** Haverfordwest 16m. On A487 to Fishguard, just off main square, 100m from Cathedral **Parking:** Car park opposite

◉◉ Warpool Court Hotel

Modern British ▲ NOTABLE WINE LIST

Spacious hotel restaurant with wonderful sea views

☎ 01437 720300 SA62 6BN
e-mail: info@warpoolcourthotel.com
web: www.warpoolcourthotel.com

CONTINUED

ST DAVID'S CONTINUED

Built in 1860 as the St David's Cathedral choir school, the hotel has an interesting history and a stunning location, set in extensive grounds overlooking one of the most beautiful stretches of coastline in Europe. Of particular note are the 3,000 hand-painted tiles to be found downstairs and in the original bedrooms. Well-coordinated design, crisp white linen and relaxed, friendly and attentive service distinguish the spacious dining room, where fine ingredients - locally sourced where possible - are used to deliver an appealing choice of imaginative dishes. Take wild sea bass fillet served with spinach-crushed potatoes and a saffron cream sauce, or perhaps roast partridge with colcannon potatoes and a white bean casserole.

Chef: Shaun Ellison **Owners:** Peter Trier **Times:** 12-1.45/7-9.15, Closed Jan **Prices:** Fixed L £24, Fixed D £39, Service included **Wine:** 101 bottles over £20, 21 bottles under £20, 4 by the glass **Notes:** Vegetarian available, Civ Wed 130 **Seats:** 50, Pr/dining room 22 **Children:** Menu, Portions **Rooms:** 25 (25 en suite) ★★★ CHH **Directions:** From Cross Sq in centre of St David's, left by HSBC bank into Goat St, at fork follow hotel signs **Parking:** 100

SOLVA   MAP 08 SM82

◉ The Old Pharmacy Restaurant

Modern International, Seafood NEW

Relaxed dining in period building with seasonal local produce and plentiful fish

☎ 01437 720005 5 Main St SA62 6UU
web: www.theoldpharmacy.co.uk

The name gives away the building's one-time occupation, with the original old pharmacy counter reinventing itself as the bar at this small, relaxed period property. Decked out in neutral tones, there's artwork decorating walls and white linen donning tables. And, though service is fittingly friendly and relaxed, the restaurant name doesn't prepare one for the menu's penchant for the fruits of the sea among its larder of quality local produce. The straightforward, ingredient-led modern approach might deliver pan-fried fillet of sea bass with tiger prawns and lobster bisque, and at dessert, perhaps Eton Mess.

Chef: Matthew Rickets, Matthew Devonald **Owners:** Martin Lawton **Times:** 5.30-10.30, Closed L all week **Prices:** Starter £3.50-£7.90, Main £15.90-£23.90, Dessert £6.20, Service optional **Wine:** 4 bottles over £20, 27 bottles under £20, 5 by the glass **Seats:** 60, Pr/dining room 20 **Children:** Menu, Portions **Directions:** 10m W of Haverfordwest **Parking:** Car park 50 yds

---

TENBY   MAP 08 SN10

◉ Penally Abbey Hotel

Traditional, Modern

Enjoy local produce in charming country-house setting

☎ 01834 843033 Penally SA70 7PY
e-mail: penally.abbey@btinternet.com
web: www.penally-abbey.com

This ivy-fronted, country-house hotel is set in 5 acres of grounds and has impressive views across Carmarthen Bay. Renovation and upgrading has done nothing to diminish the charm of the place. The restaurant is spacious, well decorated with good garden and sea views. Service is pleasant and unhurried. The menu comprises modern British dishes with good use of local produce. To start, try smoked salmon and

trout gâteau with asparagus, followed by Welsh Black beef with stilton and red wine jus. Finish with crème caramel with red berries.

Penally Abbey Hotel

Times: 12.30-2/7.30-9.30, Closed L (ex by arrangement only) **Rooms:** 12 (12 en suite) ★★★ CHH **Directions:** From Tenby take A4139 to Penally

---

POWYS

BRECON   MAP 09 SO02

◉◉ The Felin Fach Griffin

British V ◉

High-quality dining in a wonderful upland setting

☎ 01874 620111 Felin Fach LD3 0UB
e-mail: enquires@eatdrinksleep.ltd.uk
web: www.eatdrinksleep.ltd.uk

This delightful inn, with its distinctive bright red exterior and extensive garden, lies at the junction of the Brecon Beacons and the Black Mountains. Inside, the dining areas display a wealth of rustic charm, each with its own theme or colour. The modern British cooking comes underpinned by classical French influences, and local ingredients are used wherever possible. In fact, the inn's kitchen garden has recently been certified as organic. Dishes are simply prepared, letting flavours speak for themselves. Roasted diver-caught scallops with girolles, pea shoots and black pepper butter, followed by loin of local Welsh venison served with winter fruits and sweet potato purée show the style.

Chef: Ricardo van Ede **Owners:** Charles Inkin, Edmund Inkin **Times:** 12.30-2.30/6.30-9.30, Closed 24-25 Dec, few days Jan, Closed L Mon (in winter excl BHs) **Prices:** Fixed D £22.65-£29.50, Starter £4.90-£12.90, Main £13.90-£17.90, Dessert £5.75-£6, Service optional **Wine:** 45 bottles over £20, 25 bottles under £20, 9 by the glass **Notes:** Tasting menu available, Vegetarian menu **Seats:** 45, Pr/dining room 20 **Children:** Portions **Rooms:** 7 (7 en suite) ★★★★ INN **Directions:** 3.5m N of Brecon on A470. Large terracotta building on left, on edge of village **Parking:** 60

Peterstone Court Country House & Spa

Modern British, French 🍷

Accomplished modern British cooking overlooking the River Usk

☎ 01874 665387 Llanhamlach LD3 7YB
e-mail: info@peterstone-court.com
web: www.peterstone-court.com

Local ingredients are a feature of the menu at this comfortable Georgian manor - eclectically styled with a blend of traditional country-house-meets-contemporary and set on the edge of the Brecon Beacons - with meat and poultry supplied direct from the nearby family farm. It's treated sympathetically by a talented kitchen and delivered to the table in flavoursome combinations; perhaps seared diver-caught scallops with cauliflower purée, pea shoot and apple salad and a cumin foam, while parmesan and herb-crusted halibut might be accompanied by baby clam risotto, asparagus and tomato and basil coulis. Desserts don't disappoint either, as in a superb pineapple and vanilla tarte Tatin with home-made coconut ice cream and pineapple wafer. Choose from an appealing carte or plump for the seven-course tasting menu.

Chef: Mr Lee Evans **Owners:** Jessica & Glyn Bridgeman, Sean Gerrard **Times:** 12-2.30/7-9.30 **Prices:** Fixed D £30, Starter £5.50-£8.50, Main £9.95-£19.50, Dessert £6.50-£7.50, Service optional **Wine:** 30 bottles over £20, 31 bottles under £20, 12 by the glass **Notes:** Sun L 2 courses £14.50, 3 courses £18.50, Tasting menu £45, Vegetarian available, Civ Wed 120 **Seats:** 30, Pr/dining room 120 **Children:** Menu, Portions **Rooms:** 12 (12 en suite) ★★★ CHH **Directions:** 2.5m from Brecon on A40 to Abergavenny **Parking:** 40

The Usk Inn

British, French

Imaginative menu at a traditional inn

☎ 01874 676251 Station Rd, Talybont-on-Usk LD3 7JE
e-mail: dine@uskinn.co.uk
web: www.uskinn.co.uk

This traditional looking inn in the quiet village of Talybont-on-Usk was once a bank, but you'd never guess from the open log fires, polished wooden tables and flagstone floors inside. The bright, airy restaurant has a Mediterranean feel, while the bar area is more traditional. Local Welsh produce and seasonal ingredients are used to create an imaginative menu supplemented by blackboard specials. Look out for fillet of sea bass on spaghetti vegetables with walnut and cream sauce or grilled fillet steak wrapped in bacon with port and horseradish sauce.

Chef: Andrew Felix, Sean Gibbs **Owners:** Andrew, Paul & Jillian Felix **Times:** 12-3/6.30-9.30, Closed 25-27 Dec **Prices:** Fixed L £10.95, Fixed D £16.65, Starter £3.85-£6.95, Main £10.95-£16.95, Dessert £3.50-£4.50, Service optional **Wine:** 15 bottles over £20, 27 bottles under £20, 1 by the glass **Notes:** Vegetarian available, Dress Restrictions, No slogan T-shirts, etc, Air con **Seats:** 60 **Children:** Portions **Rooms:** 11 (11 en suite) ★★★★ INN **Directions:** 250 yds off A40, 6m E of Brecon **Parking:** 35

The White Swan

Modern British, Mediterranean

Charming old pub with bags of character

☎ 01874 665276 LD3 7BZ
web: www.the-white-swan.com

Originally a 17th-century coaching inn, this traditional village pub is set in a peaceful location in the heart of the Brecon Beacons. The informal bar also offers a light lunchtime snack menu, while the more spacious rustic restaurant is equally cosy with beamed ceilings, flagstone walls, inglenook fireplace and well appointed tables. Choose from the comprehensive carte or plump for a daily blackboard special. Fish is a particular speciality on the modern British menu, which makes the most of local produce. Start with Thai fishcakes with a lemon and sweet chilli drizzle, then move on to local venison sausages with creamed potato and a rich port sauce, with an excellent Bailey's brûlée to finish.

Chef: L Havard **Owners:** Richard Griffiths **Times:** 12-2/7-11.30, Closed 25-26 Dec, 1 Jan, Mon **Prices:** Starter £4.25-£5.95, Main £11.50-£15.95, Dessert £3.80-£4.95, Service included **Wine:** 6 by the glass **Seats:** 60, Pr/dining room 50 **Children:** Menu, Portions **Directions:** 3m E of Brecon, off A40. Take B4558 following signs for Llanfrynach **Parking:** 40

BUILTH WELLS   **MAP 09 SO05**

The Drawing Room

Modern British 🍷

Stylish restaurant with rooms starring local produce

☎ 01982 552493 Cwmbach, Newbridge-on-Wye LD2 3RT
e-mail: post@the-drawing-room.co.uk
web: www.the-drawing-room.co.uk

Set in the heart of Wales, near the market town of Builth Wells, this attractive restaurant with rooms is set in a graceful Georgian country residence that has been refurbished to the highest standards. The intimate dining room has a refined feel with subtle wall colours adorned with eye-catching Margaret Loxton French prints and an uncluttered atmosphere. The kitchen's modern British approach - underpinned by a classical French theme - delivers clean, unfussy flavours using quality local ingredients. Take Welsh Black beef and sautéed vegetables served with Savoy cabbage and lardons, wild mushroom and potato pavé, caramelised shallot tarte Tatin and horseradish cream, or perhaps a lemon sabayon tart with compôte of fresh late autumn berries and honey and mascarpone cream to close.

Chef: Colin & Melanie Dawson **Owners:** Colin & Melanie Dawson **Times:** 7-9, Closed 2 wks Jan, 2 wks Oct, Sun-Mon, Closed L all week **Prices:** Fixed D £45, Service added but optional 10% **Wine:** 35 bottles over £20, 15 bottles under £20, 4 by the glass **Notes:** Dress Restrictions, Smart casual **Seats:** 12, Pr/dining room 8 **Children:** Min 12 yrs **Rooms:** 3 (3 en suite) ★★★★★ RR **Directions:** From Builth Wells, take A470 towards Rhayader, 3m on left **Parking:** 14

WALES

CAERSWS MAP 15 SO09

◎◎ The Talkhouse

British, European 🍷 NOTABLE WINE LIST

Classic seasonal cooking at former coaching inn

☎ 01686 688919 Ty Siarad, Pontdolgoch SY17 5JE
e-mail: info@talkhouse.co.uk
web: www.talkhouse.co.uk

This stone-built, 17th-century inn retains much of its original character while delivering smart décor and furnishings and a warm, friendly and relaxed atmosphere. The bright, traditional-styled dining room has French windows opening on to a secluded garden for alfresco summer dining, while the comfortable sitting room comes with deep sofas and armchairs and a beamed bar with log fire. The classic seasonal cooking makes fine use of fresh local produce; think Carmarthen ham with toasted Pantysgawn goat's cheese to start, perhaps followed by Welsh pork tenderloin stuffed with local black pudding, and to finish, steamed pear and chestnut pudding with vanilla custard sauce.

Chef: Stephen Garratt **Owners:** Stephen & Jackie Garratt **Times:** 12-1.30/6.30-8.45, Closed 25 Dec, Mon, Closed L Tues-Sat, D Sun **Prices:** Starter £4.50-£6.50, Main £12.95-£17.95, Dessert £4.50-£5, Service optional **Wine:** 80 bottles over £20, 20 bottles under £20, 6 by the glass **Notes:** Dress Restrictions, Smart casual **Seats:** 35 **Children:** Min 14 yrs **Rooms:** 3 (3 en suite) ★★★★★ RR **Directions:** 1.5m W of Caersws on A470 Machynlleth road **Parking:** 40

CRICKHOWELL MAP 09 SO21

◎◎ The Bear Hotel

British, European

Quaint coaching inn offering imaginative food and a friendly welcome

☎ 01873 810408 High St NP8 1BW
e-mail: bearhotel@aol.com
web: www.bearhotel.co.uk

This historic coaching inn, purportedly built for a wealthy merchant in 1432, is furnished with antiques and retains all its original charm and character. The welcoming bar has cosy sections and there is no need to book a table to eat here. The restaurant, and at weekends the function room, offers a more formal dining experience. Here the appealing menu (bolstered by specials) offers highly accomplished British and European dishes with modern spin using bags of wonderful local produce. Take a duo of Welsh lamb (braised shoulder and rack) with a butter bean purée, dauphinoise potatoes, fig tarte

Tatin and a rosemary and red wine jus, and perhaps a classic lemon tarte finish, served with a raspberry compôte.

Bear Hotel

Chef: Stephen Hodson, John Ganeiu **Owners:** Mrs J Hindmarsh, Stephen Hindmarsh **Times:** 12-2/7-9.30, Closed 25 Dec, Mon, Closed L Tue-Sat, D Sun **Prices:** Starter £4.50-£7.95, Main £11.95-£17.50, Dessert £4.50-£6, Service optional **Wine:** 47 bottles over £20, 22 bottles under £20, 10 by the glass **Notes:** Dress Restrictions, Smart casual **Seats:** 60, Pr/dining room 30 **Children:** Min 9 yrs, Menu, Portions **Rooms:** 34 (34 en suite) ★★★ HL **Directions:** Town centre, off A40 (Brecon road). 6m from Abergavenny **Parking:** 40

see advert opposite

◎ Gliffaes Country House Hotel

Modern British

Traditional country-house setting with innovative, modern dining

☎ 01874 730371 NP8 1RH
e-mail: calls@gliffaeshotel.com
web: www.gliffaeshotel.com

This Italianate mansion stands amid 33 acres of wooded grounds by the River Usk, and has a glorious history of fly fishing. Public rooms retain elegance and generous proportions, and the richly carpeted and panelled dining room offers views over the Usk Valley. Modern British dishes include the likes of warm salad of wood pigeon with figs, fennel and balsamic and wine jus, and grilled lemon sole with marquise and crab potato, spinach mousse and prawn and dill butter. A dessert with a difference is pear pithivier with chilli and rosemary ice cream.

Chef: Stephan Trinci **Owners:** Mr & Mrs Brabner & Mr & Mrs Suter **Times:** 12-2.30/7.30-9.15, Closed 2-31 Jan, Closed L Mon-Sat **Prices:** Fixed D £30.75, Service included **Wine:** 45 bottles over £20, 33 bottles under £20, 8 by the glass **Notes:** Dress Restrictions, Smart casual preferred, Civ Wed 40 **Seats:** 60, Pr/dining room 18 **Children:** Menu, Portions **Rooms:** 23 (23 en suite) ★★★ HL **Directions:** 1m off A40, 2.5m W of Crickhowell **Parking:** 30

WALES

Manor Hotel

Traditional, International 🐾

Real food from local produce and stunning views

☎ 01873 810212 Brecon Rd NP8 1SE
e-mail: info@manorhotel.co.uk
web: www.manorhotel.co.uk

Perched high in the Black Mountains overlooking the River Usk, the impressive Manor Hotel makes a good base for exploring the Brecon Beacons National Park. Enjoy a drink in one of its comfortable bars or lounges, and then move through to the restaurant, an understated room that offers stunning views. The kitchen makes the most of local ingredients, including meats and poultry from the family farm and fresh seafood delivered daily. There's plenty to choose from, such as Cornish mussels with white wine and cream to start, as well as heartier dishes, like leg of lamb with chive mash and a red wine sauce, or Welsh Black fillet steak with mushroom and brandy sauce.

Chef: Mr G Bridgeman **Owners:** Mr G Bridgeman **Times:** 12-2.30/6.30-9.30 **Prices:** Fixed L £9.95, Fixed D £13.95, Starter £3.50-£7.95, Main £9.95-£16.95, Dessert £4.50-£5.50, Service optional **Wine:** 23 bottles over £20, 26 bottles under £20, 8 by the glass **Notes:** Sun L 2 courses £11.95, 3 courses £13.95, Vegetarian available, Civ Wed 250 **Seats:** 54, Pr/dining room 26 **Children:** Menu, Portions **Rooms:** 22 (22 en suite) ★★★ HL
Directions: 0.5m W of Crickhowell on A40, Brecon road

Nantyffin Cider Mill Inn

British, Mediterranean

Combination of old character and gastro-pub feel

☎ 01873 810775 Brecon Rd NP8 1SG
e-mail: info@cidermill.co.uk
web: www.cidermill.co.uk

Located on the main road between Abergavenny and Brecon, this 16th-century former drover's inn and cider mill is always busy, so book ahead. Chic gastro-pub décor makes the most of original features, while log fires keep things cosy - choose from a menu that draws inspiration from around the world, as well as closer to home. A great supporter of local suppliers, the owners rear their own livestock from the family farm. Mains might include lamb confit with rosemary garlic sauce or sauté scallops with rocket and chilli jam.

Chef: Sean Gerrard **Owners:** Glyn Bridgeman & Sean Gerrard **Times:** 12-2.30/6.30-10, Closed Mon, Closed D Sun(winter) **Prices:** Fixed L £12.95, Fixed D £16.95, Starter £4.95-£9.95, Main £7.50-£17.95, Dessert £4.50-£6.95, Service optional **Wine:** 50% bottles over £20, 50% bottles under £20, 8 by the glass **Seats:** 65 **Children:** Menu, Portions
Directions: 1m W of Crickhowell on A40 at junct with A479 **Parking:** 40

The Bear Hotel

The 15th century 'Bear' bristles with personality and continues its tradition of hospitality as the focal point of the market town. Evocative, busy bars have low black beams and rug strewn flagstone floors. The main dining room has recently been refurbished but still maintains a romantic and intimate atmosphere with fresh flowers and candlelit tables. Local new season lamb and welsh black beef still heads the modern British menu which covers a broad spectrum of dishes both contemporary and traditional. Starters and desserts continue to be imaginative and very popular.

CRICKHOWELL POWYS WALES
e-mail: bearhotel@aol.com   Tel: 01873 810408

Ty Croeso Hotel & Restaurant

Traditional Welsh Ⅴ

Relaxed dining with strong Welsh emphasis and stunning views

☎ 01873 810573 The Dardy, Llangattock NP8 1PU
e-mail: tycroeso@gmail.com
web: www.ty-croeso.co.uk

Translating as 'House of Welcome', Ty Croeso certainly lives up to its name. Eat in the relaxed and comfortably refurbished candlelit restaurant, while in the summer there are tables on the flower-filled terrace overlooking the Usk Valley and Black Mountains. The sensibly compact carte and excellent value Taste of Wales menus put the emphasis on quality Welsh produce. Simple, accomplished preparation hits the mark. Welsh cawl (lamb and root vegetable soup) and mussels steamed with leeks and cider are typical starters, with Welsh venison fillet served with damson sauce to follow. Finish with honey-roasted fig and almond tart.

Chef: Lisa Grenfell **Owners:** Linda Jarrett **Times:** 7-9, Closed Sun, Closed L all week ex BH wknds **Prices:** Fixed D £18, Starter £4.25-£6, Main £10.25-£18.50, Dessert £5, Service optional, Group min 12 service 10% **Wine:** 1 bottle over £20, 23 bottles under £20, 4 by the glass **Notes:** Vegetarian menu, Dress Restrictions, Smart casual **Seats:** 40 **Children:** Menu, Portions **Rooms:** 8 (8 en suite) ★★ HL
Directions: Telephone for directions **Parking:** 16

HAY-ON-WYE MAP 09 SO24

◉ Old Black Lion Inn

Modern British

International cooking in Welsh borders setting

☎ 01497 820841 26 Lion St HR3 5AD
e-mail: info@oldblacklion.co.uk
web: www.oldblacklion.co.uk

This 17th-century inn is full of original architectural features, charm and character. A French window illuminates the dining room and provides access to the patio for alfresco dining in summer. Friendly young staff serve simple starters of goat's cheese and sun-blushed tomato tart, then imaginative main courses of fillet of fallow venison on a parsnip tart with brandy and peppercorn sauce. Take a satisfying dessert such as Bailey's bread-and-butter pudding to finish. There are usually good vegetarian options and some game dishes in season.

Times: 12-2.30/6.30-9.30, Closed 24-26 Dec **Rooms:** 10 (9 en suite)
★★★ INN **Directions:** 1m off A438. From TIC car park turn right along Oxford Rd, pass NatWest bank, next left (Lion St), hotel 20 yds on right

◉ The Swan-at-Hay Hotel

British, Mediterranean NEW

Family-run hotel serving imaginative food

☎ 01497 821188 Church St HR3 5DQ
e-mail: info@swanathay.co.uk
web: www.swanathay.co.uk

This former coaching inn is now a popular family-run hotel on the edge of town, offering a choice of dining venues including a bright bar area and pleasant, more traditional restaurant overlooking lovely gardens. Service is relaxed and friendly. The menu changes seasonally, making good use of local produce and demonstrating Mediterranean style with Italian influences. Summer starters might include bresaola with mixed leaves and parmesan or spicy Mediterranean soups. Main courses include local pork and lamb, or Welsh rib-eye or sirloin beef. Italianate desserts feature Amaretto ice creams, sorbets and fresh fruit dishes.

Chef: Harry Mackintosh **Owners:** Katheryn Mackintosh **Times:** 12-2/7-9
Prices: Starter £4.25-£7.80, Main £10.90-£18.50, Dessert £4.95, Service optional **Wine:** 20 bottles over £20, 20 bottles under £20, 4 by the glass
Seats: 38, Pr/dining room 20 **Children:** Portions **Rooms:** 19 (19 en suite) ★★★ HL **Directions:** 100 yds from town centre in the direction of Brecon **Parking:** 15

KNIGHTON MAP 09 SO27

◉◉ Milebrook House

Modern, Traditional British 🍷 NOTABLE WINE LIST

Charming family-run hotel with contemporary food

☎ 01547 528632 Milebrook LD7 1LT
e-mail: hotel@milebrook.kc3ltd.co.uk
web: www.milebrookhouse.co.uk

The former home of the explorer Sir Wilfred Thesiger, this charming 18th-century dower house is set amidst typical wooded, rolling Marches landscape and was once visited by Emperor Haile Selassie. His imperial majesty would no doubt have enjoyed the exquisite formal gardens with its remarkable variety of indigenous and exotic trees and plants, and may even have partaken of a game of croquet before dinner. Nowadays the country-house hotel's kitchen garden provides virtually all the vegetables, herbs and fruits served in the elegant, traditional restaurant, complementing the local produce that makes its way on to the kitchen's imaginative modern British menus. Food is presented with real flair and panache and has high aspirations; take an excellent salad of pan-fried chicken livers with crispy pancetta, followed perhaps by a succulent rack of Welsh lamb served with dauphinoise potatoes and butternut squash purée in a rosemary jus.

Chef: Christopher Marsden, Robert Henshaw **Owners:** Mr & Mrs R T Marsden **Times:** 12-2/7-9, Closed L Mon, D Sun/Mon (open for residents)
Prices: Fixed L £11.95-£22, Fixed D £30.95, Service optional **Wine:** 30 bottles over £20, 34 bottles under £20, 34 by the glass **Notes:** Sun L 3 courses £15.50, Vegetarian available **Seats:** 40, Pr/dining room 16
Children: Min 8 yrs **Rooms:** 10 (10 en suite) ★★ HL **Directions:** 2m E of Knighton on A4113 (Ludlow) **Parking:** 24

LLANDRINDOD WELLS MAP 09 SO06

◉ The Metropole

Modern British

Stylish redesigned dining room with well-balanced menus

☎ 01597 823700 Temple St LD1 5DY
e-mail: info@metropole.co.uk
web: www.metropole.co.uk

The centre of this famous spa town is dominated by The Metropole, a large Victorian hotel, which has been personally run by the same family for well over 100 years. The lobby leads to a choice of bars and an elegant lounge, and the smart dining room exudes rejuvenated style. Relaxed, warm and modern, it's furnished with contemporary leather and suede high-backed chairs, complemented by classic ivory and white linen. Modern British dishes with a classical twist include confit shoulder of Llandrindod lamb, or carpaccio of Brecon venison, followed by Welsh Merlin whisky brûlée.

Chef: Nick Edwards **Owners:** Justin Baird-Murray **Times:** 12.30-1.45/ 7-9.30 **Prices:** Fixed L £10.95-£11.95, Fixed D £24.50-£25.50, Service optional **Wine:** 24 bottles over £20, 54 bottles under £20, 7 by the glass **Notes:** Civ Wed 200, Air con **Seats:** 200, Pr/dining room 250 **Children:** Menu, Portions **Rooms:** 120 (120 en suite) ★★★ HL **Directions:** In centre of town off A483 **Parking:** 150

LLANFYLLIN   MAP 15 SJ11

◉ Seeds

Modern British

Good honest cooking in Grade II listed building

☎ 01691 648604 5 Penybryn Cottage, High St SY22 5AP

In a property built in 1580, Seeds is a low-ceilinged parlour with an intimate dinner-party atmosphere. Original beams and slate flooring combine with curios, maps, books and original works of art to provide a truly intriguing setting. Jazz music plays in the background and friendly staff provide relaxed service. The menu offers up unfussy modern British fare. Try grilled sardine fillets with basil butter and lemon, or Welsh fillet steak with brandy and green peppercorn sauce. Comforting puddings include bread-and-butter pudding with butterscotch sauce and crème brûlée.

Chef: Mark Seager **Owners:** Felicity Seager, Mark Seager **Times:** 11-2.15/7-8.30, Closed 1 wk Oct, 1 wk Mar, 1 wk Jun, 25 Dec, Mon-Wed, Closed D Sun **Prices:** Fixed D £25.25-£27.20, Starter £3.65-£6.95, Main £10.95-£14.95, Dessert £4.25-£5.25, Service optional **Wine:** 30 bottles over £20, 81 bottles under £20, 3 by the glass **Seats:** 22 **Children:** Portions **Directions:** Village centre, on A490, 15 mins from Welshpool, follow signs to Llanfyllin **Parking:** Free car park in town, street parking

---

LLANGAMMARCH WELLS   MAP 09 SN94

◉◉ Lake Country House Hotel & Spa

British, European V ⧠ NOTABLE WINE LIST

Fine dining and old-fashioned charm

☎ 01591 620202 & 620474 LD4 4BS
e-mail: info@lakecountryhouse.co.uk
web: www.lakecountryhouse.co.uk

Imposing country house set in 50 acres of sweeping lawns, rhododendron-lined paths and riverside walks. In keeping with tradition, afternoon tea is served in the drawing room by the fire, while the spacious dining room is a luxurious affair with white-clothed tables, quality crockery and cutlery, and impeccably directed, old-fashioned service. The kitchen delivers interesting flavour combinations via a sensibly compact, four-course dinner menu, which changes daily and makes good use of locally sourced produce. Try hand-dived scallops with caramelised pork belly, a red wine and

thyme reduction, and a crab and cinnamon tuile perhaps, or whole roasted squab with fig sauce, gaufrette potato, Thai asparagus salad and cep oil. Gourmet and vegetarian menus available.

Chef: Sean Cullingford **Owners:** J Mifsud **Times:** 12.30-2/7.30-9.15 **Prices:** Fixed L £24.50, Fixed D £39.50, Service optional **Wine:** 20 bottles under £20, 7 by the glass **Notes:** Fixed L 4 courses, Fixed D 4 courses, Vegetarian menu, Dress Restrictions, Prefer no jeans, collar at all times, Civ Wed 70 **Seats:** 40, Pr/dining room 30 **Children:** Min 8 yrs, Menu, Portions **Rooms:** 30 (30 en suite)★★★ CHH **Directions:** 6m from Builth Wells on A483 from Garth, turn left for Llangammarch Wells & follow signs to hotel **Parking:** 80

LLANWDDYN   MAP 15 SJ01

◉ Lake Vyrnwy Hotel

Modern British

Stunning views and cooking presented to perfection

☎ 01691 870692 Lake Vyrnwy SY10 0LY
e-mail: res@lakevyrnwy.com
web: www.lakevyrnwy.com

Set in 24,000 acres of woodland and moors, this fine country-house hotel stands above Lake Vyrnwy. The accommodation makes the most of the views, not least the conservatory restaurant where the yield of local farms, the lake and game shoots is given pride of place on the menu. Faultless presentations whet the appetite, with options like venison Wellington and roast rack of Lake Vyrnwy lamb following roast breast of pigeon on a salad of Jerusalem artichokes, or pork and hazelnut terrine with tomato chutney. Look out for the malted milk chocolate gâteau.

Chef: David Thompson **Owners:** The Bisiker family **Times:** 12-2/7-9.15, Closed 23-27 Dec & 30 Dec-2 Jan **Prices:** Fixed L £14.50, Fixed D £33.50, Service included **Wine:** 111 bottles over £20, 19 bottles under £20, 9 by the glass **Notes:** Fixed D 5 courses, Sun L 3 courses £21.95, Dress Restrictions, Smart casual preferred, Civ Wed 125 **Seats:** 80, Pr/dining room 120 **Children:** Portions **Rooms:** 38 (38 en suite) ★★★ CHH **Directions:** Follow tourist signs on A495/B4393, 200 yds past dam at Lake Vyrnw **Parking:** 80

Carlton Riverside

LLANWRTYD WELLS MAP 09 SN84

Modern British NEW

AA Restaurant of the Year for Wales

☎ 01591 610248 Irfon Crescent LD5 4SP

e-mail: info@carltonrestaurant.co.uk

web: www.carltonrestaurant.co.uk

Now home to the friendly and enthusiastic Gilchrists (the husband-and-wife team previously at Carlton House), this small, character, three-storey restaurant with rooms is set right beside the river bridge in the centre of town. The stylish, intimate restaurant combines quality contemporary fabrics and furnishings with the charm of the house and river views. It's all very soothing, with comforts provided by high-backed chocolate-brown leather chairs and cream napery, and the diligent and attentive service of Alan Gilchrist.

Wife Mary Ann looks after the cooking, her confident, one-women act undertaken with panache, underlining her obvious passion and talent. Her fixed-price menus (the Chef's Menu a no-choice affair, while the Irfon Menu offers a compact selection) make a virtue of simplicity, the wonderful straightforward approach driven by stunningly fresh, local seasonal produce. It's honest with no gimmicks, and everything is full of flavour and perfectly timed. Take a roast cannon of Irfon Valley lamb served with a courgette, aubergine and tomato timbale, poached asparagus, crushed Jersey Royals and sauce Paloise, and to finish, perhaps a vanilla pannacotta with red-fruit jelly and blueberry and raspberry compôte.

Chef: Mary Ann Gilchrist **Owners:** Alan & Mary Ann Gilchrist **Times:** 7-8.30 (last orders) **Rooms:** 4 (4 en suite) ★★★★ RR **Directions:** Please telephone for details

LLANWRTYD WELLS MAP 09 SN84

◉◉◉ **Carlton Riverside**

see above

◉ **Lasswade Country House Hotel**

Modern British ☺

Pro-organic Edwardian country-house dining

☎ 01591 610515 Station Rd LD5 4RW

e-mail: info@lasswadehotel.co.uk

web: www.lasswadehotel.co.uk

An Edwardian house in an idyllic location with wonderful views from its lounge. The dining room feels like a traditional period home with embossed wallpaper, polished inlaid mahogany tables and elegant chandeliers. There's a great emphasis on organic and quality local produce, like smoked salmon shipped specially by train from the Welsh borders, fish fresh from Milford Haven, or Welsh Black beef reared only a quarter of a mile away. Cooking is simple without any pretension in dishes like poached wing of fresh Milford skate served with Pembrokeshire new potatoes and sauce verde. Finish with a bavarois of dark Belgium chocolate and local honey, with a compôte of gingered pear.

Chef: Roger Stevens **Owners:** Roger & Emma Stevens **Times:** 7.30-9.30, Closed 25 Dec, Closed L all week **Prices:** Fixed D £28-£30, Service optional **Wine:** 2 by the glass **Notes:** Dress Restrictions, Smart casual **Seats:** 20, Pr/dining room 24 **Children:** Portions **Rooms:** 8 (8 en suite) ★★ SHL **Directions:** On A483, follow signs for station, opposite Spar shop, adjacent to tourist info office, 400yds on right before station **Parking:** 6

LLYSWEN MAP 09 SO13

◉◉ **Llangoed Hall**

Traditional British

A classy setting for ambitious cooking

☎ 01874 754525 LD3 0YP

e-mail: enquiries@llangoedhall.co.uk

web: www.llangoedhall.com

A former home to the Laura Ashley family, this majestic Edwardian house has lost none of its grandeur, welcoming guests and diners with a distinctly upmarket décor of luxurious fabrics, duck-egg blue walls and a remarkable collection of paintings. Staff are deservedly proud of the food, and happy to spill the beans on the provenance of local ingredients that are a feature of the appealing menus. Think a rack of Breconshire spring lamb with dauphinoise potato and a tomato and thyme jus, or perhaps wild line-caught sea bass with roasted salsify and vanilla jus, while desserts might feature a blood-red orange tart with mascarpone sorbet. Whatever you choose, expect ambitious and accomplished cuisine.

Times: 12.30-2.30/7-10 **Rooms:** 23 (23 en suite) ★★★★ CHH **Directions:** On A470, 2m from Llyswen towards Builth Wells

MACHYNLLETH
MAP 14 SH70

◉ Wynnstay Hotel

Modern Welsh, Italian NEW

Ancient posting house at the heart of Machynlleth

☎ 01654 702941 Maengwyn St SY20 8AE
e-mail: info@wynnstay-hotel.com
web: www.wynnstay-hotel.com

Originally the townhouse of the Wynnstay Estates, this Georgian inn has been restored to its former glory in recent years. The comfortable, friendly atmosphere comes with a touch of quirky individualism. The restaurant offers an ambitious traditional and modern Welsh menu, with strong Italian influences, every evening using local produce, while bar meals are served at lunchtime and a traditional roast for Sunday lunch. Typical dishes from the evening restaurant menu include mains like Borth crab thermidor, tuna in 'Acqua Pazza' with bread and salad, or strips of Welsh beef fillet with cracked pepper cream. Pineapple triptych and mango salsa might feature among the desserts.

Chef: Gareth Johns, Sabrina Ballarin, Gareth Wyn Jones **Owners:** Charles & Sheila Dark **Times:** 12-2/6.30-9, Closed L 1 Jan **Prices:** Fixed L £10.95, Fixed D £27.50, Starter £3.50-£6.95, Main £10.95-£14.95, Dessert £5.50, Service optional **Wine:** 6 by the glass **Notes:** Dress Restrictions, Smart casual preferred **Seats:** 60 **Children:** Portions **Rooms:** 23 (23 en suite) ★★★ HL **Directions:** Town centre, near Clock. Car park, via Bank Lane to rear **Parking:** 40

MONTGOMERY
MAP 15 SO29

◉ Dragon Hotel

Welsh

Historic inn serving accomplished restaurant and bar food

☎ 01686 668359 & 668287 Market Square SY15 6PA
e-mail: reception@dragonhotel.com
web: www.dragonhotel.com

The nearby castle - destroyed by Cromwell - provided many of the beams and timbers for this black-and-white fronted, 17th-century coaching inn at the heart of town. The homely, traditional décor extends to the cosy beamed restaurant, which has a fireplace converted from an old bread oven. The Welsh cooking - with a nod to the Mediterranean - is via wholesome dishes that make sound use of local produce. Take roast venison with braised red cabbage, polenta and balsamic and shallot gravy, salmon suprême with béarnaise and dill potatoes, or roast sea bass on braised fennel.

Chef: Thomas Fraenzel **Owners:** M & S Michaels **Times:** 12-2/7-9, Closed L all week ex by prior arrangement **Prices:** Fixed L £14.45, Fixed D £22.50, Starter £3.95-£6.25, Main £10.50-£19.50, Dessert £3.25-£3.75, Service optional **Wine:** 7 bottles over £20, 43 bottles under £20, 12 by the glass **Notes:** Sun L 2 courses £12.50, 3 courses £14.45, Vegetarian available **Seats:** 42, Pr/dining room 50 **Children:** Portions **Rooms:** 20 (20 en suite) ★★ HL **Directions:** Behind the town hall **Parking:** 20

RHONDDA CYNON TAFF

MISKIN
MAP 09 ST08

◉ Miskin Manor Country Hotel

Traditional

Enjoyable dining in a traditional manor house

☎ 01443 224204 CF72 8ND
e-mail: info@miskin-manor.co.uk
web: www.miskin-manor.co.uk

Steeped in Welsh history and set in 22 acres of gardens, the original features of this Grade II listed property add much to its charm. The oak-panelled, silver-service restaurant provides a relaxed, romantic setting with lovely garden views, while the kitchen steers a traditional line with occasional modern detours. Great pride is taken in sourcing fresh, seasonal, quality Welsh produce - Pembrokeshire scallop with pan-fried black and white pudding, watercress salad and white truffle oil, or rack of Welsh lamb with parmesan gratin are fine examples of the fare. An undoubted highlight is the vanilla crème brûlée with pear sorbet.

Chef: Mark Beck, Ian Presgrave **Owners:** Mr & Mrs Rosenberg **Times:** 12-2.30/7-10 **Prices:** Fixed L £14.95, Fixed D £18.95, Main £23.50-£28.50, Service added but optional 10% **Wine:** 12 by the glass **Notes:** Sun L 2-3 courses £12.95-£16.95, ALC 3 courses, Vegetarian available, Dress Restrictions, Smart casual, Civ Wed 100 **Seats:** 50, Pr/dining room 20 **Children:** Portions **Rooms:** 43 (43 en suite) ★★★★ CHH **Directions:** 8m W of Cardiff. M4 junct 34, follow hotel signs **Parking:** 200

SWANSEA

LLANRHIDIAN
MAP 08 SS49

◉◉ The Welcome to Town

Traditional French

Country inn serving great local cuisine

☎ 01792 390015 SA3 1EH
web: www.thewelcometotown.co.uk

Sidebar: WALES

LLANRHIDIAN CONTINUED

Set in a rural part of the beautiful Gower peninsula, this 300-year-old whitewashed coaching inn exudes a village-pub feel. Its rich heritage includes being a former courthouse and jail, although you'll get a friendlier welcome these days. Traditional period features have been retained: blackened oak beams, simple whitewashed walls, stone fireplace and a central bar, with wooden tables and chairs, floral seat cushions and white linen continuing the unpretentious theme. The accomplished, skilful kitchen's modern approach - underpinned by classical roots - uses only the best local produce. Try pan-seared scallops with morel mushrooms and asparagus, followed by Gressingham duck breast, horseradish gnocchi and kumquats. Finish with marbled chocolate millefeuille accompanied by cinnamon chocolate mousse and cherry compôte. Good vegetarian options are available.

Chef: Ian Bennett **Owners:** Jay & Ian Bennett **Times:** 12-2/7-9.30, Closed 25-26 Dec, 1 Jan, last 2 wks Feb, 1 wk Oct, Mon **Prices:** Fixed L £15.95-£27, Fixed D £32.50-£45, Service optional **Wine:** 18 bottles over £20, 10 bottles under £20, 6 by the glass **Notes:** Vegetarian available **Seats:** 40 **Children:** Portions **Directions:** 8m from Swansea on B4231. M4 junct 47 towards Gowerton. From Gowerton take B4295 **Parking:** 12

REYNOLDSTON　　　　MAP 08 SS48

◉◉ Fairyhill

Modern British V ✦NOTABLE WINE LIST
Stylish woodland retreat with skilful kitchen

☎ 01792 390139　SA3 1BS
e-mail: postbox@fairyhill.net
web: www.fairyhill.net

Hidden away on the Gower Peninsula (Britain's first designated Area of Outstanding Natural Beauty), this Georgian house hotel with beautiful grounds has been restored with great care. A welcoming entrance hall leads on to a comfortably furnished lounge and to a dining room that extends through two rooms. The large terrace allows diners to enjoy the mild Gower climate. Service is attentive and friendly and the accurate and skilful modern British cooking makes the most of locally-sourced, often organic, ingredients. Take a fillet of Welsh Black beef served with rösti potato, and oxtail and tarragon sauce, or perhaps a suprême of Gressingham duck with pommes Sarladaise and a grape and honey jus.

Chef: Paul Davies, James Lawrence **Owners:** Mr Hetherington, Mr Davies **Times:** 12.30-2/7.30-9, Closed 26 Dec, 1-25 Jan, Closed D Sun (Nov-Mar) **Prices:** Fixed L £15.95, Fixed D £40, Service optional **Wine:** 400 bottles over £20, 50 bottles under £20, 10 by the glass **Notes:** Sun L 3 courses £24.50, Vegetarian menu **Seats:** 60, Pr/dining room 40 **Children:** Min 8 yrs, Portions **Rooms:** 8 (8 en suite)★★★ CHH **Directions:** M4 junct 47, take A483 then A484 to Llanelli, Gower, Gowerton. At Gowerton follow B4295 for approx 10m **Parking:** 45

SWANSEA　　　　MAP 09 SS69

◉◉ Bartrams @ 698

Modern European
Vibrant, modern venue with food to match

☎ 01792 361616　698 Mumbles Rd SA3 4EH
e-mail: info@698.uk.com
web: www.698.uk.com

From the groovy typographics of the frontage - which overlooks Swansea Bay - to the chic, modern interior (high-backed leather chairs, darkwood tables, artfully exposed brick, floor-to-ceiling feature radiators and a glass theatre kitchen), there's a young, funky, happening feel to this contemporary restaurant and coffee shop. Chef Bryony Jones - ex Fairyhill at Reynoldston (see entry) - shows her pedigree here via an appealing modern menu that suits the sophisticated but welcoming, friendly venue. Quality, local free-range and organic produce feature where possible; think a loin of Welsh lamb served with a black olive mash and tomato dressing. Blackboard specials reflect seasonal changes and display the dessert list (a vanilla crème brûlée might head-up the list), while diners can bring their own wine for a small corkage charge.

Times: 12-2.30/6-9, Closed 25 Dec, Mon (Winter), Closed D Sun **Directions:** From Swansea head towards Mumbles, at rdbt head for the pier for 1m, restaurant is on the right

◉ The Dragon Hotel

Modern European NEW
City-centre stylish hotel brasserie

☎ 01792 657100 & 0870 4299 848　The Kingsway Circle SA1 5LS
e-mail: enquiries@dragon-hotel.co.uk
web: www.dragon-hotel.co.uk

This central, independently-owned hotel is very modern and stylish, boasting two restaurants, the busy ground-floor Dragon Brasserie with open-plan kitchen, and the main restaurant for more formal dining. With its floor-to-ceiling windows to enable you to watch the hustle and bustle of the city, the Brasserie offers both fixed-price and carte modern European menus including a variety of interesting dishes featuring local produce. Try a starter like confit of streaky Gloucestershire Old Spot pork with shallot purée and sautéed tiger prawns, followed by local wild sea bass with roasted new potatoes, sautéed spinach and saffron sauce, or perhaps grilled Celtic Pride fillet steak with rösti potatoes, pan-fried duck foie gras and Madeira jus.

Chef: Sam Thomas **Owners:** Dragon Hotel Ltd **Times:** 12-2.30/6-9.30 **Prices:** Fixed L £9.95-£14.95, Fixed D £22.90-£31.85, Starter £4.95-£6.95, Main £12.95-£17.95, Dessert £5, Service optional, Group min 6 service 10% **Wine:** 5 bottles over £20, 24 bottles under £20, 10 by the glass **Notes:** Sun L 3 courses £15, Civ Wed 220, Air con **Seats:** 65 **Children:** Menu **Rooms:** 106 (106 en suite) ★★★★ HL **Directions:** M4 junct 42. At lights (after supermarket) turn right. Turn left into Kings Ln. Hotel is straight ahead **Parking:** 30

WALES

◉◉ The Grand Hotel

British, European 🍷 NOTABLE WINE LIST

Modern cooking and surrounds with excellent flavour combinations

☎ 01792 645898 Ivey Place, High St SA1 1NE
e-mail: info@thegrandhotelswansea.co.uk
web: www.thegrandhotelswansea.co.uk

Located next to the railway station, The Grand Hotel has been a landmark hotel in Swansea since the 1930s. Renovation has restored it to the elegance of its heyday with plenty of glass, stainless steel and, in the main restaurant, wood floors and leather, while high-backed chairs give a thoroughly contemporary spin on the original style of the building. Diners can choose between the Beeches restaurant for fine dining and the Bay bistro for more informal eating. The former is the best showcase for the capabilities of the kitchen here; there's a strong Mediterranean influence in dishes such as duck ravioli in game and redcurrant broth, or wild mushroom and chestnut risotto, although flavours from Britain and the Far East inevitably creep in.

Times: 6.30-9.30, Closed L all week **Rooms:** 31 (31 en suite) ★★★★ HL **Directions:** M4 junct 42, signed City and Train Station. Hotel opposite train station

◉ Hanson at the Chelsea Restaurant

Modern Welsh NEW

Quality cooking in relaxed surroundings

☎ 01792 464068 17 St Mary St SA1 2EA
web: www.chelseacafe.co.uk

Tucked away down a quiet side street, this contemporary restaurant may be a little hard to find, but it's well worth a detour away from the busy St Mary Street area. Set on two floors, with fireplaces and wood-panelled walls, this comfortable, relaxed place is well known for its use of local ingredients and majors on fish, with specials displayed on the chalkboard. Start with seared Cornish scallops on a trio of sauces with cockle and laverbread crumble, or maybe a tian of fresh crab, shrimp and prawns with smoked salmon and cucumber crème fraîche. Follow with Welsh beef fillet glazed with roast cherry tomato and red onion marmalade.

Chef: Mat Hole **Owners:** Mat Hole **Times:** 12-2.30, 7-11.30 Closed Sun-Mon **Seats:** 42

◉ The Restaurant @ Pilot House Wharf

Modern European

Harbourside restaurant with an emphasis on fresh fish

☎ 01792 466200 Pilot House Wharf, Trawler Rd, Swansea Marina SA1 1UN
e-mail: info@therestaurantswansea.co.uk
web: www.therestaurantswansea.co.uk

Fresh local seafood is the draw at this striking, boat-shaped building on the harbourside overlooking the River Tawe. Panoramic views, cream-painted rough-cast plaster walls and modern tables and chairs provide a light, contemporary dining space, where service proves helpful. The location ensures the promise of the freshest fish, displayed on the regularly-changing blackboard specials menu. Meat-

lovers are not forgotten, with perhaps the likes of Welsh Black beef finding its place, but the real emphasis here is fresh fish. Expect an uncomplicated, modern approach as in chargrilled wild sea bass, served with sun-dried tomato couscous and roasted Mediterranean vegetables.

Chef: Craig Gammon **Owners:** Helen Tenant **Times:** 12-2/6.30-9.30, Closed 25-26 Dec, 1 Jan, Sun, Closed L Mon **Prices:** Fixed L £12.95, Starter £4.45-£7.95, Main £10.95-£17.95, Dessert £5.45, Service optional **Wine:** 12 bottles over £20, 20 bottles under £20, 4 by the glass **Seats:** 46 **Children:** Portions **Parking:** 20

VALE OF GLAMORGAN

BARRY   **MAP 09 ST16**

◉ Egerton Grey Country House Hotel

Modern British

True country-house dining in a lovely wooded valley

☎ 01446 711666 Porthkerry, Rhoose CF62 3BZ
e-mail: info@egertongrey.co.uk
web: www.egertongrey.co.uk

This distinguished, grey-stone hotel is a Victorian former rectory where the beautifully restored gardens are a must-see in summer. The main dining room occupies the former billiard room, panelled in antique Cuban mahogany, where chandeliers, fine bone china, crystal, silverware and candlelight provide a feast for the eye. Modern British fare - underpinned by a classical French theme - is the style; think hand-dived scallops with a pea velouté, grilled fillet of turbot served with saffron-scented boulangère potatoes, wilted spinach and a lemon butter sauce, and a passionfruit cheesecake finish.

Times: 12-2.30/5-9.30 **Rooms:** 10 (10 en suite) ★★★ CHH **Directions:** M4 junct 33, follow signs for Airport then Porthkerry, then turn left at hotel sign by thatched cottage

HENSOL   **MAP 09 ST07**

◉ La Cucina at Vale Hotel Golf & Spa Resort

British, Mediterranean

Modern golf restaurant with traditional wood-fired ovens

☎ 01443 667877 CF72 8JY
e-mail: reservations@vale-hotel.com
web: www.vale-hotel.com

Part of the Hensol Castle estate, the restaurant is housed in the golf clubhouse building. It has a stunning setting above the hotel and golf course, surrounded by 600 acres of beautiful countryside. The fresh, polished interior has a vast vaulted wooden ceiling and well-spaced tables. Menus offer a good choice of Mediterranean fare, with the likes of bruschetta, breast of chicken stuffed with spinach, red pepper and ricotta cheese, or pan-roast fillet of salmon with asparagus and watercress sauce. Alternatively choose from one of the grills, or go for an authentic pizza from the wood-fired ovens.

Chef: Jamie Duncan **Owners:** Vale Hotel Ltd **Times:** 12.30-2/6-10, Closed Sun & Winter opening times vary, Closed D Sun **Prices:** Starter £4.50-£8.95, Main £9.95-£17.95, Dessert £4.95, Service optional **Wine:** 24 bottles under £20, 9 by the glass **Notes:** Sun L 1-3 courses £8.95-£15.95, Vegetarian available, Air con **Seats:** 90 **Children:** Menu, Portions **Directions:** M4, 3 mins from junct 34, follow signs for Vale Resort **Parking:** 500

WALES

687

West Arms Hotel

Wrexham LL20 7LD
Tel: 01691 600665 600612
e-mail: gowestarms@aol.com
web: www.thewestarms.co.uk

This 16th-century drover's inn is full of character with lots of exposed beams, polished brass, inglenooks and ornate fireplaces with open fires. The traditional bar with its alluring menu is popular with locals, and shooting parties also like the traditional dining here so booking is advisable. Classically-inspired and well-executed dishes use local and Welsh produce as in a starter of a warm gravad lax, mussel and leek tart or chargrilled vegetable terrine. For mains, try medallions of Welsh beef served on crushed potatoes and wild mushrooms or the panaché of grilled sea bass, red mullet and seared scallops. Maybe finish with lemon posset with sautéed strawberries.

Historic inn with good food in the beautiful Ceiriog Valley

WREXHAM

LLANARMON DYFFRYN CEIRIOG
MAP 15 SJ13

⊛⊛ West Arms Hotel

British, French
Historic inn with fine food in the beautiful Ceiriog Valley

☎ 01691 600665 & 600612   LL20 7LD
e-mail: gowestarms@aol.com
web: www.thewestarms.co.uk

This 16th-century drover's inn is full of character with lots of exposed beams, flagged floors, polished brass, inglenooks and ornate fireplaces with open fires. The traditional bar with its alluring menu is popular with locals, and shooting parties also like the traditional dining here. The restaurant's classic décor continues the theme with tables set with white and burgundy linen, while the kitchen's classically-inspired and well-

executed dishes come with a modern edge and use local and Welsh produce. Think a fillet of local Welsh lamb pan-fried with a rosemary and mint crust and served with dauphinoise potato laced in a Burgundy sauce, and to finish, perhaps a pumpkin pie with Armagnac ice cream.

Chef: Grant Williams   **Owners:** Mr & Mrs Finch & Mr G Williams
Times: 12-2/7-9, Closed L Mon-Sat   **Prices:** Fixed D £32.90, Starter £4.95-£7.95, Main £9.95-£16.95, Dessert £4.95-£5.95, Service added but optional 10%   **Wine:** 11 by the glass   **Notes:** Vegetarian available, Civ Wed 70   **Seats:** 34, Pr/dining room 10   **Children:** Menu, Portions   **Rooms:** 15 (15 en suite) ★★★   HL   **Directions:** Exit A483 (A5) at Chirk (mid-way between Oswestry and Llangollen) and follow signs for Ceiriog Valley (B4500) - 11m   **Parking:** 20   *see advert on this page*

WREXHAM   MAP 15 SJ35

⊛ Kagan's Brasserie

British V
Friendly hotel brasserie in beautiful grounds

☎ 01978 780555   Best Western Cross Lanes Hotel, Cross Lanes, Bangor Rd LL13 0TF
e-mail: guestservices@crosslanes.co.uk
web: www.crosslanes.co.uk

Built as a country house in the late 19th century and a hotel since 1959, this elegant building stands in 6 acres of beautiful grounds. Kagan's is a relaxed and friendly brasserie-style restaurant, with slate and oak floors, rustic tables, log fires in winter and patio dining in summer. The modern British menu draws inspiration from around the globe. Food is simply cooked using fresh local ingredients and might include roast rack of lamb on sweet potato and cabbage mash.

Chef: Philip Riden   **Owners:** Michael Kagan   **Times:** 12-3/6-9.30, Closed D 25-26 Dec   **Prices:** Fixed L £11.95, Fixed D £18.50, Starter £4.50-£7.50, Main £9.95-£17.50, Dessert £4.95-£6.50, Service optional   **Wine:** 34 bottles over £20, 29 bottles under £20, 20 by the glass   **Notes:** Sun D 2 courses £29, incl wine £36, Vegetarian menu, Dress Restrictions, Smart casual, Civ Wed 140   **Seats:** 50, Pr/dining room 60   **Children:** Menu, Portions   **Rooms:** 16 (16 en suite) ★★★   HL   **Directions:** On A525, Wrexham to Whitchurch Rd, between Marchwiel and Bangor-on-Dee   **Parking:** 70

Northern
Ireland

NORTHERN IRELAND CO ANTRIM

BUSHMILLS

⚛ The Distillers Arms

Irish NEW

Traditional-style inn serving hearty Irish food

☎ 028 207 31044
140 Main St BT57 8TR
e-mail: simon@distillersarms.com
web: www.distillersarms.com

The Distillers Arms is one of a number of listed buildings located in the small town of Bushmills, famous for its whiskey distillery. The spacious open-plan restaurant is laid out over two levels and finished with natural stone and a traditional beamed ceiling. In winter there's a real fire, and professional and enthusiastic staff provide relaxed and efficient table service. The style of cooking is primarily traditional Irish, so expect starters like home-cured Irish salmon with wheaten bread and horseradish mayonnaise, or perhaps Dundrum mussels served with a selection of sauces. For mains, take Irish fillet steak served with chunky chips, horseradish butter and tobacco onions.

Chef: Carl Harvey **Owners:** Simon Clarke **Times:** 12.30-3/5.30-9, Closed 25-26 Dec, Mon-Thu in winter **Prices:** Starter £3.50-£7.50, Main £10.95-£20.95, Dessert £3.95, Service optional **Wine:** 10 bottles over £20, 40 bottles under £20, 9 by the glass **Seats:** 85, Pr/dining room 30 **Children:** Menu, Portions **Directions:** On main street, 250mtrs from Old Bushmills Distillery **Parking:** 15

CARNLOUGH MAP 01 D6

⚛ Londonderry Arms Hotel

Modern

Fine dining in genteel hotel

☎ 028 2888 5255 20 Harbour Rd BT44 0EU
e-mail: ida@glensofantrim.com
web: www.glensofantrim.com

Built in the mid-19th century for Lady Londonderry - whose grandson, Winston Churchill, also owned the property at one time - this delightful hotel is set in a pretty fishing village overlooking the Antrim coast. Oak carvings, antique furniture and driftwood sculptures comprise the tasteful décor which combines with original Georgian fittings. The kitchen's modern approach contrasts with its traditional surroundings; expect simple contemporary cooking that makes good use of quality produce from the local larder, such as chargrilled fillet of hake with basil cream tagliatelle and asparagus, or prime sirloin of Irish beef with pink peppercorn sauce and horseradish mash.

Chef: Manus Jamison **Owners:** Frank O'Neill **Times:** 12.30-2.45/7-8.45, Closed 25 Dec, Closed L Mon-Sat **Prices:** Fixed L £19.95, Starter £4.50-£5.95, Main £13.75-£17.95, Dessert £4.75, Service optional **Wine:** 9 bottles over £20, 21 bottles under £20 **Notes:** Fixed L 3 courses, Vegetarian available, Civ Wed 100 **Seats:** 80, Pr/dining room 14 **Children:** Menu, Portions **Rooms:** 35 (35 en suite) ★★★ HL **Directions:** 14m N of Larne on coast road **Parking:** 30

BELFAST MAP 01 D5

⚛⚛ Aldens

Modern

Stylish restaurant serving imaginative food

☎ 028 9065 0079 229 Upper Newtownards Rd BT4 3JF
e-mail: info@aldensrestaurant.com
web: www.aldensrestaurant.com

An attractive suburban restaurant with a stylish interior. The large etched-glass screens, which match the windows, provide intimate areas, and the subtle lighting and quality table settings inspire confidence. Smart, well-informed staff provide excellent service. The modern menu takes in traditional favourites such as Caesar salad (with or without anchovies), or tiger prawns with garlic butter, while other dishes are dictated by the season as in noisettes of venison with parsnip purée and pepper sauce. Vegetarians might like to try twice-baked spinach and parmesan soufflé with chives, or red onion, spinach and ricotta tart with minted new potatoes. More unusual choices are represented by a dessert option of liquorice-scented crème brûlée.

Chef: Denise Hockey **Owners:** Jonathan Davis **Times:** 12-2.30/6-10, Closed 1 wk Jul, BHs, Sun, Closed L Sat **Prices:** Fixed D £18, Starter £4-£10, Main £6-£19, Dessert £4-£6, Service optional, Group min 6 service 10% **Wine:** 100 bottles over £20, 23 bottles under £20, 6 by the glass **Notes:** Vegetarian available **Seats:** 70 **Children:** Portions **Directions:** At x-rds with Sandown Rd **Parking:** On street

⚛ Beatrice Kennedy

Modern International V

Imaginative food in busy townhouse near the university

☎ 028 9020 2290 44 University Rd BT7 1NJ
e-mail: reservations@beatricekennedy.co.uk
web: www.beatricekennedy.co.uk

The interior of this Victorian listed building is decked out in 1940s style with rich, warm colours and lazy colonial ceiling fans, while the sounds of big-band jazz conspire to create a brasserie atmosphere. Leather chairs, white tablecloths, candles and chandeliers add to the intimate mood. Smartly turned-out staff are well informed and friendly. Good value, modern cuisine with a bistro approach is the style. Fresh local ingredients, simply cooked with flair and imagination. Sample dishes start with beetroot-cured salmon with pickled beetroot and dill, followed by Irish rump of lamb with roast garlic mash and ratatouille dressing.

Chef: Jim McCarthy **Owners:** Jim McCarthy **Times:** 12.30-3/5-10.30, Closed 24-26 Dec, 1 Jan, Etr, Mon, Closed L Mon-Sat **Prices:** Fixed L £14-£17.50, Fixed D £30-£35, Starter £4-£8, Main £12-£18, Dessert £4-£5, Group min 6 service 10% **Wine:** 20 bottles over £20, 15 bottles under £20, 4 by the glass **Notes:** Vegetarian menu **Seats:** 75, Pr/dining room 25 **Children:** Menu, Portions **Directions:** Adjacent to Queens University **Parking:** On street

IRELAND

⊛ Cayenne

Modern International

Imaginative food with global influences in innovative, buzzy surroundings

☎ 028 9033 1532 7 Ascot House, Shaftesbury Square BT2 7DB
e-mail: belinda@rankingroup.co.uk
web: www.rankingroup.co.uk

The Rankins' lively, minimalist restaurant is still the place to see and be seen, featuring a vivid colour scheme and innovative, interactive artworks by local-born artist Peter Anderson. Graphic art screened lighting with coordinated music performs alongside smartly uniformed, well-informed staff. There's a sense of theatre about the food, too, with its predominantly oriental twists (plus Pacific, Indian and Mediterranean touches) to well-sourced Irish ingredients. Imaginative cooking, well presented without over embellishment. Start with crispy pork belly and chargrilled squid, followed by Indian spiced lamb shank with curried couscous.

Chef: Paul Rankin **Owners:** Paul & Jeanne Rankin **Times:** 12-2.15/6-late, Closed 25-26 Dec, Etr Mon, May Day BH, 12-13 Jul, Closed L Sat & Sun **Prices:** Fixed L £12, Fixed D £19.50, Starter £4.50-£12, Main £10-£23, Dessert £5.75-£6, Service optional, Group min 6 service 10% **Wine:** 60 bottles over £20, 20 bottles under £20, 15 by the glass **Seats:** 150, Pr/dining room 16 **Children:** Portions **Directions:** Top of Great Victoria St **Parking:** On street, NCP

⊛ The Crescent Townhouse

Modern European

Townhouse brasserie offering creative cuisine

☎ 028 9032 3349 13 Lower Crescent BT7 1NR
e-mail: info@crescenttownhouse.com
web: www.crescenttownhouse.com

Centrally located near the Botanic Gardens and railway station, this Regency townhouse turned boutique hotel with a striking 19th-century façade, offers accomplished, creative cuisine at a wallet-friendly price. Its buzzy and cosmopolitan Metro brasserie has a globetrotting range that sets the best of traditional Irish cooking alongside more modern European ideas. Take roasted local scallops in a ginger crab bisque, or perhaps a dry-aged Irish fillet of beef on crispy potatoes with white wine, tarragon and foie gras butter. Also on the ground floor, the popular Bar Twelve complements proceedings, and comes decked out in colonial style.

Chef: Karl Taylor **Owners:** Wine Inns Ltd **Times:** 12-3/5.45-10, Closed 25-26 Dec, 1 Jan, 11-12 Jul, Closed L Sun **Prices:** Fixed D £16.95, Starter £3.95-£7.25, Main £9-£22, Dessert £4.95, Service optional **Wine:** 11 bottles over £20, 31 bottles under £20, 9 by the glass **Notes:** Vegetarian available, Dress Restrictions, Smart casual, Air con **Seats:** 72, Pr/dining room 35 **Children:** Portions **Rooms:** 17 (17 en suite) ★★★ HL **Directions:** Opposite Botanic Railway Station, on corner of Lower Crescent and Botanic Ave **Parking:** Opposite hotel

⊛⊛⊛⊛ Deanes

see page 692

⊛⊛ Shu

Modern Irish

Chic eatery for fashion-conscious foodies

☎ 028 9038 1655 253 Lisburn Rd BT9 7EN
e-mail: eat@shu-restaurant.com
web: www.shu-restaurant.com

Located in a Georgian area of the town, Shu's classical exterior belies its cool, minimalist, contemporary interior. The restaurant is decked out in warm chocolate browns and beige, with swathes of suede and leather seating, polished, well-spaced tables and wooden floors. Smartly turned-out, well-informed, confident service and a theatre-style, open kitchen give the fashionable package added edge. Shu's up-to-the-minute, lengthy Irish menu - with French influences - perfectly suits the surroundings. Serious cooking, seasonality and the use of quality local produce are key, delivering accurate, carefully presented, eclectic dishes to get the taste buds tingling. Menu samples include Clandeboye wood pigeon with mushrooms, potato fondant, chestnuts and Madeira, or perhaps Glenarm salmon served with Savoy cabbage, pancetta and thyme.

Chef: Brian McCann **Owners:** Alan Reid **Times:** 12-2.30/6-10, Closed 1 Jan, 11-13 Jul, 24-26 Dec, Sun **Prices:** Fixed L £10, Fixed D £25-£27.50, Starter £3.75-£7.25, Main £9.50-£17.50, Dessert £5, Service optional, Group min 6 service 10% **Wine:** 46 bottles over £20, 23 bottles under £20, 16 by the glass **Notes:** Tasting menu £29.50 available Mon-Wed D, Vegetarian available, Air con **Seats:** 76, Pr/dining room 22 **Children:** Portions **Directions:** From city centre take Lisburn road lower end. Restaurant in 1m **Parking:** On street

Ta Tu

☎ 028 9038 0818 701 Lisburn Rd BT9 7GU

Bar/restaurant of fashionable, modish design with global food to match.

Tedfords Restaurant

☎ 028 9043 4000 5 Donegal Quay

Seasonal and local produce with fish as a feature in 19th-century building of rich maritime history.

IRELAND

Deanes

BELFAST MAP 01 D5

Modern Irish

*Exemplary modern cooking from arguably the best
restaurant in Northern Ireland*

☎ 028 9033 1134 & 9056 6000 34/40 Howard St BT1 6PF
e-mail: info@michaeldeane.co.uk
web: www.michaeldeane.co.uk

The recently refurbished Deanes restaurant, now situated in
the larger ground floor of the Howard Street building, is
firmly established as the stylish and contemporary flagship for
the expanding Deanes Restaurant Group.
Situated just round the corner from its sibling Vin Café and
Bistro in Bedford Street, and just half a mile from the vibrant
new Deanes at Queens' bar and grill, it makes it an ideal
location for owner Michael Deane to oversee all three city-
centre operations.
The crisp linen table cloths and designer setting have proved
very popular with the dining elite of Belfast and make early
booking advisable. The open kitchen provides diners with the
theatre of chefs-on-show, though this is a calm and disciplined
brigade, while service is suitably impeccable and
knowledgeable but relaxed.
High-quality, precision cooking and clear flavours showcase
the best of the province's produce; a modern approach of the
refined and confident order. Consistency is key here, there's
nothing too overly faddish either, just quality through and
through. Take dry-aged Fermanagh beef teamed with triple-
cut chips and sauce bordelaise with bone marrow, or perhaps
pan-fried halibut served with a warm terrine of leeks and
langoustines and ginger cream. The carte comes sensibly
compact, while peripherals like breads and petits fours all hit
form, too, as might a hot chocolate pudding dessert served
with Jersey milk ice cream. An excellent wine list, including a
notable list of pudding wines, proves a fitting accompaniment.

Chef: Michael Deane,
Derek Creagh
Owners: Michael Deane,
Derek Creagh
Times: 12.30-3/5.30-10,
Closed 25 Dec, 1 Jan, 12-13
Jul, Closed Sun
Prices: Fixed L/D (5.30-
6.45pm) £15.50-£20.50,
Starter £7-£10, Main £17-
£25, Dessert £7-£8, Service
added but optional 10%,
Wine: 9 bottles over £20,
3 bottles under £20, 10 by
the glass
Seats: 60, Pr/dining room
30-40
Children: Portions
Directions: Located at rear
of city hall. Howard St on
left opposite Spires
building
Parking: On street (after
6pm)

IRELAND

CO DOWN

BANGOR   MAP 01 D5

 Clandeboye Lodge Hotel

Modern

Creative cooking in a contemporary country setting

☎ 028 9185 2500 10 Estate Rd, Clandeboye
BT19 1UR
e-mail: info@clandeboyelodge.co.uk
web: www.clandeboyelodge.com

Just 3 miles west of Bangor, this modern hotel cultivates a country-house ambience and is set beside the 200 acres of woodland, gardens, lawns and lake that make up the Clandeboye Estate. The restaurant is popular for its designer looks - think spiralling chandeliers, wood panelling and marble-topped tables - as well as for its courteous waiting team. A tempting menu features some intriguing combinations: kick off with a carpaccio of pineapple and watermelon with mint and Malibu syrup perhaps, before tucking into calves' liver with pancetta mash and onion marmalade. Presentation is simple and effective.

Chef: Dean Nickells, Ian Lyttle **Owners:** Pim Dalm **Times:** 12/9.30, Closed 25-26 Dec **Prices:** Starter £3.50-£6.75, Main £7.50-£15.50, Dessert £4.25-£4.75, Service optional, Group min 6 service 10% **Wine:** 7 bottles over £20, 24 bottles under £20 **Notes:** Sun L 2 courses £13.95, 3 courses £16.95, Vegetarian available, Dress Restrictions, Smart casual, Civ Wed 250 **Seats:** 60, Pr/dining room 300 **Children:** Menu, Portions **Rooms:** 43 (43 en suite) ★★★★ HL **Directions:** M3 follow signs for A2 (Bangor). Before Bangor turn right at junction signed to Newtownards, Clandeboye Lodge Hotel and Blackwood Golf Course **Parking:** 250

◉◉ **1614**

Modern, Traditional British

Good flavourful dining in atmospheric historic inn

☎ 028 9185 3255 Old Inn, 15 Main St, Crawfordsburn
BT19 1JH
e-mail: info@theoldinn.com
web: www.theoldinn.com

1614 is the fine-dining option in the 17th-century Old Inn. Replete with original chandeliers, oak panelling and local coats of arms, the good-quality soft furnishings, fixtures and fittings throughout complete the picture, helped along by friendly and helpful service from committed staff. Frequently-changing and keenly-priced menus rely on local seasonal ingredients to produce modern dishes

with definite local accents. Start with pan-fried pigeon breast with sautéed greens, ginger and balsamic syrup, or maybe smoked salmon, potato and chive pancake, before tucking into a main course of roast monkfish with asparagus, lobster wanton, chive and lobster velouté. Finish with praline and honeycomb cheesecake with caramel sauce, or a plate of Irish and continental cheeses.

Chef: Alex Taylor **Owners:** Danny Rice **Times:** 12.30-2.30/7-9.30, Closed 25 Dec, Closed L Mon-Sat, D Sun **Prices:** Fixed L £23, Fixed D £23-£30, Service optional **Notes:** Dress Restrictions, Smart casual, Civ Wed 85 **Seats:** 64, Pr/dining room 25 **Children:** Menu, Portions **Rooms:** 30 (30 en suite) ★★★ HL **Directions:** Take A2 E from Belfast. 5-6m turn left at Ballyrobert lights, and 400 yds to Crawfordsburn. Inn is on left **Parking:** 100

DUNDRUM   MAP 01 D5

◉ **Mourne Seafood Bar**

Seafood

Friendly fish restaurant 30 minutes from Belfast

☎ 028 4375 1377 10 Main St BT33 0LU
e-mail: bob@mourneseafood.com
web: www.mourneseafood.com

Situated in a picturesque village at the foot of the Mourne Mountains, this simply presented restaurant with wooden seats, wood flooring and basic table settings has a cracking atmosphere and, as you might expect, a preponderance of premium seafood, with most of the shellfish sourced from their own shellfish beds. There's nothing too complicated on the menu - just high-quality ingredients handled with confidence and care. Meat and poultry dishes make a cameo appearance, but fish-lovers won't want to miss tasty local mussels with pesto, or oysters au naturel. Book in advance.

Chef: Neil Auterson **Owners:** Bob & Joanne McCoubrey **Times:** 12/9.30, Closed 25 Dec, Mon-Tue (winter) **Prices:** Fixed L £7.99, Starter £3.50-£5.95, Main £6.75-£14.95, Dessert £4, Service optional **Wine:** 8 bottles over £20, 8 bottles under £20, 4 by the glass **Seats:** 50, Pr/dining room 16 **Children:** Portions **Directions:** On main road from Belfast to The Mournes, on village main st **Parking:** On street

IRELAND

The Quay's Bar & Restaurant

81 New Harbour Road Portavogie BT22 1EB
Tel: 028 4277 2225   www.quaysrestaurant.co.uk

Situated on the quay side of Portavogie fishing harbour The Quays provides a relaxed and beautiful Mediterranean themed restaurant, boasting freshly caught seafood, childrens and vegetarian dishes along side an extensive main menu and daily specials to suit all tastes. All dishes are cooked to order to maintain maximum flavour.

Opening Times
Monday – Wednesday – Thursday
12 noon until 2.30 p.m. and 5.00 p.m. until 8.30 p.m.
Tuesday closed (excepting public holidays)
Friday 12 noon until 2.30 p.m. and 5.00 p.m. until 9.00 p.m.
Saturday 12 noon until 9.00 p.m. (all day)
Sunday 12 noon until 8.00 p.m. (all day)

PORTAVOGIE   MAP 01 D5

◉ The Quay's Bar & Restaurant

British, International V

Top-quality seafood dining in quayside location

☎ 028 4277 2225 & 4277 1679 81 New Harbour Rd, Portavogie BT22 1EB
e-mail: quays@info.co.uk
web: www.quaysrestaurant.co.uk

This modern building is right on the shore with the sea in front and Portavogie Harbour behind. There's a bar, lounge and split-level restaurant specialising in seafood. Decked out in warm earthy colours, the dining room has wooden tables and comfortable chairs adding to the relaxed atmosphere. But it's the fresh local seafood that attracts the regulars. Start with Portavogie clams cooked in their shells topped with a honey mustard and spring onion sauce, before a main course

of oven-baked hake with a tomato salsa crust. Both simple, both delicious.

Chef: David Cardwell & Aaron Hanna **Owners:** Francis & Diane Adair **Times:** 12-2.30/5-9, Closed 25 Dec, Tue **Prices:** Food prices not confirmed for 2008. Please telephone for details **Wine:** 6 bottles over £20, 23 bottles under £20, 8 by the glass **Notes:** Vegetarian menu **Seats:** 95 **Children:** Menu, Portions **Directions:** Take Portaferry road out of Newtownards and head towards Greyabbey, through Kircubbin and then Portavogie **Parking:** 60

see advert on this page

CO LONDONDERRY

CASTLEDAWSON   MAP 01 C5

◉ The Inn at Castle Dawson

Traditional NEW

Period-house dining with river views

☎ 028 7946 9777 47 Main St BT45 8AA
e-mail: info@theinnatcastledawson.co.uk
web: www.theinnatcastledawson.co.uk

This large period house has undergone major renovation and sits at the heart of the village overlooking gardens and river. The front reception still has the original black-and-white floor tiles, while cosy lounges and a small bar prove ideal for aperitifs. The spacious dining room has a wall of glass to take in those views, double-height ceilings and a working stove as a focal point. The kitchen deals in quality local produce and mainly traditional dishes; take roast turbot served with braised oxtail, wilted spinach, oyster mushrooms and a red wine jus.

Chef: Simon Toye **Owners:** Simon Toye **Times:** 12-2.30/5-10, Closed 26 Dec, 1 Jan, Closed L Sat **Prices:** Fixed D £22.50, Starter £3.50-£4.95, Main £5.50-£17.95, Dessert £3.95-£4.95, Service optional, Group min 8 service 10% **Wine:** 4 bottles over £20, 16 bottles under £20, 4 by the glass **Notes:** Sun L 2 courses £13.50, 3 courses £16.50, Vegetarian available, Air con **Seats:** 80, Pr/dining room 20 **Children:** Menu, Portions **Rooms:** 12 (12 en suite) ★★★★★ GH **Directions:** Castledawson rdbt, from Belfast take 3rd exit, from Londonderry take 1st exit **Parking:** 12

LIMAVADY   MAP 01 C6

◉ The Lime Tree

Traditional Mediterranean

Solid neighbourhood restaurant with welcoming atmosphere

☎ 028 7776 4300 60 Catherine St BT49 9DB
e-mail: info@limetreerest.com
web: www.limetreerest.com

This unassuming restaurant continues to attract regulars who enjoy the consistency of the food and the friendly atmosphere. The Mediterranean menu consists largely of classics with food cooked with skill and sensitivity, and good flavour combinations. Try warm caramelised onion and goat's cheese tart to start, and follow with oven-baked suprême of salmon wrapped in smoked ham with a soya, honey and chilli dressing, or meat-lovers might go for Moroccan beef tagine. Desserts include steamed orange marmalade sponge and custard, or lemon curd cheesecake on a ginger crumb base. Look out for regular theme nights that make forays into international cuisine.

Chef: Stanley Matthews **Owners:** Mr & Mrs S Matthews **Times:** 6-9, Closed 25-26 Dec, Sun-Mon (ex Dec), Closed L all week **Prices:** Fixed D £21.95, Starter £4.25-£8.50, Main £13.50-£19.50, Dessert £5-£7, Service optional **Wine:** 11 bottles over £20, 28 bottles under £20, 5 by the glass **Notes:** Early bird menu Tue-Fri 6-7pm 2-3 courses £12.50-£14.95, Vegetarian available **Seats:** 30 **Children:** Menu, Portions **Directions:** Entering Limavady from the Derry side, the restaurant is on the right on small slip road **Parking:** 15

Radisson SAS Roe Park Resort

Modern V

Comfortable surroundings alongside a golf course

☎ 028 7772 2222 BT49 9LB

e-mail: reservations@radissonroepark.com

web: www.radissonroepark.com

This large golf resort-style hotel has a choice of dining areas. Greens restaurant is made up of two high-ceilinged rooms and offers formal dining, while the Coach House brasserie is a more informal alternative. The modern British menu - with European influences - changes seasonally and delivers straightforward fare. Expect the likes of pan-fried pork wrapped in Parma ham and served with sun-dried tomato, herb orzo and basil cream, or cod cakes with poached egg and béarnaise sauce. Desserts continue the theme - a steamed apple sponge pudding and vanilla ice cream, or After Eight crème brûlée might catch the eye.

Chef: Adrian McDaid **Owners:** Mr Conn, Mr McKeever, Mr Wilton **Times:** 12-3/6.30-10, Closed Tue-Thu in Jan, Mon, Closed L Tue-Sat, D Sun **Prices:** Fixed D £21.95, Starter £3.95-£6.25, Main £10.25-£15.50, Dessert £6.95, Service optional **Wine:** 8 bottles over £20, 23 bottles under £20, 8 by the glass **Notes:** Sun L carvery, Vegetarian menu, Dress Restrictions, Smart casual, Civ Wed 250, Air con **Seats:** 160, Pr/dining room 50 **Children:** Menu, Portions **Rooms:** 118 (118 en suite) ★★★★ HL **Directions:** On A6 (Londonderry-Limavady road), 0.5m from Limavady. 8m from Derry airport **Parking:** 250

LONDONDERRY   MAP 01 C5

Beech Hill Country House Hotel

Modern, Traditional

Elegant country house serving stylish food

☎ 028 7134 9279 32 Ardmore Rd BT47 3QP

e-mail: info@beech-hill.com

web: www.beech-hill.com

The impressive 18th-century manor house stands in 32 acres of glorious woodlands and gardens. Traditionally-styled day rooms are smartly decorated, and the dining room extends into a conservatory to make the most of the lovely view. Skilfully-cooked dishes give a modern slant to a traditional country-house style. Only carefully-sourced Irish ingredients are used, demonstrated to good effect in a risotto of Mulroy Bay mussels, chorizo and garlic peas with seared Rathmullan hand-dived scallops, or a duo of Finneborough new season Oisin venison with confit of cabbage and bacon.

Chef: Raymond Moran/Paul Curry **Owners:** Mr S Donnelly, Mrs P O'Kane **Times:** 12-2.30/6-9.45, Closed 24-25 Dec **Prices:** Fixed L £15.95, Fixed D £27.95, Starter £5.95-£10, Main £15.95-£21.95, Dessert £5.95, Service optional **Notes:** Vegetarian available, Civ Wed 80 **Seats:** 90, Pr/dining room 80 **Children:** Portions **Rooms:** 27 (27 en suite) ★★★ HL **Directions:** A6 Londonderry to Belfast road, turn off at Faughan Bridge. 1m further to Ardmore Chapel. Hotel entrance is opposite **Parking:** 50

Tower Hotel Derry

Modern Mediterranean

Bistro-style restaurant within the city walls

☎ 028 7137 1000 Off the Diamond, Butcher St BT48 6HL

e-mail: reservations@thd.ie

web: www.towerhotelderry.com

Right in the centre of the city, the Tower is the only hotel within the historic Derry walls, with fantastic views from the restaurant. The bistro is a bright, relaxing space, open-plan with the Lime Tree bar, which is ideal for pre-dinner drinks, and an increasingly popular venue with the local community. The modern dishes are a fusion of local and international ideas.

Times: 12.30-2.30/6-9.45, Closed Xmas, Closed L (booking required) **Rooms:** 93 (93 en suite) ★★★★ HL **Directions:** From Craigavon Ridge to city centre. Take 2nd exit at the end of bridge into Carlisle Rd then to Ferryquay St

MAGHERA   MAP 01 C5

Ardtara Country House

Modern International

Modern fusion cuisine in a country-house setting

☎ 028 7964 4490 8 Gorteade Rd BT46 5SA

e-mail: valerie_ferson@ardtara.com

web: www.ardtara.com

Originally built in 1896 as the Clark Linen Factory, the building was renovated as a family home and now has all the appearances of a traditional country-house hotel. Appearances can be deceptive however, and the classic décor of the dining room conceals some funky modern fusion cooking making an impact on the menu. Dishes might include a starter of cod with spicy ricotta and baby spinach millefeuille and yellow Kashmir curry sauce. A more traditional main course would be roast sirloin of McKees beef served with baked potato, Yorkshire pudding, wild mushrooms and red wine gravy. For an exotic dessert, try Guanaja dark crunchy chocolate with butterscotch sauce and crème Chantilly.

Times: 12.30-2.30/6.30-9 **Rooms:** 9 (9 en suite) ★★ HL **Directions:** Take A29 to Maghera/Coleraine. Follow B75 (Kilrea) to Upperlands. Past sign for W Clark & Sons, next left

IRELAND

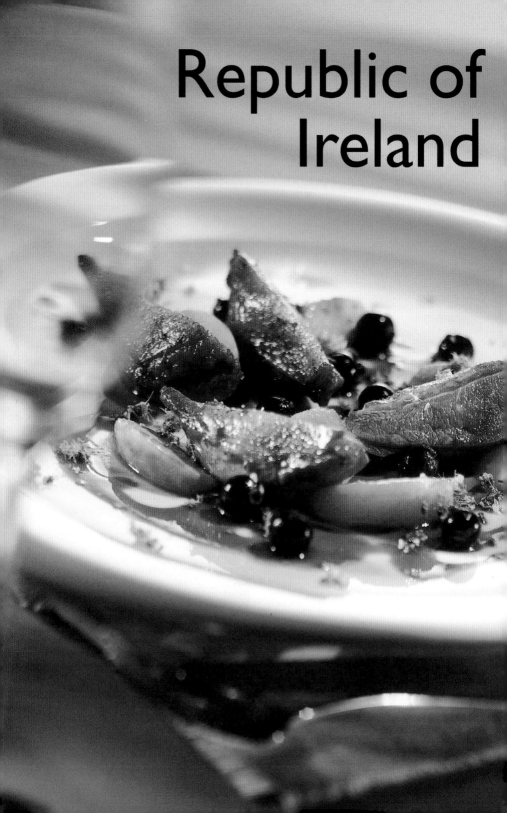

Republic of
Ireland

REPUBLIC OF IRELAND
CO CAVAN

Telephone numbers are for dialling within the ROI. If phoning from outside the ROI, please dial 00353, then drop the first '0' of the code.

BALLYCONNELL   MAP 01 C5

Slieve Russell Hotel Golf & Country Club

Modern European
Enormous hotel with a solid reputation for fine dining

☎ 049 9526 444
e-mail: slieve-russell@quinn-hotels.com
web: www.quinnhotels.com

This vast, luxurious hotel is set in over 300 acres of grounds with lakes, a popular golf course and a health spa with a wide range of pampering facilities. There are two restaurants to choose from: the Setanta with a modern European bias, and the Conall Cearnach for fine dining. Overlooking the beautifully landscaped gardens, the latter offers impressive cooking with a strong emphasis on luxury ingredients - try Mediterranean fish soup, followed by a main course of prime Irish fillet steak with leek rösti, green peppercorns and pine kernel jus.

Chef: Peter Denny **Owners:** Sean Quinn **Times:** 12.30-2.15/7-9.15, Closed L Mon-Sat **Prices:** Fixed L €27.50, Fixed D €38, Service optional **Wine:** 36 bottles over €30, 16 bottles under €30 **Notes:** Fixed L 3 courses, Vegetarian available **Seats:** 180, Pr/dining room 46 **Children:** Menu, Portions **Rooms:** 219 (219 en suite) ★★★★ HL **Directions:** From Dublin take N3 towards Cavan. At rdbt before Cavan, follow Enniskillen sign to Belturbet. From Belturbet go towards Ballyconnell. Hotel approx 6m from Belturbet on left **Parking:** 360

CAVAN   MAP 01 C4

Cavan Crystal Hotel

Modern
Innovative cooking in contemporary hotel

☎ 049 436 0600 Dublin Rd
e-mail: info@cavancrystalhotel.com
web: www.cavancrystalhotel.com

Contemporary design, matched by the use of native timber, handcrafted brick and crystal chandeliers, make this a particularly distinctive new hotel. The modern dining room is on the first floor, backed by a friendly team of professionals. There's a health and beauty clinic here, and the Cavan Crystal shop and factory are on the same site. The cuisine is innovative in style and presentation, the cooking confident and using fine-quality local ingredients with integrity and some unusual twists. Accuracy, flavour balance and texture contrast all hit the right note in dishes such as a roulade of chicken with Wensleydale cheese and Parma ham stuffing, or perhaps a lavender and honey parfait served with a berry madeleine and raspberry sorbet.

Chef: Dave Fitzgibbon **Owners:** McKenna & Quinn Partnership **Times:** 12.30-3.30/6-10, Closed 24-25 Dec **Prices:** Fixed L €15-€18, Fixed D €30-€40, Starter €4.50-€11, Main €19.20-€25, Dessert €6-€8, Service optional **Wine:** 24 bottles over €30, 26 bottles under €30, 4 by the glass **Notes:** Sun L €25, Air con **Seats:** 95 **Children:** Menu, Portions **Rooms:** 85 (85 en suite) ★★★★ HL **Directions:** Approach Cavan on N3, straight over rdbt, hotel immediately on left **Parking:** 192

VIRGINIA   MAP 01 C4

The Park Manor House Hotel

European, International
Fresh produce in former hunting lodge

☎ 049 8546100 Virginia Park
e-mail: reservations@parkhotelvirginia.com
web: www.parkhotelvirginia.com

This imposing 18th-century hunting lodge was the country estate and sporting lodge of the Marquis of Headfort (1750-1939). It enjoys a superb location in 100 acres with mature gardens and woodland. The architecturally renowned restaurants are named the Marquis and Marchionness dining rooms and here you can sample some classic cuisine with a global influence. The chef makes excellent use of local produce and fruit, vegetables and herbs from the estate's organic gardens. Try main courses like roast duckling with blackcurrant and beet jus or baked salmon with dill champ.

Chef: Sudath Peiris **Owners:** Baltimore International College **Times:** 12.30-3.30/6.30-9.30, Closed Jan, Xmas, Closed L Mon-Sat **Prices:** Fixed L €15-€20, Starter €6.50-€8.50, Main €19.50-€29, Dessert €6.50-€7.50, Service optional **Wine:** 7 bottles over €30, 19 bottles under €30 **Notes:** Vegetarian available, Dress Restrictions, Smart casual **Seats:** 45, Pr/dining room 35 **Children:** Min 12 yrs, Menu, Portions **Rooms:** 26 (26 en suite) ★★★ HL **Directions:** Follow N3 to Virginia and when in village take first left. Hotel entrance 500 yds on left **Parking:** 160

CO CLARE

BALLYVAUGHAN   MAP 01 B3

Gregans Castle

Modern French, Irish
Country-house hotel dining with splendid views of The Burren

☎ 065 7077005
e-mail: res@gregans.ie
web: www.gregans.ie

With magnificent mountain views over the unique landscape of The Burren towards Galway Bay, the appropriately austere exterior of this family-run 18th-century country house belies the comfort and style to be found within. Elegant public rooms are furnished with beautiful antiques, and window tables in the restaurant make the most of the view across the bay. Skilful cooking shows enthusiasm and good use of high-quality local and organic produce, notably lamb from the village butcher. A typical meal may feature a main of roast loin of Irish pork with mustard and herb pommade served with ravioli of pork, redcurrant jus and apple crisp. Staff are renowned for their personal service.

Times: 7-8.30, Closed 15 Oct-5 Apr 07, Closed L all week **Rooms:** 21 (21 en suite)★★★ CHH **Directions:** On N67, 3.5m S of Ballyvaughan

ENNIS	MAP 01 B3

⚜ Temple Gate

Irish, International

Modern dining in a Gothic-style building

☎ 065 682 3300 The Square
e-mail: info@templegatehotel.com
web: www.templegatehotel.com

Originally a 19th-century convent, the hotel retains much of its original Gothic style, but in a contemporary context. JM's Bistro provides a relaxed, elegant setting, with high ceilings, warm rose-coloured décor, and crisply-clothed tables. A lengthy menu of predominantly traditional Irish dishes with an international twist takes in starters like pan-fried fishcake of monkfish, cod, prawns and crabmeat, infused with chillies, spring onion and coriander and served with a sweet dipping sauce, while mains might feature chargrilled salmon darne on truffled French beans, sweet lemon and flaky crabmeat velouté. The Great Hall, once the convent's church, makes a fabulous setting for weddings and banquets.

Chef: Paul Shortt **Owners:** John Madden **Times:** 12.45-2.30/7-9.45, Closed 25-27 Dec, Good Fri, Closed L Request only Mon-Sat **Prices:** Fixed L €16.95-€25, Fixed D €30-€35, Starter €6-€9, Main €18-€28, Dessert €6-€8, Service optional **Wine:** 2 bottles over €30, 15 bottles under €30, 4 by the glass **Notes:** Sun L €19.50-€21.50, Vegetarian available, Civ Wed 150 **Seats:** 90, Pr/dining room 150 **Children:** Menu, Portions **Rooms:** 70 (70 en suite) ★★★ HL **Directions:** Follow signs for the Tourist Office, hotel is in same square **Parking:** 100

LISDOONVARNA	MAP 01 B3

⚜⚜ Sheedy's Country House Hotel

Modern Irish

Pleasant country-house cooking of the classic and modern variety

☎ 065 707 4026
e-mail: info@sheedys.com
web: www.sheedys.com

Owned by the Sheedy family since the 18th century, this former farmhouse exudes character and has a fabulous location on the edge of The Burren. Close to Lahinch golf course, Doolin and the Cliffs of Moher, it's an ideal base for touring the region. Food is strong on classic dishes with some modern influences and if some don't feature home-grown vegetables and herbs, you can be sure the produce was locally sourced. You could start with Carrigholt crab claws served in a garlic, ginger and chilli butter sauce, and follow with braised Irish lamb shank with pea purée, pearl onions and smoked bacon. Finish with a favourite: sticky toffee pudding.

Chef: John Sheedy **Owners:** John & Martina Sheedy **Times:** 6.45-8.30, Closed mid Oct-mid Mar, 1 day a week Mar-Apr **Prices:** Starter €5.50-€14.50, Main €21.50-€28, Dessert €7.80-€9, Service optional **Wine:** 11 bottles over €30, 15 bottles under €30, 2 by the glass **Notes:** Vegetarian available, Air con **Seats:** 28 **Children:** Min 8 yrs, Portions **Rooms:** 11 (11 en suite) ★★★ HL **Directions:** 20m from Ennis on N87 **Parking:** 25

NEWMARKET-ON-FERGUS	MAP 01 B3

⚜⚜ Dromoland Castle

Traditional Irish, European V

Elegant dining in historic castle

☎ 061 368144
e-mail: sales@dromoland.ie
web: www.dromoland.ie

An imposing castle turned luxury hotel, this Renaissance building is set in a 375-acre estate and is steeped in history, dating back to the 16th century. The magnificent public rooms are warmed by log fires, while the atmosphere in the elegant, fine-dining restaurant - with its Venetian silk wall hangings, crystal chandeliers and Irish linen is enhanced by the soothing cords of the resident harpist. An attentive waiting team ushers guests to their seats and an extensive menu of classic European and traditional Irish cuisine. Expect ambitious cooking from a skilful kitchen: a mosaic terrine of duck, rabbit and wild mushrooms perhaps, wrapped in cured ham and served with beetroot purée and Cassis dressing, or pot-roasted pheasant from the estate, with a pumpkin and lentil ragout and green peppercorn sauce. Vegetarian menu available.

Chef: David McCann **Owners:** Earl of Thomond **Times:** 12.30-1.30/7-10, Closed 25-27 Dec, 24 Dec, Closed L Mon-Sat **Prices:** Fixed L €45-€47, Fixed D €65, Starter €16-€25, Main €31-€40, Dessert €12-€16, Service added but optional 15% **Notes:** Fixed L 3 courses, Fixed D 4 courses, Vegetarian menu, Dress Restrictions, Jacket **Seats:** 80, Pr/dining room 40 **Children:** Menu, Portions **Rooms:** 99 (99 en suite)★★★★★ HL **Directions:** From Ennis take N18, follow signs for Shannon/Limerick. 7m follow Quin. Newmarket-on-Fergus sign. Hotel 0.5m. From Shannon take N18 towards Ennis **Parking:** 140

CO CORK

BALLYCOTTON	MAP 01 C2

⚜⚜ Bay View Hotel

Modern Irish, French

Accomplished cuisine in comfortable country house with dramatic views

☎ 021 464 6746
e-mail: res@thebayviewhotel.com
web: www.thebayviewhotel.com

The name of this country-house hotel doesn't do justice to its breathtaking coastline views, perched on a hillside near the fishing village of Ballycotton. The garden and bay views prove an irresistible

IRELAND

dining-room drawcard, and, given the location, it's unsurprising that local seafood is a speciality here, though it doesn't monopolise the repertoire. The kitchen's modern Irish approach - underpinned by a classic French theme - also makes fine use of local meats and produce, with all suppliers admirably listed on the menu. Skill, creativity, flavour and dramatic presentation parade on a balanced, well-executed repertoire; think pan-fried fillet of turbot served with saffron potato, asparagus spears, confit of vine cherry tomato and an olive oil and lemon dressing, and perhaps a trio of brûlées to finish.

Chef: Ciaran Scully **Owners:** John & Carmel O'Brian **Times:** 1-2/7-9, Closed Nov-Apr, Closed L Mon-Sat **Prices:** Fixed D €48-€52, Starter €10.50-€13, Main €28-€33, Dessert €9-€10.50, Service optional **Wine:** 6 bottles over €30 **Notes:** Dress Restrictions, Smart casual **Seats:** 65, Pr/dining room 30 **Children:** Portions **Rooms:** 35 (35 en suite)★★★ HL **Directions:** At Castlemartyr on N25 (Cork-Waterford road) turn onto R632 to Garryvoe, then follow signs for Shanagarry & Ballycotton **Parking:** 40

BALLYLICKEY   MAP 01 B2

◉◉ Sea View House

Traditional
Impressive Irish cooking in a delightful country house

☎ 027 50073 & 50462
e-mail: info@seaviewhousehotel.com
web: www.seaviewhousehotel.com

Secluded in colourful gardens close to Ballylickey Bridge, with views of Bantry Bay and the mountains beyond, this friendly, immaculately maintained hotel has earned a reputation for consistently high standards over many years. Several rooms, decorated in warm tones of green, and a delightful garden room make up the dining area, which is elegantly furnished with antiques and fresh flowers. Cooking is country-house style and shows skill, enthusiasm and sound use of top-quality local produce, with fresh fish a feature on the daily fixed-price dinner menu. Examples include fresh Bantry Bay crab salad with Marie Rose sauce, and meatier options such as roasted stuffed duckling with port and orange sauce.

Chef: Eleanor O'Donavon **Owners:** Kathleen O'Sullivan **Times:** 12.30-1.45/7-9.30, Closed Nov-Mar, Closed L Mon-Sat **Prices:** Fixed L €20-€30, Fixed D €35-€45, Starter €5-€7.50, Main €20-€30, Dessert €7.50, Service included, Group min 10 service 10% **Notes:** Vegetarian available, Dress Restrictions, Smart casual **Seats:** 50 **Children:** Menu, Portions **Rooms:** 25 (25 en suite)★★★ HL **Directions:** 3m N of Bantry towards Glengarriff, 70yds off main road, N71

BALTIMORE   MAP 01 B1

◉ Baltimore Harbour Hotel

Classic
Harbourside hotel offering enjoyable food

☎ 028 20361
e-mail: info@bhrhotel.ie

This quaint, very traditional seaside hotel in a pretty fishing village has been a fixture in the area for many years. The views across Baltimore harbour and the coastal islands are magnificent and there can be few better places to have a window table at sunset than the Clipper restaurant - the adjoining Chartroom Bar is good for a music session, too. The menu features good-quality West Cork produce and locally-landed seafood: hearty, moreish food to satisfy all comers - crab claw with citrus dressing to start for example, followed by a main course of seared tuna steak on a bed of squid ink tagliatelle and tomato herb sauce.

Times: 6.30-9.30, Closed Xmas & wkdays Nov-Mar **Rooms:** 64 (64 en suite) ★★★ HL

◉ Casey's of Baltimore Hotel

Traditional, Seafood
Enjoy fresh fish, coastal views and a warm welcome

☎ 028 20197
e-mail: info@caseysofbaltimore.com
web: www.caseysbaltimore.com

A simply-styled hotel on the outskirts of town, where the restaurant overlooks the beautiful bay offering wonderful views. A promising setting - decked out with traditional pine furniture - to enjoy the freshest of fish caught by the owner's own trawler, including mussels from his own mussel beds. In addition to this fantastic sea harvest, fresh produce includes locally-sourced vegetables and traceable meats. The restaurant menu is a fish lover's delight, with the likes of seafood platters or perhaps cod served with caper butter, stir-fried vegetables and croquette potatoes, while homely desserts - like chocolate fudge cake - provide the finale. Interesting, healthy children's menu available.

Chef: Victoria Gilshenan **Owners:** Ann & Michael Casey **Times:** 12.30-2.30/6.30-9, Closed 21-26 Dec **Prices:** Fixed L €30, Fixed D €40, Starter €8-€15, Main €18-€45, Dessert €6, Service optional **Wine:** 4 bottles over €30, 17 bottles under €30, 2 by the glass **Notes:** Fixed L 3 courses, Sun L menu available, Vegetarian available, Air con **Seats:** 100 **Children:** Menu, Portions **Rooms:** 14 (14 en suite) ★★★ HL **Directions:** From Cork take N71 to Skibbereen, then take R595. Hotel is at entrance to village on right **Parking:** 50

CLONAKILTY — MAP 01 B2

◎◎ Inchydoney Island Lodge & Spa

Modern French

Fresh West Cork food in a glorious coastal setting

☎ 023 33143
e-mail: reservations@inchydoneyisland.com
web: www.inchydoneyisland.com

Set astride two beautiful blue-flag beaches, the building enjoys panoramic views of the Atlantic Ocean from every window. There's designer furniture in the reception, a plethora of paintings for sale, and a restaurant with a contemporary look and stunning sea views. French and Mediterranean influences are evident in the menu, with fresh seafood and local organic produce used where possible, in dishes of roast rabbit loin wrapped in Parma ham with buttered linguini and vermouth cream, or pan-fried fillet of turbot on parsnip mash with orange and star anise cream. Vegetarian and various healthy options are also available, such as spinach and feta cheese parcel with oriental vegetables, basil oil and balsamic essence.

Chef: Adam Metcalf **Owners:** Des O'Dowd **Times:** 12-9/6.30-9.45, Closed 24-26 Dec, Closed L all week **Prices:** Fixed D €60, Starter €12, Main €35, Dessert €10, Service included **Notes:** Fixed D 4 courses, Dress Restrictions, Smart casual, Air con **Seats:** 90, Pr/dining room 250 **Children:** Menu, Portions **Rooms:** 67 (67 en suite) ★★★★ HL **Directions:** From Cork take N71 following West Cork signs. Through Innishannon, Bandon & Clonakilty, then follow signs for Inchydoney Island **Parking:** 250

CORK — MAP 01 B2

◎ Hayfield Manor

French, European

Simple modern cuisine in chic surroundings

☎ 021 484 5900 Perrott Av, College Rd
e-mail: reservations@hayfieldmanor.ie
web: www.hayfieldmanor.ie

Once home to the Musgrave family of Cork, the house was architect-designed with classically styled rooms and is set in secluded grounds. Period features like the original fireplaces, pillars, high ceilings and cornicing remain, alongside contemporary additions. There are two dining options: the modern glass-walled Perrotts restaurant serving an informal menu, and the more formal and elegant Orchids restaurant. Here you will find French and European dishes with a cosmopolitan feel in a room overlooking a classical garden. Simple, stylish food makes the best of the freshest Irish produce using traditional techniques; think John Dory served with tomato risotto, baby carrots, asparagus and a cep foam.

Chef: Graeme Campbell **Owners:** Mr J Scally **Times:** 12.30-2/7-10, Closed D Sun **Prices:** Fixed D €55, Starter €7-€12, Main €28-€40, Dessert €10-€12, Group min 8 service 10% **Wine:** 170 bottles over €30, 2 bottles under €30, 14 by the glass **Seats:** 80, Pr/dining room 32 **Children:** Menu, Portions **Rooms:** 88 (88 en suite)★★★★ HL **Directions:** From Cork take N22 to Killarney. On Western Rd at University gates turn left into Donovan's Rd, then right into College Rd and immediately left into Perrott Ave **Parking:** 100

◎ Maryborough Hotel & Spa

Modern European

Wide-ranging menu in a popular hotel restaurant

☎ 021 436 5555 Maryborough Hill
e-mail: info@maryborough.ie
web: www.maryborough.com

Located just outside Cork, this 18th-century country house offers a wide-ranging menu designed to suit most tastes and is popular with both locals and business travellers as a result. The split-level dining room has a contemporary feel and boasts its own walk-in wine cellar. Simpler dishes are very successful: mains such as rack of lamb with dauphinoise potato and honey-roast carrots for example, or lemon sole with shrimps, button mushrooms and a shellfish sauce. Round things off with rhubarb crème brûlée with a crystallised ginger shortbread, or vanilla pannacotta with mixed fruit compôte.

Chef: Gerry Allen **Owners:** Dan O'Sullivan **Times:** 12.30-2.30/6.30-10, Closed 24-26 Dec **Prices:** Fixed L €20-€22, Starter €6.90-€13.20, Main €26-€30, Dessert €7.50-€8.50, Service included, Group min 10 service 10% **Wine:** 44 bottles over €30, 11 bottles under €30, 4 by the glass **Notes:** Dress Restrictions, Smart casual, Civ Wed 100, Air con **Seats:** 120, Pr/dining room 60 **Children:** Min 10 yrs D, Menu, Portions **Rooms:** 93 (93 en suite) ★★★★ HL **Directions:** Telephone for directions **Parking:** 300

Jacobs

☎ 021 425 1530 30a South Mall

Skill, creativity and top-notch ingredients in an easygoing setting.

Jacques

☎ 021 427 7387 Phoenix St

Mediterranean-style décor and food, with friendly service.

GARRYVOE — MAP 01 C2

◎ Garryvoe Hotel

Modern Irish

Sea views and simply-prepared fresh local food

☎ 021 464 6718 Ballycotton Bay, Castlemartyr
e-mail: res@garryvoehotel.com
web: www.garryvoehotel.com

Redeveloped hotel standing in a seaside location with great views over Ballycotton Bay and a beautiful beach. The modern interior design extends to the restaurant with its classic look, where the choice of menus includes a bar-food option, fixed-priced dinner, carte selection and daily specials - with a strong emphasis on local produce, especially the catch from the nearby pier. Straightforward, modern Irish dishes are the forte; take golden-fried fillets of Ballycotton plaice, or roast duckling served with an orange and sage sauce, while to finish, perhaps a chocolate pudding with mixed fruit coulis.

Chef: Kevin O'Sullivan **Owners:** Carmel & John O'Brian **Times:** 1-2.30/6.45-8.45, Closed 24-25 Dec **Prices:** Fixed D €40-€44, Starter €7-€9, Main €23-€30, Dessert €7-€9.50, Service optional **Wine:** 6 by the glass **Seats:** 80, Pr/dining room 40 **Children:** Menu, Portions **Rooms:** 48 (48 en suite) ★★★ HL **Directions:** From N25 at Castlemartyr (Cork-Rosslare road) take R632 to Garryvoe **Parking:** 80

GOUGANE BARRA
MAP 01 B2

◉ Gougane Barra Hotel

Irish, French NEW

Fresh local produce in a stunning lakeside setting

☎ 026 47069
e-mail: gouganebarrahotel@eircom.net
web: www.gouganebarrahotel.com

Overlooking lakes on the edge of the National Park, this recently refurbished, traditionally-styled hotel restaurant enjoys a beautiful and peaceful setting. Service is friendly and professional, delivering a menu focused on seasonal and local produce. Starters might include succulent mussels, freshly harvested from Bantry Bay, in a reduction of white wine, with sliced wild and cultivated mushrooms and a dash of cream. Main courses feature the likes of delicious fresh lemon sole, while seasonal berries might feature in enticing desserts.

Chef: Katy Lucey **Owners:** Neil & Katy Lucey **Times:** 12.30-2.30/5.30-8.45, Closed 18 Oct-10 Apr, Closed L Mon-Sat **Prices:** Fixed L €26-€28, Fixed D €39-€41, Starter €7.50-€8.50, Main €20-€22, Dessert €5.50-€6.50, Service optional **Wine:** 10 bottles over €30, 44 bottles under €30, 6 by the glass **Notes:** Fixed L 3 courses, Fixed D 4 courses, Vegetarian available **Seats:** 70 **Children:** Menu, Portions **Rooms:** 26 (26 en suite) ★★★ HL **Directions:** Located off R584 between N22 at Muiroom and N71 at Bantry. Take the Keimaneigh junct for hotel **Parking:** 40

KINSALE
MAP 01 B2

◉ Actons Hotel

European

Georgian townhouse hotel on the waterfront

☎ 021 4772135 Pier Rd
e-mail: info@actonshotelkinsale.com
web: www.actonshotelkinsale.com

Occupying several Georgian townhouses on the waterfront, this established modern hotel overlooks Kinsale's bustling harbour. Drinks and light meals are served in the bar and adjacent garden in fine weather, while more formal fare is available in the Captain's Table restaurant - a bright, contemporary, nautically-themed room with polished tables and crisp linen. A lengthy European and modern Irish menu offers plenty of choice, including steaks as well as more elaborate dishes. Unsurprisingly, seafood is a speciality.

Times: 12.30-3/7-9.30, Closed Xmas & Jan, Closed L Mon-Sat **Rooms:** 76 (76 en suite) ★★★ HL

Longueville House

MALLOW
MAP 01 B2

Modern French V

Classical cooking in splendid Georgian manor house

☎ 022 47156 & 47306
e-mail: info@longuevillehouse.ie
web: www.longuevillehouse.ie

Set in its 500-acre estate in the heart of the Blackwater Valley, this Georgian manor house oozes period charm. Open fires, antique mirrors and glittering chandeliers evoke a bygone age of gracious living, with dinner served in the timeless elegance of the Presidents' restaurant under the gaze of former Irish presidents, the renovated Victorian Turner Conservatory, where white drapes and candlelight lend a touch of romance, or in The Library.
Chef-proprietor William O'Callaghan overseas the kitchen, his menu reflecting the top-quality produce supplied almost entirely by the estate; seasonal vegetables, fruit and herbs from the walled garden, free-range eggs from their own hens and ducks, fresh river salmon, lamb and pork from the farm. The cooking is underpinned by classical French themes, with flavourful dishes displaying high skill, balance, and plenty of enthusiasm. There might be escalope of halibut with rosemary-scented polenta and pearl onion sauce, or wild mallard duck with Jerusalem artichoke mousse and wild sloe sauce, with

caramelised apple tarte Tatin and Longueville apple brandy ice cream to finish. Peripherals like canapés, breads and petits fours hold style through to the end.

Chef: William O'Callaghan **Owners:** O'Callaghan Family **Times:** 12.30-5/6.30-9, Closed 8 Jan-17 Mar, Mon-Tue (Nov-early Dec) **Prices:** Fixed L €35-€50, Fixed D €60-€95, Service optional, Group min 8 service 10% **Wine:** 100 bottles over €30, 6 bottles under €30, 2 by the glass **Notes:** Vegetarian menu, Dress Restrictions, Smart casual **Seats:** 100, Pr/dining room 16 **Children:** Menu, Portions **Rooms:** 20 (20 en suite)★★★ CHH **Directions:** 3m W of Mallow via N72 to Killarney, right at Ballyclough junct, hotel 200 yds on left **Parking:** 35

IRELAND

KINSALE CONTINUED

Trident Hotel

Modern, Traditional European

Waterfront hotel with harbour views

☎ 021 477 9300 Worlds End
e-mail: info@tridenthotel.com
web: www.tridenthotel.com

The hotel enjoys a wonderful location on the waterfront in historic Kinsale. The Wharf Tavern is a lively bar, popular for its daily carvery lunch and evening bistro-style menu, an alternative to the award-winning Savannah Waterfront restaurant. Here you can expect to find European-style cooking, with a modern twist on traditional dishes. Starters like carpaccio of Serrano ham with exotic fruits, or local seafood chowder might be followed by roast pavé of sea trout with a spinach and saffron cream, or pan-fried sea bass with ratatouille salsa. Desserts are worth waiting for - try warm rhubarb fool. Vegetarians have an interesting selection of dishes such as red onion confit and ricotta tartlet.

Times: 1-2.30/7-9.30, Closed 24-26 Dec, Closed L Mon-Sat **Rooms:** 75 (75 en suite) ★★★ HL **Directions:** From Cork take R600 to Kinsale. Hotel at end of Pier Rd

The White House

Traditional, International NEW

Bistro-style menu served in a lively atmosphere

☎ 021 4772125 Pearse St, The Glen
e-mail: whitehse@indigo.ie
web: www.whitehouse-kinsale.ie

Situated in the town centre, this traditional-style family-run restaurant with rooms and bar was established in the 1850s. Adjacent to the bar, the restaurant is rustic in style and there is live music each night. The bistro-style menu includes starters like terrine maison - chicken, chorizo, black pudding and hazelnut wrapped in bacon - served with toast and cucumber sauce. Using lots of local fresh fish, main courses might feature Kinsale mussels with Chardonnay cream and lemongrass, while desserts include classics like chocolate gâteau.

Chef: Michael El Sahew **Owners:** Michael Fawley **Times:** 12/10, Closed 25 Dec **Prices:** Starter €5-€15, Main €12-€30, Dessert €5.95-€10.50, Service included **Notes:** Vegetarian available **Seats:** 45 **Children:** Menu, Portions **Rooms:** 10 (10 en suite) ★★★ RR **Parking:** Car park at rear of building

---

MACROOM   MAP 01 B2

Castle Hotel

European

Family-run hotel with a loyal local following

☎ 026 41074 Main St
e-mail: castlehotel@eircom.net
web: www.castlehotel.ie

There are three dining options at this popular, long-established hotel - a traditional-style Irish bar (with a good-value carvery lunch every day), a continental café, and B's Restaurant which serves up bistro-style food with a contemporary twist. The split-level main dining room

has something of an art deco feel with high-backed chairs, and grey, black and deep red tones. Local produce is high on the agenda in dishes such as warm salad of Clonakilty pudding, grilled John Dory or home-made desserts like butterscotch cream cheesecake, which may take their toll on the waistline but certainly won't disappoint the taste buds!

Times: 12-3/6-9.30, Closed 25 Dec **Rooms:** 60 (60 en suite) ★★★ HL **Directions:** On N22, midway between Cork and Killarney

---

MALLOW   MAP 01 B2

Longueville House

see page 701

CO DONEGAL

DONEGAL   MAP 01 B5

Harvey's Point Country Hotel

Modern, Traditional V

Accomplished cooking in a tranquil setting

☎ 074 972 2208 Lough Eske
e-mail: info@harveyspoint.com
web: www.harveyspoint.com

The wooded lakeside setting for this relaxing country establishment is truly idyllic. Family owned and run, the service is personal as well as professional. The split-level restaurant offers great views over the lough, while its fixed-price menus take a modern Celtic approach, and feature an alternative vegetarian option. Starters might include the likes of Clonakilty black pudding with blue cheese sorbet, Guinness glaze and crisp ham, while expect mains like a Donegal lamb shank stew served on the bone in a cider broth with butter beans and polenta. Dessert might feature a chocolate truffle cake with Calvados-soaked prunes and clotted cream. Ingredients are top quality and the cooking shows flair.

Chef: Paul Montgomery **Owners:** Marc Gysling, Deirdre McGlone
Times: 12.30-2.30/6.30-9.30 **Prices:** Fixed L €30, Fixed D €55, Service included **Wine:** 51 bottles over €30, 38 bottles under €30, 2 by the glass
Notes: Fixed L 3 courses, Fixed D 4 courses, Vegetarian menu, Dress Restrictions, Smart casual, Air con **Seats:** 100, Pr/dining room 100
Children: Min 12 yrs **Rooms:** 60 (60 en suite) ★★★★ HL
Directions: From Donegal 2m towards Lifford, turn left at Harvey's Point sign, continue to follow signs, taking three right turns to Harvey's Point gates **Parking:** 200

AA Hotel of the Year for the Republic of Ireland

RATHMULLAN   MAP 01 C6

◉ Fort Royal Hotel

Modern Irish, Seafood
Country-house dining in mature gardens sloping down to the sea

☎ 074 915 8100 Fort Royal
e-mail: fortroyal@eircom.net
web: www.fortroyal.com

No shortage of ways to raise an appetite at this friendly hotel: take a stroll around the grounds and you'll find a tennis court, a 9-hole pitch and putt course, and private access to a magnificent sandy beach. Set on the shores of Lough Swilly, Fort Royal has been run by the Fletcher family for more than 50 years and offers a high standard of hospitality. Its bright-and-airy restaurant overlooks the garden, which supplies fresh fruit, vegetables and herbs, while fish and meat come from award-winning suppliers in the region. Tuck into a warm salad of duck with croûtons and Cashel blue cheese, perfectly cooked turbot fillet with a chive hollandaise sauce, and pannacotta with mixed berry compôte.

Rooms: 15 (15 en suite) ★★★ HL **Directions:** Telephone for directions

---

ROSSNOWLAGH   MAP 01 B5

◉ Sandhouse Hotel

Traditional NEW
Coastal setting for fresh cooking and professional service

☎ 071 9851777
e-mail: info@sandhouse-hotel.ie
web: www.sandhouse-hotel.ie

Perched on the edge of the Atlantic Ocean, this hotel looks out over miles of secluded coves and sandy beaches. The split-level Seashell restaurant, with formal table settings, is a vibrant place to enjoy the catch of the day. A daily-changing fixed-price menu brings diners fish from nearby Killybegs and locally traceable meat. Try a starter of Donegal Bay timbale of white crabmeat mousse with saffron cream. Main courses might include a simple but memorable Dover sole, on the bone, served with creamy leeks, asparagus tips and new boiled potatoes.

Chef: Sid Davis, John McGarrigle **Owners:** Brian Britton **Times:** 12.30-2.30/7-9.30, Closed Nov-Feb, Closed L Mon-Sat **Prices:** Fixed L €20, Fixed D €35-€45, Starter €12.50-€17.50, Main €20-€30, Dessert €7.50-€10, Service optional **Wine:** 30 bottles over €30, 50 bottles under €30, 20 by the glass **Seats:** 80, Pr/dining room 30 **Children:** Menu, Portions
Rooms: 55 (55 en suite) ★★★ HL **Directions:** 10m S of Donegal & 7m from Ballyshannon on coast road **Parking:** 30

CO DUBLIN

DUBLIN   MAP 01 D4

◉ Clarion Hotel Dublin IFSC

Traditional Italian
Sophisticated corporate hotel with Italian cuisine

☎ 01 433 8800 I.F.S.C.
e-mail: sinergie@clarionhotelifsc.com
web: www.clarionhotelifsc.com

This well-designed, modern hotel is located in the heart of the financial service centre. The restaurant offers modern Italian dishes with some innovative ideas like 'make your own bruschetta'. Starters include carpaccio bresaola with rocket salad or one of a good selection of pasta or rice dishes. Main courses feature the signature dish of home-made agnolotti with spinach and fresh ricotta, vine ripe tomatoes and basil sauce, chicken saltimbocca alla Romana or sea bass cartoccio baked in a parcel with cherry tomatoes, olives and white wine. Desserts like pannacotta or tiramisù bring proceedings to a satisfying close. The attentive staff provide a professional service.

Times: 12-2.30/6-9.45, Closed 24-26 Dec, BHs, Closed L Sat & Sun
Rooms: 147 (147 en suite) ★★★★ HL **Directions:** Financial Services Centre

◉ Crowne Plaza Dublin Airport

American, Asian
Popular hotel restaurant with an international feel

☎ 01 8628888 Northwood Park, Santry Demesne, Santry
e-mail: info@crowneplazadublin.ie.
web: www.cpdublin-airport.com

Touzai is a bright, contemporary restaurant in a modern hotel enjoying a quiet setting overlooking 70 acres of wooded demesne. Touzai means 'east meets west' and it's a style that's reflected in both the décor and the menu, which fuses the techniques and flavours of Asia and California with those of the Pacific Rim. You might expect such temptations as wok-fried beef with lemongrass and ginger (from the Asian Delights section) or lemon sole in crisp couscous and a tomato and fennel broth (from the East and West section).

Times: 12.30-2.30/6-10.30, Closed 25 Dec, Closed L Sat **Rooms:** 204 (204 en suite) ★★★★ HL **Directions:** Telephone for directions

◉ Finnstown Country House

European, International
Crowd-pleasing country-house cooking

☎ 01 601 0700 Newcastle Rd
e-mail: manager@finnstown-hotel.ie
web: www.finnstown-hotel.ie

A short drive from central Dublin, this magnificent country house nestles in 45 acres of mature grounds and has a loyal local following. The period detail is impeccable throughout - particularly the dining room, which positively glows with Georgian-style opulence. With its foundation in simple, straightforward cooking, the menu adds influences from around the world with good seasonal awareness. Try a

CONTINUED

IRELAND

DUBLIN CONTINUED

starter of tempura of king prawns with a sweet chilli dressing, followed by a main of grilled salmon, monkfish and sole with buttered spinach and lemon and prawn beurre blanc, and chocolate banoffee pie to finish.

Chef: Steve McPhillips **Owners:** Tim Mansfield **Times:** 12.30-2.30/7.30-9.30, Closed 24-26 Dec, Closed D Sun **Prices:** Fixed L €29.95-€31.50, Fixed D €42-€45, Starter €7.95-€12, Main €17.50-€28, Dessert €7.50-€8, Service optional **Wine:** 32 bottles over €30, 32 bottles under €30, 4 by the glass **Notes:** Fixed L 3 courses, Civ Wed 200, Air con **Seats:** 80, Pr/dining room 30 **Children:** Menu, Portions **Rooms:** 53 (53 en suite) ★★★ HL **Directions:** From M1 take 1st exit onto M50 southbound. 1st exit after Toll Bridge. At rdbt take 3rd left (N4 W). Left at lights. Over next 2 rbts, hotel on right **Parking:** 150

⊚⊚ Herbert Park Hotel
Modern International
Contemporary cuisine overlooking the park

☎ 01 667 2200 Ballsbridge
e-mail: reservations@herbertparkhotel.ie
web: www.herbertparkhotel.ie

Set in an upmarket area of Dublin, this chic hotel offers leafy views of a delightful park. Enjoy a cocktail in the bar, a light meal in the lounge or lobby, or some accomplished cuisine in the airy Pavilion restaurant. Local produce forms the base of a contemporary menu, which draws on Asian and South African cooking for inspiration. You might start with beetroot and vodka cured salmon with buckwheat blinis, and then sample mains such as Thai-spiced monkfish with a mussel and lemongrass broth, or lime-crusted lamb with new potato and asparagus salad and port wine jus. Jazz buffet lunch on Sundays.

Times: 12.30-2.30/5.30-9.30, Closed 25-26 Dec, Closed D Sun-Mon & BHs **Rooms:** 153 (153 en suite) ★★★★ HL **Directions:** 5 mins from city centre. S over canal into Northumberland Rd to Ballsbridge. Turn right cross bridge in Ballsbridge, 1st right down Anglesea Rd

⊚⊚⊚⊚ Restaurant Patrick Guilbaud
see opposite

⊚ Stillorgan Park Hotel
International
Modern hotel with contemporary menus

☎ 01 288 1621 & 200 1800 Stillorgan Rd
e-mail: sales@stillorganpark.com
web: www.stillorganpark.com

Striking design is the hallmark of this modern hotel located next to Ireland's national broadcaster RTÉ (so expect to see some familiar faces). Relax in the bar over canapés before taking your table in the restaurant, with its rich colours, mosaic tiles, modern artwork and hand-painted frescoes. The best of Irish ingredients are used in a modern menu with some international influences. Recommendations include Arctic char with crayfish risotto and lobster bisque, cannon of lamb with parsnip and leek terrine and rosemary jus, or ravioli with chanterelle mushrooms, pecorino cheese and basil oil.

Chef: Enda Dunne **Owners:** Des Pettit **Times:** 12.30-3/5.45-10.15, Closed 25 Dec, Closed L Sat, D Sun **Prices:** Fixed L €20, Fixed D €35-€39, Starter €6.50-€9.50, Main €18.50-€25, Dessert €6.50-€7, Service optional **Wine:** 12 bottles over €30, 10 bottles under €30 **Notes:** Early bird menu €25, Vegetarian available, Air con **Seats:** 100, Pr/dining room 60 **Children:** Menu, Portions **Rooms:** 150 (150 en suite) ★★★★ HL **Directions:** Telephone for directions **Parking:** 300

⊚⊚ Thorntons Restaurant at The Fitzwilliam Hotel
French
Smart hotel restaurant with an extensive menu of complex dishes

☎ 01 478 7008 128 St Stephen's Green
e-mail: thorntonsrestaurant@eircom.net
web: www.thortonsrestaurant.com

Centrally located on St Stephen's Green, The Fitzwilliam is a contemporary hotel with a refurbished, first-floor restaurant. Cooking is highly seasonal using the best available local and international produce. French influences are evident in dishes of soufflé of sole and crab with red chard, chive cream sauce or roast quail with brioche, white onion purée and morel sauce, followed by ballotine of rabbit with fondant potato, Valrhona and hazelnut sauce, and then apple tarte Tatin with butterscotch ice cream. There's an eight-course surprise menu for a table of diners to experience.

Times: 12.30-2.30/7-10.30, Closed Good Fri, 17 Mar, 25 Dec-6 Jan, Sun & Mon, Closed L Tue-Thur **Rooms:** 140 (140 en suite) ★★★★ HL **Directions:** Overlooking St Stephen's Green

🍴 Chapter One
☎ 01 873 2266 18/19 Parnell Square
web: www.theaa.com/travel/index.jsp
Modern twists to consistently excellent classic French cooking.

l'Ecrivain
☎ 01 661 1919 109a Lower Baggot St
Fine French cuisine and an admirable wine list.

🍴 Les Frères Jacques
☎ 01 679 4555 74 Dame St
web: www.theaa.com/travel/index.jsp
French classic cooking with an emphasis on seafood.

Jacob's Ladder
☎ 01 670 3865 4 Nassau St
Punchy modern food with an emphasis on healthy eating.

Mermaid Café
☎ 01 670 8236 69-70 Dame St
Californian style with lovely food at this bustling venue.

Restaurant Patrick Guilbaud

DUBLIN MAP 01 D4

Modern French V 🖥

Ireland's finest restaurant

☎ 01 676 4192 Merrion Hotel, 21 Upper Merrion St
e-mail: restaurantpatrickguilbaud@eircom.net
web: www.restaurantpatrickguilbaud.ie

Chef: Guillaume Lebrun
Owners: Patrick Guilbaud
Times: 12.30-2.15/7.30-10.15, Closed 25 Dec, 1st wk Jan, Sun-Mon
Prices: Fixed L €35, Starter €20-€58, Main €32-€54, Dessert €20-€25, Service optional
Wine: 1,000 bottles over €30, 12 by the glass
Notes: Tasting menu 7 courses £180, Vegetarian menu, Dress Restrictions, Smart casual, Air con
Seats: 80, Pr/dining room 25
Children: Portions
Rooms: 143 (143 en suite)★★★★★ HL
Directions: Opposite government buildings, next to Merrion Hotel
Parking: Parking in square

IRELAND

A suitably grand stage for the city's eponymous temple of gastronomy, this generous-sized, contemporary-styled dining room is light, airy and elegantly furnished. A high-domed ceiling and glass wall along one side - overlooking an inner-courtyard garden - give a real sense of space and light, while the room is brought to life by an impressive collection of modern Irish art and a profusion of green, leafy fronds. Immaculate napery graces well-spaced tables, while service - from a veritable brigade of waiting staff - is impeccable with a friendly touch. Before descending the steps to the dining room, there's also a small - but equally stylish - bar-lounge for aperitifs. And, while the restaurant's location in the opulent Georgian splendour of the Merrion Hotel is equally fitting, it does have its own street entrance as well as access through the hotel lobby itself.

Patrick Guilbaud's modern-focused, classic French cuisine more than lives up to the billing, and focuses on the very best seasonal Irish produce to grace his intricate cooking, delivered via an impressive array of menu options that includes a good-value fixed-price lunch, extensive and enticing carte (including a vegetarian option) as well as a tasting offering. Expect plenty of sophisticated flair and innovation, silky technical skills and luxury. Think pan-roasted T-bone of turbot with Roscoff onions two ways and an ale glaze, or squab pigeon from Brittany, poached and slowly roasted, served with buttery cabbage, bread mousseline and a mead and almond jus, and to finish, perhaps a transparent Granny Smith apple with light chicory jelly and rosemary ice cream. Ancillaries, like canapés, amuse-bouche, breads, pre-desserts and petits fours also impress and add to the high-end experience factor. Reservations are essential though, as it attracts the rich and famous and the highflying business crowd.

DUBLIN CONTINUED

O'Connell's

☎ 01 647 3304 Bewleys Hotel, Merrion Rd

Carefully sourced contemporary cooking making the most of local produce.

🖳 One Pico

☎ 01 676 0300 5-6 Molesworth Place, School House Ln

web: www.theaa.com/travel/index.jsp

Sophisticated and ambitious cuisine in stylish surrounds.

Roly's Bistro

☎ 01 668 2611 7 Ballsbridge Ter

Buzzing bistro with robust retro cooking.

KILLINEY   MAP 01 D4

⊛ Fitzpatrick Castle Hotel

Traditional NEW

Fine dining overlooking Dublin Bay

☎ 01 230 5400

e-mail: reservations@fitzpatricks.com

web: www.fitzpatrickcastle.com

The Fitzpatrick Castle Hotel is an 18th-century establishment sitting on the brow of Killiney Hill overlooking Dublin Bay, just nine miles from Dublin's centre. It could be well worth a drive out of the hustle and bustle of the city to enjoy this hotel's beautiful location. PJ's is the elegant fine-dining restaurant where the style is characterised by crystal chandeliers, well-spaced tables with crisp linen and good-quality glass and silverware. The traditional menu might include roast rack of lamb on mint and spring onion mash, rosemary and Madeira jus. Dungeon Bar and Grill is a contemporary restaurant serving freshly grilled local produce. The service is professional and friendly.

Rooms: 113 (113 en suite) ★★★★ HL

PORTMARNOCK   MAP 01 D4

⊛⊛ Osborne Restaurant

Modern, Traditional

Creative cuisine in a superb location

☎ 01 8460611 Portmarnock Hotel & Golf Links, Strand Rd

e-mail: sales@portmarnock.com

web: www.portmarnock.com

Once home to the Jameson family, famous for their Irish whiskey, this imposing 19th-century mansion is perched between the sea and a magnificent 18-hole golf course designed by Bernhard Langer. A pleasant cocktail bar serves drinks, light meals and afternoon tea, but foodies should head for the Osborne Restaurant, a sophisticated dining room that offers stunning views of the garden, golf course and hills beyond. Innovative, modern dishes are the staple of the menu, conjured from the finest local ingredients, including fresh fish and seafood from Howth. Expect accomplished cooking with plenty of flair: cassoulet terrine to start

perhaps, served with sauce gribiche, fruit compôte and cress, followed by breast of Barbary duck with vanilla mash, endive and Armagnac jus.

Chef: Manuel Monson **Owners:** Hotel Partners **Times:** 11.30-3/7-10, Closed L Mon-Fri **Prices:** Fixed L €25-€39, Fixed D €25-€39, Starter €8-€16.50, Main €24.50-€34, Dessert €9.50-€12.50, Service optional **Wine:** 69 bottles over €30, 16 bottles under €30, 9 by the glass **Notes:** Tasting menu 7 courses €65, Sun L €29, Vegetarian available, Dress Restrictions, Smart casual, Air con **Seats:** 60, Pr/dining room 20 **Children:** Portions **Rooms:** 138 (138 en suite)★★★★ HL **Directions:** Follow N1 towards Drogheda. At junct with R601 turn to Malahide. 2m turn left at T-junct, through Malahide & 2.2m hotel on left. Off M1 take Malahide junct, then on to Portmarnock **Parking:** 100

SKERRIES   MAP 01 D4

⊛ Redbank House & Restaurant

Modern European

Reliable cooking in a picturesque village

☎ 01 8491005 & 8490439 5-7 Church St

e-mail: info@redbank.ie

web: www.redbank.ie

Located in a pretty fishing village some 18 miles north of Dublin, this restaurant of long standing is located in a former bank with the old bank vault now converted into a well-stocked wine cellar. The service here is faultless with a warm welcome guaranteed from friendly, accommodating staff. The food has locally-landed fish and shellfish as its central theme in a range of dishes which take a modern approach. Think monkfish 'Hampton Hall' (medallions coated in breadcrumbs, cooked in butter and served with a sauce enriched with Carrageen moss), or perhaps skate wings with a scallion sauce.

Chef: Terry McCoy **Owners:** Terry McCoy **Times:** 12.30-4/6-10, Closed 24-26 Dec, Closed L Mon-Sat, D Sun **Prices:** Fixed D €50, Starter €12-€17, Main €19-€40, Dessert €10, Service included **Notes:** Fixed D 2 courses, Sun L 2 courses €33, Vegetarian available, Dress Restrictions, Smart casual **Seats:** 60, Pr/dining room 10 **Rooms:** 12 (12 en suite) ★★★★ RR **Directions:** From Dublin, M1 N to Lissenhall interchange, take exit to Skerries **Parking:** On street

CO GALWAY

CASHEL   MAP 01 A4

⊛⊛ Cashel House

Traditional British, French

Food without fuss and a wealth of seafood in a heavenly location

☎ 095 31001

e-mail: info@cashel-house-hotel.com

web: www.cashel-house-hotel.com

This mid-19th century country-house hotel sits at the head of Cashel Bay, surrounded by 50 acres of beautiful, award-winning gardens and woodland walks. Run by the McEvilly family since 1968, it has a thoroughly established feel with assured and friendly service and an all-pervading sense of comfort. The famous Connemara lamb and an abundance of locally-landed seafood grace this extensive, traditional menu with a French bias - salad of marinated prawns and sweet chilli sauce, for example, to start, and then grilled Dover sole on the bone with herb butter or poached local salmon with dill sauce. To finish, warm rhubarb tart with ginger ice cream or sticky toffee pudding.

Chef: Arturo Amit **Owners:** Dermot & Kay Mcevilly & family
Times: 12.30-2.30/7-8.30, Closed 6 Jan-6 Feb **Prices:** Fixed D €52-€54,
Starter €7.95-€12.50, Main €12.50-€29, Dessert €8.50-€12, Service added
12.5% **Wine:** 90 bottles over €30, 4 bottles under €30, 5 by the glass
Notes: Fixed D 4 courses, Dress Restrictions, Smart casual **Seats:** 70,
Pr/dining room 10 **Children:** Menu, Portions **Rooms:** 32 (32 en
suite)★★★ CHH **Directions:** S of N59. 1m W of Recess **Parking:** 30

◎◎ Zetland Country House
Modern International
Sea views and modern, full-flavoured cuisine in refined setting

☎ 095 31111 Cashel Bay
e-mail: zetland@iol.ie
web: www.zetland.com

Built as a sporting lodge in the early 19th century, this peaceful
country-house hotel is a cultivated haven on the rugged shores of
Cashel Bay. Turf fires smoulder in the cosy lounges, while comfortable
bedrooms have wonderful sea views. The elegant dining room retains
a refined air and is the setting for sampling some excellent local
produce, including herbs and vegetables from the hotel garden. The
kitchen delivers modern, yet simple and earthy cooking, resulting in
full-flavoured dishes. The fixed-price menu reflects the seasons and
may offer deep-fried croquette of foie gras, fillet of turbot with mini
ratatouille, and buttermilk pannacotta with seasonal berries. Service is
relaxed and personal.

Chef: Samuel Lecam **Owners:** Ruaidhri Prendergast **Times:** 7-9, Closed
L all week **Prices:** Fixed D €60, Service optional **Wine:** 30 bottles over
€30, 8 bottles under €30, 6 by the glass **Notes:** Fixed D 5 courses
Seats: 75, Pr/dining room 20 **Children:** Portions **Rooms:** 19 (19 en
suite) ★★★ HL **Directions:** N59 from Galway towards Clifden, turn
right after Recess onto R340, after approx 4m turn left onto R341, hotel 1m
on right **Parking:** 40

CLIFDEN   MAP 01 A4

◎ Abbeyglen Castle Hotel
French,.International
Elegant restaurant in a fine country-house hotel

☎ 095 21201 Sky Rd
e-mail: info@abbeyglen.ie
web: www.abbeyglen.ie

Staff create a warm presence at this 19th-century country-house
hotel, where hospitality remains a key strength. The elegant first-
floor restaurant has a clubby feel with background piano music
playing each evening. The daily-changing French and international
menu makes good use of Connemara meat and game and freshly
caught seafood from the area, including lobster and crab from a
seawater tank. Typical dishes include Cleggan Bay seafood chowder,
braised shank of Connemara lamb on a bed of colcannon with
redcurrant and thyme sauce, and warm chocolate bread-and-butter
pudding.

Chef: Kevin Conroy **Owners:** Mr P Hughes **Times:** 7-9, Closed 6 Jan-1
Feb, Closed L Mon-Sun **Prices:** Fixed D €40-€47, Starter €6.20-€11.50,
Main €22-€36, Dessert €8.50, Service added 12.5% **Wine:** 23 bottles over
€30, 29 bottles under €30, 4 by the glass **Seats:** 75 **Children:** Min 12 yrs
Rooms: 45 (45 en suite) ★★★★ HL **Directions:** From Galway take
N59 to Clifden. Hotel 1km on the Sky Road **Parking:** 40

◎◎ Ardagh Hotel & Restaurant
French, Mediterranean
Assured cooking of local produce in a stunning setting

☎ 095 21384 Ballyconneely Rd
e-mail: ardaghhotel@eircom.net
web: www.ardaghhotel.com

Although modern in appearance from the road, the interior of this
quiet family-run hotel on the shores of Ardbear Bay is full of
traditional charm with turf fires and comfy couches. Stunning views
(particularly at sunset) are to be had from its first-floor restaurant,
which has a bright Mediterranean feel and - as you'd expect given the
setting - a strong emphasis on carefully cooked seafood and other
excellent local produce, with lobsters, oysters and mussels arriving
fresh from a seawater tank in the foyer. Alternatives might include pot-
roasted medallions of Irish pork with apple and potato mash and a fig
and pork jus, or grilled Barbary duck breast with red cabbage,
caramelised apples and a Calvados and duck sauce.

Chef: M Bauvet **Owners:** S & M Bauvet **Times:** 7.15-9.30, Closed end
Nov-end Mar, Closed L all week **Prices:** Fixed D €50, Starter €12.95-
€15.95, Main €22.50-€32.50, Dessert €6.95, Service optional, Group min
6 service 12.5% **Wine:** 50 bottles over €30, 6 bottles under €30
Notes: Fixed D 4 courses, Dress Restrictions, Smart casual, No shorts or
trainers **Seats:** 50 **Children:** Menu, Portions **Rooms:** 19 (19 en suite)
★★★ HL **Directions:** Galway to Clifden on N59. Signed in Clifden, 2m
on Ballyconneely road **Parking:** 40

◎ Brown's
Modern Irish, European
Welcoming hotel with a fine reputation for seafood

☎ 095 21206 & 21086 Alcock & Brown Hotel
e-mail: alcockandbrown@eircom.net
web: www.alcockandbrown-hotel.com

Brown's restaurant is housed within the very friendly, renovated hotel
at the top of the town, known as the Alcock & Brown. The dining
room has a fresh modern décor, transformed at night by dimmed
lights and candles. There's a wide-ranging carte plus daily specials
offering fairly straightforward cooking of prime ingredients, starring
locally-landed seafood (perhaps grilled fillets of sea bass served with
fresh spinach and a tomato, caper and avocado relish, or a fresh
seafood platter) and Connemara lamb (maybe roast leg with a herb
stuffing and red wine and rosemary jus). Finish with Bailey's
cheesecake or sweet cream profiteroles with chocolate sauce.

Chef: Paddy Conroy, Eddie Devane **Owners:** Deirdre Keogh
Times: 12.30-2/6-9.30, Closed 22-26 Dec **Prices:** Fixed D €25, Starter
€4.95-€11.50, Main €15.95-€23.50, Dessert €4.95-€6.95, Service optional
Wine: 2 bottles over €30, 22 bottles under €30, 5 by the glass
Notes: Fixed D 4 courses, Air con **Seats:** 100 **Children:** Menu, Portions
Rooms: 19 (19 en suite) ★★★ HL **Directions:** From Galway city take
N59 to Clifden. Follow one-way system to centre. Hotel in town square
Parking: On street parking & car park next to hotel

IRELAND

GALWAY   MAP 01 B3/4

Camilaun Restaurant

Modern International

Popular hotel with a wide-ranging menu

☎ 091 521433 Ardilaun Hotel & Leisure Club,
Taylor's Hill
e-mail: info@theardilaunhotel.ie
web: www.theardilaunhotel.ie

This 19th-century townhouse is set in landscaped grounds on the edge of Galway city and boasts a number of lounges and extensive leisure facilities. The elegant Camilaun Restaurant overlooks the garden and is a consistent performer, creating international-influenced dishes from high-quality local ingredients. The lengthy selection of mains is designed to suit most tastes and stretches from simple dishes - salmon en papillote with jumbo tiger prawns and salsa verde - to heavier fare such as cutlets of lamb marinated in honey and mustard with coriander couscous.

Chef: Nigel Murray **Owners:** John Ryan **Times:** 1-2.15/7-9.15, Closed 23-27 Dec, Closed L Sat **Prices:** Fixed L €12, Fixed D €28, Starter €5.50-€10.50, Main €20.95-€26.50, Dessert €6.25-€7.50, Service added 10% **Wine:** 21 bottles over €30, 29 bottles under €30, 2 by the glass **Notes:** Vegetarian available, Dress Restrictions, Smart dress, Air con **Seats:** 180, Pr/dining room 380 **Children:** Menu, Portions **Rooms:** 125 (125 en suite) ★★★★ HL **Directions:** 1m from Galway city centre, towards Salthill on the west side of the city, near Galway Bay **Parking:** 300

Galway Bay Hotel

International, Seafood

Light, airy restaurant with sea views and fresh Irish cuisine

☎ 091 520520 The Promenade, Salthill
e-mail: info@galwaybayhotel.net
web: www.galwaybayhotel.net

The hotel's Lobster Pot restaurant enjoys magnificent triple-aspect views over Galway Bay. The cuisine style is modern Irish with International influences and there's a strong emphasis on fresh Irish produce in creating the menus. There is a particular focus on fresh fish and seafood, including fresh lobster from the tank. Take seared fillet of cod with a coconut crust accompanied by a ragout of bacon, mushrooms, coriander and cream, or perhaps lobster grilled or thermidor, while meat options might feature grilled medallions of beef with a sauté of red onions and zucchini, red wine balsamic reduction and pâté maison.

Chef: Robert Bell **Owners:** John O'Sullivan **Times:** 12.30-2.30/6.30-9.15, Closed 25 Dec (residents only) **Prices:** Fixed L €20, Fixed D €40, Starter €6.50-€10, Main €19.95-€38, Dessert €6.95-€8.50, Service included **Wine:** 25 bottles over €30, 25 bottles under €30, 20 by the glass **Seats:** 220, Pr/dining room **Children:** Menu, Portions **Rooms:** 153 (153 en suite) ★★★★ HL **Directions:** 2m from Galway city centre **Parking:** 350

Park House Hotel & Park Room Restaurant

International

Appealing menu in bustling city-centre hotel

☎ 091 564924 Forster St, Eyre Square
e-mail: parkhousehotel@eircom.net
web: www.parkhousehotel.ie

A popular city-centre hotel built around a three-storey former grain store with its impressive, 19th-century stone façade. Paintings of old Galway line the walls of the celebrated Park Room Restaurant, which bustles with locals at lunchtime and becomes more intimate in the evening with soft lighting and elegant, linen-clothed tables. The cooking has a classical base, offering a wide choice of appealing, accomplished dishes that make good use of fresh ingredients, notably local seafood. Take baked fillets of black sole stuffed with cod, salmon and shrimp mousse accompanied by a spicy provençale and pesto sauce.

Chef: Robert O'Keefe, Martin Keane **Owners:** Eamon Doyle, Kitty Carr **Times:** 12-3/6-10, Closed 24-26 Dec **Prices:** Fixed L €24-€28, Fixed D €44.50-€45.50, Starter €7.40-€13.25, Main €15.25-€28.95, Dessert €6.75-€6.95, Service optional **Wine:** 27 bottles over €30, 56 bottles under €30, 4 by the glass **Notes:** Fixed D 4 courses, Fixed L 3 courses, Air con **Seats:** 145, Pr/dining room 45 **Children:** Menu, Portions **Rooms:** 84 (84 en suite) ★★★★ HL **Directions:** In city centre, off Eyre Sq **Parking:** 40

Radisson SAS Hotel & Spa Galway

International V

Waterfront hotel with a menu to suit most tastes

☎ 091 538300 Lough Atalia Rd
e-mail: marinasrestaurant@radissonsas.com
web: www.radissonhotelgalway.com

The décor of this split-level, waterside hotel eatery is inspired by the light and colours of nearby Lough Atalia, and teams dark wood with deep blue upholstery and panoramic views. It caters to a well-heeled business market and is often busy, with non-residents advised to book ahead. Modern dishes with international influences predominate on the lengthy menu, which makes good use of local seafood and includes a number of healthy eating options. Kick off with pan-fried diver scallops with tomato and lemon and Sévruga caviar, followed by pan-fried sea bream fillet with leek ratatouille.

Chef: Hans Prins **Owners:** Radisson SAS Hotels **Times:** 12.30-3/6-10.30, Closed L Mon-Sat **Prices:** Starter €6.50-€13.50, Main €19-€27, Dessert €6.50-€10, Service optional **Wine:** 44 bottles over €30, 8 bottles under €30, 11 by the glass **Notes:** Vegetarian menu, Dress Restrictions, Smart casual, Air con **Seats:** 220, Pr/dining room 80 **Children:** Menu, Portions **Rooms:** 238 (238 en suite) ★★★★ HL **Directions:** Take N6 into Galway city. At Hunstman Inn rdbt turn 1st left. At next lights take left fork. 0.5m, hotel at next right junct **Parking:** 250

⊛ River Room

Modern Irish, International

Modern cuisine in an 18th-century country residence

☎ 091 526666 Glenlo Abbey Hotel, Bushypark
e-mail: info@glenloabbey.ie
web: www.glenlo.com

This cut-stone abbey was built in 1740 - though today it sits in a 138-acre lakeside golf estate - and has been lovingly restored to its original glory, featuring sculptured cornices and fine antique furniture. The classical River Room restaurant is an oval affair on two levels, with high ceilings, well-spaced tables, lake views and professional but relaxed service. The modern Irish cuisine displays flair and imagination, with the skilful cooking based on quality local produce, particularly seafood. Seared Irish West Coast scallops served with potato and basil purée and warm honey truffle syrup might catch the eye.

Chef: Barry Wallace **Owners:** John F Bourke **Times:** 7-9.30, Closed 24-27 Dec, Mon-Sun **Prices:** Fixed D €40-€55, Starter €7.50-€11.50, Main €24.50-€35.50, Dessert €7.50, Service optional **Wine:** 3 bottles under €30 **Notes:** Tasting menu available, Dress Restrictions, Smart casual, Air con **Seats:** 44, Pr/dining room 30 **Children:** Menu, Portions **Rooms:** 46 (46 en suite) ★★★★ CHH **Directions:** Approx 2.5m from centre of Galway on main Clifden road **Parking:** 150

RECESS (SRAITH SALACH)   MAP 01 A4

⊛⊛ Ballynahinch Castle

Modern International

Fine dining in elegant country house

☎ 095 31006 & 31086
e-mail: bhinch@iol.ie
web: www.ballynahinch-castle.com

Standing in 350 acres of woodland and lakes and overlooking a bend in the Ballynahinch river, this splendid 16th-century mansion enjoys one of the best locations in Connemara. Log fires, stunning views, personal service and an air of casual elegance are just some of the delights of staying at this peaceful castle retreat. Crisp linen, gleaming silver and glassware and relaxing river views are features of the inviting Owenmore restaurant. The fixed-price dinner offers International cooking based on impeccable local and seasonal produce, including wild salmon from the river and locally-sourced seafood. Expect the likes of a tian of wild Atlantic salmon, layered with crème fraîche, cucumber, shallots and horseradish, followed by grilled fillets of black sole with caper berries, brioche croûtons and lemon.

Chef: Robert Webster **Owners:** Ballynahinch Castle Hotel Inc **Times:** 6.30-9, Closed 2 wks Xmas, Feb, Closed L all week **Prices:** Fixed D €55, Service added 10% **Notes:** Dress Restrictions, Smart casual **Seats:** 90 **Rooms:** 40 (40 en suite) ★★★★ CHH **Directions:** Take N59 from Galway. Turn right after Recess towards Roundstone (R331) for 2m **Parking:** 55

⊛ Lough Inagh Lodge

Irish, French

Irish country dining with lovely mountain views

☎ 095 34706 & 34694 Inagh Valley
e-mail: inagh@iol.ie
web: www.loughinaghlodgehotel.ie

This former 19th-century fishing lodge in the Connemara Mountains has the feel of a family home, with guests treated to a particularly high standard of hospitality. Set on the shores of Lough Inagh, one of the region's most beautiful lakes, it boasts comfy lounges with turf fires, a cosy oak-panelled bar, and an intimate dining room, where seafood and wild game dishes are a speciality. Fresh fish is cooked simply and served with subtle sauces that enhance rather than mask natural flavour: try local lobster or wild salmon and you're in for a treat. Meatier dishes might include fillet of beef with blue cheese topping and rosemary sauce, while apple sponge pudding is a typical dessert.

Times: 7-8.45, Closed mid Dec-mid Mar **Rooms:** 13 (13 en suite)★★★ CHH **Directions:** From Galway take N344. After 3.5m hotel on right

---

RENVYLE   MAP 01 A4

⊛ Renvyle House

Modern

Country-house dining with a romantic setting and literary connections

☎ 095 43511
e-mail: info@renvyle.com
web: www.renvyle.com

Destroyed and rebuilt over several centuries, this attractive country house is located between the Connemara Mountains and the wild Atlantic coast. Yeats honeymooned here and it was once the home of

CONTINUED

IRELAND

IRELAND

RENVYLE CONTINUED

Buck Mulligan from James Joyce's *Ulysses*. Dinner is an atmospheric occasion with turf fires and soft lighting. The menu draws on great local produce and cooking is vibrant, with dishes such as golden fried polenta-crusted calamari with tomato and chilli jam, caper and fennel dressing, or roast guinea fowl, creamed root vegetables and thyme jus.

Times: 7-9, Closed 4 Jan-14 Feb **Rooms:** 73 (73 en suite) ★★★ HL
Directions: N59 west of Galway towards Clifden, through Oughterard & Maam Cross. At Recess turn right, Keymore turn left, Letterfrack turn right, hotel 5m

---

ROUNDSTONE

MAP 01 A4

◎ Roundstone House Hotel

Modern Irish
Great sea views and cracking seafood

☎ 095 35864

This delightful, family-run hotel in its terraced-village setting enjoys magnificent sea views to the backdrop of the rugged Connemara Mountains. There are cosy, well-appointed, linen-dressed tables in Vaughan's restaurant, where service is suitably informal and friendly. The extensive carte comes brimful of quality produce from the abundant local larder, particularly seafood. Expect dishes along the lines of salmon and crab fishcake, packed with fresh fish and served with a simple hollandaise, or turbot accompanied by a light white wine sauce. The emphasis here is strictly on freshness, simplicity and clarity of flavour, allowing the main ingredients to shine.

Times: 7-9, Closed Nov-Feb **Rooms:** 12 (12 en suite) ★★ HL
Directions: Telephone for directions

CO KERRY

CAHERDANIEL (CATHAIR DÓNALL)

MAP 01 A2

◎ Derrynane Hotel

Irish, European
Enjoyable dining with spectacular Atlantic backdrop

☎ 066 947 5136
e-mail: info@derrynane.com
web: www.derrynane.com

Perched on a spectacular clifftop location on the Ring of Kerry, this friendly family-run hotel offers guests stunning ocean views of Kenmare Bay while eating in the bright, spacious dining room. The small dedicated kitchen team produces modern Irish dishes with European influences, using quality and fresh produce. Expect a five-course fixed-price dinner menu. A bar menu is also available.

Times: 7-9, Closed Oct-mid Apr **Rooms:** 70 (70 en suite) ★★★ HL

KENMARE

MAP 01 B2

◎◎ Sheen Falls Lodge

see below

Sheen Falls Lodge

KENMARE

MAP 01 B2

Irish, European V
Romantic waterfall setting for excellent cuisine

☎ 064 41600
e-mail: info@sheenfallslodge.ie
web: www.sheenfallslodge.ie

Many restaurants boast of stunning views, but few can lay claim to their own waterfall, particularly one that's floodlit at night. It's a dramatic backdrop, and the elegant La Cascade makes the most of it, spoiling its guests with vast windows and well-spaced tables that offer a chance for some salmon-spotting in between courses. The setting is a former hunting lodge on the banks of the Sheen, which was once the summer residence of the Marquis of Lansdowne, a keen gardener who filled his grounds with many of the rare trees and exotic shrubs that still grow today.

The kitchen draws plaudits, too, its modern approach - underpinned by a classical theme - focusing on fresh, top-quality produce from the abundant Irish larder. The cooking's unfussy and accomplished, arriving at the table in clear-flavoured dishes that are distinguished by well-judged combinations and bags of imagination. Try seared foie gras to start, served with kumquat caramel, pear purée, and a brioche 'doughnut', before moving on to mains such as roast Dover sole on

the bone with Kenmare mussels, seasonal wild mushrooms, vanilla-poached grapes, and white port and verjus syrup. Take a stroll before dinner to explore and you might even stumble across the ruins of a tiny church known to have witnessed the coming of Viking raiders in the 9th century.

Chef: Philip Brazil **Owners:** Sheen Falls Estate Ltd **Times:** 7-9.30, Closed 2 Jan-1 Feb, Closed L all week **Prices:** Fixed D €65, Starter €13.50-€24.50, Main €32-€38.50, Dessert €15-€17, Service optional **Wine:** 817 bottles over €30, 6 bottles under €30, 6 by the glass **Notes:** Tasting menu available, Vegetarian menu, Dress Restrictions, Smart casual (jacket), No jeans or T-shirts **Seats:** 120, Pr/dining room 20 **Children:** Menu, Portions **Rooms:** 66 (66 en suite)★★★★ CHH **Directions:** From Kenmare take N71 to Glengarriff. Take 1st left after suspension bridge. 1m from Kenmare **Parking:** 75

Lime Tree
☎ 064 41225 Sheburne St
Pretty stone building housing a bustling, seasonally-inspired restaurant.

Packie's
☎ 064 41508 Henry St
Good local ingredients treated with care and intelligence.

KILLARNEY   MAP 01 B2

Arbutus Hotel
Irish
Traditional Irish hospitality in family-run hotel

☎ 064 31037 College St
e-mail: stay@arbutuskillarney.com
web: www.arbutuskillarney.com

Family run since 1926, the Arbutus is a smart and friendly hotel in the centre of Killarney. Norrie Buckley's restaurant comprises three interconnecting dining rooms and provides locals and residents with traditional Irish cooking from the best Celtic produce available. Fish landed at Dingle, and Kerry Mountain lamb feature on the menu, together with Atlantic salmon and mussels. Alternatives include the likes of chicken liver pâté with Cumberland sauce, salmon with lemon butter, and crème brûlée served with plum coulis and home-made shortbread. A bistro menu is also served all day in the bar.

Times: 6.30, Closed 7 Dec-12 Mar, Sun, Mon **Rooms:** 35 (35 en suite) ★★★ HL **Directions:** At the rdbt on College St & Lewis Rd. Killarney town centre.

Cahernane House Hotel
Modern International
Lakeside manor-house dining

☎ 064 31895 Muckross Rd
e-mail: cahernane@eircom.net
web: www.cahernane.com

Formerly the residence of the Earls of Pembroke, this beautifully situated hotel is set in parkland on the shores of Lough Leane, with the Kerry Mountains as a backdrop. Its gracious interior teams period furniture with modern pieces to create a cosy, inviting ambience, while the restaurant is a spacious affair, boasting well-appointed tables and comfortable chairs. As you'd expect, the kitchen knows its stuff and makes the most of top-notch local ingredients in flavourful combinations that consistently impress. Dishes are simply described on the classic carte, and might include grilled fillet of black sole on the bone with toasted almond and lime butter, or pan-seared breast of Barbary duck with red onion marmalade, juniper and veal jus.

Chef: Patrick Kearney **Owners:** Mr & Mrs J Browne **Times:** 12-2.30/7-9.30, Closed Dec-Jan, Closed L all week ex by arrangement **Prices:** Fixed L €25, Fixed D €40-€52, Starter €7-€13, Main €22-€30, Dessert €7-€9, Service optional **Wine:** 98 bottles over €30, 22 bottles under €30, 20 by the glass **Notes:** Tasting menu available, Dress Restrictions, Smart casual, no shorts **Seats:** 50, Pr/dining room 18 **Children:** Menu, Portions **Rooms:** 38 (38 en suite) ★★★★ HL **Directions:** From Killarney follow signs for Kenmare, then from Muckross Rd over bridge and hotel signed on right. Hotel 1m from town centre **Parking:** 50

The Lake Room Restaurant
Modern Irish, European V
Re-branded hotel restaurant with stunning views

☎ 064 31766 Aghadoe Heights Hotel & Spa
e-mail: info@aghadoeheights.com
web: www.aghadoeheights.com

Perched on a height overlooking the lakes, mountains and golf course, the Lake Room Restaurant has been given a completely new identity following a major refurbishment and the introduction of a brand new menu. A new corner window enhances those spectacular views, and the room has been divided with timber-framed panels with sheer and linen fabric inserts. Another wonderful feature is the glass-walled wine cave. Minimal touch, maximum flavour is the philosophy behind the food. Menus are seasonal and the dishes traditional with a modern twist, such as peppered haunch of venison with parsnip purée, chilli spice risotto and chocolate sauce, followed by blancmange pudding, saffron ice cream and a trio of melon.

Chef: Gavin Gleeson **Owners:** Pat & Marie Chawke **Times:** 12.30-2/6.30-9.30, Closed 25 Dec (residents only), Jan-Mid February, Closed L all week (occasional Sun open) **Prices:** Fixed L €35, Fixed D €65, Starter €13-€18, Main €26-€34, Dessert €9-€14, Service optional, Group min 10 service 12.5% **Wine:** 132 bottles over €30, 11 bottles under €30, 21 by the glass **Notes:** Fixed D 4 courses, Vegetarian menu, Dress Restrictions, Jacket preferred, no jeans or trainers, Air con **Seats:** 150, Pr/dining room 80 **Children:** Menu, Portions **Rooms:** 74 (74 en suite)★★★★ HL **Directions:** 2.5m from Killarney, off N22. 11m from Kerry International Airport **Parking:** 120

The Park Restaurant
European
Fine cuisine in elegant hotel restaurant

☎ 064 35555 Killarney Park Hotel, Kenmare Place
e-mail: info@killarneyparkhotel.ie
web: www.killarneyparkhotel.ie

This upmarket modern hotel on the edge of town offers country-house comfort and a warm atmosphere, with its roaring fires, deep sofas and friendly Irish welcome. The elegant, classical Park Restaurant continues the theme, with well-spaced, smartly laid tables and a pianist who plays each evening. The kitchen rises to the occasion, making fine use of local seasonal produce from land and sea, its modern dishes - underpinned by classical roots - displaying skill and interesting combinations. Take a ravioli of shrimp starter with a julienne of leek, garlic and tarragon foam, followed by grilled fillets of John Dory served with caramelised fennel, tomato ragout and saffron cream, or perhaps a fillet of Irish Angus beef with red onion marmalade and potato fondant. Finish with a refreshing apricot sorbet.

Chef: Odran Lucey **Owners:** Padraig & Janet Treacy **Times:** 7-9.30, Closed 25-26 Dec, Closed L all week **Prices:** Starter €6.50-€16, Main €30-€37.50, Dessert €11, Service included **Wine:** 745 bottles over €30, 5 bottles under €30, 7 by the glass **Notes:** Fixed D 5 courses €65-70, Air con **Seats:** 130, Pr/dining room 85 **Children:** Menu, Portions **Rooms:** 68 (68 en suite)★★★★ HL **Directions:** From Cork take R22 to Killarney. Take 1st exit for town centre, then at 2nd rdbt take 2nd exit. At 3rd rdbt, take 1st exit. Hotel 2nd entrance on left

IRELAND

PARKNASILLA MAP 01 A2

◎ Parknasilla Hotel

Traditional

Formal dining in a dramatic location

☎ 064 45122
e-mail: res@parknasilla.gsh.ie
web: www.gshotels.com

A Victorian property in an extraordinary location, with stunning Atlantic, woodland and mountain views. A sweeping staircase, stained glass windows and log fires are among the period features, and the Pygmalion restaurant is suitably grand and elegant. The set-price dinner menu might offer salad of brill scaloppini, and spiced chicken breast with vegetable couscous. Alternatively there's a short carte of classic dishes: foie gras on toasted brioche, and fillet steak of Irish Angus beef. Cocktails are served in the clubby Doolittle Bar. (George Bernard Shaw was a frequent visitor.)

Times: 7-9, Closed Jan-11 Feb, Closed L all week **Rooms:** 83 (83 en suite) ★★★★ HL **Directions:** From Killarney take N71 to Kenmare. On entering town pass golf club. Hotel entrance on left at top of town

CO KILDARE

LEIXLIP MAP 01 D4

◎ Leixlip House

Modern Irish

Fine dining in charming hotel

☎ 01 6242268 Captains Hill
e-mail: info@leixliphouse.com
web: www.leixliphouse.com

Dating from 1772, this charming hotel retains its period style with Georgian furnishings and décor. The Bradaun restaurant is a bright, airy room where diners are served by friendly, professional staff. The menu makes excellent use of the finest ingredients and harmonious combinations of flavours. You might find a feuillete of mussels, clams and prawns with haricot blanc, tomato concasse and whole langoustines in seafood broth, followed by pan-fried hake with a buttered baby vegetable tartlet. Finish with a gin-and-tonic sorbet with yellow fruit salad, mango coulis and a tuile biscuit. Booking is essential, especially at weekends.

Times: 12.30-4/6.30-9.45, Closed 25-26 Dec, Mon, Closed L Tue-Sat **Rooms:** 19 (19 en suite) ★★★ HL

NAAS MAP 01 D4

◎ Killashee House Hotel & Villa Spa

Irish

Elegant dining in magnificent surroundings

☎ 045 879277
e-mail: sales@killasheehouse.com
web: www.killasheehouse.com

Luxuriously appointed Victorian manor house, once a convent and also a preparatory school for boys, set amid 80 acres of beautifully kept grounds. Turners restaurant is a magnificent room on a grand scale with pillars, chandeliers, intricate plasterwork and gold and scarlet soft furnishings. A harpist plays on Friday and Saturday nights,

adding to the sense of occasion. Excellent raw ingredients are used in the preparation of dishes such as a fillet of prime beef served with a truffled celeriac gratin and morel mushroom sauce, or perhaps grilled sea bass with stir-fried squid, purple potatoes and a fresh oyster sauce.

Chef: David Cuddihy **Owners:** Mr & Mrs Tierney **Times:** 1-2.45/7-9.45, Closed 24-25 Dec, Closed L Sat **Prices:** Fixed L €30-€35, Fixed D €55, Service optional **Wine:** 80 bottles over €30, 24 bottles under €30, 12 by the glass **Notes:** Fixed L 3 courses, Fixed D 4 courses, Dress Restrictions, Smart casual, no jeans, Air con **Seats:** 120, Pr/dining room 650 **Children:** Menu, Portions **Rooms:** 141 (141 en suite) ★★★★ HL **Directions:** 1m from Naas on old Kilcullen road. On left past Garda (police station) **Parking:** 600

NEWBRIDGE MAP 01 C3

◎◎ Keadeen Hotel

International

Stylish dining in family-run hotel

☎ (045) 431666
e-mail: info@keadeenhotel.ie
web: www.keadeenhotel.ie

Kildare's longest established family-owned and run four-star hotel has been welcoming guests for over 37 years. First opened in 1970, it has grown to meet the ever-changing needs and expectations of guests, whilst maintaining its tradition of superior quality and service. The Derby restaurant is a stylish venue for sophisticated country-house style dining. Service is formal but unobtrusive, befitting the elegant décor and fine table settings. The menu makes use of the very best local produce, typically a main course of tender cannon of lamb with dauphinoise and a honey and thyme sauce. The Club Bar is an alternative eating option, and offers a relaxing place to enjoy a drink or meal.

Times: 12.30-2.30/6-9.30 **Rooms:** 75 (75 en suite) ★★★★ HL **Directions:** N7 from Dublin to Newbridge. Hotel 1m from Curragh racecourse & 0.5m from Newbridge town centre

STRAFFAN MAP 01 C/D4

◎◎ Barberstown Castle

Irish, French

Fine dining in 13th-century castle in attractive grounds

☎ 01 628 8157
e-mail: barberstowncastle@ireland.com
web: www.barberstowncastle.ie

This one-time castle now country-house hotel features Victorian and Elizabethan dining rooms replete with period furniture overlooking the gardens. Dinner is an atmospheric, candlelit affair, while aperitifs can be taken in the elegant drawing room and informal lunch in the airy conservatory Tea Room. Service is appropriately professional, while the chef's accomplished cooking, underpinned by a classical French theme, makes the best of quality produce. Starters might include lobster, scallop and basil sausage with lobster bisque and baby leeks, followed by roast Irish beef fillet, with swede and potato purée, caramelised endive and fresh horseradish cream. Then perhaps orange and cinnamon crème brûlée to finish.

Times: 12.30-2.30/7-9.30, Closed 24-28 Dec, Jan, Mon-Tue, Closed L Wed-Sat **Rooms:** 59 (59 en suite) ★★★★ HL **Directions:** From Dublin take M50, exit for M4 at rdbt and follow signs for castle

◎◎◎ The K Club

see opposite

IRELAND

The K Club

STRAFFAN MAP 01 C/D4

Modern Irish

Luxurious golfing hotel with an impressive restaurant

☎ 01 601 7200
e-mail: hotel@kclub.ie
web: www.kclub.ie

Times: 7-9.45
Rooms: 79 (79 en suite)★★★★★ CHH
Directions: 30 minutes from Dublin. From Dublin Airport follow M4 to Maynooth, turn for Straffan, just after village on right

Sitting at the heart of a resort that includes two championship golf courses, this luxurious hotel came to global attention when it hosted the Rider Cup a few years back. The golf pavilion houses two informal eateries - Legends and Monza - but it's the fine-dining option, the gracious Byerley Turk restaurant that's the real drawcard. Dominated by a painting of the thoroughbred racehorse after which it's named, Byerley Turk boasts high ceilings, ornate chandeliers, lofty windows with lavish drapes, rich brocade wall coverings, marble columns, elegantly dressed tables and views over the gardens. Dress code is formal (strictly jacket and tie), while the silver-and-cloche service is a polished affair, yet friendly to match the tone.

The contemporary Irish cuisine - underpinned by a classical French theme - is delivered via an appealing dinner carte and tasting option, built around tip-top, fresh seasonal produce from the abundant Irish larder. Clear flavours, technical proficiency and luxury abound in highly accomplished dishes like glazed breast of Challon duck with citrus, honey and black pepper, potato galette and orange sauce, or roast loin of venison, with spätzle and five spice fennel sauce.

IRELAND

CO KILKENNY

KILKENNY
MAP 01 C3

⊚ Kilkenny River Court

International

Dining on a grand scale

☎ 056 772 3388 The Bridge, John St
e-mail: reservations@kilrivercourt.com
web: www.kilrivercourt.com

This comfortable riverside hotel boasts an impressive restaurant, designed to reflect the classical beauty of Kilkenny Castle and the surrounding area. Wonderful views of the river are framed in large picture windows and no expense has been spared with the décor, using marble flooring, crystal chandeliers and Georgian furniture. An extensive international menu repertoire showcases fresh, seasonal local produce; think beech-smoked trout layered with spinach and fresh salmon wrapped in filo pastry, a cannon of Slaney Valley lamb, Shellumsrath goose, or alternatively, perhaps lemon and coriander sea bass.

Chef: Gerrard Dunne **Owners:** Xavier McAuliffe **Times:** 12.30-2.30/6-9.30, Closed 24-25 Dec, 25-26 Jan, Closed L Mon-Sat **Prices:** Fixed L €28.50-€29.95, Fixed D €48-€49.95, Starter €10.90-€12.45, Main €19.65-€33.40, Dessert €8.50 **Wine:** 40 bottles over €30, 20 bottles under €30, 10 by the glass **Notes:** Fixed L 4 courses, Fixed D 4 courses, Vegetarian available, Smart casual preferred, Air con **Seats:** 90, Pr/dining room 200 **Children:** Menu, Portions **Rooms:** 90 (90 en suite) ★★★★ HL **Directions:** Telephone for directions **Parking:** 70

⊚⊚ Lacken House & Restaurant

Modern Irish, European

Seasonal and local produce cooked with flair

☎ 056 776 1085 Dublin Rd
e-mail: info@lackenhouse.ie
web: www.lackenhouse.ie

This fine Victorian house is located in a tree-lined residential road just a 5-minute walk from the centre of the city. Friendly service and high standards are evident in a dedicated team led by the proprietors. Dinner in the intimate restaurant is available Tuesday to Saturday from the carte, fixed-price menu or a separate vegetarian option. Particularly good presentation - on slate, glass and trenchers - interesting combinations using excellent seasonal and local ingredients and fine skill are evident throughout. Take a starter of fresh Duncannon crabmeat ravioli, scallops and a tomato and rocket compôte, or a main of Dromoland pheasant served with ballotine leg, 'spaghetti' carrot and honey-roast turnip.

Times: 12-2.30/6-9.30, Closed Mon, Closed L Tue-Sat, D Sun **Rooms:** 10 (10 en suite) ★★★★ RR

THOMASTOWN
MAP 01 C3

⊚⊚ *The Lady Helen Restaurant*

Modern French

Impressive country mansion offering superb fine dining

☎ 056 777 3000 Mount Juliet Conrad Hotel
e-mail: info@mountjuliet.ie
web: www.mountjuliet.com

Set in 1,500 acres of parkland, this elegant 18th-century Georgian mansion has its own golf course. The formal dining restaurant, with lovely panoramic views, is decorated in grand country-house style. The cooking is likewise classical, with European influences and modern interpretations, as in seared West Coast scallops with garden cauliflower purée, star anise and vanilla scallop jus, or home-cured gravad lax with marinated fennel bulb, herb salad and candied citrus zest. Mains might include line-caught fillet of turbot with a lightly poached ragout of Roma tomato and mussels, a 'study' of quail, or pan-seared fillet of sea bass with truffle leeks and chive beurre blanc. Vegetarians are in for a treat with a risotto of asparagus and artichoke served with chargrilled parmesan herb polenta demonstrating some serious culinary technique. There's good use of local ingredients, and fresh vegetables and herbs come from the kitchen gardens.

Times: 7-9.45, Closed L all week **Rooms:** 59 (59 en suite)★★★★ CHH **Directions:** Just outside Thomastown heading S on N9

CO LIMERICK

ADARE
MAP 01 B3

⊚⊚ Dunraven Arms

Modern European

Innovative dishes in an atmospheric setting

☎ 061 605900
e-mail: reservations@dunravenhotel.com
web: www.dunravenhotel.com

Behind the rustic façade of this hotel you'll find the kind of sophisticated comfort that has entertained royalty. The interior, smartly decorated and warmed by lovely open fires, looks out from large windows on to the thatched cottages of one of Ireland's prettiest villages. The country-style dining room offers modern European cuisine, with extensive use of fresh local produce. Renowned Dunraven beef is always on the menu, carved just as you like it from the trolley, and fresh fish is delivered daily. A main course that's sure to hit the spot is roast rump of lamb with braised lamb pithivier, turnip fondant and purée of root vegetables served with buttered new potatoes, while desserts include the likes of sticky toffee pudding with vanilla ice cream and caramel sauce, or choose from the selection of Irish farmhouse cheeses.

Chef: Shane McGrath **Owners:** Brian & Louis Murphy **Times:** 12.30-2.30/7-9.30, Closed L Mon-Sat **Prices:** Fixed L €27.50, Fixed D €35-€45, Starter €7.50-€10.50, Main €16-€25, Dessert €6-€7.95, Service added 12.5% **Wine:** 25 bottles over €30, 25 bottles under €30, 6 by the glass **Notes:** Fixed L 3 courses, Fixed D 4 courses, Dress Restrictions, Smart casual, Air con **Seats:** 80, Pr/dining room 30 **Children:** Min 6 yrs, Portions **Rooms:** 86 (86 en suite) ★★★★ HL **Directions:** Telephone for directions **Parking:** 60

IRELAND

LIMERICK

MAP 01 B3

⊛ Mc Laughlin's

Modern International

International dining in pretty Limerick

☎ 061 335566 Castletroy Park Hotel, Dublin Rd
e-mail: sales@castletroy-park.ie
web: www.castletroy-park.ie

This modern hotel on the outskirts of Limerick boasts a range of different eating options, including a conservatory for snacks and afternoon tea, and a bar for bistro fare. The formal restaurant does a brisk trade with locals and residents alike, conjuring a comprehensive modern menu from quality local ingredients. Dishes are flavourful creations that draw inspiration from all over the world: Scandinavian-style hot smoked salmon followed by roast crown of pigeon perhaps, or marinated fillet of monkfish. To finish, try warm pear and almond tart, or maybe ginger and lemongrass-scented crème brûlée. Lunch is by appointment only.

Times: 12.30-2.30/5.30-10, Closed 25-26 Dec, Closed L Mon-Sat
Rooms: 107 (107 en suite) ★★★★ HL **Directions:** 5 mins from Limerick on Dublin road, follow signs for University of Limerick, hotel opposite

CO MAYO

FOXFORD

MAP 01 B4

⊛ Healys Restaurant & Country House Hotel

Traditional British

Comfort cooking in a waterside setting

☎ 094 925 6443 Pontoon
e-mail: info@healyspontoon.com
web: www.healyspontoon.com

Perched on the edge of Lough Cullen, this 19th-century shooting lodge offers pretty views from its restaurant, a friendly venue with well-spaced tables and a simple blue-and-white décor. A good choice of dishes includes wild Irish oak-smoked salmon with capers and red shallots, or fresh steamed mussels with white wine and Pernod sauce to start. Mains follow up with the likes of Irish steaks, rack of spring lamb, and crisp honey-roasted duckling. Finish with ever-popular gâteau, cheesecake, or ice cream cassata.

Times: 12.30-6.30/6-10, Closed 25 Dec **Rooms:** 14 (14 en suite) ★★ HL
Directions: N26 to Castlebar turn onto R310 signed Pontoon, follow road for 5.6m

WESTPORT

MAP 01 B4

⊛ Carlton Atlantic Coast Hotel

International

West Coast dining with impressive views

☎ 098 29000 The Quay
e-mail: info@atlanticcoasthotel.com
web: www.atlanticcoasthotel.com

Behind the traditional stone façade of an old woollen mill on Westport harbour, lies a bright, modern hotel. Situated on the top floor, the Blue Wave restaurant commands spectacular views over Clew Bay. Service is friendly and attentive, while relaxing ground-floor lounge areas and a lively bar complete the package. The international cooking is as modern as the setting, with interesting combinations but no undue complication. There's good use of local ingredients, especially seafood, and the menu includes the likes of seared fillet of monkfish with Puy lentils, chorizo and tomato butter sauce, or fillet of beef on herb rösti with ratatouille and shallot jus.

Chef: Frank Walsh **Owners:** Carlton Hotel Group **Times:** 6.30-9.15, Closed 20 27 Dec, Closed L all week **Prices:** Fixed L €21.95, Fixed D €36, Service added but optional 12.5% **Wine:** 12 bottles over €30, 14 bottles under €30, 1 by the glass **Notes:** Fixed L 3 courses, Fixed D 4 courses, Vegetarian available, Air con **Seats:** 85, Pr/dining room 140
Children: Menu, Portions **Rooms:** 85 (85 en suite) ★★★ HL
Directions: From Westport take coast road towards Louisburgh for 1m. Hotel on harbour on left **Parking:** 80

⊛ Knockranny House Hotel

Modern French, International

Stunning views from an elegant restaurant

☎ 098 28600
e-mail: info@khh.ie
web: www.khh.ie

Delightfully located, this modern hotel overlooks the town with Clew Bay and Croach Patrick in the background. La Fougère is the hotel's magnificent restaurant, on two levels with many window tables and wonderful views. Local produce makes a strong showing including smoked products from the hotel's own kiln, and herbs from the kitchen garden. The menu offers modern dishes with French influences, such as pan-seared quail with mushroom ragout, pine nut and thyme monkfish tail with spinach cream, rocket and mildly smoked tomato salad, and spiced pineapple confit with coconut mousse.

Chef: David O'Donnell **Owners:** Adrian & Geraldine Noonan **Times:** 1-2.30/6.30-9.30, Closed Xmas **Prices:** Fixed D €49, Service optional **Notes:** Fixed D 4 courses, Dress Restrictions, Smart casual, Air con **Seats:** 140, Pr/dining room **Children:** Menu, Portions **Rooms:** 97 (97 en suite) ★★★★ HL **Directions:** On N5 (Dublin to Castlebar road), on the left before entering Westport **Parking:** 150

IRELAND

CO MEATH

KILMESSAN   MAP 01 D5

◉ The Station House Hotel

European, Mediterranean

Cosy, popular restaurant in converted railway station

☎ 046 902 5239

e-mail: info@thestationhousehotel.com

web: www.thestationhousehotel.com

The pretty conversion of this former railway station - which saw its last train in 1967 - into a friendly, family-run hotel with a lovely homely feel, draws a loyal local following, and has a great reputation for family celebrations. The cosy Signal restaurant delivers straightforward, uncomplicated, country-house cooking with a touch of French flair.

Top-notch ingredients are skilfully treated with respect - think roasted rack of Kilmessan lamb, served with turnip purée and balsamic and basil gravy, or perhaps baked scallops with spinach and forest mushrooms, in a creamy white wine sauce. The Platform Bar and Lounge offers informal bar food.

Chef: David Mulvihill **Owners:** Chris & Thelma Slattery **Times:** 12.30-3/4.30-10.30 **Prices:** Fixed L €27.95-€34.95, Fixed D €27.95-€44.95, Starter €4.95-€14.95, Main €12.95-€25.95, Dessert €6-€8, Service optional **Wine:** 8 bottles over €30, 29 bottles under €30, 4 by the glass **Notes:** Fixed L 4 courses, Fixed D 5 courses **Seats:** 90, Pr/dining room 180 **Children:** Menu, Portions **Rooms:** 20 (20 en suite) ★★★ HL **Directions:** From Dublin N3 to Dunshaughlin, R125 to Kilmessan **Parking:** 200

CO MONAGHAN

CARRICKMACROSS   MAP 01 C4

◉◉◉ Restaurant at Nuremore

see below

Restaurant at Nuremore

CARRICKMACROSS   MAP 01 C4

Modern French V

Innovative cuisine with bold combinations at country-house hotel

☎ 042 966 1438

e-mail: info@nuremore.com

web: www.nuremore.com

Overlooking parkland and a championship golf course, an oasis of calm and tranquillity is a phrase that sums up the restaurant at this stylish Victorian country-house hotel. The split-level dining room has a comfortable, modern country-house feel and enjoys views over gardens and lake. The imaginative menu more than befits the setting, aptly demonstrating the flair and accomplished technical skill of chef Raymond McArdle's well-motivated brigade and pleasant, attentive front-of-house service. His modern approach, underpinned by a classical French theme, utilises tip-top produce, enhanced by contemporary styling of presentation and ingredient combination. Menu descriptions don't really do justice to the intricate work that graces dishes. Nonetheless, to show the style, take an accomplished threesome of ballotine of duck foie gras with roast tranche, pear and liquorice lentil vinaigrette and balsamic, followed by roast breast of Gressingham duck cooked with twelve spices and served with a fine

tart of ceps and foie gras, carrot and orange purée and a mulled plum sauce, and to finish, a Valrhona chocolate coulant with cranberry ice cream. Peripherals like breads, amuse bouche, pre-desserts and petits fours also hold top form through to the end.

Chef: Raymond McArdle **Owners:** Gilhooly family **Times:** 12.30-2.30/6.30-9.45, Closed L Sat **Prices:** Fixed L €19.50, Fixed D €52, Service optional **Wine:** 220 bottles over €30, 30 bottles under €30, 10 by the glass **Notes:** Fixed D 4 courses, Tasting menu 8 courses, Vegetarian menu, Civ Wed 200, Air con **Seats:** 120, Pr/dining room 50 **Children:** Menu, Portions **Rooms:** 72 (72 en suite) ★★★★ HL **Directions:** 11m from M1 at Ardee turning (N33) **Parking:** 200

CO TIPPERARY

CASHEL
MAP 01 C3

⑨ Cashel Palace Hotel

Traditional French

Country-house cuisine set in former papal kitchens

☎ 062 62707

e-mail: reception@cashel-palace.ie

web: www.cashel-palace.ie

This Queen Anne house in the centre of Cashel has played home to archbishops, earls and lords in its time, and is now an elegant and inviting hotel. The Bishop's Buttery occupies the flagstoned basement and boasts vaulted ceilings, open hearths, crisp white linen and friendly, professional service. The cooking leans toward classic French cuisine and makes sound use of local produce, with game in season and fish from the Waterford coast among the specialities. A medallion of Irish Angus fillet of beef main shows the style, served with port wine jus and a wild mushroom and foie gras duxelle, or for a lighter dish, try brill with red pepper coulis and wilted spinach.

Chef: George McQuinn **Owners:** Patrick & Susan Murphy **Times:** 12-2.30/6-9.30, Closed 24-27 Dec, Closed L Sun **Prices:** Fixed L €12.50-€21.50, Fixed D €48, Starter €6-€11.50, Main €21-€31.50, Service optional **Wine:** 2 bottles over €30, 2 bottles under €30, 2 by the glass **Notes:** Fixed D 4 courses, Vegetarian available, Dress Restrictions, Smart casual **Seats:** 60, Pr/dining room 20 **Children:** Menu, Portions **Rooms:** 23 (23 en suite) ★★★★ HL **Directions:** On main street in Cashel town centre **Parking:** 60

Chez Hans

☎ 062 61177 Moor Ln

Former Wesleyan chapel offering familiar dishes.

CO WATERFORD

WATERFORD
MAP 01 C2

⑨ Athenaeum House Hotel

French, European

Innovative fare in a luxury boutique hotel

☎ 051 833 999 Christendon, Ferrybank

e-mail: info@athenaeumhousehotel.com

web: www.athenaeumhousehotel.com

Well-proportioned 18th-century house on the approach to the city, now operating as a smart, chic boutique hotel. The building, set in 10 acres of parkland on the banks of the River Suir, has been sympathetically restored in a contemporary style, and Zak's is the bright-and-airy, conservatory-style restaurant (with terrace) where innovative food is served. The modern cooking has a strong classical basis, with excellent ingredients used in interesting combinations. Take grilled whole Dover sole, perhaps pan-fried tournedos of Irish beef, or slow-braised pork belly served with glazed root vegetables. (A pianist plays at weekends.)

Chef: James Crawford **Owners:** Stan & Mailo Power **Times:** 12.30-3.30/7-9.30, Closed 25-27 Dec **Prices:** Fixed L €15-€18, Fixed D €35-€37, Starter €6-€13, Main €15-€30, Dessert €7-€9, Service optional **Wine:** 7 bottles over €30, 9 bottles under €30, 10 by the glass **Notes:** Sun L €23-€24, Tasting menu available on request, Vegetarian available, Air con **Seats:** 100, Pr/dining room 30 **Children:** Menu, Portions **Rooms:** 29 (29 en suite) ★★★ HL **Directions:** From station on N25 towards Rosslare, through lights, then right and next right **Parking:** 40

⑨⑨ Waterford Castle

Modern, Traditional

Formal dining in a romantic island castle

☎ 051 878 203 The Island

e-mail: info@waterfordcastle.com

web: www.waterfordcastle.com

Set on its own enchanting island, the hotel is accessible by chain link ferry from the mainland. The castle is an impressive 16th-century building and the 310-acre island includes an 18-hole championship golf course. There are views across the surrounding deer park from the Munster Room, an oak-panelled restaurant with ornate ceilings and mullioned windows, where a resident pianist plays most evenings. The seasonal set menu draws on excellent seafood caught at nearby Dunmore East, well-kept local cheeses, and organic vegetables where possible. Try seared scallops with pea purée, carrot and Sauternes sauce, followed by roast rump of lamb with spiced dahl, or chargrilled fillet of O'Flynn's beef with watercress mash, confit shallots, thyme butter and a Merlot jus. Private dining is available in the Leinster Room.

Chef: Michael Quinn **Owners:** Munster Dining Room **Times:** 12.30-1.45/7-9, Closed Xmas, early Jan, Closed L Mon-Sat **Prices:** Fixed L €30-€35, Fixed D €60-€70, Starter €12-€15, Main €30-€35, Dessert €10-€15, Service added but optional 10% **Wine:** 50+ bottles over €30, 8 by the glass **Notes:** Dress Restrictions, Jacket or shirt required for D **Seats:** 50, Pr/dining room 80 **Children:** Menu, Portions **Rooms:** 19 (19 en suite)★★★★ HL **Directions:** Telephone for directions **Parking:** 200

IRELAND

CO WESTMEATH

ATHLONE
MAP 01 C4

◉ Hodson Bay

Traditional, International

Smart lakeside hotel with a fine restaurant

☎ 090 644 2000 Hodson Bay
e-mail: info@hodsonbayhotel.com
web: www.hodsonbayhotel.com

With stunning views of Lough Ree and a location in the heart of some of Ireland's most beautiful countryside, this is a rural idyll that offers an exquisite taster of renowned Irish hospitality amid some fantastic scenery. L'Escale restaurant is the showcase for the hotel's fine dining and offers a menu which combines Irish cooking with international influences. Local seafood is a speciality, delivered fresh every day, with a lobster tank on the premises. A typical starter might be Atlantic lobster terrine with tomato salsa, while mains might include poached fillet of beef in Shiraz.

Chef: Kevin Ward **Owners:** John O'Sullivan **Times:** 12.30-2.15/7-9.30
Prices: Fixed L €18-€23, Fixed D €29-€32, Starter €7.50-€11.50, Main €23.50-€29.50, Dessert €7.50, Service optional **Wine:** 16 bottles over €30, 38 bottles under €30, 2 by the glass **Notes:** Vegetarian available, Air con
Seats: 180, Pr/dining room 40 **Children:** Menu, Portions **Rooms:** 182 (182 en suite) ★★★★ HL **Directions:** From Athlone follow signs for Roscommon. Approx 2.5m on entering Hodson Bay follow signs for the hotel on right **Parking:** 300

◉ Wineport Lodge

Modern, Classical

Wholesome cooking in spectacular setting

☎ 090 643 9010 Glasson
e-mail: lodge@wineport.ie
web: www.wineport.ie

A truly impressive location on the shores of the inner lakes of Lough Ree on the Shannon. Customers can arrive by road or water, and dine on the deck or in the attractive dining room. Spectacular views and friendly service reflect the highest standards of Irish hospitality. Wholesome local produce is served up in generous portions. Try a starter of spiced Thai soup, or goat's cheese and roast beetroot spring roll with thyme and maple drizzle. To follow, maybe monkfish en papillote with sundried tomato, basil, Pernod and lemon, or roast fillet of cod with honey, curry and grain mustard and red onion coriander fritters would appeal. To complement the interesting dishes there's a serious dedication to wine here.

Times: 3-10/6-10, Closed 24-26 Dec, Closed L Mon-Sat **Rooms:** 29 (29 en suite) ★★★★ RR

CO WEXFORD

GOREY
MAP 01 D3

◉◉ Marlfield House

Classic

Elegant restaurant in a country-house setting

☎ 055 21124
e-mail: info@marlfieldhouse.ie
web: www.marlfield.com

A family-operated country-house hotel with an air of luxury, from the opulent decorations and furnishings to the gracefully professional service. In the three rooms of the restaurant, the elegantly appointed tables have irresistible views over beautiful gardens. Vegetables and herbs from the kitchen garden bring fresh flavours to top-notch, mainly local ingredients including excellent beef and lamb, and the accurate cooking is reflected in succinct four-course menus. Impressive dishes might include ragout of wild mushrooms, Madeira cream, grilled potatoes and thyme focaccia, with truffle foam, followed by crab-crusted fillet of halibut, purée of watercress, roasted ratte potatoes, roma tomato ragout and beurre blanc. Enticing desserts feature the likes of Valrhona dark chocolate soufflé with pistachio ice cream.

Times: 12.30-2/7-9, Closed 24-27 Dec, 3-30 Jan, Closed L Mon-Sat
Rooms: 20 (20 en suite)★★★ CHH **Directions:** 1m from Gorey on R742 (Courtown road)

◉ The Rowan Tree Restaurant

European, International

Enjoyable dining in modern hotel spa

☎ 053 948 0500 Ashdown Park Hotel, The Coach Rd
e-mail: info@ashdownparkhotel.com
web: www.ashdownparkhotel.com

The Rowan Tree Restaurant is part of this contemporary spa hotel, situated at the edge of the picturesque town of Gorey. This modern, stylish restaurant offers both carte and fixed-price menus with efficient, yet relaxed and friendly service. In the evening, low lighting creates an intimate atmosphere. Clever use of fresh, local produce means that the simpler dishes are often the most enjoyable. Try a starter of millefeuille of smoked salmon and crabmeat, followed by a main course of seared fillet of beef, or fish-lovers might go for a brochette of French salmon, served with couscous and a citrus salsa. Don't forget to leave room for dessert - the rich chocolate fondant is especially good.

Chef: David Crossoir **Owners:** Pat & Tom Redmond **Times:** 12.30-2.30/6-9.30, Closed 24-25 Dec, Closed L Mon-Sat **Prices:** Fixed L €24,

IRELAND

Fixed D €42.50, Starter €7.50-€13, Main €18-€30, Dessert €6.50-€8, Service optional **Wine:** 19 bottles over €30, 14 bottles under €30, 10 by the glass **Notes:** Fixed L 4 courses, Fixed D 4 courses, Dress Restrictions, Neat dress, Air con **Seats:** 110, Pr/dining room 90 **Children:** Menu, Portions **Rooms:** 79 (79 en suite) ★★★★ HL **Directions:** On approach to Gorey town take N11 from Dublin. Take left signed for Courtown. Hotel on left **Parking:** 150

ROSSLARE · MAP 01 D2

⊛ Beaches

Traditional European
Classic cuisine in a Victorian seaside hotel

☎ 053 913 2114 Kelly's Resort Hotel & Spa
e-mail: kellyhot@iol.ie
web: www.kellys.ie

Founded in 1895 by William Kelly, by a 5-mile stretch of sandy beach in Rosslare, the hotel is now run by the fourth generation of the family. Beaches restaurant is traditionally opulent and the ideal home for some of the hotel's famous art collection. Chef Jim Aherne has been pleasing guests with his classic cuisine for over 30 years, and his menus reflect the value placed on fresh local produce. Pride is taken in dishes such as nettle soup, fillet of sole hermitage, and roast goose with chestnut stuffing chipolata.

Chef: Jim Aherne **Owners:** Bill Kelly **Times:** 1-2/7.30-9, Closed mid Dec-mid Feb **Prices:** Fixed L €25-€28, Fixed D €46-€48, Service optional, Group min 10 service 10% **Wine:** 170 bottles over €30, 5 bottles under €30, 15 by the glass **Notes:** Vegetarian available, Dress Restrictions, Jacket & tie, Air con **Seats:** 200, Pr/dining room 40 **Children:** Portions **Rooms:** 118 (118 en suite)★★★★ HL **Parking:** 200

WEXFORD · MAP 01 D3

⊛⊛ Ferrycarrig Hotel

Irish, International
Smart split-level restaurant overlooking the estuary

☎ 053 912 0999 Ferrycarrig Bridge
e-mail: ferrycarrig@ferrycarrighotel.com
web: www.ferrycarrighotel.ie

The two eating outlets at this smart modern hotel have been combined into one stylish split-level restaurant overlooking the Slaney River estuary. The spacious Reeds restaurant boasts bright, airy proportions, and the friendly, professional staff are particularly welcoming of families. The modern menus have been upgraded to match the stylish dining room, and draw on the freshest meats and seafood from nearby Duncannon, with many suppliers credited.

Salsas, dressings and sauces are used to good effect. If you fancy the likes of carpaccio of Irish beef with sautéed tiger prawns, and grilled Wexford Slop mallard with braised red cabbage and Cabernet Sauvignon and game jus, look no further.

Chef: Tony Carty **Owners:** Mr Griffin **Times:** 12.30-2.15/6-9.45 **Prices:** Fixed D €24.95-€28.95, Starter €5-€12, Main €17-€27, Dessert €6.50-€9.50, Service optional **Wine:** 19 bottles over €30, 50 bottles under €30 **Notes:** Fixed D 4 courses, Vegetarian available, Civ Wed 250, Air con **Seats:** 140, Pr/dining room 40 **Children:** Menu, Portions **Rooms:** 102 (102 en suite) ★★★★ HL **Directions:** On N11 by Slaney Estuary, beside Ferrycarrig Castle **Parking:** 200

⊛ Newbay Country House & Restaurant

Modern European
Popular hotel with excellent, simply-prepared dishes

☎ 053 914 2779 Newbay, Carrick
e-mail: newbay@newbayhouse.com
web: www.newbayhouse.com

Newbay just seems to get more popular and booking is essential, particularly at weekends. This elegant house sits in magnificent, mature gardens just a short drive from Wexford city and boasts an informal bistro in addition to its fine-dining restaurant. Quality ingredients are handled with confident simplicity allowing flavours to shine through, creating a range of dishes, with fish from the hotel's own trawler a speciality. Your choice might include Carne lobster in herb butter and wild garlic risotto or baked turbot fillet with chargrilled asparagus, lemon and herb butter.

Chef: Paul Wildes **Owners:** Alec Scallan **Times:** 12-3/6-9.30, Closed Xmas, New Year, Closed L Mon-Thu **Prices:** Fixed L €22.95, Fixed D €34.95, Starter €5.25-€18.95, Main €21.95-€33.50, Dessert €6.90, Service optional **Wine:** 14 bottles over €30, 15 bottles under €30, 6 by the glass **Notes:** Vegetarian available **Seats:** 75 **Children:** Menu, Portions **Rooms:** 12 (12 en suite) ★★★★ RR **Directions:** Take Cork rd from Wexford, left after Citroën garage, at x-rds turn right, restaurant on right **Parking:** 70

⊛ Whitford House Hotel Health & Leisure Club

Traditional, European
A good variety of dishes in a friendly hotel setting

☎ 053 914 3444 New Line Rd
e-mail: info@whitford.ie
web: www.whitford.ie

A long-established family-run hotel and leisure club with a strong local following, the Whitford is located a couple of kilometres from the medieval town of Wexford. Dinner is served in the spacious surroundings of Footprints restaurant, to the accompaniment of live classical music at the weekend. The European menu draws on the best of Wexford produce in dishes such as creamy Atlantic seafood chowder, followed by Irish sirloin steak with stuffed field mushroom and a choice of sauces. To finish, try seasonal fruit kebab with Malibu sabayon and raspberry ice.

Chef: Siobhan Devereux **Owners:** The Whitty Family **Times:** 12.30-3/7-9, Closed 24-27 Dec, Closed L Mon-Sat **Prices:** Fixed L €15.90-€19.95, Fixed D €27.85-€41.50, Starter €4.95-€10.95, Main €16.95-€25.50, Dessert €5.95-€7.50, Service optional **Wine:** 15 bottles over €30, 42 bottles under €30 **Seats:** 100 **Children:** Menu, Portions **Rooms:** 36 (36 en suite) ★★★ HL **Directions:** From Rosslare ferry port follow N25. At Duncannon Rd rdbt, turn right onto R733, hotel immediately on left. 1.5m from Wexford town **Parking:** 150

IRELAND

CO WICKLOW

MACREDDIN
MAP 01 D3

◎◎ The Strawberry Tree Restaurant

Modern

Dramatic dining venue specialising in organic and wild food

☎ 0402 36444 Brooklodge Hotel & Wells Spa
e-mail: brooklodge@macreddin.ie
web: www.brooklodge.com

Ireland's first certified organic restaurant is situated in a luxurious country-house hotel, part of a purpose-built village which boasts a pub, café, bakery, smokehouse, equestrian centre, 18-hole golf course, and spa. The atmospheric Strawberry Tree Restaurant is a romantic dining venue, complete with mirrored ceilings, modern lighting and dark blue décor, with tables spread across three rooms. Creativity and skill are evident on the stylish yet simple menu, which is strong on seasonality and offers the assurance of organic and wild ingredients, many from specialist suppliers. For mains, you could expect the likes of a delicious pan-fried loin of venison served with Portobello mushrooms and wild cep cream, followed by a perfect ginger and lemon crème with raspberry sorbet.

Chef: Norman Luedke/Evan Doyle **Owners:** The Doyle Family
Times: 1.30-3.30/7-9.30, Closed L Mon-Sat **Prices:** Fixed D €60, Service optional **Wine:** 10 bottles under €30, 10 by the glass **Notes:** Fixed D 5 courses, Sun L 4 courses €40, Dress Restrictions, Smart casual, Air con
Seats: 142, Pr/dining room 50 **Children:** Portions **Rooms:** 66 (66 en suite) ★★★★ HL **Directions:** From Dublin take N11, turn off at Rathnew for Rathdrum, then through Aughrim to Macreddin (2m)
Parking: 400

RATHNEW
MAP 01 D3

◎ Hunter's Hotel

Traditional French

Beautiful views and 300 years of history

☎ 0404 40106
e-mail: reception@hunters.ie
web: www.hunters.ie

Set in beautiful gardens bordering the River Varty in County Wicklow, this charming country house is Ireland's oldest coaching inn. Known as the garden of Ireland, it's the ideal base to explore the area's attractions. In the same family since 1820, spanning five generations, the hotel has developed a reputation for friendliness, hospitality and classic country-house cooking. The attentive staff serve carefully prepared dishes, utilising first-class local and seasonal produce, including home-grown fruit and vegetables. Typical dishes include smoked Irish salmon with brown bread, roast Wicklow lamb with herb stuffing and mint sauce, followed by a delicious pear almandine tartlet for dessert. Afternoon tea in the garden is a delight.

Chef: Mark Barry **Owners:** M Gelletlie **Times:** 12.45-3/7.30-9, Closed 3 days Xmas **Prices:** Fixed L €23.50-€32.50, Fixed D €45, Service optional
Notes: Fixed L 3 courses, Fixed D 4 courses **Seats:** 54, Pr/dining room 30
Children: Portions **Rooms:** 16 (16 en suite) ★★★ HL **Directions:** N11 exit at Wicklow/Rathnew junct. Take 1st left, R761. Restaurant located 0.25m before village **Parking:** 30

WOODENBRIDGE
MAP 01 D3

◎ Woodenbridge Hotel

European

Beautiful location and fine cuisine

☎ 0402 35146
e-mail: wbhotel@iol.ie
web: www.woodenbridgehotel.com

A smart family-run hotel in the Vale of Avoca, beside the Woodenbridge Golf Club. You can enjoy a pre-dinner drink in the cosy bar while you choose where to dine. The informal eating option is the Il Ruscello Mediterranean restaurant, while fine dining is found in the grand Redmond restaurant. Here diners can enjoy a range of exciting dishes with lots of fish to choose from, as well as duck, lamb, veal and beef. An impressive wine cellar stores a good collection of wines from around the globe.

Times: 12.30-3/7-9, Closed 25 Dec, Closed L Mon-Sat **Rooms:** 23 (23 en suite) ★★★ HL **Directions:** 7km from Arklow

IRELAND

Late Entries

The following restaurants were appointed to the scheme too late for us to include in the main body of the Guide (some of them had yet to be inspected at the time of going to press). For up-to-date reports and details of any changes affecting these, and all restaurants in the Guide, please see our website www.theAA.com

England

BEDFORDSHIRE

Bedford

⊛ Knife & Cleaver

01234 740387 The Grove, Houghton Conquest, MK45 3LA

Located in a pleasant village setting, this relaxing restaurant with rooms has a cosy bar and an elegant conservatory restaurant. Interesting dishes are complemented by a good wine list, and the style of cooking is modern British with an emphasis on fresh fish and seafood. Pan-fried tiger prawns with creamed leeks in a reduced celery and balsamic dressing, and grilled sea bass fillets with sautéed fennel and deep-fried chorizo curls show the style.

BRISTOL

Bristol

⊛ Mercure Brigstow Bristol

0117 929 1030 5-7 Welsh Back, BS1 4SP

A handsome purpose-built hotel beside the river, in the heart of Bristol's shopping, restaurant and trendy nightlife. The slick open-plan ground-floor bar and Ellipse restaurant enjoys superb views over the harbour, and is complemented by a further mezzanine bar and dining area for private parties, all stylishly appointed and comfortably furnished. The cooking style is modern British with continental undertones, using the freshest and most local produce available. A tian of Cornish crab served with a tomato coulis and flaked Partridge Blue cheese might be the perfect starter to a main course of Cornish hake, with hand-cut chips and delicious home-made tartare sauce.

CUMBRIA

Ravenglass

⊛ The Pennington Hotel

01229 717222 CA18 1SD

This charming beachfront hotel, a converted 16th-century coaching house in the village of Ravenglass, has a newly refurbished light-and-airy dining room with blue- and cream-coloured chairs and furnishings, and attractive flower displays. The cooking style is hearty British, so tuck into a starter of twice-baked goat's cheese soufflé with gazpacho sauce, followed by a main course of seared monkfish tail served with roast new potatoes and Savoy cabbage with smoked bacon. Finish with an excellent selection of local cheeses.

DERBYSHIRE

Risley

⊛ Risley Hall Hotel & Spa

0115 939 9000 Derby Road, DE72 3SS

This 11th-century manor house is set in 17 acres of landscaped grounds, and the formal fine-dining restaurant offers superb views across the manicured gardens through large picture windows. Friendly and attentive service complements some imaginative cuisine. Expect modern British dishes underpinned by classical French technique, as in a starter of ham hock and duck liver, perhaps followed by pan-fried turbot set on pomme matière with aromatic thyme and a demi-glace of chicken, and a classic rhubarb crème brûlée finish.

DORSET

Bournemouth

⊛ Hermitage Hotel

01202 557363 Exeter Road, BH2 5AH

Occupying an impressive position overlooking the seafront and at the heart of the town centre, the Hermitage offers friendly and attentive service. The wood-panelled lounge provides an elegant and tranquil place to relax, as

Late entries

does the restaurant where well-prepared and interesting dishes are served. Take a starter of sea-fresh pan-fried mussels in a cream, white wine, garlic and parsley sauce, and follow with a satisfying filo pastry parcel filled with goat's cheese, sun-blushed tomatoes and asparagus, and a light tomato coulis.

GLOUCESTERSHIRE

Stonehouse

◉◉ Stonehouse Court

0871 8713240 Bristol Road, GL10 3RA

Set in 6 acres of secluded gardens, this Grade II listed manor house dates back to 1601. Henry's restaurant offers a mixture of traditional and contemporary style, providing a relaxing atmosphere in which to enjoy modern British dishes with some Asian influences. Excellent use is made of fresh, local produce with suppliers listed on the seasonally-changing carte. Imaginative dishes could include the likes of chilled pressed mackerel and potato to start, with fresh herbs and mixed olive tapenade, followed by a main course of pistachio and pine kernel crusted fillet of black sea bream served on sautéed tiger prawns, with gently steamed pak choi and butternut squash. In warmer weather afternoon tea is served on the terrace.

HAMPSHIRE

Dogmersfield

◉ Four Seasons Hotel Hampshire

01252 853000 Dogmersfield Park, Chalky Lane, RG27 8TD

This elegant restaurant is set in a Georgian manor house surrounded by acres of rolling countryside and heritage listed gardens, and features a French/European menu executed with contemporary style, complemented by outstanding service and superb views across Dogmersfield Park. For starters, take Loch Fyne scallops served with a truffled French bean salad and lardons, with a brown butter foam, while for mains you might opt for seared brill with Puy lentils and glazed salsify in a red wine sauce.

Portsmouth

◉ 8 Kings Road

08451 303234 8 Kings Road, Southsea, PO5 3AH

Housed in a classic Victorian and former bank building, 8 Kings Road is only a stone's throw from Southsea's seafront and town centre. Impressive chandeliers and high ceilings create a grand atmosphere in which to enjoy some classical dishes. Fresh ingredients are in abundance, and not surprisingly given its location, fish and seafood feature strongly on the menu. A starter of seared scallops with cherry tomato vièrge might be followed by a perfectly cooked fillet of monkfish served with bacon, Puy lentils and watercress purée.

Stockbridge

◉ Peat Spade Inn

01264 810612 Village Street, SO20 6DR

Upmarket, character dining pub with rooms set in a pretty Test Valley village at the heart of fly fishing country. Aubergine-coloured walls, polished floorboards, scrubbed-wood tables and old prints engender a warm, relaxed and friendly buzz. Straightforward, accomplished modern British dishes are driven by seasonal produce; perhaps chicken liver and foie gras parfait with apple chutney, followed by confit duck leg with crushed peas and mint sauce.

Winchester

◉ The Winchester Hotel

01962 709988 Worthy Lane, SO23 7AB

Recently refurbished, Hutton's brasserie and bar has been completely rebuilt as a chic, sophisticated restaurant with walnut floors, leather banquette seating, and a stunning feature wall. Contemporary European cuisine is the order of the day, accompanied by efficient, friendly service. Kick off with a millefeuille of lobster and tiger prawn with lobster mayonnaise, and maybe take pan-fried king scallops served with pesto mash potato, a julienne of carrot and courgette and lime and vanilla foam for mains.

KENT

Maidstone

◉◉ Stone Court Hotel

01622 769769 28 Lower Street, ME15 6LX

Located in a Grade II listed former judge's residence, the Chambers restaurant is considered by many to be one of Maidstone's best-kept secrets. With a contemporary-style frontage, it combines oak-panelled walls with contemporary furnishings, including an opulent royal blue colour scheme and smartly-appointed, linen-draped tables, and bar. The intelligently simple cooking style delivers some interesting combinations using fresh local ingredients, as in gnocci and asparagus with wild mushrooms and ginger and carrot butter, followed by a more traditional dish of Scottish beef fillet with braised oxtail and a red wine jus.

LANCASHIRE

Whalley

◉ ❀ The Three Fishes

01254 826888 Mitton Road, Mitton, BB7 9PQ

This friendly 400-year-old inn has been beautifully refurbished in recent years, and comes complete with brown leather banquettes and modern décor, while losing none of its traditional feel. Run by Nigel Haworth and Craig Bancroft, it has established a well-deserved reputation for some great gastro-pub style cooking. The menu focuses on traditional specialities and British classics, all revolved around a commitment to local food heroes. Expect dishes such as heather-reared Bowland lamb Lancashire hotpot with pickled red cabbage, warm Morecambe Bay shrimps and the award-winning 'Length of Lancashire' cheeseboard comprising ten superb local cheeses. Service is friendly and attentive; the pub operates a no reservation policy, so make sure you arrive early.

LONDON NW3

XO

020 7433 0888 29 Belsize Lane, Belsize Park, NW3 5AS

Specialising in fusion cuisine, XO is Will Ricker's sixth restaurant in London and is appropriately named after a spicy seafood sauce. The sexy, softly lit bar and buzzy, brighter dining room look set to be every bit as fashionable as its Notting Hill sibling E&O (see entry), attracting affluent Belize Park residents in their droves. The Pan-Asian approach brings together Chinese, Japanese, Vietnamese and Thai dishes, delivering the likes of dim sum and sushi, Malaysian curry and Ricker's tried-and-tested classics like chilli salt squid, or miso-marinated black cod - silky, salty and sweet in all the right proportions.

LONDON SW3

Tom's Place

1 Cale Street, SW3

This third venture from Tom Aikens, located just around the corner from his two existing Chelsea restaurants, is due to open in early September 2007. An upmarket fish and chip restaurant, it will offer both eat-in and take-away with a traditional counter on the ground floor and a dining room upstairs. The fish will be scrupulously sustainable, while the whole environment will be as eco-friendly as possible using recycled materials.

LONDON W1

Ducasse at The Dorchester

020 7629 8888 53 Park Lane, W1

The legendary French chef Alain Ducasse will be executive chef at his latest forthcoming restaurant which is due to open in October 2007 in the refurbished former private dining room (The Terrace) of the Park Lane Dorchester Hotel. It is understood that the cuisine will be classic Ducasse.

Hibiscus

29 Maddox Street, W1

Hibiscus has relocated from Ludlow in Shropshire to central London and is due to open mid to late September 2007. Owned by Claude and Claire Bosi, the restaurant will retain the same menu and pricing, while Claude will be in charge of the kitchen and Claire will head-up front-of-house. The restaurant will seat around 48 people, with a 16-seater private dining room.

Late entries

La Petite Maison

020 7495 4774 54 Brooks Mews, W1K 4EG

This latest venture from Arjun Waney, co-owner of the now renowned Japanese restaurants Zuma and Roka (see entries), opened at the end of June 2007. Tucked away behind Claridge's on the former site of Teca, this is an approved copy of the original Petite Maison which opened 18 years ago in Nice and similarly features refined yet simple Niçoise/Mediterranean/Ligurian food. Think pissaladière with caramelised onions and smoked anchovies, or sea bass in salt crust with girolles, fried artichokes and tomatoes.

Rhodes W1

020 7479 3737 Marble Arch, Great Cumberland Place, W1A 4RF

Gary Rhodes' latest venture opened in May 2007 in Marble Arch's Cumberland Hotel. Described by Rhodes as the restaurant he 'has always dreamed of', the witty, glamorous interior for this 42-seater restaurant was created by celebrated designer Kelly Hoppen. Twenty-four striking Swarovski crystal chandeliers, antique French chairs and mirrors, and lush taupe, black and deep purple velvet fabrics set the luxurious and sophisticated tone. Along with head chef Brian Hughson (previously of The Savoy Grill and The Gherkin), Rhodes has developed a menu that is classically French with modern British influences. Typical dishes might include pressed foie gras with a warm duck salad, steamed turbot with buttered baby leeks and mackerel raviolis, and perhaps poached meringues with champagne rhubarb and vanilla custard to finish. The restaurant opens from Tuesday through to Saturday.

Wild Honey

020 7758 9160 12 St George Street, Mayfair, W1S 2FB

This sister restaurant to Soho eatery Arbutus (see entry), with the same menu style and pricing, opened in June 2007 on the former site of The Drones Club in Mayfair. The head chef is Colin Kelly, who has worked with Anthony Demetre for about 5 years and the restaurant is open daily for lunch and dinner.

LONDON W2

Le Café Anglais

Whiteley's Shopping Centre, Queensway, W2

Chef Rowley Leigh, who has enjoyed many years success at Kensington Place in Notting Hill (see entry), is due to open his own venture in September 2007, which will form part of a total regeneration of the shopping complex. This 170-seater informal bistrot will be in the style of a grand Parisian brasserie, but serving modern British food with a colossal rotisserie forming the centrepiece of the open kitchen.

MERSEYSIDE

Liverpool

◉ Malmaison Liverpool

0151 229 5000 7 William Jessop Way, Princes Dock, L3 1QZ

This smart, purpose-built hotel with cutting-edge, contemporary style is in a stunning location alongside the river and docks. It's particularly attractive at night with purple lights all round the dock-side illuminating the water. Inside, features like a yellow submarine suspended from the ceiling - complete with turning propeller - epitomise the sense of fun that is synonymous with this hotel group, while a champagne and cocktail bar completes the trendy, upbeat package. Expect a combination of both classic and contemporary dishes, like goat's cheese and sweet potato galette, followed perhaps by a classic Malmaison favourite, steak frites - succulent Scottish rump steak served with béarnaise sauce and accompanied by home-made chips.

NORFOLK

Fritton

◉ Fritton House

01493 484008 Church Lane, NR31 9HA

This charming 15th-century property is set amidst parkland on the banks of Fritton Lake. The dining room is contemporary in style with plain dark tables, wooden floors and smart leather chairs. The same menu is also available in the large open-plan lounge bar and outside on the terrace, and casually-dressed staff offer relaxed but very efficient service. You might start with a lovely fillet of seared tuna served on a salad with lemon dressing and Jersey Royals, and perhaps move on to lamb kofta with home-made herb flatbread, chunky chips and a refreshing mint, cucumber and yogurt dip.

Hunstanton
Sutton House Hotel

01485 532552   24 Northgate, PE36 6AP
An authentic and family-owned trattoria situated in a small hotel adjacent to the seafront in Hunstanton. Service is both attentive and very friendly, and there's an emphasis on fresh fish and seafood. You could expect to tuck into a selection of mixed bruschetta to start, followed by a hearty main course of penne in a creamy sauce, served with fresh local asparagus and smoked salmon, or maybe a lobster special, with tiramisù to close.

Norwich
St Giles House Hotel

01603 275180   41-45 St Giles Street, NR2 1JR
Located within a wonderful 19th-century Grade II listed property in the heart of the historic city of Norwich, Dimitri's bistro is the stunning art deco backdrop for some creative and modern Franco-Russian cuisine. Marble floors, black marble-topped tables and gold-plated chandeliers add to the stylish ambience. Start with a cocktail in the Romanov bar, before sampling the likes of Tsar bisque - rich and full-flavoured with brandy and cream and garnished with lobster ravioli, followed by spring lamb and tarragon pesto, served with Jerusalem artichoke and sautéed pak choi.

Swaffham
Best Western George Hotel

01760 721238   Station Road, PE37 7LJ
This smart restaurant overlooking the busy high street is situated within a Georgian hotel in the heart of this bustling market town. Crisp napery, clothed tables and traditional-style crockery set the style. Why not sit back and enjoy a delightful starter of local asparagus with home-made hollandaise, followed perhaps by slow-roasted belly pork served with caramelised red cabbage.

OXFORDSHIRE
Oxford
Aziz

01865 794945   228-230 Cowley Road, OX4 1UH
Located on the busy outskirts of Oxford city centre, Aziz offers delicious authentic Bangladeshi cuisine. The exterior is smart, while inside the décor is warm and inviting with deep red walls, long mirrors and carved wooden archways. Choose from an exciting array of dishes, all freshly cooked, such as a starter of galda chingri aar puri (sweet-and-sour king prawns with purée bread), and follow with badam gosht (lamb in mild spices with cashew nuts, cream and almond powder). Alternatively, let the restaurant team make your selection for you.

SOMERSET
Bath
Bailbrook House Hotel

01225 855100   Eveleigh Avenue, London Road West, BA1 7JD
This light-and-airy hotel restaurant with modern décor has a relaxing, contemporary feel, perfectly complemented by friendly staff who ensure guests are well looked after. The style of cooking is modern British, the kitchen using the freshest of seasonal ingredients with good use of herbs and spices to ensure a memorable dining experience. Starters might feature the likes of tuna Thai fishcakes with lime cucumber, while for mains meat-eaters will not be disappointed with rib-eye steak served with a red wine sauce, fondant potatoes and asparagus.

SUFFOLK
Eye
The Cornwallis Hotel

01379 870326   Rectory Road, Brome, IP23 8AJ
A small country-house hotel down a long, tree-lined drive is the impressive setting for this charming, recently refurbished restaurant, with neatly-clothed tables, crisp napkins and traditional crockery complemented by attentive and professional service from smart black-clad staff. Take a starter of grilled goat's cheese on toasted brioche, followed by a succulent tournedos Rossini beef fillet, set on a chicken liver parfait and served with Lyonnaise potatoes, sautéed field mushroom, roasted cherry tomatoes and a rich jus.

Late entries

Alfriston

◉ Harcourts Restaurant

01323 870248 Deans Place Hotel, Seaford Road, BN26 5TW

Situated on the southern fringe of the village in the heart of Sussex countryside, this 14th-century hotel is set in attractive gardens. The Friston bar offers an extensive bar menu, while the elegant Harcourts Restaurant is a more traditional and formal affair. The kitchen goes to great lengths to source as much local produce as possible, particularly fish from the Sussex coast. This dedication is evident in starters like Cornish sardines with rocket salad and sauce vièrge, followed by grilled Newhaven plaice fillets with lemon and caper butter, served with a warm potato salad and fresh leaves.

WARWICKSHIRE

Royal Leamington Spa

◉ The Brasserie at Mallory Court

01926 453939 Harbury Lane, Bishop's Tachbrook, CV33 9QB

This welcoming restaurant is set within an elegant Lutyens-style country manor house, surrounded by 10 acres of landscaped grounds. The Brasserie boasts a unique sense of style, with its art deco inspired interior, private gardens for alfresco dining, a stunning cocktail bar and upstairs areas for private dining. Take a starter of smoked haddock fishcakes served with sweet crayfish and a lemon butter sauce, and proceed with Casterbridge rib-eye steak accompanied by chips and a classic béarnaise sauce.

Stratford-upon-Avon

◉◉ Menzies Welcombe Hotel and Golf Course

01789 295252 Warwick Road, CV37 0NR

This Jacobean-style manor house set within 157 acres of landscaped parkland is home to the Trevelyan restaurant. The restaurant is traditional in style, and the seasonally-changing menu of English and European dishes is complemented by superb views over the Italian gardens, golf course and water features. For starters you could expect the likes of Vale of Evesham asparagus topped with a poached egg and served with asparagus velouté and chive butter, while mains might feature pan-fried halibut with creamed spinach, Montpellier butter, baby capers and a red wine jus. Save room for a dessert like pear conde - spiced poached pears served with caramelised rice and fig purée.

YORKSHIRE, SOUTH

Sheffield

◉ Whitley Hall Hotel

0114 245 4444 Elliott Lane, Grenoside, S35 8NR

This 16th-century ivy-clad country house hotel stands in 20 acres of landscaped grounds with lakes and immaculate gardens. A recent change in management has seen a renewed focus on customer care, and the use of the very freshest local produce. Imaginative and flavoursome dishes might feature a starter of stir-fried Morecambe Bay whelks with button mushrooms, served in a garlic and ginger and sesame and oyster sauce, followed by a main course of pan-fried fillet of Whitby cod served with red pimento butter, spiced couscous, charred asparagus tips and parmesan shavings.

Channel Islands

JERSEY

St Aubin

◉ The Salty Dog

01534 742760 Le Boulevard, St Aubin's Village, JE3 8AB

Located on the picturesque harbour, set back in a pleasant courtyard, this lively bistro's décor has an upbeat nautical theme with shells and driftwood complemented by colourful Caribbean prints. This relaxed, stylishly informal setting is the perfect place to enjoy Pan-Asian style dishes, with an excellent mix of seafood, spices and flavours. Kick off with the Salty Dog king prawn pana - a local favourite comprising three king prawns cooked in oyster, garlic and black bean sauce, served in a sizzling pan, and follow with pan-fried sea bass with a generous portion of perfectly cooked crab risotto. Fish-lovers will not be disappointed.

St Lawrence
◉ Hotel Cristina
01534 758024 Mont Feland, JE3 1JA
Enjoying a delightful hillside location with well-maintained gardens and stunning views over St Aubin's Bay, this modern restaurant offers simply prepared, fresh, quality local produce in a modern-style bistro atmosphere. Dishes have a distinctly Mediterranean feel, reflected in main courses like tournedos of salmon with linguine of gambas in chilli, ginger and lime salsa, or poached fillets of plaice served with a nage of oysters, scallops, crab, spring onions, lemongrass and lime leaves.

Scotland

ANGUS

Carnoustie
◉ Carnoustie Golf Hotel
01241 411999 The Links, DD7 7JE
This modern hotel is adjacent to the magnificent Carnoustie golf course, home of the 2007 British Open. Overlooking the course, the Dalhousie restaurant is attractively presented and has a modern elegance with well-appointed tables set off with quality silver and sparkling glassware. Service is attentive and friendly, and the cooking style is traditional Scottish. Shetland scallops wrapped in pancetta with saffron risotto and a julienne of sugarsnaps, followed by suprême of Scottish salmon with an oatmeal crust and lemon-glazed new potatoes show the style.

ARGYLL & BUTE

Dunoon
◉ Abbot's Brae Hotel
01369 705021 55 Bullwood Road, PA23 7QT
Perched on the hills overlooking Dunoon and the Firth of Clyde is Abbot's Brae, set in 2 acres of woodland garden with an intimate restaurant offering panoramic views of the Cowal peninsula. This is a family-run operation with a focus on Scottish cuisine, using high-quality, local and organic produce wherever possible, with suppliers admirably listed on the menu. Expect the likes of pan-fried Islay king scallops to start, and maybe squat lobster risotto with langoustine foam or smoked salmon skink for mains.

HIGHLAND

Fort Augustus
◉ Lovat Arms Hotel
0845 450 1100 Loch Ness Side, PH32 4DU
A charming country-house hotel, recently refurbished and yet brimful of original features. The bistro-style restaurant, while cosy and intimate, has a contemporary feel with subdued lighting and an informal atmosphere. Local produce is used wherever possible, including fish and seafood sourced direct from Mallaig. For starters, try langoustine and spinach mosaic herb salad with basil and lime aïoli, and follow with a main course of seared sea bass served with wilted cos and garlic salad, poached langoustine, Merlot and juniper butter sauce.

Nairn
◉ Newton Hotel
01667 453144 Inverness Road, IV12 4RX
Once a holiday haunt of Charlie Chaplin, this ancient building was established in 1640 and today offers both a traditional restaurant and a more contemporary bistro. The cooking style is traditional British, as reflected in starters like oak-smoked salmon or warm peppered mackerel with horseradish sauce, while main courses might feature steak-and-ale casserole topped with a puff pastry crust and served with new potatoes, or beer-battered haddock served with chips and traditional accompaniments. Vegetarians are well catered for.

Thurso

⊚ Forss House Hotel

01847 861201 Forss, KW14 7XY

Set in a fine country house dating from 1810, Forss House Hotel is surrounded by stunning highland scenery and 20 acres of woodland, with the beautiful Forss River running through the grounds. The restaurant has an elegant period feel, complete with family portraits, luxurious curtains, and an Adams fireplace. Uncomplicated modern Scottish dishes use the very best of the seasonal, fresh ingredients, sourced locally wherever possible. Delicious Sinclair Bay crab cakes with celeriac remoulade, hazelnut dressing and wild leaves might precede a main course of Scrabster-landed hake with saffron, spinach and sauce vièrge.

Wales

CEREDIGION

Aberystwyth

⊚ The Hafod Hotel

01970 890232 Devil's Bridge, SY23 3JL

This former hunting lodge dates back to the 17th century and is situated in 6 acres of grounds. Now a family-run hotel, it offers fine dining with an emphasis on local produce. This commitment is reflected in delicious starters such as smoked haddock, chive and Welsh cheddar cheese tart, dressed with green beans and onion marmalade, and mains such as fillet of Scottish salmon with asparagus risotto, ratatouille, parmesan biscuit and a parsley velouté.

Republic of Ireland

COUNTY DONEGAL

Dunkineely

⊚ Castle Murray House and Restaurant

00353 74 97 37022 St John's Point

Overlooking the sparkling waters of McSyne's Bay on the coast road to St John's Point, Castle Murray House offers a traditional, welcoming bar and a sun lounge where guests can watch the sun go down over the water. The restaurant makes the most of the views (floodlit at night), and not surprisingly the kitchen displays a strong commitment to seafood. The seasonally-changing carte might feature a starter of prawn and monkfish in light garlic butter, served with crumbled cheese and fresh herbs, and a main course of pan-fried black sole with clams and a cauliflower cream sauce.

COUNTY LEITRIM

Carrick-on-Shannon

⊚ The Landmark Hotel

071 962 2222

Opposite the marina on the River Shannon, CJ's restaurant is an elegant, cosy room with an impressive antique fireplace and gold and blue décor, where friendly staff serve imaginative modern dishes underpinned by classical French technique to eager diners. Think terrine of smoked duck and foie gras with confit of duck breast and a warm duck leg wonton to start, with maybe tender roast loin of lamb served with a small cottage pie in a red wine jus for mains.

COUNTY MAYO

Cong

⊚ George V Room, Ashford Castle

094 9546003

Located in the unique and magical setting of 13th-century Ashford Castle, the George V Room was originally created for a royal visit. The luxurious and sophisticated dining room is the perfect setting for refined and enjoyable cuisine, exuding an air of timeless sophistication with its high ornate ceilings and sparkling chandeliers. The cooking style reflects its surroundings - classical and elegant and based on classical French cuisine, with food prepared and presented in a light, contemporary style. You might begin with chargrilled scallop and potato-wrapped prawn tails served with rocket and gazpacho foam, and follow with a moist fillet of pan-fried turbot with creamed fresh garden peas and vanilla-scented carrots.

COUNTY SLIGO

Sligo

◉ The Glasshouse

071 919 4300 Swan Point

Situated along the river broadwalk in a cutting-edge design building, The Glasshouse's bright-and-airy dining room is intimate and luxurious with a Mediterranean vibe and fantastic views over the river; there's also a swish ground-floor bar. Contemporary interpretations of classic dishes are on offer, with some oriental influences. Starters like seared scallops served in a rich citrus orange sauce, and main courses like medallions of venison on sauerkraut in a wild berry jus, show the style.

Gibraltar

◉◉ Caleta Hotel

00 350 76501 Sir Herbert Miles Road, PO Box 73

Set above rocky cliffs and crashing waves, Nunos is the fine-dining venue at this imposing and stylish hotel, with panoramic views across the Mediterranean to Morocco, an eclectic interior and a serene and relaxing atmosphere. Service is slick and the theatre kitchen allows diners glimpses of the behind-the-scenes action. Impressive Italian dishes are flavour driven, using high-quality ingredients - particularly salads and vegetables - and include the likes of tonno orientale (seared tuna fillet with mustard, soy and balsamic marinade, with a papaya, cucumber and ginger salad), followed by nasello con vongole e lugumi (lightly poached hake fillet and clams served with chickpeas).

◉◉ The Rock Hotel

00 350 73000 Europa Road

This art deco hotel was built in 1932 by the Marquise of Bute and provides a spacious, traditionally-styled dining room with panoramic views over Gibraltar Bay to Spain and Morocco. Impeccably turned-out staff provide slick, professional service, and the cooking style is an appropriate blend of modern British with Moorish and Iberian influences; international ingredients may also feature. From the seasonally-changing carte take a starter of céviche of king prawns with lime ginger salt and Bloody Mary sorbet, and for mains tuck into a fillet of turbot set on braised fennel, and served with a prawn wafer and lobster bisque.

KEY TO ATLAS

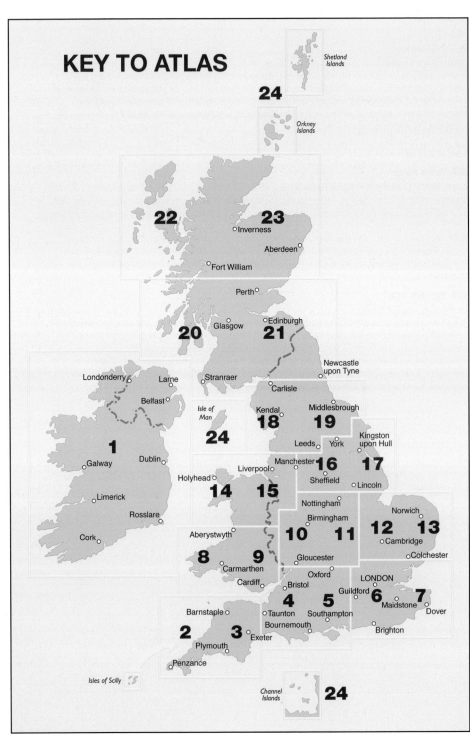

Shetland Islands

24

Orkney Islands

22 **23**
Inverness

Aberdeen

Fort William

Perth

Glasgow Edinburgh

20 **21**

Newcastle upon Tyne

Londonderry Larne Stranraer

Carlisle

Belfast Isle of Man Kendal Middlesbrough

18 **19**

Leeds York Kingston upon Hull

24

1 Dublin Liverpool Manchester **16** **17**

Galway Holyhead Sheffield Lincoln

14 **15**

Limerick Nottingham

Rosslare Birmingham Norwich

Cork Aberystwyth **10** **11** **12** **13**

Cambridge

Gloucester Colchester

8 **9** Oxford

Carmarthen LONDON

Cardiff Bristol Guildford **6** **7**

4 **5** Maidstone Dover

Barnstaple Taunton Southampton Brighton

Bournemouth

2 **3** Exeter

Plymouth

Penzance

Isles of Scilly

Channel Islands **24**

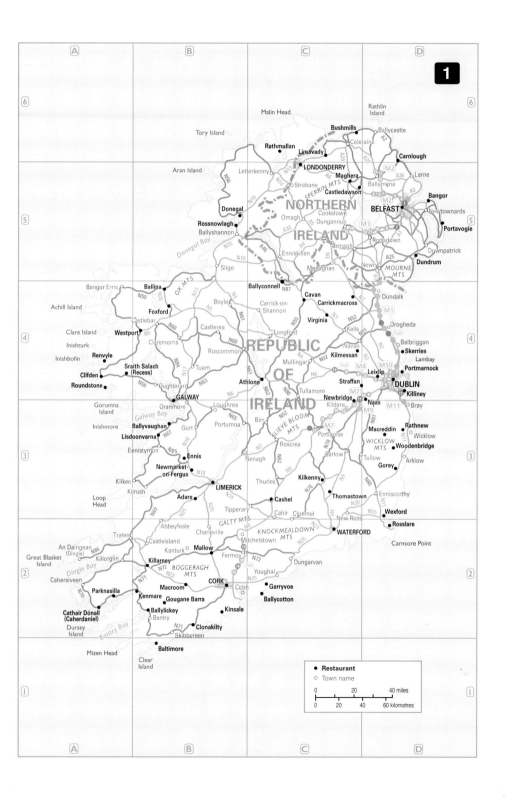

1

Malin Head
Rathlin Island
Tory Island
Bushmills
Ballycastle
Rathmullan
Limavady
Coleraine
Carnlough
Aran Island
Letterkenny
LONDONDERRY
Larne
Maghera
Ballymena
Strabane
Castledawson
Bangor
NORTHERN
BELFAST
Newtownards
Donegal
Omagh
Cookstown
Dungannon
Rossnowlagh
Ballyshannon
IRELAND
Portadown
Portavogie
Donegal Bay
Enniskillen
Armagh
Downpatrick
Dundrum
Sligo
Monaghan
Newry
MOURNE MTS
Bangor Erris
Ballina
Ballyconnell
Cavan
Dundalk
OX MTS
Achill Island
Boyle
Carrick-on-Shannon
Carrickmacross
Foxford
Virginia
M1
Clare Island
Castlebar
Castlerea
Longford
Drogheda
Westport
Claremorris
Roscommon
Navan
Balbriggan
Inishturk
Kilmessan
Skerries
Renvyle
Lambay
Inishbofin
Tuam
Mullingar
Leixlip
Portmarnock
Sraith Salach (Recess)
Oughterard
REPUBLIC
Athlone
Straffan
DUBLIN
Clifden
Roundstone
Killiney
GALWAY
OF
Tullamore
Newbridge
Naas
Bray
Gorumna Island
Oranmore
Loughrea
IRELAND
Kildare
Galway Bay
Inishmore
Ballyvaughan
Gort
Birr
Macreddin
Rathnew
Lisdoonvarna
Portumna
Portlaoise
WICKLOW MTS
Wicklow
Ennistymon
Roscrea
Woodenbridge
Ennis
Nenagh
Carlow
Arklow
Kilkee
Newmarket-on-Fergus
Tullow
Gorey
Kilrush
Thurles
Kilkenny
Loop Head
LIMERICK
Adare
Cashel
Thomastown
Enniscorthy
Tipperary
Cahir
Clonmel
Wexford
Abbeyfeale
Charleville
GALTY MTS
New Ross
Rosslare
Tralee
Castleisland
KNOCKMEALDOWN MTS
WATERFORD
An Daingean (Dingle)
Kanturk
Mallow
Mitchelstown
Carnsore Point
Great Blasket Island
Killorglin
Fermoy
Dungarvan
Killarney
BOGGERAGH MTS
Youghal
Cahersiveen
Dingle Bay
Macroom
CORK
Garryvoe
Parknasilla
Cobh
Kenmare
Gougane Barra
Kinsale
Ballycotton
Cathair Dónall (Caherdaniel)
Ballylickey
Bantry
Dursey Island
Clonakilty
Bantry Bay
Skibbereen
Mizen Head
Baltimore
Clear Island

- ● Restaurant
- ○ Town name

0   20   40 miles

0   20   40   60 kilometres

2

═══M6═══ Motorway/toll motorway	●Spalding Restaurant
Motorway junction full/ restricted. Sevice area	○Oundle Town/Village name
Primary route single/ dual carriageway	▬▬▬▬ National boundary
A34 Other A road single/ dual carriageway	**ESSEX** English county name & boundary
B3400 B road	**CONWY** Welsh county name & boundary
Unclassified road	**MORAY** Scottish county name & boundary
─Ⓥ─ Vehicle ferry	National Park
─Ⓒ─ Vehicle ferry-fast catamaran	

Lundy

Hartland Point
Hartland

Morwenstow

Kilkhampton

Bude
Bude Stra
Bay
Widemouth Bay

Crackington Haven
Week St Mary

ISLES OF SCILLY
Bryher Tresco St Martin's
New Grimsby Higher Town
Hugh St Mary's
Town
Middle Old
Town Town
St Agnes

SV

Boscastle
Tintagel

Delabole
Camelford

Port Isaac
Polzeath
Pendoggett
Harlyn Rock St Tudy Bolventor
Padstow BODMIN MOOR
Constantine Bay Blisland
Porthcothan St
Merryn Wadebridge

C O R N W A L L St Clee

Mawgan St Bodmin
Porth Mawgan
Watergate Bay St Columb Lanivet Dobwalls
Major Liskeare
Newquay Roche St
West Bugle Keyne
Pentire Sommercourt St Lostwithiel
Perranporth St Blazey Tywardreath Pelynt
Austell
St Agnes Ladock St Fowey Polperro Talla
Marazanvose Stephen Polruan Bay
Porthtowan Grampound
Portreath Pentewan
St Ives Bay Carnon Mevagissey
Truro Tregony
St Ives Gwithian St Gorran Haven
Redruth Day
Zennor Camborne Portloe
Lelant Hayle Veryan
St Just-in-
Roseland
Penryn Portscatho
Falmouth St Mawes
St Just Marazion
Penzance Perranuthnoe Constantine
Newlyn Mawnan Smith
Land's Sennen St Buryan Praa Helston Gweek
End Mousehole Sands Porthleven Manaccan
Porthcurno Treen St Keverne
Mullion
Coverack
Lizard Cadgwith
Lizard Point

SW

For continuation pages refer to numbered arrows

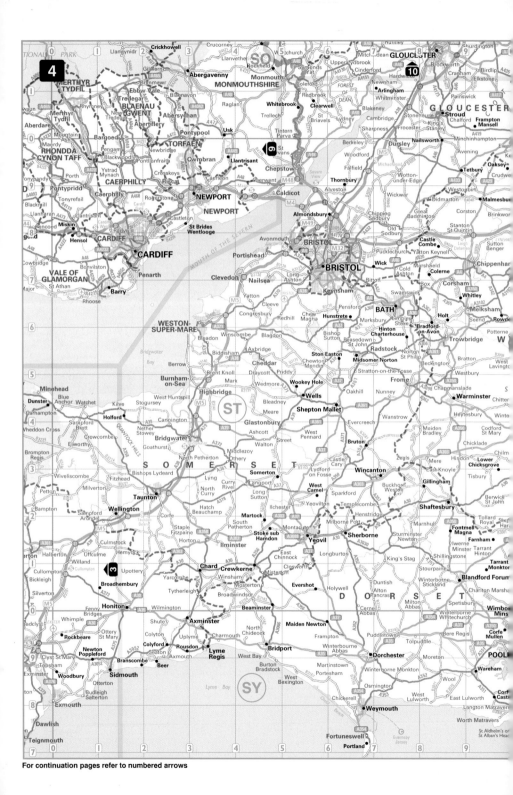

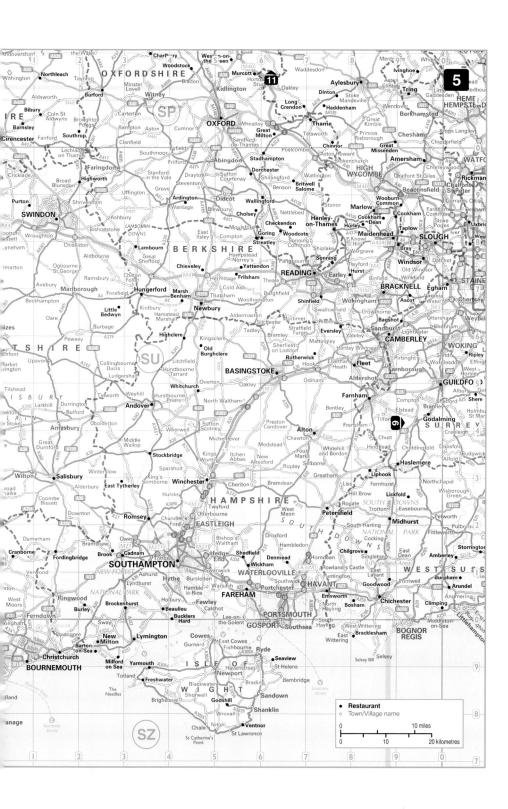

For continuation pages refer to numbered arrows

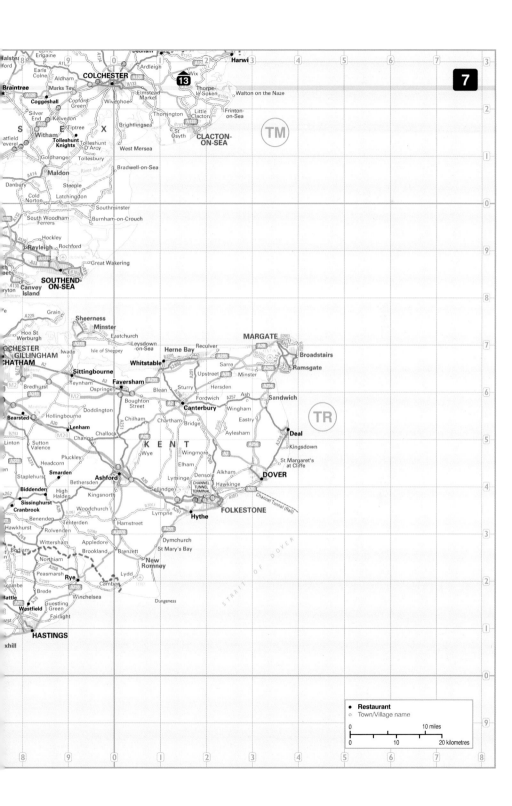

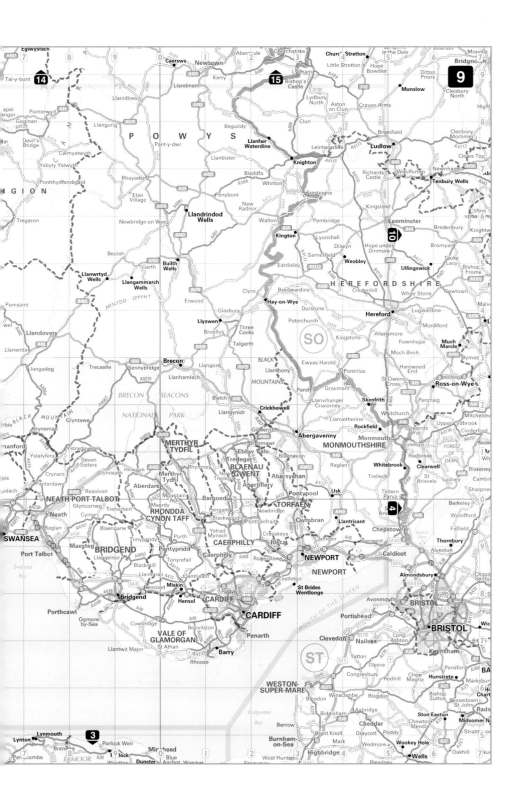

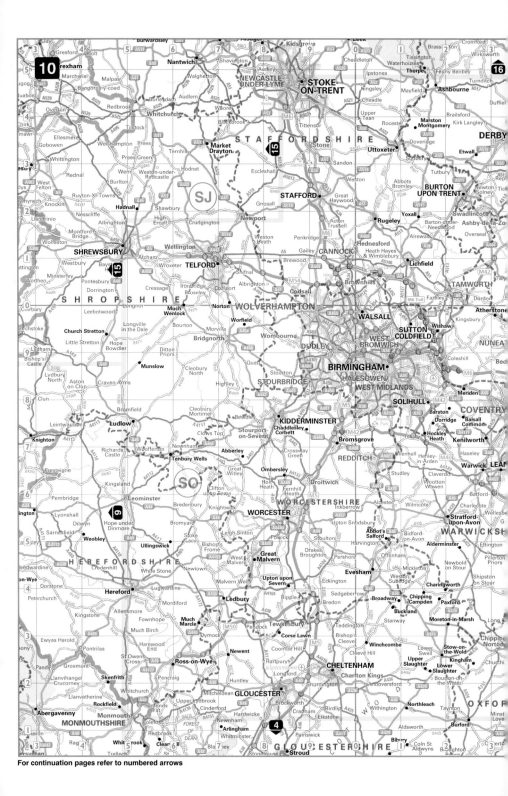

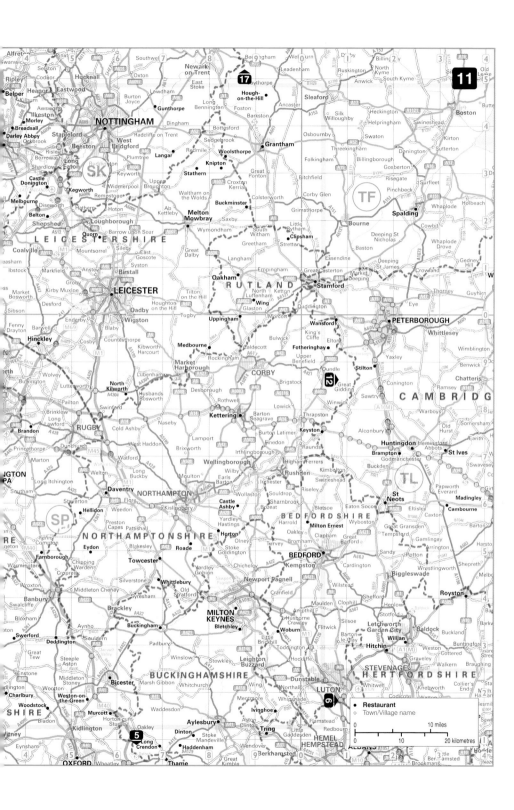

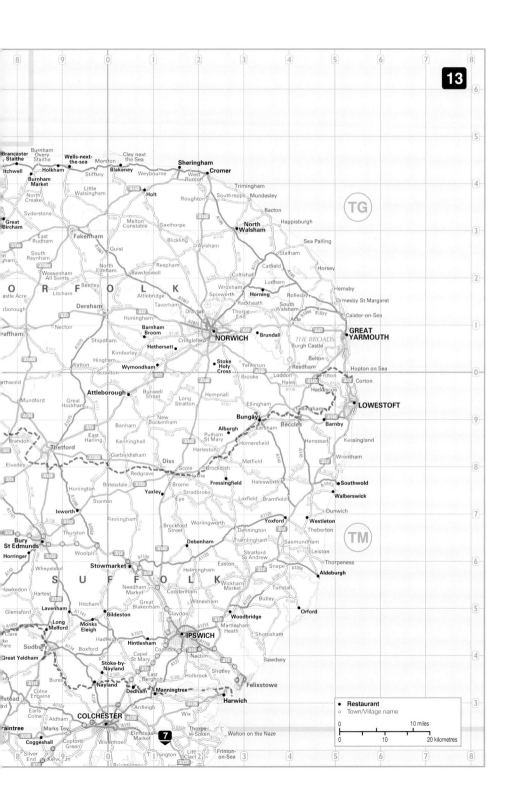

14

ISLE OF
ANGLESEY

Cemaes
Amlwch
Llanerchymedd
Holyhead
Llanfachraeth
Benllech
Red
Wharf Bay
Llangoed
Llandudno
Rhôs-
on-Sea
Rhy
Trearddur Bay
Pentraeth
Deganwy
Colwyn Bay
Aberge
Holy
Island
Llangefni
Penmaenmawr
Conwy
Llanddulas
Rhosneigr
Beaumaris
Llanfairfechan
Llansantffraid
Glan Conwy
Menai
Bridge Bangor
Llanfairfechan
Betws-yn-Rhos
Llanfair
P G
Llanilechid
Tal-y-Cafn
Llan
Aberffraw
Y Felinheli
Bethesda
Tal-y-Bont
Llanfair
Talhaiarn
He
Llangernyw
Llansanna
Newborough
Trefriw
Caernarfon
Llanrug
Llanrwst
Bylchau
Bontnewydd
Llanberis
Llanwrst
Caernarfon
Bay
Llandwrog
Llanwnda
Capel Curig
CONWY
Betws-y-Coed
Clynnog-fawr
Penygroes
Rhyd-Ddu
Dolwyddelan
Penmachno
Pentrefoelas
Cerrigydrudion
Llanaelhaearn
Beddgelert
WDONIA
Y Mae
PENINSULA
Blaenau Ffestiniog
Morfa Nefyn
Nefyn
Prenteg
Ffestiniog
Llanystumdwy
Maentwrog
Bodfuan
Tremadog
Criccieth
Porthmadog
Penrhyndeudraeth
NATIONAL
Llandde
Sarn
Borth-y-Gest
Portmeirion
Talsarnau
Bala
Pwllheli
Trawsfynydd
G W Y N E D D
Llanbedrog
Harlech
Llanuwchllyn
PARK
Aberdaron
Y Rhiw
Abersoch
Llanbedr
Ganllwyd
Bardsey
Island
Dyffryn Ardudwy
Tal-y-bont
Barmouth
Dolgellau
Dinas-Mawddwy
Fairbourne
Mallwyd
Llangadf
Llwyngwril
Corris
Cemmaes
Road
Llanbrynmair
Bryncrug
Tywyn
Pennal
Machynlleth
SN
Aberdyfi
Eglwysfach
Carno
Borth
Tal-y-bont
Llandre
9
Llanidloe
CARDIGAN BAY
Aberystwyth
Capel
Bangor
Ponterwyd

SH

- **Restaurant**
- Town/Village name

0 ———— 10 miles
0 ——— 10 —— 20 kilometres

For continuation pages refer to numbered arrows

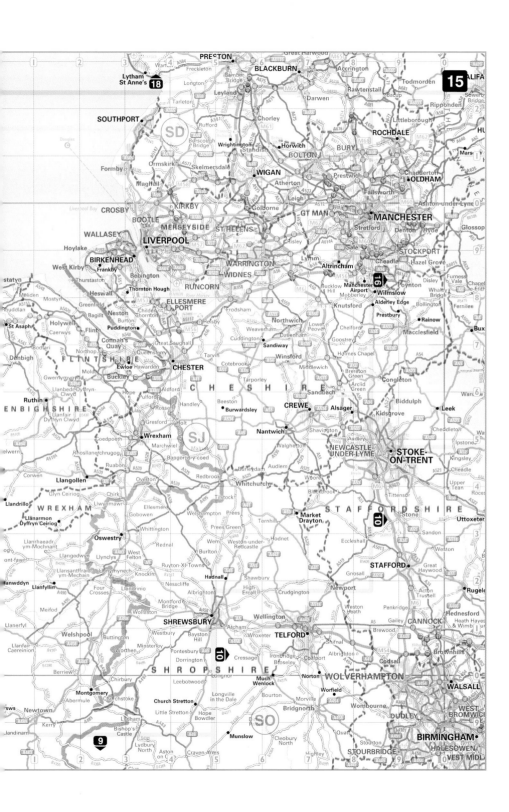

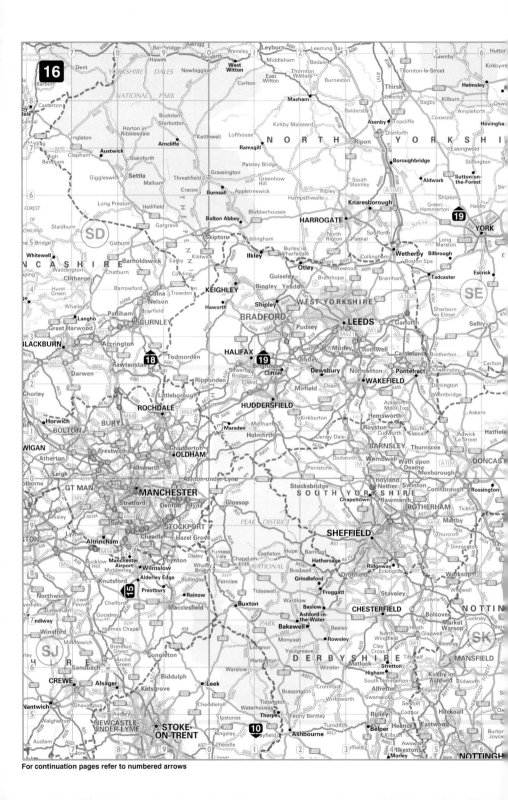

For continuation pages refer to numbered arrows

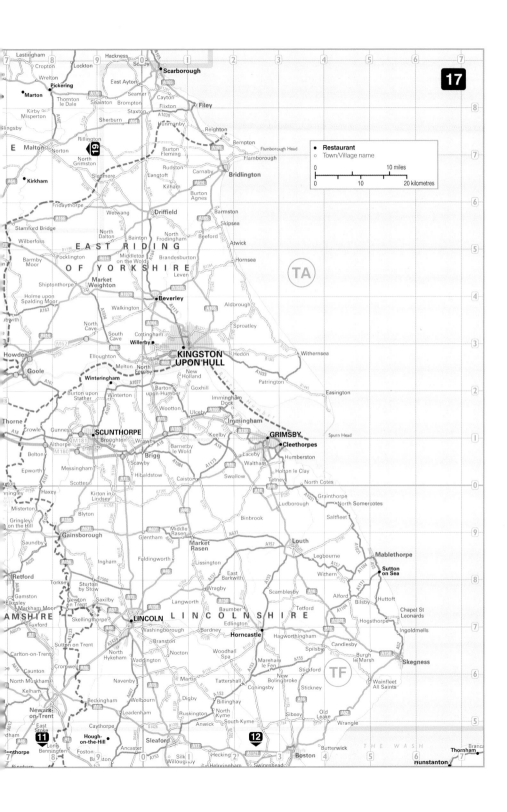

For continuation pages refer to numbered arrows

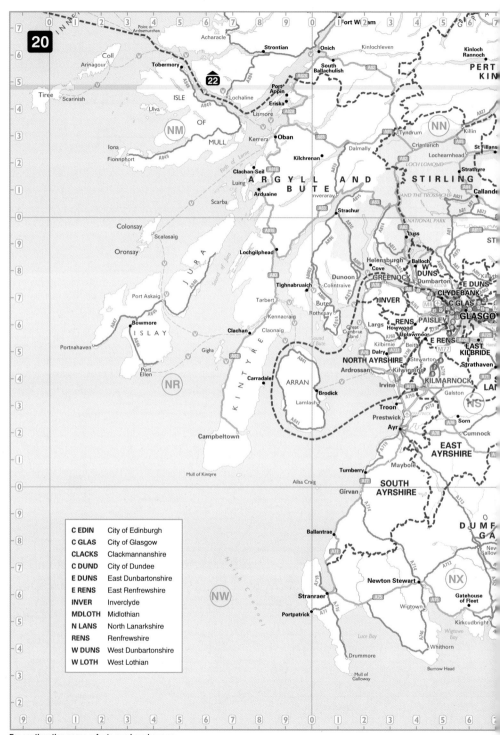

20

Point of Ardnamurchan · Acharacle · Strontian · Onich · Kinlochleven · Fort W 2 am · Kinloch Rannoch

Coll · Arinagour · Tobermory · South Ballachulish · PERTH KIN

Tiree · Scarinish · ISLE · Lochaline · Port Appin · Eriska

Ulva · Lismore · Oban

ISLE OF MULL · Kerrera · NM · NN · Killin

Iona · Fionnphort · Kilchrenan · Dalmally · Tyndrum · Crianlarich · St Fillans

Kilchrenan · Lochearnhead · LOCH LOMOND · Strathyre

Clachan-Seil · Luing · **ARGYLL AND BUTE** · **STIRLING**

Arduaine · Inveraray · AND THE TROSSACHS · Callande

Scarba · Strachur

Colonsay · Scalasaig · NATIONAL PARK · Luss · ST

Oronsay · Lochgilphead · Helensburgh · Balloch · W DUNS · Kilsyth

JURA · Cove · GREENOCK · Dumbarton · E DUNS

Dunoon · Colintraive · Tighnabruaich · **INVER** · CLYDEBANK · C GLAS

Port Askaig · Tarbert · Rothesay · Bute · **GLASGOW**

Bowmore · Kennacraig · Largs · Howwood · **RENS PAISLEY** · Uplawmoor

ISLAY · Clachan · Claonaig · Great Cumbrae Island · E RENS · EAST KILBRIDE

Portnahaven · Gigha · Kilbirnie · Beith · Stewarton

Port Ellen · **NR** · Carradale · **ARRAN** · Dalry · **NORTH AYRSHIRE** · Kilwinning · Strathaven

KINTYRE · Brodick · Ardrossan · Irvine · KILMARNOCK · LAN

Lamlash · Troon · Galston · **NS**

Campbeltown · Prestwick · Ayr · Sorn · Cumnock

Mull of Kintyre · Ailsa Craig · Turnberry · Maybole · **EAST AYRSHIRE**

Girvan · **SOUTH AYRSHIRE**

Ballantrae · DUMF GA

C EDIN	City of Edinburgh
C GLAS	City of Glasgow
CLACKS	Clackmannanshire
C DUND	City of Dundee
E DUNS	East Dunbartonshire
E RENS	East Renfrewshire
INVER	Inverclyde
MDLOTH	Midlothian
N LANS	North Lanarkshire
RENS	Renfrewshire
W DUNS	West Dunbartonshire
W LOTH	West Lothian

Newton Stewart · **NX** · Gatehouse of Fleet

NW · Stranraer · Wigtown · Kirkcudbright

Portpatrick · Wigtown Bay

North Channel · Luce Bay · Whithorn

Drummore · Burrow Head

Mull of Galloway

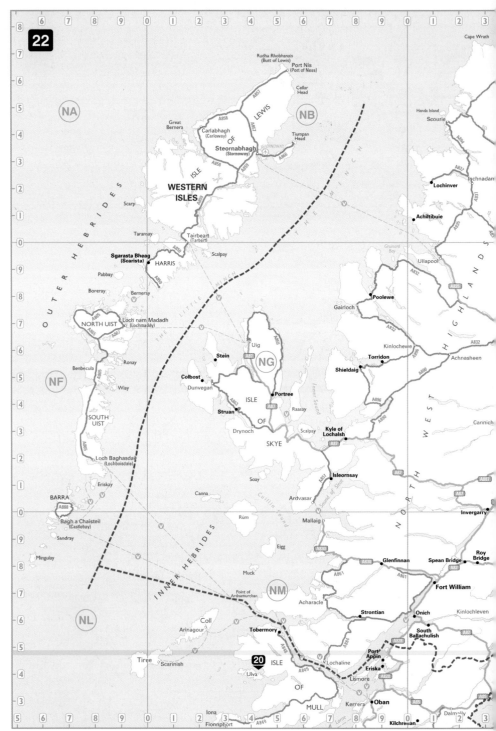

23

Restaurant
Town/Village name

0   10   20 miles
0   10   20   30 kilometres

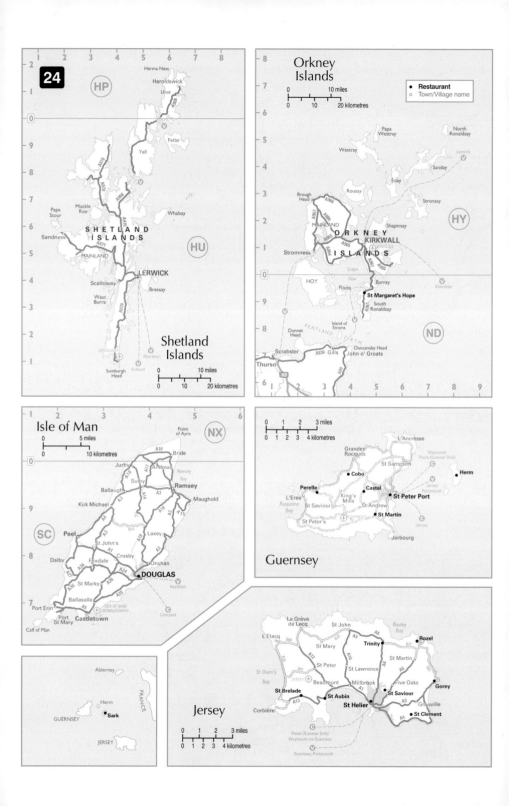

24

Herma Ness
Haroldswick
Unst
Fetlar
Yell
Whalsay
Muckle Roe
Papa Stour
SHETLAND ISLANDS
Sandness
MAINLAND
LERWICK
Scalloway
Bressay
West Burra
Sumburgh Head
Kirkwall
Aberdeen

Shetland Islands

0   10 miles
0   10   20 kilometres

HP
HU

Orkney Islands

0   10 miles
0   10   20 kilometres

• Restaurant
○ Town/Village name

Papa Westray
North Ronaldsay
Westray
Lerwick
Sanday
Eday
Rousay
Stronsay
Brough Head
MAINLAND
Shapinsay
ORKNEY
KIRKWALL
ISLANDS
Stromness
Scapa
HOY
Flow
Burray
Aberdeen
Flotta
St Margaret's Hope
South Ronaldsay
Island of Stroma
Dunnet Head
PENTLAND FIRTH
Scrabster
Gills
Duncansby Head
John o' Groats
Thurso

HY
ND

Isle of Man

0   5 miles
0   10 kilometres

Point of Ayre
Bride
Jurby
Andreas
Ramsey Bay
Sulby
Ballaugh
Ramsey
Kirk Michael
Maughold
Peel
Laxey
St John's
Dalby
Crosby
Foxdale
Onchan
DOUGLAS
St Marks
Ballasalla
Heysham
Port Erin
Port St Mary
Castletown
Liverpool
Calf of Man

NX
SC

ISLE OF MAN (RONALDSWAY)

0   1   2   3 miles
0   1   2   3   4 kilometres

L'Ancresse
Grandes Rocques
St Sampson
Weymouth Poole (Summer Only)
Cobo
Herm
Perelle
Castel
L'Eree
King's Mills
St Peter Port
Jersey Portsmouth
Roquaine Bay
St Saviour
St Andrew
St Peter's
St Martin
Jerbourg

Guernsey

Alderney
Herm
FRANCE
GUERNSEY
Sark
JERSEY

La Grève de Lecq
St John
Bouley Bay
L'Etacq
St Mary
Trinity
Rozel
St Ouen's Bay
St Peter
St Lawrence
St Martin
Beaumont
Millbrook
Five Oaks
St Brelade
St Aubin
St Saviour
Gorey
Corbière
St Helier
Grauville
St Clement
Poole (Summer Only) Weymouth via Guernsey
Guernsey, Portsmouth

Jersey

0   1   2   3 miles
0   1   2   3   4 kilometres

Index of Restaurants

Index

Index

Index

Index

Index

Index

Index

Index

The Automobile Association would like to thank the following photographers, companies and picture libraries for their assistance in the preparation of this book.

Abbreviations for the picture credits are as follows: (t) top; (b) bottom; (l) left; (r) right; (AA) AA World Travel Library.

1 Stockbyte; 3tr, 3bl AA/Clive Sawyer; 3br Photodisc; 4tl AA/Clive Sawyer; 4tr ImageState; 5tr AA/Clive Sawyer; 6tl AA/Clive Sawyer; 7tr AA/Clive Sawyer; 7b Bananastock; 8tl AA/Clive Sawyer; 9tr AA/Clive Sawyer; 10tl AA/Clive Sawyer; 11tr AA/Clive Sawyer; 14tl AA/Clive Sawyer; 15tr AA/Clive Sawyer; 16tl AA/Clive Sawyer; 16bl Photodisc; 17tl Photodisc; 17tr AA/Clive Sawyer; 17r David Wasserman/brandxpictures; 17cr Bananastock; 20tl AA/Clive Sawyer; 21tr AA/Clive Sawyer; 22tl AA/Clive Sawyer; 23tr AA/Clive Sawyer; 24tl AA/Clive Sawyer; 25tr AA/Clive Sawyer; 26/7 ImageState; 247 ImageState; 248tl AA/Clive Sawyer; 249tr AA/Clive Sawyer; 250tl AA/Clive Sawyer; 251tr AA/Clive Sawyer; 566/7 ImageState; 650/1 ImageState; 689 ImageState; 696 ImageState.

Every effort has been made to trace the copyright holders, and we apologise in advance for any accidental errors. We would be happy to apply the corrections in the following edition of this publication.

Please send this form to:
  Editor, The Restaurant Guide,
  Lifestyle Guides,
  The Automobile Association,
  14th Floor, Fanum House,
  Basingstoke RG21 4EA

or fax: 01256 491647
or e-mail: lifestyleguides@theAA.com
Please use this form to tell us about any restaurant you have visited, whether it is in the guide or not currently listed. Feedback from readers helps us to keep our guide accurate and up to date. Please note, however, that if you have a complaint to make during a visit, we strongly recommend that you discuss the matter with the restaurant management there and then, so that they have a chance to put things right before your visit is spoilt. The AA does not undertake to arbitrate between you and the restaurant management, or to obtain compensation or engage in correspondence.

Date:

Your name (block capitals)

Your address (block capitals)

....

....

....

e-mail address: ....

Restaurant name and address: (If you are recommending a new restaurant please enclose a menu or note the dishes that you ate.)

....

....

....

Comments:...

....

....

(please attach a separate sheet if necessary)   **PTO**

Readers' Report Form

The Restaurant Guide 2008

YES   NO

Have you bought this guide before? ☐ ☐

Please list any other similar guides that you use regularly...

....

....

What do you find most useful about The AA Restaurant Guide?

....

....

....

....

Please answer these questions to help us make improvements to the guide:

What are your main reasons for visiting restaurants (circle all that apply)

business entertaining   business travel   trying famous restaurants

family celebrations   leisure travel   trying new food

enjoying not having to cook yourself   to eat food you couldn't cook yourself

other ....   because I enjoy eating out regularly

How often do you visit a restaurant for lunch or dinner? (circle one choice)

once a week   once a fortnight   once a month   less than once a month

Do you use the location atlas?...

Do you generally agree with the Rosette ratings at the restaurants you visit in the guide? (if not please give examples)...

....

Who is your favourite chef? ....

Which is your favourite restaurant? ....

Which type of cuisine is your first choice e.g. French ....

Which of these factors are most important when choosing a restaurant?

Price   Service   Location   Type of food   Awards/ratings

Décor/surroundings   Other (please state):...

Which elements of the guide do you find most useful when choosing a restaurant?

Description   Photo   Rosette rating   Price   Other...

Please send this form to:
    Editor, The Restaurant Guide,
    Lifestyle Guides,
    The Automobile Association,
    14th Floor, Fanum House,
    Basingstoke RG21 4EA

Readers'
Report form

or fax: 01256 491647
or e-mail: lifestyleguides@theAA.com
Please use this form to tell us about any restaurant you have visited, whether it is in the guide or not currently listed. Feedback from readers helps us to keep our guide accurate and up to date. Please note, however, that if you have a complaint to make during a visit, we strongly recommend that you discuss the matter with the restaurant management there and then, so that they have a chance to put things right before your visit is spoilt. The AA does not undertake to arbitrate between you and the restaurant management, or to obtain compensation or engage in correspondence.

Date:

Your name (block capitals)

Your address (block capitals)

....

....

....

e-mail address: ....

Restaurant name and address: (If you are recommending a new restaurant please enclose a menu or note the dishes that you ate.)

....

....

....

Comments:..

....

....

(please attach a separate sheet if necessary)   **PTO**

We may use information we hold about you to write, e-mail or telephone you about other products and services offered by us and our carefully selected partners, but we can assure you that we will not disclose it to third parties.

Please tick here if you DO NOT wish to receive details of other products or services from the AA.

Readers' Report Form

	YES	NO
Have you bought this guide before?	☐	☐

Please list any other similar guides that you use regularly...................................

....

....

What do you find most useful about The AA Restaurant Guide?

....

....

....

....

Please answer these questions to help us make improvements to the guide:

What are your main reasons for visiting restaurants (circle all that apply)

business entertaining   business travel   trying famous restaurants

family celebrations   leisure travel   trying new food

enjoying not having to cook yourself   to eat food you couldn't cook yourself

other ....   because I enjoy eating out regularly

How often do you visit a restaurant for lunch or dinner? (circle one choice)

once a week   once a fortnight   once a month   less than once a month

Do you use the location atlas?...

Do you generally agree with the Rosette ratings at the restaurants you visit in the guide? (if not please give examples)...

....

Who is your favourite chef? ....

Which is your favourite restaurant? ....

Which type of cuisine is your first choice e.g. French ....

Which of these factors are most important when choosing a restaurant?

Price   Service   Location   Type of food   Awards/ratings

Décor/surroundings   Other (please state):.......................................

Which elements of the guide do you find most useful when choosing a restaurant?

Description   Photo   Rosette rating   Price   Other.........................

Please send this form to:
   Editor, The Restaurant Guide,
   Lifestyle Guides,
   The Automobile Association,
   14th Floor, Fanum House,
   Basingstoke RG21 4EA

**Readers'
Report form**

or fax: 01256 491647
or e-mail: lifestyleguides@theAA.com
Please use this form to tell us about any restaurant you have visited, whether it is in the guide or not currently listed. Feedback from readers helps us to keep our guide accurate and up to date. Please note, however, that if you have a complaint to make during a visit, we strongly recommend that you discuss the matter with the restaurant management there and then, so that they have a chance to put things right before your visit is spoilt. The AA does not undertake to arbitrate between you and the restaurant management, or to obtain compensation or engage in correspondence.

Date:

Your name (block capitals)

Your address (block capitals)

....

....

....

e-mail address: ....

Restaurant name and address: (If you are recommending a new restaurant please enclose a menu or note the dishes that you ate.)

....

....

....

Comments:..

....

....

(please attach a separate sheet if necessary)   **PTO**

The Restaurant Guide 2008

Readers' Report Form

	YES	NO
Have you bought this guide before?	☐	☐

Please list any other similar guides that you use regularly.................................
....
....

What do you find most useful about The AA Restaurant Guide?

....
....
....
....

Please answer these questions to help us make improvements to the guide:

What are your main reasons for visiting restaurants (circle all that apply)

business entertaining   business travel   trying famous restaurants

family celebrations   leisure travel   trying new food

enjoying not having to cook yourself   to eat food you couldn't cook yourself

other ....   because I enjoy eating out regularly

How often do you visit a restaurant for lunch or dinner? (circle one choice)

once a week   once a fortnight   once a month   less than once a month

Do you use the location atlas?...

Do you generally agree with the Rosette ratings at the restaurants you visit in the guide? (if not please give examples)...
....

Who is your favourite chef? ....

Which is your favourite restaurant? ....

Which type of cuisine is your first choice e.g. French ....

Which of these factors are most important when choosing a restaurant?

Price   Service   Location   Type of food   Awards/ratings

Décor/surroundings   Other (please state):...

Which elements of the guide do you find most useful when choosing a restaurant?

Description   Photo   Rosette rating   Price   Other...........................

Readers' Report Form

	YES	NO
Have you bought this guide before?	☐	☐

Please list any other similar guides that you use regularly.....................................
....
....

What do you find most useful about The AA Restaurant Guide?

....
....
....
....

Please answer these questions to help us make improvements to the guide:

What are your main reasons for visiting restaurants (circle all that apply)

business entertaining   business travel   trying famous restaurants

family celebrations   leisure travel   trying new food

enjoying not having to cook yourself   to eat food you couldn't cook yourself

other ....   because I enjoy eating out regularly

How often do you visit a restaurant for lunch or dinner? (circle one choice)

once a week   once a fortnight   once a month   less than once a month

Do you use the location atlas?..

Do you generally agree with the Rosette ratings at the restaurants you visit in the guide? (if not please give examples)...
....

Who is your favourite chef? ....

Which is your favourite restaurant? ....

Which type of cuisine is your first choice e.g. French ....

Which of these factors are most important when choosing a restaurant?

Price   Service   Location   Type of food   Awards/ratings

Décor/surroundings   Other (please state):...

Which elements of the guide do you find most useful when choosing a restaurant?

Description   Photo   Rosette rating   Price   Other.........................

Please send this form to:
Editor, The Restaurant Guide,
Lifestyle Guides,
The Automobile Association,
14th Floor, Fanum House,
Basingstoke RG21 4EA

**Readers'
Report form**

Readers' Report Form

or fax: 01256 491647
or e-mail: lifestyleguides@theAA.com
Please use this form to tell us about any restaurant you have visited, whether it is in
the guide or not currently listed. Feedback from readers helps us to keep our guide
accurate and up to date. Please note, however, that if you have a complaint to make
during a visit, we strongly recommend that you discuss the matter with the restaurant
management there and then, so that they have a chance to put things right before
your visit is spoilt. The AA does not undertake to arbitrate between you and the
restaurant management, or to obtain compensation or engage in correspondence.

Date:

Your name (block capitals)

Your address (block capitals)

....

....

....

e-mail address: ....

Restaurant name and address: (If you are recommending a new restaurant please
enclose a menu or note the dishes that you ate.)

....

....

....

Comments:...

....

....

(please attach a separate sheet if necessary)   **PTO**

The Restaurant Guide 2008

Readers' Report Form

	YES	NO
Have you bought this guide before?	☐	☐

Please list any other similar guides that you use regularly.....................................
....
....

What do you find most useful about The AA Restaurant Guide?
....
....
....
....

Please answer these questions to help us make improvements to the guide:

What are your main reasons for visiting restaurants (circle all that apply)

business entertaining   business travel   trying famous restaurants

family celebrations   leisure travel   trying new food

enjoying not having to cook yourself   to eat food you couldn't cook yourself

other ....   because I enjoy eating out regularly

How often do you visit a restaurant for lunch or dinner? (circle one choice)
once a week   once a fortnight   once a month   less than once a month

Do you use the location atlas?...

Do you generally agree with the Rosette ratings at the restaurants you visit in the guide? (if not please give examples)...
....

Who is your favourite chef? ....

Which is your favourite restaurant? ....

Which type of cuisine is your first choice e.g. French ....

Which of these factors are most important when choosing a restaurant?

Price   Service   Location   Type of food   Awards/ratings

Décor/surroundings   Other (please state):...

Which elements of the guide do you find most useful when choosing a restaurant?

Description   Photo   Rosette rating   Price   Other.........................

How do I find the perfect place?

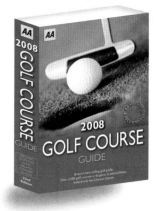

Discover new horizons with Britain's largest travel publisher